# Papers Relating to the

# Foreign Relations

## of the

# United States

# 1929

(In Three Volumes)

## Volume I

United States
Government Printing Office
Washington : 1943

DEPARTMENT OF STATE

PUBLICATION 2018

For sale by the
Superintendent of Documents, U. S. Government Printing Office
Washington, D. C.    Price $2.25 (Buckram)

# CONTENTS

# MESSAGE OF THE PRESIDENT OF THE UNITED STATES TO CONGRESS, DECEMBER 3, 1929

To THE SENATE AND HOUSE OF REPRESENTATIVES:

The Constitution requires that the President "shall, from time to time, give to the Congress information of the state of the Union, and recommend to their consideration such measures as he shall judge necessary and expedient." In complying with that requirement I wish to emphasize that during the past year the Nation has continued to grow in strength; our people have advanced in comfort; we have gained in knowledge; the education of youth has been more widely spread; moral and spiritual forces have been maintained; peace has become more assured. The problems with which we are confronted are the problems of growth and of progress. In their solution we have to determine the facts, to develop the relative importance to be assigned to such facts, to formulate a common judgment upon them, and to realize solutions in a spirit of conciliation.

## FOREIGN RELATIONS

We are not only at peace with all the world, but the foundations for future peace are being substantially strengthened. To promote peace is our long-established policy. Through the Kellogg-Briand pact a great moral standard has been raised in the world. By it fifty-four nations have covenanted to renounce war and to settle all disputes by pacific means. Through it a new world outlook has been inaugurated which has profoundly affected the foreign policies of nations. Since its inauguration we have initiated new efforts not only in the organization of the machinery of peace but also to eliminate dangerous forces which produce controversies amongst nations.

In January, 1926, the Senate gave its consent to adherence to The Court of International Justice with certain reservations. In September of this year the statute establishing the court has, by the action of the nations signatory, been amended to meet the Senate's reservations and to go even beyond those reservations to make clear that the court is a true international court of justice. I believe it will be clear to everyone that no controversy or question in which this country has or claims an interest can be passed on by the court without our consent at the time the question arises. The doubt about advisory opinions has been completely safeguarded. Our adherence to the International Court is, as now constituted, not the slightest step toward entry into the League of Nations. As I have before indicated, I shall direct that our signature be affixed to the protocol of adherence and shall submit it for the approval of the Senate with a special message at some time when it is convenient to deal with it.

In the hope of reducing friction in the world, and with the desire that we may reduce the great economic burdens of naval armament, we have joined in conference with Great Britain, France, Italy, and Japan to be held in London in January to consider the further limitation and reduction of naval arms. We hold high hopes that success may attend this effort.

At the beginning of the present administration the neighboring State of Mexico was beset with domestic insurrection. We maintained the embargo upon the shipment of arms to Mexico but permitted the duly constituted Government to procure supplies from our surplus war stocks. Fortunately, the Mexican Government by its own strength successfully withstood the insurrection with but slight damage. Opportunity of further peaceful development is given to that country. At the request of the Mexican Government, we have since lifted the embargo on shipment of arms altogether. The two governments have taken further steps to promote friendly relationships and so solve our differences. Conventions prolonging for a period of two years the life of the general and special claims commissions have been concluded.

In South America we are proud to have had part in the settlement of the long-standing dispute between Chile and Peru in the disposal of the question of Tacna-Arica.

The work of the commission of inquiry and conciliation between Bolivia and Paraguay, in which a representative of this Government participated, has successfully terminated an incident which seemed to threaten war. The proposed plan for final settlement as suggested by the neutral governments is still under consideration.

This Government has continued its efforts to act as a mediator in boundary difficulties between Guatemala and Honduras.

A further instance of profound importance in establishing good will was the inauguration of regular air mail service between the United States and Caribbean, Central American, and South American countries.

We still have marines on foreign soil—in Nicaragua, Haiti, and China. In the large sense we do not wish to be represented abroad in such manner. About 1,600 marines remain in Nicaragua at the urgent request of that government and the leaders of all parties pending the training of a domestic constabulary capable of insuring tranquility. We have already reduced these forces materially and we are anxious to withdraw them further as the situation warrants. In Haiti we have about 700 marines, but it is a much more difficult problem, the solution of which is still obscure. If Congress approves, I shall dispatch a commission to Haiti to review and study the matter in an endeavor to arrive at some more definite policy than at present. Our forces in China constitute 2,605 men, which we hope also further to reduce to the normal legation guard.

It is my desire to establish more firmly our understanding and relationships with the Latin American countries by strengthening the diplomatic missions to those countries. It is my hope to secure men long experienced in our Diplomatic Service, who speak the languages of the peoples to whom they are accredited, as chiefs of our diplomatic missions in these States. I shall send to the Senate at an early date the nominations of several such men.

The Congress has by numerous wise and foresighted acts in the past few years greatly strengthened the character of our representation abroad. It has made liberal provision for the establishment of suitable quarters for our foreign staffs in the different countries. In order, however, that we may further develop the most effective force in this, one of the most responsible functions of our Government, I shall recommend to the Congress more liberal appropriations for the work of the State Department. I know of no expenditure of public money from which a greater economic and moral return can come to us than by assuring the most effective conduct of our foreign relations.

## NATIONAL DEFENSE

To preserve internal order and freedom from encroachment is the first purpose of government. Our Army and Navy are being maintained in a most efficient state under officers of high intelligence and zeal. The extent and expansion of their numbers and equipment as at present authorized are ample for this purpose.

We can well be deeply concerned, however, at the growing expense. From a total expenditure for national defense purposes in 1914 of $267,000,000, it naturally rose with the Great War, but receded again to $612,000,000 in 1924, when again it began to rise until during the current fiscal year the expenditures will reach to over $730,000,000, excluding all civilian services of those departments. Programs now authorized will carry it to still larger figures in future years. While the remuneration paid to our soldiers and sailors is justly at a higher rate than that of any other country in the world, and while the cost of subsistence is higher, yet the total of our expenditures is in excess of those of the most highly militarized nations of the world.

Upon the conference shortly to be held in London will depend such moderation as we can make in naval expenditure. If we shall be compelled to undertake the naval construction implied in the Washington arms treaty as well as other construction which would appear to be necessary if no international agreement can be completed, we shall be committed during the next six years to a construction expenditure of upward of $1,200,000,000 besides the necessary further increase in costs for annual upkeep.

After 1914 the various Army contingents necessarily expanded to the end of the Great War and then receded to the low point in 1924, when expansion again began. In 1914 the officers and men in our regular forces, both Army and Navy, were about 164,000, in 1924 there were about 256,000, and in 1929 there were about 250,000. Our citizens' army, however, including the National Guard and other forms of reserves, increase these totals up to about 299,000 in 1914, about 672,000 in 1924, and about 728,000 in 1929.

Under the Kellogg pact we have undertaken never to use war as an instrument of national policy. We have, therefore, undertaken by covenant to use these equipments solely for defensive purposes. From a defense point of view our forces should be proportioned to national need and should, therefore, to some extent be modified by the prospects of peace, which were never brighter than to-day.

It should be borne in mind that the improvement in the National Guard by Federal support begun in 1920 has definitely strengthened our national security by rendering them far more effective than ever heretofore. The advance of aviation has also greatly increased our effectiveness in defense. In addition to the very large program of air forces which we are maintaining in the Army and Navy, there has been an enormous growth of commercial aviation. This has provided unanticipated reserves in manufacturing capacity and in industrial and air personnel, which again adds to our security.

I recommend that Congress give earnest consideration to the possibilities of prudent action which will give relief from our continuously mounting expenditures.

## FINANCES OF THE GOVERNMENT

The finances of the Government are in sound condition. I shall submit the detailed evidences and the usual recommendations in the special Budget message. I may, however, summarize our position. The public debt on June 30 this year stood at $16,931,000,000, compared to the maximum in August, 1919, of $26,596,000,000. Since June 30 it has been reduced by a further $238,000,000. In the Budget to be submitted the total appropriations recommended for the fiscal year 1931 are $3,830,445,231, as compared to $3,976,141,651 for the present fiscal year. The present fiscal year, however, includes $150,000,000 for the Federal Farm Board, as to which no estimate can as yet be determined for 1931.

Owing to the many necessary burdens assumed by Congress in previous years which now require large outlays, it is with extreme difficulty that we shall be able to keep the expenditures for the next fiscal year within the bounds of the present year. Economies in many directions have permitted some accommodation of pressing needs, the net result being an increase, as shown above, of about one-tenth of 1 per cent above the present fiscal year. We can not fail to recognize the obligations of the Government in support of the public welfare but we must coincidentally bear in mind the burden of taxes and strive to find relief through some tax reduction. Every dollar so returned fertilizes the soil of prosperity.

## TAX REDUCTION

The estimate submitted to me by the Secretary of the Treasury and the Budget Director indicates that the Government will close the fiscal year 1930 with a surplus of about $225,000,000 and the fiscal year 1931 with a surplus of about $123,000,000. Owing to unusual circumstances, it has been extremely difficult to estimate future revenues with accuracy.

I believe, however, that the Congress will be fully justified in giving the benefits of the prospective surpluses to the taxpayers, particularly as ample provision for debt reduction has been made in both years through the form of debt retirement from ordinary revenues. In view of the uncertainty in respect of future revenues and the comparatively small size of the indicated surplus in 1931, relief should take the form of a provisional revision of tax rates.

I recommend that the normal income tax rates applicable to the incomes of individuals for the calendar year 1929 be reduced from 5, 3, and 1½ per cent, to 4, 2, and ½ per cent, and that the tax on the income of corporations for the calendar year 1929 be reduced from 12 to 11 per cent. It is estimated that this will result in a reduction of $160,000,000 in income taxes to be collected during the calendar year 1930. The loss in revenue will be divided approximately equally between the fiscal years 1930 and 1931. Such a program will give a measure of tax relief to the maximum number of taxpayers, with relatively larger benefits to taxpayers with small or moderate incomes.

## FOREIGN DEBTS

The past year has brought us near to completion of settlements of the indebtedness of foreign governments to the United States.

The act of Congress approved February 4, 1929, authorized the settlement with the Government of Austria along lines similar to the terms of settlement offered by that Government to its other relief creditors. No agreement has yet been concluded with that government, but the form of agreement has been settled and its execution only awaits the Government of Austria securing the assent by all the other relief creditors of the terms offered. The act of Congress approved February 14, 1929, authorized the settlement with the Government of Greece, and an agreement was concluded on May 10, 1929.

The Government of France ratified the agreement with us on July 27, 1929. This agreement will shortly be before the Congress and I recommend its approval.

The only indebtedness of foreign governments to the United States now unsettled is that of Russia and Armenia.

During the past year a committee of distinguished experts under American leadership submitted a plan looking to a revision of claims against Germany by the various Governments. The United States denied itself any participation in the war settlement of general reparations and our claims are comparatively small in amount. They arise from costs of the army of occupation and claims of our private citizens for losses under awards from the Mixed Claims Commission established under agreement with the German Government. In finding a basis for settlement it was necessary for the committee of experts to request all the Governments concerned to make some contribution to the adjustment and we have felt that we should share a proportion of the concessions made.

The State and Treasury Departments will be in a position shortly to submit for your consideration a draft of an agreement to be executed between the United States and Germany providing for the payments of these revised amounts. A more extensive statement will be submitted at that time.

The total amount of indebtedness of the various countries to the United States now funded is $11,579,465,885. This sum was in effect provided by the issue of United States Government bonds to our own people. The payments of the various Governments to us on account of principal and interest for 1930 are estimated at a total of about $239,000,000, for 1931 at about $236,000,000, for 1932 at about $246,-000,000. The measure of American compromise in these settlements may be appreciated from the fact that our taxpayers are called upon to find annually about $475,000,000 in interest and in addition to redeem the principal of sums borrowed by the United States Government for these purposes.

## ALIEN ENEMY PROPERTY

The wise determination that this property seized in war should be returned to its owners has proceeded with considerable rapidity. Of the original seized cash and property (valued at a total of about $625,000,000), all but $111,566,700 has been returned. Most of the remainder should be disposed of during the next year.

## GENERAL ECONOMIC SITUATION

The country has enjoyed a large degree of prosperity and sound progress during the past year with a steady improvement in methods of production and distribution and consequent advancement in standards of living. Progress has, of course, been unequal among industries, and some, such as coal, lumber, leather, and textiles, still lag behind. The long upward trend of fundamental progress, however, gave rise to over-optimism as to profits, which translated itself into a wave of uncontrolled speculation in securities, resulting in the diversion of capital from business to the stock market and the inevitable crash. The natural consequences have been a reduction in the consumption of luxuries and semi-necessities by those who have met with losses, and a number of persons thrown temporarily out of employment. Prices of agricultural products dealt in upon the great markets have been affected in sympathy with the stock crash.

Fortunately, the Federal reserve system had taken measures to strengthen the position against the day when speculation would break, which together with the strong position of the banks has carried the whole credit system through the crisis without impairment. The capital which has been hitherto absorbed in stock-market loans for speculative purposes is now returning to the normal channels of business. There has been no inflation in the prices of commodities; there has been no undue accumulation of goods, and foreign trade has expanded to a magnitude which exerts a steadying influence upon activity in industry and employment.

The sudden threat of unemployment and especially the recollection of the economic consequences of previous crashes under a much less secured financial system created unwarranted pessimism and fear. It was recalled that past storms of similar character had resulted in retrenchment of construction, reduction of wages, and laying off of workers. The natural result was the tendency of business agencies throughout the country to pause in their plans and proposals for continuation and extension of their businesses, and this hesitation unchecked could in itself intensify into a depression with widespread unemployment and suffering.

I have, therefore, instituted systematic, voluntary measures of cooperation with the business institutions and with State and municipal authorities to make certain that fundamental businesses of the country shall continue as usual, that wages and therefore consuming power shall not be reduced, and that a special effort shall be made to expand construction work in order to assist in equalizing other deficits in employment. Due to the enlarged sense of cooperation and responsibility which has grown in the business world during the past few years the response has been remarkable and satisfactory. We have canvassed the Federal Government and instituted measures of prudent expansion in such work that should be helpful, and upon which the different departments will make some early recommendations to Congress.

I am convinced that through these measures we have reestablished confidence. Wages should remain stable. A very large degree of industrial unemployment and suffering which would otherwise have occurred has been prevented. Agricultural prices have reflected the returning confidence. The measures taken must be vigorously pursued until normal conditions are restored.

### AGRICULTURE

The agricultural situation is improving. The gross farm income as estimated by the Department of Agriculture for the crop season 1926-27 was $12,100,000,000; for 1927-28 it was $12,300,000,000; for 1928-29 it was $12,500,000,000; and estimated on the basis of prices since the last harvest the value of the 1929-30 crop would be over $12,650,000,000. The slight decline in general commodity prices during the past few years naturally assists the farmers' buying power.

The number of farmer bankruptcies is very materially decreased below previous years. The decline in land values now seems to be arrested and rate of movement from the farm to the city has been reduced. Not all sections of agriculture, of course, have fared equally, and some areas have suffered from drought. Responsible farm leaders have assured me that a large measure of confidence is returning to agriculture and that a feeling of optimism pervades that industry.

The most extensive action for strengthening the agricultural industry ever taken by any government was inaugurated through the farm marketing act of June 15 last. Under its provisions the Federal Farm Board has been established, comprised of men long and widely experienced in agriculture and sponsored by the farm organizations of the country. During its short period of existence the board has taken definite steps toward a more efficient organization of agriculture, toward the elimination of waste in marketing, and toward the upbuilding of farmers' marketing organizations on sounder and more efficient lines. Substantial headway has been made in the organization of four of the basic commodities—grain, cotton, livestock, and wool. Support by the board to cooperative marketing organizations and other board activities undoubtedly have served to steady the farmers' market during the recent crisis and have operated also as a great stimulus to the cooperative organization of agriculture. The problems of the industry are most complex, and the need for sound organization is imperative. Yet the board is moving rapidly along the lines laid out for it in the act, facilitating the creation by farmers of farmer-owned and farmer-controlled organizations and federating them into central institutions, with a view to increasing the bargaining power of agriculture, preventing and controlling surpluses, and mobilizing the economic power of agriculture.

## The Tariff

The special session of Congress was called to expedite the fulfillment of party pledges of agricultural relief and the tariff. The pledge of farm relief has been carried out. At that time I stated the principles upon which I believed action should be taken in respect to the tariff:

"An effective tariff upon agricultural products, that will compensate the farmer's higher costs and higher standards of living, has a dual purpose. Such a tariff not only protects the farmer in our domestic market but it also stimulates him to diversify his crops and to grow products that he could not otherwise produce, and thus lessens his dependence upon exports to foreign markets. The great expansion of production abroad under the conditions I have mentioned renders foreign competition in our export markets increasingly serious. It seems but natural, therefore, that the American farmer, having been greatly handicapped in his foreign market by such competition from the younger expanding countries, should ask that foreign access to our domestic market should be regulated by taking into account the differences in our costs of production. . . .

"In considering the tariff for other industries than agriculture, we find that there have been economic shifts necessitating a readjustment of some of the tariff schedules. Seven years of experience under the tariff bill enacted in 1922 have demonstrated the wisdom of Congress in the enactment of that measure. On the whole it has worked well. In the main our wages have been maintained at high levels; our exports and imports have steadily increased; with some exceptions our manufacturing industries have been prosperous. Nevertheless, economic changes have taken place during that time which have placed certain domestic products at a disadvantage and new industries have come into being, all of which create the necessity for some limited changes in the schedules and in the administrative clauses of the laws as written in 1922.

"It would seem to me that the test of necessity for revision is, in the main, whether there has been a substantial slackening of activity in an industry during the past few years, and a consequent decrease of employment due to insurmountable competition in the products of that industry.   It is not as if we were setting up a new basis of protective duties.   We did that seven years ago.   What we need to remedy now is whatever substantial loss of employment may have resulted from shifts since that time. . . .

"In determining changes in our tariff we must not fail to take into account the broad interests of the country as a whole, and such interests include our trade relations with other countries."

No condition has arisen in my view to change these principles stated at the opening of the special session.   I am firmly of the opinion that their application to the pending revision will give the country the kind of a tariff law it both needs and wants.   It would be most helpful if action should be taken at an early moment, more especially at a time when business and agriculture are both cooperating to minimize future uncertainties.   It is just that they should know what the rates are to be.

Even a limited revision requires the consideration and readjustment of many items.   The exhaustive inquiries and valuable debate from men representative of all parts of the country which is needed to determine the detailed rates must necessarily be accomplished in the Congress.   However perfectly this rate structure may be framed at any given time, the shifting of economic forces which inevitably occurs will render changes in some items desirable between the necessarily long intervals of congressional revision.   Injustices are bound to develop, such as were experienced by the dairymen, the flaxseed producers, the glass industry, and others, under the 1922 rates.   For this reason, I have been most anxious that the broad principle of the flexible tariff as provided in the existing law should be preserved and its delays in action avoided by more expeditious methods of determining the costs of production at home and abroad, with executive authority to promulgate such changes upon recommendation of the Tariff Commission after exhaustive investigation.   Changes by the Congress in the isolated items such as those to which I have referred would have been most unlikely both because of the concentrations of oppositions in the country, who could see no advantage to their own industry or State, and because of the difficulty of limiting consideration by the Congress to such isolated cases.

There is no fundamental conflict between the interests of the farmer and the worker.   Lowering of the standards of living of either tends to destroy the other.   The prosperity of one rests upon the well-being of the other.   Nor is there any real conflict between the East and the West or the North and the South in the United States.   The complete interlocking of economic dependence, the common striving for social and spiritual progress, our common heritage as Americans, and the infinite web of national sentiment, have created a solidarity in a great people unparalleled in all human history. These invisible bonds should not and can not be shattered by differences of opinion growing out of discussion of a tariff.

## PUBLIC BUILDINGS

Under the provisions of various acts of Congress $300,000,000 has been authorized for public buildings and the land upon which to construct them, being $75,000,000 for the District of Columbia and $225,000,000 for the country at large. Excluding $25,000,000 which is for the acquisition of land in the so-called "triangle" in this city, this public building legislation provides for a five-year program for the District of Columbia and between an eight and nine year program for the country at large. Of this sum approximately $27,400,000 was expended up to June 30 last, of which $11,400,000 has been expended in the District and $16,000,000 outside.

Even this generous provision for both the District of Columbia and the country is insufficient for most pressing governmental needs. Expensive rents and inadequate facilities are extravagance and not economy. In the District even after the completion of these projects we shall have fully 20,000 clerks housed in rented and temporary war buildings which can last but a little longer.

I therefore recommend that consideration should be given to the extension of authorizations both for the country at large and for the District of Columbia again distributed over a term of years. A survey of the need in both categories has been made by the Secretary of the Treasury and the Postmaster General. It would be helpful in the present economic situation if such steps were taken as would enable early construction work.

An expedition and enlargement of the program in the District would bring about direct economies in construction by enabling the erection of buildings in regular sequence. By maintaining a stable labor force in the city, contracts can be made on more advantageous terms.

The earlier completion of this program which is an acknowledged need would add dignity to the celebration in 1932 of the two hundredth anniversary of the birth of President Washington.

In consideration of these projects which contribute so much to dignify the National Capital I should like to renew the suggestion that the Fine Arts Commission should be required to pass upon private buildings which are proposed for sites facing upon public buildings and parks. Without such control much of the effort of the Congress in beautification of the Capital will be minimized.

## THE WATERWAYS AND FLOOD CONTROL

The development of inland waterways has received new impulse from the completion during this year of the canalization of the Ohio to a uniform 9-foot depth. The development of the other segments of the Mississippi system should be expedited and with this in view I am recommending an increase in appropriations for rivers and harbors from $50,000,000 to $55,000,000 per annum which, together with about $4,000,000 per annum released by completion of the Ohio, should make available after providing for other river and harbor works a sum of from $25,000,000 to $30,000,000 per annum for the Mississippi system and thus bring it to early completion.

Conflict of opinion which has arisen over the proposed floodway from the Arkansas River to the Gulf of Mexico via the Atchafalaya River has led me to withhold construction upon this portion of the Mississippi flood control plan until it could be again reviewed by the engineers for any further recommendation to Congress. The other portions of the project are being vigorously prosecuted and I have recommended an increase in appropriations for this from $30,000,000 of the present year to $35,000,000 during the next fiscal year.

Expansion of our intracoastal waterways to effective barge depths is well warranted. We are awaiting the action of Canada upon the St. Lawrence waterway project.

## HIGHWAYS

There are over 3,000,000 miles of legally established highways in the United States, of which about 10 per cent are included in the State highway systems, the remainder being county and other local roads. About 626,000 miles have been improved with some type of surfacing, comprising some 63 per cent of the State highway systems and 16 per cent of the local roads. Of the improved roads about 102,000 miles are hard surfaced, comprising about 22 per cent of the State highway systems and about 8 per cent of the local roads.

While proper planning should materially reduce the listed mileage of public roads, particularly in the agricultural districts, and turn these roads back to useful purposes, it is evident that road construction must be a long-continued program. Progress in improvement is about 50,000 miles of all types per annum, of which some 12,000 miles are of the more durable types. The total expenditures of Federal, State, and local governments last year for construction and maintenance assumed the huge total of $1,660,000,000.

Federal aid in the construction of the highway systems in conjunction with the States has proved to be beneficial and stimulating. We must ultimately give consideration to the increase of our contribution to these systems, particularly with a view to stimulating the improvement of farm-to-market roads.

## POST OFFICE

Our Post Office deficit has now increased to over $80,000,000 a year, of which perhaps $14,000,000 is due to losses on ocean mail and air mail contracts. The department is making an exhaustive study of the sources of the deficit with view to later recommendation to Congress in respect to it.

The Post Office quarters are provided in part by the Federal construction, in part by various forms of rent and lease arrangements. The practice has grown up in recent years of contracting long term leases under which both rent and amortization principal cost of buildings is included. I am advised that fully 40 per cent could be saved from many such rent and lease agreements even after allowing interest on the capital required at the normal Government rate. There are also many objectionable features to some of these practices. The provision of adequate quarters for the Post Office should be put on a sound basis.

A revision of air mail rates upon a more systematic and permanent footing is necessary. The subject is under study, and if legislation should prove necessary the subject will be presented to the Congress. In the meantime I recommend that the Congress should consider the desirability of authorizing further expansion of the South American services.

## COMMERCIAL AVIATION

During the past year progress in civil aeronautics has been remarkable. This is to a considerable degree due to the wise assistance of the Federal Government through the establishment and maintenance of airways by the Department of Commerce and the mail contracts from the Post Office Department. The Government-improved airways now exceed 25,000 miles—more than 14,000 miles of which will be lighted and equipped for night-flying operations by the close of the current year. Airport construction through all the States is extremely active. There are now 1,000 commercial and municipal airports in operation with an additional 1,200 proposed for early development.

Through this assistance the Nation is building a sound aviation system, operated by private enterprise. Over 6,400 planes are in commercial use, and 9,400 pilots are licensed by the Government. Our manufacturing capacity has risen to 7,500 planes per annum.

The aviation companies have increased regular air transportation until it now totals 90,000 miles per day—one-fourth of which is flown by night. Mail and express services now connect our principal cities, and extensive services for passenger transportation have been inaugurated, and others of importance are imminent. American air lines now reach into Canada and Mexico, to Cuba, Porto Rico, Central America, and most of the important countries of South America.

## RAILWAYS

As a whole, the railroads never were in such good physical and financial condition, and the country has never been so well served by them. The greatest volume of freight traffic ever tendered is being carried at a speed never before attained and with satisfaction to the shippers. Efficiencies and new methods have resulted in reduction in the cost of providing freight transportation, and freight rates show a continuous descending line from the level enforced by the World War.

We have, however, not yet assured for the future that adequate system of transportation through consolidations which was the objective of the Congress in the transportation act. The chief purpose of consolidation is to secure well-balanced systems with more uniform and satisfactory rate structure, a more stable financial structure, more equitable distribution of traffic, greater efficiency, and single-line instead of multiple-line hauls. In this way the country will have the assurance of better service and ultimately at lower and more even rates than would otherwise be attained. Legislation to simplify and expedite consolidation methods and better to protect public interest should be enacted.

Consideration should also be given to relief of the members of the Commission from the necessity of detailed attention to comparatively inconsequential matters which, under the existing law, must receive their direct and personal consideration. It is in the public interest that the members of the Commission should not be so pressed by minor matters that they have inadequate time for investigation and consideration of the larger questions committed to them for solution. As to many of these minor matters, the function of the Commission might well be made revisory, and the primary responsibility delegated to subordinate officials after the practice long in vogue in the executive departments.

## MERCHANT MARINE

Under the impulse of the merchant marine act of 1928 the transfer to private enterprise of the Government-owned steamship lines is going forward with increasing success. The Shipping Board now operates about 18 lines, which is less than half the number originally established, and the estimate of expenditures for the coming fiscal year is based upon reduction in losses on Government lines by approximately one-half. Construction loans have been made to the amount of approximately $75,000,000 out of the revolving fund authorized by Congress and have furnished an additional aid to American shipping and further stimulated the building of vessels in American yards.

Desirous of securing the full values to the Nation of the great effort to develop our merchant marine by the merchant marine act soon after the inauguration of the present administration, I appointed an interdepartmental committee, consisting of the Secretary of Commerce, as chairman, the Secretary of the Navy, the Postmaster General, and the chairman of the Shipping Board, to make a survey of the policies being pursued under the act of 1928 in respect of mail contracts; to inquire into its workings and to advise the Postmaster General in the administration of the act.

In particular it seemed to me necessary to determine if the result of the contracts already let would assure the purpose expressed in the act, "to further develop an American merchant marine, to assure its permanence in the transportation of the foreign trade of the United States, and for other purposes," and to develop a coordinated policy by which these purposes may be translated into actualities.

In review of the mail contracts already awarded it was found that they aggregated 25 separate awards imposing a governmental obligation of a little over $12,000,000 per annum. Provision had been imposed in five of the contracts for construction of new vessels with which to replace and expand services. These requirements come to a total of 12 vessels in the 10-year period, aggregating 122,000 tons. Some other conditions in the contracts had not worked out satisfactorily.

That study has now been substantially completed and the committee has advised the desirability and the necessity of securing much larger undertakings as to service and new construction in future contracts. The committee at this time is recommending the advertising of 14 additional routes, making substantial requirements for the construction of new vessels during the life of each contract recommended. A total of 40 new vessels will be required under the contracts proposed, about half of which will be required to be built during the next three years. The capital cost of this new construction will be approximately $250,000,000, involving approximately 460,000 gross tons. Should bidders be found who will make these undertakings, it will be necessary to recommend to Congress an increase in the authorized expenditure by the Post Office of about $5,500,000 annually. It will be most advantageous to grant such an authority.

A conflict as to the administration of the act has arisen in the contention of persons who have purchased Shipping Board vessels that they are entitled to mail contracts irrespective of whether they are the lowest bidder, the Post Office, on the other hand, being required by law to let contracts in that manner. It is urgent that Congress should clarify this situation.

## THE BANKING SYSTEM

It is desirable that Congress should consider the revision of some portions of the banking law.

The development of "group" and "chain" banking presents many new problems. The question naturally arises as to whether if allowed to expand without restraint these methods would dangerously concentrate control of credit, and whether they would not in any event seriously threaten one of the fundamentals of the American credit system—which is that credit which is based upon banking deposits should be controlled by persons within those areas which furnish these deposits and thus be subject to the restraints of local interest and public opinion in those areas. To some degree, however, this movement of chain or group banking is a groping for stronger support to the banks and a more secure basis for these institutions.

The growth in size and stability of the metropolitan banks is in marked contrast to the trend in the country districts, with its many failures and the losses these failures have imposed upon the agricultural community.

The relinquishment of charters of national banks in great commercial centers in favor of State charters indicates that some conditions surround the national banks which render them unable to compete with State banks; and their withdrawal results in weakening our national banking system.

It has been proposed that permission should be granted to national banks to engage in branch banking of a nature that would preserve within limited regions the local responsibility and the control of such credit institutions.

All these subjects, however, require careful investigation, and it might be found advantageous to create a joint commission embracing Members of the Congress and other appropriate Federal officials for subsequent report.

## ELECTRICAL POWER REGULATION

The Federal Power Commission is now comprised of three Cabinet officers, and the duties involved in the competent conduct of the growing responsibilities of this commission far exceed the time and attention which these officials can properly afford from other important duties. I recommend that authority be given for the appointment of full-time commissioners to replace them.

It is also desirable that the authority of the commission should be extended to certain phases of power regulation. The nature of the electric utilities industry is such that about 90 per cent of all power generation and distribution is intrastate in character, and most of the States have developed their own regulatory systems as to certificates of convenience, rates, and profits of such utilities. To encroach upon their authorities and responsibilities would be an encroachment upon the rights of the States. There are cases, however, of interstate character beyond the jurisdiction of the States. To meet these cases it would be most desirable if a method could be worked out by which initial action may be taken between the commissions of the States whose joint action should be made effective by the Federal Power Commission with a reserve to act on its own motion in case of disagreement or nonaction by the States.

## The Radio Commission

I recommend the reorganization of the Radio Commission into a permanent body from its present temporary status. The requirement of the present law that the commissioners shall be appointed from specified zones should be abolished and a general provision made for their equitable selection from different parts of the country. Despite the effort of the commissioners, the present method develops a public insistence that the commissioners are specially charged with supervision of radio affairs in the zone from which each is appointed. As a result there is danger that the system will degenerate from a national system into five regional agencies with varying practices, varying policies, competitive tendencies, and consequent failure to attain its utmost capacity for service to the people as a whole.

## Muscle Shoals

It is most desirable that this question should be disposed of. Under present conditions the income from these plants is less than could otherwise be secured for its use, and more especially the public is not securing the full benefits which could be obtained from them.

It is my belief that such parts of these plants as would be useful and the revenues from the remainder should be dedicated for all time to the farmers of the United States for investigation and experimentation on a commercial scale in agricultural chemistry. By such means advancing discoveries of science can be systematically applied to agricultural need, and development of the chemical industry of the Tennessee Valley can be assured.

I do not favor the operation by the Government of either power or manufacturing business except as an unavoidable by-product of some other major public purpose.

Any form of settlement of this question will imply entering upon a contract or contracts for the lease of the plants either as a whole or in parts and the reservation of facilities, products, or income for agricultural purposes. The extremely technical and involved nature of such contracts dealing with chemical and electrical enterprises, added to the unusual difficulties surrounding these special plants, and the rapid commercial changes now in progress in power and synthetic nitrogen manufacture, lead me to suggest that Congress create a special commission, not to investigate and report as in the past, but with authority to negotiate and complete some sort of contract or contracts on behalf of the Government, subject, of course, to such general requirements as Congress may stipulate.

## BOULDER DAM

The Secretary of the Interior is making satisfactory progress in negotiation of the very complex contracts required for the sale of the power to be generated at this project. These contracts must assure the return of all Government outlays upon the project. I recommend that the necessary funds be appropriated for the initiation of this work as soon as the contracts are in the hands of Congress.

## CONSERVATION

Conservation of national resources is a fixed policy of the Government. Three important questions bearing upon conservation of the public lands have become urgent.

Conservation of our oil and gas resources against future need is a national necessity. The working of the oil permit system in development of oil and gas resources on the public domain has been subject to great abuse. I considered it necessary to suspend the issuance of such permits and to direct the review of all outstanding permits as to compliance of the holders with the law. The purpose was not only to end such abuse but to place the Government in position to review the entire subject.

We are also confronted with a major problem in conservation due to the overgrazing on public lands. The effect of overgrazing (which has now become general) is not only to destroy the ranges but by impairing the ground coverage seriously to menace the water supply in many parts of the West through quick run-off, spring floods, and autumn drought.

We have a third problem of major dimensions in the reconsideration of our reclamation policy. The inclusion of most of the available lands of the public domain in existing or planned reclamation projects largely completes the original purpose of the Reclamation Service. There still remains the necessity for extensive storage of water in the arid States which renders it desirable that we should give a wider vision and purpose to this service.

To provide for careful consideration of these questions and also of better division of responsibilities in them as between the State and Federal Governments, including the possible transfer to the States for school purposes of the lands unreserved for forests, parks, power, minerals, etc., I have appointed a Commission on Conservation of the Public Domain, with a membership representing the major public land States and at the same time the public at large. I recommend that Congress should authorize a moderate sum to defray their expenses.

## SOCIAL SERVICE

The Federal Government provides for an extensive and valuable program of constructive social service, in education, home building, protection to women and children, employment, public health, recreation, and many other directions.

In a broad sense Federal activity in these directions has been confined to research and dissemination of information and experience, and at most to temporary subsidies to the States in order to secure uniform advancement in practice and methods. Any other attitude by the Federal Government will undermine one of the most precious possessions of the American people; that is, local and individual responsibility. We should adhere to this policy.

Federal officials can, however, make a further and most important contribution by leadership in stimulation of the community and voluntary agencies, and by extending Federal assistance in organization of these forces and bringing about cooperation among them.

As an instance of this character, I have recently, in cooperation with the Secretaries of Interior and Labor, laid the foundations of an exhaustive inquiry into the facts precedent to a nation-wide White House conference on child health and protection. This cooperative movement among interested agencies will impose no expense upon the Government. Similar nation-wide conferences will be called in connection with better housing and recreation at a later date.

In view of the considerable difference of opinion as to the policies which should be pursued by the Federal Government with respect to education, I have appointed a committee representative of the important educational associations and others to investigate and present recommendations. In cooperation with the Secretary of the Interior, I have also appointed a voluntary committee of distinguished membership to assist in a nation-wide movement for abolition of illiteracy.

I have recommended additional appropriations for the Federal employment service in order that it may more fully cover its cooperative work with State and local services. I have also recommended additional appropriations for the Women's and Children's Bureaus for much-needed research as to facts which I feel will prove most helpful.

## Public Health

The advance in scientific discovery as to disease and health imposes new considerations upon us. The Nation as a whole is vitally interested in the health of all the people; in protection from spread of contagious disease; in the relation of physical and mental disabilities to criminality; and in the economic and moral advancement which is fundamentally associated with sound body and mind. The organization of preventive measures and health education in its personal application is the province of public health service. Such organization should be as universal as public education. Its support is a proper burden upon the taxpayer. It can not be organized with success, either in its sanitary or educational phases, except under public authority. It should be based upon local and State responsibility, but I consider that the Federal Government has an obligation of contribution to the establishment of such agencies.

In the practical working out of organization, exhaustive experiment and trial have demonstrated that the base should be competent organization of the municipality, county, or other local unit. Most of our municipalities and some 400 rural counties out of 3,000 now have some such unit organization. Where highly developed, a health unit comprises at least a physician, sanitary engineer, and community nurse with the addition, in some cases, of another nurse devoted to the problems of maternity and children. Such organization gives at once a fundamental control of preventive measures and assists in community instruction. The Federal Government, through its interest in control of contagion, acting through the United States Public Health Service and the State agencies, has in the past and should in the future concern itself with this development, particularly in the many rural sections which are unfortunately far behind in progress. Some parts of the funds contributed under the Sheppard-Towner Act through the Children's Bureau of the Department of Labor have also found their way into these channels.

I recommend to the Congress that the purpose of the Sheppard-Towner Act should be continued through the Children's Bureau for a limited period of years; and that the Congress should consider the desirability of confining the use of Federal funds by the States to the building up of such county or other local units, and that such outlay should be positively coordinated with the funds expended through the United States Public Health Service directed to other phases of the same county or other local unit organization. All funds appropriated should of course be applied through the States, so that the public health program of the county or local unit will be efficiently coordinated with that of the whole State.

## FEDERAL PRISONS

Closely related to crime conditions is the administration of the Federal prison system. Our Federal penal institutions are overcrowded, and this condition is daily becoming worse. The parole and probation systems are inadequate. These conditions make it impossible to perform the work of personal reconstruction of prisoners so as to prepare them for return to the duties of citizenship. In order to relieve the pressing evils I have directed the temporary transfer of the Army Disciplinary Barracks at Leavenworth to the Department of Justice for use as a Federal prison. Not only is this temporary but it is inadequate for present needs.

We need some new Federal prisons and a reorganization of our probation and parole systems; and there should be established in the Department of Justice a Bureau of Prisons with a sufficient force to deal adequately with the growing activities of our prison institutions. Authorization for the improvements should be given speedily, with initial appropriations to allow the construction of the new institutions to be undertaken at once.

## IMMIGRATION

Restriction of immigration has from every aspect proved a sound national policy. Our pressing problem is to formulate a method by which the limited number of immigrants whom we do welcome shall be adapted to our national setting and our national needs.

I have been opposed to the basis of the quotas now in force and I have hoped that we could find some practical method to secure what I believe should be our real national objective; that is, fitness of the immigrant as to physique, character, training, and our need of service. Perhaps some system of priorities within the quotas could produce these results and at the same time enable some hardships in the present system to be cleared up. I recommend that the Congress should give the subject further study, in which the executive departments will gladly cooperate with the hope of discovering such method as will more fully secure our national necessities.

## VETERANS

It has been the policy of our Government almost from its inception to make provision for the men who have been disabled in defense of our country. This policy should be maintained. Originally it took the form of land grants and pensions. This system continued until our entry into the World War. The Congress at that time inaugurated a new plan of compensation, rehabilitation, hospitalization, medical care and treatment, and insurance, whereby benefits were awarded to those veterans and their immediate dependents whose disabilities were attributable to their war service. The basic principle in this legislation is sound.

In a desire to eliminate all possibilities of injustice due to difficulties in establishing service connection of disabilities, these principles have been to some degree extended. Veterans whose diseases or injuries have become apparent within a brief period after the war are now receiving compensation; insurance benefits have been liberalized. Emergency officers are now receiving additional benefits. The doors of the Government's hospitals have been opened to all veterans, even though their diseases or injuries were not the result of their war service. In addition adjusted service certificates have been issued to 3,433,300 veterans. This in itself will mean an expenditure of nearly $3,500,-000,000 before 1945, in addition to the $600,000,000 which we are now appropriating annually for our veterans' relief.

The administration of all laws concerning the veterans and their dependents has been upon the basis of dealing generously, humanely, and justly. While some inequalities have arisen, substantial and adequate care has been given and justice administered. Further improvement in administration may require some amendment from time to time to the law, but care should be taken to see that such changes conform to the basic principles of the legislation.

I am convinced that we will gain in efficiency, economy, and more uniform administration and better definition of national policies if the Pension Bureau, the National Home for Volunteer Soldiers, and the Veterans' Bureau are brought together under a single agency. The total appropriations to these agencies now exceed $800,000,000 per annum.

## CIVIL SERVICE

Approximately four-fifths of all the employees in the executive civil service now occupy positions subject to competitive examination under the civil service law.

There are, however, still commanding opportunities for extending the system. These opportunities lie within the province of Congress and not the President. I recommend that a further step be taken by authorization that appointments of third-class postmasters be made under the civil service law.

## DEPARTMENTAL REORGANIZATION

This subject has been under consideration for over 20 years. It was promised by both political parties in the recent campaign. It has been repeatedly examined by committees and commissions—congressional, executive, and voluntary. The conclusions of these investigations have been unanimous that reorganization is a necessity of sound administration; of economy; of more effective governmental policies and of relief to the citizen from unnecessary harassment in his relations with a multitude of scattered governmental agencies. But the presentation of any specific plan at once enlivens opposition from every official whose authority may be curtailed or who fears his position is imperiled by such a result; of bureaus and departments which wish to maintain their authority and activities; of citizens and their organizations who are selfishly interested, or who are inspired by fear that their favorite bureau may, in a new setting, be less subject to their influence or more subject to some other influence.

It seems to me that the essential principles of reorganization are two in number. First, all administrative activities of the same major purpose should be placed in groups under single-headed responsibility; second, all executive and administrative functions should be separated from boards and commissions and placed under individual responsibility, while quasilegislative and quasijudicial and broadly advisory functions should be removed from individual authority and assigned to boards and commissions. Indeed, these are the fundamental principles upon which our Government was founded, and they are the principles which have been adhered to in the whole development of our business structure, and they are the distillation of the common sense of generations.

For instance, the conservation of national resources is spread among eight agencies in five departments. They suffer from conflict and overlap. There is no proper development and adherence to broad national policies and no central point where the searchlight of public opinion may concentrate itself. These functions should be grouped under the direction of some such official as an assistant secretary of conservation. The particular department or cabinet officer under which such a group should be placed is of secondary importance to the need of concentration. The same may be said of educational services, of merchant marine aids, of public works, of public health, of veterans' services, and many others, the component parts of which are widely scattered in the various departments and independent agencies. It is desirable that we first have experience with these different groups in action before we create new departments. These may be necessary later on.

With this background of all previous experience I can see no hope for the development of a sound reorganization of the Government unless Congress be willing to delegate its authority over the problem (subject to defined principles) to the Executive, who should act upon approval of a joint committee of Congress or with the reservation of power of revision by Congress within some limited period adequate for its consideration.

## PROHIBITION

The first duty of the President under his oath of office is to secure the enforcement of the laws. The enforcement of the laws enacted to give effect to the eighteenth amendment is far from satisfactory and this is in part due to the inadequate organization of the administrative agencies of the Federal Government. With the hope of expediting such reorganization, I requested on June 6 last that Congress should appoint a joint committee to collaborate with executive agencies in preparation of legislation. It would be helpful if it could be so appointed. The subject has been earnestly considered by the Law Enforcement Commission and the administrative officials of the Government. Our joint conclusions are that certain steps should be taken at once. First, there should be an immediate concentration of responsibility and strengthening of enforcement agencies of the Federal Government by transfer to the Department of Justice of the Federal functions of detection and to a considerable degree of prosecution, which are now lodged in the Prohibition Bureau in the Treasury; and at the same time the control of the distribution of industrial alcohol and legalized beverages should remain in the Treasury. Second, provision should be made for relief of congestion in the Federal courts by modifying and simplifying the procedure for dealing with the large volume of petty prosecutions under various Federal acts. Third, there should be a codification of the laws relating to prohibition to avoid the necessity which now exists of resorting to more than 25 statutes enacted at various times over 40 years. Technical defects in these statutes that have been disclosed should be cured. I would add to these recommendations the desirability of reorganizing the various services engaged in the prevention of smuggling into one border patrol under the Coast Guard. Further recommendations upon the subject as a whole will be developed after further examination by the Law Enforcement Commission, but it is not to be expected that any criminal law will ever be fully enforced so long as criminals exist.

The District of Columbia should be the model of city law enforcement in the Nation. While conditions here are much better than in many other cities, they are far from perfect, and this is due in part to the congestion of criminal cases in the Supreme Court of the District, resulting in long delays. Furthermore, there is need for legislation in the District supplementing the national prohibition act, more sharply defining and enlarging the duties and powers of the District Commissioners and the police of the District, and opening the way for better cooperation in the enforcement of prohibition between the District officials and the prohibition officers of the Federal Government. It is urgent that these conditions be remedied.

## LAW ENFORCEMENT AND OBSERVANCE

No one will look with satisfaction upon the volume of crime of all kinds and the growth of organized crime in our country. We have pressing need so to organize our system of administering criminal justice as to establish full vigor and effectiveness. We need to reestablish faith that the highest interests of our country are served by insistence upon the swift and even-handed administration of justice to all offenders, whether they be rich or poor. That we shall effect improvement is vital to the preservation of our institutions. It is the most serious issue before our people.

Under the authority of Congress I have appointed a National Commission on Law Observance and Enforcement, for an exhaustive study of the entire problem of the enforcement of our laws and the improvement of our judicial system, including the special problems and abuses growing out of the prohibition laws. The commission has been invited to make the widest inquiry into the shortcomings of the administration of justice and into the causes and remedies for them. It has organized its work under subcommittees dealing with the many contributory causes of our situation and has enlisted the aid of investigators in fields requiring special consideration. I am confident that as a result of its studies now being carried forward it will make a notable contribution to the solution of our pressing problems.

Pending further legislation, the Department of Justice has been striving to weed out inefficiency wherever it exists, to stimulate activity on the part of its prosecuting officers, and to use increasing care in examining into the qualifications of those appointed to serve as prosecutors. The department is seeking systematically to strengthen the law enforcement agencies week by week and month by month, not by dramatic displays but by steady pressure; by removal of negligent officials and by encouragement and assistance to the vigilant. During the course of these efforts it has been revealed that in some districts causes contributing to the congestion of criminal dockets, and to delays and inefficiency in prosecutions, have been lack of sufficient forces in the offices of United States attorneys, clerks of courts, and marshals. These conditions tend to clog the machinery of justice.

The last conference of senior circuit judges has taken note of them and indorsed the department's proposals for improvement. Increases in appropriations are necessary and will be asked for in order to reenforce these offices.

The orderly administration of the law involves more than the mere machinery of law enforcement. The efficient use of that machinery and a spirit in our people in support of law are alike essential. We have need for improvement in both. However much we may perfect the mechanism, still if the citizen who is himself dependent upon some laws for the protection of all that he has and all that he holds dear, shall insist on selecting the particular laws which he will obey, he undermines his own safety and that of his country. His attitude may obscure, but it can not conceal, the ugly truth that the lawbreaker, whoever he may be, is the enemy of society. We can no longer gloss over the unpleasant reality which should be made vital in the consciousness of every citizen, that he who condones or traffics with crime, who is indifferent to it and to the punishment of the criminal, or to the lax performance of official duty, is himself the most effective agency for the breakdown of society.

Law can not rise above its source in good citizenship—in what right-minded men most earnestly believe and desire. If the law is upheld only by Government officials, then all law is at an end. Our laws are made by the people themselves; theirs is the right to work for their repeal; but until repeal it is an equal duty to observe them and demand their enforcement.

I have been gratified at the awakening sense of this responsibility in our citizens during the past few months, and gratified that many instances have occurred which refuted the cynicism which has asserted that our system could not convict those who had defied the law and possessed the means to resist its execution. These things reveal a moral awakening both in the people and in officials which lies at the very foundation of the rule of law.

## Conclusion

The test of the rightfulness of our decisions must be whether we have sustained and advanced the ideals of the American people; self-government in its foundations of local government; justice whether to the individual or to the group; ordered liberty; freedom from domination; open opportunity and equality of opportunity; the initiative and individuality of our people; prosperity and the lessening of poverty; freedom of public opinion; education; advancement of knowledge; the growth of religious spirit; the tolerance of all faiths; the foundations of the home and the advancement of peace.

HERBERT HOOVER

THE WHITE HOUSE, December 3, 1929.

# LIST OF PAPERS

[Unless otherwise specified, the correspondence is *from* or *to* officials in the Department of State.]

## GENERAL

### PROPOSED ACCESSION OF THE UNITED STATES TO THE STATUTE OF THE PERMANENT COURT OF INTERNATIONAL JUSTICE

## GENERAL

PROPOSED ACCESSION OF THE UNITED STATES TO THE STATUTE OF THE PERMANENT COURT OF INTERNATIONAL JUSTICE—Continued

GENERAL

PROPOSED ACCESSION OF THE UNITED STATES TO THE STATUTE OF THE PERMA-
NENT COURT OF INTERNATIONAL JUSTICE—Continued

GENERAL

PROPOSED ACCESSION OF THE UNITED STATES TO THE STATUTE OF THE PERMA-
NENT COURT OF INTERNATIONAL JUSTICE—Continued

## GENERAL

PROPOSED ACCESSION OF THE UNITED STATES TO THE STATUTE OF THE PERMANENT COURT OF INTERNATIONAL JUSTICE—Continued

GENERAL

INFORMAL SUGGESTIONS FOR FURTHER IMPLEMENTING THE TREATY FOR THE
RENUNCIATION OF WAR, ETC.—Continued

GENERAL

PARTICIPATION OF THE UNITED STATES IN THE WORK OF THE PREPARATORY
COMMISSION FOR THE DISARMAMENT CONFERENCE, ETC.—Continued

GENERAL

PARTICIPATION OF THE UNITED STATES IN THE WORK OF THE PREPARATORY
COMMISSION FOR THE DISARMAMENT CONFERENCE, ETC.—Continued

## GENERAL

PARTICIPATION OF THE UNITED STATES IN THE WORK OF THE PREPARATORY
COMMISSION FOR THE DISARMAMENT CONFERENCE, ETC.—Continued

## GENERAL

PARTICIPATION OF THE UNITED STATES IN THE WORK OF THE PREPARATORY
COMMISSION FOR THE DISARMAMENT CONFERENCE, ETC.—Continued

GENERAL

PRELIMINARIES TO THE FIVE-POWER NAVAL CONFERENCE TO BE HELD AT
LONDON IN 1930—Continued

## GENERAL

GENERAL

PRELIMINARIES TO THE FIVE-POWER NAVAL CONFERENCE TO BE HELD AT
LONDON IN 1930—Continued

## GENERAL

PRELIMINARIES TO THE FIVE-POWER NAVAL CONFERENCE TO BE HELD AT
LONDON IN 1930—Continued

GENERAL

GENERAL

PRELIMINARIES TO THE FIVE-POWER NAVAL CONFERENCE TO BE HELD AT
LONDON IN 1930—Continued

## GENERAL

PRELIMINARIES TO THE FIVE-POWER NAVAL CONFERENCE TO BE HELD AT
LONDON IN 1930—Continued

## GENERAL

PRELIMINARIES TO THE FIVE-POWER NAVAL CONFERENCE TO BE HELD AT
LONDON IN 1930—Continued

# GENERAL

PRELIMINARIES TO THE FIVE-POWER NAVAL CONFERENCE TO BE HELD AT
LONDON IN 1930—Continued

# LIST OF PAPERS

## GENERAL

GENERAL

PRELIMINARIES TO THE FIVE-POWER NAVAL CONFERENCE TO BE HELD AT
LONDON IN 1930—Continued

## GENERAL

PRELIMINARIES TO THE FIVE-POWER NAVAL CONFERENCE TO BE HELD AT LONDON IN 1930—Continued

## GENERAL

PRELIMINARIES TO THE FIVE-POWER NAVAL CONFERENCE TO BE HELD AT
LONDON IN 1930—Continued

# GENERAL

# GENERAL

PRELIMINARIES TO THE FIVE-POWER NAVAL CONFERENCE TO BE HELD AT
LONDON IN 1930—Continued

GENERAL

Preliminaries to the Five-Power Naval Conference To Be Held at London in 1930—Continued

GENERAL

PRELIMINARIES TO THE FIVE-POWER NAVAL CONFERENCE TO BE HELD AT LONDON IN 1930—Continued

LIST OF PAPERS

## GENERAL

### INTERNATIONAL CONFERENCE ON SAFETY OF LIFE AT SEA, LONDON, APRIL 16–MAY 31, 1929—Continued

## GENERAL

AGREEMENTS FOR EXCHANGE OF INFORMATION REGARDING THE TRAFFIC IN
NARCOTIC DRUGS—Continued

CONFERENCE FOR THE SUPPRESSION OF COUNTERFEITING CURRENCY, HELD AT
GENEVA, APRIL 9–20, 1929

## GENERAL

## GENERAL

AMERICAN REPRESENTATION IN A CONSULTATIVE CAPACITY AT THE INTERNATIONAL CONFERENCE ON THE TREATMENT OF FOREIGNERS, PARIS, NOVEMBER 5–DECEMBER 5, 1929—Continued

## GENERAL

CONTINUATION OF NEGOTIATIONS WITH CERTAIN EUROPEAN COUNTRIES FOR AGREEMENTS AND TREATIES REGARDING NATURALIZATION, DUAL NATIONALITY, AND MILITARY SERVICE—Continued

## GENERAL

CONTINUATION OF NEGOTIATIONS WITH CERTAIN EUROPEAN COUNTRIES FOR AGREEMENTS AND TREATIES REGARDING NATURALIZATION, DUAL NATIONALITY, AND MILITARY SERVICE—Continued

### DENMARK

# GENERAL

CONTINUATION OF NEGOTIATIONS WITH CERTAIN EUROPEAN COUNTRIES FOR AGREEMENTS AND TREATIES REGARDING NATURALIZATION, DUAL NATIONALITY, AND MILITARY SERVICE—Continued.

## FRANCE

## GENERAL

CONTINUATION OF NEGOTIATIONS WITH CERTAIN EUROPEAN COUNTRIES FOR AGREEMENTS AND TREATIES REGARDING NATURALIZATION, DUAL NATIONALITY, AND MILITARY SERVICE—Continued

# GENERAL

Continuation of Negotiations With Certain European Countries for Agreements and Treaties Regarding Naturalization, Dual Nationality, and Military Service—Continued

NORWAY

## GENERAL

CONTINUATION OF NEGOTIATIONS WITH CERTAIN EUROPEAN COUNTRIES FOR AGREEMENTS AND TREATIES REGARDING NATURALIZATION, DUAL NATIONALITY, AND MILITARY SERVICE—Continued

PORTUGAL

## GENERAL

Continuation of Negotiations With Certain European Countries for Agreements and Treaties Regarding Naturalization, Dual Nationality, and Military Service—Continued

### SWEDEN

### YUGOSLAVIA

Protection of Women of American Nationality Married to Aliens and Having Dual Nationality

American Participation in the Extraordinary Session of the International Commission for Air Navigation at Paris, June 10–15, 1929, To Revise the Convention of October 13, 1919

## GENERAL

### AMERICAN PARTICIPATION IN THE EXTRAORDINARY SESSION OF THE INTERNATIONAL COMMISSION FOR AIR NAVIGATION AT PARIS, JUNE 10–15, 1929, TO REVISE THE CONVENTION OF OCTOBER 13, 1919

### NEGOTIATIONS WITH CERTAIN EUROPEAN COUNTRIES TO EFFECT ARRANGEMENTS COVERING CERTAIN QUESTIONS OF AERIAL NAVIGATION

#### GREAT BRITAIN

## GENERAL

#### NEGOTIATIONS WITH CERTAIN EUROPEAN COUNTRIES TO EFFECT ARRANGEMENTS COVERING CERTAIN QUESTIONS OF AERIAL NAVIGATION—Continued

## GENERAL

### NEGOTIATIONS WITH CERTAIN EUROPEAN COUNTRIES TO EFFECT ARRANGEMENTS COVERING CERTAIN QUESTIONS OF AERIAL NAVIGATION—Continued

GENERAL

NEGOTIATIONS WITH CERTAIN EUROPEAN COUNTRIES TO EFFECT ARRANGEMENTS
COVERING CERTAIN QUESTIONS OF AERIAL NAVIGATION—Continued

# GENERAL

# GENERAL

## GOOD OFFICES OF THE DEPARTMENT OF STATE IN BEHALF OF AMERICAN INTERESTS DESIRING TO ESTABLISH AIR LINES IN LATIN AMERICA

### PAN AMERICAN AIRWAYS, INCORPORATED

# GENERAL

## GENERAL

GOOD OFFICES OF THE DEPARTMENT OF STATE IN BEHALF OF AMERICAN INTERESTS
DESIRING TO ESTABLISH AIR LINES IN LATIN AMERICA—Continued

GENERAL

Good Offices of the Department of State in Behalf of American Interests Desiring To Establish Air Lines in Latin America—Continued

# GENERAL

GOOD OFFICES OF THE DEPARTMENT OF STATE IN BEHALF OF AMERICAN INTERESTS
DESIRING TO ESTABLISH AIR LINES IN LATIN AMERICA—Continued

## GENERAL

GOOD OFFICES OF THE DEPARTMENT OF STATE IN BEHALF OF AMERICAN INTERESTS
DESIRING TO ESTABLISH AIR LINES IN LATIN AMERICA—Continued

## GENERAL

GOOD OFFICES OF THE DEPARTMENT OF STATE IN BEHALF OF AMERICAN INTERESTS
DESIRING TO ESTABLISH AIR LINES IN LATIN AMERICA—Continued

# GENERAL

# GENERAL

GOOD OFFICES OF THE DEPARTMENT OF STATE IN BEHALF OF AMERICAN INTERESTS
DESIRING TO ESTABLISH AIR LINES IN LATIN AMERICA—Continued

## GENERAL

GOOD OFFICES OF THE DEPARTMENT OF STATE IN BEHALF OF AMERICAN INTERESTS
DESIRING TO ESTABLISH AIR LINES IN LATIN AMERICA—Continued

| Date and number | Subject | Page |
|---|---|---|
| **1929** Sept. 13 (105) | *To the Ambassador in Chile* (tel.) Information concerning the inauguration, October 12, of Pan American Airways extension air-mail service. | 586 |
| Sept. 13 (148) | *From the Chargé in Venezuela* (tel.) Suggestion that Pan American Airways be informed that it would be helpful to them if Colonel Lindbergh were to include Venezuela in his next flight. | 586 |
| Sept. 14 (171) | *From the Chargé in Peru* (tel.) Report of conversation with President Leguía concerning proposed conference between the Chilean Director General of Aviation and various aviation companies to take place on September 25, in which he stated that the Peruvian Government would be unable to participate because of its existing aviation commitments; urgent recommendation that Colonel Lindbergh come to Peru, not only for the resultant favorable effect on American aviation interests in Peru, but also for the support which would be given to the President at a time when opposition to American interests will be concentrated at Lima. | 586 |
| Sept. 16 (91) | *To the Chargé in Peru* (tel.) Necessity, in order to consider plans for Colonel Lindbergh to go to Peru, of being informed how long the conference scheduled for September 25 will last. | 587 |
| Sept. 17 (173) | *From the Chargé in Peru* (tel.) Observation that it was not expected that Colonel Lindbergh could be in Lima while the conference was in session; Chargé's desire, rather, to inform the President in advance and announce about September 25 that Colonel Lindbergh is coming to Peru in connection with Pan American-Grace Airways. | 587 |
| Sept. 17 (46) | *To the Chargé in Venezuela* (tel.) Plan of Colonel Lindbergh to stop in Venezuela on return flight from Paramaribo. | 588 |
| Sept. 18 (92) | *To the Chargé in Peru* (tel.) Authorization to inform President Leguía in confidence that Colonel Lindbergh will make a flight to South America during the winter; information that the Peruvian Embassy has extended him a tentative invitation to visit Peru; inquiry whether confidential statement to President Leguía will cover the situation or whether public announcement should be made. | 588 |
| Sept. 21 (175) | *From the Chargé in Peru* (tel.) Intention to inform President Leguía confidentially; hope that official announcement of Colonel Lindbergh's trip may come first as acceptance of Peruvian invitation and be initiated from Lima; doubt, therefore, that public announcement at present would be desirable. | 589 |
| Sept. 21 (281) | *From the Ambassador in Chile* Letter to the Foreign Minister, September 20 (text printed), suggesting that, if the Chilean Government feels that original decree concession is not sufficiently clear to permit the international mails to proceed from Buenos Aires via Uspallata, Chile, to the United States, it give the necessary assurances to that effect so that the air mail service to Buenos Aires may be opened on October 12 as scheduled. | 590 |

## GENERAL

GOOD OFFICES OF THE DEPARTMENT OF STATE IN BEHALF OF AMERICAN INTERESTS
DESIRING TO ESTABLISH AIR LINES IN LATIN AMERICA—Continued

# GENERAL

GOOD OFFICES OF THE DEPARTMENT OF STATE IN BEHALF OF AMERICAN INTERESTS
DESIRING TO ESTABLISH AIR LINES IN LATIN AMERICA—Continued

GENERAL

GOOD OFFICES OF THE DEPARTMENT OF STATE IN BEHALF OF AMERICAN INTERESTS
DESIRING TO ESTABLISH AIR LINES IN LATIN AMERICA—Continued

## GENERAL

## GENERAL

GOOD OFFICES OF THE DEPARTMENT OF STATE IN BEHALF OF AMERICAN INTERESTS
DESIRING TO ESTABLISH AIR LINES IN LATIN AMERICA—Continued

## GENERAL

GOOD OFFICES OF THE DEPARTMENT OF STATE IN BEHALF OF AMERICAN INTERESTS
DESIRING TO ESTABLISH AIR LINES IN LATIN AMERICA—Continued

## GENERAL

GOOD OFFICES OF THE DEPARTMENT OF STATE IN BEHALF OF AMERICAN INTEREST
DESIRING TO ESTABLISH AIR LINES IN LATIN AMERICA—Continued

## GENERAL

GOOD OFFICES OF THE DEPARTMENT OF STATE IN BEHALF OF AMERICAN INTERESTS
DESIRING TO ESTABLISH AIR LINES IN LATIN AMERICA—Continued

## GENERAL

GOOD OFFICES OF THE DEPARTMENT OF STATE IN BEHALF OF AMERICAN INTERESTS
DESIRING TO ESTABLISH AIR LINES IN LATIN AMERICA—Continued

## GENERAL

**GOOD OFFICES OF THE DEPARTMENT OF STATE IN BEHALF OF AMERICAN INTERESTS DESIRING TO ESTABLISH AIR LINES IN LATIN AMERICA—Continued**

## GENERAL

ARRANGEMENT BETWEEN THE UNITED STATES, CANADA, CUBA, AND NEWFOUND-
LAND RELATIVE TO THE ASSIGNMENT OF HIGH FREQUENCIES TO RADIO STATIONS
ON THE NORTH AMERICAN CONTINENT—Continued

OFFICIAL STATEMENT OF AND COMMENTARY UPON THE MONROE DOCTRINE BY
THE SECRETARY OF STATE

## GENERAL

TACNA-ARICA DISPUTE: GOOD OFFICES OF THE UNITED STATES IN THE FINAL SETTLEMENT OF ISSUES BETWEEN CHILE AND PERU; REPRESENTATIONS BY BOLIVIA

## GENERAL

TACNA-ARICA DISPUTE: GOOD OFFICES OF THE UNITED STATES IN THE FINAL SETTLEMENT OF ISSUES BETWEEN CHILE AND PERU; REPRESENTATIONS BY BOLIVIA—Continued

## GENERAL

TACNA-ARICA DISPUTE: GOOD OFFICES OF THE UNITED STATES IN THE FINAL SETTLEMENT OF ISSUES BETWEEN CHILE AND PERU; REPRESENTATIONS BY BOLIVIA—Continued

## GENERAL

TACNA-ARICA DISPUTE: GOOD OFFICES OF THE UNITED STATES IN THE FINAL SETTLEMENT OF ISSUES BETWEEN CHILE AND PERU; REPRESENTATIONS BY BOLIVIA—Continued

## GENERAL

TACNA-ARICA DISPUTE: GOOD OFFICES OF THE UNITED STATES IN THE FINAL SETTLEMENT OF ISSUES BETWEEN CHILE AND PERU; REPRESENTATIONS BY BOLIVIA—Continued

GENERAL

TACNA-ARICA DISPUTE: GOOD OFFICES OF THE UNITED STATES IN THE FINAL SETTLEMENT OF ISSUES BETWEEN CHILE AND PERU; REPRESENTATIONS BY BOLIVIA—Continued

GENERAL

TACNA-ARICA DISPUTE: GOOD OFFICES OF THE UNITED STATES IN THE FINAL SETTLEMENT OF ISSUES BETWEEN CHILE AND PERU; REPRESENTATIONS BY BOLIVIA—Continued

## GENERAL

TACNA-ARICA DISPUTE: GOOD OFFICES OF THE UNITED STATES IN THE FINAL
SETTLEMENT OF ISSUES BETWEEN CHILE AND PERU; REPRESENTATIONS BY
BOLIVIA—Continued

# GENERAL

Tacna-Arica Dispute: Good Offices of the United States in the Final Settlement of Issues Between Chile and Peru; Representations by Bolivia—Continued

## GENERAL

TACNA-ARICA DISPUTE: GOOD OFFICES OF THE UNITED STATES IN THE FINAL
SETTLEMENT OF ISSUES BETWEEN CHILE AND PERU; REPRESENTATIONS BY
BOLIVIA—Continued

GENERAL

TACNA-ARICA DISPUTE: GOOD OFFICES OF THE UNITED STATES IN THE FINAL SETTLEMENT OF ISSUES BETWEEN CHILE AND PERU; REPRESENTATIONS BY BOLIVIA—Continued

# GENERAL

TACNA-ARICA DISPUTE: GOOD OFFICES OF THE UNITED STATES IN THE FINAL SETTLEMENT OF ISSUES BETWEEN CHILE AND PERU; REPRESENTATIONS BY BOLIVIA—Continued

GENERAL

TACNA-ARICA DISPUTE: GOOD OFFICES OF THE UNITED STATES IN THE FINAL SETTLEMENT OF ISSUES BETWEEN CHILE AND PERU; REPRESENTATIONS BY BOLIVIA—Continued

## GENERAL

Tacna-Arica Dispute: Good Offices of the United States in the Final Settlement of Issues Between Chile and Peru; Representations by Bolivia—Continued

# GENERAL

TACNA-ARICA DISPUTE: GOOD OFFICES OF THE UNITED STATES IN THE FINAL
SETTLEMENT OF ISSUES BETWEEN CHILE AND PERU; REPRESENTATIONS BY
BOLIVIA—Continued

## GENERAL

Tacna-Arica Dispute: Good Offices of the United States in the Final Settlement of Issues Between Chile and Peru; Representations by Bolivia—Continued

The Chaco Dispute Between Bolivia and Paraguay

ADJUSTMENT OF DIFFERENCES BY COMMISSION OF INQUIRY AND CONCILIATION FOLLOWING INCIDENTS OF DECEMBER 1928

# GENERAL

THE CHACO DISPUTE BETWEEN BOLIVIA AND PARAGUAY—Continued

## GENERAL

THE CHACO DISPUTE BETWEEN BOLIVIA AND PARAGUAY—Continued

GENERAL

THE CHACO DISPUTE BETWEEN BOLIVIA AND PARAGUAY—Continued

GENERAL

THE CHACO DISPUTE BETWEEN BOLIVIA AND PARAGUAY—Continued

# GENERAL

## The Chaco Dispute Between Bolivia and Paraguay—Continued

## GENERAL

The Chaco Dispute Between Bolivia and Paraguay—Continued

GENERAL

The Chaco Dispute Between Bolivia and Paraguay—Continued

## GENERAL

### The Chaco Dispute Between Bolivia and Paraguay—Continued

## GENERAL

### THE CHACO DISPUTE BETWEEN BOLIVIA AND PARAGUAY—Continued

## GENERAL

### THE CHACO DISPUTE BETWEEN BOLIVIA AND PARAGUAY—Continued

# GENERAL

THE CHACO DISPUTE BETWEEN BOLIVIA AND PARAGUAY—Continued

# GENERAL

## The Chaco Dispute Between Bolivia and Paraguay—Continued

GENERAL

Boundary Disputes—Continued

GENERAL

BOUNDARY DISPUTES—Continued

DOMINICAN REPUBLIC AND HAITI

GENERAL

BOUNDARY DISPUTES—Continued

GENERAL

Boundary Disputes—Continued

# GENERAL

## BOUNDARY DISPUTES—Continued

## GENERAL

### BOUNDARY DISPUTES—Continued

## GENERAL

BOUNDARY DISPUTES—Continued

HONDURAS AND NICARAGUA

GENERAL

BOUNDARY DISPUTES—Continued

GENERAL

## GENERAL

# GENERAL

## PROPOSED ACCESSION OF THE UNITED STATES TO THE STATUTE OF THE PERMANENT COURT OF INTERNATIONAL JUSTICE [1]

500.C114/445a

*The Secretary of State to the Austrian Minister (Prochnik)* [2]

WASHINGTON, February 19, 1929.

SIR: I have the honor to refer to my note of February 12, 1926,[3] with which I transmitted for the information of your Government a copy of the Resolution adopted by the Senate of the United States on January 27, 1926,[4] setting forth certain reservations and understandings as conditions on which the United States would adhere to the Protocol of Signature of December 16, 1920, of the Statute of the Permanent Court of International Justice.[5] In that note I asked to be informed whether the reservations and understandings contained in the Resolution of the Senate of the United States were acceptable to your Government as a part and condition to the adherence of the United States to the said Protocol and Statute.

Five Governments unconditionally accepted the Senate reservations and understandings, three indicated that they would accept but have not formally notified my Government of their acceptance, fifteen simply acknowledged the receipt of my Government's note of February 12, 1926, while twenty-four have communicated to my Government replies as hereinafter indicated.

At a conference held in Geneva in September 1926 by a large number of the States signatories to the Protocol of Signature of the Statute of the Permanent Court of International Justice, a Final Act was adopted in which were set forth certain conclusions and recommendations regarding the proposal of the United States, together with a preliminary draft of a Protocol regarding the adherence of the United States, which the Conference recommended that all the signatories of the Protocol of Signature of December 16, 1920, should adopt in replying to the proposal of the United States. Twenty-four of the Governments adopted the recommendations of the Conference of 1926 and communicated to the Government of the United States in the manner

---

[1] For previous correspondence, see *Foreign Relations*, 1926, vol. I, pp. 1 ff.

[2] Identic notes were delivered to the diplomatic representatives in Washington of all the nations signatories to the protocol of signature of the statute of the Permanent Court of International Justice.

[3] *Foreign Relations*, 1926, vol. I, p. 3.

[4] *Ibid.*, p. 1.

[5] For texts of the protocol of signature, the optional clause, and the statute of the Court, see *ibid.*, 1920, vol. I, pp. 17 and 18.

1

suggested by the Conference.[6] By these replies and the proposed Protocol attached thereto the first four reservations adopted by the Senate of the United States were accepted. The fifth reservation was not accepted in full but so much of the first part thereof as required the Court to render advisory opinions in public session was accepted, and the attention of my Government was called to the amended rules of the Court requiring notice and an opportunity to be heard.

The second part of the fifth reservation therefore raised the only question on which there is any substantial difference of opinion. That part of the reservation reads as follows:

" . . . Nor shall it (the Court) without the consent of the United States entertain any request for any advisory opinion touching any dispute or question in which the United States has or claims an interest."

It was observed in the Final Act of the Conference that, as regards disputes to which the United States is a party, the Court had already pronounced upon the matter of disputes between a member of the League of Nations and a State not a member, and reference was made to advisory opinion No. 5 in the Eastern Carelia case[7] in which the Court held that it would not pass on such a dispute without the consent of the non-member of the League. The view was expressed that this would meet the desire of the United States.

As regards disputes to which the United States is not a party but in which it claims an interest, the view was expressed in the Final Act that this part of the fifth reservation rests upon the presumption that the adoption of a request for an advisory opinion by the Council or the Assembly requires a unanimous vote. It was stated that since this has not been decided to be the case it can not be said with certainty whether in some or all cases a decision by a majority may not be sufficient but that in any case where a State represented on the Council or in the Assembly would have a right to prevent by opposition in either of these bodies the adoption of a proposal to request an advisory opinion from the Court, the United States should enjoy an equal right. Article 4 of the draft Protocol[8] states that "should the United States offer objection to an advisory opinion being given by the Court, at the request of the Council or the Assembly, concerning a dispute to which the United States is not a party or concerning a question other than a dispute between States, the Court will attribute to such objection the same force and effect as attaches to a vote against asking for the opinion given by a

---

[6] See note No. 817, December 23, 1926, from the British Ambassador, *Foreign Relations*, 1926, vol. I, p. 30.

[7] Given by the Court on July 23, 1923. See Permanent Court of International Justice, *Collection of Advisory Opinions*, Series B, No. 5.

[8] *Foreign Relations*, 1926, vol. I, p. 36.

member of the League of Nations either in the Assembly or in the Council", and that "the manner in which the consent provided for in the second part of the fifth reservation is to be given" should be the subject of an understanding to be reached by the Government of the United States with the Council of the League of Nations.

The Government of the United States desires to avoid in so far as may be possible any proposal which would interfere with or embarrass the work of the Council of the League of Nations, doubtless often perplexing and difficult, and it would be glad if it could dispose of the subject by a simple acceptance of the suggestions embodied in the Final Act and draft Protocol adopted at Geneva on September 23, 1926. There are, however, some elements of uncertainty in the bases of these suggestions which seem to require further discussion. The powers of the Council and its modes of procedure depend upon the Covenant of the League of Nations which may be amended at any time. The ruling of the Court in the Eastern Carelia case and the rules of the Court are also subject to change at any time. For these reasons, without further inquiry into the practicability of the suggestions, it appears that the Protocol submitted by the twenty-four Governments in relation to the fifth reservation of the United States Senate would not furnish adequate protection to the United States. It is gratifying to learn from the proceedings of the Conference at Geneva that the considerations inducing the adoption of that part of Reservation 5 giving rise to differences of opinion are appreciated by the powers participating in that Conference. Possibly the interest of the United States thus attempted to be safeguarded may be fully protected in some other way or by some other formula. The Government of the United States feels that such an informal exchange of views as is contemplated by the twenty-four Governments should, as herein suggested, lead to agreement upon some provision which in unobjectionable form would protect the rights and interests of the United States as an adherent to the Court Statute, and this expectation is strongly supported by the fact that there seems to be but little difference regarding the substance of these rights and interests.

Accept [etc.] FRANK B. KELLOGG

---

500.C114/445bbb

*The Secretary of State to the Minister in Switzerland (Wilson)*

No. 404 WASHINGTON, February 19, 1929.

SIR: I am enclosing, for transmission in the usual informal manner, a note to the Secretary-General of the League of Nations,⁹ setting

---

⁹ Not printed.

forth the text of a communication which I have addressed to each of the signatories to the Protocol of Signature of the Statute of the Permanent Court of International Justice.

I am [etc.]                                              FRANK B. KELLOGG

---

500.C114/758 : Telegram

*The Consul at Geneva (Rand) to the Secretary of State*

GENEVA, March 4, 1929—3 p. m.
[Received March 5—3 : 26 a. m.]

[Paraphrase.] From Root.[10]  I have suggested personally to those representing the signatories of the December 16, 1920, protocol the following draft for a working agreement to apply practically the second part of the fifth reservation. Opinions that have been expressed regarding this suggestion have been so far favorable that I am telegraphing the draft in full to you for your study and that of the President with the hope that you will informally advise me whether it meets with your approval and in order that you may be ready to make quick response to any request for authority which may be made by me to represent the United States in an exchange of views along the lines of this suggestion, thereby bringing about the exchange of views of an informal character which the twenty-four Governments contemplate and which is covered by the last paragraph of your letter of February 19, 1929. It may be necessary to act very rapidly as the representatives of the signatories are now here for a meeting of the Council and at the end of this week they will leave.

Before leaving here it is highly important that they reach favorable conclusions regardless of whether effect is to be given these conclusions through recommendations of Committee of Experts or through the Council's action in accordance with authority from the twenty-four Governments in the September 23, 1926, final act.

Several minor matters which can be provided for when the protocol is redrafted after removal of the main difficulty are not dealt with in this draft working agreement. [End paraphrase.]

Suggested draft for proposed working agreement:

The Court shall not, without the consent of the United States, render an advisory opinion touching any dispute to which the United States is a party.

The Court shall not, without the consent of the United States, render an advisory opinion touching any dispute to which the United States

---

[10] Elihu Root, former Secretary of State (1905–1909). Mr. Root, acting in a purely private capacity and not as representative of the Government of the United States, was appointed by the Council of the League of Nations as American member of the Committee of Jurists which had been set up to make a preliminary study of the question of revising the statute of the Permanent Court of International Justice.

is not a party but in which it claims an interest or touching any question other than a dispute in which the United States claims an interest.

The manner in which it shall be made known whether the United States claims an interest and gives or withholds its consent shall be as follows:

Whenever in contemplation of a request for an advisory opinion it seems to them desirable, the Council or Assembly may invite an exchange of views with the United States and such exchange of views shall proceed with all convenient speed.

Whenever a request for an advisory opinion comes to the Court, the registrar shall notify the United States thereof among other states mentioned in the now existing article 73 of the Rules of Court stating a reasonable time limit fixed by the President within which a written statement by the United States concerning the request will be received.

In case the United States shall, within the time fixed, advise the Court in writing that the request touches a dispute or question in which the United States has an interest and that the United States has not consented to the submission of the question; thereupon, all proceedings upon the question shall be stayed to admit of an exchange of views between the United States and the proponents of the request and such exchange of views shall proceed with all convenient speed.

If after such an exchange of views, either while a question is in contemplation or after a question has gone to the Court, it shall appear (1) that no agreement can be reached as to whether the question does touch an interest of the United States within the true meaning of the second paragraph of this article, and (2) that the submission of the question is still insisted upon after attributing to the objection of the United States the same force and effect as attaches to a vote against asking for the opinion given by a member of the League of Nations either in the Assembly or in the Council and if it also appears that the United States has not been able to find the submission of the question so important for the general good as to call upon the United States to forego its objection in that particular instance leaving the request to be acted upon by the Court without in any way binding the United States: then, it shall be deemed that owing to a material difference of view regarding the proper scope of the practice of requesting advisory opinions the arrangement now agreed upon is not yielding satisfactory results and that the exercise of the powers of withdrawal provided in article seven, hereof, will follow naturally without any imputation of unfriendliness or of unwillingness to cooperate generally for peace and good will.

[Paraphrase.] The foregoing draft is based on the following theory:

In the first place, the word "interest", as used in reservation number 5, is indefinite and vague and is obviously not meant to encompass all that the many customary uses of the term denote, such as, interest in national prosperity, interest in the preservation of all the rules of the law of nations, interest in freeing peoples suffering from oppression, interest in buyers of the products of the country, and so forth.

It is not possible, in the second place, to arrive at an abstract formula plainly distinguishing between that which the word "interest" in the fifth reservation does or does not include.

Whenever, in the third place, a specific case should arise (in the event that this ever occurs) practical experience, as well as common sense, would find no difficulty in determining whether an interest of this country was touched by that particular question.

In the fourth place, therefore, discussion should be shifted to the concrete and specific from the abstract and general and the solution of such a question should be provided for by a friendly, prompt exchange of views on that specific point.

In the fifth place, in the event that there resulted a difference of view which is irreconcilable, this will manifest a disagreement concerning the correct scope of requests for advisory opinions so fundamental as to make advisable the resumption of the *status quo ante* by exercising the right of withdrawal which the fourth reservation, as extended by the December 1926 draft protocol, article 7, provides.

In the sixth place, such a tremendous preponderance of likelihood that such a controversy would not arise and be insisted upon in order to obtain an advisory opinion on any question, whatever its nature, that it would be clearly worthwhile trying out the arrangement.

The United States, in the seventh place, has much more to gain by having a question of this sort determined by discussing it with those who are proposing a request than by its being discussed by the court under a prohibition which would prevent it from entertaining the request, for then it would be up to the court to determine whether such an interest as the fifth reservation envisages were touched by the question and the United States would thereby be forced to submit to the court's decision and to all which is implied thereby. [Root.] [End paraphrase.]

Rand

---

500.C114/759 : Telegram

## The Consul at Geneva (Rand) to the Secretary of State

[Paraphrase]

Geneva, March 5, 1929—7 p. m.<br>[Received March 5—4:27 p. m.]

From Root. If draft cabled you yesterday is approved by President, the moment seems appropriate for it to be officially transmitted to Secretary-General for the information of Council of the League of Nations in its capacity of representative of the signatory states, as being one suggestion of possible basis for a working agreement. Under the fifth reservation there will probably be approval in principle of amendments and then their reference to Committee of Experts for working out of details. May I have authority? [Root.]

Rand

500.C114/759 : Telegram

*The Secretary of State to the Consul at Geneva (Rand)*

WASHINGTON, March 6, 1929—2 p. m.

For Root. Your telegram March 4, 3 p. m. and March 5, 7 p. m. Due to the pressure of business incident to the beginning of the administration and critical condition in Mexico, it has not been possible to consult both the President and the interested Senators, especially those with whom you discussed the matter.

With reference to the plan submitted in your telegram of March 4th, after a hasty examination of the proposal by the President, the plan to us seems to be feasible and we think well of it. Do not think it advisable for this Government to undertake to negotiate through the League Council. It would I fear have disastrous effect on the Senate. We have always negotiated with the individual governments and not through the agency of the League at Geneva. If you submit the proposal to the Council for their informal approval, it should be purely on your own responsibility as a member of the Committee of Experts. President will consult Senators with whom you talked and perhaps others as soon as possible.

I am delighted that the informal sounding out which you have been able to do with members of the Council has met with such good reception and the President deeply appreciates your efforts in this matter.

KELLOGG

---

500.C114/762 : Telegram

*The Consul at Geneva (Rand) to the Secretary of State*

GENEVA, March 7, 1929—9 a. m.
[Received 9:25 a. m.]

From Root. Do not trouble about authority. I think I have arranged for referring proposal of 1926 conference to Committee of Experts thus giving them the whole subject for consideration.

Should be glad of any information about situation in Washington.

[Root]
RAND

---

500.C114/765a : Telegram

*The Secretary of State to the Consul at Geneva (Rand)*

[Paraphrase]

WASHINGTON, March 8, 1929—8 p. m.

For Root. The President and I have consulted with Senators Swanson, Walsh (of Montana), and Borah on your proposed draft.

Senators Walsh and Swanson agree to it and think that it adequately protects this Government under the last half of the fifth reservation. The President and I share their view.  We cannot make sure in any way, of course, that the Senate would adopt the proposed draft; of this, you are aware.

After he had talked with me, Senator Borah had a conference last night with the President, after which the President wrote to me as follows: [11]

"I have now had an opportunity of discussing Mr. Root's proposal with Senator Borah.  My understanding is that Senator Borah is opposed to the Court undertaking any advisory opinions, and voted against our adherence to the Court for this reason.   He also feels that Mr. Root's plan satisfies the requirements of the 5th reservation. He seems to feel that those who believe we should adhere to the Court subject to the reservations, ought to be satisfied with Mr. Root's plan.

Senator Borah still believes that the suggestion he made to Mr. Root that the statute should provide that no advisory opinions would be given in respect to non-members of the League would be a more effective method of action than the special program provided by Mr. Root."

Senator Walsh agreed with the above views, but he wishes to make some suggestions with regard to the wording.  I quote the Senator's letter to me as follows: [11]

"Agreeably to my promise of this morning, I am sending you the following on the subject of our conference:

I approve of the draft sent by Senator Root, intended as a modification of Reservation V, and am prepared to urge acceptance of it by the Senate in lieu of its draft, but the essentials could, in my judgment, be expressed in fewer words.  With great deference I offer the following:

Paragraphs 1 and 2 should be consolidated.  They express no idea not implied in the Senate language, and no reason is apparent why it should be departed from.

I appreciate that three conditions are contemplated in paragraphs 1 and 2, a dispute to which the United States is a party, a dispute between two other parties involving a question in which it is interested, and a question concerning which the advice of the Court is sought, not involved in any pending dispute.  All three conditions are covered by the Senate language.

I would cut out paragraphs 3 and 4.  Doubtless the latter was inserted as a suggestion that the course therein indicated be pursued, but it may or may not be.  The League bodies may now seek the views of our Government.  The draft puts no obligation on them to do so in any case.  Considering the circumstances of our adherence, should we adhere, it would be courtesy to do so in any case in which there would appear reason to believe we might be interested.  I see no reason for suggesting in advance that they do the courteous thing. Moreover, I believe, not being a member of the League, we should avoid making any agreement as to what the League bodies may or may not do.

If the first part of Reservation V is to be preserved—and I understand no serious objection to it is entertained—there would seem to be no occasion for Paragraph 5. Rule 73 would, by the first part of Reservation V, become permanent. I would redraft what follows as here indicated:

In case the United States shall, within the time fixed for the hearing after notice, advise the Court in writing that the request touches a dispute or question in which it has or claims an interest, and that it has not consented to the submission of the question, all proceedings upon the question submitted shall be stayed for such time as the Court may direct to admit of an exchange of views between the United States and the proponents of the request.

If at the expiration of the period of such stay, the Court shall, after giving to the objection of the United States, indicated by its appearance as aforesaid, the same force and effect as attaches to a vote against asking for the opinion given by a member of the League of Nations, either in the Assembly or in the Council, and the Court nevertheless proceeds, the objection of the United States not being recalled, such action shall be held to justify the exercise by the United States of the power of withdrawal provided for in Article seven hereof, without any imputation of unfriendliness on its part or any unwillingness to cooperate generally in the cause of peace and good-will.

I might observe that in the above proposed draft even Paragraphs 1 and 2 are omitted, there being what seems an incongruity between them and the concluding portion of the draft for which the substitute is offered. Advisory opinions under the conditions specified are forbidden by those paragraphs and yet, later, it is contemplated they will be given in which case the United States may exercise its right to withdraw."

We have worked out what Senator Walsh's letter apparently would provide for; that is, that the Court shall not, without the consent of the Government of the United States, render an advisory opinion touching any dispute to which this Government is a party, and the Court shall not render, without the consent of the Government of the United States, an advisory opinion touching any dispute to which this Government is not a party but in which it claims an interest, or touching any question not a dispute in which the United States claims an interest; and that whenever a request for an advisory opinion comes before the Court, the Registrar shall make notification of it to this Government, among the other States which are mentioned in the present article 73 of the Rules of the Court, stating a reasonable time limit fixed by the President of the Court within which a written statement by this Government on the request will be received.

The remainder of the Senator's suggestions is comprised in the two paragraphs of his letter beginning with "In case the United States shall" and concluding with "peace and good will".

I am forwarding his suggestions to you, without comment, for your information.

KELLOGG

500.C114/765c : Telegram

## The Secretary of State to the Consul at Geneva (Rand)

[Paraphrase]

WASHINGTON, March 11, 1929—4 p. m.

For Root. I have just talked with the President. He wished me to inquire from you if there were any chance to have advisory opinions eliminated entirely from the Court statute. He says elimination would remove last objection in United States, and ratification would be almost unanimous. He is very anxious for you to endeavor to see what can be done in this direction.

It is my understanding that there has been some discussion among members of League for elimination of advisory opinions in the Court statute and for the setting up of a Jurists Committee in the League itself for advisory opinions disconnected entirely from the Court. I do not know how much sentiment exists for this.

KELLOGG

500.C114/767a : Telegram

## The Secretary of State to the Consul at Geneva (Rand)

[Paraphrase]

WASHINGTON, March 12, 1929—2 p. m.

For Root. President has had several interviews on subject of your proposal, and he is convinced of validity of suggestion contained in Senator Walsh's letter (Department's telegram, March 8, 8 p. m.) that third paragraph of your draft should be omitted as there can be no question that Council of the League may consult this Government at any time. To include a provision for this purpose in any arrangement to be made would arouse bitter opposition from the anti-League of Nations Senators, signs of which have already appeared in the Hearst press.

President is anxious to have necessary changes adopted with least possible friction, and does not see any necessity, from point of view either of this Government or of the League, for inclusion of this third paragraph, which is purely permissive in character.

KELLOGG

500.C114/768a : Telegram

## The Secretary of State to the Consul at Geneva (Rand)

[Paraphrase]

WASHINGTON, March 14, 1929—noon.

For Root. Since I telegraphed you last night I have had a conference with Senator Walsh on what appears to be draft of Hurst [12]

---

[12] Sir Cecil Hurst, British member of the Committee of Jurists.

proposal which was printed in *New York Times*. From this it seems that Hurst proposed that League of Nations shall notify an agent of the United States of desire of either the Council or the Agency to request an advisory opinion from the Court, and that it is only when the League fails to give notice to this Government that the United States can obtain a stay before Court for purpose of negotiating with the proponents. That is to say, if League is giving the notice no stay can be procured, and this Government's sole remedy would be to withdraw at once. Your original proposal seems to us to be far preferable to this plan. It is very doubtful indeed if Congress would authorize appointment of such a special agent. Of course it is quite likely that Congress would give authorization to the President to decide these questions and would give him, perhaps, the authority to appoint any representative he may desire. We should think it unnecessary to have any agreement on this protocol. If League of Nations desires to communicate with this Government, it can very easily do so by cable through the usual channels.

Furthermore, under Hurst proposal, whenever a question of deciding whether or not to seek an advisory opinion from the Court, the Council or the Assembly of the League shall attach to this Government's objection the same value as that which they attach to vote of a state which is a member of the League of Nations. The Court would be excluded, by this means, from giving the same consideration, while, according to your proposition, the Council, the Assembly and the Court alike shall be required to give such value as that which they attach to vote of a member, and Court would pass on that in last resort rather than League of Nations.

You will forgive me for making so many suggestions; of course, they are not intended to be instructions, but I thought you would like to be kept fully posted with regard to objections which may be raised when matter is brought up before Senate. Senator Walsh is particularly interested in this point.

Kellogg

---

500.C114/769 : Telegram

*The Consul at Geneva (Rand) to the Secretary of State*

Geneva, March 18, 1929—7 p. m.
[Received March 19—5 a. m.]

From Root. Report of Committee of Experts to Council [13] recommends following protocol:

[Here follows the text of the protocol, except for place, date, and signatures, printed on page 53.]

---

[13] *Post*, p. 16.

Basis is acceptance of all reservations in article 1. No reservation is repeated in protocol except for the purpose of showing some modification. Thus reservations one and three are unmodified. Two is strengthened by drafting addition to make meaning clear under continental usage. Four is made reciprocal. First part of five is made definite by taking in rule adopted by court after Senate action in order to give effect to Senate views.

Second part of five is unmodified and thus becomes the rule of action leaving only questions of its application. Fifth article of protocol is intended to provide for application of fifth reservation through method of procedure by which any question [omission] whether a particular request would result in breach of fifth reservation may be disposed of in friendly discussion, with the understanding that if there is no agreement and a request for opinion which we consider in violation of reservation five is insisted upon we shall be considered to have just ground for denouncing the protocol.

This protocol carefully avoids the submission of any question to the Court. This is for absolutely conclusive reasons which I shall be glad to state when I return. Any provision for such a submission would be wholly inconsistent with the plan for settlement which I explained at Washington and here and which is embodied in this draft.

I have made thorough inquiry regarding European attitude toward advisory opinion and will explain results in person. They indicate no useful possibilities at present.

The committee report will go to the Council which can not consider it until its June meeting.[14]

Thank you for many helpful suggestions and information. Expect to sail for home by *Ile de France* April 10. [Root.]

RAND

500.C114/791½

*The Secretary of State to Mr. Elihu Root*

WASHINGTON, May 25, 1929.

MY DEAR MR. ROOT: This is to confirm and clarify my talk with you over the telephone this morning. I have just had a long talk with the President, to whom I brought our proposed *aide mémoire* in reference to the World Court.[15] He feels very strongly that if we come out unequivocally and publicly for the amended protocol now, it would be at once made the subject of bitter attacks in the Senate at a time when we are not prepared to meet the attack and when we are in the midst

---

[14] See letter of June 12 from the Secretary-General of the League of Nations, p. 15.

[15] Presumably the draft of the *aide-mémoire* transmitted in the Department's telegram No. 84, August 14, 11 a. m., to the Minister in Switzerland, p. 22.

of very serious attacks against the administration on farm relief and the tariff. He thinks this would greatly endanger the ultimate chance of successful adherence to the Court. He is particularly anxious that we shall not fail when we begin our fight for ratification because he feels that another rebuff would set back the adherence to the Court for half a generation.

Immediately after leaving the President, I saw Senator Swanson, who led the fight on behalf of the Democrats for the Court last time and is willing to lead it again this time. Swanson was very strongly of the same views as the President. He urged strongly that the Council should not take a question of the passage of protocol at the June Session, but to put it over until September. He believed it would be easier to get the matter through our Senate if most of the signatories had not acted rather than if they had acted. Swanson suggested that if you would yourself suggest to the Council such a postponement they would not attribute it to lack of enthusiasm on the part of this Government.

What I am trying to do is to think out some message that I can also send to Drummond [16] which will express our friendliness to the amended Protocol and yet not provoke public debate; and thus far I have not thought of any satisfactory way to do so. If you can assist me in that respect it would be a great help. I have therefore asked Castle to go over and discuss this matter with you; and I am also telegraphing Jessup [17] to meet Castle at your house tomorrow morning. Castle is not opposed to the Court; he has always been for it even without reservations but he doubts whether the present amended Protocol actually accepts the Senate reservations. At any rate, he is the Assistant Secretary who has had charge of this matter throughout and is the man most familiar with the political situation here whom I can send.

Faithfully yours,                                           HENRY L. STIMSON

---

500.C114/795 : Telegram

*The Secretary of State to the Minister in Switzerland* (*Wilson*)

[Paraphrase]

WASHINGTON, May 27, 1929—6 p. m.

57. If Drummond has not yet started for Madrid, I should be pleased to have you deliver to him personally the following letter, which you will sign: [18]

"My dear Sir Eric. I am instructed to acknowledge the courtesy of the Secretary General of the League of Nations in transmitting

---

[16] Sir Eric Drummond, Secretary-General of the League of Nations.
[17] Philip C. Jessup, lecturer and writer on international law, and member of the faculty of Columbia University, New York.
[18] Quotation not paraphrased.

with his informal note of May 2, 1929,[19] a copy of the report and draft protocol adopted by the Committee of Jurists at their session in Geneva, March 11 to March 19, 1929, and concerning the proposed adherence of the United States to the Protocol and Statute of the Permanent Court of International Justice. I am glad to inform you further that whenever the suggestions of the Committee have been laid before the Council and have come to the Government of the United States officially, the Government will be glad to give them most attentive and cordial consideration."

When you deliver this letter, please inform Drummond that I believe it not only inappropriate to comment in any way on the draft protocol before it has been submitted to Council of the League, but that at this time it is highly inadvisable to start any public discussion when the Government is not able to lead in that discussion. Drummond already knows the President's desire that the United States may become a member of the Permanent Court of International Justice, and he will realize that we must decide both as to best time and best method of approaching subject. In any event, the matter can not be brought before Senate until regular session of Congress in December.

STIMSON

---

500.C114/796 : Telegram

*The Minister in Switzerland (Wilson) to the Secretary of State*

[Paraphrase]

BERNE, May 30, 1929—1 p. m.
[Received 4 : 30 p. m.]

44. On eve of Drummond's departure yesterday for Lisbon and Madrid, I delivered to him letter and message transmitted in your No. 57, May 27, 6 p. m.

I think he is thoroughly conversant with situation and inadvisability of the matter's being publicly discussed until you can lead the way. He told me that three steps have been determined as definite:

1. Submission of the draft protocol to the Council at this meeting;
2. In event of agreement by Council, official transmission of the protocol to all interested governments including the United States;
3. Putting the matter on the agenda of Assembly for September meeting of that body, as its agreement is also necessary.

Drummond believes that all of the foregoing steps, certainly the first two, can be accomplished as routine matters which will furnish occasion for little or no discussion; and that official transmission immediately following the meeting of the Council will enable you to lead discussion in way you desire.

---

[19] Transmitted with the Legation's despatch No. 850, May 6; not printed.

Further procedure has not been definitely settled as yet. Sir Eric believes, nevertheless, that conference of all states which are signatories to statute of the Permanent Court of International Justice (this will include Brazil) may well be held during period of next Assembly to consider draft protocol; in this connection see fourth paragraph, page three, document C.142.M.52.1929.V. April 2.[20] This conference may well decide to open protocol at once for signature with ratification to follow. In this event, protocol would be open at once, of course, to the United States for signature with subsequent ratification.

As I stated above, Drummond left last night for Lisbon, to go from there to Madrid; any further observations which you desire to offer before the Council meets might be transmitted, therefore, through our Missions in those capitals.

WILSON

---

500.C114/808

*The Secretary-General of the League of Nations (Drummond) to the Secretary of State*

MADRID, June 12, 1929.
[Received June 24.]

SIR: On June 12th 1929, the Council of the League of Nations considered the report of the Representative of Italy, of which a copy is enclosed,[21] and adopted the following resolution:

"The Council adopts, together with the draft Protocol annexed thereto,[22] the report submitted to it by the Committee of Jurists on the question of the accession of the United States of America to the Protocol of Signature of the Statute of the Permanent Court of International Justice.[23]

Accordingly, it instructs the Secretary-General:

1) to reply to Mr. Kellogg's note of February 19th 1929, and communicate to the United States Government, together with the present Council resolution, the text of the said report and of the said draft Protocol;
2) to make the same communication to the States Signatories of the Protocol of December 16th, 1920, and to transmit also to those States the text of the resolution of the Senate of the United States, dated January 27th, 1926, embodying the latter's reservations.

In order that the Assembly, being, like the Council, a body whose procedure in regard to the method of seeking Advisory Opinions from

---

[20] Not reprinted.
[21] Document I, League of Nations publication No. A.9.1929.V; not reprinted.
[22] See telegram, March 18, 7 p. m., from the Consul at Geneva, p. 11.
[23] Enclosure, *infra*.

the Court would be affected by the adoption of the Protocol proposed by the Committee of Jurists, may have an opportunity of expressing its opinion thereon, the Council decides to instruct the Secretary-General to transmit to the Assembly the report of the Committee and the draft Protocol and to place the question on the supplementary agenda of the Xth ordinary session of the Assembly."

In execution of this decision of the Council, I have the honour to transmit to you, herewith, the document C.142.M.52.1929, which contains on page 15 and the following pages the text of the report mentioned in the resolution and that of the Protocol annexed thereto.

I venture to send these texts in this form in order that they may reach you without delay. I beg, however, to add that it is intended to print a separate document containing the report and the Protocol in question, copies of which I will not fail to transmit to you as soon as possible.

I have [etc.]                                    ERIC DRUMMOND

[Enclosure]

*Report Adopted by the Committee of Jurists on the Question of the Accession of the United States of America to the Protocol of Signature of the Statute of the Court*

On February 19th, 1929, the Secretary of State of the United States of America addressed to each of the Governments which had signed the Protocol of Signature of the Statute of the Permanent Court of International Justice, dated December 16th, 1920, and also to the Secretary-General of the League of Nations a note suggesting that an exchange of views might lead to an agreement with regard to the acceptance of the stipulations set forth in the resolution adopted by the Senate of the United States on January 27th, 1926, as the conditions upon which the United States would adhere to the said Protocol. This note was considered by the Council of the League of Nations at its meeting on March 9th, 1929, and cordial satisfaction was expressed at the prospect which the note held out that a solution might be found for the difficulties which had prevented the adherence of the United States in 1926. On the same date, a resolution was adopted by the Council, requesting the Committee of Jurists, which had been appointed by the Council at its meeting on December 14th, 1928, to consider the revision of the Statute of the Permanent Court of International Justice, to deal with this question as well as those with which it was already charged and to make any suggestions which it felt able to offer with a view to facilitating the accession of the United States on conditions satisfactory to all the interests concerned.

It has been of the greatest assistance to the Committee in the accomplishment of this additional task that among its members was to be found the Honourable Elihu Root, formerly Secretary of State of the United States, and one of the members of the Committee which in 1920 framed the original draft of the Statute of the Court. His presence in the Committee has enabled it to re-examine with good results the work accomplished by the Special Conference which was convoked by the Council in 1926 after the receipt of the letter of March 2nd of that year from the then Secretary of State of the United States informing the Secretary-General of the League that the United States was disposed to adhere to the Protocol of December 16th, 1920, on certain conditions enumerated in that letter. The United States did not see its way to participate, as it was invited to do, in the Special Conference of 1926, and, unfortunately, the proposals which emanated from that Conference were found not to be acceptable to the United States. Nevertheless, as is shown by the note of February 19th, 1929, from Mr. Kellogg, the margin of difference between the requirements of the United States and the recommendations made by the Special Conference to the Powers which had signed the Protocol of December 16th, 1920, is not great. For this reason, the Committee adopted as the basis of its discussions the Preliminary Draft of Protocol annexed to the Final Act of that Conference and has introduced into the text the changes which it believes to be necessary to overcome the objections encountered by the draft of 1926 and to render it acceptable to all parties. This revised text is now submitted to the Council of the League.

The discussions in the Committee have shown that the conditions with which the Government of the United States thought it necessary to accompany the expression of its willingness to adhere to the Protocol establishing the Court owed their origin to apprehension that the Council or the Assembly of the League might request from the Court advisory opinions without reference to interests of the United States which might in certain cases be involved. Those discussions have also shown that the hesitation felt by the delegates to the Conference of 1926 as to recommending the acceptance of those conditions was due to apprehension that the rights claimed in the reservations formulated by the United States might be exercised in a way which would interfere with the work of the Council or the Assembly and embarrass their procedure. The task of the Committee has been to discover some method of ensuring that neither on the one side nor on the other should these apprehensions prove to be well founded.

No difficulty has at any time been felt with regard to the acceptance of the conditions laid down by the United States except in so far as they relate to advisory opinions, and the task of the Committee would have been simplified if its members had felt able to recommend that the system of asking the Court for an advisory opinion upon any particular question should be abandoned altogether. The Committee, however, is of opinion that it cannot recommend any such drastic solution. The system of asking the Court for an advisory opinion has proved to be of substantial utility in securing a solution of questions which could not conveniently be submitted to the Court in any other form. It has also on occasions enabled parties to a dispute to ask for the submission of their difference to the Court in the form of a request for an advisory opinion when they were for various reasons unwilling to submit it in the form of international litigation.

The Committee has also felt obliged to reject another method by which satisfaction might without difficulty be given to the conditions laid down by the United States. It is that of recommending the adoption of a rule that in all cases a decision on the part of the Council or of the Assembly to ask for an advisory opinion from the Court must be unanimous. As is pointed out in the Final Act of the Special Conference of 1926, it was not then possible to say with certainty whether a decision by a majority was not sufficient. It is equally impossible to-day. All that is possible is to guarantee to the United States a position of equality in this matter with the States which are represented in the Council or the Assembly of the League.

Furthermore, mature reflection convinced the Committee that it was useless to attempt to allay the apprehensions on either side, which have been referred to above, by the elaboration of any system of paper guarantees or abstract formulae. The more hopeful system is to deal with the problem in a concrete form, to provide some method by which questions as they arise may be examined and views exchanged, and a conclusion thereby reached after each side has made itself acquainted with the difficulties and responsibilities which beset the other. It is this method which the Committee recommends should be adopted, and to provide for which it now submits a text of a Protocol to be concluded between the States which signed the Protocol of 1920 and the United States of America (see Annex, page 17.)[24]

The note of February 19th, 1929, from the Secretary of State of the United States makes it clear that the Government of the United States has no desire to interfere with or to embarrass the work of the Council or the Assembly of the League, and that that Government realises the difficulties and responsibilities of the tasks with which the League is from time to time confronted. It shows that there is no intention on the part of the United States Government of hampering, upon unreal or unsubstantial grounds, the machinery by which advisory opinions are from time to time requested. The

---

[24] See text of protocol, p. 53.

Committee is thereby enabled to recommend that the States which signed the Protocol of 1920 should accept the reservations formulated by the United States upon the terms and conditions set out in the articles of the draft Protocol. This is the effect of Article I of the draft now submitted.

The next three Articles reproduce without substantial change the corresponding articles of the draft of 1926.

The fifth Article provides machinery by which the United States will be made aware of any proposal before the Council or the Assembly for obtaining an advisory opinion and will have an opportunity of indicating whether the interests of the United States are affected, so that the Council or the Assembly, as the case may be, may decide its course of action with full knowledge of the position. One may hope with confidence that the exchange of views so provided for will be sufficient to ensure that an understanding will be reached and no conflict of views will remain.

The provisions of this Article have been worded with due regard to the exigencies of business in the Council of the League. The desirability of obtaining an advisory opinion may only become apparent as the session of the Council is drawing to a close and when it may not be possible to complete the exchange of views before the members if that body separate. In that case, it will be for the Council to give such directions as the circumstances may require, in order to ensure that the intentions of the Article are carried out. The request addressed to the Court may, for instance, be held up temporarily, or it may be despatched with a request that the Court will nevertheless suspend action on the request until the exchange of views with the United States has been completed. The provisions of the Article have purposely been framed so as to afford a measure of elasticity in its application. Similarly, if the Court has commenced the preliminary proceedings consequent upon the receipt of the request for an advisory opinion and has given notice of the request to the United States in the same way as to the other Governments, the proceedings may, if necessary, be interrupted in order that the necessary exchange of views may take place. What is said in this paragraph with regard to requests for advisory opinions made by the Council would also apply to requests by the Assembly in the event of the Assembly making any such request.

The provisions of this Article should in practice afford protection to all parties in all cases, but if they do not, it must be recognised that the solution embodied in the present proposal will not have achieved the success that was hoped, and that the United States would be fully justified in withdrawing from the arrangement. It is for this eventuality that provision is made in the last paragraph of the Article. It may be hoped that, should any such withdrawal by the United States materialise, it would in fact be followed or accompanied by the conclusion of some new and more satisfactory arrangement.

In order to ensure so far as possible that the parties to the Protocol of 1920 shall be identical with the parties to the new Protocol, Article 6 provides that any State which in future signs the Protocol of 1920 shall be deemed to accept the new Protocol.

The remaining provisions of the draft Protocol do not call for detailed comment, because they are in substance similar to the corresponding provisions of the draft Protocol of 1926.

It is necessary to consider what steps will be required to bring the Protocol of which the text is now submitted into force in the event of the recommendations of the Committee being accepted.

If the terms of the Protocol are approved by the Council, it will be advisable that the Secretary-General should be directed, when answering Mr. Kellogg's note of February 19th, 1929, to communicate the draft to the Government of the United States. Since the Protocol, if approved, covers the entire ground of Mr. Kellogg's note, its transmission with a statement of the Council's approval would seem to constitute an adequate reply to that note. It should at the same time be communicated to all the States which signed the Protocol of December 16th, 1920, together with a copy of the resolution of the Senate of the United States, dated January 27th, 1926, containing the reservations of the United States.

It should also be communicated to the Assembly, in which the proposal for the appointment of this Committee originated, in order that, if its terms are acceptable to that body, a resolution approving it may be passed by the Assembly in the course of its ensuing session. Any action taken by the Assembly should be communicated to the signatory States which are called upon to determine whether or not to sign the new Protocol now proposed.

If the replies from the various Governments indicate a desire for a further exchange of views with regard to the nature of the proposed arrangement with the United States or to the terms of the draft Protocol, it will be for the Council to decide whether such exchange of views should proceed through the diplomatic channel or whether it is necessary to convoke a further special conference for the purpose, at which States not Members of the League might be represented. In any event, such exchange of views should, if possible, be completed before the conclusion of the Assembly, in order that the approval by the Assembly may be obtained in 1929. A copy of the Protocol in the terms approved will then be prepared for signature and every effort should be made to secure that delegates to the meeting of the Assembly or of the special conference, if there should be one, should be authorized to sign the instrument and should actually sign it before they leave Geneva. The signature of representatives of States not Members of the League should be obtained at the same time.

As provided in Article 7 of the draft, the Protocol will come into force as soon as it has been ratified by the States which have ratified the Protocol of December 16th, 1920, and by the United States, and, as soon as it has come into force, it will be possible for the United States to take the necessary steps to become a party to the Protocol of December 16th, 1920, and to any further protocol which may have been concluded for introducing amendments into the Statute of the Court.

When that happy result has been achieved, it will be possible to feel that further progress has been made in establishing the reign of law among the nations of the world and in diminishing the risk that there may be a resort to force for the solution of their conflicts.

---

500.C114/822

*The Minister in Switzerland (Wilson) to the Secretary of State*

No. 969                                                   BERNE, July 18, 1929.
L. of N. No. 1399                                  [Received August 5.]

SIR: I have the honor to transmit herewith a note addressed to you on July 12, 1929, by the Acting Secretary General of the League of Nations,[25] communicating the text of a report on the amendment of the Statute of the Permanent Court of International Justice, made to the Council of the League by a Committee of Jurists appointed at its session of December, 1928 (document II in the enclosed publication, A.9.1929.V).[26]

Also, I quote below a communication on the same subject addressed to me on July 12 by Sir Eric Drummond:

"I am sending you officially a document about the meeting of a special conference during the first week of the Assembly to discuss the amendments of the Permanent Court Statute proposed by the Jurists Committee, of which Mr. Root was, as you know, a prominent member.

"To that official letter I should like to add a line to the effect that I am personally convinced that if your people thought it desirable to send anyone to the conference to follow the work at first hand and, should necessity arise, to put views before it, not only would no objection be raised, but the representatives of the states which have been convoked to the conference would be delighted.

---

[25] Not printed.
[26] Not reprinted.

"Please regard this as a quite unofficial and personal communication, but it may be of some interest to you to have this opinion."

I have [etc.]

For the Minister:
C. GROSS
*Third Secretary of Legation*

---

500.C114/825a : Telegram

*The Secretary of State to the Minister in Switzerland (Wilson)*

WASHINGTON, August 14, 1929—11 a. m.

84. You should see Sir Eric Drummond and discuss the matter in accordance with the following *Aide Memoire* and leave a copy with him:

"The Minister of the United States to Switzerland has been instructed to acknowledge in person the courtesy of the Secretary-General of the League of Nations in forwarding his informal note of May 2, 1929, and his formal note from Madrid dated June 12, 1929, the latter enclosing the Council's resolution of June 12, 1929, League Document C.142.M.52.1929.V, containing the texts of the report of the Committee of Jurists adopted at their session in Geneva March 11 to March 19, 1929, and the annexed draft protocol as mentioned in the resolution regarding the question of American accession to the protocol of organization of the statute of the Permanent Court of International Justice.

The Minister has been instructed at the same time to inform the Secretary General that after careful examination the Secretary of State considers that the said draft protocol would effectively meet the objections represented in the reservations of the United States Senate and would constitute a satisfactory basis for the adherence of the United States to the protocol and statute of the Permanent Court of International Justice dated December 16, 1920, and that after the draft protocol has been accepted by the states signatory to the protocol of signature and the statute of the Permanent Court, he will request the President of the United States for the requisite authority to sign and will recommend that it be submitted to the Senate for its consent to ratification."

STIMSON

---

500.C114/822 : Telegram

*The Secretary of State to the Minister in Switzerland (Wilson)*

[Paraphrase]

WASHINGTON, August 15, 1929—6 p. m.

86. Your despatch No. 969, July 18, 1929. With reference to Drummond's personal letter of July 12, 1929, to you, the feeling of the Department is that it does not desire to designate representative to attend Conference in question. Department would not wish to

have any misunderstandings arise through presence of any Americans at Geneva at time of meeting whose being there might occasion the unfounded inference that they were there to voice unofficially the views of this Government. The Department leaves it to your discretion, should you consider it advisable as means of forestalling any such possibility, to attend informally one or more of the sessions of the Conference as an observer, and to make such reply to Sir Eric's letter as you may deem necessary in circumstances. However, if you feel that circumstances in Geneva are such that no danger of the nature indicated will arise, you will then simply inform Sir Eric that the Department of State does not expect to designate a representative to attend Conference.

STIMSON

---

500.C114/826 : Telegram

*The Minister in Switzerland (Wilson) to the Secretary of State*

[Paraphrase]

BERNE, August 17, 1929—2 p. m.
[Received 5 : 30 p. m.]

60. Your telegram No. 84, August 14, 11 a. m. I delivered message to Sir Eric Drummond yesterday. He was greatly pleased with contents which he considered to be of highest importance. He will not give circulation to the information but will keep it confidential and to be used only in the most discreet manner. Should it appear to be necessary he might feel called upon to declare that he had reason to believe that draft would be acceptable to the Government of the United States. (With his reputation for cautious statement such a declaration would probably be sufficient.)

The committee of states which are signatories to the protocol of signature and the statute of the Court has been called for September 4, and should, Drummond hopes, accept the draft rapidly. In event that large number of states affix signature to draft while Assembly is still sitting, Drummond also hopes that you will see fit to cause signature of the United States to be affixed likewise, if possible, during life of the Assembly.

WILSON

---

500.C114/829 : Telegram

*The Minister in Switzerland (Wilson) to the Secretary of State*

[Paraphrase]

BERNE, August 20, 1929—3 p. m.
[Received 3 : 23 p. m.]

65. Your telegram No. 86, August 15, 6 p. m., not received at Legation until today; delay unexplained.

Inasmuch as your message to Sir Eric, cabled August 14 (Department's telegram No. 84), was indicated to be confidential, it would be difficult for me to attend session of Committee as almost certainly I, despite my quality of observer, should be asked questions on our attitude which I should not be in position to answer and which consequently might introduce new misunderstanding or embarrassment.

At the same time I recognize fully danger that unauthorized Americans in Geneva may give false impression of their standing and in regard to our attitude. After having carefully thought over matter, I respectfully submit certain considerations.

On May 27 (your telegram No. 57, 6 p. m.), you stated that earliest moment draft could be submitted to Senate would be December session of Congress. With this fact in mind and having in view your desire to inaugurate public discussion at most favorable moment and in most advantageous way, I assume that you would prefer to delay affixing signature to draft until you are ready to submit to Senate and open discussion upon it. Fact that draft as it now stands is satisfactory to us has been generally assumed by public from newspaper statements; official confirmation of this assumption probably would not cause any great surprise. Indeed, I believe that it would avoid any misrepresentation and hypothetical discussion that would be provoked by silence on our part through this session.

I venture to suggest idea that results of decisions of the Council taken at Madrid have been transmitted to us officially, and fact that we have not replied, at least as far as the delegates and the public are aware, might be misinterpreted and result in considerable speculation. In my view it follows that under these circumstances the most direct method is the most advantageous; namely, that Drummond be authorized by us to read in the opening session the communication which I delivered to him. If this be done I believe draft would be accepted practically without discussion. Any misrepresentation of our attitude by unauthorized persons would be nullified by such procedure.

Should you feel that announcement of an American policy by Secretary-General of League of Nations would have effect in United States of giving appearance of undue connection with the League, I could doubtless arrange with Drummond to make this declaration myself at opening session, being presented as American Minister to Switzerland, not as an American representative or observer on Committee.

If you perceive no difficulty in affixing signature immediately following acceptance by other states, same considerations would apply.

WILSON

500.C114/826 : Telegram

*The Secretary of State to the Minister in Switzerland (Wilson)*

[Paraphrase]

WASHINGTON, August 20, 1929—5 p. m.

88. Reference your telegram No. 60, August 17, 2 p. m. Method proposed by Sir Eric Drummond of treating message contained in my telegram No. 84, August 14, 11 a. m., relative to the Permanent Court is entirely satisfactory. You might inform Sir Eric that we do not intend at present to make any announcement of matter here; and that last evening and this morning a statement carried by the United Press with reference to this Administration's attitude toward the Permanent Court was a pure guess and not based upon information from the Department of State or elsewhere.

STIMSON

---

500.C114/832 : Telegram

*The Minister in Switzerland (Wilson) to the Secretary of State*

[Paraphrase]

BERNE, August 27, 1929—11 a. m.
[Received August 27—10 : 20 a. m.]

68. My telegram No. 65, August 20, 3 p. m. Intention now is that draft protocol shall be submitted to Assembly for acceptance before it is submitted to committee of signatory powers. It will be laid before the First Committee of the Assembly as the first item on the agenda, and as soon as it is adopted a special meeting of the Assembly will be called to vote formal approval and to turn the matter over to the committee of signatory powers. The draft protocol should reach the latter committee about September 10, barring development of unexpected opposition; in meantime, committee will initiate work on revision of statute of the Permanent Court.

WILSON

---

500.C114/833 : Telegram

*The Consul at Geneva (Blake) to the Secretary of State*

[Paraphrase]

GENEVA, August 28, 1929—5 p. m.
[Received 7 : 45 p. m.]

The Cuban Minister here, who is also his country's permanent delegate to the League of Nations, informed Mr. Everett, of this Consulate, that he had received instructions suggesting that in the committee of signatory states he favor postponement of revision of Court Statute until after accession of the United States, especially in view of the fourth Senate reservation of January, 1926. Government of Cuba wishes to facilitate, as far as possible, adherence of Government of the United States. After conversations with Mr. Root, the Minister [learned?] that Root considered the revision to be of secondary importance only, an opinion to which he himself inclines. The Minister would appreciate an expression of Department's views with regard to the importance of this consideration, so as to aid him in deciding what line of action he will take. After consultation with Minister Wilson, Mr. Everett will inform Cuban Minister that Department has already been informed of the plan of the League Secretariat to place the revision of the Statute as item one on the agenda, which will have been discussed by committee a few days before draft protocol will have received approval of Assembly and presented to committee of signatory powers. Mr. Everett will add that if no apprehension is expressed by Department on receipt of this news, then probability will be that Department does not regard the revision as of primary importance.

Mr. Wilson has suggested that if the Department is concerned with the procedure that has been proposed, it would probably be advisable to bring the matter to Drummond's attention rather than to have it introduced by the Cuban Minister, who will be regarded in the Committee as acting under influence of the Government of the United States.

Please instruct me through Legation.

BLAKE

500.C114/833 : Telegram

*The Secretary of State to the Minister in Switzerland (Wilson)*

[Paraphrase]

WASHINGTON, August 29, 1929—midnight.

95. Consul Blake's telegram of August 28. While the Department appreciates the courtesy of the Cuban Government, it considers that, in view of the non-membership of the United States in the Permanent Court, this Government could not with propriety make any suggestions either direct or indirect with regard to time and method of revision of the Court statute.

STIMSON

500.C114/835a : Telegram

*The Acting Secretary of State to the Minister in Switzerland (Wilson)*

[Paraphrase]

WASHINGTON, August 30, 1929—6 p. m.

97. Department's telegram No. 84, August 14, 11 a. m. Can you ascertain, discreetly, whether Sir Eric will show the message con-

tained in Department's telegram under reference to Council of the League, and if he will, at what moment? Is it your opinion that when Council discusses this message, there will be likelihood that its contents will become known to press at Geneva? Please give Department advance notice of this, if possible. It would be better for the situation here, obviously, if no publicity were given, as premature discussion of the matter over here might well be harmful.

CASTLE

500.C114/841 : Telegram

*The Consul at Geneva (Blake) to the Secretary of State*

GENEVA, September 4, 1929—1 p. m.
[Received 7:17 p. m.]

This morning at private session of the conference of signatory states the question of the accession of the United States was placed first on the agenda. Drummond read a statement to the effect that he had been informed by a dependable source which he could not divulge that the Executive branch of the United States Government found acceptable the terms of the draft protocol prepared by the Committee of Jurists relative to the accession of the United States.

A discussion followed the tone of which indicated that though Drummond's statement that his information was reliable was not questioned and the substance was a cause for gratification it was greatly to be regretted that the United States in a matter which was its primary concern had taken an indirect course in conveying this important information.

The question then arose as to whether Drummond's complete [statement] could be made [public]. Led by the Canadian representative the view was expressed that it might prove embarrassing to the United States Government and perhaps in some way prejudice favorable action by the Senate should the American press and the American people and the Legislative branch of our Government be first informed by the League and through a statement by a non-American of the position of the American Government in this matter. After a short debate it was decided for these reasons not to make Drummond's statement public for the immediate present.

Read to Minister by telephone.

BLAKE

500.C114/843a : Telegram

*The Secretary of State to the Minister in Switzerland (Wilson)*

WASHINGTON, September 5, 1929—noon.

100. Please see Sir Eric Drummond and tell him that I have this morning made the following statement to the press:

"I have carefully examined the draft protocol recommended by the Committee of Jurists last spring for the purpose of meeting the objections represented by the reservations of the United States Senate in regard to the entry of the United States into the World Court and I have satisfied myself that this draft protocol, if ratified by the other signatory powers, would meet the objections raised by the Senate and fully protect the United States against the dangers anticipated by the Senate. Accordingly, last month I notified the Secretary General of the League of Nations, who is presenting this to the other signatory powers, that the draft protocol met with my approval and that if it was accepted by the other states I would recommend to the President of the United States that it be signed and submitted to the Senate for its consent to ratification."

I have also made public the *aide-mémoire* of August 14 conveyed to you in my number 84. [Paraphrase.] You will please inform Sir Eric that in view of other important international matters which probably will be up before the Senate during the coming session this winter, it is not probable that it will be advisable to submit the amended protocol for that body's advice and consent for a considerable period, possibly a year. [End paraphrase.]

STIMSON

---

500.C114/848 : Telegram

*The Minister in Switzerland (Wilson) to the Secretary of State*

[Paraphrase]

BERNE, September 7, 1929—noon.
[Received 2 : 47 p. m.]

78. Your telegram No. 100, September 5, noon. Last night Gilbert[27] and I called on Drummond whom I informed as instructed by you, and with whom I left a copy of your press statement.

With regard to the possible delay in ratification, Sir Eric appreciates your notifying him, but he begged me to say nothing whatever about it in any quarter. Any statement that such possibility exists would have discouraging effect on zeal of the conference, and we have been working enthusiastically to get the draft protocol through in most prompt and satisfactory manner to us. Drummond himself will keep silent on the subject.

It is not at all easy to convey to the Department the extent of consideration being given here at present to our opinions and difficulties. Those who were at the private meeting on September 4 in which Drummond made his statement of your position have told me that the satisfaction and enthusiasm were dramatic, and that sole concern of all was to smooth our road. As was stated in the

---

[27] Prentiss B. Gilbert, assistant chief of the Division of Western European Affairs.

Consulate's telegram of September 7, noon,[28] Van Eysinga [29] earnestly assured Gilbert and me that decision of conference to leave protocol of amendment practically intact [was due to?] the fact that Root had collaborated and that text was thus presumably satisfactory to the United States.

I have sketched theme in this brief manner as background for further independent statements made by Drummond and Van Eysinga. I was urged by latter to cable my Government to point out satisfaction that would be universally felt were it possible to affix signature of draft protocol before close of the Assembly. Van Eysinga believes that large majority will sign as soon as protocol is open, and he hopes that you will not feel that it is obligatory to wait for unanimity as all the states may not have sent full powers, although agreement has been expressed by all.

As for Sir Eric, he thinks that the other powers will recognize the legislative difficulties and will understand the delay in ratification, especially if some statement of reasons for it might be made in Washington at some convenient time in future, but he hopes very earnestly that our signature may be affixed as soon as possible so that there may be no backward flow from present enthusiastic wave of cooperation.

WILSON

---

500.C114/893

*The Minister in Switzerland (Wilson) to the Secretary of State*

No. 1119                                           BERNE, October 8, 1929.
L. of N. No. 1501                                [Received October 26.]

SIR: With reference to my telegram No. 60, August 17, 2 p. m., and other correspondence relating to the Protocols touching on the Statute of the Permanent Court at The Hague and the adhesion of the United States thereto, I have the honor to transmit herewith a note, dated October 7, with enclosures, addressed to the Secretary of State by the Secretary General of the League of Nations, apprising the Secretary of State of the action taken in the Assembly in this matter and transmitting the pertinent documents.

I have [etc.]                                    HUGH R. WILSON

**[Enclosure]**

*The Secretary-General of the League of Nations (Drummond) to the Secretary of State*

GENEVA, 7 October, 1929.

SIR: On June 12th last I had the honour, on instructions from the Council of the League of Nations, to transmit to the United States

---

[28] Not printed.
[29] Vice chairman of the Committee of Jurists.

Government the text of a Protocol regarding the adherence of the United States to the Statute of the Permanent Court of International Justice subject to the reservations formulated by the United States Senate. This instrument had been drafted by a Committee of Jurists appointed by the Council, and had been adopted by the Council at its meeting of June 12th.

In accordance with a resolution adopted by the Council on August 31st, and a resolution of the Assembly of the League of Nations adopted on September 3rd, the Protocol was next referred for examination to the Conference of representatives of States parties to the Statute of the Permanent Court which the Council had convened for the purpose of considering amendments to the Court's Statute. The United States Minister at Berne left with me on August 16th last a memorandum on the basis of which I had the honour to read to the delegates at the first meeting of the Conference, the following statement:

"I thank you for giving me the opportunity of making this statement to the Conference. I am informed from a sure source, which I cannot divulge but on which the members of the Conference can absolutely rely, that the Secretary of State of the United States of America, after careful consideration, is of opinion that the draft Protocol drawn up by the Committee of Jurists would effectively meet the objections set forth in the reservations made by the United States Senate and would constitute a satisfactory basis for the United States to adhere to the Protocol and Statute of the Permanent Court of International Justice, dated December 16th 1920. After the states signatory to the Protocol of Signature and the Statute of the Permanent Court have accepted the draft Protocol, the Secretary of State will request the President of the United States for the requisite authority to sign and will recommend that it be submitted to the Senate of the United States with a view to obtaining its consent to ratification."

The Conference unanimously and without change, except for the correction of a mistake of translation in the French text, which has been notified to the United States Legation at Berne, adopted the Protocol as submitted to you in my letter of June 12th.

The Assembly on September 14th followed the Council in unanimously giving its consent to the provisions of the Protocol.

The Protocol was thereupon opened for signature on behalf of the States signatories of the Protocol of Signature of the Court's Statute and of the United States. Up to the present 50 Members of the League have given their signatures, as shewn in the list annexed.

I enclose an authenticated copy of the Protocol; [30] it is deposited in the archives of the Secretariat at Geneva, and I shall be glad to take any steps in my power to facilitate its signature on behalf of the United States, if, and so soon as, such signature had been decided

[30] Text of protocol, p. 53.

upon. I beg also to enclose, for your information, a copy of the Report upon the Protocol which was made to the Assembly of the League of Nations by its *rapporteur*, Monsieur Politis (Document A. 49.1929.V).[31]

I have at the same time the honour to transmit to you an authenticated copy of a further Protocol [32] intended to effect certain amendments in the Statute of the Permanent Court which, as the result of decisions of the above-mentioned Conference of Government representatives and of the Assembly of the League of Nations, has been opened for signature on behalf of the States signatories of the Protocol of Signature of the Court's Statute and on behalf of the United States. This instrument is deposited in the archives of the Secretariat and has up to the present received 48 signatures as shewn in the annexed list.[33]

From the report on the amendment of the Statute of the Court made to the Assembly by its *Rapporteur*, Monsieur Politis, which I enclose (Document A.50.1929.V),[31] you will see that the amendments which the last-mentioned Protocol seeks to effect in the Statute of the Court, except for certain minor changes and for certain amendments in Articles 4 and 35 of the Statute intended to establish general provisions for the participation in the election of members of the Court of States parties to the Court's Statute which are not Members of the League, without affecting the special agreements which it is proposed to make in the case of the United States of America, are identical with the amendments proposed in the report (Document A.9.1929.V), of which I had the honour to send you a copy with my letter of July 12th last. I venture to call your attention more particularly to the provisions of Articles 2 and 7 of the Protocol dealing with the position of the United States as regards the acceptance by it, and as regards the entry into force, of this instrument, and to the commentary on this matter which is to be found at the top of page 4 of Monsieur Politis' report to the Assembly.

I have [etc.]                                        ERIC DRUMMOND

---

500.C114/913a

*The Secretary of State to President Hoover*

WASHINGTON, November 18, 1929.

MY DEAR MR. PRESIDENT: There is now awaiting our decision the question of whether this Government shall sign the Protocol of Adherence to the Statute of the World Court, on the conditions set

---

[31] Not reprinted.
[32] Text of protocol, p. 44.
[33] Not printed.

out in the Resolution of the United States Senate of January 27, 1926, as this resolution was accepted by the recent protocol of September 14, 1929,[35] now open for signature in Geneva. Closely involved in this decision is the question whether the United States shall also sign the protocol revising the Statute of the World Court, also dated September 14, 1929,[36] and also open for signature at Geneva. This latter protocol provides for certain amendments to the charter statute of the Court which have an important bearing upon the question of our adherence. Practically all of the nations which are signatories to the World Court have already signed these protocols, during the past few weeks in which they have been open for signature, fifty nations having signed the former and forty-nine the latter. The only nations which have not signed the former to date are Albania, Costa Rica, Ethiopia, and Lithuania.

A brief summary of the considerations involved in this question seems advisable.

For over a half a century the United States has taken a leading part in promoting the judicial settlement of international disputes. Not only have its citizens been prominent in advocating such settlement as a substitute for war, but the Government, itself, has participated in many important arbitrations; and our Presidents, as well as our foreign ministers, have frequently acted as arbitrators in such disputes between other nations.

In 1899, the American delegation to the first Hague Conference was active in securing the establishment of the so-called Permanent Court of Arbitration, which still exists and in which we are members. Our Government, under Mr. Roosevelt, submitted to that body its first case, a controversy between the United States and Mexico.

This so-called Court, however, was but a step in the direction proposed by the American delegation. It is not constituted as a real court, holding regular meetings and sessions. It is a mere panel or list of about one hundred and fifty names of gentlemen who have been selected by the member states as qualified and available to sit as arbiters in any disputes which may be submitted to them. Whenever a controversy is desired to be referred to it, the arbitrators who are to sit are selected by the parties, are called out from their private lives, and the case is then referred to them.

In 1907, the American delegates to the second Hague Conference were instructed by President Roosevelt and Secretary of State Root to work for the development of this Court of Arbitration "into a permanent tribunal composed of judges who are judicial officers and nothing else, who are paid adequate salaries, who have no other

---

[35] *Post*, p. 53.
[36] *Post*, p. 44.

occupation, and who are devoting their entire time to the trial and decision of international cases by judicial methods and under a sense of judicial responsibility."

Owing to difficulties in agreeing upon the method of selecting the judges, they were unsuccessful then; but such a Court was finally established in 1920 under the name of the Permanent Court of International Justice, commonly referred to as the World Court. Its charter was framed by a group of distinguished jurists in which the United States was represented; and it is interesting to remember that the difficulty which had prevented the establishment of the Court in 1907 was solved by the suggestion of the American member, Mr. Root, based upon the analogy of a precedent in the creation of our own Federal Constitution, the so-called Connecticut Compromise.

Although this final movement which established the Court was initiated by the League of Nations, the Court took its existence and became effective not by the action of the League but under a statute and protocol separately signed by over fifty states, not all of whom are League members. It thus owes its existence to the independent authority of these signatory states.

This Court has now been in existence for over eight years. It has rendered sixteen judgments in controverted cases and has also delivered sixteen advisory opinions on questions which have been submitted to it. Several of these judgments have been rendered in cases which were of great importance and in which bitter international controversies had existed. Both the judgments and the advisory opinions have rendered important service in settling such controversies and, thus, in preserving peace. Confidence in the Court has so developed that its business is rapidly increasing, and one of the chief purposes of the proposed amendments of its charter statute above mentioned is to provide for more continuous sessions and in other respects to increase the importance and efficiency of the tribunal.

Unless a state has signed the so-called "optional clause", granting to the Court compulsory jurisdiction over it in certain classes of legal disputes (which it is not proposed in the present protocol that the United States shall sign), the Court can take jurisdiction only over cases which the parties themselves refer to it. It has no power to draw an unwilling suitor before it, even if that suitor be a signatory of the Court, and render judgment in respect to such suitor. The Court simply stands ready and available as a carefully chosen and experienced tribunal to which the nations of the world, if and when they choose, can refer their disputes for settlement, without the ordinary delays and difficulties which accompany the selection of arbitrators.

Under the terms of the original charter of the Court, the United

States is already a competent suitor to appear before it. The only obligation which we should assume by joining the Court is one which we ourselves have asked for in the Senate reservations, namely, that we should pay our appropriate share of the expenses of its maintenance. I am informed that the largest contribution by any state has been but little more than thirty-five thousand dollars a year; and, although these expenses will be slightly increased in the future by an increase in the number and salaries of the judges, this obligation in any event will be comparatively trivial.

The only other changes in our present status as suitor which would be effected by our joinder would be to give us new rights and privileges. If we join the Court, we shall be admitted, under the Protocol of Adherence, to participate on an equality with the other signatory states in the election of the judges of the Court. We should also be assured that no amendment of the Charter of the Court could be made without our consent.

Far exceeding the weight of these legal considerations, by joining the Court the United States would resume its time-honored place of leadership in the great movement for the judicial settlement of international controversies, and in the future, through its representatives and jurists, exercise its proper influence in the development of the kind of court which our representatives proposed to the Hague Conference more than thirty years ago.

These considerations were pointed out by my predecessor, Mr. Hughes, in his letter to President Harding on February 17, 1923,[37] advising adherence to the Court. On February 24, 1923, President Harding submitted to the Senate the proposal of adhesion. On March 3, 1925, a resolution was passed by the House of Representatives stating that it desired "to express its cordial approval of the said court and an earnest desire that the United States give early adherence to the protocol establishing the same" and expressing its readiness to participate in the enactment of such legislation as would necessarily follow such approval.

On January 27, 1926, the Senate gave its advice and consent to adherence to the Court upon five reservations. As to the first four of these reservations, no objection has been raised by any of the other signatories of the Court, and they are accepted *in toto* in the proposed Protocol of Adherence now before us.

The Fifth Reservation related to advisory opinions and was as follows:

"5. That the Court shall not render any advisory opinion except publicly after due notice to all states adhering to the Court and to all interested states and after public hearing or opportunity for

---

[37] *Foreign Relations*, 1923, vol. I, p. 10.

hearing given to any state concerned; nor shall it without the consent of the United States entertain any request for an advisory opinion touching any dispute or question in which the United States has or claims an interest."

As to the first half of this reservation, Article four of the Protocol of Adherence now open for signature provides:

The Court shall render advisory opinions in public session after notice and opportunity for hearing, substantially as provided in the now existing articles 73 and 74 of the Rules of the Court.

These rules provide for public hearings by the Court on [and?] advisory opinions after notice to all member states or states admitted to appear before the Court (which would cover the case of the United States whether we adhered or not). They provide for an opportunity for argument on the part of all states notified or asking to be heard and for a public delivery of the opinion in open court.

Furthermore, these rules will be incorporated into the Charter Statute of the Court in the second protocol revising the original statute which, as I first pointed out in this letter, is also open for our signature. By thus incorporating these rules, they become irrepealable and permanent; and, therefore, if we adhere to the Court, these provisions for notice and public hearing cannot be withdrawn without our consent.

By these provisions one of the chief dangers which has influenced American opinion in its objection to the rendering of advisory opinions by the Court has been removed. America's fear lest the opinion of the Court could be sought by some nations and rendered by the Court in private, and that other nations might thus suddenly find their interests compromised by a decision of the Court on a question in which they are involved, no longer has any foundation. The Court in rendering advisory opinions must follow substantially the same procedure as is followed in controversies, or as they are termed in the Rules of the Court "contentious cases." It must act in public; it must give general notice of its proposed hearing, in order that any one who is interested may have an opportunity to be heard; and it must hear them.

But the Court and the pending protocol go even further. In April, 1923, the Court was requested to render an advisory opinion in respect to the effect of the Treaty of Peace between Finland and Russia in reference to the autonomy of Eastern Carelia. When this request came before the Court in January, it was found that Russia, although notified of the pending hearing, refused to take any part in the proceedings. Thereupon the Court refused to go forward with the matter or to render any advisory opinion, saying that it found it to be

"well established in international law that no state can without its consent be compelled to submit its dispute[s] to [with?] other states, whether [*either?*] to mediation or to arbitration, or to any other means of pacific settlement. . . . The Court, being a Court of Justice, cannot even in giving advisory opinions depart from the essential rules guiding their activities as a court."

By this ruling the Court assimilated its practice in advisory opinions where a dispute was involved between any nations to the same rule provided by its charter to govern contentious cases. It will not act unless the parties to such dispute request it to act.

This rule of conduct laid down by the Court itself will now be made imperative and binding upon it by an amendment in the new proposed protocol of revision which is before us for signature. That protocol contains new Article 68 reading as follows:

"In the exercise of its advisory functions the Court shall further be guided by the provisions of the Statute which apply to contentious cases to the extent which it recognizes them to be applicable."

The Court, having already recognized this principle of contentious cases to be applicable, is required by this provision in its charter now to forever hereafter act accordingly.

The report of the Committee of Jurists of September 13, 1929, recommending these amendments, sets forth the reasons for these amendments as to advisory opinions. The amendments are shown to be general in character, so as to include all nations; they also show that the reason why it is proposed to assimilate the procedure on advisory opinions to the procedure on contentious cases is the fundamental reason that unless both parties to a dispute are present and heard, the opinion will not carry any weight. The report, therefore, makes it clear beyond peradventure that the consent of the disputant nations is required in every case as a pre-condition to the granting of an advisory opinion involving any dispute.

By this ruling and amendment another fear as to advisory opinions is removed. If the United States is involved in any dispute or controversy, to whatever degree, with another country, that matter cannot be brought before the World Court without the consent of the United States, even for the purpose of obtaining an advisory opinion.

It will be noticed that these last considerations fully meet the most important portion of the last half of the Fifth Reservation of the Senate. They give to the United States what amounts to an absolute veto upon an advisory opinion touching "any *dispute* . . . in which the United States has . . . an interest."

There remains only that portion of the last sentence in the Fifth Reservation, which provides that the Court shall not, without the consent of the United States, entertain a request for an advisory opinion touching any question in which the United States merely claims an interest and where the claim does not amount to a dispute or controversy. It will be obvious at once that the scope of this remaining clause is necessarily very narrow.

If the United States has an interest in any matter which another nation is seeking to bring up for an advisory opinion which is of so vital a character that the United States would not be satisfied to appear and present its interest to the Court, but desires to shut off all consideration of the Court therefrom by its objection, that matter, in all human probability, will have already attained the character of a dispute or controversy between the two nations, in which case the United States would already have a veto power under the new Article 68 of the Charter Statute, which adopts and enacts the spirit of the Eastern Carelia decision. Otherwise, we should perforce be brought to assume that the United States under this reservation was seeking rather arbitrarily to interfere with its veto in the affairs of other nations in which it had a very slight interest—a conclusion which is not lightly to be assumed. Therefore, I think it a fair assumption to say that the field covered by this last remaining portion of the Fifth Reservation is very narrow, and the need for such a prohibition unlikely ever to arise.

Yet this very slight possibility is elaborately guarded against by the new Protocol of Adherence. So anxious have the framers of this protocol been to meet even the most unlikely desires of the United States that they have devoted the major portion of the protocol to providing machinery to meet this contingency.

Advisory opinions can only be rendered by the Court on the request of the Council or the Assembly of the League of Nations. Article 5 of the proposed protocol provides that the Secretary General of the League shall inform the United States of any proposal for obtaining an advisory opinion of the Court which is pending before the Council or the Assembly, with a view to obtaining an exchange of views between the United States and the Council or Assembly as to whether an interest of the United States is affected. Then when a request for such an opinion actually comes to the Court the Registrar of the Court shall notify the United States and give a reasonable time in which a statement of the United States concerning the request will be received. If necessary, the Court will grant a stay of proceedings in respect to the request for such time as is necessary to enable an exchange of views to take place.

In considering a request for an advisory opinion, if the United States makes objection, there shall be attributed to that objection the same force and effect as attaches to a vote against asking for the opinion given by a member of the Council or the Assembly.

After all these steps have been taken, if it appears that no agreement can be reached and the request for the opinion is still persisted in, and the United States is unwilling to forego its objection, the United States can withdraw immediately from the Court "without any imputation of unfriendliness or unwillingness to cooperate generally for peace or good will".

A mere recital of these precautions makes it apparent how remote the contingency is that the United States will ever be constrained to exercise its right of withdrawal.  It may be suggested here that this contingency of withdrawal might place the United States in an awkward or embarrassing position, and thus submit it to moral pressure to permit a question to which it really objects.  The real hazard is more likely to be the other way.  The influence of the United States is so great, the effect of its mere suggestion of withdrawal would be so embarrassing to the other nations, that there is far more likelihood of their submitting to an ill-founded objection on our part than of their forcing us to withdraw when we really had a legitimate reason for opposition to a question.

If any proof on this point were needed, the extreme consideration which has been shown in this protocol to the objections of the United States and the promptness and unanimity with which the protocol for our adherence to the Court has already been signed by practically all of the nations of the world who are members of the Court, would supply it.

It seems to me, therefore, that the dangers which seemed to inhere in the rendering of advisory opinions by the Court at the time the question was last presented to this Government in 1926 have now been entirely removed, both by the action of the Court itself and by the provisions of these new protocols.  The objections which caused the Senate reservations have been met.  Advisory opinions can no longer be a matter of secret procedure but must follow the forms and receive the safeguards of all formal court proceedings in contentious cases.  Whenever a dispute to which we are a party is involved, no opinion on that dispute can be rendered unless we consent.  When we claim an interest, although no dispute exists, we can, if we so desire, bring our great influence to bear against the rendering of such an opinion with the same legal standing as if we were a member of the Council or the Assembly of the League of Nations and, in the extremely unlikely event of our being unable to persuade the majority of the Council or the Assembly that our interest is real and that the request for the opinion should not proceed, we may withdraw from membership in the Court without any imputation of unfriendliness.

The general situation in the world has also changed since 1926 in a way which renders the World Court more vitally important than ever before.  Since that date practically all the nations of the world have by the execution of the Pact of Paris renounced war as an instrument of national policy and have solemnly covenanted that

"the settlement or solution of all disputes or conflicts of whatever nature or of whatever origin they may be, which may arise among them, shall never be sought except by pacific means."

By this event not only has the need of developing judicial means instead of war to settle the inevitable controversies between nations become more pressing, but it has become even more important to establish and clarify the standards and rules of international conduct by which such controversies can be prevented or minimized. Never has there been a period in the world's history when there was such an imperative need for the development of international law by an international court. Admitting freely all that must be accomplished towards this end by the quasi-legislative action of international conferences which may meet to discuss and agree upon international compacts and codes, it is nevertheless to the judicial action of a World Court, passing upon the individual controversies which arise between nations, that we must look not only for the application and interpretation of these compacts and codes but for the flexible and intelligent development in this way of all the subsidiary principles and detailed rules which will surely be found necessary in such application.

No people are more familiar with this need than the American people, or have greater reason for confidence in this judicial method of developing the law of conduct between separate states. They have seen their own Supreme Court wisely and flexibly work out the myriad difficult and changing problems which in the course of one hundred and forty years have grown out of the compact in which thirteen sovereign states in 1787 agreed to settle their relations by pacific means. And they have seen that Court settle these problems between states with no other power or sanction than the mandate of such a compact and the force of public opinion.

We cannot frankly face the limitations which inevitably inhere in the process of enacting laws or creating public compacts—so evident even in domestic legislation; so certain under the much more difficult conditions of international conferences—without appreciating that in this process of interpretation and application, the World Court will perforce take a vital part in the development of international law. The standards set up by international conferences will hardly be able safely to go beyond the statement of broad general principles; the development of details will necessarily grow out of the application of such principles by the Court. Here again to the American brought up under the common law, patiently and intelligently evolved by six hundred years of judicial decisions, this will be familiar as the method by which a system of law can be most safely, flexibly and intelligently produced.

In this work, protected as they are now protected, advisory opinions rendered on questions before they have ripened into bitter quarrels and wounded pride, can play a most useful part. Such opinions will be rendered with all the advantages of full argument from opposing interests, but before those interests have settled into dangerous international grievances.

Not only do the records of the World Court show how useful such opinions have already proved to be, during the eight years of the Court's existence, in the interpretation of international treaty relations in Europe, but the rather similar form of obtaining declaratory judgments of courts upon domestic legislative questions is becoming a not unfamiliar practice in a number of the United States.

In the great future work of transforming the civilization of this world from a basis of war and force to one of peace founded upon justice, we today stand at the threshold. But it is already evident that in this work the World Court is destined to perform a most fruitful and important part. It is also clear that such an agency is more closely in line with the traditions and habit of thought of America, than of any other nation. And finally it is now possible for us to assist in the support and development of this judicial agent without in the slightest degree jeopardizing our traditional policy as a Government of not interfering or entangling ourselves in the political policies of foreign states or of relinquishing our traditional attitude as a government towards purely American questions with which we are concerned. Is there any reason why on such terms our Government should not join in the support, moral and financial, of such a Court, or why it should not lend its efforts towards the selection of judges who will act in this great work in accordance with the noble traditions of the American judiciary? Or why our Government's great power should not be placed in a position where it can influence for good or check against evil in the future development of the Court's charter and work? I think not.

For all of the foregoing reasons, I have the honor to advise you that, in my opinion, the United States can now safely adhere to the Permanent Court of International Justice, and to that end, that the American Minister in Berne should be immediately authorized to attach the signature of the United States to both of the protocols above mentioned now open at Geneva for our signature. Inasmuch as the signature of the United States has never been attached to the original protocol of the World Court of 1920, I recommend that he be also authorized to sign that protocol as the formal necessary preliminary to the signature of the United States.

I am [etc.]                                        HENRY L. STIMSON

500.C114/908

## President Hoover to the Secretary of State

THE WHITE HOUSE, November 26, 1929.

MY DEAR MR. SECRETARY: I have received your note of November 18th, analyzing the situation created by the almost unanimous signature on the part of the Members of the Permanent Court of International Justice to the Protocol of Accession of the United States of America and to the Protocol of Revision of the Statute, and in accordance with the request contained therein, I authorize you to make the necessary arrangements for the signature on behalf of the United States on December 9th, 1929, of

1. The protocol of Signature of the Statute of the Permanent Court of International Justice,
2. The protocol of Accession of the United States of America to the Protocol of Signature of the Statute of the Permanent Court of International Justice, and
3. The protocol of Revision of the Statute of the Permanent Court of International Justice.

For this purpose, I am enclosing the full powers [38] authorizing Mr. Jay Pierrepont Moffat, Chargé d'Affaires ad interim of the United States at Berne, to sign these documents.

Yours faithfully, HERBERT HOOVER

---

500.C114/893 : Telegram

## The Secretary of State to the Chargé in Switzerland (Moffat)

[Paraphrase]

WASHINGTON, December 2, 1929—11 a. m.

133. With reference to Legation's despatch No. 1119, dated October 8, 1929. The President in his message to Congress tomorrow, December 3,[39] is announcing that he has authorized, on behalf of the United States, the signature of the three protocols, relative to the Permanent Court of International Justice, as follows:

(1) The protocol of signature of the statute of the Court;
(2) The protocol of accession of the United States to protocol of signature of the statute of the Court;
(3) The protocol of revision of the statute of the Court.

Please inform Sir Eric Drummond confidentially of the foregoing and also that full powers have been mailed to you for signature of the documents on Monday, December 9. Department hopes that exhibition to Drummond of these present telegraphic instructions

[38] Not printed.
[39] Ante, p. v.

will be sufficient authority for you to sign.   At time of signature you should present note to Sir Eric of which text is quoted hereunder and which is answer to his note of October 7, 1929, to me.   I suggest, however, that you furnish a copy to him immediately for his confidential information.   If agreeable to Sir Eric both notes will be made public in Washington and in Geneva on December 9.

Until the President's announcement in his message on Tuesday, the whole matter should be kept confidential.   Text of note to be handed Sir Eric is as follows: [40]

"I am instructed by the Secretary of State of the United States to acknowledge with appreciation the receipt of your note of October 7, 1929, in which you informed him of the action taken with regard to the protocol concerning the accession of the United States to the Statute of the Permanent Court of International Justice, as well as the protocol to effect certain amendments in the Statute of the Permanent Court.   Note has been taken of the fact that fifty states have up to date signed the protocol of American accession to the Court.

In view of the almost unanimous acceptance of the protocol of accession by the members of the Court, it gives me pleasure to inform you that at the direction of the President of the United States I have been instructed to sign on behalf of the United States of America, the protocol of signature of the statute of the Permanent Court of International Justice; the protocol of accession of the United States of America to the protocol of signature of the statute of the Permanent Court of International Justice; the protocol of revision of the statute of the Permanent Court of International Justice.

The Secretary of State has requested me to express through you to the members of the Court who have signed the protocol of American accession, the appreciation of the Government of the United States for their friendly endeavors to meet the objections set forth in the reservations of the United States."

You will please express my personal appreciation to Sir Eric for his ceaseless efforts to obtain accession of the United States to the Permanent Court of International Justice on bases satisfactory both to the members of the Court and to this Government.

STIMSON

-------------------

500.C114/914 : Telegram

*The Chargé in Switzerland (Moffat) to the Secretary of State*

[Paraphrase]

BERNE, December 3, 1929—4 p. m.
[Received December 3—1: 22 p. m.]

114.   I have seen Drummond and conveyed to him in confidence the contents of your No. 133, December 2, 11 a. m.   Sir Eric was highly gratified.

-------------------

[40] Quotation not paraphrased.

(1) He regards your telegram as providing me with sufficient authority to sign the three protocols without waiting for arrival of full powers.

(2) Date of signature has been set for Monday, December 9, 3 p. m., Geneva time.

(3) He will release the texts of both notes on December 9, at 5 p. m., which is the equivalent of 11 a. m., Washington time.

(4) Even after message of the President has been made public, Sir Eric will give no advance intimation of either date or hour of prospective signature, but will leave such announcement to your discretion.                                                      MOFFAT

---

500.C114/938

*The Chargé in Switzerland (Moffat) to the Secretary of State*

No. 1220                                      BERNE, December 16, 1929.
L. of N. No. 1570                          [Received January 3, 1930.]

SIR: I have the honor to transmit herewith copy of a note addressed to me by the Secretary General of the League of Nations on December 14, 1929,[41] (3c/16264/279) acknowledging the receipt of a note which I addressed to Sir Eric Drummond in pursuance of the Department's telegraphic instruction No. 133, December 2, 11 a. m., on the occasion of signing the three Protocols relating to the Permanent Court of International Justice.

I likewise transmit the three enclosures to Sir Eric's note, namely, certified true copies of:

> The Protocol of Signature of the Statute of the Permanent Court of International Justice, Geneva, December 16, 1920; [41a]
> The Protocol concerning the revision of the Statute of the Permanent Court of International Justice, Geneva, September 14, 1929, and
> The Protocol relating to the accession of the United States of America to the Protocol of Signature of the Statute of the Permanent Court of International Justice, Geneva, September 14, 1929.

I feel that I should call the attention of the Department to the fact that whereas in the certified true copy of the Protocol of Signature the listing of countries is alphabetical according to French spelling, placing the United States in the third position, in reality my signature appeared last, the order of signing at least among the later signatories being one of chronology. In view of the special

---

[41] Not printed.
[41a] For texts of the protocol of signature, the optional clause, and the statute of the Court, see *Foreign Relations, 1920*, vol. I, pp. 17 and 18.

provision found in the Preamble that "the said Protocol shall remain open for signature by the Members of the League of Nations and by the States mentioned in the Annex to the Covenant of the League", the order may not prove important, but I feel that the rearrangement of signatures should not pass without comment. In the cases of the Protocol of Revision and of the Protocol of American Accession, on the other hand, all signatures were affixed according to French alphabetic listing, as appears in the certified true copies.

I have [etc.]                                    PIERREPONT MOFFAT

[Enclosure 1]

*Protocol for the Revision of the Statute of the Permanent Court of International Justice, Signed at Geneva, September 14, 1929*

1. The undersigned, duly authorised, agree, on behalf of the Governments which they represent, to make in the Statute of the Permanent Court of International Justice the amendments which are set out in the Annex to the present Protocol and which form the subject of the resolution of the Assembly of the League of Nations of September 14th, 1929.

2. The present Protocol, of which the French and English texts are both authentic, shall be presented for signature to all the signatories of the Protocol of December 16th, 1920, to which the Statute of the Permanent Court of International Justice is annexed, and to the United States of America.

3. The present Protocol shall be ratified. The instruments of ratification shall be deposited, if possible before September 1st, 1930, with the Secretary-General of the League of Nations, who shall inform the Members of the League of Nations and the States mentioned in the Annex to the Covenant.

4. The present Protocol shall enter into force on September 1st, 1930, provided that the Council of the League of Nations has satisfied itself that those Members of the League of Nations and States mentioned in the Annex to the Covenant which have ratified the Protocol of December 16th, 1920, and whose ratification of the present Protocol has not been received by that date, have no objection to the coming into force of the amendments to the Statute of the Court which are annexed to the present Protocol.

5. After the entry into force of the present Protocol, the new provisions shall form part of the Statute adopted in 1920 and the provisions of the original articles which have been made the subject of amendment shall be abrogated. It is understood that, until January 1st, 1931, the Court shall continue to perform its functions in accordance with the Statute of 1920.

6. After the entry into force of the present Protocol any acceptance of the Statute of the Court shall constitute an acceptance of the Statute as amended.

7. For the purposes of the present Protocol, the United States of America shall be in the same position as a State which has ratified the Protocol of December 16th, 1920.

DONE at Geneva, the fourteenth day of September nineteen hundred and twenty-nine, in a single copy which shall be deposited in the archives of the Secretariat of the League of Nations. The Secretary-General shall deliver authenticated copies to the Members of the League of Nations and to the States mentioned in the Annex to the Covenant.

Union of South Africa
ERIC H. LOUW

Germany
FR. GAUS

United States of America
JAY PIERREPONT MOFFAT

Australia
W. HARRISON MOORE

Austria
Dr MARCUS LEITMAIER

Belgium
HENRI ROLIN

Bolivia
A. CORTADELLAS

Brazil
M. DE PIMENTEL BRANDAO

Great Britain and Northern Ireland and all Parts of the British Empire which are not separate Members of the League of Nations.
ARTHUR HENDERSON

Bulgaria
VLADIMIR MOLLOFF

Canada
R. DANDURAND

Chile
LUIS V. DE PORTO-SEGURO

China
CHAO-CHU WU

Colombia
FRANCISCO JOSÉ URRUTIA

Denmark
GEORG COHN

Dominican Republic
M. L. VASQUEZ G.

Spain
C. BOTELLA

Estonia
A. SCHMIDT

Finland
A. S. YRJÖ-KOSKINEN

France
HENRI FROMAGEOT

Greece
POLITIS

Guatemala
LUIS V. DE PORTO-SEGURO

Haiti
LUC DOMINIQUE

Hungary
LADISLAS GAJZAGO

India
MD. HABIBULLAH

Irish Free State
JOHN A. COSTELLO

Italy
VITTORIO SCIALOJA

Japan
ISABURO YOSHIDA

Latvia
CHARLES DUZMANS.

Liberia
A. SOTTILE

Luxemburg
BECH

Nicaragua
FRANCISCO TORRES F.

Norway
ARNOLD RAESTAD

New Zealand
C. J. PARR

Panama
J. D. AROSEMENA

Paraguay
  R. V. Caballero de Bedoya

The Netherlands
  V. Eysinga

Peru
  Mar. H. Cornejo

Persia
  P. P. Kitabgi

Poland
  M. Rostworowski
  S. Rundstein

Portugal
  Prof. Doutor J. Lobo d'Avila Lima

Roumania
  Antoniade

Salvador
  J. Gustavo Guerrero

Kingdom of the Serbs, Croats and Slovenes
  I. Choumenkovitch

Siam
  Varnvaidya

Sweden
  E. Marks von Würtemberg

Switzerland
  Motta

Czechoslovakia
  Zd. Fierlinger

Uruguay
  A. Guani

Venezuela
  C. Zumeta

### Annex to the Protocol of September 14, 1929

#### AMENDMENTS TO THE STATUTE OF THE PERMANENT COURT OF INTERNATIONAL JUSTICE

Articles 3, 4, 8, 13, 14, 15, 16, 17, 23, 25, 26, 27, 29, 31, 32 and 35 are replaced by the following provisions:

New text of Article 3.

The Court shall consist of fifteen members.

New text of Article 4.

The members of the Court shall be elected by the Assembly and by the Council from a list of persons nominated by the national groups in the Court of Arbitration, in accordance with the following provisions.

In the case of Members of the League of Nations not represented in the Permanent Court of Arbitration, the lists of candidates shall be drawn up by national groups appointed for this purpose by their Governments under the same conditions as those prescribed for members of the Permanent Court of Arbitration by Article 44 of the Convention of the Hague of 1907 for the pacific settlement of international disputes.

The conditions under which a State which has accepted the Statute of the Court but is not a member of the League of Nations, may participate in electing the members of the Court shall, in the absence of a special agreement, be laid down by the Assembly on the proposal of the Council.

New text of Article 8.

The Assembly and the Council shall proceed independently of one another to elect the members of the Court.

New text of Article 13.

The members of the Court shall be elected for nine years.
They may be re-elected.
They shall continue to discharge their duties until their places have been filled.  Though replaced, they shall finish any cases which they may have begun.
In the case of the resignation of a member of the Court, the resignation will be addressed to the President of the Court for transmission to the Secretary-General of the League of Nations.
This last notification makes the place vacant.

New text of Article 14.

Vacancies which may occur shall be filled by the same method as that laid down for the first election, subject to the following provision: the Secretary-General of the League of Nations shall, within one month of the occurrence of the vacancy, proceed to issue the invitations provided for in Article 5, and the date of the election shall be fixed by the Council at its next session.

New text of Article 15.

A member of the Court elected to replace a member whose period of appointment has not expired, will hold the appointment for the remainder of his predecessor's term.

New text of Article 16.

The members of the Court may not exercise any political or administrative function, nor engage in any other occupation of a professional nature.
Any doubt on this point is settled by the decision of the Court.

New text of Article 17.

No member of the Court may act as agent, counsel or advocate in any case.

No member may participate in the decision of any case in which he has previously taken an active part as agent, counsel or advocate for one of the contesting parties, or as a member of a national or international Court, or of a commission of enquiry, or in any other capacity.

Any doubt on this point is settled by the decision of the Court.

New text of Article 23.

The Court shall remain permanently in session except during the judicial vacations, the dates and duration of which shall be fixed by the Court.

Members of the Court whose homes are situated at more than five days' normal journey from The Hague shall be entitled, apart from the judicial vacations, to six months' leave every three years, not including the time spent in travelling.

Members of the Court shall be bound, unless they are on regular leave or prevented from attending by illness or other serious reason duly explained to the President, to hold themselves permanently at the disposal of the Court.

New text of Article 25.

The full Court shall sit except when it is expressly provided otherwise.

Subject to the condition that the number of judges available to constitute the Court is not thereby reduced below eleven, the Rules of Court may provide for allowing one or more judges, according to circumstances and in rotation, to be dispensed from sitting.

Provided always that a quorum of nine judges shall suffice to constitute the Court.

New text of Article 26.

Labour cases, particularly cases referred to in Part XIII (Labour) of the Treaty of Versailles and the corresponding portions of the other Treaties of Peace, shall be heard and determined by the Court under the following conditions.

The Court will appoint every three years a special Chamber of five judges, selected so far as possible with due regard to the provisions of Article 9. In addition, two judges shall be selected for the purpose of replacing a judge who finds it impossible to sit. If the parties so demand, cases will be heard and determined by this Chamber. In the absence of any such demand, the full Court will sit. In both cases, the judges will be assisted by four technical assessors sitting with them, but without the right to vote, and chosen with a view to ensuring a just representation of the competing interests.

The technical assessors shall be chosen for each particular case in accordance with rules of procedure under Article 30 from a list of "Assessors for Labour Cases" composed of two persons nominated by each Member of the League of Nations and an equivalent number nominated by the Governing Body of the Labour Office. The Governing Body will nominate, as to one-half, representatives of the workers, and, as to one-half, representatives of employers from the list referred to in Article 412 of the Treaty of Versailles and the corresponding Articles of the other Treaties of Peace.

Recourse may always be had to the summary procedure provided for in Article 29, in the cases referred to in the first paragraph of the present Article, if the parties so request.

In Labour cases, the International Office shall be at liberty to furnish the Court with all relevant information, and for this purpose the Director of that Office shall receive copies of all the written proceedings.

### New text of Article 27.

Cases relating to transit and communications, particularly cases referred to in Part XII (Ports, Waterways and Railways) of the Treaty of Versailles and the corresponding portions of the other Treaties of Peace, shall be heard and determined by the Court under the following conditions:

The Court will appoint every three years a special Chamber of five judges, selected so far as possible with due regard to the provisions of Article 9. In addition, two judges shall be selected for the purpose of replacing a judge who finds it impossible to sit. If the parties so demand, cases will be heard and determined by this Chamber. In the absence of any such demand, the full Court will sit. When desired by the parties or decided by the Court, the judges will be assisted by four technical assessors sitting with them, but without the right to vote.

The technical assessors shall be chosen for each particular case in accordance with rules of procedure under Article 30 from a list of "Assessors for Transit and Communications Cases" composed of two persons nominated by each Member of the League of Nations.

Recourse may always be had to the summary procedure provided for in Article 29, in the cases referred to in the first paragraph of the present Article, if the parties so request.

### New text of Article 29.

With a view to the speedy despatch of business, the Court shall form annually a Chamber composed of five judges who, at the request of the contesting parties, may hear and determine cases by summary procedure. In addition, two judges shall be selected for the purpose of replacing a judge who finds it impossible to sit.

### New text of Article 31.

Judges of the nationality of each of the contesting parties shall retain their right to sit in the case before the Court.

If the Court includes upon the Bench a judge of the nationality of one of the parties, the other party may choose a person to sit as judge. Such person shall be chosen preferably from among those persons who have been nominated as candidates as provided in Articles 4 and 5.

If the Court includes upon the Bench no judge of the nationality of the contesting parties, each of these parties may proceed to select a judge as provided in the preceding paragraph.

The present provision shall apply to the case of Articles 26, 27 and 29. In such cases, the President shall request one or, if necessary, two of the members of the Court forming the Chamber to give place to the members of the Court of the nationality of the parties concerned, and, failing such or if they are unable to be present, to the judges specially appointed by the parties.

Should there be several parties in the same interest, they shall, for the purpose of the preceding provisions, be reckoned as one party only. Any doubt upon this point is settled by the decision of the Court.

Judges selected as laid down in paragraphs 2, 3 and 4 of this Article shall fulfil the conditions required by Articles 2, 17 (paragraph 2), 20 and 24 of this Statute. They shall take part in the decision on terms of complete equality with their colleagues.

New text of Article 32.

The members of the Court shall receive an annual salary.

The President shall receive a special annual allowance.

The Vice-President shall receive a special allowance for every day on which he acts as President.

The judges appointed under Article 31, other than members of the Court, shall receive an indemnity for each day on which they sit.

These salaries, allowances and indemnities shall be fixed by the Assembly of the League of Nations on the proposal of the Council. They may not be decreased during the term of office.

The salary of the Registrar shall be fixed by the Assembly on the proposal of the Court.

Regulations made by the Assembly shall fix the conditions under which retiring pensions may be given to members of the Court and to the Registrar, and the conditions under which members of the Court and the Registrar shall have their travelling expenses refunded.

The above salaries, indemnities and allowances shall be free of all taxation.

New text of Article 35.

The Court shall be open to the Members of the League and also to States mentioned in the Annex to the Covenant.

The conditions under which the Court shall be open to other States shall, subject to the special provisions contained in treaties in force, be laid down by the Council, but in no case shall such provisions place the parties in a position of inequality before the Court.

When a State which is not a Member of the League of Nations is a party to a dispute, the Court will fix the amount which that party is to contribute towards the expenses of the Court. This provision shall not apply if such State is bearing a share of the expenses of the Court.

The French text of Article 38, No. 4, is replaced by the following provision:

4. Sous réserve de la disposition de l'article 59, les décisions judiciaires et la doctrine des publicistes les plus qualifiés des différentes nations, comme moyen auxiliaire de détermination des règles de droit.

[There is no change in the English text.]

Articles 39 and 40 are replaced by the following provisions:

New text of Article 39.

The official languages of the Court shall be French and English. If the parties agree that the case shall be conducted in French, the judgment will be delivered in French. If the parties agree that the case shall be conducted in English, the judgment will be delivered in English.

In the absence of an agreement as to which language shall be employed, each party may, in the pleadings, use the language which it prefers; the decision of the Court will be given in French and English. In this case the Court will at the same time determine which of the two texts shall be considered as authoritative.

The Court may, at the request of any party, authorise a language other than French or English to be used.

New text of Article 40.

Cases are brought before the Court, as the case may be, either by the notification of the special agreement or by a written application addressed to the Registrar. In either case the subject of the dispute and the contesting parties must be indicated.

The Registrar shall forthwith communicate the application to all concerned.

He shall also notify the Members of the League of Nations through the Secretary-General, and also any States entitled to appear before the Court.

The English text of Article 45 is replaced by the following provision:

The hearing shall be under the control of the President or, if he is unable to preside, of the Vice-President; if neither is able to preside, the senior judge present shall preside.

[There is no change in the French text.]

The following new chapter is added to the Statute of the Court:

### CHAPTER IV.—ADVISORY OPINIONS

New Article 65.

Questions upon which the advisory opinion of the Court is asked shall be laid before the Court by means of a written request, signed either by the President of the Assembly or the President of the Council of the League of Nations, or by the Secretary-General of the League under instructions from the Assembly or the Council.

The request shall contain an exact statement of the question upon which an opinion is required, and shall be accompanied by all documents likely to throw light upon the question.

New Article 66.

1. The Registrar shall forthwith give notice of the request for an advisory opinion to the Members of the League of Nations, through the Secretary-General of the League, and to any States entitled to appear before the Court.

The Registrar shall also, by means of a special and direct communication, notify any Member of the League or State admitted to appear before the Court or international organisation considered by the Court (or, should it not be sitting, by the President) as likely to be able to furnish information on the question, that the Court will be prepared to receive, within a time-limit to be fixed by the President, written statements, or to hear, at a public sitting to be held for the purpose, oral statements relating to the question.

Should any Member or State referred to in the first paragraph have failed to receive the communication specified above, such Member or State may express a desire to submit a written statement, or to be heard; and the Court will decide.

2. Members, States, and organisations having presented written or oral statements or both shall be admitted to comment on the statements made by other Members, States, or organisations in the form, to the extent and within the time-limits which the Court, or, should it not be sitting, the President, shall decide in each particular case. Accordingly, the Registrar shall in due time communicate any such written statements to Members, States, and organisations having submitted similar statements.

New Article 67,

The Court shall deliver its advisory opinions in open Court, notice having been given to the Secretary-General of the League of Nations and to the representatives of Members of the League, of States and of international organisations immediately concerned.

New Article 68.

In the exercise of its advisory functions, the Court shall further be guided by the provisions of the Statute which apply in contentious cases to the extent to which it recognises them to be applicable.

[Enclosure 2]

*Protocol of Accession of the United States of America to the Protocol of Signature of the Statute of the Permanent Court of International Justice, Signed at Geneva, September 14, 1929*

The States signatories of the Protocol of Signature of the Statute of the Permanent Court of International Justice, dated December 16th, 1920, and the United States of America, through the undersigned duly authorised representatives, have mutually agreed upon the following provisions regarding the adherence of the United States of America to the said Protocol subject to the five reservations formulated by the United States in the resolution adopted by the Senate on January 27th, 1926.

## ARTICLE 1

The States signatories of the said Protocol accept the special conditions attached by the United States in the five reservations mentioned above to its adherence to the said Protocol upon the terms and conditions set out in the following Articles.

## ARTICLE 2

The United States shall be admitted to participate, through representatives designated for the purpose and upon an equality with the signatory States Members of the League of Nations represented in the Council or in the Assembly, in any and all proceedings of either the Council or the Assembly for the election of judges or deputy-judges of the Permanent Court of International Justice, provided for in the Statute of the Court. The vote of the United States shall be counted in determining the absolute majority of votes required by the Statute.

## ARTICLE 3

No amendment of the Statute of the Court may be made without the consent of all the Contracting States.

## ARTICLE 4

The Court shall render advisory opinions in public session after notice and opportunity for hearing substantially as provided in the now existing Articles 73 and 74 of the Rules of Court.

## ARTICLE 5

With a view to ensuring that the Court shall not, without the consent of the United States, entertain any request for an advisory opinion touching any dispute or question in which the United States has or claims an interest, the Secretary-General of the League of Nations shall, through any channel designated for that purpose by the United States, inform the United States of any proposal before the Council or the Assembly of the League for obtaining an advisory opinion from the Court, and thereupon, if desired, an exchange of views as to whether an interest of the United States is affected shall proceed with all convenient speed between the Council or Assembly of the League and the United States.

Whenever a request for an advisory opinion comes to the Court, the Registrar shall notify the United States thereof, among other States mentioned in the now existing Article 73 of the Rules of Court, stating a reasonable time-limit fixed by the President within which a written statement by the United States concerning the request will be received. If for any reason no sufficient opportunity for an exchange of views upon such request should have been afforded and the United States advises the Court that the question upon which the opinion of the Court is asked is one that affects the interests of the United States, proceedings shall be stayed for a period sufficient to enable such an exchange of views between the Council or the Assembly and the United States to take place.

With regard to requesting an advisory opinion of the Court in any case covered by the preceding paragraphs, there shall be attributed to an objection of the United States the same force and effect as attaches to a vote against asking for the opinion given by a Member of the League of Nations in the Council or in the Assembly.

If, after the exchange of views provided for in paragraphs 1 and 2 of this Article, it shall appear that no agreement can be reached and the United States is not prepared to forgo its objection, the exercise of the powers of withdrawal provided for in Article 8 hereof will follow naturally without any imputation of unfriendliness or unwillingness to co-operate generally for peace and goodwill.

## ARTICLE 6

Subject to the provisions of Article 8 below, the provisions of the present Protocol shall have the same force and effect as the provisions of the Statute of the Court and any future signature of the Protocol of December 16th, 1920, shall be deemed to be an acceptance of the provisions of the present Protocol.

## ARTICLE 7

The present Protocol shall be ratified. Each State shall forward the instrument of ratification to the Secretary-General of the League of Nations, who shall inform all the other signatory States. The instruments of ratification shall be deposited in the archives of the Secretariat of the League of Nations.

The present Protocol shall come into force as soon as all States which have ratified the Protocol of December 16th, 1920, and also the United States, have deposited their ratifications.

## ARTICLE 8

The United States may at any time notify the Secretary-General of the League of Nations that it withdraws its adherence to the Protocol of December 16th, 1920. The Secretary-General shall immediately communicate this notification to all the other States signatories of the Protocol.

In such case, the present Protocol shall cease to be in force as from the receipt by the Secretary-General of the notification by the United States.

On their part, each of the other Contracting States may at any time notify the Secretary-General of the League of Nations that it desires to withdraw its acceptance of the special conditions attached by the United States to its adherence to the Protocol of December 16th, 1920. The Secretary-General shall immediately give communication of this notification to each of the States signatories of the present Protocol. The present Protocol shall be considered as ceasing to be in force if and when, within one year from the date of receipt of the said notification, not less than two-thirds of the Contracting States other than the United States shall have notified the Secretary-General of the League of Nations that they desire to withdraw the above-mentioned acceptance.

DONE at Geneva, the fourteenth day of September, nineteen hundred and twenty-nine, in a single copy, of which the French and English texts shall both be authoritative.

Union of South Africa
ERIC H. LOUW

Germany
FR. GAUS

United States of America
JAY PIERREPONT MOFFAT

Australia
W. HARRISON MOORE

Austria
Dr. MARCUS LEITMAIER

Belgium
HENRI ROLIN

Bolivia
A. CORTADELLAS

Brazil
M. DE PIMENTEL BRANDAO

Great Britain and Northern Ireland and all Parts of the British Empire which are not separate Members of the League of Nations.
ARTHUR HENDERSON

Bulgaria
VLADIMIR MOLLOFF

Canada
R. DANDURAND

Chile
LUIS V. DE PORTO-SEGURO

China
CHAO-CHU WU

Colombia
 Francisco José Urrutia

Cuba
 G. de Blanck

Denmark
 Georg Cohn

Dominican Republic
 M. L. Vasquez G.

Spain
 C. Botella

Estonia
 A. Schmidt

Finland
 A. S. Yrjö-Koskinen

France
 Henri Fromageot

Greece
 Politis

Guatemala
 F. Mora

Haiti
 Luc Dominique

Hungary
 Ladislas Gajzago

India
 Md. Habibullah

Irish Free State
 John A. Costello

Italy
 Vittorio Scialoja

Japan
 Isaburo Yoshida

Latvia
 Charles Duzmans

Liberia
 A. Sottile

Luxemburg
 Bech

Nicaragua
 Francisco Torres F.

Norway
 Arnold Raestad

New Zealand
  C. J. Parr

Panama
  J. D. Arosemena

Paraguay
  R. V. Caballero de Bedoya

The Netherlands
  V. Eysinga

Peru
  Mar. H. Cornejo

Persia
  P. P. Kitabgi

Poland
  M. Rostworowski
  S. Rundstein

Portugal
  Prof. Doutor J. Lobo d'Avila Lima

Roumania
  Antoniade

Salvador
  J. Gustavo Guerrero

Kingdom of the Serbs, Croats and Slovenes
  I. Choumenkovitch

Siam
  Varnvaidya

Sweden
  E. Marks von Würtemberg

Switzerland
  Motta

Czechoslovakia
  Zd. Fierlinger

Uruguay
  A. Guani

Venezuela
  C. Zumeta

INFORMAL SUGGESTIONS FOR FURTHER IMPLEMENTING THE TREATY FOR THE RENUNCIATION OF WAR SIGNED AT PARIS, AUGUST 27, 1928 [1]

[On July 25, 1929, during the discussions arising out of the Sino-Russian controversy, the Secretary of State made a suggestion for the implementation of the Kellogg-Briand Pact, i. e., the Treaty for the Renunciation of War; see memorandum by the Secretary of State, "Suggestions for a Commission of Conciliation," volume II, page 243.]

711.0012Anti-War/968½

*The French Embassy to the Department of State*

NAVAL SITUATION OF FRANCE AND ITALY

*1. Position of France*

1°. No difficulty can arise between France and the United States.

2°. France has no fear to entertain against Great Britain, although the enormous naval superiority of the latter country might create an uneasy feeling on the part of the other.

3°. On the side of Italy France may have serious fears due to the fact that the Government of that country is constitutionally irresponsible and depends entirely upon the will of a single man. Everyday the Italian press, which relies entirely upon Mussolini, addresses threats to France and the whole Italian nation is being fed with the idea that conquests on the side of her neighbor country are possible. Likely, such threats are not serious; nevertheless they constitute a disturbing factor. History shows that an act of madness is always possible when national feelings have been systematically raised to a certain pitch.

4°. An alliance between Italy and Germany is not inconceivable and in that case France, obliged to face two fronts, would be put in a dangerous situation. In fact, free communications with Africa where she finds an important proportion of her military contingents, are vital. Italian raids against such an important artery may be extremely serious.

5°. Is it absolutely sure that in a war of that kind France could depend upon the unconditional help of Great Britain?

---

[1] For previous correspondence concerning the treaty, see *Foreign Relations*, 1928, vol. I, pp. 1 ff.

6°. As far as United States are concerned it is true that they have declared that war is a crime and that consequently the nation which causes war is criminal. But they have always declined to consider the consequences of that principle and they seem to claim the right to furnish supplies indiscriminately to the aggressive nation, and to her victim under penalty of war.

## 2. Position of Italy

1°. In case of war with France Italy would be placed in an extremely disadvantageous position. Her enormous length of coast exposes her to attacks from all sides and her main rail lines might be cut at any time.

2°. From a strategic point of view, Italy is entirely surrounded by French possessions (Bizerte, Corsica, Toulon, and on her eastern coasts, Yugo-Slavia who would probably be an allied [ally] of France).

3°. Economically speaking, Italy produces no iron, no coal, no metal, no lumber, no textiles, no oil. Her financial resources are limited. Her political situation is uncertain.

4°. Italy depends also completely upon foreign help for her food supplies. A few German submarines almost succeeded in bringing shortage of food in England. What could numerous French submarines not do?

5°. From the point of view of her resources as well as of her geographic independence, Italy finds herself, as regards France, in serious conditions of inferiority. Naval forces constitute only one factor of that disparity.

6°. Since Italy lives within the limits of a sea which it would be easy to close entirely, no country could be more attached to the principle of the freedom of the seas, a principle of which America is an ardent defender.

## 3. Conclusion

For France as well as for Italy, there are questions more vital than proportion of naval armament (neither in fact wants a race for armaments). The question of general security is the most important for them.

For France absolute security lies within a defensive entente with Great Britain and a favorable interpretation of the Kellogg Pact by the United States.

For Italy her security lies within the principles of the freedom of the sea.

Consequently nothing could be better for the peace of the Old Continent in which America is so interested, as shown by present negotiations, than an extension by the United States of the principles of Article 7 of the Washington Conference:[2]

"The contracting Powers agree that whenever a situation arises which, in the opinion of any one of them, involves the application of the stipulations of the present Treaty (the Kellogg Pact), and renders desirable discussion of such application, there shall be full and frank communication between the Contracting Powers concerned".

The United States might object that such a clause is similar to "foreign entanglements". In fact the United States have the right to protect themselves against an event which constitutes for them a serious threat. They have the right to be interested into a conference against war just as they would interest themselves into a conference against plague, against noxious insects, etc. The principle of the foreign policy of the United States was enounced by President Coolidge when he said in his Gettysburg speech: *Everywhere there is war or threat of war, something happens which is contrary to the interests of the United States.*[3] Hence the necessity for them to take measures of prophylactic nature./.

[WASHINGTON,] September 25, 1929.

---

711.0012Anti-War/982

*Memorandum by the Secretary of State*

[WASHINGTON,] October 10, 1929.

The French Ambassador came in to say that the French Government was very warmly pleased with the visit of Mr. MacDonald[4] and that they considered it a great success. I thanked him and told him that I was especially glad to see him because of the confidential note which he had sent me a few days ago.[5] I told him that that represented just the line of thought which I had been following, particularly the suggestion of the extension of the Pacific Treaty of the four powers[6] to other parts of the world. I then reminded him of the difficulties which we found under the Kellogg-Briand Pact when we reminded China and Russia of their obligations thereunder, in that there was no machinery for investigation and for enlightening the public opinion of the world as to the controversy.

---

[2] Article VII of the Nine-Power Treaty concerning China, signed at Washington, February 6, 1922; *Foreign Relations*, 1922, vol. I, p. 280.
[3] In his speech delivered on May 30, 1928, President Coolidge said in part: "It is almost impossible to conceive of any conflict anywhere on earth which would not affect us injuriously."—*Congressional Record*, vol. 69, pt. 10, p. 10729.
[4] For correspondence concerning the British Prime Minister's visit, see vol. III, pp. 1 ff.
[5] *Supra.*
[6] Treaty signed at Washington, December 13, 1921, *Foreign Relations*, 1922, vol. I, p. 33.

I pointed out that in the Kellogg-Briand Pact, unlike the League of Nations, we had no sanction except the public opinion of the world and that I felt from my experience both in China and Russia and in regard to Bolivia and Paraguay, the importance of machinery which should be invokable by the parties themselves and also by outsiders when they would not invoke it. He said he agreed with me, recalling Mr. Coolidge's analogy of plague in which outsiders were interested that it should not spread. I suggested that he ascertain Mr. Briand's[7] views on this subject and as to the possibility of taking further steps to achieve such machinery for arousing public opinion. He manifested great interest and said he would be glad to do so.

He asked me if I would give him an *aide memoire*. I told him I would be glad to draw one up as soon as possible and give it to him, but that I felt that the initiative in this really belonged to Mr. Briand because he was one of the authors of the Kellogg-Briand Pact and this was so closely related to the purpose of that Pact. The Ambassador asked whether I thought it should take the form of the extension of the Pacific Treaty or of the Kellogg-Briand Pact. I told him I had no conclusive views but that I thought that the latter pact was more in the thoughts of the world today and more popular than the Pacific Treaty; that, however, I should like to have Mr. Briand's views on it. He asked whether I thought that such a treaty would not meet opposition in the Senate. I told him I could not go so far as to say that, but I thought it would be less likely to meet opposition than any other treaty because the MacDonald visit had stimulated great interest in the Kellogg-Briand Treaty.

In the course of his felicitations on the success of the MacDonald visit I said we should be very glad to welcome Mr. Briand in a similar manner and asked him whether he thought there would be any chance of Mr. Briand making such a visit. He seemed quite interested and said he thought there would.

---

711.0012Anti-War/1002½

*Memorandum by the Assistant Secretary of State (Castle)*

[WASHINGTON,] October 25, 1929.

THE SECRETARY: The French Ambassador came to see me this morning to say that, in talking with you the other day, you had said that you felt there was a lack in the Kellogg Pact in that at least means for settling such disputes as might arise were not provided. He seemed to think that you had particularly in mind the fact that suggestions or advice might be resented as in the case of

---

[7] Aristide Briand, French Minister for Foreign Affairs.

Russia. The Ambassador said that you had asked him to get some suggestions as to what might be done from Monsieur Briand. The Ambassador has not heard from Briand, who he thinks probably did not fully understand the suggestion made by cable. He said that he himself, therefore, had drawn up something along the line of your suggestion and had shown it to the French international lawyers who happened to be here at the moment. He said he did this because he thought it was always more satisfactory to talk of something definite than to discuss a not clearly defined idea. He asked me to translate his draft and submit it to you merely as a basis of something to think about, to submit it also as a very modest contribution on his part.

W. R. C[ASTLE,] JR.

[Annex—Translation]

*Informal Draft by the French Ambassador (Claudel) of a Multilateral Declaration Relative to the Treaty for the Renunciation of War*

The high contracting parties, deeply sensible of the responsibilities imposed on them by the Pact of Paris which they signed;

Understanding that in the actual condition of international relations there can be no such thing as an isolated conflict, that a state of tension arising in any part of the world interests the entire family of nations and particularly the signatories of the Pact;

Conscious of the obligations which they have thus assumed toward their cosignatories and the practical consequences which flow from it as affecting any nation that might be placed outside the Pact, which today unites practically all civilized peoples;

Declaring that if a situation should arise where the views and the interests of one nation seem to be violently in opposition with the views and the interests of another nation, they will both make every effort to bring to the knowledge of the other states signatory to the Pact and above all those who are especially interested in the dispute and the prospective conflict, all the circumstances of fact and of law which are such as may enlighten them and assist them in forming a just opinion;

They declare further that, among the pacific methods indicated in Article II of the Pact of Paris, which might well include either arbitration or conciliation as specified in different treaties, or procedure established or envisaged by the League of Nations, or recourse to the international tribunals of the Hague, or special commissions which might be instituted with or without the collaboration of one of the bodies mentioned above,

They will not exclude such immediate measures as advice, the good offices or common consultation among the states signatory of the Pact of Paris, but that on the other hand that they will consult the wishes of all and will furnish a frank and loyal collaboration.

---

711.0012Anti-War/1031 : Telegram

*The Ambassador in France (Edge) to the Secretary of State*

PARIS, December 16, 1929—4 p. m.
[Received December 16—3 :30 p. m.]

565. On the morning of December 14, I was received by Briand in the customary audience preliminary to presenting my letter of credence. He was extremely affable and everything passed off most satisfactorily. During the course of the conversation, the Pact of Paris having been casually mentioned, Briand remarked in the more than an off hand way that he felt that Pact lacked something; that what it really needed was an extra article in the nature of that contained in the Four-Power Pacific Treaty which would justify the signatory powers in taking action in an emergency. (He apparently had reference to article 2 of the Four-Power Treaty Relating to Insular Possessions in the Pacific.) I replied that I presumed that what he meant was some article envisaging concerted action such as that initiated by you in the recent Russo-Chinese dispute. He replied, "Exactly." I added that I could see no objection to such an article provided of course it did not envisage military intervention of any kind. He said that he was quite in accord on this point. You may wish to let me have your views on this suggestion in the event that Briand should raise the point at a later meeting.

I am informed by the Foreign Office my reception by the President will take place probably Wednesday.

EDGE

## PARTICIPATION OF THE UNITED STATES IN THE WORK OF THE PREPARATORY COMMISSION FOR THE DISARMAMENT CONFERENCE, SIXTH SESSION[1]

500.A15/853

*The Minister in Switzerland (Wilson) to the Secretary of State*

No. 733                                                      BERNE, February 9, 1929.
L. of N. No. 1269                                   [Received February 21.]

SIR: I have the honor to refer to my despatch No. 715, of January 23, 1929, (L. of N. No. 1259)[2] relative to a projected visit by Mr. Colban, Chief of the Disarmament Section of the Secretariat of the League of Nations, to the various capitals of the great Powers of Europe for the purpose of discussing a preliminary agenda for the sixth session of the Preparatory Commission on Disarmament, which is scheduled to meet on April 15. Hearing that Mr. Colban had returned on the 7th instant, I at once got in touch with him, and he outlined to Mr. Rand[3] and myself in considerable detail the views which he had already expressed: in Paris (to Mr. Massigli and Mr. Loudon, Chairman of the Preparatory Committee), in Berlin (to Count Bernstorff), and in Prague. Tonight (the 9th instant) Mr. Colban intends to leave for London to consult Lord Cushendun,[4] and again to get in touch with Mr. Loudon in Paris on his return. As soon as he reaches Geneva he will communicate with me and arrange a time for visiting me in Berne to inform me of his discussions in London as well. In giving a summary of what Mr. Colban anticipates and hopes will be the agenda for the meeting, it may be that I give it in more precise and logical form than it actually shapes itself in his mind, for the reason that the conversation was of long duration, that I was unable to take notes, and therefore had to reduce the conversation to a skeleton form in my own thoughts.

Mr. Colban's plans divide themselves into certain broad categories, which I shall enumerate in the order in which he hopes that they will be taken up by the Preparatory Commission.

1. Certain work remains for the Security Committee, inasmuch as the last Assembly, at the instigation of the Hungarian delegation,

---

[1] For correspondence relating to the fifth session, see *Foreign Relations*, 1928, vol. I, pp. 235 ff. The proceedings of the sixth session are printed in League of Nations, *Documents of the Preparatory Commission for the Disarmament Conference Entrusted With the Preparation for the Conference for the Reduction and Limitation of Armaments*, Series VIII (C.195.M.74.1929.IX).

[2] Not printed.

[3] Elbridge Rand, Consul at Geneva.

[4] Massigli, Bernstorff and Cushendun were the French, German and British delegates, respectively, on the Preparatory Commission.

requested the Committee to make a study of Article 13 of the Covenant. Hungarian interest in this matter presumably results from a desire to pursue still further the optants question. Certain other purely formal business may lie before the Security Committee, but Mr. Colban is of the opinion that the Preparatory Commission, by resolving itself into the Security Committee, can accomplish such work as is before the latter Committee in one day.

2. The Russian proposal. (The Department will remember that this is a proposal for a progressive reduction of armaments. See C.P.D.–117.[5]) Mr. Colban believes that since the Committee took a resolution apropos of the first Russian proposal to continue its work along the path already indicated, the Committee will be urged by the President to adopt the position that the second Russian proposal should be split up into its component parts and treated as amendments to the pertinent sections of the draft convention. I pointed out to Mr. Colban that I had no doubt that the Russians would jump with enthusiasm at this solution; if we voted directly on acceptance or rejection of their proposal, we could probably kill it in an hour, whereas such a plan as he outlined would enable the Russians to air their views on every sentence of every clause of every chapter of the draft convention. Personally, it seems to me that if the Committee decides to follow Colban's program, it will create itself into the most perfect and sustained sounding-board for Russian propaganda that has yet been offered.

3. Count Bernstorff's proposals relative to publicity submitted in the session of March, 1928. (See C.P.D.–111.[6]) Count Bernstorff has shown entire willingness to have these proposals debated in their proper place, in the second reading of the draft convention, and it is believed that it will be found that a simple method of attacking this problem is to treat it as an amendment presumably to Chapter V of the draft convention. It is possible, however, that certain of the Powers will take the position that most of the matter covered in the German proposals is already being debated by the Special Commission on the Manufacture of Arms. However, it is needless further to discuss this matter at the present moment.

4. The second reading of the draft convention. Under this heading, according to Mr. Colban's ideas, the subjects could be treated logically and practically in the following order:

a. Those questions which were definitely reserved for second reading,—for example, the question of poison gas. Mr. Colban is earnestly desirous that some definite statement, if only a resolution, be adopted applauding the ratification by some of the states of the poison gas protocol adopted at the time of the Traffic in Arms Conference.[7]

b. Budget limitation. On this Mr. Colban expressed the view that he was heartily in sympathy with our position that it was impossible to limit budgets; nevertheless, he thought it would be of extreme value to provide for the most complete publicity in budgeting and perhaps to work out a unified method of presenting expenses.

[5] Annex 5 to minutes of the fifth session (1928), League of Nations, *Documents of the Preparatory Commission*, Series VI (C.165.M.50.1928.IX), p. 347.
[6] Annex 1 to minutes of the fifth session (1928), League of Nations, *Documents of the Preparatory Commission*, Series VI, p. 315.
[7] *Foreign Relations*, 1925, vol. I, p. 89.

*c.* War material in reserve. Mr. Colban points out that this involves those questions which I have just been discussing in the Private Manufacture Conference,[8] namely, whether an indication of the value of such material is of any use, or whether it is necessary to have more definite measure thereon. As the Department will recollect, those nations which have large arsenals have so far shown themselves entirely unwilling to furnish other than value of stock on hand.

*d.* Land effectives. On this question Mr. Colban stated that he finds an extreme reluctance on the part of the Continental Powers (by this I take it he did not mean to include Germany) to make any concessions from their point of view until they knew what form the solution of the naval question would take,—this in line, of course, with their general thesis of the inter-relation of the various arms.

*e.* The naval question.

The ground on which Mr. Colban is urging the order of events such as I have described above has some practical virtue from our point of view. The Secretariat has estimated that it would take the Commission approximately three weeks to debate as far as through 4*b*. By this time the delegates would be very ready to adjourn the session, especially when faced with the very thorny questions which follow. It might be preferred merely to adjourn the session rather than to close it, and to name a future date for the continuation of the more thorny discussions.

Mr. Colban asked me expressly whether we would have naval advisers on our delegation. I told him that the Department had not yet instructed me in this matter but that I assumed it would be necessary to have them in view of the type of agenda which he contemplated. He stated that he was very glad to hear this, since irrespective of whether naval questions were to be debated in plenary session he hoped that the presence of naval advisers would enable them, by informal discussion among themselves, to find a way out of the naval impasse. I took the liberty of stating, as a purely private expression of views, my scepticism as to the possibility of this difficulty being solved by technical conversations alone, pointing out to Mr. Colban that the naval question in all the countries of big navies had assumed such importance politically that only the most responsible authorities of the various countries could stand sponsors for any agreement, and that furthermore only such responsible authorities could make the concessions which would be necessary for the reaching of an accord. I was careful to emphasize that my Government had given me no instructions to present this view, and that it was my personal opinion only.

Mr. Colban then touched upon the proposal made by Germany in the Assembly, namely, that the Preparatory Commission resolve itself

[8] See *ibid.*, 1928, vol. I, pp. 292 ff.

into a group of subcommittees to treat the various questions on which agreement had not yet been reached. I am not able to state whether or not Mr. Colban favors such procedure, as he did not explicitly express himself on this point.

Mr. Colban emphasized several times the fact that he was speaking purely from his own point of view; that he had not discussed all of these questions in great detail even with Sir Eric Drummond; and that his view did not necessarily represent that of Mr. Loudon. He added that, while he had, of course, no objection to my reporting his views confidentially, he trusted that it would be remembered that he was secretary to this organization and could, therefore, have no official views on any question which arose.

Copy of this despatch is being furnished to the Embassies at Paris, London, and Brussels, and to the Consulate at Geneva.

I have [etc.]                                        HUGH R. WILSON

---

500.A15/855 : Telegram

*The Minister in Switzerland (Wilson) to the Secretary of State*

[Paraphrase]

BERNE, February 27, 1929—3 p. m.
[Received February 27—2 : 30 p. m.]

17. Reference my despatch No. 733, February 9. Mr. Colban has returned from his second trip. Yesterday he informed me that although he encountered no opposition to the project, he met with an entirely noncommittal attitude except from Germans. He was informed by Bernstorff that German delegation to last two sessions of Preparatory Commission had been seriously reproached, after its return home, not because of failure of Commission to reach an agreement but on ground that the German delegation had specifically failed to provoke a serious debate in effort to reach an agreement. This time, therefore, they were under the necessity of pushing the Commission into a serious discussion of all points, and under this impulsion Bernstorff intends to introduce resolution to form subcommittee to debate naval questions. Presumably this subcommittee will be composed of chief delegates of naval Powers and not of experts.

Since the Three Power Conference in 1927,[9] much propaganda has been disseminated to effect that naval difficulty of France is chief obstacle to an accord, and blame for failure has been placed on naval Powers. Colban's plan to place naval matter at end of agenda unquestionably will bring out on other points differences of opinion as profound as those existing on naval questions. From our point of view his plan would seem advisable way to approach the problem, as

---

[9] See *Foreign Relations*, 1927, vol. I, pp. 1 ff.

it would make clear that naval question is only one of many in regard to which profound differences of opinion exist.

Mr. Colban emphasized purely tentative nature of his plan, and states that it is his hope that in the next Council the representatives of the Great Powers can be induced to discuss these matters and that he will keep me advised of results of such discussions. In meantime, he was particularly anxious that any suggestion from the United States regarding our preferences on procedure should arrive as soon as possible so that he might utilize it discreetly in conversation with the representatives of the other states before the actual meeting takes place. He would appreciate having even an expression as to whether his program would, in general, meet with our approval. Considering the essentially negative attitude of almost all the other delegations, any preference we might express of a positive nature should have strong chance of adoption.

WILSON

---

500.A15/855 : Telegram

*The Secretary of State to the Minister in Switzerland* (*Wilson*)

[Paraphrase]

WASHINGTON, March 1, 1929—2 p. m.

24. Your No. 17, February 27, 3 p. m. This Government would not feel warranted in making any proposals as to procedure to be adopted. Department has examined agenda proposed by Colban. It appears to be sound and logical order for dealing with pending questions. You may inform him of Department's view.

The Government of the United States has consistently maintained that sole determining factor should be progress of the work in hand. Proposal offered by German delegates to split Preparatory Commission into committees would appear merely to be device for creating impression of activity without regard to practical considerations. In view of present status of work, the method which the German delegation has proposed would appear to lead directly to confusion and deadlock, or, at best, merely to the illusion of progress.

We are unable to see, therefore, any justification for the subordination of this primary purpose to personal political fortunes of any individual delegate. Undoubtedly the German delegation would share this view were it proposed to disrupt Commission's work in order to save American delegation from criticism at home.

These considerations should be taken into account in informal discussion with the Secretariat at your discretion.

KELLOGG

500.A15/863a

*The Secretary of State to the Ambassador in Belgium* (*Gibson*)

WASHINGTON, March 23, 1929.

SIR: The President has instructed me to inform you of his desire that you continue to act as Chairman of the American Delegation at the Sixth Session of the Preparatory Commission for the Disarmament Conference, which is to meet at Geneva on April 15, 1929.

The President has directed that the following persons be designated to assist you at this conference:

> Advisers:
>> From the Department of State:
>>> The Honorable Hugh R. Wilson;
>> From the War Department:
>>> Major John N. Greely;
>> From the Navy Department:
>>> Rear Admiral Hilary P. Jones;
> Technical Assistants:
>> Jay Pierrepont Moffat, Esquire,
>> Commander Harold C. Train, U. S. N.

On the basis of information which has reached the Department, it is assumed that before undertaking a second reading of the draft convention, the Commission will discuss certain general proposals, among them

(1) Report on the Work of the Security Committee.

(2) The proposal of the Russian Soviet Government for a progressive reduction of armaments.

(3) The proposal made by the German Delegation regarding publicity in connection with armaments.

1. Report on the Work of the Arbitration and Security Committee. While this Government has considered from the beginning that this was a purely European question and therefore did not feel warranted in accepting membership on the Committee on Arbitration and Security, it is not anticipated that the Committee will have a definite report ready for approval, but that the discussion will be confined to certain phases upon which agreement has not as yet been reached. In this event, there will presumably be no occasion for seeking an expression of the views of this Government. Should the Committee, however, have a report ready, the attitude of the American Government on the general subject of security has been very clearly developed in connection with the conclusion of the General Pact for the Renunciation of War,[10] in the statements of its attitude on the arbitration treaties and more recently in the attitude of the American Delegation

---

[10] *Foreign Relations*, 1928, vol. I, p. 153.

at the Havana Conference [11] and the International Conference of American States on Conciliation and Arbitration.[12]  On the basis of the documents which have been furnished to you, you will be enabled to point out, should occasion arise, that the United States has demonstrated its eagerness to contribute to general security by the development of the resources of arbitration, inquiry and conciliation not only in the Western Hemisphere, the region in which it is primarily interested, but likewise, throughout the world, by its solemn undertaking not to resort to war as an instrument of national policy.  The United States cannot, however, join in any pact for security containing any obligation to enforce the treaty either by economic or military sanctions; in fact, beyond what we have done in treaties already concluded, we cannot become a party to any security pact.

2. The Proposal of the Russian Soviet Government of March 23, 1928, providing for a reduction, within two years, of all land, naval, and air armaments by an amount ranging from one-half to one-fourth their present strength.  This proposal has been carefully examined by this Government, which, however, has not been able to escape the conclusion that it is essentially impracticable as a basis for further discussion.  In many respects, it remains as objectionable as the earlier proposal of the Soviet delegation looking toward the complete abolition of all military establishments, and the criticisms voiced at the Fifth Session of the Commission with regard to this latter scheme are to a large extent applicable to the present proposal.  In particular, this proposal takes into consideration no other factor than the scale of the present military establishments.  The discussions at past sessions of the Commission have clearly shown that it is impossible to base a practical solution of the disarmament question on such abstract mathematical formulas applied indiscriminately to all categories of armaments, land, sea, and air, as are contained in the second Russian proposal.  They take no account of the varying needs of individual countries as regards national security, depending on such factors as geographical position, area, population and resources.  In this connection, it may be noted that the League Covenant provides that the League Council, in formulating plans for a reduction of armaments, shall take account of the "geographical situation and circumstances of each state."

The completely impractical nature of the proposal would, in the opinion of this Government, justify setting it aside in order not to waste the time of the Commission in fruitless discussion; it has been reported to the Department that there may be a proposal to divide the Russian scheme into various parts to be treated as amendments to

---

[11] See *ibid.*, pp. 527 ff.
[12] See *ibid.*, pp. 621 ff.

the pertinent sections of the draft convention with the idea that it be discussed in proper order during the second reading. It would seem that this would be an even more wasteful procedure than a general discussion resulting in the elimination of the Russian Proposal as a whole, as it would afford the Russian Delegates an opportunity in connection with each paragraph of the draft convention for a general restatement of their views on all subjects and for publicity and propaganda. Of the three courses suggested as possible, the wisest would seem to be for a certain number of Delegations to state briefly the obvious objections to the Russian Proposal as a whole and then to call for a vote eliminating it as a matter of discussion. A less desirable alternative would be to agree to a general discussion of the Soviet Proposal with the understanding that the Committee would, after hearing what was to be said for and against it, vote upon it as a whole.

3. The Proposal made by the German Delegation, on March 15, 1928, regarding Publicity in connection with Armaments. This proposal would not seem to require any fresh instructions from the Department. Our position as favoring the fullest measure of publicity in regard to all measures of budgetary expenditure, military forces and materiel in stock has been fully set forth before the Preparatory Commission, and there would seem to be no occasion for your intervening in the debate further than to restate our position if you deem this desirable. It is not believed that the Commission would be warranted in devoting a great deal of time to the discussion of this proposal, which has been taken up in part by the Special Commission for the Preparation of a Draft Convention on the Manufacture of Arms and in part under the proposals for the control of budgetary expenditure.

Second Reading of the Draft Convention. If the Commission reaches a second reading of the draft Convention, it is assumed that it will take up at first a limited number of questions which were definitely reserved for consideration at the second reading, namely:

(a) Poison Gas,
(b) Limitation of Budgetary Expenditure,
(c) War Materiel in Stock,
(d) Land Effectives, including Trained Reserves,
(e) Limitation of Naval Armaments.

(a) Poison Gas. The American Government was a pioneer in the effort toward the abolition of the use of poison gas and concluded a treaty with Great Britain, France, Italy and Japan on February 6, 1922,[13] for this purpose. Although the United States has ratified this treaty, it has not yet entered into effect due to the failure of other Powers to ratify. It will furthermore be recalled that the American

---

[13] *Foreign Relations*, 1922, vol. I, p. 267.

Delegation at the Arms Traffic Conference in 1925 took the initiative in the conclusion of a protocol for the abolition of the use in war of asphyxiating gas, and of bacteriological methods of warfare.[14] The protocol was signed by thirty-eight nations, including the United States, but has, up to the present time, only been ratified or acceded to by Austria, Belgium, Egypt, France, Italy, Liberia, Russia and Venezuela. It is the earnest hope of this Government that further ratifications of both of these conventions will bring them into effect at the earliest possible date.

(b) Limitation of Budgetary Expenditure. This Government has seen no reason to modify its view that there is no useful purpose to be served by the conclusion of measures for budgetary limitation and that the cost of building or maintaining armament or armies varies so in each country, due to differences in exchange rates, prices of materiel and labor costs, that it could not possibly serve as a logical basis for limitation. These views have been fully set before the Commission and you will probably not find it necessary to enter into the debate further than to restate our previous position that such limitation is neither practical nor possible.

(c) War Matériel in Stock. This Government feels that agreements for the limitation of armaments would not be really complete without provisions for publicity regarding war matériel in stock. This view was set forth in the Preparatory Commission and its Technical Subcommittees in the most definite form and is a matter of record. On first reading, it was considered proper for the American representatives to state our views in this matter and to make an earnest endeavor to persuade other delegates to adopt these views. When, however, we come to second reading, it must be remembered that agreement can be reached only by a considerable measure of mutual concession. This imposes upon each participating government the obligation carefully to examine the whole field covered by the draft Convention and to make the fullest measure of concession possible upon points which are not of vital interest to it. The Department has scrutinized the draft Convention with a view to finding what concessions it can make without sacrificing fundamental American interests, and it is felt that while we should certainly prefer to have strict measures of publicity for matériel in stock, this is, after all, a matter of secondary importance and one on which we can, with some reluctance, defer to the wishes of other governments in the hope that this concession will awaken a responsive effort to meet our views in regard to those questions which we consider of primary American importance. You are therefore authorized when, in your judgment, it becomes desirable, clearly to restate the American

[14] *Ibid.*, 1925, vol. I, p. 89.

position on this subject and to state that in the desire to promote general agreement our views will not be allowed to constitute an insurmountable obstacle as regards this particular question.

(*d*) Land Effectives including Trained Reserves. The American Government is convinced that the question of trained reserves is of fundamental importance in connection with any general scheme for the limitation of armaments and that no general agreement can be thoroughly accurate and effective which fails to take account of such forces which, in many instances, comprise the major portion of the military strength of a nation. It will be remembered that this Government has maintained this point of view in agreement with certain other Governments since the first meeting of the Preparatory Commission. However, we have felt that we should discriminate between those questions which were of vital importance, and those of theoretical value to the United States. We have felt throughout that it was improbable that any agreement could be reached which would call for any reduction of the land forces of the United States. In these questions we are disposed, as a practical matter, to defer to the views of those countries whose land forces constitute their chief military interest, again in the hope that this will cause them in like manner to defer to us as regards those questions which are of primary importance to us. If it becomes apparent to you that by making a concession on this question we can contribute to an ultimate agreement, you are authorized clearly to restate our reasons for believing in the limitation of trained reserves and for supporting that view in the Preparatory Commission, and also in stating our reasons for abandoning our insistence in the hope of facilitating agreement. You may consider it advisable to take this occasion for intimating that we trust that our concessions in regard to land armaments will prompt others to display a similar spirit in making concessions on naval questions.

In accordance with your previous instructions, you should naturally refuse to countenance for the United States any measure or methods of supervision and control in connection with carrying out any of the provisions of the draft Convention.

(*e*) The Naval Question. It is the task of the Preparatory Commission to agree upon a method of naval limitation, consideration of quantitative proposals being reserved for a final conference; it is therefore unnecessary at this time to furnish you with precise figures as to tonnages, percentages, ratios, or other definite criteria which would be acceptable to this Government.

In previous discussions the American Government has been disposed to examine in the most friendly spirit any proposed methods for effecting the limitation of naval armaments. Nevertheless, it has found no reason for modifying its view that the simplest, fairest and most practical method is that of limitation by tonnage by categories,—a method which has been given practical and satisfactory application in the Washington Treaty.[15] While it is realized that this does not constitute an exact and scientific gauge of strategic strength, we have nevertheless felt that it did constitute a method which has the advantages of simplicity and of affording to each Power the freedom to utilize its tonnage according to its special needs.

The United States has supported its thesis throughout the first reading, but in view of the disparity of views presented and the unacceptability of this thesis unmodified, this Government has sought, in the various methods presented, for some solution which might offer the possibility of compromise and general acceptance. During the Third Session of the Preparatory Commission the French Delegation brought forward a method which was an attempt to combine the total tonnage with tonnage by categories, by the assignment of a total tonnage to each nation and the division, for the duration of any agreement to be signed, of this total tonnage into five categories of ships by specific tonnages. The proposal was subsequently modified so as to provide that the percentage allocated to any given category might be increased by a certain percentage to be agreed upon, such increase to be transferred from any other category or categories not already fixed by existing treaty (battleships and aircraft carriers).

In the hope of facilitating agreement as to naval armaments, this Government is disposed to accept in principle this method of effecting limitation. It is, of course, the understanding of this Government that this involves an agreement upon the method alone and not upon any proposed quantitative tonnage or, as the matter is now understood, on the percentages to be transferred from one category to another. All quantitative proposals of any kind should properly be reserved for discussion by an eventual conference.

This Government is disposed to give full and friendly consideration to any supplementary methods of limitation which may be calculated to make the application of the French thesis acceptable to other Powers and if such a course appears desirable when the time comes for considering the application of that thesis, this Government will be prepared to give consideration to the method of equivalent tonnage values. In order to arrive at the basis of comparison in the case of categories in which there are marked variations as to unit characteristics, it might be desirable in arriving at an equivalent

---

[15] Treaty for the limitation of naval armament, February 6, 1922, *Foreign Relations*, 1922, vol. I, p. 247.

tonnage to consider certain factors which produce these variations, such as displacement, age and calibre of guns. This method of comparison has been given careful consideration and this Government will be in a position to discuss the subject whenever it becomes of practical interest.

Aside from the very material concession which you have been authorized to make on land armament, this Government feels that in accepting the French thesis in regard to naval armaments it is giving unmistakable evidence of its anxiety to contribute, by all possible means, to the early achievement of general agreement. It is hoped that by the removal of obstacles in regard to land armaments the question is simplified in the sense that further discussions will be limited to those Powers directly and vitally interested in this phase of the disarmament problem, and it is hoped that unhampered by opposition from this Government they may find it possible to agree among themselves. As regards naval armaments, which are recognized as being of vital concern to this country, we have given further proof of our earnest desire to contribute to the solution of the problem by material concessions, in the hope of simplifying the issues involved and promoting the possibility of general agreement on naval matters. In the event that there is any attempt on the part of other delegates to inject into the debates a discussion of the specific problems involved in our naval relations with other countries, you will, of course, find it desirable to point out that this is a subject entirely without the scope of the Preparatory Commission.

This Government realizes, of course, that the discussions of the Preparatory Commission are merely for the purpose of agreeing on methods to be recommended to a General Conference for the limitation of armament; nevertheless, it is desirable that you bear in mind the following considerations as to our general position regarding the limitation of naval armament:

This Government believes that there can be no complete and effective limitation of armament unless all classes of war vessels, including cruisers, destroyers, and submarines, are limited, and would not agree to any method which would result in leaving any class of war vessels unrestricted. In its reply of September 28, 1928, to communications from the British and French Governments concerning an understanding reached between them as to a basis of naval limitation, this Government pointed out that this understanding applied to only one type of cruiser and one type of submarine and would leave totally unlimited a large class of effective fighting units.[16] Our note also called attention to the position we took at the Geneva Naval Con-

---

[16] See telegram No. 329, September 25, 1928, 3 p. m., to the Chargé in France, *Foreign Relations*, 1928, vol. I, p. 282.

ference and the fact that we there made a proposition for real limitation.

If the proposition, suggested by the French at the last Session of the Commission and subsequently modified, should be adopted as a basis of limitation, it will be impossible ever to make an agreement with Great Britain unless that Government very materially modifies its demands. However, rather than to insist on a plan of fixing exact tonnages for each category, it may be advisable to agree to the French plan, which, of course, we would be willing to see accepted at a final Conference, provided that the tonnages in each class should be sufficiently low to mean a real naval reduction and provided the percentages of variation from the tonnage of each of the categories should be satisfactory. Again it appears probable that the British Government will insist on two classes of cruisers and possibly of submarines. In that event, it would seem impossible to work out, to the satisfaction of the United States, the French plan of permitting the transfer from the tonnage of one category to that of another.

It should be borne in mind that in the event a final conference is called this Government feels that the principal emphasis must be placed on reduction rather than mere limitation of armaments. In all the conferences in which this Government has participated, it has consistently advocated the lowest levels of armament that could be arrived at on a relative basis.

Ever since the Three-Power Conference in Geneva,[17] this Government has felt more and more impressed with the fact that the only real contribution we could make lay in the direction of an actual drastic cut rather than the mere placing of a limit beyond which we agreed not to go. This could hardly be considered an achievement in the cause of disarmament, but merely the sanctioning of existing armaments or even a tacit encouragement to build up to still higher levels.

Moreover, it is the belief of this Government that the levels of naval armament are almost entirely a relative matter between the principal naval Powers, since the whole world, aside from the Washington Treaty Powers, does not contain sufficient cruiser tonnage to endanger any one of them. Therefore, the great burden of taxation entailed by the building and maintenance of unnecessarily large naval establishments seems wholly unjustifiable and this Government would be willing to take any steps necessary to arrive at a low level agreed upon by the remaining Powers and feels that in doing so it is meeting the ardent desire for disarmament manifested by the very meeting in which we are taking part.

---

[17] See *ibid.*, 1927, vol. I, pp. 1 ff.

Unless we can find some method of agreeing upon a genuine reduction in existing establishments, we can see no useful purpose to be served by concluding an agreement which would countenance extensive building.

This Government, in accordance with Article 21 of the Treaty for the Limitation of Naval Armaments, is obligated to call a conference during the year 1931 to consider what changes, if any, may be necessary in that Treaty, and furthermore has already expressed its willingness to call that conference as early as January in that year. Naturally this conference will only affect the five Naval Powers signatory to the Washington Treaty and will not touch on land armament. However, in view of the fact that Great Britain, although bound by the provisions of the Washington Treaty, and thus unable to effect any changes before 1931, has frequently asserted its willingness to reduce the size and extend the life of battleships, and has maintained that great saving might be effected thereby (a view not shared by this Government), it seems that if the subject is raised you should state that the American Government will be prepared in 1931 to discuss the subject of the reduction in size and armament and the extension of life of battleships and aircraft carriers.

I am [etc.]                                                   FRANK B. KELLOGG

500.A15/864

*The British Embassy to the Department of State*

### MEMORANDUM

The instructions to the British delegate on the Preparatory Committee for the Disarmament Conference which meets at Geneva on April 15th have lately been under review by His Majesty's Government.

In the opinion of His Majesty's Government it seems generally to be felt that it will be impossible at this stage to make progress with the problems of naval disarmament and, indeed, it appears to His Majesty's Government unlikely that discussions in full committee at Geneva, or even in a special naval sub-committee, would be fruitful of results until the ground has been prepared by previous consultation through diplomatic channels, particularly between the United States Government and themselves.

In these circumstances His Majesty's Government propose at the forthcoming meeting of the Preparatory Committee at Geneva to take the line that the difficulty of proceeding with the naval problem is no reason for doing nothing with regard to disarmament on land and in the air. Bound by the Washington Treaty the principal naval Powers have already accepted a very large measure of limitation and even reduction of naval armaments. On the other hand no agreement has yet been reached in the matter of armies or air forces and as it is most desirable that progress should be made in these spheres His Majesty's Government have given to their delegate instructions designed to enable him to cooperate in the most helpful manner possible. Nevertheless they fear that the possibility of no agreement being reached along the present lines of discussion must be contemplated.

His Majesty's Government have therefore been considering whether, in the event of a breakdown, any more promising compromise could be proposed.

The Committee have for two years past been trying to elaborate a convention which would in practice amount only to an agreement by the signatory Powers not to exceed certain maximum limits which would be fixed by each for themselves. This is not a very ambitious scheme. In fact, each signatory Power would only bind itself under this projected convention not to exceed a certain maximum program for a given period. Even so, however, the Preparatory Committee has been unable to agree on the headings or framework of the proposed programs. Discussion, largely theoretical, continues but no real progress is being made toward the actual limitation of armaments. In these circumstances if it becomes clear that along the present lines no real progress can be made, His Majesty's Government contemplate proposing that rather than do nothing, and since the Committee appear to be unable to agree on the exact form in which programs should be presented, each Government should be asked to submit a program in its own form in the hope that these several programs may eventually be assembled and embodied in a convention binding the signatories not to exceed them. The programs envisaged should cover a period of years.

As the United States Government are aware the French and other Continental Governments attach great importance to their theory that the naval, land and air arms must be treated alike. In these circumstances were His Majesty's Government to put forward the proposal above indicated they might be asked whether they would be willing to apply the same plan to navies as well as to armies and air forces. For their part His Majesty's Government would be willing to do so and are disposed to believe that such a procedure if applied to naval armaments might after friendly discussion between His Majesty's Government and the United States Government assist to a solution of the difficulties hitherto separating the United States Government and themselves and might render possible of realisation some, if not all, of the results which the naval powers have been seeking to obtain. Before issuing final instructions to their representative, however, His Majesty's Government desire to assure themselves that the United States Government agree with them that it would be unwise to resume the discussion of naval issues on the old lines until there has been an opportunity for further confidential discussion between the two Governments. His Majesty's Government have not interpreted Mr. Houghton's note of September 28th, 1928,[18] as implying that the United States Government would be indisposed towards such confidential discussions and they consequently hope that the United States Government will agree with them that it is desirable that the naval debate at Geneva should for the present be adjourned. If the United States Government do in fact agree with His Majesty's Government on this point His Majesty's Government would be glad to know whether, in the event of a failure to reach agreement at the forthcoming meeting at Geneva with regard to armies and air forces and in the event of the British delegate being consequently obliged to suggest procedure by programs in order to avoid a complete breakdown, and in the subsequent event of his being asked whether he would agree to the adoption of a similar procedure with regard to navies, the United States Government would see any objection.

His Majesty's Government are anxious to avoid giving any impression that they despair of the success of the Preparatory Committee on present lines and to avoid prejudicing its chances in any way. The proposal outlined above would only be made if the discussion on present lines definitely fails. In that event, the British delegate would explain his proposals to the members of the Committee before they disperse and beg them to obtain the views of their Governments thereon at the earliest opportunity. But for the moment His Majesty's Government wish only to obtain confidentially the view of the United States Government as a preliminary step and they trust that the United States will regard this communication as entirely confidential lest as above indicated the impression should be given that His Majesty's Government despair of the success of the Preparatory Committee on present lines and thereby prejudice its chances.

WASHINGTON, March 28, 1929.

---

500.A15/864

### The Department of State to the British Embassy

#### MEMORANDUM

The British Embassy's memorandum of March 28th arrived during the discussions incident to the preparation for the forthcoming meeting of the Preparatory Commission on April 15th. The American

---

[18] See telegram No. 329, September 25, 1928, 3 p. m., to the Chargé in France, *Foreign Relations*, 1928, vol. I, p. 282.

Government appreciates the candor with which the British Government has set forth its views on the slight prospect of achievement at the forthcoming meeting, and the desire of the British Government to bring about some tangible result. The American Government cordially agrees with His Majesty's Government that progress toward the settlement of naval questions would be much more probable if it could be preceded by consultation between the two Powers, and this Government would be most happy to examine in a friendly spirit any proposals which the British Government may care to put forward.

As is pointed out in the memorandum of the British Embassy, certain continental Governments have always insisted that land, naval and air limitation must be considered concurrently as part of a single program; it therefore seems unlikely that it will be possible to avoid discussion of naval questions without the risk of giving the impression that the naval Powers are preventing discussion of the problem in its entirety. It is also obvious that the time remaining before the meeting of the Commission is rather short for discussions between the two Governments.

The memorandum of the British Embassy is not clear to the American Government in its statement that the purpose of the Preparatory Commission is "to elaborate a convention which would, in practice, amount only to an agreement of the signatory Powers not to exceed certain maximum limitation which would be fixed by each for themselves". It has been the understanding of the American Government that the purpose of the Commission was to agree on a method of limitation and to prepare a draft treaty which would serve as a frame-work for ultimate quantitative limitation and reduction to be agreed upon by a plenary conference. In other words, it has always been understood that the Preparatory Commission was not authorized to deal with quantitative proposals of any character. The Commission is made up of representatives of a limited number of Powers and any decisions it reaches must receive the approval of numerous other Governments before they can be made a basis upon which ultimate agreement may be reached. This point of view has repeatedly been expressed by numerous delegations without contradiction.

This being the case, the American Government does not entirely understand the suggested proposal of the British Government that each nation should be asked to submit a program of its own in the hope that these several programs might eventually be assembled and embodied in a convention binding the signatories not to exceed them. Such a proposal would seem to call for a material modification of the functions of the Commission. It is quite true that this technical aspect of the competence of the Preparatory Commission should not be permitted to interfere with any ultimate agreement among the naval Powers, but on the other hand a complete change of the basis of discussion from that of method to that of actual quantitative proposals covering all aspects of armament so completely alters the character of the work of the Commission that the American Government doubts whether it would receive general assent. Furthermore, even if such a radical change should be made, it does not appear that the suggested proposal of the British Government, based presumably on this change, would constitute an advance in the discussion of the limitation or reduction of naval armament. The building programs of the naval Powers are, in general, matters of public record, and a mere statement of such programs would not go beyond an agreement to perpetuate existing armaments and projected increases. This could hardly be considered useful achievement in the cause of limitation and reduction. The American Government hopes sincerely that some progress toward agreement on method may be made in the course of the forthcoming meeting. On the other hand, if it should be found that agreement, even of this nature, cannot be reached, the American Government is inclined to believe that ultimate agreement would be advanced by a clear statement of the reasons for failure to agree, rather than by resort to an expedient which might disappoint the hopes of effective reduction and limitation of armaments.

If the meeting of the Preparatory Commission takes place on April 15th, the date now fixed, there will obviously be practically no time prior to the meeting for discussion with the British Government. However, the American Government welcomes the friendly spirit exhibited by the British Government in its memorandum and will at all times be disposed to examine in the most friendly spirit any suggestions that the latter Government may care to advance as a basis for discussion.

WASHINGTON, April 4, 1929.

---

500.A15/870

## The British Embassy to the Department of State

### MEMORANDUM

The substance of the memorandum communicated to His Majesty's Ambassador on the 4th instant by the Secretary of State regarding the forthcoming meeting of the Preparatory Committee on Disarmament at Geneva was duly forwarded to His Majesty's Government.

His Majesty's Government have taken note with pleasure of the renewed expressions of readiness on the part of the United States Government to examine in a friendly spirit any further proposals which His Majesty's Government may be able to formulate. They are, however, bound to discuss such questions with the Dominion Governments and they feel sure that the United States Government will appreciate that this fact and the proximity of the approaching General Election in England make it difficult for them to reach final decisions at the present moment. But they are most anxious to avoid further public discussion and possible controversy until there has been an opportunity for a full and confidential exchange of views between them and the United States Government.

His Majesty's Government have gained the impression from the memorandum from the Department of State that the United States Government have not fully understood their present proposal and they would offer the following explanations with a view to clearing up such misapprehension.

His Majesty's Government had not contemplated that the Preparatory Committee should consider programmes at all events at the present stage. Their proposal was merely that in the event of discussion on the present lines failing once more to produce any appreciable result, the Committee should be asked to consider whether alternative procedure by programmes would not be more effective. It would perhaps be too much to expect a final answer to this question at the forthcoming session. Delegates could only be invited to obtain the views of their Governments and it would in all probability be necessary to adjourn the proceedings in order to give time for consideration. While this proposal perhaps goes somewhat beyond mere procedure, the fact that the Committee itself is charged with interpreting its own mandate in a very liberal sense should be borne in mind.

The original purpose of the Committee was to prepare for a general Disarmament Conference but the conclusion was reached two years ago and a decision taken accordingly that the most practical method of preparation would be for the Committee to draw up a skeleton convention under which the signatory Powers would be bound to keep forces and armaments within figures which would be given in tables annexed to the Convention. The figures in these tables, which would be left blank in the skeleton Convention, would be filled in by each Power participating in the eventual general Conference on Disarmament.

The endeavours of the Committee have been devoted to preparing the framework of this Convention under which estimates of their requirements for the duration of the Convention in uniform tables or categories would be presented by the various Governments concerned. It would doubtless be more satisfactory if it were possible to secure general agreement in regard to the tables so that there might be uniformity in the returns of all Governments. But it has so far proved impossible to achieve this desirable result and if disagreement should persist, His Majesty's Government considered that it would be better than nothing to invite Governments to send in programmes in the fullest and best form they could devise. Something practical would thus be achieved at the sacrifice of a degree of uniformity and the point at which the Committee has been seeking to arrive would be reached by a slightly different route.

It is quite true, as the memorandum from the Department of State points out, that the Committee is not authorised to deal with "quantitative proposals" and it was not the intention of His Majesty's Government to suggest that it should. It is of course also true that the Committee is composed only of representatives of a limited number of Powers, but this limited Committee is now endeavouring to agree on a formula for uniform returns which the Council would be asked to submit to the general Disarmament Conference as a basis for its work.

It is naturally impossible to foretell what the subsequent procedure would be in the event of the Committee accepting the proposal for the submission of programmes but the idea in the mind of His Majesty's Government is merely that the Committee, if forced to recognise the difficulty of securing a completely uniform model for returns, should recommend the Council to invite Powers to send in returns in their own way. These returns could of course be based on tables insofar as agreement had been reached in regard to tables and in other cases contain the fullest and frankest information.

His Majesty's Government realise that the Committee's Convention, if it could be attained, would be more satisfactory, but they considered that, if continued disagreement prevented its attainment, the short cut to the same result—which their proposal was intended to provide—would be preferable to making no progress at all. It might at least put some check on competition in armaments, some symptoms of which can, unfortunately, be observed while the discussions of the Committee, fruitless as they have so far proved, continue.

While it is true that the proposal of His Majesty's Government might not, to quote the State Department's memorandum, "constitute an advance in limitation and reduction", it should at least achieve as much as the Committee's draft Convention, for under that Convention each signatory Power will insert its own figures in the annexed tables. This is surely nothing more than announcing its programme and undertaking to be bound by that programme. His Majesty's Government feel in any case that failing agreement along other lines this may prove the best method of preparing the ground for reduction in future.

Some Governments, if given full latitude as to the form in which they send in their programmes, might conceivably produce them in a form which was very unsatisfactory and incomplete and thus render it impossible eventually to conclude the Convention. But such Governments would find themselves placed in a very invidious position and it is natural to expect that they would be anxious to appear in the best possible light in view of the pressure of public opinion. Moreover, the same difficulty might arise in any case when the time came for Governments to fill in the tables under the Committee's Convention.

His Majesty's Government would emphasise in conclusion that they have put forward this idea with the main object of achieving something practical without loss of valuable time, rather than adjourning without accomplishing anything. It was not, however, their wish to adopt it at the forthcoming meeting of the Committee unless they could be sure that the United States Government would not oppose it. The demand for its application in naval as well as other phases might be difficult to resist, and they were anxious that further inacceptable proposals for preparing the ground should not complicate the already difficult question of naval disarmament.

The line which discussion of naval problems has taken up to the present in the Committee has led to a point where His Majesty's Government, for their part, see no immediate prospect of issue—unless their idea of submitting programmes commended itself to the United States Government as paving the way to a solution—and it is for that reason that they were desirous of avoiding public discussion at Geneva which might do no more than revive old controversies.

WASHINGTON, April 10, 1929.

---

500.A15/872 : Telegram

*The Chairman of the American Delegation (Gibson) to the Secretary of State*

GENEVA, April 15, 1929—4 p. m.
[Received April 15—11:15 a. m.]

2. Preparatory Commission met this morning and after president had made rather innocuous speech he submitted a proposed agenda which is substantially the Colban proposal slightly elaborated.

This will be discussed at tomorrow morning's meeting.

GIBSON

500.A15/876 : Telegram

*The Chairman of the American Delegation (Gibson) to the Secretary of State*

[Paraphrase]

Geneva, April 16, 1929—9 p. m.
[Received April 16—8: 35 p. m.]

4. Every indication points to proposal by Bernstorff, within next day or two, that special committee of the five principal naval powers be established to seek agreement as to methods as to naval reduction and limitation. Bernstorff's justification for this unusual course is that naval problem is principal obstruction in entire disarmament problem and that no progress is possible until it has been disposed of; he justifies limiting it to the five naval powers on ground that it is of vital concern to them alone.

Unless I shall be instructed to the contrary, I intend to say that if it is proposed to deal with all principal problems which are still to be solved, such as question of trained reserves, material in stock, budgetary limitation, supervision and control, military aviation, et cetera, we shall, of course, not have any objection to having naval question dealt with in similar manner; that we see no reason, however, for singling out naval problem for special treatment; and that furthermore it would not seem to be at all in harmony with the consistent procedure of the Commission that the other countries interested in naval questions be excluded from the debates. As this question may arise at any moment, I should appreciate immediate instructions in event Department does not approve course outlined.

Gibson

---

500.A15/876 : Telegram

*The Secretary of State to the Chairman of the American Delegation (Gibson)*

[Paraphrase]

Washington, April 17, 1929—3 p. m.

4. Your No. 4, April 16, 9 p. m. Department concurs with your point of view regarding the Bernstorff proposal for a special committee of the five principal naval powers; it trusts no arrangement will be made which will preclude possibility of your speech at an opportune time.

Stimson

500.A15/878b : Telegram

*The Secretary of State to the Chairman of the American Delegation (Gibson)*

WASHINGTON, April 17, 1929—4 p. m.

5. Am most anxious to deliver to the British Ambassador on the day before your speech is made, the following memorandum, which is a reply to his of April 10:

[Here follows the text of the memorandum to the British Embassy, April 20, printed on page 88.]

It is important that I have ample notice of when you expect to deliver your speech in order to be able to carry through the procedure outlined.

STIMSON

---

500.A15/882 : Telegram

*The Chairman of the American Delegation (Gibson) to the Secretary of State*

[Paraphrase]

GENEVA, April 18, 1929—9 p. m.
[Received April 19—1:14 a. m.]

7. Department's No. 5, April 17, 4 p. m. Appropriate time for making my general statement, so it seems to me, will be upon the opening of debate on major problems carried over from first reading. Until then the time of the Commission will be taken up by discussion of the Soviet proposals, which do not afford dignified setting for what we have to say. It is to be hoped that Soviet proposals will be disposed of tomorrow; but unless chairman shows more firmness, Russian delegation may protract the debates for several days yet to come.

If it becomes apparent that the Soviet proposals will be disposed of at session tomorrow, I shall ask Loudon to give me floor at opening of meeting at ten o'clock Monday morning. I deem it desirable to get in what we have to say as soon as possible in order to prevent our being anticipated by any other general statement along similar lines. This action on our part would necessitate presentation of Department's memorandum to British Ambassador on Saturday or Sunday; you may be disposed to do so, however, rather than to incur the risks involved through further delay here.

If you wish me to put off my statement until Tuesday morning, I can; but I am reluctant to give chairman longer notice than is necessary as he will pass the information along and the story will get about that an important statement is forthcoming with undesirable conjecture as consequence.

GIBSON

500.A15/885 : Telegram

*The Chairman of the American Delegation (Gibson) to the Secretary of State*

[Paraphrase]

Geneva, April 19, 1929—5 p. m.
[Received April 19—2:55 p. m.]

11. Soviet proposal was disposed of this morning, so I arranged with chairman of Preparatory Commission that I should have floor at opening of meeting Monday morning, ten o'clock.

If you will telegraph me when memorandum has been delivered to British Ambassador, I believe that it would tend to create air of frankness were I informally to hand copy to Cushendun on Sunday evening, stating that this was done for his convenience and adding that in view of fact that the correspondence between our Governments had reached this point and as he had made a general statement of British point of view, I proposed to make statement Monday morning on general position of the United States.

We have arranged matters definitely as possible to have speech made as has been stated but there are always elements of uncertainty in these meetings as Department realizes. When I rise I shall arrange to have Associated Press cable words "Gibson speaking" to Department. Department will then be able to determine advisability of release for morning papers or to hold for Monday afternoon. I should be glad to know in advance alternative taken.

Gibson

---

500.A15/870

*The Department of State to the British Embassy*

MEMORANDUM

The memorandum which the British Embassy was good enough to communicate to this Government on April 10, 1929, further contributes to the removal of any possible misunderstandings between the two Governments as to their attitude at the present meeting of the Preparatory Commission, and the American Government is grateful for the frankness with which the British Government has set forth its views and the considerations which it feels should be taken into account before discussion of the naval question.

If the Government of the United States rightly understands the suggestions of the Memorandum of the British Government, they may be stated thus:

That further public discussion and possible controversy regarding naval disarmament shall, if possible, be avoided until opportunity is had for a full and confidential exchange of views between the two Governments regarding their own naval situations.

From the wisdom of such a course, if it be feasible, the Government of the United States will not dissent. The problem facing the two Governments is how may the time for such an exchange of views be now found, with an actual meeting of the Preparatory Commission at present progressing at Geneva. This problem is complicated and made more difficult by the fact that, as the Memorandum is understood, the British Government must consult the Dominion Governments before acting, and final decisions must seemingly await the British general elections. However, the Government of the United States appreciates both these inhibitions and is disposed to yield to them so far as the nature of the subject and the situation will permit.

As a means of securing the necessary time, the British Government suggests, as the Memorandum is understood, that the Preparatory Commission should proceed for the present along existing lines in an effort to draft a skeleton convention embodying general principles, to which should be attached schedules or tables that when completed should lay down figures as to forces and armaments within which the powers signatory must keep; or, failing an agreement upon such a skeleton convention, the Commission should be asked to consider whether alternative procedure by programs would not be more effective, the program of each power to be in the best and fullest form it could devise. It seems to be recognized in the Memorandum that this latter proceeding would probably result in each power laying down its maximum needs, but the Memorandum suggests that this tendency would have, to offset it, the desire of each power, responsive to public opinion, to appear in the best light.

It is suggested in the Memorandum that the adoption of this latter course would require an adjournment of the Commission to give the members an opportunity to consult their Governments.

It need scarcely be pointed out that since the alternative suggestion, taken by itself, has in it no element that would certainly make for curtailment of armament, it could not command the approval of the Government of the United States which is keenly desirous actually to curtail and limit naval armament—the only armament in which it is itself directly interested. However, as an expedient, if it should prove feasible, for meeting any impasse that may arise in connection with the present plan and for gaining the time necessary for the United States and the British Governments to attempt an accord and understanding upon their own naval disarmament, the suggestion of an introduction of programs ultimately to be agreed upon at a final conference merits careful consideration, on the basis that the decision reached on the point shall not substantially sacrifice any interest involved in world disarmament.

It would seem therefore that the Preparatory Commission should now proceed pursuant to its regular program. If it shall appear, as time goes on, that progress cannot be made along that line, the Government of the United States will be glad to consult with the British Government as to whether some other plan might not be followed by the Commission to the end of avoiding any controversies between the two Governments which might disturb the full sympathy, friendship and accord of the two great peoples.

The American Government believes the essential matter at this time to be an understanding between the principal naval powers regarding the ratio in which and the extent to which they are willing to reduce naval armaments. Programs presented by the principal naval powers as the result of the agreed plan for reduction would encourage reduction throughout the world, whereas, programs drawn up on the basis of existing conditions would tend rather to encourage other nations to increase their navies. Naturally this Government regrets that there is so brief a time before the meeting of the Commission and hence it would be extremely difficult to work out in any detail a scheme for a basis of agreement, but it is most happy to suggest that as a result of a long series of studies on the subject, it is prepared whenever the occasion arises to examine with the British Government the possibility of a limitation of the naval types not already covered by the Washington Convention, which should take into account the relative value of ships of varying unit characteristics such as displacement, gun caliber and age.

These studies have convinced the American Government that a formula for estimating equivalent tonnage is possible and offers real hope of an arrangement acceptable to both countries. The studies in question which have been made during a considerable period were undertaken and carried out in an earnest desire to find some effective method for dealing with naval armaments while at the same time taking into full consideration the views put forward by the British Government as to its special naval needs.

The American Government would be most happy to be informed when the British Government feels that it can take up this suggestion which embodies the earnest hope of this Government that the naval problem may soon be settled to the satisfaction of both peoples.

WASHINGTON, April 20, 1929.

---

500.A15/885 : Telegram

*The Acting Secretary of State to the Chairman of the American Delegation (Gibson)*

[Paraphrase]

WASHINGTON, April 20, 1929—6 p. m.

9. Your No. 11, April 19, 5 p. m. Memorandum has just been handed to the Counselor of the British Embassy. The Department has no

objection to your giving Cushendun a copy. Speech will be released for Monday afternoon papers and Embassy in London has been instructed to release it there as soon as you have spoken, so that it will make the afternoon papers there too.

CLARK

---

500.A15/876½

*Address by the Chairman of the American Delegation (Gibson) Before the Preparatory Commission, April 22, 1929*[19]

MR. CHAIRMAN: I have sought your permission to make a general statement of the views of my Government in regard to the question of disarmament and have felt warranted in doing so at this stage of the proceedings because while we have not entered upon a second reading of the draft convention, we are bringing up for reconsideration various questions which have been previously discussed. It is felt therefore that in view of certain changed conditions it may facilitate the approach to these questions if I am permitted to take this occasion for stating my Government's views as to the means best calculated to promote an early agreement.

During the first reading of the draft convention, it was the duty of each one of us to put forward the views of his government on the various problems before the commission and endeavor to persuade his colleagues that those views should be adopted. It was only in this way that we were able to throw full light upon the complicated questions, the solution of which we seek. When we come to the second reading, however, a renewal of the old discussions is no longer in order. Our first duty is for each one of us to examine all phases of the problem before us with a view to discovering what measures of concession can be offered by each delegation. Agreement upon a single text can be achieved only by a maximum of such concession.

For the purposes of my presentation the disarmament problem may be divided into two parts, land and naval armaments. As regards land armaments, the American delegation will be able when we reach this question in our discussion to defer to the countries primarily interested in land armaments with such measure of concession as I trust will materially facilitate agreement among them.

My country's defense is primarily a naval problem. The American Government has found no reason for modifying its view that the simplest, fairest, and most practical method is that of limitation by tonnage by categories, a method which has been given practical and satisfactory application in the Washington treaty. While it is

---

[19] The text of this address was agreed upon while Mr. Gibson was in Washington and its delivery, with certain minor verbal changes suggested by Mr. Gibson before his departure on April 6, was authorized by telegram No. 28, April 11, 1929, 6 p. m., to the Embassy in Belgium (not printed).

realized that this does not constitute an exact and scientific gage of strategic strength, we have nevertheless found that it constitutes a method which has the advantage of simplicity and of affording to each power the freedom to utilize its tonnage within the limitation of each category according to its special needs.

The American delegation has urged this view throughout the first reading, but, in view of the inacceptability to some other delegations of our unmodified thesis, my Government has sought in the various methods presented some solution which might offer the possibility of compromise and general acceptance. During the third session of the Preparatory Commission, the French delegation brought forward a method which was an attempt to combine its original total tonnage proposals with the method of tonnage by categories. Under this method, a total tonnage was assigned to each nation, and this total divided among categories of ships by specified tonnages. If I am not mistaken, certain modifications were suggested in informal discussions, so as to provide that the tonnage allocated to any given category might be increased by a certain percentage to be agreed upon, such increase to be transferred from any other category or categories not already fixed by existing treaty.

In the hope of facilitating general agreement as to naval armaments, my Government is disposed to accept the French proposal as a basis of discussion. It is, of course, the understanding of my Government that this involves an agreement upon the method alone and not upon any quantitative tonnages or the actual percentages to be transferred from one category to another. All quantitative proposals of any kind should properly be reserved for discussion by a final conference.

My Government is disposed to give full and friendly consideration to any supplementary methods of limitation which may be calculated to make our proposals, the French thesis, or any other acceptable to other powers, and if such a course appears desirable, my Government will be prepared to give consideration to a method of estimating equivalent naval values which takes account of other factors than displacement tonnage alone. In order to arrive at a basis of comparison in the case of categories in which there are marked variations as to unit characteristics, it might be desirable in arriving at a formula for estimating equivalent tonnage to consider certain factors which produce these variations, such as age, unit displacement, and caliber of guns. My Government has given careful consideration to various methods of comparison, and the American delegation will be in a position to discuss the subject whenever it comes before the commission.

In alluding briefly to these possible methods, I desire to lay special emphasis on the fact that for us the essential thing is the achievement of substantial results. Methods are of secondary importance.

I feel that we are able to deal to best advantage with the specific questions on our agenda only if we bear clearly in mind the recent important changes in world conditions.

Since our last meeting, the nations of the world have bound themselves by solemn undertaking to renounce war as an instrument of national policy. We believe (and we hope that our belief is shared by the other nations) that this agreement affirming humanity's will to peace will advance the cause of disarmament by removing doubts and fears which in the past have constituted our principal obstacle. It has recently been my privilege to discuss the general problem of disarmament at considerable length with President Hoover, who has always been an ardent advocate of peace and good understanding. I am in a position to realize, perhaps as well as anyone, how earnestly he feels that the pact for the renunciation of war opens to us an unprecedented opportunity for advancing the cause of disarmament, an opportunity which admits of no postponement.

Any approach to the disarmament problem on purely technical grounds is bound to be inconclusive. The technical justification of armaments is based upon the experience of past wars and upon the anticipation of future wars. So long as the approach to the problem is based upon old fears and old suspicions, there is little hope of disarmament. The lessons of the old strategies must be unlearned. If we are honest, if our solemn promise in the pact means anything, there is no justification for the continuation of a war-taxed peace. Great armaments are but the relic of another age, but they will remain a necessary relic until the present deadlock is broken and that can be accomplished only by the decision of the powers possessing the greatest armaments to initiate measures of reduction.

In the opening statement at the Three Power Naval Conference in 1927 I took occasion, in suggesting certain tonnage levels as a basis of discussion, to say that the United States is prepared to agree to a plan for limitation at still lower levels which maintain the relative status of existing treaties with respect to the powers represented at that conference. This is still the attitude of my Government and I am authorized to state that on this basis we are willing to agree to any reduction however drastic of naval tonnage which leaves no type of war vessel unrestricted.

A large part of the suggestions for limitation hitherto made seem to have been of such a nature as to sanction existing armaments or even to set higher levels with tacit encouragement to increase existing establishments. This is only a timid expedient and an agreement on the basis of existing world armaments (or at higher levels) can never be justified before enlightened public opinion as a positive achievement. At best it is purely negative. Fundamentally, our purpose should be to release large numbers of men from military service to productive effort, and, second, to reduce the heavy burden of taxation. So long as the nations are burdened with increasing taxation for the maintenance of armament it is idle to pretend that the world is really advancing toward the goal of disarmament. In recent years the word "limitation" has come to be used chiefly in describing agreements at existing levels or still higher levels, and is generally looked upon as having nothing to do with actual reduction. It is useless to attempt to correct this impression by explaining that limitation may be at any level lower or higher than those existing. As a practical matter, it would seem to be best to accept the general public understanding of these terms. Let us therefore take the bold course and begin by scrapping the term "limitation" in order to concentrate upon a general reduction of armaments.

My Government believes that there can be no complete and effective limitation of armament unless all classes of war vessels, including cruisers, destroyers, and submarines, are limited. It could not agree to any method which would result in leaving any class of combatant vessels unrestricted. In its reply, under date of September 28, 1928,[20] to communications from the British and French Governments concerning an understanding reached between them as to a basis of naval limitation, my Government pointed out that this understanding applied to only one type of cruiser and one type of submarine and would leave totally unlimited a large class of effective fighting units. This note also called attention to the American position at the Geneva Naval Conference and the fact that a proposal for general reduction was urged by the American delegation.

The willingness of my Government, I may even say its eagerness, to go to low levels, is based upon the fundamental belief that naval needs are relative, namely, that what we may require for our defense depends chiefly upon the size of the navies maintained by others. Aside from the signatories of the Washington treaty, there is no conceivable combination of naval power which could threaten the safety of any of the principal naval powers. What justification can there be for the powers which lead in the respective classes of naval vessels to sanction further building programs in those classes? In the case of the United States we have already expressed our willingness to agree on a basis that would mean a substantial reduction of our present destroyer and submarine types. In the case of cruisers it is only possession by others of greatly superior strength in this class which has led to the adoption of the present building program.

[20] See telegram No. 329, September 25, 1928, 3 p. m., to the Chargé in France, *Foreign Relations*, 1928, vol. I, p. 282.

My Government can not find any justification for the building and maintenance of large naval establishments save on the ground that no power can reduce except as a result of general reduction. Let us ask ourselves honestly what these establishments are for. As regards the relations of the maritime powers among themselves, there is no such need. Even if the danger of war is admitted, it could be guarded against just as well by the maintenance of relative strength at low levels as at higher levels. The principal naval powers have nothing to fear from the naval strength of the countries nonsignatory to the Washington treaty. There is no conceivable combination of naval strength among the nonsignatory powers which need give concern. As an example, the cruiser strength of all the nonsignatory countries in the world does not attain to one half of the cruiser tonnage of the greatest single fleet.

The people of every country are crying out against the burdens of taxation and demanding the suppression of unnecessary expenditure. My Government is convinced that expenditure for disproportionate naval establishments is indefensible in that it can be avoided by a sensible agreement among the naval powers. And we must recognize that the people who pay taxes are bound to feel well-founded resentment against any policy which commits them to needless taxation through failure to reach rational agreements.

My Government believes firmly in its idea that naval needs are relative and that radical general reduction is possible only on the theory of relative needs. I trust that these views may commend themselves to other Governments and that it may be possible to agree upon such reductions. If, however, it is impossible to agree on this thesis, it is obvious that there will remain only the thesis of absolute naval needs. This would mean that all thought of reduction is abandoned, that each country retains a free hand in building with an inevitable tendency toward competition. Surely we can hardly envisage such a sequel to our solemn undertaking to keep the peace.

My Government has always felt that we need no exact balance of ships and guns, which can be based only upon the idea of conflict; what is really wanted is a common-sense agreement, based on the idea that we are going to be friends and settle our problems by peaceful means. My Government has never believed that an effective approach to the problem of disarmament could be made by methods of reduction of armaments alone. It feels that genuine disarmament will follow only from a change of attitude toward the use of force in the settlement of international disputes. It is for that reason that I venture to make this appeal that the countries here represented examine the whole problem afresh in the hope that they will find in general world conditions and in the solemn obligation they have taken among themselves a reassurance as to their security and that they will find in this the confidence to enable them to dispense with the armaments which hitherto have seemed so essential.

---

500.A15/887 : Telegram

*The Chairman of the American Delegation (Gibson) to the Secretary of State*

GENEVA, April 22, 1929—4 p. m.
[Received April 22—12 : 55 p. m.]

13. My statement made at the opening of this morning's session was received with more cordiality than I dared hope. In fact it has already given rise to a degree of optimism that may be difficult to sustain.

Replies made by Cushendun, Sato, Massigli, Riddell and De Marinis all in friendly vein.[21]

Cushendun in particular paid tribute to the spirit of our proposal and while reserving opinion on the technical points he made the categorical statement that:

1. British Government agreed with idea of reduction.
2. It accepted idea of limitation of all categories of ships.
3. It will give earnest study to idea of formula for naval equivalent.
4. The significance of the Kellogg Pact cannot be exaggerated and has given a new directive to the work of Preparatory Commission.

Litvinoff [22] then proved to his own satisfaction and the amusement of the Commission that every idea in my statement had already been included in his proposals.

GIBSON

---

500.A15/893

*The British Ambassador (Howard) to the Secretary of State*

No. 231                                    WASHINGTON, April 23, 1929.

SIR: I did not fail to transmit at once to my Government the text of the memorandum setting out the views of the United States Government in regard to naval disarmament which Mr. Castle handed to Mr. Campbell on the 20th instant. I now have the honour, under instructions from His Majesty's Principal Secretary of State for Foreign Affairs to inform you that His Majesty's Government in the United Kingdom are most grateful for this very friendly reply of

---

[21] The British, Japanese, French, Canadian, and Italian delegates, respectively.
[22] Maxim Litvinoff, head of the Soviet delegation.

the United States Government to the observations of His Majesty's Government contained in this Embassy's memorandum of April 10th.

When sending me these instructions, Sir A. Chamberlain had just received a summary of the very important statement made yesterday by the representative of the United States Government at the Preparatory Commission on Disarmament now meeting at Geneva, in which the views of the United States Government were further developed. He desires me to say that as stated at once by the British representative at Geneva, Lord Cushendun, His Majesty's Government entirely reciprocate the spirit of Mr. Gibson's declarations, which are likely to have a profound influence on the deliberations of the Commission, and that they agree that it is along the lines indicated by Mr. Gibson that the problem ought now to be investigated.

I have [etc.] ESME HOWARD

---

500.A15/905 : Telegram

*The Chairman of the American Delegation (Gibson) to the Secretary of State*

GENEVA, April 25, 1929—11 p. m.
[Received April 26—2 : 07 a. m.]

22. Chinese delegate added an amendment to be discussed under land effectives which will probably arise shortly on agenda, providing for the abolition of conscription in favor of voluntary armies. Chinese delegate has called twice to see me and states that he has not sought the assistance of any other nation but in view of ancient friendship of America for China he begs us to speak in a favorable manner of his project.

He declares that for the National Government their submission of this project is a test case. That they are under great pressure from the radical and Chauvinist elements to adopt conscription in China especially as they are threatened by military neighbors. That the modern [*moderate?*] element has been able, in view of this compromise, to hold them off hoping to be able to show that the countries desire real reduction.

I have explained that in my declaration on Monday I intimated that we were compelled to make compromise on the land questions and that I feared his project would be defeated by a large majority and therefore was reluctant to aid him actively, thus prolonging the debate and risking rendering impossible the acceptance of a unified text.

Since the thesis is congenial to us and since it is possible the Department may care to see us take a friendly attitude toward China it has occurred to me that I might declare that the Chinese proposal was in harmony with our practice and aspirations; that I should be happy if the nations assembled could see their way to acceptance but that in the spirit of compromise which I had already spoken of I was unwilling to insist upon its acceptance and therefore if the matter came to a vote I would abstain from voting.

I would appreciate urgent advice as to Department's views.

GIBSON

---

500.A15/905 : Telegram

*The Secretary of State to the Chairman of the American Delegation (Gibson)*

[Paraphrase]

WASHINGTON, April 27, 1929—1 p. m.

14. Your telegram No. 22, April 25, 11 p. m. I should avoid making any statement which might be taken to mean that principle of universal liability to service in a time of war was inconsistent with American principles. Many of our leading men feel exactly opposite way; and in the Great War we adopted the principle in question. We believe in voluntary standing army in time of peace, but further than that I should not go; and I question whether exigency is of sufficient importance to run risk of any broader statement which might be subject to serious misinterpretation.

STIMSON

---

500.A15/919 : Telegram

*The Ambassador in Germany (Schurman) to the Secretary of State*

[Paraphrase—Extract]

BERLIN, April 30, 1929—noon.
[Received 2:10 p. m.]

84. There has been quite general comment in the German press on Gibson's speech at Geneva on naval disarmament, as well as with regard to the sentiments and attitude of President Hoover on the same subject as cabled from Washington by European correspondents.

It has been the fixed belief in this country that there existed between the United States and Great Britain a dangerous naval rivalry which was running the same course and was laden with the same consequences as was the naval rivalry between Germany and Great Britain for a decade and more before the World War. From the new departure at Geneva the German press foresee a release of this tension and the reestablishment of cordial relations between the two "Anglo-Saxon" Powers.

[The remainder of this telegram consists of quotations from an article by the London correspondent of the *Frankfurter Zeitung* published in the Sunday issue, April 28, 1929.]

SCHURMAN

---

500.A15/933

## The British Embassy to the Department of State

### MEMORANDUM

His Majesty's Government are confident that as between Great Britain and the United States a settlement can be found of the difficulty which has hitherto tended in the discussions on naval disarmament to keep the two countries apart, namely, that of evolving a standard of parity in naval strength under which the special needs of each would be reconciled with the principle accepted by both.

This feeling of confidence springs not only from the public declaration made by Mr. Hugh Gibson, the United States representative at the present session of the Preparatory Commission for Disarmament at Geneva—a declaration which, as the United States Government are aware, His Majesty's Government have warmly welcomed—but also from the impressions which they have gained from private and unofficial indications of the mind and purpose of the President of the United States.

How far the United States Government intend to carry the discussion on which the Preparatory Commission are now engaged is not known to His Majesty's Government, but they feel strongly that time and opportunity for a private and confidential exchange of views should be afforded before new proposals are publicly presented in any detail. Indeed they would view the possible consequences of a premature presentation of such proposals with great anxiety. Once a broad line of agreement for the naval forces of the United States and Great Britain had been determined, His Majesty's Government feel that there would, despite the obviously greater difficulty of laying down rules capable of application to all navies equally, be more hope of reaching agreement with other great naval powers.

The impressions which they have gained from private and unofficial intercourse between the United States and British delegations at Geneva have left some doubt in the mind of His Majesty's Government as to the next step in procedure contemplated by the United States Government. They are not clear whether it is the desire of the United States Government that the British naval authorities should work out their own calculations independently, or whether the United States Government propose to communicate to them confidentially, for consideration, the calculations which they understand the United States naval authorities have made in regard to the value to be attached to the various factors mentioned in the American proposal.

His Majesty's Government are anxious to learn which of these courses the United States Government have in mind and they would observe that in their opinion the latter would be both more practical and more speedy.

Whichever course the United States Government wish to adopt, His Majesty's Government consider that it would be undesirable for any figures to be published until the two Governments have had full opportunity for confidential discussion. It is their earnest hope that the United States Government will share this view.

In that event they would suggest that such discussion which, they feel, could best be carried on through diplomatic channels, might usefully be initiated as soon as the General Election has taken place at the end of the present month.

WASHINGTON, May 3, 1929.

---

500.A15/933

*Memorandum by the Assistant Secretary of State (Castle)*

[WASHINGTON,] May 4, 1929.

I went to the Navy Department this morning to show Mr. Adams [23] the latest memorandum from the British. Mr. Adams said that it was his understanding that no actual figures would be proposed at Geneva and I told him that the Secretary had so informed the British Ambassador.

I told him that the question to be decided was whether or not we should furnish the British, for their consideration, the calculations which our naval authorities had made or whether we should ask the British to make their own independent research. Mr. Adams asked what I thought about it and I told him that I was inclined to feel that it would put us in a better position to take the initiative by showing the British our plan. I said that this seemed a stronger strategical position for us since it would be up to the British to prove wherein we were wrong. Mr. Adams said that he agreed with this entirely; that he felt, if the British drew up their own scheme, their minds would be likely to harden in favor of that scheme and that they would, as a result be less easy to deal with. He said, furthermore, that he was sure that they would be impressed with the honesty of Admiral Jones and of any plan which he might propose.

Mr. Adams then went on to say that, although this was his feeling

---

[23] The Secretary of the Navy.

with regard to showing our plan to the British, he nevertheless feared grave consequences should we hold discussions secretly with the British excluding all other interested parties. I said that, of course, I agreed with this to the extent that we could not run the risk of an outburst similar to that following the publication of the Franco-British Naval Agreement. I told him that, in my opinion, we ought not to carry on these conversations secretly but that it might not be necessary at the beginning to show our plan, before we had talked it over with the British, to the Japanese, French and Italians. I said, in support of this, that the Japanese Ambassador had remarked to me the other day that he felt an understanding between ourselves and the British was a prerequisite to any successful naval discussion. I told him that it, therefore, seemed to me that in all probability we could talk with the Japanese, French and Italian Ambassadors telling them in general what we were doing and assuring them that there was no thought of excluding them since we, after all, were not discussing final figures or ratios but merely the method of approach by which parity between Great Britain and the United States could be secured. Mr. Adams said that if we took some such action as this, he would be entirely satisfied.

W[ILLIAM] R. C[ASTLE, JR.]

---

500.A15/913

*The Secretary of State to the Chairman of the American Delegation (Gibson)*

WASHINGTON, May 6, 1929.

SIR: The British Ambassador came to see me the other day and wanted to obtain some information as to the extent of the suggestions contained in your speech of April 22, before the Preparatory Disarmament Commission. He said that there had been so many wild and detailed stories that one could not tell what to believe.

I told him that so far as I had observed those stories were wholly imaginary. I repeated my view of the proposal as to categories and explained specifically what was intended thereby so far as I knew, namely that the proposal or suggestion, which was not in any way completed, was merely to provide for the elaboration of a formula which would permit a common estimate of the strategic usefulness of a ship in one class to be made in terms of a ship in another class contained within the same category, giving as an example the cruiser question as it appears in the British and American points of view.

I took occasion to repeat that the fundamental proposition between our two countries upon which we had all been able to agree was a parity in navies and that such parity seemed absolutely essential;

that this proposition ought not to be departed from; that the whole purpose of our present suggestion was to permit sufficient flexibility within this general principle of parity so as to permit an agreement between us and to prevent us building against each other which in my opinion would be the greatest possible disaster.

He agreed and said that it was unthinkable that we should ever get into a war. He asked about the French proposal and inquired whether it applied as between cruisers and destroyers. I told him I thought it did and we examined the portion of your speech in which you came out in favor of it.

On the same day the French Ambassador came to see me on the same subject. I told him that your suggestion was really an extension of the French proposition so as to cover units in the same category of ships. He wanted to know whether it applied to anything else but cruisers and also whether it applied to naval questions between France and Italy. I told him what I understood was the suggestion. He said that it would be manifestly unfair to apply as between France and Italy the ratio 1.6 in respect to cruisers. Italy had only one sea to guard and France had two seas and some distant colonies. I told him that in making our suggestion we undoubtedly primarily had reference to our own problem with Great Britain. We had certainly no intention of increasing the difficulties for France or Italy.

I am [etc.]                                    HENRY L. STIMSON

---

500.A15/940

*Address by the Chairman of the American Delegation (Gibson) Before the Preparatory Commission, May 6, 1929*

MR. CHAIRMAN: I made my general statement [24] as to a possible method of approach to the naval problem early in our present session chiefly in order to afford other delegations an opportunity to consider it from every aspect and determine to what degree they were in a position to discuss it at the present time. After my statement we learned that certain other governments are making analogous studies which should of course be taken into account in any general discussion. Today we are told that certain governments feel that in order to deal with the matter effectively and expeditiously they require time for careful exploration of the possibilities opened by the American suggestions.

In my opening statement I said that I would be prepared to discuss the American proposals when we reached this chapter on our agenda but obviously this readiness was entirely contingent on the knowledge that other delegations felt prepared to enter upon the subject.

[24] *Ante*, p. 91.

The solution of the naval problem is in essence simple but in application complex. The technical considerations involved must be studied from many angles and the American Delegation recognizes that our best hope of agreement upon a method lies in having each country come into the discussion prepared to speak on the basis of its independent study and in possession of all the data that it desires. In view of the considerations I have indicated my Government feels that the course best calculated to lead to the successful conclusion of our labors lies in giving time for a careful study of this whole problem. It also feels that in view of other analogous studies which are being made it would not be opportune to embark upon detailed discussion of our suggested method of approach at the present moment. Perhaps the best course is for me to restate what our suggestion is in such a way as to afford a basis for the independent studies which I hope will be made by other interested governments.

In substance equivalent tonnage is an expression used to convey the idea, for comparative purposes, of the military value of individual ships and hence of the total value of any number of such units in any given category in which there may be wide divergences as to unit characteristics composing the category. In arriving at this equivalent of value it would seem advisable to take into account only factors that are simple and obvious, easy to compute and easy to understand. We feel that the problem should not be complicated by the introduction of factors which may well be considered as really no more than elements of the prime factors. In my general statement on this subject I indicated certain factors which include elements that enter into the design of effectiveness, of individual units, that is unit displacement, gun caliber, and age, as well as speed and other factors.

My Government feels that in order not to prejudice such studies as may be pursued independently by other governments it is best to go no further than to outline our suggestion in this manner. It will be clear that the American proposal is no rigid plan to be accepted or rejected. It is a suggestion that a new method of approach based on naval equivalents be explored, and it is in order that there may be complete liberty for independent studies that we have decided not to make any more specific proposals at this stage of our work.

The evidence of a popular desire in all countries to see us press on to our goal has been made abundantly clear. There could be nothing more favorable to the program of our work than the present atmosphere of enthusiasm and good will. We must proceed just as fast as may be consistent with sound and effective handling of the very important and complex problem before us and without jeopardizing the successful conduct of the work through entering precipitately upon discussions for which any of the interested powers is not prepared.

For that reason I fully concur in the proposal of the Japanese and British delegates to postpone consideration of the naval chapter until such time as the interested powers have signified to you, Mr. Chairman, their readiness to embark upon a general discussion.

---

500.A15/946 : Telegram

*The Chairman of the American Delegation (Gibson) to the Secretary of State*

GENEVA, May 6, 1929—2 p. m.
[Received 5 :40 p. m.]

40. Preparatory Commission adjourned at the conclusion of today's session.

Discussion on naval clauses was opened this morning by Sato who asked for postponement of their consideration until interested governments had completed detailed studies of American suggestion. His speech was cordial in tone and supported our contention as to reduction rather than limitation of armaments. Cushendun's speech seconded Sato's proposal. Massigli and Marinis followed with short speeches. I then made my statement [25] (see my 39, May 6, 11 a. m.[26]) after which the debate was closed and the matter [*meeting*] adjourned.

The next item on the agenda was the second reading to [*of?*] chapters three and five of the draft convention which as foreshadowed was likewise postponed on the ground that some of it was intimately related with decisions to be taken on naval clauses. Massigli however took the floor to announce the withdrawal of the French demand for international supervision and control (see my 35, May 3, 7 p. m. [26]) and promised to circulate in a short time the text of his substitute proposals dealing with exchange of information, arbitration regarding interpretation of convention, special status of states non members of the League, et cetera. In reply I stated that I knew that concessions were not always easy, that they often meant sacrificing for the common benefit beliefs held with conviction and that I wished to pay tribute to the spirit which had prompted Massigli and the French Government on this fundamental question.

I closed on a distinct note of optimism and was followed by Litvinoff who read a lengthy piece of cynical invective against the entire work of the Commission in which among other things he reiterated his unjustified charge that the Commission had scrapped the idea of "reduction" of armaments. President disposed of this accusation in a few effective phrases.

Commission agreed to reconvene at the call of the Chairman who was requested to keep in touch with principal naval powers and sum-

---

[25] *Supra.*
[26] Not printed.

mon the Commission as soon as it appeared that the time was ripe for further discussion. Next meeting will be a continuation of present (sixth) session.

GIBSON

---

500.A15/948 : Telegram

*The Chairman of the American Delegation (Gibson) to the Secretary of State*

[Paraphrase]

GENEVA, May 6, 1929—11 p. m.
[Received May 6—11 p. m.]

42. Reference to Department's telegram No. 24, May 4, 4 p. m., transmitting text of British Embassy's memorandum of May 3.[27]

The allusion in the memorandum to the impressions gained from us with regard to "mind and purpose of the President" refers obviously to the statement made informally in conversations with Cushendun to effect that President Hoover attaches great importance to finding a reasonable and sensible solution for present differences between ourselves and Great Britain.

Regarding British apprehensions as to just what the next step in the procedure will be, I think it would suffice to state that I have made it quite apparent that the United States felt that independent studies by the various naval powers should be the next move in the matter.

In answering informal British questions regarding just what further information the American Government may be willing to give them concerning the character of the American suggestions, you may be sure that I have made no statement whatever which would prejudice the Department's complete liberty in answering any such questions which it should deem to be most desirable, though I have not thought it appropriate to close the door to any overtures which they have thought best to make.

GIBSON

---

500.A15/949 : Telegram

*The Chairman of the American Delegation (Gibson) to the Secretary of State*

[Paraphrase]

GENEVA, May 6, 1929—midnight.
[Received May 7—1:16 a. m.]

43. I have been questioned by all of the various representatives of the naval powers as to just what the next step will be in dealing

---

[27] Latter *ante*, p. 99; telegram No. 24 not printed.

with the method suggested by the American delegation. My reply has been that it seems apparent that the best thing for them to do would be to conduct studies of their own and that the various powers could then reach an agreement as to what course would be most conducive to the progress of naval disarmament. Stating that this was something beyond the scope of my immediate mission, I have refused to give any opinion as to what procedure they should follow. However it is my opinion that either before or after the completion of their studies the four other naval powers will undoubtedly approach the Department requesting more particulars concerning the studies being made by our Government. In order to emphasize the fact that my instructions concern only the work of the Preparatory Commission and do not affect in any way the future course which the Department may pursue, I have deemed it necessary to refrain from making any suggestions in the matter. Until some solution of the problem existing between the United States and Great Britain is reached, Italy, France, and Japan apparently recognize that as a practical matter no progress can be achieved, though a certain uneasiness that some definite settlement may be reached which would be prejudicial to their various positions is apparent in each of them. It seems particularly important that the Japanese be assured, from all I have learned, that Japan is being kept informed regarding any progress being made in the British-American conversations, in order that all fear may be removed from their minds of having a definite agreement between Great Britain and ourselves placed before them. I have been told quite frankly by my Japanese colleague that this is his Government's greatest concern. It has been further stated by Sato that he considers it very important from the point of view of Japanese public opinion as a whole that a statement should be made from time to time that the Japanese Government is being consulted during the progress of the naval discussions between Great Britain and the United States. While I have encountered the greatest frankness and good will on the part of Sato, it has been quite apparent that both the Japanese Government and he are fearful that an impression may become current in Japan that their Government is not being consulted during the first steps of our discussions and for this reason I venture to emphasize particularly the importance of this point. Rather than that they should receive any material improvement in their ratio, their main preoccupation seems to be, so far as I can learn, that we permit them to save face with their own people. In view of past discussions, it should be borne in mind that the term "ratio" is particularly distasteful to the Japanese Government and so far as possible in the course of discussions it would be most desirable that it be avoided.

A separate problem exists in the relations between Italy and France. Their divergence of views was clearly manifest even in debates on land armaments. Concerning naval matters, the French delegation in various conversations with us have maintained that France's greater need in protecting her overseas possessions makes it untenable for them to admit parity with Italy, whereas the Italians maintain that they cannot admit any discussion of their right to full parity with France. The French furthermore have indicated that it may be necessary for them to consider the expansion of the Spanish navy and possibly to enter into a separate understanding with Spain before reaching any definite agreement. That the needs of other navies, or even that they may be factors of importance in the calculations of any of the principal naval powers, has thus far not been brought to our attention in any way. In case any of the lesser naval powers, members of the Preparatory Commission, should request additional information, the Department may desire to consider just how much general information might be given them. As I cannot foresee how soon any of the interested Governments may deem it desirable to approach the Department for consultation or further information, I am placing these considerations before you.

GIBSON

---

500.A15/983

*Memorandum by the Assistant Secretary of State (Castle)*

[WASHINGTON,] May 15, 1929.

The Japanese Ambassador said this morning that he hesitated to speak of two things in connection with the Disarmament Conference because he was convinced they were not true. However, statements had been made in the press which worried his Government and he felt it necessary to be able officially to satisfy his Government.

He called attention to an article in the *New York Times* which said that we had decided to ask for a maximum limit of 250,000 tons on cruisers. I told him that he could deny this absolutely; that, as he knew, we had not discussed tonnage or ratios; that the entire discussion had been on method.

The second point he brought up was repeated statements in the papers that the British Admiralty was now studying the American plan. He said this had given his Government the impression that a full detailed plan had already been furnished to the British Admiralty. I told the Ambassador that this idea again he could flatly deny; that undoubtedly the British Admiralty was studying the American plan as given in the broadest possible way by Mr. Hugh Gibson in Geneva. I showed him, however, that all that had been said in Geneva had been said for the entire Conference, not for any individual member of the Conference. I pointed out that Mr. Gibson had said enough as to what the plan was in general to enable the different admiralties to work out some detailed studies of this plan and that it was my belief that, in all probability, the Japanese Admiralty was doing this just as much as the British Admiralty.

W[ILLIAM] R. C[ASTLE, JR.]

---

500.A15/934

*The Secretary of State to the Chargé in Great Britain (Atherton)*

No. 1827                                          WASHINGTON, May 15, 1929.

SIR: The British Ambassador came to see me on May 3, 1929, and read a memorandum regarding the recent naval discussions at Geneva, a copy of which is enclosed for your strictly confidential information.[28]

When Sir Esme reached the words on the second page beginning "Once a broad line of agreement for the naval forces of the United States and Great Britain had been determined", et cetera, I interrupted him and inquired what that meant, saying that I thought that the broad lines of agreement such as the parity of the two navies were already agreed upon. He at once said that he concurred with me and did not think that the words referred to parity at all. He added that he would report my statement to his Government.

I told him that I thought that the doctrine of parity was not used in a military sense at all but as a doctrine of statesmanship, it being the only basis upon which two proud and independent countries could agree not to build against each other but to reduce their navies. He said he fully agreed with me.

He finished the reading of the paper and I told him that I should have to take conference on the question asked on the second page as to whether the United States Government desired that the British naval authorities should work out their own calculations independently or whether the United States Government proposed to communicate to them confidentially for consideration the calculations which they understand that the United States naval authorities have made, and stated that I would give him our answer later.

I told him that we agreed as to the next to the last paragraph of the memorandum in which the British Government states that it considers that it would be undesirable for any figures to be published until the two Governments have had full opportunity for confidential discussion.

[28] *Ante,* p. 99.

He stated that in view of my departure for New York he would report by telegraph to his Government what I had said and concluded that he would expect an answer from us after my return.

On the day following this conversation Mr. Castle, Assistant Secretary of State, discussed the British memorandum with the Secretary of the Navy; I am enclosing a self-explanatory memorandum on this subject.[29]

I am [etc.] H. L. STIMSON

500.A15/963

*The Secretary of State to the Ambassador in Belgium (Gibson)*

No. 227 WASHINGTON, May 17, 1929.

SIR: On May 9, the French Ambassador called to express his Government's appreciation of your sympathetic attitude with regard to the question of naval armaments, as set forth at the recent session of the Preparatory Commission for the Disarmament Conference. He asked me what steps we would take in the future and, in particular, whether we intended to call a new Conference in this or the following year.

I told him that we had made no definite plans as yet, but desired to bring to fruition, as soon as the opportunity presented by your initiative would warrant, the hope of President Hoover that a reduction in naval armaments might be achieved.

I am [etc.] H. L. STIMSON

500.A15/990 : Telegram

*The Chargé in Great Britain (Atherton) to the Secretary of State*

[Paraphrase]

LONDON, May 27, 1929—5 p. m.

[Received May 27—4:28 p. m.]

130. In view of Department's instruction No. 1827 of May 15, which I have just received, I am venturing to cable résumé of my despatch No. 3650,[30] forwarded to Department last Saturday by pouch. The chief of the American section, Mr. Craigie, who accompanied the British delegation to Geneva, asked me to call at the Foreign Office last Friday. During our conversation he stated conviction of the British that failure of the Anglo-American naval conversations which took place in 1927 was result of lack of preliminary preparatory agreement between Great Britain and the United States. In connection with Gibson's speech at Geneva, he referred to the existence of certain Amer-

---

[29] *Ante*, p. 100.
[30] Not printed.

ican figures, and stated that the British Admiralty on their part had reduced Gibson's formula to figures based on needs of British. Craigie stated his belief that without any hint getting to the press and without the knowledge of even any large number of officials, some sort of preliminary Anglo-American conversations between political officials (as in contradistinction to technical officials) should take place for the following reasons: (1) Possibly to lay frankly the two sets of figures prepared on Gibson's formula side by side and then see actually how far apart the two nations are; and/or (2) determine in the strictest confidence and without any possible publicity an interpretation of the Gibson formula which could be accepted by the British and the American Governments in any subsequent and less secret discussions. Craigie obviously had in mind that General Dawes,[31] on his arrival here from Washington, might well be the agent who, with least possible publicity, could initiate any preliminary conversations of strictly intimate nature which then might well be followed by the visit to the United States which it was stated is contemplated by Mr. Baldwin[32] in late summer, assuming that Conservative Party is returned to power at the forthcoming elections.

ATHERTON

---

500.A15/1049 : Telegram

*The Minister in Switzerland (Wilson) to the Secretary of State*

[Paraphrase]

BERNE, September 24, 1929—2 p. m.
[Received 4:03 p. m.]

91. I learned in Geneva yesterday that no intention exists of having the Preparatory Commission reconvene within the near future. There is a general opinion that it is necessary to await the results of the naval negotiations.

With regard to the attitude of France on the naval question, the general view is that the French belief in their thesis concerning the interrelation of sea, land and air armaments, has been intensified as a result of the introduction in the Third Committee of Lord Cecil's resolution with its implied revision of those compromises which were reached at the last session of the Preparatory Commission concerning matériel in stock and trained reserves, as well as on account of the discussion which followed this resolution. The attitude of the French officials in the League Assembly is, I have reason to believe, similar to the attitude expressed in the French newspapers to the effect that

---

[31] Charles G. Dawes, appointed Ambassador to Great Britain, April 16, 1929.
[32] Stanley Baldwin, British Prime Minister.

any agreement at the Five Power Naval Conference [33] as to figures must be merely tentative and must remain subject to a final general Conference's confirmation. The basis for this determination is the French desire that the League of Nations keep all matters of this kind, as far as possible, within its framework.

I have seen no evidence of a preliminary discussion of their joint problems on the part of the French and Italians.

Gibson has been furnished with a copy of this telegram.

WILSON

[33] The forthcoming naval conference at London in 1930.

# PRELIMINARIES TO THE FIVE-POWER NAVAL CONFERENCE TO BE HELD AT LONDON IN 1930

500.A15a3/1

*The Secretary of State to the Chargé in Great Britain (Atherton)*

No. 1821                                    WASHINGTON, May 14, 1929.

SIR: In the course of a conversation on May 9, the British Ambassador stated that he had understood me as saying that future discussions concerning Ambassador Gibson's recent naval proposals [1] would stand a better chance of success if they were placed under the control of civilians rather than naval experts. He added that he had agreed with that himself but had not felt free to write to the Foreign Office about it; he would like to do so now, however, if I had no objection. I told him that my view in general was as he had described it, but I was careful to explain that it did not have reference to any particular individuals or to any recent occurrences; on the contrary, I had definitely heard that the relations between Admiral Jones on our side and the corresponding British Admiral in the Three-Power Conference [2] had been extremely satisfactory; we had no doubt, however, that in general the service man was bound to look at these questions from the standpoint of a possible war between Great Britain and the United States and to make his plans accordingly, while the civilian statesman representing the people of the country might be able and willing to take chances which the professional service man could not take. He said he agreed with me perfectly and understood what I meant.

He asked me whether I thought that was the attitude of the President and I told him I thought it was. He said that was very encouraging. He asked me for my opinion as to the prospects for the future. I told him we are earnestly hoping to make progress in the line of actual reduction; that anybody who looked at the cost of modern battleships could not help being appalled by the expense. He joined in most emphatically, saying that when we realize that the cost of building a modern cruiser was more than that of the Library of Congress, it seemed a perfectly dreadful waste of money which could otherwise be used for constructive purposes.

In discussing the prospects for the future, I informed him that I had heard that the British representatives, prior to the Three-Power

[1] See Ambassador Gibson's address of April 22, 1929, p. 91.
[2] See *Foreign Relations*, 1927, vol. I, pp. 1 ff.

Conference, had made a study of what they thought were their naval requirements to cover all the trade routes of the Empire and had determined the minimum strength below which they would not go. I said that if this was their position, it would appear to destroy the possibility of reduction on the basis of parity and that I did not see how the British could reach any such position without considering us as a potential enemy. Sir Esme replied that he was not aware of any such position having been maintained by his Government and did not believe that any reports to that effect could be accurate. He agreed that it was wholly inconsistent with the idea of reduction and repeated that he did not think that they had ever fixed an irreducible minimum. He himself thought that the standards of one nation necessarily depended upon the standards of the other.

I am [etc.]                                    HENRY L. STIMSON

---

500.A15/996

*Address by President Hoover at the Memorial Exercises at Arlington Cemetery, May 30, 1929*

FELLOW COUNTRYMEN: Over the years since the Civil War the Grand Army of the Republic have conducted this sacred ceremony in memoriam of those who died in service of their country. The ranks of their living comrades have been steadily thinned with time. But other wars have reaped their harvest of sacrifice and these dead too lie buried here. Their living comrades now join in conduct of this memorial, that it may be carried forward when the noble men who today represent the last of the Grand Army shall have joined those already in the Great Beyond.

This sacred occasion has impelled our Presidents to express their aspirations in furtherance of peace. No more appropriate tribute can be paid to our heroic dead than to stand in the presence of their resting places and pledge renewed effort that these sacrifices shall not be claimed again.

Today, as never before in peace, new life-destroying instrumentalities and new systems of warfare are being added to those that even so recently spread death and desolation over the whole continent of Europe. Despite those lessons every government continues to increase and perfect its armament. And while this progress is being made in the development of the science of warfare, the serious question arises—are we making equal progress in devising ways and means to avoid those frightful fruits of men's failures that have blotted with blood so many chapters of the world's history?

There is a great hope, for since this day a year ago, a solemn declaration has been proposed by America to the world and has been signed by forty nations.[3]  It states that they

"Solemnly declare in the names of their respective peoples that they condemn recourse to war for the solution of international controversies, and renounce it as an instrument of national policy in their relations with one another."

They

"Agree that the settlement or solution of all disputes or conflicts of whatever nature or of whatever origin they may be, which may arise among them, shall never be sought except by pacific means."

That is a declaration that springs from the aspirations and hearts of men and women throughout the world.  It is a solemn covenant to which the great nations of the world have bound themselves.

But notwithstanding this noble assurance, preparedness for war still advances steadily in every land.  As a result the pessimist calls this covenant a pious expression of foreign offices, a trick of statesmen on the hopes of humanity, for which we and other nations will be held responsible without reserve.  With this view I cannot agree.

But, if this agreement is to fulfill its high purpose, we and other nations must accept its consequences; we must clothe faith and idealism with action.  That action must march with the inexorable tread of common sense and realism to accomplishment.

If this declaration really represents the aspirations of peoples; if this covenant be genuine proof that the world has renounced war as an instrument of national policy, it means at once an abandonment of the aggressive use of arms by every signatory nation and becomes a sincere declaration that all armament hereafter shall be used only for defense.  Consequently, if we are honest we must reconsider our own naval armament and the armaments of the world in the light of their defensive and not their aggressive use.  Our Navy is the first, and in the world sense the only important, factor in our national preparedness.  It is a powerful part of the arms of the world.

To make ready for defense is a primary obligation upon every statesman and adequate preparedness is an assurance against aggression.  But, if we are to earnestly predicate our views upon renunciation of war as an instrument of national policy, if we are to set standards that naval strength is purely for defense and not for aggression, then the strength in fighting ships required by nations is but relative to that of other powers.  All nations assent to this—that defensive needs of navies are relative.  Moreover, other nations concede our contention for parity.  With these principles before us our problem

---

[3] Treaty for the Renunciation of War, *Foreign Relations*, 1928, vol. I, p. 153.

is to secure agreement among nations that we shall march together toward reductions in naval equipment.

Despite the declarations of the Kellogg pact, every important country has since the signing of that agreement been engaged in strengthening its naval arm. We are still borne on the tide of competitive building. Fear and suspicion disappear but slowly from the world. Democracies can only be led to undertake the burdens of increasing naval construction by continued appeal to fear, by constant envisaging of possible conflict, by stimulated imaginings of national dangers, by glorification of war. Fear and suspicion will never slacken unless we can halt competitive construction of arms. They will never disappear unless we can turn this tide toward actual reduction.

But to arrive at any agreement through which we can, marching in company with our brother nations, secure reduction of armament, we must find a rational yardstick with which to make reasonable comparisons of their naval units with ours and thus maintain an agreed relativity. So far the world has failed to find such a yardstick. To say that such a measure cannot be found is the counsel of despair, it is a challenge to the naval authorities of the world, it is the condemnation of the world to the Sisyphean toil of competitive armaments.

The present Administration of the United States has undertaken to approach this vital problem with a new program. We feel that it is useless for us to talk of the limitation of arms if such limitations are to be set so high as virtually to be an incitement to increase armament. The idea of limitation of arms has served a useful purpose. It made possible conferences in which the facts about national aspirations could be discussed frankly in an atmosphere of friendliness and conciliation. Likewise the facts of the technical problems involved, and the relative values of varying national needs, have been clarified by patient comparison of expert opinions.

But still the net result has been the building of more fighting ships. Therefore we believe the time has come when we must know whether the pact we have signed is real, whether we are condemned to further and more extensive programs of naval construction. Limitation upward is not now our goal, but actual reduction of existing commitments to lowered levels.

Such a program, if it be achieved, is fraught with endless blessings. The smaller the armed force of the world, the less will armed force be left in the minds of men as an instrument of national policy. The smaller the armed forces of the world, the less will be the number of men withdrawn from the creative and productive labors. Thus we shall relieve the toilers of the nations of the deadening burden of unproductive expenditures, and above all, we shall deliver them from the greatest of human calamities—fear.  We shall breathe an air cleared of poison, of destructive thought, and of potential war.

But the pact that we have signed by which we renounce war as an instrument of national policy, by which we agree to settle all conflicts, of whatever nature, by pacific means, implies more than the reduction of arms to a basis of simple defense.  It implies that nations will conduct their daily intercourse in keeping with the spirit of that agreement.  It implies that we shall endeavor to develop those instrumentalities of peaceful adjustment that will enable us to remove disputes from the field of emotion to the field of calm and judicial consideration.

It is fitting that we should give our minds to these subjects on this occasion; that we should give voice to these deepest aspirations of the American people, in this place.  These dead whom we have gathered here today to honor, these valiant and unselfish souls who gave life itself in service of their ideals, evoke from us the most solemn mood of consecration.  They died that peace should be established.  Our obligation is to see it maintained.  Nothing less than our resolve to give ourselves with equal courage to the ideal of our day will serve to manifest our gratitude for their sacrifices, our undying memory of their deeds, our emulation of their glorious example.

———————————

500.A15a3/7 : Telegram

*The Chargé in Great Britain (Atherton) to the Secretary of State*

[Paraphrase]

London, June 11, 1929—1 p. m.
[Received June 11—10 : 10 a. m.]

154.  The press reports and it is the general belief here that the American proposals to the British Government on disarmament will be presented by General Dawes.[4]

Furthermore, Mr. MacDonald [5] has let it be known that he expects to go to Geneva for the League meeting in July at which there will be a discussion of the same subject.

In usually well-informed circles it was rumored during May that Mr. Baldwin [6] had been assured unofficially that the Prime Minister would be welcome should he proceed to Washington to discuss naval disarmament with the President and Mr. Mackenzie King [7] in Sep-

———————————

[4] Charles G. Dawes, appointed Ambassador to Great Britain, April 16, 1929.
[5] J. Ramsay MacDonald, leader of the Labor Party and British Prime Minister.
[6] Stanley Baldwin, leader of the Conservative Party and former British Prime Minister.
[7] Canadian Prime Minister.

tember. That the same unofficial assurances from Washington have been extended to Mr. MacDonald and that upon his arrival in London General Dawes will convey to Mr. MacDonald an official invitation, is the rumor at present. The latter has said "If Mr. Hoover invites me to Washington, I shall go," according to the London newspapers.

A duplicate of this telegram has been transmitted to Brussels for information of Embassy there.

ATHERTON

500.A15a3/10 : Telegram

*The Ambassador in Great Britain (Dawes) to the Secretary of State*

[Paraphrase]

LONDON, June 17, 1929—4 p. m.
[Received 5 p. m.[8]]

158. I spent two hours with MacDonald yesterday and had a most satisfactory interview. He agrees fully that it would be much wiser that the question of freedom of the seas should be discussed later. We talked over other controversial questions, stressing naval reduction as the first step to be made. My address was gone over carefully by the two of us.[9] MacDonald suggested two minor changes to which I assented as they in no way deviated from the spirit of my Washington instructions or the text of my address. The propositions authorized by the President and yourself, as set forth in my address, were most satisfactory to him, MacDonald said, adding that he would most earnestly endeavor to cooperate in every way to bring them to a fruitful conclusion. It was intimated by MacDonald that he had reason to believe that his Admiralty would be more cooperative than had been the case in the past. He expects to make an address in Scotland on the subject of naval disarmament tomorrow night, as he announced in the statement which he gave to the press. Except to state that his address in every respect would be consistent with the American proposition as outlined in my speech, he gave no intimation of what he would say. MacDonald further stated that he expected to discuss with us first any steps which he contemplated taking and that he hoped that we would place a like confidence in him. I assured him that we would most certainly do so. The President, I added, had already expressed the desire to advise him of all steps which he contemplated taking, including information as to the manner in which he was handling the naval situation of the United States.

This morning upon my return to London from Scotland I made a

[8] Telegram in two sections.
[9] Address delivered in London at the banquet of the Society of Pilgrims of Great Britain, June 18, 1929, p. 121.

call upon the Japanese Ambassador with whom in Washington I was very well acquainted. I went over my complete address very carefully with him, saying that the President had told me that it was his desire that the Japanese Government should participate with us in the most confidential and intimate manner in all discussions upon this subject and should be kept fully advised. The Japanese Ambassador expressed his satisfaction with my coming to him at this date and said that he approved heartily of all of the American suggestions contained in my speech as well as the method of their presentation. Matsudaira intimated that while his Government was most sympathetic in all regards he thought it would have been better had it been kept more intimately in touch with the discussions between ourselves and the English during the Geneva Conferences.

After my visit with Matsudaira I had a conference with Henderson, Secretary of State for Foreign Affairs, with whom I became acquainted when he accompanied me to present my credentials to the King on Saturday. I have just returned from this interview. Asking for any suggestions as to changes, I went carefully over the text of my address with Henderson. Henderson expressed himself as entirely satisfied with it and with the program outlined therein.

I would also refer to another self-assumed diplomatic endeavor before closing. MacDonald spoke of a possible visit to America during our entirely unrestrained and frank exchange of views and requested my natural reflections upon this subject. I complied with his request stating that I could qualify as a prognosticator of senatorial criticism due to my enforced contact, which had entailed some suffering. My views in general were that a portion of the Senate, which was always inclined to be exceedingly jealous of Executive initiative in international affairs, would use such a visit, should it be taken during the course of negotiations for naval disarmament, to inject into the situation discussions of a most demagogical and demoralizing character. In the discussion of the ratification of any treaty drawn up after such a conference, it would be said that the Prime Minister of England had left the United States with that nation sewed up in his pocket and there would be no material assistance in rectifying this American view by the counterclaim of many of his own countrymen that in his visit he had been seduced into surrendering British sovereignty to the United States. In view of the relations of the Senate to the situation, I further stated that any such uncommon event as a visit of the Prime Minister of England to the President of the United States would be used with diabolical ingenuity to create a fog bank, in which the real merits of the case would be completely lost to the view of the ordinary citizen. Notoriety which is not based upon an accomplishment, especially when it is acquired only at its risk, is not worth a damn, I suggested in closing. When I had finished speaking, MacDonald remarked with some emphasis: "It is my hope that I may sometime take a trip to America, but it is decided now that it will not be until after the ratification of the disarmament agreement." The President of the United States and its people, I assured him, would give him a most sincere and hearty welcome at any time he announced his plan of coming to the United States for a visit.

This morning finally I had a very agreeable visit with E. Price Bell [10] to whom I outlined the situation and gave a résumé of my conversation with the Prime Minister. The President, I told Mr. Bell, had not expressed his attitude to me on the subject, but when the question was discussed in his presence he did not openly demur when views similar to those I made to MacDonald were expressed. The fact that it was semi-officially announced from Washington that the President was awaiting information from me as to whether Mr. MacDonald planned the trip and the foregoing justified me in my judgment in stating my own personal reaction in the matter in my conversation with Mr. MacDonald. I respectfully submit all of the above to you.

DAWES

---

500.A15a3/11 : Telegram

*The Ambassador in Great Britain (Dawes) to the Secretary of State*

[Extract—Paraphrase]

LONDON, June 18, 1929—1 p. m.
[Received June 18—11:40 a. m.]

159. In pursuance of the commonsense policy of having friendly and close relations at the outset with those whose cooperation is essential at the ending of negotiations, I had very intimate and satisfactory conferences today with the French Ambassador here and with the Italian Chargé, the Ambassador being away from England, and also with Mr. Ferguson, the Canadian High Commissioner. I followed this course simply to inform them of what I should say tonight in presenting the President's suggestions for a new method of negotiation. All of them were agreed regarding wisdom of his suggestions, and promised their active support. . . .

DAWES

---

[10] Edward Price Bell, American journalist and author, who was exerting his personal efforts to advance friendly sentiment among the English-speaking peoples of the world.

500.A15a3/31

*The Ambassador in Great Britain (Dawes) to the Secretary of State*

No. 4                                         LONDON, June 18, 1929.
                                              [Received June 26.]

SIR: I have the honor to refer to the Embassy's telegram No. 158, June 17, 4 p. m., in which reference was made to my trip to Scotland for the purpose of discussing with Mr. Ramsay MacDonald the question of naval disarmament in connection with my speech to be delivered before the Pilgrim Society this evening. At the conclusion of our conference, which was most satisfactory, Mr. MacDonald read the following statement:

"General Dawes and myself have agreed to read you this as a communiqué to be issued as a result of our conversations.

"We have had a conversation regarding the present position of the question of naval disarmament as between the United States and Great Britain.

"It has been informal and general and most satisfactory.

"His Excellency proposes to refer to the subject at the Pilgrims Dinner on Tuesday next, and I shall do the same myself at the same time at Lossiemouth, and that is intended to be the beginning of the negotiations.

"We both wish to make it clear that the other naval Powers are expected to co-operate in these negotiations, upon the successful consummation of which the peace of the whole world must depend."

Although this trip for a three-hour conference necessitated altogether some thirty hours in the train, we were accompanied by a group of reporters, principally American, and the London press also evinced considerable interest. There are enclosed copies of articles appearing in the more important London journals.[11] Other editorials of possibly less moment are being forwarded to the Department in the usual manner with the Embassy's press clippings.

It may not be amiss at this moment to quote from a speech delivered by Mr. Winston Churchill to his constituents a day or so before my conversation took place with Mr. MacDonald. The entire text of this speech is appended hereto.

"If naval equality is to lead to a jealous and suspicious scrutiny of every ship and every gun and every armour-plate between the two navies, it would be much better to have no agreement at all, and for each of us to go our own way, acting sensibly and soberly and in a neighbourly fashion, but free and unfettered.

"Since Mr. Hoover became President of the United States it has seemed to me, at any rate, that a more comprehending and sympathetic spirit has been imparted to the policy of the United States, not only towards this country, but towards Europe in general."

---

[11] Not reprinted.

There was no editorial comment on this subject in either the *Daily Herald* or the *Times*, but both of these papers have extended a cordial welcome to me in recent editorials.

I have [etc.]
(For the Ambassador)
RAY ATHERTON
*Counselor of Embassy*

---

500.A15a3/40

*The Ambassador in Great Britain (Dawes) to the Secretary of State*

[Extract]

No. 12
LONDON, June 20, 1929.
[Received June 29.]

SIR: Referring to the Embassy's strictly confidential telegrams No. 158 of June 17, 4 p. m., and No. 159 of June 18, 1 p. m., I have the honor to enclose the text of my speech at the dinner given in my honor by The Pilgrims on Tuesday, June 18th, at the Hotel Victoria, London. I am sending the text published in the *Times* of June 19th. The few minor inaccuracies printed have been corrected in ink on each copy forwarded.

I have [etc.]
For the Ambassador:
RAY ATHERTON
*Counselor of Embassy*

[Enclosure]

*Speech Delivered by the American Ambassador (Dawes) at the Banquet of the Society of Pilgrims of Great Britain, June 18, 1929*

We are in a period when mankind, emerged from its greatest cataclysm—the World War—is lifting its eyes from the darkness of the past toward the sunlight of international peace and tranquillity. It is the era of effort for world construction—moral and material.

The ratification of the Kellogg Peace Treaty, which is the agreed-upon expression of a world intention, has one of its first effects in a pronounced change in the form of the international discussion of the world's peace. The closing of the discussion upon the form of the expression of the principle, and the inception of the discussion of the practical methods by which to make it effective, prove the existence of the general determination to make the treaty not a mere gesture, but the foundation of an era of "Peace on earth and good will toward men."

The matter of first importance at the present time is that the friends of the world's peace move unitedly toward that objective with a clear understanding among themselves that any effort which is not a united effort is liable to be ineffective and tending toward disintegration. To avoid confusion and delay endangering their common objective, they now should not only unitedly consider what steps should be taken toward it, but the order in which those steps are to be taken.

The importance of an early agreement on naval reduction by the nations is of outstanding importance at the present time, and it would seem to be the next step to be taken toward world peace. As to any other controverted questions between any nations or between Great Britain and the United States, their future peaceful settlement, either way, will not be endangered by the cessation of an enormously expensive naval competition in progress during their discussion.

Congress has already by law committed the United States to an immediate naval programme involving over $250,000,000, giving, however, to the President the power to suspend it in the event of an international agreement for the limitation of naval armament.

On May 31 last the Secretary of State of the United States said: "I have in my possession a memorandum from the Director of the Budget showing the cost of the programme recommended by the Navy Department in case the policy of naval reduction which the President advocates is not adopted. That memorandum shows that the authorized and contemplated naval programme for the construction of new ships alone amounts to $1,170,800,000. When it is borne in mind that the foregoing figures involve the construction programme of only one nation, and that if it proceeds other nations will be impelled to follow suit, the burden of unproductive expenditure which will be imposed upon the economic world during the next 15 years can be to a certain extent realized."

My address tonight concerns itself with suggestions as to a change in the method of future negotiations for naval disarmament. Agreement upon a method of negotiation must concern, from the very beginning, all interested naval Powers and should have not a partial, but a world, sanction. While in the course of the discussion I may refer to the principle of equality of naval power as between Great Britain and the United States, it is only because the outcome of previous conferences shows that this is the agreed policy of both Governments. My theme is what method of procedure had best be adopted to translate a policy of naval reduction into a fixed agreement between the nations—a step so important to the peace of the world and to the happiness hereafter of mankind.

Edmund Burke, in his "Observations on a Late [*the Present*] State

of the Nation," once made a profound remark about politics which
he could have made with equal truth of law, of government systems,
and of dealings with international relations of all kinds, including
methods of negotiation for reparation settlements or reduction in
naval armament. "Politics," said he, "ought to be adjusted not to
human reasonings but to human nature, of which the reason is but a
part, and by no means the greatest part."

The long time which elapsed after the ending of the Great War
before a proper method of negotiation for reparation settlements was
evolved was because the first method was adjusted to human reasoning
and not to human nature. That method was to have the recommended
settlement prepared by the continuing and concurrent work of economic experts and statesmen combined.

Since the reparation settlement involved, in each one of the nations
interested, both an economic and a political problem, it was reasonable to suppose that it would be best determined by the joint effort
of statesmen and of economists working together. This futile effort
continued so long before its abandonment that all Europe was brought
to the brink of economic and political chaos. And then only, in the
latter part of 1925, did the Reparations Commission as an experiment
decide upon the separate formation of the First Committee of Experts. This expedient, viewed at that time as almost hopeless by
most economists and entirely so by most politicians—then designated
by one great member of the Reparations Commission as the "pre-
scription of a pill for an earthquake"—proved successful.

The formation of that Committee was not a triumph of intellect—
it was the triumph of despair. It was adopted because nothing else
had worked. Its success was due to its unconscious but proper adjustment to the law of human nature. What happened thereafter demonstrated that by accident the world had discovered that the proper
method of settling an international problem, involving a separate
economic and political problem in each country, was to use independent
experts whose suggestions involved their interpretation of the correct
and fundamental economic principles involved in the situation, their
formula then to be handed over to the statesmen, who, reinforced
by general public confidence in the impartiality of expert opinion,
could better bring the respective public sentiments into acceptance of
the necessary working compromise between political expediency and
economic principles.

In committees formerly composed of co-labouring statesmen and
economists, the economists had always stood rigidly for conclusions
endangering the statesmen and the acceptance of the Plan,
and the statesmen for conclusions which would stultify the
economists and endanger the success of the Plan. Under such cir-

cumstances the arrival at a constructive compromise was well-nigh impossible. The method was not adjusted to the law of human nature.

Economic and technical problems are one thing—governmental and political problems another. The rigid attitude and determined expressions of international economic and technical specialists as to the inviolability and sacredness of technical principle is perhaps praiseworthy, but we must remember that these expressions are often incident to a doubtful embodiment of them in a personal interpretation of their applicability to international political situations, of which the experts are not always competent diagnosticians.

One who is inclined to believe that economists and technicians, claiming to be guided in their intellectual voyages by the stars and compasses and high lighthouses of fixed principles, never compromise, as do the alleged unworthy politicians, is lacking in experience in international economic negotiations. For six years after the War the unhappy Reparations Commission, besides its other misfortunes, was surrounded by an army of economic experts representing the different nations interested in the problem. These experts delivered innumerable written ultimatums as to the correct economic principles which underlay their divergent recommendations which filled vast untouched libraries and now moulder in their unruffled dust. The disagreements of these experts with each other, each swearing devotion to infallible principle, was as complete and overwhelming as those which characterized the deliberations of the supposedly less worthy, entirely confused, but fully as determined politicians and statesmen.

I remember during the last two weeks of deliberation on the part of the First Committee of Experts appointed by the Reparation Commission that, as the inside expert Committee was labouring with the formulation of its conclusions, almost all of them more or less the result of a compromise, they faced a snowstorm of protesting papers filled with the voluminous but disagreeing economic advice of outside experts removed from the field of negotiation.

What I have said has a most direct bearing upon the question of the method of conducting the great negotiation for naval disarmament soon justly to occupy the attention of the world. The question is how best to adjust the methods of negotiation to accord with the laws of human nature so that a successful outcome, so vital to the welfare of the world, may not be unnecessarily endangered.

International naval reduction is a task the successful accomplishment of which requires the cooperative employment of two distinctly unrelated talents—that of naval technical experts and of statesmen.

Important as is a preliminary expert examination of economists to report to the statesmen on an international problem involving both an economic and political phase, it is even more important where naval technicians and statesmen confront a problem involving both a technical and political phase. But here we must keep in mind the law of human nature. In the case of a preliminary use of economic experts, their prime objective is a formula which will recognize the dominance of economic law, and the success of the statesmen in reaching the second objective of accommodating the expert formula to the political conditions in the respective countries is something as much desired by the economic experts as by the statesmen themselves. That later achievement only will crown with success the preliminary expert effort. This attitude has recently been twice demonstrated. So anxious was the first Economic Committee of Experts, Reparations Commission in 1924, that their report should be the basis of a successful settlement that they were engaged continually during their work in adjusting the form of their statement to expected political repercussion.

It was their constant endeavour to frame their conclusions in such language as would make them easily understood and be as inoffensive from a political standpoint as was possible. This effort to adjust economic necessity to political expediency led them to many collateral individual conferences for advice from European statesmen during their work. As a result, when the report of the First Committee of Experts was delivered to the statesmen of the London Conference, the latter found it unnecessary to change the Plan, but only to supplement it by collateral international agreements relating to it, making it politically acceptable to all the nations concerned. And thus it was with the world-important report of the Second Committee of Experts just completed. It was their intense desire to have a constructive outcome of their work, as much as because the work itself was a diplomatic as well as an expert employment, that led them to consult constantly with the leading European statesmen during their epoch-making labours. This desire on the part of these Economic Committees accorded with the law of human nature. But in the case of naval technical experts, working for a formula for naval equality, the law of human nature runs contrary to such an attitude. It would be vastly more difficult, other things being equal, for a mixed commission of navy technicians and statesmen to agree on a plan for naval disarmament than for a mixed commission of economists and statesmen to agree upon a reparations settlement, practically impossible as history has shown the latter to be.

A naval expert is qualified to define accurately the principles which should determine abstract naval equality, but the law of human nature decrees that his opinion is relatively not as safe in a programme which he formulates as a practical interpretation of those principles applied to a partial destruction of his own navy. The proper pride of a naval officer's life is his navy. His whole professional career impels him to think of a navy only in terms of victory. He not only instinctively feels, but he is rightly taught to feel, that he must strive not for equal navies, but for a superior navy. It is difficult for him to forget that with a superior navy, victory is probable, with an equal navy doubtful, with an inferior navy almost hopeless. Other things being equal, I fear no naval officer ever inherently favours equality.

The naval officer has his duty to perform to his State, and it is primarily to secure it against attack. He therefore trusts to his ships and his armament. It is the duty of the statesman to remove from his State the danger of attack. Upon the latter primarily lies the duty of peace-making, and in these negotiations he must hold the initiative. He is the one to build up the new order and to start the new policy, guided as he goes by the advice of those competent and patriotic naval experts who serve him. What differences there are in their respective duties can be coordinated into a policy of statesmanship, and that and that alone is what I have in mind in what I now say.

I have no knowledge of the qualifications and records of any naval officers heretofore engaged in these negotiations, or acquaintance with them. I am concerned only that the methods under which this work is to be done, whoever may do it, shall be adjusted to the laws of human nature.

At the beginning of the work the contribution of the naval experts to the problem should be a definition of abstract equality. It is certainly possible for naval experts to arrive at a definition for evaluation of fighting strength of ships. Thus, for instance, one might find a yardstick with which to determine the military value of individual ships. These ships might differ in displacement, size of guns, age, speed, and other characteristics, and yet such an agreed properly weighted value might be given to each of these differing characteristics as to make it possible to compare, for example, the cruiser fleets or combined fleets of two navies, and establish a parity between them. If naval experts rise to the proper sense of their responsibility, the use by statesmen of their yardstick will not be one which will invite peril from those extreme pacifists and extreme militarists who form the "lunatic fringe."

But, again, in connexion with the method of preparing the naval yardstick, let us consider the law of human nature. Should a Commission composed of the representatives of each Navy concerned meet to reach agreement upon this yardstick, they would be asked to agree upon something the use of which will reduce in number the idols of their hearts—the ships of their navies. I am casting no reflection here upon naval officers when speaking of the law of human nature which subconsciously influences the actions of all mankind, learned or ignorant, good or bad, rich or poor, skilled or unskilled, great or humble, old or young of every race and nationality of the world.

I have already spoken of the fallibility and lack of agreement of expert and economic opinion as exemplified by the experience of the Reparations negotiations. I will say, frankly, that from a commission of naval experts of the respective nations meeting together and called to evolve a final definition of the naval yardstick, I personally should expect a failure to agree.

It would seem that, to adjust to human nature the method of arriving at naval reduction, each Government might separately obtain from their respective naval experts their definition of the yardstick and then the inevitable compromise between these differing definitions, which will be expressed in the final fixation of the technical yardstick, should be made by a committee of statesmen of the nations, reinforced from the beginning by these separate expressions of abstract technical naval opinion and able again to seek further naval advice, if necessary, before the final fixation.

These statesmen should further be the ones to draw up for the world the terms of the final agreement upon naval reduction, which should be couched in those simple terms understandable to the ordinary man in the street, which, while the pet aversion of the casuist, are the highest expression of true statesmanship. That final agreement, covering the quantitative dispositions, will go to the nations for approval or rejection.

If this should be the outcome, let those entrusted with the last draft of the conclusions of the last Conference be men born with the faculty of clear and concise statement, for that document must appeal to the composite will of the peoples of the nations, and in order to make the proper appeal it must be read generally and understood.

There, again, we remember the operations of the law of human nature, and will hope that in these men the temptation to show erudition be subordinated to writing that which, while properly covering the cause, may be understood by the audience. A clear statement of the case, understandable by all, should mean success.

And here let me anticipate the possible comments of those whom we have always with us on both sides of the ocean—the social purveyors of the trivial in international discussion who talk so continually about good relations and do so little to forward them.

In all I have said tonight I intend nothing in derogation of the absolute necessity for the consideration and presentation of the naval side of this question by its ablest experts the world over, and, on the other hand, nothing in derogation of the absolute necessity of bringing to the political side of it the highest qualities of statesmanship which the world can provide. But to properly solve the problem we must adopt a method which brings the full weight of both of these classes of men to bear upon it, without their unnecessary collisions during the first formulating period when they are primarily concerned with two separate objectives.

Again, and also anticipating certain comment, let me say that while it is the fashion of these sensational days to attribute to any statement of irritating fact by a public man some malevolent purpose towards individuals, there is nothing of this in my mind.

The Committee from the Governments which met at Geneva to agree upon naval disarmament was a mixed commission of statesmen and naval technicians, and, in my judgment, that was the reason for its failure. The method was adjusted to human reasoning, but not to human nature.

We should not look upon the failure at Geneva in 1927 as the failure of individuals, but of the method under which they were asked to function. This may be said, however, that under the laws of human nature, probably 90 per cent. of Englishmen think the American Delegation was responsible for the mistake, and 90 per cent. of Americans think that the British members of the Commission were responsible for the mistake. The great, overwhelming, and soul-satisfying fact about it is that the British and American people are a unit in agreeing that, whoever was responsible for it, a mistake was made. And of what is this significant? It means that in the inarticulate consciences and hearts of the two great English-speaking peoples there is upheld, sacred and inviolate, the principle of the equality between them of naval strength. Their attitude upon this question—unmistakable—assumed as out of the realm of debate even by the nationalistic demagogues of both countries—while decorated by reason, is based under the providence of God upon fundamental human instincts and a commingling of the blood.

In these circumstances, let us be hopeful for the cause of world peace and the progress of civilization; for in the joint hands of these same English-speaking peoples rests not only their secure guarantee, but as well the ark of the covenant of human freedom.

---

123G35/431 : Telegram

*The Ambassador in Belgium (Gibson) to the Secretary of State*

BRUSSELS, June 20, 1929—11 a. m.
[Received June 20—9 : 05 a. m.]

39. The President having told General Dawes I would be available for consultation he telegraphs he would be glad to see me in London

next week. If the Department approves I could go Monday or Wednesday. Request instructions.[12]

GIBSON

---

500.A15a3/14 : Telegram

*The Ambassador in Great Britain (Dawes) to the Secretary of State*

[Paraphrase]

LONDON, June 20, 1929—noon.
[Received 12:55 p. m.]

162. Evidently having had inquiries from his Government concerning the proposed visit of MacDonald to the United States, the Japanese Ambassador paid me a call yesterday morning. In confidence I informed him that MacDonald had told me that his visit to the States would not be made until the negotiations for naval disarmament had taken place, and the reasons therefor. He seemed relieved and expressed his gratitude for the information given.

I am very glad that the President decided to have Gibson confer with me in London. It would be well, I think, for you to announce in Washington that at your suggestion Gibson is going to London in a few days to have a conference with me; that the announcement should be made in Washington rather than in London seems advisable to me. It would appear from such a course that the United States Government realized that these negotiations should proceed without interruption, considering the conditional legislative commitment of this Congress to a large naval program. We must overcome, of course, any appearance that our desire for expediency should militate against the most careful and painstaking technical preparation. However, the whole psychology of the situation is at present in its most favorable state and the earlier we reach an agreement upon the yardstick the more confident we can be that it will receive approval.

The King's speech will be read before Parliament on July 2 and the debates in that body on this measure during the ensuing days will indicate just what support MacDonald may expect on his program of pressing for a settlement of the disarmament question in the near future from this newly elected legislative body.

My kind regards to yourself and the President.

DAWES

---

[12] The authorization requested was granted for a period not to exceed one week; Department's telegram No. 41, June 20, noon, to the Ambassador in Belgium, not printed (123G35/434).

On June 26 the Ambassador in Great Britain cabled the Department asking permission to invite Mr. Gibson to come to London from time to time for consultation on naval questions without having to obtain specific instructions from Washington. The authorization requested was granted. Embassy's telegram No. 172, June 26, 8 p. m., and Department's telegrams No. 43 and No. 159, June 27, 4 p. m., to Belgium and Great Britain, respectively; none printed (500.A15a3/29).

500.A15a3/12 : Telegram

*The Chargé in Japan (Neville) to the Secretary of State*

TOKYO, June 20, 1929—3 p. m.
[Received June 20—8:55 a. m.]

65. The Prime Minister told me yesterday that Japan was prepared to support any measures looking to further reduction of armaments; that the country wanted peace and lessened expenditure for war purposes and that he would welcome concrete suggestions; that recent reports had led him to suppose that our Government might later have something definite and he asked me to state that Japan could be counted on.

I told him that I did not know what plans, if any, were under consideration but that I should gladly inform Washington where I was sure it would cause gratification.

NEVILLE

---

500.A15a3/14 : Telegram

*The Secretary of State to the Ambassador in Great Britain (Dawes)*

WASHINGTON, June 21, 1929—3 p. m.

150. Your 162, June 20, noon. In accordance with your suggestion the Department will inform the press that Mr. Gibson is proceeding to London next week for consultation with you on the naval matter with particular reference to the present state of the affair before the Preparatory Commission. I hope that you and Gibson will make some recommendation as to what steps you think would be most effective at this time to carry on the good work which you have begun.

STIMSON

---

500.A15a3/18 : Telegram

*The Ambassador in Great Britain (Dawes) to the Secretary of State*

[Extract—Paraphrase]

LONDON, June 22, 1929—1 p. m.
[Received 1:55 p. m.]

166. . . . Gibson arrives Monday evening. Of course I have kept away completely from any naval contacts. Furthermore I have asked MacDonald to decide whether I ought to see Bridgeman,[13] as the latter wishes. If MacDonald should advise me to see Bridgeman, I shall await arrival of Gibson so that he can join in the conference. His experience and knowledge make his initiative in this situation essential in any contacts or discussions with naval people.

---

[13] William Clive Bridgeman (created Viscount Bridgeman of Leigh in June 1929), First Lord of the British Admiralty, 1924–1929.

The following is entirely tentative, and for your possible comment; it is something which I shall talk over with Gibson. It seems to me that possibly it might be wise for Gibson, MacDonald and myself to make as full use as possible of the personality of Matsudaira in these early conferences. The Japanese Ambassador is sympathetic and wise. It is clear to me that possible advantages may accrue in the future from the initiative of Japan in suggestions as to a naval yardstick, as well as in other matters. From naval interviews in Tokyo which are printed here, I take it for granted that the Japanese Government is already concerning itself sympathetically with the question of the naval yardstick which will be prepared by its own naval technicians. These conversations with the Japanese Ambassador would inevitably bring up, of course, the questions of conversations concurrently with France and Italy. This matter must be thought over very carefully.

Your No. 150, dated June 21, 3 p. m., has just been received. What I have said above will indicate to you some of the things which I plan to talk over with Gibson. I await his coming with much eagerness.

DAWES

500.A15a3/18 : Telegram

*The Secretary of State to the Ambassador in Great Britain (Dawes)*

[Paraphrase]

WASHINGTON, June 24, 1929—1 p. m.

154. Your No. 166, June 22, 1 p. m. I agree with your view that it would be wise to keep the Japanese Ambassador closely informed with regard to the subject matter of any conferences which you and Gibson may have with the British, but I do not think that he should be present personally in any such conversations as otherwise the rumor might arise that a conference was already under way to the exclusion of France and Italy.

STIMSON

500.A15a3/8

*The Secretary of State to the Chargé in Japan (Neville)*

No. 573                          WASHINGTON, June 24, 1929.

SIR: This is to inform you that I received a call on June 11, 1929, from Mr. Katsuji Debuchi, Japanese Ambassador at Washington. During the course of the conversation the Ambassador asked me whether we had any further plans in regard to a naval conference. He said he understood that Admiral Jones was preparing a formula and was at work and he asked what our procedure would be.

I told the Ambassador that we were rather waiting to see how other nations felt and asked him how he would feel toward a proposition that the authorized representatives of Great Britain, Japan and ourselves should each separately with the advice of their naval officers try to work out a formula from the lead which Mr. Gibson's speech had given, namely to work out a method by which the equivalent value of different sized cruisers could be obtained, taking into consideration their tonnage, their caliber and their age.

Mr. Debuchi said that he had supposed that we were going to do that first and then give it to them. He agreed with me that there would be small hope of agreement if the work were left to the naval representatives alone. I told him I felt very clear about this; that every such agreement upon a formula would involve sacrifices and compromise on the part of each country and that in my opinion could be better done by the work of responsible representatives of the government advised by the navy rather than by the navy alone. He agreed. I told him that we were at work on this and that when I came back to Washington I would take it up again with him; that we hesitated to impose our formula upon the others first and would rather have them do it and work simultaneously. He indicated that he thought that our country was going to do it first and seemed to prefer that way.

He then said that in this connection he hoped that I would remember that Japanese opinion was very sensitive on the question of the 5–5–3 ratio; that this had been agreed to as to capital ships but when it came to auxiliary vessels we would find their public opinion very keen, as he expressed it; that the reason for this was China; that China required the presence of a great number of auxiliary vessels of Japan in Chinese waters in the present troubled condition although it did not require any capital ships and therefore this served to affect the ratio 5–5–3 when it came to such smaller vessels. I reminded the Ambassador that we were discussing not the ultimate quantity ratio of such craft but merely a formula for determining their relative efficiency or value; that this must be taken as the first step and after we had done that then we could sit down and discuss 5–5–3. He said he recognized this.

I am [etc.]                                        H. L. STIMSON

---

500.A15a3/25 : Telegram

*The Ambassadors in Great Britain and Belgium (Dawes and Gibson) to the Secretary of State*

[Paraphrase]

LONDON, June 25, 1929—6 p. m.
[Received 11:15 p. m.]

168. With reference to your telegram No. 150, June 21, 3 p. m., suggesting that we offer recommendations concerning what steps we

consider would be most effective at the present time to carry the work forward, our opinion is that the next logical step would be to convene a meeting of non-technical Governmental representatives to consider this matter. Until the various special needs, obligations and worries of each of the five naval powers have been discussed and dealt with in a broad manner, we run the risk of striking a deadlock on purely technical questions before arriving at a discussion of the broader field upon which we must reach an agreement. From our point of view it would seem advisable that some other power should take this next step. Should we take the initiative it might be interpreted as our insistence, in the face of indifference on the part of other Governments, of consideration of our proposals. Both the Italian and French Governments may be safely eliminated as they will hardly take any initiative and therefore the choice lies between the Governments of Great Britain and Japan. Should the suggestion of the meeting be made by the British Government, it would have the advantage both in Great Britain and in the United States of showing a spontaneous desire to proceed with consideration of proposals made by us. Moreover, should the French prove obstructive they will have to justify their attitude not to the United States but to the British Government which would have a distinctive advantage from our viewpoint. While the French may prove somewhat obstructive, this attitude, if careful attention is given to the form of invitation, may be made more difficult for them. In this connection, the Department will recall that the French Government refused an invitation to the naval conference held in Geneva in 1927, on the ground that the League of Nations should be the sole agency to deal with all disarmament matters. Should agreement grow out of these propositions, incidentally, it is hard to see on what grounds the French Government could demand that these discussions be deliberately delayed until the Preparatory Commission should take general action on the question. If the invitation made it clear that the French proposal of 1927 for methods of naval limitation was to be used as a basis of discussion, French obstructiveness could be rendered still more difficult.

Some of the French naval experts, at least so I understand, express doubt as to whether a method applicable to France and Italy can be found in our suggestions. They also indicate their belief that it is possible to discover some other method which would meet their problem with Italy. The French might be told that so long as this solution keeps them within limits which cause no misgivings to the British Government the three principal naval powers would not object to a different method being adopted by them. Agreement between the five naval powers upon the two methods and their application to the different groups is, of course, desirable. Should the French and Italians decline to negotiate you may still feel that we could well go ahead in an endeavor to bring about an understanding among the three other powers. The British would probably object to a rigid agreement under such conditions on the ground that they could not bind themselves without having some knowledge as to the intentions of the French. The political clause which we suggested in 1927, as outlined hereinafter, might be used to meet such reasonable misgivings on the part of the British.

The following is a rough summary of our suggestions:

(*a*) A proposition to be made upon the initiative of Great Britain or Japan providing for the appointment of a civilian commission on naval disarmament, on which commission the five governments would be represented by two members each.

(*b*) The government which makes the proposal should, in transmitting its suggestion to the five nations, recommend that the suggestions of the United States should govern the conference regarding methods of negotiation.

(*c*) It should be made clear by the proposing government that in this conference, participated in by the five naval powers, it should be thoroughly understood that the first objective would be the full and informal exchange of views which the representatives of the five interested nations agreed upon last month as a necessary preliminary to further profitable endeavor. A treaty providing for a program of naval reduction covering all the navies represented would, of course, be the ultimate endeavor. The conclusion of such a treaty might be a logical outcome if the work progressed satisfactorily. If a longer time was needed for the consideration of the application of the principle to any particular nation or nations, any of the remaining nations in consultation with the other members of the commission would be free to consider treaties between themselves provided a reduction of their armaments was the purpose of such a treaty.

(*d*) As we suggested at Geneva in 1927, the treaty might include a provision under which, if the building program of a nonsignatory power assumes such proportions as to give concern to one of the signatories, the latter would have the right to summon a three-power conference for the purpose of examining the situation and, if unable to secure satisfactory agreement with the nonsignatory power, to relieve itself from the obligations of the treaty within a fixed period; such a provision however would only be inserted in case a treaty for naval reduction should result from the conference which involved less than all the nations there represented.

A treaty for naval reduction executed by the three principal powers alone under the above general arrangement and after full consideration and consultation with the other powers, would be feasible without awaiting a possibly delayed agreement between Italy and France which are concerned with their own questions of relativity primarily. Should these countries, that is, Italy and France, not desire to reduce their navies or settle the question of their relativity, it would seem to be of no disadvantage to them either collectively or separately in case an agreement is reached between the three great naval powers regarding their own problems of naval reduction.  If these two countries did not join in the desired treaty covering the five powers, questions of the result of an unrestricted construction program on their part and its relation to the whole question would have to be taken into consideration.  A present forward step in naval reduction could not be endangered by delays over the question of Italian and French relativity by the proposition outlined above.

It would appear that the chances for success would depend to a large extent upon initiative at this time and the adoption of the right methods of procedure.  The statesmen could begin their general discussions while the technicians were preparing the yardstick under such an arrangement.  At the present time a most favorable atmosphere exists between the three principal naval powers as concerns a settlement based on general principles in the near future, and conversations concerning the technical yardstick proceeding concurrently will not preclude a discussion of this more important matter.  Taking into consideration the importance of action while general psychology is so favorable, we should not delay too long the work of building the house when we may lose the impulse as well as the essential material for its construction by awaiting too long the completion of the minor implements of internal measurements, yardsticks, carpenter's squares, and so-forth and so-forth.  While these tools must be employed before the house is completed they are not necessarily important in the first steps of construction.  However, the whole enterprise from the beginning must be decorated with the background of the concurrent use and consideration of technical naval opinion, we all understand, as this is especially desirable for its influence upon public opinion, including that of congresses and parliaments to whom we must sell the house under construction.

Foregoing is our attempt to express our interpretation of what has been said from time to time by President Hoover during the discussions of this naval question.

DAWES and GIBSON

---

500.A15a3/26 : Telegram

*The Ambassadors in Great Britain and Belgium (Dawes and Gibson) to the Secretary of State*

[Paraphrase]

LONDON, June 25, 1929—midnight.
[Received June 25—10:40 p. m.]

169. We called upon the Prime Minister today (June 25) after sending you our long telegram No. 168.  MacDonald has decided that he will extend an invitation for a conference of nontechnical govern-

mental representatives of the five naval powers and has under consideration the form of invitation which he expects to submit to us tomorrow evening, Wednesday, at 6 o'clock. MacDonald's purposes coincide with those which we outlined to you in our longer telegram. Matsudaira also called upon us this afternoon. He is awaiting a message from his Government in full expectation of an agreement by it upon the program which we later learned MacDonald was contemplating. The Prime Minister brought up the question as to where the conference should take place, stating that if it could be held in London it would be of the greatest convenience to him. Should it take place at Paris it would be impossible for him to give his own personal and continuous attention to the progress of the work was the reason he gave for this. Furthermore, he indicated that in London the conference could be conducted with greater privacy.

DAWES and GIBSON

500.A15a3/28 : Telegram

*The Ambassador in Great Britain (Dawes) to the Secretary of State*

[Paraphrase]

LONDON, June 26, 1929—8 p. m.
[Received June 26—7:15 p. m.]

171. Reference is made to my telegram No. 169, June 25. I have just returned from a visit to the Prime Minister who had definitely decided to take some step to initiate positive work on the problem of naval disarmament. MacDonald in his address last night referred to his intention to convene a conference, but evidently since then it had been called to his attention that it would be preferable to so word his invitation as to afford no pretext to France to decline to attend with the excuse that it would not be loyal to the League of Nations to do so. MacDonald proposes to discuss the subject tomorrow with the Foreign Office and request that it draft some form of invitation which he may discuss with the representatives of the five countries interested in the naval problem. MacDonald further proposes to urge that July 22 be the date upon which this conference shall take place as he is convinced that it is impossible during the month of August to carry on serious work as a practical matter and the Assembly of the League of Nations will occupy the attention of the various powers during September. MacDonald indicated that it was his idea that the work of this conference should be confined to a discussion of certain general principles, the methods of work and the adoption of a resolution to the effect that ultimate agreement upon the naval problem must be achieved through a full adherence to the spirit of the Kellogg Pact which justifies naval reduction and that the conference should not last more than a week.

MacDonald was of the opinion that some such general resolution would serve to maintain public confidence and thus time would be gained for the careful technical studies to be carried on after the first meeting had adjourned. At a later date when the Assembly of the League of Nations was out of the way subsequent conversations could be held.

Apparently MacDonald is exploring the possibility of coming into the conference after consultation with us and making some very general public proposal to the effect that the Government of Great Britain is disposed to scrap certain construction, to abandon its present building program, and to contribute such further concessions as are possible and allow us an opportunity to reply in like manner, thus liquidating our problem but without resorting to the use of the yardstick at any time.

DAWES

500.A15a3/26 : Telegram

*The Secretary of State to the Ambassador in Great Britain (Dawes)*

[Paraphrase]

WASHINGTON, June 27, 1929—6 p. m.

160. Reference your telegram No. 171, June 26, and your telegrams Nos. 168 and 169, June 25, 1929. It is not believed by the President and myself that it is at all feasible to hold a conference for any final action on reduction of armament at the present time. The reasons for this are as follows:

First. Should any conference be called now with powers to examine naval disarmament in all its phases including those phases which are technical, it is likely that the opposition of the naval experts in all countries to any conclusions arrived at will be aroused. This would operate to add to the burdens of ratification dangerously.

Second. Our naval experts are not yet prepared to present their final views and we must be ready to digest thoroughly the technical questions. It is necessary to convince the naval experts that reduction can go further than they at present think so we must have the time to do so.

Third. The door would be left open for criticism for lack of preparation for this conference. The last conference was generally the target of such criticism.

However, it appears to us that it would greatly contribute to the solution of our difficulties and would seem to accord with Mr. MacDonald's views to have a preliminary nontechnical consultation of representatives strictly limited to examining certain broad questions of general policy. As a basis of any consultation as well as of the final conference it is assumed by us that the Government of Great Britain agrees with us accepting the general principle of parity between both our navies as axiomatic. On this point we would like to have an assurance. You should state frankly if it were declined that from our point of view no purpose would be served by a consultation.

We would suggest then if the Government of Great Britain agrees with us as to this point that the following questions be considered by a preliminary consultation to be held by representatives of the five powers:

(a) Let the technical questions which are to be submitted to the experts in development of methods for ascertaining comparative naval strength be enumerated.

(b) In order to consider whether or not the ultimate conference should deal with the whole gamut of naval strength or only with particular categories such as cruisers for instance, it is our desire that the ultimate conference should discuss the categories covered by the Washington treaty as well and deal with the entire question of all kinds of combatant ships.

(c) The problem as to whether there should be actual reduction of present or authorized construction or merely limitation which will result in the construction programs being completed. Feeling strongly that the conference must result in reduction we believe that this can be done equably among the powers.

(d) The problem of relative strength which will meet Japanese needs and also the problems of Italy and France. In case it were impossible to secure agreement with Italy and France, this fact, if developed at the consultation, would also probably determine whether they should be members of the final conference or whether it would be limited to Great Britain, Japan and the United States.

When these and possibly other questions have been settled and with the questions which are to be addressed to the naval experts determined upon, after an interval of some time for preparation and consideration the final conference, we believe, could then be called with the prospects of success immensely increased. The preliminary consultation in London would be favored by us but the location of the final conference must, it seems to us, rest naturally at our option since the movement was initiated from this country. At the present time we are not prepared to say finally whether it would be more desirable to have the conference in the United States or in some other country.

However, we wish to impress upon you strongly that there would need to be solely a preliminary consultation called for the consideration of limited and agreed questions, otherwise we are convinced that such haste is likely to bring disaster and to prevent success in ultimate and complete form. It is also felt that success from the British point of view, in view of the political balance of power, is dependent upon the Prime Minister being able to carry with him certain other strength and that if by hasty action he should have the complete opposition of the British Admiralty and should not have prepared the way carefully his defeat would not be unlikely. Such a contingency, you must realize, might not be altogether undesirable to him as an issue in his present precarious political position and might make him ready to take chances which we should not wish to bear. It is borne in mind that the British position vis-à-vis the League of Nations may necessarily influence them in the form of invitations which they are preparing to make.

STIMSON

---

500.A15a3/37 : Telegram

*The Ambassador in Great Britain (Dawes) to the Secretary of State*

[Paraphrase]

LONDON, June 28, 1929—7 p. m.
[Received 7:45 p. m.]

175. I discussed with MacDonald this afternoon the terms of your telegram, No. 160, of June 27, 6 p. m. He entirely approves, generally speaking, giving emphasis to the fact that the only idea that was ever in his mind was a preliminary conference. MacDonald said that he had no hesitation in giving assurance on the question of parity, and upon grasping the complete import of your suggestions, he stated that they were so nearly in accord with his own views that he was desirous of discussing the question with his Cabinet and that, reenforced by their views, some time next week he would give me a statement from the British Government. Of course, this will dispose of the July 22 date about which I telegraphed you in my No. 171 of June 26. We discussed the questions which might arise in the proposed preliminary conference, especially the paragraph marked "First" in your telegram No. 160, June 27. It was apparent that the technical questions to be submitted to the experts were as a matter of fact "terms of reference" requiring in case of necessity careful technical consideration and complete and strictly confidential agreement between the United States and Great Britain before the preliminary conference was held or even the invitation was extended to the other interested powers. The Foreign Office in May, during a discussion with Atherton [14] suggested that a naval mathematician, preferably without rank, having full cognizance of the figures of the American yardstick should confidentially meet his opposite number of the British Admiralty and that the two should place on the table side by side their two sets of figures and study how great the actual divergence was between the ideas of the American and British Governments. This matter was referred to the Prime Minister who said that should such a proposition be made to him he would be willing to meet it. Should such a method of approach to the Anglo-American accord seem satisfactory, I would suggest that such a meeting be held at Brussels as Gibson would then be closely in touch

---

[14] Ray Atherton, Counselor of the American Embassy.

with their labors and they would be insured an absence of publicity. I discussed with Gibson when he was here the possibility of this confidential meeting as the next preliminary step and it met with his approval.

I shall probably hear from the Prime Minister again by Tuesday or Wednesday of next week and await any comment you may wish to make for my guidance. I have telegraphed the text of this message to Gibson requesting that he telegraph you his views on the matter also.

From the above it is apparent that our next conversation with the Prime Minister will be after he has consulted with his Cabinet concerning the matter. Acquiescence was expressed as to your suggestions concerning the place of meeting for any final conference.

DAWES

---

500.A15a3/50 : Telegram

*The Ambassador in Great Britain (Dawes) to the Secretary of State*

LONDON, July 9, 1929—9 a. m.
[Received July 9—8 : 40 a. m.]

179. I received at the Embassy last evening a letter from the Prime Minister in his own handwriting as follows:

"Ten Downing Street, Whitehall, 8 July, 1929.

My dear Ambassador: I have been giving a good deal of consideration to the situation which has been clarified by the talks we have had up to now and this is what is in my mind as the result:

1. I think it would be a very useful thing if our two Governments were to announce our agreement that we are to take the pact of peace—the Kellogg Pact [15]—as a vital and controlling fact in our relations and use it as the starting point in negotiations regarding disarmament.

2. We should then proceed to declare that on that basis the object of negotiations must be reductions in existing armaments and that between us the relations are such that we both agree to parity.

3. We adopt the United States proposal that parity should be measured by an agreed 'yardstick' which enables the slightly different values in our respective national needs to be reduced to equality.

4. In order that the elements which enter into the 'yardstick' be determined I venture to ask you to send for an officer of your Navy— or Naval Department—with the requisite knowledge to come here and be at your service and act with a similar officer whom I shall appoint to guide both of us in agreeing as to the 'stick'.

5. I think it would expedite matters if your officer would take with him a proposal which your people are prepared to make as to the 'stick' in all fairness to us.

6. When we agree as to the 'stick' we can proceed as to its application and so far as I can see little trouble will arise about this between us. If it does its cause has certainly not been evident to me yet.

---

[15] Treaty for the Renunciation of War, *Foreign Relations*, 1928, vol. I, p. 153.

7. Whilst this is going on between us we must keep Japan, France and Italy generally informed in ways which we can decide from time to time.

8. We should also decide when the moment had come for the general conference to meet in London, when I should go to Washington, and when the final conference of ratification should take place. My own view is that if you got your officer over at once you and I would soon settle the preliminaries and the other conferences would follow. The stage indicated in paragraph 6 might be that when the general conference should begin, though we should know where we stand, first of all.

9. We should also agree upon the wording of the invitations to be sent to the other powers and to the scope of the discussion. I think it ought to be confined to naval matters and that we should agree that the actual negotiations should be in the hands of politicals and that officers should be in attendance or at call only for expert and technical advice.

If you will let me have your views on this note we could go ahead. I feel that time is precious and should not be lost. People are expecting much from us and I am sure we can satisfy them. I am, my dear Ambassador, yours very sincerely, Ramsay MacDonald."

[Paraphrase.] I shall await your comment before arrival of Gibson, whom I have asked to come here for a conference with me, and before seeing MacDonald again. After you have conferred with Myron Taylor,[16] paragraph 8 which refers to a trip to Washington by the Prime Minister will be clearer to you. It is my opinion, however, that it does not indicate that there has been any change in the position earlier expressed to me by MacDonald to the effect that in determining the time for crossing the Atlantic he will be guided by considerations as to whether or not such a visit would be advisable while the naval negotiations are pending.

Several questions which I should ask MacDonald concerning his letter have suggested themselves to me and I have no doubt that Gibson will think of others. If they appear to be important after conferring with Gibson I shall cable for your comment before taking further action. [End paraphrase.]

DAWES

---

500.A15a3/50 : Telegram

*The Secretary of State to the Ambassador in Great Britain (Dawes)*

WASHINGTON, July 11, 1929—6 p. m.

174. Your 179, July 9, 9 a. m., 180 and 181, July 10, 4 p. m.[17] The President and I would be glad if you would informally communicate the following to Mr. MacDonald.

[16] Myron C. Taylor, chairman of the finance committee, United States Steel Corporation, who had been traveling in England and with whom the Ambassador had talked informally regarding certain personal impressions on current matters.
[17] Nos. 180 and 181 not printed.

"We wish to express our great appreciation of the letter from the Prime Minister. It is most constructive in its tenor and practical in its proposals. We have some variants to suggest as to procedure, which by simplifying the problem would even further expedite practical results.

Referring in detail to his suggestions:

A. Paragraph 1—We are in agreement.

B. Paragraph 2—We are in agreement as to reduction of naval armaments.

C. Paragraph 3—We are in agreement—with the understanding that the expression 'slightly different values in our respective national needs' refers to characteristics of combatant ships but does not refer to reasonable equality of the respective total combatant strength.

D. Paragraphs 4 and 5—These relate to the method of developing a yardstick by our technical advisers. It seems to us that the suggestion made may perhaps, by its shortcut, lead to technical difficulties, and, more important, to conflict within and between our different Navy Departments and their experts. We believe that instead of this suggestion we should take a little more time and direct our activities on both sides to securing a common line of thought in our different Navy Departments. To bring this about we make the following suggestions to Mr. MacDonald for consideration, which we think will greatly simplify the technical questions:

E. These points are:

> *a.* We suggest that the scope of agreement shall cover all combatant ships.
>
> *b.* We suggest that combatant strength shall be considered by categories of capital ships, aircraft carriers, cruisers, destroyers and submarines.
>
> *c.* We suggest that right of limited transfer between these categories be recognized and that such transfer be made in accordance with an agreed yardstick.
>
> *d.* As our capital ship and aircraft carrier status is fixed by the Washington Treaty of 1922,[18] we suggest that these categories require no further discussion as to relative combatant strength. The only question for consideration in these categories is deferment of replacements.

F. We suggest that in measuring relative combatant strength of ships we should consider the elements of such yardstick to be

> (*a*) Displacement.
> (*b*) Guns.
> (*c*) Age.

Our general view is that protection, speed, habitability, etc., are entirely relative to the other factors and do not require special consideration.

G. We suggest that these factors may deserve different weight for different categories.

---

[18] *Foreign Relations*, 1922, vol. I, p. 247.

H. It is not expected that any yardstick will be a mathematical nicety. It would appear to us that if the suggestions in paragraphs E, F and G meet with approval we shall have enormously simplified the problem which we have to lay before naval experts and that they could quickly come to conclusions.

I. Paragraph 6—We are in agreement.

J. Paragraph 7—We are in agreement.

K. Paragraph 8—This raises the question as to the location of the final conference. We still believe that this should be held open until our progress in these preliminary steps enables us to determine these final questions with the best chances of ultimate success.

L. Paragraph 9—is affected by comment on paragraph 8. We are entirely agreeable as to the desirability of expediting matters as rapidly as we can and to do so with an assurance of success. We should hope to do this by simplifying our problem as much as possible by these direct discussions. If we could agree upon the principles in E and F we could at once send a naval expert if it is desired or we could mutually exchange views upon the weight to be given factors mentioned in F with hope of early decision."

STIMSON

---

500.A15a3/61 : Telegram

*The Ambassador in Great Britain (Dawes) to the Secretary of State*

LONDON, July 11, 1929—11 p. m.
[Received July 12—7:27 a. m.]

186. In regard to matter of MacDonald's visit it is evident that the present status is causing him much embarrassment. Would it not seem that the presence of the Prime Minister of England at the final naval conference which I infer you desire to be held at Washington would be helpful to the negotiations? The situation will be well developed at that time and the objections to a premature visit will be largely removed. The influence the Prime Minister has upon the situation will then be developed in the public mind by what he says and does at the public conference and therefore cannot be made the pretext for demagogical misrepresentation that conferences during an earlier stage of naval disarmament necessarily private might bring about—a matter which has caused our apprehension. I express these views believing we should be of assistance in this matter if possible and that inclusion in his late letter to you of a reference to a decision as to time of the trip would indicate that some such solution is in the Prime Minister's mind. I am not suggesting any public statement about this now but if the Prime Minister's suggestion about a joint announcement hereafter as to a program by the two countries is agreed to then would be an opportunity for an accompanying statement, if then advisable, that at the final con-

ference it was desirable that those in first authority should be present as far as possible. In the meantime MacDonald might say that the matter of his visit was a subject of diplomatic conversation with a view to determining how the trip might best advance the cause of naval disarmament. Any later announcement that the trip would be made for the final conference would be only by understanding of the two countries at the proper time. Later, before sending it to you and after further reflection, I took the above message and showed it to the Prime Minister. He stated that he is compelled to answer in Parliament within a few days an interpellation now in his hand as follows:

"Hansard, 10th July, 1929.
Prime Minister's visit to America:
Mr. Day asked the Prime Minister whether he is in a position to state when his forthcoming visit to America will take place and whether any representatives of the Dominions will be present at any conference that takes place.
The Prime Minister. I am not yet in a position to make any statement."

Inasmuch [as] it does not [preclude] any of the other suggestions or points in my message above and will satisfy his requirements in the situation, the Prime Minister will now answer this interpellation in substance,

"That the matter of his visit was a subject of diplomatic correspondence with a view to determining how the trip might be arranged to best advance our common interest in naval disarmament."

Later in the course of our talk, the Prime Minister then showed me private documents relative to decisions he had already arrived at as to his naval program based on our former conversations, all of which conversations have been heretofore reported to you. Then remarking that frankness was the order of the day he wrote down in his own hand the following message for transmittal to you which he handed to me:

"In view of our conversations I have just decided to slow down our preparations for laying the keels of the two cruisers in my naval program of 1928–29. I hope they need never be built. Might I presume to remark that if a corresponding step could be taken on your side it would have a fine effect. I must announce this in the course of a week or two before the House rises and a simultaneous statement of your plans would enable me to get this through without an attack on the ground that I had done something without any response. J. R. M. Handed to General Dawes by me, J. R. M., 11th June [July], 1929".

Copy to Brussels.

DAWES

500.A15a3/63 : Telegram

*The Ambassador in Great Britain (Dawes) to the Secretary of State*

[Paraphrase]

LONDON, July 12, 1929—1 p. m.
[Received July 12—10:40 a. m.]

187.  I called on the Prime Minister and delivered in person your No. 174 of July 11, 6 p. m.  He was most appreciative, giving careful attention to your telegram, with which, after reading it, he expressed himself as greatly pleased.  Further careful study will be required for paragraphs E, F and G, but in the meantime he is assuming that there is complete agreement between you and him. He accepted at once paragraph C and everything else while making a study of E, F and G, as mentioned.

MacDonald also agreed that I could communicate at once to Japanese Ambassador the substance of his letter of July 8,[19] making slight modification in paragraph No. 7 by omission of last ten words. I ask your authorization, therefore, to submit this letter of MacDonald's immediately, together with text of your No. 174, in confidence to Matsudaira.  Please inform me as quickly as possible on this point.  The Prime Minister said he would send me next week a written reply to your telegram.

Following our usual custom of transmitting all telegrams bearing on naval disarmament to Gibson, I have forwarded him text of your No. 174.

DAWES

---

500.A15a3/63 : Telegram

*The Secretary of State to the Ambassador in Great Britain (Dawes)*

[Paraphrase]

WASHINGTON, July 12, 1929—2 p. m.

176.  Our No. 174 was sent last evening after conference with the President in order that you might have as soon as possible our views on the immediately pressing steps relating to settlement of the preliminary questions between ourselves and Great Britain, and in furtherance of the Prime Minister's note.  Prior to our conference with the President he had talked with Mr. Myron Taylor and we appreciate importance of information received from him as bearing upon our own proposal, which will not be framed for bargaining purposes.

[19] See telegram No. 179, July 9, 9 a. m., from the Ambassador in Great Britain, p. 140.

We are in agreement with you that it would be unfortunate to have any publicity given MacDonald's letter, and likewise to our reply, until further progress is made in settling Anglo-American questions that are suggested in this correspondence. It is our view that the questions thus under consideration between our two Governments cannot give offense to any of the other powers as they do not infringe upon interests of the latter, and also because it is evident that these powers expect us to make this preliminary progress with the British Government before taking up the subject with them. I saw the French and the Italian Ambassadors yesterday and told them that we were engaged in threshing out these preliminary questions regarding parity between ourselves and the British, but that nothing would be done which touched their interests. Both Claudel and Martino seemed perfectly satisfied. About a fortnight ago I made a similar statement to the Japanese Ambassador, and I shall probably see him again soon.

Our intention now is to try out upon our own naval experts the possibility of framing questions as to a technical yardstick in endeavor to ascertain whether such a method would be a useful preliminary to a general conference were such questions addressed to the experts of the other powers. President is impressed with importance of such methods, and it seems desirable thus to give it a preliminary test. You will be kept informed with regard to results.

Referring to your suggestion that Gibson go to Paris in order to set at rest any suspicions which might be aroused there, this would seem to me to be unwise as his journey there would imply that the French were being taken into a confidence not enjoyed by the Italians and the Japanese. I think that the wisest course would be, therefore, to allow the French, Italian, and Japanese Ambassadors in Washington and in London to know that preliminary conferences not touching their interests are in progress between ourselves and Great Britain, and that as soon as sufficient progress has been made to warrant taking up the matter with them, it will be done.

With reference to the foregoing there will not, of course, be any objection to having Gibson give the same assurances to his colleagues from the other interested Powers in Brussels.

Since the above was dictated your Nos. 186 and 187 have been received. You may make communication to the Japanese Ambassador which you suggest in second paragraph of your No. 187. The other questions presented in these cables will be answered as soon as possible.

STIMSON

500.A15a3/61 : Telegram

*The Secretary of State to the Ambassador in Great Britain (Dawes)*

[Paraphrase]

WASHINGTON, July 12, 1929—6 p. m.

177. (1) With reference to your telegram No. 186 of July 11, 1929, the President and myself heartily concur in your views regarding the importance of Mr. MacDonald's presence at the final naval conference and the manner in which you handled the matter in your interview with him is fully approved by us. The President and I consider it of prime importance that Mr. MacDonald should head the British delegation to such a conference and are of the opinion that his doing so would contribute greatly to accomplishing the end so much desired by all of us. The Prime Minister's proposed answer to the interpellation is fully approved by the President and myself.

(2) We can cooperate with the Prime Minister's suggestion that there be a slow-down in construction. The United States has completed, or ready for early launching, eight of the new type of approximately ten thousand ton cruisers; there are two more under contract in private shipyards; in Government yards in the United States there are three undertaken for construction and Congress has authorized ten more. Fourteen cruisers of about the same type have been completed and apparently ten more are under construction or have been authorized by the British Government. The United States can reciprocate upon Mr. MacDonald's announcement by a statement that we have slowed down our preparations for laying the keels of the three cruisers which have been undertaken by the Government yards in the United States. The statement as to what we propose to do must, of course, come from the United States and can be made in response to the Prime Minister's statement in Great Britain.

STIMSON

———————

500.A15a3/66 : Telegram

*The Ambassador in Great Britain (Dawes) to the Secretary of State*

[Paraphrase]

LONDON, July 15, 1929—1 p. m.
[Received July 15—9 : 05 a. m.]

190. I received your telegrams Nos. 176 and 177, July 12, Saturday. I communicated their contents to Mr. MacDonald while on a visit to Chequers yesterday afternoon. The Prime Minister was greatly pleased and told me that in order to properly express his appreciation of your action in the premises that he wished to prepare a letter. This answer should be received by us very shortly. Mr. MacDonald said

that your response to the decision reached by him of postponing work on new cruisers was a great contribution to the progress of the common cause for which we were striving.

DAWES

---

500.A15a3/70 : Telegram

*The Ambassador in Great Britain* (*Dawes*) *to the Secretary of State*

LONDON, July 18, 1929—5 p. m.
[Received July 18—2 : 52 p. m.]

197. Received from the Prime Minister this afternoon a letter as follows:

"I must express to you my very great appreciation of the spirit and the contents of the communications you have on behalf of your Government made to me within the last day or two. The desire which your President has shown to understand us and to make possible a clearance of the points of difference that have hitherto prevented an agreement between us has been a heartening proof that we have begun conversations which will not only end happily for us but be a lead to the whole world.

The position of our conversations up to now seems to me to be as follows:

1. We both agree that the Washington arrangements regarding first class battleships and aircraft carriers will not be disturbed.

2. We agree that there will be a parity between us as regards cruisers. Hitherto there have been difficulties between our experts on this subject arising out of the distribution of tonnage between large and small craft. We have agreed however that the somewhat differing situations of our two countries will be resolved by the construction of a yardstick and I am waiting for your proposals regarding this. Pending this you and I on behalf of our Governments have agreed that we shall not allow technical points to override the great public issues involved in our being able to come to an agreement.

In this connection I should like to amend some figures which appear in the note which Mr. Atherton sent to Sir Robert Vansittart [20] on the 15th instant. He says: 'Fourteen approximately the same type of cruisers (as the United States are laying down) have been completed by the British who have apparently in construction or otherwise ten more.' These figures have been taken apparently from an out-of-date white paper. Since then alterations have been made and the position today is: number built and building, fifteen; number projected, three—these three include the two I have slowed down. I give you these figures because I am sure that they will be regarded by you and your Government as having a bearing upon our work. As I said to you in one of the interviews I had with you last week I have slowed up the preparations for laying down the two cruisers included in the 1928 program and have done so not merely for the purpose of lengthening out the time for the completion of that program but in the hope that it is the first step towards a reduction.

3. We agree to parity in destroyers and in submarines, parity in

---

[20] Private Secretary to the Prime Minister.

this case being equal gross tonnage in each of the two categories. I ought to tell you however that as soon as the Five-Power Conference meets I shall raise again the use of submarines and state my desire that they may be eliminated altogether. I know that I am in a somewhat weak debating position as regards this because the submarine is exactly the arm that can do Great Britain the most damage in the event of a naval war against us breaking out. My motive is however not that at all. I base myself on the fact that though all war is brutal and ruthless the way in which the submarine is used raises that brutality and ruthlessness to a very much greater height than has hitherto been known.

That being the position we now only need the yardstick to make our agreement complete and I still press the wisdom of striking whilst the iron is not hot and the public are expectant. I am hoping to see the French and Italian Ambassadors this week and to speak to them of what is being done within the limits of my assuring talk with the Japanese Ambassador. I had also better refer to the Five-Power Preliminary Conference which with your concurrence is to be held here and for which you and I shall agree as to the terms of the invitation. They will need at least a fortnight's notice and I am getting rather encumbered with international conferences.

First of all there is the Reparations Conference [21] which raises some very important issues for us and which is likely to require my presence if an agreement is to be reached.

Then there is the Assembly of the League at Geneva which I have promised to attend during the opening week at the beginning of [session].

Finally I must consider my visit to America which Mr. Stimson's recent message allows me to discuss with you. The House of Commons will meet at the end of October and my presence will be required here then.

We can do little now without the yardstick which I hope is being hurried, but if you would be so good as to come to see me we might discuss the next step of inviting the other naval powers to the conference and also my visit to Washington."

DAWES

---

500.A15a3/70 : Telegram

*The Secretary of State to the Ambassador in Great Britain (Dawes)*

[Paraphrase]

WASHINGTON, July 21, 1929—7 p. m.

182. Our comments to be conveyed by you to MacDonald on his position are as follows:

With reference to his first point. There is agreement between the Prime Minister and ourselves on this point and we believe that it is

---

[21] An international conference held at The Hague, August 6–31, 1929, between representatives of the German Government on the one hand and those of the several creditor powers on the other, for the purpose of liquidating questions still outstanding from the World War. A representative of the Government of the United States was present "in the capacity of Observer and with specifically limited powers." A second and final session of the conference was held at The Hague, January 3–14, 1930.

unnecessary to explore this question any further at the present time. We shall urge, however, that there shall be a postponement until 1936 of capital ship replacements.

As regards his third point. On the assumption that parity in other classes is reached, we accept parity in destroyers. As the Prime Minister states, such parity should consist of equal gross tonnage and it is our suggestion that this be achieved by the scrapping of destroyer tonnage on the part of the United States until it is equal to the present tonnage of the British. This determination may encounter public opposition in this country, inasmuch as the United States now has a clear preponderance over Great Britain in the destroyer class such as it does not have in any other. However, when fleet parity is actually in sight, this is a real contribution toward armament reduction which this Government is able and prepared to make.

We also agree with MacDonald as to parity in submarines, to consist of equal gross tonnage and to be arrived at by the scrapping of present submarine tonnage on the part of the United States until it has become equal to existing submarine tonnage of Great Britain. As to the Prime Minister's desire to abolish the use of submarines and the reasons he gives for this wish, we are in agreement. This position of the two countries as to submarines may be influenced by the attitude of other nations. The drastic steps, as to submarines and destroyers, suggested by this Government are predicated on drastic action with regard to cruisers by the British. It may be found easier to arrange to achieve equality as to destroyers, submarines, and cruisers by scrapping before 1936 rather than by scrapping immediately.

As to MacDonald's second point concerning cruisers. The nub of our difficulties lies here and we realize the real difficulty of solving this problem. It was on account of wide differences of views that the Geneva Conference failed. Both countries are now attempting to make a new beginning on the basis of the principle of cruiser parity. While this involves a real change of purpose, the fundamental practical question to be settled is at what time and at what tonnage is parity to be determined. In settling that question, it is most important that our actual tonnage situation is mutually understood. In this connection we are in some doubt whether we are fully aware of Great Britain's position and whether MacDonald has given consideration to our relative strengths and understands our own status.

The following is our general understanding of British cruiser strength:

Of larger cruisers, the British have in service fourteen, namely, *London, Devonshire, Sussex, Berwick, Suffolk, Cumberland, Cornwall, Australia, Canberra, Kent, Effingham, Vindictive, Frobisher, Hawkins;* they have in construction seven additional large cruisers, namely, *Surrey, Exeter, York, Shropshire, Northumberland, Nor-*

*folk, Dorsetshire;* finally they have three more not yet in construction but authorized. This brings the total of large cruisers to twenty-four of an aggregate tonnage of about 231,800. Is it to be our understanding that Great Britain is in a position to stop the building of eight of the ships included in the above figures and thereby to reduce to about 160,000 tons the total large cruiser tonnage?

From our tables we also gather that the British have, in addition to the above, smaller cruisers of differing ages, numbering thirty-eight and aggregating 171,000 tons. All of these are in service and none of them building. If our assumptions as described above are correct, the total cruiser tonnage of Great Britain thus amounts to approximately 402,800 tons, in service, in construction, and authorized. The age of all of this tonnage is well below twenty years. Great Britain, if we have correctly read MacDonald's letter, might limit her total cruiser tonnage to about 331,000.

Our own cruiser force consists of ten large cruisers now building and thirteen more authorized, thus making a total tonnage of 230,000. We have, in addition, ten smaller units of an aggregate tonnage of 70,500 thus raising our total cruiser tonnage to 300,000 or thereabouts. It is our intention, as a part of our arms reduction program to scrap in the near future all of our remaining cruisers consisting of twenty-two vessels all of which are more than twenty years old and aggregate more than 150,000 tons. We are anxious in addition to effect a reduction of our authorized program to such a degree as would produce equality with Great Britain; how far this can go, however, is dependent on how far the British Government itself is willing to go in limiting its own cruiser class. It is impossible to develop a yardstick which would bridge the difference between 300,000 tons and a tonnage of 402,888. Still less would it be possible to bridge a greater difference which might result from a scaling down of our program as now authorized. As soon as we have an agreement with the British, however, fixing a limit within which they are ready to maintain their cruiser strength, and to establish equality, it will be possible effectively to use the yardstick for the purpose of evaluating the two cruiser fleets whereby the apparent difference in the tonnages will be lessened.

The next steps, as we see it, are first of all to make sure that MacDonald and we agree as to what is the actual status of the cruiser tonnages of the two fleets. In the second place we would like to have a clear statement from MacDonald as to the limit within which he intends that British cruiser strength should be checked and maintained. What further steps will be necessary in order to achieve parity will then become apparent to us. From our contacts with opinion in this country and our examination of the naval figures, we have become more and more convinced that the two Governments must decide at what point cruiser strength is to be checked before we enter any general conference; this point is in the first place a question of the needs of the British inasmuch as they have a preponderance in the cruiser class. We agree that a consultation for the purpose of formulating questions to the naval experts may be called when we have agreed with MacDonald on that fundamental issue.

We feel strongly, however, that the problem of the point at which parity is to be established should not be left in such shape that it may become a matter of naval views. It is believed that we understand MacDonald's viewpoint on everything except this difficult problem of fixing the limit for the establishment of cruiser parity. When this has been approximately fixed, we are ready to leave it to the conference to thrash out the problem of how to determine the relative value, for comparative purposes, of individual ships of the various fleets and it is our opinion that in such conference it will be possible to develop a common measurement or yardstick, as applied to tonnage, of the factors of age and guns. For these reasons we wish to have an answer from the Prime Minister before going into a discussion of the specific items of the agenda outlined in your telegram No. 197 of July 18.

It is necessary that MacDonald be convinced that our sole purpose in suggesting that the speed both of us desire will best be gained by being sure of our ground is because of our desire for ultimate success. In particular, we do not wish MacDonald to feel that this insistence on our part is a freshly emphasized hindrance to swift progress and we want to be sure that he himself, with complete knowledge of the figures, arrives at a conclusion as to how far he is prepared to change the British proposals at the three power conference by a policy of cruiser equality at a feasible level which we can adopt as a basis for a conference with like certainty as to the figures.

We would like to have MacDonald's opinion as to the suggestion contained in our telegram No. 174 with regard to the yardstick. This proposal to consider only the application of certain factors was made by us for the purpose of simplifying the yardstick. Should our suggestion prove to be acceptable, the setting up of a yardstick will have been resolved into two problems; first, to make proper allowance for age and second, to make proper allowance for lesser armament as applied to tonnage of cruisers. It will be necessary for us to seek agreement between our respective naval experts on these two questions.

STIMSON

500.A15a3/75 : Telegram

*The Ambassador in Great Britain (Dawes) to the Secretary of State*

LONDON, July 22, 1929—6 p. m.
[Received 9:19 p. m.]

201. Having received word that the Prime Minister desired to see me, I called on him this afternoon taking with me sections one and two of your 182, July 21, 7 p. m.,[22] the third section not having been received then or at this time. I read to the Prime Minister the first two sections of your No. 182. He then read and discussed an address he must make in Parliament Wednesday afternoon at 5 o'clock in reply to an interpellation. Insofar as this speech affects us and relates to our position he will say the following which he gave me in writing:

"I am now in a position to make a statement of the immediate intentions of the Government regarding the naval building program. The Government's general position is that the defense of a country must be devised with two main considerations in view: first the chances of the defenses having to be used; then the efficiency and economy shown in their magnitude and character. The Government has kept in view the revolutionary changes in policy and in the problem of national security effected [*affected?*] by the Peace Pact if that pact is to be made an effective influence in international relations. To make it so is the controlling purpose of the Government and a systematic policy is being developed which will take a little time to complete to carry out that intention. In coming to decisions upon these matters no government ought to allow itself to be rushed, but at the same time it must not permit public money to be wasted by delay in applying obvious conclusions which if applied will result in economy.

As is well known, in the midst of the multifarious concerns which the formation of a new government entails and the specially pressing and complicated nature of our tasks, conversations have been actively carried on between the United States and ourselves for the purpose of opening the way for an agreement on naval matters which hitherto have defied a settlement. By a happy coincidence our assumption of office corresponded in time with the arrival in this country of the new American Ambassador, General Dawes, who has come here charged by the President of the United States of America with a mission for preparing the ground for an international agreement on the reduction and limitation of naval armaments. Already the whole field of these differences with the United States has been surveyed and the two Governments have made a fresh start on their solution. We have agreed upon the principle of parity; we have agreed that without in any way departing from the conditions of parity a measure of elasticity can be allowed so as to meet the peace requirements of two nations. We have determined that we shall not allow technical points to override the great public issues involved

---

[22] The text of telegram No. 182 does not have indicated the sections into which it was separated for cable transmission.

in our being able to come to a settlement. A visit by me to the President of the United States is now the subject of conversation so that it may take place when it will be most helpful to promote the cordial relations of our two countries and in particular advance the ends of disarmament and peace which we hold in common.

We have set up a committee to coordinate the three services for the purposes of Cabinet consideration but as that coordination is not comprehensive enough to meet the requirements of state policy the Foreign Office is also represented upon it. This will enable us to systematize our work. In the opinion of this committee, matters have progressed so favorably and the general outlook is such as to justify us in reviewing our own program. Our predecessors did this from time to time as the outlook brightened. Therefore not only as a proof of our own sincerity but as a duty imposed upon us to guard the expenditure of national money we have decided as follows:

> To suspend all work on the cruisers *Surrey* and *Northumberland*.
> To cancel the submarine depot ship *Maidstone*.
> To cancel two contract submarines.
> To slow down dockyard work [on] other naval construction.

As regards the 1929–30 program, in any event no commitments would have to be entered into before the autumn and no steps will be taken to proceed with it until the matter has received further consideration.

The Government of course recognizes that a substantial reduction in the naval building program must have a direct effect on employment in the dockyards but I am glad to say that as a result of special rearrangement suggested by the Admiralty it is hoped to secure the absorption of a large amount of labor which would otherwise be discharged from the royal dockyards. The representatives of dockyard labor will at once be consulted.

We are indebted to the Board of Admiralty for the help which they have rendered and I desire to state that, having expressed their technical view on the minimum armaments they consider to be necessary, they have furnished us with loyal help in achieving our object with the least possible dislocation and hardship.

I ought to add that it is recognized by all the powers concerned that a preliminary agreement on Anglo-American differences is essential to a general agreement on naval building and the governments of the powers represented at Washington 1921–22 have been kept informed of the conversations. So soon as the way is cleared they will be invited to a preliminary conference so that we may all together try to come to an agreement of a comprehensive kind and this will then be embodied in something of the nature of a treaty at a place which I hope will by common consent be chosen by the United States as a recognition of the splendid part played by its President in these transactions.

If these intentions are fulfilled the request of the chairman of the Preparatory Commission on Disarmament [made at Geneva on March 15, 1928,] that the naval powers should make an attempt to agree among themselves will be accomplished and we shall be in a position to pursue with that Commission the difficult but essential problems of how to reduce other forms of armaments in accordance with the pledge given by the Allies at Versailles when imposing disarmament on Germany and its associated nations and in pursuance of the Pact of Peace. To that His Majesty's Government will direct its thoughts and its energies in cooperation with other nations so soon as this more immediate work on naval agreement has been finished. A general disarmament conference will then be possible and a clearly marked achievement in the pursuit of national security through peace will have been recorded."

The Prime Minister desires to change what he expects to say as above in accordance with any suggestions you may make. Of course what he says was written without knowledge of what may be contained in the third section of your telegram which has not been received. If this is received tonight I will communicate to him such portions as you indicate in it are to be shown him and will wire any changes which the Prime Minister may make because of it. The Prime Minister expects that after the delivery of this speech he will be asked from the floor as to whether there was any agreement for a response from the United States Government in return for stopping work upon the English cruisers. To this he will reply in effect that he made the decision and will abide by the consequences. In this connection however he would greatly appreciate it if the United States made the response which you have already outlined in time to have it available before Parliament rises Friday afternoon. If you decide that any portion of the Prime Minister's address, as given above, should be changed it is urgent that word as to the change reach here tomorrow Tuesday evening.

DAWES

---

500.A15a3/75 : Telegram

*The Secretary of State to the Ambassador in Great Britain (Dawes)*

[Paraphrase]

WASHINGTON, July 23, 1929—7 p. m.

186. With reference to your No. 201, July 22, 6 p. m. MacDonald's statement appears to us wise and exactly right in feeling and tone. We feel that its generous attitude for us is admirably adapted to gain the American public's approbation. Two cautionary suggestions, however, for his consideration and for his decision may be submitted:

First. The position as we see it and as we explained in our telegram No. 182, July 21, is that if parity in cruisers is to be arrived at without necessitating the completion of the whole cruiser program of the United States, Great Britain must not only check her present program of construction but must also decide practically to give up until 1936 all further building of cruisers. MacDonald will know best in what manner to prepare the British public for such a decision; however, unless the Prime Minister is able to reach such a determination as far as he himself is concerned and unless British policy is to follow these lines, we are afraid that all the significant progress thus far achieved may be of very little avail.

Second. In our view it is difficult to see how MacDonald could visit this country before October considering his various engagements explained in his letters, if he is to have any time for consultation in this country and to receive the welcome which our people will want to give him and without which the complete purpose of his visit would not be realized. It is our earnest desire that the visit take place but a public promise of such a visit on his part would simply result in the newspapers making life a burden for him until he actually carries out the visit. Would it not be possible until the dates are fixed for him to make the matter a little more vague or, on the other hand, for him definitely to fix the month of his visit?

On receipt of the news of the Prime Minister's statement to Parliament, the President will issue a statement approving what MacDonald has said and giving voice to our pleasure at the progress made and the new departure begun. He will also state that our future naval plans will await consultation and that, specifically, there will be a slowing down in the preparations for laying the keels of the three new cruisers which, according to our program, are to be built at the navy yards.

STIMSON

500.A15a3/76 : Telegram

*The Ambassador in Great Britain (Dawes) to the Secretary of State*

LONDON, July 23, 1929—1 p. m.
[Received 1:30 p. m.]

202. Upon receipt of the third section of your 182, July 21, 7 p. m., this morning I took the same over and read it to the Prime Minister. The first two sections I had read to him yesterday afternoon as I cabled you last night.

He fully recognizes the constructive importance of the suggestions contained in the third section and that the method of procedure proposed is especially valuable as isolating and defining the problem of technical differences, thus putting it in its proper relation to the other important questions upon which we seem in substantial agreement. As I explained through Mr. Myron Taylor, the Price Minister has full confidence in the sincerity, high purpose, wisdom and competence of our President in this naval matter and a disposition to trust the men whom he trusts in connection with it. Early this morning, and of course before knowing the contents of the third section of your 182, he had written me a note which was still at 10 Downing Street when I arrived and its terms were then discussed by us after the reading of the third section of your telegram. MacDonald is about to consult his Admiralty in connection with the statement of the British cruiser situation contained in the first two sections of your 182. As I told you through Mr. Myron Taylor, he apparently lacks an adviser with the particular qualities that Gibson has in his relations to us. His First Lord of the Admiralty, Mr. Alexander, has the qualities of loyalty and trustworthiness of Gibson but not his technical competency. MacDonald of course wants to be sure that his Admiralty figures are correct, especially since his impression of what they are will be much altered if the statements as to British cruiser strength contained in your telegram are correct.

The note which he handed me is as follows:

"I have been thinking over the despatch you showed me yesterday and though I have not yet had it (I am writing this early in the morning when only the birds are up and they even are sleepy) to study, it is clear that it raises a problem which we have assumed was smaller than it appears to be. We have been waiting for the 'yardstick', but the despatch of yesterday says that the gap between us is too wide for a yardstick to span. So we must examine it and I must get advice and guidance.

I propose, if it meets your convenience, to stay in town till we settle something. This week finds me full of concerns till the House rises. Would it be possible for us to meet on Monday morning to go into whole matter of this tonnage of cruisers and go at it till we agree on how we stand. If Mr. Gibson could be with us, I would bring Mr. Alexander, the First Lord (Civil), and a day or two ought to see the end of our preliminary conversations. Then, I shall go on a holiday!"

Upon inquiry as to whether I thought in view of the third section of your telegram he should modify the suggestions of his letter, I stated that I thought it would be valuable to you to have this letter showing the run of his mind before reading the third section.

From the discussion of the matter with MacDonald after knowledge of the contents of the third section of your cable it is evident that the Prime Minister will welcome an interpretation of the representations of his Admiralty to him, as to what point the British cruiser strength is to be checked, from Gibson whom he designates because of his technical knowledge as an "honest broker". In other words MacDonald welcomes our help and suggestions in the responsibility which he must assume in fixing cruiser strength which, as you say, because of British preponderance in the cruiser class is primarily a question of British needs. I think therefore that the suggestion in his letter as to a conference between him, Alexander, Gibson and myself, on Monday is valuable but before agreeing to it would like your approval and comment. Since the conversations at such a conference, if you approve of it, would of course all be submitted to you and no decisions taken without your approval, it would at least result in some additions to our knowledge of the British position and the elements which would necessarily enter into the determination of their final attitude.

DAWES

---

500.A15a3/76 : Telegram

*The Secretary of State to the Ambassador in Great Britain (Dawes)*

[Paraphrase]

WASHINGTON, July 23, 1929—8 p. m.

187. Reference your No. 202, July 23, 1 p. m. In my opinion it will be most desirable for you to carry out MacDonald's proposal for a discussion with Alexander and Gibson next Monday for the purpose of arriving at an analysis of the problem which would permit MacDonald to clearly understand the need for a practical cessation until 1936 of all further cruiser construction on the part of the British in order that parity might be obtained by the United States. It is assumed by the Department that Gibson has been kept currently informed by you and that the repetition of this cable to Brussels will be sufficient authority for Gibson to proceed to London for this conference.

STIMSON

---

500.A15a3/78a : Telegram

*The Secretary of State to the Ambassador in Great Britain (Dawes)*

[Paraphrase]

WASHINGTON, July 24, 1929—5 p. m.

189. President and I are most anxious to have a check-up on accuracy of our figures regarding British cruiser strength as contained in Department's telegram No. 182, July 21, 7 p. m., before you confer with Gibson and MacDonald on Monday. We find it difficult to make any suggestions or plans until this matter has been cleared up.

STIMSON

---

500.A15a3/79a : Telegram

*The Secretary of State to the Ambassador in Great Britain (Dawes)*

WASHINGTON, July 24, 1929—8 p. m.

190. The President made the following statement this afternoon after reading the Prime Minister's statement.[23] The President said:

"I have read with real satisfaction the statement which the Prime Minister has made in the House of Commons. The American people

---

[23] See telegram No. 201, July 22, 6 p. m., from the Ambassador in Great Britain, p. 153.

are greatly complimented by his proposed visit and he will find a universal welcome.

Mr. MacDonald's statement marks a new departure in discussion of naval disarmament. The Prime Minister introduces the principle of parity which we have now adopted and its consummation means that Great Britain and the United States henceforth are not to compete in armament as potential opponents but to cooperate as friends in the reduction of it. The Prime Minister has stated clearly and unmistakably the principles on which he is acting. I cannot but be responsive to the generous terms in which he has spoken of the attitude and purpose of the United States. We join in his efforts in the same spirit.

Mr. MacDonald has indicated the good will and positive intention of the British Government by suspension of construction of certain portions of this year's British Naval program. It is the desire of the United States to show equal good will in our approach to the problem.

We have three cruisers in this year's construction program which have been undertaken in the Government Navy Yards, the detailed drawings for which are now in course of preparation. The actual keels would, in the ordinary course, be laid down some time this fall. Generally speaking, the British cruiser strength considerably exceeds American strength at the present time and the actual construction of these three cruisers would not be likely in themselves to produce inequality in the final result.

We do not wish, however, to have any misunderstanding of our actions and therefore we shall not lay these keels until there has been an opportunity for full consideration of their effect upon the final agreement for parity which we expect to reach, although our hopes of relief from construction lie more largely in the latter years of the program under the law of 1928." [24]

STIMSON

---

500.A15a3/79 : Telegram

*The Ambassador in Great Britain (Dawes) to the Secretary of State*

LONDON, July 25, 1929—1 p. m.
[Received 2 : 35 p. m.]

204. The statement of the Prime Minister in the House of Commons yesterday had a fine reception and the few questions which it evoked were well handled by him. Immediately after he was through with his statement on the floor, at his request, I met the Prime Minister and at that time he again expressed the hope that the President's statement would appear before Friday. The fact that this fine statement of the President appears in the morning London papers, together with the statement of the Prime Minister of yesterday, is unquestionably a great satisfaction to him, although I have not seen him as yet today.

---

[24] 45 Stat. 624, "An Act Making appropriations for the Navy Department and the naval service for the fiscal year ending June 30, 1929, and for other purposes."

This morning had long and satisfactory interview with Matsu-daira whom I am keeping informed. His mind runs parallel to ours, except for the Prime Minister's proposition to abolish entirely sub-marines to which he will dissent. He hopes in the eventual agree-ment to have a slight increase for Japan in the 5–5–3 ratio, this to apply only to ships other than capital ships.

Answering your No. 189, July 24, 5 p. m., I give below the letter received from the Prime Minister this morning:

"My dear General: I was hoping that we might have been able to proceed with a yardstick examination and test in accordance with the lines of our conversations, but the despatch you handed to me yesterday raises the whole question of tonnage in its old absolute form. A failure to escape from this led to a breakdown of the Naval Conference at Geneva. Your Government is of opinion that the differences in cruiser tonnage held or contemplated by the United States and Great Britain are so great as to defy the successful operation of the yardstick plan straight away. It gives figures to prove this and concludes that we must as a preliminary to further progress agree 'at what spot Great Britain is willing to check its cruiser strength and establish parity.' When that is done 'the yard-stick can be effectively used to make fair an evaluation of the two cruiser fleets and the apparent difference in the tonnages will be lessened.' In order to save time I was hoping that we might have cleared this up at the same time as we were considering the effect of the yardstick which you were to propose, but I see that the figures of absolute tonnage upon which your people have been working do appear to be a formidable obstacle and I am anxious to remove these and any other difficulties which lie in our way.

In a previous note I warned you not to work upon an old white paper outlining our building program of two or three years ago because the plan there laid down has not been carried out by my predecessors. In the course of conversation over the despatch which deals with the ingredients of the 'yardstick,' I also referred to the variety of ship included in cruiser category and I shall now state what information I have gathered since I saw you yesterday and the day before.

Large cruisers: We have 22, not 24, built and projected, the total tonnage being 216,200 not 231,000. From the original program upon which Washington seems working, our predecessors dropped 3 eight-inch cruisers and that has been announced for a long time and we ourselves are holding up laying the keels of other three—two in the 1928 and one in that of 1929.

The relative values of classes in the cruiser categories raise details which can best be discussed and settled over a table with authorized representatives dealing with the points there and then. But in this note I point out by way of illustration that the *Hawkins* group laid down for war purposes in 1916 cannot either in their present condition as ships or in their armament of seven 7.5-inch guns, hand-worked and throwing a projectile of 200 pounds instead of 250 pounds, really be valued on displacement tonnage alone. We regard them as being nearer to the modern six-inch cruiser than to its eight-inch companion.

This is preeminently a case for the yardstick. The despatch I am now considering includes their total tonnage of about 40,000 in the large cruiser tonnage.

Smaller cruisers: Of these we have 40 classed as six-inch with a tonnage of 179,270. But here again we really need a yardstick because the tonnage value requires to be adjusted. I am told for instance that your *Omaha* class, of which you have 10 carries 120 six-inch guns and are of a total tonnage of 70,500. They cannot be compared to our 'C' class of which we have 24 carrying 109 six-inch guns and of a tonnage of 100,250. Here again is a case for an examination round a table not of service experts in command but of statesmen working upon material supplied by service experts.

To sum up I give you a table as I have received it in reply to inquiries I have made since I have had your despatch.

Eight-inch cruisers: British 15 ships, 146,800 tons; 3 projected, 30,000; total 176,800. United States 13 building, 130,000; 10 projected, 100,000; total 230,000.

7.5-inch cruisers: Great Britain, *Hawkins* class 4, 29,400. United States none.

Six-inch cruisers: Great Britain 40, 179,270. United States 10, 70,500.

That is a somewhat complicated tangle to unravel but I am sure we can do it if we go about it in the right way and keep political and not service hands in control. When I say this, I must add that I have found my service advisers most anxious to come to an agreement. Still we must remain in control.

My view is that it will not be helpful for either of us to begin by stating absolute limits but rather to examine the present condition, working out parity within it, total the results and see what happens, examine the total and if it be satisfactory take it as the absolute limit, if it be unsatisfactory return to an examination of why it is so and continue this till we are satisfied. For I will not assume that there is any doubt about our agreeing. I have had some experience with these negotiations and all urge me to come to close grips with details and from an examination of details to come to comprehensive conclusions. We begin by assuming that our countries each has an absolute minimum enforced upon it by the present state of the world and that the settlement of details must conform to that general requirement. If the settlement of details when summed up get beyond it we must reduce the categories; if it gets us under it we must expand them. As we are both determined to agree I feel pretty strongly that that is both the surest and the quickest way to set to work.

Yours very sincerely, J. Ramsay MacDonald.

Postcript:

Since I wrote this note we have agreed to have a meeting on Monday with Mr. Gibson present, so part of it is out of date. So fast does the world move in these days! I send the note however for its figures particularly."

I have wired Gibson to meet me here Sunday.

DAWES

500.A15a3/79 : Telegram

## *The Secretary of State to the Ambassador in Great Britain (Dawes)*

WASHINGTON, July 26, 1929—4 p. m.

192. Your 204, July 25, 1 p. m. In view of the meeting of Mr. Gibson and yourself with Mr. MacDonald on Monday, it seems to us desirable to review the position of negotiations to date and explain for the guidance of yourself and Mr. Gibson our views as to the several matters.

*First point*—We may summarize accomplishments in agreement with the British up to the present moment as:

1. We have agreed that the conference shall be inaugurated as a consequence of the Kellogg Pact.

2. We have agreed on parity in combatant strength.

3. We have agreed that this parity should be separately by categories of capital ships, aircraft carriers, destroyers, cruisers and submarines.

4. We have agreed not to disturb the provisions of the Washington Treaty, thereby fixing ratios of capital ships and aircraft carriers but see paragraph (*a*) *infra* under second point.

5. We have agreed that a yardstick shall be adopted by which comparative value of the ships within the categories shall be measured.

6. The American Government agrees, subject to reaching an agreement on other questions, to scrap excess destroyers and excess submarines down to the British level either at present or by 1936.

7. We agree with Mr. MacDonald as to the principle of total abolition of submarines in international war. We realize with him that it may be impossible to secure consent of other nations, but we should make a mutual effort in this direction.

*Second point*—There are left the following points which we would like to have settled in principle as necessary to assure the success of a conference.

(*a*) We should like an agreement that all replacements of capital ships under the Washington Treaty shall be postponed until after 1936. This will give a holiday from major naval construction (capital ships and aircraft carriers) until after that date, and as at that time under that Treaty it will be necessary to revise the programs, that would be an appropriate date at which again to seek a further general revision of naval strength downward.

(*b*) Entirely in accord with the suggestion that we must have a yardstick, we consider it essential that we should agree upon certain principles upon which the yardstick shall be based before we can present a definitive series of figures. It is our suggestion that in the cruiser category, for instance, we should take the new 10,000 ton,

8-inch gun cruiser as representing the standard, and that we should in measuring the relative combatant strength of other ships in the cruiser category, consider the elements of the yardstick at

> Displacement.
> Age.
> Guns.

Our general view is that protection, speed, habitability, et cetera, are entirely relative to the other factors, and do not require special consideration. No doubt these factors may deserve different weight for other categories.

(c) We suggest that for cruisers we should adopt 20 years of age as the scrappable age, for destroyers 16 years, and for submarines, 13 years.

(d) It is our impression that we should seek to equate our cruiser, destroyer and submarine tonnage as at 1936 instead of today, as this will better accommodate the British situation.

(e) If the principles of paragraphs (b), (c), and (d) can be adopted, we have resolved technical questions purely into the question as to the discounts from the standard that are to be allowed for age and gun calibre. We realize that technical difficulties will arise over the determination of these two factors, in which there will need to be a spirit of compromise, but we think that the whole problem will be infinitely simplified if we can agree upon the principles which we are to submit to the naval experts.

(f) We are, of course, anxious to arrive at a situation which will allow us to reduce our authorized cruiser program, which would imply arriving at a theoretical tonnage in 1936 of somewhere from 200 to 250 thousand tons. We have made some rough calculations as to our own and the British fleets, taking into account age and gun calibre and taking into account the number of ships that would be scrapped by 1936 under the 20 year age limit, and taking into account the cessation of construction of the three new eight-inch cruisers and the two projected six-inch cruisers of the British Navy, and we believe that we could work it out quantitatively at about these limits.

(g) Our view is that if we can agree to these principles a preliminary conference should be had in London, representative of the Five Powers, seeking their adherence to such of these principles as concern them.

(h) Under the Washington Arms Treaty we are compelled to hold a conference of the five naval powers by 1931. We could by mutual consent merge these conferences into the one proposed for next December and avoid the necessity of holding two conferences on much the same subjects.

(*i*) A formal conference should be called in December, following Mr. MacDonald's visit. The result of that visit undoubtedly will be to further the building of good will and to pave the way for mutual understanding.

STIMSON

---

500.A15a3/86 : Telegram

*The Ambassadors in Great Britain and Belgium (Dawes and Gibson) to the Secretary of State*

[Paraphrase]

LONDON, July 29, 1929—5 p. m.
[Received 5 : 55 p. m.[25]]

209. Your clear telegram proved of great advantage as a basis for the conference which proceeded with expedition this afternoon along the following lines:

In an informal memorandum we laid before the Prime Minister and the First Lord of the Admiralty the views contained in your telegram No. 192 of July 26.

On the headings 1 to 7 in Point 1, the Prime Minister and the First Lord of the Admiralty expressed entire and unhesitating agreement. Both of them also agreed to headings (*a*), (*b*), (*c*), (*d*), and (*e*), of Point 2, but they wished heading (*e*) to be revised to read thus: "If the principles of paragraph (*b*), (*c*), and (*d*) can be adopted we have resolved technical questions into the application of the yardstick to the category of cruisers." In the following sentence strike out the words "over the determination of these two factors". They agreed to point (*f*) revised to read as follows: "Both Governments are of course anxious to arrive at a situation which will allow them to reduce their authorized cruiser program. Study will be devoted to this subject." As we were in ignorance of the facts upon which it was based, the remainder of the paragraph was deleted in the memorandum as not essential. In regard to points (*g*), (*h*), and (*i*), full agreement was expressed.

Mr. MacDonald, with the full agreement of the First Lord of the Admiralty, then stated that he felt that a minimum of 45 six-inch-gun cruisers is essential, due to the need for numbers of small vessels on distant stations and for long lines of communication and this made it difficult to comply with the idea of not replacing small cruisers which would become obsolete by 1936 under the twenty year age limit.

The following memorandum embodying his views as to how parity

---

[25] Telegram in two sections.

might be achieved in the cruiser class was then written by Mr. Mac-Donald. He emphasized the fact that this was an entirely personal and tentative proposal which he would submit tonight to his Admiralty and upon which he would be glad to have your views:

"General agreement as to cruisers:

1. The British Government would be satisfied with a large cruiser strength of 15 and would agree to the American Government building up to 18.

2. The British Government would ask for an equivalent (to be measured by the yardstick) in six-inch cruisers so that their total in that class should be 45.

3. As regards the *Hawkins* (or *Effingham*) group of 4 cruisers, an agreement will be come to that for the purposes of classification they shall, during their lifetime, be counted amongst the six-inch class and then replaced by ordinary six-inch ships. Consideration will be given to having this equation completed by 1936.

4. In order to arrive at parity the United States may construct up to 10 six-inch-gun ships".

Mr. MacDonald made it clear that in the above memorandum it was his idea that the equivalent of the 45 six-inch-gun British cruisers would be constituted by 10 additional American six-inch-gun cruisers, to be constructed should we desire them, the 3 additional American 10,000 ton cruisers and our 10 *Omaha* type cruisers.

Also the Prime Minister kept in mind, it seems evident, the possible intentions of other naval powers in laying down this minimum need for 45 six-inch-gun cruisers. Mr. MacDonald stated that he would submit his proposals to the First Sea Lord tonight and that if any material modifications were suggested he would communicate them to me before his departure for Scotland on his vacation.

The best possible spirit on the part of the British was exhibited in the conduct of the conference. Save reserving the question of replacements of small cruisers, no objection was made by them to the suggestion of abandoning all future new cruiser construction. Our readiness to support the movement for the suppression of submarines and our readiness to defer replacements of capital ships until 1936, when they agreed that an excellent opportunity would be afforded to make renewed efforts for more definite reduction, met with particular gratification on their part.

We wish also to call attention to the fact that the suggestion of our having preponderance in 10,000-ton cruisers came spontaneously from them, as did the suggestion that we be authorized, should we so desire, to build 10 additional six-inch-gun cruisers.

That reduction in all classes of ships was one of the ideas uppermost in the President's mind, we did not fail to point out and for that reason we urged that they give consideration as to how far they could go in refraining from replacing, as they became obsolete, six-inch-gun cruisers.

DAWES and GIBSON

---

500.A15a3/92 : Telegram

*The Ambassador in Great Britain (Dawes) to the Secretary of State*

LONDON, July 30, 1929—4 p. m.<br>[Received July 30—12 : 47 p. m.]

211. This morning received the following letter from the Prime Minister which I forward with much satisfaction and which should be read in connection with my telegram No. 209, July 29, 5 p. m.:

"My dear General: I have been studying the agreement which we came to yesterday and decided to send to our Governments, and the more I think of it the more satisfactory it seems. There are two small points however which we overlooked. The first is in paragraph 5. It is provided that the yardstick shall be adopted to find out comparative values of ships within each cruiser category. Later on, paragraph (*e*), it is assumed that the yardstick will only be required for cruisers because we have already come to an agreement on tonnage as regards destroyers and submarines. The latter decision I am sure is the best for both of us because if we were to go to the Five-Power Conference and say to France and Italy 'You can get for destroyers and submarines tonnage which you can save from the other categories', we shall get into endless bother and will create a new menace which will be peculiarly embarrassing for me and will give the Admiralty here a strong case for an increase in our small cruisers. As I am out for reduction all along the line I should like to avoid this without doing any other nation a real injustice.

The second point is the paragraph relating to lengthening the lives of first class battleships. We would like to do this by some arrangement which would not mean that we should have to discharge the whole of our staff by a revolutionary stroke of the pen but would enable us to keep on a sort of nucleus. This means that we should have to spread the lengthening of the life over a series of years. It is only a matter of arrangement and not of principle or object. From a businessman's point of view you will appreciate this point.

I should also like to let you know that although I agreed yesterday to the figures of 15 and 45 as my program of cruiser building I am going now to work to find out whether I cannot reduce both these figures but certainly the second one if we can get an agreement with Japan, France and Italy. So if there is any objection from America that the total reduction involved in our agreement of yesterday is a little disappointing please let it remain where it is because I think if we can extend our agreement to other powers I can offer you a still better arrangement.

With kindest regards. Yours very sincerely, J. Ramsay Mac-Donald."

DAWES

500.A15a3/92 : Telegram

*The Secretary of State to the Ambassador in Great Britain (Dawes)*

[Paraphrase]

WASHINGTON, July 31, 1929—1 p. m.

195.   Reference is made to your telegrams No. 209 and No. 211, July 29 and July 30.   Insurmountable obstacles to agreement are apparently presented by the tentative program proposed by Mr. MacDonald for the following reasons:

(1) The principle of decrease in naval armament is totally abdicated.

(2) The principle of parity and equality between the navies of Great Britain and United States, the crux of which rests in the cruiser class, is abandoned.

We may reduce the proposal of the Prime Minister to the following statement of displacement tonnage, in order to make this clear:

British Empire: A total tonnage of 146,800 in 15 large 8-inch-gun cruisers (the *Surrey* and the *Northumberland* and an unnamed author-ized cruiser would apparently be scrapped); a total of 39,426 tons in 4 cruisers of the 7½-inch-gun *Hawkins* class; a total of about 190,-000 tons in 41 cruisers of the 6-inch-gun class, or a grand total of about 376,226 tons of cruisers.   This tonnage will be maintained by replace-ment of the various classes of ships.

United States of America: A total of 180,000 tons in 18 large cruisers, also a total of 70,500 tons of ten 6-inch-gun cruisers now in service, or a grand total of 250,500 tons which it is suggested that we increase by building ten more vessels of the 6-inch-gun type which would probably amount to 50,000 or 75,000 tons, but which our Navy Department does not deem acceptable and therefore cannot be included, as was fully explained at the Geneva Conference of 1927.

We would point out, in amplification of our statement in point (1) above that while the proposal implies scrapping the *Northumber-land* and the *Surrey* as well as an unnamed large authorized cruiser, it is proposed that Great Britain shall undertake new construction of smaller cruisers to be used as replacements by 1936 of at least 70,000 tons, assuming that the tonnage of the ships replaced remains that of the vessels at present in existence.   The construction of 10 out of our recently authorized 15 large ships in order to arrive at 18 large cruisers is implied, thus making new construction of 100,000 tons on the present authorized program for the United States, together with further construction of at least 125,000 tons more, in order to compensate us for the superiority of the British.

By 1936 the total new construction will thus amount to 295,000 tons between the two countries.   When you consider that about 70,000 tons of this is replacement, there will remain a net addition to the present naval strength of the world of something like 225,000 tons, aside from the cruisers amounting to about 125,000 tons which the United States and Great Britain now have on the stocks. We would not be bringing about the reduction of naval armament should we carry out this program and the originally agreed basis of our negotiations would be completely abandoned. Attention is called to a statement in Mr. MacDonald's letter to you of July 8 [26] in which he said "we should then proceed to declare that on that basis the object of negotiations must be reduction in existing armament."

Referring to point (2) above and in further amplification thereof, we would point out that while Mr. MacDonald's program would leave the British with 15 large ships of a total tonnage of 146,800 tons as against 18 large American ships of 180,000 tons and thus with a British inferiority of 33,200 tons in this 8-inch-type cruiser, it leaves the United States with an inferiority amounting to 39,426 tons of the *Hawkins* 7½-inch-type class which more than compensates for the American superiority of 33,200 tons in 8-inch-gun cruisers above referred to.

Far beyond this, however, it leaves the British with about 190,000 tons of 6-inch-gun cruisers against the present 70,500 tons of that class held by the United States, or an inferiority of 120,000 tons which they propose, as set forth above, the United States should only partly equate by the construction of ten new cruisers of the 6-inch type which we have no intention of constructing.

These proposals are practically no real modification of those made at the Geneva Conference and it does not seem to us that they offer any hope of agreement.

STIMSON

---

500.A15a3/92 : Telegram

*The Secretary of State to the Ambassador in Great Britain (Dawes)*

[Paraphrase]

WASHINGTON, July 31, 1929—3 p. m.

196. Reference is made to telegram No. 195, July 31, 1 p. m., to which this is supplementary.

It is very difficult to tell you how keenly disappointed we are over the proposal made by the Prime Minister. We prefer no agreement in preference to his proposal, as we now see the situation. It is our belief that he has been won over by the Admiralty who have returned to all the demands originally made by them. There is no evidence that we can see that he has any understanding of the figures thus far. The only ray of daylight which we see at this time is the statement contained in his letter which you quoted in your telegram No. 211,

---

[26] See telegram No. 179, July 9, 9 a. m., from the Ambassador in Great Britain, p. 140.

July 30, that he wishes to secure reduction all along the line. It is obvious that his proposals which you quoted in your telegram No. 209, July 29, call for increases in the cruiser categories both for the United States and Great Britain and not for reductions. It is suggested that you call to Mr. MacDonald's attention the fact that, in proposing 15 and 45 as the number of cruisers he desires, he is proposing, as against 52 cruisers which are in service today, a total of 60 cruisers. Lines of communication apparently have been ably maintained by the 52 cruisers in commission at this time. The nub of the difficulty seems to have been correctly stated in our telegram No. 186, July 23. You might call to Mr. MacDonald's attention that in that telegram we stated:

"The position as we see it and as we explained in our telegram No. 182, July 21, is that if parity in cruisers is to be arrived at without necessitating the completion of the whole cruiser program of the United States, Great Britain must not only check her present program of construction but must also decide practically to give up until 1936 all further building of cruisers. MacDonald will know best in what manner to prepare the British public for such a decision; however, unless the Prime Minister is able to reach such a determination as far as he himself is concerned and unless British policy is to follow these lines, we are afraid that all the significant progress thus far achieved may be of very little avail."

The United States, you may inform Mr. MacDonald, has found itself with rapidly increasing armament costs both for its Army and its Navy and this Administration has made the statement publicly that it has set itself the task to cut these costs. Should we accept the program suggested by the Prime Minister we should find that our actual Navy costs instead of falling were rising and should we reach an agreement based on the program suggested by him it would become the laughing stock of those who, in the spirit of the Kellogg Pact, seriously desire disarmament. For this reason and because it is so apparently unfair, the proposals made by the Prime Minister fall far below the legitimate expectation which we had concerning the question. Frankly, we do not believe that Mr. MacDonald realizes that, in adopting the theory advocated by his Admiralty that Great Britain must almost match us in large cruisers and needs in addition 45 units of small cruisers to protect its long lines of communication, he is departing from the fundamental conception that the naval needs of nations are relative, which is the whole basis of our efforts to reach an agreement. It seems to us that if Great Britain needs and must have such a large number of cruisers of small calibre, which are not desired by the United States, Great Britain must be willing that the United States should have a great preponderance in cruisers of ten-thousand-ton calibre. We consider that the preponderance suggested by Mr.

MacDonald in this type of cruiser is so small as to be of no importance whatever.

Should Great Britain cease building cruisers, any fair yardstick which measures the value of tonnage, as of say 1936, in the cruiser category and makes a fair allowance for age would rate the old units of the British fleet as of less value than the newly built units of the American fleet; but if Great Britain is to continue building, it is apparent that the yardstick will not have that effect because the two fleets resulting from this would be of substantially the same age and to ascertain parity we would be back to a displacement tonnage basis. The Prime Minister will recall, should our position seem to be harshly stated, that the reason for this is that we feel so keenly that he has not given due consideration to what would be the results of the proposals made by him. Matters to be called to the Prime Minister's attention end with this paragraph.

Is it conceivable, we have been wondering, that the Prime Minister, in order to try us out, has been presenting the old Admiralty programs? Let us know what you personally think regarding the truth or falseness of this.

STIMSON

---

500.A15a3/100 : Telegram

*The Ambassador in Great Britain (Dawes) to the Secretary of State*

[Paraphrase]

LONDON, August 1, 1929—4 p. m.
[Received August 1—2 : 05 p. m.]

215. Reference your No. 196, July 31, last paragraph. The Prime Minister may possibly be presenting the old program of the Admiralty for the purpose of trying us out; but I do not believe that this is the case. I think I owe it to the Prime Minister to state that in last Monday's conference, at which we arrived at the tentative figures contained in my telegram No. 209 of July 29, my own attitude and that of Gibson was such as to give him grounds for his belief that these propositions, in our view, were a contribution to progress, although at the same time we pressed the need for more reduction. I presented to MacDonald early this morning your forcible and direct telegram No. 196 without in any way softening it, and discussed it with him. This message should induce him to send me today that statement which we now need in order that the vital issues should be clarified.

I should like to present the following reflections which have suggested themselves to me:

It will be necessary for him to take a stand for such a real reduction as will provide an opportunity, well-founded or otherwise, for an attack on the part of the opposition, with the support of the Admiralty, to the effect that the safety of the Empire is being endangered; or he must take the position, which will have some public appeal, that he must now urge, as the position most consistent with Empire safety, naval parity combined with a certain amount of limitation of construction programs and a stopping of competition, without however any substantial present reduction save as regards building programs. His statesmanship will inevitably be tested by this situation and it may be possible that without any dangerous loss of his political prestige he could risk a showdown on a basis of this sort. It will not represent a refuge for any great length of time if he suggests a delay. Up to the present he has shown himself as a statesman who is ground between the millstones of his own Admiralty propositions and the American proposals. I should add that he is entirely frank and sincere with us and that he conceals neither the facts which he receives from his Admiralty nor the reactions which they produce in him.

Athough MacDonald is leaving for Lossiemouth tonight, he will come back to confer with me on your reply to the letter he is now preparing and which will be cabled to you as soon as it is received this afternoon. This conference will probably take place on Tuesday and Gibson, who is receiving all this correspondence, will of course attend.

DAWES

---

500.A15a3/101 : Telegram

*The Ambassador in Great Britain (Dawes) to the Secretary of State*

LONDON, August 1, 1929—5 p. m.
[Received 9 : 10 p. m.]

216. Following letter just received from the Prime Minister:

"My Dear General: I am very disappointed that the proposal which came out of the conversation on Monday between you and Mr. Gibson on the one hand and the First Lord and myself on the other is not acceptable to the President and that the explanation I gave in my note of the same date to you (that if we could get agreement with the other naval powers the cruisers figures might be still further reduced) does not modify his judgment. I have been studying the despatch you left with me this morning and it seems to me that it brings us for the moment back to an objective study of the actual facts of the position.

1. The President and I are striving to do two things. He wants parity in strength with Great Britain and to this I heartily agree; we both in addition wish to reduce naval armaments. The combination of both gives us a specially difficult practical problem.

2. In the British program of building there is not one ship included to be set against American strength. Were it so my task would be

easy because you and I can just agree not to continue to build against each other and off would go the cruisers on both sides. Parity and reduction would then go hand in hand. I am in the ridiculous position therefore of appearing to be grudging in my negotiations because my country had not been assuming that yours was a potential enemy.

3. I am sure that the President, in the exercise of that fine understanding mind of his, will see that when, as a practical person, I have to face the question of the standard upon which parity is to be secured I must turn my thoughts from America and direct them to the rest of the world. These two predominant facts confront me: (1) There are three other naval powers armed very effectively and in a position to damage my country and the people for whose existence I am responsible. (2) There are our dominions with their needs and their fears. I must take these things into account. If I did not my existence as Prime Minister would soon be [apparent omission] and no agreement which I should make with your President would be worth the paper upon which it was written. He and I would be pursuing a vain thing. The standard upon which parity is to be based must therefore allow me to fulfill my obligations.

4. I am determined to make that standard low—lower than it is at present. Indeed, I wish to begin a policy which will reduce it to zero by making nations secure by other means than armament. But obviously my ability to do so depends for the moment not upon my country and yours but upon agreements which in cooperation with each other we can persuade the other powers to make mutually. The completeness of our agreement—not in spirit I hope because that so long as this Government lasts is absolute but in program details—will therefore depend upon the success of the conferences which will follow the termination of our work.

5. These are considerations which, when understood sympathetically by you, point to the inevitable conclusion that the figures upon which we now may agree must be rather high and would be subject to revision so soon as I know definitely what is to be my position as regards the other nations. In view of the difficulty which has arisen on the receipt of your last despatch, is not this the position? Whatever figures we may put before each other now must be provisional upon the agreements to be made with the other powers, and we could agree to examine them further whilst the wider negotiations are going on and settle them during that conference or at once after it.

6. As to this point I want to put on paper an assurance I have given you repeatedly by word of mouth. The figures I have put in are high but they have been used under no Admiralty pressure. There is a tremendous tide of opinion here in favor of agreement but public opinion would not stand against a rational proof that our friendship for the United States had left us exposed to any mischief-maker in the rest of the world. The Pact of Peace has crippled those mischief-makers but in the transition period public opinion will be tender and we must handle it in a statesmanlike way. Thinking of his own position I fear your President may smile at this but he will see how different my problem is from his. I only wish he were sitting by me so that we could expose that subject by continued conversation. So much for the standard of parity. Now as to reduction.

7. The figures I have given to you and which the President rejects are in fact a reduction in the British estimates of millions per annum

of actual expenditure. The cuts I have made alone amount to a gross reduction of over six million pounds sterling.

8. You are in a different position because in building to parity you will apparently have to increase your present strength.

9. As I understand it, however, you would reduce your program.

10. Now we are in this position. The programs have been devised to meet actual needs, so when we consider 'naval armaments' we must not only take into account actual floating tonnage plus the tonnage building in the yards but also the tonnage which without an agreement will inevitably be built. The proposals you put up to your Government will reduce that enormously. I emphasize that naval armaments are not what is built but what things remaining as they are must be built and when we use the word 'reduction' that must be taken into account.

11. Like your President I am not satisfied with that reduction alone but it will be a step and will set inevitabilities in motion which will lead to further reductions and I hark back to the results of the wider conference.

12. I see your President's difficulty. At the moment the bulk of your cruiser strength is in a program; ours is on the water. If you have parity you have to build a part of your program. That is an increase. Here we are two miserable men in authority determined to do the right thing and kept from it by all the devilish powers which have had a hand in making our past. How can we meet each other and overcome these powers?

13. I trusted much to your device of a 'yardstick' and I am sorry to see that it has disappeared from recent despatches. I still trust to it and wish we had it so that we could work on 'effective' and not on absolute tonnage.

14. 1936 has been suggested as the date of equation. That is good, but I must see my way clear so that any promise I make to you may be carried out to the last letter. If you say let us have a holiday in cruiser building then every naval dockyard will have to be reduced to a mere nucleus of repairing and conditioning men and after 1936 an expansion will have to take place for replacement. That does not commend itself to me as a business proposition. I agree to a date. The open question is: how is the time to be used and to what standards? Further negotiations might clear that up if we both work with the problems of each other in both of our minds.

15. Figures have been used again in our respective communications. In all my life I have never known the two sides in a naval affairs dispute to agree upon figures. I have listened to too many debates in the House of Commons. It was that we might come to a rough agreement upon them that I begged of you to have Mr. Gibson with us at our conference of last Monday. The only consideration I have is that I must look at the world with which I am in contact and the only real problem as I see it is how can I arrange strengths so as to enable Mr. Hoover to claim reductions and yet maintain parity. Can he not broaden his definition of reductions? Can he not bring up into prominence in his declarations his double problem of reduction and parity? Can he not show how he has maintained the latter whilst reducing the building which would have been necessary had he never taken the stand he has done? Before the larger

conference and certainly after that conference has been held I would give further study to the figures which our conference of Monday the 29th accepted as a basis for work.

16. This is a long and in some parts very informal communication but our last interviews have undoubtedly cast dark clouds over our prospects. Still I will not let this thing go and this is written as a general statement of our position as your President has stated his, in the hope that we shall both strive to overcome our adverse circumstances.

17. I have cancelled my arrangements to go to my home today in order to write this. I shall go up tonight by train and shall be at the end of a telephone by eleven a. m. tomorrow. On Tuesday I am ready to fly back and have made arrangements with the Air Ministry to provide a machine. So I shall be available by five p. m. that day for a further conference, Mr. Gibson being present if possible and agreeable to you. Please let my secretary here know if that will hold good and he will inform the Air Ministry and myself. Or you can speak to me direct to Lossiemouth. Naturally I shall be anxious to know what reply you get if you send this to Washington.

Yours very sincerely,  J. Ramsay MacDonald."

Am wiring Gibson to whom copies of all my cable correspondence are regularly sent that I will expect him here Tuesday.

DAWES

---

500.A15a3/101 : Telegram

*The Secretary of State to the Ambassador in Great Britain (Dawes)*

[Paraphrase]

WASHINGTON, August 2, 1929—6 p. m.

201. Your telegrams No. 215 and No. 216, August 1. We understand, at least in some degree, the difficulties which the Prime Minister is up against and we appreciate the sincerity and frank friendliness of his message. The fact that you and Gibson are to confer with the Prime Minister again on Tuesday is very satisfactory to us. Mr. MacDonald must be conscious of the fact that he has now reached the nub of the difficulty; that the actuality of figures must be dealt with by him; that a quantitative proposition is being dealt with by him and that it is a case of either increasing one or reducing the other if two unequal quantities are to be made equal. Candidly, we do not know any other method of attacking the problem, nor can we see where our analysis of the facts, as set forth in our previous telegrams, is wrong; neither have we changed our minds as to the kind of an agreement that we deem worth-while reaching. It is felt that Mr. MacDonald will not misunderstand our absolute frankness in commenting upon his letter.

1. At the conference held in Geneva in 1927 Great Britain stated its absolute need of a large number of six-inch-gun cruisers and that she

should match the United States in eight-inch-gun cruisers and it was the opinion of the American representatives that the United States was driven to a large cruiser program at Geneva. An attempt has been made by us to reexamine the basis of our difficulty and a decision has been reached by us that all these naval needs, basically, were relative and that we will accept reduction of our cruiser program if parity by classes can be obtained.

2. The Prime Minister, it appears to us, is still accepting the statement made by the British at Geneva of their need of small cruisers and it still seems to have an intrinsic basis of truth to Mr. MacDonald. Candidly we are doubtful that Great Britain's need is as great as he seems to think and also we are doubtful of the necessity, if Great Britain has a fleet of small cruisers, of her even nearly matching the United States' strength in 10-thousand-ton cruisers.

3. We have great belief in the usefulness of the yardstick which we proposed. Its essential usefulness is demonstrated by the fact that some fair allowance can be made for the difference between six- and eight-inch guns and for relative ages within the cruiser class. The United States stands ready to use this yardstick as a bridge as far as it will go, but this alone will not span the wide gap which exists between the fleets of Great Britain and the United States and it had been our hope that reduction rather than increase would be measured by it.

4. Mr. MacDonald has not yet fully considered the actual effects on tonnage, we would like to point out, if he agrees that parity is to be reached in 1936 and that the cruiser obsolescence age is to be 20 years. Assuming this to be so, without any scrapping at all it is possible that the present British fleet of effectives might remain in existence until 1934. A substantial number of the older small cruisers would be scrapped at that time owing to the 20-year period of obsolescence; and if the obsolescence age be accelerated, and when Mr. MacDonald comes to study the actual figures he will find it almost certainly must be accelerated, still more cruisers would be scrapped. Such being the conditions for the two years, 1934–36, the number of British cruiser units will be smaller than is the case at present. It is possible that under such circumstances some of the dangers which Mr. MacDonald conceives might exist for those two years. To protect against any such occurrence, has Mr. MacDonald considered the use of a political clause which would call for a revision in case a threat of naval construction was made by any power, similar to the suggestion made during the Geneva Conference?

In paragraph three of his communication Mr. MacDonald refers to three other naval powers effectively armed to which he must give consideration besides the United States. It is difficult for us to imagine such a political combination as he refers to and still more difficult to imagine that it will be balanced or made impossible by the number of units of small cruisers that he is discussing. It does not seem likely that the addition of a dozen small cruisers to Britain's existing fleet would affect the situation should he, in truth, find Great Britain surrounded by a host of enemies in 1934 when his fleet might begin to decrease in numbers.

Mr. MacDonald refers in point 14 of his note to the effect of a holiday in cruiser building which would reduce every naval dock-yard to a nucleus with later expansion for replacement, and "that does not commend itself to me as a business proposition" he states. Why it should not we utterly fail to see. The British people might be far better off that those naval docks were employed in building merchant ships and that the subsidy, if there is to be a subsidy, should be for trade and not for the expansion of naval construction. If Mr. MacDonald can keep his cruiser building down until 1936, there is a substantial chance that the expansion for replacement will never take place.

Cannot Mr. MacDonald see that he is assuming what he thinks is an actual and positive need for small cruisers as something that is true today, as it was at Geneva in 1927, and in 1936 is sure to be true also?

It is suggested that Mr. MacDonald reexamine that feeling and that he should certainly not in his own mind think there is any business argument against declaring a holiday in cruiser building in Great Britain.

We would again repeat that the problem which he faces is one of a quantitative nature. We still believe that a fair and sound solution is possible if he will hasten obsolescence and keep construction to an absolute minimum, but no solution that results in an agreement for the United States to construct to parity with an increased British cruiser fleet appears to us a worth-while result of what the two Governments have been striving to accomplish.

STIMSON

---

500.A15a3/105 : Telegram

*The Ambassador in Great Britain (Dawes) to the Secretary of State*

[Paraphrase]

LONDON, August 4, 1929—2 p. m.
[Received August 4—7:10 p. m.[27]]

220. This morning I received the following from Gibson:

"General Dawes has furnished me copies of all cable correspond-ence including the Department's Nos. 195 and 196 of July 31. If the

---

[27] Telegram in four sections.

President and Secretary had been present at our last interview on July 29th I am confident that they would feel differently on the subject. Some misapprehension, it seems to me, has arisen due to our being able to telegraph only definite facts, while we have no means of conveying adequately the atmosphere of the conversations and an understanding of the spirit. It is my belief that the Prime Minister is in no way trying on behalf of his Admiralty to put over anything on us; on the contrary, we must remember that he is a novice as far as this problem is concerned and has no knowledge of details. For this reason he has to rely on his Admiralty for his figures and in the process he inevitably becomes indoctrinated with the general Admiralty views to some extent. I believe, by the same token, that he is open to our suggestions and guidance to an almost equal extent.

It must be borne in mind, furthermore, that the proposals which he made very tentatively and which, as he clearly stated at the time, were merely for the purpose of starting the ball rolling and of discovering what points we could talk about, are by no means a return to the program of the Admiralty at the Three-Power Conference at Geneva. We never were able at that conference to squeeze their minimum demands for cruiser strength into a limitation of 400,000 tons and to keep them within that tonnage. Their figures went well above 600,000 tons at times. The old Birkenhead program was revealed in its entirety in every alternative proposal which they put forward as soon as its disguise had been removed. Not only did they, in other words, insist on preserving the effective cruiser force they then had together with a complete replacement program, but they also were adamant in their demand that they should be able to carry out their entire cruiser building program including such portions of it as had not been made public. Although we realized at the time that you would be disappointed by the present proposal, it constitutes nevertheless a considerable modification of their old position inasmuch as the abandonment of all new construction is envisaged by it.

While it did not undertake to abandon the replacement of small cruisers, it seemed clear to me that this would not constitute a final rejection of such abandonment but rather a hesitation, on the part of men who were aware of the limits of their knowledge, to commit themselves. This revolutionary change apparent in the spirit and attitude toward the whole naval question between our two countries was to my mind the one essential thing. The Prime Minister and Alexander, when making their suggestion for a slight preponderance on the part of the United States in 8-inch-gun ships, added that they did not care how great our preponderance in these ships would be. This is in complete contrast with Bridgeman's blunt repudiation of any idea that Great Britain could view our possessing a superior force of such ships with equanimity. MacDonald and Alexander both emphatically stated that as far as they were concerned they were acting on the conviction that the naval forces of the two countries would not be used by either one against the other and that to ascertain their minimum needs in relation to other powers was their only preoccupation.

Although from our standpoint the first tentative figures are plainly quite inacceptable, I do not feel for a minute that the cruiser problem constitutes an insuperable obstacle, particularly in view of the sincere desire of the Prime Minister to effect a reduction. The question however cannot be settled by simply demanding that Great Britain, in order to avoid the necessity for us to build, must come down to a specified level.   They hold to the belief in a certain 'absolute need' as a minimum, rightly or wrongly, but it is my conviction that the gap between us can be bridged by a careful examination of real needs combined with the exercise of ingenuity and resourcefulness.   To my mind it is important that before the undertaking of any general conversations the British be asked to study various possible means of combining parity and reduction in the cruiser class.   One or a combination of the following methods might achieve this:

1. Certain new construction already under way might be scrapped.

2. An agreement might be concluded to the effect that between 1931 and 1936 no replacement shall be made of small cruisers which become obsolete.

3. It might be possible to agree that obsolete small cruisers be replaced by new vessels carrying 4.7- or 5-inch guns, thus making it possible to include these cruisers in the tonnage of their destroyers.   The basis for this suggestion is the contention of the Admiralty that of these small cruisers a large number are required for work of a police nature but that their habitability and sea endurance must be greater than are afforded by destroyers.

4. It is conceivable that they would accept the idea that we should have a considerable predominance so far as eight-inch gun cruisers are concerned, a proposition which offers the best hope, I believe, for the following reasons:

(1) As I have already attempted to explain, MacDonald takes the attitude of disregarding any possibility of an Anglo-American conflict and therefore concluding logically that it is unnecessary for him to worry about exactly balancing the combat strength of the two fleets.

(2) If we had a predominance of treaty cruisers, in part at least arrived at if possible by British scrapping, the application of the yardstick to differentiated tonnage would be made easier.

(3) Inasmuch as such an arrangement would be founded on a practical carrying out of the anti-war pact between Great Britain and the United States, it would find strong political support in both countries.

We might submit to MacDonald for his consideration other possible expedients which would be combined with those already outlined.   In asking him to study these suggestions, we could point out that the successful application of the yardstick would be materially facilitated by British acceptance of concessions of this sort in a reasonable measure.

I think it would be wise that time for study be given to the Prime Minister.   Information furnished him by his Admiralty people and tempered by his desire to take our point of view into consideration and by the independence of his own mind, will of course serve as a basis for his study when completed.   It is necessary that the question of the best method of procedure be now considered.   The telegraph is not the best means of conducting negotiations between two leaders of courage and independent mind; it causes numerous irritations and errors which direct discussion can largely eliminate. For that reason I am wondering whether it would not be the most practical course for us to present a set of proposals for MacDonald to study, at the same time informing him that it is the desire of the President that these questions be reserved for oral discussions at the time of the Prime Minister's visit to the United States.

Our problem, fundamentally, is to discover some means of reducing the cruiser strength of Great Britain in cooperation with a man who, if its political practicability can be demonstrated to him, is honestly willing to carry it out. He is naturally cautious on account of the great responsibility resting upon him. I am nevertheless convinced that it will be possible, without endangering British security, to reduce British cruiser strength and that, by dealing directly with MacDonald, you and the President can give him this same conviction.

It will be the expectation of every political party in England that an agreement with us be reached before the November meeting of Parliament. It is obvious that MacDonald realizes this pressure and it is unlikely that so auspicious a time for negotiations will present itself again. For this reason I feel that this problem should be taken up directly and as soon as possible by the two leaders. Gibson."

With reference to the above letter it is obvious that comments from me as to the constructive technical suggestions made would be unnecessary. However, I would say that the letter evidences the indispensability of Gibson's technical and general advice not only to myself but to the Prime Minister, which he is giving at a cost in inconvenience, resulting from the detail away from him of his effective diplomatic staff, the extent of which I doubt the Department of State fully realizes.

Concerning Gibson's suggestion that the most practical course now is for us to lay before the Prime Minister a series of suggestions for study and say to him that the President would like to reserve these questions for direct discussion during the visit to Washington of the Prime Minister, I am somewhat undecided. Though I agree emphatically with him as to the courage and independence of mind of the two leaders in these negotiations, I do not recognize that any danger exists. In my view certain irritations may be anticipated from a continuance of this long-range written discussion between them. An exchange of comment has already been indulged in which might irritate men of lesser calibre, with only the effect of the better precipitation of the crux of the question and the demonstration of the mutual high purpose to find the real solution which depends upon a mutual understanding of the limitations which circumstances impose upon each party. Disregarding the question of the wisdom of a personal meeting between the President and the Prime Minister for a direct discussion of unsettled vital differences before the meeting of Parliament, my contacts with the Prime Minister compel me to think that the present method of discussion is the most useful, for the time being, to him. The Prime Minister's great desire for agreement to which his high purpose and idealism as well as political expediency make contribution, tempts him to quick expression of purpose before the technical difficulties have been comprehensively and completely studied. After he has given such an expression of purpose, technical difficulties are advanced by a determined Admiralty and the political opposition, with the result that the Prime Minister's attitude becomes too conservative, an attitude which is often the result of a perception of a new set of facts. Following this reaction, his constructive purpose leads him to another which results in some advance along the right lines. As an instance of this may be cited his letter addressed to me which was forwarded in my No. 211, July 30, and which was induced by his own reflections upon the position of his Admiralty.

It would appear advisable, therefore, that the Prime Minister should meet the President when he is familiar with all the facts which in a proper final attitude should have been taken into full consideration by him. In my judgment, the diplomatic exchanges which are now taking place are educating him as to the facts much better than any other method would at the present time. It would be a mistake, in my judgment, to have the negotiations postponed until the meeting of the Prime Minister and the President. Since I am myself technically ignorant I am a good judge of the methods that best contribute to a gradual emergence from that unhappy condition. Though the fog which surrounds the Prime Minister is not so dense as it is in my case, when I sympathetically read to him directly the sentence in your No. 196, July 31, which reads as follows: "There is no evidence that we can see that he has any understanding of the figures so far," he remarked upon the excellence of your understanding. In explanation, and parenthetically, I read the sentence in your telegram No. 196 to the effect that "matters to be called to the Prime Minister's attention end with this paragraph," as leaving to my judgment what preceding parts of the telegram might be transmitted to him for his assistance.

According to my belief it is just as important that the President and the Prime Minister reach an understanding before the time of their meeting has been decided, as it is that there should be substantial agreement between the two countries before a preliminary conference is called with the other powers.

Finally: I am afraid that MacDonald's attitude, which Gibson assumes means that a material preponderance of the United States in large cruisers is an accepted matter, will later be modified by the Prime Minister as another instance where his constructive purpose induced temporary thoughtlessness in some of the things said at our meeting. When I suggested that the Prime Minister's statement should propose for the United States 18 or more large cruisers and for the British 45 or less smaller cruisers it met with the immediate opposition of Alexander and this opposition was encouraged by MacDonald himself. There is not the least doubt in my mind that Gibson realizes this and also realizes that for purposes of negotiation we should assume the statement in MacDonald's letter to be his ultimate decision in the matter.[28]

DAWES

---

500.A15a3/105 : Telegram

*The Ambassador in Great Britain (Dawes) to the Secretary of State*

[Paraphrase]

LONDON, August 5, 1929—1 p. m.
[Received August 5—9 : 35 a. m.]

221. On reading my No. 220, August 4, over again, I find that the last two sentences need to be clarified; therefore please substitute for them the following:

Gibson's statement in his letter telegraphed herewith is what I have in mind: "The Prime Minister and Alexander, when making their suggestion for a slight preponderance on the part of the United States in 8-inch-gun ships, added that they did not care how great our preponderance in these ships might be."

After a consideration of the discussion which took place I was not impressed by the belief that their ultimate attitude was thus represented. However, in the negotiations it may be best to assume that this attitude exists and that such attitude is intended to be conveyed by the letter from MacDonald.

DAWES

---

500.A15a3/105 : Telegram

*The Acting Secretary of State to the Ambassador in Great Britain (Dawes)*

[Paraphrase]

WASHINGTON, August 5, 1929—3 p. m.

206. We have read Gibson's communication transmitted in your No. 220, August 4, most sympathetically and we are willing to accept your joint judgment of the negotiations of the Prime Minister and what he is trying to bring about. We do not, however, believe that to leave to any personal or later conference the determination of the

---

[28] For substitution for two last sentences, see telegram No. 221, August 5, from the Ambassador in Great Britain, *infra.*

point at which parity is to be reached would be wise nor do we believe that to call a consultation until that point shall have been arrived at between us is advisable. The present method of conducting the negotiations is generally satisfactory to us. On this side there will be the greatest difficulty in obtaining approval of any agreement unless it could be demonstrated that there had been an arrangement for quantitative parity between the fleets. A personal conference may smooth out all other difficulties once that has been arranged for. We should regard it as a disaster of the first magnitude to the cause of reduction in armament if a personal meeting or a general conference were held which failed to reach that result. The advance of peace for years to come would in fact be jeopardized by the acerbities which would now follow such a failure. We urge you for that reason to press for further consideration along the lines which have been pursued hitherto.

We suggest in view of the suggestions contained in your No. 220 that you explore the possibility of Great Britain's ability to reach an agreement with us as follows:

Not to replace the cruisers becoming obsolete by 1936, possibly to scrap one or two more large cruisers which are being constructed at present and to consider also the inclusion of a political clause which would say that if before 1934 any substantial naval war or large increase of armament by any power were to take place, Great Britain might delay the scrapping of 60,000 displacement tons or the equivalent according to the yardstick of such 60,000 displacement tons or that Great Britain might lay down replacements for an equivalent amount, giving the United States a similar right to construct the equivalent tonnage in the same period at the same time. We are trying to suggest roughly speaking that the cruiser strength be checked at 250,000 tons parity to be reached in 1936 with what is tantamount to a condition that if the conditions of world armament as viewed in 1934 tend to justify the belief of the British that their needs for small cruisers were absolute needs, Great Britain at that time may have the option to move the point at which parity should be reached up by 60,000 tons displacement more. A similar option would be given to the United States. We are trying to do something which will make it easier for the Prime Minister, although we should much prefer the bolder course of a flat agreement checking the cruiser category at about 250,000 tons.

The purpose of this proposal is not indirectly to make 300,000 tons the point of parity but to make sure that if a British need for cruisers should develop in five years to be real, the Prime Minister will not by the action he takes irretrievably fail to meet it.

COTTON

500.A15a3/109a : Telegram

*The Acting Secretary of State to the Ambassador in Great Britain*
*(Dawes)*

[Paraphrase]

WASHINGTON, August 6, 1929—5 p. m.

209. Department has been asked by British Ambassador to ascertain what time in October would be most convenient for Prime Minister's visit to the United States. Mr. MacDonald has indicated that he could spend a week here, possibly up to the 12th of October; he will have to sail for home on the 19th and thinks of going to Canada for the intervening period. Our answer to the Ambassador will be that these dates would not come into conflict with the President's engagements. It will be clear to you, however, that we consider it essential that, before he makes such a visit, and as a necessary prerequisite thereof, there should be substantial agreement on the parity question which in our earlier cables we have mentioned as the nub of our difficulties. Without this, his visit, we fear, is likely to have bad rather than good results.

COTTON

500.A15a3/109 : Telegram

*The Ambassadors in Great Britain and Belgium (Dawes and Gibson)*
*to the Secretary of State*

[Paraphrase]

LONDON, August 6, 1929—6 p. m.
[Received 8:48 p. m.[30]]

223. This afternoon Gibson and I had a conversation with the Prime Minister and Alexander which lasted two hours.

First Gibson and I handed the Prime Minister a memorandum which was based upon the pertinent sections of the Department's telegram No. 206 of August 5. The Prime Minister read the memorandum through and then stated that he considered this a very helpful approach to the problem as well as a most friendly one.

Gibson and I then outlined the problem to the Prime Minister as it appears to us and we urged upon him to explore the possible methods of effecting a material reduction of cruiser needs so that a level may be reached which we could justify as representing a reduction in naval armament. The fact was brought out by Gibson and myself that to grant us a material preponderance in 10,000 ton, 8-inch-gun vessels would perhaps be the most effective manner of bridging the gap between the cruiser fleets of the two countries. Mr. Mac-

[30] Telegram in two sections.

Donald replied in a most definite manner that so far as the United States and Great Britain were concerned he would have no hesitation in complying and that he would not feel obliged to modify his naval building program no matter how many of these larger vessels were built by the United States, but he called our attention to the fact that neither Great Britain nor the United States could show the same indifference to the building of such cruisers by other nations and that, when the negotiations had reached the point where the five naval powers would be participating, it is quite apparent that Japan would desire to base the ratio of her cruiser strength on that of the navy of whichever country should have the greatest number of cruisers of the 10,000 ton, 8-inch-gun type. Any bilateral agreement which might be reached by the United States and Great Britain must be influenced, of course, by this consideration.

Our first fundamental problem, we stated to the Prime Minister, was to determine what really constituted the lowest level which the British Government considered essential and that up to this time we had only had the assertion of the need for a definite number of 6-inch-gun cruisers without any explanation of why it was necessary for it to have such a large number and that until we knew on what they based their need for these ships it was difficult for us to discuss the justification for such levels. Mr. MacDonald then stated that while he was on his vacation at Lossiemouth he had formulated some figures of his own based upon an independent study he had made without suggestions from the Admiralty. Tomorrow he will submit a memorandum giving explanations regarding the exact use to be made of the various cruisers constituting the force together with the figures which he outlined to us.

A statement containing the Prime Minister's ideas regarding how parity may be obtained by 1936 will also be presented by him. Mr. MacDonald said that he recognized very clearly the problem which confronted the President and that he is endeavoring to devise some method of meeting him in combining parity and reduction. The Prime Minister anticipates giving definite figures in the memorandum which he will submit tomorrow and these will constitute a distinct reduction over previous figures unless they are modified in the meantime.

During the discussion, it was quite apparent that the political situation in England is giving the Prime Minister much thought in connection with this problem, not so much as regards the naval relations between the United States and Great Britain as those between Great Britain and other nations. Moreover, though the various political parties are each committed to the idea of naval reduction, if they have any ground for it, they will not hesitate to attack Mac-

Donald for having made reductions beyond the limit of safety for the Empire. In the course of the discussions, Mr. MacDonald was asked what he thought would be the effect of a visit by him to the President of the United States before the conclusion of a substantial agreement by the two powers and then there should be a failure to reach any agreement. Mr. MacDonald's reply was that he believed it would be [fatal?] and that his trip to the United States should not be taken until a practical agreement had been reached by the two nations. In the absence of a complete agreement, the trip could be considered only if minor difficulties, which reason upheld as certainly possible of adjustment, remained. On this account, he said, he was most anxious to hurry on the negotiations because if some substantial agreement was not reached by us before the end of September it would be necessary for him to postpone his visit to the United States until after next July on account of Parliament being in session and the number of engagements he has. There is no doubt that the Prime Minister is straining every effort to meet you, and any suggestions whatever as to how this can be achieved he will continue to welcome. He is leaving tomorrow for a holiday in Scotland and arrangements are being made to communicate to him there your comments upon the memorandum which he will give us tomorrow, as he does not expect to allow his holiday to interfere with his full attention to the naval problems presented by our discussions.

DAWES and GIBSON

---

500.A15a3/111 : Telegram

*The Ambassador in Great Britain (Dawes) to the Secretary of State*

[Paraphrase]

LONDON, August 7, 1929—1 p. m.
[Received August 7—9:20 a. m.]

225. I talked with the Prime Minister yesterday about his trip and covered the results of the conversation reported in telegram No. 223, August 6. The view expressed was precisely that which was covered in your No. 209, August 6.

This morning I received a long statement from the Prime Minister who later on telephoned through his secretary to ask that it not be transmitted to you until I should have received a letter from him modifying one or two paragraphs. Letter has just been received, and as explanation of earlier request Prime Minister added in postscript that he was writing in great hurry as he had decided to return to Lossiemouth tonight.

I leave for Dublin tonight and shall return Saturday night, but I have arranged for Prime Minister's revised statement to be telegraphed to you as soon as it has been received. As it will probably be sent from Lossiemouth, it will not be received here, probably, until tomorrow night or Friday.

DAWES

---

500.A15a3/113 : Telegram

*The Ambassador in Great Britain (Dawes) to the Secretary of State*

LONDON, August 9, 1929—11 a. m.
[Received 1 : 34 p. m.[31]]

228. Following is text of Prime Minister's letter just received and modified as explained in my 225, August 7, 1 p. m.

"Lossiemouth, August 8th.

My Dear General: According to my promise I put down in writing the matters of importance dealt with in our conversation of the 6th instant at which Mr. Gibson and the First Lord were present.

I have been studying very closely whilst in Lossiemouth the recent despatches sent to me in reply to my letter to you last week with a view to discovering whether I am able to meet Mr. Hoover's double desire to get parity as well as reduction. The crux of the problem is the cruiser category and upon that it is necessary for me to make one or two observations because I do not think that Mr. Hoover sees in detail what my position is and it is necessary that it should be understood.

1. Were the question of cruiser tonnage one between the United States and us alone there would be no difficulty. You could build as much as you like or as little as you like. I should not trouble, because the Government declines to make any provisions for the possibility of the United States being an enemy. Therefore I think that Washington is pressing me unduly when it asks me to reduce naval figures compiled solely on account of our needs in relation to the rest of the world.

2. American building however does affect me indirectly. Japan may say, were your cruisers much in excess of theirs, that whatever ratio it accepts must be in relation to the larger and not the smaller fleet. That owing to the United States building would compel me to retain a Japanese relationship which would impose a heavy program upon theirs [*sic*].

3. In order that an idea may be had of why our cruiser figures appear to be high, the following facts should in fairness be kept in mind.

(*a*) The British fleet is not one unit. If it were, I could reduce considerably. It is scattered into different and remote divisions each with functions to perform relating to peace and not to war conditions. I know that if war broke out concentration would naturally take place but that cannot be helped. I really cannot neglect peace duties in order to avoid the suspicion that war is in our minds all the time.

---

[31] Telegram in three sections.

Let me state what the cruiser disposition today is so that what I now say may be plain:

> First. With our two main fleets—the Atlantic and the Mediterranean—there are three 8-inch and twelve 6-inch cruisers (in September there will be four and eleven respectively).
>
> Second. On foreign stations (China and Australia) there are seven and twelve respectively.
>
> Third. Two are at home on instructional duties.
>
> Fourth. Fourteen are in reserve or undergoing large repairs.
>
> Fifth. Four are in care and maintenance.

You will at once see how this division of the whole fleet necessitates the maintenance of figures higher than if the fleet operated as one unit.

(b) Put it another way. Australia, New Zealand and the numerous islands for which we are responsible in the southern Pacific, are policed by four cruisers in commission and two in reserve, and remember these are the only resources we have in the event of civil trouble or lawlessness breaking out. India, Burma, the Malay Straits, Somaliland, Kenya, the Persian Gulf, the Indian Ocean islands are policed by three cruisers and a few sloops which barely can make one visit a year to necessary ports. When one visualizes what the function and necessary work of the cruisers are and when my high figures are apportioned to duties, one begins to see the difficulty of a drastic reduction.

(c) The cruiser category for me is therefore only partly a fighting category and is to a considerable extent a police category. (That gives us a possible chance of an agreement if we could decide upon police units which, however, must be habitable [for?] the troops as I must consider the comforts of the men.)

4. I have been working at a scheme which would make British figures in 1936 the standard of parity. Then without replacement in the meanwhile we should have fifteen 8-inch and thirty-four 6-inch ships, a total of forty-nine. I hope that you will see in the light of the above functions of cruisers that there is not much margin for reduction unless in the meantime by our united efforts we can make the world feel [differently toward?] peace. But I must deal with today and it is quite impossible for me to think of figures now which are remote from today—say beyond 1936. I shall, however, steadily reduce as national security is found by other means than arms and I shall continue to work for that other security. Whether it is possible to fix as a first resting place upon the 1936 position depends upon an international agreement.

5. If your President would agree to this 1936 position as being a temporary maximum goal to be worked for I can see my way to meet him, subject to the proviso I have made. That position is reached by the ordinary operations of scrapping, but as I really feel the practicability of an absolute naval committee [reduction?], as a business proposition I would propose to scrap each year one cruiser which I would not otherwise scrap and replace it by a scheme of building which would leave us with fifty cruisers and no more.

6. I ought to say that that will leave me in a bit of a fix between 1936 and 1940 as cruisers fall out in bunches during these years to a total of no less than twenty-three but again that would be a matter of

arrangement in manipulation of building. That might at times appear to be an increase but of course the whole scheme would be published so that mischief makers might be disarmed.

7. I again press for the production of some yardstick to let us see where we are in actual effective strength. Every text book and naval report I have consulted in order to be prepared for these conversations show that the 8-inch cruisers are worth in the event of a fight almost an infinity of smaller craft and guns. You in your 8-inch ships have more guns than are in ours and so in your *Omahas*. It is not profitable to talk of these ships as though their tons were of the same value. Let us know where we are. The constant reference to absolute tonnage in your recent messages stands in the way of a clear vision of either quantitative or qualitative negotiation. Your declaration at Geneva was very specific upon this point.

8. I emphasize the obligations placed upon me by my geographical position which the United States does not have to bear. That makes the Five-Power Conference so important to me, and I could only go as far as I have proposed if that conference is a success.

9. It has been suggested that we might come to a covering political agreement by which after settling figures between ourselves we might provide that, in the event of other powers building so as to [cause] either party disquiet, our agreement might be varied in consequence. We may have to resort to this, but (*a*) it would leave uncertainty and a possibility of serious disagreement, and (*b*) would lay both of us open to press stunts and manufactured panics. It should be used only as a last expedient.

10. I have explained the need we have for cruisers to a minimum figure irrespective of programs which compete with any other nation; I have made another suggestion for solving the problem, what the standard of parity should be, and understand that Mr. Gibson has some suggestions to advance upon that in relation to the yardstick and a transfer of destroyer tonnage to cruiser denominations that however may be dangerous in the light of the Five-Power Conference problems. I am also examining the possibility of smaller police craft. I hope I have made it clear that I shall go to the utmost possible length to meet Mr. Hoover. But there are things I cannot do. I cannot take the necessary police off the seas and I cannot make an agreement with America alone which leaves me at the mercy of powers with which I have no agreement or a very imperfect one. I believe that our somewhat different requirements can be met but give and take and a yardstick are required.

Yours very sincerely, J. Ramsay MacDonald."

DAWES

---

500.A15a3/117

*The Assistant Secretary of State (Castle) to the Under Secretary of State (Cotton)*

[WASHINGTON,] August 12, 1929.

MR. COTTON: The Japanese Ambassador came in to talk with me on August 7th about naval limitation, as usual, and also I had an opportunity to give him an answer in writing in the form of an unsigned memorandum to certain questions he had asked about the arbitration treaty.[32]

I told the Ambassador, in general, what was going on in England without, of course, giving him any details. The purpose of his coming was to say that his Government was very anxious not to have the question of ratio brought up if possible and to add to this that the Japanese felt very strongly that, on account of their long coast line and the need of boats to do police work, it would be impossible for them to accept the same ratio in cruisers which they had accepted in battleships and aeroplane carriers. He said he was merely telling me because he wanted the American Government to understand the Japanese point of view. I told him I would be glad to pass the information on to you.

I should suppose that this demand of the Japanese ought not to make any serious trouble. It seems to be, to some extent at least, justified. They do not want to build large cruisers and it might be possible to adjust matters by leaving out any question of ratio and allowing them to substitute in cruisers what they had cut down in battleships, for example.

W[illiam] R. C[astle, Jr.]

---

500.A15a3/115 : Telegram

*The Ambassador in Great Britain (Dawes) to the Secretary of State*

[Paraphrase]

London, August 12, 1929—5 p. m.
[Received August 12—3:24 p. m.]

235. This afternoon the Japanese Ambassador called on me and told me that he was under instructions from his Government to say that it was most sympathetic to the idea of reduction as touching all categories. Mr. Matsudaira also stated that the Japanese Government would ask for a readjustment of the percentages of naval strength to a 10–10–7 basis.

A message from Gibson states that illness and a possible operation will prevent his coming here for conference for some time, so I am wondering if it would be possible, in the interim, for you to send an expert like Marriner[33] here. Gibson made this suggestion to me a few days ago in explaining difficulty of leaving his work in Brussels for his trips to London.[34]

Dawes

---

[32] *Foreign Relations*, 1928, vol. III, p. 135.
[33] J. Theodore Marriner, Chief of the Division of Western European Affairs.
[34] A marginal notation on the telegram states that no answer was required.

500.A15a3/113 : Telegram

## The Secretary of State to the Ambassador in Great Britain (Dawes)

WASHINGTON, August 15, 1929—5 p. m.

217. Your 228. Following are our comments on Prime Minister's letter of August eighth:

In general we regard his letter as highly important and if we now correctly understand his position we think we see daylight and that it marks great progress toward agreement.

We recognize, as stated in his 1, that he must take into account his naval needs in relation to the rest of the world. We recognize, as stated in his 2, that he has to bear in mind the relationship to Japan although we do not entirely understand his 2 when he speaks of the larger and the smaller cruiser fleets because the fleets are to be at parity. If he means that Japan might insist she have the same ratio as to large cruiser units with the United States which she would have as to small cruiser units with Great Britain, we understand the Prime Minister's meaning but we doubt if Japan would take such a position. However, we understand Japan's wishes must be considered.

We have read Prime Minister's 3 (a), 3 (b), and 3 (c). We think we understand them and we are not disposed to question his judgment as to the functions and as to the number of units necessary for him to carry out the functions. We understand that in general he will require 50 units for the functions described which are now carried out by cruisers.

There is one particular as to the foregoing where we are inclined to see the matter rather differently. We do not see why all these functions must be carried on by the character of cruiser you [they?] are now using. This we shall comment on later.

His 4. We are in agreement that the British figures of December 31, 1936, should be the standard of parity and we understand that (without replacements in the meanwhile) Britain will then have 49 cruisers comprised of (a) 15–8″, of which 10 are already constructed, (b) 4 Hawkins class with 7.5 guns and (c) 30 armed with 6″, which will mean that Britain will before December 31, 1936, have scrapped all cruisers completed prior to 1916.

We understand that if there are no replacements there would be practically little margin for reduction unless something should have happened in the meantime which will make the world feel differently toward peace and that the Prime Minister cannot think of figures beyond 1936. We also understand that whether or not it will be possible to fix the first resting place upon the 1936 position depends upon international agreement.

His 5. We are willing to agree to take the December 31st, 1936, position as a temporary goal to be worked for subject to such provisos as either of us now find necessary to state. We understand that instead of stopping replacements as we have urged, the Prime Minister feels that there must be a minimum program of building and he proposes, as we understand it, during the period from now until 1936 to scrap six cruisers completed in 1916 plus those completed prior to that date, making a total scrapped of fourteen. (The three cruisers now on the sale list *Conquest*, *Birmingham*, and *Yarmouth* are considered as having been already scrapped and are not subject to the present discussion.) The foregoing fourteen cruisers are to be replaced by seven. We assume that the cruisers he means to scrap are the oldest cruisers then on his list, that is, those completed in 1916. Is that correct?

He does not state the particular boats to be scrapped or the tonnage of the boats to be built for replacement. That is important and we should be glad if we could be particularly advised both as to type and tonnage of replacements whether they are the new type of 6,500 ton 6-inch gun ships or whether they are 4,000 ton type. We make a further suggestion on this point later on.

His 6. We realize that he has a number of cruisers going out between 1936 and 1940 so that those years may see extensive building if the world shall not have changed.

His 7. We will deal with his inquiry later in this message.

His 8 we understand. We also understand that the arrangements which are being suggested between us are contingent upon the success of the five-power conference, although we urge and shall continue to urge that it be consummated upon agreement by Japan, Britain and the United States. It is earnestly hoped, however, that France and Italy will join but if that cannot be effected Britain, Japan and ourselves may well come to agreement containing clause covering contingency of menacing building program on part of any non-signatory power.

His 9. In regard to the covering political agreement which was suggested in our previous messages, we are willing to abide by the Prime Minister's decision to leave that question out of consideration for the moment and only resort to it if other plans fail.

His 10. We are sympathetic with what the Prime Minister says as to doubting the advisability of a transfer of destroyer tonnage to the cruiser denomination, and we agree it may be dangerous in the light of five power conference problems particularly relating to submarines, and we are willing for the present to leave that out of the attempt to reach agreement. For the purposes of this negotiation we agree, as he states, that the Prime Minister cannot take the necessary police craft off the seas and that he cannot make an agreement with the United States alone, which will leave him at the mercy of powers with which he has no agreement or a very imperfect one.

There are several additional questions raised by his letter to which we desire to explain our position. In his 10 he states that he believes our somewhat different requirements can be met by "give and take" and by a yardstick; and in his 7 he refers to our constant reference to absolute tonnage as standing in the way of clear vision. In his 7 he again presses for us to produce a yardstick "to let us see where we are in actual effective strength". The friendly frankness of the Prime Minister deserves to be met in a similarly sincere spirit and this we have been trying to do. Let us try again, even more specifically, to make our position absolutely clear. Parity from our viewpoint is not only an essential element in our negotiations but we believe it to be the underlying reform in the relations of our two countries from which we hope the greatest future benefits will be obtained. As the President pointed out in his Memorial Day address[35] it transforms the relation of Britain and America from one of competition to one of cooperation in respect to armaments. It relieves the atmosphere from the psychology of potential war and transforms it into one of friendly agreement. So long as both countries understand they are not to outbuild each other, the incentive to build is removed. It is a practical method of inculcating among the people at large of both countries the spirit which the Prime Minister describes in his 1 as being his own attitude towards the United States.

The Prime Minister can see that from this standpoint parity must not only be substantially real but must be recognizable as such by the people of both countries. It must not be a matter of such difficult technique that each people will think the other is outwitting it. For this reason we can never get very far away from the quantitative aspect of parity which has hitherto been used in such negotiations.

In previous negotiations the only criterion of comparison which the United States has used has been the easily understood criterion of displacement tonnage. Realizing that this has not succeeded in meeting existing conditions for both countries, we advanced at Geneva the suggestion of a yardstick; and we have desired that when consultations or conferences are held there might result from them substantial agreement among the naval experts of all countries to make allowances for the factors of age and gun calibre which would discount absolute tonnages. We assumed that the use of the yardstick would apply particularly to the cruiser category and felt that within that category the discounts must inevitably be somewhat in favor of Britain, simply because its cruiser fleet will in 1936 be older and will contain a larger number of small cruiser units of less gun calibre. It had been hoped in the beginning that a yardstick might perhaps be devised which would measure and make possible a marginal exchange of tonnages between categories. The Prime Minister (See

[35] *Ante*, p. 113.

his letter of July 29 contained in your 211)[36] came to the definite conclusion that it would not be wise to use the yardstick excepting within the cruiser category. In that decision, which obviously limited the use of the yardstick, we acquiesced. (See our 174, paragraph E, (c).)[37] We have hitherto made clear the simple character of this suggested yardstick and its elements. If those elements are agreed upon the only technical question remaining, as we have already pointed out, will be the values to be assigned to these elementary factors. Of course, we may be quite wrong in thinking that it is possible to obtain agreement among all naval experts on this subject. The expression in the Prime Minister's 7 gives us the impression that the naval experts with whom he has talked say very different things to him than our experts say to us, and we cannot be sure just where a yardstick, if finally agreed upon, will lead. But what we wish to make clear is that this new suggested instrument of agreement, the yardstick, in order to fulfill the purpose of its genesis cannot be allowed to be carried to such lengths as will be difficult for the ordinary citizens of either country to understand. The average citizen of both countries in comparing fleets will always be largely guided by a quantitative basis. Frankly, we do not believe the American public would ever accept such a ratio as that stated in the Prime Minister's 7, namely "that the 8-inch cruisers are worth in the event of a fight almost an infinity of smaller craft and guns." On the contrary, we are advised by our experts that inasmuch as the armor of an 8-inch cruiser is, and necessarily must be, penetrable by 6-inch guns, the ratio of the respective fighting capacity of these two classes of cruisers, particularly in fleet action, reduces substantially to the ratio of the destructive power of 8-inch guns with their greater range against that of the 6-inch guns with their much greater rapidity of fire; and this ratio is very far from infinity. We are advised that the chief governing reason which compels the United States to depend upon the larger cruisers instead of the smaller is their greater cruising radius made necessary in our case by the absence of naval bases.

Now in conducting our present negotiations, inasmuch as it has been clear from the beginning that the United States having during the past ten years allowed its cruiser program to fall behind must in any event build in order to reach any parity, we thought that we could ascertain the point at which the Prime Minister is willing to check Britain's cruiser strength and then secure what would be parity with that point in displacement tonnage, realizing that whatever discounts the yardstick would thereafter create would simply mean that the United States would have to build just so much less in order to reach parity. This still seems to us the sound method of figuring and the one most

---

[36] *Ante,* p. 166.
[37] *Ante,* p. 141.

likely to reach agreement, particularly because Britain states absolute needs and we are willing to put parity in cruisers in 1936 as low as Britain will agree. Following out this method, if we assume from the Prime Minister's last letter that his replacements to be made before 1936 will not increase his aggregate displacement tonnage beyond the amount of 330,000 displacement tons of cruisers (this assumes replacement cruisers about 4,000 tons each), we believe that speaking generally parity could only be reached by building our total program of 23 large cruisers. This means that in addition to our ten 7,050 ton cruisers of the *Omaha* class (aggregating 70,500 tons) the United States would have 23 10,000 ton 8-inch cruisers (aggregating 230,000 tons) or a total displacement tonnage of both types of 300,500 tons. The yardstick, from such light as we now have upon it, would about cover the resulting difference of 30,000 tons. Parity would then be fixed at the point stated by the Prime Minister's letter. He will understand that we are not questioning the complete sincerity of that letter when we say that such a result is to us disappointing, because we hoped to see parity placed at such a point where it would mean reduction on our part as well as on his, and would allow us to build less than our full program.

The Prime Minister may argue that the difference of 30,000 tons which we have indicated as the result of the application of the yardstick is disappointing to him because he thinks it too low. It is, however, the figure which is now reported to us. It is subject to change or reconsideration after conference if it can be shown that it is not soundly based on the true facts as to the respective fleets or if it be shown technically erroneous. When in considering the yardstick it is realized that since both fleets as of 1936 will show fifteen 8-inch units, it becomes clear that the function of the yardstick is really to measure the relative combatant strength of the remainder of the two fleets. The remainder of the United States fleet is only 150,000 tons on which a discount of 30,000 tons would amount to a discount of 20 per cent. Even if the Prime Minister should believe that the discount should be as high as 30 per cent instead of 20 per cent and our naval experts are convinced after conference that the Prime Minister's view was correct, the yardstick would result in reducing our total program only from 23 to 21 cruisers.

It is for this reason we draw hope from the words of his 10 "I am also examining the possibility of a smaller police craft". As we read his letter as a whole it is convincing as to his need of craft to perform the police functions. At this point we suggest a new idea in the creation of a new term of "police cruisers" which shall be built for that purpose alone—their character to be radically changed from the types of ships we both now use for these purposes in that they should not exceed say 4,000 tons, have limited armament, and slow speed. Such boats would have small combatant value. That the British should in this police work use the cruisers which they now have until 1936 we easily understand but if they could make replacements mentioned in this new type it would still further relax our building program,—the United States to have a right to build a like tonnage of that same type of craft. If we both had the right to build, there would be parity and if Britain would build these police cruisers not only would they serve police functions but they would greatly reduce the total offensive naval armament and thus let both of us fairly show the people of the world that we are reducing our fleets. More than that, such a course would, it seems, make the whole problem easier vis-à-vis Japan and the other nations because it would distinctly lessen the number of United States large cruisers without lessening the number of Britain's large cruisers and thus would go far to meet our problems.

We have not in the least ceased our desire to come to agreement with the Prime Minister. We find the keenest satisfaction in that he has come to grips with his figures and is dealing with his crucial questions, and in spite of some disappointment we feel that Britain and the United States are today nearer real and complete agreement in the light of the true facts understood by both of us than we have ever been.

This seems to deal with all the questions in the Prime Minister's letter save perhaps what he says about the spirit of "give and take." If by the spirit of "give and take" he means that the United States should approach conference without pettiness, we can give him a satisfactory assurance, but we do think the problem essentially a quantitative one, that we must so defend it before our people if agreement is reached, and that the spirit of give and take may ease our differences but cannot change that nature of the problem.

STIMSON

500.A15a3/147

*The Ambassador in Great Britain (Dawes) to the Secretary of State*

[Extract]

No. 179 LONDON, August 23, 1929.
[Received August 31.]

SIR: Referring to the Embassy's telegram No. 241 of August 21st, 12 noon,[38] I have the honor to transmit herewith the text of the Prime Minister's statement on Anglo-American naval negotiations, issued at Lossiemouth on August 20th and generally published in the London press on August 21st . . .

I have [etc.] For the Ambassador:
F. L. BELIN
*First Secretary of Embassy*

---

[38] Not printed.

[Enclosure]

*Statement by the British Prime Minister (MacDonald) at Lossie-mouth, August 20, 1929*

General Dawes came up to exchange views with me upon a message from Washington which I am studying, as it, with one I sent from here shortly after my arrival, marks a distinct advance in our conversations. We have been working all the time at the problems which have hitherto baffled the representatives of both countries—as, for instance, at the Geneva Naval Conference—of how to reconcile three positions: American claims for parity, which we admit; British necessities, which have no relation at all with American building (but which are determined by our relations to, and responsibilities in, the rest of the world); and the desire, common to both Governments, to reduce armaments.

If the exchange of views and arguments which have taken place are ever published, it will be seen that these questions have been discussed with great frankness, the very best of good will, and an increasing understanding of the position of both sides. Everything has been under review, from the composition and effects of a yardstick to the function of police cruisers; and the composition of fleets, from first-class battleships to submarines, has been surveyed. Everything at the moment is tentative, and it would only mislead the public if trial suggestions and proposals were disclosed.

We are examining everything that promises to be helpful. A good deal of hampering undergrowth has been cut away, and we are up against hard realities, with some valuable agreements of a general character behind them. Both of us are fully aware, however, that no agreement between us two can carry us very far unless other Powers agree, and that conditions all our work. A wide conference—say, a resumption of the Washington Conference before the date now fixed for it—is at the back of our minds all the time.

---

500.A15a3/130 : Telegram

*The Ambassador in Great Britain (Dawes) to the Secretary of State*

LONDON, August 24—2 p. m.
[Received August 25—7:30 a. m.[39]]

242. The following undated letter [40] has just been received from Lossiemouth.

"My dear General: I have now had time to study the note you sent to me on the 16th instant. The delay has been caused by my having to

---

[39] Telegram in nine sections.
[40] Letter should have been dated August 23.

consult some of my experts regarding the practical effect of certain proposals in it.

1. Once again I appreciate its frankness in dealing with our practical difficulties. I am a little disappointed by the indications in it that the yardstick is not to make very much difference in the calculations of displacement tonnage which was the rock upon which the Geneva Conference foundered. We seem to be like the fox and the stork who invited each other to dinner which each served up in turn in utensils from which only one could eat. From the yardstick with some reductions I hoped we could devise a vessel convenient for both.

2. As I should like that there should be no misunderstanding about what I wrote in my last about Japanese and American building I shall repeat it. My argument was that though Great Britain is not likely to build against America as all parties here are opposed to it, if America were to continue to build against us you might put so many cruisers upon the sea that Japan might be forced to say that whatever ratio it had to adopt that ratio had to be calculated in relation to the American fleet and not to ours. Only in this indirect way would American building affect British programs because we could not be indifferent to that.

3. I fully understand value of the word 'parity' in the minds of the American people and I have made it clear that it raises no hostility in ours. I have also made it clear that the British standard must be determined by obligations which I have described; that my task is to value these obligations in terms of a fleet just sufficient to fulfill them and that I regard that valuation as something which must fluctuate as peace conditions fluctuate. As the President knows, the President's Government has already taken great strides forward in creating a machinery for making the peace pact effective. The Government's view is that as security by pacific means advances, so security vainly sought by arms will disappear.

4. I have looked ahead as far as 1936 and have proposed to arrange programs of building so that, assuming an agreement with other powers, the British fleet of cruisers all told will be forty nine or fifty at the outside. These figures express the outlook of 1929. In the meantime eyes will be kept open and, though I can make no promises, the President may be assured that any justification which may arise for carrying out a more effective peace program will be used. Great Britain does not wish a useless or superfluous warship to sail the seas.

5. In the process of reduction we might agree to a lengthening of the life of cruisers so that the amount of rebuilding for displacement would be reduced. As regards some ships rushed through the yards during the war, this might be awkward for us as they are really not in good condition for much further sea service but the problem they present need not obstruct an agreement.

6. As regards the wider agreement with other countries which we both contemplate I have already agreed to an understanding with Japan and, us two failing, a satisfactory arrangement with France and Italy as well and in that event I have proposed and you have agreed to a proviso that if either of the parties to the tripartite agreement find that that agreement is laying it open to danger, the agreement shall be subject to an arrangement which will enable the threatened signatory to make adequate provision for its safety. I agree to this only after every effort has been made to make the others rea-

sonable because the political effect of leaving them out might be uncomfortable and have naval reactions.

7. I threw out the suggestion that our visiting and police work might be done by a type of minor craft and that is being studied. Many points have to be considered, e. g., accommodation for crews, the arm needs of a police force, tropical conditions on board small craft, their yardstick value, et cetera, and an answer to this cannot be hurried. For the moment the idea had better be kept to provide a margin within which my actions may be better than my promises.

8. In all this, the Government must carry the Dominions with it.

9. Taking all these into account I am advised that the figures I gave in my last letter go right to the bone and must be taken as the minimum to which the Government at present can commit itself.

10. For Great Britain they are a considerable reduction on the Geneva figures and on the present fleet and they are a still greater reduction in the program of building announced two or three years ago. With this reduction we should be prepared to go to the Preparatory Commission on disarmament and show that they would lead to a substantial reduction in world naval armaments if other countries would respond.

11. The note upon which I am commenting deals with the above proposals. If the United States puts equivalents on the water I am told it means building though considerably short of its full program. I should like to meet the President in no niggardly or niggling way but I really cannot go below minimum requirements under present conditions and the proposals I have indicated depend upon an agreement with the other powers.

12. Parity when all is said and done must have some quantitative expression. The President may admit that the British fleet is constructed with no thought of the United States and that its minimum requirements are fixed for purposes which would be real even if no United States lay on the map of the world. He is nevertheless committed to parity and parity he must show. Parity with the British fleet is to him the same necessity as the work I have described is to me. There is no going beyond that. But I hoped that the yardstick might have helped us to strip from our problem whatever is really nonessential in it. Your note tells me that no yardstick would make a greater difference than thirty thousand tons. That is not to be sneezed at but still it is disappointing as an equivalent for the numbers of small cruisers which we have to maintain not as possibilities for war but absorbing necessities for peace. As possibilities for war a proportion of them would be scrapped tomorrow, as necessities for peace they are barely sufficient.

13. I do not forget that in the event of a war these cruisers would be turned from police to war purposes. But,

(a) We are both working unwearyingly to remove this possibility and I have always insisted that we must take a reasonable risk that the other fellow means to honor his signature.

(b) As fighting vessels the smaller cruiser is on a much lower plane than this would imply. If your board of admiralty were to go to sea with small cruisers to meet an enemy of large cruisers how many of the former would you want in proportion to the larger to give them a dog's chance of victory? The experts in naval matters whom I have consulted and have shown the observations in your note, reply in writing 'these arguments are clearly without foundation having regard to the experience of the war'.

14. To sum up the actual questions which we have brought ourselves to face are:

(a) Can the United States accommodate itself either by building and/or by a yardstick to our minimum and what in an actual quantitative program does it mean especially in the category of cruisers?

(b) Can we agree to a program of lengthening years and replacement which would put us in a position mutually satisfactory in 1936?

15. Upon (b) it appears that we can come to an agreement quite easily. The difficulty is in (a).

16. I have put the proposals and comments of your note into a table so that we may see how we stand. This is the result in terms of the 1936 standard:

> Great Britain 8-inch cruisers, 15; *Omaha*, none; 6-inch cruisers, 35.
> United States, 23; 10; none.

A superiority of eight 8-inch cruisers is an impossible proposition to take to our people labeled 'parity' especially as supported by ten ships of your *Omaha* caliber and alternative, our fifteen being supported by thirty-five 6-inch ships. We might go to the country and say that we have found it impossible to agree, and that the United States is to build such and such a program and we might advise that our own program should make no response. But to say that we accept this table as parity would make people turn and rend us. An agreed parity must commend itself to our [people?] as well as to those of the United States.

17. I have been working upon the prospects held out at Geneva. My papers record that on the 23rd ultimo April Mr. Gibson informed our delegate at Geneva that the plan then suggested would give the American navy superiority over the British of one or two 10,000, 8-inch cruisers and give the British navy superiority over America of some thirty 6,400 tons, 6-inch cruisers. That I have met generously, and the margin of strength shown in the suggestions I have made is less than in that estimate but even as a basis of discussion it had now been completely departed from in your last note and we are back to all intents and purposes upon dead as against effective tonnage with results shown in the above table. This is the Geneva deadlock.

18. Furthermore during our conversation on the 17th June you told me that as soon as the Government at Washington had made up its mind about the yardstick formula at which it was working it would be communicated to His Majesty's Government in confidence. Now, without any indication of what the formula is, this note informs me that it provides for a margin of only 30,000 tons, e. g., eight extra 8-inch cruisers and ten *Omaha* calibers only add one-tenth to the effective strength of the United States cruisers in comparison with ours. Surely on the face of it there is something wrong in such a calculation. I should like to see the formula which gives that result. Surely, we ought to exchange views upon it before we declare its influence in determining for one of us a decision regarding parity

standards. Could I not see the formula in order to study it and comment upon it?

19. I am getting disturbed about my visit to America. I see in this one of the most beneficial moves that could be made in the present state of the world. Every one with a vision must see that the demonstration of our two countries standing side by side for fellowship and peace will greatly move the world, whereas the abandonment of the visit or its postponement till next year will have a correspondingly depressing effect. But the House of Commons meets at the end of October and I cannot be absent beyond say the first week of the session. What is done must be done quickly. On Saturday week I go to Geneva and for the 28th of September I have a "call upon" steamer accommodation for New York.

With all my best wishes, I am, my dear General, always zealous, J. Ramsay MacDonald."

As arranged (see my 240, August 19, 4 p. m.[41]) I met the Prime Minister at Elgin on Friday, August 23. Prior to the receipt by me of the letter transmitted above I received a letter from him dated Lossiemouth, August 22nd which reads as follows:

"My dear General: I have now finished my study of the last note you transmitted to me from Washington and have refreshed my memory by papers sent up to me here. The result is that I am more depressed than I have been since we began our conversations. You will remember that we started on the yardstick which was the proposal which brought back hope after Geneva. You were to give me a formula and we both agreed that it should be examined by subordinate experts. That has all gone. In your speech at the Pilgrims, you said so truly that the statesmen should handle this matter and that as there was the desire for an agreement, and as a naval conflict between the countries was unthinkable, the technicians should not thwart the statesmen. That has gone, and we are back into exactly the same atmosphere and facing exactly the same presentation of the problem as we were at Geneva. We are drifting away from the only road which offers a solution of a problem which does not consist of reality at all, but of words and appearances. Experts and lawyers make nearly all the reefs in the seas of life upon which men and states founder. I am now working at my formal reply, which I am sorry cannot be ready today, as I led you to expect. It will be ready tomorrow however. I thought I should tell you this so as to keep my promise to you.

With all my best wishes for a good time in the Highlands.

Yours very sincerely, J. Ramsay MacDonald."

[Paraphrase.] The Prime Minister was required to take part in several ceremonies Friday morning at Elgin, and our talk was necessarily limited. He said that the pessimism revealed in his letter of August 22nd was due to apprehension that British public opinion would react unfavorably to the knowledge that the United States

---

[41] Not printed.

would have preponderance in heavy cruisers. It has been assumed in these discussions that parity must be obtained through heavy cruisers. The compass of necessary technical differences was being reduced by the exchanges, I remarked, to language comprehensible to the average man; a clearer public perception of the relative insignificance of the quantities involved in comparison with the total naval strength of the two countries would result and a general public demand in both nations that for the sake of world peace the smaller technical differences be reasonably adjusted in a spirit of fair compromise would probably be encouraged. Therefore, my remarks concerning naval problems at the Elgin ceremonies in his honor [42] were made after consulting with him, as he considered they would be of value.

The situation at The Hague [43] is causing MacDonald much concern and this afternoon he will arrive by aeroplane in London. When I left him yesterday afternoon his last words to me were that he had just received news from The Hague where the situation seemed most serious, that they were trying to persuade him to go there in person but that, unless later events would justify the hope that some settlement which would be acceptable in the present state of British public opinion might be effected, he would not go. [End paraphrase.]

DAWES

---

500.A15a3/130 : Telegram

*The Secretary of State to the Ambassador in Belgium (Gibson)*

WASHINGTON, August 26, 1929—4 p. m.

57. In Dawes' 242 to us Prime Minister says

"I have been working upon the prospects held out at Geneva. My papers record that on the twenty-third ultimo April Mr. Gibson informed our delegate at Geneva that the plan then suggested would give the American navy superiority over the British of one or two 10,000 eight inch cruisers and give the British navy superiority over America of some thirty 6,400 ton six inch cruisers. That I have met generously."

Please inform us if you said it, or what you said. Are we correct in assuming that if you said anything like that you are counting four *Hawkins* as practically equivalent to three 10,000 ton cruisers and that you were limiting your British replacement program to the then announced building program?

STIMSON

---

[42] Printed in Charles G. Dawes, *Journal as Ambassador to Great Britain* (New York, 1939), pp. 58–60.
[43] See vol. II, pp. 1025 ff.

500.A15a3/135 : Telegram

*The Ambassador in Great Britain (Dawes) to the Secretary of State*

LONDON, August 27, 1929—noon.
[Received August 27—10:12 a. m.]

245. . . .

On arrival at the office this morning I found following letter from the Prime Minister.

"26th August, 1929.

My dear General Dawes: On further examination of the despatch of the 23rd instant,[44] I see that I did not make it as clear as I ought to have done in paragraph 17 that the figures I quoted as having been used by Mr. Gibson were not official figures and not binding in any way on the American Government. Since my return I have been informed that they were only used in purely personal conversation as something which might happen when we got into closer grips in making an agreement.

I am, yours very sincerely, J. Ramsay MacDonald."

The Foreign Office asks that for purposes of reference the Prime Minister's undated letter "in my 242, August 24, 2 p. m., be dated August 23rd."

DAWES

_____

500.A15a3/139 : Telegram

*The Ambassador in Belgium (Gibson) to the Secretary of State*

[Paraphrase]

BRUSSELS, August 28, 1929—noon.
[Received August 28—8:16 a. m.]

71. Department's No. 57, August 26, 4 p. m. Neither at Geneva nor elsewhere did I say anything resembling this. I explained to a British delegate in a conversation so informal that no memorandum was ever made that a recognition of the different needs of the two navies was prompted by our idea of a formula; that we hoped that a means of measuring naval strength, which in the event of real reduction would in any case give us the heavy cruisers, might be devised in some such way, and the British would be allowed the most small 6"-gun cruisers for their special needs should we balance our preponderance in these bigger ships together with our ten *Omahas*. Necessarily I explained this in a most general and obvious manner and made no quantitative speculations, this not only being without meaning but clearly premature until we could have some idea of the level where we could reach an agreement.

_____

[44] See telegram No. 242, August 24, from the Ambassador in Great Britain, p. 196.

As I recollect, a guess was hazarded by either Craigie or Cushendun to the effect that on some such basis as that indicated by the Prime Minister we could work out an agreement. This is clearly a very different matter from my having suggested it. Texts to London and Berne.

GIBSON

---

500.A15a3/141 : Telegram

*The Ambassador in Great Britain (Dawes) to the Secretary of State*

[Paraphrase]

LONDON, August 28, 1929—2 p. m.
[Received August 28—1 : 44 p. m.]

247. This morning the Japanese Ambassador called to say that on August 27 he had an interview with the Prime Minister. During the interview the Ambassador told the Prime Minister that his Government would desire the ratio of strength to be 10–10–7 in any proposed settlement and that his Government was very sympathetic toward the negotiations so far as they had progressed according to information which I had given him. The Ambassador also told the Prime Minister that his Government was hopeful that the cruiser strength agreed upon between Great Britain and the United States would be as low as possible in order that Japan could reach its ratio position without requiring so much building. Parenthetically, it may be said that his attitude in this connection is the same as that of our own. MacDonald told me in so many words to keep the Japanese Ambassador informed of his own position as he would outline it to me from time to time. Matsudaira was informed by me of the informal word which the Prime Minister had sent to the effect that he desired to forestall any attempt, at Geneva, to bring about the transfer to the Preparatory Commission of the negotiations. It is my belief that Matsudaira will be very cooperative in this matter. He leaves for Geneva on the morning of the 29th.

DAWES

---

500.A15a3/135 : Telegram

*The Secretary of State to the Ambassador in Great Britain (Dawes)*

[Paraphrase]

WASHINGTON, August 28, 1929—5 p.m.

224. Reference your telegrams No. 242, August 24, 2 p.m., and No. 245, August 27, noon. A separate telegram is being sent you from which it seems possible an agreement might be reached; but it is, in our opinion, essential that the letter of the Prime Minister,

which was included in your telegram No. 242, should be answered in detail. In our opinion in that letter he is in error and we think that some of the conclusions of his letter are a result of his errors, and that our separate telegram referred to above will not lead to results unless these errors are dispelled.

In his letter it is assumed that the four *Hawkins* type cruisers can fairly be placed in the 6-inch cruiser class. We have not concurred and do not now concur in that conclusion. This type was referred to by the Prime Minister as a group laid down in 1916 for war purposes (see your No. 204, July 25, 1 p. m.). They were completed in 1918, 1919, 1924, and 1925, respectively, according to our information. The 7.5-inch guns they carry are much nearer to 8-inch than they are to 6-inch guns. These guns can be worked by hand, according to the Prime Minister, which, it would seem, should give an advantage in being fired rapidly. The shell they fire, which weighs 200 pounds, is obviously nearer to a shell of 8 inches weighing 250 pounds than to a shell weighing 105 pounds of 6 inches. It is' difficult to understand how the *Hawkins* type can be considered by the Prime Minister or his advisers as nearer to the modern cruiser carrying 6-inch guns than to the type carrying 8-inch guns; in the opinion of our advisers the four *Hawkins* type cruisers of about 40,000 tons are comparable substantially to 40,000 tons of four 8-inch type cruisers. If the four cruisers of *Hawkins* type are compared with 8-inch gun cruisers, some deductions would, of course, have to be allowed for age and some small discount for size of guns in favor of the *Hawkins* type, but in spite of this, in our opinion, the *Hawkins* class would still remain comparable with four cruisers of 8-inch type.

It is stated by the Prime Minister in his letter, transmitted in your No. 242, that there are no ships in the British fleet of the type of the *Omaha*. It is difficult to understand why the *Emerald* and the *Enterprise*, each of which is over 7,500 standard tons, are not at least of equivalent value with two *Omaha* type cruisers.

The Prime Minister will see that more large cruisers than he has stated are possessed by Great Britain, if he takes these facts into consideration. We believe that he should figure his large cruiser units more nearly at nineteen instead of fifteen which would make considerably less than asserted in his letter, the disparity in large cruisers considered alone. He will find if he goes through the cruiser fleets and matches off units which are substantially equivalent that even if the full program of twenty-three cruisers should be completed by the United States after fifteen 8-inch cruisers of 10,000 tons have been matched off in each fleet and the *Hawkins* class has been matched off against its equivalent in 8-inch cruisers of 10,000 tons as stated above and if, also, two of the *Omaha* as stated above are matched off against the *Enterprise* and the *Emerald*, there will remain of the United States fleet as of 1936 approximately four cruisers with 8-inch guns and eight cruisers of the *Omaha* type, which makes a total of approximately twelve units to be evaluated against twenty-nine British 6-inch units. The displacement of these twenty-nine British units is not known to us now but would seem to be about one and a third times as great as that of the twelve units in the United States fleet. This way of testing whether or not the result of a yardstick is fair appears reasonable. At the moment, the point we are stressing is that the disparity deplored by the Prime Minister does not exist and that our statement that in order to reach parity, we must build our full program was not unfair. As to whether or not it is correct is a question of fact on which there should not be a very material difference between reasonable men after discussion and conference. We do not understand why great difficulty in believing in a parity so arrived at should be found by either the public or the Admiralty.

The figures given above are based on the assumption that the replacements proposed by the Prime Minister are as stated in his letter of August 8 (your No. 228, August 9, 5 p. m.) and consist of cruisers of 4,000 tons of a type which is substantially equal to the older ships. In your No. 242, we have not been furnished by him with the details we specifically asked concerning the tonnage or armament of the replacements he wishes to make.

We quite agree that Japan must have full consideration as regards the Prime Minister's paragraph 2 in your No. 242. Suggestions for a program are dependent upon the agreement of the Japanese. In our No. 217, August 15, 5 p. m., we were quite clear on that matter.

The Prime Minister's paragraph 3. There is no objection on our part to Great Britain's placing the point of parity in cruisers at fifty units if that is consistent with 330,000 tons total displacement.

We are in agreement with the Prime Minister's paragraph 4.

We are not sure we have complete understanding of the Prime Minister's paragraph 5. Should his suggestion mean that both his cruisers and ours which would reach an age of twenty years before 1936, should there be any, may be kept active and not be replaced? We are in agreement if it is understood that the amount of rebuilding for replacement purposes before 1936 should be reduced by the same extent, but we are not sure that this is his meaning. If his meaning is that cruisers becoming over-age before 1936 are to be kept active and that in spite of this vessels should be built to replace such over-age cruisers, obviously, we do not agree to this because it would mean that Great Britain would simply have so much additional tonnage.

We are in agreement with the Prime Minister's paragraph 6.

In regard to his paragraph 7, it is hoped that he will reconsider his belief that the idea of minor vessels for police purposes should be kept to allow a margin within which his promises may be surpassed by his actions. Should the Prime Minister be able to agree to make even 20,000 tons of his replacements for 1936 in vessels of this type that would shorten to an equivalent amount our present building program and bring reduction from twenty-three to twenty-one 8-inch cruisers and lessen to a great extent the apparent inequality which he fears exists in the large cruiser class.

The Prime Minister's paragraph 8. It is understood that the necessity of carrying the Dominions with him restricts him practically in his promises.

In regard to his paragraph 9. The statement in his last communication that he is cutting the unit needs of Great Britain to a minimum is acceptable because we realize that he knows how far he can go better than we do. However, it may be pointed out to him that in his last communication no attempt was made to limit the British replacement tonnage and all inquiries in this matter have not yet been answered.

The Prime Minister's paragraph 10 is accepted.

We agree to the Prime Minister's paragraph 11 as we understand it.

In regard to his paragraph 12, his disappointment is understood. We have made an attempt to express both our sympathy and our understanding of his viewpoint that the necessities for peace require a large number of cruisers for Great Britain and we comprehend entirely that many of these vessels will in 1936 be near the age for scrapping.

In regard to subsection (b) of his paragraph 13, we are not in agreement with his sentiments at the present time but we are willing to go to a consultation ready to be convinced that we are mistaken if the facts convince us. We offer the suggestion to the Prime Minister that an examination of the data concerning the two fleets does not lead, necessarily, to the pessimistic conclusions drawn by him.

We meant to answer fully in our No. 217, subsection (a) of his paragraph 14. Subsection (b) has already been answered above.

We have already replied to the Prime Minister's paragraph 15.

In our opinion, the Prime Minister is mistaken in his paragraph 16. We believe that, as stated above, his view of the two cruiser fleets is based on misunderstanding of these fleets. In our opinion, we have no superiority of eight cruisers carrying 8-inch guns to be taken before his public under the guise of equality.

Gibson's suggestion is treated in the fifth section of your No. 242.[45]

We entirely concur in what the Prime Minister says in his paragraph 19 concerning the importance of his visit here, and we insist strongly for that reason upon the importance that definite agree-

---

[45] The Prime Minister's paragraphs 17 and 18.

ment with his Government should be reached in these conversations before his arrival. As this agreement is so certain to eliminate any real danger of failure at a later date, it will not only be the base upon which other beneficial consequences of his visit as he pictures them may be constructed but practically makes certain that no disappointment in the Naval Conference itself can take place which might as an anticlimax otherwise endanger the results of his visit. We can meet with equanimity the unavoidable difficulties which will arise in the Conference due to the participation of other nations if our two Governments have reached a clear agreement upon the questions under discussion. If an agreement of this nature has not been reached, it is conceivable that these outside complications might render the Conference futile and by so doing in that way practically nullify the benefits otherwise resulting from his conversation with the President and from his visit to this country.

The stress which we lay upon the importance of a clear agreement between us will not, we feel sure, be misunderstood by the Prime Minister. This point would seem to be proved by our experience in these conversations. If negotiators who have approached their work with the enthusiasm and purposes in common which have been found on both sides of these conversations can find the difficulty we have found in working out the details of only two nations in the problem of cruisers, the dangers of leaving to the uncertainties of a larger conference the problem of finding the solution of these questions is obvious.

In looking over the situation as it now stands, there remains only one point on which we need assurance; namely, the exact tonnage of the fifty British cruiser units on December 31, 1936, including replacements which you have suggested. If this information can be given us, and is not different from our expectations of 330,000 tons displacement (see our No. 217) we feel, as has already been stated above, that we could go into a Conference.

This telegram will be followed by two other messages, one with regard to the yardstick and the other (mentioned at the beginning of this telegram) summarizing the extent of agreement with the Prime Minister which we feel we have reached.

STIMSON

---

500.A15a3/130 : Telegram

*The Secretary of State to the Ambassador in Great Britain (Dawes)*

[Paraphrase]

WASHINGTON, August 28, 1929—7 p. m.

225. Relative to your telegram No. 242, August 24, 2 p. m. The following review of our points of agreement is sent to you in an

endeavor to meet the whole situation. The phraseology of some of these has been slightly changed to meet our general discussions, with the addition of certain clauses which may, prior to the general Conference, cover the whole of the questions if Mr. MacDonald agrees. This memorandum is in order that our entire discussion may be simplified.

(1) The discussions are the result of the general pact renouncing war and of the consequent realignment of national attitudes to the position that the use of armaments is not permitted in the relations of nations with each other as an instrument of national policy; the starting point of agreement, therefore, must be taken to be that pact.

(2) Parity in combatant strength of our respective navies is agreed between ourselves.

(3) The principle that this parity shall be by categories, that is, submarines, destroyers, cruisers, aircraft carriers and capital ships, is agreed between ourselves.

(4) It is agreed that the date when parity shall be arrived at between our fleets will be considered December 31, 1936.

(5) The ratio of capital ships and aircraft carriers having been fixed to that date by the Washington Treaty, the provisions of that treaty shall not be disturbed by us, except that its replacement programs shall be reconsidered by us with a view to diminishing the amount of construction for replacement which the treaty implies.

(6) The principle of total abolition of submarines in international warfare is agreed upon, but it is realized that the consent of other nations to this proposal may be impossible to obtain.

(7) The limitation of future construction of destroyers and submarines and the reduction of their present aggregate tonnages is agreed upon. We agree to arrive at parity on December 31, 1936, as computed in standard tonnage in each of these two categories, by the construction required by either nation to reach parity, by obsolescence or by scrapping. As Great Britain retains tonnages beyond parity in the cruiser category, the United States may retain destroyers and submarines, temporarily in excess of the point of parity agreed upon and after the age of obsolescence during such parity prior to 1936.

(8) We agree to adopt a yardstick for cruisers which shall measure the comparative value of vessels in this category. The basis for this yardstick shall be the principle that the standard will be taken to be a new 8-inch gun, 10,000 standard ton cruiser, and that consideration of age, gun factor and displacement shall determine the relative comparative strength of inferior cruisers. Inasmuch as other elements are relative to the facts as above mentioned, no others are to be considered.

(9) A request for the formulation for submission to the Conference of the view of the yardstick to be applied under the prin-

ciples set out in paragraph (8) above shall be requested of each Government signatory to the Washington Treaty.

(10) Thirteen years for submarines, sixteen years for destroyers, twenty years for cruisers shall be the scrapping age of ships. Upon reaching scrapping age ships are forthwith to be scrapped except that as stated in paragraph (7) above and except that ships may be retained beyond the scrapping age as an alternative to permitted replacements.

(11) A reduction of the British cruiser strength shall be made by December 31, 1936, to fifty units whose total displacement shall not exceed a standard tonnage of 330,000. Fifteen of these fifty units shall be 8-inch cruisers with an aggregate standard tonnage of 146,800. There shall be four 7.5-inch gun cruisers, with an aggregate tonnage of 39,426, and there shall be thirty-one 6-inch gun cruisers with an aggregate tonnage of 143,774, of which, prior to 1936, not more than seven armed with 6-inch guns are to be constructed.

(12) Parity with the British cruiser strength shall be attained for the United States cruiser strength as above stated, taking into consideration the effect that the elements of age, displacement and guns as evaluated by the yardstick will have upon both navies.

(13) The Conference will give consideration to the restricting of new cruiser construction to the peace time police cruiser type of slow speed and limited armament.

(14) A provision will be contained in any agreement to be arrived at during the Conference that in the event of the inauguration by any nonsignatory power of a menacing building program, it will be open to reconsideration by any of the parties.

(15) The British Government shall call a Conference of the five powers to meet early in December 1929 in London.

(16) That this Conference will become the Conference which the Washington Treaty provides shall be called in 1931, will be proposed to the other naval powers signatory to the Washington Treaty.

STIMSON

---

500.A15a3/130 : Telegram

*The Secretary of State to the Ambassador in Great Britain (Dawes)*

[Paraphrase]

WASHINGTON, August 28, 1929—9 p. m.

226. Reference your telegram No. 242, August 24, 2 p. m. Although we have made clear the elements which we consider should enter into the yardstick and consequently its general nature, it has not yet been produced for the Prime Minister's inspection nor has an immediate agreement on such a yardstick been suggested. The preliminary conversations between the two countries should, we

consider, be limited to this.  For Great Britain and the United States to try actually to agree upon the details of such a yardstick we consider would be unwise at the moment.  The following are our reasons for this:

(1) The naval experts of the two countries may have diverging opinions, and, since complicated formulae and considerations are involved in the yardstick, we may become involved in prolonged and highly technical mathematical discussions.

(2) The only point in the conversations between the two countries directly affecting interests of other countries is the yardstick, and without keeping them informed it would hardly be fair to agree upon it.  In response to inquiries, their representatives have been told by us that as soon as the yardstick was given to anyone it would be given to them.

(3) The yardstick would inevitably become public should we do this, and public discussion and undoubtedly violent press controversy would also inevitably arise which would becloud all of the much more important matters upon which we have already reached an agreement and would render far more difficult a final agreement in the Conference subsequently to be held.  Therefore, it is sincerely hoped that the Prime Minister will be agreeable not to insist upon his request for the mathematical yardstick formulae, but to defer until the Conference the consideration of this matter.  It is our desire, however, to be absolutely frank and to keep the Prime Minister fully informed. The results of our yardstick as applied to each fleet are therefore given to him as follows: A discount of about 65,000 tons from the 330,000 ton, fifty-ship British fleet as of the 31st of December, 1936, is given by the yardstick and from the contemplated 300,000 ton American fleet which contains ten *Omahas* and twenty-three 8-inch, 10,000 ton units, the discount is similarly about 23,000 tons, or in other words this will permit the shortening by at least one 8-inch, 10,000 ton ship of the United States program.

Stimson

---

500.A15a3/145 : Telegram

*The Ambassador in Great Britain (Dawes) to the Secretary of State*

[Paraphrase]

London, August 30, 1929—noon.
[Received 4:33 p. m.[46]]

252. Late last evening, on delivering your No. 225, August 28, 7 p. m., I had a conversation with the Prime Minister.

He evidently intends to agree with your statements and after his return from Geneva will answer.  All of the figures will be checked

---

[46] Telegram in three sections.

up by the Admiralty. According to his statement, the figure of 330,000 tons is certain.

As you assume in your No. 225 that the memorandum of agreement incorporated in it may cover, if the Prime Minister agrees, the whole ground prior to the Conference itself, I urge strongly that the following changes should be made in its present form: We should omit paragraphs 8 and 9; a new paragraph 8 should be made of paragraph 11; new paragraph 9 should be formed by paragraph 12, omitting the words "by the yardstick" in this paragraph; paragraph 10 remains paragraph 10; new paragraphs 11, 12, 13, and 14 are formed of 13, 14, 15, and 16.

I advance the following reasons:

This memorandum concerning what constitutes the preliminary agreement between the United States and Great Britain will be given to the public at a future date but before the meeting of the Conference. It will become known to all members of the Conference and will publicly become known to the press during the negotiations even if its publicity should be delayed until the opening of the Conference. You are directing the general attention of the public in paragraphs 8 and 9 of your telegram in a most prominent way to the possibility of disagreement concerning a method of procedure that is a probability only. In this way a technical naval question about very few ships compared to the total number involved in the negotiations is magnified and thrust upon the center of the stage as far as public opinion is concerned, thereby lending weight to an impression that before agreement can be reached, the yardstick must be found.

If the memorandum is not changed, the press, since it finds most news value in prospective controversies, will devote little space to the agreements contained in the memorandum which are of great importance and which would have the greatest public effect if they should be made public alone. If the public has been persuaded by the press to believe that any agreement resulting from the Conference will be inadequate from a technical point of view unless a yardstick can be agreed upon and can be so persuaded in the beginning of the agreement, the effect will be most unfortunate on the later ratification of any compromise settlement agreed upon. In this, I am only paraphrasing your No. 226, August 28, 9 p. m., which contains an entirely sound argument by which you decided that it would not be safe to allow even Great Britain and the United States, to say nothing of the other powers, to introduce a discussion of the yardstick at this stage of the proceedings. If it is unwise for the United States and Great Britain to attempt to introduce an actual discussion as to the details of the yardstick at this late stage of the negotiations between two parties who are both so anxious to agree, the question as to when such a discussion will become wise naturally arises. To me the answer appears obvious—only when we have discussed questions with all of the other naval powers in the same manner we have with Great Britain and have reduced the technical differences between us and them to the simplest form of statement as we have now with the differences of this sort between Great Britain and the United States. We must keep the ultimate reactions of the public constantly in view in every stage of these negotiations. The difficult technical controversy will become of minor importance in the minds of the public if they can be made to realize the relatively small amount of technical differences.

If paragraphs 8 and 9 are eliminated, the status of the present agreement between Great Britain and ourselves concerning the yardstick will not be changed as it will be covered by paragraph 12, even if the words "by the yardstick" are eliminated from it.

Paragraphs 8 and 9 are agreed by the Prime Minister as defining the attitudes of Great Britain and the United States to be taken toward the yardstick when the Conference considers this matter. This is only an outline of a procedure for approaching this problem for our two countries which seems at the present time the most reasonable course and unquestionably will be followed; but I desire to emphasize the point that when this document or another in its place which becomes later on the ultimate form of the preliminary agreement between the United States and Great Britain is made public, it should not give the public an impression of undue importance of this controversy over a yardstick as does this memorandum. It is possible that neglect of this matter might constitute an error that would be fatal. All newspaper writers on the subject of these naval negotiations are invited by the present statement to rehash immediately their articles concerning the yardstick and the idea of cynics will be that these difficulties are inherent in the whole problem instead of only a minor part of this problem. In my opinion, the importance of the yardstick should be recognized as also the probability that its use will be necessary, but we should not forget that long and complicated negotiations are sometimes quickly brought to successful conclusion near the time of final settlement by compromises. There is a distinct possibility that discussion between the different navies of the yardstick may result in a compromise concerning it and we might then see instead of the settlement fitted to the yardstick, the yardstick drawn up to fit the settlement. The unimportance of a controversy can be realized by the public although it does not understand the question. The professional arguments of two doctors upon the correct course of medical procedure to follow may not be understandable to the man in the street, but the relative importance of this argument if it affects the life of the patient can easily be undersood when he knows whether it concerns a light case of measles or a bad case of smallpox. There is, in my opinion, no way more likely to create everywhere the false impression that these small technical controversies we are now discussing are a severe case of smallpox rather than a light case of measles, as they are in fact, than to exploit them as has been done in your No. 225, paragraphs 8 and 9.

As stated in your No. 225 [*226*], a violent controversy would undoubtedly arise in the press which would becloud all of the matters of vastly greater importance upon which agreement has already been reached and would render much more difficult a final agreement in the Conference. This was fully discussed with the Prime Minister last evening and he raised no objection.

DAWES

---

500.A15a3/146 : Telegram

*The Ambassador in Great Britain (Dawes) to the Secretary of State*

LONDON, August 31, 1929—10 a. m.
[Received August 31—9 a. m.[47]]

254. The following letter was received at the Embassy at 11:20 last night:

"August 30th, 1929.

My dear General Dawes: I am enclosing you herewith my comments[48] upon the document, which I repeat is a very valuable one, presented to me last night in the form of a draft agreement.

We are all determined to bring something out of these conversations and to do it by the beginning of next week. But in our desire to do so we may make the mistake of committing ourselves to general statements which cover unsolved problems that when we face them may wreck the further stages of our agreements. That is why those of us who met today to consider the agreement felt that it was necessary to press for a little more definiteness regarding the parity program of the United States. We cannot afford to go into the Five-Power Conference with major difficulties between ourselves unsettled. If the figures could be supplied from your side in the same measure of detail as you have inserted for us in your paragraph 11 I would not suggest that either paragraph 11 or 12 would at the moment be published. It would be an agreement between ourselves which would guide us in our action at the Five-Power Conference. Only if we have those figures in our possession can we bring the persuasion and the pressure to bear upon the other powers which we must do if the Conference is to be a real success from the point of view of disarmament. If the President could meet us on this and the other points, we could still close not later than Monday morning.

I am very sorry about the 9,000 tons which I have had to add to the 330,000 which has been the hypothetical figure appearing in your notes.

[47] Telegram in two sections.
[48] See telegram No. 255, *infra*.

I strove hard to hold it undisturbed and we worked out tonnages and units in every possible way to enable us to accept it without any alteration. The hard unfortunate thing, however, is as I have stated in the note accompanying this—there is not a single naval power building, on the same lines you have assumed to be possible, 6-inch cruisers standard tonnage.

You will recognize that I am, once again, not against you at all, but against the rest of the world minus you. I need only add that the reason why I did not give you tonnage before was that my last note was written from Lossiemouth where I could not get the advice that was necessary nor indeed the figures themselves. If we can be met now on this note I can agree without any further reference to anybody.

I should like to explain a little more than has been done in the accompanying note what has been the result of our very thorough examination of the American proposal that for our fifteen 8-inch cruisers you should have twenty-three. The ratio 5–5–3.5 which Japan asks for would mean that in relation to the twenty-three Japan could build sixteen which would be one of a superiority over us. If you fixed your 8-inch cruisers at twenty, the ratio would mean that Japan could build fourteen. I am perfectly certain that the Dominions would reject any agreement upon that basis. If on the other hand you made it eighteen for you, Japan could build 12.6 which would be thirteen. In order to get a settlement, we might get Japan to accept twelve and to that we would agree. Even supposing we got Japan to be content with a cruiser ratio of 5–5–3, on an American strength of twenty-three that would mean a Japanese building of fourteen—at least two more than there is any chance of our getting our dominions to agree to.

One very important result of an agreement which would enable Japan and ourselves to fix our actual units at twelve and fifteen is that neither of our countries until replacement is necessary would have to build any more 8-inch cruisers.

I should be glad if you would treat this letter as for the information of the American Government only.

I am, yours very sincerely, J. Ramsay MacDonald."

DAWES

---

500.A15a3/148 : Telegram

*The Ambassador in Great Britain (Dawes) to the Secretary of State*

LONDON, August 31, 1929—11 a. m.
[Received 3 : 18 p. m.[49]]

255. Following are the Prime Minister's comments mentioned in the first sentence of his letter quoted in my 254, August 31, 10 a. m.

"August 30, 1929.

My dear General Dawes: I have had a very prolonged discussion today on the three notes you left me last night and regret exceedingly that I found I could not carry out the promise I made to you to let you have my report by about tea time. As a matter of fact, some

---

[49] Telegram in three sections.

extraordinarily difficult points are involved in the draft of the memorandum of agreement. I had better go through it paragraph by paragraph:

Paragraph 5. I agree.

Paragraph 6. I agree; though I think we might use the word 'difficult' instead of 'impossible'.

Paragraph 7. I agree.

Paragraph 8. You told me last night that you were to urge that that should go out for the purpose of eliminating from the memorandum all references to a yardstick. If the President agrees to that, I shall agree. If he does not and this paragraph is retained, I agree.

Paragraph 9. I hope that this paragraph in any event will be deleted. If it remains in, it will mean that any agreement we may come to will run the risk of being sometimes upset by a yardstick constructed primarily not to meet our mutual requirements but requirements of a nature so different from ours as to call for a totally different yardstick.

Paragraph 10. We agree, but the wording would be influenced by paragraph 11 which I propose to alter as underneath. If the alteration were agreed to, the following words would require to be added to paragraph 10 'and paragraph 11 below' because we are contemplating some premature scrapping in order to make this agreement easier to come to.

Paragraph 11. This paragraph, read with your accompanying, assumes that the new 6-inch cruisers will be of a standard tonnage of 4,000 each. A consideration of this point has been one of the causes of the prolonged examination I have had to give to your note. I find that today no naval power is building a 4,000 standard ton, 6-inch cruiser and therefore unless we could get other powers to use a percentage of the tonnage of 6-inch cruiser for the construction of 4,000 ton cruiser it would be impossible for us to build such a ship.

In one of the notes accompanying the draft agreement you assume that in 1936 we shall still have our four ships of the *Hawkins* type in commission. As you will remember I have repeatedly said that I was willing to scrap these prematurely in order that this problem of distribution of tonnage within the cruiser category might be simplified.

I repeat that I am willing to include that scrapping in the provisions of this agreement. The position regarding the provisions of paragraph 11, therefore, is as follows:

I agree to fifty units in the category; but as you have assumed a 4,000 tonnage for each 6-inch cruiser to be built, and [*which?*] I find to be quite impracticable, your 330,000 maximum requires to be slightly expanded. We have worked at this very carefully with the determination to reduce it to its very minimum but it cannot be brought below 339,000.

As regards the fifteen 8-inch units, I agree.

As regards the four 7.5-gun cruisers, they will have disappeared before the end of 1936. As regards the remainder of the paragraph, it would then be worded as follows 'of the balance of thirty-five, fourteen will be 6-inch replacement construction aggregating 91,000 tons, and twenty-one will be existing older 6-inch cruisers aggregating 101,200 tons. The following ships have been scrapped in the interval, i. e., before December 31st, 1936. *Hawkins* class aggregating 39,400 tons. Eighteen old, 6-inch cruisers aggregating 76,200 tons, the total tonnage scrapped being 115,600 showing a net reduction of 24,600 tons.'

Paragraph 12. On several occasions this has also been the subject of very prolonged consideration. Were I to agree to it as it is drafted it would mean that we should go into the Five-Power Conference with no agreed standard of American strength and I think you will agree that that would place our representatives in a very awkward position. It might indeed not only render the Five-Power Conference abortive but would throw our two countries back into a state of having no agreement at all. Supposing for instance you found that you could not reduce your 8-inch units below twenty-three and that one or other of the other Governments insisted upon using that figure for the purpose of calculating what number of units it could build upon a ratio agreed to. The British Government might then be faced with a situation which meant that in terms of ships it would have to accept not the ratio agreed to but equality, then we should have to increase our fifteen and that in turn would upset your twenty-three and with that would go the whole of our agreement. We have tried every way we could conceive of getting round the difficulty and we have been unable to find one. I would therefore urge you to make this paragraph a definite statement of your conception of parity in units. If we cannot come to an agreement upon this now it only means that we postpone it and face failure in a few months. In the note commenting upon the yardstick you come to the conclusion that the yardstick on certain figures permits the shortening of the American program by at least one 8-inch ship of ten thousand tons. If I have followed the figures discussed in the latest memorandum which replies in detail to my last note, the difference between us even on your own calculation is practically equal to two 8-inch cruisers, bringing your figure of twenty-three down to twenty-one. In addition to that in the figures upon which you base your calculation is included the group of four *Hawkins* bearing a specially high valuation—in your own words (Department will realize this is taken from Embassy's paraphrase) used in the note in front of me August 29th. 'We are of the opinion that the *Hawkins* cruisers would remain well within comparative range of four cruisers of the 8-inch type' or again a few lines earlier in the same paragraph 'Our advisers look upon the four cruisers of the *Hawkins* type of 40,000 tons as substantially comparable to four 8-inch cruisers of the 10,000 type'.

As I say we propose to scrap these and to replace them by 6-inch vessels the tonnage of which is included in our 339,000 figure.

Paragraph 13. This paragraph commits us to considering that question of the police cruiser. I would go further and say that I should consider it with great sincerity but it must be understood that tonnage could not be used for this unless we could get an agreement from the Five-Power Conference. In that consideration there would have to be taken into account the points mentioned in my last note under this heading.

Paragraphs 14, 15, and 16. I agree.

I am sorry for the delay, but it could not be helped.

Yours very sincerely, J. Ramsay MacDonald."

DAWES

500.A15a3/149 : Telegram

*The Ambassador in Great Britain (Dawes) to the Secretary of State*

[Paraphrase]

LONDON, August 31, 1929—1 p. m.
[Received 4:30 p. m.]

256. Reference my telegram of August 31, 10 a. m., No. 254, which relates to the apprehension on the part of MacDonald, as expressed in his note of yesterday, of the difficulty of satisfying public opinion in Great Britain should 70 percent of the number of United States large cruisers be demanded by Japan. I long ago explained to Matsudaira that this would some time become embarrassing to the British Prime Minister. Consequently Matsudaira has been helpfully working with his Government and he said before he left for Geneva that he hoped that as they were very anxious to do so they would be able to satisfy Great Britain in this matter. MacDonald has desired that I keep the Japanese Ambassador informed until the letter sent to you in my telegram No. 255 of August 31, 11 a. m., and upon his own initiative, in anticipation of a later discussion of the matter, the Japanese Ambassador has been working in this useful way.

DAWES

---

500.A15a3/150 : Telegram

*The Secretary of State to the Ambassador in Great Britain (Dawes)*

[Paraphrase]

WASHINGTON, September 3, 1929—5 p. m.

237. Your No. 254, August 31, 10 a. m., and succeeding telegrams relating to naval disarmament proposals.

1. In view of the revolutionary changes which are involved in the new proposals of the Prime Minister, we shall need to give reconsideration to the entire situation.

2. Mr. MacDonald's proposal to scrap *Hawkins* class will be of great help in simplifying the problem, especially in presentation of it to the public. But his other proposals for the increase of British total tonnage and for the limitation of our 8-inch construction, the type to which our Navy is now committed, present a problem which to us frankly seems extremely difficult if not insoluble.

3. Mr. MacDonald thus abandons his previous proposal of seven new replacement, 6-inch ships and now proposes replacement program of fourteen new, 6,500 ton, 6-inch ships. By introduction of these fourteen new ships our previous discounts for age factor are entirely

upset and discount to the British fleet is greatly diminished, reducing amount of allowable disparity between displacement tonnage of the two fleets. In place of the figures given in paragraph 3 of our 226, August 28, 9 p. m., for the British discount of 65,000 tons for a fifty-ship, 330,000 ton fleet we would now have a discount of only 51,000 tons for a 339,000 ton fleet whereby an evaluated British tonnage of about 287,866 tons instead of about 275,000 tons is left. The difference, therefore, between the American and British fleets after the application of the yardstick would be even greater than the mere 9,000 tons which has been added in their displacement tonnage to the difference.

4. His proposals to cut down the American fleet of large cruisers by five units present even greater difficulties. The American fleet by this proposal would be given a total of only twenty-eight units as against fifty units for the British fleet; a total of 250,000 displacement tons for the American fleet as against a total of 339,000 displacement tons for the British fleet or a disparity amounting to 90,000 displacement tons. To present anything approaching this to our public and Congress would be quite hopeless. The difficulties arising out of the desires of Japan and the attitude of the Dominions we recognize but on our side it is necessary for the Prime Minister to remember that the American policy of a 10,000 ton cruiser fleet has grown out of American needs for cruising radius which are quite as peremptory as the British peace time needs for police work which was presented so forcibly by the Prime Minister and which has been cheerfully recognized by us. The very foundation of this American large cruiser policy is cut by his present proposal.

5. He can see from this that he has confronted us with proposals which if they are capable of solution can only be solved after a thorough consultation with our Naval General Board and the basis of these negotiations entirely reconsidered. A week at least will be consumed for this and we feel that it is out of the question for us to formulate any reply which the Prime Minister can make the basis of a statement at Geneva. This cable is being sent hurriedly on account of his expressed desire to make such a statement concerning this. It is hoped that under the present conditions no statement will be made. Any statement which may lead to false hopes and baseless surmises in the press, we feel, will make even more difficult our difficulties in the ultimate Conference. This matter will be taken up by us with our Naval Board with the same earnest desire for an eventual agreement which has actuated us throughout but in all frankness the difficulties seem greater today than they have for a long time.

Stimson

500.A15a3/154 : Telegram

*The Ambassador in Great Britain (Dawes) to the Secretary of State*

[Paraphrase]

LONDON, September 4, 1929—4 p. m.
[Received September 4—12 : 50 p. m.]

262. Reference is made to my telegram of August 31, 1 p. m., No. 256, and for your information. The Japanese Ambassador told me confidentially that in relation to the ratio of large cruisers their efforts to satisfy Great Britain may involve, when the time comes, a proposal to arm a limited number of their smaller cruisers with 8-inch guns in order that an increase in the number of large cruisers may be avoided to that extent.

I have also learned, in a confidential manner from the French Ambassador, that disturbing information came to them some time ago from the British Admiralty that a settlement might be reached between the United States, Great Britain, and Japan, independently of other naval powers. This situation was taken care of in the President's statement from Washington, but as an evidence of the attitude of the British Admiralty it is interesting. The contents of your telegram of September 3, 5 p. m., No. 237, will be communicated to the Prime Minister when he returns from Geneva.

DAWES

---

500.A15a3/158 : Telegram

*The Ambassador in Great Britain (Dawes) to the Secretary of State*

[Paraphrase]

LONDON, September 6, 1929—3 p. m.
[Received 3 : 14 p. m.]

263. This morning the Prime Minister arrived from Geneva and I transmitted to him your telegram of September 3, No. 237.

He summarized for me what he had learned at Geneva. Matsudaira had told him that the application of the Japanese ratio to the number of American large cruisers was desired by Japan. The point I telegraphed to you in my telegram of September 4, No. 262, was not mentioned to MacDonald by Matsudaira. I was then informed by the Prime Minister that the British Admiralty seemed willing that Japan should have twelve large cruisers in relation to Great Britain's fifteen.

Briand[50] had conversed with the Prime Minister and had been informed by him fully of the progress of the Anglo-American negotiations, and the difficulties had been frankly explained to him. Briand had been asked for his assistance; and later MacDonald asked

[50] Aristide Briand, French Minister of Foreign Affairs.

Beneš,[51] as well, to impress the necessity of French cooperation upon Briand. His conversation with Briand had been most helpful he felt.

The Anglo-American naval negotiations, he said, appeared to be uppermost in the minds of all those whom he had seen at Geneva; the results of disagreement would be as demoralizing as success would be beneficial, inasmuch as negotiations seem to be assuming such importance in the public interest in all powers. The determination to agree was again reiterated by MacDonald. In discussing his difficulties some reaction in the Dominions, particularly Australia and Canada, was mentioned. Australia possessed navy yards, he said, and it might object to a British unified naval command and propose construction in its own yards on its own account, if not satisfactory.

The Prime Minister stated in connection with Matsudaira that he had again told the Japanese Ambassador that he could consider as having come from him those statements which came from me.

DAWES

500.A15a3/162 : Telegram

*The Ambassador in Great Britain (Dawes) to the Secretary of State*

LONDON, September 10, 1929—noon.
[Received 3:30 p. m.[52]]

266. Following is text of letter referred to in my 265.[53]

"September 9th.

My dear General Dawes: Although the confidential memorandum which you handed to me last Friday [54] is of the nature of an interim note and although it states that my last note to you will have to be considered by the Navy General Board, I send you this in order that there may be no confusion as to how we stand. If you look back at the various notes I have sent you I think you will agree that the position admits of no doubt but it might be convenient for the President to have a summary in a very definite form of what I have proposed.

1. Paragraphs 2 and 3 of the confidential memorandum of Friday are not quite clear, particularly where it is stated that 'he now abandons his previous proposal of seven new replacement, 6-inch ships and proposes a replacement program of fourteen new, 6,500 ton, 6-inch ships.' This is a misapprehension and the best way to remove it is to come back upon precise figures.

I have agreed to a standard number of fifty cruisers in 1936 and this is how that number is reached: The present strength of the British cruiser fleet built and building, but for the purposes of 1936

[51] Eduard Beneš, Czechoslovak Minister of Foreign Affairs, and member of the Council of the League of Nations.
[52] Telegram in two sections.
[53] Not printed.
[54] See telegram No. 237, September 3, 5 p. m., to the Ambassador in Great Britain, p. 217.

assumed to be built, is 58. Between now and 1936 fifteen of these will disappear on account of age, reducing us to forty-three. I have proposed to scrap the four *Hawkins* group bringing us down to thirty-nine. I explained to you in a previous note that immediately after 1936, say between 1936 and 1940, cruisers were to fall out in blocks and that as I could not accept a naval holiday, because it was impracticable from the point of view of employment of labor, I proposed to scrap prematurely a number of these aged cruisers solely in order to stabilize average building. I have now fixed that number to be scrapped previous to 1936 at three. That reduces us to thirty-six. Now I propose to build between now and 1936 fourteen by way of replacement and that brings us to the fifty standard. In other words, taken as a whole, the proposal now before President Hoover is that by the 31st of December, 1936, the British cruiser fleet will be fifty and no more. Should any be in the process of building at that date, they will only be sufficient to keep the standard at fifty and no more in succeeding years.

2. As regards the tonnage and the possibility of including in the fourteen which are proposed to be built ships of about 4,500 tons, I should like the President to consider this. In 1936 we shall have thirty-five 6-inch cruisers, fourteen of which will be replacement ships built between now and then of an average of 6,500 tons each; twenty-one will be older ships; two of the twenty-one are the *Emerald* and the *Enterprise* and the remaining nineteen are all of our C and D class of an average of slightly over 4,500 tons each. Therefore over half of the 6-inch group will be 4,500 ton ships. When we come to replace, after say about 1935, we shall have to face the agreement which I am willing to make that the total of 339,000 tons will not be exceeded assuming that there is no change in the pacific conditions of the world.

This, I hope, will enable the President to visualize the character of the total group and show him how impossible it is for me to promise a smaller tonnage in the ships to be built within next seven years.

3. I had hoped that by extending the age of our cruisers I might be able to meet the President still further but I am informed that all the calculations given above assume that a cruiser is not scrapped until it has been built for two years so that we are now working upon the maximum proposed by you during our conversations.

4. I wonder if I might venture to make a suggestion to you regarding the numbers of 8-inch ships which you say you are bound to build? The conversation which I had at Geneva, and which I reported to you on Friday, is, I am sure you will agree, a very serious obstacle in the way of a superiority of as much as eight in your program. (See my 263, September 6, 3 p. m., first paragraph.) If insisted upon I am unable to see any way out of the deadlock. I notice, however, that in the memorandum the very reasonable point is made that you must have ships capable of operating within a large radius.

Could you not build ships that would satisfy the radius requirement and at the same time get me out of my difficulties in relation to other powers; for instance, would it be feasible for you to build say five 10,000 ton cruisers carrying 6-inch guns that would enable you to have the eighteen 8-inch cruisers, which I understood originally was satisfactory to you, and at the same time enable you to use effectively the tonnage which you say you require in order to enable you to satisfy your people that you have secured parity with us?   As I understand it the tonnage position will then be that we have 339,000 and you have 300,000 but for your shortage in tonnage you have a superiority of three 8-inch cruisers and possess five other 10,000 ton ships.

5. These proposals which I am making really touch bottom and expose me to risks which only the cooperative good will of other nations and even continued peace of the world will justify me in taking.  They are really in the nature of an experiment in peace making and will have to be accompanied by two conditions:

> (a) That nothing is done at the Five-Power Conference and no failure experienced there which will upset the basis of security and responsibility embodied in the program.  That means that the final ratification of our agreement would be after the Conference and not before it.
>
> (b) That we should agree to examine the situation in 1935 and see whether the experiment has been justified and to continue or otherwise the agreement beyond the end of 1936.

In this connection we should just follow the precedent of the Washington Agreement of 1922.

Very sincerely yours, J. Ramsay MacDonald."

DAWES

---

500.A15a3/162 : Telegram

*The Secretary of State to the Ambassador in Great Britain (Dawes)*

WASHINGTON, September 11, 1929—6 p. m.

242. Your 266. For Prime Minister.

1. We have now spent the past week in most earnest consideration of the Prime Minister's proposed British cruiser fleet of 339,000 displacement tons comprising 15 large 8-inch cruisers—146,000 tons; 14 new replacement cruisers—91,000 tons, and 21 of the old 6-inch cruisers, 101,000 tons, which program includes scrapping the four *Hawkins* class.

2. Our Naval Board reports to us this morning that in an endeavor to meet the British proposals just as closely as they can they will for this purpose accept as representing parity with such a program, after taking into account both the age and gun factors, an American fleet comprising 21 8-inch 10,000 ton cruisers—that is 210,000 tons; 10 of the *Omaha* class—70,000 tons; and 5 new cruisers of about 7,000 tons 6-inch class—about 35,000 tons, making a total of about 315,000 displacement tons.

3. We are repeating separately the memorandum of our 225 of the points of agreement in which we have deleted the 8th and 9th paragraphs as suggested by you and we have changed the wording of the new paragraphs 8 and 9 to coincide with the above.  We have purposely left out mentioning the total number of British and American ships in these paragraphs 8 and 9 as it seems to us it would

create less discussion and allow larger liberty of action by placing the whole question on a tonnage basis subject to the yardstick rather than upon the number of ships.

We have also simplified the memorandum by adding the words "scrapping, obsolescence and construction" to paragraph fourth and deleting the same words from paragraph seventh.

4. We have also reconstructed the new eleventh paragraph from the old thirteenth.

5. We suggest that the memorandum can be given to the other powers in issuing the call for conference and given to the public at the same time but that the contents of this and other cables should be held confidential. We expect to be consulted as to form of call for conference and as to time and form of giving publicity to memorandum.

STIMSON

---

500.A15a3/162 : Telegram

*The Secretary of State to the Ambassador in Great Britain (Dawes)*

WASHINGTON, September 11, 1929—7 p. m.

243. You will please communicate the following to the Prime Minister:

In respect to our cablegram 242 the President trusts that the Prime Minister will realize the very great advantage from the President's point of view in planning an agreement which will carry the enthusiastic and cordial support of our naval board. He understands that the Prime Minister is in exactly the same position with the Admiralty.

The final result of our cable 242 is that the Prime Minister's technical experts and ours are apart on only one point and on that point are not far apart. This particular point is represented by the question as to whether three of the American cruisers are to be of the 8-inch 10,000 ton type or whether there is to be a substitution for them of say four cruisers of the 6-inch gun type.

Or, in the more recent view of the Prime Minister, your 266, four, the question as to whether these three cruisers of 10,000 tons are to have 8-inch guns or 6-inch guns mounted on them.

The Prime Minister will note that neither we nor our Naval Board have suggested any alteration in the Prime Minister's proposal for the British fleet so that altogether out of the perfected set-up covering in all categories perhaps 1,200,000 tons in each of our respective fleets, we are down to this small difference.

The President thinks that when we consider all these things and realize that the items we are discussing are so small a percentage of our total difficulties and that we are developing the greatest problem in statesmanship of our times; and when we realize how strongly the people behind us desire disarmament and peace, he feels sure that we could between the two governments compromise these small differences.

The President earnestly wishes Mr. MacDonald to visit the United States.

STIMSON

500.A15a3/162 : Telegram

## The Secretary of State to the Ambassador in Great Britain (Dawes)

WASHINGTON, September 11, 1929—8 p. m.

244. The following principles are set down upon which the Government of the United States and His Majesty's Government propose, as relating to their own governments, to enter upon a conference of the principal naval powers for the limitation and reduction of naval armament.

First: These negotiations are the result of the general pact for the renunciation of war, and the consequent realignment of national attitudes to the position that armament may not be used as an instrument of national policy in the relations of nations with each other; therefore, that pact must be taken as the starting point of agreement.

Second: We agree on parity in combatant strength of the respective navies.

Third: We agree that this parity shall be separately by categories, of capital ships, aircraft carriers, destroyers, cruisers, and submarines.

Fourth: We agree that we shall consider December 31, 1936, as the date on which parity shall be reached between our two fleets either by scrapping, obsolescence or construction as the two navies may require.

Fifth: The Washington Treaty having fixed the ratio of capital ships and aircraft carriers to that date, we shall not disturb the provisions of that treaty except that we shall reconsider its replacement programs with view of diminishing the amount of replacement construction implied under that treaty.

Sixth: The scrapping age of ships is to be as to cruisers, twenty years, as to destroyers, sixteen years, and as to submarines, thirteen years. Ships are to be scrapped forthwith on reaching scrapping age, except that ships may be retained beyond scrapping age as an alternative to permitted replacements and except as stated in the eighth paragraph.

Seventh: As to submarines we agree to the principle of total abolition in international war but we realize that it may be difficult to secure the consent of other nations to this proposal.

Eighth: We agree upon reduction of the present aggregate tonnages of destroyers and submarines and the limitation of future construction. The United States may retain destroyers and submarines temporarily in excess of the point of parity agreed upon and after the age of obsolescence during such period prior to 1936 as Great Britain retains tonnages beyond parity in the cruiser category.

Ninth: The British cruiser strength shall be reduced to a maximum of a total displacement of 339,000 standard tons of which not to exceed 15 ships may be 10,000 ton or less with 8-inch guns.

Tenth: The United States cruiser strength shall be brought to parity with British cruiser strength as above stated taking into account in both navies the elements of displacement, age and guns, but the United States shall have not to exceed 21 of the 10,000 ton ships with 8-inch guns.

Eleventh: The standard of cruiser strength stated in paragraphs ninth and tenth are maximums which both governments desire to reduce at the conference, and it is agreed that earnest consideration will be given before and during the conference to methods by which further reduction can be accomplished, including consideration of confining a part of cruiser construction by both nations to peace type police cruisers of limited armament and speed.

Twelfth: Any agreement to be reached at the conference is to contain a provision that it is open to reconsideration by any of the parties in the event of the inauguration of a menacing building program by any non-signatory power.

Thirteenth: A conference of the five powers is to be called by the British Government to take place in London early in December 1929.

Fourteenth: It will be proposed to the other naval powers signatory to the Washington Treaty that this conference become the conference provided under the Washington Treaty to be called in 1931.

STIMSON

500.A15a3/162 : Telegram

*The Secretary of State to the Ambassador in Great Britain (Dawes)*

WASHINGTON, September 12, 1929—5 p. m.

245. The last sentence of our 243 [55] may be capable of misinterpretation. It is not our conception that the Prime Minister come over to discuss and try to end the points of difference between our naval board and your [*his?*] Admiralty which are the subject of our 243. These points of difference can best be dealt with, we think, at the conference. We think it would simply cloud the Prime Minister's visit if it were to be turned into a technical conference.

STIMSON

500.A15a3/168 : Telegram

*The Ambassador in Great Britain (Dawes) to the Secretary of State*

[Paraphrase]

LONDON, September 13, 1929—5. p. m.
[Received September 13—3 : 35 p. m.]

268. Last night your telegrams of September 11, Nos. 242, 243 and 244, were delivered to the Prime Minister. Entire satisfaction was

[55] *Ante*, p. 223.

expressed by him after reading them but he said that they would have to be discussed with his Admiralty this morning and that he hoped this afternoon a formal reply might be sent me. I have not received this as yet but I understand that it will come this evening, whereupon it will be immediately forwarded to you. Yesterday the Prime Minister was most hopeful of the negotiations when extended to the other powers and seemed much pleased with the situation. Especially did he appreciate the mutual confidence and joint constructive purpose by which these negotiations have been characterized.

The Japanese Ambassador and I have conferred today and, as agreed upon by the Prime Minister, the sense of your telegrams of September 11 above referred to were communicated to him.

The Japanese Ambassador expressed the hope that the British and ourselves may proceed to those discussions in detail with Japan which will bring about the same sort of preliminary agreement with Japan prior to the Conference as that which Great Britain has already agreed to. In my judgment, I told him, this is exactly what is desired by the United States and Great Britain. The simplification of the points which Japan is desirous of discussing with us has been contributed to by the fact that we have kept the Japanese Government so well informed of all our negotiations in detail. I was told yesterday by the Prime Minister that he would see the Japanese Ambassador personally and explain thoroughly to him the Department's attitude.

A helpful editorial appeared in the *Times* this morning in which the desire to cooperate was expressed. . . .

DAWES

---

500.A15a3/170 : Telegram

*The Ambassador in Great Britain (Dawes) to the Secretary of State*

LONDON, September 13, 1929—8 p. m.
[Received September 14—7 : 50 a. m.[56]]

269. The following is the text of the letter mentioned in my 268, September 13, 5 p. m., which has just been received from the Prime Minister.

"My Dear General Dawes: I have now had time to study the proposals which you left with me yesterday in three separate messages— one, a redraft of the proposed terms of agreement; one which conveys to me the opinions of the Naval Board; and one which gives me your President's tentative views.

The delay in my answer is owing to the fact that the First Sea Lord is up in Argyllshire shooting and before sending you this reply I felt that I ought to get his concurrence which I now have.

[56] Telegram in four sections.

1. The proposals of your Navy Board, if I understand it aright, I comment upon as follows: Your last despatch suggested, as parity with our program, twenty-three 8-inch, 10,000 ton cruisers (one of which you doubted if you could sustain on the application of a yardstick), plus ten *Omahas* of 7,000 tons each, equaling 300,000 tons. With a view to our international relationship we suggested that it might meet your requirements to take eighteen 8-inch cruisers plus five 10,000 tons, 6-inch cruisers, plus ten *Omahas* which also equaled 300,000 tons. An American strength of eighteen 8-inch cruisers is a very critical figure for us, not as regards you but as regards the rest of this world. We considered that our superiority of 39,000 tons was adequately set off by your superiority of three 8-inch cruisers, plus five 10,000 ton, 6-[inch gun] cruisers. Your Navy Board's proposal is that you should reduce your 8-inch cruisers by two making them twenty-one and that you should also build five 7,000 ton, 6-inch cruisers and retain your ten *Omahas*. This amounts to a tonnage of 315,000; in other words that a difference of 24,000 tons in our favor should be set off by a superiority of six 8-inch cruisers in yours. In your despatch dated September 11, 7 p. m., it is suggested as a way of meeting us that you should use the tonnage of three 8-inch cruisers (the President's message bringing your 8-inch cruisers strength down to eighteen) by building either four 6-inch cruisers of, I suppose, 7,500 tons each or three 6-inch cruisers of 10,000 tons each. That would give you a fleet of eighteen 8-inch cruisers, ten *Omahas*, and eight or nine 6-inch cruisers, the total tonnage being again 315,000.

2. On my side I am advised that a total tonnage difference of 39,000 tons barely compensates for the 33,000 tons superiority in 8-inch tonnage, plus the 50,000 extra 6-inch tonnage which I ventured to suggest for your consideration in my last despatch. The difference between us is only 15,000 tons or two 7,500 ton cruisers and I am prepared to leave this for adjustment as far as our relations to the United States alone are concerned. The figures of the Navy Board as regards 8-inch cruisers would present insuperable difficulties especially in view of international ratios.

3. As is remarked in one of your despatches, our conversations have brought the margin of difference to such a very small compass that it is unthinkable that it can prevent a settlement and now I am content to leave it as it is pending further conversations which in your last brief message Mr. Hoover suggests should be continued at the Five-Power Conference. I think however it would be a great pity if he and I did not exchange views on unsolved outstanding point when we are together and try to come to some agreement. We have never started a game of huckstering and these conversations would not degenerate into that. They would however tend to make the understanding between us more complete and more cordial and I am far more interested in that than in anything else. Unless, therefore, he absolutely prohibits it, I would like to conclude with him the conversations which for my part at any rate I have found so delightfully enlightening when we two were engaging in them. The danger of leaving any hiatus in our understanding to a Five-Power Conference is very great especially if we find that anybody is trying to drive a wedge between us. If either the President or

myself found that a continuation of the conversations would become embarrassing in any way I am sure we could trust enough to each other's friendship and good will to call a halt.  For myself I do not apprehend the least shadow of such difficulty.

4. In order to leave both him and myself free for the Five-Power Conference I suggest that we should agree to review the agreement we may make together after that Conference has been had, lest in consequence of it some readjustment may have to be made.  I do not anticipate that this will be necessary but it would assure opinion here if it felt that an arrangement which we were anxious to make with you would not seriously prejudice our relations with other powers.

5. I think that we ought also to agree on the lines of the Washington Conference decision that in 1935 we should review the situation of the world in relation to this agreement.  To be perfectly candid with you it comes short of what I should like but at the same time my mind is perfectly clear that it is as much as I can consent to in the light of present circumstances.  The world is not too comfortable a place for men of good will today and when they are composed of two parts—50 percent caution, 50 percent ideal desire—they have at the end of the day to admit that the good they would do they can not do fully.  If we could have a really big influence on world policy for six years I believe that some of the things which we really must make provisional now will have been dissipated and a review of this agreement in 1935 would enable us to reduce some of these figures.  It is going to be six years of hard political work to remove from the minds of the people of Europe the shadow of fear and until that has been done both America and us will have to accommodate ourselves to a disturbed world.

6. I am having prepared and will send you without delay the invitation which I think should go to the Washington Convention signatories.  Would you be so good as to ask Mr. Hoover if he places any importance upon a December meeting?  I have discussed that with the Foreign Office and the Admiralty and they both take the view that it is impossible.  We must give time for despatches to go to and come from Japan by bag, as well as cable, for governments to set up committees, to consider accommodations and for delegates to come from Japan.  Moreover it is not at all unlikely that I shall find it advisable to have preparatory conversations with some of the other powers interested so that as far as humanly possible we shall all be safeguarded against a failure.  Finally, it is inadvisable to call a meeting which may be interrupted in the middle of its work by the Christmas holidays.

I should be glad if you would put these points to your President and tell him that the opinion here this morning is that the Conference should be called for the middle or latter part of January.  I could then guarantee to take a hold on the business myself and give it more or less individual attention.  Of course, before we send out the invitations I shall let you have a copy for transmission to the President so that he may make his comments before the issue takes place.

7. I cannot tell you how relieved I am that the way has been opened up for a visit to Washington.  I know the delicacies which will have to be observed, but I am sure that with generosity and the forbearance of good will on both sides they will all be successfully

overcome. I am confident that the feeling of Europe demands that we should see each other and that our meeting should be a signal to the rest of the world to think generously and behave decently.

When I have a little more leisure I really must put on paper an expression of some of the obligations we all owe to you for what you have done since you set foot on our shores. I feel that if this were to end one's service for the world it would have been worth while.

In due course I shall send you what will appear to be, after the high importance of our previous conversations, some trivial matters—details which I propose for the distribution of my time in America.

With kindest regards, I am, yours very sincerely, J. Ramsay MacDonald."

There was also a supplementary letter received reading as follows:

"My dear General Dawes: In the note herewith no reference is made to the issue of the memorandum. One or two expressions in it require consideration but you will have a separate note on it without delay.

With kindest regards, yours very sincerely, J. Ramsay MacDonald."

DAWES

---

500.A15a3/171 : Telegram

*The Ambassador in Great Britain (Dawes) to the Secretary of State*

LONDON, September 13, 1929—midnight.
[Received September 14—11 a. m.]

270. The following additional letter was received from the Prime Minister this evening.

"My dear General Dawes: I now send you my suggestions regarding the memorandum which, when agreed to, is to be handed to the other naval powers and published.

(1) The sections to which no reference is made are agreed.

(2) Section 7. The words 'it may be difficult to secure the consent of other nations to this proposal' seem to give up the battle before we engaged in it. Would it [disturb?] the President if these words were to be substituted 'a final decision upon this must be such as the Five-Power Conference will accept'?

(3) Sections 9 and 10. These sections include a specific mention of fifteen and twenty-one 8-inch cruisers. It is true that these figures are given as maxima but as they are included in those about which we are still negotiating the mention of them is likely to be misunderstood. Would the President consider ending of section 9 at 'standard tons' and of section 10 at 'and guns'. It will be perfectly well known that these two figures have been mentioned by us and discussion will range round them but for the purposes of a published agreement I think on the whole it would be advisable to make the alterations I suggest.

(4) Section 11. I agree [to] this being put on the agenda of the business of the Conference but, as I told you, I am meeting with considerable technical difficulties which the President will easily understand when I tell him that they relate to the fact that police cruisers of slow speed in the event of any naval disturbances would be smashed to smithereens and the most friendly and helpful of my advisers, whilst favorable to the idea if it could be worked out and generally agreed to, would like to delete the final words 'of limited armament and speed' and put instead some such words as 'of [severely?] limited fighting value.' Frankly the technicians who have to design such ships are very doubtful if the idea is practicable but they will work at it. Meantime if we specify too definitely what the characteristic of a police cruiser is it will put obstacles in the way of getting them accepted and I have been advised that that objection will be taken even more strongly by some other powers than by ourselves.

(5) I should like after section 12 that a clause would be put in to run as follows. 'Thirteenth: During or before 1935 this agreement will be reviewed for the purpose of considering whether these provisions regarding naval strength could be revised so as to contribute more than is possible at the moment to general disarmament.'

(6) Section 13 (new 14). If the President agrees to my observations about date of the Conference made in my note of today '1929' should be deleted—and the words 'or January next' inserted.

(7) Section 14 would then become section 15.

(8) In order to carry out another precaution which has been referred to several times in our conversations, I think a note should be added as follows: 'Note: It is understood that if the decisions of the Five-Power Conference or its failure to come to decisions should affect this agreement, readjustments will be made in many ways so that it may conform to the conditions left by the Conference.'

The only purpose of this is to prevent arguments which may proceed on the assumption that we have bound ourselves to a program which may find us in a state of inferiority to powers upon whose building we must keep our eye. Moreover if other powers assume that you and we have fixed ourselves up before we meet them they may trade upon that assumption and give us difficulties in the further negotiations.

Perhaps the President would be so good as to let me have his decision on these points without delay and then we could simultaneously publish the document.

I am, yours very sincerely, J. Ramsay MacDonald."

DAWES

---

500.A15a3/170 : Telegram

*The Secretary of State to the Ambassador in Great Britain (Dawes)*

WASHINGTON, September 14, 1929—4 p. m.

247. Your 268 and 269.[57] Your 269 was received late today and a more careful study of it may make it advisable for me to follow this

---

[57] *Ante,* pp. 225 and 226.

cable with a further one early next week after fuller conference with the President.

While we have from the beginning endeavored to recognize and give weight to the international difficulties which might be presented by the excess in 8-inch cruiser tonnage insisted on by our Naval Board we must emphasize the difficulties which we on our own side would confront in obtaining the consent of our Senate to any reduction in large cruiser figures which were not supported by our naval advisers. This is a very real difficulty which we can not lose sight of.  The President will be quite willing to exchange views with Mr. MacDonald when he is here on these points and to try to arrive at a settlement as between himself and Mr. MacDonald.  In view of this and the difficulties which Mr. MacDonald feels he will have with our figures we make the following suggestions.

First, we think it would be well for the Prime Minister to have in this country during the time of his visit a British naval officer in whom he has confidence with whom he could consult, if necessary, as to the views of his Admiralty.  We hope that such consultation may not be necessary but we can see that such a course might have great advantages in facilitating a successful conclusion of the conversations between the President and the Prime Minister.

Second, we think there should be no publication of the agreement contained in our 244 until after the meeting between the President and the Prime Minister.  We are not satisfied with the language of No. 244 from the standpoint of publicity and we think that after the personal meeting between Mr. Hoover and Mr. MacDonald not only would it be possible to put it into better form for publication but we might possibly be able to make it more complete.

Third, for the same reason we think that the actual sending out of the invitations to the conference might also better wait until after Mr. MacDonald's visit.  The President is willing to defer to the Prime Minister's suggestion of a postponement of the conference, and that being so, would permit the postponement of the invitations.  We feel that the personal conferences during Mr. MacDonald's visit will throw so much light on the character and the date of the conference as to make it worth while to postpone the invitations until then.

STIMSON

---

500.A15a3/171 : Telegram

*The Secretary of State to the Ambassador in Great Britain (Dawes)*

WASHINGTON, September 14, 1929—5 p. m.

248. Since dictating my number 247, September 14, 4 p. m., I have received your No. 270, September 13, midnight, Mr. MacDonald's criticism of the agreement.  This reenforces my suggestion that we

allow the publication of that agreement to wait until after Mr. Mac-Donald's visit. Assuming that this can be done I will not now attempt any review of Mr. MacDonald's suggestions.

STIMSON

---

500.A15a3/172 : Telegram

*The Ambassador in Great Britain (Dawes) to the Secretary of State*

[Paraphrase]

LONDON, September 16, 1929—4 p. m.

[Received 5 : 43 p. m.[58]]

272. I received your telegrams Nos. 247 and 248 of September 14 yesterday. Realizing the bearing of these cables upon a meeting with members of the British press which I knew the Prime Minister had arranged for this afternoon, I had a conference with him yesterday evening and submitted your Nos. 247 and 248 to him. The Prime Minister will probably send me a written reply which I shall promptly transmit to you.

MacDonald and I had quite a conference over your cables. I have felt concern over the concession you make in your No. 247 in answer to Prime Minister's suggestion relative to the wise policy which you stated in your No. 245, September 12, 5 p. m. I expressed myself freely when MacDonald asked for my views with regard to effect upon public opinion of acceptance of his suggestions especially as your acceptance might involve taking a British naval representative with him to America. In reply MacDonald said that selection by him of naval officer to accompany him might cause trouble with rest of Admiralty staff, with which his relation is difficult.

I shall give you the run of my mind, as I gave the Prime Minister, regarding effect, if knowledge became public, of discussion between him and President personally of remaining technical difference with view to its settlement before Conference is convened. If this small remaining difference is not adjusted by exchange of telegrams before MacDonald leaves it would then be twisted and magnified out of its true significance. As result of methods of negotiation pursued to present moment, together with the able official public statements made at Washington relative to its insignificance, this difference is no longer regarded by the public as serious. Then why run risk of changing public's state of mind with regard to its insignificance, thereby making its final settlement by compromise more difficult?

On previous occasions I have fully expressed myself to you and to MacDonald as to the dangers of the latter's visit to the United States prior to a successful conclusion of the preliminary naval negotiations

---

[58] Telegram in two sections.

GENERAL 233

between the United States and Great Britain. In my judgment the reasons I voiced then would fully apply in this instance were it not that the present agreement is now publicly considered as an accomplished fact, even though a small technical difference is left for the conference to adjust.

Both in England and in the United States such wide public interest attaches to the Prime Minister's visit and his forthcoming personal conference with the President that the possible repercussions may be tremendous either for good or evil. Inasmuch as the public considers that the two countries have arrived at a substantial agreement and that the remaining difference is insignificant, there is grave danger of creating the impression that the small remaining difference is of such importance as to make it necessary for the Prime Minister to come to this country for the purpose of arriving at a settlement. Should this impression get out, what would be the effect of an announcement that they were unable to settle it after conference? And what is likely to be the reaction upon the naval personnel of the two countries as to the importance of their relation to a final agreement? Furthermore what is likely to be the reaction in Parliament and in the Senate, those breeding grounds of imaginative and ingenious deviltry of the rarest order? To my knowledge an international settlement has never before been guided more directly and personally by those first in authority than has this one by the Prime Minister and the President. The substance being assured, why should we endanger it by risking the appearance that might cause the visit to be regarded as an approaching joint debate on technical questions— a debate in which agreement or disagreement would equally present an invitation and an excuse for misrepresentation on the part of British and American demagogues—rather than an evidence of the constructive purpose to further the peace of the world.

Throughout all these negotiations I have kept most closely in touch with Japanese Ambassador and up to this time the Japanese Government feels that it has been properly informed. Last night at my house, however, when I was going over the present situation with Matsudaira, the Ambassador stated that his Government desired to have same direct informal conferences as those in which the American and British Governments have been engaged relative to large cruisers extended now to Japan; and that if relationship of Great Britain and the United States as to large cruisers is agreed upon in discussion between President Hoover and the Prime Minister with their naval assistants, then his Government could only regard the matter as a *fait accompli* to be presented Japan for either acceptance or rejection without the latter's having had opportunity to present and to have considered its political and technical requirements in the proper sort of informal preliminary discussion such as the United States and Great Britain have had. Pressure of work upon MacDonald has been such that to date he has had but one short interview with Matsudaira and that was at Geneva. He will see the Ambassador very soon, however, and I think that now is the time when informal preliminary discussion between the United States, Great Britain and Japan should begin.

DAWES

---

500.A15a3/176 : Telegram

*The Ambassador in Great Britain (Dawes) to the Secretary of State*

[Paraphrase]

LONDON, September 17, 1929—1 p. m.
[Received 2 : 52 p. m.]

273. The Japanese Ambassador came to see me again yesterday for the purpose of discussing the situation along the lines already reported in my telegram of September 16, No. 272.

Yesterday evening I had a further conference with MacDonald. MacDonald, realizing that, owing to the substantial agreement now arrived at between the United States and Great Britain, a growing restiveness for similar preliminary adjustments will develop on the part of other powers, is preparing a letter for transmission to the British Ambassadors in France, Italy, and Japan instructing them to inform those powers that he wishes to begin informal preliminary conversations with each of them along the same lines as those which have been going on with the United States. After the preparation of this letter and prior to its transmission he intends to hand me a copy for the purpose of submitting it to you for such suggestions or modifications as you desire to make.

With reference to your suggestion that the memorandum of agreement between our two countries should not be made public until the time of the Five-Power Conference, MacDonald, while realizing that the situation may be altered by conditions, tends to agree with you particularly since after the submission of this memorandum to his official advisers he was presented with a large damn fool exposition of several pages concerning your error in making use of the term "armament" in place of something else in the first proposition of your No. 225, August 28, 7 p. m.[59] He added that unimportant comments of a similar sort were made on almost all paragraphs of the memorandum; however, he had made use of your suggestion that the memorandum should not be given out until the conference as an excuse for not prolonging the discussions with his official advisers and

---

[59] *Ante*, p. 207.

in this connection he manifested a feeling of gratitude for your suggestion.

I think, after my talk with the Prime Minister, that, in view of his attitude, you may well consider as undisturbed your statement of policy in your telegram of September 12, No. 245,[60] unless you yourself desire to make a change. The official public statements concerning the remaining difference have, as a matter of fact, been prepared so admirably that the man in the street has been able to understand them and this particular matter has lost its public importance to a large extent as a result. However, in connection with the attitude of Japan and possibly of the Italian and French Governments, it remains very important.

I have received word from the French Ambassador that he desires to call on me after noon today.

DAWES

---

500.A15a3/177 : Telegram

*The Ambassador in Great Britain (Dawes) to the Secretary of State*

LONDON, September 17, 1929—4 p. m.<br>[Received 6 : 15 p. m.[61]]

274. I have just received the following letter from the Prime Minister together with the draft of a letter which, subject to your approval or modification, he desires to send to the French, Italian, and Japanese Ambassadors in London:

"My dear General Dawes: I saw the Italian and Japanese Ambassadors last night (the French was out of town), and told them of how matters stood between us in terms which have already been published in the press—but without the mistakes which are included in all the newspaper stories. There is however one proposal made by the Secretary of State in his last message which you might reconstruct. He proposes that no invitation should be sent to the naval powers to attend a Conference until after I have been in Washington. Both Washington and London have given it out that they are to propose such a Conference and a delay in issuing a notification to that effect would give rise to all sorts of surmises and might give time for difficulties to grow up in our way.

I am asking the Foreign Office to send you a copy of a despatch which I think ought to go at once to the Ambassadors of France, Italy, and Japan, in London. Perhaps after what has been published in the press you will be willing to agree to its being sent without referring it to Washington but if you decide otherwise I should be glad if you would let the Foreign Office have the consent of Washington as soon as you possibly can. The sooner we settle this the better for the successful completion of the work we have been doing.

I am, my dear General, yours very sincerely, J. Ramsay MacDonald."

---

[60] *Ante*, p. 225.
[61] Telegram in three sections.

Draft

"September (blank) 1929.

Your Excellency: I have the honor to inform Your Excellency that the informal conversations on the subject of naval disarmament which have been proceeding in London during the last three months between the Prime Minister and the Ambassador of the United States have now reached a stage at which it is possible to say that no point of such serious importance as to prevent an agreement now divides the two Governments.

From time to time the Prime Minister has notified Your Excellency of the progress made in these discussions and I now have the honor to state that provisional and informal agreement between His Majesty's Government and the Government of the United States has been reached on the following principles.

1. The conversations are the result of the Treaty for the Renunciation of War signed at Paris in August, 1928, and the consequent realignment of our national attitudes to the position that war may not be used as an instrument of national policy in the relations of nations with each other. The Peace Pact must therefore be regarded as the starting point of agreement.

2. It has been made abundantly clear both by His Majesty's present Government and by their predecessors in office that this country has no intention of instituting a program of naval construction in competition with the United States. The conversations have therefore been directed toward the program which both Governments could agree to be parity in the combatant strength of the two navies. Furthermore, the aim which both Governments had in view throughout has been the reduction and not merely the limitation of naval strength.

3. The conversations have covered the whole field of naval disarmament and have dealt in greater or less detail with all categories.

4. It is agreed that parity as between the two nations shall be established by December 31, 1936.

5. The main subject which has been under discussion has been the relative cruiser strength of the two navies. The position reached at present is that Great Britain has agreed to accept the following minimum cruiser strength:

Fifteen 8-inch gun ships with a total tonnage reduction to 146,800.

Thirty-five 6-inch gun ships with a total tonnage of 192,200.

Making grand total for the cruiser strength of the British Navy of 339,000 tons.

As against this the Government of the United States propose that the following should be regarded as parity in combatant strength with Great Britain.

Twenty-one 8-inch gun ships with a total tonnage of 210,000.

Ten of the existing *Omaha* class of 6-inch gun ships with a total tonnage of 70,000.

Five new 6 [-inch] gun ships with a total tonnage of 35,000.

Making a grand total of 315,000 tons.

His Majesty's Government have not accepted the above figures for the American Navy as constituting their conception of what would be parity with the British minimum figures but I am happy to state that the margin which divides the two Governments is a relatively small one. For the confidential information of the (blank) Government, I would add that His Majesty's Government are prepared to accept as parity in combatant strength a maximum figure for the United States of eighteen 10,000, 8-inch gun cruisers and a maximum total cruiser tonnage of 300,000.

6. The question of battleship strength was also touched upon during the conversations and both Governments are in agreement that, subject to the assent of the other signatory powers, it would be desirable to reconsider the battleship replacement programs provided for in the Washington Treaty of 1922 with the view of diminishing the amount of replacement construction implied under that treaty.

7. As regards other categories of ships, i. e., destroyers and submarines, His Majesty's Government and the Government of the United States are agreed that parity should be established on the basis of ton for ton. Since both Governments adhere to the attitude that they have publicly adopted in regard to the desirability of securing the total abolition of the submarine, this matter hardly gave rise to discussion during the recent conversations. They recognize, however, that no final settlement of this subject can be reached except in conference with the other naval powers.

In view of the scope of these discussions the Government of the United States and His Majesty's Government consider it as most desirable that a Conference should be summoned at an early date to replace the Conference which, under the terms of the Washington Treaty, is to be held in the year 1931. It is our earnest hope that the (blank) Government will agree as to the desirability of the Conference being antedated in this manner and will be willing to appoint representatives to attend a Conference which it is suggested by the United States as well as ourselves should be held in London at the beginning of the third week in January 1930. The Conference, it is further suggested, should be constituted in the same way as was the Washington Conference in 1922.

A similar invitation is being addressed to the Governments of (blank) and the United States. I should be grateful if Your Excellency would cause the above invitation to be addressed to the (blank) Government.

In the same way as the two Governments have kept Your Excellency informally *au courant* of the recent discussions so now His Majesty's Government will be willing in the interval before the proposed Conference to continue informal conversations with Your Excellency on any points which may require elucidation. The importance of reviewing the whole naval situation at an early date is so vital in the interests of general disarmament that I trust that Your Excellency's Government will see their way to accept this invitation and that the date proposed will be agreeable to them.

It is hoped that at this Conference the five principal naval powers may be successful in reaching agreement as between themselves on all outstanding problems of naval disarmament and that by this means a text can be elaborated which will facilitate the task of the League of Nations Preparatory Commission and of the subsequent general disarmament conference. I should like to emphasize that His Majesty's Government have discovered no inclination in any quarter to set up new machinery for dealing with the naval disarmament question; on the contrary there is a very general desire to look upon these negotiations as an effort on the part of the five naval powers to carry out the invitation given to them by the President of the Preparatory Commission to try to come to a naval agreement amongst themselves and thus facilitate the work of the Preparatory Commission of the League of Nations."

I have notified the Prime Minister that I am forwarding this to you and will let him know your views upon the same as soon as received. His letter indicates that he is anxious to have an answer soon.

DAWES

---

500.A15a3/176 : Telegram

*The Secretary of State to the Ambassador in Great Britain (Dawes)*

[Paraphrase]

WASHINGTON, September 17, 1929—7 p. m.

249. Reference your telegrams No. 269, September 13; No. 270, September 13; No. 272, September 16; and No. 273, September 17.

Over the week end it has been possible more carefully to review your telegrams No. 269 and No. 270 in connection with those which we sent and to which yours were a reply; we have also further consulted on the subject with the President. The letter to you from MacDonald of September 14 [*13*] contains several statements indicating a possible misunderstanding which it is my wish should be avoided at all costs. Our telegram No. 243, September 11, contains the following: [62]

"The final result of our cable No. 242 is that the Prime Minister's technical experts and ours are apart on only one point and on that point are not far apart. This particular point is represented by the question as to whether three of the American cruisers are to be of the 8-inch 10,000 ton type or whether there is to be a substitution for them of say four cruisers of the 6-inch gun type, or in the more recent view of the Prime Minister, your 266, four, the question as to whether these three cruisers of 10,000 tons are to have 8-inch guns or 6-inch guns mounted upon them."

I was endeavoring in these statements to clarify on the President's behalf the opposing proposals made in these negotiations between us respectively, in which our minimum offer was for the United States to have twenty-one cruisers of a tonnage of 10,000 and with 8-inch guns; all substitutions proposed for these cruisers were suggestions coming from the side of the British. It is an error for paragraph 1 of MacDonald's letter to treat our statement above quoted as though the President had accepted the Prime Minister's proposal for equipping 10,000 ton cruisers with 6-inch guns. That suggestion has been rejected by our Naval Board which considers that there would be no

---

[62] Quotation not paraphrased.

advantage in equipping 10,000 ton ships with 6-inch guns and that the tonnage of such 6-inch gun cruisers as the American Navy may accept should be approximately 7,000. Thus our minimum position as stated in paragraph 2 of our No. 242, September 11, remains and we are very anxious that no misunderstanding as to this should be in Mr. MacDonald's mind.

Unless there is a reduction in the proposed British cruiser total, we do not see any means of reducing this limit on our part. There has been an opportunity now for us to review the results of these discussions up to the present time and I am expecting a letter from the President in which he will outline his views on these results; I shall communicate it to you so that you may acquaint MacDonald with them. It is my hope that until the receipt of this letter no further public statements will be made.

For the Ambassador's confidential information and with reference to his telegrams Nos. 272 and 273 of September 16 and 17 respectively.

The dangers which might follow from having a naval expert accompany MacDonald to this country are recognized by us; however, considering the expressed desire of the Prime Minister to start a discussion of this sort, it is our opinion that to bring an officer with him with whom he could consult would be a smaller evil than to have a unilateral conversation in which it will be possible that our side would be held to responsibility while MacDonald would be enabled to advance the absence of technical advice on his side as an excuse for refusing to enter into commitments, a situation which would result in a very difficult position for us. From the beginning I have insisted on the importance of an adjustment before the Conference of all the differences outstanding between the two nations; my hand has been forced, however, by the pressure of the dates available for the Prime Minister's visit. These have left insufficient opportunity to close what, in my feeling, may at the Conference become a serious gap. The statement which he gave out yesterday relative to the extent of that cleavage has served to make the difficulty greater by drawing the public's attention to it, thereby to a certain extent stressing the position of the big navy advocates in this country who no doubt will fix their opposition to any reduction on the part of the United States unless it appears as the reply to a corresponding scaling down of British strength. All published figures prior to that statement were mere guesses on the part of the press. Therefore I wish you to understand that in my opinion the situation is still open to grave developments and although the closeness of our present position is such that it is impossible for me to believe that the Conference will leave the gap unbridged, it would nevertheless make our situation much easier if it were possible to find a solution before the Conference.

Concerning MacDonald's discussions with Japan, France and Italy, there is no objection on my part to his assumption of the burden of testing their attitude; however, I hope that until he receives the President's letter he will not proceed with such discussions.

STIMSON

500.A15a3/176

### President Hoover to the Secretary of State [63]

WASHINGTON, September 17, 1929.

MY DEAR MR. SECRETARY: I have been giving a great deal of thought over the week end to the Prime Minister's latest dispatches.

I am, of course, glad to discuss with him on his visit the gap between our two cruiser proposals, but I suggest later on a method of closing it before Mr. MacDonald's visit. I dislike the idea that Mr. MacDonald's visit might become one of negotiation or split on such a question as this for our whole great program might in public mind degenerate into a huckster's quibble; nor does it seem to me that we should fail after Mr. MacDonald's visit to call the conference because of such a gap. The purpose of the conference is to find methods for surmounting difficulties that we cannot solve otherwise.

The position as I see it, on the two proposals as to cruisers, is that the British with 339,000 tons would have a superiority of some 24,000 tons over the American 315,000 tons, a superiority to the British equal to, say, 4 medium sized modern cruisers, as against the American Navy having the advantage of two inches in gun calibre on 60,000 tons, or 30% of its fleet. It is true that part of the British cruisers will be less modern than ours, yet our *Omaha* class is in turn less modern than other important British classes. I am, therefore, convinced that we have gone as far as we can go on this line. We have on our side a great burden indeed to prove to our people that we have parity in the two programs when the American Navy will be 24,000 tons and 16 ships less than the British Navy even if it be compensated by larger gun calibre and an average more modern fleet—that is by the yardstick.

I am willing to try to carry this burden through but I do not believe if Mr. MacDonald understood the difficulties of our situation he would insist upon enlarging this margin by 15,000 tons and decreasing the compensation in gun calibre. Our situation is necessarily different from his because, having arrived in a position in which his own political colleagues have agreed to support him, he

[63] Text telegraphed to the Ambassador in Great Britain as Department's telegram No. 250, September 17, 8 p. m., for communication to the British Prime Minister.

can carry through Parliament. We, on the other hand, have to persuade an independent branch of the Government to vote with us by a two-thirds majority. I am, however, very anxious to find a way around this difficulty by mutual concession especially as the twenty-one large cruisers on our part may affect the program for the other powers.

It seems to me that the emphasis which the Prime Minister properly lays upon the importance of a second conference in 1935 to again reduce the world's naval arms, suggests a new line of thought and presents a basis to reorient our whole discussions and proposals.

Under the cruiser programs which we have been discussing the British will between now and the conference of 1935 lay down 91,000 tons in new 6-inch cruisers. We must lay down 145,000 tons further. This is in addition to the ships which we now have in construction. In other words, we shall between us have imposed upon ourselves, say 236,000 tons of new warships at an expense of, say $1,500 a ton, a total expenditure of over $350,000,000, some part of which at least would be much better invested in works contributing to real human welfare. And then after we have done all this, the whole purpose of the proposed 1935 conference and the aspirations we have with regard to it, would be that after we have built up all this tonnage and expended all this money, we shall then try to find a method by which we shall scrap it, or some large part of it. And in any event we shall then determine that some of it was not necessary.

It seems to me that there is the most profound outlook for peace today that we have had at any time in the last half century, more especially if we succeed in our conference of January next, yet in effect we are plunging along building more ships at fabulous expense only with the hope and aspiration that at the end of a period so short as 6 years we shall be able to sink a considerable part of them.

In the same line of thought it occurs to me that the dangers of war during the next six or ten years for either of our countries in any direction are inconceivably less than they have been at any period since the Great War. But I find on examination that the British Empire has apparently, during the past few years, been able to preserve peace and provide for its naval defense with a very much smaller cruiser fleet than that now contemplated.

The figures given to me indicate that the British cruiser strength actually in commission in 1922 was 285,000 tons; that it decreased to 244,000 in 1925 and that after allowing for recent disposal of three old ships it comprises only 300,000 tons actually in commission today. Yet we are proposing at this moment that the British fleet should be increased to 339,000 tons. Again in the American fleet I find that we had in commission a total cruiser tonnage of 161,000 in 1922, 153,000 in 1925, and that we have today a tonnage of 100,000 tons afloat—and we are likewise proposing to increase this to 315,000 tons by 1936. In the same breath we are promising the world that at that date we shall use our best endeavors to sink a considerable portion of these fleets. All this is illogical and is the simple negation of our own aspirations and I believe also of public opinion on both sides of the Atlantic.

This discussion between our governments has been in progress now for about three months. There has been time for public opinion to react on all sides, and there is the most extraordinary unanimity and prayer throughout both countries and the whole world that we shall succeed in actually reducing naval strength, not that we shall increase it.

The major discordant note we have is the criticism in the United States over the published statements of proposed cruiser programs—that it is not a program of reduction but a program of expansion. We are faced with the practical fact, however, that to abolish competition and to get any program accepted, we must reach what will not only be parity but what will carry to our people a conviction of parity.

In view of all this situation I am anxious that before Mr. MacDonald arrives he shall have opportunity to find whether or not it will be possible for him to reduce the proposed tonnage of the British fleet from 339,000 tons to at least 300,000 tons. I would be glad to join with him in so bold a move. On such a gross tonnage we could in turn reduce our program by 39,000 tons, thus solving the question of reduction of our 8-inch cruisers from 21 to 18, and allowing us to make a further cut of one proposed new 6-inch 7,000 ton cruiser.

I know that upon turning to his charts, Mr. MacDonald will find that with his proposed replacement program of 14 new ships, this could not be accomplished. If, on the other hand, after scrapping the *Hawkins* class, he limited his replacements so as to provide the laying down of one cruiser per annum, or a total of six replacements, he would keep constant employment in his yards and he could perhaps worry along with his policing of the British Empire by extending the life of some of his older ships for a few years and we would thus each of us arrive at 1936 with at least 39,000 tons less of new ships to deal with. Such a program could apparently be worked out to about fifty ships. I may mention that we have four cruisers now in service that are over 25 years old and one 30 years old that do most effective police duty in various parts of the world. Even a reduction of 39,000 tons in our cruiser programs seems small in the face of all our public backing in this situation, and I should like to see it down another 50,000, but I do not wish to seem impractical.

I would call your attention to the fact that if our present agreement is proposed to be binding only to 1936, if at that time the reduction of the British fleet to 300,000 tons proved too severe, it could be corrected then.

There are some other phases of the problem which seem to me also of the utmost importance and could quite well be taken up on Mr. MacDonald's arrival here with view to making an announcement after his visit of an accord much more powerful from a world point of view. At various times in these discussions we have referred to the maximum destroyer strength of somewhere about 150,000 tons for each country. If we could agree on this figure, it would in itself mark a great tonnage reduction on both sides, although we would each require some construction for replacement. Likewise on submarines, if we could agree on some maximum tonnage for each country, at say 75,000 or even 50,000 tons, it would be helpful to have such a figure declared to the world as a part of our accord.

Another still more important phase of the whole discussion that I think we should bring in, and which I would appreciate Mr. Mac-Donald's having in mind, is whether or not as a part of this preliminary accord we could not settle the proportion of replacements of battleships we should propose to the January conference that are to be undertaken prior to 1936.

By reference to the Washington Arms Treaty I find that we each of us are presumed to lay down cruisers C and D in 1931, E and F in 1932, G in 1933, H and I in 1934, and K and L in 1935. As these ships are 35,000 tons each, this amounts to each country laying down ten ships, or 350,000 tons which will represent a commitment to an expenditure to our two countries of over $1,000,000,000.

I recognize the Prime Minister's feeling that he must keep some continuous construction going in his navy yards, but it would seem to me this could be accomplished if we laid down a maximum of one ship each 18 months which would reduce the number laid down from ten to four on each side. The net effect of all this would simply be that we should maintain in service our present ships for a longer time than we contemplate in the Treaty, which would give opportunity in our second conference of 1935 to reconsider whether or not we should scrap these older ships and thus reduce the capital ships in the world. It would seem to me a most effective and comforting statement if we could arrive at some such proposal as this during Mr. MacDonald's visit and could announce it as part of the conclusions at which we have arrived.

Obviously proportionately the same reduction would need be accepted by the other signatories to the Washington agreement and they should be glad to have such an opportunity.

I shall look forward to the Prime Minister's visit as an opportunity for most distinguished accomplishment.

Yours faithfully,                                    HERBERT HOOVER

500.A15a3/177 : Telegram

*The Secretary of State to the Ambassador in Great Britain (Dawes)*

WASHINGTON, September 17, 1929—9 p. m.

251. Section 1 of your 274 has just arrived.  Please do not under any circumstances consent to the proposed invitation being sent until we have had an opportunity to receive it and state our views.  The President and I have serious objections to even the portion contained in this first section, and we think that the invitation itself had much better await the conclusion of Mr. MacDonald's visit.  I will give you our matured views after receipt of the remainder of the proposed invitation.

STIMSON

---

500.A15a3/177 : Telegram

*The Secretary of State to the Ambassador in Great Britain (Dawes)*

[Paraphrase]

WASHINGTON, September 18, 1929—6 p. m.

252. There has now been time for me to study Mr. MacDonald's complete draft of his proposed invitation to the other three powers for a Naval Disarmament Conference, and for me to confer on the subject with the President.  The Prime Minister's reasons for issuing immediate invitations and his proposed date for the Conference are acceptable to us.  However, the form which he proposes, according to your telegram, has serious objections from our point of view.  It is, we think, a grave mistake to bring up before the other powers the divergencies which still exist as a result of our discussions.  You undoubtedly have realized from the President's letter which I sent you yesterday, how important these differences are, in our view; the fact must also be clear to you that it is impossible for us to recede from our minimum position explained in my No. 249, September 17, unless the British can reduce their cruiser fleet below the aggregate 339,000 tons.  It would merely serve to crystallize public opinion in both countries upon the respective positions and to make a final settlement all the more difficult, if these differences were stated.  We are sure moreover that a statement such as appears in the fifth paragraph of MacDonald's draft relative to the cruiser strength for the United States which he would accept, would be intensely resented by the American press which would regard it as an effort on the part of his Government to determine what size the American fleet should have and to monopolize in favor of his position the opinion of the world.

We feel very clearly for these reasons that all reference to the differences still subsisting between the two countries should be omitted from the planned invitation and that there should be merely a simple invitation addressed to the other nations to meet us in conference.

We have prepared, for the purpose of assisting him as much as possible, a redraft of MacDonald's proposed invitation; [64] in this redraft the features which we consider objectionable have been omitted but it is based upon the old draft in other respects. It is our hope that he will find this of assistance.

As I told you over the telephone, neither the President nor I have given out to the American press any information in the shape of figures concerning the differences between us in our present discussions. Such figures as have appeared in the press are the result of mere guesswork, and I repeat my hope that neither the Prime Minister nor you will allow yourselves erroneously to be led to believe that such figures will in the future be given out by us without giving you full notice.

Our view has been that should the time come when another statement to the public becomes desirable dealing with the matters we have agreed on, this statement can be the result of mutual discussion. However, we have a strong feeling at present that the time best suited for issuing such a declaration will arrive only after MacDonald's visit, when the President and he will have been able to talk over the public sentiment both in America and in Great Britain.

STIMSON

---

500.A15a3/177 : Telegram

*The Secretary of State to the Ambassador in Great Britain (Dawes)*

WASHINGTON, September 18, 1929—7 p. m.

253. The following is the text mentioned in my No. 252 of our suggested revised draft of Mr. MacDonald's invitation to the Powers to the naval conference:

[The first three paragraphs are omitted since they are identical with the first three paragraphs of the final text, printed on page 263.]

(*d*) It has been agreed that the principle of parity in each of the several categories shall govern the size of the two fleets and that such parity shall be reached by December 31, 1936.

[The next paragraph is identical with the fifth paragraph, or principle three, of the final text.]

(*f*) Since both governments adhere to the attitude that they have publicly adopted in regard to the desirability of securing the total abolition of the submarine this matter hardly gave rise to discussion during the recent conversations. They recognize however that no final settlement of this subject can be reached except in conference

---

[64] *Infra.*

with the other naval powers. In view of the scope of these discussions, the Government of the United States and His Majesty's Government consider it most desirable that a conference should be summoned to consider the categories not covered by the Washington Treaty and to study the questions which, under the terms of the Washington Treaty, would otherwise be discussed in the year 1931. It is our earnest hope that the (blank) Government will agree to the desirability of such a conference. His Majesty's Government and the Government of the United States are in accord that such a conference should be held in London at the beginning of the third week of January, 1930, and it is hoped that the (blank) Government will be willing to appoint representatives to attend it.

(*g*) A similar invitation is being addressed to the Governments of (blank) and the United States. I should be grateful if Your Excellency would cause the above invitation to be addressed to (blank) Government.

[The next paragraph is identical with the eighth paragraph of the final text.]

(*i*) It is hoped that at this conference the five principal naval powers may be successful in reaching agreement as between themselves on all outstanding problems of naval disarmament and that by this means a text can be elaborated which will facilitate the task of the League of Nations Preparatory Commission and of the subsequent general disarmament conference. I should like to emphasize that His Majesty's Government have discovered no inclination in any quarter to set up new machinery for dealing with the naval disarmament question; on the contrary there is a very general desire to look upon these negotiations as an effort on the part of the five naval powers to carry out the invitation given to them by the President of the Preparatory Commission at the Conference in Geneva last Spring to try to come to a naval agreement amongst themselves. Such agreement as the five Powers may reach in the conference now proposed may then be used by the Preparatory Commission of the League of Nations as a foundation to facilitate its further endeavor.

STIMSON

---

500.A15a3/181 : Telegram

*The Ambassador in Great Britain (Dawes) to the Secretary of State*

[Paraphrase]

LONDON, September 18, 1929—9 p. m.
[Received September 18—8:53 p. m.]

275. Received your telephone call [65] before I had finished reading President's letter,[66] with all of which I am in agreement.

As I see it, the situation has become a simple one in the public mind which favors the success of a bold reduction move along the lines suggested to MacDonald by the President. The maximum quantitative difference in my judgment involving parity as it has been ex-

---

[65] No record of telephone call found in Department's files.
[66] *Ante*, p. 240.

pressed in the public figures, is regarded as most insignificant in the public mind. Public opinion is concerned only to a small extent with the relation of this small difference to the cruiser tonnage of the fleets of the two countries, but rather with its relation to the total tonnage of 2,400,000. Now, before MacDonald comes, is the best time to settle the difference that remains, or otherwise not until the Conference opens. Should it be possible to adjust this matter and therewith the question of parity now before he comes, a new agreement between the President and the Prime Minister made public from Washington, in which both would strike for additional proportional reductions on the basis of an eventual British cruiser fleet of 300,000 tons, would have throughout the world a psychological effect of great depth. As compared with the total tonnage of the fleets the reduction suggested by the President will appear to the public as insignificant as the divergence which now separates the two parity proposals. MacDonald should find the President's analysis of the real strength of Great Britain's cruiser fleet in recent years useful in overcoming his fear of the defeating consequences of opposition on the part of his Admiralty, a fear which he is likely to advance as his principal objection to accepting our proposal.

It is my hope that MacDonald will realize, as a result of the President's wider suggestions, the need for meeting before he leaves the present American proposal concerning parity, thereby opening a way for more important things during his visit. In the present psychology of the world what the President has said can be accomplished provided its leaders have his courage.

As I already telephoned, I shall see the Prime Minister on Thursday.

DAWES

---

500.A15a3/182 : Telegram

*The Ambassador in Great Britain (Dawes) to the Secretary of State*

[Paraphrase]

LONDON, September 19, 1929—1 p. m.
[Received September 19—1 p. m.[67]]

276. After having had a night in which to think over the matter, I believe I realize better the full import of the President's letter. Am sending you this, therefore, to be read in connection with my telegram No. 275, September 18, 9 p. m.

My next discussion with the Prime Minister will not be until after his return from Sandringham this afternoon, when I shall simply present the Washington correspondence to him, and shall be careful to avoid creating any atmosphere which would interfere with Mac-

---

[67] Telegram in two sections.

Donald's natural reaction from the impact of this correspondence. Unquestionably, however, MacDonald will be led by the frank and confidential relations existing between us, to ask me in time for my personal views. Of course I have no right to express these unless they are in accord with the President's and your own; it may possibly be useful to you in formulating instructions, however, to have some knowledge as to the run of my mind under the changing circumstances.

The President's plan has my enthusiastic support and I feel that we must carefully consider from now on all the steps to be taken with reference to his plan and the manner in which the powers will eventually receive and treat it. Since I am in doubt as to your wishes, I request you to instruct me now as to whether you want me to urge MacDonald to come to a settlement, before he comes to the United States, of the technical differences arising from the two propositions now before us. If you do not wish such a preliminary settlement before he goes to America please so instruct me; I can see good reasons for such a preliminary settlement inasmuch as the President is suggesting a new line of thought and is laying the basis for a reorientation of the entire proposals and discussions, to use his words.

It is possible that the President's new presentation of the matter may arouse the desire of the Prime Minister and his naval experts at once to give way in the present divergency in order to avoid having to meet the President's proposal of achieving greater reduction by reorienting the entire discussion.

A new line of thought as to methods is opened up to me by the President's letter, particularly in the event that the Prime Minister will give consideration to the President's proposal, for MacDonald of course has to face in this matter greater difficulties than we do. I think it may be assumed that the British Admiralty cannot possibly be induced to support the President's proposition and likewise that MacDonald can win if he will carry through the fight in the right way. For that reason it becomes of increasing importance to see to it that at the Conference the naval experts will not have any power to cause a delay in decisions. I can well understand that it will be embarrassing to deny to American naval experts a full recognition as members of the delegation of the United States, in view of the loyal cooperation which you are. evidently receiving from them; however to grant them such full recognition would make it necessary to include on the British delegation representatives of the Admiralty. That situation to my mind could best be handled by your suggesting that you, MacDonald, the French Premier, and a corresponding official of Italy and Japan should be the only delegates and that these delegates might select such experts as they may deem necessary to advise them. Gibson and myself, I am sure, will feel honored to act as your advisers together with our two distinguished admirals or such others as you may select, although if you do not have us in mind we will in any event forgive you. In my judgment it is important for us to follow this method of sole delegates, no matter what the subjects for consideration at the Conference will be; and this method will be imperative if the proposals of the President are to be taken up with any chance of success.

As a former director of the Budget an intimation from my subconscious self concerning the relation between our established policy of Government economy and State Department cable tolls orders me to cease.

Dawes

---

500.A15a3/182 : Telegram

*The Secretary of State to the Ambassador in Great Britain (Dawes)*

Washington, September 19, 1929—8 p.m.

255. I have discussed your 276 with the President.

1. I assume that the "two propositions" about which you ask instructions are, first, our original minimum position stated with the approval of the General Board in our 242,[68] paragraph 2, and second, the proposition of a further general cruiser reduction in both the American and British fleets contained in the President's letter to me. If I am correct in that assumption the President and I would be very glad if, with your assistance, Mr. MacDonald could be brought to an agreement along the lines of the second proposition before his visit, and we have no objection whatever to your discussing that proposition with him. We appreciate the difficulties he may be under as suggested in your 276, but the reasons for a further reduction in both navies as stated in that letter are so cogent and the disappointment of what must otherwise be the cruiser agreement, in case such reduction can not be accomplished, will be so widespread both among Mr. MacDonald's supporters and our own people that we hope he will attack it with the same courage that the President is willing to display on this side. Mr. MacDonald's difficulties in forcing such a reduction upon his Admiralty will be no greater than our difficulties with big navy people here both in the navy and in Congress. If Mr. MacDonald should be unwilling to attack this second proposition before coming to America you should use your fullest endeavors to make clear to him that our figures on the first proposition represent the minimum which, in my opinion, can be obtained with the consent of our General Board. In other words, unless we are both willing

---

[68] *Ante,* p. 222.

to cut loose from our naval advisers and depend upon the support from the undoubtedly strong public opinion which exists behind us both for reduction it would be manifestly unfair and impossible for him to ask us to cut loose from our Naval Board while he himself clings to the support of his own.

2. In reference to your suggestion as to the delegates to the conference, while I appreciate the kindness of your suggestion it was our view that that matter had better be left unsettled until after the Prime Minister's visit and for that reason in my modification of the proposed invitation I struck out the portion of the Prime Minister's draft in which he proposed to repeat the organization of the Washington Conference. This will have the effect of leaving the matter open for the present and not crystallizing it in the invitation.

STIMSON

500.A15a3/191

*Memorandum by the Secretary of State*

[WASHINGTON,] September 20, 1929.

The French Ambassador called and said that he had two communications for me, but that they were not notes and that he would like to have them considered informal. He handed me the following translation:

"On September 16th, Lord Robert Cecil presented to the Third Commission of the Assembly of the League of Nations, a resolution, the text of which appears in the *New York Times* of September 17th, concerning the limitation of armaments.

"In the opinion of the French Government such a proposal reopens the discussion of questions definitely settled last April. By claiming the limitation of material, either directly by enumeration, or indirectly by budgetary limitation, the resolution might in particular compel the French delegation to take up again before the Preparatory Committee of Disarmament, the proposals of limitation of material and limitation of expenses that they had abandoned in order to take into consideration the point of view of the American delegation.

"Besides, the adoption of the British proposal would prejudge decisions of the Preparatory Committee concerning the control of armaments while, in order to comply with the wishes of the American delegation, the French delegation, at the last session of the Preparatory Committee, declared that they would present on this special point transactional propositions.

"It is the intention of the French delegation to ask that the British resolution be rejected, stating mainly that it is impossible for a Commission to reopen now questions decided upon by the Preparatory Commission, with the cooperation of the United States delegation. The French delegation would add that if the Preparatory Commission is going to overcome the difficulties that have been encountered until now, the best procedure is to follow the attitude taken by Mr. Hugh

Gibson, that is to say, to work for a practical agreement by the way of mutual concessions.

"If the French delegation were opposed by the majority, they would ask that the text of the resolution mention the naval program, without which the work of the Preparatory Commission cannot be finished, and the French delegation would recall on the occasion the principles laid down by them in 1927 and agreed upon by the American delegation last April.

"The French Government is in favor of continuing the collaboration, started last Spring, between the American and French delegations and to limit the intervention of the Assembly of the League of Nations into the preparatory work of disarmament, to the adoption of a text expressing the wish that the Commission meets as soon as possible in order to terminate its work so that a general conference for reduction and limitation of land, sea and air armaments may be convoked during next year.

"September 19, 1929."

The Ambassador showed me the French excerpts from the proceedings of the Preparatory Commission last May where there were remarks by the presiding officer and Mr. Gibson which he thought supported the statements in the memorandum handed to me. He said he assumed that I would want to take time to look it over and consider it and I thanked him and said I would. He then handed me the following, saying it was more important:

"The program of the future naval Conference and the questions which will be discussed by it, are not quite clear to the French Government.

"It was its understanding, according to indications given on several occasions by the Honorable Secretary of State and his representatives, that the Anglo-American conversations would lead only to agreements of devolution (meaning methods and categories) without deciding officially upon figures.

"In that case, the future Conference, which should remain within the limits of the Preparatory Commission, would simply have to outline plans by application of the principles proposed by France and agreed upon by the American Government according to Mr. Hugh Gibson's declarations. The question of the figures of limitation should be left to the future General Conference, which will deal with the reduction of the three kinds of armaments (land, sea and air), and which will examine them with the aid of quantitative proposals of each Government for the limitation of its own armaments, taking into account conditions of security and special geographic or other necessities of its own national defense.

"September 20, 1929."

I told the Ambassador that it was true that we had first approached these conversations from the standpoint of discussing the proposition made by Mr. Gibson and called the "yardstick", but that we very soon found that it was impossible to confine the matter to the question of the yardstick alone and that the negotiations had taken a wider scope. I told him that the President's speeches would have indicated that, going back as far as his Memorial Day address.[69]  Then I told Mr. Claudel what we had discussed, namely, the capital ship program where we discussed the possibility of postponing the replacements from 1931 to 1936; the destroyer category and the submarine category, in both of which the American Navy was superior to the British Navy and in which our position had been that we were willing to reduce as far as Great Britain would reduce; that in the cruiser category we had found that it was impossible to confine ourselves to the yardstick alone, that the British cruiser fleet was so much larger than the American cruiser fleet that no yardstick would bridge the gap, and that therefore it was necessary to come down to concrete realities and discuss whether Britain should scrap ships and if so, how much, and whether we should construct ships and if so, how many; and that therefore it had been necessary to talk figures and we had talked figures. But I assured him that throughout the discussion, from the very beginning, it had been mutually understood that all agreements between Great Britain and ourselves should be contingent upon the action of the other three powers at the suggested five power conference.

We then discussed the character of the General Conference. I told him it had been our view that five principal naval powers might get together and agree upon naval disarmament more easily than if other powers were present and that therefore we were thinking of a general conference composed of those five powers. He stated that that was not so easy on the part of the French whose naval defense was necessarily connected with their land defense—that communication by ship was just like communication by land and that naval action played a part with their land defense. I pointed out to him that our principal object in the entire negotiations was to remove the disagreement with Great Britain which had not only broken up the Conference of 1927 but had proved such a source of irritation between the two countries; that to us the settlement of this question was so much the most important matter on our horizon that it outweighed everything else. He pleaded for more preparatory discussions with the other powers, saying that he thought such preparatory discussions of the same type which we had been having would be very important. I asked him for advice on how they should be conducted; whether France wished to have such discussions with us which I pointed out could not involve any very important questions between us because we had no issues with France, or whether she had not better hold them with Great Britain or with Italy. I told him that I fully approved of getting as many of these questions out of the way before the conference as possible. He said that that was his view. I asked him to consider it and talk it over with his Government and let us know what their suggestions were. He left me saying he felt much reassured and that he would talk over these matters with his Government.

H[ENRY] L. S[TIMSON]

500.A15a3/189 : Telegram

*The Ambassador in Great Britain (Dawes) to the Secretary of State*

[Paraphrase]

LONDON, September 21, 1929—1 p. m.
[Received September 21—9:26 a. m.]

279. I have just had unofficial information that the Foreign Office has approved the suggested revised draft of invitation contained in your 253, September 18, 7 p. m., with one minor suggested change in phraseology for the sake of clearness and a revised rendition of the last half of paragraph (*i*) to conform more closely with the English understanding on the Geneva remarks referred to. Meanwhile the suggested draft of the invitation is being submitted to the Dominions and immediately upon replies being received from them and after your approval thereof the invitations will be issued, it is hoped, before Mr. MacDonald reaches America.

I understand the Prime Minister will send for me upon his return to town on Monday.

DAWES

500.A15a3/197 : Telegram

*The Ambassador in Great Britain (Dawes) to the Secretary of State*

LONDON, September 24, 1929—noon.
[Received 12:50 p. m.[70]]

281. I received the following letter from the Prime Minister this morning. He has been at Chequers during the week end and my last interview with him was September 19th.

"23rd September, 1929.

My dear General Dawes: What I take as a personal letter from your President to myself has given me the greatest pleasure. Its candor is a proof of that trust which we must have in each other if we are to overcome the difficulties which face us. Moreover, its line of thought and its subject matter have been giving me concern and he may have comfort in knowing that before his note came I had addressed inquiries to my advisers on some of the points he discusses. Further, it is just that line of country which I hope to go over with

[70] Telegram in five sections.

323421—43—vol. I——25

the President when I see him. I want no bargaining and that sort of thing, but primarily a political talk on the world situation so that our hands may be strengthened by an understanding of each other's problems and purposes.

But it will be helpful to both of us if I make a few comments with a view to carrying the President's letter a further stage.

The minds of our European neighbors who will be invited to the Five-Power Conference is not tranquil but is suspicious that we are making some bargain with the United States against them. We have to walk warily lest we upset them, and they may decline to attend a Conference. Upon that I am now making private and unofficial inquiries, but their press is illuminating. The President is free of that troublesome part of my problems. It has been increased by the leakages which have come from Washington and which forced my hand and compelled me to prevent a stampede of the British press by seeing journalists much against my will.

When I found the contents of my notes appearing here within two days of their receipt in Washington, it was like a net about my feet. I knew my statement might give trouble but on thinking it over concluded that it would be a puff of bad weather that would soon pass over us.

This parity business is of Satan himself. I am sure it has struck the President as it has me as being an attempt to clothe unreality in the garb of mathematical reality. Opinion in the United States demands it and the Senate will accept nothing which does not look like it. On my side I am not interested in it at all. I give it to you with both hands heaped and running down. When I am forced to scrutinize your program which you say embodies it, I turn from you altogether and have to think of things which, but for my importunities, you would not think much about, viz, the fleets of other nations. Therefore, although in our talks with each other, we assume that the discussion takes place between us two, that is really not the case. There are shadowy entities behind me. A spirit photograph would show you unaccompanied, but round me would be the ghosts of the other nations. In its ultimate, the parity we are trying to devise is one between you and the rest of the world in relation to the British position in it. If the appearance of parity is to be obtained, neither of us can get away from the fact that the standard must be fixed by British needs. The tides of events swelling upwards and downwards, backwards and forwards, change our defense problems every year and with that the figures change.

Now what am I trying to do? First and foremost, I am trying to stop the daily swell so that we may fix levels which cannot be exceeded and then create a confidence which will permit those levels to be steadily lowered. I want to substitute the security of peace for that of military preparation. But if in the lowering we act impatiently there will be a break back. That psychological fact fixes my present limits. Stabilization downwards is the only road by which Europe will move to disarmament.

In consequence to [of] this the nearer our two countries come to an agreement the larger in my mind becomes the Five-Power Conference and its results. Let me illustrate by referring to what the President says about three categories.

A. The first class battleships:

Our Admiralty, I believe, would be willing to agree to reduce the replacement ships from 35,000 tons to, say, 25,000; to reduce the caliber of their guns; to increase their age and to propose that at the Conference. But I am warned that the offer will be rejected. Therefore, it will not be the fault of Great Britain if that reduction is not made.

B and C. Destroyers and submarines:

I believe I should have no difficulty in closing at once with figures in the region of the President's proposals. But the tonnage in destroyers depends largely on the tonnage put by other powers into submarines. I am warned that certain other powers will not agree to a limitation in submarines. I might be willing to support something like the President's figures, but what can I do if the Five-Power Conference were to reject them?

Under the geographical and political conditions of the British Empire, the cruiser category is that upon which public opinion can be most easily stampeded, and is also the chief concern of the Admiralty. When we came into office, we found a program of considerable expansion being built on the ground that in view of the building of other powers we were too weak. Three 8-inch cruisers were to be added at once, making eighteen. We stopped it and that must be counted as a reduction. We have stopped other expansions. The whole of my resistance to your proposal of twenty-one is that its effect upon other powers will compel me to expand whether I like it or not. The Admiralty view is that it is not parity; the political view is that it inevitably means expansion. The narrow margin which divides us does not really lie between you and us but between both of us and the rest of the world. If by hook or by crook the United States could say regarding something like 30,000 tons 'we shall not use them' or 'we shall use them in such a way as not to have world repercussions' our agreement would be pretty complete.

Involved in this is a valuation of the relative efficiency of the 8-inch and 6-inch cruiser. I find so far as I can lay my hands on discussions on the subject that in actual battle the relation is almost infinity; in the general operations of war the relation is at least 4 to 1. I have had the relation implied in the President's figures worked out for my guidance and I find that they vary, but that his latest proposal is 10 to 3 in individual ships irrespective of guns and gross tonnage. Here there might be found a way of coming still nearer and critics could be silenced by naval opinion itself on the relative value of the two classes of ships.

The major difficulty is indeed with the 8-inch cruiser. If the three biggest naval powers would agree first of all to a ratio of 6.5.4 (18.15.12) that, as I am advised, would be a world equilibrium unless some of the other powers disturbed it. But Japan wishes instead of two-thirds of the largest cruiser fleet, 70 percent, though, on an American force of eighteen, it might be induced to build no more than twelve. It would certainly want more than twelve on twenty-one and then we should have to move up our figure of fifteen by four or five and the whole plan would fall to the ground.

This is so important that I must emphasize it. If I had the shadow of dread that the United States and ourselves would ever be at war, it would be impossible for me to agree to parity being expressed by any number of 8-inch cruisers beyond our own, e. g., 15. I should be willing to refer the inclosures [*issue?*] to any body of able and impartial authorities on sea warfare to decide between us and I should be assured of their verdict. But that is not in my mind at all. Everybody here is anxious to accommodate themselves to an agreement with you on the assumption that there will be no war and no interference in which our fleets are involved. But I am not justified in making the same assumption as regards the rest of the world, and Mr. Kellogg himself used language which justifies that.[71]

He referred to the possibilities of wars of defense. I may regret it, but he did it, and if I am to get Parliament to agree to our programs I cannot at the moment overlook that fact.

As I am most anxious that the President should be fully aware of the facts as I have to look at them, let me refer to guns—a very important consideration so soon as our people examine the agreement in cold blood. On its 8-inch ships (assuming twenty-one) the United States will carry a superiority of 75 guns and on our 6-inch ships our superiority would be 47 only—a very hard bit of mathematics for me to prove to be parity. Even on our proposals my task will not be easy for they give the United States a superiority of forty-eight 8-inch guns to ours of twenty-three in 6-inch guns, but the numbers are substantially diminished.

I have spent every spare moment at Chequers this week end trying to see daylight through this entanglement and the only conclusion I can come to is that, if the United States insists upon more than eighteen 8-inch cruisers, British expansion is inevitable, especially in view of the hostile reception which the twenty-one figure has received in both the French and Japanese press.

Another point which the President has overlooked when he writes that on present proposals we shall have actually increased warship tonnage by 236,000 is that of that total 145,000 is new construction by the United States, whereas our addition of 91,000 is offset by 115,000 scrapped. This unsatisfactory result arises from the fact that your ships actually built must be increased if you now put the parity agreement on the seas and do not accept it as something you can build up to if you think it is necessary. Again and again, I had been driven back upon this fundamental difficulty. It is the insuperable problem and we must get round it somehow. I shall continue to work away at it but the peace of Chequers has yielded barren results. I am however, looking forward with hope to continuing my ponderings with the President himself in the intervals of the all too generous hospitality which, according to the President [*press?*] he is preparing for me.

Believe me to be, yours very sincerely, J. Ramsay MacDonald."

DAWES

---

[71] Frank B. Kellogg, Secretary of State March 5, 1925–March 28, 1929. On several occasions Mr. Kellogg stated his position on the question of national self-defense under the Treaty for the Renunciation of War, e. g., "Every nation is free at all times and regardless of treaty provisions to defend its territory from attack or invasion and it alone is competent to decide whether circumstances require recourse to war in self-defense."—Excerpt from an address entitled *The French Draft of the Multilateral Treaty for the Renunciation of War*, delivered before the American Society of International Law, Washington, April 28, 1928, and published in pamphlet form by the Government Printing Office, Washington, D. C., 1928.

500.A15a3/215

*Memorandum by the Secretary of State of a Conversation With the Japanese Ambassador (Debuchi)*

[WASHINGTON,] September 24, 1929.

The Japanese Ambassador said he had been instructed by his Government to convey the following messages.

First. His Government wished it to be understood that in order to permit the Japanese Government to participate in the naval conference they must receive the invitation at least three months ahead. The reason was that the distance was so great and they could no longer use the Siberian Railway. They therefore wished to know when it was likely that the invitations would be issued. I told him that I understood their necessity and that I believed the Prime Minister was considering issuing the invitations immediately, probably before he came to this country, and that the conference would be set for the third week in January and that this would allow ample time. I told him, however, that it was not a matter for which we were responsible; that I had supposed his Government would make inquiry from London. He said they would, but he said smilingly, his Government regarded us as really responsible for the conference. I told him that it was all off our shoulders now and that Mr. MacDonald had the responsibility.

Second. He asked what the chances were for further reduction in armament, expressing the hope that the reduction would go further than the press announcements. I replied that we would go as far as Great Britain; that that had been our position; that we would reduce as far as Great Britain and even further in displacement tonnage in view of the fact that we built a larger proportion of eight-inch cruisers.

Third. He asked me when he would get the figures on the agreement between Great Britain and America. I told him I was willing to give them to him now; that that agreement was limited by Great Britain's inability to go below 339,000 displacement tonnage; that their lowest figures to which they would be willing to go were fifteen eight-inch cruisers and thirty-five six-inch cruisers and that their latest proposition involved a large proportion of new replacements and a raise from 330,000 tons to 339,000 displacement tons. If Great Britain was unable to go below those figures our General Board advised us that we could not go below twenty-one eight-inch cruisers, the *Omahas*, and five new sixes as being parity with the British figures. I told him we were very sorry for this for we wanted to go much lower. He said that Japan wanted to go much lower and he brought out a slip of paper showing the following figures as to the Japanese eight-inch cruisers, viz:

Eight 10,000 ton eight-inch cruisers, aggregating 80,000 tons.

Four 7,100 ton eight-inch cruisers, aggregating 28,400 tons, or a total of twelve eight-inch cruisers aggregating 108,400 tons. Underneath this he had figures showing 70 percent of 180,000 equals 126,000 and 70 percent of 210,000 equals 147,000, and he explained that this meant that in case we built 18 of our eight-inch cruisers Japan would have to have 126,000 tons or about 20,000 additional tons of such cruisers, while if we built 21 cruisers aggregating 210,000 tons, Japan would have to build about 40,000 tons extra beyond what she now had. I asked him how about their six-inch cruisers. He replied that Japan only had 80,000 tons of six-inch cruisers.

Fourth. He then said that speaking very frankly he hoped that we would cut down to 15 eight-inch cruisers and Great Britain to 12 eight-inch cruisers, in which case Japan would not have to build any more at all.

Fifth. He then asked me how about the 10,000 ton six-inch cruisers. I told him that that had been merely a proposition of Mr. MacDonald's but that we had not accepted it and that our Naval Board had advised that putting six-inch guns on such large cruisers would be an unnecessary waste. He replied that that was exactly the position of Japan.

Sixth. He then asked me about submarines and destroyers. I told him what our position was and that we would go as low as Great Britain; that as to submarines we both would be glad, as had been our position in the Washington Conference, to abolish submarines altogether. He said he understood that but Japan, like Italy and France, felt that she required a certain number of submarines.

Seventh. He brought up again the question of the ratio of 10–10–7. He said that Japan was like Great Britain in being an island dependent upon external food supply, while at the same time she was like the United States in having long commercial lanes to protect with no naval bases and thus required large cruisers. He said he hoped we would not be harsh in regard to the desire for an increased ratio; that at the time when the matter came up at the Washington Conference there were conditions which did not maintain now; that then the question of an alliance with Great Britain was complicating matters also that the American people were more suspicious of Japan but that now he thought all of those matters had been ironed out and that the American people would not object to a 10–10–7 ratio. I told him that I agreed with him on the point that the relations between the two countries were very friendly now and we would approach this in a friendly spirit, but that we had always felt that the same ratio as had been established in regard to capital ships should be maintained all through the fleet. Any different method would complicate matters. He said he appreciated that.

Eighth. He then said that he wanted us to understand that Japan was very friendly to the conference and would stand beside Great Britain and America; that she would not be like France and Italy, who had a different attitude toward the conference. He said very emphatically that Japan would cooperate with us heartily. I told him I was very glad to hear it and thanked him for it.

H[ENRY] L. S[TIMSON]

500.A15a3/207 : Telegram

*The Ambassador in Great Britain (Dawes) to the Secretary of State*

[Paraphrase]

LONDON, September 26, 1929—3 p. m.
[Received September 26—1:47 p. m.]

283. The Italian, French and Japanese Ambassadors have called on me with regard to the delay in sending out the Conference invitations which they had expected to receive before this time from the British Government. I explained, with the Foreign Office's approval, that the delay had been caused by the necessity for the British Government to inform the Dominions as to the form of the agreement, that the United States and Great Britain were practically agreed upon the form except as regards minor details, and that upon the receipt of Dominion approval and after the United States had given its consent, the invitations would be issued. This morning I called at the Foreign Office and learned that Australia, Canada, and the Free State had not yet been heard from. It is the intention of the Foreign Office to cable them this morning, asking them, as soon as possible, to reply. As the situation is viewed from this side, it would appear to be desirable that the invitations be given out before the Prime Minister's arrival in the United States, since a delay until a later date might give rise to the impression that an essential difficulty in agreeing exists, although, in fact, there is none. I suggested the following plan of procedure, subject to your approval, which the Foreign Office finds satisfactory: Should the agreement of Australia, Canada, and the Free State not be received prior to Mr. MacDonald's departure tomorrow night the draft of the invitation should, as soon as received, be communicated to me for transmission to you; as soon as possible after its receipt you would then let me know whether or not it is satisfactory. If you find it satisfactory, it will then be issued by the Foreign Office while the Prime Minister is still crossing the Atlantic. If this procedure meets with your view please cable me, bearing in mind that its alteration rests in your hands, entirely, inasmuch as you can withhold your approval of the form of the invitation submitted to you until after the Prime Minister's arrival should you deem this desirable.[72]

My conversation with the Prime Minister this morning did not deal in any length with the present state of the negotiations since

[72] By telegram No. 285, September 27, 4 p. m. (not printed), the Ambassador reported that the Dominions had approved the revised text of the invitation without change (500.A15a3/216).

Mr. MacDonald evidently wishes the *status quo* under which the conversations in Washington will commence to be completed by his last letter. His former intimation which I cabled to you some time ago concerning the reduction of the British 10,000 ton cruisers from fifteen to fourteen, was not referred to by him and for that reason I also did not bring up that subject. However, he did speak of another possible reduction in the British proposal of some 3,000 tons. I inferred that this suggestion had some connection with a detached statement of his to me to the effect that he had discovered that of the cruisers he had been counting as having a displacement of 10,000 tons each, two had in reality a displacement each of only 8,500 tons.

While Mr. MacDonald is not taking a naval expert with him, I think it well to point out that Craigie, of the Foreign Office, who will accompany him, has a close acquaintance with the naval problem and has, during the progress of the negotiations, been kept thoroughly informed by his Government.

DAWES

---

500.A15a3/217a : Telegram

*The Secretary of State to the Ambassador in Italy (Garrett)*

[Paraphrase]

WASHINGTON, September 27, 1929—7 p. m.

62. Within a few days the British Government will issue invitations to the Five-Power Conference, and in conversations with the several Ambassadors of the interested powers, including the Italian, I have explained quite confidentially that to date Great Britain had not been willing to go below 339,000 tons displacement tonnage apportioned between fifteen 8-inch gun cruisers and thirty-five 6-inch gun cruisers. If the British Government finds itself unable to go below this figure, the American General Board has advised that this Government could not go below twenty-one 8-inch gun cruisers; ten *Omaha* class cruisers (7,100 tons each); and five new 6-inch gun cruisers which would probably approximate about 5,000 tons each. Considering the strong desire for reduction of naval armaments I have stated that the Government of the United States would regret very much not to be able to reduce that figure further. In talking with me, the Japanese Ambassador expressed his country's strong hope that it would be possible to go considerably lower than figures so far reached would indicate. Likewise, I have informed him that with respect to destroyers and submarines this Government could go to as low a figure as British Government cared to go; and that with respect to submarines both Governments would be glad to abolish submarines altogether, as they had pointed out at the Washington Conference.

Italian Ambassador has visited the Department several times and has been kept informed regarding the situation, apparently to entire satisfaction of his Government, which also received, naturally, reports from Italian Embassy in London.

STIMSON

---

500.A15a3/229

*Memorandum by the Secretary of State*

[WASHINGTON,] October 2, 1929.

The French Ambassador said he came to present me with the following *aide-mémoire* from his Government:

"The French Minister of Foreign Affairs has been sincerely touched by the frankness and loyalty of the explanations given by the Secretary of State to the French Ambassador concerning the Anglo-American negotiations and the naval agreement to be conducted with a view to the general limitation of armaments.

"It is M. Briand's understanding that the Anglo-American agreement is only of a relative value and that subsequently it will be placed within the limits of the general agreement to be reached by the Preparatory Disarmament Commission concerning the method of limitation of naval armaments. M. Briand is all the more pleased by the settlement of the difficulties which existed between the two great naval powers that up to now these difficulties were the main obstacle to the realization of a general agreement.

"In view of reaching such an agreement, the French Government still believes that the basis of compromisory proposals made by France, proposals which were received quasi-unanimously by the Preparatory Commission in March 1927, and which the American delegation made their own last April, seem to be the most appropriate ones. It is to be hoped that, if necessary at the price of slight retouching, it will be possible to conciliate the Anglo-American agreement with that proposal, the modalities of which could also be subjected to certain modifications. But in order to study the question, it will be necessary for the French Government to know shortly on what technical basis the Governments of London and Washington have reached an agreement, and especially the characteristics of the three categories of light surface units which they seem to have considered.

"As a whole the French Government would be interested in knowing the different elements, such as strategic or other considerations, protection of lines of communication etc., which have been considered for the determination of the respective needs of the English and American fleets and which have led to the fixation of the total of 340,000 tons of cruisers apparently considered by the British Empire as indispensable. Such information is important to the French Government in view of ascertaining in what measure the principles which have guided the Anglo-American agreement could be conciliated with French interests.

"Contrary to certain press comments, the French Government has no intention to raise objections of a 'procedure' nature to the proposed Conference among the five principal naval powers, provided it remains well understood that the main object of such a conference is to open the way to a final agreement at the Geneva Commission for the purpose of the conclusion of a general treaty of limitation concerning all categories of armaments.

"Washington, October 1, 1929."

I read it and told him that there were some questions in it that were very easily answered. So far as the questions in regard to the protection of lines of communication were concerned they had not been discussed in any detail. The British had stated the number of ships and the tonnage which they considered their minimum for the protection of their lines of communication. In general, they had also stated on one occasion where their cruisers were situated. No further details had been made or furnished. Their case rested upon the geographical situation of their empire, the general needs of which were fairly well understood by us.

I asked him what he meant by the question as to the characteristics of the three categories of light surface units. He said he meant the two classes of cruisers and the destroyers. I said that there was no agreement in regard to the categories of cruisers except the one which had been stated in the press and which he knew and I restated to him the minimum positions of the two governments respectively which he said he had seen in the press. I said that there was no agreement on that point but that once an agreement was entered into before, we would enter the conference with that existing gap, feeling, however, that it was narrow enough to compromise at the conference.

He spoke of the difficulties of the question of parity. I told him of its importance not in regard to a doctrine of military precision but as a doctrine of statesmanship to restore a condition or [of?] agreement instead of one of competition.

When the Ambassador handed me the *aide memoire* and I had read it he said: "You will readily see that our previous interview was very helpful and that my Government is ready to go to the conference".

H[ENRY] L. S[TIMSON]

---

500.A15a3/238 : Telegram

*The Ambassador in Great Britain (Dawes) to the Secretary of State*

LONDON, October 7, 1929—3 p.m.
[Received October 7—1: 30 p.m.]

292. My 290, October 5, 12 noon.[73] I have received today a formal note from Mr. Henderson as follows:

"Your Excellency: I have the honor to transmit to Your Excellency herewith copies of the notes [74] which I am today addressing to the

---

[73] Not printed.
[74] *Infra.*

French, Italian and Japanese Ambassadors in London inviting the French, Italian and Japanese Governments to participate in a Five-Power Conference to deal with the question of naval disarmament, which it is proposed to hold in London in the latter part of January next.

2. As I understand that the Government of the United States concur in the terms of the enclosed notes, I shall be grateful if Your Excellency will be so good as to confirm my impression that they will find it possible to participate in the Conference above mentioned."

The text, dated October 7th, of the enclosure is identical with the text submitted in my 285, September 27, 4 p. m., and amended by your 262, September 28, 12 noon, and also my 289, October 4, 1 p. m.[75] full texts to go forward by pouch tomorrow but will be cabled should Department so desire.

Instructions are requested as to what reply I shall make to Foreign Office note.

DAWES

---

500.A15a3/233

*The Identic British Notes Delivered to the French, Italian, and Japanese Ambassadors in Great Britain, October 7, 1929* [76]

YOUR EXCELLENCY: I have the honor to inform Your Excellency that the informal conversations on the subject of naval disarmament which have been proceeding in London during the last three months between the Prime Minister and the Ambassador of the United States have now reached a stage at which it is possible to say that there is no point outstanding of such serious importance as to prevent an agreement.

From time to time the Prime Minister has notified Your Excellency of the progress made in these discussions and I now have the honor to state that provisional and informal agreement has been reached on the following principles:

One. The conversations have been one of the results of the Treaty for the Renunciation of War signed at Paris in 1928, which brought about a realignment of our national attitudes on the subject of security in consequence of the provision that war should not be used as an instrument of national policy in the relations of nations one to another. Therefore the Peace Pact has been regarded as the starting point of agreement.

Two. It has been agreed to adopt the principle of parity in each of the several categories and that such parity shall be reached by December 31st, 1936. Consultation between His Majesty's Government in the

---

[75] None printed; the modifications of the draft text to which they related were mainly matters of wording and of form rather than of substance.
[76] Text as issued by the Department as a press release on October 8, 1929.

United Kingdom and His Majesty's Government in the Dominions has taken place and it is contemplated that the program of parity on the British side should be related to naval forces of all parts of the Empire.

Three. The question of battleship strength was also touched upon during the conversations and it has been agreed in these conversations that subject to the assent of other signatory powers it would be desirable to reconsider the battleship replacement programs provided for in the Washington Treaty of 1922 with the view of diminishing the amount of replacement construction implied under that treaty.

Four. Since both the Government of the United States and His Majesty's Government in the United Kingdom adhere to the attitude that they have publicly adopted in regard to the desirability of securing the total abolition of the submarine, this matter hardly gave rise to discussion during the recent conversations. They recognize however that no final settlement on this subject can be reached except in conference with the other naval powers.

In view of the scope of these discussions both Governments consider it most desirable that a Conference should be summoned to consider the categories not covered by the Washington Treaty and to arrange for and deal with the questions covered by the second paragraph of Article 21 of that Treaty. It is our earnest hope that the (blank) Government will agree to the desirability of such a Conference. His Majesty's Government in the United Kingdom and the Government of the United States are in accord that such a Conference should be held in London at the beginning of the third week of January 1930 and it is hoped that the (blank) Government will be willing to appoint representatives to attend it.

A similar invitation is being addressed to the Governments of (blank) and the United States and His Majesty's Governments in the Dominions are being asked to appoint representatives to take part in the Conference. I should be grateful if Your Excellency would cause the above invitation to be addressed to the (blank) Government.

In the same way as the two Governments have kept Your Excellency informally *au courant* of the recent discussions, so now His Majesty's Government will be willing, in the interval before the proposed Conference, to continue informal conversations with Your Excellency on any points which may require elucidation. The importance of reviewing the whole naval situation at an early date is so vital in the interests of general disarmament that I trust that Your Excellency's Government will see their way to accept this invitation and that the date proposed will be agreeable to them.

His Majesty's Government in the United Kingdom propose to communicate to you in due course their views as to the subjects which they think should be discussed at the Conference, and will be glad to receive a corresponding communication from the (blank) Government.[77]

It is hoped that at this Conference the principal naval powers may be successful in reaching agreement. I should like to emphasize that His Majesty's Government have discovered no inclination in any quarter to set up new machinery for dealing with the naval disarmament question; on the contrary, it is hoped that by this means a text can be elaborated which will facilitate the task of the League of Nations Preparatory Commission and of the subsequent general disarmament conference.

---

500.A15a3/238 : Telegram

*The Secretary of State to the Ambassador in Great Britain (Dawes)*

WASHINGTON, October 9, 1929—6 p. m.

271. Your 292, October 7, 3 p. m. You should address the following note to the Foreign Minister in reply to his note of October 7:

"I have the honor to refer to the note which you were good enough to address to me [78] October 7 and I take great pleasure in informing you that the American Government hastens to accept the invitation of His Majesty's Government to a conference on naval armaments to take place in London the latter part of January, which will unite the powers signatory to the Washington Treaty in a discussion which will anticipate the problems raised under Article 21 of that Treaty as well as broaden its whole scope by the inclusion of the other categories of ships."

The text of this communication will be released for the morning papers of Friday, October 11th.

STIMSON

---

500.A15a3/261 : Telegram

*The Ambassador in Italy (Garrett) to the Secretary of State*

ROME, October 14, 1929—10 p. m.
[Received October 14—9 : 17 p. m.]

72. My telegram No. 71.[79] Following is text of Italian acceptance of invitation to Disarmament Conference.

"The Italian Government has considered most seriously the note of the 7th instant in which the Secretary of State for Foreign Affairs,

[77] This paragraph was inserted in the final draft at the request of the British Foreign Office; Embassy's telegram No. 289, October 4, 1 p. m. (not printed).
[78] The Department was informed by the Chargé in Great Britain that in the text of the above note, which he sent to the British Foreign Office on October 10, the word "me" was changed to "the Ambassador", in view of the Ambassador's temporary departure from London; telegram No. 296, October 10, 11 a. m. (not printed).
[79] Not printed.

after having informed the Italian Government of the points upon which a provisional and informal agreement was reached between the British Government and the United States Government in the course of their conversations on the subject of naval disarmament, proposed to the Royal Government that it participate in a Conference to be held in London at the beginning of the third week of next January for the purpose of considering the categories of ships not covered by the Washington Treaty of 1922 and in order to deal with the questions covered by the second paragraph of article 21 of that treaty. The aim of this Conference to which the powers signatory to the Washington Treaty are invited, should be to elaborate a text to facilitate the task of the League of Nations Preparatory Commission and of the subsequent General Disarmament Conference.

The views of the Italian Government on the problems of disarmament in general and of naval disarmament in particular are too well known to the British Government to require further declarations with regard thereto. These views have been clearly expressed on repeated occasions and ultimately in the *note verbale* addressed to the British Embassy in Rome on October 6, 1928,[80] in reply to the communication relative to the proposed Franco-British naval agreement of the past year.[81]

Desirous as always of participating in any move whatsoever that may be proposed for the elimination of the losses and dangers of excessive armaments and entertaining the hope that the general initiative may result in real progress toward the solution of the general problem of disarmament, the Italian Government is happy to accept the invitation of the British Government to participate in the London Conference.

The Italian Government takes due notice of the British Government's proposal to communicate to it the British views on the subjects to be discussed at the Conference and, while waiting for these communications, it is considering in its turn informing the British Government of its own point of view on the matter."

GARRETT

---

500.A15a3/451

*French Note Accepting the Invitation of the British Government To Participate in a Naval Conference* [82]

[Translation]

LONDON, October 16, 1929.

The French Government has studied with great interest the letter of the Secretary of State for Foreign Affairs by which the British Government, while communicating the principles which formed the basis of provisional accord between itself and the Government of

[80] Great Britain, Cmd. 3211, Miscellaneous No. 6 (1928), *Papers Regarding the Limitation of Naval Armaments*, p. 39.
[81] *Foreign Relations*, 1928, vol. I, p. 264.
[82] Translation supplied by the editor. A copy of the French text was received by the Chargé in Great Britain from the French Ambassador and transmitted to the Department in despatch No. 435, November 21, 1929 (500.A15a3/451).

the United States of America, invites it to be represented at the Conference which will open in London beginning the third week in January, and at which will be discussed the problems relative to the categories of warships not included in the Treaty of Washington of 1922, as well as questions envisaged in the second paragraph of article XXI of that treaty.

The Government of the Republic is extremely happy that the conversations engaged in between the British Prime Minister and the Ambassador of the United States at London, following the method suggested during the deliberations of the Preparatory Disarmament Commission, have taken so favorable a turn; it is not less happy to learn that the two Governments have found in the Pact of Paris of August 27, 1928, a valuable source for the realization between them of an entente in principle on naval armaments which appears to them to respond to the needs of their security. The British Government, after having consulted with the Government of the United States, now proposes to extend these conversations to the powers particularly interested in the solution of the naval problem, and this initiative has expressly for its object, as is stated in the communication of the Foreign Secretary, the facilitation of the task of the Preparatory Commission and that of the future General Conference for the Limitation and Reduction of Armaments.

The Government of the Republic has given too many proofs of its desire to see the prompt accomplishment of the preparatory work of this Conference, whose meeting will permit the realization of the obligations of article VIII of the Covenant of the League of Nations, not to be delighted by such a proposition. It is therefore happy to accept the invitation which has been addressed to it.

The principles which have always guided French policy, both with regard to the general conditions of the problem of the limitation of armaments and on the subject of the special conditions of the problem of the limitation of naval armaments, have been too often defined, both during the work at Geneva and in related negotiations, to need any repetition.

Furthermore, the British Secretary of State for Foreign Affairs in his letter mentioned above lets it be known that it is the intention of his Government to proceed with the French Government, as with the other Governments invited to the London conference, for a preliminary exchange of views on the questions which will be entered upon the program of their common deliberations. The Government of the Republic sees only advantages in the application of such a method, which will furnish it the opportunity to set forth its viewpoint with regard to the several points outlined in the letter of His Excellency Mr. Henderson on the problems connected with them and on all the questions which may arise before the forthcoming Conference.

500.A15a3/281

*The Japanese Ambassador (Debuchi) to the Secretary of State*

WASHINGTON, October 16, 1929.

MY DEAR MR. SECRETARY: With reference to our conversation this morning, I take pleasure in sending you herewith, for your information, a copy of the reply of my Government to the British Note of October 7. I may add that the text is to be released to the press at Tokio at 9 o'clock, this Friday evening.

With best regards [etc.]    K. DEBUCHI

[Enclosure]

*Japanese Note Accepting the Invitation of the British Government To Participate in a Naval Conference*

1. I have the honour to acknowledge the receipt of your Note dated October 7, informing me of a provisional and informal agreement reached between the Prime Minister and the American Ambassador at London on the subject of naval disarmament, and inviting the Japanese Government to participate in a Conference which it is proposed to summon in London, to consider the categories of ships not covered by the Washington Treaty, and to arrange for and deal with the questions covered by the second paragraph of Article 21 of that Treaty.

2. Having laid before my Government the contents of your Note under acknowledgement, I am desired to state in reply that the Japanese Government are happy to signify their entire concurrence in the desirability of the proposed Conference, and are ready to appoint representatives to take part in that Conference. The date suggested for the opening of the Conference, namely, the beginning of the third week of January, 1930, is also agreeable to my Government.

3. The Japanese Government are further gratified to know of the willingness of the British Government to continue informal conversations with me, as hitherto, on many points which may require elucidation. They note that similar discussions conducted in London by the Prime Minister with the American Ambassador during the last three months had cleared the ground for an agreement on essential points between the British and American Governments, prior to the invitation extended to other naval Powers to meet in a Conference. My Government attach the highest importance to the same procedure being followed by the Japanese and British Governments, in order to ensure agreement between them on various questions that are to be laid before the Conference. The success of the forthcoming Conference no doubt depends in a large measure upon

the satisfactory issue of such preliminary discussions, and my Government confidently trust that the informal conversations between the British Government and myself on questions of special moment will be carried on and completed before these questions are presented to the Conference for final adjustment.

4. In your Note under review, it is intimated that the British Government propose to communicate to me in due course their views as to the subjects for discussions at the Conference. The Japanese Government are looking forward to such a communication with keen interest, and, on their part, they will be glad to furnish the British Government with a corresponding communication as desired.

5. With regard to the four points of principle mentioned in your Note as the subject of provisional agreement between the British and American Governments, the Japanese Government hope to be able to submit their observations in the course of the informal conversations which I shall shortly permit myself to hold with the British Government. They would, however, make use of this occasion to answer [assure?] you of their cordial support to the principle that the Treaty for the Renunciation of War, signed at Paris in 1928, should be taken as the starting point for all discussions on disarmament. They feel confident that the sense of national security inspired by the provision of that Treaty in the mutual relations of the contracting Powers will pave the way for the final settlement of the outstanding questions relative to naval disarmament.

6. In conclusion, I am instructed to express the sincere and earnest hope of the Japanese Government that the Conference will succeed in the adoption of plans calculated to promote international peace and goodwill, and to relieve humanity of the heavy burden of armament whether existing or contemplated. It is not merely the limitation, but also the reduction of armament, that all nations should seek to attain.

---

500.A15a3/436

*Memorandum by the Assistant Secretary of State (Castle) of a Conversation With the Italian Ambassador (De Martino)*

[WASHINGTON,] October 24, 1929.

The Italian Ambassador read me a paraphrase of a cable, sent apparently for his information, on the Italian attitude toward the Naval Conference. He said that Italy must have parity with France. The reason in favor of this is that Italy, because of its situation, has greater interest even than France in receiving supplies from overseas. This, in the opinion of the Italian Government, fully counterbalances the French claim for a larger navy because of having two shores to defend. The Italian Government feels further that the agreement as to parity between Great Britain and the United States is of great value to Italy in its claim for parity with France. One of the French arguments in favor of a larger navy than Italy is that France has more, and more widely scattered colonies which must be defended. Certainly Great Britain might well make the same argument in its discussions with the United States and the fact that Great Britain has agreed to parity with us ought to make it very easy for France to agree to parity with Italy. I told the Ambassador that what he said was interesting, but that I did not feel that his arguments had any validity whatever. I said it seemed to me France needed to receive supplies from overseas just as much as Italy did and that the very fact of having two coasts to defend would make France's need for a navy greater.

As to the American-British argument, I pointed out that one reason why, with its colonies and empire, Great Britain could still afford parity with the United States was the fact that it had naval bases scattered all over the world. I told him, of course, that I could not possibly take sides in the Italian-French controversy and that I was merely pointing out to him the obvious answers which could be made. I told him all I hoped was that both France and Italy would go into the Conference with the full determination to make it a success.

W[ILLIAM] R. C[ASTLE, JR.]

---

500.A15a3/322 : Telegram

*The Ambassador in Belgium (Gibson) to the Secretary of State*

[Paraphrase]

BRUSSELS, October 29, 1929—5 p. m.
[Received 7:43 p. m.]

84. Tyrrell and Massigli [83] came to see me while I was in Paris on my way back to Brussels.

Massigli told me that his Government was very much concerned over the forthcoming Conference since it felt that, as soon as we had come to an agreement with the British, we had disregarded our understanding that a general exchange of views would take place, and had called the London Conference without considering the convenience of the French. Massigli stated that the French Government is of the opinion that: (1) The United States has reached a definite quantitative agreement with the British, and France will be face to face with the alternative of being blamed for failure of the Conference

---

[83] Sir William G. Tyrrell, British Ambassador in France; René Massigli, Chief of the League of Nations section of the French Foreign Office, and French representative on the Preparatory Commission for the Disarmament Conference.

or of accepting the place assigned to her in the agreement; (2) America will withdraw from the Preparatory Commission and all efforts of the League of Nations towards disarmament as soon as a naval agreement has been secured. Massigli added that this belief came from official sources and his Government believed in its accuracy.

My obvious reply was that it is contrary to our methods to arrive at agreements against one country with another and that any idea of an attempt on our part to maneuver the French into an embarrassing position could be dismissed. We had, I told him, no hard and fast understanding with the British, but had merely had discussions and come to an agreement contingent on its acceptance by the other powers; he himself had insisted at Geneva that this method was an essential preliminary to any general negotiations.

Massigli then informed me that they had been unable to begin their conversations with the Italian Government and that the Cabinet crisis had temporarily delayed matters, although it was his hope that the discussions might soon begin. He said, however, that the Anglo-American difficulties were not as hard to solve as were those between France and Italy, inasmuch as the latter was worked up to a high degree of nationalistic feeling and was insistent on parity with France, while France was just as determined that Italy should not be granted parity. France's position, he explained, was based on the fact that the Italian forces were concentrated in the Mediterranean, while the French Navy was spread all over the world; ship for ship parity would amount to giving the Italians manifest superiority. I found him very pessimistic as to the possibility of a reasonable solution considering the temper existing in both France and Italy. He says that in any event they cannot hope to be ready for the Conference at the time it has been called for.

Massigli stated finally, with some show of vigor, that France was determined that the London Conference should make no final decisions, and that the French would not yield on this point inasmuch as their policy was founded on the theory of interdependence of armaments; insistence on this point was largely due to the conviction that the United States, possibly in the company of Great Britain, would withdraw from further disarmament efforts after achieving a naval agreement, unless all categories of armaments were dealt with together; all hope of general disarmament would be useless if this were to happen. I brought out the point that the French position could not be prejudiced by anything contained in the agreement which might be reached at the Conference since what was desired was an agreement which would be supplementary to the Washington Treaty and coterminous with it and which would result in restraining building until 1936; a more comprehensive agreement which might be reached by a General Disarmament Conference would thereby be facilitated. In my opinion the French Government might be reassured on this basis.

Tyrrell later came to see me and stated that he was worried over the French feeling about the Naval Conference. His outline of French feeling in various circles was similar to that which Massigli had described to me; he added that there could be no doubt that the French really thought a definite Anglo-American agreement had been reached, including, presumably, an understanding as to the forces to be allotted to France. The Franco-Italian situation, he said, was very difficult and, if left to themselves, he did not think they would be able to find a solution; in his opinion, the only hope lay in tactful mediation, a mediation which only the United States could supply since France had no confidence in the disinterestedness of the British. Finally, he stated that he had done all in his power to reassure the French concerning the nature of our understanding and our intentions toward them, but he felt that it would undoubtedly have much more effect if we were to approach them along the same lines.

How much of the state of mind now obtaining in France has resulted from inaccurate information and how much from general nervousness I cannot say, but I believe that, for your information, I should report these conversations.

Wilson [84] is sailing home this week and is fully informed as to my conversations with Tyrrell and Massigli. I have consulted with Armour [85] before sending this telegram and have sent a copy to the London Embassy.

GIBSON

---

500.A15a3/381

*The British Chargé (Campbell) to the Secretary of State*

No. 612                                    WASHINGTON, November 11, 1929.

SIR: I have the honour, under instructions from His Majesty's Principal Secretary of State for Foreign Affairs, to inform you that it is suggested that the London Naval Conference should hold its first session on the morning of Tuesday, January 21st next. I am instructed to enquire whether this date would be agreeable to the Government of the United States.

I am further instructed to state that His Majesty's Government consider that it is most desirable that no technical experts should be nominated as delegates by any of the participating Governments though experts would of course be present in the Conference room in

---

[84] Edwin C. Wilson, First Secretary of the Embassy in France.
[85] Norman Armour, Counselor of the Embassy in France.

an advisory capacity. This procedure would, as you are aware, Sir, be in conformity with previous practice and I am to express the hope that the United States Government will agree that this practice should be followed on the present occasion.

His Majesty's Representatives at Paris, Rome and Tokio have been instructed to address similar communications to the French, Italian and Japanese Governments and I understand that particulars regarding the time and place of meeting of the Conference will be communicated to me when agreement has been reached regarding its date of opening. His Majesty's Government would be glad to know at the earliest possible moment whether the date above suggested is agreeable to the Government of the United States.

I also understand that I shall be advised as soon as a definite decision has been taken in regard to the constitution of the British Delegation to the Conference.

I have [etc.]                                          RONALD CAMPBELL

---

500.A15a3/381

### The Secretary of State to the British Chargé (Campbell)

WASHINGTON, November 12, 1929.

SIR: I desire to acknowledge receipt of your note of November 11th and to inform you that it is altogether agreeable to this Government that the first session of the London Naval Conference should be held on the morning of Tuesday, January 21st next.

I desire also to assure you that, in conformity with previous practice, this Government has no intention of appointing technical experts as delegates to the conference. All such necessary experts will naturally be attached to the delegation in an advisory capacity.

Accept [etc.]                                          HENRY L. STIMSON

---

500.A15a3/387

### Memorandum by the Secretary of State of a Conversation With the Japanese Ambassador (Debuchi)

[WASHINGTON,] November 12, 1929.

After explaining that what I said was tentative and in no sense an ultimatum and that I was prepared to go to the conference with an open mind, and further, that what I said had no connection with the British, I went over the aide-mémoire [86] with the Japanese Ambassador explaining the positions throughout and pointing out clearly among the other points that the West Pacific bases question would be affected by the opening of the ratio question, and explained to him how strongly our people out there felt about the result of the

---

[86] Infra.

last conference on the base question. I told him that the last part of the *aide-mémoire* was merely an attempt to put on record for him what I never had an opportunity to put in writing but thought I had told it verbally many times, namely, the substance of our conversations with the British during the summer.

After I had finished he expressed his disappointment on the subject of the ratio and was evidently very much troubled as to how he could explain it to his people. He will come here next week and asked for at least an hour's conference. Incidentally he said that he had been at the Washington Conference and pointed out that Balfour [87] had reserved the question of small cruisers from the 5–5–3 agreement, so far as Britain was concerned; also that the question had been brought up again at Geneva in 1927 [88] by Japan and that he got the idea that America was friendly to 10–10–7. For these reasons he was afraid that our opposition to opening it, he thought, was unreasonable. I pointed out to him that he had not shown any change of situation from 1922 when I had understood the 5–5–3 ratio had been accepted by the Japanese representatives as a sufficiently defensive position for them. We talked at considerable length in a very frank way and it was agreed that he should come in next week.

H[ENRY] L. S[TIMSON]

500.A15a3/387

*The Secretary of State to the Japanese Ambassador (Debuchi)*

AIDE-MÉMOIRE

[WASHINGTON, November 12, 1929.]

You have asked me for an expression of my opinion as to the proposed ratio for Japan in the several classes to be dealt with at the London Conference, and you have suggested that Japan desires a ratio not of 5–3 but of 10–7 in the cruiser class particularly as to the type armed with 8-inch guns.

You will realize that one of the great difficulties of the conference will come in the desires of France and Italy to keep certain ratios with each other and it may well be that the word "ratio" will be an unfortunate word in the London conference. It may be possible that the eventual settlement will be made as a result of actual conditions in ships rather than ratios.

I have not reached final opinions on conference matters and hope

---

[87] Rt. Hon. Arthur James Balfour, member of the British delegation at the conference on the Limitation of Armament, Washington, November 12, 1921–February 6, 1922.
[88] Three-Power Conference; see *Foreign Relations*, 1927, vol. I, pp. 1 ff.

to go to the conference with no fixed positions on the topics that are to come up. I look forward to the personal meetings with your representatives to get a knowledge of your particular problems and wishes and recall the effective support for reduction which the Japanese delegation afforded our delegation both at Geneva and Washington. In that light you will understand my answer. You will understand also I am speaking what is in my mind with great frankness and not guardedly as if I were stating final positions.

I do not believe that a change in the attitude of the Japanese Government on its ratio in the cruiser class increasing it to 10–7 is likely to be conducive to the success of the conference. I desire to state quite frankly and at some length my reasons for my belief.

The Washington Conference was an attempt so to limit naval armament in order to remove the incentive of one nation to build against another. The formula which was proposed by that conference to end the competition was that Great Britain and the United States should agree that their fleets should be equal, the theory being that inasmuch as future building could not change that equality, the incentive to build would be gone. The formula between Japan and Great Britain and Japan and the United States was that a ratio of 5–3 would result in satisfactory naval strength in Japanese waters. If you will refer to the record of the conference you will find that the original formula proposed by this Government covered not only capital ships and aircraft carriers but also all auxiliary combatant craft, and specifically covered cruisers, destroyers and submarines. This proposition was accepted on behalf of Japan by Baron Kato.[89] He said:

"Gladly accepting, therefore, the proposal in principle, Japan is ready to proceed with determination to a sweeping reduction in her naval armament",

and again he said:

"Japan has never claimed nor had any intention of claiming to have a naval establishment equal in strength to that of either the United States or the British Empire. Her existing plan will show conclusively that she had never in view preparation for offensive war."

Later the position of Japan was greatly solidified by Article 19 of the treaty under which Japan, Great Britain and the United States undertook to maintain the *status quo* as to military stations in Pacific waters within a large radius from Japan.[90] The point I am

---

[89] See *Conference on the Limitation of Armament, Washington, November 12, 1921–February 6, 1922* (Washington, Government Printing Office, 1922), p. 106.

[90] Treaty between the United States, the British Empire, France, Italy, and Japan for the limitation of naval armament, signed February 6, 1922, *Foreign Relations*, 1922, vol. I, pp. 247, 252.

emphasizing at the moment is that the net result gave Japan a naval position in the East which more than adequately protected her interests without any increase in the 5–5–3 formula. Under these circumstances it would seem that to increase Japan's ratio to 10–10–7, would in view of these restrictions on American and British defenses in Eastern waters, tend to increase her strength beyond that which is necessary for defensive purposes. Therefore I had considered that I should accept the statements made on behalf of Japan at the Washington Conference, in view of the circumstances attending their utterance, as a considered and final statement of naval policy, largely dependent on the agreement as to bases, in the same way that the agreement as to bases is dependent on it.

After the Washington Conference, it is true, there was substantial building in the cruiser and submarine classes by various nations, and the race for armament seemed again to be forcing a needless and dangerous financial burden on the nations. To attempt to deal with that situation the Geneva Conference was called, and if you will refer to the invitations to that conference you will remember that it was called in an attempt to carry on the principles laid down at Washington. The Geneva Conference failed largely because of difficulties between Great Britain and the United States, and in that conference Japan always took the position that she desired to limit the tonnage in each class, and to put that limit down as low as other nations would agree. At that time Great Britain desired a large number of cruisers; the United States was not willing to accede.

Recently we have entered into the communications which you know about with Great Britain. In those communications and in our conferences with Mr. MacDonald we have not discussed the Japanese ratio or the Japanese position, feeling that it would not help to discuss such questions when the representatives of Japan were not present, therefore what I am now saying to you is in no wise a statement of the British position, nor am I informed whether or not the British agree with what I am saying.

The general range of our discussions with the British has been as follows:

We considered the submarine category together and found that both of us would be willing to abandon the submarine entirely. We felt doubt as to whether either Japan or France and Italy would so agree. We felt that, if submarines were not to be abolished we were willing to limit the building of them, and we expected that Japan would probably have the same idea as to submarines although we knew that Japan had, built and building, a very substantial submarine tonnage, probably above any ratio of 5–5–3.

When we came to discuss the destroyer class we found that the United States was at the moment possessed of a large number of destroyers, built for the purpose of the last war, which would become over sixteen years old by 1936, some of them are out of commission already. The United States probably would in ordinary course soon scrap a certain amount of this tonnage so that Great Britain and ourselves felt that we would be glad to put the limit of this destroyer class as low as practicable, and we talked of a limitation, between 150,000 and 200,000 tons.

In respect to capital ships, the United States suggestion was that there should be no replacements or a minimum of replacements other than those necessary to work out in 1936 the 5–5–3 ratio. That, we pointed out, would mean a large saving in money. Great Britain did not take any final position as to capital ship replacements but suggested that all nations should make some replacements in a smaller type of battleship perhaps 25,000 tons. We are not inclined to accord with this last suggestion as it is out of accord with our historic naval views. We have promised Great Britain to consider it. We regard the question as less important than the cruiser question and felt that it was a matter which could safely be left to the London Conference.

When we came to the more difficult cruiser class our effort was first to persuade the British to be satisfied with what we regarded as a smaller number of units and a lower tonnage than they asked at Geneva. They finally made a suggestion that they would be satisfied with about 50 units with a tonnage of about 340,000 tons in 1936 (this is about their present strength), with a replacement program of say two cruisers a year until 1936, making a total of 14 replacements. That would make their 1936 cruiser status fifteen 8-inch gun cruisers, a total of 146,000 tons, and about 192,000 ton smaller 6-inch cruisers, many of which would be old. Suggestions were made between us of some method of providing a common yardstick for measurement which would make due allowance for greater age and inferior gun calibre of the British fleet as compared with the American cruiser fleet which, Great Britain suggested should consist of 10 of our *Omaha* class (7,000 ton 6-inch); 18 of 10,000 8-inch class and a further number of smaller 6-inch gun cruisers to accomplish parity with Great Britain under such terms as we might agree on as constituting total cruiser equality. United States naval advisers on the other hand felt that the United States should have at least 21 of the 10,000 ton 8-inch gun type to make up for the disparity in displacement tonnage. When we reached this point we thought we were near enough agreement with Britain to leave the matter safely to the conference, and in that situation the matter has been left.

H[ENRY] L. S[TIMSON]

500.A15a/392a : Telegram

*The Secretary of State to the Ambassador in Great Britain (Dawes)*

WASHINGTON, November 12, 1929—5 p. m.

294. The Secretary of State handed the Japanese Ambassador an *aide-mémoire* this noon concerning the Japanese desires at the forthcoming naval conference which reads as follows:

[Here follows the text of the *aide-mémoire*, printed *supra*.]

You may communicate a copy of the *aide-mémoire* to the Prime Minister for his confidential information.

STIMSON

---

500.A15a3/393 : Telegram

*The Chargé in Great Britain (Atherton) to the Secretary of State*

[Paraphrase]

LONDON, November 14, 1929—3 p. m.
[Received November 14—2 : 45 p. m.]

325. Department's No. 294, November 12, 5 p. m.   I have been informally advised by the Foreign Office that your *aide-mémoire* handed to the Japanese Ambassador in Washington has been read with considerable satisfaction, and that Great Britain will follow the same line with reference to Japan's wish for a cruiser ratio of 10–10–7, although it will not take any action which might give rise to suspicion of any Anglo-American agreement against Japan.

I have been asked by newspaper reporters for comment on the story which appeared in the Tokyo press today to the effect that, as the result of the Anglo-American naval agreement, Japan's desire for a cruiser ratio of 10–10–7 had been turned down.   In reply I stated that I had no knowledge of Anglo-American conversations but could give assurances that the Anglo-American discussions would not in any way impinge upon the work of the Naval Disarmament Conference since this agreement is concerned exclusively with parity in naval strength between Great Britain and the United States.

ATHERTON

---

500.A15a3/425

*The British Chargé (Campbell) to the Secretary of State*

WASHINGTON, November 18, 1929.

MY DEAR MR. SECRETARY: As requested by you during our conversation this afternoon I send you herewith an *aide-mémoire* containing the message I was instructed to deliver to you on the subject of the Japanese Government's wish for an increase in their cruiser ratio.

As I informed you, I was to explain that my instructions to speak to you in this sense were despatched before your *aide-mémoire* on the subject of the Japanese Government's claim had been seen by His Majesty's Government. I was to add that His Majesty's Government fully agreed with the forceful arguments employed by you therein, but that it would, in their opinion, probably be unwise to use precisely the same language to the Japanese Ambassadors in Washington and London.

I should perhaps further explain that my instructions to speak in the sense of the enclosed *aide-mémoire*, resulted from my having informed my Government, after our conversation of November 7th, that you wondered what was being said by His Majesty's Government to the Japanese Government on the subject of their wish to have a cruiser ratio of 70% of the United States figure for 8″ gun cruisers,— a wish which, you had said, you found embarrassing (1) because you did not wish in your conversations with Japanese representatives to have the understanding—as far as it went—between our two Governments attacked as it were in detail, while at the same time you were under the necessity to avoid saying anything by which they might receive the impression that the understanding was in the nature of a rigid Anglo-American agreement and so conceive that they were being confronted with a *fait accompli:* (2) because you were at the same time anxious not to offend the Japanese Government, who, you considered, genuinely desired naval limitation and reduction.

In speaking to you in the sense of the enclosed *aide-mémoire* I was to enquire whether you agreed.

I should add that since the instructions to me in the sense of this *aide-mémoire* were prepared the Prime Minister has found that even on an agreement between the United States and the United Kingdom with eighteen and fifteen 8″ gun cruisers respectively, Japan as I mentioned this afternoon will claim that to her strength of twelve such vessels must be added twenty thousand tons. The Japanese claim to a 70% ratio is based on tonnage and not numbers of ships—and, as is of course known to you, the displacement of Japan's twelve 8″ gun cruisers built and building is only 108,400. If the 8″ gun cruiser tonnage of the United States can be reduced to 180,000 the settlement of the Japanese ratio difficulty will in His Majesty's Government's opinion still be difficult, but not impossible: but if the United States 8″ gun cruiser strength were to remain at a figure higher than 180,000 tons the settlement of the difficulty raised by the Japanese claim would appear to be impossible without some addition to the projected British 8″ gun cruiser tonnage.

I am reporting to my Government by telegram your request to be kept fully and early informed of any conversations carried on between His Majesty's Government and the French and Italian Governments respectively, as well as of any thing they may know of the conversations between France and Italy. I am also reporting that you would wish to learn as fully and as soon as possible what passes between His Majesty's Government and the Japanese Government.

Believe me [etc.]     RONALD CAMPBELL

[Enclosure]

*The British Embassy to the Department of State*

### AIDE MÉMOIRE

His Majesty's Government in the United Kingdom think that the answer to the three points raised by the Secretary of State is as follows:

(1) His Majesty's Government consider there would be no objection to the Japanese Ambassador being frankly informed of the understanding with the Prime Minister, namely, that the ways and means of bridging the gap of 30,000 tons which divides the Governments of the United States and of the United Kingdom would be studied by each during the period before the Five-power Conference meets in January, the actual solution of this particular problem being left to the Conference. The problem is in the opinion of His Majesty's Government of the type which is best left for treatment when the interested Powers meet round a table, since it depends to some extent on the attitude of other Powers for its solution.

(2) His Majesty's Government find difficulty in the Japanese Government's wish for a certain increase in their ratio for 8″ gun cruisers, only in so far as the Government of the United States may find it necessary to embark on a heavy programme of 8″ gun cruiser construction. On a comparison of the 8″ gun cruiser tonnage built and building for the Governments of the United Kingdom and Japan, it will be seen that the Japanese ratio will be nearly 74% of the 8″ gun cruiser tonnage of the United Kingdom. It is clear that any increase in the present building programme of Japan which might be brought about by the size of the 8″ gun cruiser programme of the United States, would impose upon His Majesty's Government however reluctantly a revision of British 8″ gun cruiser strength. If it prove possible to find a way to enable the United States to reduce the number of their 8″ gun cruisers to eighteen, this particular difficulty of the Japanese ratio will have been reduced to small proportions for the Japanese by building twelve ships would almost have achieved a 70% ratio on numbers of ships, if not on tonnage.

However the difficulty is not only the Japanese demand for a 70% ratio which causes a difficulty for His Majesty's Government with regard to the relative numbers of 8″ gun cruisers: for His Majesty's Government find that any higher American figure for such vessels than eighteen would probably involve an agitation for further British construction of 8″ gun cruisers in order to achieve parity, whence it is the more desirable for the United States strength in this type of vessels to be kept down to eighteen.

(3) His Majesty's Government agree that the Japanese Government sincerely desire reduction. They feel that that Government are clearly most anxious not to exceed their present building programme of twelve 8″ gun cruisers and that they would only do so if this necessity were imposed upon them by the size of the American building programme.

His Majesty's Government do not for their part think there would be danger of offending the Japanese Government were the position explained to them frankly, and if it were added that both the Government of the United States and His Majesty's Government in the United Kingdom feel confident of guaranteeing a solution of the problem of parity when the Conference meets, that the question of the size of the Japanese ratio is intimately associated with the bridging of the gap between the United States and the United Kingdom and that these Governments feel that both questions could most appropriately be left for final decision when the Conference meets.

WASHINGTON, November 19, 1929.

---

500.A15a3/407 : Telegram

*The Secretary of State to the Ambassador in Great Britain (Dawes)*

WASHINGTON, November 18, 1929—4 p. m.

299. In reply to the following questions handed to me by the French Naval Attaché on Friday, an *aide-mémoire* was handed him this morning.

"1. Are the categories of the modified French formula to be adhered to at the London Conference? Or shall we understand that the number of these categories is to be five instead of four?

2. Is a certain percentage of transfer between these categories to be considered?

3. What is the tentative Anglo-American agreement on the following points.:

*a*) Battleships. Abolition by age limit?

*b*) Aircraft carriers.

*c*) Cruisers. Is there a definite agreement reached for the total tonnage of this class, and for the proportion between 10,000 and smaller cruisers?

*d*) Destroyers.

*e*) Submarines."

The *aide-mémoire* reads as follows:

"November 15, 1929.    Answer to points raised in French Memorandum.

1. It is presumed that by the words "modified formula", the French Embassy refers to the proposal presented at the 26th Meeting of the Third Session of the Preparatory Commission, the 11th of April, 1927, by Mr. Paul Boncour. This proposal was subsequently modified in informal conversations in Paris between Vice Admiral Kelly and M. Saluan, Chief of Staff of the French Marine, and in similar conversations between Commander Sablé, French Naval Attaché in Washington, and Admirals Jones and Long, of the General Board, United States Navy. The conversations in Paris and Washington covered five categories, namely, capital ships, aircraft carriers, cruisers, 10,000 to 1,850 tons, destroyers, 1,850 to 600 tons, and submarines. The recent tentative discussions between Great Britain and the United States have dealt similarly with five categories, namely, battleships, aircraft carriers, cruisers, destroyers and submarines.

2. While the question of percentage of transfer between categories has not been considered in the discussions between Great Britain and the United States, this country will look sympathetically on the raising of this question at the forthcoming conference, in the hope that it will aid France and Italy in the solution of their respective problems, due to their special needs.

3. There has been no definite agreement between Great Britain and the United States on any of the points mentioned. Certain matters have been discussed and tentative understandings arrived at as follows:

(*a*) Battleships. The general principle of reduction of the battleship fleet has been agreed upon, but the question of method will be left entirely to the forthcoming conference.

(*b*) Aircraft Carriers. The question has not been discussed and will be left entirely to the forthcoming conference.

(*c*) Cruisers. A comparison of the cruiser fleets of the two Powers resulted in placing the tentative figure of 339,000 tons for Great Britain and 315,000 tons for the United States as the figures which best suited the relative needs of the two Powers. There is no agreement on a proportion between the number of 10,000-ton and the number of smaller cruisers, and the question of numbers of such units is still to be agreed upon, the United States desiring 21 and Great Britain, 15 such cruisers.

(*d*) Destroyers. No figure has been agreed upon, this question being left open to the conference. It is the desire of both Powers to reduce, however, and a figure below 200,000 tons might be expected to be satisfactory.

(*e*) Submarines. Both nations have expressed their willingness to abolish the submarine in case all other countries would do the same. It is the desire of both countries likewise to reduce the tonnage of this type if it is maintained, but no definite figures have been set, the whole question being left to the conference."

You may communicate a copy of the questions and the *aide-mémoire* to the Prime Minister for his information.

Mail copies to Paris.

STIMSON

---

500.A15a3/409 : Telegram

*The Ambassador in Italy (Garrett) to the Secretary of State*

[Paraphrase]

ROME, November 19, 1929—5 p. m.
[Received November 19—4 : 25 p. m.]

84. I was today informed by Minister for Foreign Affairs that he is most optimistic concerning the possibility of coming to an understanding on parity with France. He says this optimism is based on the report of a discussion between the Italian Ambassador in Paris and Briand; as has happened before, however, he may perhaps be forced to reduce this optimism when Briand has had further talks with Berthelot and other officials. Grandi expresses enthusiastic support of President Hoover's proposal that food ships in time of war should be free from any interference.[91] There is no thought in his mind—as he most emphatically says—of placing any obstacles in the way of the announced purposes of the Naval Conference, but he said that he is considering bringing up the food ship question himself in his opening speech at the Conference, despite the President's statement that this question will not be injected into the discussions. My answer to him, to which he readily assented, was that I assumed there would be an agenda agreed on by the five powers before the conference.

GARRETT

---

500.A15a3/417a : Telegram

*The Secretary of State to the Ambassador in Great Britain (Dawes)*

[Paraphrase]

WASHINGTON, November 20, 1929—5 p. m.

305. The President deems it wiser, until after the outcome of the forthcoming discussions with the members of the Japanese delegation on their way to London, for you to refrain from discussing the question of the Japanese ratio with Matsudaira, in order that any possible misunderstanding or confusion on this delicate subject may be avoided.

STIMSON

---

[91] See vol. III, p. 24. The President's views were publicly stated in his Armistice Day address printed in *Congressional Record*, vol. 72, pt. 1, p. 505.

500.A15a3/425

### The Secretary of State to the British Chargé (Campbell)

WASHINGTON, November 21, 1929.

MY DEAR MR. CAMPBELL: Referring to your letter of the eighteenth and the *Aide-Mémoire* contained in it, your letter correctly states the further information which I desire from your Government.

As to the three sections of the *Aide-Mémoire,*—I am in agreement with No. 1. I am not in agreement with the sense of No. 2 that it is the United States desire for a program of eight inch gun cruisers that constitutes the difficulty with Japan. I would be inclined to put the reasons for the difficulty in the British demands for total cruiser tonnage, but that difference of approach is more or less inherent in our two somewhat different points of view.

The same comment applies in a less degree to Paragraph 3 of your *Aide-Mémoire*.

Sincerely yours,

HENRY L. STIMSON

---

500.A15a3/417

### The British Embassy to the Department of State

#### AIDE-MÉMOIRE

On November 11th an interview took place between the Prime Minister and the Japanese Ambassador, when the latter expressed the hope that whatever agreement might be arrived at between Great Britain and the United States it would not be on such a basis as to necessitate further construction by Japan: for example, if Great Britain maintained fifteen 8″ gun cruisers as against eighteen for the United States, Japan would require to add 20,000 tons to her present programme while, if the United States maintained twenty-one of the above units, it would necessitate additional Japanese construction to the amount of 40,000 tons. These figures were calculated upon the American programme.

The Japanese Ambassador also expressed, on behalf of his Government, the hope that Great Britain would not object to Japan having a 70% ratio in relation to Great Britain or the United States, whichever of the two fleets was the stronger, and further that this ratio should apply to all categories of war vessels with the exception of capital ships.

In replying that he would note what His Excellency had said and would in due course furnish him with a memorandum as soon as there had been time to consider his points, the Prime Minister expressed surprise that an American strength of eighteen 8″ gun cruisers, as opposed to fifteen for Great Britain, would necessitate additional construction for Japan. In return for certain compensations in the matter of small vessels, this country would accept fifteen 8″ gun vessels as against eighteen for the United States, and regard this as parity. Mr. MacDonald also hoped that the present Japanese strength, which he understood to be twelve 8″ gun cruisers, would be accepted as an equilibrium: and that the United States, Great Britain and Japan, as the three great naval Powers, would rest content with an 8″ gun cruiser ratio of 18–15–12.

On November 18th a further interview between the Prime Minister and the Japanese Ambassador took place, when the Ambassador enquired whether Mr. MacDonald had any further communication to make regarding the Japanese claim to a 70% ratio. Mr. MacDonald said that he had not, but that he strongly advised the Japanese Ambassador to let the matter rest. The Prime Minister pointed out that the Japanese Ambassador had begged him to come to such an agreement with the United States as would not necessitate any new building on the part of Japan, and that he had taken this as a sincere request. The Prime Minister assured the Ambassador that it fitted in with his own ideas. If, however, the Japanese Ambassador wished to supplement that with a request that his Government might increase its ratio of building, he would lay himself open to the charge, or at any rate the suspicion, that their real object was to increase the relative strength of the Japanese navy. That would have a very bad effect on everybody concerned.

The Prime Minister explained to the Japanese Ambassador the general idea of His Majesty's Government. His Majesty's Government were working on tonnage figures and also on numbers of ships and that, in the end, would have to be the form which any agreement took. What they were really driving at was to get to an agreement upon what would be a state of equilibrium, and they were working on the assumption that if Japan would agree to twelve, 8″ gun cruisers, the United States to eighteen and His Majesty's Government to fifteen, they would regard those as the figures of equilibrium in that particular class of vessel.

The Japanese Ambassador emphasised the necessity of Japan possessing means of security and on this Mr. MacDonald had two observations to make:—firstly that in these modern days security was being sought for more in the effective creation of a peace organisation than in competition and comparative building and, secondly, that Japan would have to be very careful that in seeking her own security she did not upset the sense of security of other nations. Nobody wanted Japan to be insecure, nor did any nation wish to feel insecure herself.

Mr. MacDonald emphasised that the conversations he was having with the Japanese Ambassador were a kind of process of thinking aloud, and that he was not negotiating with him, but was surveying with him the elements of a problem to which His Majesty's Government and the Japanese Government were to come to close grips when the five Power conference entered upon its work.

WASHINGTON, November 21, 1929.

---

500.A15a3/426

### The British Chargé (Campbell) to the Secretary of State

WASHINGTON, November 23, 1929.

MY DEAR MR. SECRETARY: I am very much obliged to you for your letter of November 21st giving your views on the *aide-mémoire* which I sent you in my letter of November 18th.

I have informed my Government of what you say.

I have now received instructions to state that His Majesty's Government in the United Kingdom entirely share your views regarding the advisability of each of our two Governments keeping the other fully and urgently informed of their conversations with the other three interested Powers, and I am to communicate to you summaries which have been telegraphed to me of conversations that took place between the Prime Minister and the French and Italian Ambassadors on November 11th and 12th.

I annex an *aide-mémoire* containing these summaries.

Believe me [etc.]
RONALD CAMPBELL

[Enclosure]

### The British Embassy to the Department of State

#### AIDE-MÉMOIRE

The French Ambassador expressed M. Briand's hope that belligerent rights would not be raised at the conference and he was assured by the Prime Minister that so far as His Majesty's Government in the United Kingdom were concerned, the subject would not be raised, and further, that during the Prime Minister's visit to Washington he had invited Mr. Hoover's attention to obligations assumed by Great Britain under Article 16 of the League Covenant which His Majesty's Government could in no way violate. The French Ambassador, who afterwards left for Paris to consult his Government, was also informed that it was the intention of His Majesty's Government to raise at the conference the question of the size and age of capital ships as well as the calibre of their main armament. The

Prime Minister also remarked that a destroyer agreement would have to depend mainly upon an agreement regarding submarines.

In speaking to the Italian Ambassador the Prime Minister explained that both President Hoover and himself had felt that personal and informal communications had been so helpful in removing misunderstanding that they had agreed to suggest to other participating Governments that they might pursue the same method. The Italian Ambassador replied that conversations which his Government had initiated with the French Government had been temporarily suspended owing to the French Ministerial crisis, but were about to be resumed. Italy, who was not much interested in submarines, if an agreement could be arrived at, would certainly seek naval parity with France.

The Italian Ambassador left for Italy November 15th to consult his Government.

WASHINGTON, November 23, 1929.

---

500.A15a3/427 : Telegram

*The Ambassador in Great Britain (Dawes) to the Secretary of State*

[Paraphrase]

LONDON, November 23, 1929—1 p.m.
[Received 10:50 p. m.]

342. At noon today the French Ambassador called on me to report on his conversation with the Prime Minister. He had been asked by Briand to submit to MacDonald question No. 3 as contained in your telegram No. 299 of November 18 and MacDonald's answer was in effect the same as the one you gave. The Ambassador, at Briand's suggestion, asked MacDonald for what he called the "criterion" of the British Navy; I gather that this is the beginning of a Franco-British discussion as to the minimum naval needs of the two countries.

I learned from the French Ambassador that France will appoint no naval officers as delegates but that a similar procedure will be followed as in our own case through the appointment of naval officers as official advisers. It is probable, but not yet settled, that the French delegation will consist of four members. The state of health of the French Minister of Marine is causing some embarrassment and it is possible that he may not be able to attend the Conference. The delegation will include Briand and it is expected that Tardieu [92] will come to London for a few days only.

Briand's suggestion was conveyed to MacDonald by the French

---

[92] President of the French Council of Ministers.

Ambassador to the effect that the Conference be opened with a general discussion of the "criterion" as he called it; by this he meant a general discussion of relative naval needs, thereby avoiding too early precipitation of questions of a technical nature. Briand's idea, according to the Ambassador, was suggested by some of the methods which obtained at the Geneva Naval Conference—methods which had best be avoided, he thought.

DAWES

500.A15a3/465

## The Italian Embassy to the Department of State

### MEMORANDUM

[WASHINGTON, November 29, 1929.]

1. In the preliminary discussions between the United States and Great Britain has the fixing of a maximum age limit been contemplated for other types of naval vessels besides the battleships?

2. Under which principles will the line of demarcation between cruisers and destroyers be fixed?

3. Has the American Government considered the opportunity that, in view of the difficulty to fix a same and only method of limitation for all of the five participating nations, the London Conference take into consideration the possibility of applying such different principles as will be suggested by the different needs and the inequalities existing in the composition and strength of the fleets of the various nations?

4. Among the methods that may be considered by the Conference in view of the planned reduction of tonnage to replace the battleships, has the method suggested by Italy in her reply to the Anglo-French proposal of August 1928 [93] been considered, that is, that the five Powers signatories of the Washington Treaty pledge themselves to postpone until after 1936 the construction of the line vessels that the Treaty allows them to lay down during the period 1931–1936?

500.A15a3/455

## Memorandum by the Secretary of State

[WASHINGTON,] December 2, 1929.

I had a long interview with the Japanese Ambassador this morning. He said first that he was instructed by his Government to tell me two things. First, that in regard to my former note as to what took place at the Washington Conference Baron Shidehara wanted

[93] Presumably the British *note verbale* presented pursuant to instructions contained in the Foreign Office telegram of July 30, 1928, Great Britain, Cmd. 3211, Miscellaneous No. 6 (1928), p. 27; Italian reply, October 6, 1928, *ibid.*, p. 39.

to call my attention to the fact, in respect to Senator Kato's speech, that the Japanese delegates had merely wished to express their general concurrence but not to commit themselves as to anything concerning the ratio of auxiliary vessels. He pointed out that the time was so short after the Hughes' "bombshell" as he expressed it, that they could not have taken any other position.

In the second place, that in respect to cruisers specifically there had been little discussion at the time of the conference and nothing had been agreed on that.

He said that Baron Shidehara nevertheless was willing, without compromising his original proposal of the cruiser ratio of 10–10–7, to discuss the matter of actual conditions. He pointed out this phrase had been used by me.

At this point I took occasion to tell the Ambassador of my proposition to the British made through Ronald Campbell on Saturday, namely, that care should be taken not to make any announcement of the detailed position of any power during the first speeches at the conference. I pointed out how inevitably the newspapers of each country would "dig in" if any such announcement was made and subsequent compromise would become very much more difficult. I pointed out also the different conditions which existed in 1921 when Mr. Hughes made his celebrated first speech. The Ambassador said he fully understood and would communicate it to his Government.

He then brought up the conferences that were going on between Prime Minister MacDonald and Ambassador Matsudaira and stated that Matsudaira had stated to MacDonald that the ultimate aim of Japan was to have 126,000 tons of large cruisers if the United States tonnage was taken tentatively as 180,000 tons. He pointed out that this made a ratio of 70 to 100. He said that this tonnage was ultimately to be distributed in thirteen vessels aggregating the 126,000 tons. He pointed out, however, that at present Japan had four of the large cruisers completed and four under construction; that in addition she had four smaller cruisers of 7,100 tons carrying eight-inch guns; that she wanted to build two more smaller cruisers with eight-inch guns, making fourteen cruisers altogether carrying eight-inch guns. He said, however, that this was merely a temporary condition, made necessary by her possession of the four smaller cruisers and that her ultimate aim would be as above stated—thirteen vessels aggregating 126,000 tons. He asked if Mr. Dawes would not be authorized to receive communications from Mr. Matsudaira and to negotiate with him. I told him that Mr. Dawes was already authorized to receive such communications and send them to me, but that for the present I found difficulty in having him negotiating over there while we were considering the matter here and that at present I would rather have that situation stand.

He then asked my view as to Japan having seventy per cent of the total auxiliary vessels. I countered by asking him which his Government laid more stress on—having seventy per cent of the large cruisers or seventy per cent of the total auxiliary vessels. He said that if we were willing they should have seventy per cent of the large cruisers it would be very easy to settle the question of the total auxiliary vessels— evidently feeling that we would have no objection to seventy per cent of that. I laughingly told him I could see that that might follow.

He then asked me about submarines, telling me that the Japanese planned to have 100,000 tons but were willing to cut to 80,000 and would not insist on parity with us—and thus would not object to our having more than 80,000. I asked him what Japan would do supposing we only had 75,000 tons and he was not prepared to answer, evidently indicating that it would not make any change in their plans. He asked me about our negotiations on destroyers which he understood were to be 150,000 to 200,000 tons. I told him that was not settled; that all we had done with Great Britain was to agree that we would have the same number and to feel that it did not make a very difficult proposition.

He then reminded me that I had asked him at an earlier conference what the position of his Government would be as to capital ships; whether they would prefer to reduce in size of ships or in the number of ships. He told me that that matter was still under the consideration of his Government.

He then told me that he brought me a special message of thanks from Baron Shidehara; that the Baron had noticed the opinion in the United States was more friendly to Japan than it had been and regarded it as due to the leadership of this Administration and he said that Japan felt that Mr. Hoover having been in Japan and I having been in Japan, it was a good time to work for intellectual cooperation and, if possible, to solve the question of immigration. He said he realized that we had first better solve the important question of the naval conference but that he had always hoped that this Administration would work out these other matters which would put American relations with Japan on the most happy foundation. I expressed my thanks for Baron Shidehara's message but disclaimed any ability to lead the American public opinion to the extent that he mentioned.

H[enry] L. S[timson]

---

500.A15a3/449a : Telegram

*The Secretary of State to the Ambassador in Great Britain (Dawes)*

[Paraphrase]

Washington, December 3, 1929—1 p. m.

326. The Chargé d'Affaires of the British Embassy came in yesterday to discuss a tentative outline of procedure for the Naval Confer-

ence and to inquire if we agreed to this outline in principle. The proposal was that a plenary session be held for speeches of welcome, replies and for organization of the Conference on January 21, and that on Wednesday, January 22 a "private plenary session" should be held for the purpose of set speeches by the various delegates discussing the whole naval problem. I was strongly opposed to the second item concerning a private plenary session, since the President and I are both of the opinion that the chances of success will be the better the fewer set speeches are made in the early part of the Conference. I think furthermore that it is utterly impossible to keep private a plenary session, the result of which would only be that press accounts of such a session would be announced in advance and would consist of a series of rumors both ill advised and contentious. I suggested to Mr. Campbell, as an alternative, that a plenary session should take place on the first day as planned, that on the second day there should be a private meeting between the heads of the various delegations and that the third day should be occupied with a further plenary session for organizing and for dividing the work of the Conference into committees. Campbell has reported these points of view direct to the Foreign Office, but the President and I feel so strongly the need for avoiding the possibility that the various delegations might assume attitudes in public early in the Conference from which they could not recede (thereby converting what was intended to be a peaceable conference into a battleground) that I think this matter should be discussed by you as soon as possible with both the Prime Minister and with Henderson for the purpose of making sure that in the arrangement laid down before the first meeting no opportunity will be afforded for anything but speeches of a most general nature. I think the less rules and regulations laid down in advance, the better; thereby the Conference will be placed in a position to determine its own procedure in a way best suited to the circumstances obtaining at the time, after arrival of the delegates at London.

STIMSON

---

500.A15a3/462

*The British Chargé (Campbell) to the Secretary of State*

No. 643                                        WASHINGTON, December 3, 1929.

SIR: I have the honour to inform you, under instructions from His Majesty's Principal Secretary of State for Foreign Affairs, that all five Governments concerned having now accepted January 21st as the date for the opening of the Naval Conference, the opening meeting will now definitely be held on the morning of that day.

Mr. Henderson would be glad to receive, not later than December 15th next, a complete list of all advisers, experts, and secretaries who will be attending the conference. It would be convenient if this list could be drawn up in two forms, the first list indicating the technical division between the various groups of advisers and the second giving the whole list of advisers, experts and secretaries in order of their precedence.[94]

I have [etc.]                                         RONALD CAMPBELL

500.A15a3/466

### The Department of State to the Italian Embassy

#### MEMORANDUM

With reference to the memorandum from the Italian Embassy dated November 29, 1929, there is submitted the following answers to the Ambassador's questions.

(1) Yes. The discussions were on the basis that cruisers had a life of twenty years, destroyers sixteen years, and submarines thirteen years. There is no reason why other ages should not be considered by the conference. Those figures seem to be the result of general Navy opinion.

(2) While the matter has not been particularly discussed, the smallest cruiser to be included in the classification is in the neighborhood of 4,000 tons. Such cruisers are all British and it is not the intention to build American cruisers so small nor that the British shall build other cruisers so small.

(3) The matter has been talked about, but it seemed to be one fairly open to the consideration of the conference.

(4) The matter has been talked about without agreement. The United States has expressed a desire to reduce battleship replacements to the minimum. Some discussion has been had as to whether those replacements should be in tonnage of units or units, but no determination has been arrived at. The suggestion of the elimination of units has been coupled with the suggestion that the life of existing units be lengthened.

WASHINGTON, December 4, 1929.

---

500.A15a3/456 : Telegram

### The Ambassador in Great Britain (Dawes) to the Secretary of State

LONDON, December 4, 1929—1 p. m.
[Received 4:45 p. m.]

359. Department's 299, November 18, 4 p. m. The following letter, dated December 3, has been received by Atherton from Craigie of the Foreign Office:

---

[94] The information requested was communicated to the British Embassy in the Department's note of December 19, 1929, not printed. The composition of the American delegation to the London Naval Conference is printed in full in Department of State, *Press Releases*, December 21, 1929, p. 121.

"I have been asked to let you know that the *aide-mémoire* on the naval question communicated by the Secretary of State to the French Naval Attaché at Washington, a copy of which you were good enough to enclose in your letter to Vansittart, of the 19th ultimo, has been carefully considered here.

As regards categories, we are very interested to learn that in the later conversation between the French and yourselves the 'French formula' was modified so as to cover five categories, namely, capital ships, aircraft carriers, cruisers from 10,000 to 1,850 tons, destroyers from 1,850 to 600 tons, and submarines. This division of categories would be fully in accordance with our views, and it is to be hoped that the French Government will see their way to abide by the formula which emerged from the unofficial conversations at Washington and Paris.

We also agree to what you said in regard to the percentage of transfer between categories, though in anything we say to the French we shall have to make it clear that we can only agree to this proposal in principle and must safeguard ourselves against the scheme being used to upset equilibrium in strength or to produce programs of relatively unequal strength. Thus the percentage of transfer would have in any case to be a relatively small one. We also consider—and I believe that this is equally the view of the United States Government—that this principle would not apply to the two categories of capital ships and aircraft carriers. These are matters for consideration at the Conference, but it has been thought desirable that you should know our view on this point and we shall be glad to learn in due course whether the United States Government agree.

The only other observation I am asked to make relates to cruisers, and this is really merely a question of wording. The *aide-mémoire* states that 'there is no agreement on a proportion between the number of 10,000 and the number of smaller cruisers and the question of numbers of such units is still to be agreed upon, the United States desiring 21 and Great Britain 15 such cruisers.' This wording might possibly give the impression that, as things stand, we only desire to have fifteen 8-inch cruisers against the American twenty-one 8-inch cruisers, although no final agreement on the point has been reached. The wording is the more open to such an interpretation in that the sentence which introduces the discussion of the five categories of combatant ships runs as follows: 'Certain matters have been discussed and *tentative understandings* arrived at as follows' (the underlining [*italics*] is mine).

We shall, therefore, propose to say, in discussing this matter with the French Government, that there is no agreement yet on a proportion between the number of 10,000 ton and the number of smaller cruisers, that we are anxious if possible not to add to our existing program of 15 eight inch gun cruisers, but that in order to obviate this, some means will have to be found to enable the United States Government to reduce their number of eight inch cruisers from twenty-one to eighteen.

As you will see we only differ from you on points [of] detail and wording, and it is satisfactory that we can, if approached by the French or Italian Governments with the same inquiries, give them an almost identical reply to that embodied in the *aide-mémoire*."

DAWES

500.A15a3/457 : Telegram

*The Ambassador in Great Britain (Dawes) to the Secretary of State*

[Paraphrase]

LONDON, December 4, 1929—8 p. m.

[Received 8:50 p. m.]

360. Your telegram No. 326, December 3, 1 p. m.   First, I think that you are wholly right.   In the second place, the Prime Minister said to me during our conference this afternoon at 5:45 that nothing will be settled concerning methods of procedure without first consulting you and no method of procedure will be suggested which does not have your approval.   A paraphrase of your message was left with him at his request, and he will prepare an answer to it which I shall forward when received.   The Prime Minister agrees with what you say in every respect and understands the danger which exists on account of the coming juxtaposition of political motives and individual vanity in the Conference with malevolent elements among the press representatives.   Do you not think that it would be better to have no fixed program as to Conference methods in advance of the arrival of the leaders?   It would then be possible for the leaders to discuss methods on the day before the opening of the Conference and to arrange that the first plenary meeting devote itself to organization and division into committees for the work of the Conference, thus eliminating all but a short opening statement by the chairman previously submitted to the leaders of the delegations, similar to what was done in the case of our first committee of experts in 1924 in Paris.   MacDonald feels that the matter of speeches could be controlled if he could see Briand, although it would be better to abandon them entirely; he is not so sure of Tardieu however.   It would be useful to create, if possible, a public impression by departing from the conventional through having the Conference convey an evidence of the earnestness of the powers represented and of their determination to indulge not so much in declamation as in constructive work.   However, MacDonald is dealing in this situation with those first in authority in the different countries and an appearance of dictation must be avoided even in methods. The Prime Minister's mind is open and I would suggest that you freely express yourself as to anything which under the circumstances you deem wise.   MacDonald has under consideration a personal letter to Briand for the purpose of bringing about a discussion of this matter between the two of them.   It is, as you say, essential above all else that there should be no possibility of individuals on the delegations taking public stands early in the Conference.   This may not be difficult to arrange unless there is an underlying desire on the part of some of them that the Conference should not succeed. The advisors of the Prime Minister have told him that the speeches

of the opening session would probably be of a very general nature, to wit, "agin sin" and for peace.  He fully realizes however that he has no control over the delegations and that, since "the reason for the ass' bray is that the ass is built that way", accidents may happen.

DAWES

500.A15a3/457 : Telegram

*The Secretary of State to the Ambassador in Great Britain (Dawes)*

[Paraphrase]

WASHINGTON, December 10, 1929—2 p. m.

333. Your telegram No. 360, December 4, 8 p. m.  Your opinion that the forthcoming Conference should avoid all unnecessary distraction and should be devoted to the serious business in hand has also been reported by Belin.[95]  This view corresponds so exactly to my own and, I believe, to that of the rest of the delegation that I should like to encourage you in having that impression conveyed to Mr. MacDonald.  For myself, I should like to avoid entertainment, and particularly the burden of public speeches. so far as may be possible until we have completed the business in hand.  At best it is difficult for me to absent myself from this country, and every day that it is possible to save in prolonged absence is important.  We intend to remain until something is accomplished, but we want to accomplish it as speedily as we can.

STIMSON

500.A15a3/479 : Telegram

*The Chargé in France (Armour) to the Secretary of State*

[Paraphrase]

PARIS, December 11, 1929—11 a. m.
[Received 5 : 31 p. m.]

555. Last night I dined with Bunau Varilla, who is the owner of the newspaper *Le Matin;* the only other person present, other than the immediate family, was Tardieu.  After dinner the question of the London Naval Conference was raised by Tardieu, who spoke very frankly regarding the difficulties confronting France.  He referred particularly to the problem presented by the new German cruiser *Ersatz Preussen*, and also discussed France's position in the Mediterranean and the insistence of Italy on parity.  He seemed inclined to trace much of France's troubles back to the creation of ratio figures at the Washington Naval Conference.  Tardieu admitted that one of the things that did not make the work easier was what he called the "Geneva frame of mind" of his subordinates who from their work at the League seemed to have evolved a complicated and

[95] F. Lammot Belin, First Secretary of the Embassy in Great Britain.

circuitous method of approach to all problems. When Hugh Gibson's name was mentioned in the course of the conversation, Tardieu spoke in very warm terms of Gibson and his work. He made it clear to me that he would welcome an opportunity to see Gibson and talk over matters with him, should Gibson be in Paris in the near future.

I spoke with Gibson this morning by telephone. He told me that he feels sure that he could come to Paris without having his visit cause any comment, as a number of reasonable explanations for it could be offered, but he would hesitate to accept Tardieu's suggestion until he knows whether it meets with the Department's approval. I am inclined to believe from the fact that when Bunau Varilla invited me he stated that Tardieu wanted to see me and from the way the conversation was turned to the London Conference that Tardieu has something on his mind, and that a meeting with Gibson at this time might prove most useful. You may, in this connection, wish to reread Gibson's telegram No. 84 of October 29, 5 p. m.[96]

Please let me have your decision in this matter as soon as possible? Cipher mailed to Brussels.                                                                ARMOUR

---

500.A15a3/479 : Telegram

*The Secretary of State to the Ambassador in Belgium* (*Gibson*)

[Paraphrase]

WASHINGTON, December 12, 1929—4 p. m.

71. Armour's telegram No. 555, December 11, 11 a. m. I think that you should proceed to Paris in accordance with the suggestion which Tardieu made to Armour and listen sympathetically to Tardieu's statement of the French position. As the policies of the delegation are in process of being worked out, naturally you will not commit yourself on the policy which is to be followed by the United States in the Conference at London, but you will take care to reassure the French that no special agreement has been reached between this Government and that of any other nation.

Repeat to Embassies in London and Paris.

STIMSON

---

500.A15a3/486

*The British Embassy to the Department of State*

MEMORANDUM

The following personal message to the Secretary of State from the Prime Minister was delivered orally by the British Ambassador on the morning of December 12th:

---

[96] *Ante*, p. 270.

"It is the Prime Minister's intention to make the opening speech on quite general lines which will touch on no controversial points but will make a short survey of naval disarmament question and state the importance of the conference and the great issues and hope of peace it has in its keeping. An outline of this speech will be communicated to principal delegates of the other powers, and they will be asked privately and individually to keep their replies as far as possible, on the same lines and above all not to take up any unexceptional positions in these opening addresses, but to associate themselves with the purpose of the conference and to begin on a cordial note which each of the five leading delegates will strike. Prime Minister thinks this most important. Time for bringing forward plans will be when the first committee meets and the Prime Minister desires to come to an understanding with Mr. Stimson as to how this is to be done. There are two sets of exchanges of views which must decide how the opening movements of business are to be handled. First, those between United States and ourselves; second, those between France and Italy. Prime Minister is still studying how this can best be arranged, and when he knows how matters between France and Italy have progressed he will address Secretary of State further.

Prime Minister's experience at such conferences has taught him that no hard and fast plan of handling can be carried out. We ought to have a general understanding, but its application depends on the moods and nature of the actual situation which has to be faced. A short conference between the Prime Minister and Secretary of State would be desirable before the first meeting of the conference.

As regards representation on committees, the Prime Minister will bear in mind what the Secretary of State says in regard to all seven members of the American delegation being absorbed on committees, and he will cooperate cordially in meeting this and similar considerations.

As regards the Dominions there will be one delegate from each Dominion and each will, we believe, want to be represented on the first committee. He would like an exchange of views with Secretary of State nearer to the time, when he will make a definite proposal as to the composition of these committees."

WASHINGTON, 12 December, 1929.

---

500.A15a3/498 : Telegram

*The Appointed Ambassador in France (Edge) to the Secretary of State*

[Paraphrase]

PARIS, December 14, 1929—3 p. m.
[Received 4:45 p. m.]

561. Wilson and Gibson, with my approval, made an informal call this morning on Massigli. Massigli, in referring to his visit to General Dawes when he was last in Paris, stated that he was intending to take the draft of a note to London next week and, before sending it formally to the Governments interested, to submit it to the British Foreign Office and General Dawes.

He repeated the French insistence upon the interdependence of armaments without giving a complete résumé of the contents of the note. It appears from the excerpts read that the French Government's first intention at the Conference will be to work out something to further the work of the Preparatory Commission; and, second, to see if figures can be reached which, however, the French would regard as subject to reservations and only tentative.

The French insistence on interdependence of armaments was indicated by Massigli as inspired by a belief that the coming Conference would be used by the British to reassert their supremacy on the seas and, after France had been relegated as a maritime power to an inferior position, set to work to reduce the air and land force of the French. The impression was gained by Gibson and Wilson that France would endeavor to induce the British to resume their original position as regards trained reserves which Cecil [97] abandoned last September at Geneva.

With reference to Italian-French conversations, Massigli said that discussions were not progressing at the moment as the last French note had received no reply. He added that the French Government's note proposed two sets of figures, (1) the naval strength considered necessary for prestige, and (2) figures based on actual naval needs as shown by the functions of the different classes of ships. It was also stated in the note that, as the actual needs of the French were in a certain measure dependent upon the forces of other nations which are to have no representation at the Conference, if a general Mediterranean political agreement could be reached the entire situation would be considerably facilitated. Subject to your approval after the presentation of my credentials, probably Wednesday, I shall endeavor to secure more definite information, as well as reports, concerning the progress of Franco-Italian negotiations during the course of official visits.

London, Rome, Brussels, receiving copies by mail.

EDGE

---

500.A15a3/494 : Telegram

*The Appointed Ambassador in France (Edge) to the Secretary of State*

[Paraphrase]

PARIS, December 14, 1929—4 p.m.
[Received December 14—12:20 p. m.]

562. With reference to the Embassy's telegram No. 555 of December 11, 11 a. m., and your answer to the Brussels Embassy.

---

[97] Viscount Cecil of Chelwood, British representative on the Third Committee of the League of Nations Assembly, which dealt with disarmament problems.

Yesterday Gibson arrived and we agreed, after full discussion with him and Wilson, that it was wiser that Tardieu not be informed of his presence and that the suggested interview be postponed until after my relations here had been established, when, without any possible misinterpretation, it can readily be held. With this Gibson agrees fully and, subject to recall by me if it seems wise, he returns this afternoon to Brussels. We reached this decision before the Massigli visit concerning which my telegram No. 561 was sent today and we believe that the wisdom of this is confirmed, especially with regard to this matter, as we feel we have now learned what is in the French mind.

EDGE

---

500.A15a3/494 : Telegram

*The Secretary of State to the Ambassador in France (Edge)*

[Paraphrase]

WASHINGTON, December 16, 1929—6 p.m.

409. Your telegram No. 562, December 14, 4 p.m. Considering Tardieu's statement to Armour with reference to certain views held by the French subordinate staff (Embassy's telegram No. 555, December 11, 11 a.m.), it was my feeling that Massigli's views were not necessarily in conformity with those of Tardieu, and I hope that you will soon find opportunity to arrange for Gibson to go with you to see Tardieu, at which time Gibson's experience at Geneva with these intricacies may prove helpful.

STIMSON

---

500.A15a3/590

*French Memorandum of December 20, 1929, Delivered to the British Government and Communicated to the Other Interested Governments* [98]

[Translation]

In accepting, on October 16, the invitation of the British Government to take part in the London Naval Conference, the French Government reserved the liberty of defining its views regarding the problems which will be included in the agenda of the deliberations and the questions generally which may arise at that international meeting. After the exchanges of views which have already taken place, it believes that the time has come to define its attitude with respect to essential questions of principle and method which will

---

[98] Received in the Department from the French Embassy.

present themselves during the negotiations and the importance of which, transcending the technical limits of the case, deserves to be fully brought out.

# I

The French Government has already had occasion to express its appreciation of the considerations which led to the step taken by the British Government in conjunction with the American Government. It understands too well the vital character of the task of limiting armaments, it has taken too active a part in the work carried on up to the present in this direction, not to welcome a proposal which tended, as expressly stated by His Excellency Mr. Arthur Henderson in his letter of October 7, to facilitate the task of the Preparatory Commission of the League of Nations and later, that of the General Disarmament Conference.

It is, moreover, the naval disarmament problem which, since the meeting in April and May last of the Preparatory Commission of Geneva, must be considered as still presenting an obstacle to the conclusion of the work which that Commission carried on with the efficient cooperation of American delegates. Furthermore, the last Assembly of the League of Nations declared that an agreement between the principal naval powers was necessary to pave the way to a general understanding regarding the methods to be applied for the reduction of naval armaments; in fact the conversations which were already being carried on appeared to it as calculated to permit the resumption and the completion of the interrupted work of the Preparatory Commission, and, subsequently, the convocation of the General Conference.

It is, therefore, primarily in regard to principles and methods permitting the subsequent conclusion of a General Convention for the limitation of armaments that, in the opinion of the French Government, the powers meeting at London should come to an agreement.

The British Government has stated that the Government of the United States and itself had taken the Paris Pact as the basis of their conversations. The French Government, which has already had occasion to express the satisfaction with which it welcomed this statement, took so great a part in the preparation of that Pact that there is no necessity of indicating the importance which it attaches thereto. The Paris Pact is based on the force of public opinion, which is great, but its methodical application has not yet been organized; it does not settle all the questions of pacific procedure and mutual assistance against an aggressor, implied in the outlawry of war. It is undoubtedly a real step toward the maintenance of peace, but in its present state it cannot be considered as sufficient to guarantee the security of nations.

It is this consideration, no doubt, which prevented the British Government from contemplating a substantial reduction in its naval armaments and the American Government from giving up the rapid carrying out of its latest naval program. While both were in agreement in excluding any possibility of conflict between themselves, they were bound to consider that it was an essential task of their navies to assure the protection of their communications, which does not appear to exclude the hypothesis of their being led to intervene in a conflict originating in the violation of solemn pledges.

Whatever may be the importance ascribed to the Pact of Paris, it is essentially on the Covenant of the League of Nations that the French Government, as well as the other Governments belonging to the League, has undertaken to base the limitation and reduction of its armaments, of which naval armaments are but a part. However incomplete the measures taken for carrying it into effect may still be, this Covenant already provides the basis of a complete system of security based upon the application of methods of peaceful settlement and assistance to any State unjustly attacked. It is only in proportion to such outside assistance as they can rely upon that nations will be in a position actually to reduce their armaments. So true it is that a general technical agreement upon armaments implies a previous political agreement; so true it is that a complete naval agreement presupposes an agreement on the question of freedom of the seas, defining the rights of belligerents and those of neutrals and providing for the contingent cooperation of other fleets against that of an aggressor country.

However deeply it may regret this situation, the French Government is none the less determined to extend its full cooperation to the Powers meeting in London, to bring about such solutions as may be feasible at the time.

The question of methods is no less important. In accordance with the example set by the Washington Conference, the Government of the United States and the British Government would appear to have contemplated the adoption of a method of evaluation of naval armaments dealing only with the armaments of the five numerically most powerful navies, and based on mathematical tables.

The example, however, of the Naval Conference of Rome is there to remind us that the principles of the Washington treaty met with a check when the League attempted, in 1924, to extend them to all navies, and it has frequently been demonstrated at Geneva that mathematical tables did not permit of rational application, valid for all States, of the principles defined in Article VIII of the Covenant, which contemplates a general reduction of armaments compatible with the security of each State, and with international obligations which would impose upon it a common action, account being taken of its geographical position and the conditions peculiar to it.

Now, the Conference will not have completely achieved its object unless it makes it possible to reach at Geneva a general agreement as to the methods for the limitation of naval armaments.

## II

These general observations were necessary for the precise definition of the principles which will inspire the French Government in the course of the London negotiations.

1. It is upon Article VIII of the Covenant that the French Government, faithful to its signature, intends to base reduction of its armaments. It is, indeed, upon this basis alone—a basis which does not imply an a priori application of mathematical formulas, and upon which the Preparatory Commission on Disarmament has already based its work—that it would be possible, in its opinion, to prepare an agreement acceptable for the governments which will not be represented in London.

Two opposing methods, within the framework of Article VIII, were put forward at Geneva for the limitation of naval armaments, one by total tonnage and the other by classes of ships. The stronger navies were inclined to the latter method while the others declared themselves in favor of the former.

Desirous of facilitating the conciliation of these conflicting points of view, the French delegation proposed, as early as April, 1927, a compromise system which was favorably received by all the navies which will not be represented in London, and which was sympathetically considered by several others. The United States Government in particular twice had occasion to state publicly that it was willing to accept it as the basis for discussion. This system consisted in supplementing the limitation of fleets by total tonnage by publishing the distribution of this tonnage between the chief classes of ships and by regulating the transfer of tonnage from one class to another.

Such a system, which is moreover susceptible of adjustments of detail, may adapt itself all the better to the needs of the contemplated understanding between the American and British Governments in that it leaves to any States, that may desire to do so, full liberty to bind themselves more closely to each other. In spite of its preferences for the method of limitation by total tonnage, the French Government is still willing to agree to this compromise method if it permits of accomplishing the general agreement.

2. The preparatory work in Geneva established that there existed a close interdependence in the total defensive armaments of a country, between its land, naval and aerial forces. The French Government

has frequently had occasion to declare that here was a fundamental principle of its policy of national defense, the importance of which arises particularly from the geographical position of France, a power both continental and maritime and the metropolis of a colonial empire spread out over the whole surface of the earth.

The Government of the Republic does not wish to find itself obliged to raise at London questions relating to the determination of land and aerial armaments, but it must point out the fact that the tonnage required to meet the needs of its naval defense is in close relation to the level of its land and aerial armaments, computed in accordance with the methods laid down by the Preparatory Commission at its last meeting. If the decisions of the latter were to be reconsidered, the particulars which it will afford as regards its naval armaments would become utterly valueless.

The French Government, moreover, desires to add that these difficulties will not prevent it from seeking solutions which will permit powers which may desire to do so and which may believe that they can do so in complete security, to enter into a definitive and binding agreement between themselves without awaiting the conclusion of the General Convention for the limitation of all armaments.

3. In the light of the foregoing observations, the delegation of France will have no difficulty in making known the importance of the tonnage corresponding to the national needs, in view of the geographical position of France on three seas, and the extent of her colonial empire, with an area of 11,000,000 square kilometers [4,247,100 square miles],[99] a population of 60,000,000 people, and a trade amounting to 32,000,000,000 francs [about $1,280,000,000].[99]

The existence of this empire, the necessity of providing for the separate defense of each of the great groups which constitute it, the numerous political and economic ties which unite these great groups to each other and to the mother country, the need of protecting the integrity and the economic life of the latter, the task of providing for the security of more than 30,000 kilometers [18,630] [99] of coast, in all, impose upon the French Navy duties which the French Government cannot ignore when it is called upon to apply Article VIII of the Covenant. The French naval budget, moreover, is lower today than it was in 1913, and the same desire for strict moderation will continue to inspire France in the estimation of her needs and in computing the forces necessary to meet them.

In this respect the French Government will take fully into account any guarantee of security that might be set up and which would give full effect to the engagements of international solidarity against an aggressor contained in Article XVI of the Covenant.

[99] Bracketed insertion appears in file translation.

4. Moreover, remembering the beneficial effects produced by the Pacific treaty in view of the conclusion of the Washington naval agreements, the French Government considers that in a limited field, but one in which most of the European fleets are concerned, some progress might be achieved. Communications through the Mediterranean have an importance for the British Empire which the French Government does not disregard. They are equally vital for France. Could an agreement of mutual guarantee and non-aggression be effected between the Mediterranean naval powers to which those among them which will not be represented at London would be parties, and, first of all, a power like Spain, the importance of whose naval interest in the Mediterranean needs no mention? The French Government propounds this question, declaring itself in favor of the principle of such an agreement because it is earnestly desirous of bringing about reduction of naval armaments.

As the conclusion to this statement of general views, suggested to it by study of the agenda of the Conference, the French Government desires to state that none of the difficulties to which it has thought it necessary to draw attention appears to it to be insuperable.

Convinced that all the Governments that are to meet at London will enter upon these discussions with the same will as itself to cooperate sincerely in giving effect to such means as may lead to the overcoming of every difficulty, the French Government has confidence in the success of the negotiations that will pave the way for the General Conference for limitation and reduction of armaments which alone seems capable of satisfying the common will of the nations to organize for peace.

---

500.A15a3/528 : Telegram

*The Ambassador in France (Edge) to the Secretary of State*

[Paraphrase]

Paris, December 21, 1929—1 p. m.
[Received December 22—6 : 48 a. m.[1]]

575. Armour accompanied me on Thursday afternoon on my first official call on Tardieu. Almost immediately we began discussion of the London Conference. I laid stress on the deep interest which you and the President personally took in it. He categorically stated that an agreement could be arrived at in London, in fact must be arrived at. One thing, however he declared could prevent it and that would be if the British and ourselves came to London with an agreement concluded in advance by which the acceptance of our terms would be forced upon France and the other powers or else they would risk breaking up the

---

[1] Telegram in five sections.

Conference. He was assured by me that we had not advanced beyond the stage of the actual beginning of all negotiations, that further I could assure him that neither the British nor ourselves have the slightest intention of taking an unalterable formula to London, that a real reduction was our sole object. Then he repeated he could see no reason for not arriving at an accord. Two principal points that the French Government considered essential were stated to me by Tardieu:

(1) Any agreement concluded in London would be subject to the approval of the Geneva Preparatory Commission. Also he believed it should be temporary, that is, limited to an approximate period of five or six years.

(2) France desired the interdependence of land, sea, and air armaments.

The particular desire of the French Government, according to Tardieu, was to avoid a repetition of the occurrences of the 1921 Naval Conference in Washington, and their delegation would go to London with a clear outline of what they considered their necessities. It is the desire of France that its case be considered on its merits and that its position as a maritime power be sympathetically and carefully considered; its coast line included the Atlantic Ocean, the Mediterranean and the Channel; its northern and western Africa colonies, Madagascar, Indo-China and others; its colonial population of 60 million and its 12 billion franc trade. The fear of France was that we would arrive upon a figure for ourselves and for the British which might be called $x$ and that then a figure $y$ would arbitrarily be assigned to France. What France wished to have allotted was a figure to which her actual defensive needs would correspond. He repeated that battleships only had been limited by the Washington Conference. No battleships since that time had been built by France. Battleships were an offensive weapon; submarines and cruisers were defensive weapons, but France desired an adequate tonnage based on its actual need in these weapons. This seemed reasonable to me and I said I thought France should keep to a reasonable minimum requirement rather than to a maximum intended to meet some almost inconceivable danger, when she estimated what was needed for defense; that what we all desired after all was a real reduction to bring to all nations corresponding relief in taxation.

The French Premier insisted that the 1925 law stated clearly and openly the requirements of France, that a reduction was made in these figures over those of 1914, and that in reality they constituted the present minimum requirements of France. The United States, he added, was the only country which had increased its figures and these had been increased 60 per cent (it was not made clear whether this increase was in tonnage or in appropriations but I assume the latter is referred to). Laughingly I replied that this seemed a technical question, and suggested that it would be better that it be discussed at the London Conference with our experts. He then stated that he would like to ask me a question in an informal and confidential manner; certain friends in the United States had informed him that during the President's talks with MacDonald there had been discussion of the question of dismantling the British bases off the United States—Bermuda, Halifax, et cetera—but that MacDonald had received a telegram from Henderson to the effect that the British Government could not agree to the discussion of such a proposal. However, he admitted that they had told him that the Hoover-MacDonald talks reached no concrete results in this connection. That statement as an evidence of no final commitments or any details, I encouraged. I added that as already stated the British and ourselves had only discussed a starting point, consequently he could put all this out of his mind. Our effort had only been to smooth away extreme difficulties in order that the achievement of positive results in London might be made possible.

Tardieu next referred to the point which he had mentioned about ten days ago in an after-dinner conversation with Armour (reference is made to the Embassy's telegram No. 555 of December 11) that is to say, he was afraid that the practical result of parity would be that the old system of alliances would be revived; that should parity be obtained by the British and ourselves the arbiter between the two of us would be Japan and both of us would attempt to reach an understanding with the Japanese; so that if a Mediterranean party was agreed upon by the French and Italians, in this situation the British would then be made arbiters.

My answer was that I [thought there was no?] more danger of alliances with reduced armaments than with larger navies as at present.

Tardieu in conclusion asked me if I did not think further informal talks between ourselves prior to the meeting in London would serve a useful purpose, that he thought that the more such matters were discussed by laymen, rather than by technical naval experts, the better. If I agreed to the usefulness of such talks, he asked how it would be possible to get in touch with and to include Gibson or others. To me the idea seemed a good one and so I told him. He then suggested in the near future a luncheon conference. Gibson has been asked by me to be ready in case Tardieu should desire to act upon this idea and it will in fact be encouraged by me. Before leaving I again stressed the [importance] which you and the President attached to success at the London Conference.

Tardieu's answer was that we would and we must reach an accord; that it had seemed almost impossible during the war to find ships, men or munitions, but that together we had accomplished this, and our success in peace could not be less than it was during war.

My reply was that we apparently agreed as regards the real objective and there remained only an equitable means of reaching this to be worked out by our respective delegations; that if London failed, Geneva could accomplish nothing. A direct reference to the effect on British public opinion of French cooperation which has been suggested by Lord Tyrrell did not seem wise to me as it appeared that this might indicate collusion or evidence of too much of an advance understanding.

Sent to Brussels, Rome and London.

EDGE

---

500.A15a3/550

## The Department of State to the Japanese Embassy [2]

### MEMORANDUM

During the stay in Washington of the Japanese Delegates to the London Naval Conference, they attended two meetings with the American Delegates to the Conference on Tuesday December 17 and Thursday December 19, 1929, respectively.

At these meetings the Chairman of the Japanese Delegation, the Honorable Reijiro Wakatsuki and the Chairman of the American Delegation, the Honorable Henry L. Stimson presented their points of view on certain questions affecting Japan and the United States.

Mr. Wakatsuki after emphasizing Japan's great desire for the success of the London Conference and an actual reduction of naval armaments explained that Japan had always made it the fundamental principle of her national armament to hold such strength as would not disturb the sense of national security of her people. In other words, a strength insufficient for attack and adequate for defense. Japan desired to obtain agreement from all Powers concerned to her having a ratio of 70 per cent of the largest naval strength as being that necessary for defense purposes in the adjacent waters of Japan. Mr. Wakatsuki said that he understood that the Secretary of State had proposed to Ambassador Debuchi to contrive to find some means of solving this question by taking into consideration the actual conditions. He then asked for information upon which to construct such a plan. He desired particularly to be informed as to the details regarding the provisional understanding between the United States and the British Government in regard to large sized cruisers.

Mr. Stimson replied to express his great desire for the success of the London Conference and to set forth his views frankly.

---

[2] Copies also sent to the British, French, and Italian Embassies.

On the question of 10,000 ton cruisers, he said there existed no agreement except what he had told Ambassador Debuchi some time ago. The American Government demanded 21 such cruisers on the recommendation of its naval advisers while the British Government thought that the United States should be satisfied with 18 ships. The American Government thought that that was near enough to an agreement to enable the two countries to go to London with every hope of success. The difference of three ships could some how be adjusted. However, as yet he had no figures of adjustment.

As to the larger ratio suggested by Mr. Wakatsuki, he said he would reply, giving the result of his careful thought after his consultation with his colleagues and his survey of the minds of the people. He considered the Government ought to represent such opinion as the people would think just and right.

Mr. Stimson then referred to the Washington Conference which brought about the situation that led to the convening of the Conference at London. He said the American people felt that this country had been very generous and made great sacrifices in order that an agreement might be reached. America in 1921 had the largest navy program in the world but was ready to give up that position and, moreover, to pledge herself to maintain the *status quo* of the fortification in the Philippine Islands and her other Pacific possessions in order to facilitate disarmament by removing the sense of rivalry, jealousy and competition and particularly to relieve Japan of any anxiety as to her national security. He referred to the improved good feelings between America and Japan resulting from the successful outcome of the Washington Conference. The American people believed in good faith that that agreement could only have been reached by the United States giving up a very large portion of her naval strength and consenting to the maintenance of the *status quo* of fortifications in her possession in the vicinity of Japan.

Mr. Stimson commented on the regrettable renewal in the last seven or eight years of competition of naval construction in the classes of ships not covered by the Washington Treaties. There was therefore a feeling that that Conference had not altogether been a success. America had not been party to that competition in the beginning but after the failure of the Geneva Conference felt constrained to take to naval building once again, as was shown by the Acts of Congress authorizing the construction of 23 10,000 ton cruisers. The last Act was peremptory which meant that the President must build unless some international agreement as to disarmament could be arrived at. Moreover, the American navy had formulated a big plan involving an enormous expenditure to build the other classes of ships that might be necessary to complete the American fleet. He explained that in order to show the importance which the American people attached to the necessity of catching up with the navies of the other Powers unless some agreement of disarmament could be concluded.

Such being the case when asked by Mr. Debuchi as to the opinion of the United States in regard to the desire of Japan to hold a higher ratio in cruisers than in capital ships, he had replied frankly that that would give a bad impression to the American people and would not conduce to the success of the Conference. A great many Americans would feel such a change to be unfair to themselves.

The American people, the Secretary continued, strongly felt that battleships were the center of naval strength. They had never considered a battleship fleet as obsolete. However, the United States was willing to try to find a way to reduce the strength of that class. He knew also that that was Japan's wish. The United States, however, would not feel it in her interest if Japan reduced the battleship fleet in which the ratio of 5–5–3 had already been agreed upon and turned the moneys thus saved to the building of cruisers in which Japan was asking for a ratio of 10–10–7. The United States did not seek to impose a position of inferiority on any nation. He had told Ambassador Debuchi therefore that they would rather discuss matters at the Conference giving careful consideration to the actual conditions of the situation without referring to the question of ratio. He hoped that a basis for an understanding or agreement might be found in the light of what Japan had actually been doing in regard to her cruiser strength.

He had therefore been very disappointed to learn that Japan had recently increased her proposed cruisers strength from 206,000 tons to 226,000 tons. He would rather make the subject of discussion the actual strength of 206,000 tons than any figures calculated merely on account of the ratio. He could not but feel that the American people would regard the high figures with serious misgivings and that as a result it might demand a corresponding increase in the American cruiser program.

So his opinion had been that if Japan would keep her needs down to the actual existing strength, America would be willing to try to meet her on the same principle and to persuade other nations to come to an agreement. Great Britain had already shown her willingness to reduce her cruiser strength lower than what she proposed in 1927 and if the latter came down, America would go down even further. All he could promise now was to give the utmost sympathy and fair consideration to the Japanese claim.

Mr. Wakatsuki was gratified that Mr. Stimson was willing to give sympathetic consideration to the Japanese attitude. The Japanese people had a feeling that they had been pressed to accept the form of disarmament stipulated at the time of the Washington Conference. Without criticizing the results of that Conference, he mentioned that Japan had claimed from the beginning a ratio of 70 per cent and the people deeply regretted that that claim had not been accepted. The Government explanation of the benefit of maintaining the *status quo* of fortification in the Pacific had conciliated some portion of the people but the general feeling of regret had not been wiped away. Public opinion favored 70 per cent being put forward strongly at a further disarmament conference for the class of ships not covered by the Washington Conference. This had been a national conviction. He pointed out that Japan had agreed also to maintain the *status quo* of fortifications of her own islands. Japan had also made sacrifices by scrapping warships. At anything short of 70 per cent, Japan's sense of national security would be disturbed. He had no idea of reopening the 5–5–3 ratio agreed upon at the Washington Conference as to capital ships. However, as to other categories of ships not covered by the Washington Conference no agreement whatever had been completed at that Conference. It had only been agreed upon that the size of cruisers should be limited to 10,000 tons,—a size which did not exist at that time. Subsequently a number of cruisers of 10,000 tons had gradually come into existence, developments had been effected in other instruments of war and the general situation had been greatly changed since the time the Washington Treaties were concluded. Therefore, he thought it would not be adequate to make the ratio of the Washington Treaties the basis upon which to argue disarmament today.

As to capital ships, Japan had never thought that they were obsolete. They still constituted the center of armament. Japan thought that in order to meet the necessity of naval reduction it would be advisable to prolong the age, reduce the size, lengthen the period of replacements, and so on, of this class of war ships. It was the Japanese feeling that it was not Japan alone that would profit by it, but all nations concerned at the same time. Japan had no thought of utilizing the moneys saved by reducing the capital ship strength for augmenting the cruiser tonnage. This he was saying just on the spur of the moment, but he believed that it was the conviction of the Japanese people.

He would not object to studying the matter as Mr. Stimson had suggested from the point of view of actual conditions and without reference to the question of ratio. However, he was given to understand that between the United States and Great Britain the principle of parity had first been decided upon and the concrete figures taken into consideration as an application of that principle. Japan had proposed to have an agreement on the ratio first, in the sense that some standard had better be adopted as in the case of the Anglo-American arrangement. He thought that it would not be inadvisable to approach actual conditions and concrete figures, keeping the ratio always in mind. Later, he would be glad to submit for Mr. Stimson's consideration a plan conceived in that sense.

Mr. Wakatsuki referred to Mr. Stimson's disappointment in regard to the figures of 206,000 tons and 226,000 tons which Japan now proposed as cruiser strength.

The difference of 20,000 tons was calculated on the basis of the 70 per cent ratio. Therefore this suppositive tonnage might come down as tonnage to be held by the superior navies would come down. The figures stood high simply because the superior navies seemed to claim high figures. Mr. Wakatsuki said in reply to an inquiry from Mr. Stimson that he would submit his plan for consideration. If America were going to hold 18 8-inch-gun 10,000 ton cruisers, Japan would desire to possess a certain number of 10,000 ton cruisers and a certain number of cruisers of less than 10,000 tons aggregating 126,000 tons distributed among 13 ships. This represented the eventual figures but in the transitory period pending the replacements of the *Furutaka* class cruisers, Japan desired to hold fourteen ships consisting of the eight 10,000 ton cruisers, four *Furutaka* class cruisers with 7,100 tons each, and two more ships with a tonnage of less than 10,000 tons. This he considered very much inferior to a fleet consisting of cruisers with a uniform tonnage of 10,000 tons.

Mr. Wakatsuki referred to submarines, and their adequacy as weapons of defense for a country like Japan consisting of islands widely scattered on the sea and holding an inferior naval strength. Japan would be content to hold nothing more than her present strength of 78,500 tons. She would have no objection if other Powers held ten sevenths of her submarine strength.

With regard to small cruisers and destroyers, Japan stood ready to effect reduction according as the other Powers concerned decreased their holdings.

Mr. Stimson thought that it might be preferable not to discuss only the question of 10,000 ton cruisers but to take other categories of ships into consideration at the same time. He felt that if the discussion centered on 10,000 ton cruisers alone it would be quite difficult to arrive at an agreement satisfactory to the American people. It could not but feel that the amount of 226,000 tons meant that Japan desired an increase of her naval strength on one hand and demanded a reduction of American naval strength on the other.

At this point the meeting adjourned to December 19th.

Mr. Stimson referred to the good feeling existing between Japan and the United States largely as a result of the confidence which had been set up after the Washington Conference, and said that this knowledge made him enter this Conference anxious that nothing would change or diminish this feeling.

He thought that the figures relating to Japanese naval strength mentioned by Mr. Wakatsuki would cause anxiety in the American public mind. The President who is seeking reduction would be most disappointed. The President and all those who are also in touch with public opinion realize that the American people would feel that this country with its immensely long coast line on two oceans, separated by the Isthmus of Panama, would normally require a much larger defensive force than a nation situated like Japan in a compact group of islands.

Mr. Stimson said he hoped that they would be able at the Conference to find a way by which the national feeling of the Japanese people could be protected and their national sensibilities not in any way offended by anything like an attempt to impose upon them or put them in a position of inferiority to other nations.

After again stating that the American people and Congress would regard a cruiser tonnage of 226,000 tons for Japan as so high that it would necessitate counter building on the part of America, Mr. Stimson referred to the matter of submarines. He said that the American Government is very strongly opposed to the use of submarines for destroying commerce and was very glad that it was joined by Japan in the Washington Conference Treaty (unfortunately not ratified by all of the other nations) which forbade their use indiscriminately for destroying commerce.

Mr. Stimson said he felt that the danger of too great a reliance on submarines, and too large a construction of submarines, the uses of which are comparatively limited apart from commerce destroying, is that it creates a temptation to use them against merchant ships under conditions where they cannot obey the rules of war. He recognized that other nations might differ in their opinion as to the usefulness of submarines in warfare, but hoped that at least the construction of submarines might be restricted so as to avoid their use against merchant commerce in the inhuman manner which had been used in the past. Mr. Stimson said that he hoped that this Conference might successfully reaffirm the humane principles of the 1922 Treaty on the subject of commerce destroying submarines.

Mr. Stimson feared that the nearly 80,000 tons of submarines suggested for Japan by Mr. Wakatsuki would be thought by the American people to be unduly high and he feared that such large construction might tend to lessen the good feeling of which he had already spoken, and might excite a demand in America for the construction of a large force of anti-submarine craft like destroyers and light cruisers. Mr. Wakatsuki in reply said that the Japanese people have in mind only the maintenance of national security and therefore it had never entered their mind that the Japanese Navy might ever excite the mistrust of other Powers. He again said that cruiser tonnage is a relative question and that if other Powers came down in their strength, Japanese figures would naturally decrease. He also said that Japan would be most willing to conclude a treaty at the forthcoming Conference such as the kind referred to in the Treaty of 1922 forbidding illegal use of submarines.[3]

Mr. Wakatsuki, with reference to the use of submarines as a weapon of defense, suggested that if both Governments consulted experts in the matter, it would eventually become very much clearer.

Mr. Stimson and Mr. Wakatsuki both expressed their gratification of the very friendly and frank nature of the conversations and considered that a very considerable progress had been made in the direction of a mutual understanding.

WASHINGTON, December 26, 1929.

---

500.A15a3/536 : Telegram

*The Ambassador in France (Edge) to the Secretary of State*

[Paraphrase]

PARIS, December 26, 1929—11 a. m.
[Received 12 : 40 p. m.[4]]

581. Acting on his own suggestion, Tardieu called at the Embassy at five o'clock on Christmas Day. He almost immediately started a discussion of the London Conference and repeated his earlier statement that the Conference must and would be successful (reference is made to my telegram No. 575 of December 21). He remarked, with reference to the reparations meeting which is to reconvene on January 3 at The Hague, that he felt more optimistic of success at London than at The Hague. He gave no details regarding his reasons for pessimism concerning The Hague meeting beyond stating generally that, in view of the length of time since the earlier meeting [5] and with Hungary and Bulgaria still not included, he feared the introduction of some new difficulties as to assuring final payments.

He clearly indicated, returning to the subject of the London Conference, that reduction would be assured if some evidence of defensive security such as a Mediterranean pact could be evolved from the Conference.

In expressing his high regard for the Secretary of State he signified a strong desire to confer with you before the London Conference convenes. I was told by him that the French delegation now plans to arrive in London on January 18th in the afternoon. He expressed the conviction that satisfactory adjustments could be

---

[3] *Foreign Relations*, 1922, vol. I, p. 267.
[4] Telegram in three sections.
[5] August 6–31, 1929.

worked out by the French and American delegations. Some misgiving he evidenced regarding the British position, particularly as to Mediterranean security, but he gave no details.

At this time Senator King of Utah was also a caller and I presented him to Tardieu at the end of my conference. His assurance to Tardieu of his great interest in naval reduction was quite helpful. Briefly, Tardieu repeated to King his sincere desire for success in London, but in part repeated the portion of our discussion (refer to my telegram No. 575) which emphasized the needs of the French.

It seems significant to me however that while Tardieu and I were alone he did not so constantly emphasize the French position as he had on Wednesday (reference is again made to my telegram No. 575). Throughout this conversation there prevailed a note of optimism as to success and a confident feeling that United States and France would reach complete understanding.

After Senator King joined us, however, he did refer to this naval law of 1925 as generally representing the requirements of the French. While discussing submarines he repeated the French conception of global tonnage as a solution and expressed some concern over the new type German cruiser.

Tardieu has accepted my luncheon invitation for next Saturday, December 28, at the Embassy. Others to be present are Armour, Gibson, Henry Moysset, Director of Cabinet of the President of the Council of Ministers, at Tardieu's suggestion.

It has occurred to me, as a result of this conversation, that it might help if either the President or you send Tardieu an intimate confidential note while the French case is being prepared by its delegation to be presented at London. Regarding the advisability of this, however, I shall consult Gibson and after our luncheon conference on Saturday will advise you further.

Have I your approval on the policy I have been following? Your reaction and viewpoint up to the moment before Saturday's conference will be helpful.

Copies to Brussels, Rome and London.

EDGE

500.A15a3/536 : Telegram

*The Secretary of State to the Ambassador in France (Edge)*

[Paraphrase]

WASHINGTON, December 26, 1929—6 p. m.

430. Your telegram No. 581, December 26, 11 a. m. I think procedure you have followed has been very satisfactory. I do not think that it would be wise to send Tardieu a note, but I hope that you and Gibson will assure him that President Hoover and I are most pleased

over assurances which you have communicated regarding his firm intention of bringing the London Conference to successful conclusion. You may also inform him that I have had in mind at all times the various naval needs of the five powers attending the Conference.

Before the formal opening of the Conference, I hope to have the opportunity of conferring with Tardieu.

STIMSON

---

500.A15a3/558 : Telegram

*The Ambassador in France (Edge) to the Secretary of State*

[Paraphrase]

PARIS, December 31, 1929—noon.
[Received December 31—10 a. m.]

588. I conferred with Tardieu again last night for the fourth and probably the last time before he leaves on Thursday for The Hague. Except for a further confirmation that French public opinion must be placated by some concession along lines mentioned in previous telegrams, nothing new was developed. The virtual unanimity of the debate in Parliament preceding the final vote of confidence shows that the country supports the Government's program for London as outlined in the French memorandum of December 20th, which had been published and therefore was officially before Parliament and the country before the vote was cast. Tardieu's unquestioned desire for cooperation with us is made difficult by this together with the constant insistence of the French press for recognition of the national requirements as outlined in the aforesaid note.

The original view to the effect that the British-American advance understanding had ignored the necessities of the French, Tardieu frankly admits has been cleared away; I believe that a solution harmonious with the desire for ultimate reduction will actually be sought by him at the Conference.

EDGE

---

500.A15a3/579½

*The British Embassy to the Department of State* [6]

MEMORANDUM

In a memorandum presented on December 20th, the French Government, in laying down the principles by which they will be guided at the forthcoming Naval Conference, draw attention to the happy influence exerted by the Treaty relating to the Pacific which was concluded as a result of the Washington Conference of 1921, and

---

[6] This memorandum embodies the contents of a telegram which the British Ambassador had read to the Secretary of State on December 31, 1929.

suggest that it might be possible to draw up a treaty of non-aggression in which the Mediterranean Powers, including those who will not be represented at the London Naval Conference, might participate. His Majesty's Government are not disposed to enter into a regional treaty guarantee of this description, but they appreciate the motives which have inspired the French Government and they would welcome any step (short of a commitment to intervene in a dispute) which would add to the sense of security of the Mediterranean Powers.

On the occasion of his visit to Washington, the Prime Minister discussed informally with the President of the United States the possibilities of further steps being taken by international agreement for the peaceful and orderly settlement of international disputes without, however, having reached a definite conclusion. Since then there have been reports in American newspapers that the United States may propose at the Naval Conference some extension to other parts of the world of the principle of "consultation" between the signatory powers which is contained in Articles 1 and 2 of the Four Power Treaty relating to the Pacific. His Majesty's Government are unaware whether these reports have any foundation in fact, but it is clear that, taken on the initiative of the United States, any such step would exercise a beneficial influence on the course of the Naval Conference. His Majesty's Government do not feel that this question can usefully be discussed by letter and cable at this juncture but, provided the Secretary of State sees no objection, and that further enquiries in England encourage His Majesty's Government to believe that such a step would be helpful, the Prime Minister proposes to resume with Mr. Stimson as soon as he arrives in London, the private conversations on this subject which took place between Mr. Hoover and Mr. MacDonald at Washington.

WASHINGTON, January 3, 1930.

CONVENTIONS CONCLUDED AT GENEVA, JULY 27, 1929, WITH OTHER POWERS FOR (1) AMELIORATION OF THE CONDITION OF THE WOUNDED AND SICK OF ARMIES IN THE FIELD; AND (2) TREATMENT OF PRISONERS OF WAR

514.2A12/49½

*Memorandum by Mr. Rollin R. Winslow, Division of Western European Affairs*

On February 6, 1925, the Department received a note from the Minister of Switzerland at Washington [1] inquiring whether this Government would be ready to take part in a Conference for the revision of the Geneva Convention of July 6, 1906, for the amelioration of the condition of the wounded in armies in the field [2] and whether it would be willing in principle to join in the framing of a code for prisoners of war.

The Geneva Convention of 1906 contained twenty-one articles providing in detail that persons attached to armies in the field who are sick and wounded shall be respected and cared for, without distinction of nationality by the belligerent power in whose hands they may fall; that after an engagement the belligerent in possession of the field shall search for the wounded and dead and protect them from robbery and ill treatment; that lists of the sick and wounded shall be given to the enemy, et cetera.

On June 22, 1925, a reply was sent to the Swiss Minister [1] based on a communication from the Secretary of War stating that this Government "will be glad to take part in a Conference for the revision of the Geneva Convention of July 6, 1906, and will be ready in principle to join in the framing of a code for prisoners of war and to entrust the same diplomatic conference" to work out both questions.

Since the date of the above note a study has been made and an extensive correspondence exchanged between the State, War and Navy Departments, by way of formulating this Government's views on the matters to be discussed and in working out the details connected with American participation. On December 28, 1929 [*1928*], a note was sent to the Swiss Minister [1] enclosing proposals made by the War Department for the revision of the Geneva Convention of 1906 and for the framing of a code for prisoners of war.

In regard to the code for prisoners of war the War Department proposed that the provisions of Section I of the Annex to The Hague

[1] Not printed.
[2] *Foreign Relations*, 1906, pt. 2, p. 1559.

Convention of 1907 respecting the laws and customs of war on land [4] should form a basis for such a code and should be extended and amended to meet any discrepancies developed during the World War.

[WASHINGTON,] June 5, 1929.   R[OLLIN] R. W[INSLOW]

---

514.2A12/71a

*The Acting Secretary of State to the Chairman of the American Delegation (Wadsworth)*

WASHINGTON, June 17, 1929.

SIR: With reference to the Department's instruction [5] informing you of your appointment as Chairman of the American Delegation to the Conference for the Revision of the Geneva Convention of 1906 and for Framing a Code for Prisoners of War, the Department desires you to be guided by the following instructions during your participation in the meetings of the Conference:

1. In view of the understanding expressed by the Swiss Government, the two subjects to be considered are separate and distinct and should be embodied in separate and distinct conventions, even if these conventions be drafted at the same Conference and by the same personnel.

2. In the revision of the Geneva Convention of July 6, 1906, this Government has no objection to the proposed changes as submitted by the Tenth and Eleventh International Red Cross Conferences,[6] but you should request a consideration of the following points with a view to their inclusion in the revised Convention.

*a.* You may, if deemed wise, consider an extension of Article 20 by providing for a system of adequate control over the wearing of the Red Cross armlet (brassard) in the theatre of operations, by personnel of voluntary aid societies and by individuals not engaged in caring for the sick and wounded.

*b.* You are instructed to advocate a revision of Articles 14, 17 and 19, of the Geneva Convention of July 6, 1906, whereby the provisions of these articles will be made applicable to all sanitary matériel and its operating personnel devoted exclusively to the transportation of the sick and wounded by land, water or air.

The Department believes that Article 19 should be so phrased as to require the marking of all principal matériel but so as not to require the marking of all matériel of a purely accessory nature such as the tools on ambulances, kitchen utensils in a hopital, surgical instruments, et cetera.

---

[4] *Foreign Relations,* 1907, pt. 2, p. 1204.
[5] June 12, 1929; not printed.
[6] *Revue Internationale de la Croix-Rouge,* Avril, 1921, No. 28, pp. 341–347, and Août, 1923, No. 56, pp. 771–814.

It is believed that the last amendment by the International Red Cross Committee under Article 21, which reads,

The belligerents shall take such measures as may be necessary in order to render the distinctive emblems placed on the sanitary formations and establishments plainly visible to the enemy forces, terrestrial, aerial and maritime.

will cover the question of visibility of the emblems. You will make it clear, if occasion arises, that this Government believes that "sanitary formations and establishments" is a term which will cover any kind of sanitary vehicle or unit engaged in succoring the sick and wounded.

*c.* You should advocate painting or otherwise marking aircraft pertaining to the Sanitary Services so as to be distinguishable from the ground or elsewhere under all conditions. A method for this purpose might provide for percentage of area to be covered, for the determination of the dimensions and character of the marking.

*d.* You should also advocate a uniform method of effectively marking sanitary formations and establishments for aerial identification distinguishable under all conditions.

*e.* It would be desirable to incorporate a provision that combatants engaged obviously temporarily, and primarily, in the transportation or treatment of the sick and wounded shall be respected and protected while so engaged in the same degree as are permanent sanitary personnel. However, if they fall into the hands of the enemy, they shall be treated as prisoners of war.

3. This Government has no objection to the presence of representatives of the International Red Cross and the Sovereign Order of Malta at the meetings held for a revision of the Geneva Convention of July 6, 1906 and for the formulation of a code for prisoners of war.

This Government, however, is strongly opposed to granting the International Red Cross or the Sovereign Order of Malta plenipotentiary status at the Conference in question, and since these organizations are not sovereign states it would oppose any proposal destined to allow either of them to vote in the Conference or to sign any instrument emanating from the Conference. Moreover it feels that since these organizations are not sovereign states they should not be given any function in the administration of the code after its adoption by the powers. In its note of February 18, 1929,[7] this Government so informed the Swiss Government.

4. You will find annexed to this instruction a listing of the general principles along which this Government believes the code for prisoners of war should be drafted.[7] It is believed that to this code there should be annexed regulations based substantially on the provisions of the

[7] Not printed.

detailed draft code prepared by the International Red Cross Committee (which follows closely the terms of the Treaty of November 11, 1918, between the United States and Germany [9]). This Government recognizes, however, the widely varying conditions under which hostilities occur and to meet this objection to the adoption of detailed regulations it suggests that you propose, at an opportune time, the formulation or ratification of a code, which should consist only of broad principles, and further suggests after ratification of the code and regulations by certain governments, the formation of a body in each of the capitals of the ratifying governments whose duty it would be to watch over the welfare of prisoners of war if hostilities should break out, to adapt the regulations annexed to the code to suit the exigencies of the situation and to see that these general principles were applied in any question which might arise and which had not been provided for. You should endeavor to obtain insertion in any agreement of a provision embodying the principles above suggested, but should you not be successful in this regard and should no other acceptable alternative appear, you may agree to a detailed code in the form now suggested in the agenda, excluding any agency of the International Red Cross from functioning thereunder.

5. This Government believes that it should be clearly stated in both agreements that in the event that one belligerent should allege a violation or nonobservance of any one article by another belligerent the former shall not be free to regard any of the remaining articles as thereby invalidated except such articles as are directly dependent upon the one concerning which there is an alleged violation or nonobservance.

I am [etc.]

J. REUBEN CLARK, JR.

---

514.2A12/60½

*Press Release Issued by the Department of State, June 19, 1929*

THE COMPOSITION OF THE AMERICAN DELEGATION TO THE CONFERENCE FOR THE REVISION OF THE GENEVA CONVENTION OF 1906 AND FOR THE FRAMING OF A CODE FOR THE TREATMENT OF PRISONERS OF WAR, WHICH WILL MEET AT GENEVA, SWITZERLAND, ON JULY 1, 1929

*Delegates:*

The Honorable Eliot Wadsworth.

The Honorable Hugh R. Wilson, American Minister to Switzerland.

[9] *Foreign Relations*, 1918, supp. 2, p. 103.

*Technical Advisers:*

Joseph R. Baker, Solicitor's Office, Department of State.

Frederic R. Dolbeare, formerly a Counselor of Embassy in American Foreign Service.

Major Allen W. Gullion, Judge Advocate General's Office, United States Army.

Major John P. Fletcher, Medical Corps, United States Army.

Major John B. Anderson, General Staff, United States Army.

Captain Frank L. Pleadwell, Medical Corps, United States Navy.

*Assistants:*

Jay Pierrepont Moffat, First Secretary, Geneva, Switzerland.

Marc Smith, Vice Consul, Geneva, Switzerland.

---

Treaty Series No. 847

*International Convention for the Amelioration of the Condition of the Wounded and Sick of Armies in the Field, Signed at Geneva, July 27, 1929* [10]

[List of heads of states which appears at the beginning of the convention is omitted.]

equally desirous of diminishing, so far as lies within their power, the evils inseparable from war, and wishing to perfect and complete, for this purpose, the provisions agreed upon at Geneva, August 22, 1864 and July 6, 1906 to ameliorate the condition of the wounded and the sick of armies in the field,

have decided to conclude a new Convention for this purpose, and have appointed the following as their plenipotentiaries, namely:

[List of plenipotentiaries is omitted.]

Who, after having communicated to each other their full powers, found to be in good and due form, have agreed as follows:

CHAPTER I. *The Wounded and Sick*

ARTICLE 1

Officers, soldiers, and other persons officially attached to the armies who are wounded or sick shall be respected and protected in all circumstances; they shall be humanely treated and cared for without distinction of nationality by the belligerent in whose power they are.

---

[10] In French: English translation reprinted from S. Ex. Doc. F, 71st Cong., 3d sess. Ratification advised by the Senate, January 7, 1932; ratified by the President, January 16, 1932; ratification of the United States deposited with the Government of Switzerland, February 4, 1932; proclaimed by the President, August 4, 1932.

A belligerent, however, when compelled to leave his wounded or sick in the hands of his adversary, shall leave with them, so far as military exigencies permit, a portion of the personnel and matériel of his sanitary service to assist in caring for them.

### ARTICLE 2

Subject to the care that must be taken of them under the preceding article, the wounded and sick of an army who fall into the power of the other belligerent shall become prisoners of war, and the general rules of international law in respect to prisoners of war shall become applicable to them.

The belligerents shall remain free, however, to agree upon such clauses to the benefit of the wounded and sick prisoners as they may deem of value over and above already existing obligations.

### ARTICLE 3

After every engagement, the belligerent who remains in possession of the field of battle shall take measures to search for the wounded and the dead and to protect them from robbery and ill-treatment.

A local armistice or cessation of fire to enable the removal of wounded left between the lines shall be arranged whenever circumstances permit.

### ARTICLE 4

Belligerents shall mutually forward to each other as soon as possible the names of the wounded, sick and dead taken in charge or discovered by them, as well as all indications which may serve for their identification.

They shall draw up and forward to each other death certificates.

They shall collect and likewise forward to each other all objects of personal use found on the field of battle or on the dead, especially one-half of their identity plaque, the other half remaining attached to the body.

They shall see that a careful examination, if possible, medical, is made of the bodies of the dead prior to their interment or cremation, with a view to verifying their death, establishing their identity, and in order to be able to furnish a report thereon.

They shall further see that they are honorably buried and that the graves are treated with respect and may always be found again.

For this purpose, and at the outbreak of hostilities, they shall officially organize a service of graves in order to render any later exhumation possible and to make certain of the identity of bodies even though they may have been moved from grave to grave.

Upon the termination of hostilities, they shall exchange lists of graves and of dead buried in their cemeteries and elsewhere.

## ARTICLE 5

The military authority may make an appeal to the charitable zeal of the inhabitants to receive and, under its supervision, to care for, the wounded or sick of the armies, granting to persons responding to such appeals special protection and certain facilities.

CHAPTER II. *Sanitary Formations and Establishments*

## ARTICLE 6

Mobile sanitary formations, i. e., those which are intended to accompany armies in the field, and the fixed establishments belonging to the sanitary service shall be protected and respected by the belligerents.

## ARTICLE 7

The protection due to sanitary formations and establishments shall cease if they are used to commit acts injurious to the enemy.

## ARTICLE 8

A sanitary formation or establishment shall not be deprived of the protection accorded by Article 6 by the fact:

1. that the personnel of the formation or establishment is armed and uses its arms in self-defense or in defense of its wounded and sick;

2. that in the absence of armed hospital attendants the formation is guarded by an armed detachment or by sentinels;

3. that hand firearms or ammunition taken from the wounded and sick and not yet turned over to the proper authorities are found in the formation or establishment;

4. that there is found in the formation or establishment personnel or matériel of the veterinary service which does not integrally belong to it.

CHAPTER III. *Personnel*

## ARTICLE 9

The personnel charged exclusively with the removal, transportation, and treatment of the wounded and sick, as well as with the administration of sanitary formations and establishments, and the chaplains attached to armies, shall be respected and protected under all circumstances. If they fall into the hands of the enemy they shall not be treated as prisoners of war.

Military personnel which has received special instructions to be used when necessary as auxiliary attendants or litter bearers in the removal, transportation and treatment of the wounded and sick, and bearing an identification document, shall benefit by the same conditions as the permanent sanitary personnel if they are captured at the moment when they are fulfilling these functions.

## ARTICLE 10

The personnel of volunteer aid societies, duly recognized and authorized by their Government, who are employed in the same functions as the personnel contemplated in Article 9, paragraph 1, are assimilated to that personnel upon condition that the said societies shall be subject to military laws and regulations.

Each High Contracting Party shall make known to the other, either in time of peace or at the opening or during the progress of hostilities, and in any case before actual employment, the names of the societies which it has authorized to render assistance, under its responsibility, in the official sanitary service of its armies.

## ARTICLE 11

A recognized society of a neutral country may only lend the services of its sanitary personnel and formations to a belligerent with the prior consent of its own Government and the authority of such belligerent.

The belligerent who has accepted such assistance shall be required to notify the enemy before making any use thereof.

## ARTICLE 12

The persons described in Articles 9, 10 and 11 may not be detained after they have fallen into the power of the adversary.

Unless there is an agreement to the contrary, they shall be sent back to the belligerent to whose service they are attached as soon as a way is open for their return and military exigencies permit.

While waiting to be returned, they shall continue in the exercise of their functions under the direction of the adversary; they shall be assigned preferably to the care of the wounded and sick of the belligerent to whose service they are attached.

At the time of their departure they may carry with them such effects, instruments, arms and means of transport as belong to them.

## ARTICLE 13

While they remain in their power, belligerents shall secure to the personnel mentioned in Articles 9, 10 and 11, the same maintenance and quarters, pay and allowances, as to persons of corresponding rank in their own armies.

At the outbreak of hostilities the belligerents shall reach an understanding on the corresponding ranks of their sanitary personnel.

## CHAPTER IV. *Buildings and Matériel*

### ARTICLE 14

If mobile sanitary formations, whatever may be their nature, fall into the power of the adversary, they shall retain their matériel, their means of transportation, and their conducting personnel.

The competent military authority, however, shall have the right to employ them in caring for the wounded and sick; restitution shall take place in accordance with the conditions prescribed for the sanitary personnel and as far as possible at the same time.

### ARTICLE 15

Buildings and matériel of the fixed sanitary establishments of the army shall remain subject to the laws of war, but may not be diverted from their use so long as they are necessary for the wounded and sick.

However, commanders of troops engaged in operations may use them in case of urgent military necessity if, before such use, the wounded and sick treated there have been provided for.

### ARTICLE 16

The buildings of aid societies admitted to the benefits of the Convention shall be regarded as private property.

The matériel of these societies, irrespective of its location, shall likewise be regarded as private property.

The right of requisition recognized to belligerents by the laws and customs of war shall be exercised only in case of urgent necessity and after the wounded and sick have been provided for.

## CHAPTER V. *Sanitary Transports*

### ARTICLE 17

Vehicles equipped for sanitary evacuation traveling singly or in convoy shall be treated as mobile sanitary formations subject to the following special provisions:

A belligerent intercepting sanitary transportation vehicles, traveling either singly or in convoy, may, if required by military necessity, stop them and break up the convoy, charging himself in all cases with the care of the wounded and sick whom it contains. He may only utilize such vehicles in the sector wherein they were intercepted and exclusively for sanitary needs. When their local mission is at an end, these vehicles must be returned under the conditions stipulated in Article 14.

Military personnel assigned by competent orders for sanitary transportation purposes shall be returned under the conditions stipulated in Article 12 for sanitary personnel, and subject to the provisions of the last paragraph of Article 18.

All means of transportation especially organized for evacuation purposes, as well as their appurtenances attached to the sanitary service, shall be returned in conformity with the provisions of Chapter **IV**.

Military means of transportation and their teams, other than those belonging to the sanitary service, may be captured.

The civil personnel and all means of transportation obtained by requisition shall be subject to the general rules of international law.

### ARTICLE 18

Aircraft used as a means of sanitary transportation shall enjoy the protection of the Convention during such time as they are exclusively reserved for the evacuation of wounded and sick and for the transportation of sanitary personnel and matériel.

They shall be painted in white and shall bear clearly visible the distinctive sign mentioned in Article 19 alongside of the national colors on their upper and lower surfaces.

Excepting with special and express permission, a flight over the firing-line, as well as over the zone situated in front of the major medical dressing stations, and in general over any territory under the control of or occupied by the enemy shall be forbidden.

Sanitary aircraft must comply with all summons to land.

In the case of a landing thus required or made accidentally upon territory occupied by the enemy, the wounded and sick, as well as the sanitary personnel and matériel, including the aircraft, shall benefit by the provisions of the present Convention.

The pilot, mechanics, and wireless operators who have been captured shall be returned on condition of only being utilized in the sanitary service until the termination of hostilities.

### Chapter VI. *The Distinctive Sign*

### ARTICLE 19

Out of respect to Switzerland the heraldic emblem of the red cross on a white ground, formed by the reversal of the Federal colors, is continued as the emblem and distinctive sign of the sanitary service of armies.

However, for countries which already use, as a distinctive sign, in place of the red cross, the red crescent or the red lion and sun on a white field, these emblems shall likewise be recognized within the meaning of the present Convention.

## ARTICLE 20

The emblem shall appear on flags and brassards, as well as upon all matériel, appertaining to the sanitary service, with the permission of the competent military authority.

## ARTICLE 21

The personnel protected in virtue of the first paragraph of Article 9 and Articles 10 and 11 shall wear attached to the left arm a brassard bearing the distinctive sign, issued and stamped by a competent military authority.

The personnel mentioned in Article 9, paragraphs 1 and 2, shall be furnished with an identification document consisting either of an inscription in their military booklet or a special document.

Persons mentioned in Articles 10 and 11 who do not wear military uniform shall be furnished by competent military authority with a certificate of identity containing their photograph and attesting to their sanitary status.

Identification documents must be uniform and of the same type in each army.

The sanitary personnel may in no case be deprived of their insignia nor of their own identification papers.

In case of loss they shall have the right to obtain duplicates.

## ARTICLE 22

The distinctive flag of the Convention may only be displayed over the sanitary formations and establishments which the Convention provides shall be respected, and with the consent of the military authorities. In fixed establishments it shall, and in mobile formations it may, be accompanied by the national flag of the belligerent to whose service the formation or establishment is attached.

Sanitary formations which have fallen into the power of the enemy, however, shall fly no other flag than that of the Convention as long as they continue in that situation.

The belligerents, in so far as military exigencies allow, shall take such measures as may be necessary to render the distinctive emblems marking sanitary formations and establishments plainly visible to the land, air and sea forces of the enemy, with a view to preventing the possibility of any aggressive action.

## ARTICLE 23

The sanitary formations of neutral countries which, under the conditions set forth in Article 11, have been authorized to render their services, shall fly, with the flag of the Convention, the national flag of the belligerent to which they are attached.

They shall have the right during such time as they are rendering service to a belligerent to fly their own national flag also.

The provisions of the second paragraph of the preceding article are applicable to them.

### ARTICLE 24

The emblem of the red cross on a white ground and the words *Red Cross* or *Geneva Cross* may be used, whether in time of peace or war, only to protect or designate sanitary formations and establishments, the personnel and matériel protected by the Convention.

The same shall apply with respect to the emblems mentioned in the second paragraph of Article 19 for such countries as use them.

Moreover, the volunteer aid societies provided for under Article 10 may, in conformity with their national legislation, employ the distinctive emblem for their humanitarian activities in time of peace.

As an exceptional measure and with the specific authorization of one of the national Red Cross Societies (Red Crescent, Red Lion and Sun), the use of the emblem of the Convention may be allowed in peace time to designate the location of relief stations reserved exclusively to giving free assistance to wounded or sick.

## Chapter VII. *The Application and Execution of the Convention*

### ARTICLE 25

The provisions of the present Convention shall be respected by the High Contracting Parties under all circumstances.

If, in time of war, a belligerent is not a party to the Convention, its provisions shall nevertheless remain in force as between all the belligerents who are parties to the Convention.

### ARTICLE 26

It shall be the duty of the commanders-in-chief of the belligerent armies to provide for the details of execution of the foregoing articles, as well as for unforeseen cases, in accordance with the instructions of their respective Governments, and conformably to the general principles of this Convention.

### ARTICLE 27

The High Contracting Parties shall take the necessary steps to acquaint their troops, and particularly the protected personnel, with the provisions of this Convention, and to make them known to the people at large.

CHAPTER VIII. *The Repression of Abuses and Infractions*

### ARTICLE 28

The Governments of the High Contracting Parties whose legislation may not now be adequate shall take or shall recommend to their legislatures such measures as may be necessary at all times:

*a*) to prevent the use by private persons or by societies other than those upon which this Convention confers the right thereto, of the emblem or of the name of the *Red Cross* or *Geneva Cross*, as well as any other sign or designation constituting an imitation thereof, whether for commercial or other purposes;

*b*) By reason of the homage rendered to Switzerland as a result of the adoption of the inverted Federal colors, to prevent the use, by private persons or by organizations, of the arms of the Swiss Confederation or of signs constituting an imitation thereof, whether as trademarks, commercial labels, or portions thereof, or in any way contrary to commercial ethics, or under conditions wounding Swiss national pride.

The prohibition mentioned in subparagraph *a*) of the use of signs or designations constituting an imitation of the emblem or designation of the *Red Cross* or *Geneva Cross*, as well as the prohibition mentioned in subparagraph *b*) of the use of the arms of the Swiss Confederation or signs constituting an imitation thereof, shall take effect from the time set in each act of legislation and at the latest five years after this Convention goes into effect. After such going into effect it shall be unlawful to take out a trademark or commercial label contrary to such prohibitions.

### ARTICLE 29

The Governments of the High Contracting Parties whose penal laws may not be adequate, shall likewise take or recommend to their legislatures the necessary measures to repress in time of war all acts in contravention of the provisions of the present Convention.

They shall communicate to one another through the Swiss Federal Council the measures taken with a view to such repression, not later than five years from the date of the ratification of the present Convention.

### ARTICLE 30

At the request of a belligerent, an investigation must be held, in such manner as shall be agreed upon by the interested parties, concerning any alleged violation of the Convention; whenever such a violation is proved, the belligerents shall put an end to it and repress it as promptly as possible.

*Final Provisions*

### ARTICLE 31

The present Convention, which will bear the date of this day, may be signed up to February 1, 1930, on behalf of all the countries represented at the Conference which opened at Geneva on July 1, 1929, as well as by the countries not represented at the Conference which are parties to the Geneva Conventions of 1864 or of 1906.

### ARTICLE 32

The present Convention shall be ratified as soon as possible.

The ratifications shall be deposited at Berne.

A record of the deposit of each instrument of ratification shall be prepared, a duly certified copy of which shall be forwarded by the Swiss Federal Council to the Governments of all the countries on whose behalf the Convention has been signed or notification of adhesion made.

### ARTICLE 33

The present Convention shall become effective six months after the deposit of at least two instruments of ratification.

Subsequently, it shall become effective for each High Contracting Party six months after the deposit of its instrument of ratification.

### ARTICLE 34

The present Convention shall replace the Conventions of August 22, 1864 and of July 6, 1906, in the relations between the High Contracting Parties.

### ARTICLE 35

From the date on which it becomes effective, the present Convention shall be open for adhesions given on behalf of any country in whose name this Convention was not signed.

### ARTICLE 36

Adhesions shall be given by written notification addressed to the Swiss Federal Council and shall take effect six months after the date of their receipt.

The Swiss Federal Council shall communicate adhesions to the Governments of all the countries on whose behalf the Convention was signed or notification of adhesion made.

### ARTICLE 37

A state of war shall give immediate effect to ratifications deposited or adhesions notified by belligerent Powers prior to or after the outbreak of hostilities. The communication of ratifications or adhesions received from Powers at war shall be made by the Swiss Federal Council by the most rapid method.

### ARTICLE 38

Each of the High Contracting Parties shall have the right to denounce the present Convention. The denunciation shall not take effect until one year after notification has been made in writing to the Swiss Federal Council. The latter shall communicate such notification to the Governments of all the High Contracting Parties.

The denunciation shall have effect only with respect to the High Contracting Party which gave notification of it.

Moreover, such denunciation shall not take effect during a war in which the denouncing Power is involved. In this case, the present Convention shall continue in effect, beyond the period of one year, until the conclusion of peace.

### ARTICLE 39

A duly certified copy of the present Convention shall be deposited in the archives of the League of Nations by the Swiss Federal Council. Likewise, ratifications, adhesions, and denunciations of which the Swiss Federal Council has been notified shall be communicated by it to the League of Nations.

IN FAITH WHEREOF, the Plenipotentiaries named above have signed the present Convention.

DONE at Geneva, the twenty-seventh of July, one thousand nine hundred and twenty-nine, in a single copy, which shall remain in the archives of the Swiss Confederation and duly certified copies of which shall be forwarded to the Governments of all the countries invited to the Conference.

For Germany:
EDMUND RHOMBERG

For the United States of America:
ELIOT WADSWORTH
HUGH R. WILSON

For Austria:
LEITMAIER

For Belgium:
Dr. DEMOLDER
J. DE RUELLE

For Bolivia:
A. CORTADELLAS

For Brazil:
RAUL DO RIO-BRANCO

For Great Britain and Northern Ireland, and all parts of the British Empire which are not separate members of the League of Nations:

I declare that the signature which I affix to this Convention for Great Britain and Northern Ireland, and all parts of the British Empire which are not separate members of the League of Nations is given with the reservation that His Britannic Majesty interprets Article 28 of the Convention as meaning that the legislative provisions contemplated in this article may provide that the individuals, associations, firms or societies that shall, before the present Convention goes into effect, have used the arms of the Swiss Confederation, or signs constituting an imitation of the said arms, for any legal purpose, shall not be prevented from continuing to employ such arms or signs for the same purpose.

HORACE RUMBOLD

For Canada:

I declare that the signature which I affix to this Convention for Canada is given with the reservation that the Government of the Dominion of Canada interprets Article 28 of the Convention as meaning that the legislative provisions contemplated in this article may provide that the individuals, associations, firms and societies that shall, before the present Convention goes into effect, have used the arms of the Swiss Confederation, or signs constituting an imitation of the said arms, for any legal purpose, shall not be prevented from continuing to employ such arms or signs for the same purpose.

W. A. RIDDELL

For Australia:

I declare that the signature which I affix to this Convention for Australia is given with the reservation that the Government of the Commonwealth of Australia interprets Article 28 of the Convention as meaning that the legislative provisions contemplated in this article may provide that the individuals, associations, firms and societies that shall, before the present Convention goes into effect, have used the arms of the Swiss Confederation, or signs constituting an imitation of the said arms, for any legal purpose, shall not be prevented from continuing to employ such arms or signs for the same purpose.

CLAUD RUSSELL

For New Zealand:

I declare that the signature which I affix to this Convention for New Zealand is given with the reservation that the Government of New Zealand interprets Article 28 of the Convention as meaning that the legislative provisions contemplated in this Article may provide that the individuals, associations, firms or societies that shall, before the present Convention goes into effect, have used the arms of the Swiss Confederation, or signs constituting an imitation of the said arms, for any legal purpose, shall not be prevented from continuing to employ such arms or signs for the same purpose.

CLAUD RUSSELL

For South Africa:
ERIC H. LOUW

For the Irish Free State:
I declare that the signature which I affix to this Convention for the Irish Free State is given with the reservation that it interprets Article 28 of the Convention as meaning that the legislative provisions contemplated in this article may provide that the individuals, associations, firms or societies that shall, before the present Convention goes into effect, have used the arms of the Swiss Confederation, or signs constituting an imitation of the said arms, for any legal purpose, shall not be prevented from continuing to employ such arms or signs for the same purpose.
SEAN LESTER

For India:
I declare that the signature which I affix to this Convention for the Government of India is given with the reservation that the Government of India interprets Article 28 of the Convention as meaning that the legislative provisions contemplated in this article may provide that the individuals, associations, firms or societies that shall, before the present Convention goes into effect, have used the arms of the Swiss Confederation, or signs constituting an imitation of the said arms, for any legal purpose, shall not be prevented from continuing to employ such arms or signs for the same purpose.
CLAUD RUSSELL

For Bulgaria:
D. MIKOFF
STEPHAN N. LAFTCHIEFF

For Chile:
GMO NOVOA
D. PULGAR

For China:
C. Y. HSIAO

For Colombia:
FRANCISCO JOSÉ URRUTIA

For Cuba:
CARLOS DE ARMENTEROS
CARLOS BLANCO

For Denmark:
HARALD SCAVENIUS
GUSTAV RASMUSSEN

For the Dominican Republic:
CH. ACKERMANN

For Egypt:
MOHAMMED ABDEL MONEIM RIAD
H. W. M. SIMAIKA

For Spain:
  Ad Referendum

  MAURICIO LOPEZ ROBERTS Y TERRY, MARQUÉS DE LA
    TORREHERMOSA

For Estonia:
  Dr. LEESMENT

For Finland:
  A. E. MARTOLA

For France:
  H. DE MARCILLY
  J. DU SAULT

For Greece:
  R. RAPHAËL
  S. VENISELOS

For Hungary:
  PAUL DE HEVESY

For Italy:
  GIOVANNI CIRAOLO

For Japan:
  While accepting in principle the provisions of Article 28, Japan makes
reservations as to the date of enforcing the interdiction provided for under
letter *b* of the said article. Japan understands that this interdiction does
not apply to arms and signs which may have been in use or registered before
it goes into effect. The delegates of Japan sign the present Convention
with the above mentioned reservations.

  ISABURO YOSHIDA
  S. SHIMOMURA
  S. MIURA

For Latvia:
  CHARLES DUZMANS
  Dr. OSKAR VOIT

For Luxembourg:
  CH. G. VERMAIRE

For Mexico:
  FR. CASTILLO NÁJERA

For Nicaragua:
  A. SOTTILE

For Norway:
  J. IRGENS
  JENS MEINICH

For the Netherlands:
W. Doude van Troostwijk
Dr. Diehl
J. Harberts

For Persia:
Anouchirevan Sepahbodi

For Poland:
Józef G. Pracki
W. Jerzy Babecki

For Portugal:
Vasco de Quevedo
F. de Calheiros e Menezes

For Rumania:
M. B. Boeresco
Colonel E. Vertejano

For the Kingdom of the Serbs, Croats and Slovenes:
I. Choumenkovitch

For Siam:
Varnvaidya

For Sweden:
K. I. Westman

For Switzerland:
Paul Dinichert
Hauser
Züblin
De la Harpe
Schindler

For Czechoslovakia:
Zd. Fierlinger

For Turkey:
Hassan
Dr. Abdulkadir
M. Nusret
Dr. Akil Moukhtar

For Uruguay:
Alfredo de Castro

For Venezuela:
C. Parra-Pérez
I. M. Hurtado-Machado

Treaty Series No. 846

## *International Convention Relative to the Treatment of Prisoners of War, Signed at Geneva, July 27, 1929* [11]

[List of heads of states which appears at the beginning of the convention is omitted.]

recognizing that in the extreme case of a war, it will be the duty of every power to diminish, so far as possible, the unavoidable rigors thereof and to mitigate the fate of prisoners of war;

desirous of developing the principles which inspired the international conventions of The Hague, in particular the Convention relative to the laws and customs of war and the regulations annexed thereto;

have decided to conclude a Convention to that end, and have appointed the following as their plenipotentiaries, namely:

[List of plenipotentiaries is omitted.]

Who, after having communicated to each other their full powers, found to be in good and due form, have agreed as follows:

### TITLE I. GENERAL PROVISIONS

#### ARTICLE 1

The present Convention shall apply, without prejudice to the stipulations of Title VII:

1) To all persons mentioned in Articles 1, 2 and 3 of the Regulations annexed to the Hague Convention respecting the laws and customs of war on land, of October 18, 1907, and captured by the enemy.*

---

[11] In French; English translation reprinted from S. Ex. Doc. E, 71st Cong., 3d sess. Ratification advised by the Senate, January 7, 1932; ratified by the President, January 16, 1932; ratification of the United States deposited with the Government of Switzerland, February 4, 1932; proclaimed by the President, August 4, 1932.

\* *Annexed Regulations:*

ART. 1. The laws, rights, and duties of war apply not only to armies, but also to militia and volunteer corps fulfilling the following conditions:

1. To be commanded by a person responsible for his subordinates;
2. To have a fixed distinctive emblem recognizable at a distance;
3. To carry arms openly; and
4. To conduct their operations in accordance with the laws and customs of war.

In countries where militia or volunteer corps constitute the army, or form part of it, they are included under the denomination "army."

ART. 2. The inhabitants of a territory which has not been occupied, who, on the approach of the enemy, spontaneously take up arms to resist the invading troops without having had time to organize themselves in accordance with Article 1, shall be regarded as belligerents if they carry arms openly and if they respect the laws and customs of war.

ART. 3. The armed forces of the belligerent parties may consist of combatants and noncombatants. In the case of capture by the enemy, both have a right to be treated as prisoners of war. [Footnote in the original.]

2) To all persons belonging to the armed forces of belligerent parties, captured by the enemy in the course of military operations at sea or in the air, except for such derogations as might be rendered inevitable by the conditions of capture. However, such derogations shall not infringe upon the fundamental principles of the present Convention; they shall cease from the moment when the persons captured have rejoined a prisoners-of-war camp.

### ARTICLE 2

Prisoners of war are in the power of the hostile Power, but not of the individuals or corps who have captured them.

They must at all times be humanely treated and protected, particularly against acts of violence, insults and public curiosity.

Measures of reprisal against them are prohibited.

### ARTICLE 3

Prisoners of war have the right to have their person and their honor respected. Women shall be treated with all the regard due to their sex.

Prisoners retain their full civil status.

### ARTICLE 4

The Power detaining prisoners of war is bound to provide for their maintenance.

Difference in treatment among prisoners is lawful only when it is based on the military rank, state of physical or mental health, professional qualifications or sex of those who profit thereby.

### TITLE II. CAPTURE

### ARTICLE 5

Every prisoner of war is bound to give, if he is questioned on the subject, his true name and rank, or else his regimental number.

If he infringes this rule, he is liable to have the advantages given to prisoners of his class curtailed.

No coercion may be used on prisoners to secure information relative to the condition of their army or country. Prisoners who refuse to answer may not be threatened, insulted, or exposed to unpleasant or disadvantageous treatment of any kind whatever.

If, because of his physical or mental condition, a prisoner is unable to identify himself, he shall be turned over to the medical corps.

### ARTICLE 6

All effects and objects of personal use—except arms, horses, military equipment and military papers—shall remain in the possession of prisoners of war, as well as metal helmets and gas masks.

Money in the possession of prisoners may not be taken away from them except by order of an officer and after the amount is determined. A receipt shall be given. Money thus taken away shall be entered to the account of each prisoner.

Identification documents, insignia of rank, decorations and objects of value may not be taken from prisoners.

## TITLE III. CAPTIVITY

### SECTION I. EVACUATION OF PRISONERS OF WAR

#### ARTICLE 7

Prisoners of wars shall be evacuated within the shortest possible period after their capture, to depots located in a region far enough from the zone of combat for them to be out of danger.

Only prisoners who, because of wounds or sickness, would run greater risks by being evacuated than by remaining where they are may be temporarily kept in a dangerous zone.

Prisoners shall not be needlessly exposed to danger while awaiting their evacuation from the combat zone.

Evacuation of prisoners on foot may normally be effected only by stages of 20 kilometers a day, unless the necessity of reaching water and food depots requires longer stages.

#### ARTICLE 8

Belligerents are bound mutually to notify each other of their capture of prisoners within the shortest period possible, through the intermediary of the information bureaus, such as are organized according to Article 77. They are likewise bound to inform each other of the official addresses to which the correspondence of their families may be sent to prisoners of war.

As soon as possible, every prisoner must be enabled to correspond with his family himself, under the conditions provided in Articles 36 *et seq.*

As regards prisoners captured at sea, the provisions of the present article shall be observed as soon as possible after arrival at port.

### SECTION II. PRISONERS-OF-WAR CAMPS

#### ARTICLE 9

Prisoners of war may be interned in a town, fortress, or other place, and bound not to go beyond certain fixed limits. They may also be interned in enclosed camps; they may not be confined or imprisoned except as an indispensable measure of safety or sanitation, and only while the circumstances which necessitate the measure continue to exist.

Prisoners captured in unhealthful regions or where the climate is injurious for persons coming from temperate regions, shall be transported, as soon as possible, to a more favorable climate.

Belligerents shall, so far as possible, avoid assembling in a single camp prisoners of different races or nationalities.

No prisoner may, at any time, be sent into a region where he might be exposed to the fire of the combat zone, nor used to give protection from bombardment to certain points or certain regions by his presence.

## CHAPTER 1.  *Installation of Camps*

### ARTICLE 10

Prisoners of war shall be lodged in buildings or in barracks affording all possible guarantees of hygiene and healthfulness.

The quarters must be fully protected from dampness, sufficiently heated and lighted.  All precautions must be taken against danger of fire.

With regard to dormitories—the total surface, minimum cubic amount of air, arrangement and material of bedding—the conditions shall be the same as for the troops at base camps of the detaining Power.

## CHAPTER 2.  *Food and Clothing of Prisoners of War*

### ARTICLE 11

The food ration of prisoners of war shall be equal in quantity and quality to that of troops at base camps.

Furthermore, prisoners shall receive facilities for preparing, themselves, additional food which they might have.

A sufficiency of potable water shall be furnished them.  The use of tobacco shall be permitted.  Prisoners may be employed in the kitchens.

All collective disciplinary measures affecting the food are prohibited.

### ARTICLE 12

Clothing, linen and footwear shall be furnished prisoners of war by the detaining Power.  Replacement and repairing of these effects must be assured regularly.  In addition, laborers must receive work clothes wherever the nature of the work requires it.

Canteens shall be installed in all camps where prisoners may obtain at the local market price, food products and ordinary objects.

Profits made by the canteens for camp administrations shall be used for the benefit of prisoners.

CHAPTER 3. *Sanitary Service in Camps*

ARTICLE 13

Belligerents shall be bound to take all sanitary measures necessary to assure the cleanliness and healthfulness of camps and to prevent epidemics.

Prisoners of war shall have at their disposal, day and night, installations conforming to sanitary rules and constantly maintained in a state of cleanliness.

Furthermore, and without prejudice to baths and showers with which the camp shall be as well provided as possible, prisoners shall be furnished a sufficient quantity of water for the care of their own bodily cleanliness.

It shall be possible for them to take physical exercise and enjoy the open air.

ARTICLE 14

Every camp shall have an infirmary, where prisoners of war shall receive every kind of attention they need. If necessary, isolated quarters shall be reserved for the sick affected with contagious diseases.

Expenses of treatment, including therein those of temporary prosthetic equipment, shall be borne by the detaining Power.

Upon request, belligerents shall be bound to deliver to every prisoner treated an official statement showing the nature and duration of his illness as well as the attention received.

It shall be lawful for belligerents reciprocally to authorize, by means of private arrangements, the retention in the camps of physicians and attendants to care for prisoners of their own country.

Prisoners affected with a serious illness or whose condition necessitates an important surgical operation, must be admitted, at the expense of the detaining Power, to any military or civil medical unit qualified to treat them.

ARTICLE 15

Medical inspections of prisoners of war shall be arranged at least once a month. Their purpose shall be the supervision of the general state of health and cleanliness, and the detection of contagious diseases, particularly tuberculosis and venereal diseases.

CHAPTER 4. *Intellectual and Moral Needs of Prisoners of War*

ARTICLE 16

Prisoners of war shall enjoy complete liberty in the exercise of their religion, including attendance at the services of their faith, on the sole condition that they comply with the measures of order and police issued by the military authorities.

Ministers of a religion, prisoners of war, whatever their religious denomination, shall be allowed to minister fully to members of the same religion.

ARTICLE 17

So far as possible, belligerents shall encourage intellectual diversions and sports organized by prisoners of war.

CHAPTER 5. Internal Discipline of Camps

ARTICLE 18

Every camp of prisoners of war shall be placed under the command of a responsible officer.

Besides the external marks of respect provided by the regulations in force in their armies with regard to their nationals, prisoners of war must salute all officers of the detaining Power.

Officers who are prisoners of war are bound to salute only officers of a higher or equal rank of that Power.

ARTICLE 19

The wearing of insignia of rank and of decorations shall be permitted.

ARTICLE 20

Regulations, orders, notices and proclamations of every kind must be communicated to prisoners of war in a language which they understand. The same principle shall be applied in examinations.

CHAPTER 6. Special Provisions Regarding Officers and Persons of Equivalent Status

ARTICLE 21

Upon the beginning of hostilities, belligerents shall be bound to communicate to one another the titles and ranks in use in their respective armies, with a view to assuring equality of treatment between corresponding ranks of officers and persons of equivalent status.

Officers and persons of equivalent status who are prisoners of war shall be treated with the regard due their rank and age.

ARTICLE 22

In order to assure service in officers' camps, soldiers of the same army who are prisoners of war and, wherever possible, who speak the same language, shall be assigned thereto, in sufficient numbers, considering the rank of the officers and persons of equivalent status.

The latter shall secure their food and clothing from the pay which shall be granted them by the detaining Power. Administration of the mess-fund by the officers themselves must be facilitated in every way.

CHAPTER 7. *Financial Resources of Prisoners of War*

ARTICLE 23

Subject to private arrangements between belligerent Powers, and particularly those provided in Article 24, officers and persons of equivalent status who are prisoners of war shall receive from the detaining Power the same pay as officers of corresponding rank in the armies of that Power, on the condition, however, that this pay does not exceed that to which they are entitled in the armies of the country which they have served. This pay shall be granted them in full, once a month if possible, and without being liable to any deduction for expenses incumbent on the detaining Power, even when they are in favor of the prisoners.

An agreement between the belligerents shall fix the rate of exchange applicable to this payment; in the absence of such an agreement, the rate adopted shall be that in force at the opening of hostilities.

All payments made to prisoners of war as pay must be reimbursed, at the end of hostilities, by the Power which they have served.

ARTICLE 24

Upon the outbreak of hostilities, the belligerents shall, by common agreement, fix the maximum amount of ready money which prisoners of war of various ranks and classes shall be allowed to keep in their possession. Any surplus taken or withheld from a prisoner shall be entered to his account, the same as any deposit of money effected by him, and may not be converted into another currency without his consent.

Pay to the credit of their accounts shall be given to prisoners of war at the end of their captivity.

During their imprisonment, facilities shall be granted them for the transfer of these amounts, in whole or in part, to banks or private persons in their country of origin.

CHAPTER 8. *Transfer of Prisoners of War*

ARTICLE 25

Unless the conduct of military operations so requires, sick and wounded prisoners of war shall not be transferred as long as their recovery might be endangered by the trip.

## ARTICLE 26

In case of transfer, prisoners of war shall be officially notified of their new destination in advance; they shall be allowed to take with them their personal effects, their correspondence and packages which have arrived for them.

All due measures shall be taken that correspondence and packages addressed to their former camp may be forwarded to them without delay.

Money deposited to the account of transferred prisoners shall be transmitted to the competent authority of their new place of residence.

The expenses occasioned by the transfer shall be charged to the detaining Power.

### SECTION III. LABOR OF PRISONERS OF WAR

#### CHAPTER 1. *Generalities*

## ARTICLE 27

Belligerents may utilize the labor of able prisoners of war, according to their rank and aptitude, officers and persons of equivalent status excepted.

However, if officers or persons of equivalent status request suitable work, it shall be secured for them so far as is possible.

Noncommissioned officers who are prisoners of war shall only be required to do supervisory work, unless they expressly request a remunerative occupation.

Belligerents shall be bound, during the whole period of captivity, to allow to prisoners of war who are victims of accidents in connection with their work the enjoyment of the benefit of the provisions applicable to laborers of the same class according to the legislation of the detaining Power. With regard to prisoners of war to whom these legal provisions might not be applied by reason of the legislation of that Power, the latter undertakes to recommend to its legislative body all proper measures equitably to indemnify the victims.

#### CHAPTER 2. *Organization of the Labor*

## ARTICLE 28

The detaining Power shall assume entire responsibility for the maintenance, care, treatment and payment of wages of prisoners of war working for the account of private persons.

## ARTICLE 29

No prisoner of war may be employed at labors for which he is physically unfit.

### ARTICLE 30

The length of the day's work of prisoners of war, including therein the trip going and returning, shall not be excessive and must not, in any case, exceed that allowed for the civil workers in the region employed at the same work. Every prisoner shall be allowed a rest of twenty-four consecutive hours every week, preferably on Sunday.

## CHAPTER 3. *Prohibited Labor*

### ARTICLE 31

Labor furnished by prisoners of war shall have no direct relation with war operations. It is especially prohibited to use prisoners for manufacturing and transporting arms or munitions of any kind, or for transporting material intended for combatant units.

In case of violation of the provisions of the preceding paragraph, prisoners, after executing or beginning to execute the order, shall be free to have their protests presented through the mediation of the agents whose functions are set forth in Articles 43 and 44, or, in the absence of an agent, through the mediation of representatives of the protecting Power.

### ARTICLE 32

It is forbidden to use prisoners of war at unhealthful or dangerous work.

Any aggravation of the conditions of labor by disciplinary measures is forbidden.

## CHAPTER 4. *Labor Detachments*

### ARTICLE 33

The system of labor detachments must be similar to that of prisoners-of-war camps, particularly with regard to sanitary conditions, food, attention in case of accident or sickness, correspondence and the receipt of packages.

Every labor detachment shall be dependent on a prisoners' camp. The commander of this camp shall be responsible for the observation, in the labor detachment, of the provisions of the present Convention.

## CHAPTER 5. *Wages*

### ARTICLE 34

Prisoners of war shall not receive wages for work connected with the administration, management and maintenance of the camps.

Prisoners utilized for other work shall be entitled to wages to be fixed by agreements between the belligerents.

These agreements shall also specify the part which the camp administration may retain, the amount which shall belong to the prisoner of war and the manner in which that amount shall be put at his disposal during the period of his captivity.

While awaiting the conclusion of the said agreements, payment for labor of prisoners shall be settled according to the rules given below:

*a*) Work done for the State shall be paid for in accordance with the rates in force for soldiers of the national army doing the same work, or, if none exists, according to a rate in harmony with the work performed.

*b*) When the work is done for the account of other public administrations or for private persons, conditions shall be regulated by agreement with the military authority.

The pay remaining to the credit of the prisoner shall be delivered to him at the end of his captivity. In case of death, it shall be forwarded through the diplomatic channel to the heirs of the deceased.

SECTION IV. EXTERNAL RELATIONS OF PRISONERS OF WAR

ARTICLE 35

Upon the outbreak of hostilities, belligerents shall publish the measures provided for the execution of the provisions of this section.

ARTICLE 36

Each of the belligerents shall periodically determine the number of letters and postal cards per month which prisoners of war of the various classes shall be allowed to send, and shall inform the other belligerent of this number. These letters and cards shall be transmitted by post by the shortest route. They may not be delayed or retained for disciplinary reasons.

Within a period of not more than one week after his arrival at the camp, and likewise in case of sickness, every prisoner shall be enabled to write his family a postal card informing it of his capture and of the state of his health. The said postal cards shall be forwarded as rapidly as possible and may not be delayed in any manner.

As a general rule, correspondence of prisoners shall be written in their native language. Belligerents may allow correspondence in other languages.

ARTICLE 37

Prisoners of war shall be allowed individually to receive parcels by mail, containing foods and other articles intended to supply them with food or clothing. Packages shall be delivered to the addressees and a receipt given.

ARTICLE 38

Letters and consignments of money or valuables, as well as parcels by post intended for prisoners of war or dispatched by them, either directly, or by the mediation of the information bureaus provided for in Article 77, shall be exempt from all postal duties in the countries of origin and destination, as well as in the countries they pass through.

Presents and relief in kind for prisoners shall be likewise exempt from all import and other duties, as well as of payments for carriage by the State railways.

Prisoners may, in cases of acknowledged urgency, be allowed to send telegrams, paying the usual charges.

ARTICLE 39

Prisoners of war shall be allowed to receive shipments of books individually, which may be subject to censorship.

Representatives of the protecting Powers and duly recognized and authorized aid societies may send books and collections of books to the libraries of prisoners' camps. The transmission of these shipments to libraries may not be delayed under the pretext of censorship difficulties.

ARTICLE 40

Censorship of correspondence must be effected within the shortest possible time. Furthermore, inspection of parcels post must be effected under proper conditions to guarantee the preservation of the products which they may contain and, if possible, in the presence of the addressee or an agent duly recognized by him.

Prohibitions of correspondence promulgated by the belligerents for military or political reasons, must be transient in character and as short as possible.

ARTICLE 41

Belligerents shall assure all facilities for the transmission of instruments, papers or documents intended for prisoners of war or signed by them, particularly of powers of attorney and wills.

They shall take the necessary measures to assure, in case of necessity, the authentication of signatures made by prisoners.

SECTION V. PRISONERS' RELATIONS WITH THE AUTHORITIES

CHAPTER 1. *Complaints of Prisoners of War because of the Conditions of Captivity*

ARTICLE 42

Prisoners of war shall have the right to inform the military authorities in whose power they are of their requests with regard to the conditions of captivity to which they are subjected.

They shall also have the right to address themselves to representatives of the protecting Powers to indicate to them the points on which they have complaints to formulate with regard to the conditions of captivity.

These requests and complaints must be transmitted immediately.

Even if they are recognized to be unfounded, they may not occasion any punishment.

## CHAPTER 2. *Representatives of Prisoners of War*

### ARTICLE 43

In every place where there are prisoners of war, they shall be allowed to appoint agents entrusted with representing them directly with military authorities and protecting Powers.

This appointment shall be subject to the approval of the military authority.

The agents shall be entrusted with the reception and distribution of collective shipments. Likewise, in case the prisoners should decide to organize a mutual assistance system among themselves, this organization would be in the sphere of the agents. Further, they may lend their offices to prisoners to facilitate their relations with the aid societies mentioned in Article 78.

In camps of officers and persons of equivalent status, the senior officer prisoner of the highest rank shall be recognized as intermediary between the camp authorities and the officers and persons of equivalent status who are prisoners. For this purpose, he shall have the power to appoint a prisoner officer to assist him as an interpreter during the conferences with the camp authorities.

### ARTICLE 44

When the agents are employed as laborers, their activity as representatives of prisoners of war must be counted in the compulsory period of labor.

All facilities shall be accorded the agents for their intercourse with the military authorities and with the protecting Power. This intercourse shall not be limited.

No representative of the prisoners may be transferred without the necessary time being allowed him to inform his successors about affairs under consideration.

## CHAPTER 3. *Penalties Applicable to Prisoners of War*

### 1. GENERAL PROVISIONS

### ARTICLE 45

Prisoners of war shall be subject to the laws, regulations, and orders in force in the armies of the detaining Power.

An act of insubordination shall justify the adoption towards them of the measures provided by such laws, regulations and orders.

The provisions of the present chapter, however, are reserved.

### ARTICLE 46

Punishments other than those provided for the same acts for soldiers of the national armies may not be imposed upon prisoners of war by the military authorities and courts of the detaining Power.

Rank being identical, officers, noncommissioned officers or soldiers who are prisoners of war undergoing a disciplinary punishment, shall not be subject to less favorable treatment than that provided in the armies of the detaining Power with regard to the same punishment.

Any corporal punishment, any imprisonment in quarters without daylight and, in general, any form of cruelty, is forbidden.

Collective punishment for individual acts is also forbidden.

### ARTICLE 47

Acts constituting an offense against discipline, and particularly attempted escape, shall be verified immediately; for all prisoners of war, commissioned or not, preventive arrest shall be reduced to the absolute minimum.

Judicial proceedings against prisoners of war shall be conducted as rapidly as the circumstances permit; preventive imprisonment shall be limited as much as possible.

In all cases, the duration of preventive imprisonment shall be deducted from the disciplinary or judicial punishment inflicted, provided that this deduction is allowed for national soldiers.

### ARTICLE 48

Prisoners of war may not be treated differently from other prisoners after having suffered the judicial or disciplinary punishment which has been imposed on them.

However, prisoners punished as a result of attempted escape may be subjected to special surveillance, which, however, may not entail the suppression of the guarantees granted prisoners by the present Convention.

### ARTICLE 49

No prisoner of war may be deprived of his rank by the detaining Power.

Prisoners given disciplinary punishment may not be deprived of the prerogatives attached to their rank. In particular, officers and persons of equivalent status who suffer punishment involving deprivation of liberty shall not be placed in the same quarters as non-commissioned officers or privates being punished.

## ARTICLE 50

Escaped prisoners of war who are retaken before being able to rejoin their own army or to leave the territory occupied by the army which captured them shall be liable only to disciplinary punishment.

Prisoners who, after having succeeded in rejoining their army or in leaving the territory occupied by the army which captured them, may again be taken prisoners, shall not be liable to any punishment on account of their previous flight.

## ARTICLE 51

Attempted escape, even if it is a repetition of the offense, shall not be considered as an aggravating circumstance in case the prisoner of war should be given over to the courts on account of crimes or offenses against persons or property committed in the course of that attempt.

After an attempted or accomplished escape, the comrades of the person escaping who assisted in the escape, may incur only disciplinary punishment on this account.

## ARTICLE 52

Belligerents shall see that the competent authorities exercise the greatest leniency in deciding the question of whether an infraction committed by a prisoner of war should be punished by disciplinary or judicial measures.

This shall be the case especially when it is a question of deciding on acts in connection with escape or attempted escape.

A prisoner may not be punished more than once because of the same act or the same count.

## ARTICLE 53

No prisoner of war on whom a disciplinary punishment has been imposed, who might be eligible for repatriation, may be kept back because he has not undergone the punishment.

Prisoners to be repatriated who might be threatened with a penal prosecution may be excluded from repatriation until the end of the proceedings and, if necessary, until the completion of the punishment; those who might already be imprisoned by reason of a sentence may be detained until the end of their imprisonment.

Belligerents shall communicate to each other the lists of those who may not be repatriated for the reasons given in the preceding paragraph.

## 2. DISCIPLINARY PUNISHMENTS

## ARTICLE 54

Arrest is the most severe disciplinary punishment which may be imposed on a prisoner of war.

The duration of a single punishment may not exceed thirty days.

This maximum of thirty days may not, further, be exceeded in the case of several acts for which the prisoner has to undergo discipline at the time when it is ordered for him, whether or not these acts are connected.

When, during or after the end of a period of arrest, a prisoner shall have a new disciplinary punishment imposed upon him, a space of at least three days shall separate each of the periods of arrest, if one of them is ten days or more.

### ARTICLE 55

Subject to the provisions given in the last paragraph of Article 11, food restrictions allowed in the armies of the detaining Power are applicable, as an increase in punishment, to prisoners of war given disciplinary punishment.

However, these restrictions may be ordered only if the state of health of the prisoners punished permits it.

### ARTICLE 56

In no case may prisoners of war be transferred to penitentiary establishments (prisons, penitentiaries, convict prisons, etc.) there to undergo disciplinary punishment.

The quarters in which they undergo disciplinary punishment shall conform to sanitary requirements.

Prisoners punished shall be enabled to keep themselves in a state of cleanliness.

These prisoners shall every day be allowed to exercise or to stay in the open air at least two hours.

### ARTICLE 57

Prisoners of war given disciplinary punishment shall be allowed to read and write, as well as to send and receive letters.

On the other hand, packages and money sent may be not delivered to the addressees until the expiration of the punishment. If the packages not distributed contain perishable products, these shall be turned over to the camp infirmary or kitchen.

### ARTICLE 58

Prisoners of war given disciplinary punishment shall be allowed, on their request, to be present at the daily medical inspection. They shall receive the care considered necessary by the doctors and, if necessary, shall be removed to the camp infirmary or to hospitals.

## ARTICLE 59

Excepting the competence of courts and higher military authorities, disciplinary punishment may be ordered only by an officer provided with disciplinary powers in his capacity as commander of a camp or detachment, or by the responsible officer replacing him.

### 3. JUDICIAL SUITS

## ARTICLE 60

At the opening of a judicial proceeding directed against a prisoner of war, the detaining Power shall advise the representative of the protecting Power thereof as soon as possible, and always before the date set for the opening of the trial.

This advice shall contain the following information:

*a*) Civil state and rank of prisoner;

*b*) Place of sojourn or imprisonment;

c) Specification of the [count] or counts of the indictment, giving the legal provisions applicable.

If it is not possible to mention in that advice the court which will pass upon the matter, the date of opening the trial and the place where it will take place, this information must be furnished to the representative of the protecting Power later, as soon as possible, and at all events, at least three weeks before the opening of the trial.

## ARTICLE 61

No prisoner of war may be sentenced without having had an opportunity to defend himself.

No prisoner may be obliged to admit himself guilty of the act of which he is accused.

## ARTICLE 62

The prisoner of war shall be entitled to assistance by a qualified counsel of his choice, and, if necessary, to have recourse to the services of a competent interpreter. He shall be advised of his right by the detaining Power, in due time before the trial.

In default of a choice by the prisoner, the protecting Power may obtain a counsel for him. The detaining Power shall deliver to the protecting Power, on its request, a list of persons qualified to present the defense.

Representatives of the protecting Power shall be entitled to attend the trial of the case.

The only exception to this rule is the case where the trial of the case must be secret in the interest of the safety of the State. The detaining Power should so advise the protecting Power.

## ARTICLE 63

Sentence may be pronounced against a prisoner of war only by the same courts and according to the same procedure as in the case of persons belonging to the armed forces of the detaining Power.

## ARTICLE 64

Every prisoner of war shall have the right of appeal against any sentence rendered with regard to him, in the same way as individuals belonging to the armed forces of the detaining Power.

## ARTICLE 65

Sentences pronounced against prisoners of war shall be communicated to the protecting Power immediately.

## ARTICLE 66

If the death penalty is pronounced against a prisoner of war, a communication setting forth in detail the nature and circumstances of the offense shall be sent as soon as possible to the representative of the protecting Power, for transmission to the Power in whose armies the prisoner served.

The sentence shall not be executed before the expiration of a period of at least three months after this communication.

## ARTICLE 67

No prisoner of war may be deprived of the benefit of the provisions of Article 42 of the present Convention as a result of a sentence or otherwise.

## TITLE IV.   TERMINATION OF CAPTIVITY

### SECTION I. DIRECT REPATRIATION AND HOSPITALIZATION IN A NEUTRAL COUNTRY

## ARTICLE 68

Belligerents are bound to send back to their own country, regardless of rank or number, seriously sick and seriously injured prisoners of war, after having brought them to a condition where they can be transported.

Agreements between belligerents shall accordingly settle as soon as possible the cases of invalidity or of sickness, entailing direct repatriation, as well as the cases entailing possible hospitalization in a neutral country.   While awaiting the conclusion of these agreements, belligerents may have reference to the model agreement annexed, for documentary purposes, to the present Convention.

## ARTICLE 69

Upon the outbreak of hostilities, belligerents shall come to an agreement to name mixed medical commissions. These commissions shall be composed of three members, two of them belonging to a neutral country and one appointed by the detaining Power; one of the physicians of the neutral country shall preside. These mixed medical commissions shall proceed to the examination of sick or wounded prisoners and shall make all due decisions regarding them.

Decisions of these commissions shall be by majority and carried out with the least possible delay.

## ARTICLE 70

Besides those who are designated by the camp physician, the following prisoners of war shall be inspected by the mixed medical Commission mentioned in Article 69, with a view to their direct repatriation or their hospitalization in a neutral country:

*a*) Prisoners who make such a request directly of the camp physician;

*b*) Prisoners who are presented by the agents provided for in Article 43, acting on their own initiative or at the request of the prisoners themselves;

*c*) Prisoners who have been proposed by the Power in whose armies they have served or by an aid society duly recognized and authorized by that Power.

## ARTICLE 71

Prisoners of war who are victims of accidents in connection with work, except those voluntarily injured, shall enjoy the benefit of the same provisions, as far as repatriation or possible hospitalization in a neutral country are concerned.

## ARTICLE 72

Throughout the duration of hostilities and for humane considerations, belligerents may conclude agreements with a view to the direct repatriation or hospitalization in a neutral country of able-bodied prisoners of war who have undergone a long period of captivity.

## ARTICLE 73

The expenses of repatriation or of transportation to a neutral country of prisoners of war shall be borne, from the frontiers of the detaining Power, by the Power in whose armies the prisoners have served.

## ARTICLE 74

No repatriated person may be utilized in active military service.

SECTION II. RELEASE AND REPATRIATION UPON CESSATION OF HOSTILITIES

### ARTICLE 75

When belligerents conclude a convention of armistice, they must, in principle, have appear therein stipulations regarding the repatriation of prisoners of war. If it has not been possible to insert stipulations in this regard in such convention, belligerents shall nevertheless come to an agreement in this regard as soon as possible. In any case, repatriation of prisoners shall be effected with the least possible delay after the conclusion of peace.

Prisoners of war against whom a penal prosecution might be pending for a crime or an offense of municipal law may, however, be detained until the end of the proceedings and, if necessary, until the expiration of the punishment. The same shall be true of those sentenced for a crime or offense of municipal law.

On agreement between the belligerents, commissions may be established for the purpose of searching for dispersed prisoners and assuring their repatriation.

## TITLE V. DEATH OF PRISONERS OF WAR

### ARTICLE 76

Wills of prisoners of war shall be received and drawn up in the same way as for soldiers of the national army.

The same rules shall be observed regarding death certificates.

Belligerents shall see that prisoners of war dying in captivity are honorably buried and that the graves bear all due information, are respected and properly maintained.

## TITLE VI. BUREAUS OF RELIEF AND INFORMATION CONCERNING PRISONERS OF WAR

### ARTICLE 77

Upon the outbreak of hostilities, each of the belligerent Powers, as well as the neutral Powers which have received belligerents, shall institute an official information bureau for prisoners of war who are within their territory.

Within the shortest possible period, each of the belligerent Powers shall inform its information bureau of every capture of prisoners effected by its armies, giving it all the information regarding identity which it has, allowing it quickly to advise the families concerned, and informing it of the official addresses to which families may write to prisoners.

The information bureau shall immediately forward all this information to the interested Powers, through the intervention, on one hand, of the protecting Powers and, on the other, of the central agency provided for in Article 79.

The information bureau, being charged with replying to all inquiries about prisoners of war, shall receive from the various services concerned full information respecting internments and transfers, releases on parole, repatriations, escapes, stays in hospitals, deaths, as well as other information necessary to enable it to make out and keep up to date an individual return for each prisoner of war.

The bureau shall state in this return, in so far as is possible and subject to the provisions of Article 5: the regimental number, given names and surname, date and place of birth, rank and unit of the interested party, the given name of the father and the name of the mother, the address of the person to be advised in case of accident, wounds, date and place of capture, internment, wounding and death, as well as any other important information.

Weekly lists containing all new information likely to facilitate the identification of each prisoner shall be transmitted to the interested Powers.

At the conclusion of peace the individual return of the prisoner of war shall be delivered to the Power which he served.

The information bureau shall further be bound to receive all objects of personal use, valuables, letters, pay vouchers, identification marks, etc., which are left by prisoners of war who have been repatriated, released on parole, escaped or died, and to transmit them to the countries interested.

### ARTICLE 78

Relief societies for prisoners of war, which are properly constituted in accordance with the laws of their country and with the object of serving as the channel for charitable effort, shall receive from the belligerents, for themselves and their duly accredited agents, every facility for the efficient performance of their humane task within the bounds imposed by military necessities. Agents of these societies may be admitted to the camps for the purpose of distributing relief, as also to the halting places of repatriated prisoners, if furnished with a personal permit by the military authorities, and on giving an undertaking in writing to comply with all measures of order and police which the latter may issue.

### ARTICLE 79

A central information agency for prisoners of war shall be created in a neutral country. The International Committee of the Red Cross shall propose the organization of such an agency to the interested Powers, if it considers it necessary.

The function of that agency shall be to centralize all information respecting prisoners, which it may obtain through official or private channels; it shall transmit it as quickly as possible to the country of origin of the prisoners or to the Power which they have served.

These provisions must not be interpreted as restricting the humanitarian activity of the International Committee of the Red Cross.

### ARTICLE 80

Information bureaus shall enjoy the privilege of free postage on postal matter, as well as all exemptions provided in Article 38.

## TITLE VII. APPLICATION OF THE CONVENTION TO CERTAIN CLASSES OF CIVILIANS

### ARTICLE 81

Individuals who follow armed forces without directly belonging thereto, such as newspaper correspondents and reporters, sutlers, contractors, who fall into the enemy's hands and whom the latter thinks expedient to detain, shall be entitled to be treated as prisoners of war, provided they are in possession of a certificate from the military authorities of the armed forces which they were accompanying.

## TITLE VIII. EXECUTION OF THE CONVENTION

### SECTION I. GENERAL PROVISIONS

### ARTICLE 82

The provisions of the present Convention must be respected by the High Contracting Parties under all circumstances.

In case, in time of war, one of the belligerents is not a party to the Convention, its provisions shall nevertheless remain in force as between the belligerents who are parties thereto.

### ARTICLE 83

The High Contracting Parties reserve the right to conclude special conventions on all questions relative to prisoners of war, on which it seems to them expedient to have particular regulations.

Prisoners of war shall receive the benefit of these agreements until the completion of repatriation, except in the case of express stipulations to the contrary contained in the above-mentioned agreements or in later agreements, or also except in the case of more favorable measures taken by one or the other of the belligerent Powers respecting the prisoners which they hold.

In order to assure the reciprocal application of the stipulations of the present Convention, and to facilitate the conclusion of the special conventions provided for above, belligerents may, upon the commencement of hostilities, authorize meetings of representatives of the respective authorities charged with the administration of prisoners of war.

### ARTICLE 84

The text of the present Convention and of the special conventions provided for in the foregoing article, shall be posted, wherever possible in the native language of the prisoners of war, in places where it may be consulted by all the prisoners.

The text of these conventions shall be communicated to prisoners who find it impossible to get the information from the posted text, upon their request.

### ARTICLE 85

The High Contracting Parties shall communicate to one another through the Swiss Federal Council, the official translations of the present Convention, as well as of the laws and regulations which they may come to adopt to assure the application of the present Convention.

### SECTION II. ORGANIZATION OF CONTROL

### ARTICLE 86

The High Contracting Parties recognize that the regular application of the present Convention will find a guaranty in the possibility of collaboration of the protecting Powers charged with safeguarding the interests of belligerents; in this respect, the protecting Powers may, besides their diplomatic personnel, appoint delegates from among their own nationals or from among the nationals of other neutral Powers. These delegates must be subject to the approval of the belligerent near which they exercise their mission.

Representatives of the protecting Power or its accepted delegates shall be permitted to go to any place, without exception, where prisoners of war are interned. They shall have access to all places occupied by prisoners and may interview them, as a general rule without witnesses, personally or through interpreters.

Belligerents shall so far as possible facilitate the task of representatives or accepted delegates of the protecting Power. The military authorities shall be informed of their visit.

Belligerents may come to an agreement to allow persons of the same nationality as the prisoners to be permitted to take part in inspection trips.

### ARTICLE 87

In case of disagreement between the belligerents as to the application of the provisions of the present Convention, the protecting Powers must, in so far as possible, lend their good offices for the purpose of settling the difference.

For this purpose, each of the protecting Powers may, in particular, suggest to the interested belligerents a meeting of representatives thereof, possibly upon a neutral territory suitably chosen. Belligerents shall be bound to accede to proposals in this sense which are made to them. The protecting Power may, if occasion arises, submit for the approval of the Powers concerned a person belonging to a neutral Power or a person delegated by the International Committee of the Red Cross, who shall be summoned to take part in this meeting.

### ARTICLE 88

The foregoing provisions are not an obstacle to the humanitarian activity which the International Committee of the Red Cross may use for the protection of prisoners of war, with the consent of the interested belligerents.

### SECTION III. FINAL PROVISIONS

### ARTICLE 89

In the relations between Powers bound by the Hague Convention respecting the Laws and Customs of War on Land, whether it is a question of that of July 29, 1899, or that of October 18, 1907, and who participate in the present Convention, this latter shall complete Chapter II of the Regulations annexed to the said Hague Conventions.

### ARTICLE 90

The present Convention, which will bear this day's date, may be signed up to February 1, 1930, on behalf of all the countries represented at the Conference which opened at Geneva July 1, 1929.

### ARTICLE 91

The present Convention shall be ratified as soon as possible.

The ratifications shall be deposited at Berne.

A record of the deposit of each instrument of ratification shall be prepared, a duly certified copy of which shall be forwarded by the Swiss Federal Council to the Governments of all the countries on whose behalf the Convention has been signed or notification of adherence made.

### ARTICLE 92

The present Convention shall become effective six months after the deposit of at least two instruments of ratification.

Subsequently, it shall become effective for each High Contracting Party six months after the deposit of its instrument of ratification.

## ARTICLE 93

From the date on which it becomes effective, the present Convention shall be open for adherences given on behalf of any country in whose name this Convention was not signed.

## ARTICLE 94

Adherence shall be given by written notification addressed to the Swiss Federal Council and shall take effect six months after the date of their receipt.

The Swiss Federal Council shall communicate adherences to the Governments of all the countries on whose behalf the Convention was signed or notification of adherence made.

## ARTICLE 95

A state of war shall give immediate effect to ratifications deposited and to adherences notified by belligerent Powers prior to or after the outbreak of hostilities. The communication of ratifications or adherences received from Powers at war shall be made by the Swiss Federal Council by the most rapid method.

## ARTICLE 96

Each of the High Contracting Parties shall have the right to denounce the present Convention. The denunciation shall not take effect until one year after notification has been made in writing to the Swiss Federal Council. The latter shall communicate such notification to the Governments of all the High Contracting Parties.

The denunciation shall have effect only with respect to the High Contracting Party which gave notification thereof.

Moreover, such denunciation shall not take effect during a war in which the denouncing Power is involved. In this case, the present Convention shall continue in effect, beyond the period of one year, until the conclusion of peace, and, in any event, until the processes of repatriation are completed.

## ARTICLE 97

A duly certified copy of the present Convention shall be deposited in the archives of the League of Nations by the Swiss Federal Council. Likewise, ratifications, adherences, and denunciations of which the Swiss Federal Council shall be notified, shall be communicated by it to the League of Nations.

IN FAITH WHEREOF, the Plenipotentiaries named above have signed the present Convention.

Done at Geneva, the twenty-seventh of July, one thousand nine hundred and twenty-nine, in a single copy, which shall remain in the archives of the Swiss Confederation and duly certified copies of which shall be forwarded to the Governments of all the countries invited to the Conference.

For Germany:
EDMUND RHOMBERG

For the United States of America:
ELIOT WADSWORTH
HUGH R. WILSON

For Austria:
LEITMAIER

For Belgium:
Dr. DEMOLDER
J. DE RUELLE

For Bolivia:
A. CORTADELLAS

For Brazil:
RAUL DO RIO-BRANCO

For Great Britain and Northern Ireland and all parts of
the British Empire which are not separate members
of the League of Nations:
HORACE RUMBOLD

For Canada:
W. A. RIDDELL

For Australia:
CLAUD RUSSELL

For New Zealand:
CLAUD RUSSELL

For South Africa:
ERIC H. LOUW

For the Irish Free State:
SEAN LESTER

For India:
CLAUD RUSSELL

For Bulgaria:
D. MIKOFF
STEPHAN N. LAFTCHIEFF

For Chile:
  Gmo Novoa
  D. Pulgar

For China:
  C. Y. Hsiao

For Colombia:
  Francisco José Urrutia

For Cuba:
  Carlos de Armenteros
  Carlos Blanco

For Denmark:
  Harald Scavenius
  Gustav Rasmussen

For the Dominican Republic:
  Ch. Ackermann

For Egypt:
  Mohammed Abdel Moneim Riad

For Spain:
  Ad Referendum
  Mauricio Lopez Roberts y Terry, Marqués de la
    Torrehermosa

For Estonia:
  Dr. Leesment

For Finland:
  A. E. Martola

For France:
  H. de Marcilly
  J. du Sault

For Greece:
  R. Raphaël
  S. Veniselos

For Hungary:
  Paul de Hevesy

For Italy:
  Giovanni Ciraolo

For Japan:
  Isaburo Yoshida
  S. Shimomura
  S. Miura

For Latvia:
CHARLES DUZMANS
Dr. OSKAR VOIT

For Luxembourg:
CH. G. VERMAIRE

For Mexico:
FR. CASTILLO NÁJERA

For Nicaragua:
A. SOTTILE

For Norway:
J. IRGENS
JENS MEINICH

For the Netherlands:
W. DOUDE VAN TROOSTWIJK
Dr. DIEHL
J. HARBERTS

For Persia:
ANOUCHIREVAN SEPAHBODI

For Poland:
JÓZEF G. PRACKI
W. JERZY BABECKI

For Portugal:
VASCO DE QUEVEDO
F. DE CALHEIROS E MENEZES

For Rumania:
M. B. BOERESCO
Colonel E. VERTEJANO

For the Kingdom of Serbs, Croats and Slovenes:
I. CHOUMENKOVITCH

For Siam:
VARNVAIDYA

For Sweden:
K. I. WESTMAN

For Switzerland:
PAUL DINICHERT
HAUSER
ZÜBLIN
DE LA HARPE
SCHINDLER

For Czechoslovakia:
ZD. FIERLINGER

For Turkey:
HASSAN
Dr. ABDULKADIR
M. NUSRET
Dr. AKIL MOUKHTAR

For Uruguay:
ALFREDO DE CASTRO

For Venezuela:
C. PARRA-PÉREZ
I. M. HURTADO-MACHADO

## ANNEX TO THE CONVENTION OF JULY 27, 1929, RELATIVE TO THE TREATMENT OF PRISONERS OF WAR

### MODEL AGREEMENT CONCERNING DIRECT REPATRIATION AND HOSPITALIZATION IN A NEUTRAL COUNTRY OF PRISONERS OF WAR FOR REASONS OF HEALTH

### I. *Governing Principles for Direct Repatriation and Hospitalization in a Neutral Country*

#### A. DIRECT REPATRIATION

There shall be repatriated directly:

1. Sick and wounded who, according to medical opinion, are not likely to recover in one year, their condition requiring treatment and their mental or physical fitness appearing to have suffered considerable diminution;

2. Incurable sick and wounded whose mental or physical fitness appears to have suffered considerable diminution;

3. Cured sick and wounded whose mental or physical fitness appears to have suffered considerable diminution.

#### B. HOSPITALIZATION IN A NEUTRAL COUNTRY

There shall be placed in hospitals:

1. Sick and wounded whose cure within a period of one year is to be expected, such cure appearing more certain and more rapid if the sick and wounded are given the benefit of the resources offered by the neutral country than if their captivity properly so-called is prolonged;

2. Prisoners of war whose mental or physical health appears, according to medical opinion, to be seriously menaced by continuance in captivity, while hospitalization in a neutral country would probably remove this danger.

There shall be repatriated the prisoners of war hospitalized in a neutral country who belong to the following categories:

1. Those whose state of health appears to be or to be becoming such that they fall within the categories of persons eligible to repatriation for reasons of health;

2. The recovered whose mental or physical fitness seems to have suffered a considerable diminution.

## II. *Special Principles for Direct Repatriation or Hospitalization in a Neutral Country*

### A. REPATRIATION

There shall be repatriated:

1. All prisoners of war who, as the result of organic injuries, have the following impairments, actual or functional: loss of a member, paralysis, articular or other defects, provided that the loss is at least a foot or a hand, or is equivalent to the loss of a foot or a hand;

2. All wounded or injured prisoners of war whose condition is such that it renders them invalids whose cure, within a period of one year, can not be anticipated from a medical standpoint;

3. All the sick whose condition is such that it renders them invalids whose cure, within a period of one year, can not be anticipated from a medical standpoint;

The following, in particular, belong to this category:

*a*) Progressive tuberculosis of any organs which, according to medical opinion, can no longer be cured or at least considerably improved by a course of treatment in a neutral country.

*b*) Nontubercular affections of the respiratory organs presumed incurable (such as, above all, strongly developed pulmonary emphysema, with or without bronchitis, bronchiectasis, serious asthma, gas poisoning, etc.);

*c*) Serious chronic affections of the organs of circulation (for example: valvular affections with tendencies to disorders of compensation, relatively serious affections of the myocardium, pericardium of the vessels, especially inoperable aneurisms of the large vessels, etc.);

*d*) Serious chronic affections of the digestive organs;

*e*) Serious chronic affections of the urinary and sexual organs (particularly, for example: all cases of confirmed chronic nephritis with complete semeiology, and most especially when cardiac and vascular impairments already exist; likewise, pyelites and chronic cystitis, etc.);

*f*) Serious chronic diseases of the central and peripheral nervous system (such as, particularly, serious neurasthenia and hysteria, all unquestionable cases of epilepsy, serious cases of Basedow's disease, etc.) ;

*g*) Blindness in both eyes, or in one eye when the vision of the other remains below 1 in spite of the use of corrective glasses; reduction in acuteness of vision in case it is impossible to restore it by correction to the acuteness of ½ for one eye at least; other ocular affections coming in the present class (glaucoma iritis, choroiditis, etc.) ;

*h*) Total deafness in both ears, as well as total deafness in one ear in case the partially deaf ear does not discern the ordinary spoken voice at a distance of one meter ;

*i*) All unquestionable cases of mental affections;

*k*) All serious cases of chronic poisoning by metals or other causes (lead poisoning, mercury poisoning, morphinism, cocainism, alcoholism, gas poisoning, etc.) ;

*l*) Chronic affections of the organs of locomotion (arthritis deformans, gout, rheumatism with impairments clinically discoverable), provided they are serious;

*m*) All malignant growths, if they are not amenable to relatively minor operations without endangering the life of the patient;

*n*) All cases of malaria with noticeable organic changes (important chronic increase in size of the liver, of the spleen, cachexia, etc.) ;

*o*) Serious chronic cutaneous affections, in so far as their nature does not constitute a medical indication for hospitalization in a neutral country;

*p*) Serious avitaminoses (beri-beri, pellagra, chronic scurvy).

### B. HOSPITALIZATION

Prisoners of war must be hospitalized if they have the following affections:

1. All forms of tuberculosis of any organs whatever if, according to present medical knowledge, they may be cured, or at least considerably improved by methods applicable in a neutral country (altitude, treatment in sanatoria, etc.) ;

2. All forms—necessitating treatment—of affections of the respiratory, circulatory, digestive, genito-urinary, and nervous organs, of organs of the senses, of the locomotor and cutaneous apparatus provided, however, that the forms of these affections do not belong to the categories requiring direct repatriation, or are not acute diseases properly so-called susceptible to a complete cure. The affections contemplated in this paragraph are those which offer really better chances of cure for the patient by the application of means of treatment available in a neutral country than if he were treated in captivity.

Nervous troubles, the efficient or determinant causes of which are the events of the war or even of the captivity itself, such as the psychasthenia of prisoners of war and other analogous cases, should be given special consideration.

All duly verified cases of this kind should be hospitalized, provided that the seriousness or constitutional character thereof does not make them cases for direct repatriation.

Cases of psychasthenia of prisoners of war which are not cured after three months of hospitalization in a neutral country or which, after this period has expired, are not obviously on the road to final recovery, should be repatriated.

3. All cases of wounds or lesions and their consequences which offer better chances of cure in a neutral country than in captivity, provided that these cases are not either eligible for direct repatriation or else are insignificant;

4. All cases of malaria, duly verified and not presenting organic changes clinically discoverable (chronic enlargement of the liver, of the spleen, cachexia, etc.), if the stay in a neutral country offers particularly favorable prospects of final cure;

5. All cases of poisoning (particularly by gases, metals, alkaloids) for which the prospects of cure in a neutral country are especially favorable.

There shall be excluded from hospitalization:

1. All duly verified cases of mental affections;

2. All organic or functional nervous affections reputed to be incurable; (These two categories belong to those giving a right to direct repatriation.)

3. Serious chronic alcoholism;

4. All contagious affections during the period in which they are transmissible (acute infectious diseases, primary and secondary syphilis, trachoma, leprosy, etc.).

### III. *General Observations*

The conditions given above should, generally speaking, be interpreted and applied in as broad a spirit as possible.

This breadth of interpretation should be especially applied to neuropathic or psychopathic conditions caused or brought to a head by the events of the war or even of the captivity itself (psychasthenia of prisoners of war), and also to cases of tuberculosis in all degrees.

It is needless to state that camp physicians and the mixed medical commissions may find themselves confronted with a great number of cases not mentioned among the examples given under Section II, or cases not fitting in with these examples. The examples mentioned above are given only as typical examples; an analogous list of examples of surgical alterations has not been drawn up because, with the exception of cases incontestable by their very nature (amputations), it is difficult to make a list of particular types; experience has shown that a recital of these particular cases was not without disadvantages in practice.

All cases not fitting exactly into the examples cited shall be decided by invoking the spirit of the above governing principles.

580.7A3/464

## The Secretary of State to the American Delegation [1]

WASHINGTON, March 28, 1929.

SIRS: The International Conference on Safety of Life at Sea, to be held at London beginning April 16, 1929, to which you have been appointed as delegates on the part of the United States of America by the President, by Commissions issued on February 16, 1929, and already delivered to you, has as its purpose the revision of the Convention of 1914 on Safety of Life at Sea.

The Convention of 1914 [2] was drawn up at a Conference held at London, November, 1913, to January, 1914, and was signed on January 20, 1914, by representatives of Germany, Austria, Belgium, Denmark, Spain, the United States of America, France, Great Britain, Italy, Holland, Norway, Russia, and Sweden. Japan was represented at the Conference of 1913–1914, but the delegation was appointed at a late date and was not authorized by the Japanese Government to vote in the Conference or committees or to sign the Convention.

The main provisions of the Convention of 1914 relate to the safety of navigation by the destruction of derelicts, the study and observation of ice conditions, the maintenance of the ice patrol in the North Atlantic Ocean, to the construction of vessels, to radio telegraphy, life-saving appliances and fire protection on vessels, and to safety certificates. The Convention was ratified by some of the signatory States but not by all of them. It was not ratified by the United States. Owing to the war and other causes, the Convention was not brought into force completely as a Convention in any country, though parts of it have been adopted and put into force by several countries under their national law. The regulations in Section 14 of the Act of the Congress of the United States, approved March 4, 1915 (38 Stat. 1164, 1170–1184), known as the La Follette Seamen's Act, follow almost verbatim Articles XXVII to LI of the regulations annexed to the Convention of 1914, which have to do with "life-saving appliances and fire protection."

Notwithstanding the failure of the Government of the United States to ratify the Convention of 1914, this Government undertook the direction of the services of derelict destruction, study and observation

---

[1] For personnel of the American delegation, see p. 380.
[2] *British and Foreign State Papers*, vol. CVIII, p. 283.

of ice conditions, and the international ice patrol in the North Atlantic, as it was invited to do by Article 7 of the Convention. Pursuant to an Executive Order these services are performed by the vessels of the United States Coast Guard, Treasury Department, under the direction of the Interdepartmental Board on International Ice Observation, Ice Patrol, and Ocean Derelict Destruction. Foreign nations contribute pro rata shares for the maintenance of the services.

The proposal for a Conference to revise and amend the Convention of 1914 for the Safety of Life at Sea was made by the British Government in the autumn of 1927. By a note under date of September 30, of that year, the British Ambassador at Washington transmitted to the Secretary of State a memorandum [3] of suggestions for the revision of the Convention of 1914, prepared by the British Board of Trade, inquired whether in the opinion of the Government of the United States the proposals in the memorandum formed a suitable basis for the discussion of the amendment of the Convention of 1914, and requested an expression of the views of the Government of the United States as to the advisability of holding an international conference for the purpose of making such revision.

In the memorandum it was suggested that as a result of experience obtained by the maritime powers it might be advisable to modify the Convention of 1914; and certain observations, based upon the experience of the British authorities, were submitted therein concerning proposed modifications. These proposals related to the following subjects:

> Subdivision of Ships;
> Life-saving Appliances;
> Wireless Telegraphy;
> Fire Extinguishing Appliances;
> Ice Patrol;
> Collision Regulations.

The proposals received from the British Ambassador were brought to the attention of the Departments of War, Navy, Treasury, Commerce, Agriculture, and Shipping Board for an expression of their views in regard to them. All the Departments concurred in the view that the Convention of 1914 required amendment, that the proposed Conference was of vital interest to the United States, and that it should be represented at the Conference by delegates, technical advisers, and other necessary personnel.

By a note dated January 23, 1928,[4] the Secretary of State informed the British Ambassador that the Government of the United States was in agreement with the British Government that consideration should

---

[3] Neither printed.
[4] Not printed.

be given to the revision of the Convention of 1914, and suggested that, if it were decided to call a Conference, it be called for a date in the spring of 1929, subsequent to April first, in order to allow time for the making of adequate technical preparation on the various subjects which would be discussed.

On January 12, 1928, an Interdepartmental Committee was organized, composed of representatives of the Departments of State, Treasury, War, Navy, Commerce, Agriculture, and the United States Shipping Board, for the purpose of developing a plan of procedure with reference to preparation by the United States for participation in the proposed Conference. At the second meeting of the Interdepartmental Committee, held on January 21, 1928, a Resolution was adopted charging the Department of Commerce with the organization of technical committees to make the necessary preparatory studies and with the direction of the preliminary work. Under the direction of the Department of Commerce, three principal technical committees with subcommittees were organized, as follows:

1. Ship Construction Committee
   A. Subdivision of Ships
   B. Lifesaving Appliances
   C. Fire extinguishing Appliances
2. Wireless Telegraphy Committee
3. Navigation Committee
   A. Ice Patrol
   B. Meteorology
   C. Rules of the Road

Later, an Executive Committee, having the Commissioner of Navigation as Chairman, was organized to direct and correlate the work of the technical committees.

As a result of the studies made by the technical committees and on the recommendation of the Executive Committee and the Secretary of Commerce, the Secretary of State suggested to the British Ambassador in a note of December 6, 1928, that the subject of stability be added to the agenda of the Conference. The United States has not been informed as to the views of the Government of Great Britain or of the Governments of other foreign countries in regard to this suggestion. The agenda, so far as the Government of the United States is now informed, consists, therefore, of the subjects originally proposed by the British Government, listed on the third page of this instruction, which are as follows:

> Subdivision of Ships;
> Lifesaving Appliances;
> Wireless telegraphy;
> Fire extinguishing Appliances;
> Ice Patrol; and
> Collision Regulations,

with the possible addition of the subject of stability as was suggested by the United States.

The technical committees have now made and filed their final reports, which are on the following subjects:

1. Subdivision of Ships;
2. Lifesaving Appliances;
3. Fire extinguishing Appliances;
4. Wireless Telegraphy;
5. Ice Patrol and Derelict Destruction;
6. Meteorological Reports;
7. Rules of the Road.

Copies of each of these reports are herewith transmitted to you for your information and for your guidance in your capacity as delegates on the part of the United States.

Participation in the Conference on the part of the United States was authorized by Public Resolution No. 70, 70th Congress, 2nd Session, entitled Joint Resolution Providing for the participation by the United States in the International Conference for the Revision of the Convention of 1914 for the Safety of Life at Sea, approved December 7, 1928, which is as follows:

"*Resolved by the Senate and House of Representatives of the United States of America in Congress assembled,* That the sum of $100,000, or so much thereof as may be necessary, is hereby authorized to be appropriated for the expenses of participation by the United States in the International Conference for the Revision of the Convention of 1914 for the Safety of Life at Sea, to be held in London, England, in 1929, including travel and subsistence or per diem in lieu of subsistence (notwithstanding the provisions of any other Act), compensation of employees, stenographic and other services by contract if deemed necessary, rent of offices, purchase of necessary books and documents, printing and binding, printing of official visiting cards, and such other expenses as may be authorized by the Secretary of State.",

and by a provision in Public No. 1034, 70th Congress, 2nd Session, being an Act entitled an Act making appropriations to supply urgent deficiencies . . . for the fiscal year ending June 30, 1929, and for other purposes, approved March 4, 1929, which is as follows:

"International Conference for the Safety of Life at Sea: For the expenses of participation by the United States in the International Conference for the Revision of the Convention of 1914 for the Safety of Life at Sea, as authorized by Public Resolution Numbered 70, approved December 7, 1928, including travel and subsistence or per diem in lieu of subsistence (notwithstanding the provisions of any other Act), compensation of employees, stenographic and other services by contract if deemed necessary, rent of offices, purchase of necessary books and documents, printing and binding, printing of official visiting cards, and such other expenses as may be authorized by the Secretary of State, $90,000, to remain available until June 30, 1930."

The formal invitation to the Government of the United States to send representatives to the Conference was contained in a note of January 21, 1929, to the Secretary of State from the British Ambassador,[5] in which it was stated that the Conference would convene in London on April 16, next.   This invitation was accepted on behalf of the Government of the United States by the Secretary of State in a note of February 21, 1929, to the British Ambassador.[5]   It is understood that the British Government also extended invitations to the several British Dominions, India, Belgium, Denmark, Finland, France, Germany, Italy, Japan, the Netherlands, Norway, Russia, Spain and Sweden, and to the League of Nations Advisory and Technical Committee for Communications and Transit, *ad audiendum.*

It is believed that the American delegation is in a well-fortified position in respect of the work of the Conference.   A thorough study of the situation has been made in the preparatory work.   Concrete proposals which have the approval of all the American interests concerned, including the shipping and shipbuilding industries have been made in the reports of the technical committees.   Congress has passed the Load Line Bill,[6] which furnishes the necessary legislative authority for establishing standards of safety in the loading of vessels.   The United States will not, therefore, be exposed to the criticism, heretofore sometimes made, of urging high standards and of subsequently not putting into effect such standards as were adopted.

The recent loss of the steamship *Vestris* has directed public attention to and has crystallized public opinion on the necessity for a high standard for safety at sea.   The high standards of safety required of transportation facilities in the United States fortify the delegation in advocating high standards of safety at sea.   To obtain acceptance of the high standards of the proposals brought forward in the reports of the technical committees will, it is believed, require determined and combined effort on the part of the American delegation.   Decisions of the delegation should follow, as far as practicable, the recommendations agreed to in the technical reports.   Proposals leading to standards less high than the recommendations should be given most careful consideration and the delegation should not agree to them unless there is strong reason for so doing.   Unanimity of view and of action on the part of the delegates is essential.   In order that the influence of the American delegation may be effective, the individual delegates should be guided and abide by the majority decisions of the delegation, and individual opinions at variance with the delegation's decisions should not be expressed.

To assure that the American proposals are couched in well-chosen

---

[5] Not printed.
[6] Approved March 2, 1929; 45 Stat. 1492.

words which convey the exact meaning intended, it would appear that, except in informal committee discussions, such proposals, so far as practicable, should be prepared in advance of the occasion on which they will be used.

Important questions of policy and general principle not covered by the reports of the committees or the instructions to the delegation should be determined by vote of the delegation, or be made the subject of a request to the Department for instructions.

The delegation has the responsibilities:

(1) to uphold the prestige and dignity of the Government of the United States;

(2) to obtain the highest practicable standard of safety at sea for American nationals traveling in ships flying the flags of foreign nations; and

(3) to obtain an international standard commensurate with the high standard of safety now being constructed into American vessels, in order that these vessels may not suffer in commercial competition with foreign competitors.

In a letter of March 14, 1929, to the Chairman of the delegation, the President wrote:

"In connection with the International Conference for the revision of the Convention for Safety of Life at Sea, which is to convene in London on 16 April, it is my desire that the American delegation urge the international acceptance of the highest practicable standards in the various fields which affect the safety of lives of American citizens and of American vessels at sea. This is a matter of great importance to the shipping industry in this country, and is a matter of even greater importance to American citizens who are engaging in ocean voyages in increasing numbers.

"The recommendations which have been made by the technical committees organized by the Department of Commerce constitute, I am advised, a substantial basis for proposals by the United States at the forthcoming conference, and can be urged with the full assurance that the administration will do all in its power to place such standards into full effect in the event that they are incorporated in an international agreement."

You will consider what provision should be made in the Convention stipulating for subsequent conferences to consider improvements which may be suggested by invention or with reference to the adoption of such improvements by individual nations before they can be made a matter of conventional agreement.

If you deem it advisable to do so, you are authorized to arrange for preliminary and informal consultation with your colleagues of other nations, in order that those standards in regard to safety of life at sea which are held in common may be supported, if possible, with the weight which would naturally result from united effort.

It has been observed that the London treaty of 1914 is in the French language only. At the Conference for the Limitation of Armament held at Washington in the winter of 1921–22, both French and English were made official languages of the Conference and the treaties adopted were signed in the two languages. The treaties signed at the Peace Conference at Paris likewise were signed in English as well as French. Moreover, French and English were made the official languages of the League of Nations, and it is my understanding that all international acts signed under the auspices of the League are in the two languages. It would seem to be desirable that English as well as French should be the official language of the Conference on Safety of Life at Sea, not only as a compliment to the British Government, in whose territory the Conference is held, but also because of the richness of the English language in commercial and nautical terminology. For the same reasons it is believed that any Convention or other instrument signed at the Conference should be signed in English as well as in French. As, however, the Conference will be held at London, it would seem to be more appropriate for the British delegates to make proposals in regard to this matter. You may confer with them informally concerning it, and should they propose to the Conference the adoption of English as an official language of the Conference, you will give the proposal your support.

You will be assisted in your work at the Conference by the following technical assistants:

Lieutenant Commander E. L. Cochrane
Commander C. M. Austin
Captain W. E. Griffith
Mr. A. J. Smith
Mr. J. F. MacMillan
Mr. David Arnott
Mr. Edgar B. Calvert
Captain N. B. Nelson
Lieutenant E. M. Webster
Mr. J. C. Niedermair

Mr. Vinton Chapin, Foreign Service Officer, has been detailed from the State Department as Secretary to the delegation.

There is enclosed the President's instrument [6a] conferring upon you, jointly and severally, plenary powers to negotiate, conclude and sign a Convention revising the Convention of 1914 for the Safety of Life at Sea. This instrument should be deposited with the Secretariat of the Conference, or the Committee on Credentials, whichever may be the procedure adopted.

Doubtless questions which are not definitely covered in the reports of the technical committees or in these instructions will arise at the Conference, both in regard to technical subjects and in regard to

[6a] Not printed.

matters of policy. In respect of the decisions to be made and the action to be taken on such questions, reliance is placed to the fullest extent on the experience and judgment of the delegation. While it is not desired to discourage the delegation from requesting specific instructions from the Government when such instructions are necessary, it is desired that requests for instructions other than requests merely for information which the delegation may not have in its possession should, in order to avoid the delay incident to communication between the delegation and the Government, be limited as much as possible.

Expressing the hope that your mission and its duties may be pleasant, and the results gratifying to yourselves, your colleagues and the Government and people of the United States,

I am [etc.]                                                FRANK B. KELLOGG

---

580.7A3/402

### The Secretary of State to the American Delegation

WASHINGTON, March 28, 1929.

SIRS: In further reference to the International Conference for the Revision of the Convention of 1914 for the Safety of Life at Sea, which will convene at London on April 16, and as supplementing the general instructions of this date,[7] to you in regard to your duties as representatives of the United States to that Conference, you are reminded that the Government of the United States has never recognized as the Government of Russia the régime now functioning in that country, called the Union of Soviet Socialist Republics, to which an invitation to send representatives to the Conference was extended by the Government of Great Britain, as mentioned on page 7 of your general instructions.

I am not informed whether the so-called Union of Soviet Socialist Republics has accepted the invitation to send representatives to the Conference and, of course, it is not possible to foresee whether such representatives, if in attendance, will sign a Convention or other instrument resulting from the Conference or even whether you as plenipotentiaries on the part of the United States will sign such an instrument. In view, however, of the probability of the participation in the Conference of representatives of the régime now functioning in Russia and of the signature by you and by them of a Convention or other instrument drawn up at the Conference, I furnish you for your information and guidance a statement of the views of the Government of the United States with respect to the attitude which you should adopt if these events occur.

---

[7] Supra.

It is the view of the Government of the United States that neither participation of the United States through an American delegation in a Conference in which delegates representing the Soviet régime are also participants, the signing by American plenipotentiaries of a multilateral Convention which is signed also by delegates of the Soviet régime, nor the ratification of a Convention signed by plenipotentiaries of the United States and representatives of the Soviet régime constitute recognition of the so-called Government of the Union of Soviet Socialist Republics as the Government of Russia, and that such actions by the United States or its plenipotentiaries are not fairly open to construction by foreign Governments as constituting such recognition by the United States.

It may be observed in this connection that although the Allied Powers permitted the Soviet régime to sign the so-called Straits Convention, concluded at Lausanne on July 24, 1923, those Powers did not consider that they thereby gave recognition to the Soviet régime as the Government of Russia. No reservations were made by them. The Soviet Government made no effort to claim that their signature of that Convention constituted recognition of their régime as the Government of Russia by the other signatories.

It is believed that it is widely recognized that mutual participation in an international conference is of no significance as indicating reciprocal recognition of the Governments represented at the Conference, and that in respect of this matter, it is not necessary for the delegation to take any action. The Government of the United States foresees, however, that it is possible that such an act as the signing on the part of the United States of a Convention, which also is signed on the part of the Union of Soviet Socialist Republics, might, if the position of the United States is not explained at the time of signing, be construed in some quarters which are not acquainted with the views of this Government, as a recognition of the Soviet régime as the Government of Russia.

On the occasion of the signing of the Convention Revising the International Sanitary Convention of January 17, 1912, signed at Paris June 21, 1926,[8] by plenipotentiaries of the United States and the Soviet régime as well as by the plenipotentiaries of other countries, a reservation was made by the plenipotentiaries of the United States as follows:

"The Plenipotentiaries of the United States of America formally declare that their signing the International Sanitary Convention of this date is not to be construed to mean that the United States of America recognizes a régime or entity acting as Government of a signatory or adhering Power when that régime or entity is not recog-

[8] *Foreign Relations.* 1926, vol. I, p. 177.

nized by the United States as the Government of that Power. They further declare that the participation of the United States of America in the International Sanitary Convention of this date does not involve any contractual obligation on the part of the United States to a signatory or adhering Power represented by a régime or entity which the United States does not recognize as representing the Government of that Power, until it is represented by a Government recognized by the United States."

It is desired that, in the event that the plenipotentiaries of the United States and the Soviet representatives both sign a Convention or other instruments drawn up at the Conference on Safety of Life at Sea, an appropriate reservation, similar to the one above quoted, be made on the part of the United States at the time of signing, as a safeguard against any possible misconstruction of the position of the United States in regard to the question of the recognition of the present régime in Russia.

I am [etc.] FRANK B. KELLOGG

---

580.7A3/409 : Telegram

*The Chargé in Great Britain (Atherton) to the Secretary of State*

[Paraphrase]

LONDON, April 14, 1929—8 p. m.
[Received 9:08 p. m.]

84. With reference to Department's telegram No. 32, February 19, 6 p. m.[9] Chairman White orally requests me to telegraph the following:

In the draft rules of procedure which the British Government submitted yesterday there is a clause which reads: "Each country shall be entitled to one vote." It may come up morning of April 16 in first meeting of Conference. This rule will give British Empire six votes. It should be kept in mind, however, that on any question it is not certain that the votes of the British Empire would be cast as a unit. There are three possible solutions:

1. To agree to the clause.
2. To propose one vote for each sovereign state represented.
3. To throw the question into the Conference at the opening meeting and state that the American delegation cannot accept this clause without specific authorization from Washington.

Please instruct before morning of April 16.

ATHERTON

---

[9] Not printed.

580.7A3/413 : Telegram

*The Secretary of State to the Chargé in Great Britain (Atherton)*

[Paraphrase]

WASHINGTON, April 15, 1929—6 p. m.

84. Your telegram No. 84, April 14, 8 p. m. You may accept the first proposal, that is to agree to the adoption of the clause which reads: "Each country shall be entitled to one vote."

STIMSON

---

580.7A3/417 : Telegram

*The Chargé in Great Britain (Atherton) to the Secretary of State*

LONDON, May 28, 1929—noon.
[Received May 28—7 : 57 a. m.]

131. Kelly, Eastern European Division, from Congressman White. "1. Convention for the Safety of Life at Sea. Instruction March 28 concerning Russia.

2. Chairman of Russian delegation points out that United States made no reservation in respect of Convention for the Suppression of Counterfeiting Currency. Final act of Conference signed at Geneva, April 20, last. See League of Nation[s] C. F. M. 12. He makes no objection to proposed reservation to Safety of Life at Sea Convention.

3. Please instruct whether instruction of March 28 shall be carried out or whether reservation shall be dropped.

4. Delegation would appreciate receiving as complete explanation as possible.

5. Immediate reply is requested as it is hoped that convention may be signed not later than May 31st."

ATHERTON

---

580.7A3/420 : Telegram

*The Secretary of State to the Chargé in Great Britain (Atherton)*

WASHINGTON, May 29, 1929—8 p. m.

131. For White. Your 131, May 28, noon. Department considers that in order to avoid possible misunderstanding and the necessity for making explanations you should follow instructions March 28 concerning reservation.

This Government has not signed the Counterfeiting Convention."[9a]

STIMSON

---

[9a] See pp. 394 ff.

580.7A3/461

*The Chairman of the American Delegation (White) to President Hoover*

WASHINGTON, August 6, 1929.

To THE PRESIDENT: As Chairman of the Delegation of the United States of America to the International Conference for the Revision of the Convention of 1914 for Safety of Life at Sea held at London from April 16th to May 31st last, inclusive, I submit the following report on behalf of the Delegation:

The Convention of 1914 was signed by representatives of sixteen governments. It was ratified by some of the signatory governments but because of the War and for other reasons it was not brought completely into force as a convention, by any State, although parts of it were made effective by particular States by legislative enactment or otherwise. In the years following the signing of the Convention in 1914, many changes and advances were made in the types and methods of construction of ships, and additional experience and knowledge were gained with respect to many other matters covered by the Convention of 1914. For these reasons the British Government in the autumn of 1927 transmitted to other maritime nations which had signed the Convention of 1914 a memorandum by the British Board of Trade covering in some detail a study which had been carried on in Great Britain since 1914 of the subjects included in the Convention of that year, and made tentative suggestions for the revision of the 1914 Convention and for the holding of a Conference for that purpose.

As a result of these proposals from the British Board of Trade, a study of the 1914 Convention and of the respects in which it should be revised was undertaken by interested Departments of our Government and by shipbuilding and ship operating interests of the United States: An Interdepartmental Committee under the Chairmanship of one of the Assistant Secretaries of State, and an Executive Committee, under the Department of Commerce, were created for the purpose of organizing and directing these preliminary studies.

For making the detailed technical studies, three principal technical committees with subcommittees were organized, under the supervision of the Department of Commerce, as follows:

1. Ship Construction Committee
    A. Subdivision of Ships
    B. Lifesaving Appliances
    C. Fire extinguishing Appliances
2. Wireless Telegraphy Committee
3. Navigation Committee.
    A. Ice Patrol and Derelict Destruction
    B. Meteorology
    C. Rules of the Road

Representatives of the American Steamship Owners' Association, of the National Council of American Shipbuilders, and of the American Bureau of Shipping, as well as of the interested Departments of the Government, were included in the membership of these technical committees and of the Executive Committee.

The technical committees devoted a year to an intensive study of their subjects. From their earliest organization, they were aided in their work by many of the leading naval architects, shipbuilders and marine insurance authorities of the country. Their reports were submitted to the Executive Committee, and by it were transmitted through the Secretary of Commerce to the Secretary of State, who issued the instructions to the Delegates.

The holding of an international conference to convene at London on April 16, 1929, having been decided upon, an invitation to the Government of the United States to participate therein was extended through the British Ambassador at Washington on January 21, 1929, and was accepted on behalf of the United States on February 21, 1929. Participation by the United States in the Conference was authorized by Congress and Delegates were appointed by the President. The members of the Delegation were:

> Honorable Wallace H. White, Jr.,—Member of Congress, Chairman of the Committee on Merchant Marine and Fisheries, House of Representatives.
> Mr. Arthur J. Tyrer,—Commissioner of Navigation, Department of Commerce.
> Mr. Charles M. Barnes,—Chief of the Treaty Division, Department of State.
> Rear Admiral George H. Rock,—Construction Corps, United States Navy, Assistant Chief of the Bureau of Construction and Repair, Navy Department.
> Captain Clarence S. Kempff,—United States Navy, Hydrographer, Navy Department.
> Mr. Dickerson N. Hoover,—Supervising Inspector General of the Steamboat Inspection Service, Department of Commerce.
> Mr. William D. Terrell,—Chief of the Radio Division, Department of Commerce.
> Rear Admiral John G. Tawresey,—Construction Corps, United States Navy (Retired), United States Shipping Board.
> Mr. Herbert B. Walker,—President of the American Steamship Owners' Association.
> Mr. Henry G. Smith,—President of the National Council of American Shipbuilders.
> Captain Charles A. McAllister,—President of the American Bureau of Shipping.

With a single exception, the Delegates designated by the President had served upon the technical committees to which reference has been made and were familiar not only with the 1914 Convention but with all the shipping and navigational questions likely to be considered at the Conference. They were the men who had determined the principles and the policies and indeed the precise proposals which were recommended in the reports of the technical committees, and which it was believed the United States should endeavor to have adopted by the Conference.

In addition to the Delegates, the following Technical Assistants were appointed and accompanied the Delegation to London:

Lieut. Commander E. L. Cochrane,—Construction Corps, United States Navy, Bureau of Construction and Repair, Navy Department.

Mr. J. C. Niedermair,—Navy Department.

Mr. J. F. MacMillan,—American Steamship Owners' Association.

Mr. David Arnott,—American Bureau of Shipping.

Captain William E. Griffith,—United States Shipping Board.

Mr. A. J. Smith,—Marine Office of America.

Captain N. B. Nelson,—United States Steamboat Inspection Service.

Lieut. E. M. Webster,—United States Coast Guard.

Commander C. M. Austin,—United States Navy, Bureau of Navigation, Navy Department.

Mr. Edgar B. Calvert,—United States Weather Bureau.

Instructions were issued to the Delegation under date of March 28, 1929. A copy of these instructions is attached hereto and is marked "Exhibit A".[10] In addition to these general instructions, the President, in a letter to the Chairman, indicated his desire that the Delegation should strive at the Conference for the highest practicable standards of safety. A copy of this letter is attached and is designated "Exhibit B".[11]

In pursuance of these instructions, the Delegation of the United States proceeded to London, arriving there on April 12. The Conference convened on April 16. Delegates were present from Germany, the Commonwealth of Australia, Belgium, Canada, Denmark, Spain, Irish Free State, the United States of America, Finland, France, the United Kingdom of Great Britain and Northern Ireland, India, Italy, Japan, Norway, the Netherlands, Sweden and the Union of Soviet Socialist Republics. The League of Nations was represented by observers. The Conference was opened by Sir Philip Cunliffe-Lister, President of the British Board of Trade. By request, the Chairman of the Delegation of the United States placed in nomination as President of the Conference Vice Admiral Sir Herbert Richmond, of the British Delegation, who was unanimously elected. At this opening session the rules of procedure for the Conference were presented. They followed closely the rules of the 1913–1914 Conference. A change of importance was in that article of the rules which made English and French both official languages. At the previous Con-

---

[10] *Ante,* p. 368.
[11] *Ante,* p. 373.

ference French only was recognized as the official language. By vote passed at this first plenary session the duty of drafting a program for the Conference was placed upon a Committee consisting of the Chairmen of the Delegations present at the Conference. As a result of action by the Committee of Chairmen, the following technical committees of the Conference were determined upon, i. e., (1) Ship Construction, (2) Life-saving Appliances, (3) Radiotelegraphy, (4) Safety of Navigation, and (5) Certificates. A (6) Committee on General Provisions and a (7) Drafting Committee were provided for later. The Committee of Chairmen also was given authority to designate the heads of these committees and by its action Rear Admiral George H. Rock of the Construction Corps of the Navy of the United States was named as Chairman of the Committee on Ship Construction. The Chairmen of the other Committees were:

> Committee on Life-saving Appliances,—Sir Norman Hill of the British Delegation.
> Committee on Radiotelegraphy,—Mr. Hermann Giess of the German Delegation.
> Committee on Safety of Navigation,—Sir Charles Hipwood of the British Delegation.
> Committee on Certificates,—Major General F. Marena of the Italian Delegation.
> Committee on General Provisions,—Sir Charles Hipwood of the British Delegation.
> Committee on Drafting,—Senator Rio of the French Delegation.

The Chairmen of the several Delegations at the Conference were asked to designate the members of their Delegations to serve upon the Conference Committees. With the approval of the Delegation of the United States, I made assignments of Delegates and Technical Assistants to each Committee as follows:

### SHIP CONSTRUCTION

| Delegates | Technical Assistants |
|---|---|
| Rear Admiral George H. Rock | Lieut. Commander E. L. Cochrane |
| Mr. H. G. Smith | Mr. J. F. MacMillan |
| Mr. H. B. Walker | Mr. David Arnott |
| Rear Admiral J. G. Tawresey | Mr. J. C. Niedermair |
| Mr. D. N. Hoover | Mr. A. J. Smith |

### LIFE-SAVING APPLIANCES

| Delegates | Technical Assistants |
|---|---|
| Mr. D. N. Hoover | Captain N. B. Nelson |
| Rear Admiral J. G. Tawresey | Captain W. E. Griffith |
| Captain Charles A. McAllister | Mr. A. J. Smith |
| Mr. H. B. Walker | Mr. J. F. MacMillan |
| Mr. H. G. Smith | Mr. David Arnott |
| | Lieut. Commander E. L. Cochrane |

## RADIOTELEGRAPHY

*Delegates*
Mr. W. D. Terrell
Mr. H. B. Walker
Mr. A. J. Tyrer
Captain Charles A. McAllister
Mr. D. N. Hoover

*Technical Assistants*
Lieut. E. M. Webster
Captain W. E. Griffith
Mr. E. B. Calvert

## SAFETY OF NAVIGATION

*Delegates*
Captain Clarence S. Kempff
Captain Charles A. McAllister
Mr. H. B. Walker
Mr. H. G. Smith

*Technical Assistants*
Captain W. E. Griffith
Commander C. M. Austin
Mr. E. B. Calvert
Lieut. E. M. Webster
Mr. J. F. MacMillan

## CERTIFICATES

*Delegates*
Mr. A. J. Tyrer
Mr. Charles M. Barnes
Captain Charles A. McAllister
Mr. D. N. Hoover

*Technical Assistants*
Captain N. B. Nelson
Captain W. E. Griffith

## COMMITTEE ON GENERAL PROVISIONS

*Delegates*
Honorable Wallace H. White, Jr.
Mr. Charles M. Barnes

*Technical Assistants*

## DRAFTING

*Delegates*
Honorable Wallace H. White, Jr.
Mr. Charles M. Barnes

*Technical Assistants*

Upon the completion of the organization of the Technical Committees, those Committees began the study of the proposals submitted. As the several Technical Committees completed their work and made their reports to the President of the Conference, these reports were read, discussed and acted upon at meetings of the Delegation of the United States. Upon the conclusion of the work of the Technical Committees the Drafting Committee began its work. From time to time as questions arose which could not be readily solved by the Drafting Committee, they were referred to a Committee of Five appointed by the Drafting Committee. Great Britain, France, Germany, Denmark and the United States were represented on this Committee of Five by the Chairmen of their Delegations.

No alterations which appeared to result in changes in substance in the reports of the Technical Committees were agreed to by the United States members of the Drafting Committee which were not called to the attention of and which were not passed upon by the full Delegation of the United States.

The Conference concluded its work and the Convention as agreed to was signed on May 31. Every Delegate present indicated his approval of the Convention by signature thereof. The Conference adjourned in the afternoon of May 31. A copy of the Convention is attached hereto and is marked "Exhibit C".[12] It was signed in French and English texts, both of which are of equal authority. The greatest care was taken that the French and English texts should be identical in meaning. The Final Act of the Conference, signed at the same time and included in the document with the Convention, embraces certain supplementary agreements, declarations and recommendations made by the Conference or Delegations thereof.

The Convention consists of 66 articles grouped in eight chapters. It is completed by regulations which have the same force and take effect at the same time as the Convention itself.

Chapter One contains certain preliminary articles. Of first importance is the article setting forth to what ships the Convention shall apply and carrying definitions used throughout the Convention.

Chapter Two deals with ship construction. This subject was considered by and the chapter was prepared by the Committee of which Rear Admiral Rock of the Delegation of the United States was Chairman. Its work was technical in the extreme and the provisions of the chapter are of outstanding importance, for safety of life at sea in the first instance and in large degree depends upon the ship itself. The work of the Committee divided itself into four main subjects: (a) that of subdivision of ships, (b) the structure and openings, (c) stability, and (d) the voyages. In very large measure the agreements reached by the Conference with respect to these subjects were responsive to proposals urged by the Delegates of the United States and it is believed that by this chapter of the Convention world standards of construction have been substantially raised. With few exceptions the laws of the United States do not cover the requirements of this chapter, although in practice they are largely conformed to. The chapter deals with structural matters and applies in the main to ships built after July 1, 1931. With respect to existing ships, the obligation is imposed upon each government to effect upon its ships, so far as practicable and reasonable, the increased standards of safety recommended. The chapter covers in detail water-tight subdivisions, peak and machinery space bulkheads, the rules for constructing and testing bulkheads, water-tight decks, fire-resisting bulkheads, the openings in bulkheads and ships sides, exits from compartments, pumping arrangements, etc. It requires a stability test for every new ship, and initial and subsequent

---

[12] See bracketed note, p. 388.

surveys for ships. In the regulations annexed to the Convention and having reference to this chapter, will be found the detailed provisions for making effective the general requirements of the Convention dealing with this matter of ship construction.

Chapter Three of the Convention, as supplemented by regulations, deals with life-saving appliances and with fire detection and extinction. With respect to these subjects your Delegation supported those safeguards which science, nautical experience and seamanship approve. This chapter and its regulations make provision for the life boats required on passenger ships, and for additional buoyant apparatus. They provide specifically that there must be accommodations in boats for all persons on board, and in addition, buoyant apparatus for twenty-five per centum of the persons on board. They deal with the construction of life boats, with the embarkation of passengers, with life jackets and life buoys, with means of ingress and egress for passengers and crew, with dangerous goods and fire protection, and with muster rolls and drills. In many respects this chapter raises world standards and the standards of the law of the United States.

Chapter Four relates to the subject of radiotelegraphy. The provisions of the chapter are supplemented by regulations. The 1914 Convention required a radio installation only if a ship had on board 50 or more persons. Radio installation under the law of the United States is required only on steam vessels having on board 50 or more persons. The law does not apply to sailing vessels carrying either passengers or cargo. It does not apply to the modern motor ship. There are many cargo ships of the United States of a tonnage of 6,000 to 8,000 tons and possibly up to 10,000 tons, which under the present law are not required to have radio installation because of the fact that such vessels will not have on board 50 or more persons and there are many passenger ships not reached by the law of this country. The present Convention requires, subject to definite exemptions, that all passenger ships and all cargo ships of 1,600 tons gross tonnage and over engaged on international voyages, shall be fitted with radio installation. These new standards are much above those of the 1914 Convention and of the law of the United States.

An interesting problem of the Conference was with respect to authorizing the use of an automatic radio alarm receiver. The Washington Radiotelegraph Convention of 1927,[13] in Section 21 of Article 19 of the General Regulations annexed thereto, specified standards which should be attained by any such automatic alarm receiver. The present Convention recognizes the use of any automatic alarm receiver meeting the specifications of the Washington Radiotelegraph Convention. It was believed that the recognition of this instrument would increase

---

[13] *Foreign Relations*, 1927, vol. I, p. 288.

the number of ships which might hear a distress call, and so add to the margin of safety of all vessels. The general result of the provisions of the Convention relating to radiotelegraphy is that at least 1,000 vessels not now equipped with radio will be required to install radio apparatus and that many hundreds and perhaps thousands of vessels now maintaining a voluntary radio service of indifferent quality will be compelled to have an installation and to meet standards prescribed by the Convention. They make potential life savers of a vastly increased number of ships. Through the use of the automatic alarm continuous watch is assured upon many vessels not now required to maintain such watch. The whole effect of this chapter of the Convention, in the opinion of your Delegation, is to elevate the legal standards of the world and of the United States.

Chapter Five of the Convention and the articles pertinent to the chapter, deal with the general subject of navigation. The provisions refer, unless express exception is made, to all ships on all voyages. Under this chapter provision is made for the collection and dissemination of meteorological data by ships at sea and for ships. The North Atlantic ice patrol established by the 1914 Convention is continued and its activities are enlarged. The question of routes across the Atlantic is dealt with. The chapter requires the equipment of passenger ships of 5,000 tons and over with the radio compass. The chapter also covers helm orders, alarm, distress and urgency signals, the misuse of distress signals, the speed of transmission of messages of distress, the procedure in handling messages, and includes an undertaking by each government to insure that ships shall be sufficiently and efficiently manned. Of outstanding importance in this chapter is the agreement in Article 40 that alterations in the international regulations for preventing collisions at sea should be made. In Annex 2 to the Convention appear the alterations to these collision regulations which the Conference believed should be made effective. An examination of Annex 2 will disclose the importance from the standpoint of safety of life at sea of these "rules of the road," so called, and of the changes which are recommended therein. The changes recommended tend to clarity and to greater safety. As a part of its work the Technical Committee on Safety of Navigation also made various other recommendations which are included in the Final Act of the Conference, Part III, paragraphs 9–14. These recommendations have to do with radio aids to navigation, synchronized radio and under-water signals, depth sounding apparatus, life-saving signals, shore lights and collision regulations for aircraft on the surface of the water. The subject matter of Chapter Five and of the regulations bearing thereon, the changes recommended in the collision regulations and the recommendations adopted by the Conference with respect to the matters enumerated were of particular concern to the Delegation of the United States, and the advances made may be attributed in no small part to the interest and efforts of its Delegation.

Chapter Six provides for the issue of certificates by the appropriate government. A safety certificate is required to be issued after inspection and survey to every passenger ship which complies with the requirements of Chapter Two (Construction), Chapter Three (Lifesaving Appliances) and Chapter Four (Radiotelegraphy) of the Convention. In addition to this safety certificate a safety radiotelegraphy certificate is required for every ship other than a passenger ship which complies with the provisions of Chapter Four relating to radiotelegraphy, and a third certificate, called an exemption certificate, is provided for each ship to which an exemption is granted by a contracting government under specific authority of the Convention. This chapter deals with the form of certificates, their duration, and the credit to be given them by another government. The right of inspection of a foreign ship while within the jurisdiction of a contracting government is preserved.

The Convention will come into force on July 1, 1931, as between the governments which have deposited their ratifications by that date provided that ratifications of at least five governments have been deposited. Provision is made for future conferences for the revision of the Convention, the first of which conferences may not be held until after the Convention shall have been in force for five years. A government may withdraw from the Convention by denunciation thereof after the expiration of five years from the date on which the Convention came into force with respect to it.

The hope of the Delegation of the United States was to secure the adoption of rules which with respect to vessel construction would make ships as nearly unsinkable as practically possible; which would guard against fire; which would protect from the dangers of storm, of derelicts and of ice; which in time of emergency and disaster would insure adequate lifeboats, rafts and belts, and would otherwise safeguard the lives of passengers and crew; which would extend the use of radio as a protection of life and as an aid to navigation; which would make the rules of navigation responsive to the use of modern ships and changed conditions; and which would contribute in their letter and spirit to the highest standards of safety for those going down to the sea in ships. The Delegation encountered wide diversity of interest and opinion as to many of the subjects considered, but the deep sense of responsibility felt by all led to final agreements upon all matters included within the scope of the Convention.

I am convinced that the purpose which animated the Government of the United States in participating in this Conference has been realized. I believe the Convention provides for the highest standards of safety which it is now practicable to bring forward for international adoption. It represents a marked advance over the present legal standards and practices of the world and in many and important particulars it has raised the standards of our own country.

Respectfully submitted,    WALLACE H. WHITE, JR.

---

[For text of the International Convention and Regulations for Promoting Safety of Life at Sea, signed at London, May 31, 1929, see Department of State Treaty Series No. 910 or 50 Stat. 1121. Ratification of the convention was advised by the Senate, subject to understandings, June 19 (legislative day of June 15), 1936; it was ratified by the President, subject to said understandings, July 7, 1936; ratification of the United States was deposited at London, August 7, 1936; and the convention was proclaimed by the President, September 30, 1936. For amendment of the convention, proclaimed by the President, September 3, 1937, see Department of State Treaty Series No. 921 or 51 Stat. 13.]

# AGREEMENTS FOR EXCHANGE OF INFORMATION REGARDING THE TRAFFIC IN NARCOTIC DRUGS [1]

800.114N16 Information/156½

*Summary of Arrangements Entered Into Between the United States and Certain Other Governments* [2]

At the instance of the Treasury Department, the Department of the United States Government which is charged with the greater part of the administration of the laws of this Government controlling the traffic in narcotic drugs, the Government of the United States, in an endeavor to bring about a stricter control of the traffic in narcotic drugs, has concluded during the last two years, informal agreements for the direct exchange, between the enforcement officers of the United States and certain other Governments, of information regarding the traffic in narcotic drugs. The countries with which such arrangements have been made are: Belgium, Czechoslovakia, Free City of Danzig, Denmark, France, Germany, Great Britain, Greece, Italy, Japan, The Netherlands, Portugal, Rumania, Spain and Turkey.

The arrangement provides for

1) The direct exchange between the Treasury Department and the corresponding office in the foreign countries of information and evidence with reference to persons engaged in the illicit traffic, including photographs, criminal records, fingerprints, Bertillon measurements, description of the methods which the persons in question have been found to use, the places from which they have operated, the partners they have worked with, et cetera;

2) The immediate direct forwarding of information by letter or cable as to the suspected movements of narcotic drugs, or of those involved in smuggling drugs, if such movements might concern the other countries, it being realized that unless such information reaches its destination directly and speedily it is useless;

3) Mutual cooperation in detective and investigating work.

Negotiations are in progress with other countries for the conclusion of similar arrangements. [3]

---

[1] For previous correspondence concerning efforts to control traffic in narcotic drugs, see *Foreign Relations*, 1928, vol. I, pp. 444 ff.

[2] Reprinted from Department of State, *Bulletin of Treaty Information*, No. 5, July 1929, second supplement. The correspondence constituting the exchanges of notes to effect the arrangements is contained in this "second supplement" and is not reprinted here. Until October 1929, the *Bulletin* was issued in mimeographed form for distribution.

[3] Arrangements by exchanges of notes were also entered into with Austria (signed April 10 and July 24, 1931), Cuba (signed February 12 and March 7, 1930), Egypt (signed June 20 and August 26, 1930), Mexico (signed August 5 and October 2, 1930), Poland (signed August 17 and September 17, 1931), Switzerland (signed November 15 and 16, 1929), and Yugoslavia (signed February 17, 1928, and May 8, 1930). See Department of State, *Treaty Information Bulletin No. 39*, December 1932, supplement, pp. 80–83.

800.114N16 Information/134

*The Secretary of State to the Chargé in Japan (Neville)* [4]

No. 520                                     WASHINGTON, April 1, 1929.

SIR: In a communication, dated June 29, 1923, addressed to the Secretary of State, the British Embassy in Washington referred to a recommendation of the League of Nations Advisory Committee on the Traffic in Opium and Other Dangerous Drugs, passed at the fourth session held at Geneva from the 8th to the 14th of January, 1923, which reads as follows:

"That the Governments be asked to extend the arrangement for the mutual exchange of information in regard to seizures to include information in regard to the proceedings and movements of persons who are known to the authorities to be engaged in carrying on an illicit traffic in drugs."

The British Embassy stated that this recommendation had been accepted by the British Government and that a circular despatch had been sent to the Governors of all colonies and protectorates, expressing the hope that each of them would cause this recommendation to be put into force, and directing them to cause any information of the nature indicated, which might be of immediate importance to neighboring administrations, to be communicated to the British consular officers in the country concerned, for transmission by them to the local authorities. On August 7, 1923, in replying to the note from the British Embassy, the Secretary of State stated:

"I take pleasure in assuring you that the Government of the United States is deeply gratified by the action of His Majesty's Government, and is prepared to cooperate to the fullest extent in transmitting information of the character suggested. To this end, the Department of State is desirous, if agreeable to your Government, of instructing its Diplomatic and Consular Officers to cooperate with their British colleagues, or the competent British authorities (if in British territory) in collecting and forwarding information that will lead to the seizure of illicit narcotic drugs and the detection or apprehension of persons engaged in this traffic."

Attached to the reply to the British Embassy was a list of the United States local authorities to whom there might be communicated such information as might come to the attention of British Consular Officers in this country.

In a note, dated December 12, 1923, the British Embassy at Washington notified this Government that the British Government welcomed the proposal of the United States and that instructions were being issued to the competent authorities in the British Empire and

---

[4] Previous correspondence with Great Britain mentioned in this instruction is not printed.

to the British Diplomatic and Consular representatives abroad to cooperate with the United States authorities in the manner proposed. To this note was appended a list of the British officials to whom such information should be communicated in Great Britain, Ireland, India, Australia, Canada, New Zealand, the Union of South Africa, Newfoundland and the British Colonies not possessing responsible Government, in British Protectorates and in Tanganyika territory. In conformity with this arrangement, appropriate instructions were sent to the American Diplomatic and Consular Officers on December 28, 1923.[5]

By an exchange of correspondence between the American and British Governments in 1927 and 1928, the above arrangement was made applicable to the Philippine Islands and the Straits Settlements.

This Government would welcome the conclusion with the Japanese Government of an arrangement similar to that in effect with the British Government. You are requested, therefore, to present this matter to the appropriate Japanese authorities and to state that this Government is prepared, if agreeable to the Japanese Government, to instruct its Diplomatic and Consular Officers to cooperate with their Japanese colleagues, or the competent Japanese authorities (if in Japanese territory) in collecting and forwarding information that will lead to the seizure of illicit narcotic drugs and the detection or apprehension of persons engaged in this traffic.

You should add that this Government has been gratified at the recent conclusion with the Japanese Government of the informal arrangement for the direct exchange, between the enforcement agencies of the two Governments, of certain information with regard to the traffic in narcotic drugs and believes that the present proposal, if accepted, would supplement that arrangement and provide for cooperation in matters not covered by it, thus marking a further advance in the elimination of the narcotic menace.

I am [etc.]                                    For the Secretary of State:
                                               NELSON TRUSLER JOHNSON

---

800.114N16 Information/170½

*The Chargé in Japan (Neville) to the Secretary of State*

No. 1270                              TOKYO, September 9, 1929.
                                     [Received September 27.]

SIR: I have the honor to refer to the Department's instruction of April 1, 1929, informing the Embassy of the conclusion of an arrangement, with the British Government for the mutual exchange of infor-

---

[5] Not printed.

mation in regard to seizures of narcotic drugs and in regard to persons who are known to be engaged in carrying on illicit traffic in drugs.

In compliance with the Department's instructions, the Embassy addressed a note to the Foreign Office suggesting the desire of the Government of the United States to conclude with the Japanese Government an arrangement similar to that concluded with the British Government. A reply has now been received from the Foreign Office stating that the Japanese Government is prepared to welcome the conclusion of such an arrangement and to instruct its Diplomatic and Consular Officers to cooperate with their American colleagues or the appropriate American authorities (if in American territory) in collecting and forwarding information that will lead to the seizure of illicit narcotic drugs and the detection or apprehension of persons engaged in the traffic. In an annexe to its note the Foreign Office submits a list of the competent Japanese authorities to whom the information in question should be forwarded in Japan.

A copy of the note from the Foreign Office, with its annexe, is transmitted herewith.

I have [etc.]                                      EDWIN L. NEVILLE

[Enclosure—Translation]

*The Japanese Minister for Foreign Affairs (Shidehara) to the American Chargé (Neville)*

No. 86/Ts                                    TOKYO, September 6, 1929.

MONSIEUR LE CHARGÉ D'AFFAIRES: I have the honor to refer to your Note No. 481 of April 23rd last,[6] in which you were good enough to inform Baron Tanaka, my predecessor in office, of the arrangement now existing between the United States Government and the British Government for the exchange of information relating to the seizure of illicit narcotic drugs and to persons engaged in this traffic. You also stated that your Government would welcome the conclusion with the Japanese Government of an arrangement similar to that in effect with the British Government, and were prepared, if agreeable to the Japanese Government, to instruct their Diplomatic and Consular Officers to co-operate with their Japanese colleagues, or the competent Japanese authorities (if in Japanese territory), in collecting and forwarding information that will lead to the seizure of illicit narcotic drugs and the detection or apprehension of persons engaged in this traffic.

I am happy to state in reply that the Japanese Government welcome the proposal of your Government and are prepared to co-operate with them in forwarding information of the nature indicated above. The Japanese Government, for the attainment of the object in view, agree

---

[6] Not printed.

to instruct their Diplomatic and Consular Officers to co-operate with their American colleagues, or the competent American authorities (if in American territory), in collecting and forwarding information that will lead to the seizure of illicit narcotic drugs and the detection or apprehension of persons engaged in this traffic. Your Government will be so good as to issue the necessary instructions, and to inform me of the competent American authorities to whom such information should be communicated by the Japanese Diplomatic and Consular Officers in the United States. I beg to set forth in the Annexe [7] a list of the competent Japanese authorities to whom the information in question should be forwarded in this country.

I beg [etc.]        BARON KIJURO SHIDEHARA

---

800.114N16 Information/201

*The Secretary of State to Diplomatic and Consular Officers*

Diplomatic Serial
No. 887        WASHINGTON, December 7, 1929.

SIRS: Referring to General Instruction of December 28, 1923 (Diplomatic Serial No. 235, G. I. Consular No. —),[7] with regard to cooperating with your British colleagues or (if in British territory) with the competent British authorities, in collecting and forwarding information that would lead to the seizure of illicit narcotic drugs and the detection or apprehension of persons engaged in this traffic, you are informed that there has now been concluded with the Japanese Government an informal arrangement similar to that previously effected with the British Government. You will therefore cooperate with your Japanese colleagues or (if in Japanese territory) with the competent Japanese authorities, a list of which is enclosed, in the same manner as with your British colleagues or with the competent British authorities.

I am [etc.]        For the Secretary of State:
NELSON TRUSLER JOHNSON

---

[7] Not printed.

551.58B1/18

*The Minister in Switzerland (Wilson) to the Secretary of State*

No. 619                                                    BERNE, October 11, 1928.
L. of N. No. 1219                                          [Received October 29.]

SIR: I have the honor to transmit herewith a communication addressed to you on October 8 by the Secretary General of the League of
Nations,[1] forwarding three copies of the report of the Mixed Committee for the Suppression of Counterfeiting Currency and of the
draft Convention drawn up by that Committee,[2] and requesting any
observations which the Department may have to make on the proposals contained in the document. The Department will note that
Sir Eric[3] intends to postpone the general Conference on Counterfeiting Currency if possible until the month of April, 1929, in the
hope that the comments of the American Government may previously
be received and circulated.

I have [etc.]                                              HUGH R. WILSON

---

551.58B1/21

*The Minister in Switzerland (Wilson) to the Secretary of State*

No. 645                                                    BERNE, November 5, 1928.
L. of N. No. 1232                                          [Received November 30.]

SIR: Referring to my despatch No. 619, L. of N. No. 1219, of October
11, 1928, and to my telegram No. 106 [*100*], of today's date,[4] I have
the honor to transmit herewith a communication addressed to you by
the Secretary General of the League of Nations, dated November 3,[1] inviting the American Government to send duly authorized representatives to take part in an international conference for the final adoption
of an international convention for the suppression of counterfeiting
currency. The Conference is to meet at Geneva on April 9, 1929.

I have [etc.]                                              HUGH R. WILSON

[1] Not printed.
[2] League of Nations document C.523.M.181.1927.II.
[3] Sir Eric Drummond, Secretary General of the League of Nations.
[4] Latter not printed.

551.58B1/35d

*The Secretary of State to the Minister in Switzerland* (*Wilson*)

No. 426                                    WASHINGTON, March 22, 1929.

SIR: Referring to the Department's telegram No. 39 of March 18, 1929,[5] advising you that the President had designated you as the delegate to represent the United States at the Conference on Counterfeiting Currency to be held at Geneva April 9, the Department directs you to be guided by the following instructions with regard to the matters dealt with in the draft convention which has been submitted by the Secretary General of the League of Nations and which, it is understood, is to be considered by the Conference.

In paragraph I, Article 1 of the draft convention it is provided that the Contracting Parties shall agree to adopt the necessary measures for introducing the rules laid down in that Article into their respective legal and administrative systems except in so far as they may be already embodied therein. With respect to this provision it may be said that this Government would desire to have it changed so as to provide that the High Contracting Parties agree themselves to take or propose to their respective appropriate law-making bodies the necessary measures for the adoption of the rules set forth in Article 1 of the draft convention. In this relation it may be pointed out that the treaty-making power of this Government could not well agree to bind the law-making body to the adoption of specific legislation.

So far as concerns the other provisions of paragraphs I to V, inclusive, of Article 1 of the draft convention it may be observed that they appear to impose no requirements which are not covered by laws of the United States at present in force.

It is provided in paragraph VI, Article 1 of the draft convention that no distinction should be made in the scale of punishments for offenses referred to in the convention between acts relating to domestic currency on the one hand and to foreign currency on the other hand. With reference to this provision it may be stated that the penalties provided in the Federal statutes of the United States relative to the counterfeiting of foreign obligations and securities are not at present as severe as those imposed by laws denouncing the counterfeiting of obligations and securities of the United States. However, an effort might be made to remedy this position by equalizing these penalties through statutory amendments.

With respect to the provisions of paragraph VII, Article 1 of the draft convention it may be observed that confiscation of counterfeit money and material and apparatus fitted or intended for counterfeiting purposes is provided for in the Federal statutes of the United

---

[5] Not printed.

States and that the surrender of such property to the interested government in case of counterfeiting of foreign moneys can be accomplished by direction of the Secretary of the Treasury.

Concerning the provisions of paragraph VIII, Article 1 of the draft convention, it should be stated that the Federal statutes of the United States do not permit the participation of civil parties in criminal proceedings.

The Department would have no objection to the incorporation in the convention of the provisions of paragraph IX, Article 1 of the draft convention relating to political offenses.

The Department does not object to the provisions of paragraph X, Article 1 of the draft convention relating to the punishment in their own country for offenses committed abroad of nationals of that country. However, inasmuch as the United States recognizes the general rule of extraditing its nationals for offenses committed in a foreign country, subject to the provisions of existing treaties, the provisions of paragraph X would not be applicable to the United States.

The Department would have no objection to the provisions of paragraph XI, Article 1 of the draft convention relative to the punishment of foreigners for offenses committed abroad, but it should be pointed out that this country does not come within the category of those referred to in this paragraph "whose internal legislation recognizes as a general rule the principle of the prosecution of offenses committed abroad", and that, therefore, this paragraph would not be applicable to the United States.

With regard to the remaining paragraphs of Article 1 of the draft convention relative to the maintenance of central offices in each country to deal with investigations, correspondence, communications and conferences concerning the subject matter of the convention, it may be observed that a central bureau in the United States charged with the suppression of counterfeiting, namely, the Secret Service Division of the Treasury Department, has been in existence since 1864 and is in close touch with the institution issuing currency and with the police authorities throughout the country. It is believed that it will be entirely practicable for this Division to effect contact with the central bureaus abroad and with good results.

It is further believed with particular reference to the provisions of paragraph XIII, Article 1, that direct communication between these central bureaus will facilitate their activities and add materially to their effectiveness.

With regard to the provision of paragraph XIV, Article 1, for furnishing specimens of the currency issues of the several countries, it may be stated that the United States could not comply with this provision without violating the policy of its Treasury Department as established for a long period of time and that it is not believed that this policy should be changed. However, it is suggested that the same result could be accomplished if the foreign governments would obtain United States currency in exchange for legal tender, which exchange could be made directly with the Treasury of the United States so that the currency obtained will be known to be genuine.

Referring to the provisions of paragraph XV, Article 1, it may be stated that periodical conferences attended by representatives of the contracting governments might prove advantageous.

Paragraph XVI, Article 1, refers to "letters of request relating to offenses referred to" in the convention. Before giving further consideration to this matter the Department would desire to be informed exactly what is intended to be included in such "letters of request". If it is intended to refer merely to correspondence relating to counterfeiting operations and their suppression it may be stated that in the opinion of the Department such correspondence should be conducted directly between the central bureaus and confirmed by copies despatched through the usual diplomatic channels.

Article 2 of the draft convention provides that the offenses referred to in the convention "are recognized as extradition crimes" and that "extradition will be granted in conformity with the internal law of the country applied to". In the interest of clarity and since in the United States the laws do not permit the extradition of a fugitive except for a specific offense and in accordance with the requirement of a treaty or a statute, it is deemed preferable that it be stated in this Article that extradition will be granted for certain specific offenses, and an appropriate phrasing for the Article would seem to be somewhat as follows:

"Extradition will be granted in conformity with the internal law of the country applied to for the offenses of . . . . . . . and . . . . . . . and . . . . . ."

In its practical operation the provisions of the convention relating to extradition would, if entered into by the United States and other Powers, constitute an agreement to extradite without exception as to the nationals of the Contracting Parties. However, in view of the provisions of paragraph X, Article 1, relating to countries in which the principle of the extradition of nationals is not recognized and of the experience of this Government in such matters, the result of such an agreement would be that nationals of the United States would be extradited by it while nationals of most of the other Contracting Parties would not be extradited by their respective governments. The Department would be averse to attempting to commit this Government to such an arrangement and, therefore, would desire an addition to Article 2 of the draft convention providing that the Contracting Parties shall not be obligated to surrender their own citizens under the provisions of the convention. The Department might be willing to qualify this provision by a further provision that the Contracting Parties may surrender their own citizens if they see fit to do so. For your confidential information it may be stated that the practical effect of the proposed addition without the qualifying clause would be that the United States would be unable under its laws to surrender its own citizens, whereas with the addition of the qualifying clause it would have the power to surrender them. It may be argued in opposition to the inclusion of an exception in favor of nationals that countries which do not extradite their own nationals have the power to punish them for crimes committed abroad. On its face this argument has considerable force, but the experience of the Department indicates that the power to punish nationals for crimes committed abroad is exercised very leniently when exercised at all.

The extradition laws of the United States are not very comprehensive and do not cover several matters which are ordinarily dealt with in the extradition treaties which the United States has entered into. Therefore, embarrassment might be expected to be caused this Government should it enter into this proposed convention without covering some such matters which are not dealt with in the internal law of the United States. As examples may be pointed out the usual provisions contained in extradition treaties of the United States (1) that no person shall be tried for any crime or offense committed before his extradition other than that for which he was surrendered unless he shall have been given a reasonable opportunity to leave the country after trial or punishment; (2) that a fugitive shall not be surrendered when the offense with which he is charged is barred by the Statute of Limitations in the country where the offense was committed; (3) that if a person whose extradition is requested be actually under prosecution for an offense in the country where he has sought asylum, or shall have been convicted thereof, his extradition may be deferred until such proceedings be terminated or until he shall be set at liberty in due course of law; (4) that if a fugitive claimed by one of the Parties to the convention shall also be claimed by one or more Powers pursuant to treaty provisions on account of crimes or offenses committed within their jurisdiction, he shall be delivered to that State whose demand is first received unless such demand is waived; (5) that the person provisionally arrested shall be released, unless within a specified time, usually two months from the date of his commitment or arrest, the formal requisition for his surrender, with the necessary proofs, be made, and (6) that if the fugitive shall have been convicted of the crime or offense for which his extradition is requested a duly authenticated copy of the sentence of the court before which such conviction took place shall be produced and that if the fugitive is merely charged with a crime a duly authenticated copy of the warrant of arrest in the country where the crime was committed and of competent evidence in the form of affidavits or depositions making out a prima facie case of guilt shall be furnished.

So far as concerns the remaining Articles of the draft convention it may be said that they appear to be unobjectionable.

The modifications which have been set forth above as desirable from the standpoint of this Government are considered to be important and, as at present advised, the Department would not desire to have you sign a convention in which such modifications were not substantially incorporated.

You will, of course, feel free to consult the Department during the progress of the conference by telegraph or otherwise. In the event that an agreement is reached upon the terms of the convention satisfactory to this Government, the Department will authorize you by telegraph to sign the convention in accordance with the enclosed full powers.

I am [etc.] FRANK B. KELLOGG

---

551.58B1/18

*The Secretary of State to the Minister in Switzerland* (*Wilson*)

No. 430 WASHINGTON, March 22, 1929.

SIR: There is enclosed, for transmission in the usual informal manner, a note to the Secretary General of the League of Nations, in reply to his note of October 8, 1928,[7] requesting this Government's observations on the proposals contained in the report of the Mixed Committee for the Suppression of Counterfeiting Currency.

I am [etc.] For the Secretary of State:
W. R. CASTLE, JR.

---

[Enclosure]

*The Secretary of State to the Secretary General of the League of Nations* (*Drummond*)

The Secretary of State of the United States of America refers to the note of the Secretary General of the League of Nations, dated October 8, 1928, in which he requested this Government's observations on the proposals contained in the report of the Mixed Committee for the Suppression of Counterfeiting Currency.

---

[7] Latter not printed.

In reply, the Secretary of State desires to submit the following comments on the provisions of the Draft Convention:

*Article I.*

The Government of the United States suggests that the agreement for the adoption of necessary measures embodied in Paragraph 1, be modified so as to provide that the contracting parties agree themselves to take or propose to their respective law making bodies the necessary measures in question.

With this exception, Paragraphs 1 to 5, inclusive, appear to impose no requirements that are not covered by the laws of the United States at present in force.

Paragraph 6. The penalties provided in the Federal Statutes of the United States relating to the counterfeiting of foreign obligations and securities are not as severe as those imposed by laws denouncing the counterfeiting of United States obligations and securities. An effort might be made to remedy this by amending the statutes to equalize these penalties.

Paragraph 7. Confiscation of counterfeit money and material and apparatus fitted or intended for counterfeiting purposes is provided for in the Federal Statutes, and the surrender of such property in case of the counterfeiting of foreign moneys to the interested government can be accomplished by direction of the Secretary of the Treasury.

Paragraph 8. The Federal Statutes do not allow participation of civil parties in criminal proceedings.

Paragraph 9. The American Government perceives no objection to this paragraph.

Paragraph 10. The American Government approves of the provisions of this paragraph, but desires to point out that, inasmuch as it recognizes the general rule of extraditing its nationals for offenses committed in a foreign country, subject to the provisions of existing treaties, paragraph 10 is not applicable to the United States.

Paragraph 11. This paragraph is not applicable to the American Government, since the internal legislation of the United States does not recognize the principle of the prosecution of offenses committed abroad. The American Government perceives no objections to the provisions of this paragraph.

Paragraph 12. A central bureau in the United States charged with the suppression of counterfeiting, the Secret Service Division of the Treasury Department, has been in existence since 1864, and is in close touch with the institution issuing currency and with the police authorities throughout the country. It is believed that it will be entirely practicable for the Secret Service Division of the Treasury

Department to effect contact with the central bureaus abroad with good results.

Paragraph 13. It is believed that direct communication between these central bureaus will facilitate their activities and add materially to their effectiveness.

Paragraph 14. The provisions of this paragraph calling for specimens of the currency issues of the United States cannot be complied with without violating the policy of the Treasury as established for a long period of time. It is not believed that this policy should be changed and it is suggested that the same results can be accomplished if the foreign governments obtain United States currency in exchange for legal tender, which exchange can be made direct with the Treasury so that the currency obtained will be known to be genuine.

Paragraph 15. Periodical conferences attended by representatives from the contracting governments might prove advantageous.

Paragraph 16. The Government of the United States would desire further information as to the exact scope and effect of "letters of request," but may observe that mere correspondence relating to counterfeiting operations and their suppression should be conducted directly between these central bureaus and confirmed by copies despatched through customary diplomatic channels.

## Article II

The American Government is of the opinion that the offenses referred to should be recognized as extraditable offenses, and, subject to the limitations contained in existing treaties or conventions, favors the principle stated. However, it would much prefer that the offenses in question should be specifically set forth in this Article.

In view of the provisions of Paragraph 10, Article I, and of the foregoing comment thereon, the Government of the United States would desire an addition to Article II providing that the contracting parties shall not be obligated to surrender their own citizens.

Moreover, since the extradition laws of the United States are not very comprehensive and do not cover several matters which are ordinarily dealt with in the extradition treaties of the United States, the American Government considers that future embarrassment to it might be obviated by providing in the convention under consideration for such matters: as for instance, a prohibition of the trial of the extradited person for another offense until he has had a reasonable opportunity to leave the country following his trial or punishment on the charge for which he was surrendered; the effect upon the obligation to surrender of the running of the Statute of Limitations and of the current prosecution or conviction of the fugitive upon an offense committed in the territory of the surrendering government;

the rule which shall govern in case surrender is requested by two or more powers; the limit of time a fugitive shall be held after commitment or arrest and awaiting the production of the formal documents, and, finally, the nature of the evidence which it is essential to produce.

The Government of the United States does not object to the provisions of the remaining articles of the draft convention.

With reference to the recommendations numbered 1 to 8, inclusive, on page 24 of the printed report, this Government has no comments to submit at this time. However, the Government of the United States reserves the right to make such further comments as it may later deem advisable.

WASHINGTON, March 22, 1929.

---

551.58B1/49: Telegram

*The Chief of the American Delegation (Wilson) to the Secretary of State*

GENEVA, April 18, 1929—10 p. m.
[Received 11:25 p. m.]

10. Second reading of the convention terminated this afternoon and document issued with slight modifications in the same form as submitted by the small committee. Signature will probably take place coming Saturday the 20th.

In the course of the negotiations of several treaties we have established the principle that the United States will not sign at the termination of negotiations but because of its great distance and difficulty of communication must be permitted to sign subsequently with full rights as a signatory state. Article 20 of present draft accords ample lapse of time for our signature.

While I hope that the document will be such that you will find it possible to authorize me to sign, I propose, unless you instruct me to the contrary, to follow the precedent which we have already established and make an announcement in the final plenary session for signature briefly stating our reasons for not signing at the outset and adding that this does not signify on our part an intention not to sign. Fuller explanation is contained in my despatch of April 17th [9] mailed today.

WILSON

[9] Not printed.

551.58B1/56

*The Chief of the American Delegation (Wilson) to the Secretary of State*

GENEVA, April 20, 1929.
[Received May 3.]

SIR: I have the honor to transmit herewith the Final Text of the Convention for the Suppression of Counterfeiting Currency signed today at Geneva by 23 states,[10] of which a list follows:

| | |
|---|---|
| Albania | Hungary |
| Austria | India |
| Belgium | Italy |
| Colombia | Japan |
| Cuba | Luxemburg |
| Czechoslovakia | Netherlands |
| Danzig | Poland |
| France | Portugal |
| Germany | Rumania |
| Great Britain and Northern | Serbs, Croats and Slovenes |
| Ireland | Switzerland |
| Greece | U. S. S. R. (Russia) |

Four other countries enumerated below have expressed their intentions to sign in the near future:

China, Denmark, Finland, Nicaragua.

Inasmuch as this Conference worked on principles somewhat different from those which are ordinarily employed in preparing conventions, I think it well to explain that practically all the debates took place in a Special Subcommittee, to which the most difficult questions were referred. No minutes were taken of the proceedings of the Special Subcommittee. The Department will not find, therefore, any full account of these debates in the procès-verbal, and I will have to enter somewhat at length on an analysis of the argument, depending on my memory for this purpose.

In its instruction No. 426, the Department adopted a position somewhat in opposition to the draft convention on the following points:

(*a*) Paragraph 1, Article I;
(*b*) Paragraph 6, Article I;
(*c*) Paragraph 14, Article I;
(*d*) Paragraph 16, Article I;
(*e*) Article II.

For the sake of convenience I shall treat these matters seriatim.

The Department will remember that I explained in my telegram No. 2, April 9, 7 p. m.,[11] that two subcommittees were set up, Com-

---

[10] *Post*, p. 409.
[11] Not printed.

mittee A for legal questions, Committee B for administrative or enforcement questions. It was subsequently found advisable to further reduce the number of participants in Committee A and therefore a "Special Subcommittee" was instituted. In addition to the committees mentioned above a committee of Draft and Coordination was instituted, composed of the President, Dr. Posposil, myself, Vice-President, the President and Vice-President of Committee A, M. Servais (Belgium), and Sir John Fischer Williams (Great Britain), and the President and Vice-President of Committee B, M. Delaquis (Switzerland), and Count Chalendar (France). Added to this was Mr. Pella (Rumania) as *rapporteur* of Committee A.

(*a*) Article I, paragraph 1, draft convention. In an early session of the judicial committee, Mr. Pella (Rumania) moved that the words "or to recommend to their legislative bodies the adoption of" be inserted after the word "adopt" in the second paragraph. I immediately seconded this motion, whereupon the Chairman ruled that this raised a question on which debate had better be reserved and it was subsequently ordered that this should be one of the subjects of discussion in the Special Subcommittee. In the sessions of the Special Subcommittee I supported warmly Mr. Pella's proposal, using the arguments advanced in the Department's 426. It appeared at once that in the minds of the great majority of the delegates the insertion of such a clause would greatly weaken the force of the convention, since it was pointed out that this would permit the ratification of the convention without the adoption of the necessary legislation. It was clear that the states of Eastern Europe especially were unwilling to depend on the good faith of their neighbors in this connection and that it was essential if they were to adhere to the convention, to find a formula which would make ratification dependent upon legislation in conformity with the convention having been adopted. This led us after prolonged argument to the adoption of a formula which the Department will find in Article 23 of the convention, together with the elimination of the subparagraph of paragraph 1, Article I. Inasmuch as this seemed to cover the objections which the Department had raised to the original text, and at the same time to establish the principle that ratification was dependent upon laws conforming to the convention, I acquiesced in this solution and was gratified to find that the Department had approved the thought therein contained in its telegram No. 1, April 17 [*18*], 3 p. m.[12]

(*b*) The foregoing paragraph brings me, both in seriatim consideration and in logical thought, to the contemplation of paragraph 6 of Article I, concerning which paragraph the Department had informed me that our legislation was not in entire conformity with

---

[13] Neither printed.

the draft convention but that legislation designed to make it so conform might be proposed by us. Under the present drafting of the treaty, therefore, the Department would naturally consider the advisability of submitting a bill equalizing penalties in the sense of paragraph 6, Article I, now Article 5 of the Final Convention. Such legislation would, as far as I can see, and Mr. Moran shares this opinion, be the only special legislation which it would be necessary for us to adopt in order to conform with the terms of the convention. I call attention again to the foregoing paragraph—to Article 23 and its implication that legislation has been adopted before ratification.

(c) Paragraph 14, Article I, draft convention. This Article as finally adopted stands as Article 14 of the text. In a session of Subcommittee B, Mr. Moran made a statement following the lines of your instruction beginning page 4 of No. 426 and declared that the words "so far as it considers expedient" had been inserted in the draft convention to meet the objections that he had already raised in the sessions of the Mixed Committee to any obligation on the part of the United States to supply such canceled specimens. Our attitude and the nature of the obligation so far as it applies to us is thoroughly understood by the conference.

(d) Paragraph 16, Article I, now Article 16 in the final text. This Article caused me a considerable amount of perplexity since it was extremely difficult to ascertain from my colleagues exactly what was meant by "letters of request", or "commissions rogatoires" in the French text. It finally became apparent that the phrase as used was equivalent to "letters rogatory" in our terminology and I therefore caused to be inserted a foot note to page 4 of the Final Act, stating that "this expression has the same meaning as letters rogatory." There was a very evident disposition on the part of the majority of those present to simplify the procedure for the transmission of letters rogatory, since in Continental practice such letters are accepted in certain cases as evidence even in criminal procedure. The discussion on this Article occurred so late in the debates that I was forced to act without the opportunity of consulting you in detail. However, when your telegrams Nos. 4 and 5, of April 18, 4 p. m., and 6 p. m.,[13] respectively, arrived, I satisfied myself to the best of my knowledge, after consultation with some of the best jurists on the Commission that the anxieties evidenced in the Department's telegram were met by the text. The Department will note that in the four concluding paragraphs of the Article it is provided that each High Contracting Party shall notify the others of the method of transmission which it will recognize for letters rogatory, and that,

[13] Neither printed.

further, until such notification is made existing procedure shall remain in force. Also that the Article shall not be construed as an undertaking that any party will adopt in criminal methods any form or methods of proof contrary to their law. With regard to the matter of expense, as I pointed out in my telegram No. 8, April 18, 10 a. m.,[14] for such states as make the practice of the use of letters rogatory in criminal procedure it has been the custom to make no charge for such procedure other than for expert testimony. I felt that you would not wish me to prevent these states from adopting a text which might simplify their own procedure, if at the same time such text left us free to follow our ordinary practice. If there were any doubt of our position in regard to Article 16 it would appear to me that such doubt was eliminated by the phraseology of No. 4 of the Interpretations contained in the Protocol on page 8, to the effect that the High Contracting Parties are required to execute letters rogatory only in the limitations provided for by their domestic law.

(e) Article II of draft convention, now Article 10 of the final text. This Article gave rise to one of the most protracted debates which took place in the Special Subcommittee. In accordance with the suggestion which I ventured to make in my No. 1, April 8, 9 a. m. [p. m.], amended by your unnumbered, April 9, 6 p. m.,[15] I submitted an amendment dealing with this problem of extradition. In the Special Subcommittee I pointed out that the amendment had the defect which you observed in the first paragraph of your telegram which I have just mentioned, namely, that so far as concerns countries not having treaties of extradition the present situation was not relieved. The proposals were many and varied as to how we should reach a text which would embody the suggestions contained in my amendment and at the same time stop the gap which you had suggested, and the final text of Article 10 is designed to cover both cases. I believe that the Department will find it satisfactory in that it refers to definite offenses which are listed in Article 3, in that it makes extradition dependent upon treaty for countries which subject their extradition to treaty provisions, in that it supplements existing treaties in so far as they do not cover the offenses listed in Article 3, in that it provides for extradition between states which do not make extradition conditional on treaty or reciprocity, and in that such extradition shall be granted in accordance with the law of the country, including, in the case of the United States, duly ratified treaties.

A very interesting discussion arose on paragraph 9 of Article I

---

[14] Not printed.
[15] Neither printed.

of the draft convention in relation to the political motive. Many of the states, and especially the neighbors of Hungary which were still deeply under the influence of the events connected with the Hungarian counterfeiting case in which Prince Windeschgraetz played an important part, made a determined struggle to insert in the convention a declaration to the effect that in cases of counterfeiting the political motive should not afford a valid excuse either for the escape of punishment or refusal of extradition. The British Delegation and others were, on the other hand, equally determined that the traditional right of asylum should not be infringed, even though they were unable to formulate suppositious cases in which counterfeiting might be considered a political offense. Since I had no definite instructions from you on the subject, I did not play a very active part in this discussion but confined myself in the Special Subcommittee to stating that I hardly believed that my Government would go so far as to adopt measures which could be considered as a limitation on the right of asylum or upon application of internal law. A compromise was finally reached; in Article 3 of the present text it is provided that the offenses enumerated shall be punishable as "ordinary crimes", which is the nearest translation which we could reach of the French expression "droit commun", which of course can not be translated as "common law". At the same time Article 18 of the present text was added so that as far as the application of internal law is concerned it should not be assumed that the wording of Article 3 has made any change. Naturally, those states which desired to go much further were not satisfied with this solution, and they have therefore formulated among themselves an additional protocol which is found on page 22 of Document C. F. M. 12 of the final text. As far as the rest of the Articles are concerned, I believe that the Department will not consider that the changes from the draft convention are material or of great interest to ourselves. As far as the administrative clauses are concerned, Mr. Moran has expressed himself satisfied.

I made a declaration in the final plenary session in accordance with my telegram No. 10 of April 18, 10 p. m. As I indicated, Article 20 of the present convention gives us ample time to sign at our convenience. I venture to make the suggestion, however, that if the Department believes that we can with benefit sign this convention, it would be advisable to authorize me to do so at the earliest possible moment in order that the full sympathy of our Government with this movement may be shown, and in order that no doubt may arise in the participating countries as to our willingness to cooperate with them in this matter. This argument, to my mind, carries special weight, as the first state to establish a central office such as are [*is*] contemplated in this convention was the United States, and our central office has to a large measure been considered the example which should be followed by the others.

As the Department knows, the Final Act consists, in the practice current in Geneva, of a series of "voeux", or aspirations, which all those present at the Conference sign as a rule. The Final Act, however, has no force of law, is in no sense a contractual obligation, nor is it subject to ratification nor is it even to be considered in connection with ratification of the Convention and Protocol. It consists of recommendations which are pushed by divers individuals in the Conference and are often inserted to give them satisfaction in order to avoid their continuing their efforts to insert them in the body of the Convention. It might be termed the waste-basket of the Convention. Thus the Department will find in the clauses of the Final Act recommendations to the Council of the League in which I hardly think we should participate. Also there are certain recommendations of an administrative nature with which Mr. Moran is not in accord. I think it highly probable that the Department will desire, if it considers that signature can properly be affixed to the Convention and Protocol, that signature should not be affixed to the Final Act. As a matter of fact, since we have delayed signature, it will not be remarked if I fail to sign the Final Act at the time of signing the Convention and Protocol.

In asking the Department's indulgence towards the form of this despatch, which is drafted in the haste necessarily incident to the work of the Preparatory Commission of Disarmament, I have the honor to express on my own behalf and that of the Delegation, our appreciation of the Department's sympathetic cooperation.

I have [etc.]                                    HUGH R. WILSON

_____

551.58B1/56 : Telegram

*The Secretary of State to the Minister in Switzerland (Wilson)*

WASHINGTON, July 16, 1929—noon.

74. Your despatch from Geneva, April 20, 1929. Please proceed to Geneva at your early convenience and sign the convention and protocol for the suppression of counterfeiting currency. Do not sign the final act or optional protocol. Telegraph date of signature.

For your information, in connection with Article 23, this Government proposes that, before the convention is ratified, certain changes in its legislation shall be made.

STIMSON

551.58B1/62 : Telegram

*The Minister in Switzerland (Wilson) to the Secretary of State*

BERNE, July 20, 1929—noon.
[Received 1:20 p. m.]

57. Your cipher telegram 74, July 16, noon. I signed convention and the protocol for the suppression of counterfeiting on Saturday morning, July 20.

WILSON

---

551.58B1/70

*International Convention for the Suppression of Counterfeiting Currency* [16]

[List of heads of states and list of plenipotentiaries is omitted. For full text in French and English, see League of Nations Treaty Series, volume CXII, page 371.]

## PART I

### ARTICLE 1

The High Contracting Parties recognise the rules laid down in Part I of this Convention as the most effective means in present circumstances for ensuring the prevention and punishment of the offence of counterfeiting currency.

### ARTICLE 2

In the present Convention, the word "currency" is understood to mean paper money (including banknotes) and metallic money, the circulation of which is legally authorised.

### ARTICLE 3

The following should be punishable as ordinary crimes:

(1) Any fraudulent making or altering of currency, whatever means are employed;
(2) The fraudulent uttering of counterfeit currency;
(3) The introduction into a country of or the receiving or obtaining counterfeit currency with a view to uttering the same and with knowledge that it is counterfeit;
(4) Attempts to commit, and any intentional participation in, the foregoing acts;
(5) The fraudulent making, receiving or obtaining of instruments or other articles peculiarly adapted for the counterfeiting or altering of currency.

---

[16] Signed by 23 states April 20, 1929; signed on behalf of the United States July 20, 1929. Not submitted to the Senate.

## ARTICLE 4

Each of the acts mentioned in Article 3, if they are committed in different countries, should be considered as a distinct offence.

## ARTICLE 5

No distinction should be made in the scale of punishments for offences referred to in Article 3 between acts relating to domestic currency on the one hand and to foreign currency on the other; this provision may not be made subject to any condition of reciprocal treatment by law or by treaty.

## ARTICLE 6

In countries where the principle of the international recognition of previous convictions is recognised, foreign convictions for the offences referred to in Article 3 should, within the conditions prescribed by domestic law, be recognised for the purpose of establishing habitual criminality.

## ARTICLE 7

In so far as "civil parties" are admitted under the domestic law, foreign "civil parties", including, if necessary, the High Contracting Party whose money has been counterfeited, should be entitled to all rights allowed to inhabitants by the laws of the country in which the case is tried.

## ARTICLE 8

In countries where the principle of the extradition of nationals is not recognised, nationals who have returned to the territory of their own country after the commission abroad of an offence referred to in Article 3 should be punishable in the same manner as if the offence had been committed in their own territory, even in a case where the offender has acquired his nationality after the commission of the offence.

This provision does not apply if, in a similar case, the extradition of a foreigner could not be granted.

## ARTICLE 9

Foreigners who have committed abroad any offence referred to in Article 3, and who are in the territory of a country whose internal legislation recognises as a general rule the principle of the prosecution of offences committed abroad, should be punishable in the same way as if the offence had been committed in the territory of that country.

The obligation to take proceedings is subject to the condition that extradition has been requested and that the country to which application is made cannot hand over the person accused for some reason which has no connection with the offence.

### ARTICLE 10

The offences referred to in Article 3 shall be deemed to be included as extradition crimes in any extradition treaty which has been or may hereafter be concluded between any of the High Contracting Parties.

The High Contracting Parties who do not make extradition conditional on the existence of a treaty or reciprocity, henceforward recognise the offences referred to in Article 3 as cases of extradition as between themselves.

Extradition shall be granted in conformity with the law of the country to which application is made.

### ARTICLE 11

Counterfeit currency, as well as instruments or other articles referred to in Article 3 (5), should be seized and confiscated. Such currency, instruments or other articles should, after confiscation, be handed over on request either to the Government or bank of issue whose currency is in question, with the exception of exhibits whose preservation as a matter of record is required by the law of the country where the prosecution took place, and any specimens whose transmission to the Central Office mentioned in Article 12 may be deemed advisable. In any event, all such articles should be rendered incapable of use.

### ARTICLE 12

In every country, within the framework of its domestic law, investigations on the subject of counterfeiting should be organised by a central office.

This central office should be in close contact:

    (a) With the institutions issuing currency;
    (b) With the police authorities within the country;
    (c) With the central offices of other countries.

It should centralise, in each country, all information of a nature to facilitate the investigation, prevention and punishment of countterfeiting currency.

### ARTICLE 13

The central offices of the different countries should correspond directly with each other.

ARTICLE 14

Each central office should, so far as it considers expedient, forward to the central offices of the other countries a set of cancelled specimens of the actual currency of its own country.

It should, subject to the same limitations, regularly notify to the central offices in foreign countries, giving all necessary particulars:

(*a*)  New currency issues made in its country;
(*b*)  The withdrawal of currency from circulation, whether as out of date or otherwise.

Except in cases of purely local interest, each central office should, so far as it thinks expedient, notify to the central offices in foreign countries:

(1) Any discovery of counterfeit currency. Notification of the forgery of bank or currency notes shall be accompanied by a technical description of the forgeries, to be provided solely by the institution whose notes have been forged. A photographic reproduction or, if possible, a specimen forged note should be transmitted. In urgent cases, a notification and a brief description made by the police authorities may be discreetly communicated to the central offices interested, without prejudice to the notification and technical description mentioned above;

(2) Investigation and prosecutions in cases of counterfeiting, and arrests, convictions and expulsions of counterfeiters, and also, where possible, their movements, together with any details which may be of use, and in particular their descriptions, finger-prints and photographs;

(3) Details of discoveries of forgeries, stating whether it has been possible to seize all the counterfeit currency put into circulation.

ARTICLE 15

In order to ensure, improve and develop direct international cooperation in the prevention and punishment of counterfeiting currency, the representatives of the central offices of the High Contracting Parties should from time to time hold conferences with the participation of representatives of the banks of issue and of the central authorities concerned. The organisation and supervision of a central international information office may form the subject of one of these conferences.

ARTICLE 16

The transmission of letters of request * relating to offences referred to in Article 3 should be effected:

(*a*)  Preferably by direct communication between the judicial authorities, through the central offices where possible;

---

* This expression has the same meaning as "letters rogatory". [Footnote in the original.]

(*b*) By direct correspondence between the Ministers of Justice of the two countries, or by direct communication from the authority of the country making the request to the Minister of Justice of the country to which the request is made;

(*c*) Through the diplomatic or consular representative of the country making the request in the country to which the request is made; this representative shall send the letters of request direct to the competent judicial authority or to the authority appointed by the Government of the country to which the request is made, and shall receive direct from such authority the papers showing the execution of the letters of request.

In cases (*a*) and (*c*), a copy of the letters of request shall always be sent simultaneously to the superior authority of the country to which application is made.

Unless otherwise agreed, the letters of request shall be drawn up in the language of the authority making the request, provided always that the country to which the request is made may require a translation in its own language, certified correct by the authority making the request.

Each High Contracting Party shall notify to each of the other High Contracting Parties the method or methods of transmission mentioned above which it will recognise for the letters of request of the latter High Contracting Party.

Until such notfication is made by a High Contracting Party, its existing procedure in regard to letters of request shall remain in force.

Execution of letters of request shall not be subject to payment of taxes or expenses of any nature whatever other than expenses of experts.

Nothing in the present article shall be construed as an undertaking on the part of the High Contracting Parties to adopt in criminal matters any form or methods of proof contrary to their laws.

### ARTICLE 17

The participation of a High Contracting Party in the present Convention shall not be interpreted as affecting that Party's attitude on the general question of criminal jurisdiction as a question of international law.

### ARTICLE 18

The present Convention does not affect the principle that the offences referred to in Article 3 should in each country, without ever being allowed impunity, be defined, prosecuted and punished in conformity with the general rules of its domestic law.

PART II

ARTICLE 19

The High Contracting Parties agree that any disputes which might arise between them relating to the interpretation or application of this Convention shall, if they cannot be settled by direct negotiation, be referred for decision to the Permanent Court of International Justice. In case any or all of the High Contracting Parties parties to such a dispute should not be Parties to the Protocol bearing the date of December 16th, 1920,[17] relating to the Permanent Court of International Justice, the dispute shall be referred, at the choice of the parties and in accordance with the constitutional procedure of each party, either to the Permanent Court of International Justice or to a court of arbitration constituted in accordance with the Convention of October 18th, 1907,[18] for the Pacific Settlement of International Disputes, or to some other court of arbitration.

ARTICLE 20

The present Convention, of which the French and English texts are both authentic, shall bear to-day's date. Until the 31st day of December 1929, it shall be open for signature on behalf of any Member of the League of Nations and on behalf of any non-member State which was represented at the Conference which elaborated the present Convention or to which a copy is communicated by the Council of the League of Nations.

It shall be ratified, and the instruments of ratification shall be transmitted to the Secretary-General of the League of Nations, who will notify their receipt to all the Members of the League and to the non-member States aforesaid.

ARTICLE 21

After the 1st day of January 1930, the present Convention shall be open to accession on behalf of any Member of the League of Nations and any of the non-member States referred to in Article 20 on whose behalf it has not been signed.

The instruments of accession shall be transmitted to the Secretary-General of the League of Nations, who will notify their receipt to all the Members of the League and to the non-member States referred to in Article 20.

ARTICLE 22

The countries which are ready to ratify the Convention under the second paragraph of Article 20 or to accede to the Convention under

---

[17] *Foreign Relations*, 1920, vol. I, p. 17.
[18] *Ibid.*, 1907, pt. 2, p. 1181.

Article 21 but desire to be allowed to make any reservations with regard to the application of the Convention may inform the Secretary-General of the League of Nations to this effect, who shall forthwith communicate such reservations to the High Contracting Parties on whose behalf ratifications or accessions have been deposited and enquire whether they have any objection thereto. If within six months of the date of the communication of the Secretary-General no objections have been received, the participation in the Convention of the country making the reservation shall be deemed to have been accepted by the other High Contracting Parties subject to the said reservation.

ARTICLE 23

Ratification of or accession to the present Convention by any High Contracting Party implies that its legislation and its administrative organisation are in conformity with the rules contained in the Convention.

ARTICLE 24

In the absence of a contrary declaration by one of the High Contracting Parties at the time of signature, ratification or accession, the provisions of the present Convention shall not apply to colonies, overseas territories, protectorates or territories under suzerainty or mandate.

Nevertheless, the High Contracting Parties reserve the right to accede to the Convention, in accordance with the provisions of Articles 21 and 23, for their colonies, overseas territories, protectorates or territories under suzerainty or mandate. They also reserve the right to denounce it separately in accordance with the provisions of Article 27.

ARTICLE 25

The present Convention shall not come into force until five ratifications or accessions on behalf of Members of the League of Nations or non-member States have been deposited. The date of its coming into force shall be the ninetieth day after the receipt by the Secretary-General of the League of Nations of the fifth ratification or accession.

ARTICLE 26

After the coming into force of the Convention in accordance with Article 25, each subsequent ratification or accession shall take effect on the ninetieth day from the date of its receipt by the Secretary-General of the League of Nations.

ARTICLE 27

The present Convention may be denounced on behalf of any Member of the League of Nations or non-member State by a notification in writing addressed to the Secretary-General of the League of Nations, who will inform all the Members of the League and the non-member States referred to in Article 20. Such denunciation shall take effect one year after the date of its receipt by the Secretary-General of the League of Nations, and shall operate only in respect of the High Contracting Party on whose behalf it was notified.

### ARTICLE 28

The present Convention shall be registered by the Secretariat of the League of Nations on the date of its coming into force.

In faith whereof the above-mentioned Plenipotentiaries have signed the present Convention.

Done at Geneva, the twentieth day of April, one thousand nine hundred and twenty-nine, in a single copy, which will remain deposited in the archives of the Secretariat of the League of Nations, and of which certified copies will be transmitted to all the Members of the League and to the non-member States referred to in Article 20.

Albania
>   Dr. Stavro Stavri

Germany
>   Dr. Erich Kraske
>   Dr. Wolfgang Mettgenberg.
>   Vocke

United States of America
>   Hugh R. Wilson

Austria
>   Dr. Bruno Schultz

Belgium
>   Servais

Great Britain and Northern Ireland and all parts of the British Empire which are not separate Members of the League of Nations
>   John Fischer Williams
>   Leslie S. Brass

India
>   As is provided in Article 24 of the Convention, my signature does not include the territories of any Prince or Chief under the Suzerainty of His Majesty.
>   Vernon Dawson

Bulgaria
>   D. Mikoff

China
  Lone Liang

Colombia
  A. J. Restrepo

Cuba
  G. de Blanck
  M. R. Alvarez

Denmark
  William Borberg

Free City of Danzig
  F. Sokal
  John Muhl

Spain
  Mauricio Lopez Roberts, Marquis de la Torrehermosa

France
  Chalendar

Greece
  Mégalos Caloyanni

Hungary
  Paul de Hevesy

Italy
  Ugo Aloisi

Japan
  Raizaburo Hayashi
  Shigeru Nagai

Luxemburg
  Ch. G. Vermaire

Monaco
  R. Ellès

Norway
    At the time of signing the present Convention, the undersigned declares on behalf of his Government that:
    In view of the provisions of Article 176, paragraph 2, of the Norwegian Ordinary Criminal Code and Article 2 of the Norwegian Law on the Extradition of Criminals, the extradition provided for in Article 10 of the present Convention may not be granted for the offence referred to in Article 3, No. 2, where the person uttering the counterfeit currency himself accepted it *bona fide as* genuine.
  Chr. L. Lange

Panama
> J. D. Arosemena

The Netherlands
> A. A. van der Feltz
> P. J. Gerke
> K. H. Broekhoff

Poland
> F. Sokal
> Vlodzimierz Sokalski

Portugal
> José Caeiro da Matta

Roumania
> Antoniade
> Vespasien V. Pella
> Pascal Toncesco

Kingdom of the Serbs, Croats and Slovenes
> Dr. Thomas Givanovitch.

Union of Soviet Socialist Republics
> G. Lachkevitch
> Nicolas Liubimov

Switzerland
> Delaquis

Czechoslovakia
> Jaroslav Kallab

## PROTOCOL

### I. Interpretations

At the moment of signing the Convention of this day's date, the undersigned Plenipotentiaries declare that they accept the interpretations of the various provisions of the Convention set out hereunder.

It is understood:

(1) That the falsification of a stamp on a note, when the effect of such a stamp is to make that note valid in a given country, shall be regarded as a falsification of the note.

(2) That the Convention does not affect the right of the High Contracting Parties freely to regulate, according to their domestic law, the principles on which a lighter sentence or no sentence may be imposed, the prerogative of pardon or mercy and the right to amnesty.

(3) That the rule contained in Article 4 of the Convention in no way modifies internal regulations establishing penalties in the event of concurrent offences. It does not prevent the same individual, who is both forger and utterer, from being prosecuted as forger only.

(4) That High Contracting Parties are required to execute letters of request only within the limits provided for by their domestic law.

## II. Reservations

The High Contracting Parties who make the reservations set forth hereunder make their acceptance of the Convention conditional on the said reservations; their participation, subject to the said reservations, is accepted by the other High Contracting Parties.

(1) The Government of India make a reservation to the effect that Article 9 does not apply to India, where the power to legislate is not sufficiently extensive to admit of the legislation contemplated by this article.

(2) Pending the negotiation for the abolition of consular jurisdiction which is still enjoyed by nationals of some Powers, the Chinese Government is unable to accept Article 10, which involves the general undertaking of a Government to grant extradition of a foreigner who is accused of counterfeiting currency by a third State.

(3) As regards the provisions of Article 20, the delegation of the Union of Soviet Socialist Republics reserves for its Government the right to address, if it so desires, the instrument of its ratification to another signatory State in order that the latter may transmit a copy thereof to the Secretary-General of the League of Nations for notification to all the signatory or acceding States.

## III. Declarations

### SWITZERLAND

At the moment of signing the Convention, the representative of Switzerland made the following declaration:

"The Swiss Federal Council, being unable to assume any obligation as to the penal clauses of the Convention before the question of the introduction of a unified penal code in Switzerland is settled in the affirmative, draws attention to the fact that the ratification of the Convention cannot be accomplished in a fixed time.

"Nevertheless, the Federal Council is disposed to put into execution, to the extent of its authority, the administrative provisions of the Convention whenever these will come into force in accordance with Article 25."

### UNION OF SOVIET SOCIALIST REPUBLICS

At the moment of signing the Convention, the representative of the Union of Soviet Socialist Republics made the following declaration:

"The delegation of the Union of Soviet Socialist Republics, while accepting the provisions of Article 19, declares that the Government of the Union does not propose to have recourse, in so far as it is concerned, to the jurisdiction of the Permanent Court of International Justice.

"As regards the provision in the same Article by which disputes which it has not been possible to settle by direct negotiations would be submitted to any other arbitral procedure than that of the Permanent Court of International Justice, the delegation of the Union of Soviet Socialist Republics expressly declares that acceptance of this provision must not be interpreted as modifying the point of view of the Government of the Union on the general question of arbitration as a means of settling disputes between States."

The present Protocol in so far as it creates obligations between the High Contracting Parties will have the same force, effect and duration as the Convention of to-day's date, of which it is to be considered as an integral part.

IN FAITH WHEREOF the undersigned have affixed their signatures to the present Protocol.

DONE at Geneva, this twentieth day of April, one thousand nine hundred and twenty-nine, in a single copy, which shall be deposited in the archives of the Secretariat of the League of Nations and of which authenticated copies shall be delivered to all Members of the League of Nations and non-member States represented at the Conference.

Albania
DR. STAVRO STAVRI

Germany
DR. ERICH KRASKE
DR. WOLFGANG METTGENBERG
VOCKE

United States of America
HUGH R. WILSON

Austria
DR. BRUNO SCHULTZ

Belgium
SERVAIS

Great Britain and Northern Ireland and all parts of the British Empire which are not separate Members of the League of Nations
JOHN FISCHER WILLIAMS
LESLIE S. BRASS

India
VERNON DAWSON

Bulgaria
D. MIKOFF

China
  LONE LIANG

Colombia
  A. J. RESTREPO

Cuba
  G. DE BLANCK
  M. R. ALVAREZ

Denmark
  WILLIAM BORBERG

Free City of Danzig
  F. SOKAL
  JOHN MUHL

Spain
  MAURICIO LOPEZ ROBERTS, MARQUIS DE LA TORREHERMOSA

France
  CHALENDAR

Greece
  MÉGALOS CALOYANNI

Hungary
  PAUL DE HEVESY

Italy
  UGO ALOISI

Japan
  RAIZABURO HAYASHI
  SHIGERU NAGAI

Luxemburg
  CH. G. VERMAIRE

Monaco
  R. ELLÈS

Norway
  CHR. L. LANGE

Panama
  J. D. AROSEMENA

The Netherlands
  A. A. VAN DER FELTZ
  P. J. GERKE
  K. H. BROEKHOFF

Poland
  F. SOKAL
  VLODZIMIERZ SOKALSKI

Portugal
  JOSÉ CAEIRO DA MATTA

Roumania
  ANTONIADE
  VESPASIEN V. PELLA
  PASCAL TONCESCO

Kingdom of the Serbs, Croats and Slovenes
  DR. THOMAS GIVANOVITCH

Union of Soviet Socialist Republics
  G. LACHKEVITCH
  NICOLAS LIUBIMOV

Switzerland
  DELAQUIS

Czechoslovakia
  JAROSLAV KALLAB

## OPTIONAL PROTOCOL

Recognising the important progress regarding the suppression of counterfeiting currency which has been realised by the Convention for the Suppression of Counterfeiting Currency bearing this day's date, the High Contracting Parties signatory to this Protocol, subject to ratification, undertake, in their mutual relations, to consider, as regards extradition, the acts referred to in Article 3 of the said Convention as ordinary offences.

Extradition shall be granted according to the law of the country to which application is made.

The provisions of Part II of the said Convention apply equally to the present Protocol, with the exception of the following provisions:

(1) The present Protocol may be signed in accordance with Article 20 of the Convention in the name of any State Member of the League of Nations and of any non-member State which has been represented at the Conference and which has signed or will sign the Convention, or to which the Council of the League of Nations shall have sent a copy of the said Convention.

(2) The present Protocol shall come into force only after it has been ratified or adhered to in the name of three Members of the League of Nations or States which are not members.

(3) Ratification of and accession to the present Protocol are independent of ratification of or accession to the Convention.

In faith whereof the Plenipotentiaries named below have signed the present Protocol.

Done at Geneva, in a single copy, forming an Annex to the Convention for the Suppression of Counterfeiting Currency, on the twentieth day of April, one thousand nine hundred and twenty-nine.

Austria
DR. BRUNO SCHULTZ

Colombia
A. J. RESTREPO

Cuba
G. DE BLANCK
M. R. ALVAREZ

Greece
MÉGALOS CALOYANNI

Portugal
JOSÉ CAEIRO DA MATTA

Roumania
ANTONIADE
VESPASIEN V. PELLA.
PASCAL TONCESCO

Kingdom of the Serbs, Croats and Slovenes
DR. THOMAS GIVANOVITCH

Czechoslovakia
JAROSLAV KALLAB

Panama
J. D. AROSEMENA

Bulgaria
D. MIKOFF

Spain
MAURICIO LOPEZ ROBERTS, MARQUIS DE LA TORREHERMOSA

Poland
F. SOKAL

## ENTRY INTO FORCE OF THE INTERNATIONAL CONVENTION FOR THE ABOLITION OF IMPORT AND EXPORT PROHIBITIONS AND RESTRICTIONS [1]

Treaty Series No. 811

*Protocol Signed at Paris, December 20, 1929, Concerning the Entry Into Force of the International Convention of November 8, 1927, for the Abolition of Import and Export Prohibitions and Restrictions and of the Supplementary Agreement of July 11, 1928* [2]

The undersigned, being duly authorised and met at Paris at the invitation of the Secretary-General of the League of Nations, in conformity with the provisions of Article 17 of the International Convention for the Abolition of Import and Export Prohibitions and Restrictions signed at Geneva on November 8th, 1927, and of Articles C and D of the Supplementary Agreement to the said Convention signed at Geneva on July 11th, 1928;

Having noted that the instruments of ratification were deposited by their respective Governments within the time-limit provided for in the aforesaid Article C of the Supplementary Agreement, except in the case of Germany, on behalf of whom this deposit was not effected until November 23rd, 1929, and except in the case of Norway who has not yet carried out this formality;

Taking note of the annexed declaration made by the delegate of Norway;

Noting that certain of the conditions for the entry into force of the Convention and of the Supplementary Agreement mentioned above as defined in Article 17 of the Convention have not been fulfilled;

Noting furthermore that it is not possible at the moment to fulfil these conditions;

Being anxious nevertheless that the above-mentioned Convention and Supplementary Agreement should be put into force between the countries they represent, and hoping that the said conditions will be realised in the near future;

---

[1] For text of convention of November 8, 1927, and supplementary agreement of July 11, 1928, see *Foreign Relations*, 1928, vol. I, p. 336. For correspondence concerning the Second International Conference for the abolition of import and export prohibitions and restrictions, see *ibid.*, pp. 366 ff.

[2] The protocol was signed in a single copy in French and English; French text not printed.

Have agreed to the following provisions:

1. The German Government's ratification shall be regarded, exceptionally, as having the same effect as if it had been deposited before September 30th, 1929.

2. The forthcoming ratification announced by the Norwegian Government shall be regarded, exceptionally, as having the same effect as if it had been deposited before September 30th, 1929.

3. If ratifications on behalf of Czechoslovakia and Poland are deposited before May 31st, 1930, they shall be regarded, exceptionally, as having the same effect as if they had been deposited before September 30th, 1929.

4. The Convention shall be put into force on January 1st, 1930, by the countries on whose behalf the present Protocol is signed.

In the case of Hungary, the Convention will be put into force in the manner stated in the annexed declaration by the Hungarian delegate.

5. Those of the countries referred to above which have made the putting into force of the Convention conditional on its ratification by Czechoslovakia and Poland or either of these countries, shall not be bound by its provisions after July 1st, 1930, unless both or either of these countries, as the case may be, ratified the Convention before May 31st, 1930, and complies with the obligations arising out of the putting into force of the Convention on January 1st, 1930. Similarly, a country which made the putting into force of the Convention conditional, as far as it is concerned, upon its ratification for any country or countries other than Czechoslovakia or Poland shall not be bound by its provisions after July 1st, 1930, unless such other country or countries are themselves bound after that date.

If any countries waive the benefits of the provisions of the preceding sub-paragraph, they shall inform the Secretary-General of the League of Nations of this fact by a declaration addressed to him before June 20th, 1930.

6. Any of the countries referred to in paragraph 4 shall be relieved of the obligations accepted by it in virtue of the present Protocol on June 30th, 1931, or the same date in 1932, 1933 or 1934, on forwarding a declaration to that effect on any of these dates to the Secretary-General of the League of Nations. This possibility, however, will cease if and when the number of countries for which, before the signature of the present Protocol, the Convention has been ratified without its entry into force being made subject to conditions or with its entry into force being made subject to conditions which are fulfilled is not less than eighteen.

It is understood that, when a country maintains the Convention in force under the provisions of the second sub-paragraph of No. 5 of this Protocol, in spite of the fact that its conditions have not been fulfilled, those conditions shall not thereby be considered to have been fulfilled for the purpose of the application of the second sentence of the preceding sub-paragraph.

The provisions of the preceding two sub-paragraphs shall apply to Czechoslovakia and Poland in the event of the Convention being ratified on their behalf within the period mentioned in paragraph 5.

7. The provisions contained in paragraph 6 above shall be extended to any Member of the League of Nations or any non-Member State acceding to the Convention after this day's date.

IN FAITH WHEREOF the undersigned have signed the present Protocol.

DONE at Paris, on December twentieth one thousand nine hundred and twenty-nine in a single copy the French and English texts of which are both authoritative and which shall be deposited in the archives of the Secretariat of the League of Nations. Certified true copies shall be transmitted to all the Members of the League of Nations and to any non-Member States to which the Council of the League of Nations shall have communicated a copy of the Convention of November 8th, 1927.

Germany
> ADOLF REINSHAGEN

Austria
> DR. GRÜNBERGER

Belgium
> J. BRUNET

Great Britain
> I declare that my signature does not include any of His Britannic Majesty's Colonies, Protectorates or territories under suzerainty or mandate.
> S. J. CHAPMAN

Denmark
> BOECK

United States of America
> CHARLES E. LYON

France
> P. ELBEL

Hungary
> NICKL

Italy
  G. Manzoni*

Japan
  (Ad referendum)
  N. Ito

Luxemburg
  Albert Calmes

Norway
  Sigurd Bentzon

The Netherlands
  Posthuma

Portugal
  F. deCalheiros e Menezes

Roumania
  E. G. Neculcea

Switzerland
  W. Stucki

Yugoslavia
  I. Choumenkovitch

[Translation]

## Declaration by the Norwegian Delegation

The undersigned, being duly authorised by the Norwegian Government, declares that the said Government undertakes to put into force by administrative measures as from January 1st, 1930, and pending the deposit of the formal ratification of the Convention, the provisions of the Convention of November 8, 1927, and of the Supplementary Agreement of July 11, 1928.

Paris, December 20, 1929.

Sigurd Bentzon

----

* At the time of signing the Protocol, His Excellency the Royal Italian Ambassador in Paris deposited with the Secretariat of the League of Nations the following declaration which must be considered as accompanying the signature affixed by him on the said Protocol:
[*Translation*]
"In thus affixing its signature, the Royal Italian Government undertakes to put the Convention into force provided the conditions laid down in the present Protocol are fulfilled, as well as the condition specified in Article C of the Supplementary Agreement, namely that eighteen States at least which have ratified the Convention should apply it effectively as from July 1st, 1930." [Footnote on original protocol.]

## Declaration by the Hungarian Delegation

The undersigned, being duly authorised by the Hungarian Government,

In consideration of the fact that the special conditions of Hungarian legislation prevent him from appending his signature to paragraphs 4 and 5 of the annexed Protocol,

Declares that, whilst accepting the other provisions of the aforesaid Protocol, his Government will, for its part, regard the Convention as having been put into force by Hungary on January 1, 1930, provided always:

(1) That Austria, Germany, Italy, Roumania, Switzerland and Yugoslavia are as from July 1, 1930, bound by the provisions of the Convention;

(2) That Poland and Czechoslovakia have ratified the Convention before May 31, 1930, and that they conform with the obligations involved by the coming into force of the Convention on January 1st, 1930.

Paris, December 20, 1929.

Nickl

# AMERICAN REPRESENTATION IN A CONSULTATIVE CAPACITY AT THE INTERNATIONAL CONFERENCE ON THE TREATMENT OF FOREIGNERS, PARIS, NOVEMBER 5-DECEMBER 5, 1929 [1]

511.1D1/21

*The Acting Secretary General of the League of Nations (Barone) to the Secretary of State* [2]

C. L. 59 (a).1929.II.                                        GENEVA, April 10, 1929.

SIR: In my letter of December 18th, 1928, (C.L. 83(*a*)) [3] I had the honour to submit for your consideration a draft convention on the treatment of foreigners drawn up by the Economic Committee of the League of Nations in pursuance of the resolutions of the International Economic Conference of 1927. [4]

The text of this draft and the comments made upon it by the Economic Committee are reproduced in the enclosed document C. I. T. E. I. [5] This document also includes a historical introduction, the observations submitted by various Governments in reply to the letter of December 18th, and the comments made by the Economic Committee on these observations. It thus contains the preparatory documents for the International Conference, which was already in contemplation at the time when I communicated to you the draft convention (C.174.M.53.1928.II).

A resolution adopted by the Council of the League of Nations on December 14th, 1928, authorized the Secretary-General to invite the States concerned to this Conference after consulting the Economic Committee. I have since been requested by this Committee to make use of the powers thus conferred on me, and the Council at its meeting of March 7th, 1929, fixed the date of the Conference as November 5th, 1929.

I accordingly have the honour to invite your Government to send a delegation invested with the necessary powers to this Conference, the object of which is to conclude an international convention relative to

---

[1] The minutes and other records of the Conference are published in League of Nations, *Proceedings of the International Conference on Treatment of Foreigners, First Session, Paris, November 5th–December 5th, 1929* (C.97.M.23.1930.II. [C.I.T.E. 62]).
[2] Copy transmitted to the Department by the Minister in Switzerland as an enclosure to his despatch No. 813 of April 11; received April 29.
[3] Not printed.
[4] *Foreign Relations*, 1927, vol. I, p. 238.
[5] Not reprinted.

429

the treatment of foreigners. The attached draft prepared by the Economic Committee will serve as a basis for discussion.[8]

I should be grateful if you would inform me whether the United States Government is prepared to send representatives to this Conference, and, if so, to let me know the composition of its delegation, if possible before October 1st, next.

I have [etc.]

G. PAULUCCI DI CALBOLI BARONE

---

511.1D1/35 : Telegram

*The Secretary of State to the Minister in Switzerland* (*Wilson*)

WASHINGTON, October 11, 1929—7 p. m.

120. Your 33, April 11, noon.[8] You are requested to notify the Secretary General of the League of Nations in the sense of the following, referring to his communication of April 10, 1929, addressed to the Secretary of State:

The Government of the United States, being desirous of cooperating in a work which has for its object the proper treatment of foreigners, is pleased to inform the Secretary General that it has designated George A. Gordon, American First Secretary at Paris, to attend the Conference as a technical expert to cooperate in a consultative capacity.

Please request Consul at Geneva to forward immediately to Gordon League documents concerning the Conference including the draft Convention and any information which he believes will be of assistance.

STIMSON

---

511.1D1/42

*The Secretary of State to the Chargé in France* (*Armour*)

No. 4279

WASHINGTON, October 22, 1929.

SIR: The Department refers to its telegraphic instruction No. 327 of October 11, 1929,[8] designating Mr. Gordon as representative of this Government to sit in a consultative capacity at the forthcoming conference which is to convene in Paris on November 5, 1929, to consider a draft convention for the protection of foreigners abroad, and submits the following considerations for Mr. Gordon's guidance.

It is important that the impression should not be gained that the refusal of this Government at this time to become a party to the convention in question is based on a failure on its part to be interested in the subject matter thereof or because it is not in a position

---

[8] Not printed.

to assure to aliens within the jurisdiction of the United States as favorable treatment as is generally accorded by other States to aliens within their confines.

There are at present residing within the United States millions of non-naturalized aliens who not only are as well protected in their persons and property as American citizens, but who also for all intents and purposes are untrammeled in their activities, whether of commercial, educational or professional character. In this connection it should be emphasized that aliens, as well as citizens of the United States, come within the purview of the fourteenth amendment to the Constitution which provides in part that no State shall "deprive any person of life, liberty or property without due process of law nor deny to any person within its jurisdiction the equal protection of the laws". It may be pointed out in this relation that, with very few exceptions, aliens have been free to exploit the natural resources of the United States; that they have been permitted to engage in commerce and other commercial pursuits, and that even the professions, with the exception of admission to the bar, have been open to them. It is the Department's understanding that in so far as the legal profession is concerned admission thereto under the laws of most States is usually reserved to nationals of that State.

As you are aware, it has been the general policy of the Federal Government to abstain as far as possible from concluding treaties with foreign Powers, the provisions of which directly affect the police power of the several States. However, in view of the provisions of the fourteenth amendment to the Constitution of the United States, above referred to, of the existing practice of the several States in regard to the treatment of aliens as well as to the provisions of bilateral treaties concluded between the United States and foreign Powers, it may be asserted that in general the rights and privileges of aliens in the United States are as broad as those accorded by any other State to aliens within its jurisdiction.

The Department encloses for your ready reference a copy of the Treaty of Friendship, Commerce and Consular Rights between the United States and Germany [9] which, as you know, is serving as a model for the new treaties of this nature concluded by this Government with foreign countries, and your attention is especially invited to the provisions of Articles I, II, III, IV, V, VI, VII, VIII, IX, X, XI, XII, XIII and XIV, which relate particularly to the treatment of nationals of the respective parties in the territories of the other. You will note that except as to real estate, German nationals in the United States in so far as their persons, property and activities are concerned are placed on as favorable a basis as Amer-

---

[9] Treaty signed December 8, 1923; *Foreign Relations*, 1923, vol. II, p. 29.

ican citizens. Attention is especially invited to the national treatment provided in Article VIII in regard to the taxation of nationals and merchandise of one party in the territory of the other and to the broad privileges conferred upon nationals of each contracting party in Article I of the Treaty.

The Department submitted the League's draft convention to the Treasury Department, the Department of Justice, and the Labor Department, and it quotes for your information pertinent portions of the replies received to its above mentioned communications.

From the Treasury Department:

"This Department has been unable to determine in many instances the exact meaning of certain of the articles and the commentary has not always made the meaning clear. For example, the question of customs duties is stated to be beyond the scope of the convention but some of the provisions designed to secure absolute freedom of trade seem to be directed to certain of our tariff provisions. The line of demarkation is not at all clear between measures designed to prevent unfair competition and to develop particular industries, which are allowable, and measures intended to favor national products over foreign products, which are not allowable.

"Foreigners who have been admitted to this country are accorded the same fiscal treatment as nationals. Many treaties entered into between the United States and other countries contain provisions to this effect. Nationals who are not admitted to this country are accorded practically the same treatment in so far as income tax is concerned as nonresident citizens of the United States and certain domestic corporations."

From the Department of Labor:

"It is noted, first of all, that Part III, Chapter VI, declares that the provisions of the present Convention shall in no way affect the freedom of the High Contracting Parties as regards the admission of foreigners or the police measures which the Parties may take in regard to them. That provision is important, as it is consistent with the American view that the regulation of immigration is a domestic question as asserted in the Committee Report on the bill which became the Immigration Act of 1924. The statement in this provision that the Convention shall not affect the freedom of the High Contracting Parties as to police measures which Parties may take in regard to foreigners is hardly clear enough to show that the freedom of the Parties with respect to the deportation or expulsion of foreigners is not to be affected by the Convention. In view of the elaborate provisions relating to the right of resident aliens to carry on business in the territory of a Party to the Convention on an equality, with certain exceptions, with the citizens of such Party, it might be argued that it was not intended by the Parties to the Convention that the residence of the foreigners was to be terminated where it would result in embarrassment to or destruction of their business. It is believed that the freedom to expel or deport should be clearly and expressly recognized in the draft, because even though a subsequent Act of Congress would prevail over the Convention it is a fact that once a construction of a Convention is given in favor of an alien the courts would be reluctant to give an Act of Congress a construction inconsistent with the Convention unless the Act is clear and unambiguous."

In further relation to this matter, the Department encloses a copy of the American comment on the subject of "Treatment of Foreigners" at the meeting of the International Chamber in Amsterdam, received from the American section of the International Chamber of Commerce.[10] While this comment is, of course, not to be considered in any way as an official expression of this Government's views on the subject, it is believed that the information contained therein relative to the treatment of aliens in the several States will be of interest to the Embassy.

In conclusion, the Department desires to emphasize again the importance of having the position of the Government of the United States in regard to the treatment of foreigners as set forth above clearly understood. Should further information be desired concerning any of the subject matters coming within the scope of the Convention you will, of course, request further instructions by telegraph. The Department desires a full report of the proceedings of this conference, together with any comments which you deem pertinent. Should any points arise which you consider advisable to bring immediately to the Department's attention you will, please submit them in the form of a telegraphic report. In making your reports the Department requests that you bear in mind the fact that several Departments including the Treasury, Commerce and Labor Departments, all have an interest in the subject matter of the conference and you should, therefore, submit sufficient copies of your reports and any enclosures thereto, to permit their distribution to the above-mentioned Departments.

I am [etc.]

For the Secretary of State:
J. P. COTTON

---

511.1D1/47 : Telegram

*The Chargé in France (Armour) to the Secretary of State*

PARIS, November 5, 1929—10 a. m.
[Received 8:55 a. m.]

509. From Gordon. Department's instruction number 4279 of October 22, 1929. In this instruction the Department mentions "the refusal of this Government at this time to be a party to the convention." This would seem to presuppose that such refusal had already been communicated to the interested parties but I do not find that in

---

[10] Not printed.

its correspondence with the Secretary of the League of Nations or elsewhere the Department has notified this refusal or assigned any ground therefor.

Accordingly in the statement which I will presumably have occasion to make (probably tomorrow evening)[11] during the course of the general discussion which will open the Conference, I propose, in addition to setting forth the substantive points of the Department's instruction, to make reference to the reservation of powers to the several States, as set forth in the tenth amendment to the Constitution, as this would seem to support our point that while the United States does grant very liberal treatment to aliens the authority to enact laws upon a number of the important subjects dealt with by the proposed convention is reserved to the several states, and also to lend force to our other main point that our inability to become a party to the convention is in no wise due to any lack of interest. [Gordon.]

ARMOUR

___

511.1D1/48 : Telegram

*The Secretary of State to the Chargé in France (Armour)*

WASHINGTON, November 5, 1929—6 p. m.

368.  For Gordon.  Your 509, November 5, 10 a. m.  In its telegraphic instruction of October 11, 1929, to the American Legation at Berne, the Department requested Mr. Wilson to notify the Secretary General of the League of Nations in the sense of the following:

[Here follows the text of the statement embodied in the Department's telegram under reference, printed on page 430.]

Since you were assigned to attend the Conference in a consultative capacity it would seem obvious that the United States did not contemplate becoming a party to the Convention.

Department approves tenor of statement which you propose to make during course of general discussion which will open Conference.

STIMSON

___

511.1D1/49 : Telegram

*The Chargé in France (Armour) to the Secretary of State*

[Paraphrase]

PARIS, November 7, 1929—1 p. m.
[Received 3 : 30 p. m.]

515.  From Gordon.  Haitian delegate to the Conference, who is brother of Haitian Minister to France now home on leave of absence,

___

[11] The text of the statement made at the fourth plenary meeting, November 6, by the American representative was printed in *Proceedings of the Conference*, p. 49.

has stated to me that first point under article 18 of the draft convention gave him concern.[12] If the United States should ever become a party to this convention, he said, then France, for instance, could demand of Haiti under this article by a grant of reciprocal agreement (which might only be nominal and sterile) the same treatment which Haiti extends to us, and this he felt would not be to the best interest of either Haiti or ourselves. He hoped that my views met his and that I would express an opinion unfavorable to this clause which he might thereupon quote to his Government and advise the latter to authorize him to refuse to accept this provision.

In reply to the delegate I observed that the point he raised could not have any immediate application as long as the United States did not become a party to the convention. He then said that he wished to consider all possible eventualities before he agreed to any provisions which held such dangerous possibilities.

The question raised by the Haitian delegate is doubtless of interest to the Department, as the same considerations might arise with respect to our relations with certain other countries. It is my belief that the delegates to this Conference from the countries I have in mind are considering this question (the Haitian delegate has already spoken to his colleagues at the Conference from Panama and the Dominican Republic), so I should appreciate receiving an instruction regarding Department's views to guide me in any future conversations I may have with such delegates. If Department should feel inclined to set forth its views in some detail, I think that an instruction by mail, if it were sent off by end of this week, would reach me probably in sufficient time. [Gordon.]

ARMOUR

---

511.1D1/50 : Telegram

*The Chargé in France (Armour) to the Secretary of State*

PARIS, November 13, 1929—7 p. m.
[Received November 14—12 : 36 a. m.]

523. From Gordon. In connection with discussion of article 6 of draft convention, Australian delegate today circulated following proposed text for insertion as additional article to protocol:

"As regards the application of any or all of the articles of the convention, the obligations assumed by states signatories having a federal constitution binds only the federal governments and not the provincial

---

[12] Point 1 of article 18 after providing for the granting by any high contracting party, under certain limitations, of more favorable conditions to one or more of the other high contracting parties under the terms of special agreements, continues to read as follows: "These more favourable conditions may be claimed on condition of reciprocal treatment by any High Contracting Party not enjoying the benefits of the most-favoured-nation clause under a bilateral agreement and therefore unable to claim the free benefit thereof on that account."

or state governments which under federal constitutions may possess complete or partial autonomy as regards the treatment of foreigners."

He asked me particularly what I thought of it and I replied that I should like to study its possible effect and implications more carefully. In my despatch of November 7,[13] I alluded to the probability of some such development and expressed the view that my opening statement would still constitute an answer to a suggestion of this nature.

If it should become necessary to make a formal statement in this connection I should think something to the following effect would suffice:

"Even in view of the provisions of this additional article my Government, for the reasons which I set forth in my statement during the course of the general discussion, is unable at this time to become a party to this convention. Any provisions of this nature however cannot but add to the interest with which my Government proposes to study the proceedings of this Conference."

The matter may come up at any time. Will Department therefore please telegraph me if it approves. [Gordon.]

ARMOUR

---

511.1D1/51 : Telegram

*The Acting Secretary of State to the Chargé in France (Armour)*

WASHINGTON, November 15, 1929—5 p. m.

379. Your 523, November 13, 7 p. m. Department approves the first sentence of your proposed statement but feels that the second sentence thereof should be omitted. Department prefers to avoid any suggestion which might lead to the conclusion that a Convention excepting the individual States would be more acceptable to this Government.

COTTON

---

511.1D1/58½

*Dr. Manley O. Hudson*[14] *to the Under Secretary of State (Cotton)*

CAMBRIDGE, November 19, 1929.

DEAR MR. COTTON: A few days ago our newspapers carried a report of a statement by Mr. Gordon at the Conference in Paris on the Treatment of Foreigners and Foreign Enterprises. Mr. Gordon

---

[13] Not printed.
[14] Director of Research in International Law at Harvard University.

was reported to have said that the Government of the United States could not enter into such a treaty as is proposed at Paris because some of the matters in the treaty had been reserved to the states by our Constitution. (*New York Times*, November 7, 1929, p. 8.)

For several years, representatives of the Government of the United States in international conferences have taken the view that our treaty-making power is very limited because of the federal nature of our Government. This was noticeably true in the drafting of Part XIII (Labor) of the Treaty of Versailles,[15] and at the Conference on Traffic in Arms in 1925.[16] The position taken seems to me so important for the future of this country, that I should like to bring it to your special attention. Surely since the decision in *Missouri* v. *Holland* (1920) 252 U. S. 416, the Migratory Bird Case, the doubts about the extent of our treaty-making power should be allayed. There may be excellent reasons why the United States should not participate in a particular treaty, or why the Department would not care to have the question debated in the Senate; but it does seem that our Government ought not to stultify itself by placing on our constitutional situation the most limited interpretation of the treaty-making power.

I very much hope that while you are in the Department something can be done to make current a different attitude toward the treaty-making power. Won't you have the matter in mind?

Faithfully yours,                                    MANLEY O. HUDSON

---

511.1D1/55 : Telegram

*The Secretary of State to the Chargé in France (Armour)*

WASHINGTON, November 20, 1929—6 p. m.

381. Your 515, November 7, 1 p. m. As a matter of policy the Department does not seek for its nationals in foreign countries commercial privileges any more favorable than those countries accord or may be willing to accord to nationals of other countries. Department would not therefore wish to comment unfavorably upon Article 18 point one since we claim no exclusive or preferential rights in Haiti or in any other country except perhaps Cuba, where by reciprocal treaty arrangement customs preferences are received. Department feels that you should explain to the Haitian delegate for his own information that in the light of the above, you regret that you are not in a position to express an opinion on the article in question.

STIMSON

---

[15] Malloy, *Treaties*, 1910–1923, vol. III, pp. 3329, 3503.
[16] *Foreign Relations*, 1925, vol. I, pp. 26 ff.

511.51D/58⅔

*Mr. P. T. Culbertson, of the Division of Western European Affairs, to the Under Secretary of State (Cotton)*

[WASHINGTON,] November 22, 1929.

MR. COTTON: The statement which Mr. Gordon made at the opening of the Convention on the Treatment of Foreigners at Paris was in part as follows:

"This study of the draft convention has made it apparent that the right which the Constitution of the United States of America reserves to the several states to enact laws upon various matters, covers many of the important subjects dealt with by the proposed convention. For instance, the rights of foreigners with respect to real estate within their territories is a question which, under our Constitution and the system of laws flowing therefrom, falls within the exercise of their legislative powers by the several states, and in consequence the right of foreigners to own lands and to succeed thereto by inheritance is prohibited in some of the states by statute, and in others by their constitution as well. Likewise, the several states are entitled to withhold and to grant freely or conditionally the privilege of engaging in business within their borders to corporations organized under the laws of another jurisdiction . . . ."

Mr. Hudson apparently feels that the Department has determined as a matter of fact that international agreements of this sort cannot be entered into by this Government because of the provisions of our Constitution. However, it has been the general policy of the Department to abstain as far as possible from concluding treaties with foreign governments, the provisions of which directly affect the legislative power of the several states. This policy, as I understand it, has been adopted not necessarily because we could not as a Government enter into this type of agreement but because it seems preferable to avoid unnecessarily committing the states in these matters.

P[AUL] T. C[ULBERTSON]

# CONTINUATION OF NEGOTIATIONS WITH CERTAIN EUROPEAN COUNTRIES FOR AGREEMENTS AND TREATIES REGARDING NATURALIZATION, DUAL NATIONALITY, AND MILITARY SERVICE [1]

## Belgium

711.554/2 : Telegram

*The Ambassador in Belgium (Gibson) to the Secretary of State*

BRUSSELS, January 18, 1929—1 p. m.
[Received 3 p. m.]

7. Department's instruction No. 167, December 1, 1928.[2] Foreign Office asks for information as soon as possible whether American laws contain any provision which would permit children born in the United States of a Belgian father, even if they continue to reside permanently in the United States, to renounce American nationality on arriving at a certain age and to retain only the nationality of the father.

It seems to me that by virtue of section 2 of the act [of] March 2, 1907,[3] an oath of allegiance to the Belgian Government would be sufficient to divest the child of American citizenship.

Please instruct.                                                GIBSON

711.554/3 : Telegram

*The Secretary of State to the Ambassador in Belgium (Gibson)*

WASHINGTON, January 19, 1929—6 p. m.

7. Your 7, January 18, 1 p. m. Persons born in the United States may expatriate themselves only by taking an oath of allegiance to a foreign state or by being naturalized in a foreign state in conformity with its laws. See Section two of the Act of March 2, 1907. There is no other method of renouncing American citizenship provided for by the laws of the United States.

KELLOGG

711.554/4

*The Chargé in Belgium (Reed) to the Secretary of State*

No. 393                          BRUSSELS, February 23, 1929.
[Received March 7.]

SIR: I have the honor to refer to the Embassy's telegram No. 7 of January 18, 1929, and the Department's telegram in reply thereto of January 19, 6 p. m., relative to an inquiry of the Belgian Foreign

---

[1] For previous correspondence, see *Foreign Relations*, 1928, vol. I, pp. 494 ff.
[2] *Ibid.*, p. 497.
[3] 34 Stat. 1228.

Office concerning the manner in which a child born in the United States of a Belgian father may divest himself of his American citizenship with a view to retaining only the father's nationality.

The import of the Department's telegram was conveyed to the Foreign Office by a note dated January 21, 1929, a copy of which is enclosed.[4]

The Embassy has now received a further communication on the subject from the Foreign Office, from which it appears that the latter is not satisfied with the information furnished it by the Embassy and that it desires a more precise explanation of the bearing of American legislation on the point in question.

I am enclosing a copy and translation of this note, dated February 22, 1929,[4] and I should appreciate it if I might have the Department's instruction regarding the reply which should be made thereto.

I have [etc.] EDWARD L. REED

---

711.554/5 : Telegram

*The Secretary of State to the Ambassador in Belgium (Gibson)*

WASHINGTON, March 28, 1929—8 p. m.

23. Your despatch No. 393, February 23. While there seems to be no judicial decision directly in point, it is believed that a citizen of the United States cannot expatriate himself while continuing to reside permanently in American territory.

KELLOGG

---

711.554/8

*The Chargé in Belgium (Reed) to the Secretary of State*

No. 433 BRUSSELS, April 29, 1929.
[Received May 11.]

SIR: I have the honor to transmit herewith a copy and English translation of a note from the Foreign Office dated April 27, 1929, which contains the Belgian Government's reply to the suggestions looking toward the conclusion of conventions respecting dual nationality and compulsory military service, which the Embassy made in compliance with the Department's instruction No. 167 of December 1, 1928.

It will be noted that the Belgian Government, for reasons set forth in this communication, is not convinced of the necessity for entering into agreements of the nature proposed by the Department, but is nevertheless entirely disposed to carry the discussions further, should the Department so desire.[5]

I have [etc.] EDWARD L. REED

---

[4] Not printed.
[5] Negotiations for the conclusion of a convention do not appear to have been continued.

[Enclosure—Translation]

*The Belgian Minister for Foreign Affairs* (*Hymans*) *to the American Chargé* (*Reed*)

BRUSSELS, April 27, 1929.

MR. CHARGÉ D'AFFAIRES: Referring to my letter of January 11, 1929,[6] and in response to the Embassy's notes Nos. 227 and 228 of December 27, 1928,[6] I have the honor to inform you that after a thorough study of the question, the Government of the King does not think there is reason to conclude the suggested agreements concerning dual nationality and the performance of military service.

The question of dual nationality which one of these conventions seeks to remedy, finds, in fact, a perfect solution, based on individual liberties, in Belgian nationality legislation now in force.

The fact must not be lost sight of that double nationality and, consequently, the conflict to be settled, occur only in the case of the birth to Belgian parents of a child in the United States of America. This child, Belgian *jure sanguinis*, is American *jure soli*. No conflict of this nature is to be looked for in the event of the birth on Belgian soil of the child of an American father. Such a child is not a Belgian by reason of his birth and, by virtue of his foreign nationality he is not called upon for military service in Belgium.

Furthermore, Article 18, Section I, Paragraph 2, of the law of May 15, 1922, concerning the acquisition and the loss of Belgian nationality, permits a Belgian who has lawfully acquired a foreign nationality (especially by reason of *jus soli*) to make this acquisition "voluntary", by signing, on reaching 16 years of age, a declaration renouncing Belgian nationality, which declaration may be received abroad by the Belgian diplomatic or consular agents. A Belgian minor who desires thus to renounce Belgian citizenship is not competent to make his declaration without the authorization of the persons whose consent would be necessary to validate his marriage.

It is true that according to the provisions of Article 16 of the law of August 4, 1926, concerning the acquisition, the recovery and the loss of nationality, a Belgian still liable to obligations of military service for the active army and reserve, who desires to sign a declaration of renunciation, must ask, before making his declaration, the Royal permission to renounce his Belgian nationality.

The duration of military obligations in the active army and the reserve is 15 years. The King's consent is also required when the renunciation of Belgian nationality is made at any date whatever between the 31st of December of the year in which the interested party has attained the age of 19 years and the time when he is incorporated in the territorial army.

---

[6] Not printed.

Incorporation in the territorial army occurs on December 15 of the year in which the militiamen reach their 15th year of service. The period of 15 years in the active army and the reserve begins on May 1st of the year by which the class to which the recruit definitely belongs is designated. The necessity of obtaining the Royal authorization in question cannot cause any great inconvenience for the persons interested. As a matter of fact it may be noted that it is customary not to refuse the authorization to those who are definitely established outside the Kingdom.

Furthermore, if a Belgian is not yet subjected to military service obligations, for the active army and the reserve, or if he is no longer subjected to them, he may sign a declaration of renunciation without the King's authorization.

A young man who desires to regularize his position with respect to Belgium without having to solicit the Royal authorization has only to renounce Belgian nationality between the time when he reaches 16 years and the 31st of December of the year during which he reaches 19 years of age.

A Belgian who has validly and properly renounced his nationality under the above conditions severs all ties with his former country, after signing the act of renunciation. There cannot thus be any question of imposing on such an ex-Belgian any military obligation or any act of allegiance whatsoever in the event of a visit or a temporary stay in Belgium. As has been stated, a Belgian born in the United States of America of Belgian parents may therefore elect, in the light of the Belgian law, a single nationality, i. e. that which he possesses by reason of his birth on foreign soil.

The initiative in taking a decision in the matter is left to him, and it should be noted that the conclusion of an agreement imposing on such a Belgian the renunciation of his Belgian nationality would do violence to one of the primary principles of Belgian legislation concerning nationality. The Belgian nationality law cannot seek to constrain a Belgian, who is American according to the principles of the *jus soli*, to renounce the nationality which he derives from his forebears.

A Belgian born in these circumstances, who really desires to possess only American nationality would not hesitate, in view of the many inconveniences resulting from dual nationality, to decide to renounce his Belgian citizenship.

Moreover, the Belgian consular representatives in the United States do not fail to bring to the notice of persons interested that they have the choice under Belgian law itself of retaining only American nationality.

The objection might, however, be reasonably made that a Belgian minor born in the United States of America and subject to Belgian military service laws, might be prevented from signing the declaration of renunciation because of the refusal of his parents to the exercise of this option. But even in this case, it is possible for such a person to avoid all difficulties if he wishes to make a temporary stay in Belgium. All he has to do is to regularize his position temporarily by demanding that he be inscribed for the Belgian militia and by requesting suspensions until such time as when, having attained the age of majority, he can execute the act of renunciation without the approval of his legal guardians and can thus definitely regularize his position.

Such persons, whoever they may be, who, wishing to assert only their American nationality, hesitate or refuse to make their choice or to solicit the suspensions with respect to military service, in spite of the facilities furnished them in this respect, can only blame themselves if any inconvenience results from their inaction.

For various reasons, the relevancy of which will not escape the American authorities, the Government of the King considers that it is not necessary to conclude the suggested agreements, at least in so far as concerns enabling a Belgian born of Belgian parents in the United States to renounce Belgian nationality.

It appears, however, a priori, that an agreement might be entered into in favor of a Belgian, born on American soil, who might wish, although residing in the United States of America, to retain only his Belgian nationality and to divest himself of his American nationality acquired *jure soli*.

If the American authorities are disposed to conclude a convention of this nature, the Government of the King would be obliged to the Embassy if it would be good enough to transmit to it the text of a draft agreement on this basis. One may, however, wonder whether such an agreement would have any real practical value. As a matter of fact, either the Belgian in question, American *jure soli*, would desire to continue to reside permanently in the United States, and in this case it is certain that his interests and his associations in the United States would constrain him to retain the nationality of the country where he is established and to renounce his Belgian nationality, which he has the option of doing, or he would return to Belgium and establish himself there after having discharged his military service obligations in the Kingdom, and in this case, according to our information, the American authorities would subsequently refuse to consider him any longer as an American.

I would be obliged to you, Mr. Chargé d' Affaires, if you would be good enough to bring the foregoing suggestions to the attention of the American Government. The Government of the King will not fail to welcome warmly any additional proposal regarding this question and to examine any objections which the Belgian point of view might encounter from the competent American authorities.

I beg [etc.]                                        HYMANS

---

**Bulgaria**

711.744/20

*The Chargé in Bulgaria (Kodding) to the Secretary of State*

No. 1337                                        SOFIA, October 19, 1928.
                                        [Received November 10.]

SIR: I have the honor to request instructions concerning the procedure to be followed in the application of the Naturalization Treaty between the United States and Bulgaria proclaimed on May 6, 1924.[7]

It may be noted that in the Department's Instruction No. 165 of March 25, 1926,[8] it was desired that a Bulgarian emigrant to the United States who subsequently became a naturalized American citizen be relieved of the necessity of paying Bulgarian taxes from the date of his emigration to the United States. In the Department's Instruction No. 176 of July 13, 1926 [8] it was desired, however, that the Bulgarian Government remit only such taxes as had been collected from an emigrant subsequent to the date of his naturalization as an American citizen.

It may be stated that in no single case has the Bulgarian Government been willing to release its former subjects from taxation from any date previous to their naturalization as American citizens.

A case involving the above interpretations of the Bulgarian-American Naturalization Treaty is now pending and I respectfully recommend that the Legation be authorized to adopt the latter policy providing no legal objection is perceived to it.

I have [etc.]                                        T. KODDING

---

711.744/20

*The Secretary of State to the Minister in Bulgaria (Schoenfeld)*

No. 278                                        WASHINGTON, January 9, 1929.

SIR: The Department has received despatch No. 1337 dated October 19, 1928, from your office requesting instructions as to the interpretation which should be placed on the Naturalization Treaty between the United States and Bulgaria in cases of claims of naturalized American citizens of Bulgarian origin for exemption from the payment of taxes for failure to perform military service to which

---

[7] Signed November 23, 1923; see *Foreign Relations*, 1923, vol. I, p. 464.
[8] Not printed.

they became liable after emigrating to the United States. The pertinent Treaty provision reads as follows:

"Article II . . . Nationals of either country who have or shall become naturalized in the territory of the other, as contemplated in Article I, shall not, upon returning to the country of former nationality, be punishable for the original act of emigration, or for failure, prior to naturalization, to respond to calls for military service not accruing until after bona fide residence was acquired in the territory of the country whose nationality was obtained by naturalization."

It appears that the aforementioned tax is in the nature of a penalty and there can be no doubt that any punishment inflicted on naturalized American citizens of Bulgarian origin for failure to respond to calls for military service after they have taken up a permanent residence in this country is a violation of the Treaty. The language of the Treaty is clear in this regard. Therefore in taking up cases of this character with the Bulgarian Government, your representations should conform to the Department's instruction of March 25, 1926, in reference to the assessment of taxes against Mr. Saro Atanasoff on account of his son, Christo Saroff. The statement in the last sentence of the Department's instruction of July 13, 1926, is not in accordance with the Treaty provision and is therefore in error and should be disregarded.

I am [etc.]

For the Secretary of State:
WILBUR J. CARR

---

711.744/21 : Telegram

*The Chargé in Bulgaria (Kodding) to the Secretary of State*

SOFIA, April 24, 1929—3 p. m.
[Received 3:25 p. m.]

7. Department's instruction No. 278, January 9th. The Bulgarian Government releases former Bulgarians from military fines from the date of their acquisition of residence in the United States, but does not release them from road repair and other personal taxes accrued previous to naturalization. Department's telegraphic instructions requested as to whether this meets treaty obligations.

KODDING

---

711.744/21 : Telegram

*The Secretary of State to the Chargé in Bulgaria (Kodding)*

WASHINGTON, May 4, 1929—4 p. m.

5. Your telegram No. 7 April 24. Taxes mentioned, having accrued prior to naturalization and not being in lieu of military service, do not violate treaty.

CLARK

[In despatch No. 1621, March 22, 1930, The Chargé in Bulgaria reported that the Bulgarian Foreign Office had assented to an arrangement whereby in the future the notes addressed to it by the American Legation requesting liberation of American citizens from Bulgarian personal taxes would set forth (1) the type of taxes demanded, (2) the date of emigration to the United States in the case of military taxation demands, and (3) the date of naturalization in other cases; also that the Foreign Office, for its part, would simply reply that the naturalized citizen in question had been removed from the list of Bulgarian taxpayers. (711.744/23)]

---

## Denmark

711.594/3

*The Minister in Denmark (Dodge) to the Secretary of State*

No. 866
COPENHAGEN, May 23, 1929.
[Received June 11.]

SIR: Referring to my Despatch No. 699 of December 29th [*28*] last,[9] relative to the conclusion with Denmark of a Convention covering cases of military obligations of persons of double nationality and a Convention for the termination of double nationality, I have the honor to enclose herewith a copy and translation of a note from the Foreign Minister, Dr. Munch,[9] in reply to my note of December 27th last,[9] mentioned in my Despatch referred to. It will be observed that Dr. Munch's note states that, after having been examined by the Foreign Office, my note has now been referred to the Ministry of the Interior and that as soon as the latter has announced its opinion, I will be informed of the Government's attitude. The note ends with the assurance that the Foreign Office "will be entirely disposed to use its influence with the competent authorities" with a view to obtaining the exemption from military service of persons making temporary visits to Denmark.

Since the date of my Despatch No. 699, above referred to, I have brought up the subject of these Conventions in the course of numerous conversations both with the late and present Foreign Ministers, Count Reventlow, Director General of the Foreign Office and Dr. Wadsted, Director of the Bureau of the Foreign Office immediately concerned. All three have emphasized their desire to conclude Conventions of the nature indicated but have declared that as the Danish nationality legislation was extremely complicated, their conclusion

---

[9] Not printed.

would require considerable study, not only by the Foreign Office but by the Ministries of the Interior and of Justice.

Regarding the Danish nationality legislation, my Despatch No. 733 of February 10th last [10] has reported upon this subject and from it it will be seen that there are three principal nationality laws now in force none of which are retroactive: the Law of 1776 applying the *Jus Soli* and making only Danes born in Denmark Danish subjects with some exceptions, like the children of Danish officials stationed abroad, etc.; the Law of March 19, 1898, which changed the former law and made all children of Danish subjects Danes, without regard to the place of their birth, and the Law of April 18th, 1925, a translation of which was enclosed in my Despatch No. 699, above referred to, and Article 6 of which provides that a Dane born abroad, who has never resided in Denmark, loses his Danish citizenship upon ending his 22nd year, unless he has obtained the right to retain it by Royal Decree.

Dr. Wadsted informs me that he believes that there are three years not covered by the Laws of 1776 and 1925 but that these years would have also to be considered. As the desired Conventions would require a change in legislation, they would have to be passed by the Rigsdag. In view of this expected delay, I enquired whether, as stated in your Instruction, pending the conclusion of a Convention, an informal agreement in accordance with the Joint Resolution of the Congress could not be arranged. Count Reventlow informed me that although he would be glad to make such a temporary and informal agreement, he feared that it would not be possible as it would touch upon a subject which was for the decision of the Rigsdag and might be embarrassing when eventually the proposal for a formal Convention was submitted to that body. I then suggested that if no temporary agreement could be made, as by a mere exchange of informal notes, the Foreign Office might be able to write me a letter stating that, pending the negotiation of a formal Convention, the Foreign Office would agree to use its influence with the competent departments of the Government so that American citizens, whom it might be claimed also possessed Danish nationality, might not be held liable to Danish military service. Count Reventlow appeared doubtful at first as to whether even this could properly be done. However the passage quoted above in the note enclosed shows that the Foreign Office have finally complied with this suggestion.

I should add that both Count Reventlow and Dr. Wadsted assured me that, even if the Foreign Office could not give me such a written statement, I might nevertheless rest assured that it would use its influence in every case I might bring before it. They then reminded

[10] Not printed.

me that up to now the Legation had never had any real difficulty in obtaining the release from military service of any American citizens who were also claimed as Danes. It is true, that, so far as I know, all such American citizens have eventually been relieved but occasionally after considerable annoyance to them. I may also state that during the last nine months, the Legation has only had one such military case brought to its attention.

Count Reventlow informs me that it is unlikely that the Ministries of the Interior and of Justice will announce their opinions regarding the conclusion of the desired Conventions before next Autumn. I shall however continue doing what I can to hasten their decisions.

I have [etc.]                                          H. PERCIVAL DODGE

---

711.594/4

*The Secretary of State to the Minister in Denmark (Dodge)*

No. 156                                    WASHINGTON, June 19, 1929.

SIR: The Department has received your despatch No. 866 of May 23, 1929, in reply to its instruction of December 1, 1928,[11] concerning the proposed treaty with Denmark in regard to military obligations in cases of persons who are born in either country of parents having the nationality of the other, and who have the nationalities of both countries under the laws thereof.

It is noted that this matter has been referred to the Ministry of the Interior, for consideration, and that meantime the Minister for Foreign Affairs has assured you in his note of May 22, 1929, that in cases of persons of the class mentioned who visit Denmark temporarily "the Ministry for Foreign Affairs will be entirely disposed to use its influence with competent authorities with a view to obtaining their exemption from military service." The Department is gratified by this assurance and commends you for your efforts in the matter.

It is to be hoped that the Danish Government will find it possible to enter into a formal agreement upon this subject, since such an agreement would tend to promote intercourse between the two countries. It does not seem reasonable that a person who was born in either country and has a permanent residence therein should be unable to visit the other for a temporary purpose without being arrested and detained for military service.

I am [etc.]                                          J. REUBEN CLARK, JR.

[11] See instruction No. 167, December 1, 1928, to the Ambassador in Belgium, *Foreign Relations*, 1928, vol. I, p. 497.

711.60M4/4

**Estonia, Latvia, and Lithuania**

*The Minister in Latvia (Coleman)* [12] *to the Secretary of State*

No. 6220                                                RIGA, June 18, 1929.
                                                    [Received July 1.]

SIR: I have the honor to refer to the Department's Instruction No. 632, of May 29, 1929,[13] inquiring in regard to the negotiations for a Treaty of Naturalization between Latvia, Estonia and Lithuania, respectively, and the United States, as forwarded in the Department's Instructions Nos. 582, 583, and 584, of December 1, 1928.[14]

In this connection, I have the honor to state that copies of these draft treaties were sent to the governments concerned under cover of identical Notes all dated January 7, 1929, these Notes embodying the contents of the Instructions transmitting these treaties to the Legation. The Latvian and Estonian Foreign Offices acknowledged the receipt of the Legation's Note on January 25 and 28, 1929,[13] respectively. No reply has as yet been received from the Lithuanian Government. On June 10, 1929, the Legation sent Notes, copies of which are enclosed herewith, to the Latvian and Estonian Governments,[13] requesting them to expedite the consideration of the matter. A similar Note is now being forwarded to the Lithuanian Government.

If replies are not received from any of these Governments within 2 weeks, the Legation will have the matter taken up orally, and the results will be promptly communicated to the Department.

I have [etc.]                                         F. W. B. COLEMAN

---

711.60i4/5

*The Minister in Estonia (Coleman) to the Secretary of State*

No. 6440                                            RIGA, September 26, 1929.
                                                    [Received October 11.]

SIR: Referring to the Department's Instruction No. 583 of December 1, 1928, calling the Legation's attention to the Joint Resolution of Congress, approved by the President on May 28, 1928, and instructing the Legation to bring this Resolution to the attention of the Estonian Government with a view to the conclusion of an appropriate convention between the United States and Estonia, I have the honor to transmit herewith copies of a note, dated September 23, 1929, from the Estonian Foreign Office, setting forth the views of the Estonian Government concerning this subject.

I have [etc.]                                         F. W. B. COLEMAN

---

[12] The Minister was accredited to Estonia, Latvia, and Lithuania, with residence at Riga.
[13] Not printed.
[14] *Foreign Relations*, 1928, vol. I, p. 500.

[Enclosure]

*The Estonian Assistant Minister for Foreign Affairs (Schmidt) to
the American Minister (Coleman)*

TALLINN, 23 September, 1929.

EXCELLENCY: With a Note dated January 9 [7], 1929, Your Excellency kindly transmitted through the Minister for Foreign Affairs for the consideration of the Estonian Government a draft Treaty of Naturalization between Estonia and the United States. In the same Note, in compliance with instructions from Your Excellency's Government, the desire was expressed that, pending the conclusion of the treaty, the Estonian Government would permit temporarily persons born in Estonia and naturalized in the United States, as well as persons born in the United States of Estonian parents, to visit Estonia without being required to perform military service or other acts of allegiance. In reply now I have the honour to bring the following to Your Excellency's notice.

The principles set forth in the draft treaty of naturalization are on some points in disagreement with the stipulations of the existing Estonian Law on Nationality. The second paragraph of Art. 1 of the draft treaty, for instance, provides that "nationals of Estonia who have been or shall be naturalized in territory of the United States shall be held by Estonia to have lost their nationality". According to Par. 20 of the Estonian Law on Nationality the loss of Estonian nationality is conditional on obtaining authorization from the Estonian Minister of the Interior. The application itself for authorization to renounce shall be accompanied by a certificate concerning foreign naturalization. Consequently Estonian nationals who have been naturalized in the United States and have not applied for and obtained authorization to renounce their original nationality are considered under Estonian law to be Estonian nationals, while according to the provisions of the draft treaty the fact itself of their naturalization in the United States would entail the loss of their original nationality.

Further, Art. IV of the draft treaty provides that "a person born in the territory of one party of parents who are nationals of the other party, and having the nationality of both parties under their laws, shall not, if he has his habitual residence, that is, the place of his general abode, in the territory of the state of his birth, be held liable for military service or any other act of allegiance during a temporary stay in the territory of the other party". According to Par. 2, p. 3, of the Estonian Law on Nationality, children born without the territory of Estonia of a father who is Estonian national are held to be Estonian nationals. At the same time Par. 6 of the same law expressly precludes the possibility of dual nationality by refusing to admit that a person who, under the existing law, is considered an Estonian national, can simultaneously have the nationality of another Power. The Estonian Law on Military Service, Par. 1, however, stipulates that all male nationals of Estonia are held liable for military service. They have, nevertheless, the possibility, under the provisions of Par. 7 of the same law, to renounce, with the consent of the Estonian Minister of War, their Estonian nationality before they have done their military service.

The Estonian Government, in sharing the desire of the Government of the United States to reach through an agreement the settlement of questions arising from dual nationality, attach, however, great importance to the fact that the rules to be applied in cases of dual nationality between different States were of uniform character. They think it, therefore, advisable to delay further negotiations on the conclusion of a Treaty of Naturalization until the international Convention on nationality now in elaboration under auspices of the League of Nations assumes definitive form. At the same time I have the regret to inform Your Excellency that the Estonian Government, in view of the stipulations of the Estonian Laws on Nationality and on Military Service referred above to, are not in a position to permit temporarily persons born in Estonia and naturalized in the United States, as well as persons born in the United States of Estonian parents, who have not applied for and obtained authorization to renounce their Estonian nationality, to visit Estonia without being required to perform military service or other acts of allegiance. In practice persons, who have presented an appropriate certificate required under Estonian law to prove their naturalization in a foreign country, have experienced no difficulty to renounce their Estonian nationality.

I avail myself [etc.]                                     SCHMIDT

---

[Further negotiations (1930–1935) with the Governments of Estonia and Latvia failed to effect the conclusion of the treaties desired. A treaty with Lithuania was signed October 18, 1937 (Department of State Treaty Series No. 936).]

---

## Finland

711.60d4/3

*The Minister in Finland (Pearson) to the Secretary of State*

No. 1191                            HELSINGFORS, February 15, 1929.
                                         [Received March 6.]

SIR: Referring to the Department's Instruction No. 99 dated December 1, 1928,[16] I have the honor to report that in a conversation Tuesday

---

[16] See instruction No. 583, December 1, 1928, to the Chargé in Estonia, *Foreign Relations*, 1928, vol. I, p. 500.

evening, February 12, with Mr. Winckelmann, head of the Bureau of Judicial Affairs in the Foreign Office, I was informed that he had already finished his study of the proposal for a Treaty of Naturalization between the United States and the Republic of Finland, and had submitted it to the Department of the Interior for examination. Mr. Winckelmann said, "I think I can promise you that we shall be ready to report by June 1st. I see no need of a temporary arrangement, as suggested in your note, for I believe that a treaty agreement, satisfactory to both Governments, can be reached during the Summer."

I have [etc.]                                           ALFRED J. PEARSON

---

France

711.514/9

*The Ambassador in France (Herrick) to the Secretary of State*

No. 9435                                    PARIS, March 19, 1929.
                                            [Received March 27.]

SIR: I have the honor to acknowledge the receipt of the Department's Instruction No. 2993 of December 1, 1928,[17] (File No. 711.514/), directing me as to the course of action which should be pursued by the Embassy with a view to giving effect to the provisions, so far as France is concerned, of the Joint Resolution of Congress approved on May 28, 1928, relative to the status of persons born in the United States of foreign parentage and of naturalized American citizens when visiting the country of parental affiliation or of origin. The Embassy is instructed to approach the French Government in an effort to reach an accord which would cover the points raised in the Joint Resolution and other problems of dual nationality, and to that end four categories of understandings are proposed.

I am requested first, to propose agreement upon an article reading as follows:

"A person born in the territory of one party of parents who are nationals of the other party, and having the nationality of both parties under their laws, shall not, if he has his habitual residence, that is, the place of his general abode, in the territory of the state of his birth, be held liable for military service or any other act of allegiance during a temporary stay in the territory of the other party."

As the Department was advised in the Embassy's despatches No. 7344 and 8030 respectively of April 8 and November 15, 1927,[18] nonreciprocal agreements, of a nature somewhat analogous to the above, were concluded with France by Peru on March 16, 1927,[19] and by

---

[17] *Foreign Relations*, 1928, vol. I, p. 499.
[18] Neither printed.
[19] Text printed in *Journal Officiel*, April 5, 1927, p. 3794.

Paraguay on August 30, 1927.[20]   The French text, and a translation thereof, of a similar agreement concluded by Argentina on January 26, 1927, is now enclosed.[21]   By the latter agreement the French Government agrees not to hold a person born in the Argentine liable to French peace time military service if he can produce a document from the Argentine Government to the effect that he has fulfilled his military obligations in that country.   As a partial corollary, persons born in the Argentine and who have fulfilled the French military requirements are excused from military service in Argentina.   The juridical status of the person concerned, as regards nationality, is specifically excepted from the scope of the agreement.

I have been orally assured by the Ministry for Foreign Affairs that such an arrangement as that made with Argentina may easily be effected between the United States and France.   The arrangement would procure the admission of all those rights envisaged in the cited proposal of the Department with the exception that the formality must be accomplished by producing a document certifying to the performance of military service, (or that such requirement does not exist), and that the agreement does not include in its provisions immunity from "any other act of allegiance".

However, I can see no useful purpose in entering into an accord of the type signed by the Argentine and other South American countries since all the rights to be obtained thereunder are now automatically accorded (without the parallel admission of the equivalent value of French military service) by Article 99 of the French Recruitment Law of March 31, 1928.   This article provides:

"By derogation from the dispositions of Articles 2 and 98 of the present law, young men who, by the circumstances of their birth abroad, are at the same time French and subjects of a foreign country other than the countries of Europe and the neighboring countries of the Mediterranean, are exempt from military service, in time of peace, if they prove, by the production of an official document, either that they have fulfilled the military law of the foreign country of which they are subjects, or that obligatory military service is not there instituted."

It will be readily seen that, by the terms of Article 99, a person born in the United States of French parents is not held liable for French military service if he presents a document to the effect that obligatory military service is not instituted in the United States.   This simple document the Embassy has been in the habit of issuing upon request and proof of citizenship.   So far as concerns the exemption by France from military service of persons born in the United States, it should be possible to reach an agreement going a step further than the Law

[20] *British and Foreign State Papers*, vol. CXXVII, p. 499.
[21] League of Nations Treaty Series No. 1457, vol. LXII, p. 85.

of March 31, 1928, by exempting such persons from the necessity of producing the certificate of service called for by Article 99. Such understanding would not, of course, cover the point of "any other act of allegiance" envisaged by the Department, but would have the advantage of not binding the United States to corresponding concessions. In this connection, it should be stated parenthetically that, since I am confident that when the French Government is approached in the matter, a definition of "any other act of allegiance" will be asked, I should be glad to receive an expression of precisely what sense the Department intends this phrase to convey.

The proposal of the Department, being reciprocal in its nature, would by implication admit the right of France to subject the children born in France of American parents to obligatory military service. Of course such a child, upon attaining legal age may repudiate French citizenship in the manner provided for in Article 9, paragraph 2, of the Law of August 10, 1927, and as further governed by Article 2 of that law, and so avoid military service. While it is obviously the obligation of such persons, upon reaching majority, themselves promptly to clarify their position as regards nationality, it is perhaps not superfluous to remark, against the event that a controversial situation should arise from the negotiation of a reciprocal agreement of the kind, that the number of individuals who would be affected thereby is a large and constantly increasing one. It may be, however, that the Department, in contemplating this step, has in mind paving the way for the termination of the dual nationality of those born and permanently living abroad when they shall have attained legal age.

As to the Department's second proposal that, if the French Government is willing to conclude a Naturalization Treaty, it might be desirable to include therein the suggested article concerning dual nationality, it should be stated that I have ascertained from officials at the Foreign Office to whom the matter has been tentatively broached, that the French viewpoint has not altered since the conversations on the subject carried on in the years 1925 and 1926. It will be recalled from the Embassy's despatch No. 6218 of April 1, 1926,[22] that a considerable number of points of difficulty would have to be overcome before such a treaty would be acceptable to the French Government. I therefore feel that, in view of the obstacles to the negotiation of a treaty of this character, it would be preferable not to attempt it for the moment, but rather, by provisional understandings on individual points of contention, to prepare the way step by step for the broader ultimate agreement.

Thirdly, I am instructed to endeavor to obtain an informal agreement which would protect from molestation during temporary so-

---

[22] *Foreign Relations*, 1926, vol. II, p. 108.

journs in France persons born in France but naturalized in the United States, and persons born in the United States of French parents. The latter classification of persons is already covered by the terms of the Department's first proposal. In view of the provisions of Article 99 of the Law of March 31, 1928, such an agreement as applied to them should be possible of arrangement and I shall only await clarification by the Department of whether the agreement should be reciprocal or unilateral and of the phrase "any other act of allegiance", to propose the matter to the French authorities.

As to the application of such an informal agreement to naturalized Americans of French origin, it must not be forgotten that in accord with Article 9, paragraph 1 of the Law of August 10, 1927, although a Frenchman naturalized abroad loses his French citizenship, nevertheless such loss of citizenship does not become effective until the expiration of a period of ten years counted from the date of his incorporation into the active army unless the repudiation of citizenship shall have been authorized by the French Government. On account of these legal limitations it would probably be difficult to induce the French authorities to give up this ten year period of control over naturalized Americans of French origin. Possibly the period of control might be reduced or eventually the French Government might be persuaded to abandon it on the ground that the United States is a non-European country (a distinction drawn in Article 99 of the Law of March 31, 1928). When presenting such project as the Department may decide to recommend, I shall be glad to inquire concerning the possibility of reaching a provisional accord relative to naturalized citizens, but am not sanguine with regard thereto.

Finally the Department instructs me to inquire relative to the attitude of the French Government concerning the termination of one nationality or the other, in cases of a dual nationality arising at birth, upon attainment of majority or some other prescribed age. This seems to me an important issue and one that should if possible be definitely determined. I am inclined to believe that if the Government of the United States were willing to accept the domicile of such person at the age of twenty-one to twenty-two as the governing factor—of course thus alienating the children born in France of American parents and still residing in this country at that time—the French authorities would consider the proposal sympathetically. I am doubtful, however, if in the face of the legal provisions of Article 9 of the Law of August 10, 1927, the right to opt could be denied the child of French parents born in the United States. I thoroughly agree with the Department that the confusion resultant from dual nationality, whether by birth or naturalization, should be done away with through understandings to be reached with the French Government. As previously stated, however, it would seem best to accomplish the reform step by step rather than, through attempting to effect an agreement of too broad a scope, to reach an impasse. When I shall have received the further instructions herewith requested of the Department, the Embassy will be in a position informally to discuss the matter with the Foreign Office and to determine upon what questions a definite agreement may reasonably be sought.

I have [etc.] MYRON T. HERRICK

---

711.514/9

*The Secretary of State to the Chargé in France (Armour)*

No. 4089 WASHINGTON, May 7, 1929.

SIR: The Department has received the Embassy's despatch No. 9435 of March 19, 1929, in reply to its instruction No. 2993 of December 1, 1928, concerning the proposed agreement between the Governments of the United States and France in regard to the status of naturalized citizens and persons born with dual nationality, and their liability for performance of military service and other acts of allegiance.

With reference to the meaning of the phrase "other act of allegiance" in the Department's instruction of December 1, 1928, attention is called to the fact that this phrase is taken from the Joint Resolution of Congress approved by the President May 28, 1928. It is the Department's understanding that this phrase relates to any act the performance of which is required by the Government of a country upon the ground that the person of whom it is required has the nationality of such country under its law.

As it appears from the despatch under acknowledgment that it is not practicable at the present time to conclude a formal treaty upon the subject in question, you are instructed to endeavor to obtain a unilateral agreement under which the French authorities, in the case of a person born in the United States of French parents and visiting France for a temporary purpose, will not require the certificate, mentioned in Article 99 of the French Recruitment Law of March 31, 1928, to the effect that the law of the United States does not provide for obligatory military service. It would seem that, if the Embassy should furnish the French Government with a general statement to this effect, there would be no practical necessity for each person concerned to submit a separate statement. Moreover, such general statement would seem to render unnecessary a reciprocal agreement on the part of this Government.

I am [etc.] For the Secretary of State:
J. REUBEN CLARK, JR.

711.514/10

*The Chargé in France (Armour) to the Secretary of State*

No. 10059                                    Paris, December 7, 1929.
                                             [Received December 20.]

Sir: I have the honor to refer to the Department's instruction No. 4089 of May 7, 1929 (file 711.514/9), requesting the Embassy to endeavor to obtain an agreement under which the French authorities will no longer require a certificate, stating that the law of the United States does not provide for obligatory military service, from persons born in the United States of French parents, since it would appear that a general statement to this effect by the Embassy should answer the purpose.

A note has now been received from the Ministry for Foreign Affairs under date of December 2, a copy and translation of which are enclosed herewith,[23] stating that the Ministry of War does not consider the proposed general statement adequate since the Presidents of the Councils of Revision might one day lose sight of the declaration and the persons concerned would then irregularly be considered as deserters. The Foreign Office has agreed, however, to modify the decree in question so that the certificate may in future be obtained from the French representatives in foreign countries. A copy of the modified text will be sent to the Department as soon as it is received.[24]

I have [etc.]                                    Norman Armour

---

**Great Britain**

711.414/4

*The Ambassador in Great Britain (Houghton) to the Secretary of State*

No. 3323                                    London, January 26, 1929.
                                           [Received February 8.]

Sir: I have the honor to refer to the Department's instruction No. 1622, December 1, 1928,[25] more especially the latter part dealing with the question of dual nationality, and in this connection to report that the Embassy has received an informal note from the Foreign Office stating:

"While the Government of the United Kingdom view with much sympathy the general idea of agreements concerning dual nationality, the subject is one which is shortly to come up for consideration

---

[23] Not printed.
[24] No further communication on this subject appears to have been received by the Department.
[25] See instruction No. 167, December 1, 1928, to the Ambassador in Belgium. *Foreign Relations*, 1928, vol. I, p. 497.

at the proposed Conference on the Codification of International Law at The Hague,[26] and they would prefer, so far as they are concerned, to defer consideration of the proposals contained in your letter until after that Conference has met. In the meantime the Governments of the Dominions are being informed of these proposals."

In discussing the Convention proposed by the Joint Resolution of Congress, referred to in the first paragraph of the Department's instruction No. 1622 of December 1, 1928, a member of the Embassy staff was given the personal opinion of a ranking officer in the Foreign Office that it was impossible for the British Government to conclude such a convention with the United States without a special Act of Parliament. Furthermore, it was stated that, in view of the fact that there was no compulsory military service in the United Kingdom, it would seem impolitic to introduce such legislation to Parliament. As an example, the hypothesis was given that should it come about that a British subject were to become a commissioned officer of the American Embassy it would be impossible to grant him, without a special Act of Parliament, diplomatic immunity, due to his British citizenship.

I have [etc.]

For the Ambassador:
RAY ATHERTON

---

**Greece**

711.684/17

*The Minister in Greece (Skinner) to the Secretary of State*

No. 751

ATHENS, December 17, 1928.
[Received January 4, 1929.]

SIR: I have the honor to refer to the Department's instruction No. 157 of May 2, 1928 (711.684/15)[27] calling to my attention a draft Naturalization Treaty communicated to my predecessor October 21, 1925, but not accepted by the Hellenic Government. As the Department is aware, it is because of the absence of any understanding respecting naturalization with the Hellenic Government that difficult questions are arising constantly. Since my arrival in Athens, I have taken advantage of every opportunity to point out the inconvenience of the present state of affairs, and to make it clear that the unwillingness of the Hellenic Government to come to an understanding on the subject had already reduced the amount of remittances from the Greek population of the United States to this country, and was discouraging an important passenger traffic which might be made a source of consider-

---

[26] The first Conference for the Codification of International Law was held at The Hague, March 13–April 12, 1930.
[27] *Foreign Relations*, 1928, vol. III, p. 29.

able revenue. Apparently, these substantial considerations have had more weight with the present Government than with those to which it has succeeded, as I have now received a counter draft from the Minister of Foreign Affairs with an accompanying letter of transmittal.[28]

It scarcely needs to be stated that the draft now submitted is unacceptable, but I am hopeful that it can be brought into line with American legislation, and I shall be glad to have instructions on the subject from the Department as promptly as possible, as I desire to take advantage of the present favorable frame of mind of the Minister of Foreign Affairs.

Article I of the Greek draft seems to be unobjectionable as far as it goes.

Article II contravenes the Constitution of the United States, which provides that all persons born or naturalized in the United States are citizens thereof. Under Article II of the draft treaty, minor children of former Greek nationals remain nationals of Greece "even though they are residents of the United States." Obviously, we cannot deprive children born in the United States of the privilege of citizenship guaranteed in the Constitution. As to minor children of former Greek nationals, born in Greece and actually residing in the United States, they become citizens of the United States by naturalization through the naturalization of their parents, the naturalization of such children being accomplished automatically; consequently they would seem to come under the provisions of Article I of the draft treaty: If this theory is correct, then under the draft American born children of Greek nationals would be in a less favorable position than Greek born children whose fathers become American citizens by naturalization.

Article III of the draft treaty relates to nationals of Greece who have been naturalized in the United States, and who thereafter return to Greece and remain in this country for more than two years. This Article is not very different from Article III in the Department's draft, except that it deals with minor children, also, and is open to the objection that minor children, of American birth, cannot be dispossessed of their rights because of a change of status involving their father.

Nothwithstanding the several objections to the draft which I have pointed out, it marks a distinct advance in the Greek position, the military authorities having receded somewhat from their hard and fast attitude. As already stated, I hope to receive the Department's definite instructions on this subject at an early date while the Minister is still in the mood to conclude an arrangement.

I have [etc.] ROBERT P. SKINNER

---

[28] Neither printed.

711.684/18

*The Minister in Greece (Skinner) to the Secretary of State*

No. 757                                    ATHENS, December 21, 1928.
                                           [Received January 14, 1929.]

SIR: I have the honor to refer to my despatch No. 751 dated December 17, 1928, bringing to the Department's attention the counter-draft of the Naturalization Treaty submitted to me by the Minister for Foreign Affairs. I have today had a further discussion with him, as a result of which I submit the following additional comments:

ARTICLE I.—It will be observed that under the Greek draft the American naturalization of former Greeks is recognized only in the case of those who have already acquired naturalization. The naturalization of Greeks subsequent to the going into effect of the contemplated treaty is covered by Article IV, and is conditioned upon their having complied with the internal laws of the country whose nationals they are. I have asked Mr. Carapanos to give me a minute specifying the nature of the present internal laws of Greece applicable to this subject, and have intimated to him that probably we could not undertake to make our naturalization conditional upon compliance with the internal laws of a foreign country. He, on his side, impressed me as unwilling to yield the point, explaining that, as Greek legislation recognized the right of Greeks to expatriate themselves, and set forth in what manner they might acquire another nationality with the consent of the Greek Government, it was only reasonable that they should satisfy those requirements before undertaking to obtain another nationality.

ARTICLE II.—This Article lays down the rule that minor children of former Greek nationals are not affected by the naturalization of their fathers. As to this, Mr. Carapanos remarks that the rules relating to dual nationality apply; that is to say, parents who divest themselves of their original nationality have no right to impose such acquired nationality upon their children, and children, as minors, have no power to elect a nationality until they attain their majority.

ARTICLE III.—Under this article, nationals of Greece who reside two years in Greek territory after having been naturalized in the United States are held to have renounced their American nationality. I pointed out to Mr. Carapanos that, under our legislation, the naturalized citizen who resides in the land of his birth upwards of two years is "presumed" to have expatriated himself, and have suggested that, as this is in our fixed legislation, we could hardly go further in a treaty. He is giving this suggestion consideration and will let me know how far he is prepared to go.

Neither in the Greek draft nor the Department's draft of some years ago, does anything appear which regulates the status of persons born in territory which is now Greek, before its annexation, who themselves never owed allegiance to the Greek Government, and who, after acquiring American naturalization, desire to return to what has now become Greek territory. Mr. Carapanos, personally, would like to help us in cases of this kind by a treaty provision, but does not see how it can be accomplished. There are, for example, thousands of persons born in what is at present Greek territory who, under the exchange of populations arrangements, have been compelled to emigrate to Bulgaria and Turkey, and many of them wish to return to the territory in which they were born. The Greek Government feels that it must guard against any arrangement by which such persons, following upon naturalization in the United States, might return to the territory which they have been obliged to leave. Thus far, I have been unable to think of a text which would cover these cases in a satisfactory way. I have pointed out, however, that the recognition of a fact, such as the naturalization of individuals, is one thing, and admission of such individuals to territory is another, the latter being subject to police regulation. It is the common practice of all nations to refuse admission to their country, of objectionable persons, and they cannot be required to state their reasons for doing so. It would seem as though something could be accomplished by an exchange of notes, outside of a treaty, under which, for example, the Greek Government might be willing to instruct Greek consuls in the United States to grant visas to our citizens born, prior to its annexation, in territory now Greek, the granting of the visas in these cases to carry with it a guarantee that the individual would not be molested after arrival.

I have [etc.] ROBERT P. SKINNER

868.111/42

*The Minister in Greece (Skinner) to the Secretary of State*

No. 841 ATHENS, March 1, 1929.
[Received March 27.]

SIR: I have the honor to report that, pending the conclusion of the naturalization treaty with the Hellenic Government, I have recommended that temporary measures be taken which would facilitate the arrival in this country of persons of Greek origin who, under the normal application of laws and regulations, might be held for military service or the payment of fines, and I have now received a note from the Ministry of Foreign Affairs covering this matter in satisfactory form, and in the following terms:

"In reply to the Note No. 204 a. p. addressed by the American Legation to the Ministry of Foreign Affairs, the latter has the honor to state that the Government of the Republic has decided to postpone all proceedings because of military obligations, as respects excursionists departing from the United States, of Hellenic origin, during the whole of their sojourn in Greece. The measures taken in favor of the said excursionists will be applicable from March 1st to October 1st, 1929."

It is understood from the competent officials at the Foreign Office that Greek Consuls in the United States have been instructed to issue to such excursionists a special certificate upon which his Greek visa will be placed.

I suggest that the above information be communicated to the press for the benefit of the public.

I have [etc.]                     Robert P. Skinner

---

711.684/18

*The Secretary of State to the Minister in Greece (Skinner)*

No. 274                               Washington, July 2, 1929.

Sir: The receipt is hereby acknowledged of despatches Nos. 751 and 757 of December 17 and December 21, 1928, concerning the proposed naturalization treaty with Greece, which was discussed with you recently when you visited the Department.

After careful consideration the Department has reached the conclusion that it will not be desirable to enter into a formal agreement with Greece whereunder the Greek Government would recognize the loss of Greek nationality in cases of Greeks naturalized in this country prior to the conclusion of the agreement but would not grant such recognition in cases of those who might be naturalized thereafter. This Government considers that the naturalization of a Greek in this country in good faith should be regarded as terminating his prior allegiance regardless of the date of the naturalization, and believes that an agreement such as that suggested by the Greek Government would not only be inconsistent with the view of this Government concerning the effect of naturalization but would set a precedent which would make it difficult to conclude satisfactory naturalization treaties with other countries.

The Department is also unable to agree to the proposals of the Greek Government to the effect that Greeks naturalized in the United States during minority, through the naturalization of their parents, are to be regarded as retaining their Greek nationality.

The naturalization laws of the United States have always contained provisions under which minor children are naturalized through the naturalization of their parents provided they are residing in the United States at the time of their parents' naturalization or take up their residence in this country thereafter and while they are are still minors. The Department holds that such derivative naturalization has the same effect as direct naturalization in terminating the prior allegiance.

If a person of the class mentioned remains in the United States there is no apparent reason why it is to the interest of Greece for him to retain his Greek nationality.   On the other hand, if after attaining his majority, he does not desire to have American nationality and if he returns to Greece it is apparently easy for him to recover Greek nationality under the provision of Article 26 of the Greek Civil Law No. 391 of October 29, 1856.   I may add that the Department has construed the naturalization treaties concluded between the United States and other foreign states as applicable to persons naturalized during minority through the naturalization of their parents as well as to those naturalized upon their own petitions, and a specific provision concerning this matter is found in Article 1 of the Naturalization Treaty signed November 23, 1923 between the United States and Bulgaria.[29] Such provisions are also found in various other draft treaties proposed by this Government to the governments of other countries.

This Government is unable to agree that the residence of a naturalized citizen in his native land for two years shall terminate the nationality acquired through naturalization, regardless of the cause of such residence.

This Government has no desire to make agreements under which its protection shall be extended indefinitely to persons of foreign origin who obtain naturalization in the United States merely in order to evade the performance of obligations to their countries of origin, and who, after obtaining naturalization, establish themselves in those countries.   This is shown not only by provisions in various naturalization treaties to which the United States is a party but also by the provisions of the second paragraph of Section 15 of the Naturalization Act of June 29, 1906[30] and the second paragraph of Section 2 of the Expatriation Act of March 2, 1907.[31]   On the other hand, it is the desire of this Government to make it possible for naturalized citizens to visit their countries of origin for legitimate objects, such as the promotion of commerce between the United States and those countries, the settlement of estates and other family business and the pursuit of studies of a specialized character which can not be pursued to such great advantage in the United States, and it is the principal object of naturalization treaties to make this possible.   An unqualified provision to the effect that residence of two years in the native land shall terminate the nationality acquired through naturalization, regardless of the cause of such residence, is believed to be too rigid and drastic.   The provision contained in Article 3 of the proposed treaty to the effect that resumption of residence of a permanent character in the native land shall terminate the naturalization status and the further provision in the

---

[29] *Foreign Relations*, 1923, vol. I, p. 464.
[30] 34 Stat.  596, 601.
[31] 34 Stat. 1228.

same article to the effect that a residence of two years in the native land shall raise a rebuttable presumption of permanence, which provisions are similar to those found in various naturalization treaties to which the United States is a party, would seem to be sufficient to meet the just demands of the country of origin. However, the Department will be glad to consider such further suggestions as the Greek Government may see fit to make with regard to this point.

The Department desires that you avail yourself of a suitable opportunity to renew the discussion of this subject with the Greek Foreign Minister. It is hoped that it will be possible to persuade the Greek Government that the conclusion of the proposed treaty will not cause any disadvantage to Greece, while on the other hand it would serve to prevent the recurrence of incidents which are embarrassing to both of the Governments concerned and which disturb normal intercourse between the two countries.

You may, in your discretion, call attention to the action of the Greek Government in waiving temporarily its laws concerning nationality and military service in favor of Americans of Greek origin visiting Greece in connection with the conventions of the American Hellenic Educational Progressive Association (your despatch No. 841, March 1, 1929), and suggest that, if it is possible to make waivers in these cases, it would also seem possible to make similar waivers in other cases of naturalized Americans of Greek origin desiring to visit Greece temporarily for legitimate purposes.

I am [etc.]

For the Secretary of State:
J. P. COTTON

---

868.111/45

*The Minister in Greece (Skinner) to the Secretary of State*

No. 1158

ATHENS, November 26, 1929.
[Received December 13.]

SIR: I have the honor to report that by an order of the Ministry of War dated October 31, 1929, no measures will be taken during the year 1930 against Greek citizens returning to this country from America or against American citizens of Greek origin returning to Greece, by reason of alleged military obligations.

The "amnesty" originally granted for the period March 1–October 1, 1929 (reported in the Legation's despatch No. 841 of March 1, 1929) was recently extended to cover the remainder of the present year, and according to official information now received, it has been further extended to December 31, 1930. An English translation of the pertinent order of the Ministry of War is enclosed.[32]

---

[32] Not printed.

It will be observed that apart from the privilege of returning to Greece without molestation during the period mentioned, military delinquents are offered certain facilities in the event they desire to adjust their military obligations and thus remove the delinquency for all time. It will be also noted that these facilities will terminate on the same date as the "amnesty" now granted—i. e. on December 31, 1930.

I shall in the meanwhile continue to keep the question of a naturalization treaty before the attention of the competent Hellenic authorities, in the hope that it may be possible to come to a definite understanding with respect to the vexatious matters of dual nationality and military obligations.

I have [etc.]
ROBERT P. SKINNER

_____

## Italy

711.654/40

*The Ambassador in Italy (Fletcher) to the Secretary of State*

No. 2167
ROME, March 1, 1929.
[Received March 14.]

SIR: I have the honor to refer to the Department's instruction No. 1102 of December 1st, last,[33] on the subject of the proposed naturalization convention between Italy and the United States and to the Embassy's despatch No. 2119 of January 31st,[34] regarding the military obligations of Italians who expatriate themselves or reside abroad.

As soon as possible after the receipt of the Department's instruction above mentioned Mr. Kirk opened conversations on the subject with Mr. Valentino, Chief of the American Section of the Foreign Office, and submitted to him:

1. A draft of a Naturalization Treaty which was based on a prepared treaty submitted by the Department of State in February, 1926,[34] and of which certain parts were redrafted in order to conform with the Department's above-mentioned instruction of December 1, 1928.

2. A draft of an informal agreement in the sense of the Article quoted on page 2 of the Department's instruction of December 1, 1928, regarding the liability for the performance of acts of allegiance on the part of persons possessing both American and Italian nationality while residing in the territory of either country.

3. A draft of an agreement for the termination of one nationality or the other in cases of dual nationality arising at birth, as outlined in the last paragraph on page 3 of the Department's instruction of December 1, 1928.

_____

[33] See instruction No. 2993, December 1, 1928, to the Ambassador in France, *Foreign Relations*, 1928, vol. I, p. 499.
[34] Not printed.

Mr. Valentino stated that all matters relating to nationality were extremely difficult of solution in Italy owing to opposition on the part of the military authorities, but that he would study the various questions submitted and inform the Embassy of the result.

Mr. Kirk has had several subsequent conversations with Mr. Valentino but no progress has been made.

On my first call on Undersecretary Grandi after my return to Italy, I brought up this subject and he also referred to the difficulties in the way of making the arrangements we desired, but promised to give the matter further consideration.

He informed me confidentially that he feared that if Italy agreed to our proposals with regard to the nationality of those born in the United States of Italian parents, they would be placed in an embarrassing position vis-à-vis France, as his Government did not wish to recognize this principle in the case of Italians born in France.

I am informed by my Brazilian and Argentine Colleagues that they also have had this subject before the Italian Foreign Office and are experiencing the same difficulties as ourselves.

The Brazilian Ambassador informs me that he has made an arrangement whereby the Italian Government agrees not to require military service of Italian-Brazilians (if one may use this term to denote the dual nationality) who produce a certificate from the Brazilian Embassy that they have performed their military service in Brazil.

The Argentine Ambassador informs me that he is unwilling to make an arrangement of this kind as it is inconsistent with Argentine law. He has also informed me in confidence that after a very flagrant instance where Italian officials insisted that one of his nationals of Italian name and Italian paternity should provide himself with an Italian passport before being allowed to embark, he (the Ambassador) instructed all Argentine Consular Officers in Italy to suspend the certification of shipping documents etc. for vessels destined to the Argentine. This had the effect he desired. An immediate storm was raised by the Shipping Companies. After a rather hectic interview with Undersecretary Grandi his nationals were allowed to depart and the consular embargo was raised. The Ambassador told me that he was very reluctant to have had recourse to strong measures but his representations and protests in support of Argentine nationals of Italian origin and parentage visiting Italy had proven unavailing.

He also suggested the idea that joint representations or action might be taken by the Governments of the United States of America, Brazil and the Argentine to secure the recognition by Italy and all other European Governments of the *Jus soli*. I suggested that he would probably wish first to have his Government's approval of such a course and in any event I felt sure my Government would wish to discuss any proposals looking to this end directly with his Government.

I report these facts to show that notwithstanding the opposition of the War Department and the special considerations involving France, a steady pressure is being brought to bear on the Italian Government to modify its attitude regarding those who are born in American countries (at least) of Italian parents and who claim and have received American nationality under the laws of the country of their residence.

There is of course one difficulty in this connection which should be borne in mind, and that is that very often Italian born Americans or Argentines or Brazilians returning to Italy endeavor to enjoy the advantages of both foreign and native citizenship, claiming to be Italians when that is to their advantage and foreigners when that seems best, especially when called to perform military service.

I shall keep this matter steadily before the Foreign Office but can not as yet predict with what success.

I have [etc.] HENRY P. FLETCHER

---

## Netherlands

711.564/6

*The Chargé in the Netherlands (Johnson) to the Secretary of State*

No. 2010 THE HAGUE, August 29, 1929.
[Received September 9.]

SIR: With reference to this Legation's despatches Nos. 1756, of January 3rd and 1763 of January 8th and to the Department's Instruction No. 649, of March 19, 1929,[35] concerning the proposed treaty between the United States and The Netherlands in regard to the status and military obligations of naturalized persons and persons born of dual nationality,[36] I have the honor to enclose herewith a copy and translation of a note from the Foreign Office dated August 19th.[37]

This note states that the Netherland Government is not yet in a position to give precisely its attitude with respect to the entire proposal but that the Government is disposed in principle to consider the question of a treaty along the lines desired particularly in so far as naturalized citizens are concerned.

The note points out that Dutch legislation and practice is in con-

---

[35] None printed.
[36] See instruction No. 583, December 1, 1928, to the Chargé in Estonia, *Foreign Relations*, 1928, vol. I, p. 500.
[37] Not printed.

formity with the provisions of the two first paragraphs of Article 1 of the draft treaty and that therefore the negotiation of a provisional agreement with regard to these points would appear to be unnecessary. In support of this contention it is stated that Article 6 of the militia law provides that an inhabitant of the Kingdom who is not Dutch will not be required for obligatory military service if he belongs to a country where a Dutch subject who is established therein is not subject to military service. (—This provision, however, would not seem to cover the question should at any time conscription exist in the United States—)

With regard to Article 2 of the draft the note states that the right of prosecution and punishment can only be set aside by a formal treaty.

With regard to Article 3 of the draft the note states that the Netherland Government can not without thorough examination agree to a proposal so little in harmony with Dutch law.

The note states that the Netherland Government must also reserve its opinion with regard to Article 4.

The note concludes that perhaps it would be advisable to await the results of the Conference for the Codification of International Law which will be held at The Hague in 1930 before attempting to reach a solution of the general problem of dual nationality.

It will be observed that the above-mentioned note is satisfactory only in part in that the Foreign Office agrees in principle to consider a treaty applying to naturalized persons but postpones for further consideration and discussion the question of the status of persons born in the United States of Netherland parents. Articles 1 and 2 of the draft treaty have not met with any objection on the part of the Dutch authorities. Article 3 is objected to because it is not in harmony with Dutch law but a further study and discussion of this question may bring about a solution. As regards Article 4 it would not seem that an agreement is impossible for as stated in the last sentence of the fifth paragraph of the note the Minister of Defense has the power "to accord exemption for special cases which makes it possible to exonerate even persons possessing a dual nationality". In actual practice the Minister of Defense almost invariably grants exemption to persons of dual nationality when the matter is brought to his attention by the Legation.

The attitude of the Foreign Office toward an informal agreement is quite clear. They consider it unnecessary as regards Article 1 and 2 of the draft and they are not prepared to negotiate such an agreement as regards Article 4. The Minister of Defense is apparently unable by an informal agreement to waive the provisions of the militia law granting him discretionary power to set aside the obligation of military service in cases of dual nationality. The adoption of our suggestions in this respect would require a revision of certain features of the militia law. The Foreign Office would not undertake such a revision for the purpose of negotiating an informal agreement but there is nothing in its note which would deny the possibility of a revision by means of a formal treaty which would give the necessary legislative sanction.

Therefore, although it may be possible to secure a provisional agreement as regards Articles 1 and 2 it may be preferable not to press this point but to concentrate upon the negotiation of a formal treaty to which plan the Foreign Office has raised no specific objection. The Legation would be glad to be instructed by the Department in the premises.

The Chief of the Treaty Section, Mr. Beucker Andreae, is now on his vacation but is expected to return in ten days at which time I will discuss the above-mentioned note with him in detail and report further to the Department.

I have [etc.] HALLETT JOHNSON

---

711.564/7

*The Secretary of State to the Chargé in the Netherlands (Johnson)*

No. 750 WASHINGTON, October 7, 1929.

SIR: The Department has received the Legation's despatch No. 2010 of August 29, 1929, in reply to its instruction of March 19, 1929,[38] concerning the proposed treaty in regard to nationality between the United States and the Netherlands. It appears that the Dutch Foreign Office is opposed to the provision of Article 3 of the Department's draft concerning the presumed renunciation of naturalization in the case of a naturalized citizen who resumes residence of a permanent character in his country of origin, but may be willing to consider the conclusion of the proposed treaty with the omission of this article.

While Article 3 seems reasonable and desirable, especially from the point of view of the country of which a person was a national before his naturalization, the Department is not inclined to insist upon its inclusion in the proposed treaty.

As to Article 1, the Department considers that it is desirable to retain it in the treaty even though the existing Netherland law provides that Netherland nationality is lost by naturalization abroad.

Article 2 seems desirable, from the point of view of the two Governments and of the individuals concerned, since it defines the limitation upon the right of either country to punish its former nationals who have acquired naturalization in the other on account of failure to respond to calls for military service.

---

[38] Not printed.

As to Article 4, it does not appear that it would be in any sense inconsistent with the present Netherland law authorizing the Minister of Defense "to accord exemption for special cases which makes it possible to exonerate even persons possessing a dual nationality". The provisions of this article would have the effect of relieving the Minister of Defense of the burden of granting special exemptions in cases of dual nationality covered by this article. It is believed that these provisions would tend to promote normal intercourse between the two countries by giving to the persons concerned some assurance that they would be able to visit the country of their parents' nationality without molestation.

The Department desires that this matter be again brought to the attention of the Netherland Government with a view to reaching a definite agreement.

I am [etc.]

For the Secretary of State:
J. P. COTTON

711.564/8

*The Chargé in the Netherlands (Johnson) to the Secretary of State*

No. 2094

THE HAGUE, October 22, 1929.
[Received November 2.]

SIR: I have the honor to acknowledge receipt of the Department's Instruction No. 750, of October 7th (File No. 711.564/7) concerning the proposed treaty between the United States and the Netherlands, in regard to the status and military obligations of naturalized persons and persons born with dual nationality. In accordance with the Department's instruction to bring this matter again to the attention of the Netherland Government with a view to reaching a definite agreement, I called today on Mr. Beucker-Andreae, the Chief of the Treaty Section of the Foreign Office, and presented him with a note, a copy of which is enclosed herewith.[39]

Mr. Beucker-Andreae stated that the Netherland Government has no objection to the incorporation into the treaty of the first two paragraphs of the draft, relating to naturalization, and that the Government has in principle no objection to the other paragraphs of this article. In commenting on paragraphs 4 and 5 he remarked, however, that there is no provision in Dutch law prohibiting loss of nationality in time of war and that it is a principle of law in Holland that the wife assumes the nationality of the husband.

As regards Article 2 of the draft, concerning punishment for failure to respond to calls for military service, Mr. Beucker-Andreae said that this article would have to be taken up further with the military authorities but that he did not anticipate that there would

[39] Not printed.

be much difficulty in securing agreement to it. He realized that this article is a logical corollary to article 1.

I find that article 3, relating to the renunciation of naturalization, is an obstacle in these negotiations as it is not in accord with the Dutch theories of naturalization. Mr. Beucker-Andreae stated that a prolonged study of the theories involved would be necessary before any decision could be arrived at and added that it was probable that the decision would be an unfavorable one. He said that while he personally considered the American point of view reasonable and that it had much in its favor, nevertheless it would not be easy to bring about the desired change in the point of view held here. In reply I intimated to him, in accordance with the second paragraph of the Department's above-mentioned instruction, that the Department might not be inclined to insist upon the inclusion of this article in the proposed treaty.

On the other hand I emphasized the Department's desire for the inclusion of article 4, which relates to the exemption from the liability to military service of persons possessing dual nationality. I said that this article was by no means an attempt to attain a partial solution of the general problem of dual nationality but was merely an agreement that persons having dual nationality would not be called upon for military service during a temporary sojourn in either of the two countries involved. I also pointed out that this article did not appear to be inconsistent with the principles of the present Dutch laws on the subject and would merely define a condition which now largely exists in practice. I emphasized the good that would come from such an agreement in the promotion of normal intercourse between the two countries.

Mr. Beucker-Andreae agreed personally with these observations and stated that he would at once take the matter up again with the Departments concerned. He believed that it would be possible to negotiate a treaty such as is desired by the Department, with the omission of article 3, and said that he hoped to be able to take up the matter again with me in the near future.

I have [etc.] HALLETT JOHNSON

---

711.574/6a supp.

**Norway**

*The Secretary of State to the Minister in Norway (Swenson)*

No. 462 WASHINGTON, May 29, 1929.

SIR: Referring to the Department's instruction No. 442, of December 1, 1928,[40] in regard to the desired negotiation of a treaty between

---

[40] See instruction No. 167, December 1, 1928, to the Ambassador in Belgium, *Foreign Relations*, 1928, vol. I, p. 497.

the United States and Norway providing that persons born in the United States of Norwegian parentage, and naturalized American citizens, shall not be held liable for military service or any other act of allegiance during a stay in the territory subject to the jurisdiction of the Norwegian Government while citizens of the United States of America under the laws thereof, to which instruction no answer appears to have been received, I have to request a reply thereto as soon as circumstances will permit.

I am [etc.]

For the Secretary of State:
W. R. Castle, Jr.

---

711.574/7

*The Minister in Norway (Swenson) to the Secretary of State*

No. 1453

Oslo, July 3, 1929.
[Received July 17.]

Sir: With reference to the Department's Instruction No. 462, of May 29, 1929, and previous correspondence in regard to the Department's negotiations of a treaty between the United States and Norway providing that persons born in the United States of Norwegian parentage and naturalized American citizens shall not be held liable for military service or any other act of allegiance during a stay in the territory subject to the jurisdiction of the Norwegian Government while citizens of the United States of America under the laws thereof, I have the honor to transmit herewith, for the Department's information, a copy of a note addressed to me by the Norwegian Foreign Office under date of the 29th ultimo, in reply to mine of January 4, 1929,[41] conveying the instructions of the Department's No. 442.

In perusing the note from the Foreign Office I received the impression that there has been a misapprehension as to the nature of the proposal submitted by the Department. The Department of Justice, which has had the matter under consideration for the past six months, appears to have rendered its opinion on the assumption that the draft agreement had reference to natives of Norway who have become naturalized American citizens.

I suspect that the confusion has arisen from a careless reading of the Joint Resolution of Congress, which contains the words, "providing that persons born in the United States of foreign parentage, and naturalized American citizens, shall not, etc.,". Inasmuch as I wanted a preliminary report on this subject to go forward by the first pouch I called up the Chief of Bureau in the Department of Justice who had handled this case and invited his attention to the text of the draft submitted by the Department of State, which obviously contemplates an

---

[41] Neither printed.

agreement affecting persons born in the territory of one party of parents who are nationals of the other party, and having the nationality of both parties under the laws, I also pointed out the paragraph in the Department's instruction stating that in view of the provisions of the existing naturalization Treaty between the United States and Norway it is unnecessary to enter into a new agreement concerning natives of either country who, after having acquired naturalization in the other, desire to visit their native land.

The Bureau Chief admitted that there seemed to have been some misunderstanding on the part of his office. I shall take the earliest opportunity to discuss the situation with the Foreign Office with a view to a renewed consideration of the subject.

I take it, however, that the Government will adhere to its present attitude with respect to an agreement regarding the termination of dual nationality.

As regards the status of persons born in the United States of parents who are nationals of Norway I may state that under the present citizenship law, which went into effect January 1, 1925, they lose their Norwegian citizenship when they reach the age of 22 years provided they have not resided in Norway.

Persons born abroad and never having lived in Norway who had reached their 22nd year on January 1, 1925, lost their Norwegian citizenship January 1, 1928, or three years after the new citizenship law went into effect.

I have [etc.]                                          LAURITS S. SWENSON

711.574/9

*The Minister in Norway (Swenson) to the Secretary of State*

No. 1526                                        OSLO, October 19, 1929.
                                            [Received November 6.]

SIR: I have the honor to refer to my despatch No. 1453, of July 3, 1929, in regard to the proposed negotiations of a treaty between the United States and Norway providing that persons born in the United States of Norwegian parentage, and naturalized American citizens, shall not be held liable for military service or any other act of allegiance during a stay in the territory subject to the jurisdiction of the Norwegian Government while citizens of the United States of America under the laws thereof and to report that the Legation is now in receipt of a note from the Foreign Office, dated the 9th instant,[42] in which the Norwegian Government expresses the opinion that there would seem to be no need for a new treaty provision regarding exemption from military service in Norway of per-

---

[42] Not printed.

sons who visit Norway temporarily. It is pointed out that such cases are likely to be so rare that they will be of little significance and that in case a man who has acquired both Norwegian and American nationality through birth and who has his permanent residence in the United States should visit Norway temporarily he will always have the opportunity of submitting the matter of his military service to the appropriate conscription authorities and that it may be confidently assumed that the matter will be decided with due regard to his American citizenship so that he will not be required to perform military duty in Norway during the period when, pursuant to the Convention of 1871,[43] he is exempt therefrom, provided that all the circumstances governing the case point to his American citizenship.

The Department will observe that in my despatch of July 3, 1929, I stated that owing to an evident misapprehension of the Department of Justice as to the nature of the proposal submitted in my note of January 4, 1929, I would take the earliest opportunity to discuss the situation with the Foreign Office with a view to a renewed consideration of the subject.

I transmit herewith a copy of a note which I addressed to the Foreign Office under date of July 9, 1929,[44] requesting that in the circumstances referred to the matter be given renewed consideration. The note from the Foreign Office, dated the 9th instant, of which a copy with translation is enclosed, is a reply to my communication.

I have [etc.] LAURITS S. SWENSON

---

711.574/9

*The Secretary of State to the Minister in Norway (Swenson)*

No. 495 WASHINGTON, December 13, 1929.

SIR: The Department has received your despatch No. 1526 of October 19, 1929, in which you refer to your despatch No. 1453 of July 3, 1929, and previous correspondence concerning the proposal of this Government looking to the conclusion of a treaty with Norway under which persons born in either country of parents having the nationality of the other, and continuing to reside in the country of birth, may visit the country of their parents' nationality temporarily without being held for the performance of military or other national services.

Accompanying your despatch is a note of October 9 from the Norwegian Foreign Office to the effect that a formal treaty upon this subject is unnecessary. The reasons given for this view are as follows:

"Such cases will continue to be so rare as to be of little or no significance. However, should a man who has acquired both Norwegian

---

[43] Naturalization convention concluded May 26, 1869; ratifications were exchanged on June 14, 1871; Malloy, *Treaties*, 1776–1909, vol. II, p. 1758.
[44] Not printed.

and American nationality through birth and who has his permanent residence in the United States visit Norway temporarily he will always have the opportunity of submitting the matter of his military service in Norway to the highest conscription authorities, in which case it may confidently be assumed that the decision will be made with due regard to his American citizenship, so that he will not be required to perform military duty in Norway during the period when, pursuant to the Convention of 1871 he is exempt therefrom provided that all the circumstances governing the case point to his American citizenship."

The Department infers that the treaty provision to which reference is made is Article 3 of the protocol to the naturalization convention between the United States and Sweden and Norway, which was signed at Stockholm May 26, 1869, which article reads as follows:

"III.   Relating to the 3d article of the convention.
"It is further agreed that if a Swede or Norwegian, who has become a naturalized citizen of the United States, renews his residence in Sweden or Norway without the intent to return to America, he shall be held by the government of the United States to have renounced his American citizenship.
"The intent not to return to America may be held to exist when the person so naturalized resides more than two years in Sweden or Norway."

You are requested to endeavor to obtain a definite assurance from the Norwegian Government in regard to the point last mentioned. In taking the matter up with the Foreign Office you may say that this Government would still be glad to enter into a formal treaty governing cases of the kind mentioned which would state definitely the conditions upon which persons born in the United States of Norwegian parents would be able to visit Norway temporarily without being detained for the performance of military or national services.[45]

I am [etc.]                              For the Secretary of State:
                                         WILLIAM R. CASTLE, JR.

---

711.60C4/11                              **Poland**

*The Chargé in Poland (Benton) to the Secretary of State*

No. 2594                              WARSAW, September 3, 1929.
                                         [Received September 17.]

SIR: I have the honor to refer to the Department's Instructions Nos. 873 and 1026 of December 1, 1928 [46] and May 13, 1929,[47] respectively,

---

[45] A treaty between the United States and Norway regarding military service was signed at Oslo, November 1, 1930; Department of State Treaty Series No. 832.
[46] See instruction No. 2993, December 1, 1928, to the Ambassador in France, *Foreign Relations*, 1928, vol. I, p. 499.
[47] Not printed.

and to my despatch No. 2180 of February 25, 1929,[48] relative to negotiations between this Legation and the Polish Government for the conclusion of a Treaty of Naturalization.

Prior to his departure from Warsaw, Mr. Stetson [49] engaged in various conversations with the then Acting Minister for Foreign Affairs, Mr. Juljusz Łukasiewicz, and with General Piskor, Chief of the General Staff, relative to the proposed agreement. At the time, Mr. Stetson pointed out, as I did in my Note 1309 of January 8, 1929 [48] (copy of which was enclosed with my despatch referred to above), as well as in the conversations which I had with Polish officials, that we desired two things—namely, (1) an expression of their views with regard to the Treaty itself, and (2), pending the definite conclusion of the Treaty, an informal agreement which would make it possible for persons born in the United States of Polish parents, as well as those naturalized in the United States, to visit temporarily in Poland without fear of being punished for the failure to perform military service.

With regard to the Treaty itself, I beg to transmit herewith copy of an informal note, dated August 14, 1929, from Mr. Łukasiewicz to Mr. Stetson [48] with which the former encloses what he describes as an "unbinding draft" of the proposed treaty. An English translation of the draft is also attached. Mr. Łukasiewicz's "unbinding draft" should not be considered as a draft treaty, but merely as an expression of the point of view of the Polish Government to form a basis for discussion.

With regard to the informal agreement which the Department is anxious shall be reached with the Polish Government as soon as possible, I beg to state that from conversations between Mr. Stetson and Mr. Łukasiewicz it would appear that the Polish Government is now prepared to effect such an agreement by an exchange of notes. Before he left Warsaw Mr. Stetson drafted a note which I now have every reason to believe that the Polish Government will accept as a basis of exchange. The Department will note that while the Polish Government is willing to agree that persons born in the United States of Polish parents, as well as those naturalized there, may visit in Poland temporarily without fear of being punished, they insist that an exception be made of those Poles who leave Poland subsequent to having received a call to military service without, of course, first securing permission from the Ministry of War.

For the information of the Department, I enclose a draft copy of the note [48] which, if agreeable to the Department, I propose to forward to the Polish Foreign Office in return for a similarly worded note from them. While there may of course be a few minor changes in phrase-

[48] Not printed.
[49] John B. Stetson, Jr., Minister in Poland, 1925–1930.

GENERAL 477

ology so as to conform to Polish views, I believe the draft as submitted
will meet the approval of the Polish Foreign Office and that an informal agreement on that basis can be speedily reached. I should
appreciate the Department's approval by telegraph of my proposed
action.

I have [etc.] J. WEBB BENTON

## Portugal

711.534/3a

*The Secretary of State to the Minister in Portugal (Dearing)*

No. 1029 WASHINGTON, June 27, 1929.

SIR: The Department has in recent years received many complaints
from naturalized American citizens of Portuguese origin against their
being required to perform military service in Portugal or against the
payment of a military tax by such persons or their relatives for failure
to comply with the military laws of Portugal. From time to time it
has communicated with you and the American consular officers in the
Azores concerning the matter, but its efforts in behalf of these persons
have, with few exceptions, been unsuccessful. At the suggestion of
your office, consular officers in the Azores were instructed to take up
with the local Portuguese officials each case of a naturalized American
citizen of Portuguese origin who had been impressed or was about to
be impressed into the Portuguese Army or against whom a tax was being assessed for failure to perform military service. The procedure
suggested by you, however, proved to be unsuccessful except in a few
isolated cases. With respect to naturalized American citizens of Portuguese origin who were residing in the United States and against
whom a military tax was being assessed, the American Consul at St.
Michael's Azores in a despatch of May 4, 1928,[50] stated that the proper
procedure for such a person to follow would be to make an affidavit before a Portuguese Consul in the United States setting forth the basis
for his claim to American citizenship, the exact period of his residence
within the United States and the period of his service, if any, in the
army of this country during the World War, and have this affidavit
witnessed before the Portuguese Consul by two persons having knowledge of the facts, after which the affidavit and a translation of the
naturalization certificate of the person concerned should be forwarded
by the Portuguese Consul directly to the Ministry for Foreign Affairs
at Lisbon for legalization of the seal and signature of the Portuguese
consular officer and submitted by the Ministry for Foreign Affairs to

[50] Not printed.

the Civil Governor at Angra, Terceira, Azores, for reference to the High Military Authorities there. This procedure has been suggested to a number of naturalized American citizens of Portuguese origin and in almost every case the Department has subsequently been advised that when the naturalized citizen concerned consulted a Portuguese consular officer in the United States he was advised that the Portuguese consular officer knew nothing of this procedure and was of no assistance to the naturalized citizen.

The Department is being requested with considerable frequency to take some action in behalf of these persons. It is, of course, desirous of being of as much assistance as possible to them and with that end in view, it suggests that you take up with the Ministry for Foreign Affairs at Lisbon the matter of obtaining a precise statement of the Portuguese law under which naturalized American citizens of Portuguese origin are forced into the military service of Portugal or are taxed for failure to perform such service. If the law provides for the exemption of such a person from compulsory military service or from the payment of a tax in lieu of service in the Portuguese Army, it is suggested that you obtain a precise statement as to the kind of evidence required under such law.

In connection with this matter you should not fail to call the attention of the Ministry for Foreign Affairs to the provisions of Article I of the Naturalization Treaty between the United States and Portugal, signed May 7, 1908,[53] which, for your convenience, is quoted:

"Subjects of Portugal who become naturalized citizens of the United States of America and shall have resided uninterruptedly within the United States five years shall be held by Portugal to be American citizens and shall be treated as such. Reciprocally, citizens of the United States of America who become naturalized subjects of Portugal and shall have resided uninterruptedly within Portuguese territory five years shall be held by the United States to be Portuguese subjects and shall be treated as such."

You will observe from this provision of the Treaty that Portugal agreed to recognize the naturalization of Portuguese nationals in the United States if they resided uninterruptedly in this country for a period of five years. As certificates of naturalization issued prior to two or three years ago set forth the fact that the person naturalized as a citizen of the United States had resided in this country for a period of five years, it would seem that in most cases the certificate itself should be sufficient under the provisions of the Treaty of Naturalization between the United States and Portugal to warrant the exemption of the bearer from the performance of military service or from being taxed for failure to perform such service. In the case

[53] *Foreign Relations,* 1908, p. 700.

where a certificate of naturalization does not set forth the fact that the person naturalized resided in the United States for a period of five years the Portuguese authorities would, nevertheless, seem to be warranted in accepting the certificate as evidence that the holder comes within the scope of the provision of the Treaty quoted above, since, with few exceptions, an alien desiring to become naturalized as an American citizen must submit proof that he comes within the scope of the fourth subdivision of Section 4 of the Naturalization Act of June 29, 1906,[54] or Section 6 (b) of the Act of March 2, 1929,[55] which provides that, before an alien can become naturalized, he must have resided in the United States continuously for a period of at least five years immediately preceding his naturalization. The exception to the rule that an alien must submit proof that he has resided in the United States for a period of at least five years immediately preceding his naturalization, relates principally to aliens who served in the military or naval forces of the United States during the World War. This class of persons are merely not required to submit proof of their having resided in the United States for a period of five years continuously immediately preceding their naturalization. In the case of persons who, while minors, were naturalized through the naturalization of their parents as citizens of the United States, there is no requirement in the naturalization laws of this country that they must have resided in the United States for a particular period. The law merely requires that the minor reside in the United States at the time of the parent's naturalization or that he come to the United States to reside subsequent to the naturalization of the parent and prior to attaining the age of twenty-one years. It would seem reasonable for the Portuguese Government to accept in this type of case a document of nationality issued by this Government, such as a passport, the naturalization certificate of the parent, a certificate of registration or a special certificate of citizenship, accompanied, when necessary, by an affidavit or other evidence that the person concerned had resided in the United States for a period of five years.

In view of the large number of cases which have been called to the attention of the Department, you are directed to take up this matter with the Portuguese Ministry for Foreign Affairs as soon as possible and endeavor to have some simple and definite procedure adopted by the Portuguese authorities which would carry out the provisions of the Treaty above quoted.

I am [etc.]

For the Secretary of State:
WILBUR J. CARR

---

[54] 34 Stat. 596, 598.
[55] 45 Stat. 1512, 1513.

711.534/4 : Telegram

*The Minister in Portugal (Dearing) to the Secretary of State*

LISBON, July 22, 1929—11 a. m.
[Received 11:45 a. m.]

22. Department's instruction 958, December 1, 1928; [56] and 1029 June 27, 1929, military service in Portugal of naturalized citizens of the United States.

May Legation consider these instructions as dealing with two phases of same situation and seek a permanent solution for both in the treaty desired by our Government? If so, please draw and forward for use in negotiations draft text adequately covering all points.

DEARING

———

711.534/4

*The Secretary of State to the Chargé in Portugal (Magruder)*

No. 1049                                    WASHINGTON, August 22, 1929.

SIR: The Department has received your telegram of July 22, 1929, in reply to its instruction of June 27, 1929, in regard to the action of the Portuguese Government in compelling naturalized American citizens of Portuguese origin to perform military service in Portugal or to pay a tax in lieu of such service.

The Department has given attentive consideration to your suggestion that the Legation regard its instruction of June 27, 1929 and its instruction of December 1, 1928 concerning the cases of persons born in the United States of Portuguese parents as presenting two phases of the same situation and that an effort be made to solve both problems in a single treaty.

As you know, there is now in effect a treaty between the United States and Portugal governing the status of naturalized citizens, which resembles in the main treaties which have been concluded between the United States and various countries. It does not appear that any difficulty has arisen out of the provisions of the present treaty or that the two Governments have differed with regard to its meaning. The difficulties which have arisen and which have been the subject of protests by various naturalized citizens of the United States appear to have arisen, principally if not entirely, from the failure of Portuguese officials to observe the treaty and to apply its provisions. Many protests have been received in recent years because of the action of Portuguese officials in conscripting naturalized American citizens of Portuguese origin or in taxing them or members of their families in total disregard of the provisions of the treaty under which they were

———

[56] See instruction No. 167, December 1, 1928, to the Ambassador in Belgium, *Foreign Relations*, 1928, vol. I, p. 497.

required to recognize the naturalization of Portuguese in the United States as terminating their Portuguese nationality. In some of the cases mentioned the persons of whom military service or military taxes were required may have obtained naturalization in the United States during their minority, through the naturalization of their parents.

The Department considers that the provision of Article 1 of the treaty that "subjects of Portugal who become naturalized citizens of the United States of America and shall have resided uninterruptedly within the United States five years shall be held by Portugal to be American citizens and shall be treated as such", is applicable to persons naturalized during their minority through the naturalization of their parents as well as to persons naturalized upon their own petitions. It does not appear that the Portuguese Government has adopted a different construction of this treaty provision in cases of the kind mentioned and it is not believed that there are any reasonable grounds upon which it could do so.

While the Department will be glad to consider any further recommendations which you may make in this matter, it is not convinced at present that it is necessary or desirable to endeavor to conclude a new treaty which would not only be applicable to persons born in either country of parents having the nationality of the other but would cover also cases of naturalized citizens and thus take the place of the treaty of 1908 concerning the latter. It is suggested that you avail yourself of a suitable opportunity to discuss this whole question again with the Portuguese Foreign Minister with reference to particular cases in which naturalized citizens of the United States appear to have been conscripted or compelled to pay military service taxes in violation of the present naturalization treaty, and that you endeavor to ascertain as definitely as possible the grounds upon which the Portuguese officials seek to justify their action. If any differences of opinion concerning the meaning of the treaty become apparent from such discussion, it may be possible to clear them up. Meantime, the drafting of a new convention will be held in abeyance, pending a final decision as to its scope.

I am [etc.]                          For the Secretary of State:
                                          WILBUR J. CARR

---

711.534/6

*The Chargé in Portugal (Magruder) to the Secretary of State*

No. 2823                          LISBON, September 23, 1929.
                                          [Received October 5.]

SIR: I have the honor to acknowledge the receipt of the Department's instruction No. 1049 of August 22, 1929, regarding the action taken by Portuguese officials in compelling naturalized American citizens of Portuguese origin to perform military service in Portugal or to pay a tax in lieu of such service.

In view of the Department's suggestion that the Legation avail itself of a suitable opportunity to discuss this whole question again with the Portuguese Minister for Foreign Affairs, I have the honor to report that on September 21, 1929, having had occasion to call on the Minister for Foreign Affairs in order to take up another matter, I deemed it advisable to lose no time in drawing the new Minister's attention to this long pending question. In consequence, I went into the matter briefly, citing as a statement of the position of the United States the Legation's note No. 942 of July 31, 1929, a copy of which accompanied the Legation's despatch No. 2767 of August 2, 1929.[57] His Excellency assured me that he would lose no time in looking into the question, but made no pretense of being in a position to enter into a discussion thereof at the time, being frank enough to say that, having been at his desk but four days, he knew little or nothing about anything bearing on the work of the portfolio he had taken up so recently. Captain da Fonseca Monteiro was most sympathetic, however, in his general attitude and assured me of his earnest desire to cooperate in this matter, as well as in all others which the Legation might bring to his attention. The ground having been prepared in this matter, it is possible that particular cases in which naturalized citizens of the United States appear to have been conscripted or compelled to pay military service taxes in violation of the present naturalization treaty may profitably be taken up for discussion in the near future.

I have [etc.]                                              ALEXANDER R. MAGRUDER

---

### Rumania

711.714/3

*The Minister in Rumania (Wilson) to the Secretary of State*

No. 178                                        BUCHAREST, April 24, 1929.
[Received May 13.]

SIR: Referring to the Department's Instruction No. 11 of December 1, 1928,[58] and to the Legation's Despatch No. 88 of January 24, 1929,[59] in regard to a proposed Naturalization Treaty between the United States and Rumania, I have the honor to report that Mr. Djuvara of the Foreign Office came to see me this morning, and on the part of the

---

[57] Neither printed; the Legation's note No. 942 to the Portuguese Foreign Office followed closely the relevant portions of the Department's instruction No. 1029, p. 477.
[58] See instruction No. 583, December 1, 1928, to the Chargé in Estonia, *Foreign Relations*, 1928, vol. I, p. 500.
[59] Not printed.

Minister for Foreign Affairs, to explain to me the position of the Rumanian Government on this question.

The draft of the treaty prepared by the Department, Mr. Djuvara said, had been carefully studied by the Legal Council of the Ministry of Foreign Affairs, which had given a decision to the effect that certain provisions of the proposed Treaty, especially Articles II and IV, were in conflict with the existing laws of Rumania and therefore make the negotiation of such a treaty impossible at the present time.

Furthermore, Mr. Djuvara said that the question of dual nationality was in the near future to be discussed at the League of Nations, where some common accord on this troublesome problem would probably be reached, and in that case Rumania would doubtless change her laws so as to conform with any such agreement. He therefore asked me to say to my Government that the inability of the Rumanian Government to negotiate a Naturalization Treaty with the United States at this time should not be taken as a definite refusal or an unwillingness on its part to do so, but rather that the matter should be considered, for the present at least, as "in suspense," and in any case, until the discussion and settlement of the dual nationality question by the League of Nations.

I have [etc.]                                            CHARLES S. WILSON

---

### Spain

711.524/6

*The Chargé in Spain (Whitehouse) to the Secretary of State*

No. 1398                                    MADRID, November 5, 1929.
                                            [Received November 18.]

SIR: Referring to your instruction No. 491 of December 1, 1928,[60] I have the honor to transmit herewith a copy and translation of a Note — No. 171 of September 12, 1929, from the Spanish Government[61] submitting a new draft of an agreement regarding military service as a substitute for our draft.

In explanation of the delay in forwarding this Note and enclosure, I should say that it seemed to me there was obviously an error in the text as written, for it did not appear to me to make sense. I, therefore, awaited an occasion to confer personally with the official, who had charge of these matters, and saw him last week upon his return from leave.

There is no error, and the Department may think I was stupid in not understanding the text, but I still find the unilateral form in which it is written confusing, and think it requires explanation.

[60] See instruction No. 2993, December 1, 1928, to the Ambassador in France. *Foreign Relations*, 1928, vol. I, p. 499.
[61] Not printed.

Art. 1—Protects persons born of Spanish parents in the United States from military service in Spain.

Art. 2—Protects persons born of Spanish parents in the United States from having to do military service in the United States if they have in the meanwhile returned to Spain and done their military service.

Thus, only one category of persons is spoken of. No mention is made of persons born in Spain of American parents, nor of naturalized Americans.

In regard to the former, it was explained to me that such persons are not considered as Spaniards, although they have the right to opt for Spanish nationality on coming of age, and they are therefore not entitled to the privilege of performing their military service, unless, and until they have opted.

It was made quite clear to me that military service is to be regarded as a high privilege, and not as a compulsory duty, and that the Spanish War Office was unwilling to have any Article inserted in the Treaty which might lower the bars to the admission of aliens into the Spanish Army!

As regards naturalized Americans of Spanish origin, i. e., persons born in Spain of Spanish parents, they were unwilling to make any concessions in the present laws governing their military obligations, or, as I suppose I should say, privileges.

I have [etc.]    SHELDON WHITEHOUSE

---

711.524/6

*The Secretary of State to the Chargé in Spain* (*Whitehouse*)

No. 645    WASHINGTON, December 2, 1929.

SIR: The Department has received your despatch No. 1398, of November 5, 1929, in regard to this Government's proposals concerning a treaty upon the subjects of nationality and military service.

I regret to say that the counter proposal of the Spanish Government which relates solely to military obligations in cases of persons born in the United States of Spanish parents is not satisfactory to this Government. In the first place, it is not applicable to naturalized citizens nor to persons born in Spain of American parents. Furthermore, the proposed provisions concerning persons born in the United States of Spanish parents are not deemed to be desirable. With regard to such persons, the Department desires to enter into an agreement, in accordance with the Joint Resolution of Congress of May 28, 1928, under which persons born in the United States of Spanish parents and continuing to reside in this country may visit Spain temporarily without being compelled to perform military service. This Government has no desire to enter into an agreement which would be applicable to persons born in the United States of Spanish parents, if such persons have established and maintained a residence of a permanent character in Spain. The proposals of this Government are based upon the principle that in cases of persons born with dual nationality, liability for military or other national services should be dependent upon residence.

I am [etc.]                                    For the Secretary of State:
                                                          WILBUR J. CARR

---

## Sweden

711.584/1

*The Minister in Sweden (Harrison) to the Secretary of State*

No. 458                                    STOCKHOLM, January 10, 1929.
                                               [Received January 26.]

SIR: I have the honor to report that the proposals looking to the conclusion of a treaty to carry out the provision of the Joint Resolution of Congress, approved by the President May 28, 1928, and for the adoption of an agreement concerning the termination of dual nationality have, in accordance with the directions contained in the Department's instruction No. 86, of December 1, 1928,[62] been duly presented to the Minister for Foreign Affairs who has taken the matter under consideration and has promised to let me have a reply as soon as possible.[63]

I have [etc.]                                          LELAND HARRISON

---

## Yugoslavia

711.60h4/11

*The Minister in Yugoslavia (Prince) to the Secretary of State*

No. 542                                    BELGRADE, January 24, 1929.
                                               [Received February 14.]

SIR: I have the honor to report, referring to the Department's Instruction No. 165 of December 1, 1928,[64] (File No. 711.004/16 [711.60h4/10a]) regarding the proposed naturalization agreement between the United States and Yugoslavia, that I have submitted this matter both to the Acting Foreign Minister, Mr. Komanudi, and to the King, in private audience, (cf. Legation's Despatch No. 541[65]).

Both His Majesty and the Acting Foreign Minister inform me that they approve of the Department's suggestion in this connection and I urged upon these authorities the necessity of some haste, as

---

[62] See instruction No. 167, December 1, 1928, to the Ambassador in Belgium, *Foreign Relations*, 1928, vol. I, p. 497.
[63] A treaty between the United States and Sweden regarding military service was signed on January 31, 1933; Department of State Treaty Series No. 890.
[64] See instruction No. 2993, December 1, 1928, to the Ambassador in France, *Foreign Relations*, 1928, vol. I, p. 499.
[65] Not printed.

I told them that our Government was desirous of closing up the matter of such agreements regarding naturalization practically at once.

I therefore hope that any opposition which I am informed might arise from General Hadjich, the . . . Minister of War, may be removed and that the matter will soon be concluded.

I have [etc.] JOHN DYNELEY PRINCE

711.60h4/13

*The Secretary of State to the Minister in Yugoslavia (Prince)*

No. 199 WASHINGTON, September 30, 1929.

SIR: The Department refers to the Legation's despatch No. 542 of January 24, 1929, in reply to the Department's instruction No. 165 of December 1, 1928, and previous correspondence regarding the proposed naturalization agreement between the United States and the Kingdom of the Serbs, Croats and Slovenes.

As indicated by *note verbale* No. 1329 of April 23, 1928, from the Foreign Office, in reply to the Legation's *aide-mémoire* of March 15, 1928,[66] the only objection raised by the Foreign Office in answer to the Legation's inquiry for an expression of opinion as to the possibility of the conclusion of a naturalization treaty was that the then legislation of the Kingdom did not yet include an internal law concerning naturalization. As such a law was passed on September 21, 1928, the Legation might draw the attention of the Foreign Office to this fact and again enquire whether the Government is now in a position to express its views in regard to the conclusion of a naturalization treaty.

I am [etc.] For the Secretary of State:
WILBUR J. CARR

[In despatch No. 675, November 1, 1929, the Minister reported that the possible effect of the law of September 21, 1928, on negotiations for the naturalization agreement had been brought to the attention of the Yugoslav Foreign Office on several occasions (711.-60h4/16). The Department was informed by the Chargé in despatch No. 689, December 10, 1929, that a new law of September 23, 1929, regarding military service apparently represented the views of the Ministry of War, and conceded the most liberal treatment which that Ministry deemed possible to those Yugoslav subjects who had become naturalized in foreign countries (711.60h4/17). No treaty of the nature desired was concluded with Yugoslavia.]

---

[66] Neither printed.

## PROTECTION OF WOMEN OF AMERICAN NATIONALITY MARRIED TO ALIENS AND HAVING DUAL NATIONALITY

130 Bolton, Ada Reba Buchwalter

*The Secretary of State to the Vice Consul in Charge at Yunnanfu (Chamberlain)*

WASHINGTON, June 12, 1929.

SIR: The Department has received your despatch No. 31, dated November 14, 1928,[1] transmitting an application for registration as an American citizen of Mrs. Ada Reba Buchwalter Bolton, who it appears was born at Paradise, Pennsylvania, on July 1, 1893; was married on April 7, 1928, to Leonard G. Bolton, a British subject, and has resided in China since November 9, 1928. It appears from your despatch under acknowledgment that according to British law an alien woman acquires British nationality upon her marriage to a British subject and that Mrs. Bolton was, therefore, included in the British passport held by her husband. You inquire whether Mrs. Bolton has prejudiced her status as an American citizen by permitting herself to be included in a British passport and as to the attitude which you should adopt towards her and women having a like status, should they become involved in litigation and the British consular authorities should attempt to exercise jurisdiction in their cases. You also inquire whether the Department recommends that American women who were married subsequent to September 22, 1922, to nationals of foreign countries be advised to decline to be included in foreign passports issued to their husbands.

In reply you are informed that under the provisions of Section 2 of the Act of September 22, 1922,[2] an American woman who is married to an alien subsequent to the passage of that Act does not cease to be a citizen of the United States merely by reason of her marriage. However, with respect to the case of Mrs. Bolton, while she did not lose her American citizenship by reason of her marriage to a British subject, it is the understanding of the Department that, under British law, she thereby acquired the status of a British subject. The necessary result of the concurrent operation of these different laws is to confer dual nationality upon Mrs. Bolton.

With respect to your inquiry regarding the attitude the Consulate should take if British consular authorities should attempt to exercise

---

[1] Not printed.
[2] 42 Stat. 1021, 1022.

extraterritorial jurisdiction over persons having the status of Mrs. Bolton, the Department informs you that since such persons have the status of British subjects under the laws of Great Britain and since British consular officials in China have jurisdiction over British subjects in that country the right of the British authorities to assume jurisdiction over persons of the category under consideration could not be questioned as a matter of law. Legally, British authorities and American authorities would each equally have the right to assume such jurisdiction. In case there develops in your district a contingency in which the rights and duties of a person possessing dual nationality one of whose nationalities is American is involved, you are instructed to accord proper assistance to that person as an American citizen, and you will promptly submit to the Department for its consideration a report giving the details of any aspect of the matter which may be or may become controversial.

It is the understanding of the Department that an oath of allegiance to Great Britain is not required to be taken in connection with the issue of, or inclusion in, a British passport, and the Department is, therefore, of the opinion that Mrs. Bolton in nowise prejudiced her status as an American citizen by permitting herself to be included in her husband's British passport. However, it is suggested that American women who are married to aliens and who are situated as Mrs. Bolton is, be advised that if they wish to be under the protection of the Government of the United States, it is advisable for them to provide themselves with American passports. It may be added that, if in obtaining a foreign passport or in being included in such a document, an oath of allegiance to a foreign country is required to be taken, an American citizen taking such oath would expatriate himself under the provisions of the first paragraph of Section 2 of the Act of March 2, 1907.[3]

The registration application of Mrs. Bolton is approved.

I am [etc.]                                    For the Secretary of State:
                                                        WILBUR J. CARR

---

[3] 34 Stat. 1228.

# AMERICAN PARTICIPATION IN THE EXTRAORDINARY SESSION OF THE INTERNATIONAL COMMISSION FOR AIR NAVIGATION AT PARIS, JUNE 10–15, 1929, TO REVISE THE CONVENTION OF OCTOBER 13, 1919 [1]

579.6D1/267

*The Secretary General of the International Commission for Air Navigation (Roper) to the Secretary of State*

No. 229

PARIS, 15 February, 1929.
[Received March 1.]

SIR: In an article entitled "Germany and the Paris Convention relating to air navigation dated 13th October 1919", published in October 1928 in the "Zeitschrift für das gesamte Luftrecht", Dr. Wegerdt, Ministerial Counsellor of the Ministry of Communications of the Reich, set forth the reasons why the German Government has hitherto abstained from adhering to the said Convention.

The International Commission for Air Navigation (I. C. A. N.), having taken cognizance of this article, considered that it might serve as the basis for a very opportune discussion.

Desirous to facilitate the adhesion of all the States to the Air Convention of 13th October 1919 by making such amendments of the text now in force as may be warranted by the progress realized in the domain of air navigation and by the necessity of universal co-operation to ensure the unity of aerial law, the I. C. A. N., adopting the procedure suggested in the above mentioned article, has therefore decided to bring about without delay a general discussion, by holding an extraordinary session to which will be invited, side by side with the Governments of the States parties to the Convention, the Governments of all the non-contracting States.

The German Government has already announced that it is prepared to accept this invitation.

I have the honour, in the name of the Commission and consequently of the Governments which it represents, to request your Government to be good enough to take part in this Conference which will be held in Paris at the end of May 1929.

---

[1] For the text of the convention and certain correspondence relating to it, see *Foreign Relations*, 1926, vol. I, pp. 145 ff., especially p. 152.

Documents relating to the extraordinary session of the Commission were printed in the Commission's *Official Bulletin No. 16*, November 1929, pp. 36–53. A résumé of the proceedings was also published by the Department of State in *Bulletin of Treaty Information* No. 4 (June 1929), Second Supplement (mimeographed copy). The minutes of the sessions were issued in mimeographed form by the I. C. A. N., together with a compilation of certain papers entitled *Extraordinary Session of June 1929, Documents* (579.6D1/318).

The discussion will have as its basis the above mentioned article of Dr. Wegerdt, a French translation of which I send you herewith annexed to a Note [3] which I have thought fit to prepare on the question.

These negotiations must greatly interest your Government, which was a signatory to the Convention after having participated, in 1919, in its preparation; it would be deeply regrettable that modifications to be made in its text should be discussed without the presence of your Government and the entire Commission sincerely hopes that it will take an active part in the debates.

I hope consequently to receive at an early date the announcement of the acceptation of your Government and I have [etc.]

ALBERT ROPER

579.6D1/293

*The Secretary of State to President Hoover*

WASHINGTON, April 25, 1929.

MY DEAR MR. PRESIDENT: I have the honor to inform you that the Department has received a communication dated February 15, 1929, from the Secretary General of the International Commission for Air Navigation in Paris, inviting this Government to take part in an extraordinary session of the Commission to be held in Paris early in June, 1929, for the purpose of considering such changes in the text of the International Convention relating to the Regulation of Air Navigation, of October 13, 1919, as may facilitate the adherence of states which are not parties to the Convention.

Accompanying the communication from the Secretary General is a memorandum entitled "Memorandum by the Secretary General on the Origin of the Air Convention of October 13, 1919, and its Progressive Extension from 1922 to 1928 and the Problem of its Revision," together with an article by Doctor Wegerdt, Ministerial Counselor of the Ministry of Communications of the Reich,[3] in which he states further the reasons why the German Government has not adhered to the Convention in its present form. Doctor Wegerdt also discusses the development of an aerial law, and makes reference to the Paris Convention of October 13, 1929 [*1919*], the Ibero–American Convention on Air Navigation concluded on November 1, 1926,[4] and the Convention on Commercial Aviation adopted at the Sixth International Conference of American States, held at Habana, Cuba, from January 16 to February 20, 1928.[5] The Secretary General's communication of February 15 further indicates that his memorandum and Doctor

[3] Neither printed.
[4] Published in *Gaceta de Madrid*, April 23, 1927, p. 562.
[5] *Foreign Relations*, 1928, vol. I, p. 585.

Wegerdt's article will afford the basis of discussion at the June meeting of the International Commission for Air Navigation.

The International Convention Relating to the Regulation of Air Navigation was signed on behalf of this Government, with reservations, on May 1 [*31*], 1920. On October 27, 1922, the International Commission for Air Navigation approved a protocol of amendment of Article 5 of the Convention, and on June 30, 1923, the Commission approved a protocol of amendment of Article 34. The amendments came into force on December 14, 1926, after ratification by the states which were parties to the Convention at the time of the approval of the protocols by the Commission.

The International Convention Relating to the Regulation of Air Navigation was transmitted by the President to the Senate on June 16, 1926,[6] with a report from the Secretary of State [7] recommending that the Senate be requested to take suitable action advising and consenting to the ratification of the Convention with Articles 5 and 34 amended as recommended by the International Commission for Air Navigation in the protocols of amendment approved by the Commission on October 27, 1922, and June 30, 1923, respectively, on the following conditions and understandings.

"1. The United States expressly reserves, with regard to article 3, the right to permit its private aircraft to fly over areas over which private aircraft of other contracting States may be forbidden to fly by the laws of the United States, any provision of said article 3 to the contrary notwithstanding.

"2. The United States reserves the right to enter into special treaties, conventions, and agreements regarding aerial navigation with any country in the Western Hemisphere if such country be not a party to this convention, without conforming to the provisions of article 5 of the Convention.

"3. The United States reserves complete freedom of action as to customs matters and does not consider itself bound by the provisions of Annex H or any articles of the convention affecting the enforcement of its customs laws.

"4. Ratification of the present convention shall not be taken to involve any legal relation on the part of the United States to the League of Nations or the assumption of any obligation by the United States under the Covenant of the League of Nations constituting Part I of the treaty of Versailles.[8]

"5. The United States reserves its freedom of action under article 37 with respect to the submission to the Permanent Court of International Justice of any disagreement that may arise between the United States and any other State regarding the interpretation of the convention."

The Convention is still pending in the Senate, action on it having been suspended at the request of this Department which acted at the

[6] See *Foreign Relations*, 1926, vol. I, p. 152.
[7] *Ibid.*, p. 145.
[8] Malloy, *Treaties*, 1910–1923, vol. III, p. 3329.

instigation of the Department of Commerce. This Government is not a signatory of the Ibero-American Convention on Air Navigation concluded November 1, 1926. The Convention on Commercial Aviation adopted at the Sixth International Conference of American States, though signed by the delegates of the United States, has not yet been sent to the Senate for approval.

The proposed extraordinary session of the International Commission for Air Navigation which this Government is invited to attend will, it appears probable, consider the Convention of 1919, as amended, in its entirety. The result may be the adoption of such amendments as to constitute a thorough-going revision. The opportunity is presented, accordingly, to modify such provisions of the Convention as may have been in conflict with other conventions dealing with air navigation or with national laws and regulations on the subject. The possibility of reconciling these conflicts and of laying a firmer foundation for a code of air law that may commend itself for universal adoption is of practical interest to the United States. It appears that the Conference will be attended by representatives of all the nations party to the International Air Navigation Convention of 1919, as well as by Germany and other nations which have not as yet adhered to that Convention, and, accordingly, in view of the rapidly increasing development of aviation activities in general and of American aviation interests in particular, I am of the opinion that it would be appropriate and advantageous for the United States to participate in this Conference.

I have consulted the Departments of Commerce, War, Navy, Post Office, Treasury and Labor, and the National Advisory Committee for Aeronautics, all of which have concurred in the view that recommendation should be made to you favoring the acceptance by the United States of the invitation to attend this Conference and suggesting the appointment of official delegates for this purpose.

Accordingly, I have the honor to making formal recommendation that the United States accept this invitation and that a delegation be sent to represent the United States at this Conference to be composed as follows:

*Delegates:*
    William P. MacCracken, Junior, Assistant Secretary, Department of Commerce, Chairman;
    Joseph R. Baker, Assistant to the Solicitor, Department of State;
*Technical Advisors:*
    John J. Ide, European Representative of the National Advisory Committee for Aeronautics;
    Major Barton K. Yount, Assistant Military Attaché, American Embassy, Paris;
    Lieutenant-Commander William D. Thomas, Assistant Naval Attaché, American Embassy, Paris.

It is possible that I shall later recommend that an additional delegate be added.[9]

In the event that this recommendation meets with your approval, appropriate instructions for the guidance of the delegation will be prepared in the Department. Such instructions would be based upon principles embodied in the Pan-American Air Convention of 1928 and would authorize the American delegation to use its influence with a view to effecting the amendment of the International Air Navigation Convention of 1919 in a manner which would make it acceptable to all the conferring governments and which would at the same time accord adequate recognition to American rights and interests in international air navigation.

If you should approve of American participation in this Conference upon the basis set forth above, the question of meeting the expenses of the delegation would then arise. It is estimated that the cost of participation would not exceed $5,000 as there will be no expenses in connection with the attendance of the technical advisors. One of two courses would appear to be open with a view to providing this amount. Normally the appropriate course to follow would be to ask the Congress for an appropriation to cover the cost of participation in the Conference. The probable intention of the Congress to consider only a limited number of questions at the present Special Session makes it doubtful whether favorable Congressional action could be had before June 4, next, the date on which the Conference is expected to meet. The other course would be to meet the expenses of the delegation from the appropriation for Emergencies Arising in the Diplomatic and Consular Service, in which there is an unobligated balance sufficient for the purpose. In connection with this suggestion, however, there are certain other facts which appear to me to require your consideration. The Deficiency Appropriation Act approved March 4, 1913,[10] contained the following provision:

"Hereafter the Executive shall not extend or accept any invitation to participate in any international congress, conference, or like event, without first having specific authority of law to do so."

The question of the effect of the provision upon the prerogatives of the President in the conduct of the foreign relations was discussed between President Wilson and Secretary Lansing in 1917, and on February 20, 1917, President Wilson addressed a letter to Mr. Lansing in which he made the following statement:[11]

"This is an utterly futile provision. The Congress has no power to limit the Executive in this way. It can, of course, refuse the appropriations necessary to pay for this Government's part in a conference but that is the most it can do.

[9] The delegation as finally determined was identical with the above list.
[10] 37 Stat. 912, 913.
[11] The two paragraphs quoted constitute the entire text of the letter.

"I do not mean that I intend to join a conference notwithstanding this futile provision. I mean only that such a provision is entirely without constitutional validity and that we are free to consider the matter on its merits."

The Department has consistently acted in accordance with this view, and delegates have been sent to international conferences from time to time without prior authorization of Congress, notwithstanding the provision of law which I have quoted. I concur in the position taken by President Wilson to the effect that the provision under the Appropriation Act of March 4, 1913, was an encroachment upon the prerogatives of the Executive. I think the present practice, however, of having the expense of such conferences fall constantly upon the Emergency Appropriation is not desirable and that at an appropriate season it may be well to take up with Congress the provision of some other regular appropriation for the expenses of the scientific and technical conferences to which this government is being constantly invited, leaving the emergency appropriation for its original purposes. In the present situation however, inasmuch as I understand that you deem it desirable that the matters taken up by the present Special Session of Congress be restricted in scope as much as possible, I am willing to recommend that the expenses of the delegates of this conference be taken from the Emergency Appropriation. Upon receiving notification of your wishes in respect to the approval of these delegates and of my other recommendations herein I shall take appropriate action.

I am [etc.]    HENRY L. STIMSON

---

579.6D1/292

### President Hoover to the Secretary of State

THE WHITE HOUSE, April 27, 1929.

MY DEAR MR. SECRETARY: I have your letter of April 25th on the subject of the International Commission for Air Navigation in Paris. I approve of the arrangements you have made and of the appointment of Messrs. MacCracken and Baker with their technical advisors, to attend this conference.

Yours faithfully,    HERBERT HOOVER

---

579.6D1/302a

### The Secretary of State to the Chairman of the American Delegation (MacCracken)[12]

WASHINGTON, May 20, 1929.

SIR: With respect to your designation as a delegate to represent the United States at an extraordinary session of the International Com-

---

[12] An identic instruction was sent to Mr. Baker.

mission for Air Navigation to be held in Paris early in June, 1929, I may say that it is my understanding that the purpose of this meeting is to consider such changes in the text of the International Convention relative to the Regulation of Air Navigation of October 13, 1919, as may facilitate the adherence of States which are not parties to the Convention.

As you are aware, this convention was signed with certain reservations by representatives of the United States and was transmitted by the President to the Senate on June 16, 1926, with a report from the Secretary of State [13] containing recommendations that the Senate be requested to take suitable action advising and consenting to the ratification of the Convention with Articles 5 and 34 amended as recommended by the International Commission for Air Navigation in the protocols of amendment approved by the Commission October 27, 1922, and June 30, 1923, respectively, on the following conditions and understandings:

[Here follows the text of the reservations quoted in the letter to the President, printed on page 491.]

The Department considers that the foregoing conditions and understandings should still be adhered to by the United States and that an effort should be made by you to effect such changes in the text of the convention as may appear practicable in order to bring it into conformity thereto.

You are also aware that the convention in question is still pending before the Senate and that action thereon has been suspended pursuant to a recommendation of this Department made February 20, 1929, and based upon the statement that the Department of Commerce felt that it would be inadvisable for the Senate to take action on the convention before that department had had an opportunity to try out its own air regulations made under authority of the Air Commerce Act of 1926.[14]

In this relation it may be pointed out that the air regulations of the United States are much less complex and exhaustive than those included in the annexes to the international convention in question and that it may be doubted whether some of the latter regulations would be suitable to conditions existing on this continent. Therefore you will bear in mind that the simplification of the regulations contained in these annexes and their change in other respects so as to bring them into closer harmony with the air regulations of the United States would assist in rendering it advisable for this Government to ratify that convention.

In considering changes in the convention referred to you should bear in mind the provisions of the Pan American Air Convention of

[13] *Foreign Relations*, 1926, vol. I, p. 145.
[14] 44 Stat. 568.

1928 which was signed by representatives of this Government but has not yet been sent to the Senate. The provisions of the latter convention are in general satisfactory to this Department, and it would therefore be advisable for you to endeavor to bring about such changes in the first-named convention as will conform to the provisions of the Pan American Convention.

However, you will observe that the last paragraph of Article 30 of the Pan American Convention provides that "nothing contained in this convention shall affect the rights and obligations established by existing treaties". This was intended to cover the peculiar relations existing between the United States and Panama and it may perhaps be rightly held to cover such situation as regards air navigation by reason of the provisions of the treaty of 1903 between the two countries [15] and the inferences and implications to be drawn therefrom. Nevertheless that treaty does not specifically deal with the question of air navigation and therefore it was deemed advisable to insert in the convention between the two countries signed June 28, 1926,[16] the following provisions:

"ARTICLE X

"All aircraft and aviation centers in the Republic of Panama other than those pertaining to the defensive forces of the Canal and those owned and officially operated by the Government of Panama shall be subject to inspection by both the United States and the Panaman Governments to insure compliance with such rules and regulations as may hereafter be agreed upon.

"Aircraft owned and operated by the nationals of the United States or Panama may operate in the Republic of Panama, provided both the aircraft and the operators thereof hold a joint United States–Panama license issued by a board composed of representatives of the Governments of the United States and Panama and otherwise to conform to restrictions recommended in the Convention for the Regulation of Aerial Navigation signed at Paris, October 13, 1919, or such other restrictions as the two countries may from time to time jointly prescribe.

"All aircraft other than those pertaining to the defensive forces of the Canal and those owned and officially operated by the Government of Panama must follow routes prescribed jointly by the United States and Panama in flying over the Republic of Panama and must land at airports or airdromes designated jointly by the United States and Panama and must otherwise conform to such restrictions as the two countries may from time to time jointly prescribe.

"In applying and enforcing the rules and regulations regarding aircraft and aviation centers the two Governments shall regard as the deciding factor the safety of the Panama Canal.

[15] Convention signed November 18, 1903; *Foreign Relations*, 1904, p. 543.
[16] *Ibid.*, 1926. vol. II, p. 846.

"The Republic of Panama agrees not to permit flying in Panaman territory over areas near the defenses of the Canal except in agreement with the United States.

"In time of war or threatened hostilities the provisions of Article XI of this Treaty shall be applied."

The last-mentioned convention has not yet come into force and consequently it is believed that in addition to endeavoring to have incorporated in the international convention a provision similar to the one above quoted as contained in the Pan American Convention you should also try to have this provision supplemented by a clause reading somewhat as follows:

"or such rights and obligations as may later be established through the substantial coming into force of provisions already agreed upon by representatives of two or more countries and embodied in signed treaties."

It is needless to remind you that for the purposes of the maintenance and protection of the Panama Canal this Government attaches great importance to the matter of the regulation of the operation of aircraft in the Republic of Panama. In fact, this Government would not consider it advisable to enter into treaty arrangements which might tend to diminish its rights either inchoate or in being regarding this matter.

The Department has been informed by the Secretary General of the International Commission for Air Navigation that the forthcoming conference will be assembled for the purpose of examining proposals of modifications in the convention made by Dr. Wegerdt, Ministerial Counselor of the Ministry of Communications of the German Reich, and approved by the German Government. Therefore it seems advisable to consider these proposals in detail and they are taken up below with reference to the particular articles of the convention to which they respectively relate.

## ARTICLE 1

It is provided in Article 1 of the convention that for the purposes of the convention the territory of the state shall be understood as including . . . "the colonies".

The German suggestion is that the word "colonies" might be defined more clearly.

This Government would have no objection to an appropriate definition of "colonies" which would make more clear the meaning of that word.

The German proposals point out that the convention does not deal with flight over Straits and that this question might perhaps be dealt with in accordance with the Treaty of Lausanne of July 24, 1923,[17] relating to "straits" in the sense of freedom of the air space over straits.

The treaty referred to deals with the Strait of Dardanelles, the Sea of Marmora and the Bosporus.

Before consenting to an agreement with respect to straits this Government would desire to know exactly what bodies of water are understood to be comprehended under the term "straits" and the relation of such agreement to the present provision of Article 1 of the convention that each state has complete and exclusive sovereignty over its territorial waters.

The German proposals suggest that it would perhaps be advisable, as did the Inter-American Air Convention, to provide that the convention under consideration applies to private aircraft only. On the other hand the German proposals recognize that State aircraft will have to observe the same regulations concerning navigation, etc., as to private aircraft.

The Department would have no objection to the amendment of the convention so as to make it applicable to private aircraft only, but does not consider that this matter is of great importance.

## ARTICLE 3

It is provided in Article 3 of the convention that each state is entitled to establish certain prohibited areas as against aircraft of the other contracting states "subject to no distinction being made in this respect between its private aircraft and those of the other states".

The German suggestion is that it be considered whether this article should be supplemented so as to provide that national aircraft employed for special services in the service of the state should be permitted to fly over such areas and it is asked whether this principle is expressed in the provision of the Inter-American Air Convention restricting the equal treatment to be accorded to national and foreign aircraft with reference to prohibited zones, to aircraft engaged in international commercial air traffic.

The Department is of the opinion that such a provision might well be incorporated in the convention and considers that the provision of the Inter-American Air Convention referred to expresses such a principle.

The German proposals further point out that the convention does not provide for the right of the contracting parties in exceptional circumstances temporarily to restrict or prohibit air traffic above their territory wholly or in part and with immediate effect, and that

---

[17] Convention between Turkey and other powers relating to the Régime of the Straits, League of Nations Treaty Series, vol. XXVIII, p. 115.

such provision seems necessary as otherwise traffic by foreign aircraft can not be prohibited in times of internal unrest.

The Department is inclined to the opinion that it might be well to incorporate such a provision in the convention.

## ARTICLE 5

With respect to the provision of Article 5 of the convention that no contracting state shall, except by special and temporary authorization, permit the flight above its territory of an aircraft which does not possess the nationality of a contracting state unless it has concluded a special convention with the state in which the aircraft is registered, the German proposals point out that there is a "certain justification" for such provisions if they are to be understood as representing an incentive to adhere to the convention, but that otherwise such provisions should be deleted as a "contracting state should not be restricted from determining its relations with noncontracting states as it may think necessary" and that this article "contains an obligation not customary in international agreements".

It would seem that this Government might well support heartily a proposal for the deletion of the provision in question. In a sense this provision probably represents an incentive to adhere to the convention, but conceivably it may also represent an incentive to refrain from adhering in order to retain freedom of action. Deletion of the provisions in question would apparently be beneficial to the United States in its relations with Latin American States, few of which now adhere to the convention, and particularly with Panama in the event of nonadherence on the part either of the United States or Panama, but not of both. Deletion would also apparently remove the necessity of a reservation by the United States to this article which otherwise, as above indicated, it would be obliged to make.

## ARTICLE 6

In connection with Article 6 the German proposals raise the question whether the word "nationality" can properly be used in connection with an aircraft or whether this term should be reserved for persons alone.

No reason is perceived why this question should be raised. We speak of the "nationality" of a vessel and it would seem entirely appropriate to speak of the nationality of an aircraft. Furthermore, it might be difficult to conceive of an appropriate substitute for this word.

## ARTICLE 7, PARAGRAPH 1

Article 7 of the convention requires that no aircraft shall be entered on the registry of one of the contracting states unless it belongs wholly to the nationals of such state.

The German suggestion is that this article be amended so as to provide that the owner of an aircraft must be domiciled in the country in which the aircraft is to be registered.

In support of this proposal it is argued that with the article as it stands it would be impossible for a foreigner living abroad to keep an aircraft of which he is the registered owner in his country of residence, as he does not possess the nationality of that country and that consequently if he wishes to fly his own aircraft he can only do so with an aircraft registered in his home country, which means that in case of damage to any essential part of the aircraft whereby its airworthiness is affected a new certificate issued in his own country is required by the regulations.

## ARTICLE 7, PARAGRAPH 2

This paragraph provides that no incorporated company can be registered as the owner of an aircraft unless it possesses the nationality of the state in which the aircraft is registered and unless the president or chairman of the company and at least two-thirds of the directors possess such nationality.

With regard to these provisions the German proposals suggest that they be amended by providing that aircraft may only be entered in the register of a contracting state if the owner is domiciled in that state irrespective of whether the owner is an individual or a company. In this relation the German proposals refer to Article 8 of the Inter-American Air Convention which provides that the registration of aircraft shall be governed by the laws and special regulations of each contracting state (similar provisions being contained in Article 8 of the Pan American Convention), but state that in order to prevent the continued validity of the principle derived from the present provisions of Article 7, paragraph 2 of the International Convention, now adopted in the municipal legislation of most countries, it would be necessary to insert in the article a clause forbidding the contracting states to make registration dependent upon the nationality of the owner.

With relation to the German proposals for the amendment of paragraphs 1 and 2 of Article 7 it may be observed that Section 3 of the Air Commerce Act of 1926 provides that no aircraft shall be eligible for registration unless it is a civil aircraft owned by a citizen of the United States and not registered under the laws of any foreign country or unless it is a public aircraft of the Federal Government or of a state, territory, or possession or of a political sub-division thereof. In view of this provision of the laws of the United States, it is believed that you should not favor the German proposals for amendment of Article 7. However, it would appear to be prac-ticable to arrange that in case of damage to an aircraft, a certificate as to its airworthiness, after repairs, could be issued in the country where the aircraft is situated. Moreover, it is believed that the provision of Article 8 of the Pan American Convention that the reg-istration of aircraft shall be made in accordance with the laws of each State is preferable to either the German proposal or the present article of the International Convention, and that its adoption would render the Convention much more acceptable to the States of the Western Hemisphere.

## ARTICLE 9

Article 9 of the convention provides for the monthly exchange among the contracting states of copies of registrations and cancella-tions thereof.

The German proposals query whether such requirement is really necessary in view of the considerable administrative labor involved.

With reference to this proposal it would seem that it might per-haps be advisable to provide for such exchange of information at longer intervals, or that the information merely concern[s] planes to be used in international service and licensed for that purpose.

## ARTICLE 13

This article provides that airworthiness certificates must be recog-nized as valid by the other contracting states.

The German proposal is that the "expansion of air navigation would be helped if it were laid down that airworthiness certificates were to be recognized not only in the case of aircraft entering the country under a foreign nationality mark, but also in the case of imported aircraft, unless the national legislation sets higher stand-ards of airworthiness than the minimum requirements of the 'international convention' ".

The Pan American Convention provides that the contracting states reserve the right to refuse to recognize as valid the certificates of airworthiness of any foreign aircraft where inspection shows the aircraft is not reasonably airworthy in accordance with normal re-quirements of the inspecting state. (Article 12).

Section 3 (b) of the Air Commerce Act of 1926 gives wide regu-latory powers to the Secretary of Commerce with respect to the landing of foreign aircraft in the United States as to their airworthiness.

It would seem that the United States might agree to the German suggestion. If this suggestion were adopted then should the minimum requirements of the Commission for Air Navigation not be up to the standards prescribed by the Secretary of Commerce, the United States would not be obligated to recognize airworthiness certificates issued by other states.

## ARTICLE 15, PARAGRAPH 3

This paragraph provides that "the establishment of international airways shall be subject to the consent of the states flown over."

The German suggestion respecting this paragraph is that its meaning should be made clear and it is stated that Germany would be glad if it could be modified so as to provide as do her own air agreements that "the institution and operation of regular air lines from one contracting state into or over the territory of another contracting state, with or without intermediary landing, is subject to a special agreement between the two states in question." This paragraph of the Convention and the German proposal are contrary to the spirit of the Pan American Convention and seriously limit the declaration for freedom of innocent passage contained in Article 2 of the International Convention, and it would seem preferable to eliminate the paragraph in question.

## ARTICLE 18

It is proposed in Article 18 of the convention that every aircraft of one contracting state passing through the territory of another contracting state, including landings and stoppages reasonably necessary for the purpose of such transit, shall be exempt from any seizure on the ground of infringement of patent, design or model, subject to the deposit of security.

The German suggestion is that in view of the rapid development of regular air traffic it is worth while considering, to avoid interruption, the advisability of applying to aircraft the principle recognized to a certain extent, of the immunity from seizure of railroad transport material.

In view of the system of government obtaining in the United States it would seem inadvisable for this Government to agree to the German suggestion and thus assume to bind the several states upon the matters indicated.

The German proposals further suggest that it might be desirable by a clause to be inserted after Article 18 to attempt to settle the question of conflicting laws but points out in this relation that the Pan American Convention is restricted in this matter to a provision that the regulations as to entering and leaving the country, customs, police and public health, are to be observed, and to a regulation that reparation for damages caused to persons or property in the subjacent state shall be governed by the laws of such state.

It is believed that this Government would desire to adhere to the principles thus laid down in the Pan American Convention and in this relation reference is made to the reservation recommended to the Senate of the United States on the subject of customs regulations as dealt with in the International Convention.

## ARTICLE 19

This article provides that an aircraft engaged in international navigation shall be provided, if it carries freight, with a bill of lading.

The German proposals state that the expression *bill of lading* "which is a term of maritime law, should be replaced by 'air consignment note' ".

While this is apparently purely a matter of nomenclature it may be said that the term "bill of lading" as known in the United States is not only a term of maritime law but also a term generally used in commercial transfers and that it would seem to be preferable for use in the convention to the term proposed by the Germans, which, so far as the Department is aware, is not used in this country.

## ARTICLE 23

This article provides that the principles of maritime law apply in the absence of any agreement to the contrary in the case of salvage of aircraft wrecked at sea.

With regard to this the German proposals state that the regulation is burdensome to air navigation companies as they have to pay heavy salvage charges while the shipping companies find the maximum charge possible insufficient to cover the cost of salvage.

Respecting this proposal it may be said that it would seem to be difficult to remedy the situation said to exist so as to satisfy both interests involved and that perhaps the present provision is as fair to both parties as could well be arranged. In the absence of a definite proposal of substitution the Department is not prepared to sanction a change in the provisions of the convention on this point.

## ARTICLE 31

This article provides that every aircraft commanded by a person in military service detailed for the purpose shall be deemed to be a military aircraft.

The German proposals state that the word *detailed* used in this article seems not altogether clear.

The Department suggests that after the word "purpose" there be added the words "by authority of his Government."

## ARTICLE 32

This article provides that military aircraft especially authorized to fly over the territory of another contracting state shall enjoy in principle the privileges which are customarily accorded to foreign ships of war.

The German proposals question whether such privileges should be accorded and express a doubt whether the mere transference to air navigation of the rules and customs of maritime navigation is advisable.

In the absence of any concrete proposal for a change in the provisions of this article the Department is disposed to await a recommendation by the Delegation.

## ARTICLE 34

Paragraph 1 of this article states that the International Commission for Air Navigation shall be "placed under the direction of the League of Nations."

The German proposal on this point is that it might be advisable to make a clearer definition of the position of the Commission with regard to the League.

The Department is in accord with the German proposal, assuming that the clearer definition suggested would not indicate a greater subordination of the Commission to the League than is inferable from the present provisions. Bearing in mind the reservation before referred to on this point, as recommended by the President of the United States to the Senate, the Department would be glad to have the matter defined so as to render the Commission independent of the League.

Article 34 further provides that the Commission shall be composed of two representatives each from the United States, France, Italy, and Japan; one representative of Great Britain, and one from each of the British Dominions, and one representative from each of the other contracting states.

The German proposals state that if certain states have two representatives Germany would have to demand the same privilege, but would not object to an amendment providing that each state should have only one representative.

In this relation it is observed that Article 34 also provides that the expenses of the Commission shall be payable in the proportion of two shares each for the United States, British Empire, France, Italy and Japan and one share each for all the other states.

Assuming that the last mentioned provision shall remain in force and that Germany shall be placed in the same category as the United States therein, the Department would have no objection to allotting to Germany two representatives on the Commission. In this relation, the inquiry suggests itself whether it would not be equitable, in view of the representation of the British Dominions on the Commission, for the British Empire to pay a larger share of the expenses.

On the other hand, if each state is to pay an equal share of the expenses, this Government would presumably have no objection to giving each state but one representative on the Commission.

With respect to other provisions of Article 34 the German proposals suggest that the sphere of activities of the International Air Commission be extended so as to include, so far as possible, "all questions of sovereignty which require international regulation so that no international conferences of representatives of the states need be held other than those of the Commission."

If this suggestion is intended merely to enlarge the Commission's activities in the line of the collection of information and the making of recommendations to the contracting states, the suggestion would appear meritorious. However, if it is designed to give the Commission further authority to promulgate rules and regulations of a wide scope which would be binding on the contracting states, it may be said that this Government could not well agree thereto.

In connection with his suggestion to enlarge the activities of the Commission the German expert suggests that consideration be given to the question of incorporating into the Commission the Committee of Air Law Experts instituted by the Paris International Private Air Law Conference of 1926 [*1925*] [18] for the purpose of drafting conventions on international private air law.

This Government did not participate in the Private Air Law Conference of 1926 [*1925*]. However, no objection is perceived in principle to the suggested incorporation.

A further statement by the German expert with reference to Article 34 is that it would not be possible to ignore the question whether the International Commission is necessary at all and in this relation he calls attention to the fact that the Inter-American Convention makes no provision for such a body. However, he concludes that the Commission's continued existence is highly desirable.

It seems very improbable that at the forthcoming conference called by the Commission there will be a serious effort made to amend the convention so as to abolish the Commission and this Government,

---

[18] The United States was represented at the Conference by Lieutenant Commander Burg and Major Yount in the capacity of observers without power to sign any of the acts of the Conference.—Ministère des Affaires Etrangères, *Conférence Internationale de Droit Privé Aérien, 27 octobre–6 novembre 1925* (Paris, Imprimerie Nationale, 1926).

as at present advised, is not prepared to support any such step. It is recognized that the Commission apparently serves a useful purpose and its continued existence would seem desirable as a clearinghouse for information, but not as a regulatory body.

## ARTICLES 41 AND 42

These articles make a distinction with respect to adhesion to the convention between states which took part in the World War and those which did not, and the German expert states that this distinction should be eliminated, which would result in the amendment of Article 41 and the deletion of Article 42.

There would seem to be no good reason for failing to agree with the German view in this respect.

## ANNEX H

The German expert suggests that this Annex might be amended so as to "do more justice to traffic requirements."

Referring to the before-mentioned reservation as to this article recommended by the President to the Senate it is to be observed that this Government would not desire to agree to provisions for the regulation of customs procedure, which appears to be the whole purpose of this Annex, and therefore is interested not in the amendment of this Annex but in its deletion.

## LANGUAGE IN WHICH THE COMMISSION'S PUBLICATIONS ARE ISSUED

The German expert points out that the convention's publications are now issued in French, English and Italian, and says that Germany and Spain will demand equal recognition in this respect. However, he adds, that in view of the expense involved Germany would agree to publication in French only.

The Department considers that you should endeavor to arrange for an agreement to publish in English and French only, but, if such an agreement can not be reached, that you should favor the continuance of the present plan, so far as concerns publication in English.

## PRESENT GERMAN DISABILITIES

Finally, the German expert calls attention to the disabilities under which Germany labors with respect to the establishment of airdromes and traffic landings in the occupied area and the so-called evacuated area and the so-called demilitarized neutral area as the result of the provisions of Articles 42 and 43 of the Treaty of Versailles;[19] the limitations imposed upon Germany as to the construction and opera-

---

[19] Malloy, *Treaties*, 1910–1923, vol. III, pp. 3329, 3351, 3352.

tion of aircraft as result of the provisions of Article 198 of that treaty; [20] the requirements of Article 200 of the treaty that until the complete evacuation of German territory the occupying powers shall enjoy in Germany freedom of passage through the air, freedom of transit and landing; [21] and the existing requirement that the German occupied area may not be flown over except upon authority of the Rhineland High Commission.

The German proposals point out that these disabilities and limitations might interfere with German cooperation in the Air Navigation Convention and intimate that the bodies having authority in the matter should grant Germany a "measure of equality with the other states in the matter of civil aviation." With the exception below mentioned the views of the German Government last set forth will apparently not fall within the scope of the conference, and, moreover, the United States, as having refused to ratify the Versailles Treaty, is not directly concerned with such matters. Therefore you need not interest yourself therein.

Calling attention to the fact that under Section 198 of the Versailles Treaty Germany has been obliged to agree to the prohibition of the construction, importation or use of aircraft armored or arranged to take any weapon of war, the German expert seems to be of the opinion that under Article 2 of the Air Navigation Convention Germany will be obliged to permit flight over her territory of aircraft of the other contracting states even though armored or arranged to take weapons of war and that if Germany undertook to guard herself against this by national legislation she would act in opposition to Article 31 of the convention which prescribes as military aircraft only those commanded by a person in military service detailed for that purpose. Hence he argues that Germany might have to demand that if a certain definition of military aircraft remains in force for her, the definition of such aircraft in the convention be altered to correspond therewith.

In principle this German suggestion seems, on its face, to be equitable. However, it is desired that you consult the technical assistants to your delegation with reference to this matter. In any event, this would seem to be primarily a question to be dealt with by the parties to the Versailles Treaty.

It appears that the International Commission for Air Navigation desires to prepare a protocol of amendments to the text of the Convention of 1919, and the Department is informed that the representatives of the United States should be authorized to represent it "without involving the Government." Therefore, full powers will be issued to you, for use if necessary. However, the Department does not

[20] *Ibid.*, p. 3411.
[21] *Ibid.*, p. 3412.

desire you to sign any act of agreement without specific authority from it so to do, which you may request, if advisable, by telegraph. Presumably, an arrangement can be made for deferring to the future the question of the signing on behalf of this Government, of such agreement as may be reached, and may contemplate that it be signed on the part of the interested governments.

I am [etc.]               HENRY L. STIMSON

---

579.6D1/318

*The American Delegates (MacCracken and Baker) to the Secretary of State*

PARIS, June 28, 1929.
[Received July 13.]

SIR: Referring to your separate instructions to us of May 20, 1929, with regard to the action we should take as delegates representing the United States at an extraordinary session of the International Commission for Air Navigation to be held in Paris in June, 1929, we have the honor to submit the following report.

Delegate Baker arrived in Paris May 30 and Delegate MacCracken May 31, and during the time intervening between the last mentioned date and June 10, 1929, held consultations with the Technical Advisors to the Delegation and made the necessary preliminary arrangements.

It developed on our arrival that one of the rooms in the Office of the Automotive Trade Commissioner to Europe, could be made available for our use at the Chancellery of the American Embassy and that stenographic assistance could there be furnished. Consequently, it was determined to cancel the reservation which had been made for an office room at the Hotel d'Iena, and to employ no outside clerk-stenographer. Therefore, the only outside assistance employed has been that of a translator, and a considerable saving has been effected in the budget prepared by the Department.

The Conference met June 10, in a room of the Department of Foreign Affairs, and was attended by representatives of the following governments:—

*Contracting States:* Belgium, British Empire, Canada, Irish Free State, Union of South Africa and India, Bulgaria, Chile, Denmark, France, Greece, Italy, Japan, Netherlands, Poland, Portugal, Saar Territory, Kingdom of Serbs, Croats and Slovenes, Siam, Sweden, Czecho-Slovakia and Uruguay.

*Non-Contracting States:* Germany, Austria, Brazil, China, Colombia, Cuba, Spain, Esthonia, Finland, Haiti, Hungary, Luxembourg, Norway, Switzerland, Venezuela and the United States of America.

The Honorable Laurent Eynac, Air Minister of France, opened the Conference. Mr. Pierre-Etienne Flandin, head of the French delegation was chosen Chairman. He presided with the utmost fairness and his tactful efforts to compromise differences of opinion among the delegates, which arose frequently, were successful to such an extent that he earned the unqualified commendation of all. He was ably assisted in his efforts by Captain Albert Roper, Secretary General of the Commission Internationale de Navigation Aérienne. The proceedings were conducted in French and English, but the verbatim transcript of the debate was preserved only in French. It will be published later with an English translation. There were ten sessions of the Conference, and two sessions of the Drafting Committee. The delegates and technical advisors attended all the sessions of the Conference. Mr. John J. Ide was appointed as United States member of the Drafting Committee, because of his exceptional knowledge of the French language, but both delegates were permitted to and did attend the sessions of this Committee. The final session of the Conference was held Saturday morning June 15, at which the final resolutions were unanimously adopted and signed.[22] The United States Delegation signed with permission to file reservations, copy of which is attached hereto.[23] There are also attached French and English copies of the minutes of the session, including the final resolutions, the May 1929 Edition of the Convention, a copy of the Documents in French and English used at the session, a statement of the preparation of the Convention, and a copy of the press release issued by the Secretary General.[24]

On Saturday afternoon June 15, there was a regular session of the International Commission for Air Navigation. The session unanimously adopted a protocol amending the convention in accordance with the final resolutions of the Conference. We are informed that eleven nations out of the twenty-six members of the Commission have signed this Protocol, and that others will undoubtedly do so in the course of the next two weeks.[25] Before these amendments become effective, they must be ratified in accordance with the provisions of the Convention. The following comment relative to the resolutions adopted by the Conference is respectfully submitted.

*Article 3* [26]

The Conference adopted a recommendation that Article 3 be modified so as to provide that each contracting State is entitled for military

[22] The final resolutions were signed by all the delegates without engagement for their respective Governments.—Commission's *Official Bulletin No. 16*, November 1929, pp. 33–35.
[23] Embodied in the letter to the Secretary of Commerce, *infra.*
[24] Not printed; see publications cited in footnote 1, p. 489.
[25] The protocol was signed only by states parties to the convention of October 13, 1919; for text of the protocol, see Commission's *Official Bulletin No. 16*, November 1929, p. 49.
[26] The article references are to the text of the convention of October 13, 1919; see *Foreign Relations*, 1926, vol. I, p. 152.

reasons or in the interest of public safety, to prohibit the aircraft of other contracting States from flying over certain areas of its territory, subject to no distinction being made in this respect between the private aircraft of the contracting States, and as an exceptional measure and for public safety, to provide further that each contracting State might authorize flight over the areas in question by its national aircraft.

This appears to constitute some improvement over the present provisions of Article 3 of the Convention, although the improvement in question does not go so far as was contemplated in our instructions, since the Conference was disinclined to go to this extent.

As an additional provision of Article 3, the Conference recommended that there be incorporated in this article a right of reservation in each contracting State, under exceptional circumstances in time of peace, temporarily, to limit the flight over its territory or over part of its territory, of foreign aircraft.

This last mentioned addition was contained in the German proposal and approved in our instructions and we succeeded in having a further provision added to the effect that any such restriction or prohibition as should be imposed should be applicable without distinction of nationality to the aircraft of all the other States.

We proposed in this connection that an exception be made for postal aircraft, but it was explained by members of the Conference that the whole question of postal aircraft was to be considered at a Conference of the International Postal Union to be held at an early date, and in view of this situation, the Conference was unwilling to provide for an exception for postal aircraft.

*Article 5*

The present article 5 of the Convention provides that no contracting State shall, except by special or temporary authorization, permit the flight over its territory of aircraft which does not possess the nationality of any contracting State, unless it has made a special convention with the State in which the aircraft is registered and that the stipulations of such special conventions must not infringe the rights of the contracting parties and must conform to the rules laid down by the Convention and its annexes.

The recommendation made by the Conference as to article 5, states affirmatively that each contracting State is entitled to conclude special conventions with non-contracting States, and adds that the stipulations of such conventions shall not infringe the rights of the contracting parties to the present Convention. However, with regard to the question of conformity to the rules laid down by the present Convention, the recommendations provide that such special conventions "in so far as may be consistent with their object", shall not be contrary to the "general principles" of the present Convention.

The provisions of the recommendations last mentioned were inserted with a view to meeting the wishes of the Delegation of the United States, and while the Conference did not go so far in this respect as was desired by our Delegation, it is our opinion that the recommendations, if adopted, will constitute a considerable improvement, from the standpoint of the United States, to the present provisions of Article 5 of the Convention.

*Article 7*

The recommendations of the Conference with respect to the provisions of Article 7 of the Convention, are to the effect that the registration of aircraft shall be made in accordance with the laws and special provisions of each contracting State. This provision corresponds to provisions in this respect contained in the Pan-American Convention [27] and apparently should be satisfactory to the United States.

*Article 15*

The Conference recommended in accordance with a proposal of the German Delegation, an additional paragraph in article 15, dealing with flights by pilotless aircraft which appears unobjectionable.

Referring to our instructions concerning paragraph 3 of Article 15, it may be said that the Conference took a vote upon the question of freedom of innocent passage and decisively defeated the proposal that this be recommended. Therefore, the Conference's recommendation on the question of this paragraph is that every contracting State may make conditional on its prior authorization the establishment of international airways and the creation and operation of regular international air navigation lines, with or without landing on its territory.

This last mentioned provision seems to constitute a slight improvement over the existing provisions with regard to the freedom of innocent passage, but in any event, it represents the extent to which the Conference was willing to go on this point.

The Commission was authorized to recommend that the contracting states should not refuse such authorization except on reasonable grounds. (See Resolution No. 3, pages 5 and 6 of the Final Resolutions.) [28]

*Article 34*

The Conference was unwilling substantially to change the wording of paragraph 1 of article 34, relative to the connection between the

---

[27] *Foreign Relations*, 1928, vol. I, p. 585.
[28] Commission's *Official Bulletin No. 16*, p. 34.

International Commission and the League of Nations. However, it was explained by reference to a document issued by the Commission (page 71 of Documents) [29] that such relations are in fact of an unsubstantial character and that in reality they are largely confined to keeping the League advised of the doings of the Commission, which apparently constitutes a body essentially independent of the League in other respects. In this relation, reference may be made to recommendation No. 4 of the Conference, as to the future relations between the Commission and the Pan-American Union, as indicating the sense of the Conference that such relations should be similar to those between the Commission and the League of Nations. It was apparently considered by the Conference that the last mentioned recommendation would be satisfactory to the United States.

The Conference recommended changes in paragraphs 2, 3 and 4 of Article 34, so as to place each State on an equality in the matter of representation on the Commission.

With respect to the provisions of Article 34 as to the modification of any of the annexes, the Conference recommended a change in the direction of equality of States by striking out the present provision as to the favored situation of certain States in making up a majority, and in the interest of the practicability of making changes, recommended that modifications need only be approved by three fourths of the total votes of the States represented at the session, and two thirds of the total possible votes which could be cast if all the states were represented.

On the question of the provisions of article 34, regarding the payment of expenses, the Conference recommended that such expenses should be borne by the contracting States in the proportion fixed by the Commission.

It seemed necessary to avoid a recommendation for a definite allocation of expenses, especially in view of the fact that a request made by the British Delegation that representation on the Commission with vote, be given each British Dominion and India, was informally agreed to by the representatives of the contracting States as presenting an appropriate matter to be considered at an early session of the Commission.

The Chairman ruled that this request of the British Delegation was not properly before this Conference for recommendation as the British Empire was already a party to the Convention and had not given advance notice of its intention to present this subject for

---

[29] Note of June 7, 1929, by the Secretary General of the Commission on the relations between the International Commission for Air Navigation and the League of Nations, *Extraordinary Session of June 1929, Documents* (579.-6D1/318).

discussion. However, this ruling was not made until after we had cabled request for instructions on this proposal.

## Article 37, 1st Paragraph

The present Article 37, 1st Paragraph, provides that in case of a disagreement between two or more states relative to the interpretation of the Convention, the question in dispute shall be brought before the Permanent Court of International Justice.

A recommendation for a change in this respect was made to the effect that if one of the States concerned has not accepted the protocols relating to the Court, the question in dispute may, on the demand of such State, be settled by arbitration.

This recommendation, if accepted, would seem to render the Convention much more satisfactory to States not members of the Court.

The Conference recommended the amendment of Article 41 of the Convention, and the deletion of Article 42, so as to avoid any distinction between States which took part in the World War and those which did not.

It should be pointed out that the German Delegation failed to press a number of their proposals, including the following:

## Under Article 1

1. The proposal that the word "colonies" be defined more clearly in article 1 of the Convention.

2. The proposal that the Convention deal with flight over Straits.

3. The proposal that the Convention apply to private aircraft only.

## Under Article 6

The proposal that the Conference consider the question of the word "nationality" in connection with aircraft.

## Under Article 7

Paragraphs 1 and 2. The proposals that the registration of aircraft depend upon the domicile of the owner, whether an individual or a corporation.

## Under Article 9

The proposal that the Conference consider the requirement for the monthly exchange among the contracting States of copies of registrations and cancellations thereof.

## Under Article 18

The proposal of applying to aircraft immunity from seizure and the proposal that an attempt be made to settle the question of conflicting laws.

*Under Article 19*

The proposal that the expression "Bill of Lading" be replaced by "Air Consignment Note".

*Under Article 23*

The proposal that the Conference consider whether the principle of maritime law should apply in the absence of any agreement to the contrary in the case of salvage of aircraft wrecked at sea.

*Under Article 31*

The proposal that the word "detailed" is used in this article to be made more clear. The German Delegation also submitted a definition of the term "Military Aircraft" which was referred for further study.

*Under Article 32*

The proposal that consideration should be given to amending this article with respect to the extension to maritime aircraft of the privileges customarily accorded to foreign ships of war.

*Under Article 34*

The proposal that the sphere of activities of the International Air Commission be extended so as to include so far as possible all questions of sovereignty requiring international regulation, including the incorporation into the commission of the committee of air law experts instituted by the Paris International Private Air Law Conference of 1926 [*1925*].

The question of the necessity of the International Commission.

Finally, the Conference recommended the remission to the Commission, for further study at an early date, of certain questions which it did not seem practicable to deal with definitely at the Conference, including the question of the languages to be used in the documentation of the Commission, which last question aroused a lengthy argument at the Conference, as well as the further question of the simplification and betterment of the stipulations of Annex H to the Convention relating to customs matters. These recommendations for further study may be found on pages 5 and 6 of the Final Resolutions enclosed, and reference has been made above to the provisions of recommendation No. 4 concerning the possible future relations between the Commission and the Pan American Union.

The Air Minister gave a luncheon to the American Delegation on Monday June 10, also a dinner to the entire conference on Thursday June 13. The French Delegation entertained the conference at dinner on Friday June 14. The United States Delegation returned these courtesies at a luncheon on June 19. Though the reservations on behalf of the United States are dated June 15, the final draft was not filed with the Commission until June 27. In the meantime, delegate Baker left for Berlin on other business for the Department of State, and delegate MacCracken remained in Paris to conclude matters pertaining to these reservations and this report. He also participated in official ceremonies in connection with the reception to Messrs. Assollant, Lefevre and Lotti, the Frenchmen who flew from the United States to Paris, France.

Before concluding, the delegates desire to express their appreciation of the valuable assistance rendered by the Technical Advisors, Major B. K. Yount, Lieut. Commander Wm. B. Thomas, and John J. Ide, also by Mr. Norman Armour, Chargé d'Affaires at the Embassy, Mr. Williamson S. Howell and the members of the Embassy Staff, and Mr. D. J. Reagan, Acting Commercial Attaché, his assistant Mr. H. R. Buckley, Automotive Trade Commissioner to Europe, and the members of their Staff.

While it was not possible to prevail upon the Conference to adopt all the amendments proposed in our instructions, we believe that the amendments set forth in the Protocol adopted by the Commission in accordance with recommendations of the Conference, when they become effective, will constitute a substantial improvement in the Convention. However, we believe that the question of ratification by the United States should be the subject of further study by all departments concerned before reaching any definite conclusions.

Respectfully submitted,　　　　WILLIAM P. MACCRACKEN, JR.

JOSEPH R. BAKER

---

579.6D1/335a

*The Secretary of State to the Secretary of Commerce (Lamont)*[30]

WASHINGTON, November 26, 1929.

SIR: Reference is made to previous correspondence regarding the International Convention of October 13, 1919, relating to the Regulation of Air Navigation, and especially this Department's communications to you of March 27 and August 2, 1929.[31]

As you are aware, this Convention was signed with certain reservations by representatives of the United States on May 1 [*31*], 1920, and was transmitted by the President to the Senate on June 16, 1926, with a report from the Secretary of State containing recommenda-

---

[30] Also sent, *mutatis mutandis*, to the Postmaster General, the Chairman of the National Advisory Committee for Aeronautics, the Secretary of Labor, and the Secretary of the Treasury; and to the Navy and the War Departments with the addition of a final sentence reading as follows: "I would particularly like to have your advice as to whether you consider that the reservations should include one excepting the Panama Canal from the operation of this Convention."

[31] Neither printed.

tions that the Senate be requested to take suitable action advising and consenting to the ratification of the Convention with Articles 5 and 34 amended as recommended by the International Commission for Air Navigation in the protocols of amendment approved by the Commission October 27, 1922, and June 30, 1923, respectively, on the following conditions and understandings:

[Here follows the text of the reservations quoted in the letter to the President, printed on page 491.]

You are also aware that the convention in question is still pending before the Senate and that action thereon has been suspended pursuant to a recommendation of this Department made February 20, 1929, and based upon the statement that the Department felt that it would be inadvisable for the Senate to take action on the Convention before that Department had had an opportunity to try out its own air regulations made under authority of the Air Commerce Act of 1926.

I now transmit herewith for your information a photostat of a certified true copy of the protocol dated June 15, 1929, concerning amendments of several articles of this Convention established by the International Commission for Air Navigation at the conclusion of its recent extraordinary session at Paris of June 1929. These amendments were so established pursuant to recommendations embodied in resolutions passed at the session which was attended as well by representatives of States not parties to the Convention as by representatives of party States. The resolutions were signed by the representatives of the United States with the following reservations:

"1. The Delegation of the United States reserves on the part of its Government the position that the right to permit private aircraft of a contracting State to fly over areas over which private aircraft of other contracting States may be forbidden to fly, should be accorded, providing equality of treatment is assured to all aircraft engaged in international air commerce.

"2. The Delegation of the United States reserves on behalf of its Government the position that the right should be accorded to each Government to enter into special treaties, conventions and agreements regarding aerial navigation, so long as such convention or special agreement does not impair the rights or obligations of any of the States parties to this Convention.

"3. The Delegation of the United States reserves on behalf of its Government the position that complete freedom of action as to customs matters should be accorded the contracting States.

"4. The Delegation of the United States gives notice on behalf of its Government that should such Government ratify the International Convention, it would probably be with reservations that its action should not be taken to involve any legal relation on the part of the United States to the League of Nations, or the assumption of any obligation by the United States under the Covenant of the League of Nations constituting Part I of the Treaty of Versailles."

As a result of these changes effected at this recent extraordinary session, it is now in order for the Department to determine what action in the premises should be recommended to the Senate.

Unless the Department of Commerce desires that the Senate further delay its action this Department, as at present advised, is prepared to recommend that the Senate approve this Convention with reservations and it would be glad to receive from you any suggestions you may care to make as to the nature or language of such reservations, as well as an expression of your views upon the broad question as to whether it is desirable that the United States should become a party to this Convention at the present time. . . .

Very truly yours,                      For the Secretary of State:
                                          FRANCIS WHITE

[On December 11, 1929, a communication from the Department of Commerce expressed the view that ratification of the convention by the United States should be held in abeyance at least until such time as the amendments proposed at the extraordinary session of the International Commission were properly ratified by the several countries who were parties to the Convention (579.6D1/341).

On January 15, 1934, the convention and accompanying papers were returned to the President by the Senate, pursuant to a request by President Roosevelt, dated January 12, 1934.]

# NEGOTIATIONS WITH CERTAIN EUROPEAN COUNTRIES TO EFFECT ARRANGEMENTS COVERING CERTAIN QUESTIONS OF AERIAL NAVIGATION

## Great Britain

711.4127/1

### *The British Ambassador (Howard) to the Secretary of State*

No. 239                                        WASHINGTON, May 7, 1928.

SIR: I have the honour to state that the question has arisen of the grant of American Air Transport licenses for British pilots in this country. I am informed that the United States Air Commerce Regulations (Section 64) state that:

"All applicants for pilots licenses must be of good moral character. The minimum age requirements are 16 years for private pilots and 18 years for industrial pilots. Private pilots may be citizens of any country. Industrial and transport pilots must be citizens of the United States or of a foreign country which grants reciprocal piloting privileges to citizens of the United States on equal terms and conditions with citizens of such foreign country."

At the same time I beg leave to inform you that citizens of the United States are eligible in Great Britain and Northern Ireland for the issue of licenses:

(*a*) as private pilots, and
(*b*) as public transport pilots,

provided they attain the standards laid down in Section VIII of the Air Navigation directions of 1926, as amended by the Air Navigation directions of 1928. Copies of these documents are transmitted herewith for your information.[1]

I also transmit herewith copy of a letter dated December 22nd last, which was addressed to the Air Attaché to this Embassy by the United States Director of Aeronautics.[1] It will be observed from Mr. Young's letter that the Department of Commerce would be pleased to arrange for the issue of licenses to British subjects in the United States, and vice versa, but that they consider that an official exchange of correspondence through diplomatic channels is necessary first. I therefore have the honour to state officially that the above-mentioned facilities are granted to United States pilots in Great Britain and Northern Ireland, and I shall be glad to be informed

---

[1] Not printed.

at your convenience whether British subjects are reciprocally eligible to receive transport licenses in the United States.

I have [etc.]                           (For the Ambassador)
                                              H. G. CHILTON

---

711.4127/5

*The Secretary of State to the British Chargé (Chilton)*

WASHINGTON, June 14, 1928.

SIR: I have the honor to refer to the Department's note of May 21, 1928,[2] in regard to the proposed issuance on a reciprocal basis of licenses to air pilots in the United States and in Great Britain and to inform you that I am in receipt of a communication concerning this matter from the Department of Commerce.

In this communication attention is invited to the desirability of an agreement being reached between the United States and Great Britain with regard to the reciprocal recognition of airworthiness certificates. The following considerations are set forth in regard to this matter in the communication above referred to:

"Several cases are now pending which involve the granting of airworthiness certificates (or licenses) to aircraft of British manufacture which have been imported by citizens of the United States. Likewise, there are cases pending in which the validation of such certificates for aircraft manufactured in the United States and exported to subjects of the British Empire is required. The fundamental requirements in the manufacture of such aircraft are quite the same, as has been evidenced by material submitted upon the request of Commander Hetherington.

"There is an existing arrangement between Canada and the United States [3] which has proven to be decidedly practical and which recognizes aircraft and pilot. The Canadian authorities accept airworthiness certificates issued by the Department of Commerce in favor of domestic aircraft which is being exported to Canada. The same situation prevails in favor of aircraft imported by citizens of the United States from Canada. Canadian nationals are issued pilots' licenses upon accomplishing the tests prescribed by the U. S. Department of Commerce and citizens of the United States are granted like privileges in the matter of Canadian licenses.

"It is suggested that the time is propitious for a similar arrangement to be perfected with Great Britain and that it would be in order to transmit such a request to the British Ambassador.

"Meanwhile, the matter of issuing airworthiness certificates for both British and American aircraft is being held in abeyance in the respective countries."

---

[2] Not printed.
[3] A temporary arrangement between the United States and Canada was concluded in 1920 and renewed from time to time. It was superseded by a reciprocal arrangement effected by exchange of notes, August 29 and October 22, 1929; see vol. II, pp. 111 ff.

I shall be pleased to receive for transmission to the Department of Commerce such comments as the appropriate British authorities may deem relevant in this matter.

Accept [etc.]

For the Secretary of State:
FRANCIS WHITE

———————————

711.4127/7

*The British Chargé (Chilton) to the Secretary of State*

No. 322                     BEVERLY FARMS, MASS., July 17, 1928.
                               [Received July 23 (?).]

SIR: I have the honour to refer to your note of June the 14th on the subject of the proposed issuance on a reciprocal basis of licenses to air pilots in the United States and Great Britain. In his note No. 239 of May 7th, Sir Esme Howard stated that he understood that Section 64 of the United States Air Commerce Regulations provides that holders of private pilots' licenses may be citizens of any country but that applicants for licenses as industrial or transport pilots must be citizens of the United States or of a foreign nation which grants reciprocal piloting privileges to citizens of this country on equal terms and conditions with its own nationals. Sir Esme Howard pointed out that no nationality qualification exists as far as any British pilot certificate is concerned and that citizens of the United States are therefore on an equal footing with British subjects in this matter. In the circumstances, therefore, all that would seem to be necessary to regularize the position is an official exchange of correspondence as suggested by the Director of Aeronautics, of the Department of Commerce, in the letter which he addressed on December 22nd last to the Air Attaché of His Majesty's Embassy, and I have the honour to request that I may receive a note from the United States Government confirming my belief that British subjects are eligible to receive industrial and transport pilots' licenses in this country.

The reciprocal issuance of airworthiness certificates in Great Britain and the United States, which was suggested in the letter from the Department of Commerce, quoted in your despatch under reference, would seem to be a question of a distinctly different character, and one which should be dealt with separately. The possibility of such an arrangement as between the United States Government and His Majesty's Government in Australia was the subject of correspondence early this year between the State Department and His Majesty's Embassy.[4] It was finally referred to His Majesty's Government in Australia through the Foreign Office and I shall not

———————————
[4] Not printed.

fail to inform you in due course of the views of the Commonwealth Government in this matter.

The question has not hitherto been raised as between the United States Government and His Majesty's Government in Great Britain, but I shall be glad to take the matter up with my Government if the Department of Commerce desire to propose the conclusion of a separate arrangement of this nature. I should be glad to be informed of the views of the United States Government on this point in due course.

In the meantime I should be most grateful for an early reply on the subject of the issuance of pilots' certificates, as cases have been brought to my notice of the refusal of such certificates to British subjects on account of alleged absence of reciprocity, when, in fact, according to both the American and British regulations, such reciprocity would seem to exist.

I have [etc.]                                    H. G. CHILTON

---

711.4127/16

*The Secretary of State to the British Ambassador (Howard)*

WASHINGTON, January 22, 1929.

EXCELLENCY: I have the honor to refer to Mr. Chilton's note of October 10 [*September 19*] [5] and previous correspondence regarding the possibility of the issuance of licenses to air pilots in the United States and in Great Britain and Northern Ireland upon a reciprocal basis and I would likewise advert to the question raised in that correspondence of a similar reciprocal recognition of the air worthiness certificates issued by the two Governments.

In Mr. Chilton's note of May 7 and in your note of July 17, it was observed that no nationality qualification exists so far as the issuance of British pilot licenses is concerned and that citizens of the United States are therefore on an equal footing with British subjects in this matter, and the suggestion was made that the position of the two Governments on this point be regularized by an official exchange of correspondence. However, in response to the suggestion which had been put forward in the Department's note of June 14 that a similar and simultaneous agreement be adopted in respect of recognition of the air worthiness certificates by the two Governments, the reply was made in your note of July 17 that this latter question appeared to be of a distinctly different character from that of the issuance of pilot licenses and one which should be dealt with separately.

---

[5] Not printed.

It is the understanding of the Department that it is the desire of your Government to effect at this time merely an agreement regarding the issuance of pilots licenses in the United States and in Great Britain and Northern Ireland, leaving the question of the air worthiness certificates to future negotiations, and that your Government considers that the privileges now extended to American pilots in Great Britain and Northern Ireland fulfill the condition of reciprocity referred to in the Air Commerce Act of 1926 [6] and in Section 64 of the U. S. Air Commerce Regulations. However I must state that even if this Government were willing to discuss the question of pilot licenses and air worthiness certificates separately, it would still be unable to consider that the requirement of reciprocity contemplated in the Act had been met as regards the issuance of pilot licenses, unless it should be represented that equivalent privileges are likewise extended to American pilots in the British Dominions (excepting the Irish Free State and Canada, with whom the United States maintains direct diplomatic relations) and in the British oversea possessions. Accordingly, in the absence of such assurances, the aviation authorities of this Government, acting with the discretionary power provided by the Air Commerce Act of 1926, feel constrained to decline to issue pilot licenses to British subjects at the present time.

As to the question of the reciprocal recognition of the air worthiness certificates of the two Governments, this Government is unable to perceive the necessity for carrying on separate negotiations inasmuch as the issuance of pilot licenses and of air worthiness certificates are closely related and are subject to the control in each country of the same governmental authority, and as the identical principle of reciprocity is involved.

I would therefore suggest that it would be opportune to effect an agreement which shall include both the question of pilot licenses and that of air worthiness certificates, and which shall extend to the United States and its possessions on the one hand, and on the other to Great Britain and Northern Ireland, the British Dominions (excepting the Irish Free State and Canada) and to the British oversea possessions and I am advised that informal conversations on this matter are already under way. I trust that you will bring the foregoing to the attention of your Government and that the negotiations may be expedited in order that the present restrictions upon American pilots and aircraft in British territory and upon British pilots and aircraft in American territory may be removed.

Accept [etc.]                                    FRANK B. KELLOGG

[6] 44 Stat. 568.

711.4127/18

## The British Embassy to the Department of State

### MEMORANDUM

As stated in Mr. Chilton's note No. 239 of May 7th, 1928, the United States Air Commerce Regulations, Section 64, provide that:

"All applicants for pilots' licences must be of good moral character. The minimum age requirements are 16 years for private pilots and 18 years for industrial pilots. Private pilots may be citizens of any country. Industrial and transport pilots must be citizens of the United States or of a foreign country which grants reciprocal piloting privileges to citizens of the United States on equal terms and conditions with citizens of such foreign country."

As further pointed out in Mr. Chilton's note, citizens of the United States are eligible in Great Britain and Northern Ireland for the issue of licences, (a) as private pilots, and (b) as public transport pilots, provided they attain the standards laid down in the regulations, copies of which were enclosed.

Mr. Chilton also forwarded with his note copy of a letter dated December 22nd, 1927,[7] addressed by the United States Director of Aeronautics to the Air Attaché to this Embassy, stating that the issue of pilots' licenses upon a reciprocal basis in the United States and in the United Kingdom appeared to be provided for by the existing regulations, but that an official exchange of correspondence through diplomatic channels was necessary to confirm the arrangement.

As stated by Mr. Chilton, His Majesty's Government in Great Britain and Northern Ireland are anxious to have this reciprocity confirmed. It is understood, however, from State Department notes of June 14, 1928 and January 22nd, 1929, that the United States Government are reluctant to recognize the reciprocity provided for in the above regulations until an agreement has also been reached for the reciprocal recognition of airworthiness certificates.

His Majesty's Government fully understand the desire of the United States Government to conclude such an agreement, and as stated in Mr. Kellogg's note of January 22nd last, informal conversations on the question have been proceeding for some time past. At the same time, His Majesty's Government adhere to the view that the issue of pilots' licenses and of airworthiness certificates should be treated as separate and distinct questions. The one concerns personnel, the other equipment; and while they hope it will be possible to arrive at an agreement which will be satisfactory to the two Governments upon

---

[7] Not printed.

the latter point as well, they cannot but regard the connection between the two as purely arbitrary.

In his note of January 22nd Mr. Kellogg expressed the hope that negotiations might be expedited in order that the present restrictions upon American pilots and aircraft in British territory, and upon British pilots and aircraft in American territory might be removed. His Majesty's Government would observe that while informal conversations are still being held in the hope of reaching an agreement upon the question of airworthiness certificates, the reciprocal issue of pilots' licences appears to be already provided for by the regulations actually in force in the United States and in the United Kingdom, so that all that is necessary to remove the existing restrictions upon American and British pilots is a formal note from the United States Government stating, in reply to Mr. Chilton's note of May 7th last, that British subjects are reciprocally eligible to receive licences in the United States.

It is noted that the United States Government are anxious to arrange for the reciprocal issue both of pilots' licences and airworthiness certificates in the British possessions overseas, and in Australia, New Zealand, South Africa, Newfoundland and India, and the necessary steps are being taken to bring the matter to the attention of the Governments concerned. In the meanwhile, His Majesty's Government in Great Britain and Northern Ireland wish to express again their earnest hope that the United States Government may see their way in the near future to recognise, by a formal note, the existing regulations for the reciprocal issue of pilots' licences to the nationals of the two Governments.

WASHINGTON, February 7, 1929.

---

711.4127/25

*The Department of State to the British Embassy*

MEMORANDUM

The Department has received the British Embassy's memorandum of February 7, regarding the reciprocal issuance of pilots' licenses and the mutual recognition of air-worthiness certificates by Great Britain and the United States, and the views advanced therein have been given careful consideration by the appropriate authorities of this Government.

This Government notes the British Embassy's statement that it regards as purely arbitrary the connection between the two closely related questions of the reciprocal issuance of pilots' licenses and the mutual recognition of air-worthiness certificates by Great Britain and the United States. The Department takes this occasion to reiterate the suggestion made in its note of January 22, 1929, regarding the desirability of effecting an agreement which shall include both the question of pilots' licenses and that of air-worthiness certificates and which shall extend to the United States and its possessions on the one hand, and on the other to Great Britain and Northern Ireland, British Dominions (excepting the Irish Free State and Canada) and to the British oversea possessions. In this connection, there is enclosed the draft text of an agreement now under discussion between the United States and the Government of Canada [8] which it is believed might serve as a useful model for a similar agreement between the United States and the British Empire as a whole (excepting the Irish Free State and Canada with whom the United States maintains direct diplomatic relations). It may be added that an agreement on the basis of the enclosed draft is being proposed to the Irish Free State and that it is intended to make similar proposals to other nations.

It is hoped that the Embassy will bring the substance of this draft agreement to the attention of the appropriate British authorities with a view to advancing the previous discussions which have taken place upon the subject.

WASHINGTON, April 3, 1929.

---

## Italy

711.6527/1

*The Italian Ambassador (De Martino) to the Secretary of State*

WASHINGTON, December 20, 1928.

MR. SECRETARY OF STATE: I have the honor to bring to Your Excellency's knowledge that several Italian aviators, duly licensed, are coming to this Country for the purpose of piloting aeroplanes of the "Savoia Marchetti" type which have been or will be imported into the United States. The flights they are planning will be of a demonstrative character and they intend to make them also in view of the fact that the construction in this Country of aeroplanes of the above mentioned type is now contemplated.

Upon instructions of my Government, I have the honor to have recourse to Your Excellency's kindness and ask that permission be granted by the appropriate departments of the United States Government to these Italian aviators to pilot the "Savoia Marchetti" aeroplanes above referred to.

At the same time, and availing myself of this occasion, I would ask Your Excellency to consider the advisability of our two Countries

---

[8] Draft text not printed.

entering into an agreement on the basis of reciprocity, allowing aviators of either Party to pilot their own or foreign aeroplanes in the Country of the Other, such agreement possibly to be concluded through an exchange of notes.

My Government has informed me that they would consider this accord with great satisfaction, and I would therefore be very much obliged to Your Excellency if you would advise me in due course whether this proposition finds favor with the United States Government.

Will Your Excellency please accept [etc.]        G. DE MARTINO

---

711.6527/5

*The Secretary of State to the Italian Ambassador (De Martino)*

WASHINGTON, January 30, 1929.

EXCELLENCY: I have the honor to refer to Your Excellency's note of December 20, 1928, requesting permission for certain licensed Italian aviators to pilot airplanes of the "Savoia Marchetti" type in demonstration flights in this country and suggesting the conclusion of a reciprocal agreement, by exchange of notes between the two countries, whereby aviators of either of the contracting countries would be permitted to pilot airplanes in the territory of the other.

I now take pleasure in informing Your Excellency that I am in receipt of a reply from the interested Department of this Government. No objection is found to granting temporary permission to a limited number of Italian pilots to demonstrate the particular airplanes in question. It would be necessary, however, for this Government to be advised of the identity of the pilots, their pilot's license classification and numbers and for the flights to be limited to demonstration purposes, i. e., they should not engage in air commerce. Under the provisions of the Air Commerce Act of 1926,[9] it would also be necessary for the Italian Government to agree to extend a similar privilege to pilots of the United States, should occasion arise and it would be advisable at the same time to indicate the duration of the temporary period for which authority to demonstrate the planes in question is desired. Perhaps a period of three months would be sufficient for the purpose, but this is merely a suggestion and is subject to variation.

Should Your Excellency's Government desire to consider the question of complete reciprocity in the matter of pilots' licenses, this Government is entirely agreeable to a discussion of the matter. The suggestion advanced in Your Excellency's note under acknowledgment refers only to pilots' licenses, but if the subject of reciprocity

---

[9] 44 Stat. 568.

is to be discussed, it is believed advisable that it should include the reciprocal validation of airworthiness certificates for aircraft as well as pilots' licenses.

Accept [etc.]

For the Secretary of State:
NELSON TRUSLER JOHNSON

---

711.6527/6

*The Italian Ambassador (De Martino) to the Secretary of State*

WASHINGTON, March 28, 1929.

MR. SECRETARY OF STATE: I have the honor to refer to my note of December 20th, 1929 [*1928*] and the Department's reply of January 30th, 1929 in regard to a proposed agreement between the United States and Italy in the matter of pilot's licenses.

I have the honor to inform Your Excellency that the Italian Government is ready to conclude with the Government of the United States, through an exchange of notes, an accord for the reciprocal granting of the permission to the respective citizens of piloting all types of aircraft on the territory of the two Countries.

The Italian Government is willing to accept the proposals advanced by the United States Government as set forth in the Department's note mentioned above, with the following modifications and additions:

1) The number of pilots could be fixed at fifteen;
2) The length of the period for which authority is granted could be established at six months, with faculty of extension;
3) The Italian Government would recognize the American pilot's licenses provided full reciprocity be granted for Italian licenses issued by the Italian Ministry of Aeronautics both to military and civil aviators. The Italian Government would recognize the licenses issued by such American authorities as specified in the text of the agreement.

With reference to the last part of the Department's note of January 30th, 1929, I have the honor to inform that the Italian Government is ready to proceed at the same time to an agreement for the reciprocal recognition of airworthiness certificates issued to the aircraft of the two Countries.

Accept [etc.]

G. DE MARTINO

---

711.6527/13

*The Acting Secretary of State to the Italian Ambassador*
*(De Martino)*

WASHINGTON, June 12, 1929.

EXCELLENCY: I have the honor to acknowledge the receipt of your note of March 28, regarding the possibility of an agreement between the United States and Italy regarding the reciprocal recognition of pilots' licenses by the two Governments, and note that the Italian Government is prepared to proceed at the same time to an agreement for a reciprocal recognition of air worthiness certificates issued to the aircraft of the two countries.

While this Government has not as yet become a party to the International Flying Convention of 1919,[10] it fully appreciates the importance in the meantime of reaching agreements with the various nations of the world with a view to facilitating international aerial navigation with especial reference to commercial and privately owned aircraft. Since 1920 this Government has had an informal agreement on the subject with the Dominion of Canada which agreement is now under discussion between the two Governments with a view to revision to conform to present day conditions.[11]  The subject has also for some months past been under discussion with the British Government [12] and this Government has suggested the desirability of effecting a general agreement providing for the reciprocal issuance of pilots' licenses and the mutual recognition of air worthiness certificates by Great Britain and the United States, and has made a similar proposal to the Irish Free State.[13]  This Government has recently suggested to the British Government and to the Government of the Irish Free State the use of the proposed Canadian agreement as a model for this purpose and it takes the occasion offered by your note of March 28 to inquire whether your Government would be disposed to consider the adoption of a similar agreement between Italy and the United States which would extend to the United States and its possessions on the one hand and on the other to Italy and its possessions.  For your convenience, I enclose a copy of the draft text of the agreement now being discussed with the Government of Canada [14] which, as you will perceive, is based on the principle of recognition of the sovereignty of a state over the air space above its territory and upon reciprocity of treatment subject, of course, to restrictions designed to promote safety in aerial navigation and to make suitable provision for the requirements of national defense.

With regard to the three suggestions made in your note of March 28 regarding the number of pilots to be admitted, the length of the period for which their privileges would extend, and the designation of the licensing authority in Italy, it would appear that the conclusion of an agreement based on the Canadian model would obviate any necessity for specific reference in the agreement to the first point mentioned in your note.  With regard to the second point I would

[10] *Foreign Relations*, 1926, vol. I, p. 152.
[11] See vol. II, pp. 111 ff.
[12] *Ante*, pp. 518–525.
[13] *Post*, p. 530.
[14] Not printed.

say that it is my understanding that the Italian Government feels that the limitations imposed by the immigration laws of the United States upon the duration of the stay of Italian aviators in the United States make it appropriate for it to impose analogous restrictions upon the stay of American aviators in Italy. The Government of the United States fully appreciates this view and it is accordingly willing to accept your suggestion on this point. Regarding the third suggestion made in your note of March 28, it may be said that the United States will, of course, recognize the designation of the Italian Ministry for Aeronautics as the licensing authority in Italy and the agreement, if concluded, would contain appropriate references thereto in paragraphs 3, 4, 5 and 8 of the enclosed draft. However, in view of the circumstance that the proposed agreement is intended to apply only to commercial and privately owned aircraft, this Government would suggest that to avoid all possible ambiguity the term "licenses" be construed to refer only to civil licenses and that all reference to military licenses be eliminated.

It is understood, of course, that the agreement thus envisaged would not apply to military, naval, customs and police aircraft employed in the service of either state, which would continue to require special authorization to fly over or to land on the territory of the other state.

This Government is making similar proposals to other nations including France, Germany and Spain,[15] and in the meantime ventures to express the hope that the Italian Government may be disposed to conclude an agreement in the form suggested above. In such an event, this Government suggests that it be made effective by means of an exchange of notes.

Accept [etc.]                                        J. REUBEN CLARK, JR.

---

711.6527/21

*The Italian Ambassador (De Martino) to the Secretary of State*

WASHINGTON, October 10, 1929.

MY DEAR SECRETARY: I beg to refer to Your Excellency's note of June 12, 1929, in regard to the contemplated agreement between the United States and Italy and the reciprocal recognition of pilot licenses and of air worthiness certificates issued by the two Governments, and I also wish to refer to the conversations held at the Department by Count Marchetti, Counselor of this Embassy, and Mr. Vitetti, First Secretary, on this subject.

I am now in a position to state that the Italian Government con-

---

[15] See pp. 532–536, and 538–539.

siders the text of the agreement proposed between the United States and Canada regarding aerial navigation—enclosed in the above mentioned note—as apt to constitute the basis of the agreement. My Government, however, wishes to make the following propositions:

1) for the reasons which Your Excellency has fully appreciated in the above cited note, the length of the period for which authority is reciprocally granted to the pilots should be established to six months with faculty of extension;
2) the reciprocity treatment should be adopted also for what concerns the documents of test accompanying motorless aircraft or isolated engines or parts both of the aircraft and of the motor.

In case Your Excellency approves these points as proposed by my Government, I would be very much obliged to Your Excellency for causing your Department to prepare a draft taking them into consideration and to transmit it to me, so that I may obtain from my Government definite authority to conclude the agreement.

Accept [etc.]

———————

**Irish Free State**

711.41d27/2

*The Secretary of State to the Irish Minister (MacWhite)*

WASHINGTON, April 3, 1929.

SIR: As you are doubtless aware, the Government of the United States, although signatory, has not as yet become a party to the International Flying Convention of 1919 regarding international aerial navigation.[16]

However, I may say that this Government fully appreciates the importance in the mean time of reaching agreements with the various nations of the world with a view to facilitating international aerial navigation with especial reference to commercial and privately owned aircraft. Since 1920 this Government has had an informal agreement on the subject with the Dominion of Canada which agreement is now under discussion between the two Governments with a view to revision to conform to present day conditions. The subject has also for some months past been under discussion with the British Government and this Government has suggested the desirability of effecting a general agreement providing for the reciprocal issuance of pilots' licenses and the mutual recognition of air-worthiness certificates by Great Britain and the United States which would extend to the United States and its possessions on the one hand and on the other to Great

———————

[16] *Foreign Relations*, 1926, vol. I, p. 152.

Britain and Northern Ireland, the British Dominions (excepting the Irish Free State and Canada with whom the United States maintains direct diplomatic relations) and to the British oversea possessions. This Government is now suggesting to the British Government the use of the proposed Canadian agreement as a model for this purpose and it takes the same occasion to inquire whether your Government would be disposed to consider the adoption of a similar agreement between the Irish Free State and the United States. For your convenience, I enclose a copy of the draft text of the agreement now being discussed with the Government of Canada [17] which as you will perceive is based on the principle of recognition of the sovereignty of a state over the air space above its territory and upon reciprocity of treatment subject, of course, to restrictions designed to promote safety in aerial navigation and to make suitable provision for the requirements of national defense.

This Government expects to make similar proposals to other nations and in the meantime ventures to express the hope that your Government may be disposed to conclude such an agreement. In such an event, it is further proposed that the agreement be effected by means of an exchange of notes.

Accept [etc.]

For the Secretary of State:
W. R. CASTLE, JR.

---

711.41d27/4

*The Irish Minister (MacWhite) to the Secretary of State*

10–3/61/29                    WASHINGTON, 8 October, 1929.

SIR: I have the honor to refer to your Note of the 3rd of April, 1929 in regard to the proposal to conclude an agreement between the United States and the Irish Free State on the subject of international aerial navigation.

My Government have requested me to enquire whether, in view of the fact that the Government of the United States and that of the Irish Free State were represented at the Extraordinary Session of the International Commission on Air Navigation recently held in Paris,[18] a special convention between the two Governments is still regarded as desirable. Should it be that the United States Government will decide to ratify the International Flying Convention of 1919 as amended, it would seem that the necessity for a special convention between Governments which are parties to that Convention would disappear.

I have [etc.]

M. MACWHITE

[17] Not printed.
[18] See pp. 489 ff.

711.41d27/5

### The Secretary of State to the Irish Minister (MacWhite)

WASHINGTON, October 16, 1929.

SIR: I have the honor to acknowledge the receipt of your note dated October 8, 1929, inquiring on behalf of your Government whether, in view of the fact that both the Government of the Irish Free State and the Government of the United States participated in the recent Extraordinary Session of the International Commission on Air Navigation, this Government considered the conclusion of a special agreement as proposed in its note of April 3, 1929, still desirable.

In reply I may state that this Government, notwithstanding its participation in the recent Conference at Paris, believes it will be desirable, until such time when it may become a party to the 1919 Convention of International Aerial Navigation, to reach agreements with various nations providing for the reciprocal recognition of pilot licenses, airworthiness certificates and export certificates relative to commercial and private aircraft.

Accept [etc.]

For the Secretary of State:
FRANCIS WHITE

---

### France

711.5127/2

### The Acting Secretary of State to the French Ambassador (Claudel)[19]

WASHINGTON, June 12, 1929.

EXCELLENCY: As you are doubtless aware, the Government of the United States, although signatory, has not as yet become a party to the International Flying Convention of 1919 regarding international aerial navigation.[20]

However, I may say that this Government fully appreciates the importance in the mean time of reaching agreements with the various nations of the world with a view to facilitating international aerial navigation with especial reference to commercial and privately owned aircraft. Since 1920 this Government has had an informal agreement on the subject with the Dominion of Canada which agreement is now under discussion between the two Governments with a view to revision to conform to present day conditions. The subject has also for some months past been under discussion with the British Government and this Government has suggested the desirability of effecting a general agreement providing for the recipro-

---

[19] Also sent, mutatis mutandis, to the German and the Spanish Ambassadors, June 12, and to the Netherlands Minister, July 22.
[20] Foreign Relations, 1926, vol. I, p. 152.

cal issuance of pilots' licenses and the mutual recognition of airworthiness certificates by Great Britain and the United States and has made a similar proposal to the Irish Free State. This Government has recently suggested to the British Government and to the Government of the Irish Free State the use of the proposed Canadian agreement as a model for this purpose and it takes this occasion to inquire whether your Government would be disposed to consider the adoption of a similar agreement between France and the United States which would extend to the United States and its possessions on the one hand, and on the other to France and its possessions. For your convenience, I enclose a copy of the draft text to the agreement now being discussed with the Government of Canada [21] which, as you will perceive, is based on the principle of recognition of the sovereignty of a state over the air space above its territory and upon reciprocity of treatment subject, of course, to restrictions designed to promote safety in aerial navigation and to make suitable provision for the requirements of national defense.

It is understood, of course, that the agreement thus envisaged would not apply to military, naval, customs and police aircraft employed in the service of either state, which would continue to require special authorization to fly over or to land on the territory of the other state.

This Government is making similar proposals to a number of the other nations including Italy, Germany and Spain, and in the meantime it ventures to express the hope that your Government may be disposed to conclude an agreement in the form suggested above. In such an event, it is further proposed that the agreement be effected by means of an exchange of notes.

Accept [etc.]                                        J. REUBEN CLARK, JR.

---

711.5127/7 : Telegram

*The Chargé in France (Armour) to the Secretary of State*

PARIS, November 16, 1929—4 p. m.
[Received November 17—11:30 a. m.]

527. Reference Department's telegram number 376, November 14, noon.[21] Careful consideration being given proposed agreement by Air Ministry which informally states in effect that possibly favorable conclusion would be facilitated by agreement on the following points:

Would one of American lines be prepared to undertake establishment of airdromes and rescue facilities etc., at essential points be-

---

[21] Not printed.

tween Natal and Cayenne and to permit use thereof by French line, American Government to give such assurance as practicable that work would be carried out by American company? Parenthetically it is believed but not confirmed that this proviso is one of principal concessions desired by Aeropostale as requisite for granting permanent permission for American lines to fly over French possessions. (See my telegram number 513, November 5, 6 p. m.[22])

Negotiation agreement regarding factors of safety.

There is extreme dissatisfaction with regard to restriction entry into United States of flying boats of Lioré and Olivier Company. It would be desirable to furnish reasons for such restrictions since genuine resentment seems to be felt.

ARMOUR

711.5127/15

## The Secretary of State to the Chargé in France (Armour)

No. 4331                              WASHINGTON, December 14, 1929.

SIR: Reference is made to your telegram No. 527 of November 16, 4 p. m., and to your despatch No. 10024 of November 20, 1929,[23] reporting the attitude of French officials with respect to granting permission for American air transport companies to operate their planes over French territory in the Caribbean and South America.

The position taken by this Government, which you should emphasize in your conferences with French officials, is that any agreements between it and a foreign State regarding reciprocal flying rights should be limited to establishing questions of principle and not relate to private agreements to be made by individual American companies with foreign companies or corporations. This Government controls flying over American territory and hence is in a position to make agreements with a foreign State granting aircraft of that State permission to fly over American territory on the basis of reciprocal permission for American companies to fly over the territory of the State in question, and this is what has been proposed to the French Government. This Government has no authority to compel a private American company to make any agreements with any other American or foreign Company.

Furthermore, you should point out to the French authorities the obvious impropriety of the United States and France making an agreement covering Brazilian territory or territory of any other third nation. Even should American companies make an agree-

[22] Post, p. 631.
[23] Latter not printed.

ment with a French line for the establishment of airdromes, radio and rescue facilities, et cetera, between Cayenne and Natal, this Government obviously could give no assurance, such as you report the French authorities have requested, that this work would be carried out by the American company. The United States Government has no control over aviation in Brazil or in any other country outside of American territory. It will be interested to know how the French Government proposes to make such assurance effective in the Republic of Brazil.

The question at issue is whether the French Government is willing to make a reciprocal arrangement with the United States for flying privileges in the territories of the respective countries and if any further attempt is made to depart from that principle you should immediately point out in the first place, the obvious impossibility of this Government making such an undertaking as the French Government desires as it has no authority by law to compel the American company to make such an arrangement and, secondly, the impropriety of this Government entering into an agreement with France regarding the operations of American companies in Brazil or any other third country.

The point of view of this Government has been clearly set forth to Monsieur Henry, First Secretary of the French Embassy, as you were informed by the enclosures to the Department's instruction No. 4318 of December 5, 1929.[24] The Department has been advised that the French Embassy in Washington has been in telegraphic communication with the Foreign Office in this matter; that the Embassy feels that the Foreign Office now understands the position of this Government, and that the latter is taking the matter up with the Air Ministry and hopes to have the matter arranged satisfactorily. You will therefore please continue to press the matter along the lines above indicated.

As regards the question of the restriction upon the importation of Lioré and Olivier flying boats into the United States, there is enclosed for your information a copy of a self-explanatory letter from the Department of Commerce dated December 7, 1929.[24] In this connection it is pertinent to point out that the effecting of the proposed reciprocal arrangement containing a provision similar to Article 8 of the Canadian arrangement [25] will eliminate this difficulty.

Finally, the Department does not understand the statement that you report was made by a French official that France is not interested at this time in permission to operate planes commercially over United States territory on a reciprocal basis, since in the past the

---

[24] Not printed.
[25] See note of August 29, 1929, to the Canadian Chargé, vol. II, p. 111.

French Steamship Line operated a ship-to-shore service and it is the Department's understanding that it would wish to recommence this service next spring.

Please report promptly all developments in this matter.

I am [etc.]
For the Secretary of State:<br>
FRANCIS WHITE

---

## Germany

711.6227/5

### The German Ambassador (Prittwitz) to the Secretary of State

[Translation]

Q 46/29
WASHINGTON, June 20, 1929.

MR. SECRETARY: I have the honor to acknowledge receipt of Your Excellency's valued note 811.7961/27 of the 12th instant,[26] and of a draft of a convention between the United States and Canada concerning the settlement of questions about civil air navigation, and in provisional answer thereto to express my Government's readiness to conclude a similar agreement for the purpose of bringing about the reciprocal recognition of air worthiness for aircraft by way of an exchange of notes.

Inasmuch as the draft communicated by Your Excellency concerning the recognition of air worthiness certificates contemplates the settlement of further questions of the present international air navigation, I venture to hold in reserve any statement of position until I receive instructions from my Government on the subject.

Accept [etc.]
F. VON PRITTWITZ

---

## Netherlands

711.5627/7½

### The Chargé in the Netherlands (Johnson) to the Secretary of State

No. 2047
THE HAGUE, September 20, 1929.<br>
[Received October 5.]

SIR: I have the honor to refer to the Department's Instruction No. 711, of July 26th last,[27] transmitting a copy of a Note to the Netherland Legation at Washington,[28] as well as a copy of the enclosure

---

[26] See footnote 19, p. 532.
[27] Not printed.
[28] Dated July 22; see footnote 19, p. 532.

thereto, the draft of the aerial navigation agreement now being discussed with the Dominion of Canada.

As the Department was informed in the Legation's despatch No. 1887, of May 8, 1929,[29] the subject of an aerial navigation agreement with Holland has, with the approval of the Netherland Foreign Office, been tentatively discussed with the competent official of the Dutch Department of Waterstaat and upon the receipt of the Department's instruction first above mentioned Mr. Swift [30] again approached Mr. de Veer, the Dutch official in question, and went over with him the text of the agreement with Canada with the idea of the adoption of a similar agreement between the United States and Holland. There is every indication that the Netherland authorities are sincerely desirous of concluding an agreement with the United States but at the same time they are strongly of the opinion that any such agreement should approximate those concluded with other countries not parties to the International Air Convention which in turn conform, in their essential features, to the International Air Convention.

As will be seen from the enclosed translation of a Note from the Department of Waterstaat to the Foreign Office,[29] it is felt that the draft text of the agreement with Canada is lacking in detail, and furthermore that certain of the features thereof would be unacceptable to Holland. For example, in the case of Article I it is felt that it is desirable instead of referring solely to "commercial aircraft", to designate "private aircraft" or "private and commercial aircraft". Furthermore, in Holland licenses to operate are granted to a company or to the proprietor of the aircraft and not, as in the case of the American agreement with Canada, to the pilot.

These were only two instances cited by Mr. de Veer in his conversation with Mr. Swift, but it will be seen from the Ministry of Waterstaat's Note to the Foreign Office that the objections to the United States-Canada agreement are such as to make it difficult to use the latter as the basis of an air navigation agreement between the United States and Holland. Attention is also invited to the last paragraph of the Department of Waterstaat's Note, drawing attention to the fact that before it can become effective an agreement of this character must first be ratified by the States General. An exchange of notes is not sufficient.

In this relation, the Department's attention is invited to the fact that Dr. E. B. Wolff, Director of the Dutch Government Research Service for Air Navigation, is being sent by the Netherlands Government to the United States for the purpose of studying American

---

[29] Not printed.
[30] Merritt Swift, Second Secretary of Legation.

aviation methods. It is suggested that the Department may wish to discuss the proposed agreement with Dr. Wolff, who sailed for New York on September 21st on the S/S *Adriatic*.

I have [etc.]    HALLETT JOHNSON

---

711.5227/5

*The Spanish Ambassador (Padilla) to the Secretary of State*

[Translation]

No. 81/25    WASHINGTON, August 28, 1929.

MR. SECRETARY: With reference to Your Excellency's kind note of June 12 last [31] by which it was proposed that an agreement be reached on the ever increasingly important juridical and legal question of international aviation, submitting as a model therefor the agreement which the United States has concluded with Canada, I have the honor to inform Your Excellency that the Government of His Majesty, always deeply interested in the question, has already concluded broad conventions with Germany and France, and is negotiating upon similar bases with Italy, Holland, Denmark, England, etc., etc.

I transmit herewith a copy of the Convention between Germany and Spain [32] which my Government wishes to submit for Your Excellency's consideration, inasmuch as it would always be preferable for our country to have Air Navigation treaties which were basically the same, which would complement one another, thus reinforcing the union until, practically, a single convention is reached. In the accompanying text, air navigation is facilitated in almost all points, recognizing the laws which govern it, the use of wireless telegraphy from the air, limitation in the carriage of goods, regulations regarding passengers, freight, etc., etc., as well as mutual agreements concerning the use of airports and aerodromes.

For these reasons and in the greater interest of the regulated development of international air navigation, my Government would be happy if, as long as the United States is ready to study the matter in order to arrive at an agreement, it would follow the more general and broader bases which, in the opinion of the Madrid Cabinet, the texts agreed on by Spain with other Nations offer, and of which as I have already had the honor to say, the attached Spanish-German Pact is a model.

I avail myself [etc.]    ALEJANDRO PADILLA

---

[31] See footnote 19, p. 532.
[32] General convention relating to air navigation, signed at Madrid, December 9, 1927, League of Nations Treaty Series, vol. LXXIX, p. 203.

711.5227/11

*The Secretary of State to the Spanish Chargé* (*Amoedo*) [33]

WASHINGTON, December 4, 1929.

SIR: I beg to refer to the Department's note of June 12, 1929, regarding the negotiation of a reciprocal arrangement governing the admission of civil aircraft, the issuance of pilots' licenses, and the acceptance of certificates of airworthiness for aircraft imported as merchandise, and its enclosure, a copy of the proposed arrangement which this Government then had under discussion with the Dominion of Canada.

On October 22, 1929, the United States concluded with the Dominion of Canada an arrangement governing these matters, a copy of which I now take pleasure in transmitting herewith for your information [34] with the request that it be substituted in place of the model submitted with the Department's note of June 12 under reference as a basis for further discussions in the premises.

Accept [etc.] For the Secretary of State:
FRANCIS WHITE

[Agreements by exchange of notes were effected with Italy in 1931; Germany, 1932; Great Britain, 1934; Irish Free State, 1937; and France, 1939. An agreement was similarly concluded with the Netherlands in 1932 which was to become effective only after notification to the Government of the United States of its ratification by the Queen. No arrangement was entered into with Spain.]

---

[33] Similar notes, *mutatis mutandis*, were sent to the British, French, German, and Italian Embassies and to the Irish and the Netherlands Legations.
[34] See note of August 29, 1929, to the Canadian Chargé, vol. II, p. 111.

## UNOFFICIAL AMERICAN REPRESENTATION AT THE SECOND INTERNATIONAL DIPLOMATIC CONFERENCE ON PRIVATE AERONAUTICAL LAW AT WARSAW, POLAND, OCTOBER 4–12, 1929 [1]

579.6L2/1

### *The Polish Minister (Filipowicz) to the Secretary of State*

No. 1248/29 WASHINGTON, April 10, 1929.

SIR: Acting upon instructions of my Government, I have the honor to invite the Government of the United States to send official delegates to the Second International Diplomatic Conference on private aeronautical law, which will take place in Warsaw on October 7th, 1929.[2]

On the agenda of this Conference will be placed the discussion of the draft of the Convention relative to documents for air transportation and to the responsibility of the carrier in international air transportation, being the result of the discussions of the International Technical Committee of Legal Aeronautic Experts and adopted by the Committee during its Third Session in May 1928.

The text of this draft, in conformity with article 7 of the Regulations of the International Technical Committee of Legal Aeronautic Experts has been transmitted by the French Government to the interested Governments.

I sincerely hope that the Government of the United States will give its favorable consideration to this invitation, and advise me in due time of the names of the respective delegates.

Accept [etc.] TYTUS FILIPOWICZ

---

579.6L2/25

### *The Secretary of State to the Polish Chargé (Lepkowski)*

WASHINGTON, September 21, 1929.

SIR: Referring to previous correspondence relative to the participation of this Government in the Second International Diplomatic

---

[1] The First Conference was held in Paris in October 1925. It was attended by an Assistant Military Attaché and an Assistant Naval Attaché from the American Embassy as unofficial observers; they were instructed that in their attendance they were in no way officially to represent or bind the Government of the United States. During the Conference they were not made members of any official committees nor did they participate actively in any of the sessions. (579.6L2/1)

[2] On June 25 the Polish Chargé informed the Department that the date had been advanced to October 4 (579.6L2/8).

Conference on Private Aeronautical Law, to be held at Warsaw on October 4, 1929, I have to state that after a full consideration of your Government's invitation, the courtesy of which is highly appreciated, this Government finds itself unable to send official delegates to the Conference in question but will be glad to send Mr. John J. Ide, European representative of the National Advisory Committee for Aeronautics, as an observer to follow the proceedings of the Conference should this be agreeable to the Polish Government.[3]

Accept [etc.]            For the Secretary of State:
                               WILBUR J. CARR

---

[On October 29, 1929, the Chargé in Poland transmitted to the Department a copy of the convention on international air transportation signed October 12, 1929, by the majority of states officially represented at the Conference (579.6L2/37).

In 1934 the Government of the United States adhered, with reservation, to this convention, the text of which is published in Department of State Treaty Series No. 876 and 49 Stat. 3000.]

---

[3] On September 25 the Polish Chargé informed the Department that Mr. Ide's appointment was acceptable to his Government (579.6L2/28).

DIPLOMATIC SUPPORT FOR AMERICAN COMPANIES AWARDED MAIL
CONTRACTS BY THE POST OFFICE DEPARTMENT FOR CARRYING
AIR MAIL TO FOREIGN COUNTRIES

810.71211/22

*Memorandum by the Assistant Secretary of State (White)*

[WASHINGTON,] July 6, 1929.

To: The Under Secretary.
　　The Secretary.
Re: Policy of the Department regarding Aviation Companies.

These telegrams [1] present an important question of policy and if they are approved will constitute a change in the policy the Department has heretofore pursued.

The Post Office Department asks that diplomatic support be given to aviation companies which have been awarded air mail contracts by the Post Office Department in preference to companies not having such contracts. The Department's policy in the past has been not to discriminate between two or more American firms competing abroad. If there was only one American firm and it was in competition with foreign interests, our diplomatic Missions of course always supported the American company, but when there were more than one American firm involved, they limited themselves to putting all Americans in contact with the proper authorities and asking that they be given an equal opportunity to compete in the business.

In support of the proposed change, it may be said:

(1) It is most important that American mails be carried to the Latin American countries. Mails now get to Managua, for instance, in four days. Formerly it took anywhere from three weeks to a month. There will be vast savings in time, varying with each country and the special communication problems thereof, of from four or five days to three weeks. This is an immense advantage to American business and industry in filling orders quickly and also to our banking interests and merchants in saving several days' interest on drafts exchanged with those countries.

(2) It is important that American mails be carried in American planes by American companies. The strategic importance of having most of the flying in the Caribbean area and especially near the Panama Canal Zone in the hands of Americans is obvious. There

---

[1] See telegram No. 51, July 12, 6 p. m., to the Minister in Honduras, p. 545.

is a further advantage to American commerce in having our own service and not being dependent upon foreign facilities.

(3) European competition in South America is very keen. The Germans have the upper hand in aviation in Colombia and in Bolivia and these companies, whatever their local affiliation and registration, are controlled by the German Lufthansa. The French Latecoère Company is also very active, and a telegram dated July 4, 8 p. m. from the Legation at Caracas [2] states that a contract has been signed with this company for air mail service between Venezuela, the rest of South America and Europe. The French company also has contracts already in Argentina, Brazil, Uruguay and Chile.

(4) The French Government is backing the French Latecoère Company and no other in South America. The German Government seems to be following the same policy with the Lufthansa, backing the German companies in Colombia and Bolivia and trying to connect them up. If the United States Government keeps hands off and lets American companies indiscriminately fight one another for concessions in Latin America, all Americans are apt to lose out. I understand that American interests have suffered in this respect in the Far East in the past.

(5) The Administration is apt to be very severely criticized for taking such action. The disappointed companies and their backers will probably charge discrimination and that this Government is creating and supporting a monopoly. In reply to this it may be said that the Post Office Department called for public bids and as the result of public bidding picked out what it considered the strongest company and the one best able to perform this most important work, and the contract was awarded to it. No other American company for the period of the contract (10 years) can carry the United States mails over the routes covered in the contracts. Monopolies of air routes inside this country have been recognized for some time. It is more difficult to establish an air mail route abroad where various jurisdictions are entered into and the aviation companies asked that exclusive contracts be given for a reasonable period as this is pioneering work. No company wanted to go in and make the financial outlay and run the risk and, after that work had been done, have other companies get the contracts and the cream of the business after they had done the unprofitable pioneering work.

(6) There is a distinct strategic element entering into it as stated above, and it is certainly desirable and perhaps essential that the United States should, in so far as possible, control aviation in the Caribbean region.

[2] Not printed.

(7) Once the American firm having a contract with the Post Office Department for the carrying of mails to a given Latin American country has obtained operating rights in that country so it can perform effectively its duties under its contract, there is no reason why the Department should not assist any other American companies to get operating rights there provided that those rights in no wise conflict or infringe upon the rights of the American company in question. That is, there is no reason why this should not be done for any company wanting to go in for the carriage of passengers, express matter or the mails of foreign countries, providing that the latter does not conflict with the arrangement made with our Post Office Department.

(8) The French and German companies are fully subsidized and hence are in position to put up very strong competition. We are much more likely to be able to overcome their competition by having one strong American company with the Post Office subsidy behind it than several smaller American companies without unified control who are competing not only against the Germans and the French but against one another. It is one of those cases where vital national interests have to be considered and given preference over the particular interests of individual companies.

As stated above, however, there is apt to be very considerable criticism against this policy and opposition to it, and it should be adopted only after most careful consideration and after taking into full account the attacks against this policy which are bound to ensue.

F[RANCIS] W[HITE]

810.71211/23

*The Secretary of State to the Assistant Secretary of State (White)*

[WASHINGTON,] July 12, 1929.

MR. WHITE: Your memorandum was brought up at Cabinet Meeting this morning and the procedure to the extent directed in the proposed telegrams to our representatives was authorized. I have accordingly sent the telegrams. In the discussion however the President made it rather clear that he did not think that the Post Office Department should from the fact that it had made a subsidy contract with one company for the west coast of South America interfere with the diplomatic support of another American company which proposed to go down the east coast and he did not think that the Pan American Airways Company, even if it crossed over the Andes from Chile to Argentina or elsewhere, should be permitted to block another American company which proposed to go down the east coast via Venezuela and Brazil to Rio.

H[ENRY] L. S[TIMSON]

810.71211/5 : Telegram

*The Secretary of State to the Minister in Honduras (Summerlin)*[3]

WASHINGTON, July 12, 1929—6 p. m.

51. This Government considers it very important that the United States mails should be carried to the Latin American countries by air mail by American companies. You will therefore please support in every proper way American companies which have been awarded contracts by the United States Post Office Department to obtain privileges necessary for carrying mails to Cuba in accordance with contracts with the United States Post Office Department.

The Post Office Department has given the Department a list of the air mail routes into Latin America and has stated that "in rendering diplomatic assistance where concessions are involved to carry out the contracts for service on the above routes or extensions thereof, it is desired, of course, that our contractors be given preference." The following is the route which affects Honduras:

. . . . . . .

STIMSON

---

[3] Similar instructions were sent to the diplomatic missions in Argentina, Chile, Colombia, Costa Rica, Cuba, the Dominican Republic, Ecuador, El Salvador, Guatemala, Haiti, Mexico, Nicaragua, Peru, Uruguay, and Venezuela.

On July 23 mail instructions similar to the above were sent to the Consulates at Belize, Curaçao, Georgetown, and Nassau.

A similar telegram dated July 23, noon, was sent to the Vice Consul at Port-of-Spain, Trinidad.

# GOOD OFFICES OF THE DEPARTMENT OF STATE IN BEHALF OF AMERICAN INTERESTS DESIRING TO ESTABLISH AIR LINES IN LATIN AMERICA [1]

## Pan American Airways, Incorporated

810.79611 Pan American Airways, Inc./210 : Telegram

*The Secretary of State to the Minister in Colombia (Caffery)* [2]

WASHINGTON, January 18, 1929—noon.

5. Please request permission for Pan American Airways, Incorporated, to carry out survey flights along Colombian coast with a view to extending air lines from the Panama Canal Zone along the north and west coasts of South America. Company states no commercial activities of any kind will be entered into on its survey flights. Please expedite reply.

KELLOGG

---

810.79611 Pan American Airways, Inc./212 : Telegram

*The Minister in Colombia (Caffery) to the Secretary of State*

BOGOTÁ, January 18, 1929—4 p.m.
[Received 7 p.m.]

6. Department's telegram number 5, January 18, noon. I have requested permission. However, in view of previous correspondence relating to the activities of the Scadta [3] in connection with their desire to obtain permission to land in Canal Zone and especially this Legation's despatch number 1250, February 13 last,[4] I am inclined to question that a prompt reply will be forthcoming.

CAFFERY

---

810.79611 Pan American Airways, Inc./225 : Telegram

*The Secretary of State to the Chargé in Argentina (White)*

WASHINGTON, January 23, 1929—5 p.m.

11. Please endeavor to delay final consideration or action on any pending airmail contracts with non-American companies to Central America, West Indies or North America pending arrival Pan Amer-

---

[1] Continued from *Foreign Relations*, 1928, vol. I, pp. 775–830.
[2] The same, *mutatis mutandis*, on the same date to the missions in Ecuador (No. 2) and Venezuela (No. 1).
[3] Sociedad Colombo-Alemana de Transportes Aéreos.
[4] Not printed.

ican Airways representative March first with definite proposal guaranteeing through service within year. Pan American extending service Panama February fourth holds all United States international mail contracts. Company also now operating jointly with Grace Airmail service West Coast South America planning shortly extend Valparaiso.

You will be careful to avoid any discrimination between competing American interests.

KELLOGG

---

810.79611 Pan American Airways, Inc./227 : Telegram

*The Minister in Costa Rica (Davis) to the Secretary of State*

SAN JOSÉ, January 24, 1929—noon.
[Received 1:20 p. m.]

7. The President this morning signed contract with Pan American Airways, Incorporated.[5]   This contract will be submitted to Congress when it reconvenes.

DAVIS

---

810.79611 Pan American Airways, Inc./234 : Telegram

*The Minister in Ecuador (Bading) to the Secretary of State*

QUITO, February 2, 1929—11 a. m.
[Received 5:15 p. m.]

8. Department's 2, January 18, noon.[6]   Permission granted, but Government requests that official Ecuadorian pilot be taken on survey flights to be picked up at first Ecuadorian port.

BADING

---

810.79611 Pan American Airways, Inc./238 : Telegram

*The Minister in Colombia (Caffery) to the Secretary of State*

BOGOTÁ, February 6, 1929—11 a. m.
[Received 4 p. m.]

15. Department's telegram number 5 of January 18, noon.   Today's press carries sensational headlines to the effect that Lindbergh is coming to Barranquilla this week for Pan American Airways and that Mendez may be sent to meet him.

---

[5] See *Foreign Relations*, 1928, vol. I, p. 778, footnote 57; also telegram No. 51, December 12, 1928, 4 p.m., to the Minister in Costa Rica, *ibid.*, p. 798.
[6] See footnote 2, p. 546.

[Paraphrase.] The Colombian authorities apparently believe the report which will unquestionably have a bearing on their attitude toward the Pan American survey. I therefore respectfully urge that Colonel Lindbergh be prepared to proceed to Barranquilla should permission for the survey be granted tomorrow as the Minister for Foreign Affairs now hopes. [End paraphrase.]

CAFFERY

---

810.79611 Pan American Airways, Inc./239 : Telegram

*The Secretary of State to the Minister in Panama (South)*

WASHINGTON, February 7, 1929—11 a. m.

7. Please show the following to Colonel Lindbergh.
[Here follows text of telegram No. 15, February 6, 11 a. m., from the Minister in Colombia, printed *supra*.]
Legation Bogotá will advise you as soon as permission granted.

KELLOGG

---

810.79611 Pan American Airways, Inc./240 : Telegram

*The Secretary of State to the Minister in Colombia (Caffery)*

WASHINGTON, February 7, 1929—11 a. m.

7. Your 15, February 6, 11 a. m., repeated to Panama for Colonel Lindbergh. Please notify the Department and Legation at Panama as soon as permission for survey is granted.

KELLOGG

---

810.79611 Pan American Airways, Inc./241 : Telegram

*The Secretary of State to the Minister in Colombia (Caffery)*

WASHINGTON, February 7, 1929—1 p. m.

8. Your 15, February 6, 11 a. m. On account of delay in receiving permit for survey flight to Colombia, Pan American Airways had arranged for Lindbergh to remain in Panama until return flight to this country, which must start at 6 a. m. Sunday. If permission is received for the survey flight in time for Lindbergh to make flight to Barranquilla and return tomorrow, an effort will be made to have him do this. It is doubtful whether Lindbergh would be able to make the flight Saturday, in view of the necessity for starting return flight Sunday.

Please convey the situation tactfully to the appropriate authorities and communicate any further developments direct to Legation at Panama as well as to the Department.

KELLOGG

810.79611 Pan American Airways, Inc./242 : Telegram

*The Minister in Colombia (Caffery) to the Secretary of State*

BOGOTÁ, February 7, 1929—5 p. m.
[Received 7 : 45 p. m.]

19. Minister for Foreign Affairs communicates Legation permission granted Lindbergh flight to Barranquilla and has telegraphed Barranquilla to make necessary arrangements. War Department stipulates usual Colombian flight permit proviso against carrying aerial photography apparatus.

I regard Lindbergh's coming as extremely important for success of further Pan American negotiations in this country, in view of well known efforts of Scadta.

Please request Colonel Lindbergh inform me as soon as possible probable time of arrival. Repeated to Panama.

CAFFERY

---

810.79611 Pan American Airways, Inc./244 : Telegram

*The Minister in Panama (South) to the Secretary of State*

PANAMA, February 8, 1929—noon.
[Received 4 : 50 p. m.]

4. Department's 7, February 7, 11 a. m. Following message from Colonel Lindbergh sent today to American Minister, Bogota:

"Due to my spending the last two days on the *Saratoga* during maneuvers, a reply to your message has been delayed. As much as I wish to visit Colombia and other South American countries, I find it impossible at present to do so due to the fact that I must leave with air mail Sunday for the United States."

SOUTH

---

810.79611 Pan American Airways, Inc./249 : Telegram

*The Minister in Colombia (Caffery) to the Secretary of State*

BOGOTÁ, February 9, 1929—7 p. m.
[Received 10 : 15 p. m.]

22. My 21 February 8, 9 p. m.[7] Colombian Government today granted request of Pan American, as set forth in the Department's 5, January 18, 12 noon, under the following conditions:

1. Notification day and approximate hour arrival Colombian territory.

2. Type of plane and power of motor.

[7] Not printed.

3. Not to be considered inauguration commercial service between United States and Colombia pending termination negotiations between the two countries.[8]

Repeated to Panama.

CAFFERY

---

810.79611 Pan American Airways, Inc./277

*The Minister in Honduras (Summerlin) to the Secretary of State*

No. 800                              TEGUCIGALPA, February 9, 1929.
                                    [Received February 26.]

SIR: As Mr. J. D. MacGregor, representative of the Pan American Airways, Incorporated, pointed out in the enclosure to my despatch No. 680 of August 15, 1928,[9] Guillén Zelaya, editor of the *Cronista*, attacked the proposed Pan American contract from the beginning. Inasmuch, however, as it was decided to postpone endeavor to obtain the approval of the contract until after the elections, his diatribe subsided until the contract was presented last month to Congress.

I now have the honor to report that the *Cronista* has recently published three bitterly anti-American attacks on the Pan American Airways Company and that, although these editorials consist merely of acrimonious vaporizings, always mentioning the Pan American Airways Company as "affiliated" with the United Fruit Company (see the Department's telegram No. 56 of July 5, 1928, 5 [6] P. M.,[10] and my despatch No. 653 of July 14, 1928),[11] repeatedly calling the proposed contract a menace to the dignity and sovereignty of Honduras, and containing no real argument, they unfortunately appear to have considerable ill effect on some members of Congress.

I have had frequent conversations on this subject with President Mejía Colindres and other members of the Government, pointing out the earnest desire of the United States to have a mail service established in Central America with a reliable American company. The President has put the matter in the hands of General Meza Cálix, an influential member of Congress, and both of these gentlemen have told me they will do everything they properly can to have the contract approved.

I have [etc.]                        GEORGE T. SUMMERLIN

---

[8] See vol. II, pp. 879 ff.
[9] Not printed; but see instruction No. 285, September 14, 1928, to the Minister in Honduras, *Foreign Relations*, 1928, vol. I, p. 790.
[10] *Ibid.*, p. 786.
[11] Not printed.

810.79611 Pan American Airways, Inc./260 : Telegram

*The Minister in Venezuela (Cook) to the Secretary of State*

CARACAS, February 18, 1929—5 p. m.
[Received 9:35 p. m.]

19. Your 9, February 14, 11 a. m.[12] Permission to effect survey flights granted.

COOK

---

810.79611 Pan American Airways, Inc./278 : Telegram

*The Secretary of State to the Ambassador in Brazil (Morgan)*

WASHINGTON, February 21, 1929—2 p. m.

8. Pan American Airways, Incorporated, states that it is presenting a formal application to the Brazilian Government to obtain a concession to operate an air mail service for the transportation of local and international mails in Brazil. The Company's representative in Rio de Janeiro is Señor Cesar Pereira de Sousa. This Company is very well and favorably known to the Department, which desires you to extend upon request such assistance as may be consistently possible. You will of course make no discrimination between competing American interests.

KELLOGG

---

810.79611 Pan American Airways, Inc./271 : Telegram

*The Minister in Ecuador (Bading) to the Secretary of State*

QUITO, February 23, 1929—10 a. m.
[Received 3:15 p. m.]

10. Harris, Vice President of Peruvian Airways, secured personal but transferable contract for Pan American Airway service.[13] Copy of contract by mail.

BADING

---

810.79611 Pan American Airways, Inc./279 : Telegram

*The Secretary of State to the Chargé in Argentina (White)*

WASHINGTON, February 26, 1929—1 p. m.

12. Department's 11, January 23, 5:00 P. M. Pan American Airways, Incorporated, states that it has applied to the Government of

---

[12] Not printed.
[13] See telegram No. 30, December 8, 1928, 10 a. m., to the Minister of Ecuador. *Foreign Relations*, 1928, vol. I, p. 797.

Argentina for operating rights for its aircraft in Argentina, together with a contract for the transportation by air of mails to and from that country and has selected Mr. Vicente Lopez as its representative. This Company is very well and favorably known to the Department, which desires you to extend upon request such assistance as may be consistently possible. You will of course make no discrimination between competing American interests.

KELLOGG

---

817.796 Riguero, Manuel J./1 : Telegram

*The Minister in Nicaragua (Eberhardt) to the Secretary of State*

MANAGUA, February 27, 1929—4 p. m.
[Received 8:16 p. m.]

58. Manuel J. Riguero, a local Nicaraguan merchant, has recently proposed to the Nicaraguan Government a contract for the establishment of a commercial air mail and passenger service within Nicaragua and between Nicaragua and neighboring countries. This proposed agreement follows closely the lines of the Pan American Airways contract, but contains certain features which make it appear more favorable to Nicaragua than the latter and includes certain modifications which have already been made by the Chamber of Deputies in the Pan American Airways contract.

It appears that Riguero has made this proposal at this time in the hope that the Pan American Airways contract may be entirely rejected or modified in such a way that it would not be acceptable to that company so that he might then be in a position to conclude an agreement with the Nicaraguan Government for the establishment of an air service presumably with the backing of German or other foreign aviation interests.

Details will follow by mail.

EBERHARDT

---

810.79611 Pan American Airways, Inc./282 : Telegram

*The Minister in Panama (South) to the Secretary of State*

PANAMA, February 27, 1929—6 p. m.
[Received 10:30 p. m.]

12. Department's 37, May 16, 6 p. m., 1928.[14] My 9, February 25, 10 a. m.[14] MacGregor, of Pan American Airways, submitted to Panaman Government this afternoon contract for air mail and also for a general aviation concession which he hopes to have concluded

---

[14] Not printed.

at Cabinet meeting one week hence. MacGregor states contract is similar to those already concluded with Honduras, Nicaragua, and Costa Rica, of which the Department has copies. Exact copy also in hands of New York office Pan American Airways.

While MacGregor states Department has been informed of his intention to submit such a contract to Panama, I am bringing the matter to the Department's attention in view of its apparent inconsistency with plan now being studied for the joint control of aviation in the Republic. Request instructions as to my proper attitude in the premises, and MacGregor requests that his Washington office be informed of such action as Department may take.

SOUTH

---

810.79611 Pan American Airways, Inc./289 : Telegram

*The Secretary of State to the Minister in Panama (South)*

WASHINGTON, February 28, 1929—6 p. m.

14. Your 12, February 27, 6 p. m. Department not disposed to object to contract providing that it shall be subject to the Joint Regulations to Govern Commercial Aviation in the Republic of Panama.

KELLOGG

---

810.79611 Pan American Airways, Inc./294 : Telegram

*The Secretary of State to the Minister in Honduras (Summerlin)*

WASHINGTON, February 28, 1929—7 p. m.

17. Department advised by All American Cables that MacGregor, who has just reached Panama from Tegucigalpa, reports considerable opposition to ratification of aviation contract. You will please report situation fully. As this company is under contract with United States Government for carrying of mails to Panama Canal, this Government is anxious that it obtain the necessary permission in the countries through which the company has to pass.

KELLOGG

---

810.79611 Pan American Airways, Inc./301 : Telegram

*The Secretary of State to the Minister in Nicaragua (Eberhardt)*

WASHINGTON, February 28, 1929—7 p. m.

31. Your 58, February 27, 4 p. m. Pan American Airways also reports that German influences are attempting to block the ratification of its concession. As Pan American Airways is under contract

to carry United States mails to Panama Canal, this Government is most anxious that the necessary permission should be accorded in the countries through which it has to pass. Please render all appropriate assistance with a view to the ratification of the contract.

KELLOGG

---

810.79611 Pan American Airways, Inc./303 : Telegram

*The Minister in Panama (South) to the Secretary of State*

PANAMA [, March 7, 1929—6 p. m.]
[Received 9:40 p. m.]

16. Your 14, February 28, 6 p. m. I am informed that article 25 of contract has been revised to read:

"The stipulations of this are subject to the obligations which the Republic of Panama has undertaken or may undertake with the United States of America through treaties, conventions, agreements, or regulations".

I assume that this covers commercial aviation as well as provisions concerning radio in article 5.

SOUTH

---

810.79611 Pan American Airways, Inc./304 : Telegram

*The Minister in Panama (South) to the Secretary of State*

PANAMA, March 8, 1929—1 p. m.
[Received 2:45 p. m.]

17. My 16, March 7, 6 p. m. Contract signed this morning.

SOUTH

---

810.79611 Pan American Airways, Inc./352

*The Ambassador in Brazil (Morgan) to the Secretary of State*

No. 3126
RIO DE JANEIRO, March 13, 1929.
[Received March 29.]

SIR: In reply to the Department's telegram No. 8, of February 21, 2 P. M., and in accordance with the instructions therein contained, I have informed the Brazilian Government that the Pan American Airways Inc. is well and favorably known to the Department, and that Mr. Cesar Pereira de Sousa, a member of the bar of this city, is the local representative of the said company.

Mr. Pereira de Sousa advises me, and I agree with his opinion, that the Brazilian Government at present will not give a subsidy to Pan American Airways Inc. but that both the Federal and State governments will furnish valuable assistance in other directions.

Neither of the two foreign aeroplane companies now operating in Brazil enjoy a public subsidy nor will they obtain one until the Brazilian Government and people begin to think aeronautically to a greater extent than they do at present.

I have [etc.] EDWIN V. MORGAN

---

810.79611 Pan American Airways, Inc./326 : Telegram

*The Minister in Honduras (Summerlin) to the Secretary of State*

TEGUCIGALPA, March 14, 1929—5 p. m.
[Received 10:18 p. m.]

27. Your telegram No. 17 of February 28, 7 p. m. and my despatch No. 814 of February 23rd.[15] On March 12th the National Congress demanded that the Pan American Airways contract be reported out of committee. At the request of the local representative of the company and in order to prevent a vote on the measure, the Executive at once ordered the withdrawal of the contract for modification. Yesterday the Congress decided to ignore the order of the Executive and now it is reported that the contract was disapproved unanimously this morning.

SUMMERLIN

---

810.79611 Pan American Airways, Inc./336 : Telegram

*The Secretary of State to the Minister in Honduras (Summerlin)*

WASHINGTON, March 19, 1929—6 p. m.

23. Your 27, March 14, 5 p. m. What effect will rejection have upon operations in Honduras? Do you consider that it would help matters to effect an exchange of notes as was done recently with Colombia?[16] See press release of February 23.

KELLOGG

---

810.79611 Pan American Airways, Inc./337 : Telegram

*The Minister in Nicaragua (Eberhardt) to the Secretary of State*

MANAGUA, March 21, 1929—11 a. m.
[Received 1:05 p. m.]

76. Pan American Airways and All American Cables revised contracts passed by Congress and signed by President yesterday.

EBERHARDT

---

[15] Despatch not printed.
[16] See vol. II, pp. 879 ff.

810.79611 Pan American Airways, Inc./384

*The Ambassador in Brazil (Morgan) to the Secretary of State*

No. 3130    RIO DE JANEIRO, March 27, 1929.
[Received April 12.]

SIR: Continuing the subject of Embassy's despatch No. 3126, of March 13 last, I have the honor to report that Mr. John D. Summers, Second Vice President of the Pan American Airways Incorporated, is now in this city in conference with Dr. Cesar Pereira de Sousa, the local representative.

Permission to operate throughout Brazil which these gentlemen have requested will probably be granted as the Minister of Communications is well disposed to the Pan American Company. The Department's intimation that that organization was "well and favorably known" to the United States Government expressed through the Embassy has impressed the Minister and has quickened his interest in the Company's pretensions.

It is announced that the Tri-Motor Safety Airways Inc. also will seek to obtain a concession from Brazil for the operation of airplanes within the Republic. Lieutenant O'Neill, who visited this and adjacent countries last year, will arrive shortly. Mr. O'Neill addressed a telegram to the Commercial Attaché recently requesting his assistance in furthering his company's interests, a request to which due attention will be given.

I have [etc.]    EDWIN V. MORGAN

---

810.79611 Pan American Airways, Inc./361 : Telegram

*The Minister in Honduras (Summerlin) to the Secretary of State*

TEGUCIGALPA, April 2, 1929—11 a. m.
[Received 6 : 45 p. m.]

31. Your 23, March 19, 6 p. m. The local representative of the Pan American Airways now states that he hopes to be able to make some kind of a working arrangement with the Government of Honduras shortly after adjournment of the Congress April 10.

SUMMERLIN

---

810.79611 Pan American Airways, Inc./380 : Telegram

*The Secretary of State to the Chargé in France (Armour)*

WASHINGTON, April 9, 1929—5 p. m.

105. Pan American Airways, Incorporated, is planning to extend its system through the countries of the Caribbean to Cayenne and desires to obtain from the French Government permission to fly over French Guiana, also to refuel and make minor repairs, and to deliver

United States mail if awarded concession for that route by the United States Post Office. A representative of the Company is being sent to French Guiana to negotiate permanent operating concession and air mail contract. Please request the French Government to grant temporary authorization valid until replaced by formal contract.

STIMSON

---

810.79611 Pan American Airways, Inc./381 : Telegram

*The Secretary of State to the Chargé in Great Britain (Atherton)*

WASHINGTON, April 10, 1929—5 p. m.

76. Pan American Airways Incorporated, is planning to extend its system through the countries of the Caribbean to Cayenne and desires to obtain from the British Government permission to fly over Trinidad and British Guiana, also to refuel and make minor repairs and to deliver United States mail if awarded concession for that route by the United States Post Office. A representative of the Company is being sent to Trinidad and British Guiana to negotiate permanent operating concession and air mail contract. Please request the British Government to grant temporary authorization valid until replaced by formal contract.

STIMSON

---

810.79611 Pan American Airways, Inc./390 : Telegram

*The Secretary of State to the Chargé in Guatemala (Hawks)*

WASHINGTON, April 19, 1929—1 p. m.

19. The Department is informed that George L. Rihl, President of the Compania Mexicana de Aviacion will be in Guatemala within a few days to negotiate with the Government of Guatemala in the interests of Pan American Airways, Incorporated, having for that purpose been made a Vice President of that company, which itself or through subsidiaries now holds six foreign air mail contracts with the United States Post Office, namely, Miami to Habana, Nassau, Porto Rico and the Canal Zone respectively, also Brownsville to Mexico City and Canal Zone to Santiago. Please render appropriate assistance.

STIMSON

---

810.796 Pan American Airways, Inc./413 : Telegram

*The Acting Secretary of State to the Ambassador in Chile (Culbertson)*

WASHINGTON, May 6, 1929—7 p. m.

48. Post Office Department requests that you be advised for information of Chilean Government that the Attorney General has ap-

proved the contract awarded to the Pan American-Grace Airways for transporting mails south from Panama Canal to Chile, and that the contract is in effect and operations will begin immediately as far as Mollendo and will be extended to Chile as soon as necessary arrangement is made with the Chilean Government.

CLARK

---

810.79611 Pan American Airways, Inc./411 : Telegram

*The Chargé in Great Britain (Atherton) to the Secretary of State*

LONDON, May 11, 1929—noon.<br>[Received May 11—9 : 40 a. m.]

118. Department's 76, April 10, 5 p. m. Foreign Office states telegraphic report has been received from the Governor of Trinidad to the effect that he is in touch with a representative of the company and has given permission for "Pan American" seaplanes to land in Trinidad in connection with an experimental flight to explore the possibilities of a regular service. The Foreign Office adds Pan American Airways representative has been informed that no permanent proposal can be considered except after consultation with His Majesty's Government. Foreign Office hopes to furnish Embassy further information at an early date.

ATHERTON

---

810.79611 Pan American Airways, Inc./419 : Telegram

*The Ambassador in Chile (Culbertson) to the Secretary of State*

SANTIAGO, May 16, 1929—11 a. m.<br>[Received 1 : 40 p. m.]

80. Chilean Post Office authorities have stated to representative of Pan American-Grace Airways that cable from the United States Post Office to Chilean postal authorities is regarded merely as information and that they desire to negotiate directly with him with respect to rates to be paid by the Chilean Government for the carriage of mails north. I have had no part in discussion but would appreciate instructions as to how the United States Post Office desires situation to be handled.

CULBERTSON

---

810.79611 Pan American Airways, Inc./442 : Telegram

*The Secretary of State to the Minister in Venezuela (Cook)*

WASHINGTON, May 25, 1929—3 p. m.

18. If you perceive no objection please ask the Venezuelan Government to continue the temporary operating permit of Pan American

Airways, Incorporated, pending the conclusion of the formal contract and to have the Venezuelan Post Office accept at Maracay mail despatched by the United States Post Office, as requested in the latter's cablegram of May 4 to the Venezuelan Postal Administration.

STIMSON

---

810.79611 Pan American Airways, Inc./449 : Telegram

*The Secretary of State to the Ambassador in Cuba (Judah)*

WASHINGTON, May 27, 1929—6 p. m.

57. Upon request please render all proper assistance to Cyrus F. Wicker representing **Pan American Airways Incorporated**.

STIMSON

---

810.79611 Pan American Airways, Inc./454 : Telegram

*The Secretary of State to the Ambassador in Chile (Culbertson)*

WASHINGTON, May 31, 1929—2 p. m.

61. Your 80, May 16, 11 a. m. Please be guided by the following letter from the Post Office:

"This Department has made a contract with the Pan American-Grace Airways to carry the mails by aircraft from Cristobal, by intermediate points, to Santiago, and return, with the right to extend the route to Buenos Aires and Montevideo.

In order to provide service for carrying mails from this country and the Canal Zone outbound, it was necessary for this Department to pay the contracting company the cost of operating the aircraft back to the starting point. The contract calls for payment of $1.80 a mile for the flights outbound and return, for the transportation of such mails as may be dispatched up to 800 pounds, and for pay at pound rates for excess mails should more than 800 pounds be carried.

Since it was necessary for us to pay for operation of the airplanes on return trips and since it was considered very desirable to provide for a free exchange of mails if possible, that is, a return of correspondence to the Canal Zone and to this country as well as the dispatch outbound, the contract was made to cover the transportation of all mails to and from the United States and its possessions. The contract was so made with the hope that arrangements could be made with the several postal administrations for return of such air mail correspondence as they may have for dispatch to the Canal Zone and points beyond at reasonable pound rates.

The Postal Administration of Peru has found it agreeable to make such arrangements, and it may be stated that the arrangement for transportation of correspondence in this manner is not very different from arrangements that are made under postal conventions for carrying mails for other countries by steamships, where the service is provided by the government of a particular country.

Since it is necessary under our contract for this Department to pay the Pan American-Grace Airways for operating the planes on return trips, it is hoped that the Chilean Administration may see its way clear to accept service for the dispatch of its air mails to the Canal Zone and points beyond as well as receive mails from this route, under arrangement with this Administration, as proposed.

It may be stated that service for the exchange of local mails with intermediate countries on the route may be arranged with the Pan American-Grace Airways.

It is requested that the Ambassador present the facts to the Chilean authorities in the hope that upon further consideration of the matter in the light of the circumstances set forth above, the Chilean Postal Administration may see its way clear to utilize under arrangements with this Department the return service for the dispatch of its mails to the Canal Zone and beyond, as well as to accept delivery of mails dispatched by the southbound service. The good offices of the Ambassador to this end will be appreciated."

STIMSON

---

810.79611 Pan American Airways, Inc./453 : Telegram

*The Chargé in Honduras (Merrell) to the Secretary of State*

TEGUCIGALPA, May 31, 1929—10 p. m.
[Received June 1—2 p. m.]

56. Legation's telegram number 31, April 2, 11 a. m. The President of the Republic today approved a contract signed by the Postmaster General and the representative of the Pan American Airways, providing for the carrying of mail by air to and from Honduras until January 31, 1931, and renewable for two years upon the agreement of both parties. The contract, which is satisfactory to the company as a provisional arrangement pending the approval by Congress of a concession for 25 years, takes effect today.

MERRELL

---

810.79611 Pan American Airways, Inc./455 : Telegram

*The Acting Secretary of State to the Ambassador in Argentina (Bliss)* [17]

WASHINGTON, June 1, 1929—1 p. m.

46. Please request on behalf of Pan American Airways free entry contingent upon reexportation for one Fokker super universal monoplane, also permission to fly over and land in Argentina in making air mail survey flights.

CLARK

[17] The same, *mutatis mutandis*, on the same date to the Minister in Uruguay as telegram No. 9.

810.79611 Pan American Airways, Inc./456 : Telegram

*The Acting Secretary of State to the Ambassador in Brazil (Morgan)*

WASHINGTON, June 1, 1929—1 p. m.

21. Please request free entry contingent upon reexportation for one Fokker super universal monoplane with wasp engine, shipped May 31 on *Western World* by Pan American Airways, also permission for air mail survey flights along the coast of Brazil.

CLARK

---

810.79611 Pan American Airways, Inc./460 : Telegram

*The Ambassador in Chile (Culbertson) to the Secretary of State*

SANTIAGO, June 5, 1929—noon.
[Received June 7—2:30 p. m.]

86. It appeared yesterday in a conversation between representative of Pan American-Grace Airways and Director of Aviation in the Ministry of War that a proposal has been made by the representative of the Curtiss Aeroplane and Motor Corporation which the director used as an excuse for holding up the concession to the Pan American-Grace Airways. This proposal is to organize a Chilean company which will not only operate the local air service within Chile but will also establish an aviation repair and assembling plant and school. Director of Aviation argued that this proposal offered Chile full power and he proposed among other things that the Pan American-Grace Airways deliver mail and passengers for intermediate points to the Chilean line at Arica for which the former would pay the latter and that it fly direct from Arica to Santiago and beyond. It would appear that the Curtiss Company has made a proposal appealing to the national prejudices of the Ministry of War and that it may be used to hamper if not defeat the project of the Pan American-Grace Airways.

Before I see the Minister of War, will the Department please instruct me concerning my attitude towards the Curtiss proposal? Will I insist upon the right of Pan American-Grace Airways to deliver at points between Arica and Santiago international mails, as provided for in its contract with the United States Post Office?

[Paraphrase.] I believe that the activities of any American company should be opposed at any point where they interfere with the fullest development of international air ways as contracted for between the Post Office Department of the United States and the Pan American-Grace Airways. [End paraphrase.]

CULBERTSON

810.79611 Pan American Airways, Inc./461 : Telegram

*The Ambassador in Chile (Culbertson) to the Secretary of State*

SANTIAGO, June 5, 1929—1 p. m.
[Received 2 : 30 p. m.]

87. Department's telegram number 61, May 31, 2 p. m. I have conferred twice with Director of Posts who frankly says that Minister of War has final say in aviation even in air mail contracts and that therefore he is not in a position "politically" to complete arrangements with the United States Post Office. I will see the Minister of War next Friday and will endeavor to obtain his acceptance of the proposal made by the United States Post Office in its cablegram to the Chilean Post Office May 29th.

The Minister of War proposes that the contract for carrying northbound mail be made directly with the company on the theory that he can hold it responsible. In case he insists upon this position, would our Post Office contract directly for the mails north of the Canal Zone only and permit an indirect arrangement through the Pan American-Grace Airways to contract with Chilean Post Office for mail from Santiago to the Canal Zone at rate asked by United States Post Office?

CULBERTSON

---

810.79611 Pan American Airways, Inc./476 : Telegram

*The Chargé in Venezuela (Engert) to the Secretary of State*

CARACAS, June 12, 1929—6 p. m.
[Received 10 : 30 p. m.]

61. Department's 18, May 25, 3 p. m. Foreign Office in a note dated today transmits without comment letter from Minister of Fomento, also of today, granting permission for one more flight "with official correspondence".

. . . I therefore suggest the Legation be instructed to repeat request for temporary operating permit.

ENGERT

---

810.79611 Pan American Airways, Inc./477 : Telegram

*The Ambassador in Chile (Culbertson) to the Secretary of State*

SANTIAGO, June 13, 1929—10 a. m.
[Received 1 : 45 p. m.]

91. Chilean Post Office Department has accepted offer of Peruvian Post Office Department to carry Chilean air mail, ordinary and registered, to the United States and intermediate points departing from

Mollendo every Friday. Chilean Post Office has announced mail can now be sent from Chile by regular steamers to Mollendo for dispatch by air mail onward to the United States for eleven pesos 25 centavos per 20 grammes plus usual postage or by Chilean air mail to Arica, thence to Mollendo by the steamer and from Mollendo by air mail to the United States for eleven pesos 25 centavos plus a surcharge of one peso 20 centavos per 20 grammes plus 25 centavos regular postage. Air mail postage rates quoted to intermediate countries are in proportion. I am informed by Chilean Post Office Department that this agreement should not prevent subsequent arrangements with Chilean Post Office Department to deliver through mails to Pan American-Grace Airways at Santiago and other Chilean points for Canal and United States at rates per pound suggested in recent telegram from Postmaster General as soon as War Department grants permission to company to operate mail service. Foreign Office informed me yesterday that War Department will grant this permission in a few days and accept international mails at Arica, Santiago and at one intermediate point not yet determined and that a landing charge will be imposed.

CULBERTSON

---

810.79611 Pan American Airways, Inc./483 : Telegram

*The Acting Secretary of State to the Chargé in Venezuela (Engert)*

WASHINGTON, June 13, 1929—7 p. m.

23. Your 61, June 12, 6 p. m. You will extend all proper assistance to the Pan American Airways in that company's efforts to obtain an operating permit which will enable it to bring to Venezuela the mail carried in accordance with its contract with the United States Post Office Department. You may explain that this Government is much interested in the establishment of a more rapid mail service to Venezuela and would be very glad if the Venezuelan Government would cooperate with it by granting the necessary permit.

CLARK

---

810.79611 Pan American Airways, Inc./480 : Telegram

*The Ambassador in Chile (Culbertson) to the Secretary of State*

SANTIAGO, June 17, 1929—noon.
[Received 1:55 p. m.]

92. My 86, June 5, noon, and 87, June 5, 1 p. m. The discussions are progressing satisfactorily, but it will be next week before all the details can be settled.

CULBERTSON

810.79611 Pan American Airways, Inc./495 : Telegram

*The Acting Secretary of State to the Ambassador in Chile (Culbertson)*

WASHINGTON, June 19, 1929—7 p. m.

65. Your 86, June 5, noon, 87, June 5, 1 p. m., 91, June 13, 10 p. m. [*a. m.*] and 92, June 17, noon. You will please support Pan American Airways in every proper way to obtain privileges necessary for carrying mail through to Santiago in accordance with its contract with United States Post Office Department. For your information the Post Office Department is especially anxious that the line should reach Santiago in order that it may eventually be extended to East coast ports. It also desires that the Pan American Airways should be permitted to deliver and receive mail at intermediate points but one intermediate stop between Arica and Santiago will be fairly satisfactory if no better arrangement possible.

Under the terms of contract, the Pan American-Grace Airways is obligated to carry for Post Office Department all mails to and from the United States and its possessions, which may include transit mails through this country and mails connecting with steamships at the Canal Zone. Accordingly, Post Office Department requests that Chilean postal administration despatch its air mails for the Canal Zone (including mails for onward dispatch by steamship from the Canal Zone) and air mails for the United States (including mails for onward dispatch), under arrangements with Post Office Department at rates per pound. The contractors have the right to make arrangements with the countries traversed for carrying their mails to intermediate countries.

The Post Office Department states that a joint service to connect at Arica is not possible and adds "it is very important that all practicable assistance be given the Pan American-Grace Airways in securing operating arrangements in preference to any other company."

CLARK

---

810.79611 Pan American Airways, Inc./498 : Telegram

*The Ambassador in Chile (Culbertson) to the Secretary of State*

SANTIAGO, June 22, 1929—noon.
[Received 12:50 p. m.]

96. Your 65, June 19, 7 p. m. Decree signed granting concession to Pan American-Grace Airways.

CULBERTSON

810.79611 Pan American Airways, Inc./501 : Telegram

*The Ambassador in Chile (Culbertson) to the Secretary of State*

SANTIAGO, June 26, 1929—4 p. m.
[Received 7:30 p. m.]

98. My number 96, June 22, noon. Although permission granted Pan American-Grace Airways transport correspondence, passengers, freight to and from United States and also to and from countries en route on Pacific, there is one technical detail to be settled between company and War Department here before company will start operations. Company expects receive satisfactory written understanding this detail few days when I will cable Department.

CULBERTSON

810.79611 Pan American Airways, Inc./548

*The Chargé in Uruguay (Gade) to the Secretary of State*

No. 849

MONTEVIDEO, June 27, 1929.
[Received July 18.]

SIR: With reference to the Department's telegraphic instruction No. 9, of June 1 (1929) 1 p. m.,[18] regarding a Fokker Super-Universal monoplane belonging to the Pan American Airways, I have the honor to report that in a note received yesterday the Ministry of Foreign Affairs advises this Legation that the Ministry of War and Marine has accorded permission for this airplane to fly over and land in Uruguayan territory.

The Ministry of Finance has not yet granted free entry contingent upon reexportation, but the Foreign Office has promised promptly to notify the Legation as soon as a reply is received.

I have [etc.]

GERHARD GADE

810.79611 Pan American Airways, Inc./508 : Telegram

*The Ambassador in Chile (Culbertson) to the Secretary of State*

SANTIAGO, June 30, 1929—10 a. m.
[Received 1:45 p. m.]

101. My telegram number 96, June 22, noon, was sent on information furnished orally by officials at the Foreign Office, but when I received the text of the decree I found that it varied in several

[18] See footnote 17, p. 560.

substantial respects from their assurances. I recommend therefore that the plan for the extension of the service to Chile be held in abeyance until a satisfactory decree is signed. I will confer with the Minister of War and others this week and I hope that the revised decree will be signed soon.

CULBERTSON

---

810.79611 Tri-Motors Safety Airways/64 : Telegram

*The Secretary of State to the Vice Consul at Port-of-Spain, Trinidad (Demorest)*

WASHINGTON, July 2, 1929—10 a. m.

With reference to your undated despatch No. 1942 [19] the Pan American Airways is a reputable American concern with sound financial standing and you will please extend all proper assistance to that company in its efforts to obtain an operating permit which will enable it to bring to Trinidad United States mails under a contract which has been made with the United States Post Office Department. This Company also has contract to carry U. S. mails to Mexico, Central America, Panama, Colombia, Ecuador, Peru and Chile.

In view of reports indicating that there is a connection made or contemplated between New York Rio and Buenos Aires Line, Incorporated, and French interests the Department pending fuller information does not wish you to take any action which might serve to promote such foreign interests against those of other American firms.

STIMSON

---

810.79611 Pan American Airways, Inc./511 : Telegram

*The Chargé in Uruguay (Gade) to the Secretary of State*

MONTEVIDEO, July 2, 1929—noon.
[Received July 2—11 : 40 a. m.]

31. Department's telegram 9, June 1, 1 p. m.[20] Free entry and permission to fly and land granted.

GADE

---

810.79611 Pan American Airways, Inc./519 : Telegram

*The Chargé in Venezuela (Engert) to the Secretary of State*

CARACAS, July 6, 1929—2 p. m.
[Received 8 : 35 p. m.]

81. Department's 23, June 13, 7 p. m. Foreign Office informs me that Minister of Fomento states he has been unable to reach an agree-

---

[19] Received June 21, 1929 ; not printed.
[20] See footnote 17, p. 560.

ment with the representatives of Pan American Airways regarding provisional permit but that he reiterated "sincere purpose of collaborating as far as possible in the establishment of a fast and efficient mail service between the two countries upon bases beneficial to both."

ENGERT

---

810.79611 Pan American Airways, Inc./525 : Telegram

*The Vice Consul at Port-of-Spain, Trinidad (Demorest) to the Secretary of State*

[PORT-OF-SPAIN,] TRINIDAD, July 9, 1929—11 a. m.
[Received 3 : 13 p. m.]

With reference to my previous correspondence and your telegram July 2, 10 a. m., and despatch number 1942.[21] I respectfully assure the Department I have been and I am energetically extending all proper assistance to Pan American Airways to obtain operating permit to bring to Trinidad United States mails under a contract. Interview with the Governor this morning apparently assures me that the Trinidad Government desires Pan American Airways to operate here because approved by United States Government and also actually operating extensively and carrying United States mails. Furthermore proposed air service extremely popular with local business men, municipality and chamber of commerce. Governor expects to hear from Colonial Office within ten days relative to operating permit. Despatch follows.

DEMOREST

---

810.79611 Pan American Airways, Inc./520 : Telegram

*The Ambassador in Chile (Culbertson) to the Secretary of State*

SANTIAGO, July 9, 1929—4 p. m.
[Received 7 p. m.]

110. Referring to my telegram number 101, June 30, 10 a. m. Local papers today report United States Post Office Department announces inauguration air mail service to Santiago on July 16th. These reports tend to make more difficult an already difficult situation in connection with my efforts to have modified certain unacceptable conditions of decree concession. MacGregor, Vice President, Pan American-Grace Airways due to arrive here tomorrow.

CULBERTSON

---

[21] Despatch not printed.

810.79611 Pan American Airways, Inc./526 : Telegram

*The Secretary of State to the Ambassador in Chile (Culbertson)*

WASHINGTON, July 10, 1929—3 p. m.

73. Your 110, July 9, 4 p. m.   Post Office Department states that their action was taken at the urgent behest of Pan American-Grace Airways.   That company informed the Post Office Department some time ago that they were ready to begin operations and had equipment, et cetera.   Post Office Department inquired whether they had made satisfactory arrangements with Chilean Government and was informed in the affirmative.   It was on this basis that the announcement was made.   Representatives of Pan American-Grace Airways yesterday advised Post Office Department that while there is a hitch in the negotiations with Chile they expect to have it all straightened out so that service can begin on the sixteenth.   Consult with MacGregor and cable if you have any recommendations as to action to be taken by this Department or the Post Office Department.

STIMSON

---

810.79611 Pan American Airways, Inc./540 : Telegram

*The Secretary of State to the Vice Consul at Port-of-Spain, Trinidad (Demorest)*[22]

WASHINGTON, July 16, 1929—7 p. m.

The Department is informed that a Sikorsky amphibian of Pan American Airways, Inc., left Miami July 15 to survey a route between San Juan, Porto Rico and Trinidad for a United States Air Mail contract which that company holds.   The party consists of Robert G. Thatch, R. I. Dunton, and pilots B. G. Rowe and Roy Booth.

Please render all proper assistance if conditions make it necessary to enter a port in your district within the next few days.

STIMSON

---

810. 79611 Pan American Airways, Inc./547 : Telegram

*The Ambassador in Chile (Culbertson) to the Secretary of State*

SANTIAGO, July 18, 1929—5 p. m.
[Received 8 : 40 p. m.]

114. With the mails arriving tomorrow at Arica I have obtained in writing from the Chilean Government provisional permission under which Pan American-Grace Airways can fly and carry mail in Chile without prejudice to the efforts which we are now making to have

---

[22] The same, *mutatis mutandis*, on the same date to the Consul at Guadeloupe and the Consular Agent at Roseau.

the decree revised. Referring to my despatch No. 214 June 25.[23] The chief provisions of the decree to which objection is being made are:

1. The restriction on types of motors under clause 4.
2. Clause 6 because it violates article 12 of the Havana convention.
3. Clause 8 which requires that the company expend a large sum of money for night flying equipment.
4. Clause 10 which provides that 50 per cent of fares charged by company for carrying passengers within Chile must be paid to the Government.

These two last provisions are regarded . . . by the military authorities as contributions to be exacted from the Pan American for the benefit of national commercial aviation within Chile.

CULBERTSON

---

810.79611 Pan American Airways, Inc./589

*The Consul at Guadeloupe (Hunt) to the Secretary of State*

No. 72                                                                                  GUADELOUPE, July 19, 1929.
[Received August 6.]

SIR: In acknowledgment of the Department's telegram of July 16th, regarding the flight of the Sikorsky Amphibian of the Pan American Airways, a copy of which is enclosed herewith,[24] I have the honor to refer to my despatch No. 70 of July 5th, 1929,[23] and to report that following telegrams from the Pan American Airways at San Juan, Porto Rico, announcing the arrival of the Amphibian in Guadeloupe territory, a request for permission to land was addressed to the Governor of the Colony on behalf of Mr. Robert G. Thatch and his companions.

The Governor refused to grant the authorization requested, on the grounds that the request of Mr. Thatch was not received a sufficiently long time in advance to allow him to take a decision in the matter.

I have [etc.]                                                          WILLIAM H. HUNT

---

810.79611 Pan American Airways, Inc./561 : Telegram

*The Ambassador in Chile (Culbertson) to the Secretary of State*

SANTIAGO, July 25, 1929—noon.
[Received 7:25 p. m.]

120. Referring to my telegram number 114, July 18, 5 p. m. Discussions of the revised decree are proceeding with President, Min-

---

[23] Not printed.
[24] See footnote 22, p. 568.

ister of War, and Minister for Foreign Affairs. In the meantime other aviation interests are active:

(1) The Latécoère [25] has been granted a concession to fly in Chilean territory, transporting mails, passengers and freight from and to Bolivia and Peru and from and to the United States and intermediate countries under very favorable conditions.

[Paraphrase.] An invitation has been received from the Director General of the Scadta Company, transmitted by the Chilean Minister in Colombia, for a meeting with the Director General to take place at Lima. The Chilean Director of Aviation has been appointed by the Chilean Minister of War to proceed there at once by airplane to represent the Chilean Government. [End paraphrase.]

Montgomery in behalf of the aviation group which he represents has made a proposal to the Chilean Government similar to that made by Curtiss Motor and Aeroplane Corporation. See my telegram of June 5, noon.

The local representative of Pan American-Grace Airways today cabled his principals in New York requesting authorization to propose to the Chilean Government the following: His company to deliver foreign, southbound air mail at Arica, Antofagasta and Santiago and to pay Chilean Post Office five centavos per gramme, approximately equivalent to three dollars per pound, to deliver foreign mail to intermediate points by Chilean air service. This step is in line with my suggestions that some effort be made to gratify the national ambition of the military group and to offset the efforts of other aviation interests seeking to render ineffective the international mail to [Chile?] of the Pan American-Grace Airways. I recommend that, in case the New York office requests it, the Post Office Department approve this proposal. It will not only assist directly in obtaining a satisfactory decree but it will associate international mail service directly with the local service and in the long run make the former service more secure.

Copy repeated Lima.

CULBERTSON

---

810.79611 Pan American Airways, Inc./565 : Telegram

*The Secretary of State to the Ambassador in Chile (Culbertson)*

WASHINGTON, July 26, 1929—7 p. m.

85. Your 120, July 25, noon. Pan American-Grace Airways has made similar report of the situation to the Department.

---

[25] Compañía General de Empresas Aeronauticas, Lineas Latécoère.

You may say to the proper authorities that this Government feels sure that Chile will give American companies permission to fly in Chile on as favorable terms as any other foreign companies and that furthermore as the Pan American-Grace Airways has the contract from the United States Post Office Department to carry the mail to Chile it hopes the Chilean Government will be able shortly to give it the necessary permission on equitable terms.

As to the modification the Company states that with the Post Office Department's permission it has authorized its Santiago manager to negotiate on this basis subject to certain conditions necessitated by the nature of its contract with the United States Post Office Department.

STIMSON

---

810.79611 Pan American Airways, Inc./566 : Telegram

*The Secretary of State to the Chargé in Peru (Mayer)*

WASHINGTON, July 26, 1929—7 p. m.

78. Following sent to Santiago in reply to its 120, July 25, noon.

[Here follows text of telegram No. 85, July 26, 7 p. m., to the Ambassador in Chile, printed *supra*.]

Should the meeting in Lima referred to in Santiago telegram take place please follow situation very closely and report fully to the Department.

STIMSON

---

810.79611 Pan American Airways, Inc./569 : Telegram

*The Ambassador in Chile (Culbertson) to the Secretary of State*

[Paraphrase]

SANTIAGO, July 27, 1929—noon.
[Received July 28—5 : 30 p. m.]

122. My 120, July 25, and Department's 85, July 26. The proposed meeting at Lima is a part of a plan for international air service collaboration by Faucett of Peru, Scadta of Colombia, the Bolivian Lloyd Aerial (German controlled), and the Chilean military air service. The combination is obviously directed against the Pan American Airways. Active support is being given to the plan by Curtiss Company through the Faucett Company. I have also reason to believe that the New York, Rio, and Buenos Aires Company and allied interests are working with the French Latécoère Company on an air service across the Andes and then northward so as to connect

with the group which will try to elaborate program in Lima. Neither the German nor the French interests in this proposed combination acting alone or together could impair the efficiency of the international service of the Pan American operated under contract with the United States Post Office, but if aided by powerful American interests the program may succeed and the American line be destroyed to the profit of foreign aviation interests.

The Government of Chile is more liberally inclined toward a company like the Latécoère Company, which asks merely to deliver mail and passengers at particular points, than toward the Pan American which asks to carry and deliver mail within Chile. Therefore my recommendation for cooperation between the Pan American and Chilean national service. . . .

CULBERTSON

---

810.79611 Pan American Airways, Inc./567 : Telegram

### *The Chargé in Peru (Mayer) to the Secretary of State*

[Paraphrase]

LIMA, July 27, 1929—7 p. m.<br>[Received 11 p. m.]

142. Department's 78, July 26, 7 p. m. and Santiago's 120, July 25, noon to the Department.

(1) This noon I called upon the President and told him about the proposed meeting in Lima between Bauer and the Chilean Director of Aviation. I recalled to the President the fact that the Pan American Airways under its arrangement in Peru anticipated losing money for the first few years and that if Scadta were allowed to compete it might well be that neither company would be successful. This would be to the evident disadvantage of Peruvian commercial air traffic in which I knew he took such keen interest.

(2) The President's attitude was most favorable. He agreed heartily and appeared anxious to do everything possible to protect American aviation arrangements here. He made the suggestion that, as the airplane traffic situation in Peru was becoming more and more confused, I should tell him what the Government of the United States wished him to do in the matter, the sooner the better.

(3) In a short time I shall cable suggestions which I hope I may be authorized to place informally before the President.

Repeated to Santiago.

MAYER

810.79611 Pan American Airways, Inc./575 : Telegram

*The Chargé in Peru (Mayer) to the Secretary of State*

[Paraphrase]

LIMA, July 30, 1929—9 p. m.
[Received July 31—12:55 a. m.]

143. My 142, July 27, 7 p. m.

(1) I have been informed by Captain Grow [26] that the President through the Foreign Minister has instructed him to recommend a reply to a telegram which the Peruvian Government has received from its Embassy at Santiago reporting suggestion by the Chilean Government for a conference at Lima of official delegates from Bolivia, Chile, Colombia, and Peru to agree upon conditions of aeronautical navigation in the above countries.

(2) Captain Grow will advise the Foreign Minister that, since these matters were taken care of by the commercial aviation convention at the Sixth Pan American Conference [27] to which Peru is a signatory and since the proposed conference represents an effort on the part of certain foreign interests against the Pan American Airways which have established an efficient service between the United States and Peru and the West Coast of South America, he recommends that the Peruvian Government inform the Chilean Government that it sees no need for the proposed conference; that if the countries concerned find fault with the Havana regulations, they can discuss procedure at the next Pan American Conference with all the countries. A complete copy of Captain Grow's memorandum is being sent by air mail. [28]

(3) The proposed conference, which is of broader scope than previously reported, constitutes an even greater menace by Scadta against American aviation objectives on the West Coast of South America, because it would apparently seek to discuss and to determine, without our participation, questions which, in the last analysis, have a vital and direct bearing upon broader matters of aviation from the United States to and along the West Coast, which matters are of immediate concern to the United States. The proposed conference would also appear to be a further effort by Scadta against the one American aviation company which is established in Peru.

(4) The action of Captain Grow may prevent participation by Peru in the proposed conference. In order to make this as certain as possible, however, I think it would be wise for me to tell President Leguia informally, responsive to my 142, July 27, 7 p. m., that both

---

[26] Peruvian Director General of Aviation.
[27] *Foreign Relations*, 1928, vol. I, p. 585.
[28] Memorandum not printed.

President Hoover and yourself greatly appreciate his friendly interest in the maintenance of the established airplane communication between the United States and Peru; and that in these circumstances President Hoover hopes that President Leguia shares his feeling that an aviation conference of limited participation might well prove embarrassing to this service.

(5) With reference to the proper protection of the Pan American Airways, I did not fail to take carefully into account the question of the American interests which may be negotiating with Scadta regarding West Coast traffic. Unless and until Scadta is bought out by American interests I think it would be dangerous for the United States not to give our strong support to a purely American aviation company carrying mail and passengers along the West Coast of South America under contracts from the Governments of the United States and of Peru because of the association of other American aviation interests with Scadta or any other foreign company attempting to compete with this established American concern.

(6) If the Department decides to authorize me to speak with President Leguia in the manner set forth in paragraph (4), I respectfully request the earliest instruction possible since the [Pan American policy?] may have a determining effect upon Peru's action regarding the proposed conference.

MAYER

---

823.79625/2 : Telegram

*The Secretary of State to the Chargé in Peru (Mayer)*

WASHINGTON, July 31, 1929—6 p. m.

79. Your 143 July 30, 9 p. m., paragraph 4. Take action suggested.

STIMSON

---

810.79611 Pan American Airways, Inc./581 : Telegram

*The Ambassador in Chile (Culbertson) to the Secretary of State*

SANTIAGO, August 1, 1929—4 p. m.
[Received 9 : 55 p. m.]

125. President yesterday signed decree authorizing Chilean Post Office to sign with the Pan American-Grace Airways contract, necessary under Chilean law as a supplement to direct arrangement between two post offices, which includes provisions for carrying mail to intermediate countries. To the main decree transmitted with my despatch No. 214, July 25th,[29] I have made the objections summarized

---

[29] Not printed.

in my telegram of July 19 [*18*], 5 p. m., [No.] 114, and present discussions should result in revised decree. However it can now be said that the service is successfully inaugurated and its permanency depends only on whether the company accepts finally the provision which will be embodied in the revised decree. The way would now appear to be open to proceed with the Buenos Aires extension referred to in the Department's No. 61, May 31, and other cables.

CULBERTSON

810.79611 Pan American Airways, Inc./583 : Telegram

*The Secretary of State to the Ambassador in Chile (Culbertson)*

[Paraphrase]

WASHINGTON, August 1, 1929—6 p. m.

90. Information has reached the Department that the Chilean Director of Aviation has been publishing newspaper statements that the air mail contracts of the United States were designed to build up reserve military pilots and to establish a branch easily transformable to military purposes. It is stated that the opposition of the Chilean Director of Aviation to American aviation interests has been evident in other ways, but this latest report, if well founded, is the first indication that he openly questions the good faith of the United States. Please investigate the matter and report whether you feel you should be authorized to say informally to the Foreign Minister that the Department has learned with regret that an important Chilean official is circulating such rumors, which have no foundation in fact and which are obviously prejudicial to legitimate American interests.

STIMSON

810.79611 Pan American Airways, Inc./584 : Telegram

*The Ambassador in Chile (Culbertson) to the Secretary of State*

[Paraphrase]

SANTIAGO, August 2, 1929—noon.
[Received 2 p. m.]

127. Your 90, August 1, 6 p. m. When the statements first appeared in the newspapers I objected both orally and in an informal letter to the Foreign Minister. Subsequent articles which were prepared have not appeared in the press.

CULBERTSON

823.79625/3 : Telegram

### The Chargé in Peru (Mayer) to the Secretary of State

[Paraphrase]

LIMA, August 3, 1929—7 p. m.
[Received 9:30 p. m.]

147. Responsive to the message your telegram No. 79, July 31, 6 p. m., instructed me to convey, President Leguia authorized me to inform President Hoover and yourself that he was entirely of your opinion respecting the proposed conference. He will inform the Chilean Government that because of Peru's aviation commitments the Peruvian Government is not free to participate in the proposed conference.

MAYER

---

810.79611 Pan American Airways, Inc./591 : Telegram

### The Acting Secretary of State to the Minister in Guatemala (Geissler)

WASHINGTON, August 7, 1929—3 p. m.

45. United States Post Office Department is planning to extend its present air mail service subject to the consent of the Mexican and Guatemalan Governments, from Vera Cruz via Tapachula to Guatemala City. The American contractor for this route, operating through its 100% owned Mexican subsidiary, the Compania Mexicana de Aviacion, is preparing to begin service to Guatemala City, effective August 25th. Please extend every proper assistance in securing the assent of the Guatemalan Government.

COTTON

---

810.79611 Pan American Airways, Inc./598 : Telegram

### The Acting Secretary of State to the Chargé in France (Armour)

WASHINGTON, August 12, 1929—5 p. m.

258. Pan American Airways Incorporated is planning to extend its air mail service now operating between Miami, Florida, and San Juan, Porto Rico, through the Leeward and Windward Islands to Trinidad. Please request the French Government to grant necessary permission for operation in and over Martinique and Guadeloupe and to authorize the local Postal Administration in those islands to accept American air mail delivered by Pan American Airways,

pending a formal agreement to cover the company's operations and the exchange of air mail there.

COTTON

---

810.79611 Pan American Airways, Inc./612

*The Minister in Guatemala (Geissler) to the Secretary of State*

No. 2537                                    GUATEMALA, August 13, 1929.
                                           [Received August 21.]

SIR: Referring to the Department's cablegram No. 45, of August 7, 3 p. m., directing the Legation to extend every proper assistance in the matter of securing the assent of the Guatemalan Government to the extension of the Air Mail Service of the Compañía Mexicana de Aviación from Vera Cruz via Tapachula to the city of Guatemala, I have the honor to report, that, since that instruction was received, the subject has not been taken up with the Legation by any representative of that concern.

I assume that the Department does not desire me to initiate action.
I have [etc.]                              ARTHUR H. GEISSLER

---

810.79611 Pan American Airways, Inc./602 : Telegram

*The Vice Consul at Port-of-Spain, Trinidad (Demorest) to the*
*Secretary of State*

[PORT-OF-SPAIN,] TRINIDAD, August 15, 1929—4 p. m.
                                           [Received 6:23 p. m.]

I have been informed by the Acting Governor that the Trinidad Government has granted Pan American Airways Incorporated temporary authorization to operate for a period of six months and to use temporary landing place for that period of time pending negotiations with Imperial Government in regard to application for permanent operating permit. I believe that the Atlantic Airways Limited, Toronto, is now negotiating with Trinidad and British Guiana Governments to operate a similar service between Canada and West Indies on a yearly subsidy basis of 15,000 pounds (sterling) from Canada and 5,000 pounds (sterling) from Trinidad and 9,000 pounds (sterling) from British Government. I hear that the Canadian National Steamship Company will begin a seaplane service between Grenada, St. Christopher (Kitts), Dominica and British Guiana in October.

DEMOREST

810.79611 Pan American Airways, Inc./604 : Telegram

*The Minister in El Salvador (Robbins) to the Secretary of State*

SAN SALVADOR, August 18, 1929—noon.
[Received 6 : 55 p. m.]

59. Minister of War and Aviation assured me that the contract would be awarded to the Pan American Airways Incorporated. The President, Minister of Fomento and he appear to be in accord.

ROBBINS

810.79611 Pan American Airways, Inc./605 : Telegram

*The Minister in Guatemala (Geissler) to the Secretary of State*

GUATEMALA, August 19, 1929—6 p. m.
[Received 10 : 40 p. m.]

106. Referring to Department's telegram of August 7, 3 p. m. Legation's despatch of August 13 [30] reported receipt of a cablegram from Balch announcing transfer of Guatemala aviation contract from Latin American to the Pickwick Airways, a Delaware corporation.

About August 13th, Morrison, traffic manager of the Mexican Aviation Company, arrived in the city of Guatemala. On the 17th he asked me to receive him this morning for a conference. Today he telephoned postponing the conference pending an interview with his lawyer.

This evening the local representative of the Pickwick-Latin American Airways presented to the Legation a communication alleging that it is incorporated under American laws and owned by Americans; that it has been operating a regular mail service between Guatemala and Mexico since August 7th in accordance with its contract with the Guatemalan Government obtained "before the Compania Mexicana de Aviacion even applied for such a concession"; that the Compania Mexicana "through the efforts of the Mexican Embassy is endeavoring to obtain permission from the Guatemalan Government to operate on our route and bring mail from the United States"; that the Compania Mexicana "irrespective of the nationality of its present stockholders is a Mexican Company, incorporated and operated under the laws of Mexico"; that "common sense and business judgment repudiate the idea of operating two air lines over exactly the same route".

He says that "I do not hesitate to state that my company will undertake the carrying of United States mails from the Guatemalan-Mexico border to Guatemala City on the same terms as the Compania Mexicana de Aviacion". He protests "against the machinations of

[30] Despatch No. 2538, p. 652.

Mexican elements against our legitimate rights obtained through considerable expenditure of time, money and labor" and requests the Legation's "support and protection against such intrigues by opposing the granting of permission to the Compania Mexicana" to bring United States mail to Guatemala City.

It is doubtful that Fomento would at present grant a request for the Mexican Aviation Company to fly a route in Guatemala substantially paralleling the Pickwick Airways except perhaps upon an official request made on behalf of the Government of the United States.

See despatch No. 2480 June 27th.[31]

Please cable instructions.

GEISSLER

---

810.79611 Pan American Airways, Inc./611 : Telegram

*The Minister in Guatemala (Geissler) to the Secretary of State*

GUATEMALA, August 20, 1929—11 a. m.<br>[Received 3:20 p. m.]

107. Referring to the Legation's telegram of August 19, 6 p. m. Morrison told Hawks last night that the Mexican Company plans to operate through Guatemala and Salvador into Nicaragua connecting there with the Pan American or going on to Panama.

I appreciate that the Department is in better position to judge the situation in all its aspects but viewed from here it still seems undesirable that a foreign company other than one incorporated in the United States operate an air transport line in Central America and even less that the Government of the United States facilitate it.

GEISSLER

---

810.79611 Pan American Airways, Inc./619 : Telegram

*The Acting Secretary of State to the Minister in Guatemala (Geissler)*

WASHINGTON, August 24, 1929—2 p. m.

49. Your 106, August 19, 6 p. m. and 107, August 20, 11 a. m. It is evident that if Pan American Airways is to establish a two day service from Brownsville to the Canal Zone as planned it will be impracticable to change planes and crews at the Guatemalan border. This service is designed to handle mail from the eastern and central parts of the United States and would not necessarily compete with any other service covering the western part. The Department is assured that the Compañia Mexicana de Aviación will not run farther south than Guate-

---

[31] Not printed.

mala City. The Department as you know does not ordinarily support foreign corporations even when all of the stock is American owned but in this case it has been decided after careful consideration that an exception is warranted for the reasons stated and because of the direct interest of the United States Post Office therein. You will therefore please make such representations to the Guatemalan Government as you consider appropriate to obtain permission for the Compañia Mexicana de Aviación to bring the United States mails into Guatemala from Mexico.

CARR

---

810.79611 Pan American Airways, Inc./645

*The Chargé in Brazil (Schoenfeld) to the Secretary of State*

No. 3219                                     RIO DE JANEIRO, August 28, 1929.
                                             [Received September 12.]

SIR: Referring to this Mission's despatch No. 3130 of March 27, 1929 relative to the activities of American aviation enterprise in Brazil, I have the honor to enclose herewith the text of the authorization granted by the Brazilian Minister of Communications to the Pan American Airways, Inc. under date of August 10 [32] and as published in the *Official Gazette* of August 15, 1929, to operate aeroplanes over Brazilian territory in connection with the company's international air service.

There is likewise enclosed the text of a similar authorization granted the New York, Rio and Buenos Aires Line, Incorporated, under date of August 15, 1929,[32] and as published in the *Official Gazette* of August 18, 1929. Both authorizations are accompanied by English translations.

I have [etc.]                                RUDOLF E. SCHOENFELD

---

810.79611 Pan American Airways, Inc./654

*The Vice Consul at Georgetown (Brown) to the Secretary of State*

No. 212                                      GEORGETOWN, August 28, 1929.
                                             [Received September 17.]

SIR: I have the honor to refer to despatch No. 178 of May 27, 1929, file No. 879.6,[32] regarding the prohibition of flights over French Guiana and to enclose herewith a copy of a letter from His Excellency the Governor of French Guiana dated July 30, 1929, and received at this office on August 26, 1929.

I have [etc.]                                HAROLD R. BROWN

---

[32] Not printed.

[Enclosure—Translation]

*The Governor of French Guiana (Siadoies) to the American Vice Consul (Brown)*

CAYENNE, July 30, 1929.

MR. CONSUL: In answer to your letter of April 9, 1929, I have to inform you that I have just granted to a seaplane of the Pan American Airway a permit to fly over and land at Cayenne on the study trip the crew of that craft is taking to South America.

I shall look into the application for flight over and landing in Guiana that may be sent to me by the fliers of the United States of America for study trips in a friendly spirit.

Be pleased [etc.]                              SIADOIES

---

810.79611 Pan American Airways, Inc./626 : Telegram

*The Minister in Guatemala (Geissler) to the Secretary of State*

GUATEMALA, August 30, 1929—5 p. m.
[Received 11:40 p. m.]

109. August 26th I informed the Pickwick Airways of the Department's attitude expressed August 24, 2 p. m. Today its representative filed a protest asserting that no exception should be made against it since it is an American corporation; that the Mexican company would "receive a heavy subsidy" from the United States Post Office Department; that the death of his company would be unavoidable; and that he requests transmission to the State Department of his "formal protest for the unwarranted assistance rendered by the American Legation at their request to a Mexican company against a purely and thoroughly American corporation."

GEISSLER

---

810.79611 Pan American Airways, Inc./628 : Telegram

*The Minister in Guatemala (Geissler) to the Secretary of State*

GUATEMALA, August 30, 1929—7 p. m.
[Received August 31—10:50 a. m.]

110. Referring to my cable of August 30, 5 p. m. Morrison told me at noon that the Minister for Foreign Affairs had wired the Minister to Washington to ascertain the wishes of the Government of the United States regarding the request of the Compania Mexicana.

The only application the Mexican Company has pending before

the Guatemalan Government is one authorizing it to establish a general air mail and passenger and express service into and out of Guatemala.

I told Morrison that I cannot see my way clear to support such a proposal because it goes beyond the Department's telegram of August 24, 2 p. m.

On the other hand it appears that my action in interviewing Fomento had been interpreted by some people as support of the above-mentioned application of the Mexican Company. Therefore, I reiterated my position to Morrison and then to Irigoyen and then stated it to President Chacon this afternoon that the Department of State, in view of a request of the Post Office Department, would be pleased if Guatemala would permit United States mail to be brought to the city of Guatemala from Mexico by the Compania Mexicana but that that does not indicate a support of the much more far reaching pending application of that company.

GEISSLER

---

810.79611 Pan American Airways, Inc./638

*The Minister in Costa Rica (Davis) to the Secretary of State*

No. 1638                                         SAN JOSÉ, August 30, 1929.
                                                 [Received September 10.]

SIR: I have the honor to transmit herewith copy and translation of an agreement signed by the local representative of the Pan American Airways, Incorporated, and the Director of Posts of Costa Rica,[34] setting forth the conditions under which air mail service is to be inaugurated, and establishing postal rates for this service. This agreement supplements the contract of the Pan American Airways, Incorporated, which was recently approved by the Costa Rican Congress.

It will be noted that the agreement is entered into upon the condition that the Company may request an interpretation of Article 17 of the Contract.

Under this agreement, the Pan American Airways, Incorporated, can begin operations immediately and will enjoy all the rights granted by the contract until such time as the Company may find it advisable to request an interpretation of Article 17, to which it has raised some objections.

I have [etc.]                                    ROY T. DAVIS

---

[34] Not printed.

810.79611 Pan American Airways/642

*The Minister in Guatemala (Geissler) to the Secretary of State*

No. 2559                                    GUATEMALA, September 4, 1929.
                                            [Received September 11.]

SIR: I have the honor to report, that on September 1, 1929, I handed the Minister of Fomento, Colonel Daniel Hernández, a letter in which, confirming a conversation of August 29, I told him that I had been instructed by the Department of State to support a request of the Compañía Mexicana de Aviación for permission to bring the United States mails into Guatemala from Mexico. A copy of that letter has been furnished to Mr. Carlos Irigoyen, representative of the Pickwick Airways, and its contents have been communicated by me orally and verbatim to Mr. Wilbur L. Morrison of the Compañía Mexicana de Aviación, and he has been told that he may have a copy if he desires it.

Mr. Morrison told me today, that his negotiations with the Minister of Fomento are progressing very nicely and that he hopes to conclude a contract with that official tomorrow.

Meanwhile I enclose herewith a copy of a report of a conversation[35] in which, as related by Mr. Carlos Irigoyen, he was urged by a Secretary of the Mexican Embassy, in the presence of Mr. Morrison, to discontinue opposition to the application of the Compañía Mexicana for a permit to operate in Guatemala, some threats being made in that connection.

There is also enclosed, with translations, a set of clippings of advertisements[35] in which the Pickwick Airways has been presenting its attitude to the Guatemalan public.

I have [etc.]                               ARTHUR H. GEISSLER

---

823.79625/4 : Telegram

*The Chargé in Peru (Mayer) to the Secretary of State*

                                            LIMA, September 5, 1929—5 p.m.
                                            [Received 8:05 p. m.]

167. My despatch No. 344, August 20, page 3,[35] and telegram 147, August 3, 7 p.m. The following telegram was sent to the American Embassy Santiago:

[Paraphrase.] "September 5, 5 p. m. Your 120, July 25, noon, to the Secretary of State and pursuant telegraphic correspondence between the two Embassies.

In view of the Peruvian attitude toward the proposed conference, I had thought that the visit of the Chilean Director General of Aviation to Lima would not take place. I have now been informed that

---

[35] Not printed.

he has requested permission to fly here and that he expects to arrive within a few days. Have you any information on this?" [End paraphrase.]

MAYER

810.79611 Pan American Airways, Inc./633 : Telegram

*The Chargé in France (Armour) to the Secretary of State*

PARIS, September 6, 1929—4 p. m.
[Received September 6—2 : 32 p. m.]

405. Reference Department's telegram No. 105, April 9, 5 p. m. Temporary authorization granted for exploratory flight.

Matter of Department's telegram No. 258, August 10 [*12*], being given further study.

ARMOUR

810.79611 Pan American Airways, Inc./655

*The Minister in Guatemala (Geissler) to the Secretary of State*

No. 2562
GUATEMALA, September 11, 1929.
[Received September 18.]

SIR: Referring to despatch 2559 of September 4, 1929, I have the honor to report, that Mr. Wilbur L. Morrison, of the Compañía Mexicana de Aviación, has told Secretary of Legation Hawks, that Minister of Fomento Daniel Hernández has signed with him a "provisional license" or contract similar to the one granted by the Government of Guatemala to the Latin American Airways and by it assigned to the Pickwick Airways, and that the Minister of Fomento had also written him a letter, dated September 7, stating that until President Lázaro Chacón approves that contract, the Compañía Mexicana may bring "mail only" into Guatemala from Mexico.

As regards the abovementioned provisional contract, it will be recalled, that (see despatch 2557 of August 31, 1929,[37]) Mr. Morrison had asked for "authority to transport passengers, express and mail from abroad to the city of Guatemala and from this Capital abroad". A copy furnished the Legation by Mr. Carlos Bauer-Avilés of the contract said to have been signed by Colonel Hernández recites, however, as follows:—"The Republic authorizes the Company to establish a line of airplanes which shall render an international service of passengers, mail and express transportation. This line shall connect with the Mexican Republic at Mariscal or Tapachula, State of Chiapas, (according to contract already signed with the Government of Mexico), and with the United States of North America at

[37] Not printed.

Brownsville, Texas, the airplanes landing in the city of Guatemala."

The Minister of Fomento has heretofore indicated, that if, as a result of pressure, he does allow the Mexican Aviation Company to enter Guatemala, he will still be disinclined to let it operate toward the south from the Capital.

The signing of the contract of the Mexican Aviation Company was, according to *Nuestro Diario* of September 10, made the occasion of a very gay banquet offered by Mr. Morrison, and which was participated in by a group of cabinet officers, the Chargé d'Affaires of Mexico, some other Mexicans, and the Vice Consul of the United States. Secretary of Embassy Reyes-Spindola told me last night, that he imagines that in view of the opposition offered by the Pickwick Airways the situation must have been embarrassing to the Government of the United States and its representatives, but that, since the planes of the Compañía Mexicana "fly the flag of Mexico", the result is cause for great rejoicing.

I have [etc.]                                          ARTHUR H. GEISSLER

---

810.79611 Pan American Airways, Inc./648 : Telegram

*The Secretary of State to the Ambassador in Argentina (Bliss)*

WASHINGTON, September 13, 1929—5 p. m.

98. Post Office Department asks that you be informed that Pan American Grace Airways extension airmail service under contract with the United States Post Office Department will be inaugurated October 12 by a flight from Buenos Aires to Chile connecting there with northbound plane.

STIMSON

---

810.79611 Pan American Airways, Inc./647 : Telegram

*The Secretary of State to the Chargé in Peru (Mayer)*

[Paraphrase]

WASHINGTON, September 13, 1929—5 p. m.

89. Department's 88, September 9, 3 p. m.[38] It was Colonel Lindbergh's plan, after inaugurating a mail line to Paramaribo, to continue through South America on a good-will flight stopping at all Republics. The Colonel's plans now have to be changed. After returning from Paramaribo he will visit Venezuela, Colombia, and Central America to inspect Pan American Airways' operations there. It is probable that he will make a trip to South America in November but there are as yet no definite plans. You will be advised of any change of plans.

STIMSON

---

[38] Not printed.

810.79611 Pan American Airways, Inc./649 : Telegram

*The Secretary of State to the Ambassador in Chile (Culbertson)*

WASHINGTON, September 13, 1929—8 p. m.

105. Pan American Grace Airways extension airmail service under contract with the United States Post Office Department will be inaugurated October 12 by a flight from Buenos Aires to Chile connecting there with northbound plane.

STIMSON

---

810.79611 Pan American Airways, Inc./646 : Telegram

*The Chargé in Venezuela (Engert) to the Secretary of State*

CARACAS, September 13, 1929—8 p. m.
[Received September 14—3 : 10 p. m.]

148. You may desire to intimate informally to Pan American Airways that it might be very helpful to them if Lindbergh could arrange to include Venezuela in his next flight, as he was given great ovation last year. See Legation's despatch 1473, February 3rd [7th], 1928.[39]

ENGERT

---

810.79611 Pan American Airways, Inc./650 : Telegram

*The Chargé in Peru (Mayer) to the Secretary of State*

[Paraphrase]

LIMA, September 14, 1929—5 p. m.
[Received 8 : 25 p. m.]

171. Your 89, September 13, 5 p. m.

(1) I called on President Leguía yesterday and reviewed the efforts which Scadta, Latécoère, et al., were making in opposition to the American aviation company with which he had concluded a mail contract. See my 169, September 9, 2 p. m., paragraph 2.[39] I felt it was timely to make this call.

President Leguía said that he had also been informed by Santiago of the meeting of the Chilean Director General of Aviation and various commercial aviation companies planned to take place on September 25; that he had stated that while he had no objection to the meeting taking place at Lima there could be no question of the Peruvian Government's participation because of its existing aviation commitments. President Leguía said to me that he would maintain this attitude and would keep me informed of any further developments respecting the proposed conference.

---

[39] Not printed.

(2) I do not doubt the sincerity of his attitude toward our aviation interests in Peru, but I foresee strong probability that considerable pressure will be brought to bear upon him during the conference. I am frankly apprehensive of its influence despite every best intention. It is therefore a very psychological moment for Colonel Lindbergh to come to Peru not only for the favorable effect his coming would have generally on American aviation interests in Peru, but also for the support which it would give President Leguía at a time when opposition to American interests will be concentrated at Lima.

Parenthetically, I think it would be unfortunate if Colonel Lindbergh should again visit Colombia, the stronghold of Scadta, and not visit Peru where our interests have been so consistently seconded by President Leguía.

(3) I most strongly recommend to the Department that Colonel Lindbergh come to Peru directly after he concludes his inspection trip to Paramaribo.

MAYER

---

810.79611 Pan American Airways, Inc./652 : Telegram

*The Secretary of State to the Chargé in Peru (Mayer)*

[Paraphrase]

WASHINGTON, September 16, 1929—4 p. m.

91. Your 171, September 14, 5 p. m. In order to consider plans for Colonel Lindbergh to go to Peru, the Department must know how long the conference scheduled for September 25 will last. Please inform the Department as soon as possible as Colonel Lindbergh will stop in Washington for a few minutes early Wednesday morning en route to Paramaribo.

STIMSON

---

810.79611 Pan American Airways, Inc./653 : Telegram

*The Chargé in Peru (Mayer) to the Secretary of State*

[Paraphrase]

LIMA, September 17, 1929—2 p. m.
[Received 3 : 35 p. m.]

173. (1) No details of the conference are available, either as to make up or duration. Great secrecy is being maintained. The only certain information I have is that obtained by Harris in Ecuador and the comments of President Leguía on the conference. See my 171, September 14.

(2) I did not have in mind that Colonel Lindbergh could be able to be in Lima while the conference is in session. This in many ways would not seem desirable. Rather I had in mind that I could inform President Leguía in advance and make public on or about September 25th that Colonel Lindbergh was coming here in the immediate future in connection with the Pan American-Grace Airways.

(3) The capital which I could make of this news during the time of the proposed conference, culminating in Colonel Lindbergh's appearance in Lima shortly thereafter, should greatly strengthen our aviation position in Peru against such attack as I have described as impending.

(4) In the event that Colonel Lindbergh decides to come to Peru I request that I be authorized so to inform the President before any publicity which could be simultaneous in Peru and in the United States.

MAYER

---

810.79611 Pan American Airways, Inc./656 : Telegram

### The Secretary of State to the Chargé in Venezuela (Engert)

[Paraphrase]

WASHINGTON, September 17, 1929—5 p. m.

46. Your 148, September 13, 8 p. m. It is Colonel Lindbergh's plan to stop in Venezuela on his return flight from Paramaribo.

STIMSON

---

810.79611 Pan American Airways, Inc./657 : Telegram

### The Secretary of State to the Chargé in Peru (Mayer)

[Paraphrase]

WASHINGTON, September 18, 1929—4 p. m.

92. Your 173, September 17, 2 p. m. Today Colonel Lindbergh conferred at the Department. He then continued his journey to Miami to inaugurate the mail line to Paramaribo. On his return he will inspect the Pan American Airways line in Venezuela, Colombia, Panama, and Central America.

This winter Colonel Lindbergh will make a flight to South America and for this purpose he is now having constructed a special plane which, if all goes well, will be ready sometime in November so that his flight will take place probably in December or January. This flight will embrace all countries of South America and prior to making it he does not want to visit any of the countries of South America which he has not already visited. He will fly down the west coast stopping first in Ecuador and then in Peru where he will stay longer perhaps than in the other countries.

You may inform President Leguía in confidence that Colonel Lindbergh will visit Peru this winter. Sometime ago Colonel Lindbergh received a tentative invitation through the Peruvian Embassy in Washington with the statement that a formal invitation would be issued if it was known that he would accept. Colonel Lindbergh did not have all his data with him regarding this, but when he returns to the United States he will immediately take this up with the Department so that he may answer the invitation, and it may be possible to have the official announcement of his South American trip come first as an acceptance of the Peruvian invitation. Perhaps it may even be possible to have the announcement come from Lima. These questions of detail, however, will be gone into thoroughly upon his return.

Please advise the Department by cable whether you think that this confidential statement to President Leguía will cover the situation at the present time or whether it would be of material help to have a public announcement made of Colonel Lindbergh's impending visit. It is the feeling of the Department that it would be sufficient merely to inform President Leguía confidentially. The Department would prefer not to make the official announcement until Colonel Lindbergh returns unless there is other reason to do so.

STIMSON

---

810.79611 Pan American Airways, Inc./658 : Telegram

*The Chargé in Peru (Mayer) to the Secretary of State*

[Paraphrase]

LIMA, September 21, 1929—noon.
[Received 4 p. m.]

175. Your 92, September 18, 4 p. m. As authorized in the third paragraph, I am informing President Leguía confidentially. As a gesture in support of the President's attitude toward American aviation interests in Peru, I hope very much that the official announcement of Colonel Lindbergh's South American trip may come first as acceptance of Peru's invitation and be initiated from Lima. With this in mind, a public announcement at the present time of Colonel Lindbergh's impending visit would not appear to be desirable.

MAYER

810.79611 Pan American Airways, Inc./667

*The Ambassador in Chile (Culbertson) to the Secretary of State*

No. 281                                    SANTIAGO, September 21, 1929.
                                           [Received October 3.]

SIR: I have the honor to transmit herewith a copy of my Note
to the Minister for Foreign Affairs, No. 259 dated September 20,
relating to the Pan American Grace Airways Incorporated. The
immediate occasion for this Note was an intimation from the Director of Aviation that Decree No. 2001 (my Despatch No. 214 of
June 25, 1929 [41]), did not authorize the Pan American Grace Airways
Incorporation [sic] to continue its international mail service to the
Argentine. A rather clumsy effort was made to explain away
the phrase in the Decree which permits the Company to leave Chile
"on the south" by the line of the Uspallata Pass. The representative
here of the Pan American Grace Airways Incorporated asked the
Chilean Director of Aviation what reply his company would receive
to a letter, if submitted, enquiring whether the company's understanding was correct that its planes were permitted from that moment to
cross the Argentine frontier carrying international mail in transit,
and was informed that it would receive a negative reply. The Note
was also for the general purpose of reminding the Government that
the Decree requires general revision and that the Company is taking
steps to cooperate with the Chilean Government in the illumination
of the airport at Antofagasta and in the partial illumination of the
airport at Arica.

The situation, however, is far from satisfactory. The military
aviation group is constantly placing obstacles in the way of the Pan
American service and raising other irritating difficulties. It is clear
that the military people fear the efficiency of the Pan American and,
instead of showing a spirit of cooperation, desire to exploit the
Company in every possible way for the interests of the Chilean
national service. This general attitude of hostility toward the Company is stimulated by competing concerns who, while having their
own troubles with the Chilean authorities, believe it to be to their
interests to undermine the position of the Pan American which is in
a more secure position because of its contracts with the United States
Post Office.

I am sending this despatch by air mail since it may be necessary relatively soon for me to request more detailed instructions from the Department. It will be noted that I have taken a firm attitude in the enclosed note and it may be that on the basis of present instructions I

---

[41] Not printed; but see in this connection telegram No. 96, June 22, noon,
from the Ambassador in Chile, p. 564.

shall be able to handle the situation. The Department, however, should consider how far it is willing to go in insisting on fair treatment of the Pan American Grace Airways Inc., and in case the situation becomes more difficult than it is today, I shall request instructions by cable.

I have [etc.] W. S. CULBERTSON

[Enclosure]

*The American Ambassador (Culbertson) to the Chilean Minister for Foreign Affairs (Barros Castañón)*

No. 259 SANTIAGO, September 20, 1929.

EXCELLENCY: I have the honor to inform Your Excellency that the United States Post Office under its ten-year contract of March 2, 1929 with the Pan American Grace Airways, Incorporated reserved the option to extend the international airmail route to Buenos Aires and Montevideo and that now I am advised by my Government that, the Post Office of the United States having exercised this option, this extension of the international airmail service will be inaugurated by the Pan American Grace Airways, Inc. on October 12, 1929 by a flight from Buenos Aires to Santiago connecting here with the northbound planes of the Company.

In the various communications which I have had with your Government on the subject of the Pan American Grace Airways, Inc. the objective of my Government to create a fast express airmail service between the Canal and Buenos Aires and Montevideo by way of Santiago, has been referred to and so far as I knew, accepted. The permission asked by and in behalf of the Company has always been co-extensive with this objective. The petition of the Company dated May 18, 1929 on which Decree No. 2001, June 24, 1929 was based, stated:

"The Company that I represent has been favored by the Department of Post Office of the United States for a period of ten (10) years with the contract to effect the transportation of international correspondence to Santiago, Chile, susceptible of being made extensive to the Argentine and Uruguayan Republics"

and in order to be able to fulfill this commission, in so far as Chile is concerned, the Company requested at the same time, amongst other things, the following privileges:

"2nd. Permission to land for the purpose of receiving and delivering international mail and passengers, in the following points: Arica, Iquique, Antofagasta, Chañaral, Caldera, Coquimbo and Santiago, and to be permitted to cross the frontiers for the purpose of continuing to the Argentine and to Uruguay".

The permission granted to the Pan American Grace Airways, Inc. on the basis of the above mentioned petition stated in Clause I that the Company has the right to enter and fly out of Chile following "on the south the railroad line of Uspallata". This provision from its very phraseology can have no connection whatever with the service of the Company to the north and can be given only one interpretation, namely, the permission to fly out of Chile into Argentina and to enter Chile from Argentina.

No doubt this feature of the Decree needs clarification and perhaps amplification. This is true of other provisions of the Decree and your Government has recognized this by permitting the Company to operate provisionally under Decree No. 2001 (see communication of General Blanche transmitted to me by a note of your Ministry No. 8290 dated July 19, 1929).

Pending the issuance of the revised decree, however, I wish to be sure that we are in agreement on the scope of the provisional permission under which the Company is now operating in Chile. Having already set forth its requests in its petition of May 18, the Company is under no necessity to file a new petition for the extension of its service out of Chile to Buenos Aires and Montevideo and return. It should be emphasized that its original petition covered this service and that only within a few days has any doubt been raised as to the scope of the Company's permission. If the permission requested by the Company was not given with sufficient clarity in the Decree it is not the fault of the Company. Pending the issuance of the revised decree we are willing to accept the language of Decree No. 2001 as sufficiently definite for the inauguration of the extension of the international airmail service to Buenos Aires as ordered by my Government; if, however, your Government feels that further clarity is necessary I suggest the amplification of the above mentioned provisional arrangement on the basis of the Company's petition of May 18, 1929.

I feel certain at times that certain officials in the Direction of Aviation of your Government do not fully appreciate the effort which my Government is making to establish a rapid airmail service between the United States and Chile and Argentina. In competitive bidding the Pan American Grace Airways, Inc. was granted a substantial mail subvention by my Government in order to make this service possible and without this aid you will of course realize that no such rapid communications can be established for the time being between our countries. No monopolistic privileges have been requested and in accordance with the declared policy of your own Government it would seem that the permission which has been requested by the Company would be granted as a matter of course. I may be permitted to recall to Your Excellency that Chile signed the Havana Convention [38] and furthermore that she signed and ratified the Paris Convention.[39]

I have urged upon the officials of the Pan American Grace Airways, Inc. that they give generous coöperation in assisting your Government in the development of aviation in Chile. At the suggestion of General Blanche and with the knowledge and approval of His Excellency the President, the Company is bringing to Chile an expert to study the illumination of the airport of Antofagasta and a secondary installation in Arica. It is expected that his report will be ready during the first part of October and I venture to hope that at that time we may proceed to the formulation of the revised decree in terms satisfactory to your Government and to mine.

In the meantime, however, if your Government believes that Decree No. 2001 is not sufficiently clear to permit the international mails to proceed from Buenos Aires to the United States by way of Uspallata and return, I suggest that your Government give at its earliest convenience the necessary assurances on the basis of the Company's petition of May 18, 1929 and the provisional arrangement transmitted by the note of your Ministry No. 8290 of July 19, 1929, so that the extension of the airmail service to Buenos Aires may be opened on October 12 in accordance with the instructions of the United States Post Office to the Company and in accordance with the agreement reached between the Argentine Post Office and the Post Office of the United States.

I avail myself [etc.]       W. S. Culbertson

---

810.79611 Pan American Airways, Inc./663 : Telegram

*The Chargé in Peru (Mayer) to the Secretary of State*

[Paraphrase]

Lima, September 26, 1929—6 p. m.
[Received 11:30 p. m.]

178. My 175, September 21, noon.

(1) I had a very satisfactory audience with the President when conveying to him the substance of third paragraph of the Department's 92, September 18, 4 p. m.

The President was especially pleased at possibility of official announcement of Colonel Lindbergh's South American trip coming first as an acceptance of Peru's invitation. I repeat the hope that this can be arranged as a gesture in response to the President's support of our aviation interests here.

---

[38] For text of convention, see *Foreign Relations*, 1928, vol. I, p. 585.
[39] For text of convention, see *ibid.*, 1926, vol. I, p. 152.

(2) With reference to paragraph [1?] of my 173, September 17, 2 p. m. I have received the following telegram from the American Legation in Colombia in reply to my inquiry regarding Scadta's plans in connection with the proposed conference at Lima.

"Your September 23, noon. The Secretary of the Chilean Legation said that the conference would be held at Lima on September 25 with representatives of Peruvian Airways, Scadta and Chilean army officers with Von Bauer as Scadta representative."

Von Bauer arrived here on the 24th instant. There is no news as yet regarding the arrival of the Chilean Director of Aviation. Needless to say the Peruvian Airways have never received an invitation to the conference.

(3) With regard to the situation generally I have been reliably informed that President Leguía refused request of Faucett Aviation Company for permission to link up with Scadta.

(4) I have been informed by Harris in the strictest confidence that the Pan American-Grace Airways is conferring with the Curtiss interests in New York regarding the Peruvian aviation situation with the object of reaching some satisfactory understanding which for some time I have been suggesting to Harris as highly desirable.

MAYER

810.79611 Pan American Airways, Inc./665 : Telegram

*The Chargé in Venezuela (Engert) to the Secretary of State*

CARACAS, September 28, 1929 — 7 p. m.
[Received September 29 — 4:55 p. m.]

160. Your 47 [*46*], September 17, 5 p. m. Lindbergh and party arrived at Maracay and Caracas 26th from Trinidad and left this morning for Barranquilla via Curaçao, Maracaibo. I arranged for interviews with President Perez, General Gomez, the Minister of Foreign Affairs and the new Minister of Fomento, which I trust enabled the Pan American Airways to present their case fairly and adequately. I am now hopeful of the outcome.

ENGERT

823.79625/10 : Telegram

*The Chargé in Peru (Mayer) to the Secretary of State*

[Paraphrase]

LIMA, October 4, 1929—3 p. m.
[Received 7:50 p. m.]

188. My 178, September 26, 6 p. m. The proposed aviation conference at Lima has proved abortive from all I can gather.

The Chilean Director General of Aviation has not arrived, and nothing further has been heard from him since he requested permission to fly here. With regard to Von Bauer, who apparently is still in [Lima], I can only ascertain that he had several discussions with local Post Office authorities, but without result up to the present time. It appears that the President's refusal of the Faucett-Scadta request put the quietus on the conference. See paragraph (3) of my 178, September 26, 6 p. m.

MAYER

---

810.79611 Pan American Airways, Inc./684

*The Minister in Guatemala (Geissler) to the Secretary of State*

No. 2596                                      GUATEMALA, October 4, 1929.
                                             [Received October 16.]

SIR: Referring to previous despatches relating to activities of the Pan American Airways, the Mexican Aviation Company and the Pickwick Airways, I have the honor to report on a conversation I had on October 3, 1929, with Mr. John P. Trippe, President of the Pan American Airways, during which there was an exchange of information bearing on the International Aviation situation in Guatemala, and at the end of which Mr. Trippe inquired whether I should be willing to support an application of the Mexican Aviation Company for a contract under which it would carry mail for the Government of Guatemala from the Capital to the Mexican border, that inquiry being answered by me by stating that in view of the fact that the Pickwick Airways claims that it has a contract with the Government of Guatemala under which it is entitled to carry all of the mail over that route in that direction, I should not, without going into the matter further, deem it appropriate to comply with his desire unless the Department of State, in better position to judge the situation in its larger aspects than I am, were to instruct me to do so, but that, responding to another inquiry he made, I am inclined, as I view the situation now, not to give, without instructions from the Department, aid to either party, if such an application is presented. Mr. Trippe then told me, during a short talk on October 4, that he believes, upon full consideration, that my position is sound.

I beg leave to relate the following details and additional features of that conversation.

Mr. Trippe arrived at the city of Guatemala on October 3, from San Salvador, by airplane, in company of Colonel Charles Lindbergh and left with him the morning of the 4th for Belize. Upon my invitation he accompanied us, when I went with Colonel Lind-

bergh to pay respects to President Chacón, the Undersecretary for
Foreign Affairs, the Minister of Fomento and the Minister of War.
At night he attended a dinner I gave at the Legation for Colonel and
Mrs. Lindbergh. After dinner, Mr. Trippe expressed the desire for
a private talk.

The President of the Pan American told about the Company's
contract with the United States Post Office Department. He said
that it is desired, that the mail be carried between the morning and
the night of the same day from Brownsville to the city of Guatemala; that he has the impression that the Department of State
would prefer that the Pan American, being a company incorporated
in the United States, operate on the south of the Mexico-Guatemala
border in preference to its subsidiary the Mexican Aviation Company, a Mexican corporation, but that this would cause a loss of
time, since, he said, it would necessitate the changing of planes at
the border. Upon inquiries he stated, that the time required would
be about an hour; that this would not necessarily prevent observance of the schedule but might sometimes do so and would be an
inconvenience.

I said to Mr. Trippe, that, speaking frankly, as American to
American, I should prefer to see operation of this service by a company of the United States; that, however, the Department of State
is in better position to judge the situation in its larger aspects than
I am; that I had complied with its instruction that I aid in securing
permission for the Mexican Aviation Company to bring mail from
Mexico to the city of Guatemala against strong opposition of the
Pickwick Airways; that I do not mean to minimize the efforts of
the representatives of the Mexican Company, nor the aggressive help
it had from the Mexican Embassy, but that the President of Guatemala and the Minister of Fomento would undoubtedly tell him, if
he inquired of them, that they would have withheld that consent
and the subsequently granted provisional license, except for the
request I had made on behalf of the Department of State. I then
went on to remark, that perhaps he had been advised by officials of
the Mexican Aviation Company, in the beginning, that the Guatemalan Government would be more disposed to grant an aviation contract to a Mexican company than to an American concern. He
said that such was indeed the case, but that he had since concluded
that that was a mistake.

Thereupon I told Mr. Trippe, that two high officials of the Government (I was speaking of President Chacón and Minister of Fomento Daniel Hernandez) had recently given me the distinct impression, that they would much prefer to have the Pan American oper-

ate in Guatemala to having the Mexican Aviation Company, even though practically all of the latter's stock be now held by the former.

I also mentioned to Mr. Trippe, that I had heard, that there is serious talk of the organization of a Guatemalan company, to carry on an aviation service from the Mexican border on south through Guatemala and other Central American countries and from the city of Guatemala to Puerto Barrios and Key West; that the leading promoter of that idea is a man who has good financial connections; that he proposes to ask the Government of Guatemala to levy a heavy tax on foreign companies receiving subsidies; that he claims that the President and the Minister of Fomento are disposed to support the project; that I consider that it is quite possible that the idea may be carried out; that this may conceivably prove annoying to the Mexican Aviation Company, and also to the Pan American directly in the latter's effort to get a contract covering the territory south of the city of Guatemala, and that my personal opinion is, that it would be easier for the Pan American to defeat such a project, if it, instead of the Mexican Aviation Company, were operating between the city of Guatemala and the Guatemala-Mexico border. I added that, however, this is a purely personal opinion and must not in any way be regarded as a suggestion as to what he or his company should do, and that the opinion would hold even if somebody were American Minister here who does not share my personal preference for having that service operated by an American corporation.

In making to Mr. Trippe the statement set out in the first paragraph of this despatch, I had in mind the Department's instruction No. 38 of July 12, 3 [6] p. m.,[42] saying that the Legation should support in every proper way American companies which have been awarded contracts by the United States Post Office Department, in efforts to obtain privileges necessary for carrying mails to Guatemala in accordance with contracts with that Department and that the latter has stated that in rendering diplomatic assistance where concessions are involved to carry out the contracts it is desired that those contractors be given preference. However, obviously the Pickwick Airways, if the Pan American Airways asks for a contract to carry mail for the Government of Guatemala from the city of Guatemala to the Mexican border, may claim that this would be an infringement on its contract.

I shall be happy to receive such further instruction, if any, as the Department may desire to give.

I have [etc.]                                    ARTHUR H. GEISSLER

---

[42] See footnote 3, p. 545.

810.79611 Pan American Airways, Inc./675 : Telegram

*The Secretary of State to the Minister in Honduras (Summerlin)*

WASHINGTON, October 9, 1929—7 p.m.

76. Do you consider that the present time is favorable for Pan American Airways to apply for an operating concession in Honduras?

STIMSON

---

810.79611 Pan American Airways, Inc./674 : Telegram

*The Ambassador in Argentina (Bliss) to the Secretary of State*

BUENOS AIRES, October 10, 1929—4 p.m.
[Received 6 p.m.]

116. The representative of the Pan American-Grace Airways has just informed me that the President of Argentina signed their contract yesterday afternoon and that the first airplane carrying mail from Buenos Aires to the United States will leave here the morning of October 12th.

BLISS

---

810.79611 Pan American Airways, Inc./691

*The Vice Consul at Port-of-Spain, Trinidad (Demorest) to the Secretary of State*

[Extract]

No. 1986                                PORT-OF-SPAIN, TRINIDAD, October 10, 1929.
[Received October 22.]

SIR: I have the honor to state that the Pan-American Airways, Incorporated, inaugurated the United States Airmail Service to Trinidad and British and Dutch Guiana on Sunday, September 22, 1929.

.      .      .      .      .      .      .

The Pan-American Airways, Incorporated, has now an established weekly service to Trinidad and British and Dutch Guiana, and back to Miami via the Northern Islands.

The Company is now operating on a six months' special and temporary authorization, dated September 21, 1929, under articles 4, 5, and 27 (2) of the Air Navigation (Colonies, Protectorates and Mandated Territories Order, 1927). A copy of this authorization is attached.[43]

I understand that the Trinidad Post Office has so far cleared in profits on air mails over $1,500.

I have [etc.]                                ALFREDO L. DEMOREST

---

[43] Not printed.

810.79611 Pan American Airways, Inc./678 : Telegram

*The Minister in Honduras (Summerlin) to the Secretary of State*

TEGUCIGALPA, October 11, 1929—10 a.m.
[Received 2:30 p.m.]

103. Your telegram number 76, October 9, 7 p. m. Yes.

SUMMERLIN

---

810.79611 Pan American Airways, Inc. /706

*The Chargé in Chile (Lay) to the Secretary of State*

No. 298

SANTIAGO, October 15, 1929.
[Received November 4.]

SIR: Referring to the Embassy's despatch No. 281 of September 21, 1929, enclosing copy of a note to the Minister of Foreign Affairs, No. 259 of September 20, relating to the difficulty encountered by the Pan American Grace Airways, Inc., in obtaining permission to extend their international airmail route from Santiago to Buenos Aires, I have the honor to report the more recent steps that have been taken by this Embassy and the representatives of the Company here to enable it to start the extension of this service.

On October 1 the representative of the Pan American Grace Airways, Inc., here addressed a letter to the Director of Aviation announcing that his Company would inaugurate on October 12 the extension of its service to the Argentine and that this service had already been announced by the United States Post Office. To this letter a reply was received on October 5 (translation of which is attached herewith as Enclosure No. 1)[44] informing the Company's representative that only provisional permission is granted to make the first flight to Buenos Aires and that "subsequent flights will only be effected by virtue of a permission which will be studied more at length."

Inasmuch as no reply had been received to the Ambassador's note of September 20, on October 7 an informal communication was addressed by Mr. Culbertson to the Minister of Foreign Affairs,—five copies of which are enclosed (Enclosure No. 2),[44]—stating that the condition could not be accepted that the Pan American Grace Airways, Inc. must request special permission in the case of each flight with the international mails to and from the Argentine, and that it was important to know immediately whether these mails will be permitted to continue from Santiago to Buenos Aires according to schedule.

---

[44] Not printed.

Supplementing this letter, Ambassador Culbertson called on October 7 on General Blanche, the Minister of War, who controls aviation in Chile when the latter was reminded that freedom of transit of international airmails was granted by international conventions accepted by both Chile and the United States, and after reiterating the statements made in the enclosed note, the Ambassador urged that permission should be granted immediately to the Pan American Grace Airways, Inc. for the transport of international mails to and from Argentina and Chile not only for the first flight but that these mails should move regularly without encumbrance.

On the following day, October 8, the Ambassador received an informal letter (translation herewith as Enclosure No. 3)[45] from the Minister of War stating that "there is no objection on the part of the Government to authorize the Pan American Grace Airways, Inc. to fly to the Argentine Republic by way of Uspallata for the purposes of carrying to that country the international correspondence which the Company may bring via the Pacific", and that, "the provisional authorization . . . will be formalized, as is customary, by means of a Supreme Decree and in accordance with the provisions of said Decree No. 2001 which governs general permissions".

The Pan American Grace Airways, Inc. have brought an electrical expert from the United States at their expense to advise the Chilean Government on lighting for night flying and the Company proposes to contribute to the cost of the installation of lighting the airport of Arica. I believe when an understanding is reached as to the extent of the Company's contribution towards aërial navigation in Chile, the present unsatisfactory decree under which the Company is now operating, will be modified and in the revised decree the extension of the service to the Argentine will be more specifically and definitely provided for.

I have [etc.]    JULIUS G. LAY

---

810.79611 Pan American Airways, Inc./688 : Telegram

*The Minister in El Salvador (Robbins) to the Secretary of State*

SAN SALVADOR, October 19, 1929—11 a.m.
[Received 2:15 p.m.]

73. My telegram number 59 August 18, noon. Government of Salvador granted Pan American Airways Incorporated ten-year, non-exclusive operating contract. Final signatures affixed yesterday. Contract will require congressional approval which is highly prob-

[45] Not printed.

able. Pending such approval company will be granted provisional operating [permit] along general lines of contract. Separate mail contract is expected to be closed in the near future.

ROBBINS

---

810.79611 Pan American Airways, Inc./689 : Telegram

## The Chargé in Peru (Mayer) to the Secretary of State

LIMA, October 20, 1929—11 a.m.
[Received 4:25 p. m.]

201. My telegram number 188, October 4, 3 p.m. Captain Harris, local representative of Pan American-Grace Airways Incorporated, has just given me a copy of a contract between his company and Scadta signed here October 18th. This agreement is for an indefinite period subject to cancellation by either side on sixty days' notice "for a serious cause which may affect the privileged position of Scadta in Colombia on the one part and the privileged position of Pan American-Grace Airways Incorporated in Peru on the other."

2. The essence of the contract, in addition to this important admission by Scadta vis-à-vis Pan American-Grace Airways Incorporated position here, is the mutual agreement that Scadta exclusively turns over all Colombian air mail for Peru to Pan American-Grace Airways Incorporated at Buenaventura and Pan American-Grace Airways Incorporated exclusively turns over all Peruvian air mail for the interior of Colombia to Scadta at the same place.

3. Harris feels as I do that this contract satisfactorily defines the relations between Pan American-Grace Airways Incorporated and Scadta and should mean that the latter will cease its previously continuous attacks on Pan American-Grace Airways Incorporated's position in Peru.

4. It may be safely assumed that Von Bauer would never have entered into this arrangement if he had not been unsuccessful—which he frankly told Harris—in efforts to interest the Peruvian Government in opposition to Pan American-Grace Airways Incorporated's position here. I feel therefore, as I have previously expressed to the Department, that we owe a debt of genuine gratitude to President Leguia for his staunch stand in favor of American aviation interests here. I shall take the first opportunity practicable to inform the President of the fact of this agreement and convey to him again the appreciation of our Government in the sense indicated above.

5. A copy and translation of the contract will go forward in the next mail.

Repeated to Bogotá and Santiago.

MAYER

810.79611 Pan American Airways, Inc./690 : Telegram

### The Minister in El Salvador (Robbins) to the Secretary of State

SAN SALVADOR, October 22, 1929—11 a. m.
[Received 1:47 p.m.]

74. My telegram 73, October 19, 11 a. m. Provisional operating permit on basis of contract granted yesterday by Minister of War and Aviation.

ROBBINS

---

810.79611 Pan American Airways, Inc./700

### The Second Assistant Postmaster General (Glover) to the Chief of the Division of Latin American Affairs (Munro)

WASHINGTON, October 22, 1929.

MY DEAR DOCTOR: Would it be interesting for the State Department to know that the Post Office Department has several Air Mail contracts with the Pan American Airways Company which have been in operation for quite a period of time, all giving most satisfactory service from an operation record?

The line from Key West and Miami, Florida, to Havana, Cuba, is one of the outstanding contracts of the Post Office Department which has given exceptional service, having been in operation since October 19, 1927.

This Company also has in operation a line from Miami to Cristobal, Canal Zone, through the Pan American Countries, and a line from Miami to San Juan, Porto Rico, via Havana, Cuba, with its recent extension to Paramaribo, Dutch Guiana, South America. Both of these lines have contracts with the Department and are giving service equally as good as the first mentioned line.

The Department believes that, in the operation of all these lines by the Pan American Airways Company, it is giving a very high type of service and it is satisfied with the service rendered under the various contracts between it and the operating companies.

Very sincerely yours,                         W. IRVING GLOVER

---

810.79611 Pan American Airways, Inc./711

### The Minister in Guatemala (Geissler) to the Secretary of State

No. 2620                         GUATEMALA, October 25, 1929.
[Received November 6.]

SIR: I have the honor to report the following regarding the air transport situation in Guatemala, with specific reference to the present provisional license of the Mexican Aviation Company and to projects of the Pan American Airways.

Mr. Wilbur L. Morrison, Traffic Manager of the Mexican Aviation Company, called at the Legation on October 22, and stated that it had been decided that the Mexican Aviation Company will not seek to get permission to operate south of the city of Guatemala, but that he had that morning indicated to Minister of Fomento Daniel Hernández a willingness to carry mail from the city of Guatemala to Mexico and that Colonel Hernández had shown no inclination to grant any mail contract to the Compañía Mexicana.

Mr. Morrison then went on to say, that the Pan American Airways is now figuring on the establishment of two routes through the Republic of Guatemala, on one of which there would be stops at Belize, Flores (in the Department of El Petén, Guatemala), Tela (Honduras) and at Managua (Nicaragua), and that the other line would, starting with a connection at the city of Guatemala with the Mexican Aviation Company, go to San Salvador and Managua.

On October 24, I talked with the Minister of Fomento about another matter. Then he brought up the subject of aviation, by stating that it now seems probable that there will be made a contract under which the Pan American would have a route from Florida, via Belize, Flores and the city of Guatemala to San Salvador and on South, that being the line which had been proposed at one time last spring by Mr. George L. Rihl, Vice President of the Pan American and President of the Mexican Aviation Company, and in connection with which project I had spoken to Colonel Hernández at the time and was told by him that he was willing to grant such a contract, it developing afterwards, however, that Mr. Rihl changed his mind about wanting it.

Colonel Hernández said, that Mr. Morrison had called on him on October 22, and had indicated that the Pan American again desires to establish that line, and that he, the Minister, had reiterated his willingness and had added that he would like to see two permanent international services in Guatemala, namely that of the Pickwick Airways on the West side and the Pan American coming in from the East. The Minister added, with emphasis, "both of them American companies". I am not sure, whether he wanted to be understood as saying that he had also used that expression with Mr. Morrison, but it will be recalled that I mentioned on page 4 of despatch 2596 of October 4, 1929, that President Chacón and the Minister of Fomento had given me the distinct impression, that they would much prefer to have the Pan American operate in Guatemala to having the Mexican Aviation Company.

I have [etc.] ARTHUR H. GEISSLER

810.79611 Pan American Airways, Inc./698 : Telegram

*The Chargé in Venezuela (Engert) to the Secretary of State*

CARACAS, October 28, 1929—9 a. m.
[Received 3 p. m.]

174. Legation's 173, October 27, 8 p. m.; and despatch No. 1996, September 29th.[46]

[Paraphrase.] The Pan American Airways should be advised to press their proposal actively before the French service is established. The situation is now favorable to Pan American Airways but it may change later. [End paraphrase.]

ENGERT

---

810.79611 Pan American Airways, Inc./701

*The Secretary of State to the Postmaster General (Brown)*

WASHINGTON, October 29, 1929.

SIR: The Department refers to the letter of the Second Assistant Postmaster General, dated October 22, 1929, addressed to Mr. Dana G. Munro, reporting as of interest to this Department that the service rendered by the Pan American Airways under its various contracts with the Post Office Department is highly satisfactory.

In this relation permit me to inform you that the Department has been informed by a representative of the Pan American Airways that the company intends to bid for a contract to carry the Cuban mails to the United States, and that in the event the company obtains the contract they propose to carry the airmails to Cuba under one of their other contracts with the Post Office Department instead of the one under which they are now operating and that the funds received from the Cuban Government for carrying the mails to the United States will be turned into the United States Treasury. With this statement in mind, the Department will be glad to say to the Cuban Government that the service rendered by the Pan American Airways has been highly satisfactory if the Cuban Government makes inquiry along this line.

Very truly yours,

For the Secretary of State:
FRANCIS WHITE
*Assistant Secretary*

---

[46] Neither printed.

810.79611 Pan American Airways, Inc./702

*The Secretary of State to the Chargé in Cuba (Curtis)*

No. 476                           WASHINGTON, October 29, 1929.

SIR: The Department has been informed that the Cuban Government may make inquiry of the Embassy concerning the service rendered the United States Post Office Department by the Pan American Airways under its contracts to transport the United States mails. Should the Cuban Government make such inquiry you may say that the Post Office Department reports that the service rendered by the Pan American Airways under its various contracts is very satisfactory.

I am [etc.]                       For the Secretary of State:
                                          FRANCIS WHITE

---

810.79611 Pan American Airways, Inc./710 : Telegram

*The Minister in El Salvador (Robbins) to the Secretary of State*

SAN SALVADOR, November 6, 1929—5 p. m.
[Received 8:30 p. m.]

79. My number 75 [73] October 19, 11 a. m. Mail contract with Pan American Airways approved this afternoon in Cabinet meeting, will be signed tomorrow as of today's date. I beg to suggest that the Department urge president of company to make every endeavor to start service no later than December 1st. I understand company's representative here has made same suggestion.

ROBBINS

---

810.79611 Pan American Airways, Inc./713 : Telegram

*The Chargé in El Salvador (Schott) to the Secretary of State*

SAN SALVADOR, November 7, 1929—noon.
[Received 8:30 p. m.]

81. Referring to the Legation's telegram number 79, November 6, 5 p. m. Mail contract signed last night.

SCHOTT

---

810.79611 Pan American Airways, Inc./716 : Telegram

*The Chargé in Guatemala (Hawks) to the Secretary of State*

GUATEMALA, November 14, 1929—3 p. m.
[Received 10:15 p. m.]

148. Mr. Morrison, traffic manager of the Mexican Aviation Company, has informed me that he desires to obtain from the Government of Guatemala in the name of the Pan American Airways, In-

corporated, and its subsidiary or affiliated companies a contract for an air service carrying mail, express, and passengers in and out of Guatemala over any route. He also desires to enter into a mail contract for the same company over all routes, but states that with the possible exception of the route between the city of Guatemala and Tapachula, Mexico, which is now operated by the Mexican Aviation Company, all of the service will be in the name of the Pan American Airways, Incorporated. He requests that I interview the Minister of Fomento and the President in support of these projects. Please instruct by cable whether I may do so.

HAWKS

---

810.79611 Pan American Airways, Inc./719 : Telegram

*The Secretary of State to the Chargé in Guatemala (Hawks)*

WASHINGTON, November 18, 1929—3 p. m.

71. Your 148, November 14, 3 p. m. Provided that it will not conflict with any existing contracts or pending application of other American countries [*companies?*] you are authorized to do as requested on behalf of the Pan American Airways, Incorporated, but not of its non-American subsidiary.

STIMSON

---

810.79611 Pan American Airways, Inc./718 : Telegram

*The Chargé in Chile (Lay) to the Secretary of State*

SANTIAGO, November 18, 1929—4 p. m.
[Received 6:30 p. m.]

166. Referring to my despatch number 299, October 21.[47] Article 7 of enclosure which has not been promulgated officially in the *Diario Oficial* but press announces decree with this clause signed by President. Request telegraphic instructions whether the Department desires me to remind Chilean Government of uniform attitude respecting the Calvo clause in the contracts between Chilean Government and American citizens and companies. A number of purchase and other Chilean Government contracts with Americans have in the past included this clause.

LAY

---

[47] Not printed; it transmitted the draft of a decree with regard to the prolongation of the lines of the Pan American-Grace Airways, Inc., to Argentina, article 7 of which in translation reads as follows: "The company renounces all diplomatic recourse tending to the solving of difficulties that might arise from compliance with or execution of the present concession, establishing for that purpose, the jurisdiction of the Chilean tribunals. Note, register, communicate, and publish in the *Official Bulletin*." (810.79611 Pan American Airways, Inc./714)

810.79611 Pan American Airways, Inc./721 : Telegram

*The Secretary of State to the Consul at Kingston (Olivares)*

WASHINGTON, November 19, 1929—10 a. m.

Pan American Airways Incorporated desires to obtain from the Governor permission to make survey flight to Jamaica from Cuba within next three weeks for purpose of collecting operating data necessary to determine desirability of establishing air service to Jamaica. Also desires to obtain temporary operating permit in Jamaica with right to land, refuel, make minor repairs and deliver United States mail if awarded contract to Jamaica by United States Post Office. Please request the Governor to grant these temporary permissions valid until replaced by formal contract. Embassy at London similarly instructed with respect to British Government.[48]

STIMSON

---

810.79611 Pan American Airways, Inc./738

*The Chargé in Guatemala (Hawks) to the Secretary of State*

No. 2657                GUATEMALA, November 26, 1929.
                        [Received December 4.]

SIR: With reference to the Department's cablegram No. 71 of November 18, 3 p. m. authorizing the Legation to support the request of the Pan American Airways, Incorporated for an air transport contract in Guatemala, providing that it did not conflict with any existing contract or pending applications of other American Companies, I have the honor to report that after discussing this matter with Commercial Attaché Bohan, it was decided that due to the apparently exclusive air mail contract of the Pickwick Airways, Incorporated it would be impossible for the Legation to support the Pan American Airways in its desire for an air mail contract, but that, with this exception, the Legation could support the latter Company without conflicting with the rights of the former.

On November 20, I called upon the Minister of Fomento, Colonel Daniel Hernández, and afterwards upon President Lázaro Chacón and discussed with them the desire of the Pan American Airways, Incorporated to enter into a contract with the Government of Guatemala for the establishment of an air transport service between Guatemala and the United States and between Guatemala and the Panama Canal Zone, pointing out clearly to both of these officials that the Department of State was only supporting the application of the Pan American Airways, Incorporated and not of its non American subsidiary.

---

[48] Telegram No. 301 of the same date; not printed.

The Minister of Fomento said that he objected to granting the Pan American Airways a contract between Guatemala and Mexico via Mariscal, as this would mean the death of the Pickwick Airways, and that he desired that the Pan American enter Guatemala from Miami via Belize and the Petén and that the Pickwick Airways use the route through Tapachula and Mariscal. I stated that the Legation was in no way trying to work against the Pickwick Airways but that as the Government of the United States had granted an air mail subsidy to the Pan American Airways, naturally it desired to support that Company. Colonel Hernández said that he would be glad to receive Mr. Carlos Salazar, attorney of the Company, to discuss this matter and would also take it up with the President. From the conversation with Colonel Hernández, I received the distinct impression that he was absolutely opposed to the Compañía Mexicana de Aviación operating in Guatemala and only slightly less opposed to the Pan American Airways being granted a contract to operate over the same route as the Pickwick Airways.

President Chacón told me that the application of the Pan American Airways would be given every consideration, provided, of course, the terms of the proposed contract were favorable to Guatemala. I remarked to the President that I thought that the Minister of Fomento was against granting the Pan American Airways a contract over the same route as the Pickwick Airways. He replied that, if the proposal of the Pan American Airways was a good one from the viewpoint of Guatemala, it might be accepted whether Colonel Hernández liked it or not. He added that it would be in the Company's favor if it offered better terms with regard to mail, passengers et cetera, than those granted by the Pickwick Airways. I told the President that I would bring this point to the attention of Mr. Morrison. This was the only mention made, in either of the two conversations, of the question of carrying mail, as I referred to the whole matter as a question of air transport. From my conversation with the President, I gathered that he will receive favorably the proposal of the Pan American Airways and that, if the Company gave him some points of argument, as for example better rates, he will be inclined to overrule the opposition of the Minister of Fomento. However, this does not necessarily mean that he will do so.

I informed Mr. Morrison of the substance of the above conversations and he said that Mr. Salazar would go immediately to see the Minister of Fomento, after which he would request an audience with the President.

I have [etc.]

STANLEY HAWKS

810.79611 Pan American Airways, Inc./749

*The Chargé in Guatemala (Hawks) to the Secretary of State*

No. 2667                                           GUATEMALA, December 3, 1929.
                                                     [Received December 11.]

SIR: Referring to previous correspondence, I have the honor to report that, during the past ten days, I have had several conversations with the Minister of Fomento and with President Lázaro Chacón concerning the desire of the Pan American Airways, Incorporated to conclude with the Government of Guatemala an operating contract for air transport in Guatemala. Both of these officials continue to inform me that, providing the terms are favorable, they will be pleased to conclude the contract.

On the afternoon of December 3, Mr. Morrison told me that he had finally reached an agreement with the Minister of Fomento, who had said that he would sign the contract at ten o'clock on the morning of December 4. Mr. Morrison added that, while he did not wish to be too optimistic until the contract was actually signed, nevertheless he was extremely pleased over the result of the negotiations and was practically sure that now there would be no delay in definitely signing the contract, which in his opinion was extremely satisfactory to the Company.

I have [etc.]                                          STANLEY HAWKS

---

810.79611 Pan American Airways, Inc./737 : Telegram

*The Minister in Guatemala (Geissler) to the Secretary of State*

                                                GUATEMALA, December 4, 1929—5 p. m.
                                                     [Received 11 : 20 p. m.]

156. Morrison has informed the Legation that the Minister of Fomento today signed a contract granting the Pan American an air transport contract subject to approval by the Assembly and a provisional permit.

                                                                    GEISSLER

---

810.79611 Pan American Airways, Inc./740 : Telegram

*The Ambassador in Great Britain (Dawes) to the Secretary of State*

                                                   LONDON, December 5, 1929—noon.
                                                     [Received 1 : 25 p. m.]

361. Department's 301, November 19, 10 a. m.[49] Foreign Office states that the competent authorities have now sent instructions to the

---

[49] See footnote 48, p. 607.

Governor of Jamaica who has been informed that temporary permission has been granted to Pan American Airways to make a survey flight to Jamaica from Cuba with a view to examining the desirability of establishing an air service to Jamaica to land, re-fuel and make minor repairs on the Islands and, if awarded the contract by the United States Post Office, to deliver United States mail to Jamaica. The Foreign Office adds that the Governor has been instructed to issue a special and temporary authorization for these purposes under article 27, (2), of the air navigation (colonies, protectorates and mandated territories) order of 1927, subject to such conditions as he may consider necessary to impose.

DAWES

---

810.79611 Pan American Airways, Inc./743

*The Secretary of State to the Chargé in Peru (Mayer)*

No. 131                                          WASHINGTON, December 6, 1929.

SIR: Referring to your No. 384, of October 21, 1929,[50] transmitting a copy and a translation of a contract between the Pan American Grace Airways and Scadta, for the reciprocal handling and transmission of Peruvian and Colombian air mail, you are informed that copies of the despatch and its enclosures were sent to the Postmaster General, with an inquiry whether similar arrangements could be made by this Government with the Pan American Airways, Incorporated, and the Pan American Grace Airways. There is enclosed a copy of a letter from the Post Office Department, [51] stating that such an arrangement would not appear advisable at this time.

I am [etc.]                                  For the Secretary of State:
                                                     FRANCIS WHITE

---

810.79611 Pan American Airways, Inc./745 : Telegram

*The Secretary of State to the Chargé in Bolivia (Hibbard)*

WASHINGTON, December 7, 1929—1 p. m.

73. The Department is informed by Pan American-Grace Airways that the Lloyd Aero Boliviano is trying to obtain a monopoly in Bolivia. Please say to the appropriate authorities that this Government hopes that no action will be taken which would prejudice the pending application of an American company to connect La Paz with its established air route along the west coast and with the routes to be established along the east coast. Point out that the American com-

---

[50] Not printed; but see telegram No. 201, October 20, from the Chargé in Peru, p. 60.
[51] Not printed.

pany is not seeking exclusive privileges and that the adoption of a restrictive policy by any country would hamper the general development of commercial aviation with resultant detriment to all concerned. Report briefly by cable.

STIMSON

---

810.79611 Pan American Airways, Inc./748 : Telegram

*The Chargé in Bolivia (Hibbard) to the Secretary of State*

La Paz, December 10, 1929—4 p. m.
[Received 8:40 p. m.]

93. Department's 73 December 7, 1 p. m.  I am informed by Pan American-Grace representatives here that the Bolivian Government is now considering the proposals favorably and that no assistance from me is required at present.  Full report by mail.

HIBBARD

---

810.79611 Pan American Airways, Inc./760

*The Consul at Kingston (Olivares) to the Secretary of State*

No. 808

Kingston, December 17, 1929.
[Received December 26.]

Sir: I have the honor to refer to the Department's telegram dated 6 A. M. [*10 a. m.*] November 19, 1929, directing me to request the Governor of Jamaica to grant temporary permission to the Pan-American Airways, Incorporated, to make a survey flight to Jamaica from Cuba within three weeks and to land, refuel, make minor repairs and deliver United States Mail if awarded a contract by the United States Post Office Department, and to my telegram dated 6 P. M. November 26, 1929,[52] and to my despatch No. 799, dated November 27, 1929,[52] advising that the Governor was prepared to issue a special and temporary authorization to the Pan-American Airways, Incorporated, to land sea-planes in the water around the Island, there being no suitable landing place on shore for air-planes.

I now have the honor to report that I have received a letter dated the 16th December from the Colonial Secretary of Jamaica, a copy of which is respectfully transmitted herewith,[52] enclosing a special and temporary authorization, dated December 10, 1929, granted to the Pan American Airways, Incorporated, of the United States, permitting the flight within the limits of the Island of Jamaica of sea-planes, the property of the said Pan-American Airways, Incorporated, provided that such planes shall alight only in the sea around the coast

---

[52] Not printed.

of Jamaica, and that the said authorization shall expire on the 15th day of January, 1930.

I take pleasure in transmitting, herewith, the original of the special authorization herein referred to.[53]

I have [etc.]                                                    JOSÉ DE OLIVARES

---

### Tri-Motors Safety Airways [54]

810.79611 Tri-Motors Safety Airways/5

*The Liaison Officer of the Department of Commerce (Stevenson) to the Assistant Secretary of State (Carr)*

WASHINGTON, April 27, 1929.

DEAR MR. CARR: This is to confirm a request addressed to Mr. Thaw, of the Latin American Division, Department of State by Mr. York of our Aeronautics and Communications Section, on behalf of Captain Ralph A. O'Neill, Vice President and General Manager of the New York, Rio and Buenos Aires Line Inc., a division of the Trimotor Safety Airways Inc., 929 Graybar Building, Lexington Avenue and 43rd Street, New York City.

It is requested that the Department of State ask of the Cuban, Haitian, Dominican, French, British, Venezuelan, Netherland, Brazilian, Uruguayan and Argentine Governments temporary permission for three Sikorsky airplanes of the subject company to carry out survey flights over a route between New York and Buenos Aires. The stopping points were given to Mr. Thaw. The flights are to start about May 15 next.

As is known to the Department of State, the American company has obtained permission by a contract with the Argentine Government to establish an air mail line between Buenos Aires and New York, and to carry a fixed percentage of Argentine mail destined for certain countries. The company is making progress in the other countries concerned, and the proposed flights are intended for the purposes of making the necessary surveys to fix the actual route over which the line will operate and determine the places for lighting facilities, fuel and repair part stores and operating bases.

It is hoped that the Department of State will soon receive favorable replies from the governments concerned.

All cable charges in connection with this inquiry should be charged to the interested company whose spokesman authorized this arrangement in his letter to the Department of Commerce, dated April 25, 1929.

Very truly yours,                                              PERRY J. STEVENSON

---

[53] Not printed.
[54] Continued from *Foreign Relations*, 1928, vol. I, pp. 825–826.

810.79611 Tri-Motors Safety Airways/10 : Telegram

*The Secretary of State to the Ambassador in Cuba (Judah)*[55]

WASHINGTON, April 30, 1929—2 p. m.

39. Please request temporary permission, also free entry contingent upon reexportation, for three Sikorsky airplanes belonging to New York, Rio and Buenos Aires Line, Incorporated, which is a subsidiary of Trimotor Safety Airways, Incorporated, to fly over and land in Cuba on air mail survey flights beginning about May 15. Please expedite reply.

STIMSON

810.79611 Tri-Motors Safety Airways/11 : Telegram

*The Minister in the Dominican Republic (Young) to the Secretary of State*

SANTO DOMINGO, May 2, 1929—noon.
[Received 4:35 p. m.]

30. Department's April 30, 2 p. m.[56] Permission granted as requested.

YOUNG

810.79611 Tri-Motors Safety Airways/16 : Telegram

*The Chargé in Haiti (Grummon) to the Secretary of State*

PORT-AU-PRINCE, May 6, 1929—noon.
[Received 2:35 p. m.]

29. Department's 22, April 30, 2 p. m.[56] Foreign Office has granted permission landing and free entry subject to reexportation for three amphibian planes. On account of contract with Pan American Airways no other commercial planes may use Port-au-Prince landing field, part of which belongs to the above company. However suitable landing place is available in the harbor north of long wharf.

GRUMMON

[55] The same, *mutatis mutandis*, on the same date to the diplomatic representatives in Argentina (No. 35), Dominican Republic (No. 10), Haiti (No. 22), Uruguay (No. 8), and Venezuela (No. 13). Similar telegrams were sent to the diplomatic representatives in Brazil (No. 14) ; France (No. 128), with respect to Guadeloupe, Martinique, and French Guiana ; Great Britain (No. 104), with respect to Trinidad and British Guiana ; and the Netherlands (No. 11), with respect to Dutch Guiana. (Tri-Motors Safety Airways/6, 7, 8, 9.)
[56] See footnote 55.

810.79611 Tri-Motors Safety Airways/15 : Telegram

*The Ambassador in Cuba (Judah) to the Secretary of State*

HAVANA, May 6, 1929—4 p. m.
[Received 5 : 55 p. m.]

31. Referring to the Department's 39, April 30, 2 p. m.   Permission granted.

JUDAH

810.79611 Tri-Motors Safety Airways/19 : Telegram

*The Chargé in Venezuela (Engert) to the Secretary of State*

CARACAS, May 10, 1929—4 p. m.
[Received 9 : 15 p. m.]

33. Department's telegram number 13, April 30, 2 p. m.[53]   Permission will probably be granted shortly.

I strongly urge that this company and Pan American Airways be induced to arrive at an amicable agreement as to division of territory, as their present open rivalry in Venezuela is prejudicial to American aviation interests in general.   The Legation is maintaining strictest impartiality but foreign interests are very active.

ENGERT

---

810.79611 Tri-Motors Safety Airways/20 : Telegram

*The Chargé in Venezuela (Engert) to the Secretary of State*

CARACAS, May 11, 1929—10 a. m.
[Received 7 : 05 p. m.]

34. Local representative of New York, Rio, and Buenos Aires Line requests following message be transmitted :

For O'Neill, New York, Rio, and Buenos Aires Line, 929 Graybar Building, New York City :
Have Boudouy cable France to have French interests instruct its representatives here to assist my representations.   At the present time there is French mission here studying conditions and selling planes.   Thus far have made no representations whatever only sizing up situation.   Advise me what you do.   This is important.   Signed, Tennant."

ENGERT

---

[53] See footnote 55, p. 613.

810.79611 Tri-Motors Safety Airways/22 : Telegram

*The Chargé in Uruguay (Gade) to the Secretary of State*

MONTEVIDEO, May 13, 1929—11 a. m.
[Received 11 : 38 a. m.]

27. Department's 8, April 30, 2 p. m.[59]   I have been unofficially informed that permission for flights will be granted by the Ministry of War.   Ministry of Finance has not yet replied but is expected to accord free entry.

GADE

---

810.79611 Tri-Motors Safety Airways/23 : Telegram

*The Secretary of State to the Chargé in Venezuela (Engert)*

WASHINGTON, May 13, 1929—6 p. m.

14. Your May 11, 10 a. m. would indicate that any assistance rendered by the Department to the interested company might serve to promote the interests of foreign companies as against those of other American firms.   Under these circumstances the Department is unable to transmit the message to Mr. O'Neill or to extend any other assistance to the New York, Rio and Buenos Aires Line until it is fully and definitely informed regarding the apparent connection of the company with foreign interests.   You may convey this information orally to the local representative of the company.

STIMSON

---

810.79611 Tri-Motors Safety Airways/26 : Telegram

*The Secretary of State to the Chargé in Argentina (White)*[60]

WASHINGTON, May 16, 1929—6 p. m.

38. Department's 35, April 30, 2 p. m.[59]   In view of reports indicating that there is a connection made or contemplated between the New York, Rio and Buenos Aires Line and French interests the Department pending fuller information does not wish you to take any action which might serve to promote such foreign interests against those of other American firms.   Have you heard anything to confirm the reports mentioned?

STIMSON

---

[59] See footnote 55, p. 613.
[60] The same, *mutatis mutandis*, on the same date to the Ambassador in Brazil as telegram No. 16.

810.79611 Tri-Motors Safety Airways/28 : Telegram

*The Ambassador in Brazil (Morgan) to the Secretary of State*

RIO DE JANEIRO, May 17, 1929—noon.
[Received 1:05 p. m.]

18. Department's 16, May 16, 6 p. m.[62] The Foreign Office was asked on May 2nd to permit three aeroplanes, Sikorsky type, to fly over and land in Brazil. Although official reply has not been received the answer will be favorable.

There is no confirmation of report mentioned in your telegram but the character of the Tri-Motors Safety Airways Incorporated makes it not improbable.

MORGAN

810.79611 Tri-Motors Safety Airways/29 : Telegram

*The Chargé in Argentina (White) to the Secretary of State*

[Paraphrase]

BUENOS AIRES, May 20, 1929—11 a. m.
[Received 12:50 p. m.]

42. Your telegram No. 38, May 16, 6 p. m. French Latécoère and Tri-Motors negotiations are now being conducted between Paris and New York. The understanding here is that these concern (1) transportation by Tri-Motors between Martinique, French Guiana and Natal, Brazil, where Pacific [*Atlantic?*] Ocean Service lands; (2) use of Latécoère airports in the above-named places and also south to Buenos Aires; and (3) possible exchange of stock between the two companies to enhance cooperation. With respect to the success of these negotiations, it is thought that much will depend upon the attitude of the Government of France.

With respect to the somewhat ruthless competition between Pan American Airways and Tri-Motors, the Embassy has hitherto observed the strictest neutrality. It is presumed that the Department will instruct further if it desires the Embassy to alter this attitude.

WHITE

[62] See footnote 60, p. 615.

810.79611 Tri-Motors Safety Airways/30 : Telegram

*The Vice Consul at Port-of-Spain, Trinidad (Demorest) to the Secretary of State*

[PORT-OF-SPAIN,] TRINIDAD, May 22, 1929—10 a. m.
[Received 12 : 45 p. m.]

I have been informed by Governor of Trinidad that the Secretary of State for Colonies has granted temporary permission for three Sikorsky aeroplanes belonging to New York, Rio, and Buenos Aires Line Incorporated, subsidiary Tri-Motors Safety Airways Incorporated, to fly over and land in Trinidad. Urgent that line be notified immediately that there are no safe landing places for aeroplanes, extremely dangerous. Only seaplanes or amphibian planes can be used.

DEMOREST

---

810.79611 Tri-Motors Safety Airways/42

*The Ambassador in Brazil (Morgan) to the Secretary of State*

No. 3162

RIO DE JANEIRO, May 22, 1929.
[Received June 5.]

SIR: Referring to the Department's telegraphic instructions Nos. 14, of April 30, 2 P. M.[63] and 16, of May 16, 6 P. M.,[64] and to Embassy's telegram No. 18, of May 17, 12 N., I have the honor to report that when the Department's telegram of May 16 was received it was already a fortnight since I had formally requested the Brazilian Government to permit three Sikorsky aeroplanes belonging to the New York-Rio and Buenos Aires Line Incorporated to fly over Brazilian territory and to land at the principal seaports, and that the Foreign Office had consulted the Ministers of Communications, War, and Navy, two of whom had already replied in the affirmative. It appeared, therefore, too late to recall my request, especially since permission to make such flights is always granted to foreign aviation companies and is not considered a privilege of high value. Should I have canceled my application, a fact which the representative of the Tri-Motor Safety Airways Incorporated would certainly have learned on the first occasion on which he should visit Rio, a charge of discrimination against Tri-Motor might have been raised, which discretion advises should be avoided.

Where aviation competition is as keen as it is bound to be in South America, it would be advantageous if foreign governments in the beginning would support not more than one aviation company of

---

[63] See footnote 55, p. 613.
[64] See footnote 60, p. 615.

their nationals because if favors are distributed widely no one company will obtain the confidence of the foreign government in whose territory the company proposes to operate.

As already reported, the first State commercial hydroplane airport was recently inaugurated at Paranaguá in Santa Catharina. On the occasion of the inauguration a hydroplane of the Condor Syndicate in one day took a party of gentlemen from Rio de Janeiro to Paranaguá and returned, thus enabling them to be present at the ceremonies. In connection with the flight the representative of the Syndicate stated that with seven planes during the first quarter of 1929 his company had made 50 round trips between Rio de Janeiro and Porto Alegre; during these flights its planes had covered a total of 99,511 kilometers; in addition thereto 93 sight-seeing and experimental flights had been made; the total number of passengers carried was 475; the volume of postal correspondence being 20% greater than during the last quarter of 1928. So encouraging was the situation that on April 15 a new schedule went into effect under which three round weekly trips instead of two are made between this capital and Porto Alegre.

In spite of the success which the Condor Syndicate has gained, on account of financial difficulties in Germany and the diminution of the subsidy received from Lufthandle the Syndicate is inclined to reduce its Brazilian interests, and has approached informally the Pan American Airways Incorporated to inquire whether the latter would be interested in entering into an accord. If in addition to its international service the Pan American Airways should wish to establish a local service within Brazilian territory, the Condor Syndicate's plant and good will might be advantageously employed.

I have [etc.] EDWIN V. MORGAN

---

810.79611 Tri-Motors Safety Airways/43

*Memorandum by the Chief of the Division of Latin American Affairs (Munro) of a Conversation With the President of the American International Airways, Inc. (Montgomery)*

[WASHINGTON,] May 23, 1929.

Mr. Montgomery said that he happened to be in Washington to help christen the Tri-Motors survey plane, and that he had therefore stopped to inquire what progress had been made in obtaining permission from the various countries to be passed over on the American International Airways non-stop flight to Chile. I told him that I thought that we had informed his Company in each case where one of the countries concerned had granted permission. He said that he

GENERAL 619

had been so busy working on the merger of the two companies that he had not had time to go into the matter recently.

I remarked that I was interested in knowing that his company and the New York-Rio and Buenos Aires line had been merged. He said that his company had bought a large block of stock in the other corporation and would work with it in establishing air mail routes.

I remarked that we had recently received information indicating that the Tri-Motors Company was entering into some kind of an agreement with French interests, and that we were naturally interested in such a report. Mr. Montgomery said that it was true that they were "dickering" with the Latecoere but that the matter was in process of negotiation and he did not wish to say anything about it. He said that any arrangement which they might make would be entirely in accordance with the law and with the rules laid down by the Postoffice Department governing foreign participation in air mail contracts. He would tell me that they had already arranged to use all of the Latecoere fields on the east coast on a rental basis.

I said that I did not wish to ask for any information which he did not feel able to give me but that the Department always had to give careful consideration to connections with foreign interests in deciding whether or not to extend support and assistance to American concerns when they requested such support and assistance. I thought, therefore, that the Department might have to request specific information about the relations of the New York-Rio and Buenos Aires line with the Latecoere if any further assistance was desired from the Department, in order to enable it to decide how far such assistance could be extended.

Mr. Montgomery said that he would be very glad to give us the fullest information about the agreement with the French interests when the agreement was concluded. At present each party was naturally endeavoring to get as much as possible out of the other. The American interests at present had an option on a larger block of stock in the French company than the block of stock in the American company which was under option to the Latecoere. The general plan was to effect a combination by the exchange of stock and by the joint use of facilities and connection of air mail routes. The French were at present demanding, for example, that the Tri-Motors turn all mail over to them at Natal to be carried south from there by the service which the French had been operating for over a year. This was one of the points upon which an agreement had not yet been reached.

Mr. Montgomery further said that his Company proposed to buy a substantial minority interest in the Scadta. They had had an opportunity to buy the control of this company but did not do so because they were informed that its concession would be cancelled if they passed into American hands. I asked whether such information came from the Colombian Government. Mr. Montgomery replied that it came from Dr. Bauer, who had attempted to sell the control of the Company to American interests on a previous occasion but had hastily abandoned the negotiations upon being informed through grapevine channels that the Government was about to cancel his concession if the deal went through. Mr. Montgomery said that the feeling in Colombia toward us was very bad, although certain American interests like Baker, Kellogg & Co., which was one of the firms supporting them, stood well with the Government. He felt that his company could establish a foothold through its minority interest in the Scadta and later perhaps absorb it, and that it would be better that the Scadta should be partly American-owned than completely German and Colombian.

D[ANA] G. M[UNRO]

---

810.79611 Tri-Motors Safety Airways/32 : Telegram

*The Chargé in Great Britain (Atherton) to the Secretary of State*

LONDON, May 25, 1929—1 p. m.
[Received May 25—9:07 a. m.]

128. Department's 104, April 30, 2 p. m.[66] Foreign Office stated May 24th that the Governors of Trinidad and British Guiana were instructed May 17th by cable to grant temporary permission for three Sikorsky aeroplanes belonging to New York, Rio, and Buenos Aires Line, Incorporated, to fly over and land in these two British Colonies on the understanding that this permission would only hold good for one flight each way. Foreign Office stated further that the local authorities there were also authorized to admit the aeroplanes free of duty contingent upon reexportation provided that this privilege could legally be granted under the local laws.

ATHERTON

---

810.79611 Tri-Motors Safety Airways/36 : Telegram

*The Chargé in Venezuela (Engert) to the Secretary of State*

CARACAS, May 29, 1929—8 p. m.
[Received May 30—5:10 p. m.]

48. Department's 13, April 30, 2 p. m.[66] The Venezuelan Government will permit survey flight by one Sikorsky plane between Trinidad and Maracay.

ENGERT

---

[66] See footnote 55, p. 613.

810.79611 Tri-Motors Safety Airways/49

### The Chargé in Uruguay (Gade) to the Secretary of State

No. 831                                    Montevideo, May 31, 1929.
                                           [Received June 19.]

Sir: With reference to the Department's telegram No. 8 of April 30, 1929,[67] and to my telegram No. 27 of May 13, 1929, regarding three Sikorsky airplanes belonging to the New York, Rio and Buenos Aires Line, Inc., I have the honor to report that the Uruguayan Ministry of Defense has granted formal permission for the flights over Uruguayan territory.

In spite of repeated representations by the Foreign Office, the Ministry of Finance has not yet accorded permission for the free entry of the airplanes in question.

I shall continue my efforts to expedite the matter, and shall not fail promptly to advise the Department by telegraph upon the receipt of a reply from the Ministry of Finance.

I have [etc.]                              Gerhard Gade

---

810.79611 Tri-Motors Safety Airways/48

### The Ambassador in Brazil (Morgan) to the Secretary of State

No. 3169                                   Rio de Janeiro, June 3, 1929.
                                           [Received June 19.]

Sir: Continuing the subject of Embassy's despatch No. 3162, of May 22 last, and referring to previous correspondence on the subject, I have the honor to report that under date of May 28 last the Foreign Office informed me that the Brazilian Government found no inconvenience in allowing three airplanes, Sikorsky type, belonging to the New York-Rio and Buenos Aires Line to fly over Brazilian territory and to land at the principal seaports.

I have [etc.]                              Edwin V. Morgan

---

810.79611 Tri-Motors Safety Airways/40 : Telegram

### The Chargé in Argentina (White) to the Secretary of State

                                           Buenos Aires, June 5, 1929—noon.
                                           [Received June 5—11:55 a. m.]

48. Your 35, April 30, 2 p. m.[67] Permission Sikorsky planes granted.

                                                              White

---

[67] See footnote 55, p. 613.

810.79611 Tri-Motors Safety Airways/47 : Telegram

*The Chargé in Uruguay (Gade) to the Secretary of State*

MONTEVIDEO, June 19, 1929—10 a. m.
[Received 10:40 a. m.]

30. Department's telegram 8, April 30, 2 p. m.[70] Permission for free entry and flights granted.

GADE

810.79611 Tri-Motors Safety Airways/55 : Telegram

*The Chargé in the Netherlands (Norweb) to the Secretary of State*

THE HAGUE, June 22, 1929—11 a. m.
[Received June 22—7:50 a. m.]

35. Department's telegram 16, June 17, 11 a. m.[71] Permission to land and free entry accorded.

NORWEB

810.79611 Tri-Motors Safety Airways/63 : Telegram

*The Chargé in France (Armour) to the Secretary of State*

PARIS, July 8, 1929—9 a. m.
[Received July 9—7:44 a. m.]

324. Have vigorously pressed subject of Department's telegram No. 128, April 30, 2 p. m.[70] French Government now desires to know precise purpose flight, whether scientific, tour, or preparation establishment air line via French possessions. In the latter case delay and possible difficulties anticipated.

ARMOUR

810.79611 Tri-Motors Safety Airways/67 : Telegram

*The Secretary of State to the Chargé in France (Armour)*

WASHINGTON, July 10, 1929—6 p. m.

227. Your 324, July 8, 9 a. m. Flights referred to are for survey of proposed airmail route.

STIMSON

[70] See footnote 55, p. 613.
[71] Not printed.

810.79611 Tri-Motors Safety Airways/83 : Telegram

## *The Chargé in France (Armour) to the Secretary of State*

PARIS, July 29, 1929—2 p. m.
[Received 3:48 p. m.]

363. Reference Department's 227, July 11 [*10*], 6 p. m. Authorization granted. Governors being informed.

ARMOUR

---

810.79611 Tri-Motors Safety Airways/85 : Telegram

## *The Chargé in Venezuela (Engert) to the Secretary of State*

[Paraphrase]

CARACAS, August 3, 1929—2 p. m.
[Received 6 p. m.]

113. Confidentially informed that the Government of Venezuela has approved the contract with the New York, Rio, and Buenos Aires Line on essentially the same terms as the French contract. See Legation's despatch No. 1918, July 13. [72]

ENGERT

---

810.79611 Tri-Motors Safety Airways/97 : Telegram

## *The Acting Secretary of State to the Chargé in Brazil (Schoenfeld)*

WASHINGTON, August 17, 1929—3 p. m.

46. If the Brazilian Government inquires you may say for the information of the Minister of Transportation that the Department is informed that the New York, Rio and Buenos Aires Line, Incorporated, is American owned and financed solely by American money and that Trimotors Safety Airways, Incorporated, is a subsidiary of the New York, Rio and Buenos Aires Line entirely owned by it and with no foreign interest or control.

CASTLE

---

810.79611 Tri-Motors Safety Airways/101 : Telegram

## *The Vice Consul at Port-of-Spain, Trinidad (Demorest) to the Secretary of State*

[PORT-OF-SPAIN,] TRINIDAD, August 20, 1929—4 p. m.
[Received 6:04 p. m.]

The French Consul has volunteered the information to me that the French Government has offered the British Government airways con-

---

[72] Not printed.

cessions in French Indo China or French Africa in exchange of similar concessions in British West Indies to Compagnie Generale Aeropostale. The French Consul has informed Governor of Trinidad of connection French company with Tri-Motors Safety Airways, Incorporated, (New York, Rio, and Buenos Aires Line).

DEMOREST

---

810.79611 Tri-Motors Safety Airways/120 : Circular telegram

*The Secretary of State to the Chargé in Cuba (Reed)*[73]

WASHINGTON, September 18, 1929—4 p. m.

Please request permission, also free entry, contingent upon reexportation for six Sikorsky airplanes and four Commodore airplanes belonging to New York, Rio and Buenos Aires Lines, Incorporated, a subsidiary of Tri-Motors Safety Airways, to fly over and land in Cuba. Please expedite reply.

STIMSON

---

810.79611 Tri-Motors Safety Airways/124 : Telegram

*The Chargé in France (Armour) to the Secretary of State*

PARIS, September 25, 1929—2 p. m.
[Received September 25—12 : 52 p. m.]

449. Reference Department's telegram Sept. 18, 4 p. m.[74] French Government inquires whether ten planes arriving simultaneously or separately and in [if] the latter how many visits and at what intervals.

ARMOUR

---

810.79611 Tri-Motors Safety Airways/131 : Telegram

*The Secretary of State to the Chargé in France (Gordon)*

WASHINGTON, October 1, 1929—6 p. m.

316. Reference your 449, September 25, 2 p. m. Ten airplanes will go forward in separate flights at intervals of several days approximately between October 13 and December 20, touching Guadeloupe, Martinique and Cayenne.

STIMSON

---

[73] The same, *mutatis mutandis*, on the same date to the diplomatic representatives in Haiti; France, with respect to Guadeloupe, Martinique, and French Guiana; Great Britain, with respect to British Guiana, Dominica, and Trinidad; and the Netherlands, with respect to Dutch Guiana.
  Favorable replies were received by cable from the diplomatic representatives in Cuba (No. 97, September 24), Haiti (No. 71, October 4), and the Netherlands (No. 133, October 10).
  For attitude of the French Government, see telegram No. 449, September 25, 2 p. m., from the Chargé in France, *infra*.
[74] See footnote 73.

810.79611 Tri-Motors Safety Airways/153

*The Second Secretary of Embassy in France (Williamson) to the Assistant Secretary of State (White)*

PARIS, October 1, 1929.[75]

DEAR FRANCIS: The Embassy received Saturday the Department's instruction No. 4245 of September 17, 1929 [76] in relation to the agreement between the British and French Air Ministries for the development of air transport in Africa, the Near and Far East and in South America. It is not going to be, I apprehend, an easy task to secure precise and authentic information on the subject but the Embassy will at once commence its endeavors to that end. I trust, however, that with the contacts of Major Walsh, Military Attaché for Air, Commander Thomas, Naval Attaché for Air, and of Mr. Ide, and with my connections with the officials at the Foreign Office charged with aviation matters, we will be able in a discreet manner to procure reliable information.

As you know the Embassy has encountered difficulty in promptly obtaining permits for the flight of the Pan American Airways planes over Martinique and Guadeloupe, as well as for the flight of planes belonging to the New York, Rio and Buenos Aires lines over those islands and French Guiana. In discussing these requests a fortnight ago at the Foreign Office the competent official remarked that it seemed evident that American companies had in mind the project of running airways over French possessions in that hemisphere and that it should not be lost sight of that France might itself wish to extend its air lines in South America, notably those of the Aéropostale. He therefore observed that it seemed to him that the matter of commercial air expansion should be handled on a "fifty-fifty" basis and that perhaps it would be a good idea to have some understanding between the two countries in that regard,—that is if American lines were to operate over French territory France be assured of compensating privileges if desired. The views expressed by the officer in question were entirely informal and unofficial but it seemed evident that the delay in according the permits asked by the Department is caused by jealousness for French air interests in South America. I was, of course, careful to express no opinion on the topic brought up by him.

In order that the Embassy may have a proper background on the subject of the above paragraph, it is felt that it would be useful if it might be furnished with the purport of the understanding which, it is reported to me, Mr. Trippe of the Pan American Airways reached last year with the officials of the Aéropostale. Likewise, since it is understood that the New York, Rio and Buenos Aires Company and

[75] Receipt date not indicated.
[76] Not printed.

the Pan American Airways have been negotiating direct with the French officials in Martinique, Guadeloupe and French Guiana concerning mail concessions, it might be well for the Embassy to be informed with regard to the progress and precise nature of such understandings, if any, as may have developed. The commercial airways situation on the east coast of South America and in the West Indies, dovetailing as it does with the policy of the French Ministries for Air and Colonies, it would be helpful to us to be in possession of a full background on the matter even though you may wish the Embassy to preserve in the strictest confidence the data furnished it.

Very sincerely,                                   HAROLD L. WILLIAMSON

810.79611 Tri-Motors Safety Airways/146 : Telegram

*The Chargé in France (Gordon) to the Secretary of State*

PARIS, October 19, 1929—2 p. m.
[Received October 19—10:20 a. m.]

483. Reference Department's telegram 316, October 1, 6 p. m. Orally informed by Ministry for Foreign Affairs as follows:

"Authorization accorded for two months provided that during that period there shall be concluded an accord looking to cooperation between French Aeropostale and the New York, Rio, and Buenos Aires Lines and the Pan American Airways. Further the New York, Rio, Buenos Aires planes not to carry photographic apparatus nor to fly over zone of Fort de France."

GORDON

810.79611 Tri-Motors Safety Airways/148 : Telegram

*The Secretary of State to the Chargé in France (Armour)*

WASHINGTON, October 21, 1929—6 p. m.

339. Your 483, October 19, 2 p. m. It is not understood how an authorization to be availed of in the immediate future can be contingent upon an agreement to be made at any time within two months, nor why authorization in favor of one American company should depend upon an agreement to be made later to which another American company and a foreign organization must be parties. Authorization under such conditions is obviously no authorization at all.

The Department desires you to discuss the matter further with the French authorities, pointing out that no such impediments are placed in the way of French aviators desiring to fly over American territory.

In this connection please report attitude of French Government towards agreement suggested by Department to French Embassy on June 12th [77]—copy of which was sent to you in Department's instruction of September 17th.[78]

STIMSON

---

810.79611 Tri-Motors Safety Airways/154

*The Assistant Secretary of State (White) to the Second Secretary of Embassy in France (Williamson)*

WASHINGTON, October 21, 1929.

DEAR HAROLD: I have your letter of October first with regard to aviation matters. The situation seems to be about as follows:

The New York, Rio and Buenos Aires Line asked the Department last April to help it get temporary permission to operate in the French West Indies and French Guiana and it was granted after a delay of about three months, during which time an unauthorized flight to Guadeloupe was made. In a letter of July 27,[78] the New York, Rio and Buenos Aires Line said that they thought they had the permission because of some direct negotiations they had been carrying on with the local officials.

The Pan American Airways asked the Department on August ninth to help them get permission to operate in Martinique, Guadeloupe, and French Guiana, and on September sixth the French Embassy in Paris cabled that temporary permission was granted for an exploratory flight to the Islands but that the question with reference to French Guiana was further being studied. So far as we know there have been no direct negotiations between the Pan American Airways and local French officials. It is of course important for Pan American Airways to get into French Guiana because the company is actively pushing its plans to extend the line down the east coast and wishes to use Cayenne instead of Paramaribo in hopping off to Natal.

We learned from Mr. Trippe that the only conversations which he had in Paris were with the Embassy and the Air Ministry and that there was no "understanding" between him and the officials of the Aéropostale.

As for the New York, Rio and Buenos Aires Line, we have, on one hand, a rather emphatic statement from Colonel Donovan that there is no connection between it and any foreign interests and, on the other hand a despatch of September fourth from the Consul at Trinidad [78] reporting that when Colonel O'Neill, President of the New York, Rio and Buenos Aires Line, was there he mentioned a working agreement between his company and the Compagnie Generale Aéropostale. The

---

[77] *Ante*, p. 532.
[78] Not printed.

Embassy's telegram No. 483 of October 19, 2 p. m. would make it seem evident that there is at present no agreement between the French Aéropostale and either the New York, Rio and Buenos Aires Line or the Pan American Airways.  It is also evident that the French Government is proposing an impossible condition because neither line can do anything to bind the other and neither can say in advance that it will be able, within two months, to reach an accord of the kind mentioned.

I personally feel that the attitude of the French Government in this matter is most unfriendly and unjustifiable.  Whenever French aviators have requested authorization to fly over American territory, the permission has been promptly accorded.  A few months ago Count de Sibour landed from a steamer at a Pacific port and a local inspector of the Department of Commerce immediately gave him permission to fly across the United States.  Similar permission was also given immediately to the crew of the French plane "Yellow Bird".  Neither of these requests came through the French Government but were made direct.  The only case that I have been able to find on record of the French Government making a request was when Costes and Lebrix wished to fly over and land in the Panama Canal Zone.  The request was received by us on December 8, 1927 and, although Panama is a military reservation of the highest importance and the regulations for non-military flying over the Canal Zone had not yet been drawn up and promulgated, the desired permission was granted on January 17, 1928.  There has certainly been no undue delay in granting any French request such as American requests have met with from the French Government.  Even the permissions for Americans to fly over French territory, which are now in force, are only temporary so there is no assurance what will happen when they expire or that future requests will get any better treatment.

On June 12 the Department transmitted a note to the French Embassy here proposing an agreement similar to the one under consideration with Canada.  The French Embassy acknowledged the receipt of the note but has not yet answered the proposal.  A copy of this note was sent to your Embassy with instruction No. 4245 of September 17.[81]  If the French Government will accept this arrangement, all will be well.  It is purely obstruction and perhaps bad faith on the part of the French to make such a proposal as they transmitted in the Embassy's telegram No. 483 of October 19, 2 p. m.  No American company can make an agreement on behalf of its rival any more than the French Aéropostale can make such an agreement on behalf of one of its French rivals.  The important thing is to have agreements between the Governments by which we will let the Aéropostale, or any

<hr>

[81] Not printed.

other French companies, come into Panama and the United States in return for permission for American companies to fly across French territory.

In any conversations officials of the Embassy may have with the Foreign Office they might press the proposal made in the note of June 12 to the French Embassy here. If it is accepted, the present difficulty will be removed, and if it is not going to be accepted, it will be well to know it so that when the next French aviator asks for permission to fly over American territory his application can be held up and he can be told exactly why it is being held up. In this connection, see the Department's instruction to the American Diplomatic Missions concerned [82] printed on page 29 of the Monthly Political Report for July, 1929.

With all good wishes [etc.]                    FRANCIS WHITE

---

810.79611 Tri-Motors Safety Airways/149 : Telegram

*The Chargé in France (Armour) to the Secretary of State*

PARIS, October 22, 1929—7 p.m.
[Received October 23—9 : 25 a. m.]

486. Reference Department's telegram number 339, October 21, 6 p.m. Authorization unconditioned during two months save for stipulations relative photography and prohibited zone. Should subsequent operation over route cited be contemplated it is, however, provided that agreement must be reached with Aeropostale prior to termination two months' period.

Since Pan American has solicited analogous permission, French Government believes principle of cooperation should be settled simultaneously. Government evidently prepared to insist that Aeropostale receive favorable treatment as condition to granting privileges over French territory to American Airways although actual negotiation to be left to interested companies. It is pointed out that potential mail concessions envisaged are quite different from individual permits heretofore granted by the United States to French aviators.

Ministry for Foreign Affairs unaware of existence of Department's proposal of June 12 which it is presumed was forwarded to Air Ministry by Air Attaché in Washington. Will investigate and inform of attitude.

                    ARMOUR

---

[82] See telegram No. 51, July 12, 1929, 6 p. m., to the Minister in Honduras, p. 545.

810.79611 Tri-Motors Safety Airways/161

*The Chargé in France (Armour) to the Secretary of State*

No. 9957                                              PARIS, October 26, 1929.
                                                      [Received November 7.]

SIR: I have the honor to report that the authorization orally communicated to the Embassy by the French Ministry for Foreign Affairs and subsequently conveyed to the Department in my telegram No. 486 of October 22, 7 p.m., for the flight of the aeroplanes belonging to the New York, Rio and Buenos Aires Lines over Guadeloupe, Martinique and French Guiana, has now been confirmed by a note from the Ministry for Foreign Affairs dated October 24, 1929. This note is enclosed in copy and translation.[83]

Although the Ministry's note does not reaffirm the desire orally expressed that continued operation of the Line shall be conditional upon the reaching of an accord by not only the Aéropostale Company and the New York, Rio and Buenos Aires Lines, but as well upon one between the first mentioned Company and the Pan American Airways, I still feel that the French authorities are likely to insist upon a general agreement between all the operating companies concerned before permanent concessions will be granted to either one or both of the American lines.

I have [etc.]                                         NORMAN ARMOUR

810.79611 Tri-Motors Safety Airways/155 : Telegram

*The Secretary of State to the Chargé in France (Armour)*

                               WASHINGTON, October 29, 1929—1 p.m.

352. Your 486, October 22, 7 p.m. You should point out that (1) the New York, Rio and Buenos Aires Line and the Pan American Airways are private companies and that the American Government has no control or authority as to any arrangements which they may or may not wish to make with the Aéropostale or any other company and therefore can give no assurance that an agreement will be reached within a specified time if at all; (2) The American Government has merely asked on behalf of these companies permission to fly over and land on French territory in the course of their commercial operations, a permission which the American Government, as indicated in its note to the French Embassy of June 12, 1929, is prepared to grant to a French company on a reciprocal basis with respect to United States territory; also that the American Government is not asking that an air mail contract be granted to these companies; (3) Neither the Aéropostale nor any French company has

---

[83] Not printed.

yet requested similar permission to land passengers and/or cargo on United States territory from the American Government.

The note of June 12 mentioned in the last paragraph of the telegram under reference was a formal one addressed to the French Ambassador proposing an agreement between the French Government and the Government of the United States, and the Department consequently does not understand how it could reach the Air Ministry from the Air Attaché before being transmitted by the Ambassador to the Ministry for Foreign Affairs. Please endeavor to expedite the reply.

STIMSON

---

810.79611 Tri-Motors Safety Airways/160 : Telegram

*The Chargé in France (Armour) to the Secretary of State*

PARIS, November 5, 1929—6 p. m.
[Received November 6—10:25 a. m.]

513. Contents of Department's telegram number 352, October 29, 1 p. m., brought immediately to the attention French Government which however will not recede from position that continued operation of New York, Rio, and Buenos Aires Line is contingent upon agreement with Aeropostale. It is probable that duration permission would be extended if negotiations begun even though not completed prior expiration two months period. Point conceded that permission shall not be contingent upon like agreement between Pan American Airways and Aeropostale. Department's lack of authority in the matter understood, it being optional with line to make agreement if permission desired.

Embassy is urgently pressing for permission for Pan American Airways requested in Department's number 258, August 12, 5 p. m.,[84] which if granted would be subject same conditions as New York, Rio, and Buenos Aires permission but considered as entirely separate case.

French Government not interested in reciprocal treatment but frankly states in effect that it wants certain advantages for French air lines and has determined to use present requests of American lines as a lever to gain them, refusing permission if opportunity for successful competition by Aeropostale not assured through agreements above cited. Even though air mail contracts not asked it regards flight by ten planes as potentially a commercial venture and as quite different from flights by tourists, et cetera, which it will willingly accord without thought of compensating advantages.

[84] *Ante,* p. 576.

While stand is disappointing it makes clear French attitude which is one of bargaining rather than encouragement of reciprocal freedom of air navigation.

Department's note of June 12 to French Embassy not received by either Foreign Affairs or Air Ministry but telegram being sent Embassy to ascertain disposition made thereof. Meanwhile copies of proposal have been left with Foreign Office for study with request that prompt decision be reached. Despatch follows.

ARMOUR

---

810.79611 Tri-Motors Safety Airways/169

*The Chargé in France (Armour) to the Secretary of State*

No. 9991                                      PARIS, November 7, 1929.
                                               [Received November 21.]

SIR: I have the honor to amplify herewith my telegram No. 513 of November 5, 6 p. m., 1929, with regard to the permission desired by the New York, Rio and Buenos Aires Line to operate over Martinique, Guadeloupe and French Guiana and that for the Pan American Airways, Incorporated, to operate over the first two cited islands.

A definitive conversation with the Ministry for Foreign Affairs in the matter was not had until the evening of November 4, although the subject had been daily pressed, due to the fact that it was hoped the note addressed by the Department to the French Ambassador at Washington on June 12, proposing an agreement with regard to aerial navigation, would be found and the proposal furnish a basis upon which a more satisfactory arrangement for the operation of the American Companies might be had. As stated in my above cited telegram the note in question has not been received, either by the Ministry for Foreign Affairs nor by that for Air. The former Ministry had been convinced that the note must have been forwarded by the Air Attaché in Washington direct to his own Department, but it develops that such is not the case. M. Claudel was, in consequence, asked to report by telegraph with regard to the disposition made of the document. In the meantime copies of the note and its enclosure were left with the Foreign Office for study by the appropriate French authorities and the Foreign Office informed of the importance of the proposal and requested to render an early decision.

To-day the Ministry for Foreign Affairs telephoned, stating that a telegram had come from M. Claudel to the effect that he had never received the Department's note of June 12. In order to obviate further delay incident to this misunderstanding I am immediately addressing to the Ministry for Foreign Affairs a note requesting that the proposal, copies of which the Embassy has now furnished, be given earnest consideration. The Ministry promises, upon the receipt of this note, at once to study the project of agreement.

The conversation of November 4, although not productive of the results which might have been wished, was satisfactory in that it cleared the atmosphere concerning the French viewpoint and the cause of delay in according permissions of the nature envisaged. A frank statement of motives was for the first time evoked from the pertinent Foreign Office official, who said that in his remarks he reflected not only the views of his Ministry but also those of the other Ministries concerned.

He asserted that France had no present desire to secure permission for French planes to fly over American territory and that in consequence his Government was not in the least interested in the American offer of reciprocal treatment. The Embassy observed in response that while it appreciated his frankness the position assumed does not accord with the customary relationship of friendly nations which, in such matters, is predicated upon reciprocity. It was added that the trend in aerial navigation is, as in navigation of the seas, towards freedom of communication, provided of course considerations of sovereignty are observed and reciprocal privileges vouchsafed. Moreover, France has itself recognized this principle in becoming a party to the Convention of 1919 relating to the regulation of aerial navigation,[85] so that its attitude in the case of the West Indies shows a disposition to adopt towards the United States a different attitude than that demonstrated towards other nations. The official replied by recognizing the weight of some of the arguments advanced but reiterating his assertion that in the present situation his Government is not interested in considerations of reciprocity.

He stated that the matter is regarded as a commercial one, not one of reciprocal courtesies, and that France desires to receive value given for any privileges which it may give in the geographic zone in question,—in effect, that it is a matter of dollar for dollar. The Aéro-postale, he added, finds itself under heavy competitive pressure from the American air lines and it is the French Government's intention to secure for it advantages calculated to enable it to compete on a favorable basis with its "rivals". The American companies, desiring permission to fly over French possessions in the West Indies and South America, the opportunity is presented to gain for the Aéro-postale the advantages which it seeks. It is recognized that the Government of the United States has no control over the engagements entered into by American airways but the companies themselves, if they sufficiently desire to secure the flying permits, must, it is said, negotiate with the Aéropostale as a price for the privilege.

---

[85] *Foreign Relations*, 1926, vol. I, p. 152.

The French Government will persevere in utilizing the opportunity for insisting on favorable inter-company arrangements on behalf of the Aéropostale.

The Government expresses its willingness to continue to grant freely permits for tourists, explorers and others making isolated flights over its territories. It views, however, the contemplated flights by the planes of the New York, Rio and Buenos Aires Line and the Pan American Airways as falling within another category. Although the Embassy stressed the fact that no mail contracts or other concessions were being asked and that the permission requested is of merely a temporary character, the official of the Foreign Office stated that the French Government can only regard the consecutive flights by a number of planes belonging to companies engaged in commercial aviation as a commercial venture and therefore that no precedent has been set by the Government of the United States in granting permits to French planes since the conditions are not parallel, none of the French planes involved being engaged in regular aerial navigation.

Under these circumstances and the desire to assist the Aéropostale the French Government will not recede from its insistence that the continued operation after the termination of the two months period be contingent upon the negotiation of an agreement between the New York, Rio and Buenos Aires Line and Aéropostale. The Ministry for Foreign Affairs is not in a position to elucidate the nature of the projected agreement, leaving it to the Aéropostale to make known its desires in that connection. The Government, however, is prepared to concede that the permission for the New York, Rio and Buenos Aires Line shall not be contingent upon an agreement between the Pan American Airways and the Aéropostale. It was likewise induced to express the belief that it would be feasible to extend the two months permit, even though an agreement had not been reached, if negotiations were commenced within that period which gave promise of an ultimate favorable accord.

The position assumed is perhaps to be explained by the fact that the Aéropostale is not sufficiently capitalized to compete with the American Companies,—having a present capital of only 20,000,000 francs and an authorized capital of but 50,000,000 francs. Moreover, the only concession of consequence which the Aéropostale has, at least the only one which might be used for bargaining purposes with American aviation interests, is that granted by Venezuela. It is therefore assumed that the Government contemplates overcoming these deficiencies by forcing an agreement—which could not be gained by virtue of the companies' financial prestige or the inducement of important concessions held by them—with competing lines, such agreement presumably envisaging a combination of American and

French lines permitting the latter to have the benefit of the traffic over certain areas. Although at this distance it is difficult to judge the situation, it may be that it would warrant the American lines to accord minor concessions in order to create good will between French and American interests in face of what would seem to be a greater potential threat—competition by the German Luft-Hansa or its subsidiary.

The Ministry for Foreign Affairs admitted that it had been intended to delay acting upon the request of the Pan American Airways to fly over Guadeloupe and Martinique until such time as it could be ascertained what attitude the New York, Rio and Buenos Aires Line would adopt in according favorable terms to the Aéropostale. The Embassy pointed out the inequity of such procedure, not only since the Pan American request antedates that of the "Nyrba" Line but, also, because it is unfair to base the treatment accorded one company upon the action of another company with which it has no connection. The responsible character of the Pan American Airways and the fact that it possesses postal concessions from the United States Government was dwelt upon. As a result the Foreign Office promised to endeavor to cause the other ministries concerned to reconsider the matter with a view to obtaining prompt permission for the operations contemplated by the Pan American Airways. It was observed in conclusion that if the effort to secure permission was successful the permit would of necessity follow the same lines as that accorded the New York, Rio and Buenos Aires Line. That is, the carrying of photographic apparatus and flying over the region of Fort-de-France would be prohibited and permission would be temporary, limited to two months with continued operation thereafter, dependent upon entering into negotiations for an agreement with the Aéropostale. At the Ministry's solicitation, in order that it may be employed before the other pertinent authorities, I have again submitted a note asking a prompt and favorable decision in the instance of the Pan American Airways request.

I have [etc.] NORMAN ARMOUR

---

### Latin American Airways

811.79620 Boeing Airplane Co./63

*The Chargé in Guatemala (Hawks) to the Secretary of State*

No. 2349 GUATEMALA, April 3, 1929.
[Received April 10.]

SIR: I have the honor to transmit herewith a translation, furnished by the Office of the Commercial Attaché, of a proposed contract[90] for air mail and passenger service to be entered into between the Government of Guatemala and the Latin American Airways, said to be amalgamated with the Boeing Airplane Company.[91]

Mr. Lee C. Balch, representative of this Company, arrived in Guatemala about a week ago and has since been negotiating with the Minister of Fomento. He showed the Legation and the Commercial Attaché a copy of a contract, which his Company has concluded with the Mexican Government, for air mail and passenger service between Tiajuana and Mexico City and Mexico City and Mariscal, Chiapas. Upon the basis of a wire received by the Commercial Attaché from the Bureau of Foreign and Domestic Commerce, a copy of which is enclosed,[90] I presented a Memorandum to the Foreign Office stating that the Latin American Airways is a reputable American concern and requesting that the Minister of Fomento be so informed. As a representative of the Pan American Airways, Incorporated, is expected here shortly with a possible resultant competition between the two companies, the Legation will be extremely careful in any conversations it may have with the Government on this matter.

I received, today, a telegram from Mr. E. J. Goddard, representative of the National City Bank of New York, from Mexico City, stating that his bank is closely allied with the Boeing interests and asking whether Mr. A. K. Humphries, representative of the Boeing Air Transport Company, should come to Guatemala to conclude negotiations. I replied by telegraph, stating that Mr. Balch was progressing rapidly with the negotiations and suggesting that Mr. Humphries come as soon as possible.

I shall keep the Department informed as to the progress of these negotiations.

I have [etc.]                                    STANLEY HAWKS

814.796 Latin American Airways/2 : Telegram

*The Minister in Guatemala (Geissler) to the Secretary of State*

GUATEMALA, May 2, 1929—4 p. m.
[Received 11:20 p. m.]

54. Despatch 2371, April 24.[90] A note has been received from the Foreign Office requesting information regarding the financial backing and capacities of the Latin American Air Transport Company

[90] Not printed.
[91] For previous correspondence concerning the Boeing Airplane Company, see *Foreign Relations*, 1928, vol. I, pp. 818 ff.

represented by Lee Balch and "all such other data regarding the matter as may be deemed of interest to the Government of Guatemala." Please answer by telegraph.

GEISSLER

---

814.796 Latin American Airways/4 : Telegram

*The Minister in Guatemala (Geissler) to the Secretary of State*

GUATEMALA, May 7, 1929—1 p. m.
[Received 10:20 p. m.]

57. Hawks' despatch 2370 and 2371.[92] My telegram of May 2, 4 p. m.

The Latin American Air Transport Company has pending before the Assembly air mail contract granted by Fomento to carry mail between Mariscal, Mexico, and Guatemala.

Fomento has rejected Rihl[93] applications for a concession for Compania Mexicana between Tapachula, Mexico, and Guatemala and for a concession to the Pan American Airways connecting with Miami-Panama line. Rihl's representative is still negotiating.

Latin American and Rihl each fighting the other's projects. There is much opposition all three projects. It is doubtful that any one of them will be approved by the Assembly adjourning this month.

Compañia Mexicana and Latin American propose operating under Mexican charters in Guatemala and then in the other Central American countries.

I perceive no sound reason for our helping secure transport concessions for Mexican companies even though at present controlled by American stockholders. I believe that the psychological effect of the operation of air transport by a foreign corporation other than the United States would be bad.

Since the Compania Mexicana was mentioned in the Department's telegram of April 18 [19], 1 p. m.,[94] and is represented by Rihl, the Legation has felt that perhaps the Department may not want it to discriminate against Mexican companies said to be controlled by Americans.

Does the Department desire the Legation to offer to help the Pan American Airways actively even though that might mean the elimination of both of the Mexican companies? If so please cable soon as time is getting very short.

---

[92] Neither printed.
[93] George L. Rihl, president of the Compañía Mexicana de Aviación and vice president of the Pan American Airways, Inc.
[94] *Ante*, p. 557.

Pan American efforts would be more promising of success if Rihl had an American as his local representative instead of a German.

GEISSLER

---

814.796 Latin American Airways/5 : Telegram

*The Secretary of State to the Minister in Guatemala (Geissler)*

WASHINGTON, May 7, 1929—3 p. m.

21. Your 54, May 2, 4 p. m. Financial backing Latin American Air Transport Company is understood to be good but operating capacities have not been demonstrated. The original plan to have Boeing take over operation under its option appears to have been definitely abandoned due to alignment of Boeing with Pan American through Aviation Corporation of America, and the Department is not yet informed as to what other operating arrangements if any have been made. However, assuming that it is the intention to establish operations in some satisfactory way and not merely to trade off the concession, the Department sees no reason why you should not continue to support the Latin American Air Transport Company as a reputable American concern, and since it was the first in the field such action could not reasonably be interpreted as discrimination against others of similar standing. It would of course be most unfortunate if the efforts of competitors should result in the exclusion of all American interests and the Department desires you to use your best efforts to prevent any such development.

STIMSON

---

814.796 Latin American Airways/8 : Telegram

*The Secretary of State to the Minister in Guatemala (Geissler)*

WASHINGTON, May 11, 1929—4 p. m.

23. Your 57, May 7, 1 p. m. When the Department's 21, May 7, 3 p. m. was sent it was not understood that both Latin American and Pan American Airways proposed to operate under Mexican charters in Guatemala.

The policy of the Department is not to interpose its good offices with foreign Governments upon behalf of corporations organized in or chartered by foreign countries to the end of securing for such corporations advantages by way of favorable treatment or concessions from such countries even though such corporations may be controlled by American stockholders, particularly where such corporations are in competition with American companies with American owned stock. A different situation and not necessarily subject to the same policy of non-interposition arises when American stockholders in foreign corporations suffer injury as the result of illegal or confiscatory measures taken by a foreign Government against such corporation. In the latter case the Department may under proper circumstances make appropriate representations. The distinction is between securing business and protecting property. However, the Department does interpose its good offices on appropriate occasions to assist American companies with American stockholders to secure business. You may therefore upon request appropriately assist Pan American Airways, an American company, stock of which is American owned, to obtain the right to connect Guatemala with its Miami–Panama line.

STIMSON

---

814.796 Latin American Airways/6 : Telegram

*The Minister in Guatemala (Geissler) to the Secretary of State*

GUATEMALA, May 12, 1929—4 p. m.
[Received May 13—8 : 41 a. m.]

59. On the 10th I voiced to Balch hesitancy about aiding to secure a concession to be held by a non-American corporation. Yesterday morning I received from him a letter stating that the Latin American's Guatemala concession would be held and operated by a company incorporated in the United States.

Rihl returned yesterday from Mexico. I shall send for him and in view of the Department's May 7, 3 p. m., and 23, May 11, 4 p. m., I intend to say to him that, since the Latin American is an American concern and its financial backing is understood to be good and it was the first in the particular field, the Legation is inclined to give it appropriate support and that the Legation is also disposed to give appropriate assistance to the Pan American.

GEISSLER

---

814.796 Latin American Airways/11 : Telegram

*The Secretary of State to the Minister in Guatemala (Geissler)*

WASHINGTON, May 14, 1929—5 p. m.

24. Your 59, May 12, 4 p. m. Pending the receipt by it of fuller information as to the status of both parties the Department desires you to adopt a non-committal attitude and assumes that you can do so without jeopardizing the present rights of either.

STIMSON

814.796 Latin American Airways/13

## The Minister in Guatemala (*Geissler*) to the Secretary of State

[Extract]

No. 2403                        GUATEMALA, May 15, 1929.
[Received May 22.]

SIR: I have the honor to report that in consequence of unofficial action by the Legation there is now a fair prospect that air transport contracts may be entered into by the Government of Guatemala with the approval of the National Legislative Assembly with two American Companies, namely with the Pan American Airways Incorporated, providing for a connection with its Miami-Panama line, and with the Latin American Airways Syndicate, to be incorporated in the United States, providing for a connection with the projected Nogales-Mariscal line of the Compañía de Transportes Aéreos Latino Americana; and I beg leave to add that there are indications that if that program does not go through there may develop rapidly a now latent movement in favor of the establishment of a Government-owned service, perhaps in cooperation with two or three of the other Central American countries and possibly with the aid of European material and men.

. . . . . . . .

On May 13, I invited Mr. Rihl to call and, as foreshadowed by the cablegram just cited,[95] I said to him, after a discussion of the situation, that I intended to receive Mr. Balch later in the day and to say to him that, since the Latin American is an American concern and its financial backing is understood to be good and it was the first in the particular field, the Legation is inclined to give it appropriate support, but that, on the other hand, the Legation is also disposed to give appropriate assistance to the Pan American. . . .

An hour or so later, I had a talk with Mr. Balch, to whom I stated that, with a view to averting the possibility that no American Company will get a contract approved by the Assembly, I am inclined to give appropriate support to the Latin American and the Pan American; that I had already expressed myself similarly to Mr. Rihl, who, upon reflection, had stated that this might lead to such an adjustment of the matter as, on the whole, would be to the interests of both the concerns involved. Mr. Balch stated, that he liked the idea in principle. In fact he had told me, on May 9, that he would be willing for the Latin American contract to be amended so as to permit the Pan American to carry mail between the East coast of the United States and the city of Guatemala by way of Barrios, if the Pan American would stop fighting the Latin American's effort to get a Guatemala-Mariscal contract; but during that

---

[95] No. 59, May 12, 4 p. m., p. 639.

conversation of May 13, he recalled that he had also said that he is very sure that the Pan American would not agree to that and he said that he did not mean for that remark of his to be construed as a binding proposal. He added that, however, he feels that the time has come for the Latin American and the Pan American to quit fighting, but that he prefers that there be an agreement covering not only Guatemala but also the rest of Central America and Mexico. I said, that my own concern is regarding the Guatemala situation, which, as seemed to be agreed, called for immediate action. He said then that he would seek a conference with Mr. Rihl.

On May 14, Mr. Rihl came and reported that he had arrived at an oral understanding with Mr. Balch. Shortly afterwards, the latter joined the conference. They told me that they were in accord, that it would be to the interests of both parties for them both to favor the granting of a contract to the Pan American, under which it would come from Belize, British Honduras, or Barrios, Guatemala, or Tela, Honduras, to the city of Guatemala, returning then to say Tela, and a contract under which the Latin American would be permitted to operate between Mariscal, Mexico, and the city of Guatemala, and then toward Salvador. They also said, that they had orally agreed to recommend to their principals that the Latin American should not operate between the city of Mexico and Mariscal and that the Pan American and its subsidiaries should not operate between Mariscal and Managua by way of Guatemala and Salvador. From what Mr. Rihl has told me since, it seems that, as he understands it, the oral agreement to be submitted to their principals relates only to United States Mail contracts. I am not certain that Mr. Balch so understands it.

At any rate, Mr. Rihl and Mr. Balch, at this time, appear to be cooperating in a very friendly way in an effort to get contracts from the Government of Guatemala, covering the respective routes Mariscal-Guatemala-Salvador and Belize-Barrios-Tela-Guatemala, and Mr. Rihl has abandoned efforts to get a contract for the Pan American's subsidiary, the Compañía Mexicana.

On May 13, and again on May 14, I discussed the situation with Minister of Fomento Daniel Hernández, who told me that if the Compañía Mexicana abandons its application and the Pan American submits a contract substantially the same as that of the Latin American, except as to route, he would sign it and facilitate its despatch to the Assembly. He said that the cessation of the fight which the two interests have been carrying on against each other would probably result in the approval of both contracts. I have had and retain the distinct impression that he was conscious of the fact that the fight of the friends of the Pan American imperilled the Latin American's project, and that he was not inclined to contract with the Pan American so long as it was fighting the contract he had signed with the Latin American.

It should also be mentioned, that the Latin American Syndicate will now presumably operate under an American instead of a Mexican charter in such of the other Central American countries as may grant it concessions.

As regards the prospective establishment of a Government-owned service in cooperation with other Central American countries, the Department will recall communications from the Legations at San José, San Salvador and here, showing that the subject has recently been discussed. One of the enthusiastic proponents of the idea is said to be Dr. Eduardo Aguirre Velásquez, Guatemalan Minister to Costa Rica, who as reported confidentially in despatch 2377 of April 29, 1929,[96] may very soon be appointed Minister for Foreign Affairs. French aviation interests have indicated anxiety to sell planes to the Guatemalan Government, and it is very possible that Germans may renew efforts to become identified with the operation of aviation in the Republic. A Government supported operation would conceivably not prove profitable, but local pride would probably cause the country or countries concerned to pay any resulting deficit cheerfully, however imprudent that might seem.

The proposed Pan American and Latin American contracts may still encounter considerable opposition inspired by stockholders and friends of the Empresa Guatemalteca de Servicios Aéreos, Morales y Compañía, organized by Victor D. Gordon. According to an article published in El Excelsior of May 15, Mr. Gordon has purchased "four powerful airplanes and two hydroplanes", special mention is made of a tri-motor, and he is quoted as having said at San Francisco with reference to a rumor that the quality of the airplanes he has acquired is defective, that the "report of the Department of Commerce was based on airplanes which were *not* purchased", and that the planes he bought "are authorized by license of the American Government". The same article states that the concern has presented a project of a contract to the Minister of Government in Salvador.

Making reference to the Department's cablegram of May 14, 5 p. m., saying that pending the receipt of fuller information as to the status of both parties it desires me to adopt a noncommittal attitude and assumes that this can be done without jeopardizing the present rights of either, I respectfully beg leave to express the hope that the foregoing report regarding the situation shows that the action already taken by the Legation has the tendency of being productive of the greatest benefit possible to each one of the two American groups involved.

I have [etc.]    ARTHUR H. GEISSLER

[96] Not printed.

814.796 Latin American Airways/14

*The Minister in Guatemala (Geissler) to the Secretary of State*

No. 2416                                    GUATEMALA, May 22, 1929.
                                            [Received May 29.]

SIR: Referring to despatch 2403 of May 15, 1929, I have the honor to report that Mr. George L. Rihl has withdrawn from the agreement he made, on May 14, with Mr. Lee C. Balch, to the effect that the Pan American Airways, Incorporated, and the Mexican Aviation Company will no longer seek to get a contract from the Government of Guatemala granting air transportation privileges between Tapachula, respectively Mariscal, and the city of Guatemala and that on the other hand Mr. Balch will aid the Pan American in an effort to obtain a contract under which it would carry passengers and mail from Belize, Barrios or Tela to the city of Guatemala, returning thence to say Tela; and that, according to Mr. Balch, a revised contract between the Government and the Latin American Airways has been recommended by the Council of State, signed by the Minister of Fomento and the President and transmitted to the National Legislative Assembly, whereas the projects of the Pan American and its subsidiary are still pending before the Minister of Fomento.

There is enclosed herewith a copy of a Memorandum of conversations Secretary of Legation Hawks had with Mr. Rihl, on May 20, and also a copy of a Memorandum by Commercial Attaché Bohan,[97] regarding conversations he had with Mr. Balch on May 21 and 22.

I also beg leave to report that Mr. Bohan has received a cablegram from the Bureau of Foreign and Domestic Commerce, dated May 21, 1929, 6:30 p. m., which reads as follows:

"Latin American Airways incorporating for three million dollars purchasing first ship a trimotored to be sent to Guatemala according to contract if it is approved finally. According to report contract favorably reported by Legislature Committee please try to verify report."

I have [etc.]                              ARTHUR H. GEISSLER

[Enclosure]

*Memorandum by the Third Secretary of Legation in Guatemala*
*(Hawks)*

Mr. George L. Rihl, Vice President of the Pan American Airways, Incorporated, called at 2:30 this afternoon, Monday, to see the Minister, who however, was not in. He informed Secretary Hawks as follows:

On Saturday night, May 18, Mr. Rihl received a telegram from

---

[97] Commercial Attaché's memorandum not printed.

Mr. Trippe, President of the Pan American Airways, Incorporated, from New York stating that the Post Office Department of the United States had ordered the Pan American Airways to extend, with the consent of both Governments, i. e. the Governments of Mexico and Guatemala, their air service from Mexico City to Guatemala, establishing a regular weekly service. Mr. Rihl explained, that under the contract which the Pan American Airways has with the United States Post Office Department, for the Brownsville–Mexico City line, the latter can demand, at any time, that the Pan American Airways extend its service farther south. The telegram also said that nothing would be done until Mr. Rihl could have a conference with Mr. Trippe. Mr. Rihl hopes to leave Guatemala, on May 22, Wednesday morning for Vera Cruz, taking the train that night to Mexico City, telephoning the next morning to New York and arranging for this conference, and proceeding there probably Friday. Due to this order of the Post Office Department, the Pan American Airways would now have to extend its service from Tapachula, Mexico to Guatemala and this would mean that the Compañía Mexicana de Aviación would be the organization used for this purpose. He had told Mr. Geissler that he would use an American company in Guatemala, which now is impossible, due to the fact that commercially he could not have an American organization simply for the trip between the city of Guatemala and the Mexican border, since this would not be profitable and also it would in reality be a local company and would thus run into difficulties in connection with the Gordon contract, et cetera.

In reply to a question by Mr. Hawks, he said that if the Post Office Department of the United States ordered the Pan American Airways to extend its lines farther South through Salvador to Managua, then it would be possible to organize an American corporation to carry on this service between the Mexican border and Nicaragua.

When he and Mr. Balch of the Latin American Airways had come to an agreement, that the Latin American Airways be allowed to have the service on the West coast and the Pan American Airways would come in from Tela or British Honduras, he had told Mr. Balch that that agreement was subject to the approval of his principals and that, of course, if the Post Office Department ordered the Pan American Airways to extend the service which it is now running between Brownsville and Mexico City and Vera Cruz to Guatemala, then there would remain nothing for him to do but endeavor to obtain a contract with the Government of Guatemala for the Compañía Mexicana de Aviación for service from Mexico City to Guatemala.

He had tried to find Mr. Balch this morning but had been unable to do so, as the latter was busy in conference with the Council of State but that as soon as he saw him he would inform him of the abovementioned telegram.

He stated that while Mr. English and Mr. King Gillette were reliable people and while Mr. Balch had been very fair in attempting to get an air mail contract here, nevertheless, it was his, Mr. Rihl's, absolute opinion that the Latin American Airways would not operate its own service here, in the event that it did get a contract. . . .

He said that he had given the Minister of Fomento a short flight around the city this morning and had an appointment with him for 3:30 this afternoon, at which time the Minister had promised to definitely conclude the contract with the Pan American Airways. Despite this promise, he did not believe that the Minister would settle this matter and, according to his feeling, his contract would not be agreed upon in time to be submitted to the Assembly prior to May 25, the last date upon which new business could be brought before it according to a recent extension of time ordered by that body. Also, that although the Latin American contract might reach the Assembly before that date, he did not think that it would be approved by that body.

The contract which Mr. Rihl is now proposing to the Government is made out in the name of the Pan American Airways, Incorporated, and its subsidiary companies. There is no definite route prescribed for the service and, therefore, if this contract be approved, the Compañía Mexicana de Aviación would be able to extend its service from Mexico City and Vera Cruz via Tapachula to the city of Guatemala. However, as he does not believe that this contract will be approved, he said that he would probably merely request the Government to give him a permit so that planes of that Company could enter Guatemala and bring in mail.

The Government had requested that he amend his contract so as to make it read for four years instead of twenty; so as to enable the Government to cancel it at any time it desired, and also so as to allow the Government to take over the airplanes of the Company in time of war or national disturbance. He said, that while certain other points had been accepted by him, these last three he had refused definitely to accept.

He did not know whether the Latin American Airways had accepted these points or not. In his contract he agreed to carry mail for the Guatemalan Government but added a clause under which he would conclude a separate contract with the Guatemalan Post Office Department providing that the mail would be carried but only if it were paid for and if all the matter of the issuing and sale of stamps were taken care of by the Post Office Department.

I saw Mr. Rihl in the lobby of the Palace Hotel at seven o'clock this evening and he said that he had not yet seen Mr. Balch and, therefore, had not told him concerning the telegram which he said he had received from Mr. Trippe saying that the Post Office Department of the United States had ordered the Pan American Airways to extend its service to Guatemala.

He said that he and the Minister of Fomento had again discussed the contract that afternoon and had agreed upon all points and that he was having the final draft typed out tomorrow morning and would give the Legation a copy of it. I asked him if my impression was correct that the contract did not provide for any specific route. He replied that the contract provided for a connection with the lines of the Pan American Airways to the North. I asked whether that would authorize him to connect at his choice with Mexico or the Miami-Belize line. He said that this had been his impression, but that now he had been told that in Guatemala to the North does not mean Mexico, as this was considered as being to the West and, therefore, it would only mean the permission to connect with the Miami-Belize line. He said that he had asked the Minister of Fomento concerning a landing permit for the establishment of a weekly service with Mexico, as ordered by the Post Office Department of the United States, and that the latter had told him to apply for two permits, one to bring in the planes and the other to bring in the mail. He said that he would do so.

GUATEMALA, May 20, 1929.

---

814.796 Latin American Airways/16

*The Minister in Guatemala (Geissler) to the Secretary of State*

No. 2426                                    GUATEMALA, May 29, 1929.
                                           [Received June 5.]

SIR: With reference to despatch 2416 of May 22, 1929, and previous correspondence, I have the honor to report that the President of Guatemala and the Minister of Fomento today informed Mr. George L. Rihl, of the Pan American Airways and Mr. Lee C. Balch, of the Latin American Airways, that it would be difficult to obtain approval of their respective air transport contracts before the Legislative Assembly adjourns on May 31; that, therefore, the Government will not press for action prior to a special session likely to be called for July or August, and that meanwhile the Executive, as soon as the Assembly has adjourned, will grant their respective companies permits to fly.

I also beg leave to report that Mr. Rihl has told me that he will urge the Minister of Fomento to let his permit read "the Pan American Airways and affiliated companies" which is meant to include the Compañía Mexicana de Aviación, a Mexican corporation, and to word it so that his Company may enter Guatemala from Mexico as well as from the East. Mr. Balch still acquiesces in the granting of a permit or contract to the Pan American to enter Guatemala from the East proceeding thence from the Capital to Salvador, but he asserts that if more than one concern were to conduct an international aviation service between Guatemala and Mexico City, the business would not be profitable to either. The correctness of that contention is freely admitted by Mr. Rihl. Mr. Balch takes the position that since his contract was signed by the Minister of Fomento before anybody else had even applied for a Mexico-Guatemala air transport concession, he is entitled to a preference. Minister of Fomento Hernández concurs in that view.

. . . . . . . .

Mr. Rihl said to me today that he feels that since the contract of Mr. Balch is in the name of the Compañía de Transportes Aéreos Latino Americana, a Mexican corporation, he feels that I should support his request that the Pan American's permit include affiliated companies and that it be worded so as to allow one of those affiliated companies, namely the Compañía Mexicana de Aviación, a Mexican corporation, to fly between Tapachula, Mexico, through Guatemala to Salvador. He said that he appreciates that Mr. Balch has informed the Legation that the contract of the Latino Americana will be operated by the Latin American Airways, a company incorporated in the United States, but that the company might find it inconvenient to comply. I said that I should inquire of Mr. Balch on behalf of which corporation he will ask for a permit. Mr. Rihl meanwhile reiterated that it would be inconvenient for any international air transport company to operate in Guatemala under a charter other than the one under which it does business in Mexico. From previous conversations I knew, that he had made much of it in Mexico that the Compañía Mexicana de Aviación would every day be carrying the name and the flag of Mexico through Guatemala and thence through other states of Central America and that he has been accepting the aid of the Mexican Embassy in Guatemala for the project of the Compañía Mexicana. It is evident that he feels that he cannot now very well undertake to change that program. I told him, that I have not undertaken to say to either him or Mr. Balch under what charter they should operate in Guatemala.

Later in the day Mr. Balch informed me that his application for a permit would be presented on behalf of the Latin American Airways. The Minister of Fomento says that that is very agreeable to him and that he will request the Legislative Assembly to translate the name of the Company in the concession from Spanish into English and to specify that it is a company incorporated in the United States.

When I informed Mr. Rihl of what Mr. Balch had said to me, he stated that he appreciates the interest that I have taken in his matter and that he feels that without my help he probably would not have accomplished as much as he has and that he regrets that he did not appear in Guatemala ahead of Mr. Balch.

I have [etc.]                                    ARTHUR H. GEISSLER

---

814.796 Latin American Airways/18

*The Minister in Guatemala (Geissler) to the Secretary of State*

No. 2433                                    GUATEMALA, May 31, 1929.
[Received June 12.]

SIR: Referring to despatch No. 2426 of May 29, 1929, I have the honor to report that Mr. George L. Rihl, of the Pan American Airways, informed me today, that, on May 30, the Minister of Fomento, Colonel Daniel Hernández, received him and Mr. Lee C. Balch, of the Latin American Airways, and informed them, that, as soon as the National Legislative Assembly has, on May 31, adjourned its regular session, he will grant the Latin American a provisional permit to fly between the Mexican border town of Mariscal and the Republic of Salvador, via the city of Guatemala; that he will then also be ready to grant a permit to the Pan American to fly from the eastern, respectively northern, coast of Guatemala via the Capital to Salvador or Honduras and return, and that he will not grant a permit to the Compañía Mexicana or any concern other than the Latin American to establish an international air service between Mexico and the city of Guatemala.

Mr. Rihl also stated, that until about two weeks ago, such an arrangement would have been very satisfactory to him, but that now, in view of word received since from the President of the Pan American, he deems it advisable to go immediately to New York for a conference, before deciding whether the Company's attorney here should be authorized to agree to operate under a permit not permitting it to fly between the city of Guatemala and Mexico. . . .

The Legation has indirect information to the effect, that the Latin American Airways has completed its incorporation, under the laws of Delaware, with a capital of $3,000,000; that it is pleased with the position taken by the Minister of Fomento and that it will in view of it begin operations under the permit at an early date, between Mariscal and the city of Guatemala.

Reverting to the Pan American, I beg leave to state that it is extremely unlikely that it would have made much progress toward getting a permit and later on a contract, but for the support given it by the Legation. On the other hand, since Mr. Rihl and Mr. Balch concurred in saying that only one Company could operate an international service between Mexico and Guatemala without loss, I deemed it my duty not to comply with the desire of Mr. Rihl, reported on page 2 of despatch 2426, that I support his request that the Government grant to a subsidiary of the Pan American Airways, namely the Compañía Mexicana de Aviación, a Mexican corporation, a permit or a contract, in the face of the contract entered into by the Executive with the Latin American before the Pan American and its subsidiary had asked for a contract or a permit covering that route.

I have [etc.] ARTHUR H. GEISSLER

814.796 Latin American Airways/19

*The Minister in Guatemala (Geissler) to the Secretary of State*

No. 2443 GUATEMALA, June 11, 1929.
[Received June 20.]

SIR: Referring to despatch 2426 of May 29, 1929, I have the honor to enclose a copy of a letter [98] in which, in confirmation of a conversation, Mr. Lee C. Balch informed the Legation that, on June 8, 1929, he had signed with the Minister of Fomento a provisional contract, to be valid until the Legislative Assembly of Guatemala approves or disapproves the contract now pending before it, each of those contracts granting the Latino Americana transport privileges for a line between Mariscal, on the Mexican border, via the city of Guatemala to Salvador.

It will be observed, that Mr. Balch also expressed thanks for assistance rendered in the matter.

Mr. Balch said that, not having yet received formal power of attorney from the Latin American Airways, the provisional contract was signed in the name of the Compañía de Transportes Aéreos Latino Americana, but that, on June 10, he had filed with Minister of Fomento Daniel Hernández a request for authorization of the transfer of that contract to the Latin American Airways, of Delaware, as shown by the enclosed copy, and that he was informed by that official that the authorization would be granted as soon as the Latin American Airways, of Delaware, has been registered in Guatemala as required by law, which Mr. Balch said will be accomplished within a week or two.

[98] Not printed.

The representative of the Latin American Airways added, that he is leaving on June 12, for the city of Mexico and will proceed from there to California, to confer with his associates, and that his Company intends to begin flying in Guatemala under its concession within thirty days.

At this time it seems probable, that the Legislative Assembly will approve of the Latin American's contract, at its extra session likely to be held in August.

I have [etc.]　　　　　　　　　　　　　　　ARTHUR H. GEISSLER

814.796 Latin American Airways/22

*The Minister in Guatemala (Geissler) to the Secretary of State*

No. 2500　　　　　　　　　　　　　　　GUATEMALA, July 9, 1929.
　　　　　　　　　　　　　　　　　　　　　[Received July 17.]

SIR: Referring to previous correspondence, I have the honor to report, that Commercial Attaché Bohan has been informed by Mr. Carlos Irigoyen, who is connected with the Latin American Airways, that, according to cablegraphic advices, that Company is merging with another company now in operation, but whose name he did not give, and that it expects to have five airplanes delivered on July 12, and expects to commence operations between July 20 and 25. According to the same source, the Latin American Airways has been informed by the Minister of Fomento of Honduras, that he would be willing to give it a contract between the city of Guatemala and Tegucigalpa.

I have [etc.]　　　　　　　　　　　　　　　ARTHUR H. GEISSLER

814.796 Latin American Airways/23

*The Minister in Guatemala (Geissler) to the Secretary of State*

No. 2535　　　　　　　　　　　　　　　GUATEMALA, August 7, 1929.
　　　　　　　　　　　　　　　　　　　　　[Received August 14.]

SIR: I have the honor to report, that the Compañía de Transportes Aéreos Latino Americana inaugurated, under its temporary contract with the Government of Guatemala, mentioned in despatch 2443 of June 11, 1929, a twice-a-week air mail and passenger service with a plane which left the city of Guatemala this morning, August 7, for the city of Mexico, and in that connection I beg leave to relate some statements made to me, on August 6, by the President of the Company, Captain Daniel E. Ellis, regarding its pending merger with the Pickwick Airways Incorporated of Los Angeles, California.

Mr. Ellis came to the Legation, accompanied by Mr. Carlos Irigoyen, local representative of the Company, and said that Mr. Lee C. Balch, who had negotiated the contract with the Guatemalan Government, would probably be here again in a few days, and had asked him to call meanwhile, to reiterate appreciation of assistance given by the Legation and to give information regarding the present status of their Company.

Mr. Ellis stated, that they had had much trouble because of some actions of one of the organizers of the Compañía Latino Americana and of the Latin American Airways of Delaware . . . that . . . was eliminated, and that thereupon the stockholders had entered into a contract with the Pickwick Airways, in which concern the Southern Pacific Railway is understood to be interested, under which contract, by about October 15, would be organized an American corporation, with a capital stock of $3,000,000.00, half of which stock is to go to each of those two groups, it being agreed that meanwhile the Pickwick Airways will furnish the material and money for the inauguration of the air service between Los Angeles and the city of Guatemala. He said, that the new concern, in process of incorporation, owns all of the stock of the Latino Americana, which has the air transport contracts in Mexico and Guatemala. He remarked, that under the laws of Mexico, operations in that Republic must be by a Mexican corporation, and that therefore it might be more convenient to have the Mexican corporation operate also between Tia Juana and Los Angeles and between the southern frontier of Mexico and the city of Guatemala and possibly in Salvador and Honduras. He asked whether I would have objection to that. I replied, that it is not for me to pass on that question. Then he said, that he would like to have my advice. I answered, that I should say to him what I had stated, on previous occasions, to Mr. Balch and also to a representative of the Pan American Airways, namely that I prefer not to advise regarding that point. Then I related to him, that, in May, Mr. Balch had quite voluntarily informed me that he believed it would be better for his syndicate to transfer the contract with the Government of Guatemala, when obtained, to an American corporation for operation and that this would be done. I added, that if now Mr. Balch and his associates have decided or decide on a different course, it would be interesting information. He then stated, that no decision had been reached and that Mr. Balch would be in Guatemala in a very few days, to look after legal matters and the like; the branch of the business under his own charge being that of operations.

I believe, that Mr. Balch will carry out the written statement he made to me. See enclosure 2 [99] with despatch 2403 of May 15, 1929,

[99] Not printed.

and also despatch 2443 of June 11, 1929. Whether he does or does not, it seems now possible that, sooner or later, the Pan American group will decide that it prefers to operate in Guatemala under an American charter. Please, see in this connection despatch 2530 of August 3, 1929.[1]

I enclose a copy of a report made, under date of August 7, 1929, by Commercial Attaché Bohan to the Department of Commerce,[1] on the subject of the establishment of the "Latin American Airways" service, which report includes, beside other pertinent details, the flying schedule.

I have [etc.]                                          ARTHUR H. GEISSLER

---

814.796 Latin American Airways/25

*The Minister in Guatemala (Geissler) to the Secretary of State*

No. 2538                                        GUATEMALA, August 13, 1929.
                                                    [Received August 21.]

SIR: Referring to despatch 2535 of August 7, 1929, I have the honor to report, that the Legation has been informed, that, on August 9, 1929, Mr. Carlos Irigoyen, local representative of the Latin American Airways, filed with the Minister of Fomento an application for permission to transfer the concern's contract with the Government of Guatemala to the Pickwick Airways Incorporated, of California, and that he was told that the permission would be granted promptly upon receipt of an authenticated copy of the transfer. I beg leave to add, that today I received a cablegram from Mr. Lee C. Balch, Mexico City, saying that "transfer of Guatemala contract from Cia. Transportes Aéreos Latino Americana S. A. to Pickwick Airways a Delaware Corporation effected today before Notary Ramón Cosio González".

I have [etc.]                                          ARTHUR H. GEISSLER

---

[1] Not printed.

INTERNATIONAL CONFERENCE OF AMERICAN STATES ON CONCILIA-
TION AND ARBITRATION, HELD AT WASHINGTON, DECEMBER 10,
1928–JANUARY 5, 1929:[1] CONVENTIONS

Treaty Series No. 780

*General Convention of Inter-American Conciliation, Signed at
Washington, January 5, 1929* [2]

The Governments of Venezuela, Chile, Bolivia, Uruguay, Costa
Rica, Perú, Honduras, Guatemala, Haiti, Ecuador, Colombia, Brazil,
Panamá, Paraguay, Nicaragua, Mexico, El Salvador, the Dominican
Republic, Cuba, and the United States of America, represented at the
Conference on Conciliation and Arbitration, assembled at Washing-
ton, pursuant to the Resolution adopted on February 18, 1928, by
the Sixth International Conference of American States held in the
City of Habana:

Desiring to demonstrate that the condemnation of war as an
instrument of national policy in their mutual relations, set forth in
the above mentioned resolution, constitutes one of the fundamental
bases of inter-American relations;

Animated by the purpose of promoting, in every possible way,
the development of international methods for the pacific settlement
of differences between the States;

Being convinced that the "Treaty to Avoid or Prevent Conflicts
between the American States", signed at Santiago de Chile, May 3,
1923,[3] constitutes a notable achievement in inter-American relations,
which it is necessary to maintain by giving additional prestige and
strength to the action of the commissions established by Articles III
and IV of the aforementioned treaty;

Acknowledging the need of giving conventional form to these

---

[1] For previous correspondence concerning the Conference, see *Foreign Relations*,
1928, vol. I, pp. 621 ff.

For the proceedings of the Conference, see *Proceedings of the International
Conference of American States on Conciliation and Arbitration, Held at Wash-
ington, December 10, 1928–January 5, 1929* (Washington, Government Printing
Office, 1929).

[2] In English, Spanish, Portuguese, and French; English text only printed.
Ratification advised by the Senate, February 20 (legislative day of February
15), 1929; ratified by the President, February 26, 1929; ratification of the
United States deposited with the Government of Chile, March 27, 1929;
proclaimed by the President, April 4, 1929.

[3] *Foreign Relations*, 1923, vol. I, p. 308.

653

purposes have agreed to enter into the present Convention, for which purpose they have appointed Plenipotentiaries as follows:

Venezuela:
Carlos F. Grisanti.
Francisco Arroyo Parejo.
Chile:
Manuel Foster Recabarren.
Antonio Planet.
Bolivia:
Eduardo Diez de Medina.
Uruguay:
José Pedro Varela.
Costa Rica:
Manuel Castro Quesada.
José Tible-Machado.
Perú:
Hernán Velarde.
Victor M. Maúrtua.
Honduras:
Rómulo Durón.
Marcos López Ponce.
Guatemala:
Adrián Recinos.
José Falla.
Haiti:
Auguste Bonamy.
Raoul Lizaire.
Ecuador:
Gonzalo Zaldumbide.
Colombia:
Enrique Olaya Herrera.
Carlos Escallón.
Brazil:
S. Gurgel do Amaral.
A. G. de Araujo-Jorge.
Panamá:
Ricardo J. Alfaro.
Carlos L. López.
Paraguay:
Eligio Ayala.
Nicaragua:
Máximo H. Zepeda.
Adrián Recinos.
J. Lisandro Medina.
México:
Fernando González Roa.
Benito Flores.
El Salvador:
Cayetano Ochoa.
David Rosales, Jr.
Dominican Republic:
Angel Morales.
Gustavo A. Díaz.

Cuba:
    Orestes Ferrara.
    Gustavo Gutiérrez.
United States of America:
    Frank B. Kellogg.
    Charles Evans Hughes.

Who, after having deposited their full powers, which were found to be in good and due form by the Conference, have agreed as follows:

## ARTICLE 1

The High Contracting Parties agree to submit to the procedure of conciliation established by this convention all controversies of any kind which have arisen or may arise between them for any reason and which it may not have been possible to settle through diplomatic channels.

## ARTICLE 2

The Commission of Inquiry to be established pursuant to the provisions of Article IV of the Treaty signed in Santiago de Chile on May 3, 1923, shall likewise have the character of Commission of Conciliation.

## ARTICLE 3

The Permanent Commissions which have been established by virtue of Article III of the Treaty of Santiago de Chile of May 3, 1923, shall be bound to exercise conciliatory functions, either on their own motion when it appears that there is a prospect of disturbance of peaceful relations, or at the request of a Party to the dispute, until the Commission referred to in the preceding article is organized.

## ARTICLE 4

The conciliatory functions of the Commission described in **Article 2** shall be exercised on the occasions hereinafter set forth:

(1) The Commission shall be at liberty to begin its work with an effort to conciliate the differences submitted to its examination with a view to arriving at a settlement between the Parties.

(2) Likewise the same Commission shall be at liberty to endeavor to conciliate the Parties at any time which in the opinion of the Commission may be considered to be favorable in the course of the investigation and within the period of time fixed therefor in Article V of the Treaty of Santiago de Chile of May 3, 1923.

(3) Finally, the Commission shall be bound to carry out its conciliatory function within the period of six months which is referred to in Article VII of the Treaty of Santiago de Chile of May 3, 1923.

The Parties to the controversy may, however, extend this time, if they so agree and notify the Commission in due time.

## ARTICLE 5

The present convention does not preclude the High Contracting Parties, or one or more of them, from tendering their good offices or their mediation, jointly or severally, on their own motion or at the request of one or more of the Parties to the controversy; but the High Contracting Parties agree not to make use of those means of pacific settlement from the moment that the Commission described in Article 2 is organized until the final act referred to in Article 11 of this convention is signed.

## ARTICLE 6

The function of the Commission, as an organ of conciliation, in all cases specified in Article 2 of this convention, is to procure the conciliation of the differences subject to its examination by endeavoring to effect a settlement between the Parties.

When the Commission finds itself to be within the case foreseen in paragraph 3 of Article 4 of this convention, it shall undertake a conscientious and impartial examination of the questions which are the subject of the controversy, shall set forth in a report the results of its proceedings, and shall propose to the Parties the bases of a settlement for the equitable solution of the controversy.

## ARTICLE 7

Except when the Parties agree otherwise, the decisions and recommendations of any Commission of Conciliation shall be made by a majority vote.

## ARTICLE 8

The Commission described in Article 2 of this convention shall establish its rules of procedure. In the absence of agreement to the contrary, the procedure indicated in Article IV of the Treaty of Santiago de Chile of May 3, 1923, shall be followed.

Each party shall bear its own expenses and a proportionate share of the general expenses of the Commission.

## ARTICLE 9

The report and the recommendations of the Commission, insofar as it may be acting as an organ of conciliation, shall not have the character of a decision nor an arbitral award, and shall not be binding on the Parties either as regards the exposition or interpretation of the facts or as regards questions of law.

## ARTICLE 10

As soon as possible after the termination of its labors the Commission shall transmit to the Parties a certified copy of the report and of the bases of settlement which it may propose.

The Commission in transmitting the report and the recommendations to the Parties shall fix a period of time, which shall not exceed six months, within which the Parties shall pass upon the bases of settlement above referred to.

## ARTICLE 11

Once the period of time fixed by the Commission for the Parties to make their decisions has expired, the Commission shall set forth in a final act the decision of the Parties, and if the conciliation has been effected, the terms of the settlement.

## ARTICLE 12

The obligations set forth in the second sentence of the first paragraph of Article I of the Treaty of Santiago de Chile of May 3, 1923, shall extend to the time when the final act referred to in the preceding article is signed.

## ARTICLE 13

Once the procedure of conciliation is under way it shall be interrupted only by a direct settlement between the Parties or by their agreement to accept absolutely the decision *ex aequo et bono* of an American Chief of State or to submit the controversy to arbitration or to an international court.

## ARTICLE 14

Whenever for any reason the Treaty of Santiago de Chile of May 3, 1923, does not apply, the Commission referred to in Article 2 of this convention shall be organized to the end that it may exercise the conciliatory functions stipulated in this convention; the Commission shall be organized in the same manner as that prescribed in Article IV of said treaty.

In such cases, the Commission thus organized shall be governed in its operation by the provisions, relative to conciliation, of this convention.

## ARTICLE 15

The provisions of the preceding article shall also apply with regard to the Permanent Commissions constituted by the aforementioned

Treaty of Santiago de Chile, to the end that said Commissions may exercise the conciliatory functions prescribed in Article 3 of this convention.

## ARTICLE 16

The present convention shall be ratified by the High Contracting Parties in conformity with their respective constitutional procedures, provided that they have previously ratified the Treaty of Santiago, Chile, of May 3, 1923.

The original convention and the instruments of ratification shall be deposited in the Ministry for Foreign Affairs of the Republic of Chile which shall give notice of the ratifications through diplomatic channels to the other signatory Governments and the convention shall enter into effect for the High Contracting Parties in the order that they deposit their ratifications.

This convention shall remain in force indefinitely, but it may be denounced by means of notice given one year in advance at the expiration of which it shall cease to be in force as regards the Party denouncing the same, but shall remain in force as regards the other signatories. Notice of the denunciation shall be addressed to the Ministry for Foreign Affairs of the Republic of Chile which will transmit it for appropriate action to the other signatory Governments.

Any American State not a signatory of this convention may adhere to the same by transmitting the official instrument setting forth such adherence, to the Ministry for Foreign Affair of the Republic of Chile which will notify the other High Contracting Parties thereof in the manner heretofore mentioned.

In witness whereof the above mentioned Plenipotentiaries have signed this convention in English, Spanish, Portugese and French and hereunto affix their respective seals.

Done at the city of Washington, on this fifth day of January, 1929.

[SEAL]

CARLOS F. GRISANTI
FR. ARROYO PAREJO

Chile makes exception in this convention of questions which may arise from situations or acts prior thereto.

A. PLANET                                MANUEL FOSTER

[SEAL]

[SEAL]                                   E. DIEZ DE MEDINA
[SEAL]                                   JOSÉ PEDRO VARELA
[SEAL]                                   MANUEL CASTRO QUESADA
[SEAL]                                   JOSÉ TIBLE-MACHADO
HERNÁN VELARDE                                      [SEAL]
VICTOR M. MAÚRTUA                                   [SEAL]

Rómulo E. Durón [SEAL]
M. López Ponce [SEAL]
Adrián Recinos [SEAL]
José Falla [SEAL]
[SEAL] A. Bonamy
[SEAL] Raoul Lizaire
[SEAL] Gonzalo Zaldumbide
[SEAL] Enrique Olaya Herrera
[SEAL] C. Escallon
S. Gurgel do Amaral [SEAL]
A. Araujo-Jorge [SEAL]
R. J. Alfaro [SEAL]
Carlos L. López [SEAL]
Eligio Ayala [SEAL]
[SEAL] Máximo H. Zepeda
Adrián Recinos
J. Lisandro Medina
[SEAL] Fernando González Roa
[SEAL] Benito Flores
Cayetano Ochoa [SEAL]
David Rosales, hijo
A. Morales [SEAL]
G. A. Díaz [SEAL]
Orestes Ferrara [SEAL]
Gustavo Gutiérrez [SEAL]
[SEAL] Frank B. Kellogg
[SEAL] Charles Evans Hughes

Treaty Series No. 886

*General Treaty of Inter-American Arbitration, Signed at Washington, January 5, 1929* [4]

The Governments of Venezuela, Chile, Bolivia, Uruguay, Costa Rica, Perú, Honduras, Guatemala, Haiti, Ecuador, Colombia, Brazil, Panamá, Paraguay, Nicaragua, Mexico, El Salvador, the Dominican Republic, Cuba, and the United States of America, represented at the Conference on Conciliation and Arbitration, assembled at Washington, pursuant to the Resolution adopted on February 18, 1928, by the Sixth International Conference of American States held in the City of Habana;

---

[4] In English, Spanish, Portuguese, and French; English text only printed. Ratification advised by the Senate, with an understanding, April 1 (legislative day of March 13), 1935; ratified by the President, with the said understanding, April 16, 1935; ratification deposited April 16, 1935; proclaimed by the President, April 16, 1935.

In accordance with the solemn declarations made at said Conference to the effect that the American Republics condemn war as an instrument of national policy and adopt obligatory arbitration as the means for the settlement of their international differences of a juridical character;

Being convinced that the Republics of the New World, governed by the principles, institutions and practices of democracy and bound furthermore by mutual interests, which are increasing each day, have not only the necessity but also the duty of avoiding the disturbance of continental harmony whenever differences which are susceptible of judicial decision arise among them;

Conscious of the great moral and material benefits which peace offers to humanity and that the sentiment and opinion of America demand, without delay, the organization of an arbitral system which shall strengthen the permanent reign of justice and law;

And animated by the purpose of giving conventional form to these postulates and aspirations with the minimum exceptions which they have considered indispensable to safeguard the independence and sovereignty of the States and in the most ample manner possible under present international conditions, have resolved to effect the present treaty, and for that purpose have designated the Plenipotentiaries hereinafter named:

Venezuela:
Carlos F. Grisanti.
Francisco Arroyo Parejo.
Chile:
Manuel Foster Recabarren.
Antonio Planet.
Bolivia:
Eduardo Diez de Medina.
Uruguay:
José Pedro Varela.
Costa Rica:
Manuel Castro Quesada.
José Tible-Machado.
Perú:
Hernán Velarde.
Victor M. Maúrtua.
Honduras:
Rómulo Durón.
Marcos López Ponce.
Guatemala:
Adrián Recinos.
José Falla.
Haití:
Auguste Bonamy.
Raoul Lizaire.
Ecuador:
Gonzalo Zaldumbide.

Colombia:
Enrique Olaya Herrera.
Carlos Escallón.
Brazil:
S. Gurgel do Amaral.
A. G. de Araujo-Jorge.
Panamá:
Ricardo J. Alfaro.
Carlos L. López.
Paraguay:
Eligio Ayala.
Nicaragua:
Maximo H. Zepeda.
Adrián Recinos.
J. Lisandro Medina.
Mexico:
Fernando González Roa.
Benito Flores.
El Salvador:
Cayetano Ochoa.
David Rosales, Jr.
Dominican Republic:
Angel Morales.
Gustavo A. Díaz.
Cuba:
Orestes Ferrara.
Gustavo Gutiérrez.
United States of America:
Frank B. Kellogg.
Charles Evans Hughes.

Who, after having deposited their full powers, found in good and due form by the Conference, have agreed upon the following:

## ARTICLE 1

The High Contracting Parties bind themselves to submit to arbitration all differences of an international character which have arisen or may arise between them by virtue of a claim of right made by one against the other under treaty or otherwise, which it has not been possible to adjust by diplomacy and which are juridical in their nature by reason of being susceptible of decision by the application of the principles of law.

There shall be considered as included among the questions of juridical character:

(a) The interpretation of a treaty;
(b) Any question of international law;
(c) The existence of any fact which, if established, would constitute a breach of an international obligation;
(d) The nature and extent of the reparation to be made for the breach of an international obligation.

The provisions of this treaty shall not preclude any of the Parties, before resorting to arbitration, from having recourse to procedures of investigation and conciliation established in conventions then in force between them.

## ARTICLE 2

There are excepted from the stipulations of this treaty the following controversies:

(a) Those which are within the domestic jurisdiction of any of the Parties to the dispute and are not controlled by international law; and

(b) Those which affect the interest or refer to the action of a State not a Party to this treaty.

## ARTICLE 3

The arbitrator or tribunal who shall decide the controversy shall be designated by agreement of the Parties.

In the absence of an agreement the following procedure shall be adopted:

Each Party shall nominate two arbitrators, of whom only one may be a national of said Party or selected from the persons whom said Party has designated as members of the Permanent Court of Arbitration at The Hague. The other member may be of any other American nationality. These arbitrators shall in turn select a fifth arbitrator who shall be the president of the court.

Should the arbitrators be unable to reach an agreement among themselves for the selection of a fifth American arbitrator, or in lieu thereof, of another who is not, each Party shall designate a non-American member of the Permanent Court of Arbitration at The Hague, and the two persons so designated shall select the fifth arbitrator, who may be of any nationality other than that of a Party to the dispute.

## ARTICLE 4

The Parties to the dispute shall formulate by common accord, in each case, a special agreement which shall clearly define the particular subject-matter of the controversy, the seat of the court, the rules which will be observed in the proceedings, and the other conditions to which the Parties may agree.

If an accord has not been reached with regard to the agreement within three months reckoned from the date of the installation of the court, the agreement shall be formulated by the court.

## ARTICLE 5

In case of death, resignation or incapacity of one or more of the arbitrators the vacancy shall be filled in the same manner as the original appointment.

## ARTICLE 6

When there are more than two States directly interested in the same controversy, and the interests of two or more of them are similar, the State or States who are on the same side of the question may increase the number of arbitrators on the court, provided that in all cases the Parties on each side of the controversy shall appoint an equal number of arbitrators. There shall also be a presiding arbitrator selected in the same manner as that provided in the last paragraph of Article 3, the Parties on each side of the controversy being regarded as a single Party for the purpose of making the designation therein described.

## ARTICLE 7

The award, duly pronounced and notified to the Parties, settles the dispute definitively and without appeal.

Differences which arise with regard to its interpretation or execution shall be submitted to the decision of the court which rendered the award.

## ARTICLE 8

The reservations made by one of the High Contracting Parties shall have the effect that the other Contracting Parties are not bound with respect to the Party making the reservations except to the same extent as that expressed therein.

## ARTICLE 9

The present treaty shall be ratified by the High Contracting Parties in conformity with their respective constitutional procedures.

The original treaty and the instruments of ratification shall be deposited in the Department of State of the United States of America which shall give notice of the ratifications through diplomatic channels to the other signatory Governments and the treaty shall enter into effect for the High Contracting Parties in the order that they deposit their ratifications.

This treaty shall remain in force indefinitely, but it may be denounced by means of one year's previous notice at the expiration of which it shall cease to be in force as regards the Party denouncing the same, but shall remain in force as regards the other signatories.

Notice of the denunciation shall be addressed to the Department of State of the United States of America which will transmit it for appropriate action to the other signatory Governments.

Any American State not a signatory of this treaty may adhere to the same by transmitting the official instrument setting forth such adherence to the Department of State of the United States of America which will notify the other High Contracting Parties thereof in the manner heretofore mentioned.

In witness whereof the above mentioned Plenipotentiaries have signed this treaty in English, Spanish, Portuguese, and French and hereunto affix their respective seals.

Done at the city of Washington, on this fifth day of January, 1929.

The Delegation of Venezuela signs the present Treaty of Arbitration with the following reservations:

First. There shall be excepted from this Treaty those matters which, according to the Constitution or the laws of Venezuela, are under the jurisdiction of its courts; and, especially, those matters relating to pecuniary claims of foreigners. In such matters, arbitration shall not be resorted to except when, legal remedies having been exhausted by the claimant, it shall appear that there has been a denial of justice.

Second. There shall also be excepted those matters controlled by international agreements now in force.

CARLOS F. GRISANTI                   FR. ARROYO PAREJO        [SEAL]
                                                              [SEAL]

Chile does not accept obligatory arbitration for questions which have their origin in situations or acts antedating the present treaty nor does it accept obligatory arbitration for those questions which, being under the exclusive competency of the national jurisdiction, the interested parties claim the right to withdraw from the cognizance of the established judicial authorities, unless said authorities decline to pass judgment on any action or exception which any natural or juridical foreign person may present to them in the form established by the laws of the country.

MANUEL FOSTER                                                 [SEAL]
A. PLANET                                                     [SEAL]

The Delegation of Bolivia, in accordance with the doctrine and policy invariably maintained by Bolivia in the field of international jurisprudence, gives full adherence to and signs the General Treaty of Inter-American Arbitration which the Republics of America are to sanction, formulating the following express reservations:

First. There may be excepted from the provisions of the present agreement, questions arising from acts occurring or conventions concluded before the said treaty goes into effect, as well as those which, in conformity with international law, are under the exclusive jurisdiction of the state.

Second. It is also understood that, for the submission to arbitration of a territorial controversy or dispute, the zone to which the said arbitration is to apply must be previously determined in the arbitral agreement.

[SEAL]                                              E. DIEZ DE MEDINA

I vote in favor of the Treaty of Arbitration, with the reservation formulated by the Delegation of Uruguay at the Fifth Pan American Conference, favoring broad arbitration; and with the understanding that arbitration will be resorted to only in case of denial of justice, when the national tribunals have jurisdiction, according to the legislation of their own country.

[SEAL]                                          JOSÉ PEDRO VARELA

Reservations of Costa Rica:

(a) The obligations contracted under this Treaty do not annul, abrogate or restrict the arbitration conventions which are now in force between Costa Rica and another or others of the high contracting parties and do not involve arbitration, disavowal or renewed discussion of questions which may have already been settled by arbitral awards.

(b) The obligations contracted under this Treaty do not involve the arbitration of judgments handed down by the courts of Costa Rica in civil cases which may be submitted to them and with regard to which the interested parties have recognized the jurisdiction of said courts.

MANUEL CASTRO QUESADA                                    [SEAL]
JOSÉ TIBLE-MACHADO                                       [SEAL]

HERNÁN VELARDE                                           [SEAL]
VICTOR M. MAURTUA                                        [SEAL]

The Delegation of Honduras, in signing the present Treaty, formulates an express reservation making it a matter of record that the provisions thereof shall not be applicable to pending international questions or controversies or to those which may arise in the future relative to acts prior to the date on which the said Treaty goes into effect.

[SEAL]                                          RÓMULO E. DURÓN
[SEAL]                                          M. LÓPEZ PONCE

The Delegation of Guatemala makes the following reservations:

1. In order to submit to arbitration any questions relating to the boundaries of the nation, the approval of the Legislative Assembly must first be given, in each case, in conformity with the Constitution of the Republic.

2. The provisions of the present Convention do not alter or modify the conventions and treaties previously entered into by the Republic of Guatemala.

[SEAL]                                          ADRIÁN RECINOS
[SEAL]                                          JOSÉ FALLA

A. BONAMY                                                [SEAL]
RAOUL LIZAIRE                                            [SEAL]

The Delegation of Ecuador, pursuant to instructions of its Government, reserves from the jurisdiction of the obligatory arbitration agreed upon in the present Treaty:

1. Questions at present governed by conventions or treaties now in effect;

2. Those which may arise from previous causes or may result from acts preceding the signature of this treaty;

3. Pecuniary claims of foreigners who may not have previously exhausted all legal remedies before the courts of justice of the country, it being understood that such is the interpretation and the extent of the application which the Government of Ecuador has always given to the Buenos Aires Convention of August 11, 1910.

GONZALO ZALDUMBIDE                                       [SEAL]

The Delegation of Colombia signs the foregoing Convention with the following two declarations or reservations:

First. The obligations which the Republic of Colombia may contract thereby refer to the differences which may arise from acts subsequent to the ratification of the Convention;

Second. Except in the case of a denial of justice, the arbitration provided for in this convention is not applicable to the questions which may have arisen or which may arise between a citizen, an association or a corporation of one of the parties and the other contracting state when the judges or courts of the latter state are, in accordance with its legislation, competent to settle the controversy.

[SEAL]                                        ENRIQUE OLAYA HERRERA
[SEAL]                                                       C ESCALLÓN

[SEAL]                                             S. GURGEL DO AMARAL
[SEAL]                                                  A ARAUJO JORGE

R. J. ALFARO                                                        [SEAL]
CARLOS L. LÓPEZ                                                     [SEAL]

Reservation of the Delegation of Paraguay:

I sign this treaty with the reservation that Paraguay excludes from its application questions which directly or indirectly affect the integrity of the national territory and are not merely questions of frontiers or boundaries.

ELIGIO AYALA                                                       [SEAL]

MÁXIMO H ZEPEDA
ADRIÁN RECINOS                                                     [SEAL]
J LISANDRO MEDINA

Mexican Reservation:

Mexico makes the reservation that differences, which fall under the jurisdiction of the courts, shall not form a subject of the procedure provided for by the Convention, except in case of denial of justice, and until after the judgment passed by the competent national authority has been placed in the class of *res judicata.*

[SEAL]                                               FERDO GONZÁLEZ ROA
                                                          BENITO FLORES

The Delegation of El Salvador to the Conference on Conciliation and Arbitration assembled in Washington accepts and signs the General Treaty of Inter-American Arbitration concluded this day by said Conference, with the following reservations or restrictions:

1. After the words of paragraph 1 of Article 1 reading: "Under treaty or otherwise", the following words are to be added: "subsequent to the present Convention." The article continues without any other modification.

2. Paragraph (a) of Article 2 is accepted by the Delegation without the final words which read: "and are not controlled by international law", which should be considered as eliminated.

3. This Treaty does not include controversies or differences with regard to points or questions which, according to the Political Constitution of El Salvador, must not be submitted to arbitration, and

4. Pecuniary claims against the nation shall be decided by its judges and courts, since they have jurisdiction thereof, and recourse shall be had to inter-

national arbitration only in the cases provided in the Constitution and laws of El Salvador, that is, in cases of denial of justice or unusual delay in the administration thereof.

[SEAL]     DAVID ROSALES, HIJO                    CAYETANO OCHOA
[SEAL]

The Dominican Republic, in signing the General Treaty of Inter-American Arbitration, does so with the understanding that controversies relating to questions which are under the jurisdiction of its courts shall not be referred to arbitral jurisdiction except in accordance with the principles of international law.

A MORALES                                                        [SEAL]
G A DÍAZ                                                         [SEAL]

ORESTES FERRARA                                                  [SEAL]
GUSTAVO GUTIÉRREZ                                                [SEAL]

FRANK B KELLOGG                                                  [SEAL]
CHARLES EVANS HUGHES                                             [SEAL]

[The Senate resolution of April 1, 1935, giving advice and consent to the ratification of the treaty, contained the following understanding, made a part of such ratification, "that the special agreement in each case shall be made only by the President, and then only by and with the advice and consent of the Senate, provided two-thirds of the Senators present concur."—*Congressional Record*, volume 79, pages 4753–4754.]

---

Treaty Series No. 886

*Protocol of Progressive Arbitration, Signed at Washington, January 5, 1929* [5]

Whereas, a General Treaty of Inter-American Arbitration has this day been signed at Washington by Plenipotentiaries of the Governments of Venezuela, Chile, Bolivia, Uruguay, Costa Rica, Perú, Honduras, Guatemala, Haiti, Ecuador, Colombia, Brazil, Panama, Paraguay, Nicaragua, Mexico, El Salvador, the Dominican Republic, Cuba and the United States of America;

Whereas, that treaty by its terms excepts certain controversies from the stipulations thereof;

Whereas, by means of reservations attached to the treaty at the time of signing, ratifying or adhering, certain other controversies have been or may be also excepted from the stipulations of the treaty or reserved from the operation thereof;

[5] In English, Spanish, Portuguese, and French; English text only printed.

Whereas, it is deemed desirable to establish a procedure whereby such exceptions or reservations may from time to time be abandoned in whole or in part by the Parties to said treaty, thus progressively extending the field of arbitration;

The Governments named above have agreed as follows:

## ARTICLE 1

Any Party to the General Treaty of Inter-American Arbitration signed at Washington the fifth day of January, 1929, may at any time deposit with the Department of State of the United States of America an appropriate instrument evidencing that it has abandoned in whole or in part the exceptions from arbitration stipulated in the said treaty or the reservation or reservations attached by it thereto.

## ARTICLE 2

A certified copy of each instrument deposited with the Department of State of the United States of America pursuant to the provisions of Article 1 of his protocol shall be transmitted by the said Department through diplomatic channels to every other Party to the above-mentioned General Treaty of Inter-American Arbitration.

In witness whereof the above-mentioned Plenipotentiaries have signed this protocol in English, Spanish, Portuguese, and French and hereunto affix their respective seals.

Done at the city of Washington, on this fifth day of January, 1929.

| | |
|---|---|
| [SEAL] | CARLOS F. GRISANTI |
| [SEAL] | FR. ARROYO PAREJO |
| [SEAL] | MANUEL FOSTER |
| [SEAL] | A. PLANET. |
| [SEAL] | E. DIEZ DE MEDINA |
| JOSÉ PEDRO VARELA | [SEAL] |
| MANUEL CASTRO QUESADA | [SEAL] |
| JOSÉ TIBLE MACHADO | [SEAL] |
| HERNÁN VELARDE | [SEAL] |
| VICTOR M. MAURTUA | [SEAL] |
| RÓMULO E. DURÓN. | [SEAL] |
| M. LÓPEZ PONCE | [SEAL] |
| ADRIÁN RECINOS | [SEAL] |
| JOSÉ FALLA | [SEAL] |
| A. BONAMY | [SEAL] |
| RAOUL LIZAIRE | |

| | |
|---|---|
| [SEAL] | GONZALO ZALDUMBIDE |
| [SEAL] | ENRIQUE OLAYA HERRERA |
| [SEAL] | C. ESCALLÓN |
| [SEAL] | S. GURGEL DO AMARAL |
| [SEAL] | A. ARAUJO JORGE |
| [SEAL] | R. J. ALFARO |
| [SEAL] | CARLOS L. LÓPEZ |
| [SEAL] | ELIGIO AYALA |
| | MÁXIMO H. ZEPEDA |
| [SEAL] | ADRIÁN RECINOS |
| | J. LISANDRO MEDINA |
| FERDO GONZÁLEZ ROA | [SEAL] |
| BENITO FLORES | |
| CAYETANO OCHOA | [SEAL] |
| DAVID ROSALES, HIJO | |
| A. MORALES | [SEAL] |
| G. A. DÍAZ | [SEAL] |
| [SEAL] | ORESTES FERRARA |
| [SEAL] | GUSTAVO GUTIÉRREZ |
| FRANK B KELLOGG | [SEAL] |
| CHARLES EVANS HUGHES | [SEAL] |

CONVENTION AND PROTOCOL BETWEEN THE UNITED STATES AND OTHER AMERICAN REPUBLICS RESPECTING TRADE MARK AND COMMERCIAL PROTECTION AND REGISTRATION OF TRADE MARKS, SIGNED FEBRUARY 20, 1929

Treaty Series No. 833

*General Inter-American Convention for Trade Mark and Commercial Protection, Signed at Washington, February 20, 1929* [1]

The Governments of Peru, Bolivia, Paraguay, Ecuador, Uruguay, Dominican Republic, Chile, Panama, Venezuela, Costa Rica, Cuba, Guatemala, Haiti, Colombia, Brazil, Mexico, Nicaragua, Honduras and the United States of America, represented at the Pan American Trade Mark Conference at Washington in accordance with the terms of the resolution adopted on February 15, 1928, at the Sixth International Conference of American States at Habana, and the resolution of May 2, 1928, adopted by the Governing Board of the Pan American Union at Washington,

Considering it necessary to revise the "Convention for the Protection of Commercial, Industrial, and Agricultural Trade Marks and Commercial Names," signed at Santiago, Chile, on April 28, 1923,[2] which replaced the "Convention for the Protection of Trade Marks" signed at Buenos Aires on August 20, 1910,[3] with a view of introducing therein the reforms which the development of law and practice have made advisable;

Animated by the desire to reconcile the different juridical systems which prevail in the several American Republics; and

Convinced of the necessity of undertaking this work in its broadest scope, with due regard for the respective national legislations,

Have resolved to negotiate the present Convention for the protection of trade marks, trade names and for the repression of unfair competition and false indications of geographical origin, and for this purpose have appointed as their respective delegates,

> Peru:
>> Alfredo Gonzalez-Prada.
> Bolivia:
>> Emeterio Cano de la Vega.

---

[1] In English, French, Portuguese, and Spanish; English text only printed Ratification advised by the Senate, December 16 (legislative day of December 15); ratified by the President, February 11, 1931; ratification of the United States deposited with the Pan American Union, February 17, 1931; proclaimed by the President, February 27, 1931.

[2] *Foreign Relations*, 1923, vol. I, p. 297.

[3] *Ibid.*, 1910, p. 50.

Paraguay:
  Juan V. Ramirez.
Ecuador:
  Gonzalo Zaldumbide.
Uruguay:
  J. Varela Acevedo.
Dominican Republic:
  Francisco de Moya.
Chile:
  Oscar Blanco Viel.
Panama:
  Ricardo J. Alfaro.
  Juan B. Chevalier.
Venezuela:
  Pedro R. Rincones.
Costa Rica:
  Manuel Castro Quesada.
  Fernando E. Piza.
Cuba:
  Gustavo Gutierrez.
  Alfredo Bufill.
Guatemala:
  Adrian Recinos.
  Ramiro Fernandez.
Haiti:
  Raoul Lizaire.
Colombia:
  Roberto Botero Escobar.
  Pablo Garcia de la Parra.
Brazil:
  Carlos Delgado de Carvalho.
Mexico:
  Francisco Suastegui.
Nicaragua:
  Vicente Vita.
Honduras:
  Carlos Izaguirre V.
United States of America:
  Francis White.
  Thomas E. Robertson.
  Edward S. Rogers.

Who, after having deposited their credentials, which were found to be in good and due form by the Conference, have agreed as follows:

CHAPTER I.—*Equality of Citizens and Aliens as to Trade Mark and Commercial Protection*

ARTICLE 1

The Contracting States bind themselves to grant to the nationals of the other Contracting States and to domiciled foreigners who own a manufacturing or commercial establishment or an agricultural development in any of the States which have ratified or adhered to the present Convention the same rights and remedies which their laws extend to their own nationals or domiciled persons with respect to trade marks, trade names, and the repression of unfair competition and false indications of geographical origin or source.

## CHAPTER II.—*Trade Mark Protection*

### ARTICLE 2

The person who desires to obtain protection for his marks in a country other than his own, in which this Convention is in force, can obtain protection either by applying directly to the proper office of the State in which he desires to obtain protection, or through the Inter-American Trade Mark Bureau referred to in the Protocol on the Inter-American Registration of Trade Marks, if this Protocol has been accepted by his country and the country in which he seeks protection.

### ARTICLE 3

Every mark duly registered or legally protected in one of the Contracting States shall be admitted to registration or deposit and legally protected in the other Contracting States, upon compliance with the formal provisions of the domestic law of such States.

Registration or deposit may be refused or cancelled of marks:

1. The distinguishing elements of which infringe rights already acquired by another person in the country where registration or deposit is claimed.

2. Which lack any distinctive character or consist exclusively of words, symbols, or signs which serve in trade to designate the class, kind, quality, quantity, use, value, place of origin of the products, time of production, or which are or have become at the time registration or deposit is sought, generic or usual terms in current language or in the commercial usage of the country where registration or deposit is sought, when the owner of the marks seeks to appropriate them as a distinguishing element of his mark.

In determining the distinctive character of a mark, all the circumstances existing should be taken into account, particularly the duration of the use of the mark and if in fact it has acquired in the country where deposit, registration or protection is sought, a significance distinctive of the applicant's goods.

3. Which offend public morals or which may be contrary to public order.

4. Which tend to expose persons, institutions, beliefs, national symbols or those of associations of public interest, to ridicule or contempt.

5. Which contain representations of racial types or scenes typical or characteristic of any of the Contracting States, other than that of the origin of the mark.

6. Which have as a principal distinguishing element, phrases, names or slogans which constitute the trade name or an essential or characteristic part thereof, belonging to some person engaged in any of the other Contracting States in the manufacture, trade or production of articles or merchandise of the same class as that to which the mark is applied.

## ARTICLE 4

The Contracting States agree to refuse to register or to cancel the registration and to prohibit the use, without authorization by competent authority, of marks which include national and state flags and coats-of-arms, national or state seals, designs on public coins and postage stamps, official labels, certificates or guarantees, or any national or state official insignia or simulations of any of the foregoing.

## ARTICLE 5

Labels, industrial designs, slogans, prints, catalogues or advertisements used to identify or to advertise goods, shall receive the same protection accorded to trade marks in countries where they are considered as such, upon complying with the requirements of the domestic trade mark law.

## ARTICLE 6

The Contracting States agree to admit to registration or deposit and to protect collective marks and marks of associations, the existence of which is not contrary to the laws of the country of origin, even when such associations do not own a manufacturing, industrial, commercial or agricultural establishment.

Each country shall determine the particular conditions under which such marks may be protected.

States, Provinces or Municipalities, in their character of corporations, may own, use, register or deposit marks and shall in that sense enjoy the benefits of this Convention.

## ARTICLE 7

Any owner of a mark protected in one of the Contracting States in accordance with its domestic law, who may know that some other person is using or applying to register or deposit an interfering mark in any other of the Contracting States, shall have the right to oppose such use, registration or deposit and shall have the right to employ all legal means, procedure or recourse provided in the country in which such interfering mark is being used or where its registration or deposit is being sought, and upon proof that the person who is using such mark or applying to register or deposit it, had knowledge of the existence and continuous use in any of the Contracting States of the mark on which opposition is based upon goods of the same class, the opposer may claim for himself the preferential right to use such mark in the country where the opposition is made or priority to register or deposit it in such country, upon compliance with the requirements established by the domestic legislation in such country and by this Convention.

## ARTICLE 8

When the owner of a mark seeks the registration or deposit of the mark in a Contracting State other than that of origin of the mark and such registration or deposit is refused because of the previous registration or deposit of an interfering mark, he shall have the right to apply for and obtain the cancellation or annulment of the interfering mark upon proving, in accordance with the legal procedure of the country in which cancellation is sought, the stipulations in Paragraph (a) and those of either Paragraph (b) or (c) below:

(a) That he enjoyed legal protection for his mark in another of the Contracting States prior to the date of the application for the registration or deposit which he seeks to cancel; and

(b) that the claimant of the interfering mark, the cancellation of which is sought, had knowledge of the use, employment, registration or deposit in any of the Contracting States of the mark for the specific goods to which said interfering mark is applied, prior to adoption and use thereof or prior to the filing of the application or deposit of the mark which is sought to be cancelled; or

(c) that the owner of the mark who seeks cancellation based on a prior right to the ownership and use of such mark, has traded or trades with or in the country in which cancellation is sought, and that goods designated by his mark have circulated and circulate in said country from a date prior to the filing of the application for registration or deposit for the mark, the cancellation which is claimed, or prior to the adoption and use of the same.

## ARTICLE 9

When the refusal of registration or deposit of a mark is based on a registration previously effected in accordance with this Convention, the owner of the refused mark shall have the right to request and obtain the cancellation of the mark previously registered or deposited, by proving, in accordance with the legal procedure of the country in which he is endeavoring to obtain registration or deposit of his mark, that the registrant of the mark which he desires to cancel, has abandoned it. The period within which a mark may be declared abandoned for lack of use shall be determined by the internal law of each country, and if there is no provision in the internal law, the period shall be two years and one day beginning from the date of registration or deposit if the mark has never been used, or one year and one day if the abandonment or lack of use took place after the mark has been used.

## ARTICLE 10

The period of protection granted to marks registered, deposited or renewed under this Convention, shall be the period fixed by the laws of the State in which registration, deposit or renewal is made at the time when made.

Once the registration or deposit of a mark in any Contracting State has been effected, each such registration or deposit shall exist independently of every other and shall not be affected by changes that may occur in the registration or deposit of such mark in the other Contracting States, unless otherwise provided by domestic law.

## ARTICLE 11

The transfer of the ownership of a registered or deposited mark in the country of its original registration shall be effective and shall be recognized in the other Contracting States, provided that reliable proof be furnished that such transfer has been executed and registered in accordance with the internal law of the State in which such transfer took place. Such transfer shall be recorded in accordance with the legislation of the country in which it is to be effective.

The use and exploitation of trade marks may be transferred separately for each country, and such transfer shall be recorded upon the production of reliable proof that such transfer has been executed in accordance with the internal law of the State in which such transfer took place. Such transfer shall be recorded in accordance with the legislation of the country in which it is to be effective.

## ARTICLE 12

Any registration or deposit which has been effected in one of the Contracting States, or any pending application for registration or deposit, made by an agent, representative or customer of the owner of a mark in which a right has been acquired in another Contracting State through its registration, prior application or use, shall give to the original owner the right to demand its cancellation or refusal in accordance with the provisions of this Convention and to request and obtain the protection for himself, it being considered that such protection shall revert to the date of the application of the mark so denied or cancelled.

## Article 13

The use of a trade mark by its owner in a form different in minor or non-substantial elements from the form in which the mark has been registered in any of the Contracting States, shall not entail forfeiture of the registration or impair the protection of the mark.

In case the form or distinctive elements of the mark are substantially changed, or the list of goods to which it is to be applied is modified or increased, the proprietor of the mark may be required to apply for a new registration, without prejudice to the protection of the original mark or in respect to the original list of goods.

The requirements of the laws of the Contracting States with respect to the legend which indicates the authority for the use of trade marks shall be deemed fulfilled in respect to goods of foreign origin if such marks carry the words or indications legally used or required to be used in the country of origin of the goods.

Chapter III.—*Protection of Commercial Names*

## Article 14

Trade names or commercial names of persons entitled to the benefits of this Convention shall be protected in all the Contracting States. Such protection shall be enjoyed without necessity of deposit or registration, whether or not the name forms part of a trade mark.

## Article 15

The names of an individual, surnames and trade names used by manufacturers, industrialists, merchants or agriculturists to denote their trade or calling, as well as the firm's name, the name or title legally adopted and used by associations, corporations, companies or manufacturing, industrial, commercial or agricultural entities, in accordance with the provisions of the respective national laws, shall be understood to be commercial names.

## Article 16

The protection which this Convention affords to commercial names shall be:

(*a*) to prohibit the use or adoption of a commercial name identical with or deceptively similar to one legally adopted and previously used by another engaged in the same business in any of the Contracting States; and

(*b*) to prohibit the use, registration or filing of a trade mark the distinguishing elements of which consist of the whole or an essential part of a commercial name legally adopted and previously used by another owner domiciled or established in any of the Contracting States, engaged in the manufacture, sale or production of products or merchandise of the same kind as those for which the trade mark is intended.

## ARTICLE 17

Any manufacturer, industrialist, merchant or agriculturist domiciled or established in any of the Contracting States, may, in accordance with the law and the legal procedure of such countries, oppose the adoption, use, registration or deposit of a trade mark for products or merchandise of the same class as those sold under his commercial name, when he believes that such trade mark or the inclusion in it of the trade or commercial name or a simulation thereof may lead to error or confusion in the mind of the consumer with respect to such commercial name legally adopted and previously in use.

## ARTICLE 18

Any manufacturer, industrialist, merchant or agriculturist domiciled or established in any of the Contracting States may, in accordance with the law and procedure of the country where the proceeding is brought, apply for and obtain an injunction against the use of any commercial name or the cancellation of the registration or deposit of any trade mark, when such name or mark is intended for use in the manufacture, sale or production of articles or merchandise of the same class, by proving:

(a) that the commercial name or trade mark, the enjoining or cancellation of which is desired, is identical with or deceptively similar to his commercial name already legally adopted and previously used in any of the Contracting States, in the manufacture, sale or production of articles of the same class, and

(b) that prior to the adoption and use of the commercial name, or to the adoption and use or application for registration or deposit of the trade mark, the cancellation of which is sought, or the use of which is sought to be enjoined, he used and continues to use for the manufacture, sale or production of the same products or merchandise his commercial name adopted and previously used in any of the Contracting States or in the State in which cancellation or injunction is sought.

## ARTICLE 19

The protection of commercial names shall be given in accordance with the internal legislation and by the terms of this Convention, and in all cases where the internal legislation permits, by the competent governmental or administrative authorities whenever they have knowledge or reliable proof of their legal existence and use, or otherwise upon the motion of any interested party.

CHAPTER IV.—*Repression of Unfair Competition*

ARTICLE 20

Every act or deed contrary to commercial good faith or to the normal and honorable development of industrial or business activities shall be considered as unfair competition and, therefore, unjust and prohibited.

ARTICLE 21

The following are declared to be acts of unfair competition and unless otherwise effectively dealt with under the domestic laws of the Contracting States shall be repressed under the provisions of this Convention:

(*a*) Acts calculated directly or indirectly to represent that the goods or business of a manufacturer, industrialist, merchant or agriculturist are the goods or business of another manufacturer, industrialist, merchant or agriculturist of any of the other Contracting States, whether such representation be made by the appropriation or simulation of trade marks, symbols, distinctive names, the imitation of labels, wrappers, containers, commercial names, or other means of identification;

(*b*) The use of false descriptions of goods, by words, symbols or other means tending to deceive the public in the country where the acts occur, with respect to the nature, quality, or utility of the goods;

(*c*) The use of false indications of geographical origin or source of goods, by words, symbols, or other means which tend in that respect to deceive the public in the country in which these acts occur;

(*d*) To sell, or offer for sale to the public an article, product or merchandise of such form or appearance that even though it does not bear directly or indirectly an indication of origin or source, gives or produces, either by pictures, ornaments, or language employed in the text, the impression of being a product, article or commodity originating, manufactured or produced in one of the other Contracting States;

(*e*) Any other act or deed contrary to good faith in industrial, commercial or agricultural matters which, because of its nature or purpose, may be considered analogous or similar to those above mentioned.

ARTICLE 22

The Contracting States which may not yet have enacted legislation repressing the acts of unfair competition mentioned in this chapter, shall apply to such acts the penalties contained in their legislation on trade marks or in any other statutes, and shall grant relief by way of injunction against the continuance of said acts at the request of any party injured; those causing such injury shall also be answerable in damages to the injured party.

CHAPTER V.—*Repression of False Indications of Geographical Origin or Source*

### ARTICLE 23

Every indication of geographical origin or source which does not actually correspond to the place in which the article, product or merchandise was fabricated, manufactured, produced or harvested, shall be considered fraudulent and illegal, and therefore prohibited.

### ARTICLE 24

For the purposes of this Convention the place of geographical origin or source shall be considered as indicated when the geographical name of a definite locality, region, country or nation, either expressly and directly, or indirectly, appears on any trade mark, label, cover, packing or wrapping, of any article, product or merchandise, directly or indirectly thereon, provided that said geographical name serves as a basis for or is the dominant element of the sentences, words or expressions used.

### ARTICLE 25

Geographical names indicating geographical origin or source are not susceptible of individual appropriation, and may be freely used to indicate the origin or source of the products or merchandise or his commercial domicile, by any manufacturer, industrialist, merchant or agriculturist established in the place indicated or dealing in the products there originating.

### ARTICLE 26

The indication of the place of geographical origin or source, affixed to or stamped upon the product or merchandise, must correspond exactly to the place in which the product or merchandise has been fabricated, manufactured or harvested.

### ARTICLE 27

Names, phrases or words, constituting in whole or in part geographical terms which through constant, general and reputable use in commerce have come to form the name or designation itself of the article, product or merchandise to which they are applied, are exempt from the provisions of the preceding articles; this exception, however, does not include regional indications of origin of industrial or agricultural products the quality and reputation of which to the consuming public depend on the place of production or origin.

## Article 28

In the absence of any special remedies insuring the repression of false indications of geographical origin or source, remedies provided by the domestic sanitary laws, laws dealing with misbranding and the laws relating to trade marks or trade names, shall be applicable in the Contracting States.

### Chapter VI.—*Remedies*

## Article 29

The manufacture, exportation, importation, distribution, or sale is forbidden of articles or products which directly or indirectly infringe any of the provisions of this Convention with respect to trade mark protection; protection and safeguard of commercial names; repression of unfair competition; and repression of false indications of geographical origin or source.

## Article 30

Any act prohibited by this Convention will be repressed by the competent administrative or judicial authorities of the government of the state in which the offense was committed, by the legal methods and procedure existing in said country, either by official action, or at the request of interested parties, who may avail themselves of the rights and remedies afforded by the laws to secure indemnification for the damage and loss suffered; the articles, products or merchandise or their marks, which are the instrumentality of the acts of unfair competition, shall be liable to seizure or destruction, or the offending markings obliterated, as the case may be.

## Article 31

Any manufacturer, industrialist, merchant or agriculturist, interested in the production, manufacture, or trade in the merchandise or articles affected by any prohibited act or deed, as well as his agents or representatives in any of the Contracting States and the consular officers of the state to which the locality or region falsely indicated as the place to which belongs the geographical origin or source, shall have sufficient legal authority to take and prosecute the necessary actions and proceedings before the administrative authorities and the courts of the Contracting States.

The same authority shall be enjoyed by official commissions or institutions and by syndicates or associations which represent the interests of industry, agriculture or commerce and which have been legally established for the defense of honest and fair trade methods.

## CHAPTER VII.—General Provisions

### ARTICLE 32

The administrative authorities and the courts shall have sole jurisdiction over administrative proceedings and administrative judgments, civil or criminal, arising in matters relating to the application of the national law.

Any differences which may arise with respect to the interpretation or application of the principles of this Convention shall be settled by the courts of justice of each State, and only in case of the denial of justice shall they be submitted to arbitration.

### ARTICLE 33

Each of the Contracting States, in which it does not yet exist, hereby agrees to establish a protective service, for the suppression of unfair competition and false indication of geographic origin or source, and to publish for opposition in the official publication of the government, or in some other periodical, the trade marks solicited and granted as well as the administrative decisions made in the matter.

### ARTICLE 34

The present Convention shall be subject to periodic revision with the object of introducing therein such improvements as experience may indicate, taking advantage of any international conferences held by the American States, to which each country shall send a delegation in which it is recommended that there be included experts in the subject of trade marks, in order that effective results may be achieved.

The national administration of the country in which such conferences are held shall prepare, with the assistance of the Pan American Union and the Inter-American Trade Mark Bureau, the work of the respective conference.

The Director of the Inter-American Trade Mark Bureau may attend the sessions of such conferences and may take part in the discussions, but shall have no vote.

### ARTICLE 35

The provisions of this Convention shall have the force of law in those States in which international treaties possess that character, as soon as they are ratified by their constitutional organs.

The Contracting States in which the fulfillment of international agreements is dependent upon the enactment of appropriate laws, on accepting in principle this Convention, agree to request of their legislative bodies the enactment of the necessary legislation in the shortest possible period of time and in accordance with their constitutional provisions.

## ARTICLE 36

The Contracting States agree that, as soon as this Convention becomes effective, the Trade Mark Conventions of 1910 and 1923 shall automatically cease to have effect; but any rights which have been acquired, or which may be acquired thereunder, up to the time of the coming into effect of this Convention, shall continue to be valid until their due expiration.

## ARTICLE 37

The present Convention shall be ratified by the Contracting States in conformity with their respective constitutional procedures.

The original Convention and the instruments of ratification shall be deposited with the Pan American Union which shall transmit certified copies of the former and shall communicate notice of such ratifications to the other signatory Governments, and the Convention shall enter into effect for the Contracting States in the order that they deposit their ratifications.

This Convention shall remain in force indefinitely, but it may be denounced by means of notice given one year in advance, at the expiration of which it shall cease to be in force as regards the Party denouncing the same, but shall remain in force as regards the other States. All denunciations shall be sent to the Pan American Union which will thereupon transmit notice thereof to the other Contracting States.

The American States which have not subscribed to this Convention may adhere thereto by sending the respective official instrument to the Pan American Union which, in turn, will notify the governments of the remaining Contracting States in the manner previously indicated.

In witness whereof the above named delegates have signed this Convention in English, Spanish, Portuguese and French, and thereto have affixed their respective seals.

Done in the City of Washington, on the twentieth day of February in the year one thousand nine hundred and twenty-nine.

| | |
|---|---|
| [SEAL] | A. GONZÁLEZ PRADA |
| [SEAL] | EMETERIO CANO DE LA VEGA |
| [SEAL] | JUAN VICENTE RAMÍREZ |
| [SEAL] | GONZALO ZALDUMBIDE |
| [SEAL] | VARELA |

[SEAL]    FRANCISCO DE MOYA
[SEAL]    OSCAR BLANCO VIEL
    I sign this convention in so far as its provisions are not contrary to the National Legislation of my country, making express reservation with regard to the provisions of this convention regarding which there is no legislation in Chile.

[SEAL]    R. J. ALFARO
[SEAL]    JUAN B. CHEVALIER
[SEAL]    P. R. RINCONES
[SEAL]    MANUEL CASTRO QUESADA
[SEAL]    F. E. PIZA
[SEAL]    GUSTAVO GUTIÉRREZ
[SEAL]    A. L. BUFILL
[SEAL]    ADRIÁN RECINOS
[SEAL]    RAMIRO FERNÁNDEZ
[SEAL]    RAOUL LIZAIRE
[SEAL]    PABLO GARCÍA DE LA PARRA
[SEAL]    CARLOS DELGADO DE CARVALHO
[SEAL]    F. SUÁSTEGUI
[SEAL]    VICENTE VITA
[SEAL]    CARLOS IZAGUIRRE V.
[SEAL]    EDWARD S. ROGERS
[SEAL]    THOMAS E. ROBERTSON
[SEAL]    FRANCIS WHITE

## PROTOCOL ON THE INTER-AMERICAN REGISTRATION OF TRADE MARKS

WHEREAS, The Governments of Peru, Bolivia, Paraguay, Ecuador, Uruguay, Dominican Republic, Chile, Panama, Venezuela, Costa Rica, Cuba, Guatemala, Haiti, Colombia, Brazil, Mexico, Nicaragua, Honduras and the United States of America have this day signed at Washington through their respective delegates a General Inter-American Convention for Trade Mark and Commercial Protection;

WHEREAS, the maintenance of an international American agency is considered desirable that manufacturers, industrialists, merchants and agriculturists may enjoy the trade mark and commercial protection which that Convention grants them, and that it may serve as a center of information, and cooperate in the fulfillment and improvement of the provisions of the Convention;

WHEREAS, the adoption of a general convention and a protocol may facilitate ratification among the Contracting States and adherence among the American Republics which have not taken part in the negotiations, since acceptance of the Convention does not imply acceptance of this instrument,

The above mentioned governments have agreed as follows:

## ARTICLE 1

Natural or juridical persons domiciled in or those who possess a manufacturing or commercial establishment or an agricultural enterprise in any of the States that may have ratified or adhered to the present Protocol, may obtain the protection of their trade marks through the registration of such marks in the Inter-American Trade Mark Bureau.

## ARTICLE 2

The owner of a mark registered or deposited in one of the Contracting States who desires to register it in any of the other Contracting States, shall file an application to this effect in the office of the country of original registration which office shall transmit it to the Inter-American Trade Mark Bureau, complying with the Regulations. A postal money order or draft on a bank of recognized standing, in the amount of $50.00, as a fee for the Inter-American Trade Mark Bureau, plus the amount of the fees required by the national law of each of the countries in which he desires to obtain protection for his mark, shall accompany such application.

## ARTICLE 3

Immediately on receipt of the application for the registration of a mark, and on determining that it fulfills all the requirements, the Inter-American Trade Mark Bureau shall issue a certificate and shall transmit by registered mail copies of the same accompanied by a money order for the amount required by the respective Offices of the States in which protection is desired. In the case of adhesions or ratifications of additional states after the registration of a mark, the Inter-American Bureau shall, through the respective offices of their countries, inform the proprietors of marks registered through the Bureau, of said adhesions or ratifications, informing them of the right that they have to register their marks in the new adhering or ratifying States, in which registration shall be effected in the manner above mentioned.

## ARTICLE 4

Each of the Contracting States, through its Trade Mark Office, shall immediately acknowledge to the Inter-American Bureau, the receipt of the application for registration of each mark, and shall proceed to carry through the proceedings with every possible dispatch, directing that the application be published at the expense of the applicant in the usual official papers, and at the proper time shall notify the Inter-American Bureau of the action that it may have taken in accordance with its internal legislation and the provisions of this Convention.

In case protection is granted to the mark, it shall issue a certificate of registration in which shall be indicated the legal period of registration; which certificate shall be issued with the same formalities as national certificates and shall have the same effect in so far as ownership of the mark is concerned. This certificate of registration shall be sent to the Inter-American Trade Mark Bureau, which shall transmit it to the proprietor of the mark through the proper office of the country of origin.

If, within seven months after the receipt by a Contracting State of an application for the protection of a trade mark transmitted by the Inter-American Trade Mark Bureau, the administration of such State does not communicate to the Bureau notice of refusal of protection based on the provisions of its domestic legislation or on the provisions of the General Inter-American Convention for Trade Mark and Commercial Protection such mark shall be considered as registered and the Inter-American Trade Mark Bureau shall so communicate to the applicant through the country of origin, and shall issue a special certificate which shall have the same force and legal value as a national certificate.

In case protection of a mark is refused in accordance with the provisions of the internal legislation of a State or of the General Inter-American Convention for Trade Mark and Commercial Protection, the applicant may have the same recourse which the respective laws grant to the citizens of the state refusing protection. The period within which the recourse and actions granted by national laws may be exercised shall begin four months after receipt by the Inter-American Trade Mark Bureau of the notice of refusal.

The Inter-American registration of a trade mark communicated to the Contracting States, which may already enjoy protection in such States shall replace any other registration of the same mark effected previously by any other means, without prejudice to the rights already acquired by national registration.

## ARTICLE 5

In order to effect the transfer of ownership of a trade mark or the assignment of the use of the same, the same procedure as that set forth in the foregoing articles shall be followed, except that in this case there shall only be remitted to the Inter-American Bureau $10.00, to be retained by said Bureau, plus the fees fixed by the domestic legislation of each one of the countries in which it is desired to register the transfer or assignment of the mark, it being understood that the use of trade marks may be transferred separately in each country.

## ARTICLE 6

If the applicant claims color as a distinctive element of his mark he shall be required to:

1. Send a statement attached to the application for registration declaring the color or the combination of colors which he claims; and

2. Attach to the application for registration copies or specimens of the mark as actually used, showing the colors claimed, which shall be attached to the notifications sent by the Inter-American Bureau. The number of copies to be sent shall be fixed by the Regulations.

## ARTICLE 7

Trade marks shall be published in a bulletin edited by the Inter-American Bureau, wherein shall appear the matter contained in the application for registration and an electrotype of the mark supplied by the applicant.

Each administration of the Contracting States shall receive free of charge from the Inter-American Bureau as many copies of the above mentioned publication as it may ask for.

The publication of a mark in the bulletin of the Inter-American Bureau shall have the same effect as publication in the official journals or bulletins of the Contracting States.

## ARTICLE 8

The Inter-American Bureau, on receipt of payment of a fee to be fixed by the Regulations, shall furnish to any person who may so request, copies of the entries made in the register with reference to any particular mark.

## ARTICLE 9

The Inter-American Trade Mark Bureau shall keep a record of renewals which have been effected in compliance with the requirements of the domestic laws of the Contracting States, and after payment of a fee of $10.00 to the Inter-American Trade Mark Bureau and the customary fees required by the States where said renewal is effected.

Six months prior to the expiration of the period of protection, the Inter-American Bureau shall communicate this information to the administration of the country of origin and to the owner of the mark.

## ARTICLE 10

The owner of a trade mark may at any time relinquish protection in one or several of the Contracting States, by means of a notice sent to the administration of the country of origin of the mark, to be communicated to the Inter-American Bureau, which in turn shall notify the countries concerned.

## ARTICLE 11

An applicant for registration or deposit, transfer or renewal of a trade mark through the Inter-American Bureau, may appoint by a proper power of attorney at any time, an agent or attorney to represent him in any procedure, administrative, judicial or otherwise, arising in connection with such trade marks or application in any Contracting State.

Such agents or attorneys shall be entitled to notice of all the proceedings and to receive and present all documents that may be required by the Trade Mark Bureau of each country under the provisions of this Protocol.

## ARTICLE 12

The administration in the country of origin shall notify the Inter-American Bureau of all annulments, cancellations, renunciations, transfers and all other changes in the ownership or use of the mark.

The Inter-American Bureau shall record these changes, notify the administrations of the Contracting States and publish them immediately in its bulletin.

The same procedure shall be followed when the proprietor of the mark requests a reduction in the list of products to which the trade mark is applied.

The subsequent addition of a new product to the list may not be obtained except by a new registration of the mark according to the provisions of Article 2 of this Protocol. The same procedure shall be followed in the case of the substitution of one product for another.

## ARTICLE 13

The Contracting States bind themselves to send through their respective national trade mark offices, as soon as they are published, two copies of the official bulletins or publications in which judicial or administrative decisions or resolutions, laws, decrees, regulations, circulars, or any other provisions emanating from the executive, legislative or judicial authorities may appear and which refer to the protection of trade marks, the protection of commercial names, the repression of unfair competition and of false indications of origin, whether of an administrative, civil or penal nature.

## ARTICLE 14

In order to comply with this Protocol, and to facilitate the inter-American registration of trade marks, the Contracting States establish as their international agency the Bureau located in Habana, Republic of Cuba, referred to as the "Inter-American Trade Mark Bureau," and confer upon its official correspondence the postal frank.

## ARTICLE 15

The Inter-American Trade Mark Bureau shall perform the duties specified in this Protocol and in the Regulations appended hereto, and shall be supported in part by the fees received for handling trade marks and in part by the quotas assigned to the Contracting States. These quotas shall be paid directly and in advance to the Bureau in yearly installments and shall be determined in the following manner:

The population of each Contracting State ratifying this Protocol shall be determined by its latest official census, the number of inhabitants to be divided into units of 100,000 each, fractions above 50,000 to be considered as a full unit, and those under to be disregarded. The annual budget shall be divided by the total number of units, thereby determining the quota per unit. The contribution of each State to the Inter-American Bureau shall be determined by multiplying the quota per unit by the number of units allotted to each State.

Upon receipt of new ratifications and adhesions to this Protocol, the same procedure shall be followed with respect to such States, the quota of each to be determined by adding these additional units and thus determining the quota per unit.

It is expressly agreed that this annual contribution will continue to be paid only so long as the other revenues of the Bureau are not sufficient to cover the expenses of its maintenance. So long as this situation exists, the latest census of population will be used each year and, on the basis of official data furnished by each Contracting State, the changes in population shall be made and the quotas determined anew before fixing the contributions to be paid by those States. Once the Bureau becomes self-supporting through its own receipts, the balance remaining from the quotas shall be returned to the States in proportion to the amounts received from them.

At the end of each year the Inter-American Bureau shall prepare a statement of fees and contributions received and after making provision for its budgetary requirements for the following year and setting aside a reserve fund, shall return the balance to the Contracting States in proportion to the quotas paid by them.

The budget of the Bureau and the reserve fund to be maintained shall be submitted by the Director of the Bureau and approved by the

Chief Executive of the State in which the Bureau is established. The Director of the Bureau shall also submit an annual report to all ratifying States, for their information.

## ARTICLE 16

In case the Bureau should cease to exist, it shall be liquidated under the supervision of the Government of Cuba, the balance of the funds remaining to be distributed among the Contracting States in the same proportion as they contributed to its support. The buildings and other tangible property of the Bureau shall become the property of the Government of Cuba in recognition of the services of that Republic in giving effect to this Protocol; the Government of Cuba agreeing to dedicate such property to purposes essentially inter-American in character.

The Contracting States agree to accept as final any steps that may be taken for the liquidation of the Bureau.

## ARTICLE 17

The provisions of this Protocol shall have the force of law in those States in which international treaties possess that character, as soon as they are ratified by their constitutional organs.

The Contracting States in which the fulfillment of international agreements is dependent upon the enactment of appropriate laws, on accepting in principle this Protocol, agree to request of their legislative bodies the enactment of the necessary legislation in the shortest possible period of time and in accordance with their constitutional provisions.

## ARTICLE 18

The Contracting States agree that, as soon as this Protocol becomes effective, the Trade Mark Conventions of 1910 and 1923 shall automatically cease to have effect in so far as they relate to the organization of the Inter-American Bureau; but any rights which have been or which may be acquired in accordance with the provisions of said Conventions, up to the time of the coming into effect of this Protocol, shall continue to be valid until their due expiration.

## ARTICLE 19

The present Protocol shall be ratified by the Contracting States, in accordance with their respective constitutional procedure, after they shall have ratified the "General Inter-American Convention for Trade Mark and Commercial Protection."

The original Protocol and the instruments of ratification shall be deposited with the Pan American Union, which shall transmit certified copies of the former and shall communicate notice of such ratifications to the Governments of the other signatory States and the Protocol shall become effective for the Contracting States in the order in which they deposit their ratifications.

This Protocol shall remain in force indefinitely, but it may be denounced by means of notice given one year in advance, at the expiration of which it shall cease to be in force as regards the State denouncing the same, but shall remain in force as regards the other States. All denunciations shall be sent to the Pan American Union which will thereupon transmit notice thereof to the other States.

The American States which have not signed this Protocol may adhere thereto by sending the respective official instrument to the Pan American Union which, in turn, will thereupon notify the Governments of the remaining Contracting States in the manner previously indicated.

ANNEX

REGULATIONS

### Article 1

The application to obtain protection under the Protocol of which the present Annex is a part shall be made by the owner of the mark or his legal representative to the administration of the State in which the mark has been originally registered or deposited in accordance with the provisions in force in that State, accompanied by a money order or draft payable to the Director of the Inter-American Trade Mark Bureau in the sum required by this Protocol. The application and money order shall be accompanied by an electrotype (10 x 10 centimeters) of the mark reproducing it as registered in the State of original registration.

### Article 2

The National Bureau of such State having ascertained that the registration of the mark is legal and valid shall send to the Inter-American Trade Mark Bureau, as soon as possible:

A. The money order;
B. The electrotype of the mark;
C. A certificate in duplicate containing the following details:
  1. The name and address of the owner of the mark;
  2. The date of the application for registration in the State of original registration;
  3. The date of registration of the mark in such State;
  4. The order number of the registration in such State;
  5. The date of expiration of the protection of the mark in such State;
  6. A facsimile of the mark as used;
  7. A statement of the goods on which the mark is used;
  8. The date of the application to the National Bureau of the State of the original registration to obtain protection under the Convention and this Protocol.

D. When the applicant wishes to claim color as a distinctive element of his mark, thirty copies of the mark printed on paper, showing the color, and a brief description of the same.

### Article 3

Within ten days after receipt from such administration of the matter required by Article 2, the Inter-American Trade Mark Bureau shall enter all information in its books and inform the National Bureau of such State of the receipt of the application and of the number and date of the inter-American registration.

## Article 4

Within thirty days after such receipt, detailed copies of the inter-American registration shall be sent to the National Bureaus of those States which have ratified the Protocol.

## Article 5

The Inter-American Trade Mark Bureau shall publish a periodic bulletin wherein shall appear the data included in the certificate provided for by Section C of Article 2 of these Regulations and also all other information which may be appropriate concerning registration of such marks in the various States.

The Inter-American Trade Mark Bureau may also publish in its bulletin or separately, books, documents, information, studies, and articles concerning the protection of industrial property.

## Article 6

The acceptance, opposition, or refusal of a mark by the National Bureau of any one of the Contracting States shall be transmitted within ten days following the date of its receipt by the Inter-American Trade Mark Bureau to the administration of the State of origin of the application with a view to its communication to whom it may concern.

## Article 7

Changes in ownership of a mark communicated by the Bureau of the country of origin to the Inter-American Trade Mark Bureau and accompanied by the required fees shall be examined, entered in the register, and corresponding notice sent to the Bureaus of the other Contracting States in which the transfer is to take place, accompanied by the proper fees, all within the time herein fixed with respect to application.

## Article 8

The Director of the Inter-American Trade Mark Bureau shall be appointed by the Executive Power of the State in which the Bureau is located, from among lawyers of experience in the subject matter and of recognized moral standing. The Director, at his discretion, may appoint or remove the officials or employees of his Bureau, giving notice thereof to the Government of Cuba; adopt and promulgate such other rules, regulations and circulars as he may deem convenient for the proper functioning of the Bureau and which are not inconsistent with this Protocol.

## Article 9

The Inter-American Trade Mark Bureau may carry on any investigation on the subject of trade marks which the Government of any of the Contracting States may request, and encourage the investigation of all problems, difficulties or obstacles which may hinder the operation of the General Inter-American Convention for Trade Mark and Commercial Protection, or of this Protocol.

## Article 10

The Inter-American Trade Mark Bureau shall cooperate with the Governments of the Contracting States in the preparation of material for international conferences on this subject; submit to those States such suggestions as it may consider useful, and such opinions as may be requested as to the modifications which should be introduced in the inter-American pacts or in the laws concerning these subjects and in general facilitate the execution of the purposes of this Protocol.

### Article 11

The Inter-American Trade Mark Bureau shall inform the signatory Governments at least once a year as to the work which the Bureau has done or is doing.

### Article 12

The Inter-American Trade Mark Bureau shall maintain as far as possible relations with similar offices and scientific and industrial institutions and organizations for the exchange of publications, information, and data relative to the progress of the law on the subject of the protection of trade marks, defense and protection of commercial names and suppression of unfair competition and false indications of origin.

### Article 13

These Regulations may be modified at any time at the request of any of the Contracting States or the Director of the Bureau, provided that the modification does not violate the General Convention or the Protocol of which the Regulations form a part, and that the modification is approved by the Governing Board of the Pan American Union, after having been circulated among the Contracting States for a period of six months before submission for the approval of the Pan American Union.

In witness whereof the above named delegates have signed this Protocol in English, Spanish, Portuguese and French, and thereto have affixed their respective seals.

Done in the City of Washington on the twentieth day of February in the year one thousand nine hundred and twenty-nine.

[SEAL]   A. González Prada
[SEAL]   Emeterio Cano de la Vega
[SEAL]   Juan Vicente Ramírez
[SEAL]   Gonzalo Zaldumbide
[SEAL]   Francisco de Moya
[SEAL]   R. J. Alfaro
[SEAL]   Juan B. Chevalier
[SEAL]   P. R. Rincones
[SEAL]   Manuel Castro Quesada
[SEAL]   F. E. Piza
[SEAL]   Gustavo Gutiérrez.
[SEAL]   A. L. Bufill
[SEAL]   Raoul Lizaire
[SEAL]   Pablo García de la Parra
[SEAL]   Carlos Delgado de Carvalho
[SEAL]   F. Suástegui
[SEAL]   Vicente Vita
[SEAL]   Carlos Izaguirre V.
[SEAL]   Francis White
[SEAL]   Thomas E. Robertson
[SEAL]   Edward S. Rogers

# ARRANGEMENT BETWEEN THE UNITED STATES, CANADA, CUBA, AND NEWFOUNDLAND RELATIVE TO THE ASSIGNMENT OF HIGH FREQUENCIES TO RADIO STATIONS ON THE NORTH AMERICAN CONTINENT

574.H1/2

*The Canadian Minister (Massey) to the Secretary of State*

No. 194                                     WASHINGTON, 27 December, 1928.

SIR, I have the honour to refer to your note of December 7th. 1928,[1] in which you inform me of the desire of the Federal Radio Commission that a further conference, in continuation of the conference which was held at Washington from August 20th. to August 25th, should be held at an early date to discuss the allocation of short wave radio channels on this continent. I now take pleasure in informing you that, in view of the considerations advanced in the note to which I have referred, His Majesty's Government in Canada desires to extend an invitation for this conference to take place at Ottawa, and suggests that January 9th. next would be a suitable date. His Majesty's Government in Canada is taking steps to ascertain the views of the Governments of Mexico and Cuba concerning representation at a conference on this date.

I shall be glad if you will be good enough to inform me as soon as may be convenient to you whether the proposal that the conference should meet at Ottawa on January 9th. is acceptable to the Government of the United States.[2]

I have [etc.]

H. H. WRONG
(For the Minister)

---

574.H1/58

*Suggestions for an Arrangement Between the United States, Canada, Cuba, Mexico, and Other North American Nations Relative to the Assignment of Frequencies on the North American Continent* [3]

(1) The sovereign right of all nations to the use of every radio channel is recognized.

---

[1] Not printed.

[2] The Conference was held at Ottawa January 21–25, 1929, with delegations from the United States, Canada, Cuba, and Newfoundland participating. Mexico was invited, but was not represented.

[3] This draft, prepared by a subcommittee of Committee No. 2 of the Conference, was transmitted to the Department in a letter of February 11, 1929, from E. O. Sykes, the chairman of the American delegation. For texts of appendixes and chart mentioned as attached, see Department of State Treaty Series No. 777–A.

Nevertheless, until technical development progresses to the stage where radio interference can be eliminated, it is agreed that special administrative arrangements are essential in order to promote standardization and to minimize radio interference.

(2) The Governments agree that each country shall be free to assign any frequency to any radio station within its jurisdiction upon the sole condition that no interference with any service of another country will result therefrom.

(3) It is agreed that each Government shall use Appendix I attached hereto, as a general guide in allocating channels to the various services specified therein.

(4) Channels are divided into two classes (1) common channels which are primarily assigned to particular services in all countries, and (2) general communication channels which are assigned for use in specific areas.

(5) With regard to the general communication channels, it is considered that at the present stage of the art, the use of radio channels below 3500 K/C will not normally cause interference at distances greater than 1000 miles and such channels may, therefore, be used with freedom from interference by stations separated by such distance. It is further recognized that stations operating on frequencies above 3500 K/C may become sources of interference at distances in excess of 1000 miles, particularly at night.

(6) The Governments agree to take advantage of the physical facts just explained, and by suitable geographical distribution of these two classes of channels throughout North America and the West Indies, to make available for general communication services, the total number of channels set forth in Appendix 2 attached hereto.

(7) Each Government shall have the right to assign to stations under its jurisdiction, in the manner it deems best, such general communication channels as are allocated to that Government under this agreement, as set forth in Appendix No. 2. The Governments agree not to assign to stations within their respective jurisdiction any of the general communication channels allocated to other Governments, unless it can be accomplished without causing interference.

(8) The marine calling frequency of 5525 K/C shall be used until superseded by an international assignment.

(9) In addition to the frequencies assigned specially for experiments (1604, 2398 and 4596 K/C) the Governments agree that experimentation by particularly qualified experimenters, may be authorized on any other channel provided no interference is caused with established services, as provided in Regulation No. 11 of the International Radio Convention of Washington 1927.[4]

---

[4] *Foreign Relations*, 1927, vol. I, p. 288; also Department of State Treaty Series No. 767.

(10) The Governments agree to adopt a radio frequency standard based on the unit of time, and to compare at least once every six months, the actual radio frequency measuring standards.

(11) The Governments agree to require all stations, other than mobile and amateur stations, under their jurisdiction, to tune their transmitters with an accuracy of 0.025 percent, or better, of their national frequency standard.

(12) The Governments agree to require all stations, likely to cause international interference, other than mobile and amateur stations, to maintain their frequency with an accuracy of 0.05 percent, or better, at all times.

(13) For the purpose of this agreement a channel shall be regarded as a band of frequencies the width of which varies with its position in the range of frequencies under consideration, but which progresses numerically from the lower to the higher frequencies, as shown in the following table:—

| Frequency (K/C) | Channel Width (K/C) |
| --- | --- |
| 1500–2198 | 4 |
| 2200–3313 | 6 |
| 3316–4400 | 8 |
| 4405–5490 | 10 |
| 5495–6000 | 15 |

(14) The Governments agree to adopt for the present in their national plan of allocation a separation of 0.2 percent between radio frequency channels; and to permit stations under their respective jurisdiction to occupy the assigned frequency and the adjacent frequencies to the limit permitted by the frequency maintenance tolerances and necessitated by the type of emission the station may be authorized to use. For commercial telephony a band width of six kilocycles shall be permitted. For the present, a 100 kilocycle band width shall be considered standard for television.

(15) The Governments agree to require stations under their jurisdiction to use transmitters which are as free as practicable from all emissions (such as those due to harmonics, decrement, spacing waves, frequency modulation, key clicks, type of keying, mush, etc.) not essential to the type of communication carried on, and which would be detrimental to communication being carried on by stations in other countries.

(16) Appendices Numbers 1 and 2, together with the chart showing graphically the distribution of the frequencies which are attached hereto, shall constitute a part of this agreement.

(17) This agreement shall go into effect on March 1st, 1929, and shall remain in force until January 1st, 1932, and thereafter for an indeterminate period and until one year from the day on which a denunciation thereof shall have been made by any one of the contracting parties.

574.H1/103 : Telegram

*The Chairman of the Canadian Delegation (Johnston) to the Chairman of the American Delegation (Sykes)[7]*

OTTAWA, 1 February, 1929.

In accordance with the undertaking given by the Canadian delegation at the closing session of the Conference on Friday last, I now have the honour to advise that the proposals for the distribution of channels as set forth in detail in appendices Numbers One and Two and graphic chart attached to draft of document headed "Suggestions for an agreement between United States, Canada, Cuba, Mexico and other North American nations relative to the assignment of frequencies on the North American continent", as per copy transmitted to you by Commander Craven, are approved and accepted by the Canadian delegation. The United States delegation, having already by majority vote approved of these proposals as generally outlined at the final session of the Conference, it is our understanding that there but remains for approval the Articles of Agreement as suggested in draft document in question. As soon as we are advised that this is confirmed by the United States delegation and that these Articles of Agreement are approved and accepted by them, the whole may be considered as approved and accepted by the Canadian authorities.

A. JOHNSTON

---

574.H1/103

*The American Minister in Canada (Phillips) to the Canadian Secretary of State for External Affairs (Mackenzie King)[7]*

No. 314

OTTAWA, February 26, 1929.

SIR: With regard to the recent short length radio conference at Ottawa, I am instructed by my Government to inform you that it approves the recommendations of the delegates at the conference and will announce the agreement effective March 1, 1929.

I avail myself [etc.]

WILLIAM PHILLIPS

---

574.T1/103

*The Canadian Secretary of State for External Affairs (Mackenzie King) to the American Minister in Canada (Phillips)[7]*

No. 16

OTTAWA, 28 February, 1929.

SIR: I have the honour to acknowledge your Note of February 26th, 1929, regarding the recent Short Wave Radio Conference at Ottawa.

---

[7] Copy transmitted to the Department by the Minister in Canada as an enclosure to his despatch No. 1033, June 13; received June 17.

It is gratifying to the Government of the Dominion of Canada to learn that the Government of the United States approve the recommendations of the delegates at the Conference. The Canadian Government have pleasure in stating that they also accept these recommendations.

It is noted that your Government will announce the agreement effective March 1st, 1929. I have the honour to request that you be good enough to inform them that we will accordingly announce the agreement as effective on the same day.

Accept [etc.]                                             O. D. SKELTON
For the Secretary of State for External Affairs

---

574.H1/77

*The Canadian Secretary of State for External Affairs (Mackenzie King) to the American Minister in Canada (Phillips)* [8]

No. 21                                             OTTAWA, 6 March, 1929.

SIR: With reference to my Note of February 28th, 1929, regarding the recent Short Wave Radio Conference at Ottawa, I have the honour to state that according to a telegraphic communication received from the Newfoundland delegate, the Government of Newfoundland accept the recommendations of the delegates at the Conference and consider the agreement to be effective as from March 1st, 1929.

I may add that we have not yet received any information from the Governments of Cuba and Mexico as to their views on the same subject.

Accept [etc.]                                             O. D. SKELTON
For the Secretary of State for External Affairs

---

574.H1/84

*The Canadian Secretary of State for External Affairs (Mackenzie King) to the American Chargé in Canada (Mayer)* [9]

No. 23                                             OTTAWA, 15 March, 1929.

SIR: With reference to my Note of March 6th, 1929, regarding the recent Short Wave Radio Conference at Ottawa, I have the honour to state that, according to a Note received from the Consul General of Cuba, the agreement on this subject is accepted by the Government of the Republic of Cuba.

Accept [etc.]                                             O. D. SKELTON
For the Secretary of State for External Affairs

---

[8] Copy transmitted to the Department by the Minister in Canada as an enclosure to his despatch No. 886, March 7; received March 11.
[9] Copy transmitted to the Department by the Chargé in Canada as an enclosure to his despatch No. 902, March 16; received March 19.

## OFFICIAL STATEMENT OF AND COMMENTARY UPON THE MONROE DOCTRINE BY THE SECRETARY OF STATE

710.11/1306a

*The Secretary of State to American Diplomatic Officers in Latin America*

WASHINGTON, February 28, 1929.

SIRS: The discussions in the United States Senate incident to its consideration of the Multilateral Peace Pact,[1] and the report of the Senate Committee on Foreign Affairs[2] which dealt briefly but specifically with the Monroe Doctrine, have given rise to questions regarding the true meaning given by the United States to that Doctrine. The present seems a propitious opportunity to prepare for communication to the countries of Latin America when the occasion shall be thought by the Department to be opportune, the views of the Government of the United States on the scope and purpose of that Doctrine.

The Monroe Doctrine is sometimes conceived as a policy formulated by President Monroe and his Cabinet solely as a result of the formation in Europe of the Holy Alliance, and the operations, through France, of that Alliance against Spain. This is not a true appraisal of the Doctrine. The formation of the Holy Alliance and its subsequent activities constituted the occasion for casting into definite formula the principles behind the Doctrine, and for announcing such formula when made; but the principles of the Doctrine are as old as the nation itself. They were understood and, from time to time, announced, as occasion required, by the Revolutionary Fathers themselves.

The fundamental concept of the Doctrine is the peace and safety of the Western Hemisphere through the absolute political separation of Europe from the countries of this Western World, subject to this exception that the principle was not to be operative as against those American possessions which were held by European powers at the time the Doctrine was announced. A mere statement of this principle shows that while announced by the United States, in 1823, and by it since maintained for the primary purpose of protecting

---

[1] Treaty for the Renunciation of War, signed at Paris, August 27, 1928, *Foreign Relations*, 1928, vol. I, p. 153.

[2] *The General Pact for the Renunciation of War:* Hearings Before the Senate Committee on Foreign Relations, 70th Cong., 2d sess. (Washington, Government Printing Office, 1928).

the interests, integrity, and political life of itself, yet all the other independent republics of the Western Hemisphere have, for a century, been equal beneficiaries with the United States in the advantages which have flowed from the complete political separation of Europe from the Republics on the Western Hemisphere.

A brief survey, first, of certain significant events of the colonial experience of the British colonies in America, and, next, of matters connected with the development of the principles finally embodied in Monroe's formulae, makes entirely clear the purpose and scope of the Doctrine as announced by President Monroe in his message to Congress of December 2, 1823.[3]

Prior to the War of Independence the British colonies in America had been involved in four major wars between themselves and the French colonies. No one of these wars arose by reason of conditions in colonial America; each was but an echo of some European conflict, in the causes and with the issues of which the colonies had no concern whatever. After each of these wars, except the last, and notwithstanding what the colonies lost by waging them, in treasure and men, to say nothing of the burnings, tortures, scalpings, and murders incident to the outlying frontier operations of Indian war-parties, the respective European mother countries resumed as to the colonies practically the pre-war status,—all the suffering, privation, hardship, and loss of the colonists going for naught. The American colonies were in fact mere pawns in the game of European politics, to be taken or sacrificed as the immediate interests of the parent countries appeared to require.

All of this was an incident of the mere neighborhood of the colonies of the two Powers upon this continent and was so well understood by the Revolutionary Fathers of the United States that Washington in his Farewell Address warned and admonished his fellow citizens in these words:[4]

"The great rule of conduct for us in regard to foreign nations is in extending our commercial relations to have with them as little *political* connection as possible. . . .

"Europe has a set of primary interests which to us have none or a very remote relation. Hence she must be engaged in frequent controversies, the causes of which are essentially foreign to our concerns. Hence, therefore, it must be unwise in us to implicate ourselves by artificial ties in the ordinary vicissitudes of her politics or the ordinary combinations and collisions of her friendships or enmities.

[3] James D. Richardson, *A Compilation of the Messages and Papers of the Presidents*, 1789–1897 (Washington, Government Printing Office, 1896), vol. II, pp. 207–220.
[4] September 17, 1796; Richardson, *Messages and Papers of the Presidents*, vol. I, pp. 213, 222–223.

"Our detached and distant situation invites and enables us to pursue a different course.

. . . . . . . .

"Why forego the advantages of so peculiar a situation? Why quit our own to stand upon foreign ground? Why, by interweaving our destiny with that of any part of Europe, entangle our peace and prosperity in the toils of European ambition, rivalship, interest, humor, or caprice?"

Three years before Washington's address Jefferson, writing to our representatives in Spain, visualized the same principle,[5] and one year after the address (1797), President Adams, in a special message to Congress dealing with the relations between the United States and France, again affirmed that "we ought not to involve ourselves in the political system of Europe, but to keep ourselves always distinct and separate from it if we can, . . . "[6]

In the years which immediately followed, the representatives of the United States in London, Paris, and Madrid, carrying out the policies and instructions of their Government, announced and re-announced principles which Monroe a quarter of a century later incorporated in his famous declaration.

Nor were certain of these principles peculiar to the United States. Great Britain, for reasons of her own (which indeed were, in certain aspects, not unlike the considerations which moved the United States) entertained, equally with the United States, certain of those fundamental views. As early as 1798, Great Britain, not wishing France to have the advantage of an augmentation of Spanish American resources, intimated to the American Minister to Great Britain that she desired with our cooperation to separate South America from Spain.[7]

Speaking of the Floridas, Mr. King, American Minister to Great Britain, advised Lord Hawkesbury, in the same year (1798), that "we should be unwilling to see them transferred except to ourselves;" and speaking of Louisiana, King declared we should be unwilling "it should pass into the hands of new proprietors."[8]

The correspondence between ourselves and Great Britain, France, and Spain immediately preceding the Louisiana purchase, and the negotiations between ourselves and France leading to the cession to the United States of the Louisiana territory, brought out that the United States had not favored, and could not favor the transfer

[5] See John Bassett Moore, *A Digest of International Law*, vol. VI, p. 369.
[6] Richardson, *Messages and Papers of the Presidents*, vol. I, pp. 233, 238.
[7] Cf. *The Life and Correspondence of Rufus King*, ed. by his grandson, Charles R. King (New York, G. P. Putnam's Sons), vol. III, p. 561.
[8] The first quotation appears to be from Mr. King's despatch No. 20 of June 1, 1801; the second quotation from Mr. King's memorandum book, September 22, 1798. *Ibid.*, pp. 469, 572.

to Great Britain of the Spanish possessions on the Mississippi; that the cession of the Floridas and Louisiana worked "most sorely on the United States" and reversed "all the political relations of the United States"; that by securing Louisiana France had "assumed to us the attitude of defiance" and made "it impossible that France and the United States can continue long friends".[9] It was repeatedly declared during this period that "mere neighborhood could not be friendly." In 1803 Jefferson in a message to Congress called attention to the fact that

". . . Separated by a wide ocean from the nations of Europe and from the political interests which entangle them together, with productions and wants which render our commerce and friendship useful to them and theirs to us, it can not be the interest of any to assail us, nor ours to disturb them. We should be most unwise, indeed, were we to cast away the singular blessings of the position in which nature has placed us, the opportunity she has endowed us with of pursuing, at a distance from foreign contentions, the paths of industry, peace, and happiness, of cultivating general friendship, and of bringing collisions of interest to the umpirage of reason rather than of force."[10]

In 1811 the Congress of the United States itself in a resolution which dealt primarily with the foreign possessions lying immediately south of its southern borders, said:

"Taking into view the peculiar situation of Spain, and of her American provinces; and considering the influence which the destiny of the territory adjoining the southern border of the United States may have upon their security, tranquillity, and commerce; therefore

"*Resolved by the Senate and House of Representatives of the United States of America, in Congress assembled,* That the United States, under the peculiar circumstances of the existing crisis, can not, without serious inquietude, see any part of the said territory pass into the hands of any foreign power; and that a due regard to their own safety compels them to provide, under certain contingencies, for the temporary occupation of the said territory; they, at the same time, declare that the said territory shall, in their hands, remain subject to future negotiation."[11]

The threatening European events of this period, which had so stirred the American people, had even a greater repercussion in Spanish America. News of the enthronement of Joseph Bonaparte in Spain, under the fiat of Napoleon and with the support of his armies, threw Spanish America into political turmoil and while action was taken towards formally recognizing Ferdinand in Mexico

---

[9] The excerpts are from a despatch from Jefferson to Livingston, April 18, 1802; see Moore, *Digest*, vol. I, pp. 435–436.

[10] October 17, 1803; Richardson, *Messages and Papers of the Presidents*, vol. I, pp. 357, 361–362.

[11] Approved January 15, 1811; 3 Stat. 471.

City, Caracas, Bogotá, Chuquisaca, and Buenos Aires, yet as early as 1809 incipient separatist movements occurred in Chuquisaca, La Paz, Quito, Bogotá, Caracas, and Valladolid (in Mexico). The movement for independence so begun was destined not to fall but to continue until all the Spanish colonies upon the mainland of the Western Hemisphere were free and independent. Out of the woe and suffering of the civil wars which drenched the Spanish Americas in blood for the next decade, arose the great national heroes, Bolivar, San Martin, O'Higgins, Moreno, Artigas, Sucre, Hidalgo, and Morales, who, together with the patriots of the United States, gave to men in modern times free political institutions and made the Western World the home of popular, democratic government.

In the midst of this conflict which, beginning in 1809, was virtually concluded by 1823, the great powers of Europe called the Conference of Aix-la-Chapelle. On the Agenda for this Conference was the proposal to discuss mediation between Spain and her revolted American colonies.

Prior to the meeting of the Conference the Duc de Richelieu of France approached the Minister of the United States at Paris, Mr. Gallatin, concerning the possibility of the United States joining in the Conference to discuss this question. Mr. Gallatin advised the Duc that so far as he was able to judge

" . . . no expectation could be entertained that the United States would become parties in the proposed mediation, much less that they would accede to any measures having for object the restoration of the supremacy of Spain over the colonies which had thrown off her yoke." [13]

To the suggestion of the Duc that the revolted colonies were unfit for liberty or for forming any permanent government, and that therefore some prince of the Spanish family should be sent to America as an independent monarch, Gallatin affirmed

" . . . that with the form of government which suited the colonies, or which any of them might select we had nothing to do; that it was only to the preservation of their independence that I had alluded; and that it appeared to me doubtful whether a Spanish prince would be considered as securing that. As to the capacity of the colonists to form a government sufficient to carry on their business and to entertain foreign relations I expressed my astonishment that any doubt could exist on that point and mentioned San Domingo as a proof that even slaves could establish governments of their own, totally independent, at least of their masters." [13]

---

[13] Gallatin to Adams, August 10, 1818; *The Writings of Albert Gallatin*, ed. by Henry Adams (Philadelphia, J. B. Lippincott & Co., 1879), vol. II, p. 73.

The position of Britain (regarding the Spanish American colonies) at the Conference of Aix-la-Chapelle has been described by an able British author as follows:

"The matter was finally settled in an interview between Alexander and Castlereagh. Castlereagh was entirely opposed to the use of force. The Alliance, he said, was not competent to *arbitrate* or *judge*, and was therefore not competent to enforce any such judgment directly or indirectly; it could only mediate or facilitate, but not compel or menace. As for the commercial boycott (to use a word of later date), which had been suggested, Great Britain could be no party to it. We had had a large direct trade with France during the war, and had suffered her armies to be clothed by our manufactures; how could we interdict commerce with South America in time of peace? Since Russia could not fight either by arms or by an interdict on trade, it would be better to tell Spain so at once than to buoy her up by false hopes in the maintenance of a false attitude. There was, besides, the *moral responsibility* involved in forcing the colonies to submit to such a Government as that of Spain.

"It was the last argument, wrote Castlereagh, which made Alexander's mind 'shrink from the subject.' He expressed his regret that he had not taken the British minister's advice before the matter had been carried so far. As it was, he at once conferred with his ministers, with the result that at the next conference their tone was so altered that Richelieu withdrew his project. Thus ended the question so far as the Conference of Aix-la-Chapelle was concerned." [14]

Thus forewarned as to the attitude of the United States and advised of Great Britain's unwillingness to participate, the powers took no action at Aix-la-Chapelle with reference to Spain and her revolted American colonies.

Two years later, John Quincy Adams, Secretary of State, instructing the American Minister to Russia, Mr. Middleton, declared on July 5, 1820,

"The political system of the United States is also essentially Extra-European. To stand in firm and cautious independence of all entanglement in the European system, has been a cardinal point of their policy under every administration of their Government from the Peace of 1783 to this day. If at the original adoption of their system there could have been any doubt of its justice or its wisdom, there can be none at this time. Every year's experience rivets it more deeply in the principles and opinions of the Nation." [15]

Speaking of the system of the Holy Alliance and of the principles upon which it worked, Mr. Adams continued:

". . . But independent of the prejudices which have been excited against this instrument in the public opinion, which time and an

[14] Walter Alison Phillips; *The Confederation of Europe*, (London, etc., Longmans, Green, and Co., 1914), p. 258.
[15] Moore, *Digest*, vol. VI, p. 378.

experience of its good effects will gradually wear away, it may be observed that for the repose of Europe as well as of America, the European and American political system, should be kept as separate and distinct from each other as possible." [16]

In the year following, 1821 the Emperor Alexander of Russia issued an imperial ukase [17] which barred all non-Russians from the Aleutian Islands and the northwestern coast of America appertaining to Russia, and reserved the pursuits of commerce, whaling, and fishery exclusively to Russian subjects. Vessels approaching these coasts within less than 100 Italian miles would be subject to confiscation along with all their cargoes.

Against this action the British Government protested as early as January 1822. In the spring of 1823 the matter was taken up between Secretary Adams and Baron Tuyll, the latter representing Russia in the United States. In the course of the discussion which followed, Secretary Adams on July 17, 1823, advised Baron Tuyll specifically

". . . that we should contest the right of Russia to any territorial establishment on this continent, and that we should assume distinctly the principle that the American continents are no longer subjects for any European colonial establishments." [18]

At Aix-la-Chapelle (1818) Alexander of Russia, still fired with zeal for human rights as he conceived them, and eager to use the army and resources of Russia to the furtherance of those rights, exclaimed to Metternich, "My army as well as myself is at the disposal of Europe." At Troppau, in October of 1820, in a conversation between the same men, Alexander declared: "Tell me what you desire, and what you wish me to do and I will do it." Two years later, at Verona, Alexander, now thoroughly reactionary, proposed to march 150,000 men through Germany into Piedmont where they would be available as a police force for keeping the peace of Europe, and specifically where they might be used either against France or Spain as occasion might require. [19]

The great powers of Europe were by this time thoroughly suspicious, not so much of the actual designs which Alexander might have, as of the uses to which he might be induced to devote his resources and army.

Unable to agree with the plan of the other great powers at Verona (1822), Great Britain's representative, the Duke of Wellington, with-

[16] Moore, Digest, vol. VI, p. 379.
[17] The ukase is printed in translation in Alaskan Boundary Tribunal: Appendix to the Case of the United States (Washington, Government Printing Office, 1904), vol. II, p. 25.
[18] Memoirs of John Quincy Adams, ed. by Charles Francis Adams (Philadelphia, J. B. Lippincott & Co., 1875), vol. VI, p. 163.
[19] See Phillips, The Confederation of Europe, pp. 168, 219, 270.

drew from the Congress on the ground that Great Britain could not be a party to any declaration against Spain nor to any hostile interference in her internal affairs nor to any defensive alliance between the powers.

However, the Conference determined that France might intervene in the domestic affairs of Spain; and on April 7, 1823, a French army of 95,000 men under the Duc d'Angoulême crossed the Bidassoa and, entering Spain, placed Ferdinand VII upon the throne.

This act of high political intervention in the domestic concerns of another power, coupled with the avowed disposition of the four great powers of Europe, (Russia, Prussia, Austria, and France) to use their military forces for similar purposes in other countries offending their will, and the known preferences of those same powers with reference to the Spanish possessions in America, aroused apprehension not only in the United States and the Spanish Americas but in Great Britain also. The result was that in August of 1823, British statesmen reverted to the position announced on February 15, 1798, by Lord Grenville to Mr. King, Minister of the United States, when Grenville intimated a desire to enter upon negotiations with the United States to prevent Spanish America from falling into the hands of France.[20] Canning now affirmed

". . . that as His Britannic Majesty disclaimed all intention of appropriating to himself the smallest portion of the late Spanish possessions in America, he was also satisfied that no attempt would be made by France to bring any of them under *her* dominion, either by conquest or by cession from Spain. . . . that Great Britain certainly never again intended to lend her instrumentality or aid, either [*whether*] by mediation or otherwise, towards making up the dispute between Spain and her colonies, but that if this result could still be brought about she would not interfere to prevent it. . . . he too believed that the day had arrived when all America might be considered as lost to Europe so far as the tie of political dependence was concerned. . . . that he hoped that France would not, should even events in the Peninsula be favorable to her, extend her views to South America for the purpose of reducing the colonies, nominally, perhaps, for Spain, but in effect to subserve ends of her own; but that, in case she should meditate such a policy, he was satified that the knowledge of the United States being opposed to it, as well as Great Britain, could not fail to have its influence in checking her steps." [21]

Two days later (on August 20, 1823,) Canning addressed a "private and confidential" communication to Mr. Rush, Minister of the United States, in which Mr. Canning inquired whether or not Mr. Rush was, under his powers, authorized to enter into negotiations with Great

[20] Cf. *The Life and Correspondence of Rufus King*, vol. III, p. 561.
[21] See despatch No. 323, August 19, 1823, from the Minister in England (Rush) to the Secretary of State (Adams), Moore, *Digest*, vol. VI, pp. 386, 387, 388.

Britain with reference to the Spanish Americas, and declared as to Great Britain:

"For ourselves we have no disguise.

"1. We conceive the recovery of the colonies by Spain to be hopeless.

"2. We conceive the question of the recognition of them, as independent states, to be one of time and circumstances.

"3. We are, however, by no means disposed to throw any impediment in the way of an arrangement between them and the mother country by amicable negotiation.

"4. We aim not at the possession of any portion of them ourselves.

"5. We could not see any portion of them transferred to any other power with indifference." [22]

Within the next two days, other communications of the same tenor passed between Mr. Canning and Mr. Rush, and on August 23, 1823, Mr. Rush forwarded all of them to Mr. Adams.

They were received in Washington on October 9, 1823, and on October 17 President Monroe sent copies of them to Mr. Jefferson for his comments. In the transmitting communication, President Monroe, after raising certain questions with reference to the situation created by this correspondence, continued:

"My own impression is that we ought to meet the proposal of the British govt., & make it known that we would view an interference on the part of the European powers, and especially an attack on the Colonies, by them, as an attack on ourselves, presuming that if they succeeded with them, they would extend it to us." [23]

To this communication Mr. Jefferson replied on October 24, 1823, stating:

"The question presented by the letters you have sent me, is the most momentous which has ever been offered to my contemplation since that of independence. That made us a nation, this sets our compass and points the course which we are to steer through the ocean of time opening on us. And never could we embark upon it under circumstances more auspicious. Our first and fundamental maxim should be, never to entangle ourselves in the broils of Europe; our second, never to suffer Europe to intermeddle with cis-Atlantic affairs. America, North and South, has a set of interests distinct from those of Europe, and particularly her own. She should therefore have a system of her own, separate and apart from that of Europe. While the last is laboring to become the domicile of despotism, our endeavor should surely be, to make our hemisphere that of freedom. . .

. . . . . . . .

"I could honestly, therefore, join in the declaration proposed, that we aim not at the acquisition of any of those possessions, that we will not stand in the way of any amicable arrangement between them

[22] Moore, *Digest*, vol. VI, p. 389.
[23] *Ibid.*, p. 393.

and the mother country; but that we will oppose, with all our means, the forcible interposition of any other power, as auxiliary, stipendiary, or under any other form or pretext, and most especially their transfer to any power by conquest, cession or acquisition in any other way." [24]

These communications from Mr. Rush were sent also to Mr. Madison, who on October 30, 1823, transmitted to President Monroe his observations which included the following:

"From the disclosures of Mr. Canning it appears, as was otherwise to be inferred, that the success of France against Spain would be followed by an attempt of the holy allies to reduce the revolutionized colonies of the latter to their former dependence.

"The professions we have made to these neighbours, our sympathies with their liberties and independence, the deep interest we have in the most friendly relations with them, and the consequences threatened by a command of their resources by the great powers, confederated against the rights and reforms of which we have given so conspicuous and persuasive an example, all unite in calling for our efforts to defeat the meditated crusade." [25]

This was the situation when on October 7, 1823, President Monroe began a consideration of the question with his Cabinet. It is unnecessary to deal with their deliberations regarding this matter, for as seems clear from the message of President Monroe to Congress of December 2, 1823, the Cabinet merely framed certain formulae embodying the principles that had been for years in the minds of every American statesman and that had on many occasions been declared and acted upon by the Government of the United States and to some extent by the Government of Great Britain.

So much misconception of the import and scope of the principles declared by Monroe has crept in to the popular mind not only of the United States but of other countries, that it will be useful to repeat here the exact language of Monroe's declarations which have come to be known as the Monroe Doctrine. These declarations were embodied in the following paragraphs of the message:

"At the proposal of the Russian Imperial Government, made through the minister of the Emperor residing here, a full power and instructions have been transmitted to the minister of the United States at St. Petersburg to arrange by amicable negotiation the respective rights and interests of the two nations on the northwest coast of this continent. A similar proposal has been made by His Imperial Majesty to the Government of Great Britain, which has likewise been acceded to. The Government of the United States has been desirous by this friendly proceeding of manifesting the great value which they have invariably attached to the friendship of the Emperor and their solicitude to cultivate the best understanding with

---

[24] Moore, *Digest*, vol. VI, pp. 394–395.
[25] *Ibid.*, p. 396.

his Government. In the discussions to which this interest has given rise and in the arrangements by which they may terminate, the occasion has been judged proper for asserting as a principle in which the rights and interests of the United States are involved, that the American continents, by the free and independent condition which they have assumed and maintain, are henceforth not to be considered as subjects for future colonization by any European powers." (Par. 7) [26]

It will be observed that this paragraph deals with the question of future colonization by any European powers of the American continents. While the occasion for this was the encroachment of Russia only and on the northwest coast of America alone, yet the declaration as made referred to *any European powers* and covered the whole of the *American continents*. Thus was implemented the statement made by Secretary Adams on July 17, 1823, to Baron Tuyll "that the American continents are no longer subject for any European colonial establishments." [27] President Monroe declared that the "rights and interests of the United States are involved" in this principle.

It is most essential to observe that the principles announced in this paragraph relate entirely to the relationship between the American continents and European powers; there is no word in the statement that relates to the inter-relationships of the independent states of the American continents; and the "rights and interests of the United States" which were involved, were the rights and interests as against Europe and not against the Latin Americas.

The succeeding portions of President Monroe's message which deal with this subject are embraced in paragraphs 48 and 49 and read as follows:

"It was stated at the commencement of the last session that a great effort was then making in Spain and Portugal to improve the condition of the people of those countries, and that it appeared to be conducted with extraordinary moderation. It need scarcely be remarked that the result has been, so far, very different from what was then anticipated. Of events in that quarter of the globe with which we have so much intercourse, and from which we derive our origin, we have always been anxious and interested spectators. The citizens of the United States cherish sentiments the most friendly in favor of the liberty and happiness of their fellow-men on that side of the Atlantic. In the wars of the European powers in matters relating to themselves we have never taken any part, nor does it comport with our policy so to do. It is only when our rights are invaded or seriously menaced that we resent injuries or make preparation for our defense. With the movements in this hemisphere we are, of necessity, more immediately connected, and by causes which

---

[26] Paragraph 7, message of December 2, 1823; Moore, *Digest*, vol. VI. pp. 401–402.

[27] *Memoirs of John Quincy Adams*, vol. VI, p. 163.

must be obvious to all enlightened and impartial observers. The political system of the allied powers is essentially different in this respect from that of America. This difference proceeds from that which exists in their respective Governments. And to the defense of our own, which has been achieved by the loss of so much blood and treasure, and matured by the wisdom of their most enlightened citizens, and under which we have enjoyed unexampled felicity, this whole nation is devoted. We owe it, therefore, to candor, and to the amicable relations existing between the United States and those powers, to declare that we should consider any attempt on their part to extend their system to any portion of this hemisphere as dangerous to our peace and safety. With the existing colonies or dependencies of any European power we have not interfered and shall not interfere. But with the governments who have declared their independence and maintained it, and whose independence we have, on great consideration and on just principles, acknowledged, we could not view any interposition for the purpose of oppressing them, or controlling in any other manner their destiny, by any European power, in any other light than as the manifestation of an unfriendly disposition toward the United States. In the war between these new governments and Spain we declared our neutrality at the time of their recognition, and to this we have adhered and shall continue to adhere, provided no change shall occur which, in the judgment of the competent authorities of this Government, shall make a corresponding change on the part of the United States indispensable to their security.

"The late events in Spain and Portugal show that Europe is still unsettled. Of this important fact no stronger proof can be adduced than that the allied powers should have thought it proper, on any principle satisfactory to themselves, to have interposed, by force, in the internal concerns of Spain. To what extent such interposition may be carried, on the same principle, is a question in which all independent powers whose governments differ from theirs are interested, even those most remote, and surely none more so than the United States. Our policy in regard to Europe, which was adopted at an early stage of the wars which have so long agitated that quarter of the globe, nevertheless remains the same, which is, not to interfere in the internal concerns of any of its powers; to consider the government *de facto* as the legitimate government for us; to cultivate friendly relations with it, and to preserve those relations by a frank, firm, and manly policy, meeting in all instances the just claims of every power, submitting to injuries from none. But in regard to these continents circumstances are eminently and conspicuously different. It is impossible that the allied powers should extend their political system to any portion of either continent without endangering our peace and happiness; nor can anyone believe that our southern brethren, if left to themselves, would adopt it of their own accord. It is equally impossible, therefore, that we should behold such interposition, in any form, with indifference. If we look to the comparative strength and resources of Spain and those new governments, and their distance from each other, it must be obvious that she can never subdue them. It is still the true policy of the United States to leave the parties to themselves, in the hope that other powers will pursue the same course." [28]

---

[28] Moore, *Digest*, vol. VI, pp. 402–403.

Of the matters covered by the foregoing paragraphs the following are to be specially noted.

*a.* Referring to the "allied powers" (at that time Russia, Austria, Prussia, and France) it is declared that the United States would consider any attempt on the part of those powers "to extend their system to any portion of this hemisphere as dangerous to our peace and safety."

This declaration, like the one regarding colonization, visualized a United States against Europe, not a United States against Latin America. It is not confined to the continents only, nor, explicitly to the areas then known; it covers the whole Western Hemisphere, then discovered or thereafter to be discovered. It declares that the extension of the allied "system to any portion of this hemisphere" would be "dangerous to our peace and safety". In other words, here is the reannouncement of the principles proclaimed by Washington, Adams, and Jefferson, that the Americas must be politically independent of Europe. This general principle was subject to one reservation as follows:

*b.* "With the existing colonies or dependencies of any European power we have not interfered and shall not interfere."

But in this there is no suggestion of the United States against Latin America; it deals solely with the relationship which the United States has to the possessions of Europe on this hemisphere.

*c.* As to the revolted Spanish colonies which had declared their independence and maintained it and the independence of which the United States had recognized, it was declared "we could not view any interposition for the purpose of oppressing them, or controlling in any other manner their destiny by any European power, in any other light than as the manifestation of an unfriendly disposition toward the United States."

Again, the relationship set out is one between Europe and the United States as the attitude of Europe might affect the revolted Spanish colonies. There is no suggestion of interference by the United States with the Latin Americas as between and among themselves nor as between them and the United States; there is no suggestion that the United States would itself undertake to control the growth, the development, or the destiny of any Latin American state. The full scope of this announcement is that the United States would as a measure of self defense, protect the weak and struggling revolted Spanish colonies trying to make good their independence, from "any interposition" by European powers "for the purpose of oppressing them or controlling in any other manner their destiny."

This inhibition was levelled not only at the allied powers but at *any European power.* It did not exclude Spain; it certainly included

Great Britain. At the same time we pledged continued neutrality in the war between Spain and the new Governments.

The language held in these various declarations,—"dangerous to our peace and safety", "manifestation of an unfriendly disposition toward the United States", "endangering our peace and happiness",— is one of the formulae used when nations, speaking among themselves, refer to matters involved in their self-preservation, their self-defense, or the warding off of imminent danger. I again reiterate that there is no word or intimation in the entire declaration which visualizes a hostility or aggression or an intent to control or direct the affairs of Latin American States by the United States, save only (as must be implicit in the Doctrine as to a situation difficult to conceive) where an American State should join with a European State in carrying forward any of the matters against which the inhibitions were raised.

On the other hand, any measures which the United States might take, under and pursuant to the principles laid down by Monroe, must inevitably react to the distinct and positive advantage of Latin American States; and whatever may be the situation after a hundred years of growth and development on the part of Latin American Republics, in which they have acquired strength and defensive power, no reasonable question can exist but that at the time the doctrine was announced it was and is to them a shield of utmost value, for, as Canning said, with reference to the suggestion that France might take part in "reducing the colonies, nominally, perhaps, for Spain, but in effect to subserve ends of her own", if France "should meditate such a policy, he was satisfied that the knowledge of the United States being opposed to it, as well as Great Britain could not fail to have its influence in checking her steps." [29]

Furthermore, though after the announcement of the Doctrine the contest between Spain and her colonies was as to various regions, either continued or renewed, and while half a century later the conflict was actually renewed by Spain against certain of her former South American colonies, yet an intimation in each case from the Government of the United States of the principles announced by Monroe was sufficient to protect the Latin American States involved from a subversion of their government or an occupation of their territories.

Just as these principles (in their development) guided the United States in its interrelations with Europe, from Washington's administration to Monroe's declaration, so have they been followed by the United States during the hundred years since the Doctrine was announced.

---

[29] Moore, *Digest*, vol. VI, p. 388.

It is history that the overtures of Canning in 1823 contained a suggestion that the United States and Great Britain should enter into a convention embodying the substance of the five points covered by Mr. Canning in his letter to Rush of August 20, 1823.[30] Notwithstanding Mr. Jefferson seemed not unfriendly to this suggestion, nor apparently was Mr. Madison, nor even President Monroe in the first instance, yet it was finally decided not to make a joint declaration with Great Britain, nor a conventional arrangement with her, but instead to make for the United States a declaration of its own international, political policy with reference to matters which the United States regarded as "dangerous to our peace and safety", as a "manifestation of an unfriendly disposition towards the United States", or as "endangering our peace and happiness", that is, matters which involved the self-defense of the United States, its self-preservation, or its protection from imminent danger.[31] The declaration was made upon the responsibility of the United States alone and as involving the interests of the United States only. Suggestions since made by other States for some conventional understanding regarding the Doctrine, have been politely but firmly declined.

While appreciating the strength which Great Britain's attitude on the matter gave to the position which the interests of the United States required it to take, and while the United States was encouraged, at least in part, to make the declaration by reason of this attitude of Great Britain, nevertheless the declaration when made, was the declaration of the United States only; it defined a policy of the United States speaking for itself alone; and from the day of its announcement until the present time it has been, as it remains, a unilateral declaration of policy by the United States of America. The United States alone determines when actions violative of the principles have been taken; it alone determines what, if any, measures, and the kind and extent of the measures which shall be used to combat the aggression inhibited by the Doctrine.

The Doctrine served, at the time, the significant, important, and useful purpose of declaring to the world certain acts which the United States would regard as inimical to its welfare, its self-defense, its self-preservation, or its protection from imminent danger. Europe, thus forewarned, did not, at the time, and has never since, pushed to extremes any ambitions it, or any of its component nations, may have had against the Republics of this hemisphere. The Doctrine has, as upheld by the United States, given to those same Republics a feeling of security they could not otherwise have possessed; it has given to them a freedom from anxiety of possible aggression

[30] See Moore, *Digest*, vol. vi, p. 389.
[31] See *ibid*, pp. 393–401.

and a relief from actual restraint that has enabled them to go forward steadily in a great, forward-looking growth and development, free from European menace even to the highest destiny great nations may carve for themselves.

Not only was Monroe's declaration a unilateral act of high policy on the part of the United States in so far as determining when and where actions, violative of the precepts of the Doctrine, were under consideration or actually under way, and in so far as carrying out measures for the implementing of the Doctrine, but it was very early declared that by announcing the Doctrine the United States created no obligation against itself and in favor of other countries. As the result of certain loose expressions used by Mr. Poinsett, while representing the United States in Mexico, Henry Clay, then Secretary of State, in reporting to the House of Representatives certain correspondence under date of March 29, 1826, used the following language:

"That The United States have contracted no Engagement, nor made any Pledge to the Governments of Mexico and South America, or to either of them, that The United States would not permit the interference of any Foreign Powers, with the Independence or form of Government of those Nations; nor have any Instructions been issued, authorizing any such Engagement or Pledge. It will be seen that the Message of the late President of The United States of the 2d December, 1823, is adverted to in the Extracts now furnished from the Instructions to Mr. Poinsett, and that he is directed to impress its principles upon the Government of The United Mexican States.

"All apprehensions of the danger, to which Mr. Monroe alludes, of an interference, by the Allied Powers of Europe, to introduce their Political Systems into this Hemisphere, have ceased. If, indeed, an attempt by force had been made, by Allied Europe, to subvert the Liberties of the Southern Nations on this Continent, and to erect, upon the ruins of their Free Institutions, Monarchical Systems, the People of The United States would have stood pledged, in the opinion of their Executive, not to any Foreign State, but to themselves and to their posterity, by their dearest interests, and highest duties, to resist, to the utmost, such attempt; and it is to a Pledge of that character that Mr. Poinsett alone refers." [32]

As I have already said, the Doctrine laid down principles which were to be operative as between the United States and Europe, not as between the United States and the Latin American Republics save in the most unlikely event of a Latin American Republic being involved in a conspiracy with a European power to run counter to the principles of the Doctrine. The Doctrine did not lay down any principles that should govern the relationships between the United States and Latin American Republics, nor between and among the Latin American Republics themselves, nor between the Latin Amer-

[32] Gale and Seaton's *Register of Debates in Congress*, 19th Cong. 1st sess., vol. II, pt. 2, Appendix, p. 83.

714 FOREIGN RELATIONS, 1929, VOLUME I

ican Republics and European countries save only in those matters specifically inhibited by the terms of the Doctrine.

As President Roosevelt said:—

" . . . The Monroe Doctrine is a declaration that there must be no territorial aggrandizement by any non-American power at the expense of any American power on American soil. It is in no wise intended as hostile to any nation in the Old World. Still less is it intended to give cover to any aggression by one New World power at the expense of any other." [33]

In accordance with this conception, it was very early declared that the principles of the Doctrine had no application to wars between American States themselves; nor were the principles considered to apply (at least immediately after their promulgation) to a war confined to a parent country and its former colony, though later (by the middle of the last century) it was specifically declared that the United States would deny the rightfulness of Spain's re-annexation of certain territory which, though once a Spanish colonial possession, had established and maintained its independence from the time of the announcement of the Doctrine.

It has been many times affirmed by the appropriate authorities of the United States that the principles of the Doctrine are challenged by wars between American States and European powers, only when such wars threaten the subversion or exclusion of the self-determined government of a free American State, or the acquisition by a non-American power of the territory of one of these States.

As Mr. Roosevelt said:

"We do not guarantee any state against punishment if it misconducts itself, provided that punishment does not take the form of the acquisition of territory by any non-American power." [34]

An analogous rule was stated by Mr. Sherman, who instructed Mr. Powell, the Minister of the United States to Haiti in 1898, that

"You certainly should not proceed on the hypothesis that it is the duty of the United States to protect its American neighbors from the responsibilities which attend the exercise of independent sovereignty"; [35]

or as the general principle had been earlier stated by Secretary Cass—

"It is the established policy of this country not to interfere with the relations of foreign nations to each other and that it would be

---

[33] Annual message, December 3, 1901, *Foreign Relations*, 1901, pp. ix, xxxvi.
[34] *Ibid.*, pp. xxxvi–xxxvii.
[35] Moore, *Digest*, vol. VI, p. 476.

both improper and impossible for the United States to decide upon the course of conduct towards Venezuela which Spain may think required by her honor or her interests." [36]

Nor is the Monroe Doctrine to be understood, nor has it ever been so interpreted by the United States, as inhibiting any form of government which any American Republic might desire to establish for itself. The United States has willingly yielded to the peoples of this hemisphere the right to set up any form of government they wished; it has recognized and dealt equally and freely with the monarchies in Haiti, Santo Domingo, Mexico, and Brazil, and with the Republics in those and other Latin American countries. Its attitude toward Emperor Maximilian in Mexico was, as expressed by Secretary Seward to Mr. Adams, the Minister of the United States to Great Britain (March 3, 1862) that the United States owed a

". . . duty to express to the allies, in all candor and frankness, the opinion that no monarchical government which could be founded in Mexico, in the presence of foreign navies and armies in the waters, and upon the soil of Mexico, would have any prospect of security or permanence." [37]

Later Mr. Seward, in reply to a communication from the French Minister of November 29, 1865, said:

"The real cause of our national discontent is, that the French army which is now in Mexico is invading a domestic republican government there which was established by her people, and with whom the United States sympathize most profoundly, for the avowed purpose of suppressing it and establishing upon its ruins a foreign monarchical government, whose presence there, so long as it should endure, could not but be regarded by the people of the United States as injurious and menacing to their own chosen and endeared republican institutions." [38]

Thus the Monroe Doctrine has nothing whatever to do with the domestic concerns or policies or the form of government or the international conduct of the peoples of this hemisphere as among themselves. Each of the Republics of this half of the world is left free to conduct its own sovereign affairs as to it seems fit and proper. The principles of the Monroe Doctrine become operative only when some European power (either by its own motion or in complicity with an American state) undertakes to subvert or exclude the self-determined form of government of one of these Republics or acquire

[36] *Ibid.*, p. 530.
[37] See J. Reuben Clark, *Memorandum on the Monroe Doctrine*, December 17, 1928 (Washington, Government Printing Office, 1930), p. 138.
[38] Moore, *Digest*, vol. VI, p. 501.

from them all or a part of their territory; and the principles of the Doctrine are then vitalized solely because the aggression of the European power constitutes a threat against the United States, not because of its effect upon the other American state.

It has sometimes been said that the treaty and conventional relations which have been created between the United States and certain Caribbean powers are the fruition of the application of the principles of the Monroe Doctrine. Nothing could be farther from the truth. These relations have been built between the United States and those powers by the free and voluntary act of the parties concerned; they have in each case been created either for the protection of these powers from foreign aggression which, had it taken place, might have been violative of the Monroe Doctrine, or to insure a domestic tranquillity which was to make for the peace, prosperity, and happiness of the people concerned. But the treaty and conventional obligations incurred, the treaty and conventional rights created, being wholly between and relating solely to American powers, have nothing whatever to do with the Monroe Doctrine which, by definition, is concerned only when a European power is involved in some aggression upon this hemisphere.

At times effort has been put forth to make it appear that on the rare occasions when the United States has been forced to land forces in areas of this hemisphere for the protection of American life, it has done so pursuant to the principles of the Monroe Doctrine. This is not true. The United States has landed troops for the same purpose in other parts of the world with perhaps at least equal frequency, and no one has suggested or would suggest that such landing was pursuant to the presumed mandates of the Monroe Doctrine. The historical fact is that, under principles universally recognized as justifying such an act, troops have been landed by all the great powers in temporarily disturbed areas in which local governments were not able, for the moment, to protect foreign life. These occupations are always temporary and terminate so soon as the local sovereign becomes able to maintain peace and order and to protect the lives of foreigners within the disturbed areas. Such landings do not constitute intervention in the domestic affairs of nations. They are merely interpositions, police measures taken to assist the local sovereign where his own power is, for the time being, inadequate to afford necessary protection.

As I have repeatedly affirmed, the Monroe Doctrine is a unilateral Doctrine; the principle of self-defense on the part of the United States was implicit in the Doctrine, and has been repeatedly declared by American statesmen from the time of its announcement until the present time. It would be superfluous for me to list here the expressions to this effect of statesmen of the earlier days of the Republic, but I may call to your attention the expressions of American Statesmen during this century,—a period during which there have been voiced some false interpretations of the Doctrine to the effect that instead of being a Doctrine of self-defense, it was a Doctrine of excuse and justification for armed aggression.

Secretary Knox, speaking in 1912 [*1911*], affirmed:

"The maintenance of the Monroe Doctrine is considered by us essential to our peace, prosperity, and national safety." [39]

Senator Lodge, speaking of a Resolution which he had introduced into the Senate of the United States, (July 31, 1912) stated:

". . . It rests on the principle that every nation has a right to protect its own safety, . . . The Monroe Doctrine was, of course, an extension in our own interests of this underlying principle—the right of every nation to provide for its own safety." [40]

Mr. Root, speaking in 1914 on the subject of the Monroe Doctrine, affirmed:

"It is a declaration of the United States that certain acts would be injurious to the peace and safety of the United States and that the United States would regard them as unfriendly. . . .

"The Doctrine is not international law, but it rests upon the right of self-protection and that right is recognized by international law. . . .

"We frequently see statements that the Doctrine has been changed or enlarged; that there is a new or different doctrine since Monroe's time. They are mistaken. There has been no change. . . .

"Since the Monroe Doctrine is a declaration based upon this nation's right of self-protection, it can not be transmuted into a joint or common declaration by American States or any number of them." [41]

On January 9 [*6*], 1915 [*1916*], President Wilson declared:

"The Monroe Doctrine was proclaimed by the United States on her own authority. It always has been maintained, and always will be maintained, upon her own responsibility. But the Monroe Doctrine demanded merely that European governments should not attempt to extend their political systems to this side of the Atlantic." [42]

---

[39] *The Pending Arbitration Treaties:* Address of Hon. Philander C. Knox before the American Society for the Judicial Settlement of International Disputes, Cincinnati, Ohio, November 8, 1911 (n. p., n. d.), p. 31.

[40] *Congressional Record*, vol. 48, pt. 10, p. 10045.

[41] Speaking before the American Society of International Law, April 22, 1914, on the subject, "The Real Monroe Doctrine", *Proceedings of the American Society of International Law*, 1914, pp. 6, 10, 11, 12, 19.

[42] Address to Pan American Scientific Congress, Washington, January 6, 1916, on "What is Pan-Americanism", in *The Public Papers of Woodrow Wilson: The New Democracy*, ed. by Ray Stannard Baker and William E. Dodd (New York, Harper & Brothers, 1926), vol. I, p. 443.

Mr. Hughes, writing in 1923, declared:

"The Monroe Doctrine is not a policy of aggression; it is a policy of self-defense. . . . It still remains an assertion of the principle of national security. . . .

"The decision of the question as to what action the United States should take in any exigency arising in this hemisphere is not controlled by the content of the Monroe Doctrine, but may always be determined on grounds of international right and national security as freely as if the Monroe Doctrine did not exist. . . .

"The Monroe Doctrine rests 'upon the right of every sovereign state to protect itself by preventing a condition of affairs in which it will be too late to protect itself.' "[43]

Speaking to the American Academy of Political and Social Science on November 30, 1923, Mr. Hughes declared:

"It should be recognized that the doctrine is only a phase of American policy in this hemisphere and the other phases of that policy should be made clear. . . . The principle of exclusion embodies a policy of self-defense on the part of the United States; it is a policy set up and applied by the United States. While the Monroe Doctrine is thus distinctively a policy of the United States maintained for its own security, it is a policy which has rendered an inestimable service to the American Republics by keeping them free from the intrigues and rivalries of European powers."[44]

It is high time that misunderstanding as to the meaning of the Monroe Doctrine shall cease; that international trouble makers shall find so clear a conception of the Doctrine in the minds of the people of this hemisphere that false representations concerning it shall no longer find lodgment in the prejudices upon which such misrepresentations have heretofore lived; that irresponsible exploiters of great economic resources shall not be able hereafter to invoke an untrue concept of the Doctrine to justify and induce unwarranted international attitudes and actions; that poorly visioned, grandiose schemes of the dreamers of unrighteous dominion shall no longer be built upon erroneous principles unknown to the Doctrine.

The Monroe Doctrine is not now and never was an instrument of aggression; it is and always has been a cloak of protection. The Doctrine is not a lance; it is a shield.

I submit the foregoing to you as an official statement of and commentary upon the Monroe Doctrine which it is hoped may tend to clear up past uncertainties, remove hitherto existing apprehensions, if any, and so open the way for such a mutual understanding and

[43] "Observations on the Monroe Doctrine" by Hon. Charles E. Hughes, Secretary of State of the United States, *American Journal of International Law*, vol. 17 (1923), pp. 611, 615, 616, 619.
[44] On the subject, "The Centenary of the Monroe Doctrine," International Conciliation, *Documents for the Year 1924*, No. 194, pp. 14–15.

appreciation of the Doctrine as shall serve to augment between the United States and Latin American countries that existing good will which already binds us together as members of the great sisterhood of Republics which, as time goes on, constantly embraces new peoples of the world.

You will be prepared to communicate the foregoing to the Minister of Foreign Affairs at such time and in such manner as the Secretary of State shall direct; in the meanwhile you will hold this instruction strictly confidential.[45]

I am [etc.] FRANK B. KELLOGG

---

[45] Apparently the foregoing was never communicated to the respective Ministers for Foreign Affairs.

In a letter of June 25, 1930, to his successor, Mr. Henry L. Stimson, Mr. Kellogg with respect to this instruction wrote (710.11/1449) : "It seems to me that . . . the note ought to be delivered to the various countries and published."

To this letter the Secretary of State replied on June 28, 1930 (710.11/145) : "I have now read the note and it seems to me an excellent statement of the history and scope of the Monroe Doctrine.

"I have called its attention to the President with a view to releasing it but he has requested me to continue to hold it for awhile, thinking that at the present moment it might cause embarrassment in other matters."

## TACNA-ARICA DISPUTE:[1] GOOD OFFICES OF THE UNITED STATES IN THE FINAL SETTLEMENT OF ISSUES BETWEEN CHILE AND PERU; REPRESENTATIONS BY BOLIVIA

723.2515/3242½

*Memorandum by the Secretary of State of a Conversation With the Chilean Ambassador (Davila)*

[WASHINGTON,] December 1, 1928.

The Chilean Ambassador informed me today that his Government had instructed Figueroa, the Chilean Ambassador to Peru, to offer to Peru all the territory north of a line on an average of about ten kilometers north of the railroad. The line could not be exactly ten kilometers because it would not in every place conform with the line of the railroad but it would be as near as could be. Also that Chile would complete all public improvements in Tacna at its own expense, estimated at about six million Chilean pesos.

The Chilean Ambassador also said that Chile would be willing to make Arica a free port to Peru the same as Bolivia has at the present time and they would have their own Customs House and the same duties in the port that Chile and Bolivia now have. Chile now has a preferential duty. In this way Peru would have the same preferential low duties which Chile and Bolivia now enjoy; that Peru would enjoy the same tariffs on the railway and the Arica Tacna provinces would have access to the same ports and the same rights that they now enjoy.

---

723.2515/3235a : Telegram

*The Secretary of State to the Ambassador in Peru (Moore)*

[Paraphrase]

WASHINGTON, December 1, 1928—4 p. m.

84. Have you had an interview with President Leguia relating to a settlement of the Tacna-Arica matter along the lines you were talking to me, and with what result? Please make a full report.

KELLOGG

---

[1] Continued from *Foreign Relations*, 1928, vol. I, pp. 660–672.

723.2515/3243 : Telegram

## *The Ambassador in Peru (Moore) to the Secretary of State*
### [Paraphrase]

LIMA, December 13, 1928—7 p. m.
[Received 11:45 p. m.]

141. Your 84, December 1, 4 p. m.  Colonel Moore of the American Naval Mission is being sent by President Leguia to examine the port of Arica and vicinity to find out if another port could be established north of and near the port of Arica, or if a small part of the north end of the Arica port would meet Peru's requirements for an outlet from Tacna.  If this can be done, there is a possibility of a settlement of the entire Tacna-Arica question within a short time.  I promised this would be regarded as confidential.  It will probably be two weeks before a report can be made.

MOORE

723.2515/3243 : Telegram

## *The Secretary of State to the Ambassador in Peru (Moore)*
### [Paraphrase]

WASHINGTON, December 14, 1928—6 p. m.

87. Your 141, December 13, 7 p. m.  As the authorities of Chile are bound to find out about the visit of Colonel Moore, and most likely the reasons therefor, I think it would be well for me to inform the Chilean Ambassador at Washington confidentially regarding his going, requesting him to ask the Government of Chile to give Colonel Moore all possible facilities as we think it will help in the solution, and we are certain it will not be objected to if we take the matter up. Please inquire if there is any objection as we are anxious to do everything we can to be helpful.

KELLOGG

723.2515/3244 : Telegram

## *The Ambassador in Peru (Moore) to the Secretary of State*
### [Paraphrase]

LIMA, December 15, 1928—11 p. m.
[Received December 16—5:04 a. m.]

143. Your 87, December 14, 6 p. m.  Today I saw President Leguia. The President agrees with you that the authorities of Chile would probably find out about Colonel Moore's visit and the reasons therefor.  Since he does not wish anyone to know what is in his mind,

and he has not even told one of his Ministers, he has decided not to send Colonel Moore. I will keep you informed of any later developments. President Leguia may send someone else.

MOORE

723.2515/3249 : Telegram

*The Ambassador in Peru (Moore) to the Secretary of State*

[Paraphrase]

LIMA, December 30, 1928—10 p. m.
[Received December 31—2:45 a. m.]

148. Your 87, December 14, 6 p. m. I succeeded in getting President Leguia to accept your point of view in this matter. Could you secure permission from the Government of Chile for Ralph Cady, an American citizen, and his assistants to make a survey or examination of the coast of Tacna and Arica? Mr. Cady is the chief engineer of the Frederick Snare Corporation. President Leguia prefers to have it appear that survey project originated with you rather than with him. In any circumstances he wishes the request to be made. A prompt reply would be most helpful.

MOORE

723.2515/3250

*Memorandum by the Chief of the Division of Latin American Affairs (Morgan) of a Conversation Between the Secretary of State and the Chilean Ambassador (Davila), December 31, 1928*

The Secretary explained to the Ambassador the recent correspondence between Ambassador Moore and the Department relative to the sending of a representative by President Leguia to examine the port of Arica and vicinity to ascertain if another port could be established north of and near the port of Arica, or if a small portion of the north end of the Arica port would meet the requirements of Peru for an outlet from Tacna. The Secretary said that he had not wished Colonel Moore to go on this mission and had so informed the Ambassador. Now President Leguia desired to send Mr. Ralph Cady, chief engineer of the Frederick Snare Corporation, if permission could be obtained from the Chilean Government. Ambassador Davila after some hesitation said that he thought this could be arranged and that he would telegraph his Government accordingly. He said, however, that he thought it would be impossible to set aside a part of the port of Arica, as this port was too small. He also said that Chile planned to spend sixty million pesos in developing the port of Arica, and it seemed unnecessary for Peru to go to the expense of developing a separate port. He thought it would be better, if anyone went, that it should be Mr. Cady rather than Colonel Moore. The Secretary said he hoped that the Chilean Government would not raise any objection and would give Mr. Cady all facilities to make his investigation, in the interest of justice and the settlement of the Tacna-Arica problem. The Ambassador said that he thought it would be best that Mr. Cady should not make any public announcement of the purpose of his visit.

Referring to the Chilean Ambassador's proposal for a settlement of the Tacna-Arica problem, the Secretary pointed out that the Chilean line reached the ocean ten miles north of Arica. He thought this was pretty far, and saw no reason why the line should not be drawn down so as to meet the ocean much nearer the city. He thought this would be much more acceptable to Peru. The Ambassador said he understood that the line could not be drawn very close to the city without leaving the workshops of the Arica-La Paz Railway in Peru. After consulting the maps of the city the Secretary and the Ambassador thought that possibly a line could be drawn around the workshops and down between the Arica-Tacna and the Arica-La Paz Railways so as to reach the ocean quite near the city of Arica. This could not be decided with certainty as the workshops were not shown on the maps which were available for consultation.

MORGAN

---

723.2515/3249 : Telegram

*The Secretary of State to the Ambassador in Peru (Moore)*

[Paraphrase]

WASHINGTON, January 3, 1929—8 p. m.

1. Your 148, December 30, 10 p. m. The Chilean Ambassador informed me that the Government of Chile would give every possible facility to Mr. Cady to make the examination desired by President Leguia and he requested that the latter be so informed.

The Chilean Ambassador also informed me that this compliance on the part of the Government of Chile was not to be taken as in any way encouraging the pretensions of President Leguia to obtain an entry into the city of Arica. The Ambassador thinks that if Mr. Cady reports favorably on the possibilities of a Peruvian port north of Arica, much will have been accomplished toward bringing about a settlement; but if he reports recommending the sharing of the present port between Chile and Peru, there will be danger of another deadlock.

KELLOGG

723.2515/3251 : Telegram

*The Ambassador in Peru (Moore) to the Secretary of State*

[Paraphrase]

LIMA, January 4, 1929—3 p. m.
[Received 5:55 p. m.]

2. Your 1, January 3, 8 p. m. On January 9, Ralph Cady and assistant, Julio del Pino, will sail from Callao for Arica. Señor del Pino is a Peruvian citizen.

MOORE

---

723.2515/3252a : Telegram

*The Secretary of State to the Ambassador in Peru (Moore)*

[Paraphrase]

WASHINGTON, January 18, 1929—1 p. m.

7. I wish you would find out what the Government of Peru is willing to do to make a settlement. As you know, it is useless to talk of turning the city of Arica over to Peru. They have always understood that it could not be done. If there is to be a settlement, I should like to have it accomplished before I go out of office, and the time is very short.

KELLOGG

---

723.2515/3253 : Telegram

*The Ambassador in Peru (Moore) to the Secretary of State*

[Paraphrase]

LIMA, January 20, 1929—11 a. m.
[Received 2:20 p. m.]

6. Your 7, January 18, 1 p. m. I saw President Leguia and urged him to make some proposition. The President stated that he could not make any proposition until the Boundary Commissioners returned from Arica and reported. The Boundary Commissioners are expected to arrive in Lima on January 30. The President stated that he would try to make one at that time although he felt that if he could not get Arica, it would be just as well for Peru not to have the matter settled. There is a remote prospect, however, that he may make some proposition not including Arica. I am urging him almost daily, and I have stressed the importance of having something done before March 4.

MOORE

723.2515/3254 : Telegram

### The Ambassador in Peru (Moore) to the Secretary of State

[Paraphrase]

LIMA, January 22, 1929—6 p. m.
[Received 7:20 p. m.]

8. My 6, January 20, 11 a. m. The engineers will not return to Lima until February 6. Their preliminary report will probably be ready for presentation by February 9.

MOORE

723.2515/3254 : Telegram

### The Secretary of State to the Ambassador in Peru (Moore)

WASHINGTON, January 24, 1929—noon.

8. Your 8, January 22, 6 p. m. In view of this delay on the part of Peru please tell President Leguia that I suggest that the work of the Boundary Commission be suspended for two more months, or until April 17, 1929, in order to give time for a possible settlement after President Leguia has received the report of the engineers sent by him to Arica. Please cable immediately his answer. A similar request is being made of Chile.

KELLOGG

723.2515/3255 : Telegram

### The Ambassador in Peru (Moore) to the Secretary of State

LIMA, January 25, 1929—3 p. m.
[Received 4 p. m.]

9. Your telegram number 8, January 24, noon. President Leguia says that further suspension until April 17th is satisfactory to him.

MOORE

723.2515/3261

### The Chief of the Division of Latin American Affairs (Morgan) to the Secretary of State

[WASHINGTON,] January 30, 1929.

DEAR MR. SECRETARY: The Bolivian Minister called to say that his Government was naturally much interested over the rumors, which appeared to be well substantiated, to the effect that Chile and Peru were carrying on direct negotiations in Lima looking to a settlement of the boundary dispute. Naturally he had heard various reports as to the form that these negotiations were taking, but nothing which he could consider authentic. His Government was expecting him to keep it informed of developments in this problem of such vital importance to Bolivia, and he was somewhat at a loss to know what to report. He did not ask for any information which was confidential; of course he appreciated the fact that certain information which you received in your capacity as mediator could not be divulged, but he thought that probably there was something which you could tell him for the information of his Government, in order that they might have a slight idea of the nature of the settlement which might be expected. For example, whether there was any chance that it would follow the lines of the Kellogg Formula of 1926,[2] which of course would be very satisfactory to Bolivia. Or whether it would follow some other form. Bolivia did not wish to raise any obstacles in the way of any settlement which might be on the point of being brought about, but would like to know what was to be expected, and of course his Government was relying upon him to report. He found himself in a very embarrassing position vis-à-vis his own Government when he could tell them nothing whatever. He asked me to bring this matter to your attention and inquire whether he might have a brief conversation with you in which you might be able to give him frankly some indication of the actual situation with regard to the possible settlement of the Tacna-Arica question.

MORGAN

---

723.2515/3257a : Telegram

*The Secretary of State to the Ambassador in Peru (Moore)*

WASHINGTON, February 11, 1929—6 p. m.

10. The engineers have doubtless returned to Lima now and have presented their report on the situation at Arica to President Leguia. I sincerely hope that he will be able to make a generous and practicable proposal without delay.

KELLOGG

---

723.2515/3258 : Telegram

*The Ambassador in Peru (Moore) to the Secretary of State*

[Paraphrase]

LIMA, February 12, 1929—3 p. m.
[Received 6:20 p. m.]

12. Your 10, February 11, 6 p. m. This morning I saw President Leguia and informed him of the contents of your telegram. The engineers returned the latter part of last week; but Sunday, Mon-

---

[2] See minutes of meeting of the Plenipotentiaries, June 4, 1926, *Foreign Relations*, 1926, vol. I, p. 462.

day, and today are national holidays and President Leguia does not expect a preliminary report until the latter part of this week. The President intimated that he would make a proposal if the report was as he expected.

The situation in my opinion is simply this: Chile desires 10 kilometers north of the Arica–La Paz railroad and Peru does not want to give Chile any. I think that if a proposal is made by President Leguia, it will be based on the proposition of Chile's receiving only one quarter of a kilometer north of the railroad line at certain points. At other points they could have the ten. I will keep you posted. I am urging haste.

MOORE

---

723.2515/3264 : Telegram

*The Ambassador in Peru (Moore) to the Secretary of State*

[Paraphrase]

LIMA, February 21, 1929—4 p. m.<br>[Received February 22—12:15 a. m.]

19. Newspaper reports from Santiago published in Lima this morning regarding a settlement of the Tacna-Arica dispute have not the slightest foundation in fact. For the past five or six weeks President Leguia has not discussed the matter with any Chilean. Several weeks ago engineers went to Arica to survey the port and to find out if the suggestion which had been made concerning an extra port there was practicable. The engineers have now returned and yesterday they made their report to President Leguia.

President Leguia has not yet examined their report and consequently he could not possibly have made any proposal to Chile. If he approves the report, it is his intention to submit it to the Government of Chile through their Ambassador here.

The report indicates the following:

(1) There could be established a new port about one and a half kilometers north of the more northerly of the two existing Arica piers.
(2) It would be entirely within the present territory of Arica.
(3) The new port would form a new terminus for the Tacna railroad, and a part of this railroad (about two kilometers) at present entering the town of Arica would be abandoned.
(4) The line of the Arica–La Paz railroad would not be touched.
(5) Peruvian customhouses and warehouses would be located on grounds from dredged material. It would be necessary to dredge the port at this place.
(6) The new port would be wholly north of the present city of Arica.

In addition to this, there would be a division of territory by which arrangement Peru would receive Tacna, and Chile, Arica, as originally suggested, except a small piece of Arica territory which Peru would receive for the new port.

With regard to the Morro, President Leguia would insist that it be demilitarized and placed in charge of the Pan American Union which would supervise the erection of a peace monument there.

My personal belief is that President Leguia will approve this report and plan. If Chile agrees to it, the matter will be settled shortly.

MOORE

---

723.2515/3264 : Telegram

*The Secretary of State to the Ambassador in Peru (Moore)*

[Paraphrase]

WASHINGTON, February 25, 1929—4 p. m.

15. Your 19, February 21, 4 p. m. I think it very advisable for President Leguia to make the proposition set forth in the report outlined in your 19, February 21, 4 p. m. If this is done, I shall strongly urge Chile to accept. Can you tell when President Leguia will make his proposition?

KELLOGG

---

723.2515/3268 : Telegram

*The Ambassador in Peru (Moore) to the Secretary of State*

[Paraphrase]

LIMA, February 26, 1929—3 p. m.<br>[Received 3 : 50 p. m.]

21. This morning I saw President Leguia. The President said that he would submit a report to Ambassador Figueroa on February 28. President Leguia is not submitting the report as a proposition, but I personally believe that he would settle the Tacna-Arica question on the basis I suggested and in conformity with my 19, February 21, 4 p. m., if, in addition thereto, Chile would pay $3,500,000 for the construction of a new port in lieu of damages to Peruvian citizens.

MOORE

---

723.2515/3268 : Telegram

*The Secretary of State to the Ambassador in Peru (Moore)*

[Paraphrase]

WASHINGTON, February 27, 1929—noon.

16. Your 21, February 26, 3 p. m. Telegraph us immediately when President Leguia submits the report to Ambassador Figueroa.

I assume that it will be the same as your 19, February 21, 4 p. m. How is he going to get the proposition of $3,500,000 before Ambassador Figueroa?

I am obliged to you for your prompt message.

KELLOGG

---

723.2515/3269 : Telegram

*The Ambassador in Peru (Moore) to the Secretary of State*

[Paraphrase]

LIMA, February 27, 1929—8 p. m.
[Received 9 : 18 p. m.]

22. Your 16, February 27, noon. President Leguia will probably discuss cost of new port when he delivers engineers' report to Ambassador Figueroa. I will telegraph immediately when President Leguia submits it.

MOORE

---

723.2515/3270 : Telegram

*The Ambassador in Peru (Moore) to the Secretary of State*

[Paraphrase]

LIMA, February 28, 1929—1 p. m.
[Received 3 p. m.]

23. My 22, February 27, 8 p. m. President Leguia will deliver report to Ambassador Figueroa at the Government Palace at 5 p. m. today.

MOORE

---

723.2515/3272a : Telegram

*The Secretary of State to the Ambassador in Chile (Culbertson)*

[Paraphrase]

WASHINGTON, March 1, 1929—1 p. m.

18. I have been advised that President Leguia was to present to Ambassador Figueroa yesterday, at 5 p.m., the report of the engineers who recently visited Arica. Although this report is not presented by President Leguia as a proposal of settlement, nevertheless, it serves as a basis for discussion, and I understand that it was the intention of the President to discuss the matter with the Chilean Ambassador.

Although I do not know all the details of the matter, nevertheless, the synopsis which I have received leads me to feel that the report offers a very equitable basis for a settlement. This report is given by President Leguia to the Chilean Ambassador after most painstaking, thorough, and careful investigations, and is the result of the long and persistent friendly influence which I have exercised for a period of months. I very much hope, therefore, that the Government of Chile will give most careful consideration to this proposal, and will study it in the most sympathetic manner. You will understand, of course, that it has not been an easy matter to persuade President Leguia to go even this far, which very closely approaches the point of view which the Government of Chile has expressed. It is my personal feeling that this offers a fair basis of settlement, and I trust that Chile will consider it so.

KELLOGG

723.2515/3271 : Telegram

*The Ambassador in Peru (Moore) to the Secretary of State*

[Paraphrase]

LIMA, March 1, 1929—4 p. m.
[Received 7 p. m.]

24. My 23, February 28, 1 p. m. During a conference with President Leguia this morning he said that yesterday he had turned over the engineers' report to the Chilean Ambassador with the statement that in addition to this Peru would want $3,500,000 in lieu of damages to Peruvian citizens. This, I am convinced, is Peru's irreducible minimum.

I forwarded a copy of the engineers' report in the pouch due to reach Washington on March 12.

MOORE

723.2515/3271 : Telegram

*The Secretary of State to the Ambassador in Peru (Moore)*

[Paraphrase]

WASHINGTON, March 2, 1929—10 a. m.

17. Your No. 24, March 1, 4 p. m. Unless your No. 19, February 21, 4 p. m., is an accurate statement of the engineers' report which was furnished to the Chilean Ambassador, please telegraph it. I have assumed that it contained all the provisions on the subject of negotiation except the payment of the three and a half million dollars.

KELLOGG

723.2515/3272 : Telegram

*The Ambassador in Peru (Moore) to the Secretary of State*

[Paraphrase]

Lima, March 2, 1929—1 p. m.
[Received 2 : 25 p. m.]

25. Your 17, March 2, 10 a. m. My 19, February 21, 4 p. m., is an accurate statement of the engineers' report. Items (1) to (6) were written by the chief engineer.

MOORE

---

723.2515/3272 : Telegram

*The Secretary of State to the Ambassador in Peru (Moore)*

[Paraphrase]

Washington, March 2, 1929—6 p. m.

18. Your No. 25, March 2, 1 p. m. Thanks for the reply. In No. 19, February 21, following item (6), you say: "In addition to this, there would be a division of territory by which arrangement Peru would receive Tacna, and Chile, Arica, as originally suggested, except a small piece of Arica territory which Peru would receive for the new port." My understanding of this is that the line of division will run just north of the railroad all the way from the Bolivian boundary down to the sea; the line will not in any place exceed 10 kilometers and in many will be very much less. In any event, it is to be just north of the railway. Was this suggestion handed to the Chilean Ambassador on Thursday, February 28?

KELLOGG

---

723.2515/3274 : Telegram

*The Ambassador in Peru (Moore) to the Secretary of State*

[Paraphrase]

Lima, March 2, 1929—11 p. m.
[Received March 3—4 : 10 a. m.]

26. Your 18, March 2, 6 p. m. Your understanding of the matter is correct. The greatest distance is 10 kilometers and the smallest is 30 meters. This suggestion was handed to the Chilean Ambassador on Thursday, February 28.

MOORE

723.2515/3273 : Telegram

*The Ambassador in Chile (Culbertson) to the Secretary of State*

[Paraphrase]

SANTIAGO, March 3, 1929—noon.
[Received March 4—8:45 p. m.]

27. Your 18, March 1, 1 p. m. The Foreign Minister is absent but President Ibanez happens to be in Santiago. I am personally convinced that he and his advisers believe that a basis of final settlement has been outlined and that from now on it is only a question of working out the details. The expense connected with the new port presents a difficulty, and a request that the monument on the Morro be erected under the supervision of the Pan American Union would be regarded by Chile as a reflection on her good faith.

President Ibanez is sending you a telegram.[3] He expresses a sentiment universal in this city. You may feel confident that in this work for peace, as in others, your patient and constructive statesmanship has been decisive.

CULBERTSON

---

723.2515/3273 : Telegram

*The Secretary of State to the Ambassador in Chile (Culbertson)*[4]

[Paraphrase]

WASHINGTON, March 5, 1929—11 a. m.

20. Your 27, March 3, noon. I expect to remain as Secretary of State until about March 25 at which time my successor, Mr. Henry L. Stimson, will arrive. I wish to do everything in my power during this time to further a complete settlement.

KELLOGG

---

723.2515/3276 : Telegram

*The Ambassador in Peru (Moore) to the Secretary of State*

[Paraphrase]

LIMA, March 5, 1929—8 p. m.
[Received 9:50 p. m.]

27. If you believe it wise and can put this question up to President Hoover and can procure a favorable reply, it might go a long way toward securing a prompt settlement. The question is as follows:

---

[3] Telegram dated March 3, not printed; in it the President expressed his gratitude for Mr. Kellogg's part in restoring the ties of friendship between Chile and Peru (723.2515/3279).
[4] The same, *mutatis mutandis*, on the same date to the Ambassador in Peru as telegram No. 19.

"If President Leguia was ready to make a settlement, and if he felt it necessary, would President Hoover object to President Leguia's saying that he had made the settlement at the suggestion of, or on the advice of, the President of the United States?"

President Hoover made a very strong impression on the people of Peru, and President Leguia thinks that a statement of this kind might be most helpful.

MOORE

723.2515/3273 : Telegram

*The Secretary of State to the Ambassador in Chile (Culbertson)*

[Paraphrase]

WASHINGTON, March 6, 1929—10 a. m.

21. Your 27, March 3, noon. I very much hope that the Government of Chile will not permit the question of the erection of the monument on the Morro or the expense of the port to stand in the way of a definitive settlement.

KELLOGG

723.2515/3278 : Telegram

*The Ambassador in Chile (Culbertson) to the Secretary of State*

[Paraphrase]

SANTIAGO, March 6, 1929—noon.<br>[Received 1:45 p. m.]

28. Opposition of Chile to a separate port at Arica under the sovereignty of Peru is due in part to the fear that Peru might extend the Tacna-Arica railroad to connect with the La Paz railroad at a point beyond the Bolivian frontier, thus making possible an agreement between Bolivia and Peru which would destroy the trade of Arica. Furthermore, Chile asserts that Chile's claim for damages is as large as Peru's.

Copy sent to Embassy in Peru.

CULBERTSON

723.2515/3278 : Telegram

*The Secretary of State to the Ambassador in Chile (Culbertson)*

[Paraphrase]

WASHINGTON, March 7, 1929—7 p. m.

22. Your 28, March 6, noon. I cannot understand why there should be opposition to a separate port at Arica for Peru for the reasons set forth in your telegram. The construction of such a railroad would be so very difficult and expensive and would require such a long time that I do not feel that there is any reasonable danger to Chile on that score. The entire difficulty has been the sentiment

regarding Arica, and the proposed plan seems to be an admirable solution by permitting each country to have a port of Arica. The original port of Arica remains Chilean, and the arrangement, therefore, is very advantageous to Chile from every point of view.

Only after months of painstaking negotiations has President Leguia consented to go as far as he has in meeting Chile's point of view. The very fact that President Leguia has consented to a division of the territory is a great advance over the position he has consistently taken in the past, and his agreement now not only to the division, but also to the division on such terms as to give to Chile the greater part of the territory and the railroad to Bolivia intact, is more than I had been able to hope for for months. The payment of $3,500,000 in lieu of any damages is not a large amount, and if this most difficult question could be settled on that basis, it would appear extremely advantageous. The expenses of Chile in the plebiscite alone were probably not much, if any, short of that amount.

It is my earnest hope that the result of these long months of negotiation will not be lost now because of objections such as these.

The foregoing is for your information and informal use in conversations should a suitable opportunity present itself, but it is not to be used as a basis for making any representations.

KELLOGG

---

723.2515/3276 : Telegram

*The Secretary of State to the Ambassador in Peru (Moore)*

[Paraphrase]

WASHINGTON, March 9, 1929—1 p. m.

20. Your 27, March 5, 8 p. m. I have been unable to present this matter fully to President Hoover owing to the pressure of the first few days of the administration and especially to the Mexican situation. I am to do so the first of next week. I personally feel that President Hoover will be willing to aid along the lines suggested. I am sending this telegram to you in order that you may realize that I am not neglecting the matter.

KELLOGG

---

723.2515/3281 : Telegram

*The Ambassador in Chile (Culbertson) to the Secretary of State*

SANTIAGO, March 9, 1929—7 p. m.
[Received March 10—11:05 a. m.]

31. Minister for Foreign Affairs after a conference with the President has just sent a cable to the Peruvian [*Chilean?*] Ambassador in Lima in the following words:

"I reply to despatch No. 45. I am aware of interview with President Leguia. You will request an immediate audience with President Leguia and express regret in the first place and with much feeling at the absolute impossibility for us of accepting his (President Leguia's) idea of constructing a port on the northern side of the mouth of the River San Jose for the following reasons:

It would be situated 20 meters from the Arica-La Paz railway line at the foot of the Chinchorro yard of the same company, almost in front of the barracks of the Velazquez regiment, 1500 meters from the first pier of the bay, and finally would limit the future development of the city to the north. All these circumstances and the almost immediate vicinity to places of so much activity would give rise to constant conflicts and would create friction in a nascent friendship which we are seeking sincerely and in a definite form. For these reasons, always inspired by the hope of reaching an agreement advantageous to both, I propose to you the following ideas which you will submit to President Leguia.

1. There would be conceded to Peru anywhere within 1575 meters north of the Bay of Arica a pier, a building for her customs, and a modern station for the railway from Arica to Tacna. All constructed at our cost, and moreover there would be handed over to her $2,000,000.

The dividing line between Tacna and Arica would leave from the point on the coast known as Escritos, 16 kilometers from Arica and would continue therefrom in the form now agreed on, or that is, 10 kilometers to the north and in a line parallel in its entirety with the line of the Arica-La Paz railway. This formula is in my judgment the only one which would bring us to an effective friendship and union with Peru.

2. We would accept the port which President Leguia wishes to construct to the north of the mouth of the River Lluta or, that is, 10 kilometers from the Bay of Arica. We would give for that the sum of $3,500,000. It would be set forth in the treaty that the port could not be ceded to a third party and that no railway would be constructed to Bolivia. In accordance with our national sentiment this is the limit of our sacrifices and in no case can we go further."

[Paraphrase.] I understand from this telegram that Chile rejects the proposal of a port under the sovereignty of Peru as near as 1500 meters to Arica and proposes alternatives: (1) To give new railroad and customhouse facilities to Peru at any place between where the station now is and 1575 meters north, and to commence the international boundary on the coast about 16 kilometers north of Arica and to run it parallel to and 10 kilometers north of the railroad; (2) to give the port to Peru under Peruvian sovereignty which President Leguia asks, but to locate it 10 kilometers north of Arica at a place stated by Chilean engineers to be suitable. In this case the international boundary line would necessarily run south of the new port. The stipulation that the port could not be ceded to a third party might, I suggest, be softened by a proviso that neither Chile nor Peru shall cede all or any portion of their respective parts of the provinces without the consent of the other. With reference to my telegram No. 28, March

6, noon, I have been reliably informed that the President of Peru will agree never to extend the Tacna railroad to Bolivia. This stipulation might also have been put in general terms; for example, Chile and Peru agree not to extend or change the course of existing railroads in their respective parts of the provinces. Attention is also invited to the fact that the second proposal of Chile is to construct at Chile's expense the port that Peru asks, locating it not at the place selected by President Leguia but nevertheless within the limits of Arica so that it can be called Arica. I am convinced that the foregoing objections to a port under the sovereignty of Peru near Arica are made in good faith. There is real fear that the proximity will breed conflict.

A copy is being sent to the Embassy in Peru. [End paraphrase.]

CULBERTSON

723.2515/3281 : Telegram

*The Secretary of State to the Ambassador in Peru (Moore)*

[Paraphrase]

WASHINGTON, March 11, 1929—11 a. m.

21. I have just received from Ambassador Culbertson a copy of a telegram which the President of Chile sent to his Ambassador at Lima, repeated to you. Please telegraph as soon as possible the reaction of President Leguia to this proposition of Chile.

KELLOGG

723.2515/3283 : Telegram

*The Ambassador in Peru (Moore) to the Secretary of State*

LIMA, March 11, 1929—5 p. m.
[Received 11:11 p. m.]

28. The Chilean Ambassador today showed me the proposal from Chile. It is evident that the Chileans have not seen the engineers' report.

While on the face of it, it appeared that the shortest distance between the La Paz and Tacna railroads was 20 meters, this conclusion was reached because the engineers figured that the present tracks of the Tacna railroad would still continue to Arica. This is not the case. With the new port a part of the Tacna railroad from the new terminal to the present Arica station would be abandoned.

Assuming the port as proposed in engineers' report to be built, the following would be the distance:

1. The shortest distance between the Tacna railroad and the La Paz railroad is 230 meters.
2. The distance from the south end of the port terminal to Velasquez barracks is 300 meters.

3. The distance from the last (farthest south) track of the Tacna railroad entering the port terminal, to the Velasquez barracks is 1,030 meters.

4. The distance from the existing north pier in Arica Bay to the southern end of the new port terminal is 1,300 meters.

It would be possible to move the proposed port 300 meters north in which case the distances would be as follows:

1. The shortest distance between the Tacna railroad and the La Paz railroad will be 350 meters.

2. The distance from the south end of the port terminal to the Velasquez barracks will be 550 meters.

3. The distance from the last (farthest south) track of the Tacna railroad entering the port terminal, to the Velasquez barracks will be 1,330 meters.

4. The distance from the existing north pier in Arica Bay to the southern end of the new port terminal, will be 1,600 meters.

This answers at least to some extent the objections set forth in the Chilean proposition. The engineers say that it is not possible to locate a port farther north.

Am repeating this cable to Santiago.

MOORE

---

723.2515/3282 : Telegram

*The Ambassador in Peru (Moore) to the Secretary of State* [6]

[Paraphrase]

LIMA, March 11, 1929—9 p. m.
[Received 11:21 p. m.]

29. Your 21, March 11, 11 a. m. I saw President Leguia. He said that he must have a port for Tacna. The American engineers state that the only place where one is possible is the one they have indicated, which, they state, could be moved 300 meters north.

If the Chilean engineers can prove to President Leguia that a port can be constructed at the place they suggest for $3,500,000, I have no doubt that President Leguia will agree to it.

MOORE

---

723.2515/3283 : Telegram

*The Secretary of State to the Ambassador in Chile (Culbertson)*

WASHINGTON, March 12, 1929—1 p. m.

24. Please give Minister for Foreign Affairs copy of Ambassador Moore's cable to me No. 28, March 11, 5 p. m., which was repeated to you.

KELLOGG

---

[6] Repeated to Chile as Department's telegram No. 25, March 12, 2 p. m.

723.2515/3286 : Telegram

*The Ambassador in Peru (Moore) to the Secretary of State*

[Paraphrase]

LIMA, March 12, 1929—7 p. m.
[Received 9:15 p. m.]

30. I saw President Leguia today. He stated that he would meet the Chilean Ambassador tomorrow at 5 p. m. and would inform him that if Chile could guarantee the erection of a proper port at the place suggested in their proposal and at the figure named ($3,500,000) he would accept the proposition. President Leguia said that he would also tell the Chilean Ambassador at the same time that the American engineers had said that a port at that location was impossible. President Leguia will ask for the plans of the Chilean engineers.

MOORE

723.2515/3288a : Telegram

*The Secretary of State to the Ambassador in Chile (Culbertson)*[7]

[Paraphrase]

WASHINGTON, March 13, 1929—11 a. m.

26. I desire to know at the earliest possible time the final points on which Chile and Peru disagree as to the settlement. From all the cables, it seems to us that only the question of where the harbor will be located remains to be settled. President Hoover is anxious for an immediate settlement and he will do anything he can to further it. I desire the above information so as to advise him just what steps to take in communicating with the two Governments.

KELLOGG

723.2515/3289 : Telegram

*The Ambassador in Chile (Culbertson) to the Secretary of State*

[Paraphrase]

SANTIAGO, March 13, 1929—4 p. m.
[Received 10 p. m.]

33. (1) The Foreign Office is pleased with Ambassador Moore's report that President Leguia will accept a port near the mouth of the Lluta River if the Chilean engineers can prove that such a port is possible. This morning the engineers were working at the Foreign Office.

(2) I have emphasized to the Government of Chile that the final settlement now depends on their making good on this assertion. I

---

[7] The same, *mutatis mutandis*, on the same date, to the Ambassador in Peru as telegram No. 22.

suggest that you point out to Ambassador Davila the difficult position that Chile will be in if she fails. If Chile succeeds, we have a solution; if Chile fails, we are in a strong position from which to urge Peru's formula.

(3) Except for sentiment, Chile's proposal No. 1 in my 31, March 9, 7 p. m., is the better. The statistics in Ambassador Moore's 28, March 11, 5 p. m., and my despatch No. 106, February 11, 1929,[8] show that an independent port under the sovereignty of Peru located 1500 meters more or less north of Arica would have no hinterland for development without running into vital interests of Chile. Moving it 300 meters farther north would not help. It places it opposite and near the shops of the La Paz railroad. A new station under Chilean sovereignty and a new customhouse which will fly the Peruvian flag would give Peru all the terminal facilities which she needs. It should be obvious that there is no commercial reason for a separate port for Tacna. If it is constructed, it will become a monument to sentimental folly—a port without trade. Nevertheless, if that is the way to get the question settled, I am for it.

(4) The Peruvian Ambassador in Chile is in a state of hopeful skepticism. I have urged him to procure and study the information of the Chilean engineers regarding the practicability of a port near the Lluta River, and to report his conclusions to President Leguia.

(5) I suggest that we work toward a joint declaration by Chile and Peru to be made through you before you go out of office, embodying the vital and essential points of the settlement. The Foreign Minister approves this procedure and thinks that it is possible. I hope that we can make it sufficiently concrete so that nothing will remain to be done except the elaboration of the details in the final treaty. Your 26, March 13, 11 a. m., will be answered as soon as possible.

I am sending a copy to the American Embassy in Peru.

CULBERTSON

---

723.2515/3290 : Telegram

*The Ambassador in Peru (Moore) to the Secretary of State*

[Paraphrase]

LIMA, March 14, 1929—1 a. m.<br>[Received 10:25 a. m.]

31. I saw the Chilean Ambassador just after his conference with President Leguia. He told me that President Leguia had stated to him that if a suitable port could be constructed at the point suggested by Chile, he would accept the proposition, and he asked for a copy of the plans of the Chilean engineers. The Chilean Ambassa-

---

[8] Latter not printed.

dor informed President Leguia that he had no plans but that he would telegraph President Leguia's request to the Government of Chile. I asked Ambassador Figueroa how long it would take to get the plans here. He replied that it would probably take a month.

According to the best information I possess no survey has been made by any Chilean engineers, and my conviction is that it was just assumed that a port was possible at the place they suggested.

When the President of Peru agreed to my suggestion to establish a Peruvian port near Arica, he sent engineers to me for instructions. I accordingly requested the engineers to ascertain if it was possible to locate a port at least 10 to 15 kilometers north of Arica, and if not, to go down the coast and ascertain where it was possible to locate a port the farthest away from Arica. The engineers surveyed the coast from 15 kilometers north of Arica to the proposed location, and they told the President of Peru, and they also told me, that it was impossible to locate any port more than 300 or 400 meters north of the selected location, and they told me that the location 10 kilometers from Arica, selected by the Chileans, is just on the open sea, and that no port could be constructed there under any circumstances without the expenditure of from ten to fifteen million dollars, and perhaps not even for that sum.

The willingness of President Hoover to cooperate to the extent of having the final suggestion for settlement come from him is most helpful. I do not think that any settlement could be made without his cooperation, as both President Leguia and the Chilean Ambassador asked me to ascertain whether,—meters being in agreement,—President Hoover would make the suggestion embodying the settlement already agreed upon by them.

It is apparent to me that neither Government is certain how its people will take any settlement, and they desire to have the prestige of President Hoover's judgment back of them.

MOORE

---

723.2515/3291a : Telegram

*The Secretary of State to the Ambassador in Chile* (*Culbertson*)[9]

[Paraphrase]

WASHINGTON, March 14, 1929—1 p. m.

27. I had a long talk with Mr. Cady, the engineer who studied the situation at Arica regarding a port. He told me that while of course a port could be built anywhere, provided one had the money to do so, nevertheless, a port at Lluta would be most inadvisable. The port which he proposed at the San José River could be built satisfactorily

---

[9] Repeated to the Ambassador in Peru, for his information only, in telegram No. 23 of the same date; not printed.

for $3,500,000, and it could be moved 300 meters north as suggested in Ambassador Moore's 28, March 11, 5 p. m. Mr. Cady confirmed the distances and measurements given in that telegram. The port could not be constructed much more than 300 meters to the north or at any point between there and the Lluta River on account of the absence of water. There is water again when one gets to the Lluta River and a port could be built, but it would be greatly exposed to the sea and would be more costly because of the need for stronger breakwaters and the material would have to be transported a greater distance and hence the cost would be increased. Also, it would require probably 8 or 10 kilometers of new railroad construction to bring the Tacna railroad to a new port at Lluta at approximately the same grade as to Arica. No change in grade would be needed on the Tacna railroad to bring it into the new port proposed at the San José River, but very costly grading would be needed near Lluta where, Mr. Cady said, the character of the soil, sand and gravel is constantly changing after the yearly floods in the river and much bridging might be required.

While Mr. Cady disliked to make an estimate of cost without additional data before him, nevertheless, he said that to construct a port somewhat like the one proposed for the San José River at Lluta would probably come to two or three million dollars more than at San José, and that even then it could not be guaranteed against weather conditions, and that when the surveys are made at Lluta it may be discovered that conditions are such that an entirely different type of construction would be needed, which would greatly increase the cost. Mr. Cady referred in this connection to the costly breakwater at Antofagasta, in which there is already a breach, and to the costly construction at Valparaiso. Neither from an engineering nor from an economic point of view is a port at Lluta to be recommended, and Mr. Cady added that the site proposed on the San José River was the best in that vicinity. The proposed port would be protected by the Morro and Alacran Island and the breakwaters proposed would give protection but, on an open point as at Lluta, no guarantee could be given against damage.

Please communicate this at once to the Government of Chile and say that in view of these conditions I very much hope that it will find it possible to accept the proposal of President Leguia, which seems to be most advantageous. You may say that Mr. Cady stated that the distance from the northernmost dock at Arica to the proposed breakwater was 4000 feet, and from the same pier to the southernmost proposed pier of the new port 6400 feet, and that this port would not appear to interfere in any way with the shops of the railroad or the Velazquez barracks. The shops north of San José River have apparently been abandoned and used simply by Chilean army officers. Again, the Arica-La Paz railway rises rather sharply after it crosses the San José River and there is a natural division formed by the cliff at that point between the Tacna and La Paz railroads, so there appears to be no obstacle but rather every facility for constructing the port at that point and have the dividing line come in between the port and the La Paz railroad. Please telegraph the result of your conversation. Ambassador Davila is now in New York but he will return to Washington tonight, and tomorrow will have an interview with Mr. Cady and me at the Department.

KELLOGG

---

723.2515/3289 : Telegram

*The Secretary of State to the Ambassador in Chile (Culbertson)*[10]

[Paraphrase]

WASHINGTON, March 14, 1929—2 p. m.

28. Your 33, March 13, 4 p. m., paragraph (5). It appears to me that some time next week the Governments of Chile and Peru could make a brief memorandum setting forth that a settlement had been effected and outlining the principal points, even though certain details had to be worked out. President Hoover and I would then telegraph them, congratulating them on the settlement and expressing our gratification. I go out of office on March 26. I hope that you will work toward that end as I think such statements would have a good deal of influence with public opinion in South America.

KELLOGG

---

723.2515/3292 : Telegram

*The Ambassador in Chile (Culbertson) to the Secretary of State*

SANTIAGO, March 14, 1929—3 p. m.
[Received 8 : 35 p. m.]

35. Minister of Foreign Affairs gave me today the following information:

"Port on the River San José:—In order to find a depth of 10 meters it is necessary to go 1600 meters out to sea. The bottom is of oceanic rock which makes dredging impossible.

Port north of the River Lluta:—It can be constructed at the place called Punta Chacota, which is protected from the southern winds. In order to find a depth of 10 meters it is necessary to go only 600 meters out to sea. Its distance from the embankment of the Arica-La Paz railway is 7,230 meters.

Port north of River Molles:—According to technical opinion this is the best port. In order to find a depth of 10 meters it is only

---

[10] The same, *mutatis mutandis*, on the same date to the Ambassador in Peru as telegram No. 24.

necessary to go 402 out to sea. Its maintenance would cost very little because it is very sheltered. The Tacna-Arica railway can follow a direct line to this point thus economizing 34 kilometers of railroad. If Peru were to accept this port the frontier could be in the sea at Punta Chacota. Today there is a fishermen's cove and from there fish is sent to Tacna. Distance to the embankment of the Arica-La Paz railroad 29,730 meters."

Copy to Lima.

CULBERTSON

---

723.2515/3293 : Telegram

*The Ambassador in Chile (Culbertson) to the Secretary of State*

[Paraphrase]

SANTIAGO, March 15, 1929—1 a. m.<br>[Received 7:39 a. m.]

37. Your 26, March 13, 11 a. m. The location of the port is the only important point in disagreement. Peru accepts the second proposal quoted in my 31, March 9, 7 p. m. The Foreign Minister now says, however, that the location of a port near the mouth of the Lluta River, as in that proposal and in the second paragraph of his written memorandum which I telegraphed in my 35, March 14, 3 p. m., is not practicable because of dredging difficulty, and that the Chilean engineers now recommend that the port be located at a point opposite Escritos, 16 kilometers from Arica, which was mentioned in telegram to Ambassador Davila dated December 14. On March 15 a technical report will be cabled to the Chilean Ambassador in Peru.

Chile asks that the international boundary be located 10 kilometers north of the railroad. I do not know what President Leguia's view on this point is. Nor do I know whether President Leguia accepts the conditions specified in Chile's second proposal quoted in my 31, March 9, 7 p. m.

I have the assurance of the Foreign Minister on the following points:

Chile will pay $3,500,000 to build the port; the Government property north of the boundary will be turned over to Peru without charge; Chile will voluntarily, but not by any treaty stipulation, return to Peru certain trophies taken in the War of the Pacific; the removal of the fortifications from the Morro and the erection thereon of a monument to be dedicated by the Presidents of Chile and Peru, and the conversion of the Morro into a public park; reciprocal guarantees of personal and commercial rights; compulsory arbitration of all disputes regarding the interpretation of the treaty provisions.

If we allow the matter of the location of the port to become a wrangle among engineers, delay will result. I feel reasonably certain that Chile will never agree to a port under the sovereignty of Peru anywhere south of the Lluta River. Because of this, if Peru wants terminal facilities in that area, she must accept Chile's proposal No. 1 in my 31, March 9, 7 p. m. If she insists on a port, we might avoid the dispute over location by giving the money to Peru and leaving her free to construct a port at any place she might select north of Punta Chacota. She could then construct the port wherever she desired or use the money for something else. Perhaps we could persuade Chile to increase the payment so as to cover such items as the re-laying of the [railroad?]. In the declaration to be issued next week the provision on the port could read:

"Chile will pay to Peru the sum of $3,500,000 which sum Peru may use, if she so elects, to construct a port at any point selected by her engineers north of Punta Chacota."

The views set forth in your 27, March 14, 2 [1] p. m., just received, will be vigorously presented by me.

CULBERTSON

---

723.2515/3296 : Telegram

*The Ambassador in Chile (Culbertson) to the Secretary of State*

SANTIAGO, March 15, 1929—3 p. m.
[Received 9 : 30 p. m.]

39. The Minister for Foreign Affairs this morning after he had considered the information in your 27, March 14, 1 p. m., prepared in writing a memorandum on "reasons for not building San José port".

It reads as follows:

"1. Chile cannot accept grant of sovereignty to Peru in the vicinity of the Morro and within the Department of Arica, except north of the Lluta River from the point called Escritos and which is the same one as that of which Mr. Kellogg took notice on December 15th through Ambassador Davila as appears in official despatches.

2. The Government cannot accept this port because its acceptance is contrary to national sentiment and because it has been represented to the public that the territory would be divided into two equitable parts; while according to the Peruvian claim Peru would remain more or less 1,000 meters from the Morro with a port.

3. This would be neither a political nor commercial solution for Chile. It would not be political because Arica would remain with the knife in the side of Chile; and it is not commercial because a foreign port 1,000 meters from ours limits the development of the latter. Furthermore it should not be forgotten that we are being asked to build it ourselves.

4. The Government cannot accept even to discuss any port which Peru may wish to situate within the section of coast between the Lluta River and the San José River,—an idea which unfortunately is of

neither Peruvian nor of Chilean origin—was unanimously rejected in the Council of Ministers on Saturday the 9th, with the vote of the President of the Republic and of the Minister of Foreign Affairs."

Copy to Peru.

CULBERTSON

723.2515/3292 : Telegram

*The Secretary of State to the Ambassador in Chile (Culbertson)* [11]

WASHINGTON, March 15, 1929 — 3 p. m.

29. Your 35, March 14, 3 p. m.   I have discussed the contents of this telegram with Mr. Cady who states the following:

1. As regards the port on the San José River, the bottom of this area was thoroughly investigated and found to be gravel and sand and dredging is entirely feasible.   There is no solid rock.   Distance to ten meter counter line is not necessarily important since the cost of dredging and the cost of breakwaters must be balanced one against the other.

2. Mr. Cady states that from a general inspection of the coast north of Arica there was no place found that was worthy of a more detailed study.

3. As regards the economizing of thirty-four kilometers of railroad on the Tacna-Arica railway to a port north of the River Molles, Mr. Cady says that this would be impossible, maintaining the grade of the railroad.   The railroad from Arica rises at a uniform grade and to bring it down to the Coast at the same grade would require about the same amount of trackage.

4. Mr. Cady states that he thinks that what the Chileans have in mind in suggesting a port at these places is a small lighterage port and not a real port in the sense of one to which ships can go to dock.   It is possible that there may be small coves along this coast in which a lighterage pier could be built but nothing which would be suitable for a larger port such as he contemplated at the River San José.

KELLOGG

723.2515/3297 : Telegram

*The Ambassador in Peru (Moore) to the Secretary of State*

[Paraphrase]

LIMA, March 15, 1929 — 11 p. m.
[Received March 16 — 3:50 a. m.]

33. Your 24, March 14, 2 p. m.[12]   Today I saw President Leguia and used every argument I could think of to have him accept your proposition but he was adamant.   As nearly as I can quote him, he spoke as follows:

It is impossible.   Evidently Secretary Kellogg does not fully appreciate our proposition.   Peru must have a port for Tacna, and if

[11] Repeated to the Ambassador in Peru as telegram No. 29.
[12] See footnote 10, p. 742.

that is refused, then no settlement is possible. All other questions are of minor importance to this one. I have suggested the location of a port which I know can be constructed for $3,500,000 because the Snare Corporation has agreed to take its chances on the dredging. Chile has offered two sites which Peru's engineers state are impracticable—almost impossible. They cannot be constructed at anywhere near the cost of the port [which I have?] suggested. I am willing, however, to send the American engineers to make an investigation of these two sites, and if they agree that a suitable port can be constructed at either place, and if Chile will pay for the port and any necessary railroad connections to it, I am willing to accept the proposition. However, if and when Peru comes to an agreement with Chile and all the details are arranged satisfactory to both countries, I intend to have that agreement sent to President Hoover, and to request President Hoover to send it to Peru and Chile as a suggested settlement coming from him. Otherwise I fear the reaction of our people. We must have the prestige of the United States and of President Hoover behind any settlement. I think that Chile entertains the same opinion.

I told President Leguia that I had no authority to say, or even to intimate, what President Hoover would do under these circumstances, and all that I could say was that President Hoover wished to be as helpful as possible to both Peru and Chile.

Finally, after much urging, President Leguia replied that he would not object to discussing the proposal which you suggested in your 24, March 14, 2 p. m., with the Chilean Ambassador, if the latter brought up the subject.

MOORE

---

723.2515/3299 : Telegram

*The Ambassador in Chile (Culbertson) to the Secretary of State*

SANTIAGO, March 16, 1929 — 10 a. m.
[Received 12:25 p. m.]

41. With reference to paragraph 4 in your 29, March 15, 3 p. m., remind Cady that all the ports of Peru and Chile north of Valparaiso including the present Arica any [are?] lighterage ports. I have assumed that the port either at San José or Escritos would be of the same character.

Copy furnished Lima.

CULBERTSON

---

723.2515/3300 : Telegram

*The Ambassador in Peru (Moore) to the Secretary of State*
[Paraphrase]

LIMA, March 16, 1929—1 p. m.
[Received 3:15 p. m.]

35. Ambassador Culbertson, in his 37, March 15, 1 a. m., stated that Chile would pay $3,500,000 to Peru to build a port, and added that

perhaps we could persuade Chile to increase the payment to cover such items as re-laying the railroad. Could you ascertain how much additional Chile would pay for railroad construction if a port is found wholly north of Escritos and perhaps altogether outside the Province of Arica? I think a deal might be made if the sum is sufficient.

MOORE

723.2515/3299 : Telegram

*The Acting Secretary of State to the Ambassador in Chile (Culbertson)*

WASHINGTON, March 16, 1929—5 p. m.

31. Your 41, March 16, 10 a. m. Mr. Cady's report envisages a port with docks that ships can tie to and discharge cargo and not merely a lighterage port as at other places along the coast. He states such a port can be built at San José for three and a half million dollars and Mr. Cady's company is willing to contract to construct it for that sum.

CLARK

723.2515/3303 : Telegram

*The Ambassador in Peru (Moore) to the Secretary of State*

[Paraphrase]

LIMA, March 17, 1929—7 p. m.
[Received March 18—12 : 37 a. m.]

36. Your 27, March 16, 4 p. m.[13] I am deeply grateful for your more than kind telegram, and I will certainly work—work day and night, if necessary—to bring about an early settlement.

I was in conference for an hour with President Leguia on Saturday, March 16, before he met Ambassador Figueroa. President Leguia assured me that he would tell the Chilean Ambassador that he was willing to accept a suitable port at any place selected by the Chilean engineers if an investigation by American engineers proved it feasible, and if it could be constructed for $3,500,000. He stated that he would select Mr. George Seeley, vice president of the Frederick Snare Corporation, of New York City, and his assistants as the Peruvian engineers.

Following his conference with President Leguia, Ambassador Figueroa called and thanked me for my assistance. He said that the President had told him what I have outlined above. The Chilean Ambassador was very happy and more than profuse in his thanks.

Later I saw President Leguia again and I explained to him the delay necessary in going to Arica by steamer. At my request he

[13] Not printed.

stated that he would send his engineers by airplane. Subsequently I saw the Chilean Ambassador a second time and he said he would request the Government of Chile to send its engineers by airplane also so that no time would be lost.

Mr. Seeley will examine the plans submitted to him by Figueroa on Monday. There is a possibility that they will take off for Arica on March 18 or 19.

At present Chile and Peru are closer to a settlement than they have ever been, and for the first time I feel that a real settlement will come. The American engineers state that a real port is not feasible at any of the places suggested by Chile. But even if subsequent investigation confirms this opinion, you should not lose hope as there is yet a way out—a real solution.

I desire personally to assure you that for the past six weeks President Leguia, Ambassador Figueroa, and I have been in accord. Both President Leguia and the Chilean Ambassador are more than anxious for a settlement. Both have some obstacles to overcome. Both understand what the United States wants. I have been preaching to them that a settlement of any kind will be a good one. To use a Wilson expression, I have intimated to these gentlemen that to be a satisfactory settlement, it must be a peace without victory.

MOORE

---

723.2515/3302 : Telegram

*The Ambassador in Chile (Culbertson) to the Secretary of State*

[Paraphrase]

SANTIAGO, March 17, 1929—7 p. m.<br>[Received March 18—12 : 50 a. m.]

42. Referring to the Department's 31, March 16, 5 p. m. Of course Chile will not permit a port at the San José River superior to the port at Arica. A port at that place under the sovereignty of Peru at which oceangoing vessels can [dock?] may be an engineering possibility, but it is commercially absurd and politically impossible. Trade with Tacna would never justify it. Moreover, any attempt to use such a port to compete with Chile for the Bolivian trade would not bring the peace for which we are working. I do not think that President Leguia expects more than a lighterage port. President Leguia knows that world opinion would not uphold him in insisting, as the price of final settlement, upon a port superior not only to Arica but also to any port in Peru. If Engineer Cady will assure President Leguia that a suitable lighterage port can be built at or north of Escritos, he will do nothing less than settle the Tacna-Arica question without alteration, I think.

CULBERTSON

723.2515/3301 : Telegram

*The Ambassador in Chile (Culbertson) to the Secretary of State*

SANTIAGO, March 17, 1929—8 p. m.
[Received March 18—2 : 18 a. m.]

43. The following points are suggested unofficially for consideration in preparing the joint declaration of Chile and Peru:

1. The boundary between Chile and Peru will be fixed parallel to the Arica–La Paz railroad and 10 kilometers, more or less, north of it.

2. All government and municipal property north of this boundary will be turned over to Peru without charge.

3. Chile will pay to Peru $3,500,000 United States currency, which Peru may use, if she so desires, to build a port at any point selected by her engineers at or north of Escritos and to connect the Tacna railroad therewith.

4. Except as provided for in the treaty of settlement, Chile and Peru agree not to extend or change the course of railroads under their respective jurisdiction in the Provinces of Tacna and Arica.

5. Chile and Peru agree never to alienate to a third party all or any portion of their respective parts of the Provinces of Tacna and Arica without the consent and approval of the other.

6. If Peru decides to continue to maintain railway connections between Tacna and Arica, Chile will grant to Peru free port privileges at Arica and free transit in bond to Peruvian goods shipped into Bolivia by the Arica–La Paz railway.

7. Fortifications will be removed from the Morro promontory and a monument will be erected there in commemoration of the permanent peace established between the two countries, and the promontory will be converted into a park to which everyone will have free access.

8. Chile and Peru will agree to reciprocal guarantees of personal and commercial rights in the Provinces of Tacna and Arica.

9. Chile and Peru will embody in the final treaty of settlement specific and detailed provisions for compulsory arbitration of all disputes over the interpretation of treaty provisions.

As an alternative reading to point number 3, I suggest the following as possibly more acceptable to Peru:

3. Chile and Peru agree to appoint engineers to deal concerning the location of a suitable port for Peru at or north of Escritos and concerning the establishment of railroad connections between such port and Tacna. If and when the location of such a port is agreed upon, Chile will pay Peru the cost of construction of such port and of the establishment of railroad connections between it and Tacna but not to exceed 3,500,000 United States currency. Chile and Peru agree however that if investigation fails to convince Peru that a suitable port can be erected at or north of Escritos, the present settlement will nevertheless stand and Peru will accept in lieu of said port the sum of $3,500,000.

The Chilean Government has been [*sic*] considered and will accept all of the points suggested above. It will accept either number 3 or the proposed alternative as altered.

CULBERTSON

723.2515/3297 : Telegram

*The Secretary of State to the Ambassador in Peru (Moore)*

[Paraphrase]

WASHINGTON, March 18, 1929—1 p. m.

28. Your 33, March 15, 11 p. m. I am at a loss to understand what the President means by stating that evidently I do not fully appreciate his proposition; that he must have a port for Tacna and that if that is impossible then no settlement is possible. I made no such statement in my 24, March 14,[14] that President Leguia should not have a port; in fact, that is what I meant when I asked them to come to an agreement as to the principles, that is, including the port. He must know that I have used every possible influence with Chile to obtain a port at the site proposed by the engineers. Of course, I urged both Peru and Chile, to the extent I felt I was justified, to make a reasonable settlement. I understand President Leguia's proposition about President Hoover, and my suggestion about agreeing on principles was that, as soon as the formula of settlement was telegraphed, the President would not only endorse it but would propose it as a settlement to Peru and Chile. I do not believe I would experience any difficulty in getting him to do that if Peru and Chile came to a preliminary understanding as to what they were willing to accept. The proposal which I suggested in my 24, March 14, was along the same lines as the proposal of President Leguia contained in your 33, March 15, 11 p. m.

KELLOGG

723.2515/3301 : Telegram

*The Secretary of State to the Ambassador in Chile (Culbertson)*

[Paraphrase]

WASHINGTON, March 18, 1929—3 p. m.

32. Your 43, March 17, 8 p. m. It is my feeling that the difficulty in reaching a prompt agreement may arise from the feeling in Chile that Peru will accept a port at Escritos. The position seems to be as follows:

President Leguia insists upon a port for Tacna, and with Chile's permission sent engineers to make a survey of the coast and report if it would be possible to construct another port north of Arica. The coast was examined separately from a launch and by airplane by two American engineers who both arrived independently at the very definite conclusion that the only feasible port is at the San José River. A detailed investigation was then made there including soundings and an investigation of the bottom. After assembling all

---

[14] See footnote 10, page 742.

the data they made a comprehensive study of it and reported that a port could be made there for $3,500,000. President Leguia then presented this to Chile.

The Government of Chile replied that it would give Peru a dock, warehouse, customhouse, and railroad station in Arica and have the boundary line come to the sea at Escritos, or would give them $3,-500,000 for building a port at Lluta. The Government of Chile apparently had no surveys indicating the feasibility of such a port. President Leguia replied that, according to his information, a port could not be built at Lluta but, if Chile could show that it could be built there for $3,500,000, he would accept, and he asked for the plans of the Chilean engineers. The Chilean engineers later admitted that a port could not be built at Lluta and suggested that one be constructed at Escritos, but so far have offered no evidence that competent studies had been made there which indicate the feasibility of such a port. After this the Foreign Minister in his memorandum to you definitely stated that Chile would not accept a Peruvian port south of the Lluta River. This was the first intimation received of such a position on the part of Chile. No such intimation was made by Chile when it gave permission for the engineers to visit Arica or during the time of their investigations over a period of some weeks or while they were preparing their report. The fact that Chile made no objection to the coming of the engineers and the making of the survey seemed to indicate that Chile was willing to discuss a port south of the Lluta River. Mr. Cady states definitely that a port cannot be constructed at Escritos and the Department of State has been advised by the president of the Frederick Snare Corporation that its other engineers at Lima, including a vice president of the corporation, hold the same opinion.

While a lighterage pier might perhaps be constructed further north, its cost and that of the breakwaters, together with the very extensive railroad construction necessary to bring the Tacna railroad to such a port, would be vastly more than $3,500,000. Therefore, should Peru accept a port further north, of which we have no assurance, it would presumably want the payment of $3,500,000 by Chile augmented to such a sum as may be required to meet the increased cost.

President Leguia countered Chile's proposal by requesting evidence that such a port could be constructed for $3,500,000 and this has not been forthcoming and the American engineers say that it cannot be constructed for that sum. There is, therefore, a settlement possible by accepting the port of the San José River and a remote possibility, of which I have no assurance, that a settlement might possibly be reached if Chile would agree to construct the port further north whatever it might cost. We have no evidence that Peru would accept such a proposal nor have we been advised that Chile has agreed to pay the larger sum, whatever it might be.

You may discuss this matter fully with the Chilean authorities and report the result by cable.

KELLOGG

---

723.2515/3305 : Telegram

*The Ambassador in Peru (Moore) to the Secretary of State*

[Paraphrase]

LIMA, March 18, 1929—7 p. m.
[Received March 19—9 : 40 a. m.]

37. It is evident that my 33, March 15, 11 p. m., was not clear. President Leguia did not mean to infer that you did not desire him to have a port. Not only that, but, as I told the President in my interview, after you had talked to Mr. Cady, you had made every effort to have Chile accept the San José port. What President Leguia intended to convey was this:

(1) Chile refused to consider the San José port.
(2) Chile offered two other ports, which President Leguia's engineers state are impossible.
(3) If President Leguia's engineers are correct, then he would have no Peruvian port for Tacna.
(4) Therefore, President Leguia states that without a Peruvian port for Tacna, no settlement appears to be possible.
(5) However, as stated in my 36, March 17, 7 p. m., President Leguia is going to send engineers to investigate the sites offered by Chile, and the solution will depend upon their [report?].
(6) To put the matter concisely, it is not merely the question of obtaining $3,500,000 to construct a port, but the question of finding a location for a port.

Will you kindly telegraph me the agreement you [say?] President Leguia should sign, and I will do all in my power to have him agree to it.

MOORE

---

723.2515/3306 : Telegram

*The Ambassador in Peru (Moore) to the Secretary of State*

LIMA, March 19, 1929—1 p. m.
[Received 4 : 08 p. m.]

39. Ambassador Figueroa has notified President Leguia that additional plans and a more detailed report are on their way up from Chile and will arrive here shortly. This will delay departure of

the Peruvian engineers until the papers arrive. Anything that can be done to expedite the presentation of these plans will be helpful.

MOORE

---

723.2515/3309 : Telegram

*The Ambassador in Chile (Culbertson) to the Secretary of State*

[Paraphrase]

SANTIAGO, March 20, 1929—7 p. m.
[Received 10:32 p. m.]

45. Again I urged the Foreign Minister to give Peru a port at the San José River. I received in reply the same objections which I have already telegraphed to you. I then asked him to submit the entire question once more to President Ibanez, following the points in your 32, March 18, 3 p. m. I impressed upon him the responsibility which Chile assumes in rejecting a port at San José and pointed out the obligation that the Government of Chile is under not only to prove that a port is feasible at or north of Escritos but to pay for it whatever the cost may be. The Foreign Minister feels confident that the report and plans of the Chilean engineers now in Lima and the conference this week between the Chilean and Peruvian engineers on the ground north of Arica will satisfy Peru that a suitable port can be constructed.

To the question as to whether Chile was willing to reconsider the request of Peru for a port under Peruvian sovereignty at the San José River, the Foreign Minister after his conference with President Ibanez replied in writing:

"Never! It cannot be granted for reasons already known to Secretary Kellogg, not only through Ambassador Culbertson in Chile but also through the Chilean Ambassador in the United States."

To the question whether Chile was willing to pay for the construction of a port northwest or north of Escritos, and for the connections of it with the Tacna Railroad, even if the cost exceeded $3,500,000, he replied in writing:

"The time for raising this question has not arrived. It would not be convenient for Chile to express an opinion regarding it before the final report which we await."

In my opinion Chile is willing to pay more than $3,500,000 but [the Foreign Minister?] will not commit himself as to the amount until Chile receives the report of the engineers who are now consulting at Arica, and to which reference was made in the above answer. The Foreign Minister has made a long written explanation of the points mentioned in your telegram, and he has telegraphed it to Ambassador Davila. I will not repeat it unless you instruct me to do so.

CULBERTSON

723.2515/3308 : Telegram

## The Ambassador in Peru (Moore) to the Secretary of State

[Paraphrase]

LIMA, March 20, 1929—8 p. m.
[Received 10:32 p. m.]

40. Today Ambassador Figueroa notified me that the Chilean engineers would reach Arica today or tomorrow. The Peruvian engineers will leave Lima on the morning of March 22 by airplane for Arica.

I believe the Tacna-Arica question will be practically settled if a suitable port with proper railroad connections can and will be constructed by Chile for Peru at either place suggested by Chile, and if President Hoover will consent to present the agreement as his proposed solution.

MOORE

723.2515/3309 : Telegram

## The Secretary of State to the Ambassador in Chile (Culbertson)

[Paraphrase]

WASHINGTON, March 21, 1929—noon.

33. . . .

With regard to your 45, March 20, 7 p. m. I think that under the circumstances there is nothing else to do now except to await the report of the engineers and find out what Chile and Peru agree upon.

I am familiar with the long written explanation to Ambassador Davila so you do not need to repeat it. I do not think it would be advisable to press Chile any further; but desire your opinion as to whether there is any prospect of anything being done while I am Secretary of State.

KELLOGG

723.2515/3312 : Telegram

## The Ambassador in Chile (Culbertson) to the Secretary of State

[Paraphrase]

SANTIAGO, March 22, 1929—6 p. m.
[Received 9:40 p. m.]

46. Your 33, March 21, 11 a. m. [noon]. The Foreign Minister is heartily in favor of a joint declaration of settlement to be given publicity. He will, as I have stated, accept the declaration quoted in my 43, March 17, 8 a. m. [p. m.], or he will accept the following shorter declaration which we drafted in conference:[15]

[15] Quotation not paraphrased.

"Chile and Peru have settled the Tacna-Arica question and the following provisions are the principal features of the settlement:

1. The boundary between Chile and Peru will be fixed parallel to the Arica-La Paz railroad and 10 kilometers, more or less, north of it.

2. Fortifications will be removed from the Morro promontory and a monument will be erected there in commemoration of the permanent peace established between the two countries and the promontory will be converted into a public park.

3. A separate port for Tacna located at or north of Escritos will be constructed at the expense of Chile. Chilean and Peruvian engineers are now consulting on the exact location of this port and on its cost and when Chile and Peru have agreed on these two remaining points the final settlement will be embodied in a formal treaty and the Presidents of the two countries will unite in dedicating the peace monument on the Morro promontory."

The above declaration was telegraphed to the Chilean Ambassador in Peru with instructions to obtain the approval of President Leguia to its publication or, failing this, to inquire what modifications in the declaration would make it acceptable to Peru. The Foreign Minister strongly urges that you also submit this declaration to President Leguia tomorrow morning, either through the Peruvian Ambassador in the United States or the American Ambassador in Peru.

CULBERTSON

---

723.2515/3312 : Telegram

*The Secretary of State to the Ambassador in Peru* (*Moore*)

[Paraphrase]

WASHINGTON, March 23, 1929—11 a. m.

31. I have been informed that the Chilean Foreign Minister telegraphed to the Chilean Ambassador in Peru the following declaration with instructions to obtain the approval of President Leguia to its publication or, failing this, to inquire what modifications in the declaration would make it acceptable to Peru. The declaration is as follows:

[Here follows quoted portion of telegram No. 46, March 22, 6 p. m., from the Ambassador in Chile, printed *supra*.]

I do not desire you to urge this particular declaration on President Leguia until I know more or less of his views. He might think we are crowding him too hard. Should he favor it, or should he favor it with modification, which may be acceptable to Chile, I shall, of course, welcome the issuance of such a statement before I go out of office, and I have no doubt that the President would willingly make this, or any other agreement between Chile and Peru, as a proposal to both.

KELLOGG

723.2515/3311 : Telegram

### The Ambassador in Peru (Moore) to the Secretary of State

[Paraphrase]

LIMA, March 23, 1929—8 p. m.
[Received 9 : 30 p. m.]

44. Up until 7 p. m. the Chilean Ambassador has not asked for any conference. At that time I saw President Leguia and informed him that I had it on good authority that Chile would make a new proposition to him at once. President Leguia replied that he would be glad to see the Ambassador and promised me that immediately after his conference with Ambassador Figueroa he would send for me and let me know the result.

MOORE

723.2515/3313b : Telegram

### The Secretary of State to the Ambassador in Chile (Culbertson)[16]

WASHINGTON, March 25, 1929—11 a. m.

34. I shall remain in office until Friday.[17]

KELLOGG

723.2515/3314b : Telegram

### The Secretary of State to the Ambassador in Chile (Culbertson)[18]

WASHINGTON, March 26, 1929—10 a. m.

35. Have the engineers reported yet the results of their investigation at Escritos and to the north thereof? When may we expect to hear something definite from them?

KELLOGG

723.2515/3317 : Telegram

### The Ambassador in Chile (Culbertson) to the Secretary of State

SANTIAGO, March 27, 1929—noon.
[Received 1 : 10 p. m.]

51. Your 35, March 26, 10 a. m. The Governor of Arica reports that Chilean and Peruvian engineers have examined proposed ports at and north of Escritos; that Chilean engineers made clear that Chile would not under any conditions permit a Peruvian port at the mouth of the River San José; that the engineers representing Peru,

[16] The same, mutatis mutandis, on the same date to the Ambassador in Peru as telegram No. 32.
[17] March 29.
[18] The same, mutatis mutandis, on the same date to the Ambassador in Peru, as telegram No. 33.

who left Arica for Lima this morning, did not indicate the nature of the recommendations which they would make to President Leguia.

CULBERTSON

723.2515/3318 : Telegram

*The Ambassador in Peru (Moore) to the Secretary of State*

LIMA, March 27, 1929—5 p. m.
[Received 5 : 35 p. m.]

51. The Peruvian engineers arrived here from Arica by aeroplane this afternoon at 4 : 30.

MOORE

723.2515/3321 : Telegram

*The Ambassador in Peru (Moore) to the Secretary of State*

[Extracts—Paraphrase]

LIMA, March 31, 1929—4 p. m.
[Received April 1—7 : 12 a. m.]

55. I am sending you the following résumé of the Tacna-Arica negotiations since Chile and Peru resumed diplomatic relations [19] thinking that such a résumé may be helpful to you.

. . . . . . . .

8. At the same time President Leguia informed me that he could not agree to any solution unless the suggestion was made by President Hoover to the Governments of Peru and Chile. (I transmitted this information to Secretary Kellogg in telegram No. 27, March 5, 8 p. m. and although Secretary Kellogg said he thought he could get President Hoover to agree to it,[20] no direct answer has been received. I have referred to it several times since as being an absolute essential to any settlement of the problem. Would it be possible to obtain a definite answer?)

. . . . . . . .

MOORE

723.2515/3322 : Telegram

*The Ambassador in Peru (Moore) to the Secretary of State*

LIMA, April 1, 1929—8 p. m.
[Received April 2—6 : 58 a. m.]

56. The following report in connection with the investigation of the ports suggested by Chile was submitted today to President Leguia by Mr. George Seeley, vice president of the Frederick Snare Corporation:

[19] See *Foreign Relations*, 1928, vol. I, pp. 647 ff.
[20] See telegram No. 20, March 9, 1 p. m., to the Ambassador in Peru, p. 734.

"April 1, 1929.

Dear Mr. President: I take pleasure in reporting to you as follows the result of the trip made to Arica recently to investigate further on the proposed port.

On our arrival we were met by the Governor of the Province together with the secretary of the provincial government; the two Chilean engineers, one of whom was the one who sent in the report that was given to you recently by the Chilean Ambassador, and others. All of these gentlemen were at all times more than courteous and all facilities of every kind were placed at our disposal to help in the execution of our mission.

On discussing our mission with the Chilean engineers, I found that the report which they had sent in and which was transmitted to you through the Chilean Embassy, was based entirely on the statements that had been made to these engineers by others and on data obtained from maps in the Ministerio de la Marina and was not based on any personal investigation or knowledge. They have made no plans of any kind; in fact, they had no projects, except a verbal description which they gave me of what they had in mind. As far as I could gather, no investigation of any kind had ever been made, nor had any plans of any kind been worked up.

In company with these Chilean engineers, and on two occasions with the Governor of the Province, an examination was made of the coast in detail by automobile, launch, on foot and by aeroplane along the whole length from Arica to the mouth of the River Sama, a distance of about 3 kilometers south—or toward Arica—from the mouth of the River Lluta. This whole coast stretches in almost a straight line running about southeast to northwest and without a single point or indentation worthy of the name in the whole distance. Part of the coast is a low sandy beach, part rocky, and on the lower portions indications show that in very recent years the ocean has covered the coast line for a distance of about 2 kilometers back from the beach. As this coast lies almost directly facing the Pacific Ocean swell and as it is without natural protection of any kind, it would be difficult to find a coast line more exposed and less appropriate for the construction of the type of port that you desire.

The locations proposed by the Chilean engineers, and which were mentioned in their original report, were all looked into in detail, as also other sites proposed. The same general statement applies to all—none were in any way suitable.

With the exception of the mouth of the River San José at Arica and the mouth of the River Lluta about 14 kilometers north of Arica, there is no water to be found at any point along this coast, other than some springs located at a point named Las Yaradas.

These springs are of doubtful quantity and while the quality is subject to analysis, it has a very distinct salty taste.

The administrator of the Tacna-Arica railway also told us that these springs were entirely dry for more than three months of this year.

At all of these points lengths of railway would have to be built, varying from about 7 kilometers to 21 kilometers, in order to connect the existing Tacna-Arica line; also, as all of these locations are in desert country, it would mean the building of a complete town, together with the electric light and power plant, sewerage system, water supply, etc., all of which would considerably increase the cost.

It is our opinion that no port could be built at any point along this coast north of the River Lluta which would have the least chance of proving successful. The Chilean engineers, recognizing the nature of coast, also stated that in their opinion the locations were unsuitable. They, however, made the statement that they believed a port could be constructed at a cost of about eight million to nine million dollars but at the same time admitted that even at this expenditure such a port would not have proper protection from storms that might come from the north or northwest. We believe that even with such an excessive expenditure it would be a most improper piece of construction; one, in fact, that I do not believe our company would want to assume any responsibility for.

We believe that the only point on this coast at which a proper port could be built is in or approximately in the location picked out by us and mentioned in our previous report; viz, just to the north of the River San José, and we believe that this, in general, applies to any port whether it be a port to accommodate ships or whether it be a port for the lighterage only.

Signed, Frederick Snare Corporation, George Seeley, Vice President."

Please do not transmit this report to Santiago as it has not yet been submitted to the Chilean Ambassador here. He will send it to his Government.

[Paraphrase.] The report was very disappointing to President Leguia, for he had hoped that it would be favorable and that the controversy would be settled. He stated to me that he believed he had gone as far as he could. [End paraphrase.]

MOORE

---

723.2515/3322 : Telegram

*The Secretary of State to the Ambassador in Peru (Moore)*

WASHINGTON, April 8, 1929—2 p. m.

41. Your 56, April 1, 8 p. m. Chilean Ambassador left at Department on Saturday a telegram from his Government dated April 4, reading in translation as follows:

"Conclusions which Chilean engineers reach in their report in open disagreement with the American report. Engineers Lira and Quezada declare: First, that the data contained in the charts are in conformity with the soundings made in front of Lluta, Escritos, Hospicio and Yaradas. Second, that the waves which come from the high sea arrive at the beach perpendicularly and leave breakers which cover an area of 150 meters from the San José River to the north, being more gentle in the neighborhood of this river. Third, that the above circumstance has made the American engineers believe that a port at San José would not need important protective works. Fourth, that this advantage disappears when the sea is raging because the violence of the waves is the same as at the north of the Lluta River. Fifth, that the American Engineers, together with the Chileans, could verify the existence of fresh water at Yaradas. Sixth, that the only disadvantage at Yaradas with regard to the rest of the coast is the non-existence of rocks in the vicinity for use, which increases the cost of the works by ten per cent, at the most. Seventh, that Engineer Seeley stated to his Chilean colleagues that the commission which he had received from Leguia was to give a report on the possibility of constructing a protected port north of Lluta and that it be commercially justified. Eighth, that all agreed that there was no port from Arica to Sama in which the natural conditions would make the construction of a port commercially justifiable. Ninth, that Engineer Seeley agreed with the Chileans that the port at San José offered more favorable conditions during its construction, because the breakers were more gentle than north of Lluta, but that it would require very substantial protective works for ocean storms, with the result that the cost would be at least equal to Yaradas. Tenth, Finally Engineer Seeley declared that the port at San José had not sufficient natural conditions and that it was easier to find them at the present port of Ilo, at which the cost of the works would not be disproportionate.

As you see, the conclusions which the two reports reached are very different and contradictory."

STIMSON

---

723.2515/3325 : Telegram

*The Ambassador in Chile (Culbertson) to the Secretary of State*

[Paraphrase]

SANTIAGO, April 8, 1929—4 p. m.
[Received 8 p. m.]

57. While Peru has made no proposal, the Foreign Minister said this morning that President Leguia will accept either a port at Las Yaradas which engineers stated would cost eight or nine million dollars or a port 3 kilometers north of the most northerly pier of Arica which would cost $3,500,000. Tomorrow the Chilean Cabinet will consider these solutions. The Foreign Minister was unwilling to express an opinion as to what the decision would be.

CULBERTSON

---

723.2515/3326 : Telegram

*The Ambassador in Peru (Moore) to the Secretary of State*

LIMA, April 9, 1929—3 p. m.
[Received 7:10 p. m.]

62. Your 41, April 8, 2 p. m. President Leguia is at a loss to know how the American engineers' report could have been answered April

4th by Chile when he did not deliver it to the Chilean Ambassador here until April 6th.

Engineer Seeley will today prepare an answer to the Chilean engineers' statements.

MOORE

---

723.2515/3328 : Telegram

*The Ambassador in Peru (Moore) to the Secretary of State*

LIMA, April 8 [9?], 1929—6 p. m.
[Received April 10—6 : 23 a. m.]

63. The following memorandum commenting on the Chilean Government engineers' report, transmitted in your telegram 41, April 8, 2 p. m., has been submitted to President Leguia by Engineer Seeley.

"This cable (41) refers to a telegram dated April 4th which was left at the Department of State on Saturday April 6th by the Chilean Ambassador.

According to reports the Chilean engineers, Lira and Quesada, had an interview with the President of Chile on April 3rd at which time it is to be supposed they rendered to him a report on the investigation made jointly with us at Arica.

We believe that this cable and the telegram which the Chilean Ambassador in Washington left at the State Department must refer to our original report on the San José location and is not an answer to our more recent report dated April 1st which was, we understand, not transmitted by the Chilean Ambassador in Lima to Santiago until Saturday, April 6th.

We would comment on this telegram in detail as follows: (Numbers refer to numbered points in Chile engineers' report):

1. Altogether there were probably not over ten to fifteen soundings made along the stretch of coast examined. While it is very possible that these check up with data contained in charts, we do not believe that this is any indication that a port location exists at any of these points nor that it would in any way justify the construction of a port at any of these locations. We did not attempt to check any charts; our only object was to find a suitable location.

2. This would seem to bear out completely what we have already stated, that the closer one gets to the San José River, the more natural protection there is and consequently the less wave effect from the open sea.

3. We have at no time considered the construction of a port at the San José River location without the protection of breakwaters. These breakwaters, as designed, would be of similar construction to the one already built at Colon and while similar to those in Callao would be of heavier cross section and would be, we believe, amply heavy for the protection of any port built at this point.

4. While it is true that the San José location offers very little natural protection against storms coming from the north and northwest, it is in this regard no worse than any other point on the coast

and is at the same time protected by nature somewhat from storms coming from the south or west, which protection does not exist at any other point between Arica and the River Sama. According to the Chilean engineers, storms from the north and northwest occur very seldom along this coast. If such is the case such natural protection as there is in the San José location would be of great advantage to this port during a very large portion of the time.

5. It is true that at the point named Yaradas there is one well which, when we visited the site, contained water. There is no way of telling what the quantity of water might be. The manager of the Tacna-Arica railroad advised us that this well was dry for probably three months of this year. Without having the water actually analyzed, we cannot say whether the quality is suitable for construction purposes and afterwards for town and port use. The water itself had a distinctly salty taste in which statement I believe the Chilean engineers will also agree. It is unnecessary to call attention to the fact that in the construction of a port a large amount and a constant supply of water is required for use in boilers, concrete, etc., and that after the construction is completed, a large amount and a constant supply of water is required for everyday use, the supplying of ships etc.

6. No stone suitable for breakwater purposes was found anywhere near the Yaradas location. The Chilean engineers agreed that stone for this purpose would have to come from the quarry behind Arica. In order to bring stone from there it would be necessary to transport this material over the branch line running from the quarry into Arica then transport it over approximately 24 kilometers of the Tacna-Arica railway and then over approximately 17 kilometers of a new railway construction which would have to be put in. The manager of the Tacna-Arica railway advised us that in accordance with their concession, they had the sole right for the transporting of goods between Arica and Tacna, and if any materials were transported over their line freight to them would have to be included. The rate which he gave us for this material over that portion of their line which would have to be utilized was ten (10) pesos per ton, which is the equivalent of approximately sixty five cents gold [$2.50] [21] per cubic meter. He said that it was possible that through negotiations with their board of directors in London this rate might be lowered somewhat. I think it unnecessary to call attention to the fact that even though it were cut in half the total of this rate plus the other haulage charges would certainly increase by more than 10 percent the cost of stone brought up to this location. I believe there is very little question but that the increased cost of rock at this point would be at least twenty [fifty] [21] percent over the cost of the same material at the San José site.

7. Instructions received from President Leguia were to report on the possibility of constructing a protective port north of the River Lluta and to see if this port could be built for approximately the same figure as the one at San José, having at the same time the same facili-

---

[21] Corrected by telegram No. 65, April 10, 6 p. m., from the Ambassador in Peru (723.2515/3330).

ties which we had offered in our original report at a cost of approximately $3,500,000.

8. In this statement we agree. I would also add that we would not consider it proper from a construction standpoint.

9. This is quite true except that no statement was made by me that the port works at San José would result in a cost at least equivalent to Yaradas. I think the real answer to this is in our offer to construct a port at San José at a cost of $3,500,000.

10. No statement of this kind was made by me. There was no reason for a discussion of Ilo as there is already a port there and there is no physical connection with Tacna.

In general we believe that this telegram does not refer to the report made President Leguia on our trip of investigation. Even though it did refer to this report, we see nothing in this telegram which is particularly different or contradictory to our report of April 1st. I see nothing in this telegram which points out a proper location or any statement that a proper port can be built at any location. There are certain statements criticizing the San José location. I think a general answer to this is that we would be willing to build and guarantee a port at that point while we would be very hesitant about doing so at any other location between Arica and the Sama River. Inasmuch as no one is infallible, we would be very glad to look over and report on any plans and definite projects which the Chilean engineers might propose. So far we have seen nothing in the way of definite suggestions."

MOORE

---

723.2515/3327 : Telegram

*The Ambassador in Chile (Culbertson) to the Secretary of State*

SANTIAGO, April 9, 1929—10 p. m.
[Received April 10—1 : 35 a. m.]

59. Referring to my telegram No. 57, April 8, 4 p. m. Consideration by the Cabinet adjourned pending further discussion with the Chilean engineers. A cable was sent tonight to Figueroa at Lima in which Chilean engineers—those who designed the port of San Antonio, Antofagasta and Constitution and who have just returned from an investigation of the coast north of Arica—state:

1. That the type of construction recommended by Cady for Las Yaradas will not withstand the sea and that they disagree with Seeley as to the cost of construction at this place;

2. That following the type of construction at San Antonio they will assume the responsibility of constructing a port at Las Yaradas with warehouses, customhouse, railroad connection, et cetera, for a little under six million dollars.

Minister of Foreign Affairs concludes his cable to Figueroa as follows:

"You may tell Leguia about our desire to arrive as soon as possible at a final solution in order to avoid further cablegraphic discussions of a technical character. If he wishes, the Chilean engineers may go to Lima to show him their estimates, plans, maps, et cetera. You may add that if he accepts that Chile assumes the responsibility of the construction in Las Yaradas, he need only declare it and appoint a controller in order to initiate the works immediately. We have all the necessary equipment. In any case we would give Peru six million dollars for the port at Las Yaradas or at Ilo in southern Peru in case Leguia should choose the latter place. In this way the Tacna Arica question may come to an end without any more difficulties and with great advantage for both countries."

I understand from this cable that Chile is willing to pay Peru six million dollars to be used for any purpose Peru may choose and that, if Leguia decides to use it to build a port at Las Yaradas, Chile is willing to send her engineers to Lima for conference and that they are willing to assume the responsibility of constructing the port and facilities at this point for under six million dollars.

CULBERTSON

---

723.2515/3329 : Telegram

*The Ambassador in Peru (Moore) to the Secretary of State*

[Paraphrase]

LIMA, April 10, 1929—3 a. m.
[Received 9:05 a. m.]

64. Tonight I received the following self-explanatory note from President Leguia, dated April 9:

"Dear Mr. Ambassador: With reference to this morning's conversation I beg to say as follows:

At the various interviews which I have had with the Chilean Ambassador we have definitely agreed on two points: first, that Tacna shall have a port of its own and second, that the cost of constructing such a port will be defrayed by Chile.

As you know the Frederick Snare Corporation experts were requested to study the most suitable place for constructing the port. They have gone thoroughly into the subject, but so far the selection made by them has been objected to by Chile. Now they appear to be entangled in a discussion as to the suitability or otherwise of the sites recommended by the Chilean engineers in lieu of the site suggested by the Snare Corporation. I fear that nothing will come of it.

In order, however, that you should see clearly into the matter, I desire to tell you that as far as we are concerned it is immaterial whether the contemplated port is near to or some kilometers distant from the present port of Arica, provided that the port to be built is guaranteed by a reputable concern, and that the contract therefor insures the construction of a port similar to the one which the Snare Corporation is willing to undertake to construct at San José. In short, I do not desire any quibbling on this score, and I should be greatly obliged to you if you would kindly so convey it to

President Hoover and Secretary Stimson, if you deem it necessary to do so. I am, dear Ambassador, yours very truly, (signed) A. B. Leguia."

I suggest that the negotiations dealing with this matter be undertaken directly with Ambassador Davila because I have been informed on excellent authority that he is very close to the President of Chile and has much influence with him.

MOORE

---

723.2515/3331 : Telegram

*The Ambassador in Peru (Moore) to the Secretary of State*

[Paraphrase]

LIMA, April 11, 1929—4 a. m.<br>[Received 6:07 a. m.]

68. Tonight I saw Ambassador Figueroa. He said that on Thursday, April 11, 1 p. m., he would present the proposal from his Government to President Leguia. He outlined this as follows:

Chile will offer to build a port at the site selected by its engineers near Las Yaradas. He said that the cost would be around $6,000,000, to be paid by Chile. Tomorrow he will present the details of the proposed port, and the engineers' plans will follow by mail from Chile. If desired by Peru, the Chilean engineers will also come to Lima.

Tonight President Leguia told me that he would accept [it?] only if a reputable firm would contract to construct it and guarantee its stability, Chile to pay for it and the necessary railroad connection.

MOORE

---

723.2515/3332 : Telegram

*The Ambassador in Peru (Moore) to the Secretary of State*

[Paraphrase]

LIMA, April 11, 1929—noon.<br>[Received 1 p. m.]

69. Supplementing my telegram No. 68, April 11, 4 a. m. All of President Leguia's propositions or acceptances are predicated on the assumption that if and when Chile and Peru agree, President Hoover will offer the compromise as coming from him and both countries will accept it. The understanding, of course, is that before President Hoover makes the final proposition both countries agree to accept its terms.

MOORE

723.2515/3321 : Telegram

*The Secretary of State to the Ambassador in Peru (Moore)*

[Paraphrase]

WASHINGTON, April 11, 1929—5 p. m.

44. Your 55, March 31, 4 p. m., eighth paragraph. In your discretion you may communicate the following orally and confidentially
to President Leguia. When the time comes, President Hoover is
ready to make a suggestion of settlement to both Peru and Chile on
the condition that the settlement which the President is to suggest
has the prior approval of both Peru and Chile.

STIMSON

723.2515/3333 : Telegram

*The Ambassador in Peru (Moore) to the Secretary of State*

[Paraphrase]

LIMA, April 11, 1929—7 p. m.
[Received 11:55 p. m.]

70. This afternoon I saw President Leguia after his conference
with Ambassador Figueroa. The conference turned out as predicted
in my 68, April 11, 4 a. m. The details regarding the proposed port
were turned over to President Leguia, who in turn gave them to
Engineer Seeley for examination and report.

MOORE

723.2515/3335 : Telegram

*The Ambassador in Peru (Moore) to the Secretary of State*

LIMA, April 12, 1929—6 p. m.
[Received April 13—3 a. m.]

72. My number 70, April 11, 7 p. m. Engineer Seeley this afternoon filed with President Leguia his answer to the Chilean details
of the proposed port at Yaradas which were submitted to the President yesterday by Ambassador Figueroa.

Seeley's report reads as follows:

"April 12.
Dear Mr. President: Regarding the cable from Santiago to the
Chilean Ambassador dated April 9th, which you gave me yesterday
afternoon, I would comment as follows.

As stated in my memorandum of April 10th, there was no reason
for discussing Ilo. It already has a port belonging to Peru and
has no physical connection with Tacna.

In regard to changes deemed necessary by the Chilean engineers
in the San José project and their statement as to cost, I believe
the best answer is the one already given you; i. e., we will contract

for the construction of this port and guarantee the physical results for approximately $3,500,000 as stated in our original report.

As to their statement regarding the Yaradas location, we have been unable to work out any plans for a port at that place which we could unreservedly guarantee and which would come within their estimated cost of $6,000,000.

We would respectfully suggest, Mr. President, that the Chilean Government be requested to send, as soon as possible, their project with detailed plans and specifications showing what they have in mind and the type of construction proposed. We would be only too pleased to examine these and make a report, sending them to New York to be examined by our engineers there and by other recognized authorities in New York with whom we are in almost daily contact, submitting to you their opinions and estimates of cost. We believe this would avoid further discussions and that it would be the quickest way of satisfying all concerned as to whether the proposed scheme is really feasible or otherwise and whether it would meet with your requirements.

Very respectfully yours, Frederick Snare Corporation, (Signed) G. P. Seeley, Junior, Vice President."

President Leguia will request the Chileans to present their plans as soon as possible. Ambassador Figueroa just informed me that they are on their way and would arrive here in about 10 days.

Personally I think the expenditure of $6,000,000 for a port to take care of 1600 tons of freight (which was total tonnage of Tacna last year) is almost a financial crime.

From what the American engineers tell me and from what I learn from other Americans who have visited Tacna-Arica, the whole territory is almost worthless except in the small valleys surrounding the cities of Tacna and Arica. The whole situation reminds me of two baldheaded men fighting over a comb. However, pride is playing such an important part that a really practical and economic settlement will be hard to reach. I am using all my efforts for a solution and I believe that eventually something will be worked out.

From a purely commercial standpoint I believe Peru would be better off to accept the free port, customhouse, railroad station and pier offered by Chile with the addition of $6,000,000 for damages which I believe Chile would pay. On the other hand I think Chile would be commercially better off to accept the San José proposition. It may be possible that between these two propositions something can be worked out.

I am rather inclined to think a port at Yaradas is almost impossible for the reason that the Snare Corporation, who would naturally be most interested in securing the contract for its construction, state positively that a practical and proper port cannot be built there within the limits suggested.

MOORE

723.2515/3336 : Telegram

## The Ambassador in Peru (Moore) to the Secretary of State

[Paraphrase]

LIMA, April 14, 1929—11 p. m.
[Received April 15—1 : 45 a. m.]

73 Do not pay any attention to the newspaper report from Santiago. The conditions this evening are exactly as outlined in my 72, April 12, 6 p. m. President Leguia has asked for the plans and specifications of the proposed port at Las Yaradas. When they are received they will be turned over to Engineer Seeley who will examine them and send copies to New York City for expert opinion there. If a feasible and practical port can be constructed, Peru will accept it.

This will take time. President Leguia told me in an emphatic manner that he would not sign any papers until the question of the feasibility of the port has been thoroughly demonstrated. He requested me to inform you that he would sign no agreement until such agreement had been submitted to you and President Hoover.

MOORE

---

723.2515/3337 : Telegram

## The Ambassador in Chile (Culbertson) to the Secretary of State

[Paraphrase]

SANTIAGO, April 16, 1929—4 p. m.
[Received 9: 33 p. m.]

61. My 59, April 9, 10 a. m. [p. m.] Referring to the Chilean proposal summarized in the above telegram, President Leguia is said to have replied that the Tacna-Arica question would be virtually settled if the Government of Chile will obtain a guarantee to construct a port at Las Yaradas from an American engineering concern. The Government of Chile is now consulting the J. G. White Engineering Corporation and other American concerns, all of which are willing to guarantee the construction of the port. Ulen and Company and Fred T. Ley and Company, working together, offer to construct and guarantee the port on a cost plus basis. While the Government of Chile has now fixed the amount which it is willing to pay at $6,000,000 more or less, I feel confident that if money becomes the only question standing in the way of settlement, Chile will pay.

I am not pressing the Foreign Minister in any way. As a matter of fact, I have not seen him personally for several days in view of the fact that direct negotiations appear to be progressing nicely.

CULBERTSON

723.2515/3338 : Telegram

*The Ambassador in Peru (Moore) to the Secretary of State*

[Paraphrase]

LIMA, April 16, 1929—7 p. m.
[Received April 17—4:43 a. m.]

75. Today I had two conferences with President Leguia. At the first conference he asked me if President Hoover would make the suggestion of settlement of the Tacna-Arica question if both countries agreed beforehand to accept the suggestion.

I informed President Leguia that you had stated that President Hoover would do so, but only under the conditions mentioned in your 44, April 11, 5 p. m. He then told me of a suggestion he was going to make to Ambassador Figueroa and requested me to return at 5 p. m.

When I saw him at that time he said in substance:

"I had a conference with the Chilean Ambassador. I asked the Ambassador for the plans and specifications of the proposed port at Yaradas. The Ambassador replied that he had no plans at present but that Chile would guarantee the construction of the port.

I answered that I was unable to take this guarantee from Chile because it would only lead to future disputes, and that no one could guarantee himself.

I then informed the Chilean Ambassador that as it appeared to be impossible for Chile's engineers and mine to agree, I would consider the proposition of Peru's taking the customhouse, railroad station, and pier at Arica—all constructed at the expense of Chile for the free use of Peru in perpetuity—and $6,000,000 to connect Tacna by railroad with other portions of Peru. I stated that I would accept this proposal only on condition that the suggestion for settlement come from the President of the United States, Herbert Hoover."

. . . . . . .

President Leguia has the idea that if the proposed solution comes from the President of the United States of America, it will carry more prestige, will be more binding and will save any disputes which might arise in the future.

MOORE

---

723.2515/3340 : Telegram

*The Ambassador in Chile (Culbertson) to the Secretary of State*

[Paraphrase]

SANTIAGO, April 17, 1929—11 a. m.
[Received 3:20 p. m.]

62. My 31, March 9, 7 p. m. The Government of Chile has received a telegram from its Ambassador in Peru reporting a conversation with President Leguia. President Leguia expressed lack of confi-

dence in the possibility of constructing a port at Las Yaradas, where-upon the Chilean Ambassador asked him to speak frankly and definitely regarding the solution of the Tacna-Arica question. President Leguia replied as follows:

"I accept the proposal of the memorandum which you recently presented to me, namely, the concession to Peru within the Bay of Arica of a pier, customhouse, and station for the Arica-Tacna railway all constructed at the expense of the Government of Chile and where Peru will enjoy complete freedom of the port. In addition to this Chile must pay $6,000,000 in cash to Peru. The boundary line will commence at a point on the coast 10 kilometers north of Arica and run parallel to the railway line from Arica to La Paz up to kilometer 160. From this point to kilometer 190 the line must include in the Peruvian territory the Usuma [*Uchusuma?*] and Aguada Canals and Laguna Blanca. President Leguia added that it was not necessary to make any declaration about new railways and the concession of a port of the territory to a third party; but with regard to the last point, however, if Chile insists, Peru will accept it."

Finally, President Leguia stated that as a condition to this agreement the proposition must come from the Government of the United States inviting both countries to accept. President Leguia desires that this entire proposition be kept strictly secret until the matter is settled.

Although I have no official statement from the Foreign Minister, my impression is that the proposition will be acceptable to the Government of Chile.

CULBERTSON

723.2515/3342 : Telegram

*The Ambassador in Chile (Culbertson) to the Secretary of State*

[Paraphrase]

SANTIAGO, April 17, 1929—8 p. m.
[Received April 18—1:28 a. m.]

63. My 62, April 17, 11 a. m. This evening the Government of Chile transmitted to Ambassador Figueroa for submission to President Leguia the following suggestions to be incorporated in the proposal of settlement to be made by the President of the United States of America to Chile and Peru:

"(*a*) The division of the territory in two parts, Tacna for Peru and Arica for Chile. The dividing line shall commence at Escritos on the coast and continue 10 kilometers to the north of the Arica-La Paz railroad and run in its entirety parallel to that railroad, and follow the geographical features of the land as far as the frontier of Bolivia. The Uchusuma Canal will remain in Peruvian territory, and the Azufre tributary (Tacora) in Chilean territory, and the line shall divide Laguna Blanca in equal parts. A commission of engineers to delimit the frontier shall be named by Chile and Peru and, in case of disagreement, the President of the United States of America shall appoint a third as referee.

(*b*) The Government of Chile will give to Peru within the Bay of Arica a pier, a building for a custom house, and a station for the railway from Arica to Tacna with absolute control by, and the rights of a free port for, Peru. These works shall be constructed at the expense of the Government of Chile.

(*c*) The Government of Chile will turn over to Peru the sum of 40,000,000 pesos in Chilean currency (in the legal money of Chile) or $5,000,000.

(*d*) All real estate and public works belonging to the Government of Chile shall be turned over to the Government of Peru by Chile without cost.

(*e*) The Government of Chile shall recognize the concession which the Arica-Tacna railway enjoys in Arica.

(*f*) The Government of Chile shall turn over the territory of Tacna to Peru 30 days after the treaty is ratified.

(*g*) The Government of Chile shall construct a monument on the Morro at Arica commemorative of the peace.

(*h*) Chile and Peru shall not without previous agreement amongst themselves concede to a third party any part of the territory or alter the actual system of international railways."

The above information was brought to the Embassy by the Assistant Secretary of State, who added that the withdrawal of the Morro fortifications is not mentioned because the Government of Chile does not want to include this clause in the treaty but that it is understood that these fortifications shall be withdrawn. The Assistant Secretary of State recommended that the information conveyed in this telegram be kept strictly confidential until a reply has been received from Peru.

CULBERTSON

---

723.2515/3344 : Telegram

*The Ambassador in Peru (Moore) to the Secretary of State*

[Paraphrase]

LIMA, April 19, 1929—10 p. m.
[Received April 20—6 : 41 a. m.]

76. I saw President Leguia after his conference with Chilean Ambassador Figueroa today. President Leguia stated that they had reached an agreement as per my 75, April 16, 7 p. m. (paragraph 3 of my quotation of the President), except that the Chilean Ambassador said that his Minister for Foreign Affairs wanted the suggestion to come from him instead of from President Hoover.

Thereupon President Leguia told Ambassador Figueroa (as he had stated before) that the only way he would make a settlement would be to have hte compromise suggestion come from President Hoover.

Ambassador Figueroa said he would take it up with the Government of Chile and give President Leguia an answer as soon as possible.

President Leguia stated to me that he felt that his only protection was to have the suggestion come from the President of the United States. He said that he desired no friction over interpretation at any time, and that when the proposal came from President Hoover there could be no disputes. In addition, a suggestion from President Hoover would be more popular with the people of Peru than a suggestion from Chile. For all these reasons, therefore, President Leguia said that he must insist on this point.

If Chile agrees to it, President Leguia and the Chilean Ambassador will agree on the details and the text of the agreement will be sent to you to be submitted to President Hoover.

I emphasized to President Leguia that the question would have to be put up to President Hoover in such a manner that would in no way embarrass either him or you. President Leguia assured me that he would be quite willing to take suggestions as to the manner of presenting it. I personally think that I have a suggestion for submitting it which will make quite easy.

MOORE

---

723.2515/3346 : Telegram

*The Ambassador in Chile (Culbertson) to the Secretary of State*

[Paraphrase]

SANTIAGO, April 20, 1929—3 p. m.
[Received 8:32 p. m.]

65. Peru accepts the settlement summarized in my 63, April 17, 8 p. m., with the exception of the following changes which Foreign Minister says Chile accepts:

(1) President Leguia insists on six million dollars.

(2) President Leguia insists on boundary line commencing at coast 10 kilometers north of Arica instead of farther north at about Escritos, but he will accept decision of engineers as to starting point as well as to boundary line following railroad in accordance with the contour of the country.

(3) President Leguia insists on warehouse for merchandise in addition to customhouse at Arica.

Two other points were mentioned over which there will be some discussion but concerning which there is no doubt about agreement.

(1) President Leguia wants written clause in the treaty that the Morro of Arica will be demilitarized and that Chile will erect a peace monument thereon, or at least a separate protocol to that effect.

(2) President Leguia desires that consideration be given to the liability to military service of Peruvians born in Tacna and Arica.

President Leguia will insist that the President of the United States of America continue his good offices for the sake of public opinion and Chile is in accord. It seems that President Leguia wants it to appear publicly that the settlement has the approval of the United States of America.

The Foreign Minister is now preparing a draft of the proposal of settlement which Chile and Peru hope President Hoover will be willing to submit to them. It will contain certain whereases, the terms finally agreed upon, and it may mention the former disagreement of the two countries over the port at Las Yaradas. It is to be sent to Lima and when it is in final form it will be transmitted to Washington.

You will, of course, desire to consider fully the wisdom of such a proposal by the President of the United States and its phraseology in case its issuance meets with your approval.

CULBERTSON

---

723.2515/3347 : Telegram

*The Ambassador in Peru (Moore) to the Secretary of State*

[Paraphrase]

LIMA, April 21, 1929—11 p. m.
[Received April 22—3 a. m.]

78. This afternoon Ambassador Figueroa told President Leguia in my presence that Chile would accept President Leguia's proposition to have President Hoover make the compromise suggestion for the settlement. He stated that Chile's formal acceptance would be handed to President Leguia on Thursday, April 25. When the formal acceptance is received, the papers will be immediately drawn up, and when they are completed they will be sent to you at once for submission to President Hoover for his approval.

I do not think this will take long as all the points have been agreed upon.

If you have any suggestions, I will be glad to receive them.

MOORE

---

723.2515/3349 : Telegram

*The Secretary of State to the Ambassador in Peru (Moore)*

[Paraphrase]

WASHINGTON, April 23, 1929—6 p. m.

46. The exact scope of the proposal by the President of the United States to Chile and Peru contemplated and desired by President Leguia is not clear to the Department from your telegrams. Your 55, March 31, 4 p. m., mentions a "suggestion" by the President. Your 27, March 5, 8 p. m., also mentions a suggestion. Your 69, April

11, noon, speaks of the President offering the compromise as coming from him which both countries would accept. Your 73, April 14, 11 p. m., states that President Leguia would sign no agreement until it had been "submitted" to the President. Your 75, April 16, 7 p. m., contemplates that the President would make "the suggestion of settlement" if both countries agreed beforehand to accept the suggestion, and twice subsequently in the same telegram President Leguia mentions the "suggestion for settlement" as coming from the President of the United States. Your 76, April 19, 10 p. m., speaks of "the compromise suggestion" coming from the President. Your 78, April 21, 11 p. m., states that when the formal acceptance of the Government of Chile is received to the proposal of Peru the papers will be drawn up and will then be transmitted to Washington "for submission to President Hoover for his approval".

It is important that we should know the intention of the parties as soon as possible. Is it (1) that the President of the United States shall make a suggestion in detail to both countries, giving them the exact wording of the agreement reached by them, or (2) is it contemplated that the President of the United States should merely give an outline of the proposal, or (3) will the proposal in detail be submitted to the President of the United States as Arbitrator by the parties requesting his approval or sanction of the agreement as ending the arbitral proceedings?

STIMSON

---

723.2515/3348 : Telegram

*The Ambassador in Peru (Moore) to the Secretary of State*

[Paraphrase]

LIMA, April 24, 1929—4 a. m.
[Received 5:41 a. m.]

79. Your 46, April 23, 6 p. m. Peru and Chile were unable to agree on a port at Yaradas, and they came to an impasse. President Leguia then stated that he would be willing to accept a compromise (as outlined in my 75, April 16, 7 p. m., paragraph 3 of my quotation from President Leguia) if that compromise was suggested by President Hoover.

In answer to second paragraph of your 46, April 23, 6 p. m., number (1), it is President Leguia's idea that the President of the United States shall make the suggestion to both countries in detail, giving them the exact wording of the agreement reached between them.

I am sorry that my telegrams were confusing. I will see President Leguia immediately after Ambassador Figueroa has had his conference, and I will keep you informed.

MOORE

723.2515/3350 : Telegram

## The Ambassador in Peru (*Moore*) to the Secretary of State

LIMA, April 24, 1929—2 p. m.
[Received 2:50 p. m.]

80. Your 46.[23] Saw President Leguia at 1 o'clock today. He told me that proposition number (2) of your telegram 46 of April 23rd would also be satisfactory and might be less complicated. He said that he would consult with the Chilean Ambassador at 5 o'clock this afternoon and at 6:30 he would let me know just what the Chilean Ambassador and himself agreed on and what they would ask President Hoover to do.

MOORE

---

723.2515/3351 : Telegram

## The Ambassador in Peru (*Moore*) to the Secretary of State

[Paraphrase]

LIMA, April 24, 1929—10 p. m.
[Received April 25—6:55 a. m.]

81. I had an interview with President Leguia after his conference with Ambassador Figueroa this afternoon. President Leguia stated that the Chilean Ambassador had presented a proposed draft of the agreement for the settlement of the Tacna-Arica dispute, but that in the proposed draft the boundary lines which they had previously agreed upon had been changed, and that he could not accept this, not at least until he had time to study these matters with his engineers and experts. President Leguia told Ambassador Figueroa that he could not give him a definite answer before April 27.

The President also stated that they had a clause that the port of Arica was not to be fortified, and this was omitted. The Chilean Ambassador explained that they would be willing to agree to this in a separate note.

President Leguia and Ambassador Figueroa then discussed the question as to how the matter would be put up to President Hoover, and Ambassador Figueroa replied that Ambassador Davila had suggested that the Peruvian and Chilean Ambassadors in the United States together present the agreement to Secretary of State Stimson, and that he would in turn transmit it to President Hoover for his approval. President Leguia stated that as long as President Hoover made the decision he was satisfied, but that he wanted to be certain that it was satisfactory to the President of the United States.

President Leguia requested me to inform you that so far as this feature of the settlement is concerned he desires to do just what you feel will be best for all concerned, and the easiest for you and the President. President Leguia's one desire is to have the decision made by President Hoover.

MOORE

_____

723.2515/3351 : Telegram

*The Secretary of State to the Ambassador in Peru (Moore)*

WASHINGTON, April 25, 1929—7 p. m.

47. Before answering your 81, April 24, 10 p. m., the Department would like to know results of the interview between President Leguia and the Chilean Ambassador regarding the scope of the suggestion of settlement to be made by the President which your 80, April 24, 2 p. m., promised.

STIMSON

_____

723.2515/3352 : Telegram

*The Ambassador in Peru (Moore) to the Secretary of State*

LIMA, April 26, 1929—3 p. m.
[Received 5 : 50 p. m.]

82. Your 47, April 25. Owing to the dispute over the boundary line, President Leguia and the Chilean Ambassador did not agree on the scope of the settlement to be made by the President.

Saw President Leguia today and he showed me the draft of the proposal he was going to make tomorrow to Ambassador Figueroa. It contains about a thousand words and the President told me that if this draft was acceptable to Chile he would then give me a copy of the paragraph of it which refers to President Hoover. The President of Peru does not want to give it to you until it has been agreed to, because the Chileans may want to make some slight changes.

The only thing that seems in dispute now is the boundary line. President Leguia says that all along they have agreed to a boundary 10 kilometers north of the Arica–La Paz railway and that he would not submit to any change. The Chilean proposition practically makes it 18 kilometers.

MOORE

_____

723.2515/3364

*Memorandum by the Assistant Secretary of State (White)*

[WASHINGTON,] April 26, 1929.

The Bolivian Minister,[24] accompanied by Doctor Boyd, Counselor of the Legation, called on the Secretary on Friday afternoon, April 26.

_____

[24] Eduardo Diez de Medina.

The Minister stated that he had come about a matter of great importance to his country. His Government had learned from very reliable sources that an agreement has been practically arrived at between Chile and Peru. He said he thought that Mr. White would bear him out in the statement that Bolivia had never attempted to interfere with any direct negotiations between Chile and Peru, and that it would be glad to see a proper arrangement concluded. There was one provision in the agreement which he understood provided that neither party would transfer any portion of the territory in dispute accorded to it without the previous agreement of the other, and that there would be no change made in the international railroad system without the agreement of the other.

This matter was of the greatest importance to Bolivia as it would definitely shut out Bolivia from the seacoast. During the forty years that this question has been pending, Peru has told Bolivia that she would be willing to give Bolivia a seaport on the basis of an alliance between Peru and Bolivia and, similarly, Chile had promised Bolivia a seaport on the basis of an alliance between Chile and Bolivia. Bolivia had not wanted to make any such arrangement but wanted an arrangement concluded between the three interested parties. This suggested proposal would effectually close the door on Bolivia's aspirations of an outlet to the sea because Peru's interests with respect of Bolivia were contrary to those of Chile and vice-versa, and any arrangement Bolivia might be able to make with either party would be vetoed by the other.

Furthermore, the Minister stated that Bolivia is very anxious to extend its railroad south of Lake Titicaca through Puno in order to have a direct outlet to the sea, but this of course would be contrary to Chile's interest as she would want to have traffic come over the Arica-La Paz railroad. This provision, therefore, would damage Bolivia commercially and is also considered by Bolivia as contrary to her sovereignty. These facts, the Minister thought, justified the request of Bolivia that she should be heard in the matter.

The Minister stated that the question of an outlet to the sea for Bolivia was of such importance to his country that it had taken the matter up in the League of Nations and also in Washington. This aspiration is a very just one. The War of the Pacific had robbed Bolivia of its seacoast. Now this settlement was being made to liquidate that war which was a war not merely between Chile and Peru but between three countries, Bolivia, Peru and Chile. Now the two countries, the one that had lost the least, and the one that had gained the most, were making an arrangement utterly disregarding Bolivia. . . .

Bolivia feels that its only hope is in the United States. It knows that the United States only champions just and honorable causes and it feels that it can come to the United States, lay its position before it, and be assured that the United States, on account of its high moral authority throughout the continent, will not see this injustice perpetrated on Bolivia. Bolivia has the more reason to believe this because Secretary Kellogg suggested to Chile and Peru that the whole territory should be turned over to Bolivia.

The Secretary told the Minister that the situation then was quite different—this was a case between Chile and Peru and this Government could not bring in any third party unless the two parties directly interested should request it. Mr. Kellogg had made a number of suggestions to Chile and Peru at the direct request of those countries and this request for suggestions had made it possible for him to propose turning over the territory to Bolivia. This has not been accepted and the situation was now different. The negotiations were going on directly between Chile and Peru at Lima and Santiago and he did not see how this Government could make any suggestions regarding an outside country.

The Minister stated again that his Government did not wish to hamper a settlement but that the provisions he had mentioned were so palpably unjust to Bolivia in definitely closing the door on the hope of Bolivia's receiving a seaport that Bolivia felt it could come to the United States as its one and only hope of having its rights respected. He did not think that a great powerful nation like the United States, which had once suggested the turning over of the provinces to Bolivia, could sit by with its arms crossed and see such an injustice done.

In the course of the conversation, the Minister also referred to the economic interest of the United States in Bolivia on account of the developments going on there largely through American capital which would be greatly hampered if Bolivia were cut off from direct access to the outside world. He also stated that Bolivia desires a pacific solution of this matter; that Bolivia is a young nation with great resources, and that when it is more fully developed, unless it has an outlet to the sea, the demand on the part of the people for such an outlet would be so great that nothing would stop it from obtaining its just rights.

The Secretary thanked the Minister for his frank statement of the matter and said that he did not see exactly what he could do at the present moment but that he would carefully bear in mind what the Minister had said. The Minister said he was not asking for an immediate answer—he would like the Secretary to think it over and let him know at his convenience. The Secretary said that he would give the matter his most careful consideration.

WHITE

723.2515/3342 : Telegram

## The Secretary of State to the Ambassador in Peru (*Moore*)

[Paraphrase]

WASHINGTON, April 26, 1929—7 p. m.

48. The text of the proposed settlement has not yet been received by the Department except telegram No. 63, April 17, 8 p. m., from Ambassador Culbertson stating that the Government of Chile had on that day transmitted to its Ambassador in Peru for transmittal to the President of Peru certain suggestions to be embodied in the proposed settlement to be made by the President of the United States to both countries. There were eight suggestions. The last one was as follows: "(*h*) Chile and Peru shall not without previous agreement amongst themselves concede to a third party any part of the territory or alter the actual system of international railways."

This afternoon the Bolivian Minister called on me and made an impassioned plea that the above-mentioned proposal be stricken out because it would work irreparable . . . injustice to Bolivia, closing the door forever on Bolivia's aspirations for an outlet to the sea. He said that Bolivia's only hope was in the United States.

As you know the Government of the United States has consistently taken the position that it could not bring Bolivia into the negotiations with Chile and Peru without the request of those countries; and, while the Government of the United States has always stated that any agreement for a settlement of the Tacna-Arica question would be acceptable to it, it naturally understood that no such arrangement would be inimical to the interests of third parties.

In view of the fact that Chile and Peru desire this suggestion to come from the President of the United States, you will readily appreciate the delicacy of the situation. The Government of the United States has left the negotiations entirely in the hands of Chile and Peru, and it has been most gratified that those countries have about come to an agreement; but, as that agreement is then to come from the President of the United States, and a third country has made a vehement protest against one of the reported provisions therein, a country with which the Government of the United States maintains and has always maintained the friendliest relations, it is of the utmost importance that the Department be immediately informed of the exact text of this proposal. Please telegraph the exact text as soon as possible. Also, discreetly explore the situation to ascertain how much importance is attached to it by President Leguia and by Chile, as the Government of the United States, in the light of its present information, would not be prepared to make a suggestion containing such a stipulation.

STIMSON

723.2515/3353 : Telegram

*The Ambassador in Peru (Moore) to the Secretary of State*

LIMA, April 27, 1929—3 a. m.
[Received 7 : 12 a. m.]

83. Your telegram 48, April 26. I have seen President Leguia's draft of the proposed settlement and it contains the same provision. Will cable the exact text as soon as the President gives it to me.

MOORE

---

723.2515/3354 : Telegram

*The Ambassador in Peru (Moore) to the Secretary of State*

LIMA, April 27, 1929—noon.
[Received 1 : 50 p. m.]

84. My telegram number 83.[25] Saw President Leguia at 11:30 this morning. He said:

"Under no circumstances or conditions would I do anything in the slightest way to embarrass President Hoover for whom I have the greatest admiration. I shall ask to have the clause withdrawn immediately."

He thoroughly agrees with your viewpoint, which he says is most logical. He will see the Chilean Ambassador at 12:30 today. Have you any further instructions or suggestions?

More to follow.

MOORE

---

723.2515/3342 supp. : Telegram

*The Secretary of State to the Ambassador in Peru (Moore)*

[Paraphrase]

WASHINGTON, April 27, 1929—1 p. m.

49. With further reference to my 48, April 26, 7 p. m., I desire to state that when I made the suggestion to the President that he might with propriety and with the approval of both Chile and Peru suggest the terms of final settlement between them, I had in mind only the terms in dispute when the matter was brought before me, namely, the location and conditions of the proposed port or facilities to be allowed in Peru in the settlement. It was not my intention that the President should recommend any provisions in a settlement which might affect adversely a third power, such as Bolivia. Bolivia has strongly contended that such would be the result of such an agree-

---

[25] *Supra.*

ment not to concede any part of the territory or alter the actual system of international railways without previous agreement between both parties. You can readily understand how under such circumstances any suggestion which would cover this proposal might be deemed by Bolivia as a most unfriendly act on the part of the United States. If President Leguia or Señor Figueroa have any different intentions or views, I desire to be informed immediately, because I am certain that the President would be unwilling to recommend over Bolivia's objection any agreement which that nation asserts will unfavorably affect her interests. You will recall that the President only agreed to make suggestions with the understanding that his so doing was agreeable to the parties involved. If the scope of the agreement is now to be extended so as to affect the interests claimed by a third power, such an agreement must, of course, be acceptable to such power if the President is to propose it.

STIMSON

---

723.2515/3355 : Telegram

*The Ambassador in Peru (Moore) to the Secretary of State*

[Paraphrase]

LIMA, April 27, 1929—2 p. m.
[Received 4 p. m.]

85. My telegram 84, April 27, noon. Below is a translation of President Leguia's draft of that part of the proposed agreement which refers to President Hoover: [26]

"Memorandum which the Governments of Peru and Chile agree to submit to the President of the United States:

His Excellency, Mr. Herbert C. Hoover, The President of the United States, impressed by the cordial progress which the negotiations between the two Governments of Chile and Peru have followed in relation to the direct agreements which they have reached on almost all points in order to end the Tacna-Arica problem, and in the knowledge also of the resolution of both to submit to him the single difficulty which has arisen on account of differing opinions regarding the proposed port at Las Yaradas, summarizing at the same time all that has been accomplished, proposes the following stipulations as the definitive bases of solution."

The remaining clauses are the same as you received from Santiago [27] except that clause 8 has now been eliminated by President Leguia.

MOORE

---

[26] Memorandum not paraphrased.
[27] See telegram No. 63, April 17, 8 p. m., from the Ambassador in Chile, p. 770.

723.2515/3356 : Telegram

*The Ambassador in Peru (Moore) to the Secretary of State*

LIMA, April 27, 1929—8 p. m.
[Received 10 p. m.]

86. I assume that my telegram number 84[29] which probably reached you after you had sent your 49[29] to me answers this telegram and also your 48.[30]    Am I correct?

MOORE

723.2515/3356 : Telegram

*The Secretary of State to the Ambassador in Peru (Moore)*

[Paraphrase]

WASHINGTON, April 29, 1929—6 p. m.

50.    Your 84, April 27, noon, 85, April 27, 2 p. m., and 86, April 27, 8 p. m., answer my 48, April 26, 7 p. m., and 49, April 27, 1 p. m., as to paragraph 8 or (*h*) if the deletion of provision mentioned is accepted by Chile.    As soon as possible I should like to see the full text of the proposal which President Leguia will desire the President of the United States to make in the exercise of informal and unofficial good offices, paragraph 1 of which is quoted in your 85, April 27, 2 p. m.    I want to determine as soon as possible whether there are any other provisions which it would be either inopportune or unwise for the President of the United States to suggest.

One of the proposals transmitted from Chile is that Chile and Peru would name a commission of engineers to delimit the frontier, and that in case of a disagreement the President of the United States would appoint "a third as referee".    If this stipulation is in the agreement, is there any definition in the agreement itself, or in a subsidiary agreement, defining the powers and authority of this third engineer?

STIMSON

723.2515/3357 : Telegram

*The Ambassador in Chile (Culbertson) to the Secretary of State*

[Paraphrase]

SANTIAGO, April 29, 1929—6 p. m.
[Received 11 p. m.]

68. Today the Foreign Minister informed me that the Tacna-Arica negotiations were progressing favorably.    Leguia approves

[29] *Ante,* p. 780.
[30] *Ante,* p. 779.

the procedure that the basis of settlement when finally agreed upon be sent to the Chilean and Peruvian Ambassadors in the United States for discussion with the Department of State and then that the proposal of settlement be submitted by the President of the United States to Chile and Peru through the respective American Embassies in Chile and Peru.

The Foreign Minister is informing Leguia that Chile will concede very liberal free port privileges and control of the terminal buildings of the Tacna-Arica railway at Arica to facilitate Peruvian export import trade, but will not agree to nullify sovereignty over port property at Arica.

Chile agrees that the boundary shall be so fixed to include certain canals, water rights, and sulphur properties within Peruvian territory.[31]

Leguia desires that there be a provision in the treaty for the cancelation of old debt owed by Peru to Chile amounting with interest to thirty million pesos. Chile will agree to this, and also to a provision in the treaty or protocol for the establishment of a commission to settle private war claims. The President of Chile desires to announce definite settlement on May 21 next, and he suggests that all details be agreed to by May 15. Leguia stated that he had no objection to this.

Leguia requires details as to dismantling the Morro at Arica and the kind of monument to be erected there, all of which Chile will communicate. Leguia is anxious to have some reference made to this in the treaty or protocol.

CULBERTSON

---

723.2515/3360 : Telegram

*The Ambassador in Peru (Moore) to the Secretary of State*

LIMA, April 30, 1929—3 p. m.
[Received 4:33 p. m.]

87. Your telegram No. 50, April 29th.

1. President Leguia and Ambassador Figueroa had a conference this morning. It is necessary to change the wording but not the substance of the agreement. They have both agreed on the wording and tomorrow, after a further conference between the President and the Chilean Ambassador, President Leguia will give me the full text of the agreement. He does not want to do it until it is absolutely settled.

---

[31] For correction of this point, see telegram No. 69, May 1, 7 p. m., from the Ambassador in Chile, p. 785.

2. President Leguia told me that Ambassador Figueroa had informed him that Ambassador Davila had telegraphed to his—the Chilean—Government that President Hoover had no objection to the retention of paragraph 8 or (*h*). President Leguia told the Chilean Ambassador that his information was different and that therefore he would insist upon the elimination of this paragraph.

3. As to paragraph two of your telegram number 50, President Leguia told me that this would be changed to read "a third as referee,—his decision to be final." This was agreed to.

MOORE

---

723.2515/3386 : Telegram

*The Bolivian Minister for Foreign Affairs (Elio) to the Bolivian Minister (Diez de Medina)* [32]

[Translation]

[LA PAZ,] April 30, 1929.

Yesterday, Saturday, I had a conference with the Chilean Minister, telling him that Bolivia knows of the initiative of his Government to limit the right of Peru and Chile to transfer territory, and to establish international railroads. I told him that the proposition contained an unfriendly tendency because it limited free contract in the future both regarding the territory and international railroads.

The Bolivian attitude of indifference towards the Chile and Peru arrangement has been abandoned to protest against the restrictive convention which signifies an entente against Bolivia whose right to have her own port we will see satisfied in the future by a political-economic solution with one State or the other.

Both nations said on various occasions to Bolivia that they would satisfy her right to free maritime communication immediately the sovereignty of Tacna and Arica was defined.

If the Chilean proposal is accepted, the future situation will be more difficult.

We desire that both nations maintain complete liberty to treat with Bolivia regarding sovereignty and international communications.

I replied to him that a condominium directed against Bolivia would produce a very unfavorable impression on public opinion.

You may inform that friendly Government (the United States) regarding this conversation.

ELIO

---

[32] Handed to Assistant Secretary White by the Attaché of the Bolivian Legation, May 1, 1929.

723.2515/3361 : Telegram

*The Ambassador in Peru (Moore) to the Secretary of State*

LIMA, May 1, 1929—3 p. m.
[Received 4:05 p. m.]

88. President Leguia and Ambassador Figueroa met this morning and agreed on all points of the proposed treaty except the wording of the clause referring to the boundary line. Chile changed the reading of it but claimed it did not change the sense. President Leguia said he was not altogether convinced and has sent for his engineers. If they decide this clause does not alter the sense of the agreement he will give me a copy of it tonight which I will transmit immediately to you in translation. He will send a copy to his Ambassador in Washington tomorrow for official presentation to you.

MOORE

---

723.2515/3360 : Telegram

*The Secretary of State to the Ambassador in Peru (Moore)*

WASHINGTON, May 1, 1929—4 p. m.

51. Your 87, April 30, 3 p. m., paragraph two. There must be a mistake regarding this as Ambassador Davila has not called at the Department for over a week, that is not since prior to the time this question came up.

STIMSON

---

723.2515/3362 : Telegram

*The Ambassador in Chile (Culbertson) to the Secretary of State*

SANTIAGO, May 1, 1929—7 p. m.
[Received 10:20 p. m.]

69. Foreign Office informs me Leguia has asked a day or two to consider certain points, but that probably the draft of the settlement will be sent to Davila Friday. The press here has published several times the main provisions of the settlement and they have met with almost universal approval.

Correcting paragraph 3, my 68, April 29, 6 p. m., I am now informed that the sulphur properties will be included in Chile and the canals in Peru. It is now expected that it will be possible to announce the settlement before May 21st as mentioned in the fourth paragraph of the cable referred to above.

CULBERTSON

723.2515/3342 supp. : Telegram

### The Secretary of State to the Ambassador in Chile (Culbertson)

[Paraphrase]

WASHINGTON, May 1, 1929—8 p. m.

46. Your 63, April 17, 8 p. m., paragraph (h). The following telegrams which were sent to the Ambassador in Peru are quoted for your information.

[Here follow the texts of telegrams Nos. 48, April 26, 7 p. m., and 49, April 27, 1 p. m., printed on pages 779 and 780.]

The Ambassador in Peru in his telegram No. 87, April 30, 3 p. m., stated, among other things, the following:

[Here follows the text of paragraph two of telegram No. 87, printed on page 783.]

Today the Department replied as follows:

[Here follows the text of telegram No. 51, May 1, 4 p. m., to the Ambassador in Peru, printed on page 785.]

STIMSON

---

723.2515/3363 : Telegram

### The Ambassador in Peru (Moore) to the Secretary of State

LIMA, May 2, 1929—3 a. m.
[Received 8:20 a. m.]

89. At midnight Ambassador Figueroa informed me that he had received a telegram from his Government accepting President Leguia's draft of paragraph 3 of article number 1.

They have now agreed on all questions and at 3 o'clock today, Thursday, both countries will telegraph their respective Ambassadors in Washington the draft of the agreement which will be handed to you for transmission to President Hoover.

Our translation of the full text follows, minus the preamble which was transmitted in my telegram 85, April 27, 2 p. m.:

[Here follows text of memorandum. For translation as presented to President Hoover by the Governments of Chile and Peru on May 14, see page 798.]

MOORE

---

723.2515/3373

### Memorandum by the Assistant Secretary of State (White)

[WASHINGTON,] May 2, 1929.

The Bolivian Minister, accompanied by Senor de la Barra, Secretary of the Legation, called on the Secretary on Thursday, May 2. He said that on the previous day he had not wanted to bother the

Secretary and had delivered to Mr. White a copy of a cable received from his Government [33] which set forth a conversation between the Minister for Foreign Affairs of Bolivia and the Chilean Minister in La Paz. The Bolivian Minister for Foreign Affairs told the Chilean Minister that Bolivia had taken no part in the negotiations between Chile and Peru but, having learned that Chile had suggested limiting the rights of Chile and Peru to transfer any part of the territory now in dispute or to change the existing system of international railroads, Bolivia could not remain aloof any longer, as such a restriction would signify an understanding contrary to Bolivia's interests. He said that Bolivia desired both countries to maintain their freedom to negotiate with Bolivia.

The Bolivian Minister told the Secretary that he had been instructed to bring this matter to the attention of the Government of the United States and point out the great importance of the matter to Bolivia, and to express the hope that the United States would do something for Bolivia in the matter. Bolivia felt that as a settlement between Chile and Peru would be made under the auspices of the United States they should make their position very clear to the Secretary of State. The Minister added that this proposal was a virtual reversal of the policy in the Kellogg formula for turning over the provinces to Bolivia, and would close the door on any such solution for the future.

The Secretary stated that he had supposed, when the Minister spoke to him last Friday, that the Minister was acting under instructions from his Government, and was glad to know now that it was under direct instructions from his Government. He said that he was giving the matter careful thought and would be glad to bear in mind the Bolivian situation in so far as the matter might come before him. He added that he would like the Minister to bear two things in mind: first, that the negotiations were being carried on directly between Chile and Peru and, secondly, he thought it very important that there should be no outbreak of popular feeling while this matter is under consideration. He thought it would be most unfortunate should any irresponsible person start an attack on Chile which would stir up public feeling in Bolivia.

The Minister stated that he agreed fully with the Secretary and could give him assurances that his Government would see that there was no outbreak. He thanked the Secretary for his promise to bear in mind the Bolivian contention and point of view.

F[RANCIS] W[HITE]

---

[33] See telegram, April 30, 1929, from the Bolivian Minister for Foreign Affairs to the Bolivian Minister, p. 784.

723.2515/3367 : Telegram

### The Ambassador in Peru (Moore) to the Secretary of State

LIMA, May 4, 1929—2 a. m.
[Received 6 : 52 a. m.]

91. President Leguia tonight handed me the following memorandum:

"The memorandum suggested by Chile and Peru [34] is so worded that it admits of two decisions by the President of the United States:

> First, recommendation to the parties to accept the conditions as embodied in the memorandum. This of course, will be accepted by both parties but will leave the figure of the President of the United States somewhat short of the brilliancy with which, as the head of the greatest nation now existing, he should always be surrounded.
> Second, that instead of a recommendation his decision should have all the character and be in essence an award. This will leave his great figure intact, will allow of no evasion by the parties from the most faithful compliance with it, and the authority of the Government of the United States will be so enhanced as to facilitate the solution of any new difficulties that may arise in the future, whatever their nature or origin may be.

For the foregoing reasons, it is of the utmost importance that his pronouncement on the memorandum with regard to the Tacna-Arica question should be an award, both in its spirit and its wording."

The President added that he believed that, for the sake of pan-Americanism and the rightful position the United States should hold, President Hoover should make his suggestion an award, thus terminating the whole arbitral proposition. Such action he said would be beneficial to both countries and would be enthusiastically received by their respective peoples. President Leguia stated that of course he would be satisfied with anything President Hoover might do, but he desired to bring the matter to his attention before he made his decision.

Would it be possible to get an answer transmitted that I can present to President Leguia?

MOORE

---

723.2515/3381

### The Bolivian Minister (Diez de Medina) to the Secretary of State

[Translation [35]]

WASHINGTON, May 4, 1929.

MR. SECRETARY OF STATE: Confirming what I had the honor of expressing to Your Excellency at my two last interviews, I am pleased

---

[34] See telegrams No. 53, May 8, 6 p. m., to the Ambassador in Peru and No. 53, May 10, 6 p. m., to the Ambassador in Chile, pp. 794 and 796.
[35] Supplied by the editor.

to enclose with this note a brief confidential Memorandum with some references which the undersigned takes the liberty of bringing to the knowledge of the Secretary of State.

I renew [etc.]                                          E. Diez de Medina

[Enclosure]

## Memorandum [36]

The Governments of Chile and Peru have expressed in different opportunities their inclination to restore to Bolivia—who was the principal party to the War of the Pacific, which resulted in the loss of her whole sea coast and of the ports which she owned—her inalienable rights to an access to the sea.

It is sufficient to briefly recall the facts that prove the above assertion, all of which date back as from the War of 1879; otherwise it would be too long to enumerate the multiple occasions that Bolivia had—since her establishment—to acquire the territory over which ownership Chile and Peru have now an exclusive controversy, absolutely prescinding of Bolivia.

The War of 1879 had not yet come to an end when Chile began negotiations directed toward the delivery of Tacna and Arica to Bolivia. Having failed this desire solely for the honest and loyal sentiments that have characterized the international policy of Bolivia.

Among the basis offered by the Chilian Government to Bolivia, in May 1879, the following is drawn: "Inasmuch as the Republic of Bolivia will need a part of the Peruvian territory to regulate her own and obtain an easy access to the Pacific—which she lacks at the present time—without being subjected to the bonds imposed at all times by the Peruvian Government, Chile will not hinder the acquisition of that part of territory nor will oppose to its permanent occupation by Bolivia. But on the contrary will lend her at the present the most effective support."

The above referred overtures were not even considered by the Bolivian Government. An honest and evident loyalty to Peru, its allied, prevented that the Chilian initiative should thrive at the very moment of the armed conflict. In the same year of 1879, the President of Chile Santamaria wrote to his compatriot Victoriano Lastarria the following: "Landlords ourselves of all the Bolivian shore and of the entire Department of Tarapaca, we must necessarily give to Bolivia a vent and an outlet, placing her between Peru and Chile. Otherwise we would choke her and would force her to seek attachments with Peru or the Argentine Republic."

In January of 1882, the Chilian negotiator Lillo approached the

---

[36] In Spanish and in English; Spanish text not printed.

Bolivian Plenipoteniary Baptista on the subject of the transfer of Tacna and Arica. These provinces according to Lillo, Chile was ready to cede to Bolivia in exchange for an alliance with her.

The Chilian Historian Gonzalo Bulnes, recently Ambassador to Argentina, carries the following statement in his important work "La Guerra del Pacifico" (The War of the Pacific): "Santamaría shortly after authorized Novoa to modify the method of the sale of Tacna and Arica although not essentially. The form did not worry him much. Santamaría considered easy to substitute Peru and Chile for Bolivia in Tacna and Arica and was convinced that this would happen soon after."

Luis Aldunate former Minister of Foreign Relations of Chile stated that from the beginning of the negotiations in 1882, it was a popular policy in Chile to induce Bolivia to break away her alliance with Peru and to get an understanding with Chile.

The idea of the transfer of Tacna and Arica to Bolivia was neither strange to some of the eminent Diplomatic Representatives of the United States of America. Mr. Partridge proposed in January of the year 1883 the following suggestions for peace: 1—Unrestricted transfer of Tarapacá to Chile; 2—Cession, sale or transfer of Arica and Tacna to Bolivia, or should this prove inacceptable, to neutralize this territory; 3—Arica cannot be fortified.

Prior to this, Mr. Logan, also Minister of the United States in Chile, tried to promote an accord between the belligerent countries, offering among other suggestions the cession of Tacna and Arica to Bolivia.

On his side the Peruvian Plenipotentiary to Bolivia accredited by President Iglesias, together with the Peruvian Minister of Foreign Relations, visited the Chilean Minister Novoa to request his authorization to enable the Peruvian Plenipotentiary to offer Tacna and Arica to Bolivia in exchange of compensations to Chile. At the same time the former Executive of Peru Sr. Garcia Calderon expressed in a reply to the communication of Mr. Logan, that if the idea of ceding Tacna and Arica to Bolivia had been submitted to him, he, as President of Peru—would have accepted the proposal without delay.

Short time afterwards and on the occasion of signing Chile and Peru the Protocol of 1883, the Minister of Foreign Relations for the Government residing at Arequipa, added in a Circular addressed to the Diplomatic Corps, in connection with the cession of Tarapacá: "That cession should have placed Bolivia in the possibility of losing her sea-coast and then, without an access to the Pacific, she could not have carried an independent commerce of her own. Such condition is not in accord with the Peruvian policies in the American Continent. It is essential that Bolivia should have a free access to the Pacific." In closing he specified: "For that reason I believe that peace, giving Bolivia the participation that she must have in the negotiations, would have the approval of the people."

In the same year the representatives of President Iglesias of Peru, among the modifications which they had attempted for the settlement of peace with Chile, stated thus: "Chile remains in possession of Tacna and Arica for ten years at the expiration of which a plebiscite should determine the nationality to which they wish to belong permanently, whether Chile, Bolivia or Peru."

Some years later, in 1895, Bolivia and Chile reached an accord for the settlement of the war signing three treaties. One of these dealt with the transfer of the territories by virtue of which Chile made its duty to transfer Tacna and Arica to Bolivia. On this occasion the Minister of Foreign Relations of Chile negotiator of these treaties, made the following public statement:—"The granting of a port to Bolivia has been considered at all times as the fundamental foundation of every definite settlement of peace between the two nations."

In this connection it must be remembered that in 1919 the Minister of Chile Bello Codecido was offering to Bolivia an inlet north of Arica, which could not satisfy the aspirations nor the necessities of the latter. It must also be remembered among the declarations of each one of these countries, some of the more recent ones.

On the delivery of his Letters of Credence by the undersigned appointed Bolivian Minister to Peru in 1927, President Leguia stated in his remarks of reply: "Bolivia knows, because I have promised it since 1925, that Peru is determined to cede her, South of Arica, without expecting compensations, a strip of land for her communication with the sea. This promise disclosing the friendship of Peru for her younger sister nation—the preferred of Bolivar—interprets effectively our purpose that Bolivia should obtain an access to the ocean which she needs to facilitate her economical development."

Some years back, in 1910, the Peruvian Minister in La Paz, Sr. Solon Polo, had indicated to the La Paz Foreign Office: "In the estimation of the Government of Lima it would not be difficult to find out the means for an agreement, provided that the Province of Tacna should belong to Peru."

Furthermore: upon entering into the pacts of Peace between Chile and the Republics of Peru and Bolivia—though separately arrived at—Chile as much as Peru acknowledged the right of Bolivia to recover her access to the sea, offering on their part to contribute to such legitimate right. It will be enough to mention recent occurrences and declarations from each one of the two Governments.

While Chile solemnly stated in 1921, before the League of Nations, that she was ready to contemplate directly with Bolivia the best means to assist her in her development through direct negotiations freely accorded, and in 1926 agreed to accept in principle the proposition offered by the Secretary of State Mr. Frank B. Kellogg to cede to Bolivia in perpetuity the territories of Tacna and Arica, Peru through his Chief Executive Leguia—as in various other occasions—also offered to Bolivia his assistance to regain her maritime entity. Later Peru declared in reply to Mr. Kellogg's suggestion that the rejection did not carry with it the intention of obstructing any other solutions. She also left in record that Peru had accepted the partial or complete internationalization of the provinces and had accepted also their division giving Bolivia gratuitously an outlet to the shore and there an inlet whose conditions would allow it to be converted into a large, suitable and safe port. Finally declared that was disposed to listen to all suggestions, but under the condition that the towns of Tacna and Arica be returned to Peru.

It cannot be overlooked that in that reply to Mr. Kellogg, Peru clearly states: "It would not had [have] meant a moral victory for either Peru or Chile to make a division of the territory in the form above indicated (by Peru). because such a division would have taken into consideration reciprocal and equitable concessions in respect to the interest of both countries and might even lead to the cession of a port to the Republic of Bolivia."

In that same year of 1926, the President of Peru expressed in his Message to Congress: "The Problem of the Pacific can only be resolved by invoking the rights of Peru, and in every case our fraternal good-will to assist Bolivia in obtaining an outlet to the sea which she so necessarily reclaims."

The above antecedents and several others which are not herein considered for the sake of briefness, prove therefore that Peru as well as Chile have publicly declared their readiness to contemplate suggestions leading to the attainment of the legitimate desire for a port by Bolivia.

Instead, the clause which seemingly Chile intends to include in the negotiations being carried out in Lima to determine that neither Chile nor Peru shall be able—without previous and mutual consent—to cede to a third party any portion of the territory referred to in this agreement, nor to construct new international lines, is decidedly in contradiction with those declarations as well as with the policy pursued by both countries in connection with the maritime problem of Bolivia, fundamental for the development and the ulterior life of this Republic.

Such stipulation would render impossible or would delay every free accord with either one of the two countries once established such hateful joint-ownership intended to last indefinitely and in evident detriment of the nation that had to bear the greatest portion of the burden as one of the belligerents in the contest of 1879.

That limitation of sovereignty of the contracting parties effectively restricts the rights of Bolivia to freely and separately contract with each of the two countries also parties in the international conflict which final settlement is desired.

In regard to the obligation that Peru and Chile should contract to build no new international lines without the previous and mutual consent of both parties, it would be detrimental not only to their sovereignty and to their own conveniences, but to the rights and interests of other countries—not a part to this agreement—who are seeking their development by means of systems of communication which would firmly tie them fostering their importance and increasing the yield of the foreign capitals invested there. That clause will also injure to a great extent and indirectly even the interest of nations such as the United States who have large capitals invested in Bolivia.

If Bolivia showing an unrestricted spirit of harmony and Americanism has never intended to upset the course of the negotiations started between Chile and Peru absolutely ignoring her—because she has rested assured by the most formal and renewed declarations of the two friendly nations—she cannot refrain any longer from respectfully calling the attention of the Government who is propitiating a final settlement between those countries, to the inconvenient and unsuitable clause already referred to as this would be in contradiction with their renewed offers and would also destroy or at least impend the most noble intentions which originated the suggestion for its solution of Mr. Frank B. Kellogg, Secretary of State of the United States of America.

WASHINGTON, May 3, 1929.

---

723.2515/3367 : Telegram

*The Secretary of State to the Ambassador in Peru (Moore)*

WASHINGTON, May 7, 1929—5 p. m.

52. Your 91, May 4, 2 a. m.

1. The memoranda submitted by the Peruvian and Chilean Ambassadors is not in the form of an award. On the contrary, the preamble definitely states that it is a proposal submitted by the President to the two Governments as the final bases of a solution.

2. Furthermore, and more important, the President has no authority as Arbitrator to issue an award of this sort. The Protocol and Supplementary Act signed by Chile and Peru on July 20, 1922,[37]

[37] *Foreign Relations*, 1922, vol. I, p. 505.

specifically set forth the scope of the Arbitrator's functions, power and authority. In his Award the Arbitrator stated his duties to be:

"1. To decide whether in the present circumstances a plebiscite shall or shall not be held to determine the definitive sovereignty of the territory in question as between Chile and Peru.

2. If the Arbitrator decides in favor of a plebiscite to determine the conditions of that plebiscite, including the terms and time of the payment to be made by the nation succeeding in the plebiscite as provided in Article 3 of the Treaty of Ancon.[38]

3. If the Arbitrator decides against the plebiscite to take no further action as Arbitrator, except that—

4. Whether the decision be for or against a plebiscite, the Arbitrator is to decide the pending questions with respect to Tarata and Chilcaya arising respectively on the northern and southern boundaries of the territory."

For the Arbitrator to hand down an award as suggested by President Leguia would require a new submission to the Arbitrator and this would require a previous agreement by Chile and Peru.

In these circumstances the only course open would appear to be the proposal to the two Governments by the President in the exercise of informal and unofficial good offices of certain stipulations to form the final bases of a solution.

STIMSON

---

723.2515/3370a : Telegram

*The Secretary of State to the Ambassador in Peru (Moore)*

WASHINGTON, May 8, 1929—6 p. m.

53. The Peruvian and Chilean Ambassadors on the afternoon of May third presented identic memoranda in Spanish and English to the Department regarding the Tacna-Arica settlement. The preamble of the English texts reads as follows:

"The President of the United States having been informed of the cordial progress of the negotiations between the Governments of Chile and of Peru, with reference to the direct agreements reached on nearly all the questions involved in the solution of the problem of Tacna and Arica and having also been informed of the decision of both governments to submit to him the only difficulty that has arisen with reference to the respective viewpoints relating to the projected port of Las Yaradas:

The President of the United States summarizing the points agreed upon proposes to the two governments as the final bases of a solution the following stipulations:"

It was immediately suggested to both Ambassadors that this preamble be modified to read as follows:

"Having been informed of the cordial progress of the negotiations between the Governments of Chile and of Peru, with reference to

---

[38] Signed October 20, 1883, *Foreign Relations*, 1883, p. 731.

the direct agreements reached on nearly all the questions involved in the solution of the problem of Tacna and Arica;

The President of the United States summarizing the points agreed upon proposes to the two governments in the exercise of informal and unofficial good offices as the final bases of a solution the following stipulations:"

The delay in taking further action in this matter is caused by the lack of an answer regarding this suggestion.

STIMSON

---

723.2515/3371 : Telegram

*The Ambassador in Peru (Moore) to the Secretary of State*

LIMA, May 9, 1929—2 p. m.
[Received 3 : 05 p. m.]

94. Your telegram Number 53, May 8, 6 p. m. President Leguia stated to me this morning that the elimination from the first paragraph of the preamble of the following "and having also been informed of the decision of both governments to submit to him the only difficulty that has arisen with reference to the respective viewpoints relating to the projected port of Las Yaradas" takes the heart out of the whole agreement. This was the one thing that was essential to him in order to get the proposition past his people.

He hopes that you and President Hoover will permit this clause to remain. Otherwise it will be very difficult for him and he does not know what the real outcome may be as it will be necessary to consult many interests and practically go over all the ground covered in the last few weeks before he can come to a decision.

The President further stated that before he finally agreed to any of these propositions with Chile he understood that President Hoover would accept the compromise reached between Chile and Peru and use it as his suggestion of settlement to them.

So far as the addition of the words "in the exercise of informal and unofficial good offices" in the second paragraph of the amended preamble is concerned, there is no serious objection on the part of President Leguia and he believes that the addition of these words will meet the objection to retaining the clause he desires.

Personally, I know that the President of Peru is in a difficult position and his one and sole object in my opinion is to get something which will meet with the approval and endorsement of the majority of his people.

President Leguia is anxious to learn of your reaction to this as soon as possible. The President told me that he had not received either from his own Ambassador in Washington or from Ambassador Figueroa the change suggested by the Department of State on Friday.

MOORE

723.2515/3372 : Telegram

*The Secretary of State to the Ambassador in Chile (Culbertson)*

WASHINGTON, May 10, 1929—6 p. m.

53. The Civilian and Peruvian Ambassadors on May third left at the Department identic memoranda regarding proposed settlement. The Department suggested elimination of reference to the port of Las Yaradas in paragraph one of the preamble and the insertion of the words "in the exercise of informal and unofficial good offices" in paragraph two of the preamble. President Leguia insists upon the retention of reference to the port at Las Yaradas and asks that the words "informal and unofficial" be deleted with reference to the exercise of good offices, and this is being agreed to. The Department therefore hopes that the Peruvian Ambassador here will receive instructions in the next day or two definitely to conclude the matter with the modification proposed. In order to save time and avoid any possible misunderstanding, there is quoted herewith the Department's translation of the Spanish text of the agreement which is the text which is proposed to be used by the President. Please submit this to the Chilean Government and obtain its concurrence.

[Here follows text of memorandum identic with translation of memorandum presented to President Hoover by the Governments of Chile and Peru on May 14, printed on page 798.]

STIMSON

---

723.2515/3371 : Telegram

*The Secretary of State to the Ambassador in Peru (Moore)*

WASHINGTON, May 10, 1929—6 p. m.

56. Your 94, May 9, 2 p. m. You may tell President Leguia that I of course do not wish to cause him difficulty regarding my proposal which was made merely because the question of a port at Las Yaradas has already been settled by agreement between the two parties. If President Leguia considers the insertion of this clause necessary in order to win the support of public opinion in Peru to the arrangement, I would be willing to leave the first paragraph of the proposed preamble as submitted by the Peruvian Ambassador.

With regard to the insertion of the words "in the exercise of informal and unofficial good offices" the Peruvian Ambassador called today and, after stating that President Leguia was most anxious to have paragraph one of the preamble remain as presented, said that he was most insistent upon the deletion of the words "informal and unofficial" in the phrase quoted above. If President Leguia insists on this point, you may agree to it also, and the insertion in the second paragraph would then read "in the exercise o good offices". When this has been

GENERAL 797

agreed upon you will please suggest that the Peruvian Ambassador in Washington be authorized to make this change and submit to the Department a new memorandum either containing the modification or agreeing to the insertion of the words above quoted in the memorandum presented by him on May third.

In order to avoid any possible misunderstanding, the following is the English translation of the agreement between Peru and Chile which the President proposes to use in making his proposal:

[Here follows text of memorandum identic with translation of memorandum presented to President Hoover by the Governments of Chile and Peru on May 14, printed on page 798.]

Please obtain President Leguia's agreement to this translation.

STIMSON

---

723.2515/3372 : Telegram

*The Ambassador in Peru (Moore) to the Secretary of State*

LIMA, May 11, 1929—noon.
[Received 12:20 p. m.]

97. Your telegram No. 56, May 10, 6 p. m. President Leguia has asked me to say to you that he is deeply grateful to you and President Hoover.

He says the English translation is excellent and he agrees to it.

He will at once notify his Ambassador in Washington to agree immediately to the insertion of the words, "in the exercise of good offices".

Congratulations. Please accept my sincere thanks for your courtesy to me.

MOORE

---

723.2515/3374 : Telegram

*The Ambassador in Chile (Culbertson) to the Secretary of State*

SANTIAGO, May 11, 1929—5 p. m.
[Received 8:05 p. m.]

77. Referring to your telegram number 53, May 10, 6 p. m. I presented in person a note transmitting the English translation. In his written reply the Minister for Foreign Affairs said that

"Having examined and compared carefully the original Spanish and English text[s] of the agreement, I have not found any substantial differences between them, and therefore, I have the honor to state my concurrence (*conformidad*) in this latter text, to be used by the President of the United States in the exercise of his good offices."

CULBERTSON

723.2515/3391, 3392

*Memorandum Which the Governments of Chile and of Peru Place in the Hands of His Excellency, the President of the United States, the Honorable Herbert Hoover* [39]

Having been informed of the cordial progress of the negotiations between the Governments of Chile and of Peru, with reference to the direct agreements reached on nearly all the questions involved in the solution of the problem of Tacna and Arica and having also been informed of the decision of both governments to submit to him the only difficulty that has arisen with reference to the respective viewpoints relating to the projected port of Las Yaradas:

The President of the United States summarizing the points agreed upon proposes to the two governments in the exercise of good offices as the final bases of a solution the following stipulations:

*First.*—The territory will be divided into two parts: Tacna for Peru and Arica for Chile. The dividing line shall start at a point which shall be designated with the name, "Concordia", situated ten kilometers to the north of the bridge over the river Lluta, and shall continue parallel to the Arica-La Paz Railroad following as far as possible the topographic features which may make easier the demarcation of the line. The sulphur deposits of Tacora shall remain in Chilean territory, and the Canals of Uchusuma and Mauri, also known as Azucarero, shall remain the property of Peru, with the understanding, however, that wherever these canals pass through Chilean territory they shall enjoy the most complete servitude in perpetuity in favor of Peru. This servitude includes the right to widen the actual canals, change their course, and appropriate all waters that may be collectible in their passage through Chilean territory.

The boundary line shall pass through the center of Laguna Blanca, dividing it into two equal parts. Peru and Chile shall each designate an engineer and the necessary assistants to proceed to the demarcation of the new frontier in accordance with the points herein agreed upon, and shall indicate the dividing line by means of boundary monuments. In case of disagreement, such disagreement shall be decided by a third person designated by the President of the United States, whose decision shall be final.

*Second.*—The Government of Chile will grant to the Government of Peru within the One Thousand Five Hundred and Seventy-Five meters of the Bay of Arica, a wharf (Malecón), a customhouse and a station for the railroad from Tacna to Arica, where Peru shall enjoy

---

[39] Identic notes in Spanish and in English handed to Assistant Secretary of State White by the Peruvian and Chilean Ambassadors on May 14, 1929.

independence within the most ample free port. All the aforementioned works shall be constructed by the Government of Chile.

*Third.*—The Government of Chile will deliver to the Government of Peru the sum of Six Million Dollars.

*Fourth.*—The Government of Chile will deliver without cost of any kind to Peru all the public works already constructed, together with all government owned real property in the Department of Tacna.

*Fifth.*—The Government of Chile will maintain in the Department of Arica the franchise granted by the Government of Peru in the year 1852, to the Arica-Tacna Railroad Company.

*Sixth.*—The Government of Chile shall proceed to deliver the Department of Tacna thirty days after the exchange of ratifications of the Treaty.

*Seventh.*—The Governments of Chile and Peru will respect private rights legally acquired in the territories that remain under their respective sovereignties.

*Eighth.*—The Governments of Chile and Peru, in order to commemorate the consolidation of their friendly relations, agree to erect on the Morro de Arica a monument, the design of which shall be the subject of agreement between the parties.

*Ninth.*—The children of Peruvian nationals born in Arica shall be considered as Peruvians until they attain the age of twenty-one years, at which age they shall have the right to elect their definitive nationality; and the children of Chileans, born in Tacna, shall enjoy the same right.

*Tenth.*—Chile and Peru will reciprocally release any obligation, engagement or indebtedness between the two countries, whether derived or not from the Treaty of Ancón.

---

723.2515/3371supp : Telegram

*The Secretary of State to the Ambassador in Chile (Culbertson)* [40]

WASHINGTON, May 14, 1929—8 p. m.

55. You will please transmit immediately to the Minister for Foreign Affairs the memorandum quoted in my No. 53 of May 10, 6 p. m., under cover of the following note:

"Excellency: Under instructions from my Government I have the honor to present to Your Excellency, with the request that you be so good as to transmit it to His Excellency the President of Chile, certain stipulations which the President of the United States of America, not as Arbitrator, but in the exercise, at the request of both parties, of good offices, proposes to the Governments of Chile and Peru as the final bases of a solution of the problem of Tacna-Arica.

---

[40] The same, *mutatis mutandis*, on the same date to the Ambassador in Peru as telegram No. 58, mentioning Department's telegram No. 56 of May 10, 6 p. m.

In presenting this proposal to Your Excellency's Government I am directed by the Secretary of State to say that, in making it, the President of the United States of America has been guided by agreements reached directly between Chile and Peru on questions involved between them in the solution of the problem of Tacna-Arica. The proposal is therefore not to be interpreted as indicating that either the President or the Government of the United States of America expresses any opinion or view or makes any suggestion in any way whatever regarding any future disposition by either party of that portion of the territory in dispute which will be in its possession should the proposal enclosed herewith be accepted by the Governments of Chile and Peru."

You will please say that the terms of this proposal will not be made public by the President until the answers of Chile and Peru have been received and it is therefore requested that no publicity be given to this matter at this time. When the replies of both Governments have been received you will be advised. Cable Chilean reply.

STIMSON

---

723.2515/3393

*The Chilean Minister for Foreign Affairs (Rios Gallardo) to the American Ambassador in Chile (Culbertson)* [41]

[Translation]

SANTIAGO, May 15, 1929.

EXCELLENCY: I have the honor to acknowledge the receipt of the note dated today by which Your Excellency, in compliance with instructions from your Government, sends me for transmission to His Excellency the President of the Republic the stipulations which the President of the United States of America in the exercise of good offices sought by the Parties and guided by the direct agreements arrived at by Chile and Peru proposes as the final bases of a solution of the Tacna-Arica problem.

It affords me satisfaction to declare to Your Excellency that these bases, having been transmitted to His Excellency the President of the Republic, the Government of Chile has decided to accept them in the terms and scope of the note which I now have the pleasure to answer.

My Government believes, therefore, that the Treaty which is to be concluded between Chile and Peru in accordance with those bases will wholly and finally decide the only pending question arising from the War of the Pacific and with it the last of the boundary questions of the Republic.

The people of Chile, placing confidence in their destiny and concen-

---

[41] Copy handed to Assistant Secretary of State White by the Chilean Ambassador May 17, 1929.

trating their energies on work, note the utmost importance of this action which guarantees their safety and promotes their progress.

In thanking, by direction of His Excellency the President of the Republic and through Your Excellency, the President of the United States of America for his lofty and friendly cooperation towards removing the obstacle which for half a century has kept Chile and Peru apart, I avail myself of the opportunity to renew to Your Excellency the sentiments of my highest and most distinguished consideration.

CONRADO RIOS GALLARDO

723.2515/3384 : Telegram

*The Ambassador in Peru (Moore) to the Secretary of State*

[Translation]

LIMA, May 16, 1929—3 p. m.
[Received 3:55 p. m.]

104. My 103.[42]

"No. 28. Lima, May 16, 1929.

"Excellency: I have the honor to inform Your Excellency that I have received your important communication No. 88 dated yesterday in which you were good enough to inform me that, following instructions from your Government, you are pleased to transmit to the President of Peru certain stipulations set forth in the enclosure, which the President of the United States of America, not in his capacity as Arbitrator, but in the exercise of good offices, and at the request of both parties, proposes to the Governments of Peru and Chile, as the final bases of a solution of the problem of Tacna-Arica.

"Your Excellency states that in presenting this proposal to my Government, you have been instructed by the Secretary of State of the United States of America to inform me that, in making it, the President of the United States of America was guided by agreements reached directly between Chile and Peru on questions involved between them, in the solution of the problem of Tacna-Arica.

"Your Excellency adds that nevertheless the proposal is not to be interpreted as indicating that either the President or the Government of the United States of America expresses an opinion or view or makes a suggestion in any way whatever regarding any future disposition which either of the parties may make of that portion of the territory in dispute which will remain in its possession should the proposal enclosed in your note be accepted by the Governments of Peru and Chile.

"Your Excellency stated that you were charged by your Government to inform me that the terms of the said proposal would not be made public by the President of the United States of America until the replies of Peru and Chile had been received and therefore you requested that no publicity be given to this matter for the present.

[42] Undated, received May 16, 2:37 p. m.; it reads: "Peru's answer handed to me at 2:10 this afternoon, text follows." (723.2515/3383)

"In reply I take pleasure in informing Your Excellency that immediately upon receipt of your important note I hastened to bring it to the attention of the President of the Republic, Senor Augusto B. Leguia, who has instructed me to inform Your Excellency and, through you, the President of the United States of America, that the Government of Peru accepts each and every one of the bases proposed by the President of the United States of America, for a final settlement of the question of Tacna-Arica and that, with the acceptance of them by both parties, it considers this question absolutely and finally settled.

"I comply likewise with instructions from the President in asking Your Excellency to be so good as to express to the President of the United States of America the most cordial thanks for the eminent service which he has rendered, contributing at the opportune moment, with his high authority as friendly mediator in the solution of the grave international conflict whose termination is of importance not only to the countries directly concerned in the arrangement but also to the peace of the continent.

"It is likewise a pleasure for me to express to Your Excellency the thanks of the President of the Republic, Don Augusto B. Leguia, and of his Government, to your good self for the notable participation which you have had in the termination of this most important matter.

"In this historic moment which redounds so to the prestige not only of Peru and Chile but of America, I reiterate to you, Mr. Ambassador, the sentiments of my highest and most distinguished consideration. (Signed) Pedro Jose Rada y Gamio.[43]

MOORE

723.2515/3387

*Memorandum by the Assistant Secretary of State (White)*

[WASHINGTON,] May 17, 1929.

The Bolivian Chargé d'Affaires, Señor George de la Barra, called on the Secretary on Friday morning, May 17, at the latter's request.

The Secretary advised the Chargé that he called him in to give him the information before it is published that the Tacna-Arica question has been settled. The Secretary added that he was glad also to be able to inform him that the provision regarding the future disposition of the territories and the question of the railways about which Bolivia had protested had, at the instance of the Secretary, been eliminated.

The Chargé expressed his great gratification and said he knew his Government would be very pleased. The Secretary stated that he hoped that the Bolivian Government would remember this service rendered to it by the United States because Bolivia had, more or

---

[43] Peruvian Minister for Foreign Affairs.

less behind its back and over its head, gone to the League of Nations not only in this matter but also in the Bolivia-Paraguay boundary matter.

Señor de la Barra said he felt sure that that was merely a supplementary action on the part of his Government which felt that such matters should be settled in Washington and had always looked to the United States for help in the matter. He said that the Minister here especially felt that way and when he had been Minister in Paraguay, long before the recent outbreak between the two countries, he had suggested to Paraguay that the boundary question be brought to the United States for a settlement. The Secretary stated that he had not referred to the Bolivian Minister here particularly but to the Bolivian Government. The Secretary added that it is the firm purpose of this Government to be helpful and deal fairly with all Governments of this hemisphere, and even such action as he had described had not deterred this Government from rendering a friendly service to Bolivia.

F[rancis] W[hite]

---

723.2515/3394

*Press Release Issued by the Department of State, May 17, 1929*

[Extract]

The President is happy to be able to announce an agreement between the Governments of Chile and Peru relative to the nearly half century old question of Tacna-Arica.

As a result of the high statesmanship and lofty ideals of the Presidents and Governments of Chile and Peru, diplomatic relations were renewed between those countries last September at the suggestion of the Secretary of State, and rapid progress toward a settlement satisfactory to both was made. However, when the President, as President-elect, visited Peru and Chile last December he was advised of the difficulties of a definitive settlement and gladly consented to lend any proper assistance, upon assuming office, with a view to bring about, if happily it might be, a final agreement between the parties.

Accordingly, on May 14, the President, not as Arbitrator but in the exercise of good offices at the request of the parties, transmitted to the Presidents of Peru and Chile, through the American Ambassadors at Lima and Santiago, a proposal suggesting the final bases of a settlement. This proposal was presented to the two Governments on May 15 and was immediately accepted by them.

723.2515/3395

*Press Release Issued by the Department of State, May 18, 1929*

## TACNA-ARICA

In discussing the settlement of the Tacna-Arica problem in his press conference today, Secretary Stimson said:

"This is the solution of a forty-five year old problem which has been the only serious source of discontent in South America. Mr. Kellogg's administration is entitled to very great credit for bringing it about. Through many vicissitudes he brought the matter along by the kindly exercise of good offices to a point where both countries have directly settled the problem. It was through Mr. Kellogg's good work that these countries, which for many years had had no diplomatic relations, were induced to appoint, respectively, ambassadors to the other country, and since that was done they have been able to get together in normal and easy communication, and this settlement has followed.

I was in a position to observe Mr. Kellogg's work and I know how hard and earnestly he worked to bring that about. He deserves the greatest credit.

President Hoover himself also shared in the responsibility and the credit for bringing about the settlement, by having taken steps on his visit to Peru and Chile, last December, to smooth out and settle certain difficulties which had arisen at that time."

---

723.2515/3398 : Telegram

*The Secretary of State to the Ambassador in Chile (Culbertson)*

[Paraphrase]

WASHINGTON, May 22, 1929—6 p. m.

58. Yesterday afternoon the Chilean Ambassador called to say that some concern had been caused in Chile by published versions of a statement that I made at a recent press conference which, it is said, had been so interpreted in Chile as to give the impression that the claims of Bolivia affecting the littoral had been taken into consideration in connection with the proposal made by the President for the settlement between Chile and Peru. The Chilean Ambassador intimated that these reports had placed him personally in an embarrassing position because he had assured the Government of Chile that the Government of the United States considered the Tacna-Arica question one to be dealt with exclusively by Chile and Peru.

At the press conference in question, in response to a statement made by a press correspondent that the Legation of Bolivia had given out a statement which indicated that the settlement might interfere with the friendly relations of the countries which participated in the War of the Pacific, I said that no one else had made any such comment. Being further pressed by the correspondents I read to them the last paragraph of the note which transmitted to Chile and Peru the settlement proposed by the President, as sent to you in my 55, May 14, 8 p. m. I then pointed out that this left open to Chile and Peru to make any arrangements or disposition with regard to the portion of the territory in dispute which came to each of them which they might wish to make. That is as far as the United States of America is concerned it was left so that Chile and Peru could give Bolivia a seacoast if Chile and/or Peru so desire. Such was the full effect and purport of the statement I made to the press. Other than those which I have already reported to you in my 46, May 1, 8 p. m. there have been no communications, formal or informal, with the Government of Bolivia. We have done nothing and said nothing during this negotiation which affects or bears upon any claim or feeling which Bolivia may have regarding the territories involved in the settlement other than has been communicated to you. As a matter of fact, Bolivia did lodge a formal written protest with the Department of State against the provision in the original suggested agreement, and she also enumerated occasions on which the United States, Chile, and Peru had in her opinion appeared to recognize the validity of the demands of Bolivia for an outlet to the sea. No answer was made to this protest because it was felt that the publication of the settlement and the covering notes of the Department was sufficient answer.

I also told the Ambassador during my conversation with him that the Government of the United States had no intention of taking any further steps than had already been taken.

You may in your discretion bring the foregoing informally to the attention of the Foreign Minister.

STIMSON

723.2515/3412

*Memorandum by the Assistant Secretary of State (White)*

[WASHINGTON,] May 29, 1929.

The Bolivian Chargé d'Affaires [44] called on the Secretary of State on Wednesday, May 29. He stated that, in view of the well-known interest which the United States takes in Latin America and its friendly disposition towards them, as well as the consideration shown to Bolivia in the past with respect to her aspirations for a seaport, he had been instructed to inquire of the Secretary whether he would be willing to join with other countries of this hemisphere in endeavoring to obtain a seaport for Bolivia and, if so, whether the United States would lead the movement.

The Secretary said that the Tacna-Arica question had been settled

[44] George de la Barra.

by Chile and Peru; that Secretary Kellogg had initiated negotiations and had very ably brought them almost to a conclusion, and that the Secretary himself had had the honor of bringing them to a conclusion. The matter is now concluded except for the formalities. It was difficult enough to obtain this happy result, dealing with but two countries, and had a third country come into it a settlement would have been impossible. The Secretary stated that the only way to accomplish results is to take one step at a time and that he very much hoped Bolivia would not do anything which would prevent the final conclusion of the Tacna-Arica matter. When that question is settled, it will be time enough to discuss any further steps. The Secretary thought that after a time, when passions had cooled down, there would be much more of a chance for Bolivia to take up the question of a port. Especially would this be the case if Bolivia, in the settlement of the present dispute with Paraguay,[45] shows restraint and dignity. By so doing and making possible a settlement of the Chaco matter, Bolivia will increase her prestige and standing in the eyes of the world and will greatly promote her cause. The Secretary stated that in the case of nations, as in individuals, restraint and dignity in the representation of their claims always wins out, and that time is always on the side of the fair-minded. The Secretary therefore very earnestly urged on the Chargé that his Government should not rush into the matter now but let the Tacna-Arica question between Chile and Peru be definitely settled and out of the way; that Bolivia should exercise patience, restraint and dignity in the handling of its dispute with Paraguay, and should let time heal the breach which now exists between Bolivia and Chile, and that he thought Bolivia would gain more in the end by such tactics than by jumping in now and disturbing and upsetting the situation.

The Chargé thanked the Secretary and said that he was glad to have his opinion and advice in the matter and was sure that his Government would be guided thereby.

F[RANCIS] W[HITE]

723.2515/3444

*Memorandum by the Assistant Secretary of State (White)*

[WASHINGTON,] June 12, 1929.

The Bolivian Minister called on Wednesday, June 12, accompanied by Mr. de la Barra, Secretary of the Legation. The Minister stated that the Secretary's recent conversation with Mr. de la Barra had been duly transmitted to the Bolivian Government and that he was now instructed to say that the Bolivian Government much appreciated the interest of the Secretary in their problems and that, in

[45] See pp. 818 ff.

accordance with the Secretary's suggestion, Bolivia would drop the question of a port on the Pacific for the time being and would wait until the Tacna-Arica matter was definitively settled and out of the way. In the meantime, in view of the Secretary's view regarding the controversy between Bolivia and Paraguay, and the importance which the Secretary attaches to its prompt settlement, the Bolivian Government has instructed its delegates on the Commission of Inquiry and Conciliation to discuss with the other members of the Commission the question of a complete settlement of the dispute and to transmit to the Bolivian Government any proposals to this end which the Commission may make.

The Minister stated that his Government duly appreciates the interest which the Secretary is taking in the problems of Bolivia and is glad in this way to show its hearty appreciation and its desire to follow the suggestions made by the Secretary. The Minister added that the question of a port is a primordial one for Bolivia and that later on, when the proper moment arrives, Bolivia will take this question up again.

F[RANCIS] W[HITE]

---

723.2515/3459

## The Ambassador in Peru (Moore) to the Secretary of State

No. 301

LIMA, June 25, 1929.
[Received July 9.]

SIR: I have the honor to transmit herewith a copy of the treaty between Peru and Chile settling the Tacna-Arica question.[46] It was handed to me by President Leguia at Government Palace this morning, and it will be noted that there are several changes from the text of the original agreement as proposed by President Hoover.

I am not sending an English translation because the Department has better facilities therefor than the mission, and because the Spanish text of the original agreement is already on file in Washington.

I have [etc.]

ALEXANDER P. MOORE

---

723.2515/3452

## Memorandum by the Assistant Secretary of State (White)

[WASHINGTON,] July 3, 1929.

The Bolivian Minister, accompanied by Señor de la Barra, Secretary of the Bolivian Legation, called on Wednesday morning, July 3. He stated that he had received word a day or two ago that the clause in the Tacna-Arica arrangement which Bolivia had protested about

---

[46] Signed June 3, 1929. For text, see League of Nations Treaty Series, vol. XCIV, p. 402.

has been inserted in a secret protocol attached to the Treaty. This seemed unbelievable but he this morning received a further cable from his Government, which he showed me, stating that the Lima newspaper *Comercio* published under a Santiago headline that the Chilean Senate had approved the secret protocol by twenty-three votes to six with two abstentions. This, he said, proves the existence of the secret protocol.

I told the Minister that we had no information about the matter whatsoever; that this was the first we had heard of a secret protocol. I told him that we had received a cable yesterday [47] which confirmed what appeared in the American press to the effect that the Chilean Senate had approved the Treaty by twenty-seven votes to two with two abstentions and that this morning we had a cable from Lima [47] stating that last night the Peruvian Congress in joint session approved the Treaty with only one dissenting vote. Nothing was said about a secret protocol or the vote regarding it, nor had we information from any other source regarding such a secret agreement. I told the Minister that while this certainly was not conclusive, I did think that we were likely to hear should there be such an agreement. I briefly reviewed the position of this Government in the matter and read to him our note transmitting the President's proposal to Chile and Peru which clearly set forth this Government's attitude with respect to Bolivia. I told the Minister that even should his news be true I did not think that it altered Bolivia's position in any way and that I thought the best course for Bolivia to follow was one of patience—to let Chile and Peru settle their dispute between themselves; for Bolivia to continue to endeavor to arrive at a settlement with Paraguay over the Chaco dispute, and the way would still be open for Bolivia to take up the question of a port at a later favorable opportunity, and that I thought it would be very unwise to inject this question into the situation at present.

The Minister stated that he fully concurred and that his Government was not contemplating any action. Some had advised protest before the League of Nations but he felt sure his Government would not do so. He stated that certain neighboring nations, . . . had tried to push Bolivia into making a protest or asking the neighboring countries to use their good offices to try to obtain a port for Bolivia, but that the Bolivian Government intended to follow the advice given by the Secretary of State and would not agitate this question now. The Bolivian Government merely wanted to advise this Government of the situation. I thanked the Minister for keeping the Department informed and told him I would immediately inform the Secretary of our conversation.

---

[47] Not printed.

The Minister then stated that he had seen editorials in the *Diario Ilustrado* and the *Mercurio* of Santiago, the most important papers there (the Edwards papers), stating that the clause about the transfer of territory to a third nation is pure imagination on the part of Bolivia as no such clause was in the proposal presented to the Department of State by Chile and Peru which, in turn, had been transmitted to those countries as the President's proposal without changing a comma. I told the Minister that it was correct that when the official draft was handed to us this clause was not in it and that it was because the Department, after hearing Bolivia's complaint, had taken the matter up with both Chile and Peru that this clause had been omitted when the proposal was officially made.

The Minister stated that he would like to come in some other day and discuss with me, unofficially, the whole problem of the Pacific, not with a view to having this Government take any action, but just to give me the background from Bolivia's point of view. I told him I should of course be glad to hear anything he had to say. The Minister expressed the hope that the Department would make inquiries of our Embassies in Santiago and Lima regarding the truth of the report that there is a secret protocol. I made no commitment on this point.

F[RANCIS] W[HITE]

---

723.2515/3462

*Memorandum by the Assistant Secretary of State (White)*

[Extract]

[WASHINGTON,] July 5, 1929.

The Bolivian Minister called on Friday morning, July 5. He stated that he received last night a telegram from his Government which was a copy of an instruction sent to the Bolivian Legation in Lima. He handed me a copy of the telegram which reads, in translation, as follows:

"La Paz, July 4, 1929.

"Legation Bolivia. Lima.

"From various sources we have received rumors stating that a secret protocol concluded between Chile and Peru annexed to the principal Treaty contains stipulations contrary to Bolivian maritime reintegration and its future commercial development.

"Call on President Leguia carrying to him this despatch and state to him that we desire to put aside these rumors and to build up on permanent friendly bases the future of our international relations to which any Chilean-Peruvian entente seeking a hegemony of the South Pacific will be an obstacle.

"The sovereignty of Arica being determined, our future policy to recover an outlet to the sea can never hurt the rights nor expectations of Peru, upon whose help we hope to count.

"Similarly a Chilean-Peruvian entente which is rumored in foreign international circles would raise up a grave obstacle to the friendly future of America, to which we desire to contribute, as we have demonstrated in terminating all our differences with Atlantic nations which today extend to us frank sympathy and as we shall demonstrate, endeavoring to bring about a territorial arrangement with Paraguay in Washington.

(Signed)   Elio."

The Minister stated that I would see that this was a very temperate statement and that Bolivia is following the advice of the Department and is not stirring up this question now.

F[RANCIS] W[HITE]

723.2515/3456 : Telegram

*The Ambassador in Chile (Culbertson) to the Secretary of State*

[Paraphrase]

SANTIAGO, July 6, 1929—noon.<br>[Received 4 p. m.]

106. This morning I was orally informed by the Foreign Office that the Treaty of Lima carries a protocol which is an integral part of the treaty and ratified with it providing:

(1) That neither Chile nor Peru will cede to a third country any portion of their respective parts of the provinces of Tacna and Arica nor will they change or extend the lines of railroads in the provinces without the consent of the other.

(2) That Peru has the right to [free transit of] arms through the port of Arica to and from Peruvian territory.

(3) That the Morro will be demilitarized.

CULBERTSON

723.2515/3474

*The Ambassador in Chile (Culbertson) to the Secretary of State*

No. 225
SANTIAGO, July 8, 1929.<br>[Received July 31.]

Sir: Referring to my despatch No. 218 of July 1, 1929,[49] I have the honor to transmit herewith the Spanish text of the Protocol of the Tacna-Arica Treaty between Chile and Peru. Until released by the Governments this Protocol should be held strictly confidential.

I have [etc.]
W. S. CULBERTSON

---

[49] Not printed.

### ADDITIONAL PROTOCOL TO THE TACNA-ARICA TREATY BETWEEN CHILE AND PERU

The Governments of Chile and Peru have agreed to sign an additional Protocol of the Treaty which is signed on this day and their respective Plenipotentiaries, duly authorized thereto, have in effect agreed on the following:

ARTICLE 1.—The Governments of Chile and Peru shall not, without a previous agreement between them, cede to a third Power all or part of the territories which in accordance with the Treaty of this same date are under their respective sovereignties, neither shall they, without that requisite, build across them any new international railway.

ARTICLE 2.—The harbor facilities which the Treaty in its Article Five accords to Peru shall consist in the most absolutely free transit of persons, merchandise and armament to the Peruvian territory and from that territory across the Chilean territory. The shipping and landing operations shall, during the construction and until the completion of the works referred to in Article Five of the Treaty, take place on the Arica-La Paz railway pier, which is reserved for the service of the Arica-Tacna Railway.

ARTICLE 3.—The Arica Morro shall be dismantled and the Government of Chile will erect at its own expense the monument agreed to in Article Eleven of the Treaty.

The present Protocol forms an integral part of the Treaty of this same date and consequently shall be ratified and its ratifications shall be exchanged at Santiago de Chile as soon as possible.

In faith whereof the undersigned Plenipotentiaries sign and seal the present additional Protocol in duplicate at Lima on the third day of the month of June one thousand, nine hundred and twenty-nine.

E. FIGUEROA        [SEAL]        PEDRO JOSÉ RADA Y GAMIO        [SEAL]

---

723.2515/3477

*Final Ruling of the Arbitrator in the Matter of the Tacna-Arica Arbitration, August 2, 1929* [51]

On March 4, 1925, there was handed down the Opinion and Award of the Arbitrator in the matter of the Arbitration between the Republic of Chile and the Republic of Peru,[52] with respect to the unfulfilled provisions of the Treaty of Peace of October 20, 1883,[53] under

---

[50] Translation made in the Department.
[51] Transmitted to the Diplomatic Representatives of Chile and Peru in Washington on August 2, 1929.
[52] *Foreign Relations*, 1925, vol. I, p. 305.
[53] *Ibid.*, 1883, p. 731.

the Protocol and Supplementary Act signed at Washington on July 20, 1922.[54]

In accordance with the provisions of this Opinion and Award a Plebiscitary Commission was appointed and proceeded with its labors until June 14, 1926 when it adopted a resolution terminating the plebiscitary proceedings [55] for the reasons set forth in the resolution of the Commission. Further proceedings in connection with the action taken by the Plebiscitary Commission were held in abeyance pending the result of the good offices looking toward a direct settlement which the Secretary of State of the United States had tendered the Parties in April, 1926.[56]

A Special Commission on Boundaries was also appointed under the provisions of the Award and proceeded with its work until October 17, 1928 when, at the suggestion of the Secretary of State in the further exercise of good offices, its activities were suspended for a period of four months,[57] which was subsequently extended for fixed periods from time to time, until the suspension was made indefinite by the Arbitrator's Ruling of May 17, 1929.

Pursuant to a suggestion of the Secretary of State, in the course of his good offices, the Party Governments agreed in September, 1928, to a renewal of diplomatic relations which was actually brought about on the third of October, 1928,[58] and subsequent to that time direct negotiations for settlement proceeded between the two Governments.

As a result of these negotiations on May fourteenth the President of the United States of America, not as Arbitrator but in the exercise of good offices, at the request of both Parties, summarizing the points agreed upon in the direct negotiations between them, submitted to the two Governments a proposal for the final bases of the solution of the problem of Tacna and Arica. This proposal having been accepted by the two Governments a Treaty was concluded by them on June 3, 1929, Article I of which provides that the controversy arising from Article 3 of the Treaty of Peace and Friendship of October 20, 1883, which was the sole difficulty pending between the two Governments, is definitely settled. This Treaty was ratified by both Governments and the exchange of ratifications took place on July 28, 1929.

The Arbitrator is therefore of the opinion that the controversy between Chile and Peru concerning the provinces of Tacna and Arica

---

[54] *Foreign Relations*, 1922, vol. I, p. 505.
[55] See telegram, June 14, 1926, 8 p. m., from the Consul at Arica, *ibid.*, 1926, vol. I, p. 482.
[56] See telegram, April 1, 1926, 7 p. m., to the Consul at Arica, *ibid.*, p. 369.
[57] See *ibid.*, 1928, vol. I, pp. 663–665.
[58] See *ibid.*, pp. 647 ff.

having thus been settled by direct negotiation between the Parties themselves, all proceedings of whatsoever nature incident to the arbitration under the Protocol and Supplementary Act of July 20, 1922, should be and they are hereby terminated, except the settlement of the accounts of the Disbursing Officer as provided for in the Arbitrator's Ruling of May 17, 1929, and the functions of the Arbitrator will be completely terminated when the Disbursing Officer shall have been discharged in accordance with the Arbitrator's Ruling of May 17, 1929 from any further responsibility in respect of his accounts.

The Arbitrator takes this occasion to express his high appreciation of the services rendered by General John J. Pershing and Major General William Lassiter who served successively as Presidents of the Plebiscitary Commission under the appointment of the Arbitrator, and of the services rendered by their able assistants, and likewise his high appreciation of the services rendered by General Jay J. Morrow who was designated by the Arbitrator as the third Member of the Special Commission on Boundaries and chosen as Chairman of that Commission by his colleagues.

In conclusion the Arbitrator desires to express most especially to the two Governments concerned his grateful appreciation of the cooperation and broadminded statesmanship manifested in the direct negotiations leading up to the definitive solution of the delicate and difficult questions which have disturbed the relations of two great peoples for so many years.

HERBERT HOOVER
*Arbitrator*

By the Arbitrator
HENRY L. STIMSON
*Secretary of State.*

---

723.2515/3494

*The Bolivian Minister (Diez de Medina) to the Secretary of State* [59]

[Translation]

WASHINGTON, August 28, 1929.

EXCELLENCY: The Government of Bolivia has addressed the following Circular to its Legations abroad which, on its instructions, I make known to the Government of the United States of America:

"Circular No. 327.    La Paz, August 1, 1929.

Mr. Minister: Confirming the rumors which have been circulating that a secret protocol had been agreed upon between Chile and Peru which would fundamentally affect Bolivia in her policy of maritime restoration, the said agreement has just been officially published, the

[59] Acknowledged September 5, 1929.

secrecy of which was frustrated by the knowledge thereof which American public opinion succeeded in gaining.

The recently published protocol reestablishes one of the clauses of the Treaty regarding the division of the provinces of Tacna and Arica, a clause the text of which is given below and which was withdrawn from the Preliminary Agreement on account of timely suggestions from the Government of the United States of North America which, having mediated in the solution of the dispute, believed its maintenance inexpedient for the future of the negotiations which Bolivia might open.

According to the additional agreement, the Governments of Chile and Peru shall not be able, without a previous accord, to transfer to A Third Power the whole or a part of the territories which, in conformity with the Treaty of the same date, remain under their respective sovereignties, nor shall they be able, without this prerequisite, to construct new international rail routes across them.

This provision was covenanted directly against Bolivia, for which reason the additional agreement arouses our formal reservations, which we wish to make known to the chanceleries of sovereign States, and to international organizations, confident that they must find them rightful and legitimate.

Bolivia, who was forced into the war of 1879 by the military occupation of its port of Antofagasta by Chile, shared the vicissitudes of the campaign with her ally Peru, and Chile being victorious, our country, as a result of an unjust war which it did not provoke, suffered the dismemberment of all its coast along the Pacific Ocean, which amounted to an extent of two hundred miles.

Since that time she has never, on any occasion, renounced her right to have her maritime sovereignty restored, always appreciating that the free communication of nations by the sea—which is common to all the people of the earth—is an inalienable and imprescriptible attribute of the sovereignty of every independent State. This principle, applicable today in International Law, even to nations which do not have seaports of their own, is applicable with greater reason to a State such as ours which had had an extensive and rich littoral withdrawn from its dominion as the result of a war of conquest.

The fact that, as a consequence of the same war, the territories of Tacna and Arica had remained in the possession of Chile, without defined sovereignty, caused Bolivia, who always considered herself a principal party in the settlement of the dispute which had occasioned her so much injury, to open various diplomatic negotiations to recover her maritime sovereignty through Arica.

The Republic always took into consideration the fact that, through the Treaty of Peace signed at Ancón between Chile and Peru, in 1883, Chile, who acquired sovereignty over Tarapaca, would not be likely to consent easily to the restoration of our maritime sovereignty, through a zone which was not north of the conquered territory.

These negotiations, more than once met with a favorable reception with the Governments of Lima and Santiago, the aspirations and rights of Bolivia culminating in the suggestion which the Secretary of State of the United States of North America, Mr. Kellogg, made on November 30, 1926, proposing that the territories of Tacna and Arica should be transferred as a whole to Bolivia by the two countries which were contesting their jurisdiction.

Chile accepted this suggestion in principle, declaring that the proposal of the Department of State "involves the definitive cession of the disputed territory to the Republic of Bolivia" "and harmonizes with the often repeated desire expressed by the Government of Chile, to assist in the satisfaction of Bolivian aspirations."

Peru did not accept the Kellogg suggestion, but, in referring thereto, expressed the following ideas: "This rejection, however, does not mean an intention to obstruct any other solutions. Far from that, Peru has accepted the partial or complete internationalization of the provinces and has accepted the division of them, freely giving a narrow passage to the shore to Bolivia and an inlet on it, on conditions which permit of its being converted into a large, convenient and safe port."

President Leguia, in his Message to Congress in 1926, stated further: "The problem of the Pacific can not be solved without invoking the right of Peru and, in any case, our fraternal willingness to aid Bolivia in securing an exit to the sea which she claims with such great need."

Such eloquent and solemn declarations, coming from the Governments which participated in the struggle of 1879, did not seem destined to be cast into oblivion.

It may, however, be observed that these acknowledgments of our right encountered a serious obstacle in the indetermination as to the sovereignty of Tacna and Arica. For that reason, when Chile and Peru concluded the Treaty recently ratified, which provides for the division of those territories, we Bolivians thought that the obstacle of indivision and the lack of a definite sovereignty was finally disappearing, it being always easier and more possible to come to an understanding with the State possessing the port of Arica, which should expedite the solution of the problem of our maritime restoration, because therein lie the historical and economic antecedents which have their root in the war of 79, and which have created the landlocked situation of Bolivia which keeps, and will always keep alive the fire which feeds her ideals for the recovery [of her maritime sovereignty].

If the negotiators of the recent factum had been seeking the reign of peace, harmony and justice on the continent, they should not have closed their eyes to the case of Bolivia, forgetting their former solemn declarations, and a high American duty imposed on them the obligation freely to open the way to the satisfaction of our rights and needs. If they were endeavoring to settle the consequences of the war of 1879, as Bolivia participated in it, losing extensive and rich territories, and her maritime sovereignty, there was nothing more essential than to have taken care of that reparation.

Far from acting thus, they have given new life to the obstacle which was formerly invoked as insurmountable for any just solution. They have agreed upon an imperfect condominium of the territories in question, meant to have efficacy only when Bolivia is concerned.

Peru has chosen to limit her sovereignty over the province of Tacna, renouncing in perpetuity the right to construct an international railroad towards Bolivia, in order to have the right of veto in any negotiation which we may attempt regarding Arica; and, reciprocally, Chile has given this right to Peru in order to maintain her influence over the two contiguous regions, as well as the advantages which the key to the Arica-La Paz railroad secures to her.

This policy is not one of real international cooperation, and is capable of producing profound resentment in Bolivian consciousness in the present and in the future.

The unfriendliness of the agreement is made patent by the very secrecy with which it was wished to surround it, in spite of the fact that both contracting States, as members of the League of Nations, have promised not to make secret treaties.

Withal, and in spite of the new difficulties created for Bolivia by the additional Chilean-Peruvian pact, we want world opinion to know that we are persisting and shall persist in the policy of restoration of our maritime sovereignty. We are not renouncing the repossession of our free communication with the world, by way of the Pacific Ocean. We proclaim before the juridical consciousness of the world, today already quite strong, where yesterday it was imperfect and weak, that we do not consider the situation created by an unjust war, not provoked by us, to be juridically irrevocable or intangible, and that, either through direct negotiations, if there is occasion for them, or through the means which International Law and new organizations recognize, we shall maintain our right in all its entirety and, with the assistance of just spirits, we shall resort to the channels for reparation which international justice may point out to us. The postulates of that justice, in condemning wars of conquest, open up the revision of indefensible pacts and the rule of removing, through pacific means, every notorious injustice, the basic principle of private law, and which, if it does not govern between nations, will make peace impossible of realization, which, in order to be unalterable, must be founded on justice, and justice will not be justice as long as all States may not co-exist as persons in their own right and with the fullness of their attributes—that rule will not be long in taking root on the field of International Law, so plentifully nourished by the thousands of victims of the last great war.

Please forward these considerations for the information and examination of the friendly Government near which you are accredited, and of the organizations which may be interested in the reign of peace and justice in the world. (Signed) Tomas Manuel Elio—Minister of Foreign Affairs."

Please accept [etc.]                     E. Diez de Medina

---

723.2515/3500

*Memorandum by the Secretary of State of a Conversation With the Peruvian Chargé (Bedoya)*

[Washington,] September 12, 1929.

The Peruvian Chargé read me a translation of a message in which Peru expressed the hope that I would not do anything to encourage Bolivia in her agitation for a port on the Pacific side. He said that Bolivia was planning a campaign of agitation, et cetera. I told him that I had no intention of doing any such thing, on the contrary, when Bolivia had protested against the action of Chile and Peru in making a compact between themselves not to transfer any part of Tacna Arica without the consent of the other I had told the representative of Peru that that settlement was entirely the action of the two countries, and that we had had no part in it except to extend our good offices in order to bring them together. I told him that I had counseled moderation in all such matters, and that I had had occasion to point it out to both Bolivia and Peru in regard to their negotiations for the settlement of their troubles in the Chaco and that he might rest assured that I would not do anything to excite or further any other course. I said to him that "the settlement of the question of the port rests entirely between you three countries in South America. I am sorry that there should be any cause for irritation to any one of you, but you may rest assured that I am not going to intrude myself into the affair".

# THE CHACO DISPUTE BETWEEN BOLIVIA AND PARAGUAY [1]

### Adjustment of Differences by Commission of Inquiry and Conciliation Following Incidents of December 1928 [2]

724.3415/299b : Telegram

## *The Secretary of State to the Minister in Bolivia (Kaufman)* [3]

WASHINGTON, December 19, 1928—6 p. m.

40. At a meeting this morning of a special committee appointed by the conference,[4] the following resolution was adopted.

"The Special Committee named by the Conference to inform it fully with regard to the incident which occurred between Bolivia and Paraguay, desires to obtain on its own behalf certain data that are necessary for its report to the Conference and, therefore, asks:

1. Could each one of the Parties agree to sign a Protocol by virtue of the good offices of the Conference?

2. What would be the basis of said Protocol?

3. Would the two Governments name one or more Delegates for a Commission of Inquiry and Conciliation which would be constituted?

4. Would neutral delegate or delegates be selected by the Conference?

5. What would be the extent and jurisdiction of said Commission?

6. Would the Parties bind themselves to cease all concentration of troops on the frontier and all hostilities until the pronouncement of the Commission of Inquiry and Conciliation?

7. Where would the Commission be convened?

8. Would the Republics of Bolivia and Paraguay be disposed to renew their diplomatic relations?"

Copies of this were given to the Bolivian and Paraguayan Ministers who are making inquiries of their Governments concerning each of these points.

You will understand the importance of prompt and satisfactory answers to these inquiries so that Committee can advise the Conference and its good offices may be useful to both parties in the interest of peaceful adjustment.

KELLOGG

---

[1] For previous correspondence, see *Foreign Relations*, 1928, vol. I, pp. 672 ff.

[2] See also *Proceedings of the Commission of Inquiry and Conciliation, Bolivia and Paraguay, March 13, 1929–September 13, 1929* (Washington [1929]).

[3] The same, *mutatis mutandis*, on the same date to the Minister in Paraguay as telegram No. 17.

[4] International Conference of American States on Conciliation and Arbitration, held at Washington, December 10, 1928–January 5, 1929; see *Foreign Relations*, 1928, vol. I, pp. 621 ff. For the proceedings of the conference, see *Proceedings of the International Conference of American States on Conciliation and Arbitration, Held at Washington, December 10, 1928–January 5, 1929* (Washington, Government Printing Office, 1929).

724.3415/303 : Telegram

*The Minister in Bolivia (Kaufman) to the Secretary of State*

La Paz, December 21, 1928—6 p. m.
[Received 7 p. m.]

64. Department's telegram 40, December 19, 6 p. m.

1. Bolivia willing to sign protocol.

2. Basis of protocol covered in points 3 to 8.

3. Bolivia would probably name two delegates.

4. Delegates from the United States, Argentine, Brazil, Uruguay and Peru or Cuba are acceptable to Bolivia.

5. Bolivia is willing to have Commission settle the boundary dispute after the present difficulty is disposed of.

6. Bolivian army has already received orders not to advance or attack but to maintain defense only.

7. Bolivia favors Washington as a meeting place for the Commission.

8. Bolivia is not disposed to renew diplomatic relations at present but prefers to await opportune time after the Commission convenes.

The foregoing information is the personal opinion of Minister for Foreign Affairs.

KAUFMAN

724.3415/307 : Telegram

*The Minister in Paraguay (Kreeck) to the Secretary of State*

Asunción, December 22, 1928—8 p. m.
[Received December 25—10 p. m.]

39. The Paraguayan Government transmitted the following note to the Legation December 22, 7 p. m.:

"I have had the honor of receiving from the hands of Your Excellency a questionnaire formulated by the special commission of the Conference of Arbitration and I am pleased to answer it in the following terms:

My Government has no objection to signing a protocol by virtue of the good offices of the Conference but as the determination of its basis depends on a previous agreement between the parties, it may be permitted to suggest that the commission of inquiry be constituted immediately, with two delegates from each party and other delegates of the neutral countries that the Conference may elect and whose number it shall itself determine.

Within this commission would be studied the basis of the protocol in order to determine the matter of its jurisdiction and its attributes.

In this respect my Government takes the lead in saying that the investigation and decision of said entity should devolve not only upon the incidents of Fort Vanguardia but also upon all the other acts which have occurred and their legal antecedents.

My Government desires that effective guarantees be established in order that the decision of the Commission will be complied with and loyally respected. It also wishes to suggest that only the neutral delegates have a vote in this decision.

This Government would be pleased if the seat of the Commission were one of the South American capitals and in this respect it is permitted to indicate the city of Buenos Aires because of it being nearest to the scene of the events and to facilitate the consultation by the delegates of both parties with their respective governments.

Paraguay has no objection to cease the concentration of its troops and hostilities if Bolivia is disposed to do the same and if it be given guarantees that it will not be again attacked.

This Government believes that the propitious moment has not yet arrived for the renewing of diplomatic relations between the two countries which have been broken by the initiative of Bolivia.

In answering in this manner the above-mentioned questionnaire I am pleased to salute Your Excellency, etc. Signed, Zubizarreta".

Minister of Foreign Affairs would welcome selection of other capital than Buenos Aires but believed it policy to mention that capital in the note.

The Minister is favorable to renew diplomatic relations but believes present moment not propitious in which I can concur.

Mobilization has been suspended and instructions given restraining the forces in the field from all acts of violence. With opposing forces near, unfortunate circumstances may occur however irrespective of instruction.

KREECK

---

724.3415/343

*Reply of the Bolivian Government to the Note Sent by the Special Committee of the International Conference of American States on Conciliation and Arbitration*

[Translation]

WASHINGTON, December 25, 1928.

First: Bolivia agrees to sign a Protocol formally accepting the good offices of the Conference.

Second: The bases of said Protocol would be as follows:

a) The Commission on Investigation shall verify that it is true that within a status of pacific relations existing between Bolivia and Paraguay and in spite of the Convention signed at Buenos Aires on June [*July*] 12, 1928,[5] whereby both countries bound themselves to decide their territorial differences through pacific means, Paraguay, violating said obligations, without a prior declaration of hostility and in an uncalled for and violent manner, ordered the attacking and

---

[5] See Act of Suspension, Conference of Buenos Aires, in *Proceedings of the Commission of Inquiry and Conciliation, Bolivia and Paraguay*, p. 403.

destruction of the Bolivian outpost Vanguardia, by regular forces of the Paraguayan army on the fifth of this month.

*b)* It shall be expressly set forth that the basic questions relative to territorial litigation pending between the two countries shall not be the subject of conciliatory proceedings or inquiry, since there are obligations to submit this matter to strictly legal arbitration.

Third: Bolivia would appoint two or three delegates to the Commission of Investigation and Conciliation.

Fourth: The Conference shall appoint representatives of five neutral States to complete the Commission, they to be acceptable to both Parties.

Fifth: The Commission shall establish the facts and fix the moral and material responsibilities of the aggressor, in accordance with the provisions of international law.

Sixth: Bolivia will agree to cease all concentration of troops along the line of forts near the Paraguayan forts and all hostilities until the Commission of Investigation and Conciliation gives its decision.

Seventh: The Commission shall meet in Washington.

Eighth: Bolivia does not consider the renewal of diplomatic relations to be opportune.

Bolivia expressly states that, in conformity with the *uti possidetis juris* of 1810, her territorial dominion extends to the confluence of the Paraguay and Pilcomayo Rivers, sustains in all its integrity, her right over El Chaco and declares herself ready to submit the litigation to the decision of juridical arbitration. The arbitrator shall be the International Court of Justice of The Hague, but it is indispensable that, in conformity with existing Protocols, the territorial zone subject to arbitration shall be fixed.

---

724.3415/342 : Telegram

*The Bolivian Minister and the Paraguayan Delegate to Their Respective Governments*

[Washington,] December 25, 1928.

The Committee on Conciliation met to consider the cablegrams transmitted by the Governments of Bolivia and Paraguay and after a full deliberation thereon resolved that we, the delegates of both nations, should consult our respective governments whether they would agree to authorize the signing of the following Protocol:

"There assembled at the Building of the Pan American Union, His Excellency the Chairman of the Conference, His Excellency the Minister Plenipotentiary of Bolivia and the Honorable Chargé d'Affaires of Paraguay. The Chairman of the Conference stated that the Conference being animated by a spirit of peace, of harmony and of American fraternity, has offered its good offices to the governments of the

Republics of Bolivia and Paraguay, which, animated by the same spirit, have accepted them.

The two representatives, of Bolivia and of Paraguay, acting in full accord with their respective governments, deem it proper that a Commission of Investigation and Conciliation shall establish the facts which have given rise to the recent conflict which has unfortunately taken place on the frontiers of both countries.

The representative of Bolivia declares that the Commission on Investigation shall verify that it is true that within a status of pacific relations existing between Bolivia and Paraguay and in spite of the convention signed at Buenos Aires on June [*July*] 12, 1928, whereby both countries bound themselves to decide their territorial differences through pacific means, Paraguay, violating said obligations, without a prior declaration of hostility and in an uncalled for and violent manner, ordered the attacking and destruction of the Bolivian outpost Vanguardia, by regular forces of the Paraguayan army on the fifth of this month.

The representative of Paraguay declares, in turn, that his nation has committed no aggression, and that the Commission should investigate and give its findings not only with respect to the incident of the Vanguardia outpost but upon all the events which have occurred and their legal antecedents with effective warranty that its findings shall be fulfilled.

As a consequence, the Governments of Bolivia and Paraguay agree upon the following stipulations:

First: To constitute a Commission of Investigation and Conciliation to be made up as follows:

(*a*) Of two delegates from each of the Governments of Bolivia and Paraguay;

(*b*) Of a delegate appointed by the Governments of each of the following five American republics:

Second: The Commission on Investigation and Conciliation shall be entrusted with investigating the events which have occurred on the frontier by hearing both sides, taking into consideration the allegations made by both parties.

Third: The Commission shall make an effort to fulfill its mission within a period of six months commencing from the date of its organization. It may, if necessary, increase this period to another six months.

Fourth: The procedure of the investigation shall be that agreed upon by the Commission.

Fifth: Once the events have been investigated the Commission shall make proposals and efforts to have the incident settled amicably in such a manner that both parties shall have full satisfaction.

If this is not possible, the Commission shall draft its report setting forth the result of its investigation and the efforts it has made to settle the incident.

Sixth: The Commission is empowered, in the event that it has not been possible to arrive at conciliation, to establish at the same time that it determines the facts, the liabilities derived therefrom, in accordance with international law.

Seventh: The Commission shall be installed in Washington and after its first meeting it shall decide upon the seat of its sessions.

Eighth: The Governments of Bolivia and Paraguay bind themselves to suspend all hostilities and to cease all concentration of troops until the findings of the Commission shall have been made.

Ninth: It is understood that the procedure contained in this Protocol does not affect the bases of the controversy existing between Bolivia and Paraguay, nor the agreements now in force.

Tenth: The High Contracting Parties, nevertheless, reiterate their firm intention that said controversy be solved, at all events, through juridical methods and in perfect peace and amity between the two nations."

724.3415/309 : Telegram

*The Minister in Bolivia (Kaufman) to the Secretary of State*

La Paz, December 27, 1928—7 p. m.
[Received December 28—8:40 a. m.]

70. In a conversation this afternoon the Foreign Minister informed me that the Bolivian Government had received and was considering the protocol drafted by the Washington Conference. He said that while his Government found the draft satisfactory in the main yet he wished to point out that Bolivia could not accept the use of the word "frontier" as applied in the protocol to the present line of defense in the Chaco. He urged me to explain to the Department that Bolivia was not unappreciative and was not attempting to put obstacles in the way of the Conference; on the contrary his country was merely defending its rights to the entire territory lying between the Paraguay and Pilcomayo Rivers which he declared was the true frontier, the Paraguayans having systematically encroached upon Bolivian territory. I suggested that the difficulty might be obviated by substituting for the word frontier some such phrase as "the present line of defense". The Minister replied that he had in mind telegraphing a like suggestion to Washington tomorrow clarifying at the same time several minor points which he found obscure.

With reference to the five countries constituting the Commission, the Minister stated his belief that the Argentine would not agree to serve. In that event he said that Bolivia would request that Peru or Colombia be represented on the Commission which Bolivia desired to function in Washington where the atmosphere was more impartial than in Buenos Aires.

Kaufman

724.3415/310 : Telegram

*The Secretary of State to the Minister in Bolivia (Kaufman)*

Washington, December 28, 1928—1 p. m.

45. Paraguayan Government has transmitted to the Secretary in his character as Chairman of the Conference on Arbitration and Con-

ciliation a note[6] charging that the Bolivian forces have again occupied Fort Vanguardia; that they retain Fort Boquerón, and that their troops have made a new advance into Paraguayan territory, and that this has all been done since the acceptance of the good offices of the Conference of Arbitration.

Please immediately call on proper Bolivian authorities and, without expressing any view as to the merits of this charge, express the earnest hope of this Government that no action of a provocative nature will be taken, and that no further military activities will be undertaken while this question is pending a peaceful settlement.

Please state that I feel that it is of the utmost importance that authorization be sent immediately to the Bolivian representative here to sign the protocol suggested by the Special Committee of the Conference and emphasize that time is of the essence and that I sincerely hope that such authorization be sent without delay.

KELLOGG

724.3415/314a : Telegram

*The Secretary of State to the Minister in Paraguay* (*Kreeck*)

WASHINGTON, December 28, 1928—1 p. m.

20. In order that the efforts of the Conference to bring about a peaceful adjustment between Paraguay and Bolivia may accomplish their object, I consider it of the utmost importance that Paraguay should authorize her representative in Washington without delay to sign the protocol drawn up by the Special Committee of the Conference in conjunction with the representatives of Paraguay and Bolivia. Please call immediately upon the proper Paraguayan authorities and express to them my views as stated above, and state that I earnestly hope that they will find it possible to give this authorization without delay. I am advised by the Bolivian Minister that he has been informed by the Minister for Foreign Affairs of Bolivia that the latter is in favor of the protocol and is submitting the matter immediately to the consideration of the Bolivian Government. The Bolivian Minister expects to receive a favorable reply today. You will of course appreciate that the Conference can not adjourn with this matter pending and, as it is now on the point of bringing its labors to a successful conclusion, it is urgently necessary that both parties authorize their representatives to sign the protocol.

KELLOGG

[6] Not printed.

724.3415/316a : Telegram

*The Secretary of State to the Minister in Bolivia (Kaufman)*[7]

WASHINGTON, December 29, 1928—1 p. m.

44. Please call on Minister of Foreign Affairs and inquire of him when the Special Committee will have Bolivia's answer. We had understood it was to be here today. Every day delay endangers peace. The Protocol is simple and it is, therefore, difficult to understand this delay. I hope very much the Government of Bolivia will join this in a broad sense of conciliation of this matter. Please reply earliest possible moment as Committee is waiting.

KELLOGG

---

724.3415/318 : Telegram

*The Minister in Bolivia (Kaufman) to the Secretary of State*

LA PAZ, December 29, 1928—3 p. m.
[Received 11:30 p. m.]

72. With reference to the points set forth in the Department's 45, December 28, 1 p. m., the Foreign Minister this morning made the following oral statements:

1. Fort Vanguardia was reoccupied by Bolivian forces three weeks ago.
2. Bolivia held Fort Boquerón at the time the good offices of the Conference were accepted. Nothing was then said about relinquishing said Fort, the retention of which was considered essential to calm popular passion and to avoid a revolution.
3. Having accepted the good offices of the Conference the President telegraphed instructions the same night to the Bolivian forces to cease advancing. The Minister for Foreign Affairs stated that he was convinced that the instructions had been obeyed. . . .

Concerning Bolivia's authorization to sign protocol, the Minister for Foreign Affairs assured me that after referring the draft of the protocol to Foreign Relations Committees of the House and Senate this afternoon at 4 o'clock and to the Council of State tonight at 9 o'clock he would telegraph appropriate instructions to the Minister at Washington. He added that if any change is made he would discuss it with me tomorrow. In that event, I shall telegraph the Department.

KAUFMAN

---

[7] The same, *mutatis mutandis*, on the same date to the Minister in Paraguay as telegram No. 21.

724.3415/322 : Telegram

*The Minister in Paraguay (Kreeck) to the Secretary of State*

ASUNCIÓN, December 30, 1928—11 a. m.
[Received December 31—10 p. m.]

44.  Paraguay has telegraphed authorization to its representative in Washington to sign the protocol in view of the threatening Bolivian advances although it is confident that the investigation of recent events will not permit conciliation and lasting peace.  It feels that the Conference has taken the responsibility for the cause.  Until the entire question is determined, which Argentine mediation will not do, Paraguay will be insecure and continuous peace defeated.

KREECK

---

724.3415/319 : Telegram

*The Minister in Bolivia (Kaufman) to the Secretary of State*

LA PAZ, December 30, 1928—7 p. m.
[Received December 31—12:53 a. m.]

73.  The Foreign Office telegraphed to the Bolivian Minister at Washington at 3 p. m. this afternoon authorizing him to sign protocol with the following modifications:

Substituting for the word "frontier" substantially the phrase used in my telegram No. 70, December 27, 7 p. m.

Modifying the phraseology without essentially changing the meaning of clause 2 of the protocol.

Fixing at six months without any extension the period mentioned in clause 3.

Substituting in clauses 5 and 6 the word "fact" for "facts".

Insisting that the Commission meet at Washington.

Modifying clause 8 to read as follows: "The Governments of Bolivia and Paraguay agree to cease all hostilities and to discontinue all concentration of troops along the present line of defense until the award of the Commission is made."

Changing clause 9 to read as follows: "It is understood that the procedure outlined in this protocol does not include nor affect the basis of the territorial controversy between Bolivia and Paraguay nor the agreements of both countries to submit the question to arbitration."

Striking out the word "nevertheless" from clause 10.

KAUFMAN

724.3415/320 : Telegram

*The Minister in Paraguay (Kreeck) to the Secretary of State*

Asunción, December 30, 1928—7 p. m.
[Received December 31—2 : 34 a. m.]

45. Your telegram No. 21 [8] received December 30, 6 p. m. Paraguayan Minister for Foreign Affairs telegraphed its representative December 29, 3 p. m. to sign protocol. Delay arises from consideration of the meager provisions for the investigation they being limited to incidents other than the real cause of conflict thus permitting aggressions and molestations to continue as formerly thereby causing no real benefit to Paraguay by such investigation.

I am convinced this view is well established and that permanent peace will not be found until the cause has been removed which can only be done by the Conference.

KREECK

724.3415/322a : Telegram

*The Secretary of State to the Ambassador in Argentina (Bliss)* [9]

Washington, December 31, 1928—7 p. m.

72. The representatives of the Governments of Bolivia and Paraguay in attendance at the Conference of Conciliation and Arbitration of the American States are about to sign a Protocol providing for the constitution of a Commission of Investigation and Conciliation for the purpose of undertaking an inquiry by hearing both parties as to what has taken place in order to determine which of them brought about a change in the peaceful relations between them and also the responsibilities thereby incurred.

The Commission is to be composed of two delegates appointed by each of the Governments of Bolivia and Paraguay and of a Delegate designated by each of the Governments of the following states to wit, Argentine Republic, Brazil, Cuba, Uruguay and the United States.

The Commission is to be installed in Washington but its further procedure will be determined by the Commission itself. The work of the Commission is to be completed within six months unless the Commission finds that it needs a longer time. The Commission is empowered to determine the measures pending the inquiry which may be necessary on the part of each country to prevent a recurrence

[8] See footnote 7, p. 825.
[9] The same, *mutatis mutandis*, on the same date to the Ambassador in Brazil as telegram No. 43 and to the Minister in Uruguay as telegram No. 19. A similar invitation was presumably extended to the Government of Cuba but neither the copy of the invitation nor the acceptance has been found in Department files.

of hostilities. The Protocol and the action of the Commission are not to affect the territorial question as contended by Bolivia or the question of boundary as contended by Paraguay and are not to modify or affect existing agreements.

Please go at once to the Foreign Minister and ascertain whether his Government will be willing to appoint a representative to serve on this Commission. It is desired that the Protocol with the names of the Governments which are to act in constituting the Commission shall be approved at the earliest possible moment by the Conference in Plenary Session and it is earnestly hoped that the immediate establishment of this Commission will obviate any further difficulty between the two countries concerned. I am sending this telegram as Chairman of the Conference, and at the request of the special Committee of the Conference through which the Conference has been exercising its good offices to bring the Parties into accord. You may express my deep interest in the purpose of the Protocol and the desire that it may become effective by the appropriate action of the Governments named.

FRANK B. KELLOGG

---

724.3415/324 : Telegram

*The Minister in Uruguay (Grant-Smith) to the Secretary of State*

MONTEVIDEO, January 1, 1929—11 p. m.<br>[Received January 2—12 : 55 a. m.]

1. Department's telegram 19, December 31, 7 p. m.[10] Uruguayan Minister for Foreign Affairs accepts on behalf of his Government and states that the Uruguayan delegate to the Conference on Conciliation and Arbitration, Dr. José Pedro Varela, will probably be designated.

GRANT-SMITH

---

724.3415/327a : Telegram

*The Secretary of State to the Minister in Bolivia (Kaufman)*

WASHINGTON, January 2, 1929—11 a. m.

1. On December 31 the Bolivian Minister and Paraguayan representative drew up a protocol for the investigation of the differences between them. The Special Commission was in session for nearly five hours helping to draw up a protocol that would fall within the instructions of both Governments in order to obviate the necessity of further telegraphic exchanges, as each time the Governments have been consulted it has required six days to get an answer.

---

[10] See footnote 9, p. 827.

The protocol was finally agreed upon and at the suggestion of the Bolivian Minister the Committee met at six o'clock last night for the signing of the protocol. The Bolivian Minister did not come to the meeting and when he was finally located and prevailed upon to come, stated he could not sign without instructions from his Government. The Paraguayan representative stated that he had no instructions from his Government either but as all the labor of the preceding day had been to draw up a protocol that would fall within the instructions of both parties, he was willing and ready to sign. Please take the matter up orally immediately with the Bolivian authorities, urging that they lose no time in cabling the Minister in Washington authorization to sign the protocol, the text of which he cabled to them on the night of December 31. You may, in your discretion, point out that any undue delay now or quibble over the wording of the protocol might well cause considerable misunderstanding in the Conference regarding Bolivia's position.

The preamble of the protocol contains two paragraphs, one with the allegations of Bolivia and the other with the allegations of Paraguay. These are ex parte statements and apparently neither party should object to any allegations made by the other as these allegations are ex parte statements and the matter will be subject to impartial examination. The verbal changes in the rest of the protocol do not alter its substance and most of them were made at the request of Bolivia. It is therefore hoped that instructions will be sent without delay as the work of the Conference is now rapidly drawing to an end.

KELLOGG

724.3415/334a : Telegram

*The Secretary of State to the Minister in Bolivia (Kaufman)*

WASHINGTON, January 2, 1929—4 p. m.

2. Department's January 2, 11 a. m. Conference will hold a plenary session on Friday [11] morning at eleven o'clock and it is hoped that protocol may be signed before that time. The Conference will probably adjourn on Saturday.

KELLOGG

724.3415/329 : Telegram

*The Ambassador in Argentina (Bliss) to the Secretary of State*

BUENOS AIRES, January 2, 1929—7 p. m.
[Received 9:30 p. m.]

2. In compliance with your telegram of December 31, 8 [7] p. m. I saw this afternoon, accompanied by the Minister for Foreign Affairs,

[11] January 4.

the President of Argentina who informed me what had been the policy of Argentina in the Bolivian-Paraguayan conflict.

Dr. Irigoyen said to me that as soon as he took over the Government he received a communication from the Argentine Minister in La Paz according to which the relations between Paraguay and Bolivia had become very grave. Immediately on receipt of that telegram and as he was already preoccupied at the time of assuming the Presidency by the conflict existing between the two friendly countries, he thought it his duty to offer his services to both nations as an amicable adjuster, not as arbiter, in order thus to solve with the collaboration and agreement of the parties themselves the dispute which divides them. This offer of President Irigoyen was made before there occurred between Bolivians and Paraguayans the subsequent regrettable encounters. Paraguay replied, frankly and freely accepting the offer of Dr. Irigoyen; while Bolivia, which also did so immediately and in the most exalted terms as regards Dr. Irigoyen and Argentina, made reservations with relation to the dispute itself. Dr. Irigoyen, with sentiments of natural delicacy, believed then as he does now, that his mission and that of Argentina had terminated, since previous to the acts of bloodshed between Bolivia and Paraguay, he had offered his services to reconcile both sister nations.

President Irigoyen believes moreover that no reason exists for the moment for him to change his attitude, especially when the signing of the forthcoming protocol entrusts the solution of the latest conflict to entities as important and honorable as the United States, Uruguay, Brazil and Cuba which gives assurance that the peace of the continent will happily not be disturbed since such a disturbance would be inconceivable to contemplate after the tragic and sorrowful experience which humanity has recently undergone.

For the reasons given President Irigoyen, expressing thanks for the summons, declined to have the Argentine Republic participate in the Commission for Investigation and Conciliation.

BLISS

---

724.3415/331 : Telegram

*The Minister in Bolivia (Kaufman) to the Secretary of State*

LA PAZ, January 2, 1929—8 p. m.
[Received 9: 30 p. m.]

1. Department's telegram of January 2, 11 a. m. Foreign Minister informs me that Bolivian Minister's telegram requesting authority to sign protocol was not received until eleven o'clock this morning and that at six o'clock he cabled the Minister at Washington to sign with the following modifications:

1. To omit from the preamble an unauthorized statement included therein by the Minister on his own initiative.

2. To add at the end of clause 2 that the neutral commissioners shall continue their labors except in case of illness until the end of the period of investigation.

3. To insist under instructions from the President upon fixing the period of investigation at six months without extensions.

4. To amend clause 8 as follows: "The Commission shall be empowered to advise the parties concerning measures designed to avoid a renewal of hostilities."

KAUFMAN

---

724.3415/335 : Telegram

*The Ambassador in Brazil (Morgan) to the Secretary of State*

RIO DE JANEIRO, January 3, 1929—6 p. m.
[Received January 4—12 : 30 a. m.]

2. Embassy's telegram 1, January 2, 4 p. m.[12]   I have received this afternoon the following note from the Brazilian Minister of Foreign Affairs:

"Rio de Janeiro, January 2nd, 1929.

Excellency: I acknowledge the receipt of note No. 1404 of today's date wherein Your Excellency informs me of the communication which the Secretary of State of the United States of America as chairman of the Conference of Conciliation and Arbitration now convened at Washington requested you to transmit me.[13]

It is proposed to constitute a Commission composed of nine members, five of which are to be designated by the Governments of five American states to wit: Argentina, Brazil, Cuba, Uruguay, and the United States, two by each of the Governments of Bolivia and Paraguay. The Commission shall have no powers to take up the question of boundary between Paraguay and Bolivia. The resulting protocol shall not affect the boundary question itself nor shall it affect or modify any existing agreements. The Commission shall only verify in the serious incident which recently occurred in the disputed territory which of the two countries in disagreement brought about a change in the peaceful relations between them, place the responsibilities and determine if necessary the steps which shall be taken to avoid a recurrence of hostilities. A period of six months which may be extended has been prescribed for the work of the Commission which will be installed in Washington. His Excellency the Secretary of State of the United States of America would like to know if my Government would be disposed to designate at the earliest opportunity a representative to serve on the said Commission.

Were there not, Mr. Ambassador, as regards Brazil, the entirely special conditions which I hereafter mention, the Brazilian Government, which has not spared nor will it spare efforts towards the maintenance of peace, would accept immediately the honor which it is intended to confer upon it. Being bounded, however, as it is bounded, by the very territory where the incident took place, having

---

[12] Not printed.
[13] See footnote 9, p. 827.

just negotiated in the most perfect cordiality both with Paraguay and Bolivia boundary treaties which are at the present time going through constitutional procedure, and as either one or the other might have a reaction upon the territory in question, Brazil does not conceal the scruples which render impossible for her to accept any function as a judge of a case in which it might be argued, however unjustly, that she had any interest direct or indirect, immediate or remote. Other states which in this respect are free, as Brazil would like to be, can bring to a successful conclusion the undoubtedly beneficent task which it is planned to realize. They can, through their delegates, count not only upon the sincere wishes but also upon the full collaboration that Brazil may be able to contribute in the circumstances explained for the success of the high mission which they are called upon to discharge.

Accept Excellency et cetera."

MORGAN

---

724.3415/336a : Telegram

*The Secretary of State to the Minister in Colombia (Caffery)*[14]

WASHINGTON, January 3, 1929—8 p. m.

1. The representatives of the Governments of Bolivia and Paraguay in attendance at the Conference of Conciliation and Arbitration of the American States signed this afternoon a protocol providing for the constitution of a commission of investigation and conciliation for the purpose of undertaking an inquiry by hearing both parties as to what has taken place in order to determine which of them brought about a change in the peaceful relations between them and also the responsibilities thereby incurred.

The Commission is to be composed of two delegates appointed by each of the Governments of Bolivia and Paraguay and of a Delegate designated by each of the Governments of the following states to wit: Colombia, Cuba, Mexico, Uruguay and the United States.

The Commission is to be installed in Washington but its further procedure will be determined by the Commission itself. The work of the Commission is to be completed within six months unless the Commission finds that it needs a longer time. The Commission is empowered to determine the measures pending the inquiry which may be necessary on the part of each country to prevent a recurrence of hostilities. The protocol and the action of the Commission are not to affect the territorial question as contended by Bolivia or the question of boundary as contended by Paraguay and are not to modify or affect existing agreements.

Please go at once to the Foreign Minister and ascertain whether his Government will be willing to appoint a representative to serve on this

[14] A similar invitation was presumably extended to the Government of Mexico but neither the copy of the invitation nor the acceptance has been found in Department files.

Commission. It is desired that the protocol with the names of the Governments which are to act in constituting the Commission shall be approved at the earliest possible moment by the Conference in Plenary Session and it is earnestly hoped that the immediate establishment of this Commission will obviate any further difficulty between the two countries concerned. I am sending this telegram as Chairman of the Conference, and at the request of the Special Committee of the Conference through which the Conference has been exercising its good offices to bring the Parties into accord. You may express my deep interest in the purpose of the protocol and the desire that it may become effective by the appropriate action of the Governments named. Conference closes Saturday.

KELLOGG

---

724.3415/339 : Telegram

## *The Ambassador in Brazil (Morgan) to the Secretary of State*

RIO DE JANEIRO, January 4, 1929—3 p. m.<br>[Received 4 : 35 p. m.]

4. The Brazilian Minister for Foreign Affairs called me to the Foreign Office today and read me a telegram which he had prepared for the Brazilian Ambassador in Washington, the contents of which he wished me to communicate to you, exposing in further detail than in his note, a copy of which was contained in Embassy's telegram 2, January 3, 6 p. m., the reasons why Brazil is compelled to decline the invitation to join the Commission. The Minister for Foreign Affairs asked me to assure you of Brazil's desire to cooperate as far as possible with you in adjusting the Bolivian-Paraguayan dispute. He believes he may be able to effect more unofficially outside the Commission than within it.

These assurances appear to me to be sincere and coupled with the reasons contained in the Minister's aforesaid note are explanatory of Brazil's rejection of the invitation.

MORGAN

---

724.3415/338 : Telegram

## *The Minister in Colombia (Caffery) to the Secretary of State*

BOGOTÁ, January 4, 1929—4 p. m.<br>[Received 5 : 55 p. m.]

2. My telegram number 1, January 4, noon.[15] Minister for Foreign Affairs telephones me Colombian Government accepts the invitation.

CAFFERY

---

[15] Not printed.

724.3415/347 : Telegram

*The Minister in Paraguay (Kreeck) to the Secretary of State*

Asunción, January 5, 1929—10 a. m.
[Received January 6—6 : 55 a. m.]

2. Heavy rains have forced the Bolivians to relinquish Paraguayan Fort Vanguardia withdrawing their troops to Bolivian territory. It should not be occupied.

The Conference should insist Bolivia and Paraguay demobilize or withdraw their troops to distant points; for example, northern Bolivian forces withdraw to Robore and Suarez, northern Paraguayan forces to Bahia Negra, all Bolivian forces interior and south Chaco should be withdrawn outside of territory awarded Paraguay by President Hayes[16] to Villamonte, chief Bolivian Pilcomayo center, demobilization preferable. Without some such measures unfortunate circumstances will arise for Paraguay cannot support an army upon the frontiers for six months without affecting the economic conditions of the country.

Recent Bolivian northern concentration of troops reports following regiments at Vitiones: Infantry, four regiments, the first, the ninth, the twelfth, the thirteenth; fourth regiment engineers with aeroplanes.

Interior Chaco concentration of troops at Muñoz: Infantry, two regiments, the sixth, the eighth; cavalry, the fifth regiment engineers, the second and the third regiments.

Concentration at Villamonte, artillery, third regiment; cavalry, third regiment.

Argentine Legation reports large shipment of armament consisting of aeroplanes, 24,000 rifles, et cetera, has been received in Argentina from Germany consigned to the Bolivian Government for use southern Chaco. Part of the shipment said to be detained by Argentina. I am investigating through independent sources and will report.

Kreeck

724.3415/394

*The Secretary General of the International Conference of American States on Conciliation and Arbitration (Meyer) to the Secretary of State*

[Washington,] January 6, 1929.

Sir: At the direction of the Chairman of the International Conference of American States on Conciliation and Arbitration, I have the honor to transmit herewith the Protocol signed by the representatives of Bolivia and Paraguay, at Washington, January 3, 1929.

[16] On November 12, 1878; see *Foreign Relations*, 1878, p. 711.

This action is in accordance with the Tenth Provision of the above-mentioned Protocol, which stipulates that it shall be deposited in the archives of the Government of the United States of America.

I have [etc.]
For the Secretary General:
PIERRE DE L. BOAL

[Enclosure—Translation [17]]

### Protocol, Signed at Washington, January 3, 1929

His Excellency, Mr. Frank B. Kellogg, Chairman of the International Conference of American States on Conciliation and Arbitration, His Excellency, Mr. Eduardo Diez de Medina, Envoy-Extraordinary and Minister Plenipotentiary of Bolivia, and Hon. Dr. Juan Vicente Ramírez, Chargé d'Affaires of Paraguay, having met at the Pan American Union Building, the Chairman stated that, being animated by a spirit of peace, of harmony, and of American brotherhood, the Conference has offered its good offices to the Governments of the Republics of Bolivia and Paraguay, who, being animated by the same spirit, have accepted the same.

The two representatives of Bolivia and Paraguay, in accord with their respective Governments, deem it desirable that a Commission of Inquiry and Conciliation establish the facts which have caused the recent conflicts which have unfortunately occurred.

The representative of Bolivia states that the Commission of Inquiry should ascertain how it happened that, notwithstanding the pacific relations existing between Bolivia and Paraguay and in spite of the agreement signed at Buenos Aires on July 12, 1928, whereby both countries obligated themselves to settle their territorial differences by pacific means, Paraguay, in violation of those obligations, without previous declaration of hostilities, and in an unfounded and violent manner ordered that the Bolivian outpost "Vanguardia" be attacked and razed by regular forces of the Paraguayan Army on the 5th of the past month of December.

The representative of Paraguay denies that his country has committed any aggression whatever and affirms that Paraguay has always maintained itself within juridical standards and the loyal fulfillment of pacts in force. He adds that it was Bolivia that committed acts of provocation and of aggression by penetrating with its armed forces into the territory possessed by Paraguay, not only in the case of the "Vanguardia" outpost, in which said forces were the first to open fire upon the Paraguayan troops, but that, before that time, it made several incursions in said territory, establishing new outposts. That

---

[17] Reprinted from *Proceedings of the Commission of Inquiry and Conciliation, Bolivia and Paraguay*, p. 2.

after the events which took place at the "Vanguardia" outpost forces of the Bolivian regular Army invaded the territory possessed by Paraguay, attacking outposts and bombarding Paraguayan positions. That the Commission should fully investigate all these facts and the legal antecedents in order to establish upon which country the responsibility falls and which of them is bound to make the proper reparations.

Therefore, the Governments of Bolivia and Paraguay agree upon the following stipulations:

First. To organize a Commission of Inquiry and Conciliation which shall be composed as follows:

(a) Two delegates each from the Governments of Bolivia and Paraguay, and

(b) One delegate appointed by the Governments of each of the following five American Republics: United States of America, Mexico, Colombia, Uruguay and Cuba.

All of the said delegates, once they have entered upon the discharge of their duties, shall remain in office until the procedure contemplated in this Protocol is carried out, except in the case of proven illness. In case of said illness or because of any other reason of *force majeure*, the incapacitated delegate shall be replaced, as soon as possible, by the Government of his nation.

Second. The Commission of Inquiry and Conciliation shall undertake to investigate, by hearing both sides, what has taken place, taking into consideration the allegations set forth by both Parties, and determining in the end, which of the Parties has brought about a change in the peaceful relations between the two countries.

Third. The Commission shall fulfill its mission within the period of six months from the date of its organization.

Fourth. The procedure of the investigation shall be that agreed upon by the Commission itself.

Fifth. Once the investigation has been carried out, the Commission shall submit proposals and shall endeavor to settle the incident amicably under conditions which will satisfy both Parties.

If this should not be possible, the Commission shall render its report setting forth the result of its investigation and the efforts made to settle the incident.

Sixth. The Commission is empowered, in case it should not be able to effect conciliation, to establish both the truth of the matter investigated and the responsibilities which, in accordance with International Law, may appear as a result of its investigation.

Seventh. The Commission shall begin its labors in Washington.

Eighth. The Governments of Bolivia and Paraguay bind themselves to suspend all hostilities and to stop all concentration of troops at the points of contact of the military outposts of both countries, until the Commission renders its findings; the Commission of Inquiry and Conciliation shall be empowered to advise the Parties concerning measures designed to prevent a recurrence of hostilities.

Ninth. It is understood that the procedure contained in this Protocol does not include nor affect the territorial question, as contended by Bolivia, and the boundaries, as contended by Paraguay, which exists between both countries, nor does it include or affect the agreements in force between them.

Tenth. The High Contracting Parties reiterate their firm purpose of having said controversy settled, in any event, by juridical means and in perfect peace and friendship between the two countries.

The present Protocol shall remain deposited in the archives of the Government of the United States of America.

In witness whereof the above-mentioned representatives of Bolivia and Paraguay have signed this Protocol.

Done at the City of Washington this third day of January, one thousand nine hundred and twenty-nine.

EDUARDO DIEZ DE MEDINA<br>JUAN VICENTE RAMÍREZ

724.3415/393

*Memorandum by the Chief of the Division of Latin American Affairs (Morgan) of a Conversation With the Paraguayan Chargé (Ramírez)*

[WASHINGTON,] January 12, 1929.

Dr. Ramirez said he desired to discuss the question of the exchange of prisoners with Bolivia, which had been mentioned in the conference with the Secretary day before yesterday. He had now received a telegram from his Government stating that the Bolivian prisoners are concentrated near Asunción and are being well treated. The Paraguayan Government is perfectly willing to arrange an exchange, but first it desired to know how many Paraguayan prisoners are held by the Bolivians, where they are, and to be sure that they are being well treated. Dr. Ramirez said that as he had no communication with the Bolivian Legation he would ask me to use my good offices as intermediary. I said I would be glad to do this and immediately called up the Bolivian Minister and repeated what Dr. Ramirez had told me. Dr. Diez de Medina said that he was of the opinion that there were no Paraguayan prisoners in the hands of the Bolivians; but certainly the Paraguayan Government should know best whether there were or not as they must know if their men were missing. However, he would immediately telegraph his Government for exact information on the subject, and would let me know as soon as a reply was received.

With regard to the treatment of the prisoners, the Bolivian Minister said he felt sure that if there were any Paraguayan prisoners they would be well treated, but it was precisely because there were rumors in La Paz that Bolivian prisoners held by Paraguay were being very badly treated that he was anxious to push the exchange of prisoners, and had also suggested that a representative of a neutral country should be named to investigate the matter and supervise the exchange.

I repeated what Diez de Medina had said to Dr. Ramirez.

MORGAN

---

724.3415/393

*Memorandum by the Chief of the Division of Latin American Affairs (Morgan) of a Conversation Between the Secretary of State and the Bolivian Minister (Diez de Medina), January 17, 1929*

The Secretary said that now that all the neutral countries represented on the special commission concerned with the Paraguay-Bolivia dispute had named their delegates he thought it was high time that Bolivia and Paraguay named theirs as well and asked whether the Minister had any information. Dr. Diez de Medina said that he was much disturbed by the delay; that he had received no reply or word of any kind from his Government, either about the appointment of the delegates or about the exchange of prisoners. The Secretary mentioned the fact that it would take some time for the delegates to arrive and it was highly desirable the delegates should be named and start for Washington as soon as possible. The Bolivian Minister commented on the fact that his own Government had set a six months limit for the commission to do its work and he thought under those circumstances Bolivia should not delay the appointment of delegates but should be one of the first to name them. He asked whether the Secretary would authorize him to make such a statement as coming from the Secretary and the Secretary said that he might do so. The Minister said that possibly his Government was waiting for Paraguay to appoint its delegates, but this would be very unfortunate, as Paraguay would also wait for Bolivia and thus nothing would be accomplished at all. In conclusion he said that he would telegraph his Government immediately on the matter and urge immediate appointment of Bolivian delegates.

The Secretary then mentioned the possibility of ordering the military attachés accredited to Bolivia and Paraguay now at Lima and Buenos Aires to proceed to La Paz and Asunción, where they might be of some service in the exchange of prisoners. The Minister saw no objection to this but thought it might be well first to ascertain whether there were any Paraguayan prisoners to be exchanged. The Secretary said that even if the attachés could not be of any particular assistance in connection with the exchange of prisoners they were accredited to Bolivia and Paraguay and might as well be in those countries as elsewhere, to which the Minister agreed. In conclusion the Secretary said that he was seeing the Paraguayan Chargé d'Affaires a little later and he would speak to him along the same lines.

MORGAN

---

724.3415/393

*Memorandum by the Chief of the Division of Latin American Affairs (Morgan) of a Conversation Between the Secretary of State and the Bolivian Minister (Diez de Medina) January 22, 1929, and of a Subsequent Conversation Between Himself and the Paraguayan Chargé (Ramírez)*

The Bolivian Minister stated that, with regard to the appointment of delegates to the Bolivian-Paraguayan Commission, his Government had encountered difficulty in persuading party leaders to accept this appointment. All those to whom it had been offered so far had refused, but he felt sure that appointments would be made within the next few days.

The Minister said that he had received word about the prisoners. Bolivia held one Paraguayan officer and twelve soldiers prisoners at Villa Montes, and was prepared to exchange them for the Bolivian prisoners in Paraguay—all the prisoners on one side being exchanged for all the prisoners on the other.

The Secretary then asked the Bolivian Minister whether he knew anything about the reported shipments of arms to Bolivia. The Minister said he had no information of this subject, but felt sure that any shipments that might be made were simply ordinary replacements necessary for the army, and were being made not with any aggressive intentions but simply in order that Bolivia might be in a position to defend herself from attack. The Minister pointed out that a nation which is prepared to defend itself is much less likely to be attacked than a defenseless one. The Secretary said that he did not wish to interfere, and naturally had no right to attempt to control Bolivian arms purchases. Nevertheless, he felt that the excessive purchase of arms at this time might have a bad effect on the situation; be far from helping along a peaceful settlement; arouse suspicions and resentment in neighboring countries, and make a settlement more difficult. The Secretary said that we had received confidential information to the effect that Bolivia was importing large quantities of arms from England—some forty thousand rifles, a dozen or more airplanes, and several million cartridges had been mentioned. The Secretary did not know whether this information was accurate; but if it was, the amount seemed excessive in view of the fact that the Vickers' contract of 1927 had been cut down last summer by £670,000; it seemed as though the contract had either been restored to its first form, or a new contract must have been concluded. The Secretary only wished to make a friendly suggestion, but he did feel that any new large purchases of arms by Bolivia at this time might have a very bad effect on the situation. The Minister said he entirely agreed with the Secretary; he did not have any information as to the arms purchased by his Government, but he would forward the Secretary's suggestion and remarks to his Government by telegraph, stating that they were merely a friendly suggestion, and he felt sure that such a suggestion would be very well received in Bolivia.

Mr. Morgan subsequently saw the Chargé d'Affaires of Paraguay and asked him about the Paraguayan delegates. Dr. Ramírez said his Government was having great trouble in finding party leaders who were willing to accept. All those who had so far been approached had declined to serve, but he felt sure that the appointments would be made within the next few days.

Mr. Morgan then informed Dr. Ramírez what the Bolivian Minister had said about the exchange of prisoners. Dr. Ramírez stated that he would communicate with his Government at once and ask them to try to find some place where the exchange could take place mid-way between Villa Montes and Asunción, where the Bolivian prisoners were being held.

MORGAN

724.3415/393c : Telegram

*The Secretary of State to the Minister in Paraguay (Kreeck)*

WASHINGTON, January 22, 1929—5 p. m.

2. The Bolivian Minister has informed me that Bolivia holds one Paraguayan officer and twelve soldiers prisoners, who are all at Villa Montes. The Bolivian Government proposes the immediate exchange of all Paraguayan prisoners held by Bolivia for all Bolivian prisoners held by Paraguay. Please communicate this proposal to Paraguayan authorities, and informally urge that the exchange be consummated without delay.

KELLOGG

724.3415/401

*Memorandum by the Chief of the Division of Latin American Affairs (Morgan) of a Conversation With the Paraguayan Chargé (Ramírez)*

[WASHINGTON,] January 29, 1929.

Dr. Ramírez informed me that he had received a reply from his Government with regard to the proposed exchange of prisoners with

Bolivia. Paraguay suggests the town of Formosa in Argentina as the place for the exchange. Paraguay also requests to be informed as to the names of the Paraguayan prisoners in Bolivia. I asked Dr. Ramírez if he did not think this last request might lead to considerable unnecessary delay and further complicate the question without being of any great importance. He said they were anxious to find out whether any prisoners were missing, but I suggested that they could very quickly ascertain the names of the prisoners when they reached Formosa and discover whether any were missing, and to try to get the names from Villamonte to Washington by cable through the Bolivian Government would undoubtedly delay the matter a long time.

I then telephoned the Bolivian Minister and informed him of Dr. Ramírez' message. He said that he would at once communicate with his Government and inquire whether Formosa would be acceptable as the place for the exchange. With regard to ascertaining the names of the prisoners he made practically the same comment that I had— that it would cause considerable and apparently unnecessary delay. I then told him, with the concurrence of Dr. Ramírez, that the really important question was whether Formosa would be acceptable to Bolivia for the place of exchange; that he might also ask his Government to inform us the names of the prisoners if they were in a position to do so, but if it seemed as though this were going to cause any unnecessary delay perhaps we could persuade the Paraguayan Government to drop that point. Dr. Diez de Medina asked again for assurances that the proposal was to exchange all the prisoners on one side for all those on the other at one and the same time and Dr. Ramírez confirmed this understanding.

Dr. Ramírez informed me that while he believed the newspaper reports as to the appointment of the Paraguayan delegates to the Commission were undoubtedly correct, he had not yet been officially informed by his Government of these appointments.

MORGAN

---

724.3415/421

*Memorandum by the Chief of the Division of Latin American Affairs (Morgan) of a Conversation With the Bolivian Minister (Diez de Medina)*

[WASHINGTON,] January 29, 1929.

The Minister called and handed me a telegram from his Government, a copy of which is attached,[18] stating that Bolivia accepts Formosa as the place for the exchange of prisoners, and also forwarding the list of the names of Paraguayan prisoners asked for by

---

[18] Not printed.

the Paraguayan Legation. Señor Diez de Medina also asked that the Paraguayan Government transmit as soon as possible a list of the names of Bolivian prisoners in Paraguay.

I communicated the information in this telegram immediately to Dr. Ramírez and handed him a list of the names of the prisoners, and also requested on behalf of the Bolivian Government, the names of the prisoners in Paraguay, which he said he would endeavor to procure from Asunción. It was decided that the Bolivian Minister should communicate with his Government in order to arrange an approximate date for the exchange to take place, since Formosa is much farther from Villa Montes, where the Paraguayan prisoners are, than it is from Asunción.

MORGAN

723.2515/3260

*Memorandum by the Assistant Secretary of State (White)*

[WASHINGTON,] February 13, 1929.

The Bolivian Minister called on the Secretary of State on Wednesday morning, February 13, and inquired regarding the present status of the Tacna-Arica negotiations between Chile and Peru.[19] What he especially wanted to know was whether the negotiations are now on the basis of a division of the territory or on some other basis.

The Secretary replied that he had told the two countries when they reestablished diplomatic relations that of course he would be glad to have them carry on direct negotiations to see if they could not agree upon terms of a settlement. The Secretary had understood that negotiations were taking place principally in Lima. The Secretary was kept informed of the progress of negotiations from time to time but this information was given to him strictly confidentially and, as the United States was not a party to the negotiations and was merely kept informed confidentially through courtesy on the part of Chile and Peru, the Secretary did not feel that he was authorized to say anything regarding the matter. The Secretary suggested that the Bolivian Minister in Lima might well be able to find out the status of the matter and report it to the Bolivian Government.

The Minister thanked the Secretary and stated that he fully appreciated the situation.

The Minister then stated that his Government was perfectly willing to discuss in Washington the solution of the difficulties between Bolivia and Paraguay but that Bolivia would be willing to do so only if there were no pressure brought to bear to force her to do so, and that, should any attempt be made to put an embargo on arms against Bolivia, Bolivia would simply cut herself off and remain isolated and take

---

[19] See pp. 720 ff.

no part in any negotiations. The Minister stated that such action would be considered as derogatory to the sovereignty of Bolivia. He added that his Government had been informed that the United States was endeavoring to line up the other countries to prohibit the transit of arms to Bolivia, and he inquired regarding it.

The Secretary replied that there had been no such action taken by the United States. One country had made inquiries some time ago of the United States of the action which it should take in the matter and the Secretary had declined to make any suggestion. The Secretary had seen in the press that Argentina had stopped certain shipments but he had made no inquiries of Argentina regarding the matter nor had the Argentine Government advised him regarding it, so all he knew was what he had seen in the papers. Similarly, there had been statements in the papers that Chile had prohibited the transit of arms and, in a conversation shortly after, the Chilean Ambassador had confirmed this. This was the only authentic information which the Secretary had on the subject.

The Bolivian Minister stated that he understood the matter fully and that he had been sure that this was the case because the United States Government, he knew, always acted in a perfectly proper manner, and that he would report this to his Government. He said the supplies that have been bought were bought under contract signed over two years ago and there have been no new contracts; that the armament was for a replacement merely to put Bolivia in a position to defend herself and not for hostile motives against any country, as Bolivia was not in an economic position to carry on such an undertaking, even should she so desire.

The Bolivian Minister went on to say that he hoped the Secretary would send for him if at any time he thought that Bolivia was not acting the way she should, to see if the matter could not be straightened out. The Secretary said he would be very glad to do so and added that the Minister would recall that when there were press statements from Paris and London regarding large shipments of arms to Bolivia he had discussed the matter with the Minister and had stated that any large acquisition of arms at this time would be most inopportune. The Minister said that that was quite right and that he had passed this word on to his Government, and that he would be very glad if the Secretary would call him at any time.

The Minister stated that he and the Paraguayan Chargé d'Affaires had agreed some time ago upon the text of an arrangement by which an exchange of prisoners would take place between Bolivia and Paraguay at Formosa in Argentina. He had received word three or four days ago that the Argentine Government consented to have the exchange take place in her territory and he was at a loss to understand why the Paraguayan Chargé would not sign. He said that the

Chargé had stated that as the agreement said that both countries had obtained the permission of Argentina, he wanted to be sure that Paraguay had obtained the permission before signing that statement, but the Minister thought this rather strange as it was Paraguay that had suggested that the exchange take place at Formosa and Paraguay must have known then that Argentina would give her consent. He asked Mr. White, who was present, if he would discuss the matter with the Paraguayan Chargé. Mr. White stated that he would do so and that he would see Señor Ramírez in fifteen minutes, in any event, at a meeting of the Trade Mark Conference at the Pan American Union.[20]

Mr. White saw Señor Ramírez at the Pan American Union and the latter stated that he was expecting a reply from his Government at any moment; that he wanted to be sure that he was making a correct statement in signing the agreement and for this reason had consulted his Government three or four days ago, and that he would have an answer any moment.

F[RANCIS] W[HITE]

---

*Press Release Issued by the Department of State on March 11, 1929*

The Commission of Investigation and Conciliation created by the Protocol signed January 3, 1929, at Washington by representatives of Bolivia and Paraguay "to establish the facts which have caused the recent conflicts which have unfortunately occurred" in the Chaco region will hold its first meeting at the Pan-American Union Building at 11 o'clock a. m., March 13, 1929.

The Secretary of State will preside.

The Commission is expected to elect a Chairman and a Secretary at this session.

Membership of the Commission is as follows:

| | |
|---|---|
| Bolivia | Dr. David Alvestegui |
| | Dr. E. Enrique Finot (Minister to Chile). |
| Colombia | Dr. Raimundo Rivas. |
| Cuba | Dr. Manuel Marquez Sterling. |
| Mexico | Lic. Fernando Gonzalez Roa. |
| Paraguay | Dr. Enrique Bordenave |
| | (Dr. Pablo Ynsfran, secretary)[21] |
| | Dr. Francisco C. Chaves. |
| Uruguay | Gen. Guillermo Ruprecht. |
| | (Dr. Campora, secretary). |
| United States | Brig. Gen. Frank R. McCoy. |

Copies of the complete text of the Protocol are available.

---

[20] Pan American Trade Mark Conference held at Washington, February 11–20, 1929. See pp. 670 ff.

[21] Dr. Ynsfran was replaced by Dr. Ramírez on April 1, 1929.

724.3415/513 : Telegram

*The Minister in Paraguay (Kreeck) to the Secretary of State*

ASUNCIÓN, May 6, 1929—1 p. m.
[Received May 7—8 : 20 a. m.]

26. Paraguayan Minister for Foreign Affairs informs me as follows: Upon request of Investigating Commission for exact place of Vanguardia, the Paraguayan Government sent by aeroplane technicians with instruments to ascertain data and seek information cited in my despatch numbered 806.[22] While making a survey at Vanguardia May 4th a number of Bolivian soldiers attacked the technicians. Again May 5th while the technicians were surveying, a force of Bolivian troops estimated at three hundred men fired upon them killing two of their horses. Technicians withdrew under orders not to provoke complications. Foreign Office considers incident grave.

KREECK

---

724.3415/512a : Telegram

*The Acting Secretary of State to the Chargé in Bolivia (Martin)*[23]

[Paraphrase]

WASHINGTON, May 6, 1929—7 p. m.

22. This afternoon the Bolivian delegate handed General McCoy a telegram from the Foreign Minister which reads in translation as follows:[24]

"Protest energetically to Investigation Commission the following happening: Our military detachment situated in the zone of the Vanguardia fortress which was destroyed by Paraguayan forces was attacked on the 4th instant by Paraguayan patrol, our sentinel being wounded. Our detachment despite having been able to capture the enemy strictly maintained a defensive position without advancing a single step. The Committee may rest assured that Bolivian forces will not change their defensive attitude and have been honoring the national good faith pledged in the existing protocol, despite new Paraguayan aggressions."

Are you able discreetly to secure any additional information which would throw any light on this incident?

CLARK

---

[22] Not printed.
[23] The same, *mutatis mutandis,* on the same date to the Minister in Paraguay as telegram No. 11.
[24] Quotation not paraphrased.

724.3415/518 : Telegram

*The Minister in Paraguay (Kreeck) to the Secretary of State*

ASUNCIÓN, May 8, 1929—8 a. m.
[Received May 9—3 : 25 p. m.]

27. Answering the Department's telegram 11, May 6, 7 p. m.[25] Minister of War permitted me to read original confidential despatches received from Commander of Bahía Negra concerning late Vanguardia incident; my telegram No. 26, May 6, 1 p. m., gave full information. Later despatch to the Minister stated Bolivians are concentrating troops at Fort Vitrone and have also established a new fort or encampment near to Vanguardia.

I am inclined to believe Paraguayan presentation, and am convinced other incidents will occur as long as opposing troops face each other.

Peruvian Minister has information from Peru [omission?] insists that Bolivia will rupture Commission negotiations, while Uruguayan Chargé d'Affaires states his Government reports that Bolivian forces have destroyed every indication of the Fort Vanguardia.

Cabinet meeting tomorrow will probably treat of the proposal stated in my telegram No. 25, April 22, 10 a. m.[26]

KREECK

---

724.3415/514 : Telegram

*The Chargé in Bolivia (Martin) to the Secretary of State*

LA PAZ, May 8, 1929—noon.
[Received 3 p. m.]

41. Department's 22, May 6, 7 p. m. No publicity given to reported attack until last night when chief of police of La Paz sent a small detachment of troops to guard Chilean Legation against which a demonstration was organized but not carried out. Official version published this morning coincides with report quoted in Department's telegram except that no mention is made of capture of Paraguayan patrol. Several of my colleagues and an official of the Foreign Office with whom I talked last night are inclined to make light of the matter.

*El Diario* of this morning carries an editorial in which a statement is made that the Paraguayan patrol was not justified in approaching the zone of Fort Vanguardia and that the Bolivian detachment "could not receive the Paraguayans in any other manner than they actually did."

[Paraphrase.] While it is very difficult to secure information on which to base an opinion, my belief is that only a few shots were exchanged, that there was no bloodshed, and that the charge that the

---

[25] See footnote 23, p. 845.
[26] Not printed.

Paraguayan patrol was the aggressor should be carefully examined. [End paraphrase.]

MARTIN

---

724.3415/525 : Telegram

*The Secretary of State to the Chargé in Argentina (White)*[27]

WASHINGTON, May 11, 1929—6 p. m.

37. Formal action is to be taken May 13 by the Commission of Inquiry and Conciliation, Bolivia and Paraguay, with regard to the repatriation of prisoners. The plan will probably call for the services of the Military Attaché at your mission. Please ask him to be ready.

STIMSON

---

724.3415/527

*The Secretary General of the Commission of Inquiry and Conciliation (Schoenfeld) to the Assistant Secretary of State (White)*

MEMORANDUM

[WASHINGTON,] May 13, 1929.

The Chairman desires me to inform you that the Commission of Inquiry and Conciliation, Bolivia and Paraguay, to-day adopted the following resolutions:

RESOLUTION FOR THE REPATRIATION OF BOLIVIAN AND PARAGUAYAN NATIONALS

"In view of the initiative of the neutral Commissioners, seconded by those from Bolivia and Paraguay with the consent of their respective Governments, authorizing the Commission to undertake the exchange of nationals from one country detained by the Government of the other, as a result of the happenings of December last,

The Commission resolves:

To take over the negotiations for the repatriation of the Bolivian nationals detained by the Government of Paraguay, and the Paraguayan nationals detained by the Government of Bolivia, as a result of the happenings of December last."

NOTE: The Chairman thereafter appointed a Sub-Committee on repatriation, under the Chairmanship of the Commissioner for Uruguay, General Ruprecht, and with the Commissioner for Bolivia, Dr. Finot, and for Paraguay, Dr. Chaves, as members, and Captain Ridgway, of the Secretariat General, as Secretary. This Sub-Committee will determine the manner in which the repatriation shall be effected, reporting the result of its work to the Commission.

---

[27] The same, *mutatis mutandis*, on the same date to the Ambassador in Brazil as telegram No. 15.

RESOLUTION CONCERNING THE INCIDENT OF MAY 4, 1929 IN THE VICINITY OF "FORTIN VANGUARDIA"

"Having received from the Government of Bolivia, through its Delegation, a protest concerning the incident which took place on the 4th instant, in the vicinity of "Fortin Vanguardia", due to the presence thereon of a Paraguayan detachment, and in view of the explanations and of the protest submitted, in turn, by the Paraguayan Delegation regarding indications of the establishment of a new Bolivian military post, the Commission of Inquiry and Conciliation, Bolivia and Paraguay, is of the opinion that the Governments of Bolivia and Paraguay should assure themselves that completely effective measures have been taken to prevent any sort of friction between their respective forces, in any region for which purpose it would be desirable that they should issue categorical orders in the sense that no advances of any kind and for any purpose take place in that territory.

The Commission feels certain that the terms of the Protocol to which both Governments have pledged their faith, will be scrupulously complied with and that all necessary measures will be taken to preclude the possibility of subordinate commanders in the more inaccessible regions of the Chaco from jeopardizing the successful and pacific settlement of the matters now pending between the said Governments.

It is the sense of the Commission that any action the Commission may take under the terms of the Protocol can not be affected by the occupancy of any area by either country during the sessions of the Commission, but, on the other hand, that the Commission in determining its final action might properly take into consideration the circumstances surrounding any incidents occurring during the sessions of the Commission.

The Commission requests the delegations of Bolivia and Paraguay to communicate the text of this resolution to their respective Governments."

COMMUNICATION ON BEHALF OF THE NEUTRAL MEMBERS SENT BY THE SECRETARY GENERAL TO THE COMMISSIONERS FOR BOLIVIA AND PARAGUAY

"In view of the foregoing resolution (adopted to-day by the Commission of Inquiry and Conciliation, Bolivia and Paraguay, with reference to a recent encounter in the Chaco between the forces of Bolivia and Paraguay), the members from Mexico, Colombia, Uruguay, Cuba and the United States of the said Commission request the delegates from Bolivia (Paraguay) to inquire of their Government what measures have already been taken and what further measures will promptly be taken to prevent friction of any kind between forces of Bolivia and Paraguay in any region; and, with the consent of the Government of Bolivia (Paraguay), to transmit to the Commission the reply which may be made in response to this inquiry."

H. F. ARTHUR SCHOENFELD

724.3415/525 : Telegram

*The Secretary of State to the Chargé in Argentina (White)*

WASHINGTON, May 20, 1929—6 p. m.

40. Department's 37, May 11, 6 p. m.   The Commission of Inquiry and Conciliation has arranged for the repatriation of prisoners held respectively by Bolivia and Paraguay.   The prisoners held by Bolivia will be brought to Formosa if the Argentine Government consents to a request already made through the Argentine Embassy here for this purpose.   When Argentine consent is received the Military Attaché at your Mission will be asked to proceed with an Argentine officer to Formosa to assist in connection with the repatriation.   Further instructions will be sent for this purpose.

STIMSON

724.3415/525 : Telegram

*The Secretary of State to the Ambassador in Brazil (Morgan)*

WASHINGTON, May 20, 1929—6 p. m.

17. Department's 15, May 11, 6 p. m.[28]   The Commission of Inquiry and Conciliation has arranged for the repatriation of prisoners held respectively by Bolivia and Paraguay.   The prisoners held by Paraguay will be brought to Corumba, if the Brazilian Government consents to a request already made through the Brazilian Embassy here for this purpose.   When Brazilian consent is received the Military Attaché at your Mission will be asked to proceed with a Brazilian officer to Corumba to assist in connection with the repatriation. Further instructions will be sent for this purpose.

STIMSON

724.3415/812

*The Bolivian Delegation, Commission of Inquiry and Conciliation, to the Secretary General of the Commission (Schoenfeld)[29]*

WASHINGTON, May 21, 1929.

MR. SECRETARY GENERAL: We take pleasure in referring to your courteous note of the 13th instant which contains the text of the

[28] See footnote 27, p. 847.
[29] Printed from mimeographed minutes of Commission of Inquiry and Conciliation, Bolivia and Paraguay, Meeting of June 17, 1929, p. 2.

Resolution adopted by the H. Commission of Inquiry and Conciliation at its meeting of even date with regard to new happenings in
Vanguardia which this Delegation, complying with explicit instructions of the Bolivian Government, denounced as the result of new
incursions by Paraguayan troops in the region of the aforesaid outpost.

In connection with the foregoing Resolution you are also kind
enough to inform us that the Commissioners for Mexico, Colombia,
Uruguay, Cuba and the United States request that we inquire of
our Government what measures have already been taken and what further measures will be taken to prevent friction of any kind between
forces of Bolivia and Paraguay in any region.

In reply we are glad to reiterate the prior statement to the effect
that the Government of Bolivia has established no new outpost in
Vanguardia and that the happenings of the 4th and 5th instant have
not been provoked by the Bolivian garrisons in that zone.

With regard to the request of the Commissioners for Mexico,
Colombia, Uruguay, Cuba and the United States, we also take pleasure
in stating that the Bolivian Government deems that the Paraguayan
forces should refrain from advancing beyond their present positions
and from approaching those of Bolivia, under any pretext whatever, if they do not wish to provoke an encounter with the Bolivian
forces charged with exacting respect for the Nation's sovereignty
in the Chaco and Oriente regions. Our Government, on its part,
shall continue to fulfill, loyally, all commitments concerning the
matter made in the Protocol of January 3, of the present year.

In the hope that the foregoing statements may meet the wishes
of the Commissioners requesting them, we take pleasure in conveying
to you, Mr. Secretary General, the assurances of our highest and
most distinguished consideration.

DAVID ALVÉSTEGUI      ENRIQUE FINOT

724.3415/812

*The Paraguayan Delegation, Commission of Inquiry and Concilia-
tion, to the Secretary General of the Commission (Schoenfeld)* [30]

WASHINGTON, May 22, 1929.

MR. CHAIRMAN: I have the honor of transmitting, for the information of the H. Commission under Your Excellency's worthy chairmanship, the cable in code that the Delegation of Paraguay has
received from the Foreign Office of its country in reply to the inquiry submitted to the Paraguayan Government, at the request of

---

[30] Printed from mimeographed minutes of Commission of Inquiry and Conciliation, Bolivia and Paraguay, Meeting of June 17, 1929, p. 2.

the Commission, concerning the measures which will be taken to prevent friction between Paraguayan and Bolivian forces:

"Asunción, May 21. Paraguayan Delegation. Washington, D. C. In reply to the recommendations and queries transmitted in cablegrams of May 14 and 15, you will please inform the Honorable Commission that this Government. faithful to their pledge, have reiterated to the Commanders of our forces in all zones, unqualified instructions to abstain from any act which may cause friction between the forces of Paraguay and Bolivia. These are under capable and prudent Commanders who have instructions to submit any doubt to the Minister of War. Nevertheless, the prevention of new incidents does not rest only upon us. The proximity of the forces of both countries makes it easy for them to arise, and the Chaco desert stimulates their outbreak because it favors concealment of the true facts, thus permitting Bolivia, who provokes them, to exhibit herself as a victim, while knowing beforehand that there will always be doubts in the minds of the Plenipotentiary Commissioners as to who was the aggressor."

I avail myself [etc.]                                    FRANCISCO C. CHAVES

724.3415/558

*The Secretary General of the Commission of Inquiry and Conciliation (Schoenfeld) to the Secretary of State*

WASHINGTON, May 24, 1929.

SIR: I have the honor to enclose for the Department's information a copy of the Spanish text of a resolution passed at a session of this Commission yesterday, outlining the procedure to be followed in effecting the repatriation of the Bolivian and Paraguayan nationals, respectively, now held by the Government of the other as a result of the events of December last. I have the honor further to enclose a copy of an English translation of this resolution.

In pursuance of the resolution mentioned, the Commission has directed me also to transmit to the Department, as I do herewith, a memorandum [31] embodying the substance of an instruction which it is desired that the Department send to the American Embassies at Rio de Janeiro and Buenos Aires, respectively, on behalf of the Commission, regarding the constitution of two committees under the supervision of the Military Attachés at the two Embassies mentioned charged with the duty of carrying out the repatriation in question. The Commission respectfully requests the Department to cause this instruction to be forwarded to the two Embassies mentioned, substantially in the terms set forth in the enclosed memorandum.

I have [etc.]                                    H. F. ARTHUR SCHOENFELD

[31] Memorandum not printed; but see telegram No. 44, May 25, 5 p. m., to the Chargé in Argentina, which was based upon this memorandum, p. 854. The memorandum is printed in *Proceedings of the Commission of Inquiry and Conciliation, Bolivia and Paraguay,* p. 44.

[Enclosure—Translation]

*Resolution of Repatriation Approved by the Commission of Inquiry and Conciliation, May 23, 1929*

The Commission unanimously agrees to adopt the Report of the Sub-Committee on Repatriation under the chairmanship of the Commissioner for Uruguay, and to take such steps as are necessary for effecting the repatriation of Bolivian and Paraguayan nationals pursuant to the provisions of said Report which is hereinafter reproduced verbatim:

The Sub-Committee entrusted with the question of repatriating the nationals now being held, after several exchanges of views, has been able to secure a perfect and happy understanding between the Commissioners of the parties, and is able to report the result of its endeavors as follows:

The Delegations of Bolivia and Paraguay, with the consent and under authority of their respective governments, agree to have the repatriation of their respective nationals now being held by the other Government as a consequence of the events of December, last, effected in the following manner.

1. The exchange covers all Paraguayan nationals now being held by the Government of Bolivia and all the Bolivian nationals now being held by the Government of Paraguay.

2. The Government of Bolivia shall take all necessary steps in order that the Paraguayan nationals, now being held at Villa Montes, leave for Formosa, on the date to be determined by the Commission.

3. Those nationals shall be escorted by a representative of the Bolivian Government.

4. The route to be followed is subject to the authorization granted by the Argentine Government, from which it shall be requested, together with measures for the guarding of the nationals detained throughout their trip on Argentine territory and during their stay in Formosa and until they are delivered to the Paraguayan authorities by the Commission.

5. A Committee named by this Commission shall arrange with the Governments of Bolivia and of the Argentine Republic to receive in Formosa the nationals now held by Bolivia, and in turn shall deliver them to the representative of Paraguay to be conducted to their own country.

Said reception shall take place in the presence of a representative of the Paraguayan Government for the purpose of identifying the nationals detained.

That deputized Committee shall be formed by the Military Attaché to the United States Embassy in Argentina and by a representative of the Argentine Government.

6. The Government of Paraguay shall take all the necessary steps in order that the Bolivian nationals, now being held at Villa Hayes, leave for Corumbá on the date to be determined by the Commission.

7. These nationals shall be escorted by a representative of the Paraguayan Government, under whose guard they will remain until their arrival in Corumbá.

8. The determination of the place in Corumbá where the transfer will be effected is subject to the authorization to be granted by the Brazilian Government, which will also be requested to adopt measures for guarding the Bolivian nationals during their stay at Corumbá until the Committee turns them over to the Bolivian authorities.

9. In Corumbá the representative of the Paraguayan Government shall proceed to turn over the nationals detained to a Committee deputized by the Commission, under whose guard they shall remain until further decision by the Commission, which shall in turn deliver them to the Bolivian representative for transportation to their own country.

Said delivery shall take place in the presence of a representative of the Bolivian Government for the purpose of identifying the nationals detained.

That deputized Committee shall be formed by the Military Attaché to the United States Embassy in Brazil and by a representative of the Brazilian Government.

10. Both the expenses incident to the transportation to and stay in Formosa of the detained Paraguayan nationals, until they are turned over to the Paraguayan authorities, and those arising from the transportation to and stay in Formosa of the deputized Committee, shall be defrayed by the Government of Bolivia.

11. Both the expenses incident to the transportation to and stay in Corumbá of the detained Bolivian nationals until they are turned over to the Bolivian authorities, and those arising from the transportation to and stay in Corumbá of the deputized Committee, shall be defrayed by the Government of Paraguay.

12. The delivery of all nationals detained to their respective Governments shall be made on behalf of the Commission through each of the deputized Committees to one representative from each Government, after taking the depositions which the deputized Committees may require of the detained nationals under instructions they will receive from the Commission.

In order to carry out the foregoing resolution and with the consent of the Governments of the Argentine Republic, Brazil and the United States of America, the Commission unanimously agrees to appoint the following Committees:

To effect the repatriation of the Bolivian nationals detained by Paraguay, a Committee formed by the Military Attaché to the United States Embassy in Brazil and a representative of the Brazilian Government.

To effect the repatriation of Paraguayan nationals detained by Bolivia, a Committee formed by the Military Attaché to the United States Embassy in Argentina and a representative of the Argentine Government.

In order to carry out the foregoing, the Commission unanimously agrees to authorize the Chairman to issue the instructions which, with the consent of the Government of the United States of America, will be given to its Military Attachés at the Embassies in Buenos Aires and Rio de Janeiro.

724.3415/549b : Telegram

## *The Secretary of State to the Chargé in Argentina (White)* [32]

WASHINGTON, May 25, 1929—3 p. m.

44. The Bolivian and Paraguayan Governments have agreed to place in the hands of the Commission of Inquiry and Conciliation, Bolivia and Paraguay, the repatriation of their respective nationals now detained as a result of the events of December, last, and the Commission has accepted the task of carrying out said repatriation. The Governments of the Argentine Republic and Brazil have also consented to the repatriation taking place through their territories, and Formosa and Corumbá, respectively, have been designated as the places at which delivery of these nationals will be made to the neutral committees hereinafter provided for.

The Commission has unanimously agreed that the actual repatriation shall be effected by neutral committees. The Commission has appointed as a Committee to carry out the repatriation of the Bolivian nationals now held by Paraguay in Villa Hayes, the Military Attaché to the United States Embassy in Rio de Janeiro and an official or officials to be named by the Brazilian Government; and as a Committee to carry out the repatriation of the Paraguayan nationals now held by Bolivia in Villa Montes, the Military Attaché to the United States Embassy in Buenos Aires, and an official or officials to be named by the Argentine Government. You will conclude arrangements for designation of such official or officials which has been requested officially by the Commission through the Brazilian and Argentine Embassies in Washington. The Commission hereby delegates to these two Committees full powers to arrange all details in general conformity with the instructions which follow, and authorizes them to communicate directly with the Governments of Argentina, Brazil, Bolivia and Paraguay, and with the Commission directly or through any American Diplomatic Mission.

Repatriation shall be carried out as follows: All the Paraguayan nationals now held by Bolivia shall be delivered in Formosa to the neutral committee there. The Committee charged with effecting the repatriation of the Paraguayan nationals now held by the Bolivian Government is hereby empowered to arrange with the Governments of Bolivia and of the Argentine Republic to receive these nationals in Formosa in the presence of a representative of Paraguay, and in turn shall deliver them to the representative of Paraguay for transportation to their own country. [33] The journey of the Bolivian and

---

[32] A similar telegram was sent to the Ambassador in Brazil as telegram No. 19 of the same date.

[33] This sentence was not included in telegram No. 19 to the Ambassador in Brazil.

Paraguayan nationals from their present places of detention at Villa Hayes and Villa Montes, respectively, will begin when directed by the neutral committee concerned. The Government of Bolivia will furnish to the proper committee on its request an official list by name, rank, etc. of the one officer and twelve men it now holds, and the Government of Paraguay will similarly furnish a list of the two officers and nineteen men detained by it. The Bolivian nationals shall be received in Corumbá by the neutral committee concerned which shall satisfy itself that the identity of the individuals delivered corresponds with the official list. If and when further so instructed, the two neutral committees will, on behalf of the Commission, take the depositions of the repatriates of Bolivia and Paraguay, respectively, on the interrogatories to be furnished you by cable. In that event, the Argentine and Brazilian Governments will be asked to arrange for the taking of these depositions in accordance with their respective civil procedures and under the supervision of the neutral committee. The duly designated representatives of the Bolivian and Paraguayan Governments may be present at this time only as observers of the proceedings. The replies to the interrogatories will be telegraphed to the Commission. Pending delivery of the repatriates to the representative of their own Government and prior to the taking of their depositions, no unauthorized person shall be permitted access to them.

The expenses of the Committees will be paid by the Governments of Bolivia and Paraguay through the Commission and will include travel and other essential expenses duly certified to by the members of the Committee and subsistence of $10 gold per diem for the whole period of this duty.

Please direct the Military Attaché at your Embassy to carry out the repatriation as outlined above and to return to his post upon the conclusion thereof. When delivery of the nationals is made to the representative of their own country, that fact will be cabled to the Commission. A report of the action of the neutral committee will be submitted to the Commission by the Military Attaché. Request him to cable immediately estimate of advance of funds he will require for his committee.

STIMSON

---

724.3415/573 : Telegram

*The Chargé in Argentina (White) to the Secretary of State*

BUENOS AIRES, June 11, 1929—3 p. m.
[Received 3:45 p. m.]

55. Legation at Asunción informs Paraguay ready to deliver Bolivian nationals prisoners at any moment. Military attaché proceed-

ing Formosa as soon as flying conditions permit. He is telegraphing La Paz to have prisoners delivered Formosa June 20th and notifying Asunción accordingly.

WHITE

---

724.3415/574 : Telegram

*The Chargé in Bolivia (Martin) to the Secretary of State*

LA PAZ, June 12, 1929—noon.
[Received 1 p. m.]

49. Military attachés at Rio de Janeiro and Buenos Aires have telegraphed me that they are proceeding to Corumbá and Formosa to receive Bolivian and Paraguayan nationals held prisoners. At their request I have asked Bolivian Government for advance lists of prisoners.

Major Fleming has suggested June 20th as appropriate date for delivery of Paraguayans at Formosa. I assume that the exchange should be simultaneous. If the Commission expects to fix a date, please instruct.

MARTIN

---

724.3415/575d : Telegram

*The Acting Secretary of State to the Chargé in Bolivia (Hibbard)*

WASHINGTON, June 13, 1929—7 p. m.

29. Your 49, June 12, noon. Commission accepted charge of repatriation of Bolivian and Paraguayan Nationals as independent operations. Arrangements and dates to be made by the Governments concerned and American Military Attachés at Formosa and Corumba without reference to Commission. Major Baker Military Attaché at Rio de Janeiro together with Brazilian official should arrive at port Esperanza June fifteenth and Corumbá June sixteenth.

. . . . . . . .

CLARK

---

724.3415/577 : Telegram

*The Chargé in Argentina (White) to the Secretary of State*

BUENOS AIRES, June 17, 1929—4 p. m.
[Received 6:25 p. m.]

57. My 55, June 11, 3 p. m. American Chargé d'Affaires at La Paz telegraphs that Bolivian general staff has arranged to deliver Paraguayan nationals prisoners at Formosa June 20th and that

the Bolivian Government hopes that the exchange can be effected simultaneously, that is to say, repatriation of its nationals prisoners in Paraguay.

WHITE

---

724.3415/622

*The Chairman of the Commission of Inquiry and Conciliation (McCoy) to the Secretary of State*

WASHINGTON, July 10, 1929.

SIR: Having just been informed by cable that the repatriation of the Bolivian and Paraguayan nationals held by the Governments of Paraguay and Bolivia, respectively, as a result of the events of December, last, has been successfully completed,[34] and under direction of the Commission of Inquiry and Conciliation, Bolivia and Paraguay, I have the honor to convey to you its cordial appreciation of the efficient and constant assistance rendered by the Government and the Department of State of the United States of America, and the civilian and military officers thereof, in terminating an issue which had in the recent past called for the mediation of the Department in an endeavor to bring about an understanding of the two Governments concerned.

The Commission undertook the task in a sincere desire to assist both countries in removing all obstacles to the fulfillment of their earnest aspiration, and indeed that of the Americas, to consolidate their neighborly relations through the pacific settlement of any controversies between them. To discharge this duty it appointed a Sub-committee on Repatriation, which under the able chairmanship of the Commissioner for Uruguay, General Guillermo Ruprecht, and through the Neutral Committees deputized at Formosa and Corumba, acquitted itself in a manner deserving of the highest commendation.

I have [etc.]

FRANK McCOY

---

724.3415/622

*The Secretary of State to the Chairman of the Commission of Inquiry and Conciliation (McCoy)*

WASHINGTON, July 12, 1929.

SIR: I have the honor to acknowledge the receipt of your note of July 10, 1929, informing me that the repatriation of the Bolivian and Paraguayan nationals held by the Governments of Paraguay and

[34] For details of the repatriation, see *Proceedings of the Commission of Inquiry and Conciliation, Bolivia and Paraguay,* pp. 129-173.

Bolivia, respectively, has been successfully completed under the direction of the Commission of Inquiry and Conciliation, Bolivia and Paraguay, and expressing the Commission's appreciation of the assistance rendered by the Government of the United States, the Department of State, and certain officers of the War Department, in bringing about the termination of this issue.

Permit me, through you, to thank the Commission sincerely for this communication, and at the same time express to the Commission, the Committee, which, under the able Chairmanship of the Commissioner for Uruguay was charged with the work of repatriation, the Neutral Committees at Formosa and Corumbá, and yourself hearty congratulations upon the consummation of this splendid service. The wholehearted cooperation and inspired interest of the members of the Commission and of the two Governments concerned stand forth as an example of the spirit of conciliation and friendship prevailing among the nations of the Americas.

I have [etc.]                                             H. L. STIMSON

724.3415/688a : Telegram

*The Secretary of State to the Minister in Paraguay (Kreeck)*

[Paraphrase]

WASHINGTON, September 9, 1929—9 p. m.

37. This afternoon the Bolivian Commissioners stated orally, but officially, to the neutral Commissioners that they were authorized by the Government of Bolivia unconditionally to accept the bases of conciliation proposed by the neutral Commissioners in the week of August 26 and the points to be set forth in the statement of the Commission to accompany the bases of conciliation. The Bolivian Commissioners promised to confirm their unconditional acceptance by note.

Immediately after the above meeting with the Bolivian Commissioners and after they had departed, the chairman of the Commission in behalf of the neutral Commissioners invited the Paraguayan Commissioners into the meeting. After they had arrived the chairman informed them of the unconditional acceptance of Bolivia and urged them likewise to accept unconditionally the neutral proposal on conciliation. The chairman of the Commission added that the neutral Commissioners were prepared, if the Paraguayan delegation so chose, to hold an oral acceptance of the Paraguayan delegation strictly confidential pending a receipt of confirmation from Asunción. The Paraguayan delegation then consulted privately, after which the Paraguayan Commissioners authorized the chairman to state to the other neutral Commissioners that the Paraguayan delegation for its part accepted the proposal unconditionally and would immediately communicate with the Government of Paraguay to secure confirmation and that pending the receipt of the same it was to be understood that the acceptance of the Paraguayan delegation was to be treated as confidential.

You may state to the Government of Paraguay that it is the earnest hope of the neutral Commissioners that the Government of Paraguay will lose no time in approving of the above-described action of the Paraguayan delegation, which will result in conciliation under the protocol and open the way for a sympathetic consideration of the Paraguayan note delivered today [36] answering the neutral proposal of August 31 [37] touching the fundamental question.

Also, you are authorized to state that the Government of the United States earnestly hopes that the Government of Paraguay will accept the plan for conciliation unreservedly, thereby demonstrating its devotion to the highest interests of the American Republics and contributing to the honorable disappearance of this long-standing dispute.

STIMSON

---

724.3515/690 : Telegram

*The Minister in Paraguay (Kreeck) to the Secretary of State*

ASUNCIÓN, September 11, 1929—10 a. m.
[Received 8 : 40 p. m.]

81. After conference with the President, Paraguay will confirm their delegates' unconditional acceptance of conciliation and agree to rebuild Fort Vanguardia if the supplementary explanations do not form a part of the signed agreement of conciliation but conditions understood.

Paraguay does not wish to obstruct or impede the progress of the negotiations and is in accord with the Commission, desiring only that the supplementary explanations delivered following the memorandum of August 26th [38] respecting Boquerón and Vanguardia, be conditions to be complied with but not form a part of the signed bases of the conciliation.

The President considers this condition absolutely necessary because of the internal situation (with which I agree although I did not comment). He will proclaim an *estado de sitio* tonight following meeting of Congress this afternoon in order to establish control and meet all emergencies. The President hopes that the Commission will

---

[36] See note dated September 9, 1929, from the Paraguayan delegation to the chairman of the Commission, p. 884.
[37] See note dated August 31, 1929, from the chairman of the Commission to the delegations of Bolivia and Paraguay, p. 874.
[38] Not found in Department files.

appreciate the situation and permit the above mentioned condition so that Paraguay may give at once its confirmation and acceptance.

KREECK

724.3415/696a : Telegram

*The Secretary of State to the Chargé in Bolivia (Hibbard)*[39]

WASHINGTON, September 12, 1929.

50. Following is translation of resolution passed unanimously by the Commission of Inquiry and Conciliation at today's plenary session:

"Whereas Article 5 of the Protocol signed at Washington, January 3rd of this year, by the plenipotentiaries of Bolivia and of Paraguay provides that the Commission of Inquiry and Conciliation, Bolivia and Paraguay, which was created in conformity with the said Protocol, shall make proposals and endeavor to secure the friendly settlement of the incident arising from the events of December, last, in the Chaco Boreal, under conditions satisfactory to the two Parties;

Whereas it is necessary that the Parties should be placed in a position to negotiate an agreement on their controversy in an atmosphere of cordiality and good understanding;

Whereas the historical account of the facts reveals that the incidents at Vanguardia preceded the events which took place in the Boqueron sector;

Whereas the employment of coercive measures on the part of Paraguay in the Vanguardia incident caused the reaction of Bolivia;

Whereas the Governments of Bolivia and of Paraguay, at the unanimous suggestion of the neutral Commissioners, have agreed upon the following:

1. Mutual forgiveness of the offenses and injuries caused by each of the Republics to the other;

2. Reestablishment of the state of things in the Chaco on the same footing as prior to December 5, 1928, though this does not signify in any way prejudgment of the pending territorial or boundary question; and

3. Renewal of their diplomatic relations;

Whereas the Governments of Bolivia and of Paraguay have agreed to proceed to the reestablishment of things to the state which existed prior to December 5, through

(*a*) Restoration of the buildings of Fort Vanguardia by Paraguay; and

(*b*) the abandonment of Fort Boquerón by Bolivian troops without the presence of Paraguayan authorities, leaving it in the same state in which it was occupied by the said Bolivian troops;

Whereas in order to prevent disagreements which might make difficult the carrying out of the foregoing measures, the Governments have agreed to carry them out in the presence of an army officer of a neutral nation;

[39] The same, *mutatis mutandis*, on the same date to the Minister in Paraguay as telegram No. 41.

Therefore, The Commission of Inquiry and Conciliation, Bolivia and Paraguay, resolves:

1. To consider that conciliation of the Parties has been effected in the terms stipulated by the Protocol of January 3, 1929;

2. Likewise to acknowledge that the Parties being conciliated, the Commission, in accordance with the provisions of Article 6 of the said Protocol, has not established responsibilities;

3. To record its satisfaction at the lofty spirit of concord which has been shown by the Governments of Bolivia and of Paraguay in removing the difficulty which arose from the incidents of the month of December, 1928;

4. To recommend earnestly to the Governments of Bolivia and of Paraguay that they carry out the conciliatory measures above set forth without delay; and

5. To ask the Government of Uruguay to be so kind as to designate two officers of its army to proceed, with the consent of the Governments of Bolivia and of Paraguay, to Fort Vanguardia and Fort Boqueron, respectively, and to be present at the execution of the measures designed to restore the state of things which existed prior to December 5, 1928."

Following remarks were made by the Chairman after unanimous approval of foregoing resolution:

"I believe that I am a faithful interpreter of the feelings of the members of this Commission and of all generous minded men throughout the Continent, in extending our cordial congratulations to the Governments of the Republics of Bolivia and Paraguay on the new evidence of well advised cooperation and devotion to peace they have just given the world. Their example constitutes a solemn demonstration that in the Americas conciliation has been added to the other methods for settling satisfactorily and without injury to the paramount interests of nations, those occasional controversies that sometimes divide them."

STIMSON

---

724.3415/825

*The Chargé in Uruguay (Gade) to the Secretary of State*

No. 918

MONTEVIDEO, October 16, 1929.
[Received November 7.]

SIR: With reference to the Department's instruction No. 195, of September 24, 1929, and its telegram No. 19, of October 9th, and in confirmation of my telegram No. 47 of October 10, 1929,[40] regarding the Chaco Boreal dispute. I have the honor to report that in a conversation on the tenth instant the Minister for Foreign Affairs informed me that about a month ago he had sent an identic note to Bolivia and Paraguay designating two majors, assisted by two lieutenants, to carry out the terms of the Protocol signed at Washington by Bolivia and Paraguay on September 12th. Both Governments

---

[40] None printed.

323421—43—vol. I——63

accepted the designations, but Paraguay suggested that the officers be sent forthwith to Asunción. This, the Uruguayan Minister for Foreign Affairs felt, could not well be done for two reasons: First, if the Uruguayan officers were entertained in Asunción, the Bolivian Government might subsequently accuse them of displaying partiality. Second, it would be manifestly impossible for them to proceed to carry out the terms of the Washington Protocol without definite and very detailed instructions regarding the means of reaching the forts in question, the manner in which Fort Vanguardia should be restored, the procedure of transferring the forts, etc. Since the Uruguayan Government has been requested merely to assist in the execution of the measures stipulated in the Protocol of September 12th "with the consent of the Governments of Bolivia and of Paraguay," the Minister for Foreign Affairs believed that appropriate instructions for the Uruguayan officers should be drafted by the two contending Governments. About ten days ago he therefore proposed, in a second identic note to Bolivia and Paraguay, that their respective ministers at Montevideo be instructed to reach an agreement on this question. The Bolivian Government accepted this proposal on the 9th instant. The Paraguayan Government has not yet answered the note, but an affirmative reply is expected shortly.

I have [etc.]
GERHARD GADE

724.3415/897 : Telegram

*The Chargé in Uruguay (Gade) to the Secretary of State*

MONTEVIDEO, December 10, 1929—noon.<br>[Received 2 : 45 p. m.]

56. Ministers of Bolivia and Paraguay and Uruguayan Minister for Foreign Affairs held unsuccessful meeting regarding Chaco Boreal yesterday.

After the meeting the Minister for Foreign Affairs made the following statement:

"In view of the position taken by the representatives of the contending parties, I thought it advisable to present in the name of the Uruguayan Government a formula of conciliation which was submitted to the Paraguayan and Bolivian Governments for study. Certain objections were made by the latter and many of the conclusions were rejected by the former. Tomorrow the Uruguayan Ministry of Foreign Affairs will submit for the consideration of the Governments of both countries a formula which is enlarged and in part revised, taking into consideration the desires of each in such a manner that without friction or injury to susceptibilities we might arrive at a definite agreement.

This formula provides that the Uruguayan officers divide their tasks, one proceeding to Fort Vanguardia and the other to Fort Boquerón where the latter will await the reconstruction of the structures destroyed in that military post. Upon completion of this, the Bolivians will take possession of Vanguardia and the Paraguayans of Boquerón on the same day.

As the nonacceptance of this formula would signify a lack of good will, since there is only opposition to unimportant details, the Uruguayan Ministry of Foreign Affairs in that event would withdraw from any further intervention. This would be most deplorable, for all the high aspirations of confraternity which have been manifested in the consideration of the problem and all the extensive work done to reach a happy solution in the meetings of the neutrals held in the United States capital, would fall to the ground.

The discrepancies consist, I repeat in slight details, regarding the form in which the evacuation of Boquerón and the delivery of Vanguardia should be carried out. Our Government understands that as a proof of friendship and as the first act of a new era of peace this should be effected simultaneously.

It is to be hoped that the Uruguayan proposal will be accepted, since to refuse it would mean a return to the moment of the beginning of the conflict and this would be a constant menace to continental harmony."

Bolivian Minister informed the press that his Government was ready to accept the proposal of the Uruguayan Government. Paraguayan Minister declined to comment.

GADE

---

**Proposals for Settlement of the Basic Question**

724.3415/623

*The Chairman of the Commission of Inquiry and Conciliation (McCoy) to the Secretary of State*

WASHINGTON, July 10, 1929.

SIR: I have the honor to transmit herewith for the Department's information copies of correspondence read into the minutes of the latest meeting of the Commission of Inquiry and Conciliation, Bolivia and Paraguay, on July 2nd, at the Pan American Union, together with the remarks made on the same occasion by Dr. David Alvéstegui of the Bolivian Delegation and by myself as Chairman.

The correspondence and remarks record the proposal and acceptance of a plan whereby the neutral members of the Commission may now proceed toward a final settlement of the fundamental question affecting the Chaco, between Bolivia and Paraguay. The plan does not restrict the Commission in the performance of its duties as defined in the Protocol of January 3, 1929.[41]

The Department will, doubtless, be gratified to learn that during the negotiations which led to the adoption of this plan the Commissioners of Mexico, Colombia, Uruguay and Cuba lent the indispensable assistance of their united efforts and the prestige of their

[41] *Ante,* p. 835.

Governments, and that the delegates of Bolivia and Paraguay, keeping always in mind the interests of their respective Governments, cooperated in the most broadminded way, as members of the Commission.

I have [etc.]                                        FRANK McCOY

[Enclosure 1—Translation]

*Draft Note From the Chairman of the Commission of Inquiry and Conciliation (McCoy) to the Delegations of Bolivia and Paraguay* [42]

EXCELLENCIES: On May 31st last, the undersigned had the honor to make to Your Excellencies, through His Excellency Dr. David Alvéstegui (Dr. Enrique Bordenave), as well as to their Excellencies the Commissioners of Paraguay (of Bolivia), through His Excellency Dr. Enrique Bordenave (Dr. David Alvéstegui), the following statement:

The neutral Commissioners consider it indispensable, in order to prevent further conflicts and establish conciliation on firm and permanent bases, to procure a settlement of the fundamental question between the two countries.  They trust that Their Excellencies the Commissioners of Bolivia and Paraguay (of Paraguay and Bolivia), duly empowered by their Governments, authorize the neutral Commissioners to prepare in a spirit of amity such plans for a settlement as they may consider appropriate to submit to them, it being understood that the adoption of this procedure does not imply the abandonment of the process of investigation now being conducted by the Commission in pursuance of the Protocol of January 3, 1929.

His Excellency Dr. David Alvéstegui (Dr. Enrique Bordenave) was kind enough then to inform me orally of his agreement with the foregoing.  Accordingly, I now have the honor to request Your Excellencies to be so kind as to confirm that oral statement, in order that the neutral Commissioners, who are animated by the deepest desire to aid in establishing perfect harmony between the two countries, may undertake that task, thus interpreting the unanimous and cordial aspiration of the Republics of this Continent.

Accept [etc.]

[Enclosure 2—Translation]

*The Bolivian Delegation to the Chairman of the Commission of Inquiry and Conciliation (McCoy)*

WASHINGTON, July 1, 1929.

MR. CHAIRMAN: We have received the note that Your Excellency was kind enough to address to us on the 28th of the past month, re-

---

[42] The notes when sent were dated June 28, 1929.

questing us to confirm the verbal assent given to you by one of the undersigned Commissioners, at the interview held May 31st, last, to the suggestion of Their Excellencies the neutral Commissioners that they make friendly proposals for the settlement of the territorial question at issue between Bolivia and Paraguay, since they consider it indispensable in order to prevent further conflicts and establish conciliation on firm and permanent bases.

In reply to Your Excellency, and in view of the commendable intention expressed by Their Excellencies the neutral Commissioners to offer suggestions to the Governments of Bolivia and Paraguay for the purpose of defining the territorial question, without thereby hindering, in any wise, the procedure arising from the Protocol of January 3rd of this year, the Delegation of Bolivia, duly empowered by its Government, states:

1. The Protocol of January 3, 1929, shall be continued in full force, the activities of investigation to proceed uninterruptedly.

2. The friendly proposals of Their Excellencies the neutral Commissioners bearing on the fundamental question shall only have unofficial and informal character and will be conducted outside the scope of the aforementioned Protocol.

3. The negotiations for an understanding shall be carried out within the term of six months fixed in the Protocol to complete the task of the Commission, after the expiration of which it shall render its verdict in accordance with the provisions of the Protocol, whatever the result of the informal endeavors of Their Excellencies the neutral Commissioners.

We thus confirm and explain, in its true scope, the verbal statement recalled by Your Excellency and we take pleasure in emphasizing the special deference with which the Bolivian Government is willing to hear the friendly proposals of Their Excellencies the neutral Commissioners, whose noble efforts and cordial aspirations it acknowledges and highly appreciates.

We avail ourselves [etc.]

DAVID ALVÉSTEGUI        ENRIQUE FINOT

[Enclosure 3—Translation]

*The Paraguayan Delegation to the Chairman of the Commission of Inquiry and Conciliation (McCoy)*

WASHINGTON, July 1, 1929.

MR. CHAIRMAN: We have the honor to acknowledge receipt of your note dated June 28 as follows:

[Here follows the text of the note from the chairman of the Commission, printed on page 864.]

Witnesses as we are, until now, of the active endeavors of the neutral Commissioners to restore the good friendship at present unfortunately shaken between our country and Bolivia; reliable witnesses as we are also of the equanimity and prudence with which they are carrying on their high and noble mission, our Government and its Delegation accredited in Washington, not only grant the authorization requested in the terms of the note which we are answering, but we must be allowed again to acknowledge the generous sentiments which inspire the conduct of the Commissioners.

Confirming, therefore, the assent above expressed the Delegation of Paraguay maintains categorically all the views formulated in the memorials it presented and if it does not now mention them in detail it is because, with the amplification of the powers of the Commission, the matters that it deems to have been in its jurisdiction are not only not affected but on the contrary can be studied and decided more effectively and through a more comprehensive and broader procedure.

We believe it is both our duty, and an obligation of justice, also to state on this occasion that all the Governments which have succeeded each other in directing the destinies of Paraguay have always shown their desire and made efforts for the definitive determination of the dividing line between the respective sovereignties of the two Republics in the vast territory of the Chaco, and the firm and lasting consolidation of the friendship and solidarity that should exist between the two for reasons of identity of origin and of common interests which must bind them inescapably in the future.

Expressing our wishes that the distinguished neutral members of the Commission may obtain in their task the entire success to which their great purposes entitle them and promising our loyal cooperation within the standards indicated to us by our duty, we renew [etc.]

FRANCISCO C. CHAVES  ENRIQUE BORDENAVE

[Enclosure 4—Translation]

*The Chairman of the Commission of Inquiry and Conciliation (McCoy) to the Delegations of Bolivia and Paraguay*

WASHINGTON, July 2, 1929.

EXCELLENCIES: I have the honor to acknowledge receipt of the note dated July 1st, wherein Your Excellencies were kind enough to answer mine of June 28th, last.

In the name of the Commissioners for Mexico, Colombia, Uruguay and Cuba, and in my own, it affords me great pleasure to acknowledge the new evidence of a lofty spirit of Americanism given by your Government, through Your Excellencies, in accepting our friendly offer. At the moment of undertaking the task of preparing, for submission to Your Excellencies, plans for a settlement of the fundamental question between Bolivia and Paraguay, for which purpose we regard the two nations as being in the same position, we entertain the hope of thus contributing to the lasting understanding between these Republics which the neutral Commissioners are actively seeking.

The neutral Commissioners have noted carefully the matters set forth in the note of Your Excellencies which are considered pertinent to the work undertaken by them and they deem this task to be distinct from the work which belongs to the Commission as a whole.

I avail myself [etc.]                                    FRANK R. McCOY

[Enclosure 5—Translation]

## Remarks by the Bolivian Commissioner (Alvéstegui)

The Bolivian Commissioner, Dr. Alvéstegui, said that he wished solely to express, once more, the deep satisfaction with which the Government of Bolivia, and its Delegates in Washington, had followed the course of the friendly negotiations undertaken by the neutral Commissioners, in their praiseworthy desire to assist in the settlement of the pending territorial dispute, because, due to her historical past, Bolivia's attitude toward the controversy with Paraguay was the same that always led her to procure the termination, by pacific means, of her differences with neighboring sister countries.

He added that Bolivia had taken the initiative of promoting the settlement of the territorial dispute with Paraguay, and that, notwithstanding the little success of her first efforts, she does not hesitate in making new ones to that end whenever appropriate opportunity offers.

He further said that when incidents she had not willed cast shadows upon the international horizon, Bolivia had given again renewed evidence of her pacific spirit, by participating in the Commission of which she is a member, and that consequently, when the neutral Commissioners believed it advisable to seek for a formula to settle the territorial question with Paraguay, which it has been impossible to agree upon through direct negotiations, both the Bolivian Government and its Delegation had given ample support to and expressed appreciation of that commendable initiative.

Finally, he said that since the noble purpose of the informal negotiations had been achieved, he wished to reiterate the appreciation of the Bolivian Government and of its Delegation, to the neutral Commissioners, for their generous and well meaning efforts, and to express the earnest and sincere hope that they may be fully successful in the endeavors, to which the Government of Bolivia and its Delegation in Washington offered the assistance of a loyal and frank cooperation.

[Enclosure 6]

*Remarks by the Chairman of the Commission of Inquiry and Conciliation (McCoy)*

I am particularly happy to be able today to congratulate my distinguished colleagues, the Commissioners for Bolivia and Paraguay, for having made possible this decisive step toward conciliation of the differences between them. I believe that they have thereby interpreted in its true meaning the purpose of the Pan American Conference on Conciliation and Arbitration,[43] under the good auspices of which the Protocol was signed creating this Commission. May I be allowed also to express to my neutral colleagues my cordial felicitations on the loyalty and lofty spirit with which they have approached the negotiations that have led to this happy consummation, and on their constant solicitude for the honor and respective interests of the two countries. The American Republics, especially those having Commissioners here, have cause to look upon the work of my neutral colleagues with particular satisfaction and I am delighted to make public acknowledgment of this debt of gratitude owed to you and your respective countries.

724.3415/623

*The Secretary of State to the Chairman of the Commission of Inquiry and Conciliation (McCoy)*

WASHINGTON, July 12, 1929.

SIR: I have the honor to acknowledge the receipt of your letter of July 10, 1929, transmitting for the information of the Department copies of correspondence read into the minutes of the meeting of the Commission of Inquiry and Conciliation, Bolivia and Paraguay, held on July 2, 1929, at the Pan American Union, together with the remarks made on the same occasion by Dr. David Alvéstegui of the Bolivian Delegation, and by yourself as Chairman, recording the proposal and acceptance of a plan whereby the neutral members of the Commission may now proceed toward a final settlement of the fundamental question affecting the Chaco, between Bolivia and Paraguay.

I have duly noted that this plan does not restrict the Commission in the performance of its duties as defined in the Protocol of January 3, 1929. I have also noted with gratification the highly commendable spirit of cooperation of the Delegates of Bolivia and Paraguay, and the endeavors of the Commissioners of Colombia,

---

[43] See *Foreign Relations*, 1928, vol. I, pp. 621 ff.

Cuba, Mexico, and Uruguay in lending their assistance and united efforts and the high prestige of their respective Governments to bring about the proposal and acceptance of this plan.

I have [etc.]                                                HENRY L. STIMSON

---

724.3415/632 : Telegram

*The Minister in Paraguay (Kreeck) to the Secretary of State*

ASUNCIÓN, July 26, 1929—1 p. m.
[Received July 28—9:30 a. m.]

53. The Minister for Foreign Affairs expressed surprise that the Commission has not initiated proceedings for the prolongation of the time for the negotiations. He believes more time should be granted so that the work of the Commission may be efficient and effective and that to discontinue or close the negotiations this coming September too soon and prejudicial to the cause of peace.

KREECK

---

724.3415/659a : Telegram

*The Acting Secretary of State to the Chargé in Bolivia (Hibbard)*[44]

WASHINGTON, August 19, 1929—6 p. m.

30. The following statement was given to the Press today by General McCoy. Please communicate it to the Government of the country to which [you] are accredited:

"The Chairman of the Commission of Inquiry and Conciliation, Bolivia and Paraguay, desires to state that the neutral Commissioners have been actively engaged since the beginning of July in studying the historical, juridical, diplomatic, economic, geographic and other scientific factors involved in any proposal for a settlement of the controversy between Bolivia and Paraguay affecting the Chaco Boreal. Since the time when the neutrals undertook the task in question, they have had the cooperation not only of the technical experts who have been consulted, but they have had the benefit also of conversations with the Delegates of the interested countries. In none of these conversations with the Delegates of the interested countries, however, have the latter made any commitment of any kind though they have spoken with commendable frankness of the positions and aspirations of their respective countries.

The neutral Commissioners are now proceeding to the formulation of their proposal to be submitted to the interested Governments through their respective Delegations on the Commission. The Chairman of the Commission hopes that this task will shortly be completed.

Intensive and careful studies have also been made of all the documentation submitted by the Delegations of the interested coun-

---

[44] The same, *mutatis mutandis*, on the same date to the Minister in Paraguay as telegram No. 40.

tries with reference to the events of December, last. The result of these studies will shortly be considered by the neutral Commissioners with a view to carrying out the conciliatory functions of the Commission under the Protocol of January 3, 1929."

CASTLE

724.3415/661 : Telegram

*The Minister in Paraguay (Kreeck) to the Secretary of State*

ASUNCIÓN, August 20, 1929—9 p. m.
[Received August 22—10 : 30 a. m.]

63. Following a long discussion with the Minister for Foreign Affairs, I feel there is apprehension and uncertainty respecting the decision of the Commission of Inquiry and Conciliation in that the proposals of settlement may not be acceptable to either or both.

The negotiations must not fail. Press reports have unfortunately prejudiced the public mind against the acceptance of any published suggestions of settlement so that to terminate negotiations September 13th would be a grave mistake. . . .

Therefore, permit me to suggest that the Commission send to Paraguay experts of river transportation to view sites and suggest location for a serviceable port. Certainly those sites suggested in the press will not serve the purpose. Only the investigations of an expert can locate a port satisfactorily. Such would require time, hence a basis for prolonging the negotiations to which Bolivia could not object, the investigation being in her interest.

I doubt the acceptance of any solution offered at this time even though just and equitable; it is premature and more time is needed for success.

KREECK

724.3415/660b : Telegram

*The Secretary of State to the Chargé in Brazil (Schoenfeld)*

WASHINGTON, August 21—6 p. m.

50. You will request an interview with the Minister for Foreign Affairs and inform him confidentially that the neutral members of the Commission of Inquiry and Conciliation, Bolivia and Paraguay, expect in the near future to present to the Bolivian and Paraguayan Governments respectively a proposal for a general settlement of the dispute regarding the Chaco. This Government is not informed as to the precise nature of the proposal and will not be responsible therefor, but it is deeply interested in seeing that the proposal receives careful and dispassionate consideration from the two governments concerned. In view of the prominent part which the Brazilian Ambassador to Washington took in connection with the formulation of the pro-

tocol under which the Commission is working it is believed that it would be especially appropriate for the Brazilian Government, if it is disposed to do so, to exert its friendly influence both at Asunción and at La Paz on behalf of an objective and moderate consideration of the Commission's proposal by both governments.   Brazil's influence in this matter would be especially helpful because of that Government's disinterested position and friendship with both of the countries directly concerned, and it would therefore be most gratifying if the Brazilian Government were disposed to cooperate in the event that it should appear after the proposal has been submitted that it is not being received in such a spirit of moderation in one or both of the two interested countries.   You will inquire whether the Brazilian Government would be disposed to take action along the lines suggested, should the occasion for such action arise, making it clear that the action contemplated would be taken only after the actual submission of the proposal, and that you are not of course suggesting that the Brazilian Government commit itself in any way to the merits of the proposal at this time.

STIMSON

---

724.3415/663 : Telegram

*The Chargé in Brazil (Schoenfeld) to the Secretary of State*

RIO DE JANEIRO, August 22, 1929—6 p. m.
[Received 6 : 30 p. m.]

39. Brazilian Minister for Foreign Affairs personally and confidentially informed this afternoon of the contents of the Department's telegram number 50, August 21, 6 p. m., and stated that his Government would be glad to cooperate fully along the lines suggested.

SCHOENFELD

---

724.3415/667c : Telegram

*The Acting Secretary of State to the Minister in Paraguay (Kreeck)*

[Paraphrase]

WASHINGTON, August 24, 1929—11 a. m.

31. Legation's 63, August 20, 9 p. m.  The Department has been informed that the neutral members of the Commission soon expect to make their proposal for a fundamental settlement and desires that you should not express yourself regarding the merit of the proposal even after it shall have been made.  At that time you should take occasion discreetly to counsel an attitude of moderation in order that the feeling of apprehension and uncertainty which you report as now existing may not prevent a calm consideration of the proposal.

It is understood that the life of the Commission is limited under the protocol to a term of six months ending on September 13 next, and that the term can only be extended by the two Governments directly concerned. Should it be found, after presentation of the proposal of the neutrals and upon the conclusion of the conciliatory functions entrusted to the Commission by the protocol, that an extension is desirable in the view of either Government, it is presumed that the delegation of that Government on the Commission will be the appropriate channel for making this fact known.

Regardless of the merits of the proposal to be made for a fundamental settlement, concerning which the Department of State, of course, assumes no responsibility, it is hoped that the interested Governments, including that of Paraguay, will accord the proposal, when made, that consideration due any impartial and sincere effort by five neutral Commissioners to find a fair solution of this long-standing dispute.

CARR

---

724.3415/667a : Telegram

*The Acting Secretary of State to the Chargé in Bolivia (Hibbard)*

WASHINGTON, August 24, 1929—11 a. m.

43. Following extracts from telegram No. 63, August 20, 9 p. m., from Legation at Asunción are repeated for your information.

[Here follows the text of telegram No. 63, August 20, 9 p. m., from the Minister in Paraguay, printed on page 870.]

[Paraphrase.] In its telegram No. 31, August 24, 11 a. m., the Department sent the following answer:

[Here follows the text of telegram No. 31, August 24, 11 a. m., from the Acting Secretary of State, printed *supra*.]

If in your discretion it seems necessary, you may speak to the Government of Bolivia in the same sense and under the same circumstances. [End paraphrase.]

CARR

---

724.3415/667b : Telegram

*The Acting Secretary of State to the Chargé in Bolivia (Hibbard)*[46]

[Paraphrase]

WASHINGTON, August 24, 1929—1 p. m.

44. American Embassy in Brazil reports that the Government of Brazil will be disposed to cooperate in counseling moderation at Asunción and La Paz in the circumstances set forth in the Department's telegram 43, August 24, 11 a. m.

CARR

---

[46] The same on the same date to the Minister in Paraguay as telegram No. 32, mentioning Department's telegram No. 31, August 24, 11 a. m.

724.3415/668 : Telegram

*The Minister in Paraguay (Kreeck) to the Secretary of State*

ASUNCIÓN, August 26, 1929—10 a. m.
[Received 3 : 20 p. m.]

65. The Minister for Foreign Affairs informs me that the Paraguayan Minister to the Argentine Government is now en route to Paraguay to deliver personally a message to this Government from Irigoyen. The Foreign Minister believes that this message has relation to the Chaco negotiations. He has promised me information.

Referring to your telegrams number 31 and 32 of August 24th.[47] At all times I have counseled faith in the Commission and the necessity of solving the boundary controversy in some manner. The Paraguayan Government is so disposed and will give the decision of the Commission sincere and a conciliatory consideration, perhaps even desiring its acceptance, yet may be unable to do so because of the present unfavorable public opinion, hence my telegram number 63 August 20, 9 p. m.

KREECK

724.3415/682a : Telegram

*The Acting Secretary of State to the Minister in Paraguay (Kreeck)*[48]

WASHINGTON, August 30, 1929—3 p. m.

33. Department's telegram No. 31, August 24, 11 a. m.

1. The Chairman of the Commission of Inquiry and Conciliation, Bolivia and Paraguay, is delivering to the Delegations of the interested countries today a formal note on behalf of the neutral Commissioners transmitting a draft treaty of arbitration and a supplementary protocol, all of which represents the proposal of the neutral Commissioners to the interested Governments of a plan for a fundamental settlement of the controversy between the two countries.

2. On August 26, last, the Chairman of the Commission handed to the Delegations of the interested countries a confidential memorandum[49] embodying the basis for conciliation of the incidents of last December under the Protocol of January 3, this year.

3. These bases of conciliation with certain supplementary explanations which have been made to the interested Delegations since the delivery of the memorandum of August 26 are expected, if agreed

[47] See footnote 46, p. 872.
[48] The same on the same date to the Chargé in Bolivia as telegram No. 46, mentioning Department's telegram No. 43, August 24, 11 a. m.
[49] Not found in Department files; but see telegram No. 37, September 9, 9 p. m. to the Minister in Paraguay, p. 858.

to by the interested parties, to make it unnecessary for the Commission to establish responsibilities under Article 6 of the Protocol.

4. The proposal of the neutral Commissioners for the conclusion of an arbitration treaty and a supplementary protocol is given below in full.[50]

5. You will be guided by the Department's telegram above referred to in discussing with the Government to which you are accredited both the bases of conciliation and the proposal for a fundamental settlement.

JOHNSON

724.3415/688

*The Chairman of the Commission of Inquiry and Conciliation (McCoy) to the Delegations of Bolivia and Paraguay* [51]

WASHINGTON, August 31, 1929.

EXCELLENCIES: Under date of July first of this year, Your Excellencies were good enough to transmit to me the authority granted by the Government of Bolivia (Paraguay) to the neutral members of the Commission of Inquiry and Conciliation, Bolivia and Paraguay, Commissioners for Mexico, Colombia, Uruguay, Cuba and the United States of America, to prepare and submit, in a friendly spirit, such plans for the settlement of the fundamental question between Bolivia and Paraguay (Paraguay and Bolivia) concerning the Chaco, as they might think appropriate in order to prevent new conflicts and to establish conciliation on firm and permanent bases. The reply of Your Excellencies and that of Their Excellencies the Commissioners for Bolivia (Paraguay), together with my identical notes acknowledging receipt thereof on behalf of the neutral members, were read into the Minutes of the Plenary Meeting held by the Commission on July 2.[52]

After careful consideration of the problem with the interested Delegations, and their respective statements concerning the matter, we, the neutral Commissioners, have reached the conclusion that it is not possible, at the present time, to reconcile the divergent viewpoints of the parties to the controversy through a formula for direct settlement, and they have empowered me to submit to Your Excellencies the draft of a "Convention of Arbitration" and of a "Supplementary Protocol", attached hereto, with the request that you

[50] See note from the chairman of the Commission to the Delegations of Bolivia and Paraguay, August 31, 1929, *infra.*
[51] Transmitted to the Department by the Secretary General of the Commission on September 5.
[52] See letter dated July 10, 1929, from the chairman of the Commission to the Secretary of State, p. 863.

be kind enough to bring them to the attention of your Government, for appropriate decision.

In view of the fact that, as provided in the Protocol of January 3, 1929, the term for the work of the Commission will come to an end on September 13, we, the neutral Commissioners, express the hope that the Government of Bolivia (Paraguay) will be kind enough to transmit to us its decision with regard to the drafts attached hereto, as soon as may be possible.

I avail myself [etc.]                                    FRANK R. McCOY

[Enclosure 1]

## Proposed Convention of Arbitration

The Governments of Bolivia and Paraguay (Paraguay and Bolivia), represented in the Commission of Inquiry and Conciliation, Bolivia and Paraguay, established in the Protocol signed by their Plenipotentiaries January 3, 1929, desirous of promoting the final settlement of their controversy regarding the Chaco Boreal, have decided to effect the Convention of Arbitration which has been submitted to them by the neutral members of the Commission, to wit:

His Excellency Frank R. McCoy, Commissioner for the United States of America and Chairman of the Commission;

His Excellency Fernando González Roa, Commissioner for Mexico;

His Excellency Raimundo Rivas, Commissioner for Colombia;

His Excellency Guillermo Ruprecht, Commissioner for Uruguay, and

His Excellency Manuel Márquez Sterling, Commissioner for Cuba, for which purpose they have appointed as their Plenipotentiaries the Commissioners for Bolivia, His Excellency Dr. David Alvéstegui and His Excellency Enrique Finot, and the Commissioners for Paraguay, His Excellency Dr. Enrique Bordenave and His Excellency Dr. Francisco C. Chaves, respectively, who, after having deposited their full powers, which were found in good and due form, have agreed on the following:

### ARTICLE I

The Republics of Paraguay and Bolivia submit to arbitration the juridical difference, of a territorial nature, as contended by the first, and of boundaries, as contended by the second, which exists between both nations with regard to the Chaco Boreal.

### ARTICLE II

Within a month, to be reckoned from the time of exchange of ratifications of the present Convention, each of the High Contracting

Parties shall appoint two Arbitrators, of whom only one may be its own national, and shall agree to the designation of a fifth Arbitrator, who shall be the President of the Court. In default of this agreement, each Party shall designate a member of the Permanent Court of Arbitration at The Hague, not its own national, and the two so appointed shall immediately select a fifth Arbitrator hereinbefore mentioned.

All the designations referred to in this Article shall be bestowed upon citizens of any of the Republics of America.

The Court shall meet, for the purpose of its installation, one month after the fifth Arbitrator has been appointed.

## ARTICLE III

The High Contracting Parties shall formulate by common accord a special agreement which shall clearly define the particular subject matter of the controversy.

## ARTICLE IV

Should the High Contracting Parties fail to reach an accord on the agreement referred to in the preceding Article within a term of three months to be reckoned from the date of the exchange of ratifications of this Convention, the agreement shall be formulated by the Court within the three months following. The Court shall determine the form in which it will hear the Parties before formulating the agreement.

## ARTICLE V

It is agreed that, in any event, the following provisions will be included in the formulation of the agreement:

(a) The territory adjudicated to Paraguay by the Award of President Hayes,[53] is excluded from the province of the Court.

(b) In any case and whatever may be the arbitral decision, there shall be adjudicated to Bolivia the port of Bahía Negra, on the Paraguay River, and the territorial extent that the Court may consider appropriate for the free use and protection of said port.

(c) The Court shall decide *ex aequo et bono* all those points which could not be decided by the express application of the terms of the agreement or of principles of law.

## ARTICLE VI

Should the Court render the decision referred to in Article IV, the members constituting it shall cease in their functions; the provision

---

[53] On November 12, 1878; see *Foreign Relations*, 1878, p. 711.

in the foregoing clause shall not be so construed as to prevent the later reappointment by the High Contracting Parties of one or more of said members to the Court.

## ARTICLE VII

The Court shall adopt the provisions concerning nationality and rights acquired by lawful title, by individuals or corporations, national or foreign, in the territory under dispute which might be affected by its Award.

## ARTICLE VIII

The High Contracting Parties agree on the city of . . . . . . . . . as the seat of the meetings of the Arbitrators and of the operation of the Court; they also empower the Court to change its seat, whenever it may deem advisable to so decide.

## ARTICLE IX

The Court is authorized to appoint, from its first meeting, a Secretary and such Staff as it deems indispensable for the discharge of its duties.

## ARTICLE X

In case of death, resignation or incapacity, of one or more of the Arbitrators, and in the case provided for in Article VI, vacancies shall be filled in the same manner as the original appointment.

## ARTICLE XI

The High Contracting Parties shall be represented before the Court by Agents who may be assisted by such counsel and experts as they may deem necessary.

## ARTICLE XII

The decision containing the agreement referred to in Article IV, and the Award fixing the subject matter of the controversy, as set forth in Article I, duly pronounced and notified to the Agents, and in lieu thereof to the Governments, shall be final.

## ARTICLE XIII

The differences which may arise with regard to the interpretation and execution of this Convention and of the decisions of the Court, shall be submitted to the Court itself.

## ARTICLE XIV

The expenses incident to the arbitration shall be borne equally by both High Contracting Parties; each contending Party shall defray the expenses connected with the Arbitrators and the Staff of its exclusive appointment.

## ARTICLE XV

Should the Court be unable to establish a majority of votes, the opinion of the President of the Court shall prevail; but if the scattering of votes were to take place in connection with the decision referred to in Article IV or in connection with the final Award, a new vote shall be taken after the respective Agents have been heard on the point at issue.

## ARTICLE XVI

The Court is empowered to adopt and amend its own rules of procedure by a majority vote of the Commission.

## ARTICLE XVII

The terms established in the procedure, with the exception of those pertaining to the organization of the Court, may be extended, if necessary, by a simple exchange of notes between the High Contracting Parties.

## ARTICLE XVIII

Each High Contracting Party undertakes not to carry out any hostile action against the other as long as the present Convention is in force.

## ARTICLE XIX

The President of the Court shall advise the High Contracting Parties as to the measures of a military nature intended to avoid all kinds of hostilities.

## ARTICLE XX

The present Convention shall be signed in nine original copies which shall be deposited in the Departments of Foreign Affairs of the nations constituting the Commission of Inquiry and Conciliation, Bolivia and Paraguay.

The High Contracting Parties agree to effect the exchange of ratifications of the present Convention, with the least possible delay, through their diplomatic representatives accredited in Washington, who will communicate the respective Act and the instruments of ratification, in a joint note, to the Department of Foreign Affairs of the neutral countries represented in the Commission.

In witness whereof, the Plenipotentiaries of Bolivia and Paraguay (Paraguay and Bolivia) have signed the present Convention in nine copies, and have hereunto affixed their seals, under the auspices of the Commission of Inquiry and Conciliation, Bolivia and Paraguay, whose members also have set their hands and seals thereto.

Done in the City of Washington, District of Columbia, United States of America, this . . . . . day of the month of . . . . . . ., 1929.

[Enclosure 2]

## Proposed Supplementary Protocol

Whereas the Governments of Bolivia and Paraguay (Paraguay and Bolivia) have signed today in this City of Washington a Convention of Arbitration, under the auspices of the Commission of Inquiry and Conciliation, Bolivia and Paraguay, their Plenipotentiaries have agreed upon the following supplementary Protocol which shall be considered as an integral part of said Convention:

Article 1. The High Contracting Parties agree to extend the life of the present Commission of Inquiry and Conciliation, Bolivia and Paraguay, until the moment of the installation of the Court, for the purpose of deciding the differences which may arise between the Parties concerning the interpretation of the Convention and such other measures of conciliation as it may deem pertinent. The Commission shall recess, and during this period all decisions may be taken by mail or by cable, the Secretariat General to poll the votes and to make an official record of the decisions in such case.

Article 2. The High Contracting Parties will bear an equal share of the expenses of the Secretariat General, the organization thereof to be determined by the Chairman of the Commission of Inquiry and Conciliation, Bolivia and Paraguay.

Article 3. The Chairman may call a meeting of the Commission if conditions so require.

Article 4. The High Contracting Parties agree that upon the issuance of the Award by the Court they shall proceed to organize a Delimitation Commission composed of three expert topographical engineers or surveyors, one of whom shall be appointed by the Bolivian Government, one by the Paraguayan Government, and the third, who shall be the President of the Commission, by the Geographical Society of (Buenos Aires, Rio de Janeiro or New York), to determine the course of the boundary line in accordance with the provisions of the Award. The President of the Commission shall not be a national of either High Contracting Party.

Each High Contracting Party and the Geographical Society appointing a member of the Delimitation Commission shall appoint a

Deputy Commissioner who may be called upon in case of need, to take the place of the member of the Commission whose alternate he is.

The members of the Delimitation Commission shall be appointed within one month from the date of the Award of the Court. In the event of death or resignation of any member of the Commission, the vacancy shall be filled within one month in the manner in which the original appointment was made.

In the course of its work in the field, the Delimitation Commission may agree upon such compensations as may be necessary in order to demarcate the boundary line in a logical and natural manner.

The decisions of the Delimitation Commission shall be final and binding upon the two High Contracting Parties.

The Delimitation Commission shall be empowered to adopt and amend its own rules of procedure and to decide the manner in which it will carry out the task with which it may be entrusted by the Court.

ARTICLE 5. The High Contracting Parties will endeavor not to defer the exchange of ratifications of the Convention of Arbitration more than six months to be reckoned from the date of its signature.

ARTICLE 6. This Protocol shall be signed in nine original copies and will become effective on the date of its signature by the Plenipotentiaries of Bolivia and Paraguay (Paraguay and Bolivia).

In witness whereof the Plenipotentiaries of Bolivia and Paraguay (Paraguay and Bolivia) have signed the present Protocol in nine copies and affixed hereunto their seals, under the auspices of the Commission of Inquiry and Conciliation, Bolivia and Paraguay, whose members have also set their hands and seals thereto.

In the City of Washington, District of Columbia, United States of America, this . . . . . day of the month of . . . . . . . 1929.

---

724.3415/684 : Telegram

*The Minister in Paraguay (Kreeck) to the Secretary of State*

ASUNCIÓN, September 6, 1929—1 p. m.
[Received 8:40 p. m.]

74. This morning the Minister for Foreign Affairs asked me to inquire informally and confidentially of General McCoy what procedure is necessary for Paraguay to obtain a prolongation of the negotiations. The Minister is not favorable to the Argentine Government or the League of Nations interference for he believes a solution can be found in Washington. . . .

KREECK

724.3415/684 : Telegram

*The Secretary of State to the Minister in Paraguay (Kreeck)*

WASHINGTON, September 7, 1929—8 p. m.

36. Your telegram No. 74, September 6. General McCoy requests you to be informed that he knows of no suggestion any neutral Commissioner can properly make to the Paraguayan Government for obtaining a prolongation of negotiations if by that phrase the Minister of Foreign Affairs refers to an extension of the life of the Commission. General McCoy points out that the Commission had its origin in the will of the Paraguayan and Bolivian Governments who concluded the Protocol of January 3 establishing the Commission for the purposes specifically set forth in the Protocol. He feels that either of the two Governments therefore can initiate steps looking to continuance of the functions of the present or of a new group of Commissioners for any purpose growing out of the controversy. But the present Commission goes out of existence under the Protocol on September 13 and can act prior to that time merely as a channel of communication so far as an eventual extension of the Commission's life is concerned. It would seem that the Delegation of either Government may properly be employed for apprising the Commission and through it the other Government of the wishes of the initiating Government.

STIMSON

------

724.3415/685 : Telegram

*The Minister in Paraguay (Kreeck) to the Secretary of State*

ASUNCIÓN, September 8, 1929—4 p. m.
[Received September 9—2:08 a. m.]

77. Minister for Foreign Affairs informs me he has requested the diplomatic representatives of Mexico, Uruguay and Cuba in Asunción to make known to their Governments by cable that the Paraguayan Government desires an extension of the life of the Commission that the negotiations may continue and the controversy be settled. The Minister states that his Government sent instructions more than a week or more [ago?] to Dr. Bordenave to request an extension of the Commission's life and receiving no reply acted as above mentioned to make certain that the negotiations will not terminate September 13th.

KREECK

724.3415/714½

*The Bolivian Delegation to the Chairman of the Commission of Inquiry and Conciliation (McCoy)* [54]

[Translation]

WASHINGTON, September 9, 1929.

MR. CHAIRMAN: We have the honor to refer to the note which Your Excellency saw fit to place in our hands on August 31st, last, informing us that "after a careful consideration of the problem with the interested Delegations, and their respective statements concerning the matter, we, the neutral Commissioners, have reached the conclusion that it is not possible, at the present time, to reconcile the divergent viewpoints of the Parties to the controversy through a formula for direct settlement", adding that Their Excellencies the said Delegates had authorized Your Excellency to submit to us the draft Convention on Arbitration and the draft Supplementary Protocol which you also delivered to us with the request that we bring them to the attention of our Government "for appropriate decision".

Although on that occasion we were able to inform Your Excellency that we did not deem it in order to receive a premature proposal, contrary to the terms of the oral agreement with which Your Excellency is familiar, according to which any proposal for settlement could not be formally made without previous consultation of and acceptance by the Parties, we refrained from formulating any objection, because of the confidence with which the attitude of Their Excellencies the neutral Delegates has always inspired us, and as a matter of courtesy to Your Excellency we did not hesitate to receive the above mentioned documents, which were transmitted immediately to the Government of Bolivia.

In consequence and by virtue of instructions which we have just received, we beg Your Excellency to inform Their Excellencies the neutral Delegates of the following statements:

1. The Government of Bolivia renews, on this occasion, its invariable adherence to the principle of arbitration as an effective means of settling international controversies.

2. It expresses its willingness to settle its territorial differences, with the Republic of Paraguay by such juridical means, and is of the opinion, in this connection, that the bases for arbitration cannot be other than those formulated by the Argentine observer, Mr. Isidoro Ruiz Moreno, at the Buenos Aires Conference, and which read verbatim as follows: [55]

"1. That the settlement of the controversy should be based upon the *uti possidetis* of 1810.

[54] Transmitted to the Department by the Secretary General of the Commission on September 16, 1929.
[55] See *Proceedings of the Commission of Inquiry and Conciliation, Bolivia and Paraguay*, p. 403.

"2. That, in the event that it proves impossible to arrive at a direct understanding, it will be necessary to determine the bases of legal arbitration.

"3. That the advances that may have been made by either country have created a *de facto* situation that confers no right and that cannot be submitted to the arbitrator in order to support their respective contentions."

3. It maintains in all its force the reservation made to the General Treaty of Inter-American Arbitration signed in Washington on January 5, 1929,[56] which reads as follows:

"Second. It is also understood that, for the submission to arbitration of a territorial controversy or dispute, the zone to which the said arbitration is to apply must be previously determined in the arbitral agreement".

The foregoing statements having been made, the Government of Bolivia has charged us to inform Your Excellency, so that you may in turn so inform Their Excellencies the neutral Delegates, that the fourth and fifth articles of the Convention of Arbitration which has been submitted to its consideration, being contrary to the reservation previously made by Bolivia, are also at variance with all the international precedents on arbitration and embody a principle that is destructive of the right of sovereignty, since it does not place any limitation whatever upon any claims which Paraguay may wish to make to the territory of Bolivia. There is surely no country that will submit to an arbitration in which the specific matter to be covered by the award is not clearly determined.

In this respect there is, furthermore, a very valuable antecedent: the Protocol signed in Buenos Aires on April 22, 1927, in Article IV of which the Governments of Bolivia and of Paraguay agreed to the following:[57]

"IV. Should it prove impossible to arrive at an agreement respecting the definite determination of the international frontier, the Plenipotentiaries will state the reasons for the disagreement and fix the limits of the zone which will form the subject of the decision of an Arbitral Tribunal to be appointed by mutual agreement."

On the other hand, the exclusion in favor of Paraguay of the zone covered by the Award of President Hayes, while no zone was excluded in favor of Bolivia, signifies the establishment of an unjustified inequality and is equivalent to prejudging the validity of a title, invoked by Paraguay and challenged by Bolivia, and the weighing of which is incumbent upon the arbitrator. There does not seem to be, and in fact there is not, any strict logical relation between this stipulation and those contained in the third and fourth articles of the draft.

Finally, it is necessary to record that the return of Puerto Pacheco to Bolivia, unlawfully retained by Paraguay since 1888, in which year it was occupied by force, constitutes an act of reparation, which should

[56] *Ante,* p. 659.
[57] *Proceedings of the Commission of Inquiry and Conciliation, Bolivia and Paraguay,* p. 270.

be effected immediately, but which is not a solution of the principal controversy which, as is known, includes territory situated much further to the south of said port.

In view of the considerations above set forth, the Government of Bolivia has instructed us to express to Your Excellency that it would have been pleased to be able to respond to the generous and persevering efforts, thus far made with such marked disinterestedness and impartiality by Their Excellencies the neutral Delegates, by accepting the bases for arbitration contained in the Convention which they were good enough to draft, but it regrets that it is unable to do so owing to the well known antecedents recalled and to the necessity of safeguarding the high interests of our country.

We avail ourselves [etc.]

DAVID ALVÉSTEGUI          ENRIQUE FINOT

---

724.3415/714½

*The Paraguayan Delegation to the Chairman of the Commission of Inquiry and Conciliation (McCoy)* [58]

[Translation]

WASHINGTON, September 9, 1929.

MR. CHAIRMAN: We had the honor to receive, in due time, the note dated August 31, 1929, with which Your Excellency kindly sent us a proposal for an Arbitral Convention and one for a Supplementary Protocol prepared by the neutral members of the Commission over which Your Excellency presides, in accordance with the power granted to them by the Delegations of Paraguay and of Bolivia.

Duly authorized by our Government, the Delegates of Paraguay have the honor to announce to Your Excellency the following points of view regarding the aforesaid proposals:

Once again and taking into account the stage which the Commission has now reached, after self-denying and praiseworthy efforts to find methods for a solution of a long-standing and grave boundary question, Paraguay reaffirms her sincere and firm devotion to the principle of arbitration as a means for settling international conflicts.

Since the Commission began its work, our attitude as Delegates for Paraguay has been directed, even though it became necessary at times to curb expressions of very deep feeling, toward a loyal cooperation in the intelligent and noble efforts of the neutral Commissioners to harmonize interests and to find just formulae in connection with the controversy which was the object of their study.

In that same spirit we will express the thought of our Government

---

[58] Transmitted to the Department by the Secretary General of the Commission on September 16, 1929.

regarding the proposals which have been submitted to it, trusting that this thought may be judged as the expression of the state of mind of a people which, conscious of its duties and responsibilities, is a fervent promoter of the peace and brotherhood of the Continent, with no limitations other than those set by its dignity as a nation and its faith in its own destiny.

Article V, subhead a), of the draft Arbitral Convention establishes that: "The territory adjudicated to Paraguay by the Award of President Hayes, is excluded from the province of the Court." We are pleased to note, in the insertion of this clause, an unchallengeable acknowledgment of a *de facto* and *de jure* condition. The territory submitted to the arbitration of President Hayes legitimately belongs to Paraguay, by reason of her historical titles which constitute the immovable foundations of the Award, according to the pronouncement itself, and by reason of the peaceful, uninterrupted, patent, and undisturbed possession which Paraguay has exercised for more than fifty years and still continues to exercise over the zone adjudicated to her by the Award since it was announced.

The spirit of the clause referred to conforms with the fact, only, of the existence of a legal and just title, consolidated by possessions, both of which elements are of insurmountable force in legalizing the domain.

And we would have nothing to add to the foregoing observations, if it were not that the subhead b) of the said Article V introduces a modification as to the spirit which no doubt inspired the draft of the preceding subhead.

"In any case and whatever may be the arbitral decision, there shall be adjudicated to Bolivia the port of Bahía Negra, on the Paraguay River, and the territorial extent that the Court may consider appropriate for the free use and protection of said port", reads the aforesaid subhead b).

Is it possible to explain, on the basis of the previous subhead, a reason which justifies this amendment?

Has Bolivia by any chance such a title, juridically inspired, as is suggested by the verdict, and which would assert her rights to the North of the Chaco, or can she claim a restful, manifest or long-lasting possession of same?

We wish to maintain respectfully that, aside from her demands, the bases of which required the preceding study, we do not deem substantiated the reason which, recommend[s] a cession, in advance, to Bolivia of a part of the territory to be submitted for arbitration in accordance with the decisions of the Court.

In addition to the preceding opinion, would it not be appropriate to meditate on the extent of the authority which would be granted the Court if it be decided that it may also award to Bolivia whatever territorial extension it deems adequate for the development and protection of a ceded port?

The uncertainty as regards territorial sovereignty is a factor which should be attentively and thoroughly considered, above all because, as in the present case, it might eventually become a cause for renewed and pitiful complications and anxieties.

If the criterion which prevailed in behalf of an Award, in advance, of Bahía Negra be the actual or assumed need on the part of Bolivia of a gateway, our country might in all justice invoke her own requirements, together with a desire to assert her titles in their entirety.

All these reasons have impelled the Government of Paraguay to make the respective pertinent objections and to suggest some changes in the terms of the draft Convention, always inspired by the desire to cooperate in the efforts which the Commission is so earnestly making to bring about a solution.

In that sense, the Government of Paraguay, extremely desirous of finding a solution for our boundary differences with Bolivia, begs leave to suggest the following bases:

First—That the question be decided in two consecutive juridical arbitrations stipulated in one and the same Treaty. The first arbitration to determine the specific matter of the controversy, that is to say the zone in dispute; and the second, to decide who has a better right to the same.

Second—The territory adjudicated to Paraguay by the Award of President Hayes is at the outset to be eliminated from all arbitral jurisdiction.

Third—By reason of the first arbitration, proceedings are to be instituted before the Arbitrator, in the course of which the Parties shall assert their respective points of view by submitting memorials, records and evidence.

Fourth—With all those types of evidence in view, the Arbitrator shall decide without recourse, establishing the boundary lines of the zone which has been declared to be in dispute. The Award shall be accompanied by a statement of the reasons therefor.

Fifth—By reason of the second arbitration, which shall be undertaken as soon as a decision has been rendered in the first arbitration, ample proceedings shall be instituted in the course of which the Parties shall present memorials, records and evidence, with a view to demonstrate their better right. The Award rendered shall be without recourse, as in the previous case, and shall set forth its juridical grounds.

Sixth—The Judge shall be the same Arbitrator who rendered the decision in the first arbitration, or some other person, as may be agreed upon.

The most important bases for the draft of an Arbitral Convention thus summed up, the Delegation of Paraguay takes the liberty of suggesting, in the name of its Government, the advisability of reasonably extending the period fixed for the labors of the Commission by the Protocol of January 3rd of this year, and would like to request that Your Excellency submit for the study of the Commission the consideration of such a measure.

In the absence of an adequate study of the same and commensurate with the importance of their contents, the formulae prepared by the neutral Commissioners after careful thought and arduous labor and submitted on the eve of the termination of the period fixed by the Protocol would not produce the effect contemplated. The term thus extended, the Commission could assign itself the time necessary for considering, together with the formulae already before it, the projects or suggestions which are submitted and to which said formulae have given rise.

No one knows better than the Commissioners what efforts have so far been made, nor is anyone in a better position to realize the unquestionable need there is for these efforts to be deservedly crowned with success, in an atmosphere foreign to the haste induced by the briefness of time, in the case of a matter the magnitude and complexity of which would justify any delay.

We avail ourselves [etc.]

FRANCISCO C. CHAVES    ENRIQUE BORDENAVE

––––––––––––––––––

724.3415/714½

*The Chairman of the Commission of Inquiry and Conciliation (McCoy) to the Delegations of Bolivia and Paraguay* [59]

[Translation]

WASHINGTON, September 12, 1929.

EXCELLENCIES: I have had the honor to receive the note of Your Excellencies and that of Their Excellencies the Commissioners for Paraguay (Bolivia), both dated September 9 of this year, wherein you (they) were good enough to answer the note I addressed to you (them) dated August 31, last, transmitting to you (them) in the name of the neutral Commissioners a proposal for a Convention of Arbitration and another for a Supplementary Protocol.

Their Excellencies the Commissioners for Bolivia are good enough to state that the Government of Bolivia renews its adherence to the principle of arbitration; states that it is disposed to settle by that juridical method its territorial controversy with the Republic of Paraguay on the bases proposed by the Argentine observer during the Conferences of Buenos Aires; maintains in full force the reservation formulated to the General Treaty of Inter-American Arbitration

––––––––––––––––––

[59] Transmitted to the Department by the Secretary General of the Commission on September 16, 1929.

signed at Washington and states that Articles IV and V of the draft Arbitration Convention are not in accordance with international precedents regarding arbitration and contain a principle destructive of the right of sovereignty since they place no limit whatever on the claims which Paraguay might wish to make against the territory of Bolivia; considers that the exclusion in favor of Paraguay of the zone covered by the Hayes Award, while no zone whatever is included in favor of Bolivia, signifies the establishment of an unjustifiable inequality and is equivalent to prejudgment as to the validity of a title invoked by Paraguay and challenged by Bolivia, a title the validity of which it is incumbent upon the arbiter to weigh; establishes that the return to Bolivia of Puerto Pacheco constitutes an act of reparation which should be effected immediately, and ends by stating that the Government of Bolivia regrets being unable to accept the bases of arbitration in the draft Convention.

For their part, Their Excellencies, the Commissioners for Paraguay, say that their Government reaffirms its sincere and firm devotion to the principle of arbitration as a means of settling international conflicts; that they are pleased to see set forth in subhead *a*), Article V, recognition of a *de facto* and *de jure* condition that is not open to objections namely, that the territory adjudicated to Paraguay by the Hayes Award is excluded from the competence of the Court; that they take the liberty, respectfully, of asserting that the adjudication in advance to Bolivia of the port of Bahía Negra means the cession of a part of the territory which can be submitted to arbitration; that the Government of Paraguay suggests submitting the question to two arbitrations of law in succession, and stipulated in one and the same treaty, the first of which would determine the specific matter in controversy, that is to say, the zone of litigation, while the second would decide who had the better right thereto, excluding from the competence of the arbitrator the territory adjudicated to Paraguay by the Hayes Award; and that, in order to give sufficient time duly to consider so important a matter, the Delegation of Paraguay in the name of its Government begs leave to indicate the convenience, as a matter of prudence, of extending the term fixed by the Protocol of January 3 of this year for the operation of the Commission.

The neutral Commissioners have taken note of both documents with deep satisfaction because from their contents there is evidence of a conformity of principle on the fundamental points and, moreover, because the said documents are sufficiently enlightening to the neutral Commissioners for any study of the suggestions made by the Parties with a view to removing obstacles that stand in the way of their acceptance of the proposed arbitral process.

Before going into the details of the matter, I desire to ask Your

Excellencies to be so good as to take into consideration the following statements:

1. The neutral Commissioners have intended to place the Parties on a footing of absolute equality, both with regard to the study of the fundamental points and with regard to the mere procedure followed in prior negotiations.

2. It has never been the purpose of the neutral Commissioners to prejudge the territorial or boundary question and, in that respect, when they have referred to the territory which was the subject matter of the Hayes Award and to the port of Bahía Negra, they have done so without expressing any opinion as to the extent and the force of the titles alleged by the two nations. What induced the neutral Commissioners to consider these aspects of the question were motives of a completely different order than juridical, as the juridical aspects will have to be contemplated by the arbitrators.

The neutral Commissioners declare that, under the Protocol, there exists no power to alter the juridical conditions existing in the Chaco. Both in the documents related to the principal question and in those referring to conciliation, mentioning the reestablishment of the state of things in the Chaco on the same footing as prior to December 5, there has been carefully avoided any prejudgment as to the juridical validity of the situation, both with reference to the facts and the diplomatic instruments.

3. The neutral Commissioners presented the foregoing proposals to the Delegations in view of the fact that, as Your Excellencies are aware, the claims of both Parties were, for the moment irreconcilable and, therefore, closed the road to any solution by a direct agreement.

Turning to the main part of the two notes, the neutral Commissioners beg leave to point out the following:

1. Both nations renew their invariable adherence to the principle of arbitration as a means for settling the pending question as to the sovereignty over territories in the Chaco Boreal. The difficulty lies, then, in agreeing upon the form for giving practical application to the principle accepted.

2. The two Delegations make formal criticism of subheads a) and b) of Article V which refer to the territory adjudicated to Paraguay by the Hayes Award and to the adjudication of the port of Bahía Negra to Bolivia. There is attributed, in good faith, to those subheads an intention which was not meant to be given them by the neutral Commissioners, who take this opportunity to clear up any misunderstanding based upon the supposition that it was intended to enter upon a determination of the territory or boundary litigation. Consequently, since these subheads do not meet with the favor of either of the two Parties, the neutral Commissioners believe that a cause of disagreement would be removed by simply suppressing the said subheads.

3. The Bolivian Delegation reiterates its adherence to the bases for arbitration contained in the formula of the Argentine observer during the Conferences of Buenos Aires, expressed as follows:

"1. That the settlement of the controversy should be based upon the *uti possidetis* of 1810.

"2. That, in the event that it proves impossible to arrive at a direct understanding, it will be necessary to determine the bases of legal arbitration.

"3. That the advances that may have been made by either country have created a *de facto* situation that confers no right and that cannot be submitted to the arbitrator in order to support their respective contentions."

As these bases were accepted in principle by the Delegation of Paraguay at Buenos Aires, as appears on pages 205, 212 and 213 of the "Libro Blanco" (White Book) of the Government of Paraguay (Asunción 1928), the neutral Commissioners consider that there is no obstacle in the way of substituting for the subheads which are eliminated from Article V, the first and third points in the suggestion of the Argentine observer.

In reiterating the reservation formulated by its Government to the General Treaty of Inter-American Arbitration signed at Washington, the Delegation of Bolivia expresses its point of view by citing Article IV of the Protocol signed at Buenos Aires on April 22, 1927, by the Plenipotentiaries of Paraguay and of Bolivia, as follows:

"IV. Should it prove impossible to arrive at an agreement respecting the definite determination of the international frontier, the Plenipotentiaries will state the reasons for the disagreement and fix the limits of the zone which will form the subject of the decision of an Arbitral Tribunal to be appointed by mutual agreement."

Since that Protocol was signed by the two Governments, there is no obstacle to inserting substantially the said Article IV in the draft Convention, changing Article III of the same draft which refers to the formulation of the special *compromis*.

The fundamental objections of the two contending Governments having thus been met, the only questions which might divide them relate to the extent of the provisions in the formula of the Argentine observer and those which refer to the nature of the difference, since Bolivia maintains that it is a territorial question and Paraguay that it is a boundary question, these being aspects of the controversy which the neutral Commissioners deem appropriate for arbitral consideration, because they involve the study of questions of fact and of law belonging to a judicial determination by means of an organism especially constituted for that purpose.

The expressions of approval of both nations for the principle of arbitration give the neutral Commissioners hope that the two nations will entertain, for the natural methods leading towards the arbitral solution of the controversy, the same approval which they entertain for the application of the principle to the main question, because it would be inexplicable why the nations should be in agreement as to settling their differences by an Award and should refuse an appropriate *compromis* or, in case they cannot agree on such *compromis*, should decline to submit the difference to the same arbiters, as stipulated in the Treaty of Washington which bears the signature of the Delegate for Bolivia. It is to be noted that Bolivia does not consider that its reservation closes the road to arbitration, inasmuch as by a circular to its Legations abroad, dated January 8, 1929, that Government contrasts its attitude with that of the Government of Paraguay, the latter having made a reservation to the application of the Treaty of Washington which, according to His Excellency the Minister for Foreign Affairs of Bolivia, "will constitute an insurmountable obstacle to the arbitral solution which Bolivia desires", an insurmountable obstacle which has already been removed by the statement of His Excellency the President of Paraguay, in his message to the Honorable National Congress in April of the present year.

Nevertheless, in a desire to contemplate to the last extremity the possibility that the Government of Bolivia may not wish to resort to an arbitral Court without first agreeing to the determination of the zone which will be the subject matter of the arbitration, and the fact that the Government of Paraguay may not agree on the nature of the other elements which must be considered, the neutral Commissioners believe that the insertion of a clause giving an optional character to the further procedure for formulating a *compromis* would be satisfactory and, to this end, they beg leave to submit a provision which would require, as is natural, some slight changes in the phraseology of other Articles of the draft Convention, as follows:

"When the *compromis* has been formulated by the Court, the Parties remain free to state whether the said *compromis* is satisfactory or not. In the former case the procedure shall be subject to the stipulations agreed on in this Convention. In the contrary case the Party which may not be satisfied shall have power to withdraw from the Court, the procedure thus being closed."

The obstacles being thus removed and all doubtful points elucidated, the neutral Commissioners reiterate their proposal that the controversy be submitted to arbitration, there being introduced in the draft Convention and Protocol which were submitted by them such changes as may be necessary to make them acceptable to the two Parties.

The neutral Commissioners make this new suggestion in the most friendly spirit and inspired by sentiments of the greatest cordiality with no other thought than the welfare of two peoples who, because they are a part of the American family, have interests as dear to them as if they were their own; they cherish the hope that their new endeavor will be received with the same friendly spirit that induces them to make it and that the two Governments will deem it another proof of the intense solicitude for the peace of the Continent which dominates the American peoples.

I take [etc.] FRANK R. McCoy

724.3415/697a : Telegram

*The Secretary of State to the Minister in Paraguay (Kreeck)* [60]

WASHINGTON, September 13, 1929—1 p. m.

42. Please address a note to the Government to which you are accredited embodying the following message from the Secretary of State to the Minister for Foreign Affairs:

"It affords me great pleasure to congratulate Your Excellency on the notable success achieved by the Commission of Inquiry and Conciliation, Bolivia and Paraguay. The successful accomplishment of the mission entrusted to this body in effecting conciliation on the unfortunate incidents which took place last December [61] has been due largely to the efficacious manner in which Your Excellency's Government and its Delegation on the Commission have interpreted the constant solicitude of all the American Republics represented by the five neutral Commissioners for the peaceful adjustment of any controversy arising among them. This achievement marks an epoch in the historical development of conciliation as a practical method for advancing the cause of Pan American peace."

You will add that the Government of the United States has been informed of the view expressed by the Government of Paraguay in its note of September 9 answering the note of August 31 from the Chairman of the Commission submitting a proposal for a settlement of the fundamental controversy by arbitration that the work of the Commission should "have a worthy consummation in an atmosphere removed from the haste occasioned by shortness of time in a matter the magnitude and complexity of which justify any delay." The Government of the United States will be glad to tender to the two Governments directly interested the services of its Commissioner and of the Secretary General in a continued effort to assist the two interested Governments in finding an adequate solution of the fundamental controversy.

STIMSON

---

724.3415/696b : Telegram

*The Secretary of State to the Chargé in Mexico (Johnson)* [62]

WASHINGTON, September 13, 1929—1 p. m.

468. Following telegram has been sent to the American Legations at La Paz and Asunción today:

[Here follows the text of telegram No. 42, September 13, 1 p. m. to the Minister in Paraguay, printed *supra*.]

---

[60] The same, *mutatis mutandis*, on the same date to the Chargé in Bolivia as telegram No. 51.
[61] See telegram No. 50, September 12, to the Chargé in Bolivia, p. 860.
[62] The same, *mutatis mutandis*, on the same date to the diplomatic representatives in Colombia (No. 47), Cuba (No. 106), and Uruguay (No. 17).

Please inform the Government to which you are accredited of the foregoing action and express this Government's hope that the Government to which you are accredited will make a similar offer to the Governments of the two interested countries with a view to assuring the continued cooperation of the neutral Commissioners in assisting the two interested Governments to find a solution of their fundamental controversy.

You will bear in mind the fact that the Commission of Inquiry and Conciliation yesterday unanimously passed a resolution recording the effecting of conciliation between Bolivia and Paraguay on the incidents of last December.[63] You will have in mind also the fact that both interested Governments have accepted the principle of arbitration as being applicable to the fundamental controversy between them and differ only as to the details of its application. In a note delivered to the Delegations of the interested countries last night by the Chairman of the Commission on behalf of the neutral Commissioners these details of application are discussed and the neutral Commissioners have hope that further negotiation would assure a settlement.

STIMSON

724.3415/704 : Telegram

*The Chargé in Bolivia (Hibbard) to the Secretary of State*

[Paraphrase]

LA PAZ, September 17, 1929—9 a. m.

[Received 1:25 p. m.]

68. Legation's No. 66, September 16, 2 p. m.[64] Yesterday afternoon the Minister for Foreign Affairs read to me the text of the note sent to the Bolivian Minister in the United States for delivery to the Secretary of State.[65] The Minister for Foreign Affairs added that Bolivia desired a direct understanding with Paraguay and he thought this would be possible with a renewal of diplomatic relations between Bolivia and Paraguay. Should it be impossible to reach a direct agreement, perhaps the zone to be arbitrated could be decided upon and another arbitral commission set up. Should this fail, the matter would be referred to a commission similar to the commission just terminated. In no case would the Government of Bolivia resort to belligerent action since Bolivia fully realized the folly of such a course. The Minister for Foreign Affairs stated that the Government of Bolivia felt that the Commission in Washington had finished its duties under the protocol and that Bolivia

---

[63] See telegram No. 50, September 12, to the Chargé in Bolivia, p. 860.
[64] Not printed.
[65] *Infra.*

had previously stated that such recommendations as the neutral Commissioners might make on the settlement of the basic controversy could have only an informal character. However, in the coming negotiations with Paraguay, Bolivia would be guided by the opinión of the neutral Commissioners of the last Conference. The Minister for Foreign Affairs entertains the hope that Bolivia and Paraguay can reach an agreement as satisfactory as Peru and Chile. It is quite evident that Bolivia does not wish the present Conference to be prolonged. This, I believe, is due to the present domestic political situation, as well as the feeling that an arrangement more satisfactory to Bolivia can thus be obtained. . . .

HIBBARD

724.3415/768

*The Chargé in Bolivia (Hibbard) to the Secretary of State*

No. 242                                       LA PAZ, September 17, 1929.
                                              [Received October 8.]

SIR: I have the honor to refer to my telegram No. 66, September 16, 2 p. m.,[66] quoting a portion of a note received from the Bolivian Foreign Office in reply to one which I sent in accordance with the Department's instructions contained in its telegram No. 42, September 13, 1 p. m., and to transmit herewith a copy and translation of the note partially quoted in the telegram above referred to.

I have [etc.]                          FREDERICK P. HIBBARD

[Enclosure—Translation]

*The Bolivian Minister for Foreign Affairs and Worship (Chávez) to the American Chargé (Hibbard)*

D/P No. 364                                   LA PAZ, September 14, 1929.

MR. CHARGÉ D'AFFAIRES: I take pleasure in answering your kind note No. 104 of yesterday's date, received today, by which Your Excellency transmitted the telegraphic message from the Secretary of State of the United States of America, His Excellency, Henry L. Stimson, in regard to the happy result reached by the Commission of Investigation and Conciliation, stating that the success of the mission entrusted to that body is due largely to the efficacious manner in which the Government of Bolivia and its Delegates in Washington have interpreted the constant solicitude and interest of all the American Republics, represented by the five neutral Commissioners who have peacefully adjusted the controversy between Bolivia

---

[66] Not printed; the full text of the note which it quoted was transmitted to the Department in telegram No. 69, September 18, noon, but that text has not been used since some parts of the telegram were garbled.

and Paraguay, an achievement which marks an epoch in the historical development of conciliation as a practical method for advancing the cause of Pan American peace. You add that you have been instructed by your Government to say that, as there exists a proposition for the settlement of the fundamental controversy, the work of the Commission should have a worthy consummation in an atmosphere removed from the haste occasioned by shortness of time in a matter the magnitude and complexity of which justify any delay.. And you conclude stating that the Government of the United States will be glad to offer to the two Governments directly interested the services of its Commissioner and of the Secretary General "in a continued effort to assist the two interested Governments in finding an adequate solution of the fundamental controversy."

In reply I am pleased to inform you that the Government of Bolivia appreciates fully the congratulations of His Excellency, the Secretary of State of the United States of America, both for the success of the Commission of Inquiry and Conciliation, and for the manner in which this Government and its Delegates contributed to the notable success achieved by that Commission.

The Government of Bolivia feels that the Commission has completely fulfilled its duty under the terms of the Protocol of January 3rd of this year and has therefore instructed its delegates in the sense that the friendly and informal propositions for the settlement of the fundamental controversy, to which the President of the Commission referred in his note to our delegates of May 31 to which the note of August 31, last, is only a consequence, should be differently [*deferentemente:* deferentially] heard and studied without this meaning "the modification or weakening" of said protocol.

As in accordance with the bases of conciliation accepted by Bolivia and Paraguay, diplomatic relations between the two countries are shortly to be renewed, the Government of Bolivia will be very pleased to take into consideration the esteemed suggestions of the Commission of neutrals at the time of renewing the negotiations to which the last Conference of Buenos Aires referred.

While the new peaceful efforts which the Government of Bolivia is disposed to carry through are being realized, by means of its Foreign Office, I have the honor to present to the Government of the United States of America, through Your Excellency, the expression of the most grateful appreciation of the Government of Bolivia for the eminent services which the illustrious President of the Commission of Inquiry and Conciliation, General McCoy, gave to the cause of American peace.

I avail myself [etc.] F. VACA CHÁVEZ

724.3415/705 : Telegram

*The Minister in Paraguay (Kreeck) to the Secretary of State*

ASUNCIÓN, September 17, 1929—4 p. m.
[Received September 18—2 : 37 a. m.]

88. Minister for Foreign Affairs asks that I officially notify the United States Government that the Paraguayan Government accepts with great pleasure the good offices tendered by the United States in its note of September 14th,[67] and that the official note of acceptance will follow.[68]  Acceptances have been given to the other neutral countries with the exception of Uruguay which until fifteenth has not offered to continue its good offices.

. . . . . . . . .

KREECK

---

724.3415/704½

*Memorandum by the Assistant Secretary of State (White)*

[WASHINGTON,] September 17, 1929.

The Bolivian Minister telephoned and said that he had a message from his Government which he would like to deliver to the Secretary and wanted to know if the Secretary could see him before the appointment which is already arranged for 10 : 45 on Thursday.  I told the Minister that the Secretary was frightfully busy and I was afraid that he would not be able to do so and asked if I could see him in his stead.  The Minister came down and read me the telegram from his Government and left me an English translation thereof reading as follows :

"Lay before Secretary of State that the Bolivian Government understands spectacular conferences have the inconvenience of exciting national spirit, it being preferable to promote negotiations that could thrive within resumption of relations such as has happened short time ago between Chile and Peru.

"In discreet atmosphere offices of chancellors it will be possible to attempt again direct settlement on mutual convenient bases which parties must study calmly.

"In any case we will count help friendly Governments in accordance diplomatic precedents already established, and specially that of the Government of that great republic.  These thoughts have inspired our answer of day before yesterday to the American Legation."

F[RANCIS] W[HITE]

---

[67] See telegram No. 42, September 13, 1 p. m., to the Minister in Paraguay, p. 892.
[68] Transmitted to the Department by the Minister as an enclosure to his despatch No. 916, September 23; neither printed.

724.3415/713

*Memorandum by the Assistant Secretary of State (White) of a Conversation Between the Secretary of State and the Representatives of the Neutral Nations, September 18, 1929*

The Secretary asked the Mexican Ambassador, the Colombian Minister and the Cuban and Uruguayan Chargés d'Affaires to call on him on Wednesday morning, September 18.

The Secretary stated that he had asked the gentlemen to call on him as the representatives of the neutral nations represented on the Commission of Inquiry, Bolivia and Paraguay. The Secretary stated that he felt that the Governments could be very pleased with the results obtained by the Commission in conciliating the difference between the two countries as the result of the incidents of last December. The Secretary had been kept informed by General McCoy of the very effective work which had been done by the neutral members and great credit was due to each of them for the happy outcome of the conference. Much had been accomplished but there was still a great deal more to be done in bringing about a definitive settlement.

In such matters it was necessary to have some machinery to bring this about. The Secretary had been very much impressed by this in connection with the Briand-Kellogg Pact.[69] It was the purely fortuitous circumstance that the Pan American Arbitration Conference was in session when this trouble arose that steps were able to be taken immediately to prevent hostilities and to offer the contending parties a peaceful means of settlement.

The Commission has accomplished what it was set up to do, namely, the conciliation of the incidents of last December so that relations between the countries are now back on the basis prior to those incidents but should the Commission go out of being there will be no machinery should further crises arise, and the Secretary had been informed by General McCoy that in the past a crisis arose about once a week. The Secretary had therefore called in the diplomatic representatives of the neutral governments to advise them of the action which he had taken so far and the recommendations of the Neutral Commissioners, which had been communicated to him by General McCoy.

On September 13, the Secretary instructed the American Legations in Asunción and La Paz to tender to those Governments the good offices of the United States which in this case would be represented by the services of the American Commissioner and of the Secretary General of the Commission. On the same day the Secretary had informed the respective neutral governments of his action and had

[69] *Foreign Relations*, 1928, vol. I, p. 153.

urged those governments to make a similar offer of the service of the Commissioner representing each country. The Secretary had been advised that the Colombian Government had already tendered its good offices to Bolivia and Paraguay and that Cuba would do likewise and he expressed the hope that Mexico and Uruguay would take similar action.

Inasmuch as the Commission's term came to an end under the Protocol of last January on September 13, the Secretary felt that if the neutral governments represented on that Commission should continue to interest themselves in behalf of a settlement of the fundamental question pending between Bolivia and Paraguay it would be helpful and if those governments agreed he would like to suggest that an endeavor be made to secure agreement by Bolivia and Paraguay to continue the existence of a Commission for this purpose. The Secretary made it clear that the same Commission would not have to be maintained; that he understood that most of the Neutral Commissioners had made their plans to be here only until September 13, and were anxious to return to their respective countries for various personal reasons. It was not necessary to maintain the same Commissioners but merely to maintain a Commission composed of a representative of the five neutral governments selected by the Pan American Conference on Arbitration and Conciliation and that those Governments could send other representatives.

The situation had changed since the Secretary originally invited these gentlemen to meet with him. Paraguay has accepted the offer made but Bolivia has not. Bolivia has indicated that it thought the negotiations could best be carried on directly between the two Governments when diplomatic relations are established as they have agreed to do in the conciliation agreement.

The Secretary pointed out that Bolivia had objected to the proposal of arbitration contained in General McCoy's note of August 31. As a matter of fact both countries had done so but both had reiterated their firm intention of seeking a solution by arbitration. The objections raised by both countries had been met by what the Secretary thought was a very wise and clever suggestion, that, as the two countries could not agree on a delimitation of the territory to be submitted to arbitration and certain other preliminary considerations, the scope of the arbitration be submitted to a preliminary arbitration. This was done in a note dated September 12. This note has not been answered by Bolivia. The proposal contained therein has been accepted by Paraguay and the Secretary wanted to consult with these gentlemen as to further action that could be taken.

A brief discussion followed in which suggestions were made by the Mexican Ambassador and by the Colombian Minister and it was thereupon agreed that as the Commission is legally out of existence it would be better for it to make no suggestions as such but for General McCoy to call together his neutral colleagues, discuss the situation with them, and that their recommendation would then be transmitted to the Secretary by General McCoy who would then communicate it to the diplomatic representatives of the other neutral governments who would transmit it to their Government in order that joint representations might be made at La Paz. They felt that this would be the most effective way of handling the matter and that it would be inadvisable for the diplomatic representatives of the neutral governments to discuss the matter in Washington with the Bolivian Minister. General McCoy said that he would immediately call together his neutral colleagues and discuss the matter with them.

F[RANCIS] W[HITE]

724.3415/716

*Memorandum by the Assistant Secretary of State (White)*

[WASHINGTON,] September 20, 1929.

Señor Mora, Uruguayan Chargé d'Affaires, called on me Friday afternoon, September 20. He read me a telegram from his Government stating that Uruguay did not make the representations at La Paz and Asuncion that General Ruprecht had agreed to on the 14th instant because before they could do so Bolivia had informed them that that Government preferred to carry on direct negotiations with Paraguay. The Minister had called in the Bolivian Minister in an endeavor to have him have his Government change its attitude and after taking it up with his Government the Bolivian Minister had said that his Government was definitely decided in the matter and could not change. The offer of good offices had not been made by Uruguay as they had been definitely informed in the matter beforehand by Bolivia that the offer would be rejected.

The Chargé stated that he had been instructed to inform the Secretary of this as his Government wanted to cooperate with the other neutral governments and let them know the reason why the offer of good offices on the part of Uruguay had not been made.

I thanked the Chargé d'Affaires and told him that the Secretary would much appreciate the action of his Government in informing him and asked him to express to his Government the Secretary's appreciation. The Chargé said that he would do so.

Señor Mora then inquired regarding the situation and I told him that as agreed in the meeting at which Señor Mora was present in the Secretary's office the other day the Neutral Commissioners are discussing the matter in order to make recommendations to their Governments for further action. I pointed out to Señor Mora that there had as yet been no replies to the note of the Neutral Commissioners to the Party Commissioners on September 12, and that as this note met all the objections raised by both Bolivia and Paraguay to the draft convention of arbitration submitted to them by the neutrals on August 31, I hoped that it would be possible to make an arrangement on that basis and that I very much hoped that the position taken by Bolivia had been taken before they had received the note of September 12, and that this change in the situation would induce them to modify their attitude and accept the proposal.

I pointed out to him the serious situation that would arise should hostilities reopen and the great importance which the Secretary attached to the continuance of some friendly neutral machinery to help overcome the obstacles that inevitably arise in any negotiations and pointed out that it was merely the most fortunate chance that the Pan American Arbitration Conference was in session last December when the hostilities broke out between Bolivia and Paraguay and could thus extend its good offices with a view to a peaceful settlement.

Doctor Mora agreed entirely and said that any hostilities would be disastrous and certainly most unwelcome to the countries of South America. He expressed his readiness to cooperate in any possible way, for which I thanked him.

F[RANCIS] W[HITE]

724.3415/712a : Telegram

*The Secretary of State to the Chargé in Bolivia (Hibbard)*

[Paraphrase]

WASHINGTON, September 21, 1929—11 a. m.

56. On September 19, the Bolivian Minister, accompanied by the Bolivian Delegates, called on the Secretary of State. The Bolivian Minister thanked the Secretary for the aid of the United States in the recent conference and also for the services of General McCoy. The Minister then made a statement along the lines indicated in Legation's telegram number 68, September 17, 9 a. m. He said that the Government of Bolivia desired a complete settlement, but it felt that this could best be accomplished by direct negotiations between Bolivia and Paraguay. The Secretary replied that he appreciated Bolivia's position in the matter, that a direct settlement was sometimes the easiest, but that in many cases it was of greatest advantage to have some kind of neutral machinery set up to which appeal could be made for aid in surmounting obstacles and difficulties which might arise during the course of negotiations. An example in point is the

events of last December. Fortunately the International Conference of American States on Conciliation and Arbitration was in session and it was able immediately to tender its good offices to the contending parties. Otherwise, very serious consequences might have arisen. The Secretary of State felt, therefore, that it was well to maintain some sort of friendly neutral machinery. The Bolivian Minister said that he held the same opinion, and that he would advise the Bolivian Government of the views of the Secretary and support them.

The Secretary said he hoped that a definitive solution of the problem could be reached. He said that he did not believe any solution would be final in which the settlement was not considered just and equitable by both countries. If the Government of the United States or the Secretary personally could be of any assistance to the Governments concerned in bringing about a solution, he was ready at all times to be of service. The Secretary indicated that if a solution should not be reached, and hostilities ensue, the results would be disastrous for both countries. World opinion would be so unfavorable, especially now that so much progress has been made toward a settlement, that this would perhaps do more harm to the two countries than the actual effect of the war itself.

The Bolivian Minister said that he could assure the Secretary that there would be no resort to hostilities, and that the attitude of Bolivia should not be considered as a rejection of the good offices of the United States, but simply as indicating that in deference to Bolivian public sentiment an attempt at direct settlement was being made. Should this result in failure the Secretary could rest assured that Bolivia would again request the good offices of the United States in reaching a settlement. The Secretary expressed his gratification and readiness to be of help and he stressed again the advantage of having some machinery available in case of difficulties, such as the last conference provided.

STIMSON

---

724.3415/718

*Memorandum by the Assistant Secretary of State (White)*

[WASHINGTON,] September 23, 1929.

The Secretary on the afternoon of September 23, asked the Mexican Ambassador, the Colombian Minister and the Cuban and Uruguayan Chargés d'Affaires to call on him regarding the Bolivia-Paraguay matter.

The Secretary stated that he had been kept in touch with the situation by General McCoy and Mr. White and also by the neutral members of the Commission and that he was very much impressed by the necessity of taking some measures that might eliminate the great possibility of a conflict presented by the presence of large forces of Bolivian and Paraguayan troops in the Chaco and in the fifty odd forts facing one another there. The Secretary felt that it is essential that there should be some machinery set up which will tide over the innumerable crises that are bound to arise in the future as they have in the past.

This matter has been considered by the neutral Commissioners and the Secretary had read a memorandum of their views.[70] He wanted to emphasize, however, that while the action which he was going to propose is, he feels convinced, in harmony with the views of the Neutral Commissioners the responsibility for it is his. The Secretary has drafted a communication which he would suggest should be made by the five neutral governments separately to the Governments of Bolivia and Paraguay and he would of course be glad to have any suggestions which any of the Governments may care to make with respect thereto.

The Secretary then read the draft communication, a copy of which is attached hereto. While reading it the Secretary emphasized first that Bolivia has not definitely rejected the idea of a Commission of Neutrals and that there is therefore a basis for bringing the two parties together. He further emphatically emphasized that the essential point is that there shall be machinery established and that it is immaterial where the deliberations shall take place. He also pointed out that there are two distinct needs and functions for the Commission, one, to lend its good offices in bringing about a settlement should the direct negotiations break down, and also the need of such a disinterested neutral body to help overcome difficulties that may arise during the course of direct negotiations. The Secretary stated that he felt it very important not to have a long hiatus between the two Commissions as trouble might arise at any time.

The four diplomatic representatives in question stated their readiness to cooperate and said that they would advise their Governments immediately of the Secretary's proposal. The Colombian, Mexican and Cuban representatives stated that they felt sure their Governments would take the action suggested. The Uruguayan Chargé said that he would transmit the matter immediately to his Government; that the Minister would return tomorrow and carry on the work from that date.

---

[70] Two documents both identical and without title are attached to the document in hand. The first document is presumably the "memorandum of their views" and the second "the draft communication", mentioned in the next (fourth) paragraph. Both are the same as the quoted part of the Department's circular telegram of September 23 to the diplomatic representatives in Bolivia and Paraguay, *infra.*

The Mexican Ambassador suggested that it would be helpful to the Governments to have the report of the work of the Commission mentioned in their last meeting in order to put the neutral governments *au courant* with the present situation in the matter. General McCoy stated that the report is now ready and would be available later in the day. Copies were later sent to the four representatives in question.

F[RANCIS] W[HITE]

724.3415/716b : Circular telegram

*The Secretary of State to the American Diplomatic Representatives in Bolivia and Paraguay*

WASHINGTON, September 23, 1929—6 p. m.

I handed to the Mexican Ambassador, Colombian Minister, and the Cuban and Uruguayan Chargés d'Affaires this afternoon the following suggested communication for the representatives in La Paz and Asunción of the five neutral governments to make to the Bolivian and Paraguayan Governments. You will please be prepared to transmit this communication on behalf of this Government to the Government to which you are accredited upon receiving further instructions from the Department to that effect. You will understand that it is not to be presented without further instructions. Text follows:

"My Government is impressed with the vital importance of maintaining some friendly neutral machinery for dealing with difficulties that may arise between Bolivia and Paraguay pending the definitive settlement of the question now unhappily existing between them. It was clearly brought out last December that only the fortunate circumstance that the Pan American Conference of Arbitration and Conciliation was in session prevented an armed conflict between these two sister nations of this hemisphere. As a result of the good offices of that Conference a Commission was set up to lend its good offices to the parties in terminating the conflict and this Commission succeeded in overcoming many obstacles and in conciliating the events of last December in accordance with the protocol of January 3, 1929. The fundamental question, however, remains and while it is unsettled there is almost as much danger as there was last December that further unfortunate incidents may occur. In this connection it may be mentioned that there are some fifty-two forts belonging to the two parties facing one another in the Chaco and that relatively large bodies of troops from both sides are concentrated there.

In examining the statements made by both parties it is seen that they are in agreement in many respects. Paraguay has suggested the continuance of the Commission to help in a solution of the fundamental question, while Bolivia has suggested that direct negotiations be resorted to. Bolivia, however, states its willingness to take into consideration the suggestions of a Commission of neutrals at the time of renewing the negotiations for a settlement of the fundamental question. It would seem therefore that the wishes of both parties may be met by their agreement to enter immediately into direct negotiations for a settlement, at the same time establishing a Commission composed of members of the five neutral nations represented on the Commission whose labors terminated on September 13th, this Commission to be available not only to take up the work should the direct negotiations unfortunately not succeed but also to render its good offices with a view to overcoming obstacles which may arise during the course of the direct negotiations thereby being in a position perhaps to help those direct negotiations to a successful conclusion.

The United States Government has offered its capital as a place for holding the direct negotiations and for establishing the Commission, in view of the fact that the Pan American Conference of Arbitration and Conciliation and the Commission of Inquiry and Conciliation emanating therefrom were held in that city where there is already established the Secretariat General and other machinery for facilitating this work. It should be distinctly understood, however, that the preoccupation of the five neutral governments in harmony with the views of the American nations embodied in the General Convention of Inter-American Conciliation concluded on January 5, 1929,[71] is solely that there should be machinery immediately established that may be used in helping the negotiations and in preventing conflicts. It is immaterial where this machinery shall be established and should the contending parties agree on any other capital than Washington this will be eminently satisfactory to the five governments concerned.

As to the composition of the Commission it may be stated that certain of the delegates have other duties to perform which would make it a great hardship on them to continue on the new Commission and therefore it may be necessary for certain of the neutral governments to appoint new delegates. All the governments stand ready to do so should either or both of the two contending parties express such a desire."

STIMSON

---

724.3415/716b : Circular telegram

*The Secretary of State to the American Diplomatic Representatives in Colombia, Cuba, Mexico, and Uruguay*

WASHINGTON, *September 23, 1929—6 p. m.*

This afternoon I handed to the Mexican Ambassador, Colombian Minister, and Cuban and Uruguayan Chargés d'Affaires a draft of a suggested communication for the five governments to make separately to the Governments of Bolivia and Paraguay.

All the Neutral Commissioners on the Commission of Inquiry and Conciliation feel very strongly as I do that a very serious situation will almost inevitably arise should the negotiations between the two contending parties drift on without definite direction and without continuing some friendly neutral machinery that can use its good offices not only in promoting a direct settlement between the parties but in avoiding conflicts which must otherwise almost surely arise.

---

[71] *Ante,* p. 653.

In discussing this matter with the diplomatic representatives of the neutral governments concerned I was gratified to find that they also share my feeling and that of the Neutral Commissioners. I am encouraged to hope therefore that this proposal will meet with the support of the four other neutral governments concerned in order that the communications may be made to the two contending parties without delay. As time is of the essence I desire you to hold yourself ready to discuss the matter at once with the Minister for Foreign Affairs as soon as he shall receive this communication from his Ambassador here and to get his suggestions and cable me if he agrees in order that a time for making the communications may be mutually agreed upon at the earliest possible moment.

The text of the communication is as follows:

[Here follows the text as quoted in the Department's circular telegram of September 23, 6 p. m., to the American diplomatic representatives in Bolivia and Paraguay, printed *supra*.]

STIMSON

---

724.3415/739f : Telegram

*The Secretary of State to the Chargé in Bolivia (Hibbard)*[72]

WASHINGTON, September 30, 1929—10 a. m.

57. Department's circular September 23, 6 p. m. Please transmit communication quoted therein to Bolivian Government on Tuesday morning, October first.

STIMSON

---

724.3415/742d : Telegram

*The Secretary of State to the Minister in Paraguay (Kreeck)*[73]

WASHINGTON, September 30, 1929—5 p. m.

52. Department's Circular, September 23, 6 P. M. and No. 51, today.[74] For your information. The Mexican, Colombian and Uruguayan Governments have agreed to deliver a communication to the Governments at La Paz and Asunción, in the same sense, tomorrow. The Cuban Government, through a misapprehension, has already delivered such a communication, but the Department is not informed of the exact date when this action was taken. The Uruguayan representations will be made in Montevideo.

STIMSON

---

[72] The same, *mutatis mutandis*, on the same date to the Minister in Paraguay as telegram No. 51.

[73] The same on the same date to the Chargé in Bolivia as telegram No. 58, mentioning Department's circular telegram, September 23, 6 p. m., and telegram No. 57, September 30, 10 a. m.

[74] See footnote 72.

724.3415/742b : Telegram

*The Secretary of State to the Chargé in Bolivia (Hibbard)*

WASHINGTON, September 30, 1929—6 p. m.

59. Department's telegram No. 57 today. Upon delivery by you of the communication to the Bolivian Government which was embodied in the Department's telegram of September 23rd, 6 p. m., you may say to the Minister of Foreign Affairs that this Government earnestly hopes the Bolivian Government will give most serious consideration to the communication which is being made to it on behalf of the five neutral Governments who were represented on the Commission of Inquiry and Conciliation.

The Government of Paraguay unreservedly accepted the original tender of the neutral Governments and there is every reason to believe that Paraguay will accept the Bolivian suggestion reported in your telegram No. 69 of September 18th [75] for direct negotiations if these can be conducted with the disinterested and friendly assistance of the neutral Governments. This Government has every confidence in the pacific disposition of the Bolivian Government but the facts of the situation to which attention is invited in the communication which the neutral Governments are making cannot be overlooked. They point to the possibility that unfortunate incidents may arise at any time, threatening consequences more far reaching than can now be foreseen. Under these circumstances, the Bolivian Government I feel sure will want to keep in view the advantageous position in which Bolivia will place herself by spontaneous cooperation with the neutral Governments, which will avoid misapprehension on the part of public opinion in the American Republics as to her purpose to secure a real settlement of the controversy with Paraguay by peaceful means. You should keep in mind the fact that negotiations under the auspices of the Commission of Inquiry and Conciliation for a direct settlement proved no less futile than the previous direct negotiations extending over many years for such a settlement. It was because of the failure of this latest attempt to promote a direct settlement that the neutral Commissioners made their proposal for a settlement by arbitration. After examining the objections raised by both interested Governments to the application of the method of arbitration, which the interested Governments accepted in principle, the neutral Commissioners also indicated in the note of September 12 from the Chairman of the Commission the manner in which these objections could be overcome.

[Paraphrase.] With reference to the first of the two reasons adduced in Legation's 74, September 25, 4 p. m.,[76] for doubting the willingness

---

[75] Not printed; see despatch No. 242, September 17, from the Chargé in Bolivia, p. 894.
[76] Not printed.

of the Government of Bolivia to cooperate with the neutral Governments, I should be pleased to have some further explanation of the statement that the Bolivian internal political situation is such as to induce a postponement of a settlement with Paraguay.

With regard to the suggestion that Argentine influence is being exerted adversely, I wish to inform you that the American Embassy in Argentina has been instructed to make clear to the Government of Argentina the direct continuity which exists in the opinion of the neutrals between the proposals made for an arbitral settlement in the note of September 12 from the chairman of the Commission to the delegations of Bolivia and Paraguay, and the suggestions of the Argentine observer at the last Buenos Aires Conference on the same subject.[77] [End paraphrase.]

STIMSON

---

724.3415/742c : Telegram

*The Secretary of State to the Ambassador in Argentina (Bliss)*

WASHINGTON, September 30, 1929—6 p. m.

101. The American Legations at Asunción and La Paz will present to the Paraguayan and Bolivian Governments on Tuesday, October first, the following communication:

[Here follows the text of note transmitted in circular telegram, September 23, 6 p. m., to the American diplomatic representatives in Bolivia and Paraguay, printed on page 903.]

Please hand the Minister for Foreign Affairs on Tuesday, October 1st, a copy of the above communication and inform him that the five neutral countries represented on the Commission of Inquiry and Conciliation, that is to say, Mexico, Cuba, Colombia, Uruguay and the United States, have given very careful thought to the situation at present existing between Bolivia and Paraguay, and feel that it is fraught with very grave danger. While the Commission accomplished a conciliation of the incidents of last December under the terms of the Protocol, it was not empowered by that instrument to settle the fundamental question. As long as this exists there is very grave danger of clashes in the Chaco where there are fifty-two forts of the two Parties facing one another and where very considerable forces of troops are concentrated. An outbreak may occur at any time. The five neutral Governments felt that it is essential to have in being immediately some machinery which, through the exercise of friendly neutral good offices, can prevent outbreaks.

On August 31 the neutral Commissioners made a proposal of arbitration to the two countries. Objections were made by both Parties

---

[77] See telegram No. 101, September 30, to the Ambassador in Argentina, *infra.*

on September ninth and a modified proposal, meeting all objections of both Parties, was submitted on September 12. The Commission expired by limitation the following day before answers could be received from the Parties.

The neutral Governments offered the good offices of their Commissioners for the continuance of the work. This was accepted by Paraguay but Bolivia stated a preference for direct negotiations, expressing however its willingness to take into consideration the suggestions of a Commission of neutrals at the time of renewing the negotiations for a settlement of the fundamental question.

It therefore seemed to the five neutral Governments that the points of view of both contending Parties could be met by suggesting the opening of immediate good offices and the immediate setting up of a neutral Commission. This neutral Commission could exert its influence for the maintenance of peace before direct negotiations are entered into and after their termination, should they unfortunately prove unsuccessful, and also extend its good offices for a settlement in the latter eventuality. Furthermore, this Commission, it is felt, could be of the utmost assistance to the Parties during the course of the direct negotiations in overcoming obstacles which must invariably arise. The essential thing is the establishment of the machinery of conciliation. The place where this machinery shall be established is of secondary importance. This Government has offered Washington as a place for holding the meetings in view of the fact that the Pan American Conference, which first took this matter up, was held here and because the Commission of Inquiry and Conciliation emanating therefrom also held its sessions in Washington where there is already established a Secretariat and a very extensive collection of documents, et cetera, pertaining to this matter. However, if the two Governments agree on some other place for the holding of the meetings, this will be eminently satisfactory to the five neutral Governments. The other neutral Governments are making analogous suggestions to the two countries. You will please make this full and frank explanation of the situation to the Minister for Foreign Affairs.

[Paraphrase.] According to reliable reports that have come to the attention of the Department, Argentina is exerting every influence with Bolivia not to continue the negotiations in the city of Washington but to transfer them to Buenos Aires under the sole auspices of the Government of Argentina. The Government of the United States does not desire to make the matter a question of prestige between Washington and Buenos Aires, and for this reason it was suggested that any other capital acceptable to the two Parties would be eminently satisfactory to the five neutral Governments. The diplomatic representatives in Washington of the four neutral countries, their Commissioners and the Secretary of State are very much impressed with the danger of the situation, and the likelihood of further outbreaks unless some conciliatory machinery is established. For that reason we have made this last proposal in the endeavor to conciliate the points of view of both contending Parties. It is essential that machinery be set up to prevent any outbreak. [End paraphrase.]

In a note to the Argentine Chargé d'Affaires here on September 24, transmitting to him for the Argentine Government, at the request of the Chairman of the Commission of Conciliation, the latter's report of the results of the Commission's labors, I stated as follows:

"I have been specially requested by the Chairman of the Commission of Inquiry and Conciliation, Bolivia and Paraguay, to inform your Government that in the course of the study of the background of the Chaco dispute the Neutral Commissioners were deeply impressed by the many earnest efforts that the Government of the Argentine Republic has made to bring about the final settlement of the longstanding controversy between Bolivia and Paraguay. They were particularly gratified by the well advised action of the Argentine Government during the recent Conferences of Plenipotentiaries held at Buenos Aires and, in view of the fairness of the formula there advanced by the Argentine observer, they decided to incorporate it in their arbitral counter-proposal of September 12. They feel that the method of arbitration proposed by the Neutral Commissioners to the Republics of Bolivia and Paraguay thus becomes closely related to and is a continuation of that advanced by the Argentine Government."

STIMSON

---

724.3415/742a : Telegram

*The Secretary of State to the Chargé in Brazil (Schoenfeld)* [78]

WASHINGTON, September 30, 1929—6 p. m.

58. The American Legations at Asuncion and La Paz will present to the Paraguayan and Bolivian Governments on Tuesday, October first, the following communication:

[Here follows text of note transmitted in circular telegram, September 23, 6 p. m., to the American diplomatic representatives in Bolivia and Paraguay, printed on page 903.]

Please hand the Minister for Foreign Affairs on Tuesday, October 1st, a copy of the above communication. Similar communications are being made to the Bolivian and Paraguayan Governments by the other neutral nations represented on the Commission of Inquiry and Conciliation, that is to say, Mexico, Colombia, Cuba and Uruguay.

STIMSON

---

[78] The same, *mutatis mutandis*, on the same date to the diplomatic representatives in Chile (No. 106) and Peru (No. 97).

724.3415/747 : Telegram

*The Chargé in Bolivia (Hibbard) to the Secretary of State*

LA PAZ, October 1, 1929—4 p. m.
[Received 11 p. m.]

75. Department's telegram No. 59, September 30. I delivered the note embodied in the Department's telegram of September 23 at 2:30 this afternoon. The Colombian Minister delivered a similar note yesterday afternoon at 5 and the Mexican Minister this morning at 9.

In delivering the note I spoke to the Minister for Foreign Affairs in the sense of the Department's telegram of today's date and was informed that the Bolivian Government would give the communication its most serious consideration. I pointed out that Paraguay would probably undertake direct negotiations with Bolivia if these were conducted with the assistance of friendly and neutral governments and asked if Bolivia would be averse to such an agreement. The Minister was noncommittal in his reply, stating that this would be one way of reaching an agreement and referred to the recent agreement between Chile and Peru [79] which while arrived at directly was aided by the friendly cooperation of the United States. However he repeated his belief in the possibility and desirability of direct negotiations, adding that commissions aroused public opinion unduly, created congressional inquiries and that such questions were more easily settled in the quiet of a Foreign Office. He added that at least the zone to be arbitrated might be decided upon directly and then the matter referred to an arbitral commission.

I then asked if any arrangements had been made for renewing the diplomatic relations between the two countries as it would be impossible to carry on any direct negotiations until relations had been resumed. He replied in the negative but said he was looking for a suitable representative to send to Asunción. I then asked how Bolivia intended to resume these relations. He answered that as the recent commission had not set a definite date for pacific relations it would be necessary to ask some friendly government to inquire in Asunción whether the Bolivian representative was acceptable and vice versa. I asked if he could tell me what country this would be and whom he was considering as a possible minister. He replied in the negative. I believe from what I have heard from other sources that Argentina will be the country chosen and that Alvestegui is being considered for Minister with Guachalla, former Chargé d'Affaires in Chile, as assistant. I do not think Bolivia will take the initiative as it is desirable for reasons of internal politics that the Government does not appear too eager to resume relations.

---

[79] See Tacna-Arica dispute, pp. 720 ff.

I pointed out the danger of delay, stating that while my Government had every confidence in the pacific intentions of Bolivia there were 52 forts in the Chaco and many troops concentrated there and that it was possible for subordinates without the knowledge of their Government to create incidents the consequences of which might be both far reaching and serious. He admitted this comparing the possibilities to those of Sarajevo but assured me that Bolivia would not resort to arms under any circumstances as she firmly believed in peaceful methods and realized the folly of war from the financial viewpoint.

In closing the interview I asked what Bolivia proposed to do should Paraguay refuse direct negotiations. He said that he had not considered the matter but that Bolivia would certainly seek some other method of amicable settlement.

HIBBARD

---

724.3415/764

### Memorandum by the Assistant Secretary of State (White)

[WASHINGTON,] October 2, 1929.

The Bolivian Minister called on the Secretary on Wednesday, October 2, at the latter's request. The Secretary stated that he had asked him to come in as he had very much on his mind and heart the situation in South America and, while the five neutral Governments represented on the Commission of Inquiry and Conciliation had yesterday made representations at La Paz and Asuncion to the Bolivian and Paraguayan Governments, his personal interest in the matter was so great that he wanted to emphasize the matter by expressing very frankly and fully to the Minister his views which he hoped he would transmit to his Government.

The Secretary then read to the Minister an *Aide Memoire*, a copy of which is attached hereto,[79a] and then handed it to him. The Secretary stated that he had taken the matter up with the Minister because he knew of his friendly and sympathetic feeling toward a settlement. The Minister replied that he fully concurred with what the Secretary had just read to him and that he felt that the whole matter should be settled. At the time of signing the Protocol of January 3, last, he had said to his Government that while the wording of that Protocol limited the scope of the Commission of Inquiry and Conciliation to a determination of the responsibility for the happenings of last December, he felt that the Commission should not be limited in practice in that way but that it should study and resolve the fundamental question at issue.

---

[79a] *Infra.*

The Minister then said that while it is possible that direct negotiations may result in a settlement, he felt that there is much more chance for the success of an arbitration. Arbitration, he said, has much more support behind it and will of course be accepted by both countries, whereas a direct settlement is subject to the weakness that those opposed to it may stir up popular opinion to such an extent that a weak Government, such as he said existed in Paraguay, might be overthrown should it attempt to ratify the agreement or be forced to abandon it. For this reason he was in favor of arbitration.

The Minister then stated that he wanted to give the Secretary some of the background regarding the Commission which would explain some of the resistance on the part of Bolivia to accepting the proposal of August 31. Messrs. Marquez Sterling and Rivas were the neutral members of the Commission who were most in contact with the Bolivian representatives and these gentlemen had led the latter to believe that no proposal would be made without first submitting it to them and discussing it informally in order to get their views. They were very much astonished, therefore, when suddenly the proposal of arbitration was sprung on them. Had the matter been submitted to them first, they would have been able to point out certain objections to it which they thought could have been removed and thus make it acceptable to Bolivia.

He pointed out that the proposal for arbitration limited the scope of the arbitration in the southern part of the Chaco territory by eliminating from consideration by the Arbitrator the territory adjudicated to Paraguay in the Arbitral Award of President Hayes. Bolivia would reconcile itself to this limitation had there been a corresponding limitation in the north in favor of Bolivia but this was not done. The Bolivian delegates had become alarmed when they saw this and had cabled to the Bolivian Government which, in turn, had become alarmed, and hence the opposition to the project.

The Secretary pointed out that while there was no territory in the north excluded from the arbitration the agreement did provide that Bolivia should have a port on the Paraguay River with the necessary hinterland. The Minister stated that this was true but as the Arbitrator was not limited to the north in the boundary he might fix, he might accede to the very exaggerated claims of Paraguay and hence isolate this port. The Secretary stated that in his conversations with the Commissioners, while he was not thoroughly familiar with the geography of the Chaco, he nevertheless had very definitely understood that in giving a port definitely to Bolivia and the necessary land thereto, a zone had as a practical matter been set aside in the north which would have to be excluded in any event.

The Bolivian Minister said that his Government now understood that this was the intention of the Commissioners but it had not been definitely stated and Paraguay's pretensions went very far to the north. When the matter was under consideration in Buenos Aires, the Argentine representative had suggested drawing a line somewhat midway between the maximum pretensions of both Parties, but this line had never been drawn and Paraguay had fallen back on an earlier protocol which Bolivia felt was void and in which there was no limit placed on Paraguayan pretensions to the North, and the Bolivian Government had therefore felt that they would have to take measures to protect their interests.

The Secretary replied that he did not think that Bolivia need fear that an Arbitrator would accede to the maximum pretensions of either Party. As a matter of fact, these pretensions are very old and have, as a practical matter, been considerably limited by subsequent developments such as the establishment of centers of population from both countries and that therefore any Arbitrator must draw a medium line and not one along the maximum pretensions of either country, and he felt sure that Bolivia was perfectly safeguarded in going to arbitration.

The Bolivian Minister said that that also was his view and, such being the case, it would be a very great pleasure to him to transmit to his Government the text of the *Aide Memoire* and to support it and, as sufficient time has now elapsed since the matter first came up, he thought that public opinion had calmed down and that it would be easier for his Government to accept. He did not know, of course, what their decision would be but if it should be the Secretary's desire he would urge a prompt reply. The Secretary said he thought it very important to have a prompt reply as further outbreaks are apt to occur while there is uncertainty and delay.

F[rancis] W[hite]

---

724.3415/756a

*The Secretary of State to the Bolivian Minister (Diez de Medina)*[80]

AIDE-MÉMOIRE

Since my conversation with you on September 19th[81] the following developments have taken place:

(a) The diplomatic representatives of the neutral Governments represented on the Commission have conferred with me to consider the manner in which we could best assist in meeting the desires of the interested Governments with regard to the next step in the negotiations for the fundamental settlement. We have been informed that the Paraguayan Government unreservedly accepted the original ten-

---

[80] Handed by the Secretary of State to the Bolivian Minister on October 2, 1929.
[81] See telegram No. 56, September 21, 11 a. m., to the Chargé in Bolivia, p. 900.

der of their assistance by the neutral Governments for reaching a settlement. We have carefully considered also the position of your Government both as expressed in its note of September 16th to the American Chargé d'Affaires [82] and as stated by yourself, and we have come to the conclusion that there is no essential difficulty in the way of meeting the desires of your Government as well as those of Paraguay.

(*b*) As a result of our consultations the neutral Governments have, on October 1st, sent a communication to the two interested Governments along the lines of the memorandum which I am glad to hand you attached hereto.[83]

The five neutral countries represented on the Commission gave very careful thought to the situation and could not escape the feeling that it is fraught with very grave danger. The incidents of last December have been conciliated but the Commission was not empowered to settle the fundamental question and as long as this exists there is very grave danger of clashes in the Chaco where there are fifty-two forts of the two parties facing one another and where very considerable forces of troops are concentrated. There is the grave possibility that another outbreak may occur at any time. Consequently the five neutral Governments felt that it is essential to have in being immediately some machinery which through the exercise of friendly neutral good offices can prevent outbreaks.

It was this consideration that prompted the neutral Governments to offer the good offices of their Commissioners for the continuance of the work. This offer was accepted by Paraguay but Bolivia stated a preference for direct negotiations expressing however its willingness to take into consideration the suggestions of a Commission of Neutrals at the time of renewing the negotiations for a settlement of the fundamental question.

It would therefore seem that the points of view of both contending parties may be met by suggesting the opening of immediate direct negotiations and the immediate setting up of a neutral Commission. This neutral Commission could exert its influence for the maintenance of peace before direct negotiations are entered into, and after their termination, should that unfortunately prove unsuccessful. The neutral Commission could also extend its good offices for a settlement in the latter eventuality. Furthermore, this Commission can be of the utmost assistance to the parties during the course of the direct negotiations in overcoming obstacles which must inevitably arise and hence make far more probable the success of the direct negotiations.

The essential thing for the maintenance of peace is the establish-

---

[82] See note dated September 14 from the Bolivian Minister for Foreign Affairs to the American Chargé in Bolivia, p. 894.

[83] See quoted portion of Department's circular telegram of September 23, 1929, 6 p. m., to the diplomatic representatives in Bolivia and Paraguay, p. 903.

ment of machinery which can use its friendly neutral good offices should a crisis arise. In view of the commitments of both Governments for a peaceful settlement it is felt that both parties will welcome this means to its accomplishment and that neither party would want to assume responsibility for delaying a peaceful settlement and for losing what has already been gained through the negotiations which were interrupted when the Commission of Inquiry and Conciliation expired by limitation.

724.3415/752 : Telegram

*The Ambassador in Argentina (Bliss) to the Secretary of State*

BUENOS AIRES, October 2, 1929—6 p. m.
[Received 8 : 57 p. m.]

106. Your 101 of September 30, 6 p. m. Yesterday afternoon I presented to the Minister for Foreign Affairs the text of the note to Bolivia and Paraguay and read to him that part of your telegram intended for his information. He was not disposed to make any comment, undoubtedly desiring to consult with the President; but today I handed him at his request a memorandum of what I said to him yesterday. He then said that when the good offices of President Irigoyen had been rejected last autumn by Bolivia [84] the President considered he had done everything in his power to bring about an agreement between Paraguay and Bolivia and that he did not feel disposed to make further advances. The President's reason, he stated, for not accepting the invitation to participate in the Commission of Inquiry at Washington was to avoid being placed in the position of seeking to accomplish by circuitous means what he had failed to do by direct offer. The Minister added that the suggestion contained in the American Government's note to Bolivia and Paraguay was most laudable and intimated that the Argentine Government for the reasons stated above could take no part in the movement although it looks with favor on any effort or action taken to prevent hostilities between the two countries.

[Paraphrase.] Both the Bolivian Minister, with whom I have talked repeatedly on this subject, and his Paraguayan colleague have indicated that the President has shown indifference with respect to the Washington Conference although lately he congratulated the Bolivian Minister on the satisfactory work of the Conciliation Commission. The Bolivian Minister has stressed to me the opinion that the Conciliation Commission should continue its good offices. [End paraphrase.]

BLISS

[84] See telegram No. 93, December 10, 1928, from the Ambassador in Argentina, *Foreign Relations*, 1928, vol. I, p. 684.

724.3415/823

*The Minister in Paraguay (Kreeck) to the Secretary of State*

No. 923                                      ASUNCIÓN, October 7, 1929.
                                             [Received November 7.]

SIR: I have the honor to submit copy of the official note of the Paraguayan Foreign Office, in Spanish and translation, accepting the good offices of the United States and the neutral countries as outlined in the Department's Circular telegram of September 23, 6 p. m., and transmitted by a note to the Paraguayan Foreign Office on October 2nd by this Legation.

The Minister of Foreign Affairs on October 4th., requested that telegraphic acceptance be sent the Department, which was done by my telegram No. 101 of October 4, 4 p. m.[85]  I am happy to make this report.

I have [etc.]                                    GEO. L. KREECK

[Enclosure—Translation]

*The Paraguayan Minister for Foreign Affairs (Zubizarreta) to the American Minister (Kreeck)*

No. 679                                      ASUNCIÓN, October 5, 1929.

MR. MINISTER: I have had the honor to receive your communication of the 2nd of October in which you advise me that your Government is convinced of the vital importance of maintaining some friendly neutral organization to treat of the difficulties which may arise between Paraguay and Bolivia while they are settling the question which separates them.

In examining the declarations of both parties you will remember that my country suggested the continuation of the Commission of Neutrals and that Bolivia expressed her preference for the method of direct negotiations.

Notwithstanding this you state that Bolivia would agree willingly to take into consideration the suggestion of a Commission of Neutrals at the time of renewing direct negotiations.  From which fact it appears to result—your note continues—that the desires of both parties are united in their assent to enter immediately into direct negotiations for the solution of the principal question and to establish at the same time a Commission composed of members of the five Neutral Nations.

This Commission would lend its valuable assistance if the direct negotiations did not succeed, and if obstacles should occur during the course of the negotiations.

[85] Not printed.

Your Government kindly offers its Capital as the place of holding said negotiations and for establishing the Commission because of the advantages which the interested parties would find there, as expressed in your note, which, in another part, states that if the interested parties agree to decide upon another Capital for the object indicated, the five friendly Neutrals would have no objections.

I have, Mr. Minister, instructions from my Government to manifest to you, that it looks with pleasure upon the new initiative of which your communication informs and that it accepts it without objections, reiterating its sincere acknowledgement to the Government of the United States of America and to the other Neutral countries for their cordial interest shown by them all in solving the fundamental question between Paraguay and Bolivia by pacific means.

My Government charges me to express to you that it desires the seat of the conferences be at Washington.

In replying to you to this effect I am pleased [etc.]

G. ZUBIZARRETA

---

724.3415/769 : Telegram

*The Chargé in Bolivia (Hibbard) to the Secretary of State*

LA PAZ, October 8, 1929—4 p. m.
[Received 9:20 p. m.]

79. I called on the Minister for Foreign Affairs this morning who explained to me that no formal answer had been made to my note sent in accordance with the Department's circular September 23, 6 p. m., because the disturbed internal situation had not permitted the President to study the matter carefully. However there is to be a Cabinet meeting today at which Bolivia's reply will be discussed and when the decision is reached I am to see the President personally before a note is sent.

I believe the President still favors direct negotiations between the two countries but that he will accept the good offices of one of the neutral countries, probably the United States, to assist in the negotiations as was done in the settlement between Chile and Peru. Señor Luis Abelli has been very useful in persuading the President to consider the offer of good offices. After a conference with the President, Abelli asked me if the United States would undertake such a role in the negotiations. I replied that I was sure the United States was ready to assist in any way possible in reaching an amicable settlement but that I could not answer definitely. I would, however, be glad to cable the President's suggestions to the Department as soon as I received them.

Should such an arrangement be made, Abelli will probably represent Bolivia and the meetings will be held in Washington if direct negotiations are begun without the assistance of a neutral government. Abelli or Mercado, former Bolivian Minister to Paraguay but now in Mexico, will be sent to Asunción.

.     .     .     .     .     .     .     .

There is a feeling among a certain element here, particularly in Congress, that General McCoy has not been impartial toward Bolivia. The Minister for Foreign Affairs informs me that this feeling arises from a confidential report of the Bolivian delegates which reached Congress to the effect that they were not consulted before the formula for the settlement of the fundamental question was announced. The impression seems to be that an attempt was made to force them to accept a settlement without ample discussion. Abelli tells me the President shared this feeling but has now been persuaded that such was not the case.

HIBBARD

---

724.3415/777 : Telegram

*The Secretary of State to the Chargé in Bolivia (Hibbard)*

WASHINGTON, October 9, 1929—5 p. m.

64. Your telegram No. 79, October 8. General McCoy is at a loss to understand the statement in the last paragraph of your telegram that the Bolivian Delegates reported to the Minister of Foreign Affairs that "they were not consulted before the formula for the settlement of the fundamental question was announced". While it seems probable that any such impression results from a possible misinterpretation by the Bolivian Government of the reports received from its Delegates, nevertheless, it may be helpful in clearing away such misunderstanding as exists for you to have an understanding of the circumstances from which the neutral Commissioners concluded with great reluctance that a direct settlement of the fundamental question was impossible. This will enable you to rectify the impressions which you mention, whether they spring from a misunderstanding by the Bolivian Government or from a difference in the deductions of the Bolivian Delegates and of the neutral Commissioners drawn from the circumstances of the negotiations which were equally known to all members of the Commission.

After the powers of the neutral Commissioners were amplified they proceeded with a program, first, to effect a direct settlement and, next, if that were impossible, to propose a solution by arbitration. This program was made known to and approved by the Bolivian Delegation July 12. Thereafter constant negotiations for a direct settlement were carried on, in the course of which the outline of a formula thought by the neutrals likely to meet with the approval of both parties was insinuated and its purport modified to conform as much as possible with their observations. This negotiation was only abandoned by the neutral Commissioners on August 26 on which day the neutral Commissioners were convinced that a final deadlock was established. They felt themselves forced to this conclusion because on August 16 the Bolivian Delegation expressed to the Chairman on behalf of its Government what the neutrals regarded as a final position on an essential element of the formula then under discussion, while on August 26 the Paraguayan Delegation by direction of its Government, expressed in equally final terms a position irreconcilable with that previously stated on behalf of Bolivia. Each interested Delegation was informed of the position taken by the other and neither gave any intimation that its own position was not a final one.

However, the most important consideration in this connection is that all the neutral Commissioners then concluded that a direct settlement was impossible. The Department believes that, unless some new and favorable factor should appear, such a conclusion represents a more accurate estimate of the prospects of direct settlement than any which can be reached by either interested Government without the intervention of friendly and disinterested third parties.

Another possibility of misunderstanding is contained in the reported statement of the Bolivian Delegates above referred to. Before August 31, when the formula for arbitration was presented to them, they had been informed that the neutral Commissioners were preparing such a formula. The surprise shown by the Bolivian Delegates at the time of its presentation could have arisen only from the terms of the formula but not from the fact of its presentation or the fact that it was a formula for a settlement by arbitration rather than for direct settlement.

The foregoing considerations and any existing misunderstanding as to how the neutrals came to make their proposals are now secondary. Of primary importance at the present time is the fact that the proposals made present a practical method of reaching a solution of the basic question and the only method deemed possible by the five neutral Commissioners. The Department is therefore glad to note that the President of Bolivia has already been persuaded of the complete impartiality and loyalty of the neutral Commissioners, and especially of the American Commissioner, towards Bolivia. And this Government hopes earnestly that nothing will be permitted to obscure the point now under consideration, which is fully set forth in the communication sent to the Bolivian Government on October 1 by the neutral Governments, and in the *Aide Memoire* handed to the Bolivian Minister here on October 2 which is quoted in the Department's telegram No. 60.[86]

---

[86] Dated October 2, 6 p. m.; not printed.

The Department desires you carefully to avoid giving any impression that this Government would be willing to act as sole arbitrator. The five neutral Governments are cooperating closely and loyally and it would be embarrassing to this Government to have such a suggestion made. Please do everything you properly and discreetly can to have the offer of the five neutral Governments accepted.

STIMSON

---

724.3415/846 : Telegram

*The Chargé in Bolivia (Hibbard) to the Secretary of State*

LA PAZ, November 15, 1929—6 p. m.
[Received November 16—12 : 12 a. m.]

85. I have been handed the following note by the Bolivian Foreign Office [87] in reply to the offer of good offices made by the five neutral Governments on October 1st. The Spanish text is being transmitted by today's pouch. . . . I have some important comment to make on this which will follow immediately.

"On October 1st, last, the office in my charge received from Your Excellency the note by means of which the Government of the United States, in conjunction with those of Colombia, Mexico, Cuba, and Uruguay was kind enough to renew the offer which the neutral members of the extinct Commission of Inquiry and Conciliation, Bolivia [and] Paraguay, formulated in Washington on September 12th suggesting the advantage of arriving at a definite agreement in the question of the Chaco Boreal and continuing the project of a treaty of arbitration formulated on August 31 in view of the fact that the replies of the Bolivian and Paraguayan delegations contained in the opinion of the neutral delegates certain 'conformity of principle on the fundamental points' of the proposition giving hope for a possible understanding for the adoption of an arbitral formula 'the obstacles being removed and the doubtful points elucidated which were objectionable to the parties in the project submitted to them'.

I consider necessary to establish, to the end that the proceedings may be regularized, that Your Excellency's note and the analogous communications of the other four neutral Governments have given an official character to the offer of good offices of the neutral delegates who in reality presented their new proposition at the very moment when ending the powers conferred on them by the protocol of January 3rd, 1929, and when there also lapsed, by reason of its end, the special authority which they received from the interested parties on July 1st to propose formulae for settlement of the territorial litigation between Bolivia and Paraguay of an unofficial character and within the limits of the protocol mentioned. This circumstance determined the sense of the reply of the Bolivian delegates, dated in Washington, on September 14 in which they declined to continue intervention in the procedure for the settlement of the fundamental question as they were not authorized to do so.

From the tenor of Your Excellency's courteous note which I am

---

[87] Note No. 146, November 13, 1929.

answering, it is judged that the Government of the United States, in conjunction with those of the four friendly countries which assisted on the Commission in Washington, believes it desirable that a previous agreement be reached between Bolivia and Paraguay 'to enter immediately into direct negotiations looking to an agreement at the same time establishing a commission composed of members from the five neutral countries represented on the Commission the work of which terminated on September 13th last'.

The Government of Bolivia believes that although the functioning of this commission would be impractical and premature during the period of direct negotiations which will be held in La Paz or Asunción as soon as diplomatic relations are renewed in accordance with the conciliation agreed upon in Washington, this commission on the other hand would have a very useful and important role in case these negotiations should be abandoned because of the difficulties which may unfortunately present themselves, the moment then having arrived to utilize the good offices generously offered by the five Governments actually engaged in placing their valuable strength in the service of that harmony which should reign between the nations of this continent. The previous formation of any kind of permanent tribunal empowered to 'remove the obstacles which may present themselves during direct negotiations in order that a happy solution may be reached,' as Your Excellency's note states, or, what is the same, the immediate renewal of work by the organization which functioned in the capital of the United States of America with its seat either in the same place or any other to supervise the direct negotiations and avoid all danger of new incidents in the Chaco where as Your Excellency says there are a great number of forts of both parties situated at a short distance from one another, is not necessary in any sense and would be vexatious to the dignity and sovereignty on [of?] these nations since then,[88] as the countries in dispute are reconciled and the incidents of December 1928 have been amicably settled, the honor and faith of Bolivia and Paraguay must remain committed to maintain a peaceful and prudent situation which will make possible a final settlement of the litigation between them without recourse for this purpose to the assistance of [a mediating] organization, a method indicated by international practice only [in cases] where imminent danger of war exists.

It is opportune to point out that the menace of armed encounters in the Chaco does not exist on the part of Bolivia if it is realized that it has been demonstrated before the Commission in Washington that she had no responsibility whatever for the rupture of good relations which occurred at the end of last year. Moreover it would not be logical to continue harboring the fear that the events of December 1928 may recur solely because of the proximity and number of forts when it is remembered that this situation is not new in the Chaco but dates back many years and has never given occasion for dangerous collisions except for the deliberate attack of the Paraguayan army on the Bolivian possession of Vanguardia.

But if, unfortunately, the moment arrives when direct negotiations are abandoned and the loyal propositions of Bolivia for reach-

---

[88] The word "then" is omitted in the translation transmitted with despatch No. 298, November 18, 1929.

ing an agreement with Paraguay are not duly seconded, my Government expects to state to the Government of the United States of America through the medium of Your Excellency that it accepts with pleasure the good offices which the five brother nations so nobly offer and that in such a case it will be disposed to enter into an agreement which will create the organization proposed. The Government of Bolivia also accepts and proclaims as the fundamental basis for the work of the commission so created the juridical rules established by the principle of *uti possidetis* of 1810, the standard of American international law, which, when formulated by the Argentine observer at the Conference of Buenos Aires, was accepted by Paraguay and the authority of which was expressly recognized by the neutral delegates of the Commission at Washington according to the note of September 12th above mentioned. My Government fully agrees with the criterion that in treating a litigation of the character of that sustained by Bolivia and Paraguay, it is inevitable to adopt that juridical standard as the only adequate one to define the possession of a territory over which both parties claim rights emanating from historical titles.

The formal and express condition which my Government considers it indispensable to make in such a case and which must be included in the convention arranged for the acceptance of the good offices in an essential character forming an indivisible whole with the other conditions which the arrangement includes is that Bolivia will not admit under any circumstances the submission to arbitration of an undetermined portion of national territory, nor is she disposed to adopt the process of double arbitration suggested by Paraguay and accepted by the neutral members of the extinct Commission with the object of circumscribing first the material of the litigation and later resolving the best right to the territory thus determined. The Government of Bolivia reaffirms the reservation with which it agreed to the general treaty of arbitration signed on January 5th last year, a reservation which had as its object to exclude the procedure mentioned in the second part of article 4 of this treaty in order to define the specific material of the controversy in case of failure to agree among the interested parties. With this full knowledge [*this idea?*] the Bolivian Foreign Office corroborated the antecedent established in the conference[s] at Buenos Aires [where the] Bolivian delegation refused expressly the procedure of double arbitration suggested by the Paraguayan delegation.

A former agreement between Bolivia and Paraguay celebrated in 1927 (the Gutierrez–Diaz Leon protocol) also established in article 4 that the interested parties 'would fix a determined zone on which the judgment of an arbitral tribunal chosen by common consent should be accepted.'

As the determination of the zone may possibly be the difficulty on which the negotiations entered into to make possible an arbitral solution may break, either during the direct conversations or during the work of the proposed commission, the Government of Bolivia, sincerely desirous of avoiding difficulties, is disposed to propose a mean which will serve as a guide in delimiting the territory which shall be submitted to arbitration.

This mean, which should be accepted prior to placing the settlement of the question in the hands of a commission of neutrals, is none other than that derived from conversational [*conventional*] right or derived from treaties and consists in taking the middle point of those points of demarcation established by the three treaties celebrated in 1879, 1887, and 1894, treaties, which although they were not duly perfected, constitute the only real and worth while antecedents with regard to the opinion of the statesmen of both countries at three different episodes on the old controversy of the Chaco. Taking the middle point of the three points marked [by] these treaties of [*on*] the River Paraguay as the frontier between the two countries the corresponding parallel would be fixed as the northern limit of material [*matter*] in litigation leaving all territory situated to the south of this line to be submitted to arbitration with the limitation which Paraguay cares to place and by virtue of mutual consent.

In proposing this method for determining the demarcation of the territory in dispute, the only one which appears logical and reasonable, the Government of Bolivia believes that it is giving evident proof of the broad and generous spirit with which it is animated in obtaining a decorous solution of this question, and it hopes that the Government of Paraguay, inspired by the same feelings will come to adopt this attitude. As the Governments of the neutral countries, this Chancery hopes that they, persuaded by the just reasons which have caused Bolivia to place herself beyond the excessive and unfounded pretensions which have so often been manifested in the course of this controversy, will lend their valuable moral support toward securing an understanding which will be the first step toward the realization of those earnest hopes for peace and justice by which they are inspired. They will also understand that Bolivia in presenting this indispensable condition in the form above stated for the determination of the zone in litigation, is only endeavoring to prevent contingencies which may permit the fixation of lines or the proposal of bases of settlement fully attributed to an international commission the acts of which always establish precedents. In order that the organization charged with the good offices may have the high respect, which is indispensable in the opinion of my Government for it completely to fulfill its important task, it is necessary that it enjoy to the fullest the absolute confidence of both parties, free from fears, and this reason has influenced the condition imposed by the Government of Bolivia and stated in writing in the present communication.

In requesting Your Excellency to be kind enough to bring the tenor of the preceding considerations to the knowledge of the Government of the United States of America with the renewed expression of the gratitude of the Government of Bolivia for the laudable efforts which it has exerted in this matter, I am pleased to renew to Your Excellency the assurance of my most distinguished consideration."

HIBBARD

724.3415/849 : Telegram

*The Chargé in Bolivia (Hibbard) to the Secretary of State*

LA PAZ, November 16, 1929—noon.
[Received 11:30 p. m.]

87. My telegram No. 85, November 15, 6 p. m. During the past two weeks I have had almost daily conversations with officials of the

Foreign Office and Mr. Luis Abelli on the reply of the Bolivian Government to the offer of good offices by the five neutral Governments which composed the recent Commission and I believe the following comment forms a necessary background for the Department's future use.

Abelli has been chosen by President Siles to handle the matter and will represent Bolivia both in direct negotiations or on an arbitral commission should this be organized. He is a man of exceptional intelligence, fair-minded, and entirely divorced from politics. He has secured the entire confidence of the President, and the recent turn of events is due to him entirely.

President Siles has always favored direct negotiations between the two countries for the following reasons:

1. The question could thus be kept from internal politics and his administration protected.
2. Other South American countries of which Bolivia is suspicious could have no hand in settling the matter.
3. If necessary for internal reasons delay could be resorted to.
4. An arrangement more acceptable to Bolivia could be secured.

Before October 8th (see my telegram 79, October 8, 4 p. m.) the President was considering direct negotiations with the possible unofficial assistance of the United States. Abelli was strongly urging this course. Meantime as mentioned in the last paragraph of the telegram above referred to, there had arisen dissatisfaction with the conduct of the Commission in Washington as far as the suggestions for a fundamental settlement was concerned. This feeling arose primarily I believe from the character of the Bolivian delegates but also from the fact that Bolivia has never been willing to take into consideration any settlement not based on the *uti possidetis* of 1810. I also believe that some of the other neutral delegates have not been as guarded in their statements to the Bolivian delegates as might have been expected.

The President was alarmed by the reports he received of the suggestions of the experts as they all seemed based on economic and geographic phases of the question rather than on historic titles. He became convinced that General McCoy was responsible for these suggestions and that such was the policy of the United States. At this time the internal situation was very complicated as I have reported and party feeling very intense. Some influential members of the Government were violently opposed to the acceptance of good offices or even to direct negotiations and the answer was delayed while the exchange of notes concerning General McCoy's alleged attitude took place.[89]

---

[89] Not printed.

With the help of Abelli the President has now been convinced that whatever may have been the attitude of General McCoy he was given an entirely free hand and that any action taken by the Commission does not represent the policy of the Department or President Hoover. The President believes his mistake to be a natural one as he says that no Latin country would ever have permitted its representative to act without interference. The blame for whatever objectionable suggestions may have been made has now been shifted to Mr. Schoenfeld and the experts.

The fear remains however that should the offer of good offices be accepted and another commission created, suggestions of a similar character would be made and pressure exerted on Bolivia to accept them. As under no condition will she accept arbitration on an undetermined zone or on any other basis than historic titles, this would place her in an arbitrary and unfavorable light. This has determined her refusal of the good offices.

Bolivia's argument as explained to me is as follows:

1. According to the *uti possidetis* of 1810, the entire Chaco up to the confluence of the rivers Pilcomayo and Paraguay belong[s] to Bolivia.

2. After the war in which Paraguay lost much territory to Brazil, Argentina and Uruguay, she sought an extension of her territory in the Chaco just across the river when Bolivia was unable to protect herself due to the enormous distance from her base of supplies, lack of transportation facilities, the character of the territory and the war with Chile, going as far north as 19 degrees 50 minutes and extending along the Pilcomayo River as far as the 61st meridian.

3. Bolivia's only resource, therefore, was to endeavor to arrange a treaty with Paraguay, thus stopping her advance. In this effort three treaties were proposed in 1878, 1887, and [18]94, but although these were accepted by Bolivia they have never been ratified by Paraguay due to political maneuvering in Congress and a desire for delay.

4. The logical action therefore would be to take into consideration the points on the Paraguay River determined by these three proposed treaties and selecting an intermediary point as far south as possible in order to give Bolivia a port and possibility for its development to submit the zone between the point selected and the River Apa to arbitration.

This latter point is the suggestion made in the tenth paragraph of Bolivia's reply. I believe that if the point chosen on the River Paraguay is appropriately [*approximately?*] at parallel 21 degrees 40 minutes Bolivia will concede the territory south without arbitration and in any case will permit Paraguay to choose the other terminus of line on the Pilcomayo River. This, however, is a personal opinion.

[Paraphrase.] As soon as diplomatic relations are resumed Bolivia will propose the conditions indicated in the note to Paraguay, and from what I am able to gather from conversations with those close to the

Government, Bolivia would be very grateful if the United States would take the initiative in immediately suggesting them to Paraguay, indicating the equity and desirability of accepting them. This would greatly facilitate the entire negotiations and would make it unnecessary to inconvenience the other friendly countries who have offered their good offices, permitting the settlement of the matter directly with only the friendly presence of the United States Government as was done in the last part of the Tacna-Arica negotiations.

This last statement was made to me by Mr. Luis Abelli who informs me that it has the approval of President Siles and the Foreign Minister who are the only persons who are aware that it has been made. I believe that it is being made thus informally as President Siles wishes to know the attitude of the Government of the United States before making a formal request. He is apparently convinced of the impartiality and fairness of the United States and he believes that if President Hoover would consent to help, Paraguay would be more willing to cooperate. He definitely does not desire the assistance of any other country or commission. Should the United States consent to assist, diplomatic relations will be resumed at once.

I think that he is sincere and if he can settle the matter, it will be a triumph for him and will remove an irritating problem from internal politics, thus permitting him to devote more time to other problems . . .

I have every confidence in Mr. Abelli who has consented to help in the matter only as long as it is kept out of politics. Mr. Abelli is an ardent admirer of the United States and he thinks that an arrangement can be secured only in this way.

In all these conversations I have followed the instructions of the Department, and I have never indicated in any way that the United States desired or would be willing to assume the sole role in assisting toward any settlement. I have indicated that the offer of good offices was made jointly by the five friendly neutral powers, and that it would be perhaps embarrassing and difficult for the United States to take any initiative alone. Mr. Abelli has the feeling, and I am sure that he represents President Siles in this, that the answer has been so drafted that the other Governments can take no offense. It has been emphasized to the other representatives in La Paz that should direct negotiations fail meantime, good offices will be accepted with the reservation stated. This appeal to the United States is being kept in strict confidence. An early answer would be appreciated. [End paraphrase.]

HIBBARD

724.3415/890a : Telegram

## The Secretary of State to the Chargé in Mexico (Johnson) [90]

WASHINGTON, December 6, 1929—4 p. m.

536. I have discussed with the diplomatic representatives in Washington of Mexico, Colombia, Uruguay and Cuba the reply of the Bolivian Government [91] to the note of the neutral Governments of October first [92] and as the result of these conversations a draft reply has been drawn up which meets with their approval subject of course to the approval of their Governments. They are communicating with their Governments and in order that they may have the same English text as has been considered in Washington they have requested that this Government transmit a copy thereof to their respective Governments. You will please, therefore, hand informally to the Minister for Foreign Affairs the following copy of the note discussed in Washington. The Department will be glad to have any comment made regarding it.

"The Governments of Mexico, Colombia, Uruguay, Cuba, and the United States of America have given very careful thought to the reply received November 16 from the Bolivian Government to their notes of October first, suggesting an agreement between the Bolivian and Paraguayan Governments to enter immediately into direct negotiations for a settlement of the dispute between them, and to establish at the same time a Commission to be appointed by the Governments represented on the recent Commission of Inquiry and Conciliation.

The five Governments desire at the outset to express the great satisfaction with which they have received the statement of the Government of Bolivia that the honor and faith of Bolivia remain committed to maintain a peaceful and prudent situation which will make possible a final settlement of the litigation and that the menace of armed encounters in the Chaco does not exist on the part of Bolivia.

The five Governments concerned have noted with pleasure the feeling of the Government of Bolivia that this Commission would have a very useful and important role in case direct negotiations between Bolivia and Paraguay should be abandoned and that in that case the Bolivian Government expects to accept the good offices tendered. The neutral Governments mentioned have learned with regret, however, that the Government of Bolivia considers the functioning of the proposed Commission impractical and premature during the period of direct negotiations which the Bolivian Government states will be held in La Paz or Asunción as soon as diplomatic relations are renewed in accordance with the conciliation agreed upon in Washington.

---

[90] The same, *mutatis mutandis*, on the same date to the diplomatic representatives in Colombia (No. 59), Cuba (No. 134), and Uruguay (No. 23).

[91] See telegram No. 85, November 15, 6 p. m., from the Chargé in Bolivia, p. 920.

[92] See Department's circular telegram, September 23, 6 p. m., to the diplomatic representatives in Bolivia and Paraguay, p. 903, and telegram No. 57, September 30, 10 a. m., to the Chargé in Bolivia, p. 905.

As the Bolivian Government, in this connection, states that the previous formation of any kind of 'permanent tribunal' empowered to remove obstacles which may arise during the course of the direct negotiations is not necessary and would be vexatious to the dignity and sovereignty of Bolivia and Paraguay, the five neutral Governments fear that their notes of October first have not been completely understood by the Bolivian Government. The fact that the Government of Paraguay has already accepted the plan suggested by the neutral Governments would indicate that this interpretation was not given the proposal by that Government and encourages the neutral Governments to think that, when rightly understood, the plan will commend itself to Bolivia. No permanent tribunal was suggested but merely the setting up of a Commission to use its good offices in overcoming difficulties which the Bolivian note under acknowledgment states may unfortunately arise. The use of friendly neutral good offices in the carrying through of delicate international negotiations is a recognized and usual international practice and is one that is not necessarily resorted to only where imminent danger of war exists. It has been used in many cases in the past in negotiations between American nations where there was not only no imminent danger of war but no remote danger of war, and it certainly was not considered and is not now to be considered as in any wise derogatory to the dignity and sovereignty of the nations concerned.

Both Bolivia and Paraguay have affirmed their adherence to the principle of arbitration in its application to their present controversy. The question that remains to be settled, therefore, is the basis of that arbitration. It may be that this question can happily be arranged in direct negotiations between the two countries. The Bolivian Government however very aptly points out in its note under acknowledgment that the determination of the zone or the scope of the arbitration may possibly be, as it has been in the past, the difficulty in the way of a successful outcome. It was to avoid any such result that the neutral Governments suggested the setting up of a friendly neutral Commission which, far from impeding direct negotiations, would assist in overcoming any obstacles and through such direct negotiations facilitate an agreement between the two contending nations for a peaceful solution of their difficulties by arbitration.

The five neutral Governments have noted that the Government of Bolivia devotes a portion of the note under acknowledgment to establishing the conditions under which the Commission which is to be constituted shall operate. The suggestion that the Bolivian Government deems it indispensable formally and expressly to propose conditions for inclusion in a convention to be arranged for the purpose of governing the operations of this Commission indicates some misapprehension as to the tender of good offices which the neutral Governments hasten to remove. Their action in tendering their good offices arose from a sincere desire to assist both interested Governments in equal degree, without partiality either as to the facts of the controversy or as to the diplomatic instruments which have heretofore been formulated in connection therewith or may hereafter be elaborated to define the method of reaching or the achievement of the final settlement. It was not their understanding that a convention would be required to bring about the establishment of the Commission. Such a Commission will necessarily be guided by the accepted standards of international law in exercising its function of bringing the parties into agreement by any method acceptable to them and in harmony with the principles of the law of nations. But the Bolivian Government would not, they feel sure, desire the neutral Governments, in advance of the constitution of the Commission, to lay down conditions for its operation that would amount to prejudgment on the part of the neutral Governments of some of the very questions at issue between Bolivia and Paraguay. The neutral Governments have cherished the hope that the two contending Governments would enter into negotiations with an open mind and without stipulating indispensable conditions, thus showing their sincere desire of reaching an agreement for the mutual accommodation of their interests. If the negotiations can be entered into on this basis, the five neutral Governments feel convinced that a satisfactory agreement can be speedily arrived at.

The five neutral Governments observe the special reference made by the Bolivian Government in its note under acknowledgment to the note of September 12, 1929, addressed by the Chairman of the extinct Commission of Inquiry and Conciliation on behalf of the neutral Delegates to the Commissioners for Bolivia. They desire to take this opportunity to clear up an evident misunderstanding as to the nature of the proposal therein made which the note under consideration describes as involving a process of double arbitration. The neutral Governments do not so understand the note of September 12 in conjunction with the draft arbitration treaty submitted to the Bolivian Delegation on August 31 by the Chairman of the extinct Commission on behalf of the neutral Delegates, and are glad to state their understanding of the matter:

As modified by the note of September 12, the arbitration plan contemplated three distinct possibilities for formulating the *compromis*, namely, (1) a direct agreement between Bolivia and Paraguay as to the subject matter of the litigation to be submitted to arbitration; (2) in the event of failure to reach such an agreement directly, the determination of the *compromis* by arbiters; and, (3) the right of either Party to withdraw from the proceedings should the formula of the *compromis* determined by the arbiters be unsatisfactory. This broad method of settlement, it will be noted, affords all possible latitude to the Parties in furthering the process of arbitration and holds high hope of successfully reaching a peaceful adjustment of the existing difficulty.

Noting with pleasure that the Government of Bolivia expects to inform them of its acceptance of their offer of good offices, should the direct negotiations fail, the five Governments are glad to state their readiness to appoint at that time members to form a friendly neutral Commission whose good offices it hopes will be of service to the two Governments concerned. In the meantime, in order that their services may be the more easily available to the two contending Governments, they take pleasure in stating that they are willing that their diplomatic representatives in Washington keep in touch with the situation as it develops in order to be of immediate service in case of necessity. The neutral Governments would also be willing to have their diplomatic representatives constitute, in the absence of specially appointed delegates, the Commission above referred to.

It has been noted with satisfaction by the five Governments concerned that Bolivia proposes that direct negotiations should be held in La Paz and Asunción as soon as diplomatic relations are renewed in accordance with the conciliation agreed upon in Washington. The five neutral Governments are hopeful that as little delay as possible may ensue in formally resuming diplomatic relations in pursuance of the agreement to that effect reached last September.

However, over two months have elapsed since the agreement was made for the reestablishment of diplomatic relations and as this step will in any event necessarily entail further delay the five Governments venture to suggest that the diplomatic representatives of Bolivia and Paraguay in Washington be authorized to enter now into direct negotiations for a definitive settlement of the question outstanding between them. The neutral Governments are pleased to make this suggestion, as the Government of Paraguay has already accepted their tender of good offices made on October 1.

Accordingly, I am instructed to inquire whether, in the light of the above considerations, coupled with the explanation of the understanding as to the proper function of the Commission to the creation of which the Bolivian Government agrees, and in view of the readiness of the five neutral Governments to cooperate as indicated, the Government of Bolivia would consider that it can now favorably act upon either the tender of good offices made on October 1, last, or the suggestion now made by the neutral Governments."

STIMSON

---

724.3415/888a : Telegram

*The Secretary of State to the Chargé in Bolivia (Hibbard)*

WASHINGTON, December 6, 1929—4 p. m.

72. As a result of conversations in Washington with the representatives of the other neutral governments, the following note has been drawn up which has been submitted to those Governments for their comment and suggestions. Do not transmit this to the Bolivian Government until you receive further specific instructions to do so.

[Here follows the text of the note transmitted in telegram No. 536, December 6, 4 p. m., to the Chargé in Mexico, printed *supra*.]

STIMSON

---

724.3415/898a : Telegram

*The Secretary of State to the Chargé in Mexico (Johnson)* [93]

WASHINGTON, December 9, 1929—7 p. m.

538. Department's 536, December 6, 4 p. m. It is of course understood that the communication in question will not be sent to the

---

[93] The same on the same date to the diplomatic representatives in Colombia (No. 60), Cuba (No. 137), and Uruguay (No. 24).

Bolivian Government until it has been agreed to by all the neutral Governments. When this is done a date will be fixed by mutual agreement on which to transmit it.

STIMSON

724.3415/912 : Telegram

*The Chargé in Mexico (Johnson) to the Secretary of State*

MEXICO CITY, December 23, 1929—5 p. m.
[Received December 24—2 : 28 a. m.]

386. Your 536 December 6, 4 p. m. The following note was received today from the Foreign Office:

"In reply I take pleasure in informing you that the proposed note appears to be perfectly well suited to the purpose aimed at by the Governments of the neutral countries, and therefore the Government of Mexico is very happy to express its agreement with the ideas contained therein, for said Government, wishing to cooperate towards a friendly solution of the Chaco question, desires to omit no effort which might aid in effecting the conciliation of the contending countries.

The Mexican Government believes it very suitable that the chiefs of mission at Washington be kept constantly informed of the progress of the negotiations which may be carried on between the plenipotentiaries of the two countries, accredited to the Government of the United States.

Nevertheless, with regard to the role which the chiefs of mission of the neutral countries are to play, the wisdom of organizing those plenipotentiaries into a friendly neutral commission, according to the provisions of the Gondra Convention,[94] is questioned.

The Chaco question being so complicated, it is difficult for the chiefs of mission to find the time necessary for the unceasing study of the documents which are presented and for taking part constantly in negotiations as laborious as those of the extinct Commission of Inquiry and Conciliation, should they be called upon to officiate in a manner requiring a thorough and complete knowledge of the case.

Moreover, if the plenipotentiaries should function as a friendly neutral commission, the Governments would be besieged by continuous representations of the representatives of Bolivia and Paraguay, requesting instructions for the plenipotentiaries, and the latter Governments might also make recriminations for some attitude, however just, taken by the members of said commission, believing that as diplomats they acted under definite instructions.

For these reasons it is suggested that the ninth paragraph, which begins: 'Noting with pleasure that the Government of Bolivia expects to inform them of its acceptance of their offer of good offices, should the direct negotiations fail, the five Governments' be retained *in toto* until the words 'in order to be of immediate service' are reached and that instead of these words there be inserted 'in order that when

---

[94] *Foreign Relations*, 1923, vol. I, p. 308; see also *ibid.*, 1928, vol. I, pp. 644 ff.

proper they may be utilized for the organization of the commission in question, which should be composed of delegates especially appointed thereto.' With these words the paragraph would end, the closing sentence which says 'the neutral Governments would also be willing to have their diplomatic representatives constitute, in the absence of specially appointed delegates, the commission above referred to' being suppressed."

Full text and translation being forwarded by pouch today.

JOHNSON

724.3415/912 : Telegram

*The Secretary of State to the Chargé in Mexico (Johnson)*

WASHINGTON, December 27, 1929—6 p. m.

559. Your 386, December 23, 5 p. m. The Department concurs in the change proposed by the Mexican Government and is making inquiry of the other neutral Governments to see if it meets also with their approval. You will be informed of their replies.

STIMSON

724.3415/914a : Telegram

*The Secretary of State to the Ambassador in Cuba (Guggenheim)*[95]

WASHINGTON, December 27, 1929—6 p. m.

145. Department's 134, December 6, 4 p. m.[96] All the neutral Governments have now agreed to the proposed note with the exception of Mexico. That Government expresses its agreement with the ideas contained in the note and its wish to cooperate towards a friendly solution of the question and its desire to omit no effort which might aid in effecting the conciliation of the contending countries. It states that while it believes it very suitable that the Chiefs of Mission in Washington be kept constantly informed of the progress of the negotiations which may be carried on between the Plenipotentiaries of the two countries it feels that the Chaco question is so complicated that it would be difficult for the Chiefs of Mission to find the time necessary for the unceasing study of the documents presented and for taking part constantly in negotiations as laborious as those of the extinct Commission of Inquiry and Conciliation. Furthermore, if the Plenipotentiaries should function as a friendly neutral Commission, the Governments would be besieged by numerous representations of the Governments of Bolivia and Paraguay, requesting instructions for the Plenipotentiaries, and that those Governments might also make recriminations for some attitude, however just, taken by the

---

[95] The same on the same date to the diplomatic representatives in Colombia (No. 62) and Uruguay (No. 25).

[96] See footnote 90, p. 927.

members of the said Commission, believing that as diplomats they acted under definite instructions. The Mexican Government therefore suggests that the ninth paragraph which begins "Noting with pleasure that the Government of Bolivia expects to inform them of its acceptance" et cetera be modified to read as follows: "Noting with pleasure that the Government of Bolivia expects to inform them of its acceptance of their offer of good offices, should the direct negotiations fail, the five Governments are glad to state their readiness to appoint at that time members to form a friendly neutral Commission whose good offices it hopes will be of service to the two Governments concerned. In the meantime, in order that their services may be the more easily available to the two contending Governments, they take pleasure in stating that they are willing that their diplomatic representatives in Washington keep in touch with the situation as it develops in order that when proper they may be utilized for the organization of the Commission in question, which should be composed of delegates especially appointed thereto."

Please communicate as quickly as possible to the Government to which you are accredited this proposed modification and advise it that this Government is agreeable to the change suggested by the Government of Mexico and that if this change is agreeable to the other neutral Governments as well it will suggest the forwarding of the notes to the Bolivian Government at a date mutually agreeable to the five neutral Governments. Please endeavor to expedite a reply and inform the Department thereof by cable.

STIMSON

# BOUNDARY DISPUTES

## Colombia and Nicaragua [1]

717.2114/82 : Telegram

### The Secretary of State to the Minister in Nicaragua (Eberhardt)

[Paraphrase]

WASHINGTON, February 2, 1929—8 p. m.

23. Your telegram No. 33, January 30, 4 p. m.[2] It is a matter of regret to the Department that President Moncada is personally opposed to the treaty between Colombia and Nicaragua [3] and that there is strong opposition to the treaty in the Nicaraguan Congress and in the country at large. The Department is unable to understand why such opposition should exist, since Nicaragua, in giving up her claim to the San Andres Archipelago (which Nicaragua never occupied) without monetary compensation, obtains in return, likewise without monetary compensation, the renunciation of Colombia's claim to the Mosquito Coast and Great and Little Corn Islands.

The Government of the United States has more than an academic interest in this adjustment, since it involves Great and Little Corn Islands, leased to the United States by Nicaragua in the convention of 1914,[4] and therefore the Government of the United States would be much concerned if the treaty between Colombia and Nicaragua should fail.

Please discuss this subject again with the President and request him to urge approval of the treaty during the present session of the Nicaraguan Congress. You may say that the Department feels sure that neither Nicaragua nor Colombia could have expected a more advantageous treaty, and that no more favorable terms can be expected in the future if the present treaty is not approved.

KELLOGG

---

717.2114/85 : Telegram

### The Minister in Nicaragua (Eberhardt) to the Secretary of State

MANAGUA, February 8, 1929—noon.
[Received 2:55 p. m.]

43. Department's 23, February 2, 8 p. m. In compliance with the Department's instructions I have again discussed the matter with the

---

[1] Continued from *Foreign Relations*, 1928, vol. I, pp. 701–706.
[2] Not printed.
[3] Signed March 24, 1928; *Foreign Relations*, 1928, vol. I, p. 703.
[4] *Ibid.*, 1916, p. 849.

President and he told me that he would urge approval of the treaty during the present session of Congress.

EBERHARDT

717.2114/94

*The Minister in Colombia (Caffery) to the Secretary of State*

No. 564                                   BOGOTÁ, September 10, 1929.
                                          [Received October 5.]

SIR: I have the honor to state that the Ministry of Foreign Affairs has informally brought to my attention the situation in regard to their treaty with Nicaragua; it has been approved by the Colombian Congress but no action has been taken by Nicaragua: the Minister would be very appreciative of any good offices on our part looking to the ratification of the treaty by the Managua Congress at its approaching December sessions.

I respectfully suggest that the Legation at Managua be authorized to exert its good offices in the premises.

I have [etc.]                             JEFFERSON CAFFERY

717.2114/92

*The Chargé in Nicaragua (Hanna) to the Secretary of State*

No. 1161                                  MANAGUA, September 21, 1929.
                                          [Received September 25.]

SIR: With reference to my despatch No. 1038 of June 14, 1929,[5] and previous correspondence regarding the pending treaty negotiations between Nicaragua and Colombia, I have the honor to report that I recently received a letter from the Colombian Minister in Nicaragua, Mr. Manuel Esguerra, who is temporarily conducting his Mission in Guatemala, in which he discusses the subject.

Mr. Esguerra stated in his letter that Dr. Cordero Reyes, Nicaraguan Minister for Foreign Affairs, told him on repeated occasions that the Nicaraguan Government would appoint a commission prior to the next regular session of the Nicaraguan Congress, which would study the matter and make a report for the information of the Congress and the public. Mr. Esguerra requested that this Legation use its good offices to bring about the appointment of this commission without delay, and expressed his fear that if this is not done neither the Congress nor the Nicaraguan Government will be able to form an opinion in the matter and there will be no action on the treaty at the next session of the Congress.

I recently inquired of Dr. Cordero Reyes as to the present status of the treaty negotiations and he told me in reply that this Govern-

_____
[5] Not printed.

ment had been considering the creation of a commission to make a study of the matter and to report to Congress but that President Moncada thought that this would involve an expense which the Government can ill-afford at this time and that consequently nothing has been done towards the creation of the commission. I asked Dr. Cordero Reyes if the expense might not be obviated in part at least by using a commission of Senators and Deputies which might also have the additional advantage of greater influence with the Congress. He said that this might be done and he would give it consideration. If such a commission is to make a thorough study of the question before the Congress convenes it should be appointed without further delay.

I have never discussed this matter with President Moncada but I have touched upon it incidentally on one or two occasions with Dr. Cordero Reyes, and I have formed the opinion that the Administration continues to be opposed to ratification of the treaty. Dr. Cordero Reyes has told me that there was a great outburst of public indignation over the terms of the treaty when they first became known and that this opposition would be renewed if the treaty should be again brought up for consideration. He said that it certainly would fail of ratification unless it should be strongly recommended by a commission of the character mentioned above and that he thought it would be futile for the Administration to attempt to secure ratification without such support.

I pointed out to Dr. Cordero Reyes that the Administration would appear to be in a particularly favorable position because the treaty is the product of negotiations initiated and conducted by a Conservative Administration and asked him to give this phase of the matter his careful consideration. My conversations, however, with Dr. Cordero Reyes in connection with the treaty have been of a very general nature and not directed towards obtaining some specific action by this Government.

I have replied to the letter of the Colombian Minister with a mere acknowledgment of its receipt and the statement that I will not fail to give the matter attention and have consulted the Department in this connection.

I have [etc.] MATTHEW E. HANNA

717.2114/92

*The Secretary of State to the Chargé in Nicaragua (Hanna)*

No. 573                    WASHINGTON, October 7, 1929.

SIR: Reference is made to the Legation's despatch No. 1161, of September 21, 1929, reporting the receipt of a letter from the Colombian Minister to Nicaragua in which he requests the good offices of the American Legation in bringing about the appointment of a commission to study the Treaty of March 24, 1928, between Colombia and Nicaragua to the end that its ratification by Nicaragua be facilitated.

As was stated in the Department's telegram No. 23, of February 2, 8 p. m., 1929, this Government is interested in the settlement of the territorial litigation between Colombia and Nicaragua by the Treaty in question since it involves Great and Little Corn Islands, leased to the Government of the United States by the Government of Nicaragua under the provisions of Article 2 of the Nicaraguan Canal Route Convention of August 5, 1914. Apart from this consideration, however, the Department is of the opinion that the solution contemplated by the Treaty is reasonable and just, and that it would appear to make possible a dignified and simple termination of a controversy that has extended over a long period of time. In so far as this Government is aware, the Mosquito Coast of Nicaragua and Great and Little Corn Islands have not in recent times been in the possession of Colombia, nor has the San Andrés Archipelago been held by Nicaragua. Unqualified reciprocal recognition of sovereignty over those territories accordingly seems to be proper, and it is not believed that Nicaragua can negotiate or otherwise obtain a better settlement or one which involves the payment by Colombia of any monetary consideration.

In these circumstances, the Department has no objection to your compliance with the request of the Colombian Minister to the extent which, in your discretion, such action is advisable. In any conversation you may hold on this subject, it is desired that you shall refrain from discussing the treaty arrangements affecting the Corn Islands to which this Government is a party, although you should, of course, make it clear that the Government of the United States has no ulterior motive for its interest in the ratification of the Treaty, and entertains no desire to acquire possession of any of the islands of the San Andrés Archipelago to which it pertains.

I am [etc.]
For the Secretary of State:
FRANCIS WHITE

---

717.2114/94

*The Secretary of State to the Minister in Colombia (Caffery)*

No. 96                                    WASHINGTON, October 14, 1929.

SIR: Reference is made to your despatch No. 564, dated September 10, 1929, reporting that the Colombian Minister for Foreign Affairs has informally brought to your attention the situation with respect to the Treaty of March 24, 1928, between Colombia and Nicaragua, and has stated that he would be appreciative of any efforts made by the Government of the United States to bring about ratification of the Treaty by the Nicaraguan Government.

In reply you are advised that similar informal representations were made to the American Legation at Managua by the Colombian Minister to Nicaragua, and that the Department as a result thereof advised the American Chargé d'Affaires at Managua that it had no objection to his compliance with the request of the Colombian Minister to the extent which in his discretion such action might be advisable. A copy of the Department's instruction to the American Chargé d'Affaires at Managua, No. 573 dated October 7, 1929, is transmitted herewith for your information and guidance.[6]

I am [etc.]

For the Secretary of State:
FRANCIS WHITE

---

### Costa Rica and Panama [7]

718.1915/846

*The Minister in Costa Rica (Davis) to the Secretary of State*

No. 1554

SAN JOSÉ, June 5, 1929.
[Received June 17.]

SIR: I have the honor to report that the President's private and confidential Secretary, Mr. Ruben Castro, recently called at my office at the request of President González to inform me of the activities of the Chilean Government in connection with the Panaman-Costa Rican boundary controversy. The following is a summary of the information given to me by Mr. Castro:

Mr. Castro stated that several weeks ago the Chilean Chargé d'Affaires in Costa Rica, Mr. Irarrazabal, called on the Minister for Foreign Affairs and offered the mediation of the Chilean Government in the Costa Rica-Panaman boundary controversy, suggesting that Costa Rica and Panama appoint envoys before the Government of Chile with instructions to enter into negotiations for a settlement of the boundary controversy, with the mediation of the Chilean Minister for Foreign Affairs.

The proposal was presented to President González who instructed the Minister for Foreign Affairs to express appreciation for the interest of the Chilean Government but, at the same time, to express doubts as to the advisability of sending an expensive mission to Chile without some advance indication regarding the proposals which the Panaman Government would present. The President also instructed the Minister for Foreign Affairs to state that, since direct negotiations had been in progress with the Panaman Minister in

---

[6] *Supra.*
[7] For previous correspondence, see *Foreign Relations*, 1926, vol. I, pp. 539 ff.

Costa Rica, Mr. Tomás Arias, and since it has been reported that Mr. Arias will soon return to Costa Rica to continue these negotiations, the acceptance of the Chilean proposal might reflect unfavorably upon Mr. Arias and his negotiations.

The Chilean Chargé d'Affaires later discussed the matter with the President's Secretary and was again given the reply previously communicated to him through the Minister for Foreign Affairs.

Shortly thereafter the Chilean Chargé visited the President's Secretary and proposed that the negotiations for the settlement of the controversy be conducted in San José between Minister Arias of Panama and a representative of the Costa Rican Government, the Chilean Minister in San José to act as mediator.

The Costa Rican authorities wishing to ascertain whether the initiative for this movement came from the Chilean Government or the Panaman Government, were informed by the Chilean Chargé that the suggestion came from the President of Panama. At the request of Costa Rican authorities, the Chilean Chargé submitted, in writing, to the Costa Rican Government, excerpts from a confidential report transmitted to the Chilean Government by its representative in Panama which purport to indicate that the initiative came from the President of Panama. . . .

After hearing the above report on the activities of the Chilean Government in this matter, I discreetly inquired as to the attitude of the Costa Rican Government towards the proposal and was informed by Mr. Castro that President González is not enthusiastic about considering the boundary controversy at this time. Mr. Castro also informed me that President González hesitates to consider the proposal for fear that the mediation of Chile might be interpreted as a reflection upon the good offices previously extended by the Government of the United States in this matter, and that he would not wish to take any action that could be interpreted as showing a lack of consideration for and appreciation of the valuable service previously rendered by the United States. My impression is that President González is willing to accept the mediation of the Chilean Legation should he receive some indication that the Department, on its part, perceives no objection to the mediation of Chile. Mr. Castro indicated that the President desires to discuss the matter with me with an idea of ascertaining the attitude of the Department.

I shall be pleased if the Department will instruct me by cable as to the attitude I should take in this matter when the President confers with me about it.

In discussing the proposed Chilean mediation Mr. Castro stated that the President would be pleased if the Department of State could be a party to any negotiations that may be entered into. He also discussed the possibility of conducting negotiations in Washington with the joint mediation of a representative of the Department and the Chilean Ambassador or in San José with the joint mediation of the American and Chilean Ministers. He also discussed the possibility of negotiations in Washington with the joint mediation of a representative of the Department and of the Peruvian and Chilean Ambassadors, no doubt having in mind the idea that since Peru and Chile have recently settled their controversy by mutual accord,[8] their participation in the negotiations might have a sentimental value. These observations on his part, however, were quite informal.

It appears possible that the President of Panama may desire to effect a settlement of the controversy without the assistance of the United States, because of the attitude assumed by the Department when an armed conflict between Panama and Costa Rica developed in 1921 over the boundary question. At that time the Department recognized the validity of the boundary award of Chief Justice White to which Panama had objected.[9]

I am transmitting herewith a brief history of the boundary controversy between Costa Rica and Panama [10] which may be of interest to the Department.

I have [etc.]                                          Roy T. Davis

718.1915/847 : Telegram

*The Minister in Costa Rica (Davis) to the Secretary of State*

San José, June 21, 1929—noon.
[Received 4:20 p. m.]

45. Legation's despatch number 1554 of June 5, 1929. President González today informed me that the Panaman Government has proposed boundary negotiations here between Minister Arias and Costa Rican representative under good offices of the Chilean Minister.

At a Cabinet meeting yesterday it was decided to accept the proposal with the understanding that negotiations are to be held under the joint good offices of the Ministers of the United States and Chile.

While it is possible that the Panaman Government may not accept this suggestion, please instruct me as to the attitude I should assume in this matter.

Davis

[8] See Tacna-Arica dispute, pp. 720 ff.
[9] See *Foreign Relations*, 1921, vol. i, pp. 175 ff.
[10] Not printed.

718.1915/851

*The Minister in Costa Rica (Davis) to the Secretary of State*

No. 1568                                    SAN JOSÉ, June 21, 1929.
                                            [Received July 2.]

SIR: Referring to my cablegram No. 45 of June 21, 12 noon, with reference to the information given me by President González relative to the proposed boundary negotiations between the Governments of Panama and Costa Rica, I have the honor to report as follows:

Mr. Rubén Castro, the President's private secretary, called me this morning under instructions of the President, to inform me that the Panaman Government had proposed that negotiations relative to the Panama-Costa Rica boundary controversy be conducted in San José between the Panaman Minister to Costa Rica, Mr. Tomás Arias, and a representative of the Costa Rican Government, these negotiations to be conducted under the good offices of the Chilean Minister in San José. This proposal was transmitted to the Costa Rican Government through the Chilean Legation here.

Mr. Castro informed me that the proposal was discussed at a Cabinet meeting yesterday and that it decided to accept the proposal with the understanding that the negotiations are to be carried on under the joint good offices of the Ministers of the United States and Chile in Costa Rica. He stated that it was the consensus of opinion of the Cabinet that a representative of the Department should participate in these negotiations because of the friendly interest previously manifested by the Department in the controversy. He also stated that the President entertains serious doubts as to the success of the negotiations, since it appeared probable that Panama will insist upon material concessions which cannot be accepted by Costa Rica.

I am under the impression that President González, because of disturbed political conditions in Costa Rica, may feel that negotiations at this time are inopportune and his suggestion that a representative of the Department shall participate in the negotiations may have been made for the purpose of delaying these negotiations.

In my despatch No. 1554 dated June 5, 1929, I observed that the Government of Panama may feel disposed to carry on the negotiations without the coöperation of the United States because of the attitude assumed by the Department at the time of the conflict between Panama and Costa Rica in 1921.

I have not at any time suggested that a representative of the Department should participate in these negotiations.

I have [etc.]                                    ROY T. DAVIS

718.1915/847 : Telegram

*The Secretary of State to the Minister in Costa Rica (Davis)*

WASHINGTON, June 22, 1929—3 p. m.

25. Legation's 45, June 21, noon. You may in your discretion advise President González that the Government of the United States would view with pleasure a satisfactory solution of the boundary dispute between Costa Rica and Panama, and that it would have no objection should that settlement be arrived at by direct negotiations between the two Governments or by negotiations conducted under the good offices of the Chilean Minister.

The Department however does not desire to enter into any joint action in this question.

STIMSON

718.1915/853

*The Minister in Costa Rica (Davis) to the Secretary of State*

No. 1641

SAN JOSÉ, September 2, 1929.
[Received September 16.]

SIR: Referring to this Legation's confidential despatches No. 1554 and 1568 dated June 5 and June 21, 1929, respectively, and the Department's cablegram No. 25 dated June 22, 3 p. m., with reference to the proposed mediation of the Government of Chile in the boundary controversy between Costa Rica and Panama, I have the honor to submit the following report on recent developments in this matter:—

When Mr. Tomas Arias, Panaman Minister in Costa Rica, returned to Costa Rica on August 21st after a leave of absence in Panama, he was quoted in the local press as having stated that the Government of Chile had offered to act as mediator in the boundary dispute, but that the Government of Panama desired to treat with the Government of Costa Rica in this matter in an effort to settle the controversy by direct negotiations. The following day, Minister Arias gave out an interview in which he rectified this statement.

In the meantime, however, the Chilean representative in Costa Rica informed the Costa Rican Government of the first statement made by Minister Arias. The Private Secretary of President González has informed me that the Chilean Government has now informed its representative here that it will make its good offices available only in case both governments jointly request the cooperation of the Chilean Government.

I have [etc.]

ROY T. DAVIS

738.3915/398

### Dominican Republic and Haiti [11]

*The Haitian Secretary of State for Foreign Affairs (León) to the Secretary of State*

[Translation]

PORT-AU-PRINCE, March 15, 1929.
[Received April 12.]

MR. SECRETARY OF STATE: On January 21, 1929, the Government of the Republic of Haiti and the Government of the Dominican Republic signed a Treaty in the city of Santo Domingo,[12] for the purpose of arriving at the settlement of the frontier differences which have long existed between the two States, and to establish the definitive delimitation of their respective territories. To accomplish this delimitation, the Treaty provides for the appointment by the two High Contracting Parties of a Commission charged with undertaking the necessary labors; and, in order to assure every guarantee for the execution of the proposed line, and to remove every obstacle capable of paralyzing the work of the Commissioners, the Treaty likewise sets up a special mixed commission to arbitrate supremely and finally the difficulties of every kind which the tracing of the frontier line may occasion. This second Commission will be composed of five members, the nationals respectively of the Republic of Haiti, the Dominican Republic, the United States of North America, the United States of Brazil and the United States of Venezuela. The two interested Governments, with the idea of surrounding the appointment of the arbitrators with all desirable precautions, have agreed to request, if it should be necessary, the chief of each of the three last named States to select the citizen of his country who will be summoned to fulfill this delicate mission. Article 7 of the Treaty, a copy of which I send Your Excellency, under this cover, has confirmed the agreement of the two Governments in this respect.

In informing Your Excellency of these facts I take the liberty of hoping that you will be so good as to advise the President of the United States of America of the communication which the President of the Republic of Haiti reserves for himself the honor of sending him if later circumstances necessitate the meeting of the Arbitration Commission.

I take [etc.]        CAMILLE A. LEÓN

---

[11] Continued from *Foreign Relations*, 1928, vol. I, pp. 706–712.
[12] For text of the treaty, see League of Nations Treaty Series, vol. cv, p. 193.

738.3915/400

*The Secretary of State to the High Commissioner in Haiti (Russell)*

No. 416                                           WASHINGTON, May 9, 1929.

SIR: In a note of March 15, a copy of which in translation is enclosed herewith,[12a] the Haitian Government requested the Department to ascertain if the President would be willing to appoint an American member to the Mixed Commission, which may be established under certain conditions, in accordance with the Haitian Dominican Boundary Treaty of January 21, 1921 [*1929*].

The Department desires you to transmit the enclosed reply to the Haitian Secretary of State for Foreign Affairs and to endeavor to determine informally what the conditions are to be for the payment of the members of the Mixed Commission, should such a Commission be formed.

I am [etc.]
                                       For the Secretary of State:
                                                  FRANCIS WHITE

[Enclosure]

*The Secretary of State to the Haitian Secretary of State for Foreign Affairs (León)*

                                                 WASHINGTON, May 9, 1929.

EXCELLENCY: I have the honor to acknowledge your note of March 15, enclosing a copy of the recent Boundary Treaty between the Republic of Haiti and the Dominican Republic, and requesting me to ascertain whether the President would be willing to appoint the American member of the Special Mixed Commission, should the President of Haiti find it necessary to request the President of the United States to designate such a member.

I take pleasure in informing you that the President will be glad to make such an appointment in the event that the formation of the Mixed Commission becomes necessary.

Accept [etc.]
                                                  HENRY L. STIMSON

738.3915/408

*The Dominican Minister (Morales) to the Secretary of State*

[Translation]

                                               WASHINGTON, August 14, 1929.

MR. SECRETARY OF STATE: I have the honor to forward herewith to Your Excellency the letter sent to you through this Legation by the Secretary of State for Foreign Relations of the Dominican Republic, and also copies of the Treaties of Peace, Friendship, Arbitra-

[12a] *Supra.*

tion [13] and Boundary [14] recently concluded with the Republic of Haiti to which the letter has reference.

Accept [etc.] A. MORALES

[Enclosure—Translation]

*The Dominican Minister for Foreign Affairs (Sanchez) to the Secretary of State*

No. 295 SANTO DOMINGO, July 9, 1929.

MR. SECRETARY OF STATE: As is doubtless already known to Your Excellency, the boundary dispute long standing between the Dominican Republic and the Republic of Haiti has happily been settled through a treaty that was signed on January 21, 1929, at Santo Domingo, and was subsequently approved by the legislative bodies of the two countries, the ratifications being exchanged at Santo Domingo on the 29th of April of this year.

Article 7 of that treaty provides that if the boundary commission should be unable to agree there shall be organized a commission consisting of five members elected as follows:

One Dominican by the President of the Dominican Republic; one Haitian by the President of the Republic of Haiti; one North American by the President of the United States of North America; one Brazilian by the President of the United States of Brazil; and one Venezuelan by the President of the United States of Venezuela, upon requests made by the two high contracting parties.

I have, therefore, the honor to forward herewith to Your Excellency a certified copy of the Dominican-Haitian Boundary Treaty of January 21, 1929, with a request that you kindly take note of the provisions in Article 7 above mentioned, which is prompted by lofty ideals of American solidarity.

I avail myself [etc.] RAFAEL AUGUSTO SANCHEZ

---

738.3915/408

*The Secretary of State to the Dominican Minister (Morales)*

WASHINGTON, August 21, 1929.

SIR: I have the honor to acknowledge your note of August 14 with which you were good enough to forward to me a letter from the Secretary of State for Foreign Relations of the Dominican Republic with which he enclosed a certified copy of the Treaty for Peace, Friendship and Arbitration and of the Haitian-Dominican

[13] Signed February 20, 1929; League of Nations Treaty Series, vol. cv, p. 215.
[14] Signed January 21, 1929; *ibid.*, p. 193.

Boundary Treaty recently concluded between the Dominican Republic and the Republic of Haiti.

I desire to thank you for transmitting this letter, and I have the honor to request that you be so kind as to forward the enclosed reply to the Secretary of State for Foreign Relations of the Dominican Republic.

Accept [etc.]

For the Secretary of State:
NELSON TRUSLER JOHNSON

[Enclosure]

*The Secretary of State to the Dominican Minister for Foreign Affairs (Peynado)*

WASHINGTON, August 21, 1929.

EXCELLENCY: I have the honor to acknowledge the note of August 14 of Your Excellency's predecessor, with which he was kind enough to enclose a certified copy of the Treaty for Peace, Friendship and Arbitration and of the Haitian-Dominican Boundary Treaty recently concluded between the Dominican Republic and the Republic of Haiti and to call attention particularly to Article 7 of this Boundary Treaty.

I have taken note of the text of Article 7 of the Boundary Treaty which provides for the organization of a Mixed Commission, in the event that there is a disagreement on the part of the Boundary Commission, one member of which Commission shall be appointed by the President of the United States.

I desire to avail myself of this opportunity of expressing my pleasure at the successful outcome of the negotiations entered into between the Dominican Republic and the Republic of Haiti for the settlement of the long standing boundary difficulty.

Accept [etc.]

HENRY L. STIMSON

---

**Guatemala and Honduras** [15]

714.1515/872 : Telegram

*The Chargé in Honduras (Merrell) to the Secretary of State*

TEGUCIGALPA, May 23, 1929—3 p. m.
[Received 11:06 p. m.]

52. My despatch No. 886 of May 10.[16] The Minister for Foreign Affairs sent me last evening a lengthy confidential memorandum the substance of which follows:

1. The Government of Honduras recently protested that the Government of Guatemala has violated the *status quo* of 1918 [17] by the

---

[15] Continued from *Foreign Relations*, 1928, vol. I, pp. 712–775.
[16] Not printed.
[17] See *Foreign Relations*, 1918, pp. 32–34.

undertaking of new agricultural works in the region of the Motagua and by the establishing of an auxiliary post at Chachahualia. Guatemala denied both these allegations and protested because Honduras is disposed to reestablish a police outpost at Chachahualia where it had established a military outpost in 1917 without protest from Guatemala. In 1928 a dispute took place over Chachahualia which ended in Guatemala's recognition of Honduranean jurisdiction over that place and acceptance that Honduras establish a police outpost there. Honduras informed Guatemala last March it was an opportune moment again to establish an outpost there but has refrained from doing so because it was learned that Guatemala had regular forces there and it was desired to avoid a conflict.

The Honduranean Government now insists upon establishing a police outpost and constructing a government building at Chachahualia and "in proceeding to such acts is confident that it can count on the good offices of the Government of the United States of America in case there should be opposition or hostility on the part of Guatemala."

2. In July 1928 Honduras protested against the construction of two Guatemalan public buildings at El Cinchado in the zone of the Motagua and the work was discontinued. It has recently been renewed, however, and fresh protests have been made, Honduras invoking Secretary Kellogg's telegram of February 16, 1928, to the Honduranean Minister for Foreign Affairs.[18] Guatemala maintains this construction does not violate the *status quo* (see despatch No. 886). Both countries claim El Cinchado and Chachahualia as integral parts of their territory.

The memorandum ends with the following statement:

"My Government hopes that the Government of the United States of America will be good enough to lend its good offices with a view to causing Guatemala to demolish quickly that part which it has completed of the house it is constructing in El Cinchado or the houses themselves in case they are already constructed, and that it suspend any other class of works in the zone of Motagua, which belongs unquestionably to Honduras, while a definite solution of the pending boundary question is being arrived at, maintaining without any alteration the *status quo* of 1918.

In submitting to your consideration the points of this memorandum in connection with which my Government desires the good offices of the Government of the United States of America, I have had in mind that the arbitration agreement solemnly accepted by Guatemala in the Central American Conference of 1923[19] in which the President of the United States was accepted as arbitrator is still in force."

A copy of the memorandum and its annexes will be forwarded in the next pouch.[20]

---

[18] *Ibid.*, 1928, vol. I, p. 716.
[19] See *Conference on Central American Affairs, Washington, December 4, 1922–February 7, 1923* (Washington, Government Printing Office, 1923), p. 296.
[20] Not printed.

The President of the Republic has assured me that if the Department can find it convenient to reply in the near future Chachahualia will not be occupied until that time.

Repeated to Guatemala.    MERRELL

---

714.1515/874 : Telegram

*The Chargé in Honduras (Merrell) to the Secretary of State*

TEGUCIGALPA, May 28, 1929—3 p. m.
[Received 9:10 p. m.]

53. My telegram No. 52, May 23, 3 p.m. Last evening a group of more than five hundred, mainly students, paraded the streets carrying Honduranean flags, singing the national anthem and shouting pro-Honduranean cries and insults to Guatemala. They were deterred from reaching the Guatemalan Legation by the police, but went to the President's palace where the President counseled them to dissolve, not to insult Guatemala or Guatemalans, and to have confidence in the Government's ability to settle the matter satisfactorily.

While the demonstration, which was probably started by rumors that a reply had been received to Honduras' third note in the form of an ultimatum, was orderly it appeared more than a mere outburst of patriotism.

It is reported that the Chief of Protocol and the Chancellor of the Foreign Office were among the demonstrators but I am reliably informed this is not true.

Repeated to Guatemala.    MERRELL

---

714.1515/882

*The Minister in Guatemala (Geissler) to the Secretary of State*

No. 2428    GUATEMALA, May 29, 1929.
[Received June 5.]

SIR: I have the honor to report that President Lázaro Chacón today mentioned to me the incident of the anti-Guatemala demonstration which occurred at Tegucigalpa, on May 27. See the cablegram of the Legation in Honduras of May 28, 3 p. m. General Chacón deplored the incident. He said that there was no occasion for it and that he hopes that Honduras will not commit any act of aggression. He also stated, that he has instructed Minister Adrián Recinos, to urge upon the Secretary of State the hope that, in the interest of concord between Guatemala and Honduras, it may be possible to bring about at an early date the arbitration suggested by the Department of State in June 1928.

I have [etc.] ARTHUR H. GEISSLER

714.1515/872 : Telegram

*The Secretary of State to the Chargé in Honduras (Merrell)*[21]

WASHINGTON, May 29, 1929—5 p. m.

41. Legation's confidential 52, May 23, 3 p. m. Please seek an interview with President Mejia Colindres and inform him that this Government would view with much regret any action by the Government of Honduras or by the Government of Guatemala in the disputed territory which might result in aggravating the boundary dispute.

Please report results by telegraph together with a statement of your opinion of the attitude of the present Honduran Government toward the definitive adjustment of this question.

STIMSON

714.1515/876 : Telegram

*The Minister in Guatemala (Geissler) to the Secretary of State*

GUATEMALA, May 31, 1929—10 a. m.
[Received 10:30 p. m.]

65. Yesterday evening I conferred with President Chacón, Minister for Foreign Affairs Designate Aguirre, and Minister to Washington Recinos. I communicated orally the complaint of Honduras as reported by the Legation at Tegucigalpa, May 23, 3 p. m., and I made the representations instructed by the Department's May 29, 5 p. m.

They said that the Government of Guatemala has aimed to refrain from any action which might aggravate the boundary dispute and will continue to do so.

Regarding Cinchado, they stated that Guatemala has exercised jurisdiction there since ancient times and that the two buildings replacing houses destroyed by cyclone have been completed.

Recinos stated the attitude of the Government on behalf of the President in an informal memorandum [which] reads as follows:

"Guatemala has no military nor civilian force in Chachagualilla nor has it had such since the first part of the year 1928.

"Guatemala has done no new agricultural work in the zone of the *status quo*. According to reports in the possession of the Government of Guatemala, Honduras is the one which is doing new agricultural work in that zone.

"Guatemala accepted the arbitration proposal of June last year submitted by the Department of State. Guatemala has no official

[21] Repeated to the Minister in Guatemala in telegram No. 27 of the same date with added instruction: "Please make similar representations to President Chacón and report results."

information regarding the attitude of the Government of Honduras. Guatemala entertains the hope that Honduras will accept that proposal at an early date to the end that the boundary question be settled as soon as possible."

Repeated to Honduras.

GEISSLER

714.1515/879 : Telegram

*The Chargé in Honduras (Merrell) to the Secretary of State*

TEGUCIGALPA, June 3, 1929—8 p. m.
[Received June 4—1 : 35 a. m.]

57. In compliance with your telegram number 41 of May 29, 5 p. m., I spoke with President Mejia Colindres on May 30.

He seemed assured and pleased with the message and said that his Government was doing, and would continue to do, everything it could to avoid aggravating the boundary dispute.

He and part of his Cabinet left the next morning for an inspection of the road between here and Siguatepeque and their absence from the capital has had a tranquilizing effect on the public. Upon his return this morning however he informed me that he had received a report from the Comandante at Cuyamel that the Guatemalan military outposts at Cinchado, La Tienda, and Entre-Rios, have been doubled, that three military chiefs have arrived at Cinchado where the troops within the last few days have been organized for an active campaign, and that on June 2 a detachment of 25 men was about a mile from Cacao.

In my opinion the present Honduran Government greatly desires a definite settlement of the boundary dispute but I believe it will be little if any more favorably disposed toward accepting the Department's proposal of June 4 last [22] than the Government was last year, inasmuch as at least two members of the Cabinet are opposed to it and the President stands in great awe of the editor of *El Cronista* who will doubtless reopen a bitter campaign against it if its consideration is resumed.

Repeated to Guatemala.

MERRELL

714.1515/909

*The Assistant Secretary of State (White) to the Minister in Honduras (Summerlin), Temporarily in New York*

WASHINGTON, July 18, 1929.

DEAR SUMMIE: Here is the statement that the Secretary told you yesterday he would like to have prepared for you to deliver verbally

[22] See telegram No. 51, June 4, 1928, 4 p. m., to the Minister in Guatemala, *Foreign Relations*, 1928, vol. I, p. 746.

to the Minister for Foreign Affairs. It has been approved by the Secretary.

With best wishes for a *bon voyage* and hoping that all will go well,

Yours very sincerely, FRANCIS WHITE

[Enclosure]

*Oral Statement To Be Delivered by the American Minister (Summerlin) to the Honduran Minister for Foreign Affairs (Ulloa)*

I am charged by the Secretary of State to convey to Your Excellency his most cordial greetings. As you know, Mr. Stimson was in Nicaragua a little over two years ago and, as a consequence thereof, has a very particular interest in the Central American countries and in promoting prosperity and peaceful relations among them. He feels that the unsettled boundary questions present the only obstacle to assuring the prosperity of and peaceful relations among the Central American countries. He has therefore instructed me to express not only his great interest in this matter but also his ardent desire that these boundary questions will be promptly settled to the complete satisfaction of all parties. I am instructed by the Secretary of State to say that he is happy to note that there appears to be a reasonable prospect of a definite settlement of the boundary between Honduras and Nicaragua [23] at a not distant date, and that he very much hopes that the Honduran Government will again consider most carefully all matters connected with the boundary dispute with Guatemala, with a view to arriving at a prompt solution of that question also. Mr. Stimson feels that it will be to the great advantage of both countries to dispose of this matter as rapidly as possible and he will consequently welcome any suggestions Your Excellency's Government may have to make with this end in view.

---

714.1515/923

*The Minister in Honduras (Summerlin) to the Secretary of State*

No. 932　　　　　　　　　TEGUCIGALPA, August 19, 1929.
[Received September 4.]

SIR: In confirmation of my telegram No. 77, August 17, 11 a. m.,[24] in regard to the delivery of your verbal message to the Minister for Foreign Affairs [25] and his formal reply thereto, I have the honor to enclose herewith a copy and translation of the Foreign Office note, dated August 16, 1929.

[23] See pp. 975 ff.
[24] Not printed.
[25] *Supra.*

I called at the Foreign Office on the morning of August sixth and delivered your message to Doctor Durón, who was acting Minister for Foreign Affairs during the temporary absence of Doctor Ulloa, and at his request I left with him a copy of the message. In behalf of Doctor Ulloa, Doctor Durón expressed thanks for the message and stated that it would be brought to the attention also of the President of the Republic without delay. It will be noted that in the first paragraph of the Foreign Office reply the copy of the verbal message left with Doctor Durón is referred to as a "Confidential note".

I understand that the reply of Doctor Ulloa has received the approval of the Cabinet in Council.

I have had several private conversations with President Mejía Colindres, since my return, but aside from expressing an earnest desire for the early settlement of this boundary question, he has been noncommittal.

. . . . . . . .

I have [etc.] GEORGE T. SUMMERLIN

[Enclosure—Translation]

*The Honduran Minister for Foreign Affairs (Ulloa) to the American Minister (Summerlin)*

TEGUCIGALPA, August 16, 1929.

MR. MINISTER: I have the honor of directing myself to Your Excellency in order to inform you that I have read with the greatest interest the courteous confidential note which, upon your arrival in Tegucigalpa, on the 5th instant, you were good enough to hand to me personally.

I am extremely grateful for the cordial greeting which His Excellency the Secretary of State of the United States of America was good enough to present to me in that note, and I am delighted to return it.

I see with profound satisfaction the statements of His Excellency Mr. Stimson, that he has particular interest in favor of the Central American countries, in promoting prosperity and peaceful relations among them, to which there is no other obstacle than that presented by the still unsettled boundary questions, and his ardent desire that they be settled as soon as possible to the complete satisfaction of all parties.

The statement of His Excellency Mr. Stimson, that he feels happy to note that there appears to be a reasonable prospect of a definite settlement of the boundary question between Honduras and Nicaragua at a not distant date is equally satisfactory to me.

And in expressing that he very much hopes that the Honduran Government will again consider most carefully all matters connected with the boundary dispute with Guatemala, with a view to arriving at a prompt solution of that question also, feeling that it will be to the great advantage of both countries to dispose of this matter as rapidly as possible, and will consequently welcome any suggestions my Government may have to make with this end in view, offers Honduras a fine opportunity to carry forward its proposals which are in harmony with those of His Excellency the Secretary of State.

In effect, Mr. Minister, the Government of Honduras, which believes, with His Excellency Mr. Stimson, that a satisfactory solution of the boundary question with Nicaragua will soon be arrived at, in view of the statements which its distinguished Governor [Gobernante] made to the effect that it should comply with the Award of H. M. the King of Spain,[26] and which to judge by the message I am answering have merited the approbation of the Department of State, [the Government of Honduras] cherishes the most ardent desire that the question of the Guatemalan frontier may be settled also as soon as possible; and now, taking advantage of the generous offer of His Excellency Mr. Stimson of receiving any suggestions which it might make to him in this respect, [the Government of Honduras] has much honor in informing Your Excellency, through me, that its proposal is for its part to take at once, the necessary steps that the question may be solved by arbitration, the arbitrator being His Excellency the President of the United States, as Honduras and Guatemala have already agreed in the Treaty of 1914[27] and in statements which His Excellency Charles Evans Hughes, Secretary of State, made public solemnly on February 7, 1923, in Washington, in the closing session of the Conference on Central American Affairs;[28] since my Government believes that the Chief of the most powerful nation of America, interested in the peace and harmony of the other American nations, being the arbitrator, would have to be confided in on account of his proverbial sense of right and justice, the Decision which he pronounces will be recognized by the contesting parties as rights which by equity and justice belong to them, taking into consideration the documents and other proofs which each of them may have produced in favor of their pretensions, and in this way Guatemala should have complete faith that it will not be prejudiced in any way. So that, if by means of the good offices of the United States, Guatemala should adopt the same attitude as that of Honduras, my Government will be ready to sign the protocol of

---

[26] Of December 23, 1906. *British and Foreign State Papers*, vol. c, p. 1096.
[27] *Foreign Relations*, 1917, p. 786.
[28] See *Conference on Central American Affairs*, p. 56.

arbitration and to do whatever is necessary to obtain the decision.

If His Excellency Mr. Stimson does Honduras the honor of accepting the suggestion relative to the good offices of the Department of State with Guatemala in order that the arbitration may be constituted, and if he moreover lends his cooperation in the question with Nicaragua, he will incur the gratitude of the Hondurans and will see realized his ardent desire of promoting prosperity and peaceful relations to which, as he so aptly says, only the unsettled boundary questions are opposed.

Begging Your Excellency to be good enough to transmit the above to His Excellency the Secretary of State it gives me pleasure to reiterate assurances of my highest and most distinguished consideration.

JESUS ULLOA

714.1515/924

*The Minister in Honduras (Summerlin) to the Secretary of State*

No. 936    TEGUCIGALPA, August 24, 1929.
[Received September 7.]

SIR: With reference to my despatch No. 932 of August 19, 1929, transmitting to the Department, the reply of the Honduran Minister for Foreign Affairs to your verbal message which I delivered on August 6th, I have honor to report that in an informal conversation with the Acting Minister for Foreign Affairs yesterday, Doctor Durón volunteered the statement that his Government would be glad to receive, and to give careful consideration to, any further suggestions or proposals the Department might wish to make in connection with the Honduran-Guatemalan boundary question.

I have [etc.]    GEORGE T. SUMMERLIN

714.1515/928a : Telegram

*The Secretary of State to the Minister in Honduras (Summerlin)* [29]

WASHINGTON, September 21, 1929—11 a. m.

63. Your despatches 932 of August 19 and 936 of August 24.

Please inform the President of Honduras that this Government has given careful and sympathetic consideration to the note delivered to you on August 16 by the Minister for Foreign Affairs and to the Minister's subsequent informal statement that the Honduran Government would be glad to give consideration to any further suggestions or proposals which this Government might wish to make. In view

---

[29] Second and third paragraphs repeated to the Minister in Guatemala for his information only in telegram No. 52, of the same date (not printed).

of this latter statement, you may inquire informally whether the Government of Honduras would be willing to modify its proposal that the Guatemala boundary question be submitted to arbitration by the President of the United States and propose instead that it be arbitrated by a jurist named by the President of the United States from among the United States Members of the Permanent Court of Arbitration, established by The Hague Convention of 1899. These members are Elihu Root, John Bassett Moore, Charles Evans Hughes and Newton D. Baker. If the Honduran Government wishes to make a proposal to this effect the Department would be willing to present it to the Government of Guatemala and subsequently to exercise its good offices, if desired, in an effort to find a formula for the arbitration which would meet the views of both parties.

The Senate has confirmed your appointment as Minister to Venezuela but the Department hopes that you will remain in Tegucigalpa for the present, in order to carry on the negotiations if they can be resumed with any prospect of success.

STIMSON

---

714.1515/949

*The Guatemalan Minister for Foreign Affairs (Aguirre) to the Secretary of State* [30]

[Translation]

No. 09858                                 GUATEMALA, September 24, 1929.
227/224.I (73–69) (02)                    [Received October 8.]

MR. SECRETARY OF STATE: The Government of Guatemala wishes to ask the Government of the United States through the worthy medium of the Department of State that it kindly continue lending its friendly mediation, on the questions of territorial boundaries between Guatemala and Honduras, which were suspended in September of last year, 1928, because of the election period in which the last named country entered and the change of Government which was the immediate consequence of that event.

The Government of Guatemala is moved to make this request by the conviction that it will find in the Government of the United States the consistent upholder of the highest principles of justice, embodied in the last altruistic initiative which culminated in the Multilateral Pact that outlaws war [30a] and seeks the civilized way of averting it, so as to realize the kingdom of peace in the world.

And as the North American nation has done that, well may the Republic of Guatemala ask it to continue its interrupted mediation

---

[30] Handed to Assistant Secretary White by the Guatemalan Minister on October 8, 1929.
[30a] Treaty for the Renunciation of War, *Foreign Relations*, 1928, vol. I, p. 153.

and again do that further service to the cause of good harmony between two Central American nations, unfortunately kept apart by the boundary dispute which has not found the proper solution which my Government keenly desires.

In April of last year the mediation of the Department of State brought about the Cuyamel Conference intended to bring about a course which would permit of a truce for a final settlement of the border. Guatemala took to Cuyamel its firm purpose to promote a satisfactory arrangement and in order to do so put forth every effort consistent with the justice of its cause and the uprightness of its intentions. The Honorable Mr. Davis who represented the mediator realized the difficulties of the present time and displayed his striking gifts of goodness and fairness, so as to bring to an agreement the representatives of the two contending republics, but he could not do so; and it is not for Guatemala to say whether it cooperated sincerely and righteously with the views of the representative of the Department of State nor where the blame for the failure of that generous mediation can be placed.

In that condition of affairs the Department of State addressed the Governments concerned and proposed that they submit their boundary question to the decision of the Central American International Tribunal, under the Convention signed in Washington on February 7, 1923, providing for the creation of that tribunal so as to refer to it precisely as its text says "all controversies or questions now existing between them or may supervene, whatever their nature and origin may be." [31]

The Government of Guatemala unreservedly accepted the suggestion of the Department of State because it believed it to be fair, wise, and even compulsory within the Arbitration Convention signed by the two republics and approved and ratified by their constitutional organizations.

Honduras did not accept the discreet suggestion of the American Government and it was impossible to make it then depart from its obstinate denial, notwithstanding the obvious reasonings with which the Department of State fought the mistaken assertions of the Honduran Chancellory.

The formula which the Department of State proposed to have considered together with the colonial law the vital interests residing in the country in dispute for a just determination of the border meant an accurate conception of the worth of what goes as the fundamental conditions of life, as compared with the actual facts of

---

[31] See *Conference on Central American Affairs*, pp. 296, 297. The portion quoted from article 1 should read: "all controversies or questions which now exist between them or which may hereafter arise, whatever their nature or origin."

good faith, of devotion to work, of the cooperation of the economic forces that give birth to the great interests which constitute the mother country that have tilled its soil, brought its railways and ports into existence; which promoted the colonization of its waste lands in which the dead [*desafiaron:* they defied] the harsh climate of the tropics and there left their bones to enrich the lots inherited by their children; neither was it to be left out of the account that since 1796, Guatemala created the first stock company for the navigation of the Motagua, the needed money being subscribed by the trade of the City of Guatemala; and that four later attempts also were made in the same sense with the principal national river which takes its source in the center of the Republic; and there should also be considered the interests that Honduras might have created and might have created bonds [*vincularlos*] on the land that is disputed to us. And all is to be pondered over, considered and measured with the sound judgment of a court that would embody the conscience of Central America and in which the representatives of the mediator Government and the highest Latin-American jurists would have a seat. Guatemala has made no objection to the tribunal listening, as is Honduras' wish, to the opinion of the Conquerors [*conquistadores*], the geographical maps made under the empirical methods of the Seventeenth and Eighteenth centuries; or to the Royal Orders and Cedulas of Philip II and other Spanish monarchs being taken into consideration. The Government of Guatemala did not and does not object to there being brought before the court every element that may throw light and end injustice; but it believes that the Department of State visualizes what is the present life of the old provinces of the Kingdom of Guatemala and that that truth can not and must not be lost sight of unless it be intended to ignore the genesis of nationalities.

When Honduras rejected the proposition of the Department of State made through the illustrious medium of Secretary Kellogg the Honduran country was in the midst of the election period. Professional politicians were hoisting as their flag the conquest of the Motagua; and the popular passions aroused by the jingo speeches and partisan press called upon their followers to win the election. No one was behind in political platforms to offer at least the nearest valley, but those who pinned their prestige on the future holding of the Puerto Barrios and Guatemala railway were in the majority.[32]

The general situation has now undergone a change and it is possible that more equanimity in the views of the Honduran politicians will make it possible for them to take a more reasonable course.

---

[32] The Spanish reads: "pero sobraron quienes afirmaran sus prestigios sobre la futura posesión del ferrocarril de Guatemala al Atlàntico y de Puerto Barrios."

In the meanwhile the situation of the boundary question has continued comparatively grave; the Cuyamel Fruit Company bringing into play a moral force, which can not be resisted and seems to challenge the most sacred rights and the signed Conventions, is moving farther forward every day into the land of Guatemala, under the protection of Honduran concessions. Every party of its workers carries the usurping flag of Honduras in usurpation and although there be a *status quo* which is invoked to prevent Guatemala from moving within its house that same *status* is that which is used by Honduras through the North American Company in order to move deeper and deeper into the [*our*] land.

The Government of Guatemala has protested against the acts committed in violation of the *status quo* but the Government of Honduras will not even go to the trouble of returning an answer which courtesy demands.

The Government of Guatemala, aware of its rights and responsibilities has maintained a cautious attitude as far as it is humanly possible and does not wish to leave that path unless compelled to do so by the necessities of a needful defense.

The Government of Guatemala believes that the Government of the United States must see in the Guatemala gesture which I now have the honor to make a keen desire to arrive at a satisfactory and fair settlement of the boundary question through the interposition of the friendly offices of the Department of State. It may be that the Government of Honduras in a sentiment of legality and sound judgment may now give more attention to the friendly suggestion of the Government of the United States and refer its differences with Guatemala to the International Central American Tribunal for a decision.

My Government would have had recourse [*habria deseado acudir*] to the means afforded by Article 13 of the Convention for the creation of the International Central American Tribunal by compelling Honduras to sign the protocol for the organization of the tribunal in the form prescribed by the Convention, and file its case, but the fact that the Government of Honduras has not made up the list of its judges as prescribed by Article 2 of the Convention and the list of thirty jurists for the organization of the tribunal is not ready, stands in the way.

The Convention of February 7, 1923, was approved and ratified by the Government of Honduras; but it has not been properly executed with regard to the appointment of judges thus defeating the purposes that were taken into account when the treaty was signed.

Please accept, Mr. Secretary of State, the earnest thanks of the Government of Guatemala for the kind reception you will be pleased to give to this matter and especially the assurances of my highest consideration and particular esteem.

ED. AGUIRRE V.

714.1515/941 : Telegram

*The Minister in Honduras (Summerlin) to the Secretary of State*

TEGUCIGALPA, October 11, 1929—9 p. m.
[Received October 12—2 : 50 p. m.]

104. In an informal note dated September 23, I transmitted textually to the Minister for Foreign Affairs the instructions contained in your telegram No. 63, September 21, 11 a. m.

I am now in receipt of a reply dated today in which after repeating the substance of my note the Minister for Foreign Affairs continues:

"I informed His Excellency the President of the content of Your Excellency's courteous note, and he has given me instructions to answer it, advising you that the Government of Honduras accepts with the greatest pleasure as arbitrator in the boundary question with Guatemala any one of the above-named jurists and designated by the President of the Republic of the United States of America, with the understanding that the arbitration must be juridical, taking into account limit defined in public documents not contradicted by others of the same or weightier category, giving each of them fitting importance, according to their antiquity and juridical efficacy; the comprehension of the territory which constituted the ancient provinces of Guatemala at the date of its independence; the provisions of the royal ordinance of the intendants which was then in force; and in general all of the documents, maps, plans, et cetera, which may lead to the enlightening of precise truth, preference being given to those which by their nature should have more weight, by reason of their antiquity, of being clearer, more just and more impartial or for any other established reason, according to the principles of justice, and also taking into account the observations and studies of the mixed commission which accomplished some labors and had been organized in conformity with the boundary conventions between Honduras and Guatemala of 1895 [33] and 1914;[34] it being necessary to give importance to it only when it may be judicially legitimate and established, in conformity with the general principles of law and with the rules of justice which in connection with this case are sanctioned by law of peoples. The Government of Honduras believes that the Government of Guatemala will have no reason to decline the suggestion which the Secretary of State of the United States now makes; but in the lamentable case that it may not accept any of the jurists mentioned my Government would be excessively gratified if the arbitrator might be the President of the Republic of the United States of America or the Chief Justice of the Supreme Court of the same nation.

In replying in these terms to Your Excellency's courteous note I take pleasure in expressing the gratitude of my Government to the Government of the United States of America for the good will and generous interest with which it has been good enough to offer its

---

[33] Signed March 1, 1895, *British and Foreign State Papers*, vol. LXXXVII, p. 530.
[34] Signed August 1, 1914, *Foreign Relations*, 1917, p. 786.

important cooperation in this matter whose solution would insure forever the peace of Central America; and I avail myself of, et cetera."

Repeated to Salvador and Guatemala.

SUMMERLIN

---

714.1515/946a : Telegram

*The Secretary of State to the Minister in Guatemala (Geissler)* [35]

WASHINGTON, October 16, 1929—noon.

57. The Guatemalan Minister has presented to the Department a note dated September 24 from the Guatemalan Minister for Foreign Affairs requesting this Government to continue its friendly mediation of the boundary dispute between Guatemala and Honduras. You may inform the Minister for Foreign Affairs that a reply to this communication will be forwarded to you for delivery within the near future.

Referring to telegram No. 104, October 11, 9 p. m., from Tegucigalpa, you are directed to discuss informally with the Minister for Foreign Affairs the proposal for settlement submitted by the Government of Honduras and report by telegraph the views of the Government of Guatemala with respect to (1) the acceptance of one of the jurists referred to as arbitrator and (2) the formula proposed by Honduras. The Department would be glad to have an agreement at least as to the arbitrator, subject, if necessary, to a subsequent accord regarding the conditions of the arbitration.

You should discreetly urge upon the Government of Guatemala the importance at this time of avoiding any action or the public expression of any views which might impede the initiation of negotiations which in the Department's opinion now offer some prospect of a satisfactory conclusion.

STIMSON

---

714.1515/947 : Telegram

*The Minister in Guatemala (Geissler) to the Secretary of State*

GUATEMALA, October 18, 1929—3 p. m.
[Received October 19—12:50 a. m.]

125. Yesterday I informed the Minister for Foreign Affairs unofficially and informally of the Honduran proposal as reported October 11, 9 p. m., by the Legation at Tegucigalpa.

I also urged that the Government of Guatemala avoid any action or expression which might impede negotiations.

---

[35] Repeated to the Minister in Honduras in telegram No. 77 of the same date.

We discussed the situation very unofficially and again today.

The gist of his expressions is that he considers the situation very grave, that he will discuss it this evening with the President and the Cabinet, and that meanwhile he can with definiteness say only that the position of the Guatemalan Government is as defined in his note to the Secretary of State of September 24th.

Repeated to Honduras.

GEISSLER

---

714.1515/950 : Telegram

*The Minister in Guatemala (Geissler) to the Secretary of State*

GUATEMALA, October 20, 1929—7 p. m.
[Received October 21–12:20 p. m.]

128. Referring to Legation's telegram of October 18, 3 p. m. I had a long talk yesterday with Minister for Foreign Affairs Aguirre Velasquez. He is deeply disappointed because the Government of the United States did not, as suggested in his note of September 24th, insist that Honduras accept the State Department's proposal of June, 1928. He told me that on the 18th the President and the Cabinet instructed him to ask the Council of State, the Faculty of Lawyers and the Boundary Commission for their respective opinions on the Honduran proposal.

At this moment submission to those bodies of any concession to Honduras without the previous approval of the Executive would be fatal.

. . . . . . . . .

I urged the Minister for Foreign Affairs to postpone carrying out that instruction. He assented very reluctantly even though I had pointed out that our conversations are wholly unofficial and that the Honduran proposal, although I had informed him of it unofficially and confidentially, has not been put before the Guatemalan Government and hence cannot be submitted by it.

Afterwards I called on President Chacon who said that he will instruct the Minister for Foreign Affairs to suspend action and that they will talk with me again before taking any action. Then I conferred with Carlos Salazar whose opinion in boundary matters Guatemalans regard highly.

Unfortunately press despatches from Honduras and the United States instead of indicating that the Government of the United States is willing to present to Guatemala a proposal if made by Honduras that an American judge be arbitrator, have conveyed the impression that the Government of the United States made the proposal to Honduras. For example, an Associated Press despatch from Tegucigalpa said: "Assembly notables on behalf of the President Mejia Colindres approved Hoover's proposal appoint new arbiter *de jure pro* settlement Honduras-Guatemala boundary dispute."

Guatemalans comment with astonishment that such proposal was not simultaneously submitted to Guatemala. I have informed a number of people of the true facts, but at least with others a false impression lingers.

Furthermore, Guatemalan public men recall that certain Hondurans in past years were said to have asserted in effect that United States authorities are only seeking to find a method of securing confirmation of the title Honduras claims to the region in which the Cuyamel operates north of the Merendon. See in that connection despatch 1892.[36] There is much fear among public men that the State Department may in due course support the entire Honduras formula of October 11th.

Salazar recalled to me how hard we had to work last year to obtain popular acquiescence in arbitration proposed by the United States and legislative approval of the tribunal and of the formula then proposed by the State Department and that in that connection faith in the proposal and its proponent was slowly but effectively built up and that Guatemala took pride in finally accepting without reservation. He said that Honduras . . . injected and even now adds an "impossible" reservation before availing itself of a suggestion that the Department would be willing to present a proposal if made by Honduras that a Hague Court judge be arbitrator. He expressed the opinion that the Assembly, partly for reasons of internal politics, would probably reject any proposal submitted at this time that a Hague judge be arbitrator even if the formula of June 1928 were accepted, and that the effect on the tenure of the Government would probably be disastrous.

President Chacon today expressed himself to me similarly as had Mr. Salazar.

Repeated to Honduras.

GEISSLER

---

714.1515/952 : Telegram

*The Minister in Guatemala (Geissler) to the Secretary of State*

GUATEMALA, October 21, 1929—5 p. m.
[Received October 22—12:17 a. m.]

131. The Minister for Foreign Affairs called today and presented to me an unofficial and confidential memorandum stating "that he considers unacceptable the proposition of the Government of Hon-

---

[36] Dated April 24, 1928; not printed.

duras which comprises two different points, that is to say: (1) To submit to the arbitration of one of the American judges of the Hague Court to be selected by the President of the United States the boundary question existing between Guatemala and Honduras; (2) a condition of that arbitration is that it be exclusively *de jure*."

He contends in the memorandum that Honduras is, by the 1923 convention, bound to submit the controversy to the Central American Tribunal [37] and that Honduras could waive its reservation to the inter-American arbitration treaty of the present year.[38] He adds that "if it were possible" for him to do so he would accept one of the American judges of the Hague Court or the President of the United States or the Chief Justice as the presiding member for the Central American Tribunal.

He makes arguments against an arbitration *de jure* and closes by predicting that acceptance of the formula proposed by Honduras "would produce great public excitement tending toward revolution".

Repeated to Honduras and Costa Rica.

GEISSLER

714.1515/952 : Telegram

*The Secretary of State to the Minister in Guatemala (Geissler)*

WASHINGTON, October 25, 1929—5 p. m.

60. Legation's 131, October 21, 5 p. m. Please address a note to the Minister for Foreign Affairs in the following terms:

"Excellency: I have the honor to acknowledge the receipt of your note dated September 24, 1929, wherein, on behalf of the Government of Guatemala, you bespeak the continuance of the friendly mediation of this Government in the effort to bring about a settlement of the controversy which unfortunately exists between the Governments of Guatemala and Honduras with respect to their mutual boundary.

I am deeply sensible of the honor the Government of Guatemala does the Government of the United States in thus requesting its continued cooperation in this effort toward a better understanding between the two neighboring Republics, and it affords me especial pleasure to be able to inform Your Excellency of the readiness of the Government of the United States to continue to lend its aid in connection with this matter as heretofore.

As Your Excellency has been informally advised by the American Minister at Guatemala City the Government of Honduras recently expressed its willingness to modify its proposal that the boundary dispute be submitted to arbitration by the President of the United States, and to propose instead that it be arbitrated by a jurist named by the President of the United States from among the United States members of the Permanent Court of Arbitration at The Hague, it being stipulated that such arbitration should be juridical, taking into

[37] See *Conference on Central American Affairs*, p. 296.
[38] Treaty signed January 5, 1929, *ante*, p. 659.

account certain specified classes of evidence. While the results of this discussion have afforded grounds to hope for an eventual settlement of the question on a basis satisfactory to both parties, it is evident that further progress can best be achieved by a frank and friendly exchange of views. The Government of the United States is encouraged by the repeated evidences of the earnest desire which animates Your Excellency's Government and that of Honduras to find a solution of this important problem, to hope that a basis for a satisfactory settlement can be found through such a conference, and it accordingly takes pleasure in extending hereby to the Government of Guatemala an earnest invitation to authorize its Minister at Washington or to name another delegate, or delegates, duly empowered, to meet with a delegate, or delegates, from the Republic of Honduras in a conference at which representatives of the Government of the United States will, if so desired by the two Governments concerned, be present. A similar invitation is being addressed to the Government of Honduras.

Trusting that Your Excellency's Government may find it possible to accept this invitation, and that in doing so there may be initiated negotiations whose outcome will be satisfactory to the two Governments for whom the Government of the United States entertains sentiments of the highest regard, I avail myself of this opportunity to extend to Your Excellency the renewed assurances of my most distinguished consideration. Henry L. Stimson."

STIMSON

---

714.1515/952 : Telegram

*The Secretary of State to the Minister in Honduras* (*Summerlin*)

WASHINGTON, October 25, 1929—5 p. m.

78. Legation's 104, October 11, 9 p. m. Please present the following note to the Minister for Foreign Affairs:

Excellency: I have the honor to advise Your Excellency that I learned with pleasure from Mr. Summerlin of the willingness of the Government of Honduras to modify its proposal that the boundary dispute with Guatemala be submitted to arbitration by the President of the United States and to propose instead that it be arbitrated by a jurist named by the President of the United States from among the United States members of the Permanent Court of Arbitration at The Hague, it being stipulated by Your Excellency's Government that such arbitration should be juridical, taking into account certain specified classes of evidence.

The new proposal of the Government of Honduras has been discussed informally with the Guatemalan Government by the American Minister to Guatemala. While the results of this discussion have afforded grounds to hope for an eventual settlement of the question on a basis satisfactory to both parties it is evident that further progress can best be achieved by a frank and friendly exchange of views. The Government of the United States is encouraged by the repeated evidences of the earnest desire which animates Your Excellency's Government and that of Guatemala to find a solution of this important problem, to hope that a basis for a satisfactory settlement can be found through such a conference, and it accordingly takes pleasure in extending hereby to the Government of Honduras an earnest invitation to authorize its Minister at Washington or to name another delegate, or delegates, duly empowered, to meet with a delegate, or delegates, from the Republic of Guatemala in a conference at which representatives of the Government of the United States will, if so desired by the two Governments concerned, be present. A similar invitation is being addressed to the Government of Guatemala.

Trusting that Your Excellency's Government may find it possible to accept this invitation, and that in doing so there may be initiated negotiations whose outcome will be satisfactory to the two Governments for whom the Government of the United States entertains sentiments of the highest regard, I avail myself of this opportunity to extend to Your Excellency the renewed assurances of my most distinguished consideration. Henry L. Stimson."

STIMSON

714.1515/958 : Telegram

*The Minister in Guatemala (Geissler) to the Secretary of State*

GUATEMALA, October 28, 1929—7 p. m.
[Received October 28—1 : 25 p. m.]

133. Referring to Department's telegram of October 25, 5 p. m. In a note dated the 26th the Minister for Foreign Affairs acknowledges the note of the Secretary of State and requests that I transmit the following reply:

"The communication of this office of last September the 24th expresses the general points of view of the Government of Guatemala regarding the boundary matter with Honduras and its warm desire that the Government of the United States on this occasion, as it has always done, lend the valuable support of its aid and counsel.

Guatemala on all occasions has been disposed toward any settlement having as basis a principle of justice. For that reason it accepted, subscribed and ratified the Central American treaties of 1923, among which is the one creating the Tribunal of International Central American Arbitration and it approved and ratified also the treaty of January 1929 which establishes the inter-American Tribunal of Arbitration and means of conciliation. Absolute respect for treaties and their faithful observance has been a rule of conduct of the Government of Guatemala, wherefore on the present occasion it informed Your Excellency confidentially and unofficially in view of the plan proposed by Honduras that it is (era) not possible for the Government of Guatemala to depart from the obligations contained in the international pacts in force between Guatemala and Honduras but that in the desire of demonstrating its good will for finding legal and just ways in their procedure it would suggest to Your Excellency that there could be designated as president of the International Central American Tribunal one of the American jurists of the Permanent Court of The Hague.

Given those antecedents the Government of Guatemala takes

pleasure in accepting the courteous invitation of the Government of the United States to cause itself to be represented at the proposed conference and for that purpose it will opportunely designate a delegate in order that within the international treaty [*treaties*] in force [40] there can be studied the form leading the two states to a satisfactory solution of their differences, it being understood that representatives of the Government of Your Excellency will do us the honor to preside over the sessions of the delegates for the purpose of imparting their guidance and counsel of which the Government of Guatemala hopes so much for the happy termination of the existing conflict with Honduras.

Begging Your Excellency to be the faithful interpreter of the Government of Guatemala in presenting to that of the United States its gratitude for the benevolence with which it proceeds in this distressing matter, I am pleased to assure" et cetera.

GEISSLER

714.1515/959 : Telegram

*The Minister in Guatemala (Geissler) to the Secretary of State*

GUATEMALA, October 29, 1929—11 a. m.
[Received 2 : 40 p. m.]

134. Referring to paragraph four of Legation's telegram of October 28, 7 p. m. I am orally urging that the Government substitute for its acceptance of the invitation a note omitting the reservation "within the international treaties in force."

Since that phrase is very strongly insisted upon by a select group with whom the President had consulted I suggested as a last resort that in lieu of using the phrase in the acceptance of the invitation the Government could instruct its delegate in that sense.

It is extremely doubtful that the change can be effected but I shall report tonight.

My calculation is that such an instruction need not prevent the delegate from unofficially discussing a tribunal other than the one to which Honduras has so strongly objected and he could eventually recommend that the Guatemalan Government modify the instruction.

GEISSLER

714.1515/960 : Telegram

*The Minister in Guatemala (Geissler) to the Secretary of State*

GUATEMALA, October 29, 1929—6 p. m.
[Received 11 : 38 p. m.]

135. Following conferences I had today, I was finally told by the President and the Minister for Foreign Affairs that the Minister for

[40] For substitution of phrase reading "preferably within the international treaties in force," see telegram No. 135, October 29, 6 p. m., from the Minister in Guatemala, printed below.

Foreign Affairs will tomorrow morning substitute for his note of the 28th [*26th?*] one in the same terms as by the Legation's telegram of October 28, 7 p. m., except that the word "preferably" will be inserted before the words "within the international treaties in force," which amendment appears to leave the delegate free to consider any tribunal which may be suggested although they made it clear orally that he will be instructed to insist on the Central American Tribunal.

The President told me that Carlos Salazar will probably be appointed delegate.

GEISSLER

714.1515/961 : Telegram

*The Minister in Guatemala (Geissler) to the Secretary of State*

GUATEMALA, October 30, 1929—11 a. m.
[Received 2:45 p. m.]

136. Referring to the Legation's telegram of October 29, 6 p. m. The amended note has been received dated October 28th.

I am now telegraphing the Legation in Honduras with insertion of the amendment the summary of the text contained in the telegram of October 28, 7 p. m.

GEISSLER

714.1515/962 : Telegram

*The Minister in Honduras (Summerlin) to the Secretary of State*

TEGUCIGALPA, October 30, 1929—6 p. m.
[Received October 31—1:43 a. m.]

105. The Minister for Foreign Affairs stated to me today that Honduras will accept the proposal contained in your telegram No. 78, October 25, 5 p. m., but that the acceptance may not be forwarded until next week.

Repeated to Guatemala.

SUMMERLIN

714.1515/971 : Telegram

*The Minister in Honduras (Summerlin) to the Secretary of State*

TEGUCIGALPA, November 7, 1929—4 p. m.
[Received November 8—12:47 a. m.]

107. In reply to the Department's telegram 78, October 25, 5 p. m. I have received today a note dated November 6 from the Minister for Foreign Affairs addressed to the Secretary of State in which, after re-

peating the substance of your note of October 25, he continues as follows:

"In reply I am happy to inform Your Excellency according to instructions from the most excellent President of Honduras that my Government confirms the information with which the most excellent Minister Summerlin has been good enough to furnish Your Excellency to the effect that it is disposed to accept that our boundary dispute with Guatemala instead of being decided by the most excellent President of the United States of America as arbitrator in conformity with its most fervent desire, be decided by an arbitrator which that high functionary may choose from among the distinguished United States members of the Permanent Court of Arbitration at The Hague, it being stipulated that such arbitration should be a condition [*juridical*],[41] taking into consideration the specific classes of evidence of which Your Excellency is aware; that my Government is happy that the new proposal accepted by it had been discussed informally with the Government of Guatemala, [through] the most excellent American Minister in that republic, and that the result of that discussion had afforded grounds to hope for an eventual settlement of the question on a basis satisfactory to both parties; and therefore agrees with Your Excellency that it is evident that further progress can best be achieved by a frank and friendly conference; and that my Government, [profoundly grateful] to Your Excellency's for the invitation to the proposed conference it has been good enough to extend, accepts it and will opportunely authorize its Minister in Washington and name one or more delegates to meet in that capital with the delegate or delegates of Guatemala solemnly to undertake negotiations, it being understood that these negotiations will have as a basis the proposal of Your Excellency's Government that the arbitrator in this connection may be one of the members of the United States of America on the Permanent Court of Arbitration at The Hague and that the reservations which my Government made to the effect that the decision shall repose on a juridical basis will be taken into consideration. My Government will view with satisfaction if representatives of the Government of the United States may be present at this conference.

In replying in these terms to Your Excellency's courteous note, I cannot omit mentioning the eagerness with which my Government has received your proposal, as much on account of its origin in a respectable [*respected*] Government which has given to Honduras proofs of true friendship and obtained interest in favor of the peace and tranquillity of this Republic and of the respect for its rights, as on account of being animated with sentiments of fraternal affection for Guatemala with whom it one day formed part of the Federation of Central America and with whom it again hopes to unite in order to constitute with the other Central American countries a single nation. In case the conference should obtain no result, my Government states in advance that the question will remain in the same status that it was on August 5 of this year, that is, before the steps undertaken by Your Excellency's Government in favor of the new formula suggested for the settlement and favoring [*having*] the most excellent President of the United States as arbitrator; failing him, accepting also with the greatest pleas-

---

[41] "debiendo ser juridico el arbitraje."

ure that the arbitrator be the President of the honorable Supreme Court of the same nation.

With the hope that Your Excellency may inform me for all practical purposes of the decision of the Government of Guatemala in regard to the above-mentioned invitation, I avail myself of this opportunity, et cetera."

In his note transmitting the above note, the Minister for Foreign Affairs added:

"Also I beg Your Excellency confidentially to inform the most excellent Secretary of State, as an amplification of the reply which I have today the honor of addressing to him, that my Government seeing that the Government of the United States of America is generously preoccupied to the end that a solution of our boundary question be arrived at under the conditions expressed in the above-mentioned note of October 25, would be grateful if it would interpose its good offices with the Government of Guatemala so that for its part the *status quo* may be maintained as it was determined in 1918; thereby assuring that the conference may have a spirit of cordiality which may contribute to its success."

Repeated to Guatemala.

SUMMERLIN

714.1515/971 : Telegram

*The Secretary of State to the Minister in Honduras (Summerlin)*[42]

WASHINGTON, November 12, 1929—5 p. m.

82. Legation's 107, November 7, 4 p. m. The Department desires to fix a date for the convening of the boundary conference which will be most convenient to the Governments of Honduras and Guatemala. Please ascertain and report by telegraph the approximate time when Honduras will be prepared to be represented at the conference.

A similar telegram is being addressed to the Legation at Guatemala.

STIMSON

714.1515/973 : Telegram

*The Chargé in Guatemala (Hawks) to the Secretary of State*

GUATEMALA, November 13, 1929—noon.
[Received 3 : 35 p. m.]

146. Referring to Department's telegram of November 12, 5 p. m.[43]

The Minister for Foreign Affairs has informed me that it will be convenient for Guatemala to have the conference convened on De-

---

[42] The same, *mutatis mutandis*, to the Chargé in Guatemala as telegram No. 69, referring to Legation's telegram No. 133, October 28, 7 p. m.
[43] See footnote 42.

cember 15th. The Guatemalan delegation will consist of Carlos Salazar as delegate and Carlos Salazar, Junior, and Silva Pena as secretaries.

Repeated to Honduras.

HAWKS

714.1515/974 : Telegram

*The Chargé in Guatemala (Hawks) to the Secretary of State*

GUATEMALA, November 16, 1929—noon.
[Received 11 : 30 p. m.]

149. Referring to the telegram of November 7, 4 p. m., from the Legation in Honduras. At the request of the Minister for Foreign Affairs I called on him this morning and he told me that he had just received from the Guatemalan Legation at Tegucigalpa a copy of the text of the acceptance of the Government of Honduras as published in a newspaper of Tegucigalpa. He said that if this text was correct the terms of the acceptance were such that they absolutely closed the door to the discussion of any other viewpoint than that of Honduras, namely, that the boundary question be submitted to one of the American members of The Hague Court and be decided on a purely juridic basis and that under these circumstances it was absolutely useless to convene the conference as, unless Guatemala accepted in its entirety the point of view of Honduras, no result could be obtained.

The Minister for Foreign Affairs said that he desires (1) that the acceptance of Honduras be so written as to leave the way open for the discussion of points of view other than that of Honduras, this having already been done by Guatemala and (2) that the instructions given to both delegations be communicated to the Department of State prior to the calling of the conference in order that the latter may decide whether these instructions were flexible enough to admit possibility of a successful termination of the conference.

The Minister for Foreign Affairs said that he had telegraphed the Legation in Washington this morning to inform the Department that if the text of the Honduranean acceptance was as he had been informed the Government of Guatemala feels that it is useless to call the conference.

Mr. Salazar, who was present at this interview, stated that he was in complete accord with the position taken by the Minister for Foreign Affairs.

The terms of the Honduranean acceptance have undoubtedly intensified the feeling already strong here that Guatemala has in the negotiations of the past year and a half made all the concessions while Honduras has made none.

Repeated to Honduras.

HAWKS

714.1515/975 : Telegram

*The Minister in Honduras (Summerlin) to the Secretary of State*

TEGUCIGALPA, November 17, 1929—4 p. m.
[Received 9:55 p. m.]

112. Your telegram No. 82, November 12, 5 p. m. In a note dated November 16 the Minister for Foreign Affairs requests me to inform the Department that his "Government's delegation will be ready January next."

Repeated to Guatemala.

SUMMERLIN

714.1515/974 : Telegram

*The Secretary of State to the Chargé in Guatemala (Hawks)*[44]

WASHINGTON, November 20, 1929—8 p. m.

74. Your 149, November 16, noon. It is this Government's opinion that the prospects for the success of the approaching conference will be far better if both delegations are left free by their Governments to explore all proper methods of settlement of the controversy in informal and friendly exchanges of views. They cannot do this if they are restricted by their instructions to a discussion on any given basis. This Government wishes, therefore, to suggest to both of the Governments concerned the desirability of giving their delegates the greatest practicable freedom of action. This will not, of course, prevent either Government from setting forth fully its point of view and will not commit either Government to the acceptance of any agreement which it does not consider satisfactory.

You may inform the Guatemalan Government that this Government's views as above expressed are being communicated to the Government of Honduras and that the Legation at Tegucigalpa is being instructed to urge upon that Government the desirability of withdrawing any conditions or reservations made in its note of acceptance. It is hoped that the Guatemalan Government, as an indication of its willingness to cooperate, will likewise accede to the idea of a frank and friendly exchange of views upon all phases of the boundary question and will not give to its delegates any instructions which might prevent such an exchange.

STIMSON

[44] The same, *mutatis mutandis*, to the Minister in Honduras as telegram No. 85, referring to his telegram No. 107, November 7, 4 p. m.

714.1515/978 : Telegram

*The Chargé in Guatemala (Hawks) to the Secretary of State*

GUATEMALA, November 21, 1929—5 p. m.
[Received November 22—12:17 a. m.]

150. Referring to the Department's telegram of November 20, 8 p. m. I conveyed verbally to the Minister for Foreign Affairs the information contained therein and he stated specifically that I could notify the Department that the Government of Guatemala would so instruct its delegate that he will be able to discuss all phases of the problem.

Repeated to Honduras.

HAWKS

714.1515/980 : Telegram

*The Minister in Honduras (Summerlin) to the Secretary of State*

TEGUCIGALPA, November 26, 1929—10 a. m.
[Received 1:53 p. m.]

114. The Department's telegram number 85, November 20, 8 p. m.[44a] The Acting Minister for Foreign Affairs assures me in a note dated November 25 that his Government will not give its delegate any instructions which might prevent a frank and friendly exchange of views upon all phases of the boundary question. He said, however, that the conditions and reservations contained in its note of acceptance would be brought out in the explanation of its points of view and that those of Guatemala would be given due consideration.

The President of the Republic has stated to me that he will name Dr. Mariano Vasquez, former Minister for Foreign Affairs, as Honduran delegate.

Repeated to Guatemala.

SUMMERLIN

714.1515/981 : Telegram

*The Chargé in Guatemala (Hawks) to the Secretary of State*

GUATEMALA, November 27, 1929—3 p. m.
[Received 9:20 p. m.]

152. The following telegram was sent to the Legation in Honduras:

"November 27, 3 p. m. With reference to your telegram of November 26, 10 a. m. to the Department.

The Minister for Foreign Affairs informed me today that he did not consider that the Honduran reply makes it sufficiently clear that the Honduran delegate will be given absolute freedom to discuss any

---

[44a] See footnote 44, p. 971.

phase of the boundary question and that therefore the Government of Guatemala feels that under these conditions it is useless to call the conference."

HAWKS

---

714.1515/982 : Telegram

### The Chargé in Guatemala (Hawks) to the Secretary of State

GUATEMALA, November 28, 1929—10 a. m.<br>[Received 5 : 30 p. m.]

154. Referring to the Department's telegram of November 27, 2 p. m.[45] The Minister for Foreign Affairs still maintains the position that unless the Government of Honduras makes the same clear cut statement without any reservations, as has already been made by the Guatemalan Government, to the effect that its delegate will be able to discuss all phases of the problem it will be useless to hold the conference.

Repeated to Honduras.

HAWKS

---

714.1515/980 : Telegram

### The Acting Secretary of State to the Minister in Honduras (Summerlin)[46]

WASHINGTON, November 29, 1929—7 p. m.

89. Legation's 114, November 26, 10 a. m. and Guatemala's telegrams 152 and 154. Please transcribe fully by telegraph pertinent sections of the note from the Honduran Minister for Foreign Affairs dated November 25.

The Department earnestly hopes that the plan to hold the conference at Washington will not meet with failure through the inability of the Governments of Honduras and Guatemala to agree beforehand to leave their delegates complete freedom of action in dealing with the question at issue. Any concrete proposals emanating from the conference must of course be submitted to the respective Governments for approval and this fact should constitute a sufficient safeguard to both Governments.

Please informally discuss the matter in this sense with the Honduran Government and endeavor to obtain a modification of the terms upon which its attendance at the conference is based.

CARR

---

[45] Not printed; it requested the Chargé to inquire whether it would be satisfactory to the Guatemalan Government to have the delegates meet at Washington on January 15, 1930. (714.1515/973)

[46] Repeated to the Chargé in Guatemala in telegram No. 78 of the same date.

714.1515/985 : Telegram

*The Minister in Honduras (Summerlin) to the Secretary of State*

TEGUCIGALPA, November 30, 1929—11 a. m.
[Received 4 : 11 p. m.]

117. Your telegram No. 89, November 29, 7 p. m.  After repeating the substance of my note, the Acting Minister for Foreign Affairs' note of November 25 continues as follows:

"In reply I am gratified to inform Your Excellency, under instructions of His Excellency the President of the Republic, that my Government will confer upon its delegate the most ample power to examine informally, in a frank and friendly manner, with the delegate of Guatemala, all appropriate methods for such settlement of the controversy, without the conditions and reservations which the Chancellery under my charge made in its note of the 6th instant,[47] which it can but maintain, being an obstacle to his freedom of action, so that the object of the conference may not be defeated and that, explaining in the conference the points of view of Honduras in which are included the said conditions and reservations, and duly appreciating those of Guatemala, a solution may be arrived at satisfactory to the two Republics; but it is understood that if my Government considers that solution prejudicial to the rights of Honduras it is not obligated to accept it as Your Excellency with such ability expresses it.

Begging Your Excellency to inform the Honorable Government of the United States of America of the above I avail myself of this opportunity, et cetera."

Repeated to Guatemala.

SUMMERLIN

714.1515/986 : Telegram

*The Chargé in Guatemala (Hawks) to the Secretary of State*

GUATEMALA, December 2, 1929—11 a. m.
[Received 5 : 25 p. m.]

155. With reference to the telegram from the Legation in Honduras of November 30, 11 a. m.  The Minister for Foreign Affairs informed me this morning that the terms of the Honduranean note appear satisfactory to the Government of Guatemala and it will therefore with pleasure attend the conference on January 15.

Repeated to Honduras.

HAWKS

---

[47] See telegram No. 107, November 7, 4 p. m., from the Minister in Honduras, p. 967.

714.1515/987 : Telegram

*The Minister in Honduras (Summerlin) to the Secretary of State*

TEGUCIGALPA, December 3, 1929—6 p. m.
[Received December 4—12:12 a. m.]

118. In a memorandum dated December 3, after referring to the observations made in the Department's telegram No. 89, November 29, 7 p. m., the Minister for Foreign Affairs states:

"The Government of Honduras, taking into consideration that all proper methods for the settlement of the controversy will be examined in the conference in informal and friendly exchange of views, will confer upon its delegate ample powers in order to give him complete freedom of action in the conference, with the understanding that any concrete resolution which may emanate from the said conference must be submitted to the Government of Honduras for its approval or disapproval."

Repeated to Guatemala.

SUMMERLIN

714.1515/986 : Telegram

*The Secretary of State to the Chargé in Guatemala (Hawks)*[48]

WASHINGTON, December 31, 1929—6 p. m.

85. Department's 79, December 5, 1 p. m.[48a] As the proposed date for the convening of the boundary conference would conflict with a highway conference being held at Atlantic City which the Guatemalan and Honduran Ministers should attend, it has been agreed by them and the Department that the boundary conference shall be postponed until January 20. It is understood that both Ministers are communicating with their Governments in this sense.

STIMSON

**Honduras and Nicaragua**[49]

715.1715/316a : Telegram

*The Secretary of State to the Chargé in Nicaragua (Hanna)*

WASHINGTON, July 1, 1929—5 p. m.

94. Legation's despatch No. 1025.[50] Please say to President Moncada that I have learned with much satisfaction of the statements made by him when receiving the new Honduran Minister with respect to the settlement of the dispute concerning the Honduras-Nicaragua

---

[48] The same to the Minister in Honduras as telegram No. 95, referring to Department's telegram No. 92, December 5, 1 p. m.
[48a] Not printed.
[49] For previous correspondence, see *Foreign Relations*, 1923, vol. I, pp. 362 ff.
[50] Dated June 6, 1929; not printed.

boundary, and that I heartily congratulate him for the stand he has taken in this matter. As boundary disputes are the most likely to cause friction between the Latin American countries this Government has exerted its efforts in the past for their peaceful settlement. Especially since my visit to Nicaragua I am deeply interested in the settlement of Central American boundary disputes and earnestly hope that the pending question between Nicaragua and Honduras may be speedily adjusted by the formal acceptance on the part of Nicaragua of the award of the King of Spain.[51]

STIMSON

715.1715/317 : Telegram

*The Chargé in Nicaragua (Hanna) to the Secretary of State*

MANAGUA, July 5, 1929—3 p. m.
[Received 8 : 15 p. m.]

180. Your telegram 94, July 1, 5 p. m. President Moncada expressed his thanks for your message and requested me to convey to you the assurance that he accepts the award of the King of Spain and hopes to be prepared to appoint a commission to locate the boundary as soon as public order has been restored along the frontier.

HANNA

715.1715/322 : Telegram

*The Chargé in Nicaragua (Hanna) to the Secretary of State*

MANAGUA, September 17, 1929—7 p. m.
[Received September 18—12 : 15 p. m.]

226. The Minister for Foreign Affairs called upon me this morning and showed me two notes he has received from Honduran Minister in this capital. The first, dated September 12, reviews the history of the Nicaraguan attitude favorable to compliance with the award of the King of Spain in the Nicaraguan-Honduran boundary controversy and quotes the statements of President Moncada and the Minister for Foreign Affairs transmitted with my despatch No. 1025 of June 6, 1925 [*1929*].[52] He also quotes a statement attributed to the Minister for Foreign Affairs to the effect that conversations in the matter cannot be initiated until the northern regions of Nicaragua have been pacified. The note assumes that such pacification has been accomplished and proposes that steps be initiated to comply with the award. Finally the note suggests that, pending the determination of

[51] Award of December 23, 1906; *British and Foreign State Papers*, vol. c, p. 1096.
[52] Not printed.

the boundary by a commission, Honduras should be given immediate possession of all the left bank of the Coco River.

It appears that, at about the same time the foregoing note was delivered to the Nicaraguan Government, the left bank of the Coco River was occupied by some garrisons of Honduran armed forces, presumably by the orders of the Honduran Government, and that they proceeded to exercise jurisdiction over the territory thus occupied which it seems has long been under the jurisdiction of Nicaragua. I had been led to believe until today that this occupation was through error and that it would be terminated by Honduras without serious incident. The second note, dated September 16, refers specifically to this occupation and transcribes a telegram from the Honduran Minister for Foreign Affairs. Orders had been given for the withdrawal of armed forces from the occupied places "with the understanding that our (Honduran) territorial rights over these places are expressly recognized because they are in the region which the award of the King of Spain allots to Honduras". Continuing, the note states the Honduran Government accepts the suggestion of the Nicaraguan Minister at Tegucigalpa that a commission of three engineers, one named by Nicaragua, one by Honduras, and the third by the Government of the United States be created to establish the boundary line as fixed by the award, and requests the Government of Nicaragua to agree that the Government of the United States be asked to tender its good offices for the solution of this boundary dispute.

These notes threaten to create a serious crisis in this matter. When the Minister for Foreign Affairs saw me this morning he was agitated and said he had instructions from the President to inform the Honduran Minister that the Nicaraguan Government could not accede at this time to the pretension of the Honduran Government that it has territorial rights over the places in dispute and to demand the immediate evacuation of the occupied territory. He said further that the commission proposed by this Government was an arbitral commission, the American member of which would be the arbiter, and not a commission of engineers as stated by the Honduran Government. He desired me to submit the matter to the Department and to state that his Government would appreciate the Department's advice and assistance. I reminded him that precipitate and ill-considered action by the Nicaraguan Government at this moment might bring about a crisis and counseled him to make no reply to the notes or to take any action which might result in an impasse before I received the Department's reply. He assented.

Subsequently I saw President Moncada at his request and he also requested the Department's assistance and assured me that his Government would delay further action in the matter pending Department's advice. He seems to appreciate the consequences which probably would follow a demand by this Government that Honduras withdraw her forces from the occupied territory, but he thinks those forces must be withdrawn and the *status quo* reestablished if a crisis is to be avoided and if negotiations in the boundary matter are to be resumed.

[Paraphrase.] President Moncada said he feared that the Honduran Government had taken advantage of his recent friendly gesture in this matter and of the circumstance that the armed forces of Nicaragua are under the command of American officers, and he observed that under this circumstance he is in a quandary with regard to the use he might make of the national guard to meet such a situation. [End paraphrase.]

Repeated to Tegucigalpa.

HANNA

---

715.1715/322 : Telegram

*The Secretary of State to the Minister in Honduras (Summerlin)*

WASHINGTON, September 19, 1929—6 p. m.

62. Refer to telegram No. 226 of September 17, 7 p. m., from Managua. Please inform the President of Honduras that this Government is much concerned at the situation which has apparently been precipitated by the action of Honduras. The Government of the United States had confidently hoped that the Honduras-Nicaragua boundary question could be settled in the very near future in an atmosphere of cordiality and good will but it fears that the occupation by Honduras of territory which has long been held by Nicaragua, if indeed the fact of this occupation is confirmed, combined with the tone of the communications which have been addressed by the Honduran Government to the Nicaraguan Government, will make a satisfactory settlement far more difficult. It desires therefore that you should urge upon the President the importance of withdrawing from any territory hitherto held by Nicaragua as a preliminary to any further negotiations. Report by telegraph.

STIMSON

---

715.1715/322 : Telegram

*The Secretary of State to the Chargé in Nicaragua (Hanna)*

WASHINGTON, September 19, 1929—6 p. m.

131. Your 226, September 17, 7 p. m. The following telegram has been sent to Tegucigalpa:

[Here follows the text of telegram No. 62, September 19, 6 p. m., to the Minister in Honduras, printed *supra.*]

You may advise President Moncada informally of the action which the Department has taken without giving him the text of the above message and you may express to him my hope that he will continue to deal with this matter in a spirit of patience and moderation and that the incident will not prevent a satisfactory termination of the boundary dispute in the very near future.

STIMSON

715.1715/323 : Telegram

*The Chargé in Nicaragua (Hanna) to the Secretary of State*

MANAGUA, September 20, 1929—3 p. m.
[Received 6 : 52 p. m.]

229. Department's urgent telegram 131, September 19, 6 p. m. I have just seen President Moncada. With reference to the first paragraph of your telegram, I only told the President that instructions have been given the American Minister in Tegucigalpa to make representations to the Government of Honduras in behalf of a speedy and friendly termination of the conflict. I expressed textually the message contained in the second paragraph. I added as a personal observation that I have noted with great satisfaction that the newspapers of Managua are not discussing the matter and that it is to be hoped that they will remain ignorant of what is taking place because otherwise the efforts of the Department would be made more difficult and might be unsuccessful. I have also personally communicated the foregoing to the Minister of Foreign Affairs.

The President responded favorably to your designs. He will continue to deal with this matter in a spirit of patience and moderation and said he would do everything possible to prevent undesirable interference by the local newspapers. Concerning the settlement of the boundary dispute, he said that it is his desire to entrust the demarcation of the boundary established by the award of the King of Spain to an arbitral commission with an American arbiter as soon as banditry along the border is sufficiently under control to permit the commission to work in safety. He said the principal question for the decision of the commission will be the location of portions of the boundary not clearly defined in the award. He added that he hopes it may be possible by mutual small concessions of territory to substitute a natural boundary along a river for a portion of the ill-defined boundary as fixed in the award.

Repeated to Tegucigalpa.

HANNA

715.1715/325 : Telegram

*The Minister in Honduras (Summerlin) to the Secretary of State*

TEGUCIGALPA, September 22, 1929—11 a. m.
[Received 9 : 30 p. m.]

89. In carrying out the instructions in the Department's telegram No. 62, September 19, 6 p. m., I addressed a note to the Foreign Office and last evening received a reply thereto, dated September 21, in which the Minister for Foreign Affairs, after repeating the substance of my note, continues as follows:

"In reply I have the honor of informing Your Excellency that the Government of Honduras, in decreeing martial law in the zone which was specified in the decree itself, did so with the knowledge of the Government of Nicaragua, without any protest, and with the principal object of cooperating, as a Government friendly to Nicaragua, in the pacification of the Segovias which for so long were suffering the consequences of the Sandinista rebels, Honduras having given its effective cooperation, notwithstanding the economic and other sacrifices on its part. With this end in view my Government ordered that armed details should watch the frontier of both countries so as to pursue and capture the rebels, but without ordering any violent act against Nicaraguan forces, nor the capture of any person, other than rebels. I must inform you also that my Government has already ordered the withdrawal of these Honduran soldiers and the liberation of the prisoners, in case that which is said is true. In these circumstances, according to the suggestion of Your Excellency, there will now be no difficulty in carrying to a conclusion the proceedings indispensable to the execution of the award of His Majesty the King of Spain amid the cordial and friendly relations which fortunately exist between Honduras and Nicaragua. And my Government heeding the suggestion which, in the name of the Government of the United States, Your Excellency was good enough to make that, Honduras withdraw[ing] from any territory hitherto occupied by Nicaragua, as a preliminary step, there will be no difficulty to any further negotiations, I must inform you that His Excellency the Minister of Nicaragua, General Augusto J. Caldera, has proposed informally to His Excellency the President of this Republic the naming of a commission of engineers, one by Honduras, another by Nicaragua and another by the Government of the United States, the third named at the request of the Governments of those two republics in order that they might proceed to the definite tracing of the boundary line, taking as a base the above-mentioned award; in this conception I am happy to inform you that Honduras would be glad if the enlightened Government of Your Excellency, interested as it is in the removal of causes which impede the maintenance of the tranquillity of the two countries, would have the goodness to interpose its good offices with the Nicaraguan Government with the object that this commission may be named with the shortest possible delay, to the above mentioned end, so that this matter may be concluded as soon as possible, offering in advance the gratitude of the Government and people of Honduras to Your Government for its efforts.

I avail myself of this opportunity, et cetera."

Repeated to Nicaragua.

SUMMERLIN

---

715.1715/323 : Telegram

*The Secretary of State to the Chargé in Nicaragua (Hanna)*

[Paraphrase]

WASHINGTON, September 25, 1929—6 p. m.

132. Your 229, September 20, 3 p. m. Please confer with the brigade commander and report to the Department whether in his opinion and yours, it would be safe for a commission of engineers to survey the Honduras-Nicaragua boundary during the coming dry season. It would seem that the Guardia Nacional should be able to afford all necessary protection on the Nicaraguan side. The Department desires to have this information in order to consider what its next step should be.

Do you think the President of Nicaragua would really be prepared to go forward with a survey of the boundary if he felt that the work could be safely done?

STIMSON

---

715.1715/327 : Telegram

*The Chargé in Nicaragua (Hanna) to the Secretary of State*

[Paraphrase]

MANAGUA, September 26, 1929—5 p. m.
[Received 9:15 p. m.]

233. Department's 132, September 25, 6 p. m. I conferred with the brigade and guardia commanders and they, as well as I, are of the opinion that the guardia could afford the necessary protection in Nicaraguan territory to the proposed commission under existing conditions on the border and our expectation that conditions will be even more favorable during the coming dry season.

My information indicates that the President of Nicaragua will be glad to have this matter submitted to an arbitral commission at the earliest practicable moment, and I think he will be disposed to accept General McDougal's assurance that the work can be done with safety. I think this is an opportune moment to create the commission and if done it may relieve the tension caused by a specific answer from the Government of Honduras to this Government's objections to those notes.

Repeated to Tegucigalpa.

HANNA

715.1715/337 : Telegram

*The Chargé in Nicaragua (Hanna) to the Secretary of State*

MANAGUA, November 1, 1929—4 p. m.

[Received 8 : 30 p. m.]

259. My 253, October 17, noon.[53] The Acting Minister for Foreign Affairs called at the Legation late yesterday and showed me a telegram received by President Moncada from Dr. Cordero Reyes, dated Tegucigalpa, October 30th, reporting a conversation he had with the President of Honduras. The pertinent portions of the telegram in translation follow:

"He reiterated assurances of his cooperation but at the same time stated that said cooperation would be decisive only in case it could be announced that the mixed commission to fix the boundary will begin work immediately in order thus to overcome obstacles of his adversaries. I spoke on this point in accordance with your instructions and added that to facilitate the formation of the commission, the pacification of Segovia is indispensable not only for material security but also because you need Liberal support in order to proceed with the frontier matter and this is possible only on the basis of prior cooperation of Honduranean Government in exterminating the bandits."

The Acting Minister for Foreign Affairs also showed me President Moncada's brief reply to the foregoing, dated October 31st, which reads in translation as follows:

"Please state to the President of Honduras that my Government will not settle the boundary matter under conditions [*sic*] and that the moment has arrived for definitely settling these things for the good of both republics."

I saw President Moncada this morning and discussed with him the situation created by this exchange of telegrams and pointed out the dangerous consequences they might have on the continuance of the negotiations.

The following telegram was then drafted and will be sent to the Nicaraguan representative in Honduras today:

"Please communicate that the Government of Nicaragua proposes to the Government of Honduras as an effective means to terminate the frontier difficulties, as it has heretofore proposed, the formation of a commission made up of a representative of each country and another as president appointed by the Department of State. The last telegram sent yesterday by the President is not opposed in any manner to the appointment of the commission, which commission will be organized immediately and will begin to function insofar as circumstances permit. The President understands that the preliminary arrangements for the commission and the appointment of the representative of the Department of State will require two months more or less and that meanwhile, with the effective cooperation of both countries, banditry will cease."

---

[53] Not printed.

[Paraphrase.] If the Government of Honduras accepts the fore-going proposal, the chances for continuing the negotiations will be greatly improved . . . [End paraphrase.]

Repeated to Tegucigalpa.

HANNA

715.1715/338 : Telegram

*The Minister in Honduras (Summerlin) to the Secretary of State*

TEGUCIGALPA, November 5, 1929—9 p. m.
[Received November 6—1 : 29 a. m.]

106. With reference to Managua's telegram November 1, 4 p. m. The Minister for Foreign Affairs has just sent me confidentially a copy of his reply, dated November 4, to the Minister of Nicaragua in which Honduras accepts the proposal of Nicaragua regarding the formation of a commission of three engineers, the third member to be named by the Department of State, to fix the boundary between the two countries in conformity with the award of the King of Spain.

The reply suggests that an appropriate protocol be signed here at once giving names of Honduranean and Nicaraguan engineers and containing a clause obliging both countries to request the appoint-ment of an engineer who as president of the proposed commission will represent the United States.

The reply adds that under the above conditions Honduras will co-operate adequately in the prosecution of the outlaws on the border.

I am closely in touch with the authorities here in regard to these matters and this reply would indicate that the two Governments are progressing satisfactorily for the moment and I consider that the pro-posed visit of Beaulac suggested in Hanna's telegram November 5, 2 p. m.,[54] is not necessary.

Managua advised.

SUMMERLIN

715.1715/341 : Telegram

*The Chargé in Nicaragua (Hanna) to the Secretary of State*

MANAGUA, November 8, 1929—3 p. m.
[Received 7 p. m.]

266. My telegram No. 259, November 1, 4 p. m. The Minister of Nicaragua in Tegucigalpa has telegraphed President Moncada that the Government of Honduras accepts Nicaragua's proposal to carry out the award of the King of Spain providing the commissioners are engineers, and proposes that a protocol be immediately signed in Tegucigalpa naming the engineers appointed by the two Governments

---

[54] Not printed.

and binding both Governments to request the Government of the United States to name an engineer for president of the commission, and proposes further that the commission shall begin work immediately protected by armed forces of both countries. The telegram states that under the above conditions the Government of Honduras will cooperate with Nicaragua until peace is restored "as it has done during the present year."

In informing me of the foregoing, President Moncada said he would insist that the commission should have arbitral powers to settle obscure points in the award and other questions which may arise. He said that without such powers there is no assurance that the commission would succeed in its mission.

Repeated to Tegucigalpa.

HANNA

---

715.1715/338 : Telegram

*The Secretary of State to the Minister in Honduras (Summerlin)*

WASHINGTON, November 8, 1929—6 p. m.

81. Reference Legation's telegram No. 106.[56] Please inform the Government of Honduras that the Department is gratified to learn that it has accepted the proposal of President Moncada for the formation of a Commission to establish the boundary between the two republics and hopes that a complete agreement may now speedily be reached.

You may say to President Mejia Colindres that upon the conclusion of a protocol providing for the establishment of the Commission and for the cooperation of this Government the Government of the United States will, upon request, gladly consider the designation of a competent American engineer to serve as President of the Commission.

[Paraphrase.] It is assumed by the Department that the protocol will set forth clearly the duties to be entrusted to the Commission and will provide that the demarcation of the boundary shall be effected in accordance with the award of the King of Spain.

A similar telegram is being sent to the Chargé in Nicaragua.[57] [End paraphrase.]

STIMSON

---

[56] *Ante*, p. 983.
[57] As telegram No. 155 of the same date; not printed.

## ATTITUDE OF THE DEPARTMENT OF STATE WITH REGARD TO TARIFF LEGISLATION INCONSISTENT WITH CERTAIN TREATY OBLIGATIONS OF THE UNITED STATES [1]

611.003/1472

### The Secretary of State to Representative Willis C. Hawley [2]

WASHINGTON, February 26, 1929.

DEAR MR. HAWLEY: Certain difficulties in the conduct of the foreign relations of this Government have arisen by reason of the existence in the Tariff Act of 1922 [3] of provisions which are inconsistent with the established policy and with the treaty obligations of this Government. Other provisions in the Act have proved to be a source of international friction. In view of the fact that revision of the Act is now under consideration I feel that I should bring these matters to the attention of your Committee.

The Tariff Act of 1922 contains in eight paragraphs of its schedules provisos the effect of which is to cause the duty levied upon the products mentioned therein to vary in accordance with the amount of import duty placed by the country of origin upon similar products. Such a proviso is found in paragraph 369 which reads as follows:

"Automobiles, automobile bodies, automobile chassis, motor cycles, and parts of the foregoing, not including tires, all of the foregoing whether finished or unfinished, 25 per centum ad valorem: Provided, That if any country, dependency, province, or other subdivision of government imposes a duty on any article specified in this paragraph, when imported from the United States, in excess of the duty herein provided, there shall be imposed upon such article, when imported either directly or indirectly from such country, dependency, province, or other subdivision of government, a duty equal to that imposed by such country, dependency. province, or other subdivision of government on such article imported from the United States, but in no case shall such duty exceed 50 per centum ad valorem."

Provisos of similar effect are also embodied in paragraphs 371, 1302, 1536, 1541, 1543, 1548 and 1585. In addition there are provisos in three other paragraphs, namely, 401, 1301 and 1700, which are similar

---

[1] Communications from foreign governments relative to proposed changes in customs laws were printed in *Tariff Act of 1929:* Hearings before the Committee on Finance, United States Senate, 71st Cong., 1st sess., on H. R. 2667 . . . vol. XVIII (Washington, Government Printing Office, 1929).

These communications were transmitted to the Senate Committee through the Department of State.

[2] Chairman of the Ways and Means Committee of the House of Representatives.

[3] 42 Stat. 858.

in character and intent to those mentioned, differing only in certain particulars.

These provisions are open to serious objection on the ground that the imposition of increased duties under the terms thereof conflicts with the stipulations for most-favored-nation treatment found in practically all our comprehensive commercial treaties with foreign countries. The following stipulation in the Treaty of Friendship, Commerce and Consular Rights with Germany, signed December 8, 1923,[4] is typical of the provisions of similar treaties recently concluded.

Article VII (Paragraph two) :

"Each of the High Contracting Parties binds itself unconditionally to impose no higher or other duties or conditions and no prohibition on the importation of any article, the growth, produce or manufacture, of the territories of the other than are or shall be imposed on the importation of any like article, the growth, produce or manufacture of any other foreign country."

Duties imposed pursuant to the provisions of paragraph 369 and other similar paragraphs of the Tariff Act apply without regard to whether the foreign country discriminated against subjects the American products in question to discriminatory treatment. Under these provisions the Treasury Department has considered it necessary, despite the obligations imposed on this Government by treaties containing stipulations of the above character, to impose on certain products imported from particular countries higher duties than those applicable to importations of the products in question from other countries.

The fact that none of the provisos of the above mentioned paragraphs of the Tariff Act can be applied in the case of importations from the numerous countries with which the United States has treaties containing the most-favored-nation clause without violating our treaty obligations would seem to be sufficient ground for the repeal of the provisos in question.

I should also point out that even though the application of these provisos were limited to importations from countries which are not entitled by treaty to most-favored-nation treatment, they would still be open to the objection that they are inconsistent with the general policy of this Government envisaged in Section 317 of the same Act. Section 317 authorizes the President to impose penalty duties on importations from countries which discriminate against the commerce of the United States. Yet the provisos in question require that the commerce of foreign countries be subjected in certain circumstances to discriminations which, if employed by the same foreign countries against

---

[4] *Foreign Relations*, 1923, vol. II, p. 29.

the commerce of this country, would render their trade liable to customs penalties by the United States.

These inconsistencies with the general policy of equality of treatment envisaged in Section 317 of the Tariff Act have in fact proved to be a source of embarrassment to this Department in important negotiations having in view the removal of discriminations against American trade.

I desire to invite your further attention to the provisions of the Tariff Act pursuant to which inspections are made of the books of foreign exporters and in particular to Section 510 which provides as follows:

"If any person manufacturing, producing, selling, shipping, or consigning merchandise exported to the United States fails, at the request of the Secretary of the Treasury, or an appraiser, or person acting as appraiser, or a collector, or a general appraiser, or the Board of General Appraisers, as the case may be, to permit a duly accredited officer of the United States to inspect his books, papers, records, accounts, documents, or correspondence, pertaining to the market value or classification of such merchandise, then while such failure continues the Secretary of the Treasury, under regulations prescribed by him, (1) shall prohibit the importation into the United States of merchandise manufactured, produced, sold, shipped or consigned by such person, and (2) may instruct the collectors to withhold delivery of merchandise manufactured, produced, sold, shipped or consigned by such person. If such failure continues for a period of one year from the date of such instructions the collector shall cause the merchandise, unless previously exported, to be sold at public auction as in the case of forfeited merchandise."

The inspection of private records of foreign business concerns by officials of this Government has caused widespread criticism and resentment in foreign countries. In addition to formal protests by the Governments of Great Britain, France and Italy against such inspections and informal representations to officials of this Government by representatives of one or two other countries, strong resentment has been expressed by the press and by public officials in a very considerable number of other foreign countries.[5] One of the consequences of the tariff controversy with France in the fall of 1927[6] was that, owing to the latter's insistence, this Government discontinued inspections of the books of French business concerns.

In the case of certain countries complaint has been made on the ground that in virtually compelling exporters to permit the inspection of their private books officials of this Government seek privileges

[5] See "Unsuccessful efforts to have American customs attachés accorded diplomatic status," *Foreign Relations*, 1925, vol. I, pp. 211 ff. For representations by the Italian Government, see *ibid.*, 1928, vol. III, pp. 104 ff.

[6] See *ibid.*, 1927, vol. II, pp. 631 ff.

which could be denied under the laws and policy of the foreign country to officials of the government in whose jurisdiction such inspections are made.    There also appears to be apprehension on the part of foreign business concerns that in consequence of such inspections of their private records, trade secrets may find their way into the possession of their American competitors.

Regardless of the opinion which may be held concerning the validity of these complaints, the fact that such activities on the part of officers of this Government have caused widespread dissatisfaction and resentment abroad argues strongly for some steps being taken to remove this source of international friction and ill-feeling.    The Committee on Ways and Means will doubtless wish to consider whether some suitable basis of dutiable value or some method of verifying declarations by foreign exporters can not be found which will obviate the necessity of compelling foreign business concerns to submit to the inspection of their private records by officials of this Government.

Representations have been made to this Government by the Governments of Spain and Portugal against a recent ruling of the United States Customs Court handed down in *Armstrong Cork Company* vs. *United States*, the Boucher Cork Company appearing as a party in interest, T. D. 42993.    The Court held in that case that tapered corks imported into the United States are capable of being marked without injury within the meaning of Section 304 of the Act of 1922, and assessable with additional duty therein provided for, if not so marked. The Spanish Embassy, in a note dated June 15, 1927,[7] contended that "the expense of marking these corks and cork discs would be disproportionate to the cost and the selling price of the article and would amount to an embargo on these articles, to the detriment of an important Spanish industry".    The existence of regulations and restrictions of this character upon goods imported into the United States makes it difficult for this Department to assist American exporters adversely affected by analogous foreign regulations and restrictions.

It is desirable for obvious reasons that the views of the Department of State on the above matters should not be made public.

I am [etc.]                                                 FRANK B. KELLOGG

611.003/1511

*Memorandum by the Assistant Chief of the Treaty Division (McClure)*

[WASHINGTON,] March 30, 1929.

MR. SECRETARY: During recent months information has multiplied to the effect that the commercial policy of the United States, as expressed in its laws and treaties, is exciting increased antagonism in

---

[7] Not printed.

certain other countries. The exact extent of such opposition is difficult, perhaps impossible, to measure, but sufficient evidence of it has reached the Department to make it seem incumbent upon the Treaty Division, which has the duty of negotiating commercial treaties for the purpose of furthering this policy, to bring the situation to your attention.

The immediate occasion for so doing is the receipt of a despatch from the American Embassy at Berlin discussing several elements of opposition.[8] Among them is the suggestion, appearing in a Berlin newspaper, that other countries might retaliate against the United States by enacting provisions in their tariff laws which would result in the duty on the importation of goods into such other countries from the United States being measured by the import duties which the United States imposes upon their goods.

The Department is on record as holding that duties differentiated in this manner violate the most-favored-nation clause in commercial treaties whenever applied to the disadvantage of the goods of a country which is a party to such a treaty.

It is true, however, that in respect of a number of tariff items, such provisions occur in the tariff law of the United States. Consequently, this Government could hardly protest the violation of the treaty through the application of such provisions, no matter how disadvantageous such application might become to products originating in the United States.

By a letter of February 26, 1929, Mr. Kellogg requested the Chairman of the Ways and Means Committee to take steps to repeal the provisions in question. There is little doubt that such repeal can take place without affecting any American interest. So important is the matter, however, from the point of view of the integrity of our commercial policy, that it is thought you may care to take advantage of the present occasion again to lay the matter before the Committee and to urge the repeal.

The question of the compatibility of these provisions of the tariff act and the most-favored-nation clause has been referred to the Department of Justice by the Secretary of the Treasury for a ruling. It is understood informally that those who have considered the matter in the Department of Justice are in accord with the Department of State in considering that the application of the provisos to the disadvantage of the goods of another party to a most-favored-nation treaty contravenes such treaty. An additional question has, however, emerged in connection with the case. Some of the experts of the Department of Justice take the position that a most-favored-nation clause in a commercial treaty is not self-executing, and accordingly can not supersede

---

[8] Despatch of March 6, 1929; not printed.

a provision of a tariff law unless both houses of Congress enact a statute for the purpose of giving execution to the treaty. The case was put before the Department of Justice at the instance of Germany. This fact seems to give a certain significance to discussion of the question in Germany.

Were the European discussion of our tariff and most-favored-nation policy confined to the foregoing considerations, our concern might be relatively little. Unfortunately, however, this discussion is only one item concerning which opposition to American policy is being felt.

The practice of the United States from the beginning of our national history has usually been to maintain a uniform tariff equally applicable to the products of all countries. That practice was written into our stated policy and into our treaties beginning with the year 1923. The underlying cause was the vast increase in the surpluses of manufactured goods which must find a market, if at all, outside the United States. The process of increasing production of manufactured goods has been going on for more than a generation. Such increase was particularly rapid during the World War period and resulted in careful study of our treaty policy by the United States Tariff Commission and the subsequent decision of President Harding to base the commercial treaty system of the country upon the unconditional most-favored-nation clause. President Harding felt authorized to do so particularly because of the provisions of Section 317 of the Tariff Act of 1922 which empowered him to retaliate against commercial practices of other countries which might discriminate against the United States. Since that date eight treaties containing the most-favored-nation clause have been signed, five of them have been put into effect, and this Government has entered into executive agreements with more than a dozen other countries for the purpose of maintaining unconditional most-favored-nation treatment reciprocally in respect of customs and other commercial matters.

The program of commercial treaties included not only their conclusion with all countries with which treaties were not in effect, but the revision of old treaties so as to put them in line with the new policy. The progress of this program has been painfully slow. In the first place, the Department itself lacked the personnel to take advantage of the opportunities which were presented to it to push forward its own policy. In the second place, serious opposition has been encountered in a number of quarters. In Latin America offers to enter into unconditional most-favored-nation treaties have, on the whole, been coolly received and in a number of instances have been flatly turned down. In Europe, efforts to enter into such a treaty with Spain early proved unsuccessful, though a *modus vivendi* with that country has been maintained.[9] The center of opposition has, however, been in France.

France, though according most-favored-nation treatment to a considerable number of countries, refuses to endorse most-favored-nation treatment as a policy and contends that it will negotiate separately with each country, and arrive at a separate bargain with each as to the application of its tariff. The United States offered to France a most-favored-nation treaty in 1927 [10] but has made no progress whatever toward negotiating the same. France stands strongly by the proposition that it will not promise most-favored-nation treatment to a country which maintains a tariff that is generally more obstructive to the importation of French goods than is the French tariff to the importation of the goods of such other country. The French argue that the American tariff is decidedly higher than their own and that it falls with particular weight upon the characteristic products of France.

Recent despatches from the Consulate General and from the Embassy at Berlin give evidence of considerable dissatisfaction in Germany with the most-favored-nation treaty in force with the United States and suggest the growth of sentiment in favor of a commercial policy such as that of France. Should this attitude become dominant, the commercial treaty signed in 1923 would probably be denounced as soon as the fixed term has expired. It is true that termination could not be effected until 1935 but the growth of dissatisfaction in so important a country as Germany, and any threat to subscribe to a policy contrary to that of the United States, must be viewed with concern by this Government. There is every reason to believe that the policy of equality of treatment, as put into effect by the most-favored-nation clause, is not only of advantage to American exporters but is from almost every point of view the fairest commercial policy that a country can maintain and the one that is best calculated to promote peace and good will among nations.

The situation evidenced by despatches from Germany is confirmed by documents emanating from Geneva. The Economic Committee of the League of Nations has for some time been giving very careful consideration to commercial policy in general and to the most-favored-nation clause in particular. While the report of the World Economic Conference of 1927 [11] and other expressions of opinion through the League indicate a prevailing sentiment in favor of the most unconditional and unrestricted policy of most-favored-nation treatment,

[9] See *Foreign Relations*, 1923, vol. II, pp. 831 ff.
[10] See *ibid.*, 1927, vol. II, pp. 631 ff.
[11] See *ibid.*, vol. I, pp. 238 ff.

it is also evident that the French doctrine is receiving wide support throughout the continent of Europe and that it was directed particularly against the tariff of the United States. It would be impossible to maintain that such an attitude is wholly unreasonable. Obviously, the advantages of most-favored-nation treatment are greater where a tariff is moderate than where it is extremely high.

There is at present a movement, though apparently not a very strongly supported one, to enter into multilateral treaties for the purpose of reciprocally reducing tariff duties. In connection with this movement there has been some insistence that duties reduced by such multilateral agreements ought not to be subject to generalization to countries which are the other parties to bilateral most-favored-nation agreements in force with those countries that might subscribe to multilateral agreements. Such a doctrine is wholly at variance with the policy of the United States, and the influence of the United States should be directed against it in every way practicable. What the United States needs for the furtherance of its policy is not multilateral treaties for the purpose of altering tariff duties, but a multilateral treaty containing the most-favored-nation clause, such treaty to be accepted by the largest possible number of the countries of the world.

The International Chamber of Commerce is giving consideration to these problems and the American Section has recently taken strong ground against any limitation of the most-favored-nation clause in the event that multilateral treaties reducing tariffs should by any chance be entered into.

In view of the foregoing considerations, it is recommended:

(1) That careful consideration be given by the Department to the attitudes of other countries which may endanger the accomplishment of its commercial treaty program and that care be taken to avoid in all practicable cases increasing such opposition by unnecessary provisions of its tariff laws, either provisions inconsistent with the policy of equality of treatment or tariff rates that are unnecessarily high and provocative. Some of the administrative features of our tariff laws have excited bitter opposition and should be repealed wherever not absolutely essential to the enforcement of the law.

(2) That the Department give particular attention to strengthening its personnel where necessary to take full advantage of every opportunity to hasten the development and completion of its most-favored-nation treaties. The more treaties entered into the more difficult it will be for the enemies of the most-favored-nation principle to gain acceptance for their opposing policies.

The difficulties which the United States faces in carrying out its commercial policy are well recognized. A good example is found in the discussion contained in a recently published book by Professor Benjamin H. Williams, of the University of Pittsburgh, entitled

"Economic Foreign Policy of the United States." He concludes his discussion (page 302) with the remark that "it appears that in building a worldwide commercial treaty system incorporating unconditional most-favored-nation treatment the Department of State has encountered a formidable task".

W[ALLACE] McC[LURE]

611.003/1526

*Memorandum by the Assistant Chief of the Treaty Division (McClure)*

[WASHINGTON,] April 15, 1929.

The question has arisen whether, in view of the tariff legislation that is expected from the extraordinary session of Congress convening to-day, this Government should discontinue its program of concluding with other countries treaties containing the most-favored-nation clause.

The effect of agreeing with another country to accord most-favored-nation treatment to its commerce is to prevent this Government from levying tariff duties which discriminate against such country's commerce. Technically, at least, that is the only point of contact between tariff legislation and treaties containing the most-favored-nation clause. Whether the treaty program should be discontinued, pending the action of Congress in determining what tariff legislation it will enact, would seem to depend on whether, in reasonable contemplation, there will be enacted discriminatory duties.

So far as the Treaty Division is aware, no suggestion whatever has been made that Congress either should or would enact such duties. It is believed that Congress will not enact such duties:

1. Because it could not do so without violating numerous existing treaties and other agreements to which the United States is a party;
2. Because, since the foundation of the Government, the traditional American practice (to which exceptions have been few and relatively unimportant) has been the maintenance of tariff duties uniformly applicable regardless of the country of origin of goods imported into the United States;
3. Because, after most careful consideration, this Government has decided that the economic interests of the country are best served by such uniformity and the consequent ability of the Government effectively to insist upon equality of treatment for American commerce in other countries. This policy is indicated by Section 317 of the Tariff Act of 1922 and written into all succeeding agreements on the subject with other countries.

The present policy of the Government of the United States to obtain assured equality of treatment for its commerce in other countries by means of treaties containing the unconditional most-favored-nation clause appears to have met with practically universal public approval.

Certainly no perceptible body of opinion has expressed itself against it. Moreover, its acceptance and practice in the majority of other countries would make its discontinuance by the United States difficult, if not dangerous.

The tariff program of the present Congress is commonly expected to be essentially one of higher duties, especially upon agricultural products. As the duties are, with all but certainty, to be of uniform application, connection with the most-favored-nation clause appears at first to be non-existent. It is non-existent so far as conflict between treaty and statute is concerned. But in another sense there is a very close connection, one that may have a profound effect upon the accomplishment of our treaty program—and one which very urgently argues in favor of pushing all negotiations for most-favored-nation treaties with the utmost possible rapidity.

Under the leadership of France the idea that countries of relatively low tariffs are not, in view of their own interests, justified in granting most-favored-nation treatment to countries of relatively high tariffs appears to be gaining ground, at least on the continent of Europe. That a certain amount of correctness attaches to this idea can not be denied. While it is believed that few national tariff levels exist or are likely to exist that vary so greatly as to invalidate the argument for equality of treatment, there can be no doubt that a conspicuous increase in the level of the American tariff would arouse increased antagonism in other countries to American commercial policy in general and render more difficult, if not, indeed, wholly impossible, negotiations with other countries having in view treaty guaranties of equality of treatment for American goods in their customhouses. Accordingly, the conclusion of treaties ought to be pushed, not discontinued.

When, following the passage of the Tariff Act of 1922, this Department commenced the negotiation of agreements with other countries containing the unconditional most-favored-nation clause, it did so with the express consent and approval of the President. Accordingly, any step by the Department definitely affecting the pursuit of that policy ought, it would seem, to be taken only with the consent and approval of the President. In view of Mr. Hoover's well-known interest in all matters pertaining to commercial policy, it seems especially inappropriate to discontinue negotiations of this character without consulting him.

In addition to the foregoing consideration, an examination of the negotiations actually in progress affords additional reasons—reasons that are, in the opinion of the Treaty Division, unanswerable—against discontinuance, even temporarily:—

*Australia.* The Australian Government desires a treaty at this time and a favorable opportunity presents itself to obtain guaranties of most-favored-nation treatment. A draft note accepting the proposal has been prepared in the Treaty Division, but has not been signed.[12] Delay might mean the loss of an awaited opportunity.

*Austria.* A treaty containing the most-favored-nation clause has been signed, but ratifications have not been exchanged.[13] A treaty of this sort with a Central European country is of such importance as, seemingly, to preclude the idea of delay, pending tariff revision.

*Bolivia.* A draft treaty has been submitted to the Bolivian Government for negotiation.[14]

*Brazil.* A draft treaty has been presented to the Brazilian Government and negotiations have been commenced.[15] To fail to continue negotiations would be embarrassing.

*Chile.* Negotiations with Chile have been long and difficult.[16] Final agreement upon the text appears to be imminent. Two telegraphic instructions have been prepared and await signature. The early conclusion of the treaty is of the utmost importance to the future development of our commercial policy. Delay might well spell failure. It would certainly put this Government in a most awkward position vis-a-vis a country with which the best relations are especially desirable. It would be most embarrassing to the Ambassador and would have an almost certainly adverse effect upon our efforts to promote commerce with South America.

*Colombia.* The proposal to negotiate made by the United States has been accepted by the Colombian Government.[17] As in the case of other Latin American countries, the importance of hastening negotiations is increased by the danger that special discriminatory arrangements might be entered into with some European commercial nation.

*Costa Rica.* The two Governments have agreed to negotiate and a draft treaty has been presented by this Government to the Government of Costa Rica.[18]

*Czechoslovakia.* Negotiations are under way.[19] An instruction which should enable the Legation at Prague to proceed with them is nearly ready for signature. Delay in obtaining a treaty with a Central European power would be very unfortunate.

*Ecuador.* An instruction with draft treaty for negotiation is ready for signature.[20] It is important to hasten negotiations with any Latin American country.

---

[12] Not printed; the conclusion of a treaty was not effected.
[13] See *Foreign Relations*, 1928, vol. I, pp. 924 ff.
[14] See *ibid.*, 1927, vol. I, pp. 477 ff.
[15] See *ibid.*, 1926, vol. I, pp. 569 ff.
[16] See *ibid.*, 1927, vol. I, pp. 517 ff.
[17] See *ibid.*, 1926, vol. II, pp. 1 ff.
[18] See *ibid.*, 1927, vol. II, pp. 500 ff.
[19] See *ibid.*, pp. 539 ff.
[20] No treaty was concluded with Ecuador.

*Finland.* A draft treaty has been transmitted by the Government of Finland for negotiation.[21] An answer to counter proposals is in preparation. To give evidence now that we don't want such a treaty would be embarrassing.

*Greece.* Negotiations have made considerable progress and early continuance is expected on both sides.[22] Withdrawal or undue delay by this Government would be exceedingly embarrassing.

*Guatemala.* The American Minister to Guatemala, now in this country, has just been in conference with the Treaty Division regarding instructions which are expected to bring negotiations to a conclusion.[23] The Minister urges immediate action so as to get action by the Guatemalan Assembly before adjournment in May. Otherwise there would probably be a delay of a year.

*Irish Free State.* This Government has agreed in principle to negotiate.[24]

*Netherlands.* An unusually favorable opportunity for obtaining from the Netherland Government a treaty containing the most-favored-nation clause has been recently presented. It would be unfortunate to delay taking advantage of this opportunity.[25]

*Norway.* A treaty containing the most-favored-nation clause has been signed and has been ratified by Norway.[26] It is before the Senate. Only the President can withdraw it.

*Paraguay.* This Latin American country has agreed in principle to a treaty.[27] A draft for presentation is being prepared.

*Persia.* The American Legation at Teheran has been instructed to present a treaty to the Persian Government. The existing *modus vivendi* with Persia may be terminated on thirty days' notice.[28]

*Peru.* A treaty, long under negotiation with Peru,[29] is ready for signature excepting one or two disputed provisions. To cut off negotiations at this stage would certainly put this Government in a most awkward and embarrassing position with a country with which the most friendly relations maintain and ought to be confirmed and with which a treaty is of more than usual importance.

*Poland.* Negotiations have reached final stages.[30] Withdrawal would not only be an act of something very much like bad faith but would gravely injure American export interests, trade with Poland

---

[21] A treaty of friendship, commerce and consular rights with Finland was concluded on February 13, 1934.
[22] See *Foreign Relations*, 1928, vol. III, pp. 18 ff.
[23] See *ibid.*, 1926, vol. II, pp. 393 ff.
[24] No treaty was concluded with the Irish Free State.
[25] No treaty was concluded with the Netherlands.
[26] See *Foreign Relations*, 1928, vol. III, pp. 593 ff.
[27] See *ibid.*, 1926, vol. II, pp. 871 ff.
[28] See *ibid.*, 1929, vol. III, pp. 682 ff.
[29] See *ibid*, 1927, vol. III, pp. 594 ff.
[30] Signed June 15, 1931, but not in force.

being intimately concerned with the conclusion of a treaty assuring to imports by way of a third country complete most-favored-nation treatment.

*Salvador.* The treaty awaits exchange of ratifications.[31]

*Kingdom of the Serbs, Croats and Slovenes.* Negotiations are well advanced.[32] An elaborate instruction to the Legation at Belgrade awaits signature. It would be especially embarrassing to the Legation not to receive these instructions promptly, in view of danger of presentation of Serbian counter draft which the Legation has been instructed to endeavor to avoid if possible.

*Sweden.* Negotiations have long been under way[33] and the Minister of Sweden is pressing the Department for final conclusion. To withdraw now would be extremely embarrassing.

*Turkey.* This Government has committed itself to the negotiation.[34] To withdraw or to delay unduly would be imputed bad faith and would prejudice important interests.

The foregoing instances do not exhaust the cases of embarrassment and loss that would result if negotiations of treaties containing the most-favored-nation clause were suddenly suspended, but they give an idea of the effect of such suspension.

It has been asserted that provisions of our customs laws authorizing special anti-dumping duties and countervailing duties against bounties are not in harmony with most-favored-nation obligations. Such provisions are not uncommon in other countries and are usually interpreted as outside the implications of the most-favored-nation clause. The reason is that the extraordinary duties fall not upon the goods in general of a country but upon particular shipments of goods regardless of the country of origin. There is thus an analogy to exclusions under quarantine regulations, which appear to be universally excepted from most-favored-nation obligations. The same is true of additional duties or exclusions under Section 316 of the Tariff Act of 1922. Dumping is regarded as an unfair practice, as are the practices against which Section 316 is directed. The practice is always that of the individual exporter, not of the country or the other exporters of the country.

Section 315 of the Tariff Act of 1922 provides for alterations in duties, but such alterations are always made general and never in respect of any particular country or countries. The fact that one country may be the chief source of supply can not affect the situation when, if importation from another country does in fact take place, the duty would be the same.

[31] See *Foreign Relations*, 1926, vol. II, pp. 912 ff.
[32] See *ibid.*, 1927, vol. III, pp. 828 ff.
[33] See *ibid.*, pp. 740 ff.
[34] See *ibid.*, 1928, vol. III, pp. 950 ff.

The Treaty Division recommends that the negotiation of treaties containing the most-favored-nation clause be not stopped but expedited with the utmost possible vigor and without cessation.

W[ALLACE] McC[LURE]

---

611.003/1916

### The Secretary of State to President Hoover

WASHINGTON, June 8, 1929.

MY DEAR MR. PRESIDENT: I am enclosing a copy of a preliminary memorandum drawn up in the Office of the Economic Adviser of the State Department on the subject of foreign political reaction to the proposed tariff. The most serious of the dangers to which attention is called in this memorandum are, I think, the further building up of the imperial preference system in the British Empire and the possible creation of an European economic bloc against the United States. Both these points I know you have had in mind.

Faithfully yours,                                    HENRY L. STIMSON

[Enclosure—Memorandum]

[WASHINGTON,] June 5, 1929.

An analysis of the studies prepared by the Geographic Divisions on the probable foreign reaction to the rates proposed in the Tariff Bill now before Congress suggests that, if the Bill becomes law, it will confront this Department with serious political problems and may work substantial injury to American economic interests, entirely out of proportion to the incidence of the proposed rates and to the possible foreign acts of direct retaliation which they may provoke.

In general, the most considerable effects are anticipated with respect to Western Europe and France, in particular: in the British Empire, especially Canada; and in Latin America, principally in Cuba, Argentina and Uruguay. No very serious repercussions are forecast with respect to the countries whose relations with the United States are handled in the Eastern European, Near Eastern, Mexican and Far Eastern Divisions.

### WESTERN EUROPE

(1) *Commercial Treaties.* The negotiation of commercial treaties on an unconditional most-favored-nation basis will be rendered more difficult in the case of France and Holland. In Spain a strong impetus will be given to the current tendency to denounce the *modus vivendi*.

(2) *Geneva Convention.*[35] There is an indication, voiced by Czechoslovakia and France, to make the new rates an excuse for failure to

---

[35] Convention and protocol for the abolition of import and export prohibitions and restrictions, *Foreign Relations*, 1928, vol. I, p. 336.

ratify or apply fully the Geneva Convention ending import and export restrictions. This would imply the renewal or extension of the quota or contingent system from which certain typical American products—notably automobiles—have suffered in the past.

(3) *Films.* The State Department's protest to France,[36] Germany,[37] Spain, Italy, Czechoslovakia, Austria and Hungary against existing or contemplated film quotas may be merged with the general subject of tariff retaliation and accordingly may be rendered ineffective or be politely ignored.

(4) *European Economic Solidarity.* Powerful impetus will be given to the present tendency to build up in Europe, through a system of international cartels and tariff concessions, a solid economic front on a definitely anti-American basis. The League of Nations may be used as a center of idealistic criticism of the United States to justify economic action along Pan-European lines.

(5) *British Imperial Preference.* A similar and very powerful impetus will be given to strengthening the present system of preference in tariff rates between the component parts of the British Empire. Canada, in particular, may be driven away from her neighborly and natural commercial intercourse with the United States into an attitude of economic hostility and of corresponding British political solidarity. Other British American possessions may be driven into closer economic relations with Canada. Similar forces may orientate New Zealand, the Commonwealth of Australia and the Union of South Africa into closer preferential relations with the United Kingdom.

(6) *Anti-American Commercial Propaganda.* Opportunity will be created in the British Dominions, the Latin American, the Far Eastern and other Asiatic markets to exploit local resentment against the new rates so as to enable our competitors to recapture lost markets. Anti-American commercial propaganda may be stimulated from European competitive sources, principally British. It is interesting to note that at this time the British Government is sending a trade mission to the Argentine Republic and to Brazil.

(7) *Debts and Loans.* Some difficulty may be experienced by American financiers in the negotiation of foreign loans, both through local resentment and through the argument that by putting high duties on imports we render it impossible for our debtors to repay us. The effect of this situation would be to make London, Amsterdam and Paris the appropriate agencies for international finance and to compel our financiers to transact their foreign loans through competitive banking agencies.

[36] *Ibid.*, vol. II, p. 844.
[37] *Ibid.*, p. 918.

## Latin America

The Chief of the Division of Latin American Affairs observes:

"If the proposed increases in the tariff are adopted the political effect on our relations with Latin America will be out of all proportion to any probable effect on our actual importations from the countries involved. The feeling in the majority of the Latin American countries towards the United States is more unfriendly now than at any time for many years past. It has been skillfully fomented by our commercial competitors and by those elements which from conviction or for political reasons have been active in magnifying the bogie of American imperialism. Any action which can be represented, reasonably or not, as an injury to the interests of a Latin American country will play into the hands of these unfriendly elements and will afford them a pretext for a new campaign against us. The seriousness of this possibly can not be appreciated unless one has followed the violent and almost hysterical press comment in such countries as Argentina, Uruguay and Cuba during the past few months.

"In Argentina and Uruguay the threatened increase in the tariff on certain agricultural products has taken the place of the Nicaraguan question as the chief weapon of propaganda against the United States. The sensational campaign of the *Sociedad Rural Argentina* with its slogan "Buy from those who buy from us" is an example of the use which foreign, and particularly British, commercial interests have made of this weapon. Although this campaign has been carried to a point where it seems to have produced some measure of opposition in the Argentine itself, it will receive a new impetus when duties on such products as meat, poultry and flax seed are actually increased. The reaction in Uruguay will be very similar to that in Argentina.

"In Cuba the entire community seems to have reached a state of mind where it regards the proposal for an increase in the American sugar tariff as a matter of life and death for the Cuban Republic.

"The feeling in other Latin American countries will be unfavorably affected to a less extent. The increase in the duty on corn, for example, will injure if not kill a new and very promising industry in the Dominican Republic. Brazil will be hit by the increase on Brazil nuts. Fortunately the proposal for an increase in the duty on bananas, which would have hurt nearly all of our closest neighbors, seems to have been abandoned."

## Eastern Europe

It does not appear that the proposed changes in the tariff will have on the exports to the United States of Finland, Poland, Estonia, Latvia or Lithuania, an effect sufficient to evoke protest or to give rise to a feeling of ill will.

## Near East

Owing to the fact that our commercial rights are guaranteed in the Near Eastern countries held under mandate and by the Capitulatory regime in Egypt, while Greece for financial and Turkey for political reasons does not desire to offend us, no special reaction is anticipated in this area. However, the Prime Minister of Egypt stated to the American Minister in Cairo that the imposition of a customs duty on cotton by the United States would depress the prices of cotton in Egypt, thus causing a financial crisis in that country and might result in an anti-American feeling which would no doubt seriously affect the sale of American goods in Egypt.

## Mexican

No serious reaction is anticipated.

## Far East

No serious reaction to the proposed rates is anticipated in China, Japan or Siam. It is pointed out that the duties substantially affect only $12,000,000 out of $47,000,000 dutiable products imported from China in 1927, as against $104,000,000 non-dutiable; and $17,000,000 out of $47,000,000 dutiable products imported from Japan in 1927, as against $354,000,000 non-dutiable.

---

611.003/1673a

### The Secretary of State to Senator Reed Smoot [38]

Washington, June 26, 1929.

My Dear Senator: Certain provisions of the pending Tariff Bill (H. R. 2667) which require on certain conditions mandatory increases in the standard tariff rates established by the Bill, will, if that Bill becomes law and such increases take place, cause violation by the United States of the Treaty between Germany and the United States proclaimed October 14, 1925,[39] and other similar treaties between the United States and other countries which contain unconditional most-favored-nation clauses as to tariff relations.

The result of such violation would be either to permit the offended country (1) in case of serious breach to assert a claim of right to terminate the treaty in question at once (such treaties usually run for a fixed term of years) or (2), without terminating the treaty, to assert a plausible claim for damages against the United States equal to the amount of such excess duties collected.

Either result would be obviously unfortunate. Such most-favored-nation clauses in treaties are deemed a potent defense for the United States against possible tariff retaliation by foreign nations.

[38] Chairman of the Senate Finance Committee.
[39] Treaty signed December 8, 1923; *Foreign Relations*, 1923, vol. II, p. 29.

I respectfully suggest that the pending Bill be amended in this regard. Any question of treaty violation would be obviated if such provisions for mandatory increases were eliminated or if the mandatory feature were eliminated and the enforcement of such increases were made discretionary with the President (instead of mandatory on him or other officers).

I enclose a memorandum showing

1. A list of sections of the Bill deemed contrary to the treaties;
2. A quotation from the German Treaty showing what the United States has promised to Germany in this regard and a list of similarly situated treaties.

You will understand that this letter does not at all deal with the effect of the proposed tariff revision on our foreign relations in general, but is confined to the legal question of the effect on existing treaties.

It is desirable that the views of this Department expressed in this letter should not be made public.

I am [etc.]                                                     H. L. STIMSON

[Enclosure]

MEMORANDUM

1. A list of sections of the Bill deemed contrary to the treaties: Paragraphs 369, 371, 812, 1402, 1640, 1649, 1686, Section 303.

2. A quotation from the German Treaty showing what the United States has promised to Germany in this regard and a list of similarly situated treaties.

"Art. VII . . . Each of the High Contracting Parties binds itself unconditionally to impose no higher or other duties or conditions and no prohibition on the importation of any article, the growth, produce or manufacture, of the territories of the other than are or shall be imposed on the importation of any like article, the growth, produce or manufacture of any other foreign country.

.        .        .        .        .        .        .

"Any advantage of whatsoever kind which either High Contracting Party may extend to any article, the growth, produce, or manufacture of any other foreign country shall simultaneously and unconditionally, without request and without compensation, be extended to the like article the growth, produce, or manufacture of the other High Contracting Party."

Countries with whom the United States has similar treaties of Friendship, Commerce and Consular Rights:

Hungary [40]          Latvia [42]
Honduras [41]         Estonia [43]

[40] Foreign Relations, 1925, vol. II, p. 341.
[41] Ibid., 1927, vol. III, p. 101.
[42] Ibid., 1928, vol. III, p. 208.
[43] Ibid., 1925, vol. II, p. 70.

611.003/1854

*Senator Reed Smoot to the Assistant Secretary of State (Castle)*

[WASHINGTON,] August 27, 1929.

DEAR MR. CASTLE: This will acknowledge the receipt of your letter of August 26, 1929,[44] reminding me of Mr. Stimson's letter of June 26 calling attention to certain sections of the pending tariff bill deemed contrary to existing treaties of the United States.

It is true that no change has been made in paragraphs 812, 1402, 1641, 1650 and 1687.

Kindly let me know if any foreign country has made a protest to our State Department against the paragraphs named in your letter. If so, please give me the name or names of the countries doing so. I shall then ask the Finance Committee for the consideration of the paragraphs named in your letter of the 26th.

Yours sincerely,                                       REED SMOOT

---

611.003/1854

*The Assistant Secretary of State (Castle) to Senator Reed Smoot*

WASHINGTON, September 4, 1929.

MY DEAR SENATOR: Your letter of August 27 regarding certain provisions of the pending tariff bill deemed contrary to existing treaties of the United States has been received.

There appear to have been no formal protests by foreign governments respecting the particular contingent duty provisos tentatively retained by the majority members of the Senate Finance Committee in paragraphs 1402, 1641, 1650 and 1687 of the pending bill. However, the inconsistency of provisos of this character and the most-favored-nation clause of treaties has on several occasions been informally commented upon by representatives of foreign governments.

May I suggest that the absence of formal protests would not, of course, relieve this Government of the obligation faithfully to execute the provisions of its treaties. Moreover, there is no assurance that if these provisos are reenacted and discriminating duties are applied thereunder to products of countries entitled by treaty to most-favored-nation treatment, formal protests would not later be received.

No protests appear to have been received regarding the provisions of 812 of the pending bill.

With reference to contingent duty provisos of the kind above referred to there are certain aspects of the matter to which you may wish to give further consideration. The policy represented by such provisos tends to place this Government in an inconsistent position in its relations with foreign countries on tariff matters. The provisos

---

[44] Not printed.

in question do not apparently have in view protecting the domestic producers of the products affected from foreign competition in the American market but are apparently designed to facilitate the exportation of such products by bringing pressure to bear on foreign governments to reduce their duties thereon.

Our success in protecting American foreign trade from discriminatory treatment abroad depends on the extent to which we succeed in making precisely the opposite tariff principle prevail, namely, that the tariff being solely a domestic matter a country may impose whatever level of non-discriminatory duties it deems necessary for the protection of domestic producers and standards of living, without affording foreign countries any ground for complaint or justification for discriminations against its trade.

Opposing tariff theories are gaining considerable support abroad and departures from our declared policy on tariff matters thus assume particular importance at this time. The principle embodied in the provisos in question has recently received considerable attention abroad and was recently given prominence in the French and German press.

You may wish to consider whether the gains to American producers of the products covered by the provisos in question are sufficient to offset the disadvantages arising from the inconsistent position in which they tend to place this Government and their tendency to hamper this Department's efforts on behalf of American exporters generally.

Sincerely yours, W. R. CASTLE, Jr.

611.003/1958

*The Acting Secretary of State to Senator Reed Smoot*

WASHINGTON, January 22, 1930.

MY DEAR SENATOR: I am gratified to note from the *Congressional Record* of January 20 the action of your committee in striking out of the Tariff Bill, H. R. 2667, certain provisions in Sections 1402, 1641, 1650 and 1687 regarded by the Department as inconsistent with existing treaties of commerce between the United States and certain other countries.

This action will greatly assist the Department in its efforts to protect and promote our foreign trade.

Sincerely yours, J. P. COTTON

# REPRESENTATIONS BY FOREIGN GOVERNMENTS WITH RESPECT TO SENATE BILL RELATING TO PAYMENT OF ADVANCE WAGES TO SEAMEN ON FOREIGN VESSELS[1]

196.6/1094

## The Netherlands Legation to the Department of State

No. 1776           NOTE VERBALE

The Netherland Legation has noticed that a bill (S. 314) has been introduced by Senator LaFollette relating to the payment of advance wages and allotments in respect to seamen on foreign vessels and making further provision for carrying out the purpose of the Seamen's Act, approved March 4, 1915,[2] which bill is a copy of the bill introduced during last session by the same Senator and passed by the Senate on April 24, 1928.

The Royal Legation has the honor to inform the State Department that the remarks made on behalf of the Netherland Government by its note of May 3, 1928, No. 1413,[3] are in the same way applicable to the new bill.

WASHINGTON, May 15, 1929.

---

196.6/1093

## The German Embassy to the Department of State[4]

### MEMORANDUM

### Senate Bill S. 314

Relating to the payment of advance wages and allotments in respect of seamen of foreign vessels and making further provisions for carrying out the purposes of the Seamen's Act, approved March 4, 1915.

The Bill would in the opinion of the German Government, if enacted, jeopardize the rights and interests of German shipping companies in contracting with their crews, as provided under the German law.

The passing of the Bill would therefore be regarded with apprehension.

[1] Continued from *Foreign Relations*, 1928, vol. I, pp. 830–838.
[2] 38 Stat. 1164.
[3] *Foreign Relations*, 1928, vol. I, p. 835.
[4] Left at the Department by the Secretary of the German Embassy (Putlitz), May 17, 1929.

196.6/1093

### The Secretary of State to Senator Wesley L. Jones [5]

WASHINGTON, June 10, 1929.

SIR: I have the honor to refer to previous correspondence concerning the enactment into law of an amendment to the Seamen's Act of March 4, 1915, which was passed by the Senate on April 24, 1928, and re-introduced in that body on April 22, 1929, as Senate Bill 314 and to enclose for your consideration, copies of two memoranda received from the Royal Netherland Legation and the German Embassy at this capital in which apprehension is voiced at the possibility of the enactment into law of the above-mentioned Bill. As you may be aware the diplomatic representatives at this capital of Great Britain, Italy and Denmark have already made representations to the Department relative to the concern of the Governments which they represent at this proposed legislation.

The amendment in effect appears to declare illegal contracts for the payment of advance wages concluded by aliens without the jurisdiction of the United States in connection with the employment of alien seamen on board alien vessels and declares that "the courts of the United States shall be open to seamen for suits for payment of wages, irrespective of whether the wages were earned upon a vessel of the United States or a foreign vessel, or within or without the United States or territory subject to the jurisdiction thereof . . .".

If the proposed amendment be adopted, it is not improbable that foreign Governments might regard it as contrary to international comity, thereby causing embarrassment to this Government in the conduct of its foreign relations. Moreover, the enactment into law of the amendment in question may render the American Merchant Marine subject to retaliatory measures by foreign Governments which in their effect may far outweigh any advantages which might be secured by this legislation. For the reasons stated, the Department considers that the passage of the bill under discussion would be undesirable.

I have [etc.] H. L. STIMSON

_____

196.6/1099

### The British Ambassador (Howard) to the Secretary of State

No. 338

His Britannic Majesty's Ambassador presents his compliments to the Secretary of State and has the honour to refer to his memorandum of April 26th, 1928,[6] in which he drew attention to certain aspects of

_____

[5] Chairman of the Senate Committee on Commerce.
[6] *Foreign Relations*, 1928, vol. I, p. 832.

Senate Bill S. 2945 relating to the payment of advance wages and allotments in respect of seamen of foreign vessels and making further provisions for carrying out the purposes of the United States Seamen's Act. The memorandum in question was left by Sir Esme Howard with Mr. Phenix.[7]

Sir Esme Howard's attention has been drawn to the fact that the Bill, to which his above-mentioned memorandum referred, having failed of enactment by Congress during the last session, has now been reintroduced in the Senate under the number S. 314. In these circumstances Sir Esme Howard has the honour again to draw attention to the considerations set forth in his above-mentioned memorandum which, he is instructed to state, still appear to hold good.

WASHINGTON, June 18, 1929.

---

196.6/1102

## *The Norwegian Legation to the Department of State*

### MEMORANDUM

On May 11, 1928, the Norwegian Legation delivered to the Department of State a Memorandum [8] relative to a Bill No. "S. 2945" regarding the payment of advance wages and allotments in respect of seamen on foreign vessels and making further provisions for carrying out the purposes of the Seamen's Act of March 4, 1915.

In the Memorandum mentioned, the following statement was i. a. made:

"The effect of this Bill as understood by the Legation, will be to make unlawful the advance payment of wages in foreign ports to seamen engaged on Norwegian or other foreign ships. The Legation has been instructed to draw the attention of the appropriate authorities of the United States of America to the fact that Norwegian seamen who in the exercise of their profession have got to live for years outside their native country, in frequent cases are under the necessity of demanding advance wages in order to be able to accept engagements for longer terms. Advance wages which, consequently, are perfectly lawful under the Norwegian Seaman's Act, are a standing feature in the economy of families of Norwegian seamen and a change in this long ago established practice would contribute to the breaking up of family ties and to detach seamen from their homes in Norway. The provisions of the Bill, if enacted, would therefore be detrimental to the welfare and interests of seamen on board Norwegian ships engaged in the trade between the United States and foreign countries.

The Norwegian Government can therefore only look upon the measure contemplated in the bill with deep concern.

---

[7] Spencer Phenix, Assistant to the Under Secretary of State.
[8] Not printed.

Moreover it seems to the Norwegian Legation that the effect of the bill declaring unlawful provisions of contracts, valid under Norwegian law and made within Norwegian jurisdiction, would be contrary to the general recognized principles of international law."

As, however, the Senate Bill No. "S. 2945" failed of consideration in the House of Representatives, it did not become law.

The Legation is now informed that Senator La Follette on April 22, 1929, introduced a Bill No. "S. 314", which in fact is identical with the Bill No. "S. 2945", introduced by him and passed by the Senate in April 1928. As the considerations set forth in the Legation's Memorandum mentioned above, against the provisions of the Bill No. "S. 2945", still hold good, the Legation takes the liberty to draw the renewed attention of the appropriate authorities of the United States to the detrimental consequences which the passing of the bill will have for seamen on board Norwegian ships.

WASHINGTON, June 27, 1929.

---

196.6/1104

*The Danish Minister (Brun) to the Secretary of State*

No. 95 BAR HARBOR, MAINE, July 9, 1929.
[Received July 12.]

MY DEAR MR. SECRETARY: Referring to previous correspondence relative to the bill (S. 2945) of Senator La Follette, relating to the payment of advance wages and allotments in respect of seamen on foreign vessels, to wit: my letter to you of June 12, 1928,[9] and the reply from Mr. Secretary of State Kellogg of June 20, 1928,[10] I beg to state as follows:

You will remember that this bill was passed by the Senate on April 24, 1928, but was not passed by the House before the close of the 70th Congress on March 4 [*3*], 1929.

It consequently failed, but, as you are no doubt aware, has been reintroduced in the now sitting 71st Congress by Senator La Follette as S. 314.

As the text of this new bill is identical with the former bill, I beg leave to say, that the misgivings with respect to the effect of such legislation if adopted on the trade between Denmark and the United States, which I submitted on behalf of the Danish Government in my letter to you of June 12, 1928, are equally applicable to the new bill S. 314.

---

[9] *Foreign Relations*, 1928, vol. I, p. 836.
[10] Not printed.

I would therefor be greatly obliged to you, if you could see your way to advise the appropriate Committees of the Senate and the House of the present Congress accordingly.

Believe me [etc.] C. BRUN

196.6/1104

### The Secretary of State to the Danish Minister (Brun)

WASHINGTON, July 19, 1929.

MY DEAR MR. MINISTER: I take pleasure in acknowledging the receipt of your note of July 9, 1929, in which you informed me that the misgivings of your Government with respect to the effect of the enactment into law of Senate Bill No. 2945, relating to the payment of advanced wages and allotments in respect of seamen on foreign vessels, are equally applicable to the new Senate Bill No. 314, which was reintroduced by Senator LaFollette in the Seventy-first Congress.

In reply I have to inform you that the Department has taken due note of the position of your Government as set forth in your communication under acknowledgment. In view of the fact, however, that the Congress is not at present sitting, the Department deems it preferable to wait the reconvening of Congress before bringing the considerations set forth in your communication to the attention of the appropriate committees of the Senate and House of Representatives.[11]

I am [etc.] HENRY L. STIMSON

---

[11] Similar replies were made by the Department to the British and Norwegian memoranda.

CONFIRMATION BY CONGRESS OF INSTRUMENTS OF CESSION OF CERTAIN ISLANDS OF THE SAMOAN GROUP, SIGNED BY THE NATIVE CHIEFS ON APRIL 17, 1900, AND JULY 14, 1904 [1]

*Instrument of Cession Signed on April 17, 1900, by the Representatives of the People of Tutuila*

[Translation]

To All To Whom These Presents Shall Come, Greeting ! !

WHEREAS the Governments of Germany, Great Britain, and of the United States of America have on divers occasions recognized the sovereignty of the government and people of Samoa and the Samoan Group of Islands as an independent State: AND WHEREAS owing to dissensions, internal disturbances, and civil war the said Governments have deemed it necessary to assume the control of the legislation and administration of said State of Samoa: AND WHEREAS the said Governments have on the sixteenth day of February 1900 by mutual agreement [2] determined to partition said State: AND WHEREAS the Islands hereinafter described being part of the said State have by said arrangement amongst the said Governments been severed from the parent State and the Governments of Great Britain and of Germany have withdrawn all rights hitherto acquired claimed or possessed by both or either of them by Treaty or otherwise to the said Islands in favor of the Government of the United States of America: AND WHEREAS for the promotion of the peace and welfare of the people of said Islands, for the establishment of a good and sound Government, and for the preservation of the rights and property of the inhabitants of said Islands, the Chiefs, rulers and people thereof are desirous of granting unto the said Government of the United States full power and authority to enact proper legislation for and to control the said Islands and are further desirous of removing all disabilities that may be existing in connection therewith and to ratify and to confirm the grant of the rule of said Islands heretofore granted on the 2nd day of April 1900 Now KNOW YE:—

1. That we, the Chiefs whose names are hereunder subscribed, by virtue of our office as the hereditary representatives of the people of said Islands in consideration of the premises hereinbefore recited and for divers good considerations us hereunto moving, have Ceded, Transferred, and Yielded Up, unto Commander B. F. Tilley of U. S. [S.]

---

[1] The originals of the papers in this section are filed in The National Archives with Department of State Treaty Series 314.
[2] For text of convention, see *Foreign Relations*, 1899, p. 667.

"Abarenda" the duly accredited representative of the Government of the United States of America in the Islands hereinafter mentioned or described for and on behalf of the said Government All Those the Islands of Tutuila and Aunuu and all other Islands, rocks, reefs, foreshores, and waters lying between the thirteenth degree and the fifteenth degree of south latitude and between the one hundred and seventy first degree and the one hundred sixty seventh degree of west longitude from the Meridian of Greenwich together with all sovereign rights thereunto belonging and possessed by us To Hold the said ceded territory unto the Government of the United States of America To Erect the same into a separate District to be annexed to the said Government to be known and designated as the District of "Tutuila".

2. The Government of the United States of America shall respect and protect the individual rights of all people dwelling in Tutuila to their lands and other property in said District, but if the said Government shall require any land or any other thing for Government uses, the Government may take the same upon payment of a fair consideration for the land or other thing to those who may be deprived of their property on account of the desire of the Government.

3. The Chiefs of the towns will be entitled to retain their individual control of the separate towns, if that control is in accordance with the laws of the United States of America concerning Tutuila, and if not obstructive to the peace of the people and the advancement of civilization of the people, subject also to the supervision and instruction of the said Government. But the enactment of legislation and the General Control shall remain firm with the United States of America.

4. An investigation and settlement of all claims to title to land in the different divisions or districts of Tutuila shall be made by the Government.

5. We whose names are subscribed below do hereby declare with truth for ourselves, our heirs, and representatives by Samoan Custom, that we will obey and owe allegiance to the Government of the United States of America.

IN WITNESS WHEREOF We Have Hereunto Subscribed Our Names And Affixed Our Seals On This 17th Day of April 1900 A. D.

*Fofo and Aitulagi*

x TUITELE OF LEONE
x FAIIVAE OF LEONE
x LETULI OF ILIILI
x FUIMAONO OF AOLOAU
x SATELE OF VAILOA
x LEOSO OF LEONE
x OLO OF LEONE

x Namoa of Aitulagi
x Malota of Aitulagi
x Tunaitau of Pavaiai
x Lualemana of Asu
x Amituagai of Ituau

*Sua and Vaifanua*

| | |
|---|---|
| Pele | x |
| Mauga | x |
| Leiato | x |
| Faumuina | x |
| Masaniai | x |
| Tupuola | x |
| Soliai | x |
| Mauga | x |

The foregoing Instrument of Cession [3] was duly signed by Leoso in the presence of and at the request of the Chiefs and representatives of the Division of Fofo and Aitulagi and by Pele in the presence of and at the request of the Chiefs and representatives of the Division of Sua and Vaifanua in Tutuila in conformity with a Samoan Custom as to signatures to documents in my presence at Pagopago on the 17th day of April 1900 A. D. immediately prior to the raising of the United States Flag at the United States Naval Station, Tutuila.

E. W. Gurr
*A Barrister of the Supreme Court of Samoa*

---

*Reply of President Roosevelt to the Chiefs and People of Tutuila and Other Islands, July 21, 1902*

To the Chiefs and the People of the Islands of Tutuila, Aunuu, and Other Neighboring Islands.

Greeting: Whereas the Chiefs and People of the Islands of Tutuila, Aunuu and neighboring small Islands have, of their own free will and pleasure, for the promotion of the peace and welfare of the people of said islands, for the establishment of a good and sound government, and for the preservation of the rights and property of the inhabitants of said islands, solicited of the United States of America its supervision and protection; and,

Whereas this desire has been expressed by the hereditary representatives of the people of said islands in a Declaration dated the seventeenth day of April, A. D. 1900, executed according to Samoan custom and pledging allegiance to the Government of the United States of America;

---

[3] Received by the Secretary of the Navy on August 1, 1900; filed in the Department of State on March 1, 1902.

THEREFORE, I, THEODORE ROOSEVELT, President of the United States of America do hereby express to the Chiefs and People of said islands the gratification of the Government and people of the United States in receiving from the Chiefs and People of the said islands this token of their friendship and their confidence in the just and friendly intentions of the United States. The local rights and privileges mentioned in said Declaration will be respected and it is our earnest hope that peace, happiness, and prosperity may make their permanent abode with the good people of these islands.

White House, Washington,

July the twenty-first, in the year of our Lord one thousand nine hundred and two.

THEODORE ROOSEVELT

By the President:

DAVID J. HILL, *Acting Secretary of State.*

---

*Instrument of Cession Signed July 14, 1904, by the Representatives of the People of the Islands of Manua*

TO ALL TO WHOM THESE PRESENTS SHALL COME, GREETING :—

WHEREAS, the Islands of the Samoan Group lying east of longitude 171 west of Greenwich were, on the 16th day of February, 1900, by arrangement between the Governments of Germany, Great Britain, and the United States of America, placed under the protection of the Government of the United States of America;

AND WHEREAS, on the 17th day of April, in the year 1900, the Islands of Tutuila and Aunuu, being portion of said Islands of the Samoan Group lying east of longitude 171 west of Greenwich, were, by the chiefs and rulers of Tutuila and Aunuu, ceded to and placed under the sovereignty and protection of the United States of America, and the government of said Islands was thereupon assumed by said United States;

AND WHEREAS, in administering said government, the Islands hereinafter described, known as the Manua Islands, being the remainder of said Islands of the Samoan Group lying east of longitude 171 west of Greenwich, have been under the protection of the United States of America, and controlled and governed in conjunction with the Islands of Tutuila and Aunuu;

AND WHEREAS, at the request of Tuimanua, the King of Manua, and his chiefs, the United States Flag was, on the 5th day of June, 1900, raised on the Island of Tau, of the Manua Group, for the purpose of granting protection to the people of the Manua Islands;

AND WHEREAS, Tuimanua and his chiefs, being content and satisfied with the justice, fairness, and wisdom of the government as hitherto administered by the several Commandants of the United States Naval Station, Tutuila, and the officials appointed to act with the Commandant, are desirous of placing the Islands of Manua hereinafter described under the full and complete sovereignty of the United States of America to enable said Islands, with Tutuila and Aunuu, to become a part of the territory of said United States;

Now KNOW YE (1) That we, Eleasara Tuimanua and the chiefs whose names are hereunder subscribed, in consideration of the premises hereinbefore recited, have ceded, and, by These Presents Do Cede, unto the Government of the United States of America, All Those, The Islands Of The Manua Group, being the whole of eastern portion of the Samoan Islands lying east of longitude 171 west of Greenwich and known as Tau, Olosega, Ofu, and Rose Island, and all other, the waters and property adjacent thereto, together with all sovereign rights thereunto belonging and possessed by us.

To HOLD the said ceded territory unto the Government of the United States of America; to erect the same into a territory or district of the said Government.

(2) It is intended and claimed by These Presents that there shall be no discrimination in the suffrages and political privileges between the present residents of said Islands and citizens of the United States dwelling therein, and also that the rights of the Chiefs in each village and of all people concerning their property according to their custom shall be recognized.

Done at the place of Faleula in Tau, in triplicate, in both the Samoan and the English languages, on this 14th day of July, in the year 1904, A. D.

| | | |
|---|---|---|
| *King of Manua* | | |
| *and District Governor* | TUIMANUA | [SEAL] |
| *County Chief of Fitiuta* | TUFFLE | [SEAL] |
| *County Chief of Ofu* | MISA | [SEAL] |
| *County Chief of Olosega* | TUIOLOSEGA | [SEAL] |
| *County Chief of Faleasao* | ASOAU | [SEAL] |
| *District Clerk.* | P. LOGOAI | [SEAL] |

UNITED STATES NAVAL STATION, TUTUILA.

District Court of Tutuila, No. 5,
Held at Tau, in Manua

I HEREBY CERTIFY that on this 16th day of July, in the year 1904, before me, Edwin W. Gurr, Judge of the District Court of Tutuila, personally appeared Tuimanua, the Governor of Manua, Tufele, County Chief of Fitiuta, Misa, County Chief of Ofu, Tuiolosega, County Chief of Olosega, Asoau, County Chief of Faleasao, and Logoai, District Clerk of Manua, personally known to me to be the

Tuimanua, high chiefs, and representatives of the people of the Islands of Manua, who, each for himself, acknowledged that he executed the attached Instrument of Cession,[4] and affixed his seal thereto, freely and voluntarily, for the uses and purposes therein mentioned.

IN TESTIMONY WHEREOF I have caused the seal of the Court to be affixed this 16th day of July in the year 1904.

[SEAL]

E. W. GURR
*District Judge of Tutuila*

---

*Reply of President Roosevelt to the Chiefs and People of the Islands of Manua, August 19, 1904*

To Tuimanua, Governor of Manua; Tuiolosega, County Chief of Olosega; Misa, County Chief of Ofu; Asoau, County Chief of Faleasao; Tufele, County Chief of Fitiuta; Logoai, District Clerk of Manua, and the People of the Islands of Manua, Greeting:

WHEREAS, The Governor and Chiefs and people of the Islands of Manua, of their own free will and pleasure, have expressed their satisfaction with the justice, fairness, and wisdom of the Government administered by the United States since the flag of the United States was raised over their islands June 5, 1900, and,

WHEREAS, The people of said islands ceded unto the Government of the United States of America, on July 16 [*14*], 1904, all the islands of the Manua Group, being the whole of the eastern portion of the Samoan Islands lying east of longitude 171 west of Greenwich, and known as Pau [*Tau*], Olosega, Ofu, and Rose islands, and all other, the waters and property adjacent thereto, together with all sovereign rights thereto belonging, the same to be erected into a Territory or District of the United States, with a view to the promotion of the peace and welfare of the people of those islands, for the establishment of good and sound government, and for the preservation of the rights and property of the inhabitants of said islands, without discrimination; now,

THEREFORE, I, THEODORE ROOSEVELT, President of the United States of America, do hereby express to the Governor, Chiefs, and People of said islands the gratification of the Government and people of the United States in receiving from the Governor, Chiefs, and people of the said islands this token of their friendship and their confidence in the just and friendly intentions of the United States. The local rights and privileges mentioned in said declaration will be respected, and it is our earnest hope that peace, happiness, and prosperity may make their permanent abode with the good people of these islands.

---

[4] Received by the Secretary of the Navy on August 15, 1904; filed in the Department of State on October 31, 1904.

White House, Washington August 19, in the year of our Lord one thousand nine hundred and four.

THEODORE ROOSEVELT

By the President:
JOHN HAY,
    *Secretary of State*

---

*Public Resolution No. 89, 70th Congress, 2d Session, Approved February 20, 1929*

Joint Resolution To provide for accepting, ratifying, and confirming the cessions of certain islands of the Samoan group to the United States, and for other purposes.

WHEREAS certain chiefs of the islands of Tutuila and Manua and certain other islands of the Samoan group lying between the thirteenth and fifteenth degrees of latitude south of the Equator and between the one hundred and sixty-seventh and one hundred and seventy-first degrees of longitude west of Greenwich, herein referred to as the islands of eastern Samoa, having in due form agreed to cede absolutely and without reserve to the United States of America all rights of sovereignty of whatsoever kind in and over these islands of the Samoan group by their acts dated April 10[*17*], 1900, and July 16[*14*], 1904: Therefore be it

*Resolved by the Senate and House of Representatives of the United States of America in Congress assembled,* That (*a*) said cessions are accepted, ratified, and confirmed, as of April 10, 1900, and July 16, 1904, respectively.

(*b*) The existing laws of the United States relative to public lands shall not apply to such lands in the said islands of eastern Samoa; but the Congress of the United States shall enact special laws for their management and disposition: *Provided,* That all revenue from or proceeds of the same, except as regards such part thereof as may be used or occupied for the civil, military, or naval purposes of the United States or may be assigned for the use of the local government, shall be used solely for the benefit of the inhabitants of the said islands of eastern Samoa for educational and other public purposes.

(*c*) Until Congress shall provide for the government of such islands, all civil, judicial, and military powers shall be vested in such person or persons and shall be exercised in such manner as the President of the United States shall direct; and the President shall have power to remove said officers and fill the vacancies so occasioned.

(*d*) The President shall appoint six commissioners, two of whom shall be members of the Senate, two of whom shall be members of the

House of Representatives, and two of whom shall be chiefs of the said islands of eastern Samoa, who shall, as soon as reasonably practicable, recommend to Congress such legislation concerning the islands of eastern Samoa as they shall deem necessary or proper.

(*e*) The sum of $25,000, or so much thereof as may be necessary, is hereby authorized to be appropriated, out of any money in the Treasury not otherwise appropriated, to be expended at the discretion of the President of the United States of America, for the purpose of carrying this joint resolution into effect.

Approved, February 20, 1929.

---

*Public Resolution No. 3, 71st Congress, 1st Session, Approved May 22, 1929*

Joint Resolution To amend Public Resolution Numbered 89, Seventieth Congress, second session, approved February 20, 1929, entitled "Joint resolution to provide for accepting, ratifying, and confirming the cessions of certain islands of the Samoan group to the United States, and for other purposes."

*Resolved by the Senate and House of Representatives of the United States of America in Congress assembled*, That paragraph (*d*) of Public Resolution Numbered 89, Seventieth Congress, second session, approved February 20, 1929, entitled "Joint resolution to provide for accepting, ratifying, and confirming the cessions of certain islands of the Samoan group to the United States, and for other purposes," is hereby amended as follows: In line 1, strike out the word "six" and substitute therefor the word "seven"; in line 3, strike out the word "two" and substitute therefor the word "three"; and in line 3, between the words "chiefs" and "of," insert the words "or high chiefs", so that the said paragraph (*d*) will then read as follows:

"(*d*) The President shall appoint seven commissioners, two of whom shall be Members of the Senate, two of whom shall be Members of the House of Representatives, and three of whom shall be chiefs or high chiefs of the said islands of eastern Samoa, who shall, as soon as reasonably practicable, recommend to Congress such legislation concerning the islands of eastern Samoa as they shall deem necessary or proper." [5]

---

[5] See *American Samoa:* Hearings before the Commission appointed by the President of the United States in accordance with Public Res. No. 89, 70th Cong. and Public Res. No. 3, 71st Cong. (Washington, Government Printing Office, 1931); and the American Samoan Commission, *Report* (Washington, Government Printing Office, 1931).

# INDEX

# INDEX

# 1028

INDEX

Great Britain—Continued.

Safety of Life at Sea, International Conference, invitation to United States to participate, and U. S. acceptance, 372, 380

U. S. Senate bill relating to payment of advance wages to seamen on foreign vessels, representations to United States concerning, 1006–1007; U. S. reply, 1009n

Greece, negotiations with United States for naturalization treaty, 458–465; temporary measures of Greek Government pending conclusion of treaty, 461–462, 464–465

Guatemala (see also under Boundary disputes), aviation: Latin American Airways, negotiations and signing of contract, 635–650; French interests, 642; German interests, 642; Pan American Airways, negotiations and signing of contract, 557, 576, 577, 578–580, 581–582, 583, 584–585, 595–597, 602–603, 605–606, 607–609; Pickwick Airways interests, 578–579, 581, 583, 595, 597, 607, 608, 650–652

Haiti (see also Boundary disputes: Dominican Republic–Haiti): Interest in certain provisions of draft international convention on the treatment of foreigners, 434–435, 438; U. S. aviation interests, 613, 624n

Honduras (see also Guatemala–Honduras and Honduras–Nicaragua under Boundary disputes), Pan American Airways contract, 550, 553, 555, 556, 560, 598, 599

Hoover, Herbert: Arbitration of Guatemala–Honduras boundary dispute, Honduran insistence, 947, 953–954; Memorial Day address, May 30, 113–116; message to Congress, Dec. 3, v–xxx; submission to Chile and Peru of terms of settlement of Tacna-Arica dispute, arrangements, 732–733, 734, 738, 739, 740, 742, 744, 745–746, 750, 754, 754–755, 757, 765–766, 768, 769, 770, 771–772, 773–775, 775–776, 779, 780–784, 786, 788, 794–797

Import and export prohibitions and restrictions, abolition of, text of protocol, signed Dec. 20, concerning the entry into force of the international convention of 1927 and supplementary agreement of 1928, 424–428

Irish Free State, negotiations and agreement with United States covering certain questions of aerial navigation, 530–532, 539n, 539

Italy (see also London Naval Conference):

Aviation: Demonstration flights in United States, U. S. permission, 525, 526; negotiations and agreement with United States covering certain questions of aerial navigation, 525–530, 539n, 539

Franco-Italian naval parity, question of, 59–60, 107, 133–134, 134–135, 269–270, 271, 272, 283, 287, 298, 306

Naturalization, dual nationality, and military service, negotiations with United States for convention concerning, 465–467

Japan (see also London Naval Conference; Narcotic drugs), attitude toward U. S.–British naval conversations during sixth session of Preparatory Commission for the Disarmament Conference, 101, 106, 107–108

Kellogg-Briand Pact. See Treaty for the Renunciation of War.

Latin American Airways. See under Aviation: U. S. interests.

Latvia, inconclusive negotiations with United States for convention concerning naturalization, dual nationality, and military service, 449–451

League of Nations (see also Counterfeiting Currency, Conference for the Suppression of; Permanent Court of International Justice; Preparatory Commission for the Disarmament Conference; Treatment of Foreigners, International Conference): Advisory Committee on Opium and Other Dangerous Drugs, recommendation cited, 390; relation to the International Commission for Air Navigation, question of, 504, 511–512

Lithuania, negotiations with United States for treaty concerning naturalization, dual nationality, and military service, 449–451; conclusion of treaty (1937), 451

London Naval Conference to be held in 1930, preliminaries, 112–316

Address by President Hoover, May 30, text, 113–116

Address by U. S. Ambassador in Great Britain before Society of the Pilgrims, June 18:

Attitude of British Prime Minister and Foreign Secretary, 117, 118; of Japanese Ambassador in Great Britain, 117–118

Text, 121–128

VOLUMES II AND III ARE INDEXED SEPARATELY

# 1034

Trade Mark Bureau, Inter-American, 683–692

Treaties, conventions, etc.:

Amelioration of condition of the wounded and sick of armies in the field, international convention for, text signed *July 27*, 321–335

Arbitration. *See under* Arbitration.

Aviation. *See* Aviation: Conventions.

Boundary treaties. *See* Boundary treaties.

Conciliation. *See under* Conciliation.

Counterfeiting currency. *See* Counterfeiting Currency, Conference for the Suppression of: Convention.

Four-power treaty relating to insular possessions in the Pacific (*1921*), cited, 61, 64

Friendship, commerce, and consular rights, U. S.–Germany, *1923*, 431–432, 986, 1001, 1002

Geneva Convention of *1906*. *See* Conference for Revision of the Geneva Convention of *1906*.

Import and export prohibitions and restrictions. *See* Import and export prohibitions.

Kellogg-Briand Pact. *See* Treaty for the Renunciation of War.

Narcotic drugs, informal agreements. *See* Narcotic drugs.

Naturalization, dual nationality, and military service. *See* Naturalization, dual nationality, and military service.

Nine-power treaty relating to China (*1922*), cited, 61

Permanent Court of International Justice, protocols relating to. *See* Permanent Court of International Justice: Statute of the Court.

Prisoners of war, international convention relative to treatment of, text signed *July 27*, 336–367

Radio arrangement between Canada, Cuba, Newfoundland, and United States. *See* Radio Conference.

Radiotelegraph Convention of *1927*, cited, 385–386, 694

Renunciation of war. *See* Treaty for the Renunciation of War.

Safety of life at sea. *See* Safety of Life at Sea, International Conference: Convention.

Sanitary Convention of *1926*, cited, 376–377

Trade mark and commercial protection and registration of trade marks, convention and protocol

Treaties, conventions, etc.—Continued.

between United States and other American Republics, text signed *Feb. 20*, 670–692

Treatment of foreigners. *See* Treatment of Foreigners, International Conference on: Convention.

U. S.–Panama, unperfected treaty for the settlement of points of difference, *1926*, cited, 496–497

Versailles Treaty, 506–507

Washington Naval Treaty of *1922*, cited, 75, 78, 142, 148, 162, 163, 208, 224, 243, 264

Treatment of Foreigners, International Conference on, Paris, *Nov. 5–Dec. 5*, 429–438

American representation in a consultative capacity (*see also* Convention, *infra*):

League of Nations invitation and U. S. acceptance, 429–430

Representative: Instructions, 430–433, 434; opening statement, and comments thereon, 434, 436–438

U. S. position in regard to treatment of foreigners, 430–433

Convention, international:

Haitian concern in connection with provision under *art. 18*, 434–435; U. S. views, 438

U. S. signature, question of:

Australian suggestion for facilitating, 435–436; U. S. attitude, 436

Inability to sign, based on policy of nonconclusion of treaties with foreign powers which affect legislative power of the several states, 430–431, 433–434, 436–438

Treaty for the Renunciation of War (*1928*):

Cited, 38–39, 114, 121, 136, 140, 153, 162, 208, 224, 263, 300

U. S.–French informal discussions concerning further implementation, 59–64; French draft of a multilateral declaration, 63–64

Tri-Motors Safety Airways. *See under* Aviation: U. S. interests.

Union of Soviet Socialist Republics. *See* Russia.

Uruguay (*see also* Chaco dispute: Commission of Inquiry and Conciliation), aviation: French interests, 543; U. S. interests, 565, 566, 615, 621, 622

U. S. Congress:

Deficiency appropriation act, *1929*, cited, 371